CONTINENTAL AMBITIONS

KEVIN STARR

CONTINENTAL AMBITIONS

Roman Catholics in North America

The Colonial Experience

IGNATIUS PRESS   SAN FRANCISCO

English Scripture verses from the
Second Catholic Edition of the Revised Standard Version of the Bible
© 1965, 1966, and 2006 by the Division of Christian Education of the
National Council of the Churches of Christ in the United States of America.
All rights reserved.

Cover illustrations by Matthew Alderman

Cover design by John Herreid

© 2016 by Ignatius Press, San Francisco
All rights reserved
ISBN 978-1-62164-118-6
Library of Congress Control Number 2016933905
Printed in the United States of America ∞

For Sheila Gordon Starr,
research companion and editor,
who never lost faith in this book

CONTENTS

Preface   ix

Prologue: Garðar 1126
Bishop Eric Gnupson arrives in Greenland as Scandinavians advance
Christianity across the North Atlantic   1

Part One: Las Floridas

1   Santo Domingo 1511
    Resistance grows against the genocide and enslavement of indigenous peoples   21

2   Quivira 1527
    Dreams of empire mingle with evangelical ambition   44

3   Saint Augustine 1565
    Evangelization falters amid violence, slavery, and revolt   68

4   Apalachee 1595
    Friars and soldiers hold the Florida frontier   93

Part Two: The Spanish Borderlands

5   Ácoma 1599
    New Mexico, anchor kingdom of the Borderlands, begins with a massacre   115

6   San Fernando de Béxar 1718
    Texas is organized as a buffer province   142

7   Loreto 1767
    The Society of Jesus gains and loses its Pacific domain   173

Part Three: Las Californias

8   San Blas 1768
    New Spain launches an entrada into Alta California   203

9   The Bay of San Francisco 1776
    New Spain secures a strategic harbor on the Pacific coast   226

10   Santa Barbara 1842
    Secularization brings a bishop to the Californias   247

Part Four: New France

11   Port-Royal 1606
    Humanism inspires the foundation of New France   279

12   Quebec 1615
    The Counter-Reformation and Catholic Revival take hold in New France   299

13   Ville-Marie (Montreal) 1642
      Dévots found a city on the far frontier   321

14   Saint-Ignace 1649
      Iroquois destroy Huronia and threaten the survival of New France   342

15   The Abbey of Saint-Germain-des-Prés 1658
      *The secret consecration of a vicar apostolic for Quebec brings Roman
      Catholicism to new maturity*   364

16   New Orleans 1722
      A Jesuit savant reconnoiters French North America   397

17   Natchez 1729
      The Mississippi valley and Louisiana are explored and evangelized   430

Part Five: British North America

18   The River Boyne 1689
      A king and a peer lose their colonies   463

19   Annapolis 1704
      Catholic settlement spreads through the Chesapeake region   500

20   London 1763
      *Catholic Maryland seeks education abroad while Philadelphia prefigures an
      American Catholic future*   526

      Envoy
      John Carroll returns to Maryland   551

      Acknowledgments   557
      Notes   559
      Essay on Sources   567
      Index   607

PREFACE

In the early modern era and throughout the eighteenth century, Spain, France, and England sought with mixed results to colonize and evangelize the North American continent. These ambitions involved heroic feats of exploration and invasive conquest, followed by efforts to establish settlements and missions that frequently met the resistance of indigenous peoples. Ironically—given the hostility, violence, and social disruption accompanying missionary endeavors—the evangelization of indigenous peoples remains the aspiration most praised by Roman Catholic historians prior to recent times. True, in many cases, Spain's colonizing efforts—especially in early years but later in Alta California as well—included deliberate acts of warfare, rapine, and massacre and led to the destabilization of local cultures and the destruction of native peoples' health due to imported diseases. But the worldly ambitions of Spain, France, and England, being carried out in the name of religion also brought to the North American continent European Catholics in search of a better life, along with indigenous peoples converted to Catholicism and Catholics of mixed racial heritage who came into being. Motivated by Catholic values and according to their faith and culture, great men and women—both clerical and lay—did their best to improve conditions for the indigenous peoples of the continent. Those who say they were mistaken in these ambitions are not only judging them from contemporary perspectives; they are also branding them as hypocritical in their own time.

This narrative, however, frequently chronicles behavior that would be considered both hypocritical and offensive in any time or place, given the professed beliefs of Catholic Christianity—or the tenets of humane conduct by people of any tradition. The fact is, the arrival of Roman Catholic peoples in North America, starting with the Norse of a thousand years ago, brought with it terrible figures as well as admirable ones. Most of them, though, were simply men and women in extraordinary circumstances who struggled to behave well in the face of temptation and weakness.

Still, however mixed the motivations for settlement were, or however we judge the successes (or failures) of the efforts described in this volume, the institutional record is clear. Roman Catholicism has major standing in the North American story. In 1886 John Gilmary Shea justifiably opened *The Catholic Church in Colonial Days*—the first installment of his pioneering four-volume history of Catholicism in the United States—on a serene and confident note. "The Catholic Church", Shea wrote, "is the oldest organization in the United States, and the only one that has retained the same life and polity and forms through each succeeding age. Her history is interwoven in the whole fabric of the country's annals."[1]

Few, if any, contemporary historians of American Catholicism would open a similar history with the same confidence. Still, everything that Shea claimed of the Catholic Church in her American context remains true. Catholicism was the first form of Christianity to reach the Americas, and, as Shea pointed out in his preface, Catholic names dominate the region, Catholic missionaries evangelized its indigenous peoples, Catholic colonists developed its resources, and Catholic patriots established its republics in Latin America and Mexico and assisted in the creation of the provinces of Canada and the United States. And whereas in 1886 Shea could note that ten million of his fellow American citizens were Catholic, today a historian can cite seven times that number, fully a quarter of the population of the United States. A contemporary demographer analyzing present and future trends, moreover, might even claim that by some point in the mid- to late-twenty-first century half the population of the United States will describe itself, in one way or another, as Catholic—Americans for whom the narratives in this volume constitute a usable past.

The variability of degree just suggested underscores the differences between the sure assertions of John Gilmary Shea in 1886 and the troubled and chastened mood of Catholic people today in these United States. At its deepest theological level, so Catholicism teaches, the Church remains the Mystical Body of Christ in time and eternity; no human force, no sins of error or omission on the part of the hierarchy or the faithful, can prevail against this identity. But in addition to her transcendent and mystical nature, the Church (and no one is more aware of this than her members) is a human society, and hence liable to mistakes on the part of her nearly one and a quarter billion members across the planet.

Even the most cursory reading of Catholic and secular publications presents the challenges facing contemporary Catholicism on all continents, with the possible exception of Antarctica. It is self-indulgent for Catholics of the developed world to equate their issues and concerns with those of Catholics in developing countries, who struggle daily to obtain food and water; in certain places in the Middle East and Africa, they confront the threat of genocide. Still, Catholicism is anchored in the doctrine of the Incarnation: the belief, as the prologue to the Gospel according to Saint John puts it, that the Word became flesh and dwelled among us. Catholicism teaches that Jesus Christ was both God and man. He ate and drank in the company of outcasts and sinners, and sat with Mary in the cool of the evening in the home she shared with her sister and brother, discussing the things of God. Catholics tend to stay close to history and the sacramental specifics of everyday life. As the English Jesuit poet Gerard Manley Hopkins writes, "The world is charged with the grandeur of God." The world is our only pathway to salvation, provided we renounce its false promises. Catholicism, then, is enmeshed in and dependent on culture and society. It blesses through physical things—water, oil, incense, beeswax candles, palm branches. Its central and unifying rites, baptism and the Eucharist, are dependent on water, bread, and wine. It anoints its infants, teenagers, clergy, and dying with oil. Catholicism prizes art, architecture, and music as windows on divinity. It values community, sacred and secular and admixtures thereof, as well as the principle of subsidiarity: keeping things as local as possible. Catholicism considers itself an essential component of human life and society and the history that is being forged.

In certain sectors of the American Church, the Second Vatican Council unleashed a flood of expectations (some of them erroneous and unwarranted) that destabilized the liturgy, which had reached a high point of reform, theological depth, and connection to worship, community, and social engagement. Decades of experimentation followed, running from presumptuous to naïve to tasteless, which in turn lowered the tone of Roman Catholic worship. "We English Catholics once died for the Mass", novelist Anthony Burgess remarked to me in astonishment as the Tridentine Latin Mass, the creation of centuries, was jettisoned—not because the Second Vatican Council demanded this (it did not). Yet altars were dismantled, rubrics were ignored, and preaching devolved into anecdote. Thousands of priests left the ministry during this era. An untold number rejected its mandatory celibacy; some believed that the reforms called for by the Second Vatican Council were being thwarted; the majority departed for these reasons and others connected to a loss of faith in the Roman Catholic priesthood as a professional identity.

The papal encyclical *Humanae Vitae*, meanwhile, played a central role in this narrative of confusion and loss. Issued by Pope Paul VI in 1968 against the advice of the majority of a specially convened panel of lay and clerical consultors, *Humanae Vitae* (which included the prohibition of all artificial forms of birth control) resulted in a near-wholesale jury nullification of its prohibitions by laity and their parish clergy alike. This unprecedented rejection of papal teaching caused a further drift in the direction of cafeteria Catholicism, in which an increasing number of Catholics felt free to pick, choose, and assemble Church teachings into a personalized portfolio of belief without feeling the necessity to leave the Church. By the turn of the twenty-first century, the very understanding of certain basic doctrines, much less their acceptance—previously instilled in young Catholics for more than one hundred years through the various editions of the *Baltimore Catechism*—had decreased in significant portions of the younger population. Church attendance among the same age group had also declined.

The sexual abuse of minors and its all-too-frequent cover-up by hierarchy, moreover, eroded the laity's confidence in their bishops and clergy, forming a fault line of mistrust. Lives were destroyed. Laws were broken at the highest levels of authority. Dioceses went into bankruptcy paying justified legal judgments. The Roman Catholic priesthood lost the professional luster it had taken more than a century to attain.

In addition, the scandal unleashed a dragon of anti-Catholicism that seemed to have retreated to its lair. Never in the history of this republic—not even in the decades of Know Nothingism—has such prejudice from the anti-Catholic dragon breathed anti-Catholic fire throughout the land. This time, however, evangelical Protestants were not responsible for the aggression; indeed, evangelicals increasingly found themselves lumped together with practicing Catholics as objects of scorn. Anti-Catholicism now played itself out as part of a larger warfare against Christian belief. Furthermore, the culture of American Catholicism—once treated with respect by Hollywood—became a target of ridicule in popular entertainment, which affected sizable portions of the Catholic population.

Roman Catholicism thus entered the new millennium facing a number of challenges: the erosion of trust in the clergy; the alienation of Catholics on the left and the right; the anti-Catholicism flourishing at every level of academia, media, and entertainment; the apparent indifference of many young people; and the garbled pronouncements of Catholic politicians. Purists with an antiquarian bent can with justification cavil at one or another aspect of contemporary American Catholicism: the disappearance of philosophy and theology from sermons, the loss of cultural identity, the slavishness to popular culture. More serious still are the ongoing cases of clerical sex abuse, now being adjudicated by the courts and the criminal justice system—where bishops should have placed them decades ago.

Yet the center has managed to hold in this Church, whose motto might well be, as James Joyce put it, "Here comes everybody!" Nearly seventy-six million Americans call themselves Catholic, and thus Catholicism—however changed, however attacked, however ambiguous its hold on the population—remains a force in American life. Indeed, despite everything, the splendor of the Church endures alongside her sins and confusion. Her current pontiff, Pope Francis—an Argentinean Jesuit, the first pope from the Americas, who describes himself with total sincerity as Francis, a sinner—has encouraged a renewed spirit of humility and service in laity and clergy alike and has acknowledged institutional and personal transgressions.

The history of Catholicism in America is not simply Catholic history. It is American history and has increasingly been researched and written as such since John Gilmary Shea's pioneering work a century and a half ago. Many fine histories of Catholicism in the United States explore national, state, regional, and local perspectives. This volume is intended to be the first part of a larger narrative written at a time of crisis and renewal. Previous studies have emphasized Catholic immigrants' struggle for acceptance. This book and those that follow return to the first premise of Shea's four-volume chronicle: namely, there can be no understanding of American culture and history without an understanding of the role played by Catholic peoples in the unfolding drama of the American experience. This text uses narrative segments to present the American Catholic experience as Perry Miller presented the Puritan experience and Irving Howe presented the American Jewish experience: as part of the warp and woof, the very fabric and meaning, of American life.

As they seek renewal, American Catholics need to regain their sense of being a historical people. Conversely, in their efforts to renew a sense of American identity, Americans must understand that this fine republic has been profoundly Judeo-Christian in its formation and now struggles to incorporate other great world religions. Ecumenism and interfaith efforts require not an abandonment of doctrine, but the abandonment of the desire to impose that doctrine on others. American Catholics do not have to repudiate or vitiate their faith traditions to be acceptable Americans. Still, a recognition of the Church's achievements and failures on this continent is fundamental. It is time for American Catholics to repossess and to learn from the story of their North American pilgrimage—and for Americans of every persuasion to come to a better understanding of each other.

PROLOGUE

Garðar 1126

*Bishop Eric Gnupson arrives in Greenland as Scandinavians
advance Christianity across the North Atlantic*

The first bishop to arrive in Greenland, Eric Gnupson, is a shadowy figure. The one saga in which he appears said he continued westward, never to return. From this perspective, Bishop Eric was either a dedicated missionary surveying North American lands to the west that were part of his charge or a wandering cleric in episcopal orders. Eric remains a mystery. By the early 1100s, in any event, Greenlanders, after one hundred years of Catholic Christianity, desperately wanted a bishop of their own, which was why chieftain Sakki Thorisson sent his son Einar Sokkason to Norway in 1125 to petition King Sigurd Jorsala-Ari for a diocese and a bishop for the colony. Sakki sent a polar bear along with Einar to present to the king once a bishopric was granted. Approving of the appointment, the king sent Einar to Asser, archbishop of Lund, and metropolitan for all of Scandinavia. The archbishop approved of, and duly consecrated, the king's candidate, the priest Arnold, who expressed no desire whatsoever to be sent to the outer edge of the known world but was eventually persuaded to go.

And so, in the summer of 1126, Bishop Arnold arrived at Garðar in the East Settlement, where by common agreement his diocesan seat had been established. Ironically, the mass murderer Freydís and her husband, Thorvard—outcasts, as Leif Ericsson had predicted—had spent their last years there. (That tale is elaborated below.) In fact, remnants of the couple's home may have been absorbed into Bishop Arnold's first episcopal residence, offering posterity an opportunity to see a redemptive pattern at work, at least as far as Catholic Greenland was concerned.

Over time, Garðar developed into an impressive episcopal establishment of cathedral, bishop's house, and farm, all of it in stone and of Romanesque or sturdy Scandinavian design. The bishop's house featured a 427-square-foot ceremonial hall, the largest in Greenland and two-thirds the size of the ceremonial hall of the archbishop's house in Trondheim. Warmed by an oversized fire pit, its walls covered in tapestries, and connected to the cathedral sacristy by a stone-paved path, the bishop's house at Garðar possessed comfort and ecclesiastical flair. It remained in use for nearly 250 years. The thirty-seven-acre farm eventually developed into the largest one in Greenland, splendid in its array of sandstone cow byres, barns, and storehouses in the Anglo-Irish building tradition.

The cathedral and its bell tower conferred on the Garðar complex its deepest meaning as an outpost of Western European Catholicism a week's sail from North

America. Consecrated bishop of Greenland in 1188 or 1189, Jón Árnason—also known as Smyrill (falcon or hawk)—rebuilt and enlarged the Garðar cathedral and was interred in its north chapel around 1209, the only bishop to be thus buried. The skeleton of Jón Smyrill Árnason has been recovered, one finger still bearing a Norman-style episcopal ring. The remnants of an episcopal crozier topped in walrus ivory lay near the remains. Ring and crozier signified Bishop Jón Smyrill's authority over the ten to twelve parish churches of Greenland by the year 1200, along with the churches of the Benedictine abbey at Siglu Fjord and the house of Augustinian canons regular at Ketils Fjord, a training center for secular clergy.

A Scandinavian advance

Between 870 and 930, some ten thousand or so Scandinavians migrated by ship from Norway across six hundred miles of North Atlantic waters to Iceland, a 39,758-square-mile island just below the Arctic Circle. There the Norse voyagers and their dependents established a free state that lasted from 930 to 1262, when it was absorbed into Norway. Known as Vikings in their marauding mode—which was nearly continuous during the previous centuries—these Icelanders worshipped Thor, god of farmers and seafarers; Frey, god of fertility; and Odin, god of warriors and aristocrats. Chieftains were cremated atop pyres or burned at sea in ceremonies intended to equip the deceased for a safe and enjoyable afterlife.

More than a century before the Norse arrived in Iceland, Irish monks had reached the island in seagoing curraghs, wicker-framed vessels covered in animal skins and propelled by oars or a single sail. These curraghs, each of which carried up to eighteen passengers, have been praised by the maritime historian Samuel Eliot Morison for their ability to ride the waves like a cork and negotiate the heaviest of seas. The monks established hive-shaped coastal hermitages, similar to the ones they had already built on the rocky promontories and islets of the Irish coast and the Hebrides, Orkney, and Shetland island groups. In time, later lore would claim, these same Irish monks or their successors sailed farther west to Greenland and then even farther, to Labrador and Newfoundland, arriving there long before the Norse landed in the late tenth or early eleventh century. No historian has proven this claim. Yet few historians have totally denied it, either, given the navigational skills of the Celtic monks, the seaworthiness of the curragh, and a lingering suspicion created by a passage in the thirteenth-century *Saga of Eric the Red* in which native people captured in Vinland described to their Norse captors white-robed men walking in procession and holding banners aloft, calling out in a strange language. However, Admiral Morison points out, no Irish artifacts have ever been discovered in North America. He admits, though, that "all this was long, long ago, when one feels that anything might have happened."[1]

Iceland becomes Christian

Fusing the techniques of literature with historical memory, clerics wrote the sagas in the thirteenth or early fourteenth century. By this time, Iceland had long since become Christian, its three diocesan bishops in union with Rome through the metropolitan see of Trondheim in Norway. Leif Ericsson—son of Eric the Red,

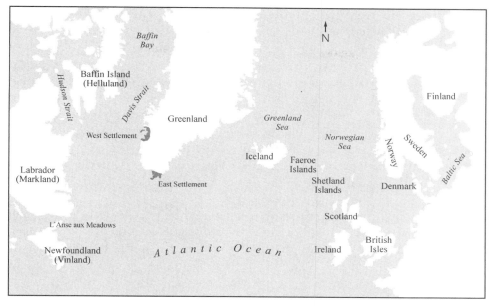

Map 1. North Atlantic.

and the official discoverer of Vinland—played a crucial role in the island's Christianization, which in the year 1000 was formalized by the Icelandic *Althing*, the parliamentary body governing the free state. Young Ericsson had been converted to Catholic Christianity while attached to the court of King Olaf Tryggvason, who sent Ericsson back to Iceland with the specific charge of converting the free state, which the king had been trying to do for some time with little success. For the writer of the *Saga of Eric the Red*, a Catholic priest living in Catholic Iceland or Norway, to evoke the pre-Norse presence of Irish monks in Iceland (or Greenland or Vinland, for that matter) was to suggest that Celtic monastics had earlier prepared for the progress of Catholic Christianity across the North Atlantic to the outer edges of the known world.

This same ambition—the creation of a prologue to Christianization and the Latin Catholic West—animates the *Navigatio Sancti Brendani Abbatis* (Voyage of Saint Brendan the Abbot). The Latin prose narrative was anonymously composed in the tenth century by a learned monk or a nonmonastic cleric of Lotharingia, the Franco-German province that stretched from Lorraine northward along the Rhine to the Dutch lowlands and the channel. The region's monastery-centered ecclesiastical and literary culture owed its vitality in great measure to the Irish monks who had been laboring there for the past two centuries.

Celtic Christianity and Brendan the Voyager

The Christianity carried to Ireland by the British-born missionary bishop Patrick between 430 and 460 brought Ireland into union with the Latin Christian West—but on its own terms. While Patrick himself established an episcopal see at Armagh in the northern part of the island, and bishops remained important in

Celtic Christianity regarding ordinations to the priesthood, conferral of confirmation, blessing of the holy oils, and other liturgical functions, the social organization of the Christian community was not centered on the bishop and his *sedes* (seat or see) in an urban complex, as was the case in western Europe. Ecclesiastical polity, rather, was based on communities of monks under the direction of an elected abbot and attached communities of lay dependents. For one thing, Ireland had few, if any, urban centers, and an extended monastic community better expressed the tribal nature of Irish society. Hence the monk and the monastery replaced the urban-based episcopal see as the organizing element, and the abbot elected by the monks became the dominant prelate of the region. This structure explains the plethora of monks, monasteries, and abbots in the first centuries of Celtic Christianity and the virtual absence of bishops and diocesan clergy.

Of these abbots, many of whom were canonized by popular acclaim after their deaths, none was better known or more revered than Saint Brendan the Voyager. Born in the late 480s near the present city of Tralee, County Kerry, and dying sometime between 570 and 583, Brendan led a long and productive life as the abbot founder of monasteries, episcopal sees, schools, and parish churches in Ireland, Wales, Scotland, and the other islands. He was also a renowned maritime missionary and explorer at a time when Irish monks were busy establishing offshore hermitages around the British Isles prior to crossing over to the continent itself, where they pursued the evangelical and educational labors that helped western Europe refound itself in the late patristic and early medieval eras.

Brendan's life, in brief, was the stuff of legend, which it became soon after his death: the legend of a great saint who was a great sailor as well, who sailed into western seas with his monks and discovered many islands, where he established hermitages. Just exactly which islands Brendan and his monks reached as they sailed into the Atlantic in their hidebound curraghs is a matter of speculation. Brendan's voyages, however, survived as legend, which for the medieval imagination constituted a mode of historical recovery. Through the early modern era, islands associated with discovery by Brendan continued to be featured on contemporary maps. One of these islands, moreover, the Isle of Saint Brendan—also known as the Promised Land of the Saints, fusing history and myth—grew in importance as Christian Catholic civilization matured in Lotharingia, a province that by the tenth century stood at the heart of the Holy Roman Empire that Irish monks had helped bring into being.

From Atlantis onward, lost or imagined islands enjoyed a special niche in the collective imagination of classical and Christian Europe. Into this niche the Promised Land of the Saints and the other islands described in the *Navigatio* fit easily. Such islands were always to the west, where the known world ended and the imagined world began, and they tended to embody ideal states of being or, at the least, to promise improved conditions for those who voyaged there. And so, during the very years in which Norway—an outpost of Europe—was pushing westward, the Latin narrative *Navigatio Sancti Brendani Abbatis* made its appearance and was translated or recast into Anglo-Norman, Dutch, German, Venetian, Occitan (Languedoc), Catalan, Norse, and English. Perhaps this arrival of a narrative about sailing west into the unknown at the very time the Norse were launching westward into the North Atlantic was mere coincidence. If so, the coincidence was fortunate indeed, for the ultrapopular *Navigatio* imaginatively prefigured a western Europe on the move even farther to the west across the northern (and later the southern) Atlantic in search of a better life and perhaps redemption itself.

From this perspective, the *Navigatio* functioned as an early-medieval *Aeneid*, a scenario of a society renewing itself through a voyage across open seas to a new place. The *Navigatio* likewise evoked the islands through which Catholic Christianity had been advancing westward. Thanks to the Irish monks settled on the Hebrides, Orkney, and Shetland island groups, and the Norse settlers advancing from the Faroes to Iceland, Greenland, and Vinland beyond (centered on an island later called Newfoundland), the archipelago conjured in the *Navigatio* became a reality within decades of the Latin narrative's debut.

Hundreds of years later, Spain and Portugal would extend that archipelago of Catholic outposts into the South Atlantic via settlements on the Azores, Canary, Madeira, and Cape Verde island groups; Columbus took it farther west across the Atlantic into the Caribbean. For the time being, though, an emergent Scandinavian, recently Catholic Christian people braved the seas in broad-beamed ships called knarrs bearing freight, cattle, sheep, and horses. These Norsemen advanced Catholic Christianity—briefly, courageously, violently, with moments of redemptive achievement—onto the North American continent.

The Norse diaspora

Well before their migration to Iceland, Norsemen—sailing as Viking marauders, settling into coastal colonies, and taking hold of larger fiefdoms that extended inland—had long since been equaling the ancient Phoenicians as masters of maritime adventure. Norse culture and social psychology exhibited two sides: one was attached to the ownership of land and cattle and the practice of agriculture; the other was enamored of coastal and open-sea sailing in deftly crafted longboats as merchants and marauders. By the late ninth century, northern Europe and coastal Ireland, Scotland, and northeastern England, as well as Normandy, southern Italy, Sicily, and various other Mediterranean places, were dotted with Norse settlements in the process of intermingling with local peoples.

Norway, meanwhile, was in the process of being unified into a Christian kingdom. Reigning from 935 to 996, King Haakon the Good initiated this transformation, which continued through the reign of King Olaf Tryggvason (995–1000) and was completed in the reign of the saintly King Olaf Haraldssön (1025–1030), who was canonized for his efforts. In 1152, Cardinal Nicholas Breakspear, the papal delegate—an Englishman who was soon to reign as Pope Adrian IV (1154–1159)—negotiated the creation of Trondheim as the metropolitan see for Norway, the Orkneys, the Faroes, the Hebrides, the Isle of Man, Iceland, and Greenland.

By the year 1000, the population of Iceland reached fifty thousand due to a slow but steady influx of settlers and a birth rate strengthened by a quasi-polygamous culture in which established Norsemen as well as free retainers and thralls in bondage practiced concubinage. As Norway developed along feudal Christian lines, land-ownership became increasingly defined and stratified as a prerogative of nobility, church, and crown. Growing numbers of the middle ranks of society were being edged out, men who were both land-owning, land-loving farmers and sea-roving

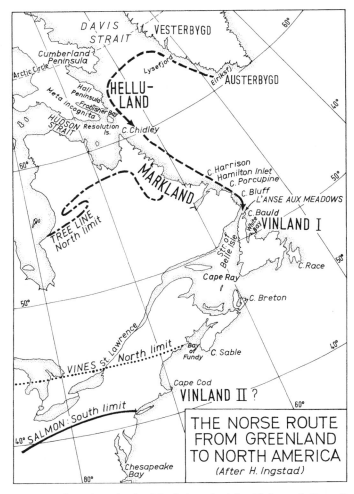

Map 2. The Norse Route from Greenland to North America (after H. Ingstad). From David B. Quinn, *North America from Earliest Discovery to First Settlements: The Norse Voyages to 1612* (New York: Harper and Row, 1977), 25. © *David B. Quinn. Reprinted by permission of HarperCollins Publishers.*

Vikings ready for the next expedition. Migration to Iceland reestablished this generation as *landnámsmenn* (men of land) on a remote mid-Atlantic island, where they settled with their families, retainers, and thralls—Norse men and women, yet possessed of a strong admixture of Celtic blood (wives and slaves, especially), given the long sojourn of the Norse in Ireland, Scotland, and the Hebrides. A number of Icelanders thus had Celtic or part-Celtic wives who were Christians; whatever their level of practice in their newfound circumstances, these women communicated some of their religion's teachings and values to family members. For most of the tenth century, however, their husbands and children remained pagan despite the Christianization of their homeland and the desire of the Norwegian kings that Icelanders replace the worship of Thor and Frey with fealty to Jesus Christ.

Christian missionaries did their best to bring about such a conversion. Thorvald Kodransson arrived in the 980s, accompanied by Fridrek, a missionary bishop who established an apostolic church once a sufficient number of converts had been gathered. Yet Fridrek disappears from the sagas without a trace, and Thorvald—a hot-tempered Norseman as well as a missionary priest—got into an altercation in which two men were killed, according to the sagas, and Thorvald's proselytizing ended.

Still, King Olaf Tryggvason sustained hopes of Christianizing Iceland, and to that end he sent two more missionaries to the island. The first, Stefnir Thorgilsson, was an Icelander—a promising start—but Stefnir, the sagas tell us, so violently assaulted the pagan religion that he provoked a protective response from the Althing, which declared it a crime to blaspheme the old gods. King Olaf then sent the experienced missionary priest Thangbrand, a German or Flemish veteran of conversion campaigns in Norway and the Faroes. While Thangbrand was a devoted missionary, his style of proselytization—roaming the countryside with a *posse comitatus* of converts, spoiling for a fight—was decidedly old-school Teutonic. Though a priest, Thangbrand remained a warrior skilled in weaponry, and the sagas say that in the course of his ministry from 997 to 999, he participated in a dustup or two in which people were killed, including a poet who wrote verses satirizing Thangbrand. Not surprisingly, the warrior-priest returned to Norway, Iceland unconverted.

King Olaf now turned to the laity—specifically, the recent convert Leif Ericsson, son of Eric the Red. On the verge of the new millennium, Leif received a mandate from the king to convert Eric the Red and thereby create leverage for the conversion of Iceland. Arriving in the free state, Leif got down to the business of convincing his father that Iceland would be better off if it converted to Christianity. Eric the Red remained dubious, but not Leif's mother, Thjodhild, who soon converted and, with a display of equality typical of Norsewomen, banished her husband from her bed—indeed, she moved out of his house—until he saw the light.

Back in Norway, King Olaf closed all ports to Icelandic trade and took into custody a number of prominent Icelanders residing in Norway at the time, whom the king promised to maim, or perhaps execute, if Iceland persisted in remaining pagan. Christianizers gained momentum from Olaf's threat, and by the year 1000 Iceland was divided into two camps, pagan and Christian, and on the verge of civil war.

Fortunately, instead of armed conflict, the matter came before the Althing for debate, followed by—according to Norse custom—a decision from the elected law-speaker, one Thorgeir Thorkelsson, a farmer from the north. After a day and night of solitary deliberation, lying completely covered by a great blanket, Thorgeir made his decision. Iceland would become Christian. Everyone not yet baptized should be so, but certain old laws (including the exposure of deformed infants) would remain permitted, and the old religion could still be practiced in private, as long as it did not provoke scandal.

The mass conversion of the free state by parliamentary fiat testifies to the power of politics and culture in the conversions of the first millennium. Religion was a political and cultural choice. Catholic Christianity could be imposed on a society through political force, the conversion of a king, a decision by a parliament—as had often been the case on the continent—without much damage either to Christian orthodoxy or to the culture of the people whose religion was changing. Prior religiosities, however, survived beneath the surface or occasionally erupted, as happened the year Iceland converted, when King Olaf died and parts of Norway temporarily reverted to paganism.

The Icelandic Church

The Catholic Christianity that came to Iceland did not involve a strong sense of the Church as a transcendent institution, juridically distinct from the rest of society. Until the Reformation, Iceland remained in union with Rome via its ecclesiastical allegiance to the archbishop of Hamburg-Bremen in northern Germany, a jurisdiction transferred to the archbishop of Lund in 1104, when that Danish city was designated as the archiepiscopal see for all of Scandinavia. It was later transferred to Nidaróss, then to Trondheim, when the archbishop there was given jurisdiction over Norway, the Orkneys, the Hebrides, the Faroes, Iceland, and Greenland. No great heretics arose in Iceland, and at least one Icelander in this era made a pilgrimage to Rome: Gudrid Thorbjarnardóttir, the thrice-widowed daughter-in-law of Eric the Red. In her long life, Gudrid crossed the North Atlantic twice, was shipwrecked off Greenland, bore a son while in Vinland (Snorri, the first European child born in North America), made a pilgrimage to Rome in late middle age, and then spent the rest of her years as an independent anchorite, one of Iceland's first. She died in 1050, the ancestor of three twelfth-century Icelandic bishops.

Up until the Reformation, many Icelandic bishops were the sons of bishops or were themselves fathers of bishops or priests. While celibate monasticism was established in Iceland in the twelfth century—three Benedictine monasteries and four houses of Augustinian canons regular were founded, as well as one nunnery—clerical celibacy was not the norm for the bishops and clergy of Iceland's three dioceses. Christianity was brought to Iceland by the laity, not by clerics, and was decided upon by a secular organization, the Althing. During the first two centuries of Icelandic Catholic Christianity, the *godar* chieftain class controlled the episcopacy, and the sons of *godar* bishops also took orders and frequently succeeded their fathers as bishops. In addition, public officials of lesser rank were ordained priests or deacons. Bishops and priests built and owned cathedrals and parish churches at their own expense and maintained them as part of their estates. Bishops and clergy married and supported their families from farming and trading revenues.

The clergy, in short, were in union with Rome but fused into secular society. Iceland functioned as the Church, and the Church functioned as Iceland, and the archbishop in Denmark or Norway left it that way—at least until the thirteenth century, when resistance to clerical marriage surfaced. The situation in Iceland was similar to that of the rest of Norway, where clerical marriage (or clerical concubinage, as critics described it) persisted among the rural parish clergy (and most of Norway was rural) until the Reformation, when clerical marriage was formally reestablished.

Bold, direct, lay centered, defining itself by actions more than by contemplation: this was the Catholic Christianity brought to Greenland in this neo-Homeric age, although colonization occurred in the pagan era.

The settlement of Greenland

Greenland was settled from Iceland in the summer of 986 in a *landnám* (land-taking) expedition organized by Eric the Red, then under a sentence of temporary exile from Iceland for manslaughter. The *Landnámabók* collection of exploration and settlement sagas notes that of the twenty-five vessels—containing men, women, children, retainers, thralls, livestock, and farming equipment—only fourteen arrived safely, testimony to the dangers of open-sea voyaging at that time. The colonists settled on the fjords, lowlands, and valleys of the southeastern and western sides of the peninsula, establishing an Eastern and a Western Settlement. A solitary Christian from the Hebrides joined this first expedition. At least two smaller excursions followed. The sagas, as well as mid-twentieth-century archaeological excavations, suggest the evolution of the first-generation turf-wall farmhouses to more ambitious stone structures such as the longhouse—several rooms, including a ceremonial hall, built along a longitudinal axis—found at Eric the Red's Brattahlíð in the Eastern Settlement. Dairy products constituted an important component of the Greenlander diet; during the long winter, cows and sheep were housed in snug stone barns, along with stores of dried fish, seal, walrus, reindeer, hares, and the occasional polar bear or stranded whale. The rocky soil and harsh climate made agriculture extremely difficult, although some barley was raised and adequate pasturage was available part of the year.

Setting up its own Althing, the Greenland colony immediately became autonomous. It received its own bishop in the mid-1120s and in 1261 was included in the North Atlantic federation being consolidated by King Haakon the Elder. Greenland was remote and environmentally challenging. Its population peaked at around two or three thousand. The colony was an afterthought of Iceland, which itself was an afterthought of Norway. In Normandy, by contrast, Norse immigrants were coming of age as Normans, an imperial people soon to advance into England, Ireland, and Sicily. No one envisioned such a future for the folk of Iceland or Greenland—Greenland especially, where holding on seemed to be conquest enough.

Then there was the question of the land to the west, Vinland, explored and ever so briefly settled in the first years of the Greenland colony and visited thereafter on expeditions to harvest wood for both Greenland and Iceland, where few trees grew. Eric Gnupson, the first bishop of Greenland, may have been there in 1121. During the years that Greenland maintained its vigor—into the mid-fourteenth century, when the Black Death decimated Norway—Norsemen were generally familiar with the lands a five to seven days' sail to the west. Leif Ericsson had divided them into three sectors: Helluland (southern Baffin Land and northern Labrador); Markland (northern Newfoundland), named for the trees growing there; and, farther south, Vinland the Good (Nova Scotia), which might have extended as far as northern New England, with a number of nineteenth- and early-twentieth-century enthusiasts arguing for even more southerly voyages to Cape Cod, Long Island, and Chesapeake Bay.

North American settlements

A Norwegian by the name of Bjarni Herjólfsson was trading between Norway and Iceland in the 980s. In 986 Bjarni set sail for Greenland to visit his father, who had migrated there. His ship was blown off course to the west. Although Bjarni's crew did not go ashore, they sailed for days past the wooded flatlands of Labrador and Newfoundland before turning eastward back to Greenland. Upon his return, Bjarni reported what he saw to Eric the Red and other Greenland leaders and then resumed trading in the North Atlantic, most likely making occasional trips back to Greenland. Bjarni's description of timber-rich country especially impressed tree-deprived Greenlanders, dependent as they were on driftwood and other miscellaneous sources for construction, heat, and cooking.

An ordinary trader, not a warrior or chieftain, Bjarni Herjólfsson received only one fragmentary mention in the sagas for his discovery of the lands to the west. Credit for the discovery of Vinland, as these lands were commonly called, went to a much more glamorous figure: Leif Ericsson, son of Eric the Red. Handsome, high-born, honorable, and a Christian, Leif was the type of figure of whom legends are made—and they were, almost immediately, following his death in the mid-1020s. In his early and pivotal conversion, his exploration of Vinland, and his general probity, Leif Ericsson provided Scandinavia with a knightly hero worthy of celebration in later chronicles. Two other sons of Eric, Thorvald and Thornstein, also figured prominently in the Vinland sagas, along with Eric the Red's illegitimate daughter Freydís, the Lady Macbeth of the saga series.

According to historical record, Vinland was first documented around the year 1070 by Adam of Bremen, a cleric on the staff of the archbishop of Bremen and Hamburg, then serving as metropolitan of Scandinavia. In his *Descriptio insularum aquilonis*, Adam described Vinland as an island on the frozen and fog-bound edge of the world, where wild grapes and self-sown wheat grew. Sixty years later, in 1130, Vinland received a second mention, this time in the *Islendinga Book* by the priest Ari Frode, who noted that Greenlanders sailed there in pre-Christian times and encountered *skrælings*, as the Greenlanders called indigenous Eskimos and Indians alike.

Yet it is through the sagas that the North American experiences of Norse men and women are primarily—and vividly—documented. Written in the thirteenth or early fourteenth century by clerical men of letters attached to church or court, the sagas are, in contemporary terminology, docudramas that present historical experience by means of dramatized narratives. Prior to the twentieth century, the sagas were regarded as largely fictive in content as well as technique. In the twentieth and twenty-first centuries, by contrast, scholars have been moving in the direction of accepting the fundamental veracity of the sagas, while remaining skeptical of their chronologies. Particularly dubious, of course, is a reference to the one-legged monster skræling who brought down the leader of an expedition with a well-placed arrow. Lively and laconic, the sagas feel authentic, however their inconsistencies must be reconciled.

In their various manifestations, the sagas tell of five Norse expeditions from Greenland to North America between 1003 and 1013. Visits in subsequent years went unrecorded, which does not mean they did not occur. The offspring of Eric the Red dominate these sagas. All of the sagas describe the purposes and economics of exploration; conflict with skrælings, the fertility of Vinland the Good, as evident in its grapes, wheat, and wood; and yet the failure to found a permanent colony. Christian sentiment or behavior is absent among the protagonists, who were, one must remember, in their early years of the conversion to Catholic Christianity brokered in Iceland by the Althing. Instead, a nonreflective reticence characterizes the responses of the explorers as they define themselves through action in an unforgiving environment.

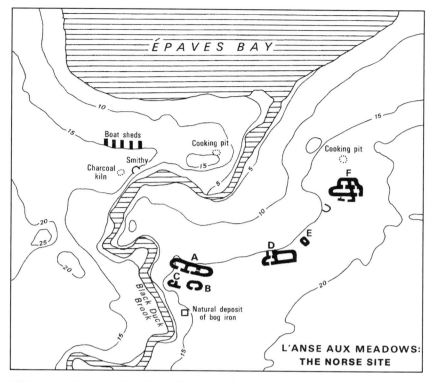

Map 3. L'Anse aux Meadows: The Norse Site. From David B. Quinn, *North America from Earliest Discovery to First Settlements: The Norse Voyages to 1612* (New York: Harper and Row, 1977), 38. © *David B. Quinn. Reprinted by permission of HarperCollins Publishers.*

Leif Ericsson

Bjarni Herjólfsson's voyage to North America was accidental. It engendered next to no response in a Greenland barely under way as a Norse settlement. The voyage of Leif Ericsson, by contrast, dated 1003–1004, represented a deliberate act of exploration planned by Leif and his father for economic reasons. The woodlands to the west featured in Bjarni's report, if successfully lumbered, could make Leif and his father a fortune. Eric the Red was originally scheduled to accompany Leif but at the last minute declined due to an injury and a sense of being too old for the rigors of the expedition. For the voyage, Leif purchased the very same knarr in which Bjarni had been blown off course in 985: a beamy vessel, Admiral Morison tells us, capable of negotiating the North Atlantic swells while carrying a generous cargo of people, animals, and freight. The famed dragon-prowed longboats of the Vikings were for marauding, but by the early eleventh century, marauding was largely a thing of the past. It was not on swift longboats but on broad, capacious knarrs that Norwegians had settled Iceland and Greenland and would now set forth on reconnaissance to North America.

Leif Ericsson's expedition made landfall on Baffin Island, north of Labrador. Going ashore, the Norsemen explored the rocky coast. Leif named the region Helluland (Country of Flat Stones). No coveted woodlands here, that was certain, and no gold, either. And so Leif and his crew sailed farther south and landed on a thirty-mile-long stretch of beach on the Labrador coast, where they discovered an abundance of black spruce, prompting Leif to call the area Markland (Land of Forests). Venturing even farther south, Leif's party alighted on Belle Isle, where they slaked their thirst on the dew of grass, finding it sweet and satisfying.

Still farther south, the Norsemen landed on the northern tip of Newfoundland—a most congenial place, says the *Groenlendinga thattr* (Tale of the Greenlanders), the mid-thirteenth-century narrative that after long debate has been accepted as the most authoritative source of information about Leif Ericsson's voyage of discovery. The great white sandy beach was pristine and accessible. A river and lake teemed with the largest salmon the men had ever seen. There was pasturage for the few runty cattle they had brought with them. Wintering on the site, the Greenlanders marveled at the frost-free days and the daylight that lasted into late afternoon. At the interface of a bay and a meadow (later called Epaves Bay and L'Anse aux Meadows), Leif Ericsson and his men constructed two houses, the larger one an impressive seventy by fifty-five feet. Made of clay floors, turf walls, and timber roofs, it contained a great hall lined with benches for sitting or sleeping under polar-bear skins, a fire pit for warmth and cooking, and adjacent rooms, some of which had fire pits of their own. In later years, Leif Ericsson would lend these two great houses to subsequent expeditions, who expanded and improved upon them, including the construction of a forge to process locally found iron ore into useful articles.

Excavating the site in the 1960s, archaeologist Helge Ingstad estimated that seventy-five to ninety people were at L'Anse aux Meadows at the height of its usage. With such numbers as this (the population of Greenland, as noted earlier, peaked at two to three thousand), L'Anse aux Meadows must be considered a settlement, though not a permanent one. Greenland was not ready for something that ambitious. Leif Ericsson called his houses *booths*, meaning temporary structures, yet he maintained jurisdiction over them following his return to Greenland. These houses and attendant buildings—these *Leifsbooths*—are described by Morison as a small village, and as such they suggest a future of more Greenlanders arriving and making a go of Vinland as a Norse Catholic colony.

Equally symbolic were the grapes, self-sowing wheat, and abundant wood they found there. Scholars have more or less agreed that the grapes described in the saga were black cranberries, the self-sown wheat was Lyme grass (which Icelanders baked into a bread-like product), and the *mosür* trees were the white or canoe birch that once grew in these regions. Yet no less a figure than Leif Ericsson himself seized upon the misidentified grapes—from which came wine, and hence all that wine suggests regarding human culture—as proof that these western lands under exploration might indeed have a future. Vinland (Wineland) the Good, he named it, blessed with timber for construction, and wheat and grapes for bread and wine: the latter two not simply for the table, it is tempting to speculate, but for use as well in the commemorative ritual at the heart of Greenland's new religion. Bread and wine were scarce, imported items in Greenland, and centuries later a bishop there actually requested of Rome that beer be used in the Mass. Request denied! How poignant—and revelatory of how bad things became in Greenland in the years following the Black Death.

No mention of sacramental implications, however, surfaces in the Tale of the Greenlanders or other sagas written by learned clerics, who might be expected to seize upon such imagery. Thus Leif Ericsson's naming of Vinland the Good remains interpreted as a public relations gesture. Yet the voyage of Saint Brendan the Abbot, which functions as overture to an age of Norse discovery, suggests that the recent Christian convert Leif Ericsson may have been aware of the power of the extended symbolism of grapes and wheat as he entered these tokens into the North American narrative.

Thorvald Ericsson

The central event of the next expedition—that of Leif's brother Thorvald in 1005–1006, as related in the Tale of the Greenlanders and the *Saga of Eric the Red*—was equally paradigmatic, albeit in a negative (one might say disastrous) way. Thorvald intended to build a home in Vinland, as his brother had done, which suggests that he had settlement in mind, eventually, although no women are recorded as having accompanied his crew. The knarr Thorvald borrowed from his brother was the one Leif had bought from Bjarni; the vessel was now making its third trip to North America. Crossing to Newfoundland, the Thorvald Ericsson party wintered in the Leifsbooths Thorvald also borrowed from his brother. Salmon and other fish kept them hale and hearty through the winter. In the spring, several members of the party headed south in a launch. In the summer, Thorvald took the knarr eastward along the coast. A gale forced the ship ashore with a broken keel, which the crew replaced with a new one constructed from local wood. Continuing east, Thorvald and his men explored a series of fjords, then landed on a wooded headland. "Here it is beautiful," Thorvald noted, "and here I should like to build my house."

So far, so good: exploration, followed by a desire for settlement. Returning to their knarr, however, Thorvald and his men happened upon three overturned boats made of animal skins. Beneath each boat, three Eskimos were sleeping. On their expeditions, the Norsemen had never encountered people before, although they had previously come upon a wooden shed for grain storage. Thorvald's crew divided into three sections and crept up on the sleeping Eskimos. With axes—their primary weapon—as well as a broadsword or two, the Norsemen hacked to death eight of the nine men. One Eskimo escaped by kayak.

Why this wanton murder? Were the Norsemen reverting to dormant Viking behavior in response to instinctive fearfulness? How could they so instantly demonize and kill these men, immobilized in the vulnerability of sleep? *Skrælings*, the term of contempt the Norse would soon apply to the native people, suggests the answer: the contempt of the strong for the weak—or, rather, those whom they believed to be weak. Yet it was no flotilla of weaklings who returned in their boats a few hours later and let fly a fusillade of deadly arrows upon, as poetic justice would have it, the Norsemen sleeping on the shore. Fleeing to their ship, the Greenlanders affixed their shields to the gunwales of the knarr in full battle mode and retreated from the shore. Thorvald ordered against a counterattack.

No Norse were wounded in the melee, except Thorvald himself. An arrow that penetrated between the shields on the gunwales struck Thorvald beneath his armpit. The wound was fatal. Before dying, Thorvald told his men, "Now I give you the advice that you prepare to return as soon as possible; but you shall take me to the headland, where I thought it best to settle; it may prove true what I said, that I should stay there a while. There you shall bury me, and place a cross at my head, and another at my feet, and the headland shall be called Crossness ever after."[2]

One of the two sagas to report on Thorvald's death claims that he was murdered by a one-legged man who emerged from the forest and, without provocation, shot Thorvald with the fatal arrow. This fabulous tale—which is unusual for a saga—was obviously intended to mask the Norsemen's murder of the Eskimos that motivated the Eskimo retaliation. Or Thorvald's men might have fabricated the story upon their return in an effort to cover their tracks. Then again, a later generation of Greenlanders might have made up the mythical uniped in an effort to objectify the Eskimo as the Other, worthy of attack, or to portray Vinland as a place fraught with danger. In any event, the insertion of such a creature into the tale represented a significant departure from the minimalist objectivity of saga presentation.

The fourth and fifth voyages

The fourth Vinland expedition ended inconclusively. The fifth witnessed yet another representative event: the first birth of a European child in North America—575 years, as Morison points out, before Virginia Dare was born in the ill-fated English colony Roanoke on the coast of North Carolina.

Returning from his voyage of discovery, Leif Ericsson rescued a foundering ship off Greenland owned by a Norwegian named Thorer, who was sailing in the company of his wife, Gudrid Thorbjarnardóttir. The rescued couple settled in Greenland. When Thorer died, Gudrid married Eric the Red's son Thorstein. When news of his brother Thorvald's death reached Greenland, Thorstein vowed to retrieve Thorvald's body from Vinland for burial at the family home at Brattahlíð. Thorstein sailed in 1007, accompanied by Gudrid. His mission ended in failure, and Thorstein died upon his return.

His widow, however, remained alert to the possibilities of Vinland. Remarried to Thorfinn Karlsefni, a wealthy merchant sea captain from Norway, Gudrid persuaded her husband to mount a trading venture to Vinland. Thorfinn promised his crew of sixty men and five women equal shares in revenue; the voyage would last from 1009 to 1011. Reaching the Leifsbooths, the Karlsefni party feasted on meat and blubber from a whale stranded ashore, pastured their cows and a feisty bull in the meadow, and began lumbering operations in the woodlands, drying their harvested timber on flat rocks. *Skrælings* came by to trade—an improvement over the violence of the Thorvald expedition three years earlier. Although the trading went well, as the skrælings exchanged pelts for dairy products, Karlsefni was suspicious and forbade the sale of weapons to the skrælings. He also had a palisade fence built around the Leifsbooths encampment.

In such generally propitious circumstances, Gudrid bore a son, whom she and her husband named Snorri. This European child, born to one of six Norse women on the expedition, suggested that in time the Norse might gain a foothold in Vinland: men, women, and children, with at least one priest, hence creating a Catholic Christian community in the distinctive Norse manner.

When the skrælings returned for a second trading session, however, one of them tried to seize a Norse weapon and was killed. The skrælings fled but returned in force. A melee ensued, and a number of skrælings fell before an onslaught of Norse axes. Capturing an axe, a skræling leader examined it curiously. Experimentally, he tried out the axe on a nearby Eskimo. The man fell dead. The leader threw the axe into the nearby lake and ordered a retreat.

The Karlsefni party wintered at L'Anse aux Meadows, but the bright prospect of a thriving settlement was replaced by the prospect of ongoing warfare. In the spring, Karlsefni and his crew loaded their knarr with wood, berries, pelts, and vines (to be used in caulking ships) and sailed to Norway via Greenland, where they sold their products at good prices. Karlsefni and Gudrid resettled in Iceland.

A fateful expedition

Gudrid's successor as first lady of Vinland, Freydís Ericsson, illegitimate daughter of Eric the Red, represents a swing of the pendulum—indeed, a swing of the axe—in a different direction. In the behavior of Freydís, Norse Vinland witnessed a stark drama of greed, ambition, and cold-blooded fury worthy of the saga format at its most remorseless. In 1101, the year Karlsefni returned from Vinland, two Icelanders, the brothers Helgi and Finnbogi, wintered in Greenland, where they met Freydís Ericsson.

Among the Norse, concubinage had been commonplace during the pagan era. Given human nature and the need to populate Iceland and Greenland as energetically as possible in the face of a small population and a high rate of child mortality, this form of de facto polygamy lasted well into the Christian era. Besides, Eric the Red spent his life as a pagan and only reluctantly accepted Christianity (if he did at all) at the end of his life. Freydís, then, had a place in Greenland society as the daughter of its founder and was most likely raised in his household or in a household attached to it. She was of the *godar* class, with the same rights, privileges, and mindset that class brought to her three half brothers, Leif, Thorvald, and Thorstein. Freydís was presumably also a Christian, although recently converted and, like her father, a continuing admirer of the old ways.

Freydís and her husband, Thorvard, lived at Garðar in the Eastern Settlement. Thorvard survives in the sagas as the kind of unassertive, malleable husband Freydís might be expected to have, given her rank and personality. In any event, Freydís, whose three half brothers had already been to Vinland, proposed to the brothers Helgi and Finnbogi that she, Thorvard, and they form a partnership and visit Vinland on a logging expedition. The brothers agreed, and the expedition—the sixth and final to be chronicled in a saga—set sail in mid-1012.

Already, however, Freydís was proving troublesome. It had been agreed that each of the two crews was to be limited to thirty men and a few women, but Freydís sneaked five extra crewmen aboard her ship. Arriving at L'Anse aux Meadows, she refused to allow the brothers' party to use the Leifsbooths, forcing them to build a separate house by the lake, farther from the shore. The two parties spent the fall cutting timber and loading logs onto their ships. Then came the long winter, and tensions rose between the crews, who stopped visiting each other's establishments for storytelling and games, as was the Norse custom.

Early one very cold, wet morning Freydís rose from her bed, got dressed as Thor-vard lay sleeping, and in bare feet trudged over to the brothers' shelter, where she stood at the door until Finnbogi, lying awake on the inner side of the room, asked her what she wanted. To talk, Freydís replied. Finnbogi joined Freydís near a tree trunk lying on the ground nearby, and they talked. "How satisfied are you here?" Freydís asked. "I am well satisfied with the country," Finnbogi replied, "but I do not like the ill-feeling that has come between us, for I think there is no reason for it." As for herself, Freydís replied, she wanted to go home. "Let's make a deal", she continued. "Your ship is larger than mine. Let's exchange ships, and I will go back to Greenland." "This I will grant you," Finnbogi replied, "if you will then be satisfied."

With this agreement reached, Freydís retraced her steps and crept back into bed. Her cold feet awoke her husband. Why was she so chilled and wet? Thorvard asked. "I have been to the brothers," Freydís replied angrily, "to buy their ship, for I wished to have a larger ship. Yet they took that so badly that they struck me and handled me very roughly. But you, miserable man, will neither avenge my shame nor your own; I feel now that I am not in Greenland, and I shall part from you unless you avenge this."

Freydís further enraged her husband by suggesting that the brothers' mistreat-ment of her involved an element of sexual aggression. Succumbing to these taunts, Thorvard led his men to the shelter by the lake. Entering the hall and rooms of the sleeping people, Thorvard had them seized and bound and presented to Frey-dís, who stood outside. Freydís demanded that the two brothers and a number of other men be killed, which they were, bound and with no opportunity to defend themselves.

That left five women, bound and standing before the corpses of their menfolk, with whom they had just been sleeping under warm protection of fur coverlets. Freydís ordered the men to kill them. The men refused. There had been enough killing, and these were Norse women, capable of bearing children, protected by the Norse custom and the new religion alike. "Hand me an axe," Freydís demanded. One of the men did so. Freydís proceeded to hack to death the five females.

To this day it remains a horror to contemplate: the cries of fear and disbelief as Freydís proceeded from one woman to the next, chopping them to the ground in cold-blooded fury, iron thudding against flesh and bone, the agonized twitching of those not yet dead, the glassy stares of those who were, blood spattered on the snow. Was this what Vinland had come to, this butchering? Freydís Ericsson engi-neered the massacre for material gain. The sexual dimension of her charges was ambiguous. Why was she barefooted on such a cold, wet morning? Was she solic-iting Finnbogi? Their conversation beside the tree trunk seems amicable enough, but did a conversation of another sort go wrong? Was Freydís a woman scorned, taking horrible revenge? Writers of the saga could tell only so much, dependent as they were on memory and received report. Perhaps it was (and remains) more complimentary to remember Freydís as a mercantile Lady Macbeth, as brutal as any of her Viking ancestors when riches were concerned. In any event, she is depicted as showing no remorse after the slaughter. "If it be ordained for us to come again to Greenland," she told her men, "I shall contrive the death of any man who speaks of this event; we shall say that they remained living here when we went away." Vinland now had a Norse settlement of sorts, founded in shame and sin.

In the spring of 1013, Freydís and Thorvard returned in their two ships manned by intimidated crews, whom Freydís liberally rewarded upon homecoming to ensure their continuing silence. When rumors of the killings reached Leif Ericsson, he had three men of Freydís' crew tortured and learned the entire story. "I have no heart," Leif stated, "to treat my sister Freydís as she deserves, but this I will predict of them, that there is little prosperity in store for their offspring."[3]

Garðar

For more than 250 years, Garðar stood at the center of Catholic Greenland, outpost of Catholic Europe. *Ubi episcopus ibi ecclesia* (Where the bishop is, there is the church), went a time-tested adage, and Greenland had its bishop, and in Norway its archbishop, and in Rome its pope. Had prosperity continued, trade among Norway, Iceland, and Greenland would have increased, as would have logging expeditions to North America. Given Greenland's environmental limitations—with the eastern shore too chilled by the Arctic Current to make settlement possible, and only two other places habitable—the population would have soon reached its limits, and a new era of *landnám* (land-taking) might have ensured migration to the west, to Vinland the Good. The mix of Norse, Celtic, and Germanic peoples might have been augmented from those of greater Scandinavia, the British Isles, and mainland Europe. New bishops would have been sent forth, and new Garðars founded.

Yet this was not to be. In the mid-fourteenth century, bubonic plague struck Norway along with the rest of Scandinavia and western Europe. The population of Norway dropped from two million to three hundred thousand, and social and economic institutions fell into steep decline. Far from peopling the North Atlantic, Norway required more than a century to rebuild its own population. The papacy, meanwhile, stood divided into two factions, headquartered in Rome and Avignon, and Garðar increasingly became a forgotten place during this time of plague and schism, a remote see on the fringe of the known world. Bishops assigned there delayed their arrivals or did not arrive at all, tarrying in more pleasant places, or they held the Greenland see on a titular basis, as if it were a diocese *in partibus infidelium*—in the lands of unbelievers.

And so the Catholic people of Greenland had no bishop on hand, and fewer and fewer priests. Still, de-Christianizing took time. As late as 1408, when maritime trade with Greenland was infrequent, visiting traders described a wedding in the parish church of Hvalsey on Cross Mass Sunday, 16 September. Everything—banns, the consent of parents, the nuptial Mass itself—was carried on in proper order, the traders chronicled. There was in 1411 one more documented connection with Greenland from Scandinavia, followed by eighty years of silence, according to one interpretation, or, according to another, interrupted only by a letter from Pope Nicholas V in 1448 to a Norwegian bishop asking for help for the Christians of Greenland; Greenlanders, the pope lamented, had been without a bishop for thirty years and had been devastated by raids from heathens—by which the pope meant Eskimos—who destroyed their churches and took many of them into bondage. Later in the century, in 1492, the Vatican noted that it had not heard from Greenland in eighty years. The pope that momentous year was Rodrigo Borgia, reigning as Alexander VI, on the verge of apportioning between Spain and Portugal the newly discovered lands to the west. The curia, the pope noted, had informed him that the people of Greenland had lost the Catholic faith.

The curia was correct. Catholic Greenland was no more. A combination of factors ended Greenland as a Christian Norse settlement. Trade declined, then disappeared. The weather grew colder, transforming what little arable land and available pasturage there was into resistant permafrost. Marginal at best, standards of nutrition sank even lower, and life in Greenland became even more brutal, nasty, and short. Incoming waves of migrating Eskimos raided the sparse settlements, as Pope Nicholas V had indicated, but English marauders came as well: payback time, perhaps, for the Viking raids on England centuries earlier.

At the same time, a process of going native was under way. Whereas the skrælings could be foes, they could sometimes be allies as well, especially when Norse hunters ventured farther and farther north into Eskimo territory in an increasingly desperate effort to feed their families and began to acquire Eskimo hunting skills. The skrælings, after all, had long since learned to survive in the harsh Arctic environment, and now the Norsemen must also learn to do so. No records were kept of this process of assimilation, which lasted for more than a century, but it proceeded apace among the dwindling number of Norse survivors. A cache of clothing recovered from Eastern Settlement graves by archaeologists shows that Greenlanders wove cloth and cut their clothes in Scandinavian style into the late fourteenth century. By the mid-fifteenth century, however, they were dressing in furs, Eskimo-style, and spending increasing amounts of time away from the land that no longer supported them. Indeed, an observer surveying the Norse settlements from offshore in this late era marveled at the emptiness of the farmsteads, although he could still see cattle grazing in some places. Norse men and Eskimo women began to cohabit. With Garðar abandoned and Greenland priestless, Catholic Christianity went into eclipse, along with its prohibitions against intermarriage with heathens. Surviving Norse and half-Norse women took Eskimo or half-Eskimo men as mates, and genetic assimilation ran its course. At some point in the late fifteenth century, the last of the residually Norse Greenlanders packed their meager belongings into makeshift backpacks and headed north to join their skræling relatives. Brattahlíð stood empty on its treeless meadow, and the snowcapped Mountain of Igdlerfigsalik kept watch over an abandoned cathedral at Garðar.

PART ONE

Las Floridas

I

Santo Domingo 1511

Resistance grows against the genocide and the enslavement of indigenous peoples

On 30 November and 2 December 1511 in Santo Domingo, capital city of the recently settled Caribbean island of Española and administrative center of the Spanish Empire in the Indies until 1526, the Dominican friar Antonio de Montesinos preached against Spaniards' genocide of the indigenous peoples. Although he had been in the Indies little more than a year, Fray Montesinos—a member of the first band of Friars Preachers to arrive in the New World—had much to talk about; the conquests of Española, Puerto Rico, and Jamaica, as well as the current subjugation of Cuba, had decimated the Arawak, Taíno, Lucayo, Carib, and other Caribbean peoples and enslaved the survivors. Montesinos took as his text John 1:23, which echoed Isaiah: "I am the voice of one crying in the wilderness." Preaching to a congregation that by deliberate invitation included Diego Columbus, viceroy and admiral of the Indies, colony treasurer Miguel de Pasamonte, and other officials, the friar (trained in the famed Dominican convent of San Esteban in Salamanca) courageously condemned the treatment of local peoples as a crime, a mortal sin, worthy of sentencing to hell.

Montesinos' sermon caused an uproar. An angry deputation of colony officials called on the Dominican prior, Fray Pedro de Córdoba, and demanded a retraction. Córdoba replied that the entire Dominican community stood behind the sermon. Unless Montesinos retracted his charges the following Sunday, the deputation protested, the friars would be sent packing back to Spain. With the support of his brethren, Montesinos preached an even more condemnatory sermon, this time taking Job 36:4 as his text: "For truly my words are not false; one who is perfect in knowledge is with you." Montesinos went so far as to dare his detractors to return him to Spain, where he would defend his case. In the weeks that followed, the Dominicans were castigated, severed from support to the point of going hungry, and threatened with violence. In two outspoken sermons, Montesinos had cut to the cruel and contradictory core of Spanish colonization.

In seeking to explain the paradoxical behavior of Spaniards in the New World—professing a desire to evangelize the very peoples they were destroying—historians have referenced a Spanish Catholic mindset born of more than seven hundred years of crusade against Islam for control of the Iberian Peninsula, during which the Catholic cause was aggressively militarized. As they advanced their seaborne empire into the Indies, runs this narrative, Spaniards brought with them their crusading habits, especially when (as in the case of the Caribs) Spanish incursions met with an equally warlike response. Fray Montesinos and his fellow Dominicans in Española saw things differently. Indians were fully human, they believed, and possessed the universal attributes of human nature—reason, primarily, as well as souls redeemed by Christ on the cross—and thus were not to be slaughtered, enslaved, or forcibly converted. Rather, they were owed fair-minded and peaceful treatment.

For the majority of Spaniards, the Indies represented more than a chance to extend Spanish Catholic culture and civilization into new regions. The isles also constituted a highly regulated franchise that provided an opportunity for the Crown, the ambitious, and the upwardly mobile to get rich, acquire titles, and stake out a better life while paying lip service to related evangelical ambitions. If indigenous peoples got in the way, as frequently happened, they were to be eliminated. Or, if they survived, they were to be enslaved and put to work as miners of gold and silver, pearl divers, laborers, personal servants, or concubines. Not every Spaniard felt this way, as the record of resistance to this attitude would soon show, but it was built into the system of *encomienda*—repayment in land and the Indian labor on that land to pioneering settlers. Under this system, Indian tribute and labor was granted to individuals in exchange for past, present, or expected service to the Crown. Indians were by definition serfs attached to land, semislaves at best, but more frequently slaves to be used at will, which in the early years of the empire meant slaves to be worked to death. From Indian labor was derived a pyramid of tithes paid from individual to local official to the Council of the Indies and the Crown, part of an intricate, closely monitored system of licenses and contracts supervised by the Casa de Contratación, a centralized board of trade in Seville. Serving as the base of this system's pyramid of payment—its fundamental economic premise—was enforced Indian labor. Without such labor, indeed, there would be no wealth in the Indies. There would not even be food on the table. Spaniards' physical efforts played no part in the economic formula. The Indies were inextricably dependent on the indigenous peoples forced to do the work.

The Laws of Burgos

Any attribution of fundamental humanity to Indians as put forth by Fray Montesinos in his two sermons stood as a braking mechanism to the theory and practice of encomienda. For those enforcing and benefiting from the system, if brute labor was necessary to make the Indies profitable, then it was easier if Indians were considered brutes. Indian resistance and rebellion compounded this tendency to dehumanize, especially when such self-defense was temporarily successful or involved cruelties by Indians against Spaniards. To the credit of Fray Montesinos and his Dominican colleagues led by Prior Córdoba, they argued against this notion—that the Indian lacked humanity—at the highest levels of the empire and won a victory that, no matter how pyrrhic in the short run, set the stage for second, third, and fourth efforts at reform.

As threatened, Fray Montesinos was summoned to Spain in 1512 by the Council of the Indies to explain himself to the council, the Dominican provincial, Fray Alfonso de Loaysa, and King Ferdinand. The colonists sent a Franciscan, Fray Alonso del Espinal, to represent their position. Meanwhile (so the Casa de Contratación later claimed), the king complained to the Dominican provincial that his friars in Santo Domingo seemed to be launching an attack against Spain's right to be in the Indies. Provincial Loaysa accordingly sent a letter of reproof to Prior Córdoba in Española.

All this would seem to prejudge Fray Montesinos' case as he and the Franciscan Espinal argued before King Ferdinand. Yet the king was so shocked by what Montesinos told him that he convened a special *junta* (council of advisors) of jurists and theologians to review the situation. Irrepressible and unintimidated, Montesinos testified so effectively before the junta that he recruited his opponent Espinal to his side of the argument and won from the junta a seven-point declaration.

1. The Indians are free.
2. They should be instructed in the faith with all possible diligence.
3. The Indians can be obliged to work, but in such manner as not to impede their religious instruction and to be useful to themselves, the republic, and the king; and this is by reason of the king's lordship and the service due him to maintain them in the faith and in justice.
4. This labor should be such as they can stand, with time to rest every day and all through the year at convenient times.
5. They should have houses and property of their own, such as seem fit to those who govern them now and henceforward, and they should be allowed time to farm and keep their property in their own manner.
6. It should be provided for them always to have contact with the settlers, so that they may be better and more rapidly instructed in the holy faith.
7. They should be given suitable wages, not in money but in clothing and other things for their houses.[1]

So ran the conclusions of the junta. They were benevolent, to be sure, but they said nothing about the system of encomienda. Inserting himself more directly into the proceedings, a Dominican member of the junta, Fray Matías de Paz, in fifteen days wrote a Latin treatise attacking the premise of encomienda, involuntary servitude. The Indians were a free people, Paz argued, and should be governed as such. Encomienda constituted a form of theft, and Spaniards owed the Indians full restitution for what had been taken from them.

This contention was taking matters too far, and the junta reacted. After all, council members included Juan Rodríguez de Fonseca, chaplain and advisor of the late Queen Isabella, bishop of Burgos (where the junta was sitting), royal minister for the Indies, and a wealthy *encomendero* (holder of an encomienda); his arch foe, Bartolomé de Las Casas, would later claim that Fonseca owned an estimated twenty-six hundred Indians on lands in Española, Cuba, Puerto Rico, and Jamaica. Another member of the junta, the Dominican Bernardo de Mesa, did not see eye to eye with Montesinos or his confreres in Santo Domingo. While he agreed that humane treatment was called for, Mesa claimed the Indians required supervision. "The Indians", he opined in a draft for the Laws of Burgos, "are not slaves by war, purchase, or birth. The only reason for [their] servitude is a natural lack of understanding and capacity and perseverance in the faith and good customs, and perchance the nature of the country (there are some lands which the aspect of the heavens makes servile). They cannot be called slaves, but for their own sake must be ruled in some sort of servitude." Nor, Mesa continued, could the Indians in any way be considered free.

Map 4. *Occidentalis Americae partis* ... (Johann Feyerabend and Theodor de Bry, Fran

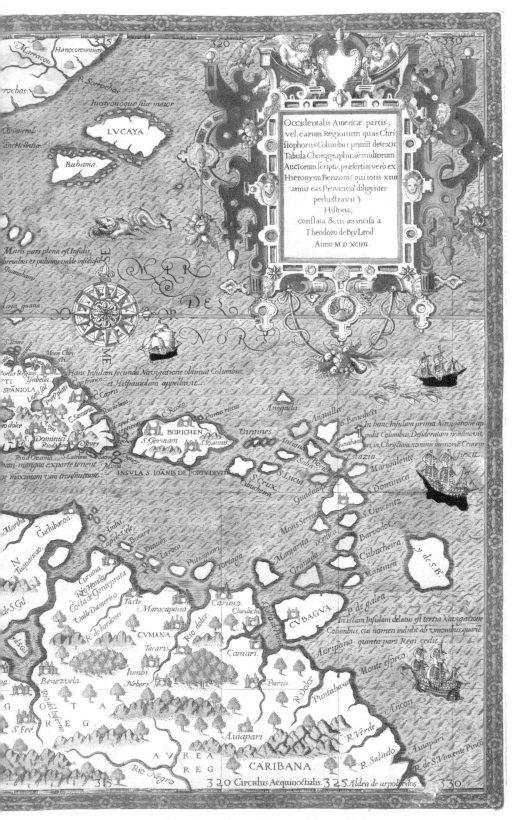

They were, rather, "given to the king for their own good, and idleness is their worst possible vice (and all others flow from it). So the king should with great care order them occupied in spiritual and corporal exercises, and to this end he may apportion them among the faithful of good conscience and customs."[2]

Promulgated on 27 December 1512, the Laws of Burgos, however compromised and incomplete, constituted a beginning for a reform movement and a victory of sorts for the Santo Domingo Dominicans leading the crusade for better behavior toward native peoples. The laws could very well have made a difference, had they been enforced and not run into the attitude of *obedecer y no cumplir* (obedience without execution) so endemic in the administration of the Indies. Having acquitted himself well in Burgos, Montesinos returned to the Indies and resumed a missionary vocation that most likely ended in his martyrdom at a later date. Soon the courageous friar would help recruit to the reform movement its iconic leader, spokesman, priest, bishop, and historian.

Bartolomé de Las Casas

In October 1498 the father of Bartolomé de Las Casas, Pedro, returned from Santo Domingo on one of five ships loaded with three hundred Indian slaves. In Santo Domingo, before the ships sailed, no one less than Christopher Columbus himself, Admiral of the Ocean Sea, had presented Pedro with an Indian boy as his slave and personal servant. Pedro, a returning veteran of Columbus' second voyage, in turn presented the boy to his twenty-four-year-old son as a companion and attendant. Bartolomé had come of age in a Seville family of remote *converso* (Jewish) and immediate Old Christian (all four grandparents) lineage involved in trade and, in the case of Pedro and his three brothers, an effort to improve their fortunes in the Indies. Bartolomé had been educated in Latin and liturgical music in the cathedral school, the Colegio de San Miguel, and the cathedral itself, under the charge of a relative on his mother's side, Luis Peñalosa, a prebendary canon, and his mother's brother Francisco de Peñalosa, an eminent musician and choirmaster by royal appointment. Such an education normally led to ordination to the diocesan priesthood, and perhaps a career in the cathedral itself.

Though not resistant to ordination as a secular priest, Bartolomé demonstrated other ambitions and capacities. As a member of the Seville militia, he took part in a brief campaign against a Morisco uprising in Granada in 1497. For the rest of his life, he would remember the luxuriant plain of Carmona through which the militia marched and his first breathtaking view of sunlit Granada. The Indies had also cast their spell on the young man: the Indians Columbus brought with him when he returned to Seville on 31 March 1493; the exotic green and red parrots; the golden and bejeweled masks and belts displayed by the Discoverer; the latex ball the Indians used in their games. A mere four months later came the departure of the second expedition, on which sailed his father and his late mother's three brothers. Nor were the Indies incompatible with the secular diocesan priesthood, for he could go there as a *doctrinero*, a priest supported by the Crown to run an Indian pueblo while permitted to engage in enterprises intended to advance his personal fortunes.

Furthering Bartolomé's interest in the Indies was this lively and bright Indian boy, his slave but a companion as well. For a year or more he remained in Bartolomé's care, until a royal *cédula* (administrative order) from Queen Isabella in June 1500 ordered the boy to be repatriated to the Indies along with twenty other slaves in an expedition under the supervision of royal commissioner and governor Francisco de Bobadilla, sent by the sovereigns Ferdinand and Isabella to investigate a rising tide of complaints against the administration of Española by Christopher Columbus and his brothers Bartholomew and Diego. A knight of the Order of Calatrava, a no-nonsense monk-warrior formed by the final campaigns of the Reconquest, Bobadilla would soon go down in history as the man who sent Christopher Columbus home in chains. In the interim, however, he was concerned with returning slaves to Española, given Queen Isabella's dislike of the slave trade.

Departure for the Indies

One year later, Bartolomé de Las Casas sailed for the Indies alongside his father as a member of an expedition under the command of yet another religious order knight, Fray Nicolás de Ovando, *comendador* (knight commander) of the Order of Alcántara, who replaced Bobadilla as governor and further Hispanicized Santo Domingo through an ambitious program of public construction. While he received tonsure and minor orders before his departure, Las Casas was not yet concerned with a clerical career. By his own account, after landing on Española in April 1502, he spent his first months on campaign against rebellious Indians in the Higuey region on the eastern end of the island, which culminated in a massacre at Xaragua ordered by Fray Ovando. Las Casas received an Indian slave, his second, for his services. Forty years later, in 1542, writing his *Brevísima relación de la destrucción de las Indias* (*Very Brief Account of the Destruction of the Indies*), published in Seville in 1552 (and thereafter reprinted in Flemish [1578], French [1579], English [1583], German [1597], Latin [1598], and Italian [1626]), he drew upon his memories to describe the massacre.

The suppression of Indians on Española offered Fray Ovando a reprise of the centuries-long epic of fierce fighting and seizure of castles, towns, and property that had been the Reconquest of the Iberian Peninsula in which Cistercian military orders such as Calatrava and Alcántara had played such a vigorous part. The saga of the Reconquest had come to an end with the fall of Granada in 1492, followed by the expulsion of Muslims and Jews from Spain, or their forced conversion. The Reconquest accomplished, Calatrava, Alcántara, and such other military orders as Aviz, Montessa, and the Order of Christ were entering the twilight of their existence as monastic organizations. In 1540, for example, the Holy See would release Calatrava from the requirement of celibacy and the common life. On crusade in Española, however, Fray Ovando envisioned one last campaign on behalf of Hispanicization and Reconquest, one last province to be wrested from the Moors—an island kingdom to be ruled by religious knights, more Spanish perhaps than Spain itself, as symbolized in the public buildings and governor's palace he had constructed in stone at Santo Domingo.

The indigenous peoples of Española divided the island into five kingdoms, Las Casas tells us in his *Brevísima relación*, which he arranged in numbered paragraphs. In paragraphs 11 through 14 of the chapter on Española, Las Casas relates what he saw, remembered, or later learned of what went on in the Indian kingdom of Xaragua.

The fourth Kingdom is that which is called Xaragua. This was as the marrow, or the Court of all this island. It surpassed all the other kingdoms in the politeness of its more ornate speech as well as in generosity of the nobles. For there were lords and nobles in great numbers. In their costumes and beauty, the people were superior to all others. The king and lord of it was called Behechio and he had a sister called Anacaona. Both rendered great services to the King of Castile, and immense kindnesses to the King of Castile, and immense kindnesses to the Christians, delivering them from many mortal dangers: and when the King Behechio died, Anacaona was left mistress of the kingdom. The governor who ruled this island [Fray Ovando] arrived there once, with sixty horsemen and more than three hundred foot. The horsemen alone were sufficient to ruin the whole island and the *terra firma*. More than three hundred Indian lords were assembled, whom he had summoned and reassured. He lured the principal ones by fraud, into a straw house, and setting fire to it, he burnt them alive. All the others, together with numberless people, were put to the sword, and lance. And to do honor to the Lady Anacaona, they hanged her. It happened that some Christians, either out of compassion or avarice, took some children to save them, placing them behind them on their horses, and another Spaniard approached from behind or ran his lance through them. Another, if a child was on the ground, cut off its legs with his sword. Some, who could flee from this inhuman cruelty, crossed to a little island lying eight leagues distant in the sea; and the said governor condemned all such to be slaves, because they had fled from the carnage.[3]

Having witnessed the massacre at Xaragua—a replay of earlier slaughters on Española and, before that, in Spain during the Reconquest—Las Casas returned to gold mining, agriculture, and related activities. That, at least, is according to the record. He must have suppressed or put aside as best he could the horror of what he observed as, with the assistance of his Indian slaves, he got down to the business of bettering his own prospects and helping his financially strapped family regain its economic footing. Still, as he would later document in his *Memorial de los abusos* (most likely prepared in 1515 when he returned to Spain as a reformer), he remained disturbed by conditions in the mines in his first years on Española: Taíno slaves being worked to death at an appalling rate, and no one—certainly not any royal officials— seeming to care about the fate of these gracious, gentle, intelligent people.

Doctrinero and encomendero

At some point during this time, a desire for priestly ordination returned. Las Casas had been oriented toward the Church since his education at the cathedral school of Seville. Most secular diocesan clergy did not possess his proficiency in Latin, which he could read and write fluently, or his skills in liturgical music, reading, and singing. To what purpose had he received the tonsure before his departure for the Indies if he did not foresee a clerical career?

He was in Rome as of January 1507, which suggests a passage to and through Spain. With the appointment of his father and uncles' friend and patron Diego Columbus—brother of the Discoverer, who died at Valladolid on 20 May 1506— as viceroy and admiral of the Indies, he might have returned to Spain for personal reasons, perhaps to present himself to the admiral and his wife, María de Toledo, niece of the Duke of Alba, before their departure for Santo Domingo. Historian Manuel Giménez Fernández speculates that Las Casas was in Rome on ecclesiastical business, namely, the establishment of the Española diocese decreed by the bull *Illius Fulciti* in November 1504, later rectified in August 1511 by the bull *Romanus Pontifex*. Fernández also argues that Las Casas was ordained to the priesthood while in Rome, based on Las Casas' assertion in 1534 that he had been confessing and preaching for the past twenty-eight years, which would date his ordination to sometime in late 1506.

And yet Las Casas did not celebrate his inaugural Mass—in the city of La Vega, the first such Mass in Española history—until 1512. Fernández explains the late date as a delay between Las Casas' ordination in Rome and the establishment of the Diocese of Santo Domingo in 1511, from which Las Casas received his faculties or permission to practice as a priest. Hence his first Mass was well remembered. Admiral Columbus himself attended, and after Mass a crowd of settlers showered Las Casas with silver *reales* and gold ducats. His ordination, however, remains undocumented.[4]

If such is the case, Las Casas put his priesthood on hold from 1506 or 1507 until his first Mass in 1512, then kept it on semihold for two more years as he devoted himself to gold mining, agriculture, stock raising, and related enterprises on the *repartimiento* (land grant) and Indians he now owned, thanks to Diego Columbus. He was also at some point named doctrinero to the Indian community governed by the cacique Manicaotex, who was attached to the viceregal court of La Concepción in the Vega Real district.

In 1513 Las Casas served in Cuba as chaplain and copacifier to the forces under Pánfilo de Narváez who were subduing the island. His duties were to negotiate and seek peaceful settlements with the Indians, but after the cruel and treacherous execution of the cacique Hatuey, who had already fled from Española with his people, and the gratuitous massacre of Indians at the pueblo of Caonao, he quit the expedition in disgust.

As with the massacre at Xaragua on Española, Las Casas presents in his *Brevísima relación* an eyewitness account of Hatuey's death by burning. "When he was tied to the stake," Las Casas writes, "a Franciscan monk, a holy man, who was there, spoke as much as he could to him, in the little time that the executioner granted them, about God and some of the teachings of our faith, of which he had never before heard; he told him that if he would believe what was told him, he would go to heaven where there was glory and eternal rest; and, if not, that he would go to hell, to suffer perpetual torments and punishment. After thinking a little, Hatuey asked the monk whether the Christians went to heaven; the monk answered that those who were good went there. The prince at once said, without any more thought, that he did not wish to go there, but rather to hell so as not to be where Spaniards were, nor to see such cruel people."[5]

Las Casas' account of the massacre at Caonao is equally representative and horrific. The Indians of the pueblo, Las Casas relates, came out to greet Narváez's party as it approached, bearing fish, bread, other provisions, and gifts. "All of a sudden the devil entered into the bodies of the Christians, and in my presence they put to the sword, without any motive or cause whatsoever, more than three thousand persons, men, women, and children, who were seated before us. Here I beheld such great cruelty as living man has never seen nor thought to see."[6]

But even this horror did not engender in Las Casas a change of mind and heart. Leaving the Narváez expedition, the *Clérigo* (cleric), as he would later call himself, accepted a large repartimiento on the banks of the Arimao River near the port of Xagua, Cuba, and devoted himself—again with the labor of enslaved Indians—to agriculture, mining, and cattle raising, exporting his products via caravel to Española, Puerto Rico, and Jamaica.

What was this lust for wealth that made this ordained priest put aside all the horror he had witnessed during the years of encomienda? Nothing less, one suspects, than the driving force behind the entire Spanish conquest of the New World: a fear born of poverty in the unyielding west-central provinces of the Iberian Peninsula— the treeless and austere region that Spaniards called a Land of Boulders and Saints— from which so many conquistadors and settlers came. In such places, there was never enough. Even hidalgos feared the wolf at the door. Poverty, hunger, and dire circumstances in part motivated the aggressive militarism of the Reconquest and the devastation of the Indies. The Spanish Empire in the Old and New Worlds required wealth to run. From court to countryside, everything that was needed was in short supply.

Las Casas—the talented son of a family recovering lost status and gaining even higher rank—felt this hunger as much as he felt the values and imperatives of the Spanish Catholicism that were fundamental to his identity. He had not heard Montesinos' two sermons of late 1511, but in Española Montesinos' equally militant prior, Pedro de Córdoba, had at one point denied the Clérigo absolution following confession on the grounds that Las Casas was neglecting his obligations to instruct the Indians under his supervision as a doctrinero in favor of devoting his time to getting rich. The priest's refusing him absolution must have stung deeply, and at some point after this rejection he began to read, study, and meditate on the book of Ecclesiasticus, chapter 34 in particular. Written around 180 B.C. by Jesus, the son of Sirach, a professional teacher of Jewish law in Jerusalem, and later translated into Greek, Ecclesiasticus (also known as the book of Sirach) is both one of the last examples of Hebrew wisdom literature and one of the early prototypes of a new style of Jewish teaching that led to the emergence of the rabbinical schools of Pharisees and Sadducees. In chapter 34, verses 1 through 12 inveigh against false dreams and hopes and the deceptions thereof. Verses 13 through 17 urge abandoning such deceptive ambitions and turning to the Lord for the strength to resist their blandishments. Verses 18 through 26 conclude the chapter with a theologized economic argument against the hypocrisy of those who seek to worship God while oppressing others.

Verses 18 through 22 must have proven especially challenging to the worldly Clérigo.

> If one sacrifices from what has been wrongfully obtained, the offering
>   is blemished;
>   the gifts of the lawless are not acceptable.
> The Most High is not pleased with the offerings of the ungodly;
>   and he is not propitiated for sins by a multitude of sacrifices.
> Like one who kills a son before his father's eyes
>   is the man who offers a sacrifice from the property of the poor.
> The bread of the needy is the life of the poor;
>   whoever deprives them of it is a man of blood.
> To take away a neighbor's living is to murder him;
>   to deprive an employee of his wages is to shed blood.[7]

By June 1514 Bartolomé de Las Casas, priest of the Diocese of Santo Domingo, had experienced his road to Damascus. He would renounce his encomienda, he proclaimed in a sermon that month, and devote himself to priestly duties.

The Clérigo had even more ambitious plans. He would struggle to end the enslavement and genocide of Indians. Wisely, he kept his counsel as he sold his assets (including the Indians and their labor attached to the lands he owned), claiming that the proceeds would support three years of study in Paris, and he did not leave before he secured a letter from the governor of Cuba, Don Diego Velásquez, testifying to his good services. Returning to Santo Domingo, he told the Dominican prior, Pedro de Córdoba, his real plans, a presentation to King Ferdinand himself, and Córdoba promised to write to the archbishop of Seville, the Dominican Fray Diego de Deza, to request his assistance in getting Las Casas presented at court.

Clérigo on crusade

For eight years, Bartolomé de Las Casas fought as a secular priest to halt encomienda and the killing of Indians. His key support in this effort were the Friars Preachers of Santo Domingo and Seville. The Dominicans of Santo Domingo had begun the campaign against genocide and slavery, had quickened his conscience by refusing him confession, had harbored and counseled him for his mission to Spain, and had supplemented his eyewitness accounts with their own arguments regarding the "destruction of the Indies," a slogan Las Casas quickly appropriated and made famous. As of 1515, on Española alone, argued the Dominicans of Santo Domingo, the native population had been reduced from one million to less than eighteen thousand in two decades. Las Casas later raised the former figure to more than three million. Recent scholarship has tended to favor higher numbers—up to as many as six million for the entire Caribbean at the time of Discovery—and vastly lower numbers by the end of the first thirty years of Spanish occupation, after disease, warfare, massacre, malnutrition, and slavery had done their work. The thoughts of the colonists then began to turn to Africa as a new and populous source of slaves. The Dominican who in one sense started the resistance movement, Antonio de Montesinos, was sent along with Las Casas when he sailed for Spain in September 1515, commissioned by Prior Córdoba to act as a backup for Las Casas as well as to solicit funds for the Santo Domingo priory. In relatively short order the Dominican archbishop of Seville, Diego de Deza, secured for Las Casas an audience with the king two days before Christmas at Placentia, where the king was staying.

How astonishing this first audience seems in retrospect, so quickly arranged between the monarch and the as-of-yet-obscure Clérigo from the Indies, who had such a startling story to tell Ferdinand (whose late wife, Queen Isabella, horrified by a similar tale, had ordered the repatriation of surviving slaves, including Las Casas' young attendant, to their homeland). Las Casas' ability to present his case convincingly to the king suggests the Clérigo's sincerity, preparation, verbal skills, and personal magnetism; the king responded positively to the disturbing presentation and promised Las Casas another audience before Easter, after the Clérigo had taken the matter up with the Council of the Indies in Seville. Mortally ill at the time of the meeting (he died a month later), Ferdinand was perturbed by Las Casas' bold suggestion that the king's spiritual well-being was at stake in the matter of how the Indians under his jurisdiction were being treated. Still, the question would first have to be considered by the Council of the Indies as a matter of governance and protocol.

Appearing before the council, Las Casas received an entirely different reception as he sought to win the council's president over to his position by focusing on one particular atrocity, the deaths of some seven thousand Indian children within a period of three months. "Look what an ignorant fool you are!" exclaimed Juan Rodríguez de Fonseca, bishop of Burgos and president of the council. "What is this to me or to the king?" Shocked by such indifference from a bishop of the Church, the leading minister for the Indies, Las Casas shouted in reply: "That all these souls should perish is nothing to you and nothing to the king! O Eternal God! Then to whom is it anything?" Turning in anger, Las Casas left. The Clérigo had bearded the very Lion of the Indies in his den. Fonseca would have been his enemy in any event. Now the bishop-president would devote his every effort to counter this meddlesome priest.[8]

Far from withdrawing after the disastrous confrontation with Fonseca and the death of the king on 23 January 1516, Las Casas took his case directly to the leading churchman of the kingdom, Francisco Ximénez de Cisneros, cardinal archbishop of Toledo, inquisitor general, governor of Castile, and, until the arrival of the new young king from Flanders, regent of Spain. Like Las Casas, Ximénez had begun his career as an ambitious, worldly secular priest but, nearing fifty, had resigned as vicar general of the Diocese of Sigüenza to enter the rigorously ascetical Observantine Franciscans. In the fateful year 1492, Queen Isabella I of Castile chose Ximénez as her confessor upon the recommendation of Cardinal Pedro González de Mendoza, archbishop of Toledo. This privileged pastoral appointment returned the austere Observantine Franciscan to the active life as, successively, vicar provincial of the Observantines in Castile and archbishop of Toledo following Mendoza's death in 1495. As archbishop, Ximénez plunged into the center of Spanish politics, ecclesiastical and civil (if such a distinction can be made in Spanish Catholic society). On the ecclesiastical front, he reformed his diocese and a number of religious orders, saved the ancient Mozarabic Rite from extinction, and had the Moors of Granada forcibly baptized and their Korans burned. Less controversially, he commissioned the Complutensian Polyglot Bible (six volumes in folio; Hebrew, Latin, Greek, and Aramaic in parallel columns) and founded the University of Alcalá and the Major College of San Ildefonso as well as numerous homes for the orphaned young, the poor, and the aged.

Following the death of Queen Isabella in 1504, Ximénez became increasingly involved in political and military affairs. After he served as mediator in the dispute regarding succession to the throne of Castile, he was created cardinal and inquisitor general in 1507. As an ardent agriculturalist, Ximénez lightened farmers' tax loads and worked to improve drainage, irrigation, and land use. As a military strategist, he donned armor and directed the defense of Navarre against French attack and prosecuted the war in North Africa. In the midst of it all—the power, the glory, the achievement—Ximénez continued to live as much as possible as an Observantine Franciscan in his private life.

Unfortunately, Ximénez was turning eighty when named regent and would die in November 1517 after a brief regency of twenty-two months. Who knows what Las Casas—in many ways a reflection of the great cardinal at a similar time of life—might have achieved had he enlisted the great and vigorous churchman's energies when he was younger. As it was, Las Casas won the confidence of both Ximénez and his coregent and successor, Adriaan Florensz Dedal, a Fleming by birth, who had been chancellor and twice *rector magnificus* of the University of Louvain and was the personal tutor and trusted confidant of Charles, future king and emperor. Created cardinal archbishop of Utrecht in June 1517, Dedal was brought to Spain as viceroy and bishop of Tortosa. Las Casas managed to impress Dedal despite the language barrier (Dedal was desperately trying to learn Spanish). Like Ximénez—whom he admired, befriended, and willingly took second place to while Ximénez lived—Dedal was a learned academic and a reformer of blameless life, formed in his youth by the Brothers of the Common Life, a Dutch reform movement that included the renowned spiritual writer Thomas à Kempis. In 1521, following the death of Leo X, a pleasure-loving de' Medici ("God has given us the papacy, let us enjoy it"), the cardinals would assemble in conclave in Rome and, feeling the weight of the Lutheran revolt, would elect Dedal in absentia. As Adrian VI, the last non-Italian pope before John Paul II, the reform-minded Dutchman would wear himself out in a futile twenty-month effort to reform Rome and launch a Counter-Reformation.

Speaking, then, to the reform instincts of two powerful cardinal-regents, Las Casas argued for the economic and spiritual reform of the Indies. At one point, appalled at what the Clérigo was claiming, Dedal personally called upon his fellow regent. Could such things be possible? he asked. Yes, Ximénez answered. His fellow Franciscans had corroborated everything Las Casas was saying.

As a result of these negotiations, Ximénez and Dedal came to a decision. They would send a delegation of Hieronymite commissioners to the Indies to investigate. Organized in 1374 at the royal court of Castile by the royal chamberlain Pedro Fernández Pecha, the Hermits of Saint Jerome developed as a network of Spanish monastic communities following the rule of Saint Augustine, which called for a blend of active and contemplative engagements. Created by the Crown, the Hieronymites never lost their political connections in either Spain or Portugal; throughout the fifteenth and sixteenth centuries, they constituted the order of choice for key assignments as confessors, royal advisors, and monastic communities for such royal centers as the Monastery of Belém in Lisbon, the Monastery Yuste in the province of Guadalajara (to which Emperor Charles V would eventually retire), and the Monastery of San Lorenzo del Escorial outside Madrid, from which Charles V's son Philip II would govern the Spanish Empire. In commissioning Hieronymites to look into the treatment of Indians in the Indies, the coregents were calling upon the highest and most respected resources of the Crown, as Ximénez emphasized in a commissioning ceremony at the Monastery of Saint Jerome outside Madrid. Las Casas was given the title protector general of the Indians, which he bore proudly for the rest of his life.

Meanwhile, the Council of the Indies, the members of the Casa de Contratación, and others highly placed and invested in the encomienda system organized resistance against Las Casas in an effort to destroy his reputation, especially after Ximénez ruled that no member of the Council of the Indies could hold a grant of repartimiento with Indian slaves, which particularly inflamed the slave-holding president of the council, Bishop Fonseca. The campaign against Las Casas was effective. Even before the three Hieronymite commissioners set sail for the Indies from Sanlúcar on 11 November 1516, they were distancing themselves from the Clérigo to the point at which they forced him to embark on another vessel. By the time Las Casas arrived in Santo Domingo, followed three months later by the regent-appointed legal advisor, licentiate Alonso de Zuazo, the Hieronymite commissioners had had ample opportunity to be further lobbied, this time by a coterie of local officials and wealthy colonists involved in the encomienda system. Within seven months of his departure from Sanlúcar, Las Casas was back on the high seas en route to Spain, his hopes for the Hieronymite mission in a shambles of hostile testimony, contested facts, evasion, calumny, and physical threats against his person that led the Dominicans to offer him refuge in their priory in Santo Domingo.

A regretted suggestion

With Cardinal Ximénez deceased and the young King Charles I now resident in Spain, surrounded by and ruling through a Flemish court, Las Casas was forced to embark upon a new round of lobbying, this time across a language barrier. Aided by Dominicans such as Fray Reginaldo de Montesinos, brother of Fray Antonio, and certain Franciscans won over to the cause, the Clérigo experienced a second success. Fray Reginaldo organized a panel of Dominican theologians, who produced signed affidavits stating that, in their opinion, denying the humanity of Indians—specifically, that they possessed the mental and moral faculties required for conversion to Christianity as free agents and did not require enslavement first, as some were arguing—constituted heresy. Hence those who propagated such a notion deserved to burn at the stake. Thus Las Casas, although he never used this decree, went so far as to enlist the Inquisition in the antislavery crusade. Yet his success alienated the Clérigo even further from high-placed Spanish interests, who loathed the new king's Flemish retainers and were themselves invested in the encomienda system.

In the course of this second round of lobbying, Las Casas stumbled into an endorsement that he would regret for the rest of his life. Asked by the Flemish chancellor Juan Selvagio to write up an alternative plan for providing the Indies with labor, Las Casas argued for the subsidized immigration of free Spaniards and their families. In the same memorandum, he suggested that slaves from Africa also be introduced.

African slavery had been a fact of life in Spain and Portugal since the 1440s; both Lisbon and Seville maintained slave marts. A royal ordinance of 3 September 1500 allowed Spaniards in the Indies to bring or acquire African slaves. As historian and jurist John Noonan would later outline so tellingly in *A Church That Can and Cannot Change: The Development of Catholic Moral Teaching* (2005), moreover, it took nearly two millennia for the Catholic tradition to hold contemporary forms of slavery as immoral and to condemn them unambiguously. As late as the 1860s, a number of Catholic bishops in the Confederacy argued on its behalf. The charge would later surface—in Antonio de Herrera's *Historia de las Indies Occidentales*, written in 1598 by the official historiographer of the realm, and again for an English-language audience in William Robertson's *History of the Discovery and Settlement of America*

(1777)—that Las Casas actively promoted the expansion of African slavery into the Indies to save his beloved Indians.

Untrue. Las Casas was merely resorting to an existing institution. Quite soon, however, he recognized the hypocrisy of his position. To enslave one race was morally equivalent to enslaving another. Like Saint Peter, Las Casas wept in the years to come when the cock of this hasty suggestion crowed. "The cleric Las Casas", he explains in his *Historia general*, "first gave this opinion that license should be granted to bring negro slaves to these countries [the Indies] without realizing with what injustice the Portuguese captured and enslaved them, and afterward, not for everything in the world would he have offered it, for he always held that they were made slaves by injustice and tyranny, the same reasoning applying to them as to the Indians."[9]

Rather than qualifying his recommendation, Las Casas repented of it almost immediately, "judging himself", as he put it, "guilty of inadvertence; and as he saw—which will be later perceived—that the captivity of the negroes was quite as unjust as that of the Indians, the remedy he had counseled, that negroes should be brought so that the Indians might be freed, was not better, even though he believed they had been rightfully procured; although he was not positive that his ignorance in this matter and his good intention would exculpate him before the divine justice."

There had to be a better way, one free from the qualifications of trying to reform the system from within and free from the trap of moral compromise he had just fallen into. The solution, Las Casas decided, was the establishment in the Indies of a counterexample based on respect, benevolence, free labor, and voluntary conversion: an ideal colony, from which might be leveraged the reform of the entire system.

A utopian experiment

Las Casas now devoted himself to establishing a reform colony on the Pearl Coast of Tierra Firme—as the South American continent was called—founded on rational, humanistic, Catholic principles and governed thusly. Two years earlier, in 1516, the English Catholic humanist Thomas More had published *Utopia*, a description of an imagined island nation organized according to reason and natural law. Although no evidence shows that More's work directly influenced Las Casas, More was certainly writing within the context of New World discovery as he probed the nature of a rational, just, and monotheistic (albeit non-Christian) society, while Las Casas was grappling with all-too-real commonwealths falling woefully short of reason, justice, and religion. At the core of Las Casas' crusade, moreover, was the same question of law, natural and applied, of More's *Utopia*. How should rational human beings (Indians) be treated in the newly founded Spanish Empire in the Indies by other rational human beings who were much more powerful? What would a New World society based on correct first principles and best practices look like? A hundred years later another Spaniard, the Jesuit philosopher and theologian Francisco Suárez, would systematically develop such speculations in *De Legibus* (1612), an early installment on a workable theory of international law.

Las Casas' effort to found a model Christian colony on the Caribbean coast of South America began in the second half of 1518. In the first phase of his plan, Las

Casas sought to recruit Spanish peasant farmers and their families for immigration
to the Indies. The idea seemed simple yet pertinent, given that since 1492 Spaniards
in the Indies had shown themselves inept in the vital matter of feeding themselves
through agriculture (and, unfortunately, would remain that way through the seventeenth century) and thus were dependent on Indian slaves or raiding expeditions into Indian territories for provisions. A skilled agriculturalist and cattleman,
Las Casas knew that a productive peasantry, working for itself in a regulated but
open market, would simultaneously advance its own cause and help solve chronic
shortages of foodstuffs. Drawn up by Las Casas, the capitulations for the Venezuela
settlement signed by Charles V in the city of Coruña on 19 May 1520 abound in
specificities about agriculture: the promise of the soil in that part of the world; the
fruit trees and vegetable crops that could flourish there; the premiums to be paid for
the cultivation of cloves, ginger, cinnamon, and other spices, as well as for silk, rice,
and olive oil. As much as possible, the document states, the local economy should
depend on trade-based exchanges between Spaniards and Indians. Rice, grains, salt,
spices, gold and pearls (humanely mined or harvested), and other products would
be exported to the Caribbean colonies or Spain, with fixed percentages on all profits
returned to the Crown. Encomienda and repartimiento are not mentioned; hence
Indian slavery is not discussed, although Knights of the Golden Spur—Las Casas'
proposal for a founding gentry, discussed below—would be allowed (as would Las
Casas himself) to import up to ten black slaves apiece once pueblos were established, provided, the king cautioned, "this does not prejudice the grant and license
We have given to the Governor of Bresca to transport 4,000 [African] slaves to the
Indies and the continent."[10]

In addition to farmers, the text goes on, more varied and talented types of colonists should be recruited: carpenters, masons, shipwrights, merchants (such as Las
Casas' parents)—colonists capable of making a colony work through work, through
craft and a commitment to craftsmanship, rather than through slave labor. Furthermore, by bringing families of self-respecting, religious working people to the Indies,
the degeneration of sexual morality—which coarsens the tone of society—might
be avoided; such families would offer a counterexample to the criminal rapine of
Indian wives and daughters by colonists and soldiers.

Developing his paradigm even further by returning to a medieval ideal of religiously inspired chivalry, Las Casas proposed the creation of a new knightly order,
the Knights of the Golden Spur, fifty or more hidalgos of faith, goodwill, and
financial resources who would make a monetary and personal investment in the
colony and serve as its founding gentry. Historians have generally treated this proposal with irony or passed over it as rapidly as possible: a confraternity of upper-
class volunteers, attired on ceremonial occasions in white robes with red crosses
at the breast and golden spurs on their boots, migrating to South America to form
the nucleus of a protective and fair-minded nobility. How silly, how unrealistic!
The criticism is valid. Yet since Las Casas was envisioning the proposed colony
as a religiously inspired crusade by example, it is not surprising that he should
hearken back to the medieval knightly orders of the Reconquest. The Cistercian-
based Order of Calatrava and its Cistercian affiliates—Alcántara, Aviz, Montessa,
and the Order of Christ—not only reconquered but also governed the territories
they reconquered. The Knights Hospitaller of Saint John of Jerusalem, a major

naval power, governed the island of Rhodes from 1310 to 1522. In 1530 Emperor Charles V (King Charles I of Spain) conferred on the Hospitaller Knights sovereignty over the islands of Malta, Gozo, and Camino as well as Tripoli in North Africa. By command of its grand master, Prince Henry the Navigator, the Order of Christ was given spiritual jurisdiction over all Atlantic islands and African regions explored and colonized by Portugal, beginning with the Azores. From this perspective, Las Casas' call for the creation of a new knighthood for jurisdiction in the Indies—to which Charles V gave his approval, making the new order hereditary—was not so far-fetched. Improbable may better describe it, and somewhat poignant, as things turned out.

Regarding clergy, Franciscans and Dominicans are cited in the cédulas as missionaries to the Indians. However, a secular diocesan clergy is suggested as well in the stipulation that, as a mature Creole Spanish society developed and a parish structure was established, all parish-related benefices or other forms of income would remain local rather than be appropriated by politically connected churchmen living elsewhere.

The cédulas connected to the Venezuelan project reveal a measured utopianism, although the license to import eventually up to five hundred African slaves from Spain remains a disturbing foretaste of things to come, once Indian slave labor was exhausted in the Caribbean. A rigid and enumerated fiscalism—what the Crown expected in return—pervades every paragraph. An experienced encomendero, Las Casas knew full well that his proposed colony had to pay its own way. And yet, if not exactly utopian, Las Casas' proposal to import to the Indies free labor as well as free artisans and merchants was radical, given the system in operation, in which free labor and free markets were scarce. The avoidance of Indian slavery, moreover, constituted a grave threat to the feudal order in Spain and the encomienda system in the Indies. It was opposed accordingly by land-owning nobles on the Iberian Peninsula fearful of losing their peasants and by encomenderos, starting at the top with Bishop Fonseca. Fonseca—re-empowered by the new king and his chief minister, Guillaume de Croy Seigneur de Clièvres, a Fleming preoccupied with European affairs—had dismissed the Hieronymite commission and begun to harass the reforming judge Alonso de Zuazo.

Point by point, month by month, as Las Casas prepared his venture, Fonseca was doing everything in his power to scuttle it on the home front. Overtly, he opposed the Clérigo at a number of sessions of the Council of the Indies, including one meeting to which Las Casas brought eight court preachers (three of them doctors of theology) to argue against Indian slavery. Fonseca succeeded in allowing only one of them, Fray Miguel de Salamanca, a Dominican with a doctorate from the University of Paris, to speak. Fonseca also drew up a memorandum listing thirty reasons the king should not take counsel of Las Casas. The ever resourceful Clérigo, however, neutralized Fonseca's memo with his own written reply, prompting the king to invite Las Casas to debate in his presence an opposing Franciscan, Fray Juan Quevedo, first bishop of Darien in Central America. In the course of the debate, Las Casas brought Quevedo around to an anti-encomienda point of view.

With the help of his crony, Captain Luis de Berrio, Fonseca managed in a tour de force of double-dealing to subvert Las Casas' efforts to recruit skilled peasant farmers and artisan colonists. Foolishly, Las Casas retained Berrio as his recruiting agent without doing what is today known as a thorough background check, which perhaps would have revealed Berrio's connection to Fonseca, who was paying the soldier for hire as a double agent sworn to secrecy. Double-dealing on two fronts, Berrio forewarned land-owning grandees of Las Casas' intention to recruit their peasant farmers, which allowed the nobles to organize resistance. Instead of recruiting skilled artisans and other upright folk as colonists, moreover, Berrio assembled a cadre of ne'er-do-wells, layabouts, and adventurers eager to secure free passage to the Indies for all the wrong reasons.

Even worse, Las Casas lost the support of Admiral and Viceroy Diego Columbus, when Las Casas—who wanted all authority invested in himself as protector general of the Indians and chaplain to the king—rejected the request of Diego's brother Fernando that Fernando be appointed judge and legal administrator of the Pearl Coast colony; this, Las Casas feared, would have rendered himself a mere figurehead. Affronted, Fernando complained to his brother, who thereupon withdrew his previous offer to construct and man a string of coastal forts for military protection and centers of trade for the colony.

Cumaná

Las Casas, then, was on his own, although diocesan organization and the appointment of a bishop would be forthcoming when the colony had sufficiently progressed. As it now stood, the colony was to extend 260 leagues (Las Casas had originally requested a thousand) on the Pearl Coast of present-day Venezuela fronting the Caribbean. Only friars and colonists personally selected by Las Casas were allowed to settle there. However, between 1515 and 1518 Spanish Dominicans and French Observant Franciscans from Picardy had established convents seven leagues apart on the coast at Chiribichi and Maracapana, respectively. These developments met with Las Casas' approval, since he planned to bring with him twenty-one Observant Franciscan friars charged with establishing and staffing five Indian pueblos.

Yet slavers were also operating on the Pearl Coast. When their captain, Alonso de Ojeda, ordered the massacre of fifteen peaceful Indian porters and the kidnapping and enslavement of another thirty-five from the same group, he provoked an attack by Carib and Guayqueri Indians in September 1520 that killed Ojeda, several other Spaniards, and, worse, the Dominican priest and lay brother at Chiribichi.

Arriving in Puerto Rico on 10 January 1521, Las Casas learned of the troubles on the Pearl Coast and that his old friend Gonzalo de Ocampo was en route from Cuba as the head of a punitive force. When Ocampo arrived in San Juan, Las Casas showed him the cédula granting him authority on the Pearl Coast and asked him to cancel his expedition. Courteously, Ocampo acknowledged the cédula, but—as yet another example of *obedecer y no cumplir* (obedience without execution)—he informed Las Casas that he was operating under orders of the Audiencia (administrative council) in Santo Domingo, with whom the Clérigo would have to take up the issue. In the meantime he would continue on to the Pearl Coast.

Las Casas now made another mistake. In retrospect, it seemed clear that he should have gone with Ocampo and his soldiers to the Pearl Coast and monitored events from there. Instead, he decided to protest in person to the Audiencia in Santo Domingo. There, certainly, his authority would be recognized. Was this a sin of overweening pride or, at the least, overconfidence in his ability to persuade councils at any level? Leaving the colonists he had brought from Spain among various planters in Puerto Rico, Las Casas spent an enormous sum of money on a barely seaworthy salt freighter and sailed to Española.

There he learned that of the twenty-one Franciscan friars who had earlier set sail for the colony, only five had reached Española. The rest were either lost or dispersed in a violent storm shortly after departure from Sanlúcar. The proposed colony was now seriously understaffed with clergy. Nor had Las Casas managed to bring any Knights of the Golden Spur with him, delaying the recruitment of these investor gentry. More bad news: the Audiencia in Santo Domingo did not recall the Ocampo expedition from the Pearl Coast, but it ordered Las Casas' ship dismantled as unseaworthy. The Clérigo, who had left Spain as the de facto governor of a new colony, stood stranded in Santo Domingo, where—aside from the Dominican community there—he was universally distrusted. He was the founder of a colony with no colonists, no ships, no Knights of the Golden Spur, and a military expedition wreaking havoc among the Indians for whom he had hoped to establish a model colony.

Even as Las Casas was negotiating with the council, a cargo of Indian slaves arrived in Santo Domingo from the Pearl Coast. This first installment of human treasure from Ocampo was sorely needed, according to common report, given the dwindling supply of natives who could be enslaved elsewhere in the Caribbean. Arriving on the Pearl Coast, Ocampo and his men had wasted no time in getting to work. They began by luring the cacique who had led the uprising to approach their ship in a canoe, whereupon a Spanish sailor swam over to his canoe and stabbed him to death. The Spaniards then landed in full force and captured their first shipload of Indians to be enslaved after the usual round of torture, rapine, and murder. Afterward, having traveled inland on the Cumaná River, Ocampo's three hundred Spaniards established a camp, which they poetically named New Toledo.

When the slave ship arrived in Santo Domingo, the Clérigo went into a rage. How dare the Audiencia so blatantly defy the king's wishes! He would return to Spain and report this outrage to the king himself! Impressed and somewhat intimidated by these threats, the leading men of Santo Domingo made Las Casas a counteroffer they claimed would be to everyone's benefit. The colony would be reconfigured as a joint venture of twenty-four shares: six for the Crown, six for Las Casas and his fifty knights, three for Admiral Diego Columbus, one each for the four auditors of the Audiencia, and the remaining five for treasurer Pasamonte and four other officials. Each shareholder was to pay equally per share and to receive profits equally per share. Ocampo's brigantines and barques would serve as the colony's fleet, and half of his three hundred soldiers would remain in the colony under Ocampo's command as its military force. Friendly Indians would be treated fairly. Should Las Casas indicate, however, that any Indian group practiced cannibalism—and only Las Casas could make such a designation—said Indians could be fought, captured, and enslaved.

Las Casas agreed, even to the slave-taking under specified circumstances. Later he would claim to be double-dealing the double-dealers. "Great was the blindness", he later wrote in his *Historia*, "—if indeed it was not malice—of those gentlemen to believe that the Clérigo would ever fulfill those horrible and absurd conditions, knowing him to be a good Christian, not covetous, and ready to die to liberate and help in saving those people from the condition in which they were held."[11] The very vehemence of this denial, however, masks remorse over making such a deal in the first place, even if he was forced to be double-dealing.

Yet for the time being, the Clérigo signed on, thinking he could outwit the double-dealers who were so desperate for slaves that they would do their best to find cannibals everywhere. Barring success in that direction, they would leverage another ambiguous clause into the agreement—that Indians proving unfriendly to Spaniards or repulsing missionaries and refusing to become Christians could also be warred against and enslaved.

Stopping off at Puerto Rico with his newly acquired fleet en route to the Pearl Coast, Las Casas suffered yet one more shock. The peasant farmers and artisan colonists he had temporarily left behind were nowhere to be found. No life of patient, redemptive toil for them! They had vanished into the headlong ambitions and enterprises of the Indies, including, most likely, the slave trade.

The Pearl Coast

Arriving at the Franciscan friary at Cumaná on the Pearl Coast in August 1521, Las Casas was greeted by the Picard friars in procession chanting the Te Deum hymn of praise and greeting him with "Benedictus qui venit in nomine Domini" (Blessed is he who comes in the name of the Lord), echoing Christ's entry into Jerusalem the week before His Passion and death. Las Casas marveled at the friars' garden—orange trees heavy with fruit, a small vineyard, rows of vegetables and melons—planted five or six years earlier by Dominican friars, two of whom were later martyred. Brought back to life by their Franciscan successors, the friary and the garden suggested what the entire colony might one day become, if its five proposed pueblos were properly developed and peacefully cultivated.

Behind the garden—as if to continue a paradigm of proper development—Las Casas had a warehouse erected, into which he brought ashore the provisions and equipment shipped from Española. Once again, as in Cuba, he was functioning as the faithful steward of land and property, this time not for his own gain but, he hoped, ultimately for the welfare in this world and the next of the Indians who were helping him to construct the storage facility. His translator, an Indian woman named Doña María, had introduced him to the workers. The Clérigo, Doña María stated, had been "sent by the King of the Christians, who was then newly reigning in Spain, to see that they received good works rather than harm from the Christians there and could live in peace and friendship with them, as they would see later on." Writing of this encounter at a later date, Las Casas sounded almost biblical in his hopes for the native people and his efforts to form with them a new covenant. "And he worked to win them over," he wrote, "and gain their good will by giving them presents from the things he had brought, and forbidding those who were with him from giving them any cause or occasion, however small, for offense."[12]

Farther inland at the soldiers' settlement of New Toledo, however, or among the Spaniards on the offshore island of Cubagua seven leagues away (where pearls were brought to the surface by enslaved Indian divers, who frequently drowned in the effort or subsequently died from exhaustion), Las Casas' peaceable kingdom was the last thing on anyone's mind. Weary of slaving raids into Indian territory, more than half of the soldiers at New Toledo chose to return to Española on the ship that carried Las Casas to the Pearl Coast. Their departure momentarily decelerated slaving but also left the colony unprotected from Indian uprisings. In an effort to protect the Indians of the Cumaná settlement from the pearl-gathering Spaniards, Las Casas had brought a master mason and put him to work supervising the construction of a small fort at the mouth of the river, but the pearlers bribed the mason to abandon the project. In short order, the Spanish pearlers of Cubagua were infiltrating the Cumaná settlement in search of fresh water, women, and Indian pearl divers, and the Indians were getting drunk on wine, which they exchanged for gold or other valuables, to the point that deadly quarrels were breaking out among the Indians when they were inebriated.

An ominous mood of impending violence began to pervade the colony. With the bitter taste of frustration and failure in his mouth—so he would later write—Las Casas traveled to Cubagua to demand that the chief magistrate there enforce better behavior, but he received no response. Fray Juan Garceto, prior of the Franciscans, urged Las Casas to return to Santo Domingo and protest to the Audiencia the blatant violations of the king's wishes as expressed in the cédula signed by Charles V at La Coruña in May 1520. Without the Audiencia's intervention, Garceto argued, the colony was doomed. Las Casas did not want to abandon his post, but Garceto persisted, and Las Casas agreed to pray about the matter at his daily Mass until the time when two salt freighters would be returning to Santo Domingo.

Acceding to Garceto's pleas, Las Casas left for Española on one of the salt freighters. He placed Captain Francisco de Soto in command with strict instructions: the two ships under military control were to remain anchored off the mouth of the Cumaná River in case of an Indian uprising and the need to evacuate the Franciscans and the colonists. As soon as Las Casas was at sea, however, de Soto sent one ship to barter for gold and pearls and the other on a slaving expedition. Rumors of an impending insurrection reached the Franciscans and were confirmed by Doña María through hand and eye signals given while she was officially translating the denials of local caciques being interviewed by the friars.

Now began a three-day countdown to insurrection. The two military ships remained absent. A passing trader ship refused to land and evacuate the friars and colonists. Late on day two, the friars and colonists at Cumaná found that their gunpowder was damp and would not ignite. At sunrise, day three, they spread it out to dry in the sun.

At this point, the Indians attacked, killing two and setting fire to the friary and the warehouse, where the friars and colonists had taken refuge. As the Indians were lighting their torches, the trapped friars and colonists punched a hole in a rear wall and fled to the embankment, where they escaped by canoe. A lay brother who had gotten separated from the main party during the attack was left behind, but he waved them from the shore to continue their flight when he saw the Indians coming in pursuit in their own canoes.

Miraculously, the friars and colonists escaped massacre when they landed on a shore dense with thorny thickets their pursuers could not penetrate. After hiding for a time in the underbrush, they reached a salt freighter anchored close to shore and escaped—all except Francisco de Soto, who had caused this disaster. Wounded in the attack by a poisoned arrow, de Soto expired on the deck of the salt freighter, having drunk too much water.

In the meantime, the salt freighter carrying Las Casas to Española landed on the western end of the island, forcing him to hike overland to Santo Domingo. While the Clérigo was en route, travelers from Santo Domingo joined his party. From them Las Casas learned of the trouble at Cumaná, including a report of his own death.

Becoming a Dominican

Now ensued the second great crisis of Bartolomé de Las Casas' career as a reformer. The Cumaná venture had failed, miserably, and he had played the leading role in this sad drama when he accepted the restructuring of the colony as a profiteering expedition in the belief that he could outwit and control partners who did not share his ideals. At nearly forty-eight, the Clérigo had been a secular priest and courtier, honored by the Crown as protector general of the Indians and chaplain to the king, a confidant of archbishops and cardinals, a brilliant debater before court and council, an experienced entrepreneur and farmer and man of affairs, the designated founder of a colony and a knightly order. And yet he had failed.

Why? Because he had overrelied on his skills and the economic ambitions and forces they served. Not that economic ambitions—trade, commerce, exchange, profit, stewardship—were dispensable when it came to creating a just and livable society in the Indies. But without the anchorage and guidance of theology, philosophy, and law, these earthly involvements could easily become ends in themselves or, worse, subversions of higher value. Unless the builder built in the Lord, the Scripture taught, the builder built in vain. Las Casas was not a university man. He held no degrees. Yet in his consultations with the Dominicans of Española and Spain, the theologians and jurists among the court preachers, and the other learned clerics from whom he had received support, he had been guided in his development as an advocate and had glimpsed the strengthening power of faith and reason as the basis for corrective action.

Old habits did not die easily. Even while under a cloud in Santo Domingo, living with the Dominicans who had once again offered him refuge, Las Casas had written the king to defend himself and ask for further instructions. He had even been approached by possible investors ready to give him and his colony another try. But when the prior of the convent of Santo Domingo, Fray Domingo de Betanzos, asked him, "Tell me, Your Reverence, if you should meanwhile die, who will receive the instructions of the king?" the Clérigo began to meditate on the implications of what Betanzos was saying. First of all, should he die, what would be the condition of his soul? Second, no one would be there to receive the king's instruction. He was alone, a clérigo without a parish, a reformer without a model colony, a protector general of the Indians in need of confreres and a larger vision.

And so Bartolomé de Las Casas asked to be received into the Order of Friars Preachers, which meant adding vows of obedience and poverty to his existing promise of priestly celibacy. He who so believed in the efficacy and redemptive power of economic activity, properly pursued, would be required to return to the royal treasury any money advanced to him for his support or the support of the proposed colony. He who throughout his life had taken and obeyed his own counsel on most matters would put himself under a vow of obedience. A rugged individualist would be promising himself to the common life.

In return, he would no longer be alone in a crusade in which Dominicans had been involved since the beginning. Fray Antonio de Montesinos had first launched the antislavery crusade. Fray Pedro de Córdoba had denied him absolution on the grounds of his use of slave labor in Cuba and thus precipitated his first conversion. Fray Diego de Deza, archbishop of Seville, had facilitated his entrance into court circles. Fray Tomás de Matienzo, confessor to the king, had secured for him his crucial interview with King Ferdinand. Fray Alonso de Medina, a court preacher, had set up the meeting with his fellow court preachers at the Dominican convent of Santa Catalina in Barcelona, where Las Casas had enjoyed an enlightening tutorial on the theological, philosophical, and legal dimensions of Indian enslavement. And now, defeated, mocked, physically threatened, he had found refuge with the Friars Preachers of the convent of Santo Domingo.

He remained semicloistered in the convent of Santo Domingo for a year of novitiate and three years of academic study, a member of an influential academic and missionary order with a commitment to theology, philosophy, and scriptural study. In May 1526 he emerged from his retreat to reengage with the world and the cause that defined his life as prior of a Dominican establishment in Puerto de Plata on the north coast of Española. There he completed the first drafts of the *Historia de las Indias* and the *Apologética historia*, which he would revise, expand, and edit for the next thirty-eight years of his long, productive life. In the decades to come, he would function in Española, Mexico, Nicaragua, Rome, Guatemala, and Spain as a force for good on behalf of his order and the indigenous peoples of the Indies. In 1541–1543, at the height of his political career as a councilor to the regent Prince Philip, soon to reign as Philip II, he would play a decisive role in reforming the Council of the Indies and promulgating of New Laws for the Indies, outlawing the enslavement of indigenous peoples. Turning down the offer of an appointment as bishop of the fabulously wealthy Diocese of Cuzco in the recently conquered Peru, he accepted instead the impoverished Diocese of Chiapas in southern Mexico, which he hoped to transform into a model of social justice for indigenous peoples and Spaniards alike. Once again, however, he failed and was driven from his diocese by a violent and almost universal resistance to reform. Resettled back in Spain by his seventy-fifth birthday at the Colegio de San Gregorio de Valladolid, he devoted the remaining sixteen years of his life to the education of future Dominican missionaries to the Indies and to further writing on behalf of his beloved Indians.

2

Quivira 1527

Dreams of empire mingle with evangelical ambition

Between 1527 and 1536, three Spaniards and a Moor—Álvar Núñez Cabeza de
Vaca, Alonso del Castillo Maldonado, Andrés Dorantes de Carranza, and Estebanico, a slave of African descent from the coastal town of Azamor, Morocco—sailed,
trekked, rafted, suffered enslavement, escaped, and then trekked once more across
two-thirds of the southern edge of the North American continent. In the course
of this odyssey, the men sailed past or traversed the present-day states of Florida,
Georgia, Alabama, Mississippi, Louisiana, Texas, New Mexico, and Arizona, and
skirted the Gulf of California on their way south to Mexico City. Their journey served (albeit unwillingly) as a reconnaissance for Spanish involvement in the
region: its dangers, its peoples, and—in the case of Cabeza de Vaca—the religious
and moral meaning of these Borderlands. When he returned to Spain after his nine-
year ordeal, Cabeza de Vaca in 1542 published *La relación* (*The Narrative*), an account
of his experiences. In 1555 he expanded the text into *La relación y comentarios*. The
commentary consisted of an account of his controversial governorship of the province of Río de la Plata, which included parts of present-day Argentina, Uruguay,
and Paraguay. A concurrent edition used the title *Naufragios* (Shipwrecks), which
suggested the catastrophic origins of the epic trek.

Set powerfully at the very beginnings of the Spanish American experience in
North America, *The Narrative* of Cabeza de Vaca is difficult to categorize. It is
a memoir most obviously, a first-person record, written for Emperor Charles V
during the period when Cabeza de Vaca was lobbying for a governorship. Drafted
in haste five to six years after the experience was over, however, and up to fifteen
years since it began, the work must be read with caution as a historical document.
The 1555 edition, moreover, intended for King Philip II at a time when Cabeza de
Vaca was facing charges regarding his administration of Río de la Plata, included
new material and modified or otherwise recast previous statements. *The Narrative*
was a living document, a work in progress across thirteen or more years. Its vital and
continuing connection to events unfolding in the Indies and the moral meaning of
these events increase, rather than diminish, its value. *The Narrative* functions as imaginative literature, its factual content upgraded to higher levels of moral meaning and
symbolic statement. Many critics consider *The Narrative* the founding text of Latin
American literature: a fragmented but effective *Odyssey* or *Aeneid* that relates an epic
journey into the unknown or a *Divine Comedy* of a middle-aged public servant lost
in a dark and foreboding place, encountering a succession of infernal, purgatorial,
and theologized experiences. To use another medieval comparison, Álvar Núñez

Cabeza de Vaca moves through his *Narrative* as an Iberian Everyman—tempted, tested, reborn in the wilderness of Florida and the lower tier of North America that reaches and embraces, via the Gulf of California, Las Californias, and the Pacific.

By birth, Cabeza de Vaca was yet another hidalgo or semihidalgo in reduced circumstances. In the early 1400s his great-grandfather Pedro de Vera had led the conquest of Gran Canaria, largest of the Canary Islands, and died poor but honored with entombment in the Dominican monastery of Santo Domingo el Real in Jerez de la Frontera. From his mother (also a native of Jerez de la Frontera), Cabeza de Vaca inherited his distinctive name—head of a cow—an honorific conferred on a medieval ancestor, a shepherd by the name of Martín Alhaja, who in 1212 set up a series of cows' skulls to guide a Christian army escaping an envelopment by Moors. Cabeza de Vaca's rank, then, was enough to allow him to enter the service of the dukes of Medina Sidonia as a *camarero* (a personal attendant with access and privileges), and to test himself as a soldier in Italy in the 1512 Battle of Ravenna during Spanish efforts to assist Pope Julius II, under attack from the French. During the Comunero Revolt of 1520, a popular uprising in Seville against conversos, he again served the ducal house of Medina Sidonia in helping to put down the rebellion. His wife, María Marmolejo, was most likely of converso stock.

Thus, like Bartolomé de Las Casas—whom he would come to resemble in an important way—Cabeza de Vaca came from a background of reduced gentry with connections to the rich and powerful. Each served as a soldier. Each had connections to conversos. Las Casas, however, educated by and for the Church, possessed not only the calling but also the temperament of a clérigo. No credible question was ever lodged against his celibacy, while Cabeza de Vaca was a gentleman's gentleman with larger ambitions, not above—so goes the only story to surface regarding his years of ducal service—securing the assistance of two or three female therapists in a failed effort to cure the duke of erectile dysfunction.

To receive an appointment as royal treasurer of a six-hundred-man expedition of conquest under the command of the grizzled, one-eyed Pánfilo de Narváez represented a big step up in the world for Cabeza de Vaca. The military campaign also offered Narváez a chance to reassert himself as a conquistador after being bested in battle, imprisoned, and expelled from Mexico by Hernán Cortés when Narváez tried to displace Cortés as the would-be conqueror of the Aztecs. Now Narváez was returning to the Indies as commander of a conquering expedition and governor of a proposed province to extend westward from La Florida to Baja California and as far south as the Río de las Palmas in northern Mexico.

A tragedy of mishaps and errors

Instead of a triumphant return at the head of six hundred soldiers, however, Narváez experienced an accelerating succession of disasters. The expedition that was intended to restore his fortune instead left him dying adrift on a raft in the Gulf of Mexico, having informed the few survivors that nothing more could be done and it was each man for himself.

Departing the port of Sanlúcar de Barrameda at the mouth of the Guadalquivir River on 17 June 1527, the Narváez fleet reached Española in late July. The most successful part of the expedition—indeed, the only successful part—was over.

While Narváez's ships were anchored in the Santo Domingo harbor, some 140 men (approximately one in every four) deserted to the gold fields or pearl fisheries. When two of his ships were sailing from Cuba to Trinidad to take on further provisions, a hurricane destroyed them, with a loss of sixty men and twenty horses. As the expedition wintered in the port of Xagua, Cuba, Narváez recruited a chief pilot by the name of Diego Miruelo to guide them along the gulf coast en route to the Río de las Palmas, their destination on the Mexican coast. While the expedition was circling Cuba, it was forced to confront three more storms before heading to the mainland. There Miruelo, unfamiliar with the gulf stream and other currents, piloted by dead reckoning and made landfall near Tampa Bay on the west side of the Florida peninsula on the opposite side of the gulf, nine hundred miles from the Río de las Palmas. Miruelo and his fellow pilots, however, believed that they had landed a mere ten to fifteen leagues—thirty to forty-five miles—south of their intended landfall.

At this point in the cumulative tragedy of errors, Narváez made an extraordinary decision. As a soldier, he preferred land maneuvers, the kind of forced marches he had employed in his earlier conquest of Cuba. He proposed to his staff that they put their military ashore to march to the Río de las Palmas; the remaining colonists would travel north by ship. Cabeza de Vaca opposed the plan. Even before the expedition left Spain, he argued, a Moorish woman had predicted disaster on land for the Spaniards. Why test fate? This report of a prophecy might have been authentic, or Cabeza de Vaca may have fabricated it at a later date, for the Moorish woman, he related, had also predicted that a few would survive the destruction of the expedition and no less than the Almighty Himself would work great things through them. In any event, Narváez prevailed, and so disembarked some three hundred men, including the Franciscan chaplain, Fray Juan Suárez, bishop designate of the new colony, and at least one other chaplain, a secular priest from Asturias.

With this decision—to go ashore on the wrong side of the gulf, believing it to be the Mexican coast, in hopes of a short march north—Narváez doomed three hundred men to death by starvation and thirst, exposure, Indian attack, lingering wounds, drowning, exhaustion, and despair. But this disaster would take time to unfold; meanwhile, Narváez sent Miruelo back to Cuba in the lead ship for supplies. Upon Miruelo's return, the remainder of the fleet spent more than a year unsuccessfully searching the coast for the land party. Even before the colonists gave up the effort and returned to Cuba, a number of the ten women aboard, supposing their husbands were dead, had formed new relationships.

Of the extensive scholarship devoted to the subject, Andrés Reséndez has most meticulously researched and reconstructed the debacle. Trekking north through the western edge of Florida, the Spaniards turned west into the panhandle, then southwest through wooded marshland to the coastal region of Saint Mark's River and Apalachicola Bay, a maze of swamps and coves. Camped on a shallow estuary they named the Bay of Horses, Narváez's men ate their remaining horses and constructed five thirty-five-foot rafts from local hardwood logs, harvested and prepared with axes and saws created from the little metal they had—weapons, stirrups, spurs, crossbows—melted down in makeshift forges of hollowed-out logs with bellows of deerskin. On 22 September 1528 they embarked on their improvised rafts.

Propelled by currents and sails of stitched-together shirts, guiding by oars, the Spaniards sailed past the southern shores of present-day Florida, Alabama, Mississippi, and Louisiana before coming ashore south of Galveston Bay on the gulf coast of what is now Texas, with one raft landing 155 miles farther south at Corpus Christi Bay. Its famished crew was immediately slaughtered by Camones Indians.

Intensities of meaning

At this point, *The Narrative* of Cabeza de Vaca begins an ascent up a steep curve of importance as a religious document: to become, that is, the *Navigatio* of the Spanish Borderlands. Slowly, then gaining momentum, Cabeza de Vaca—the self-authenticating, self-documenting courtier petitioning king and council for a South American governorship—increasingly remembers himself as a naked pilgrim in an unknown wilderness. There he encounters the flora, the fauna, and, most important, the people of this new place, giving names to them as Adam did in the Garden and, like Adam, walking with God in the cool of the evening. Was it true? The substance of it was, most likely, if not the details. But in its literary dimension—in its imaginative and evangelical scope, *The Narrative* seemed totally true in its central argument, which was linked to the message of Bartolomé de Las Casas. What Las Casas absorbed as a priest, friar, and bishop and augmented through theological, philosophical, and legal study as well as missionary zeal, Cabeza de Vaca—a layman with little learning who was certainly no saint—acquired through experience and intuition: namely, however desired its gold and jewels and pearls, its fabled cities, might be, the enduring wealth of the region was to be found in its indigenous peoples. Fully human in their faculties and sentiments, capable of good and evil, they were waiting only to have shared with them the message of God's love for and redemption of them as proven by the death, Resurrection, and gospel of Jesus Christ.

The Indians in the opening portion of *The Narrative* are the enemy, vicious and murderous foes on beaches and in the forests of the interior. The first Indians Cabeza de Vaca and his companions encountered in Texas proved no exception to this rule, and the Spaniards, lured by a false promise of hospitality, found themselves in a fierce fight from which they barely escaped to their rafts; many of them were wounded, including Narváez. The Indians continued to harass the flotilla until the exhausted Narváez encouraged each captain to do the best he could on his own—every raft for itself—before he and his raft disappeared into a gloomy mist. Narváez's raft later made landfall, but he was too weak to disembark. While some Spaniards were on shore, Narváez's raft drifted away with its sole passenger, never to be seen again. The Spaniards who landed soon died or were killed.

Cabeza de Vaca's raft made it to shore farther on, and another group of Indians approached the Spaniards as they lay naked and fatigued on the beach. These Indians showed a completely different reaction. Learning of the Spaniards' plight, they wept in sympathy. They then built a series of fires back to their village and carried the survivors from fire to fire, rewarming them at each stop. Some Spaniards feared they would be sacrificed, but they were instead fed fish and roots and allowed to rest. Through these Indians, Cabeza de Vaca's crew was united with the crews of Andrés Dorantes and Alonso del Castillo. A Castilian captain of infantry in his mid-twenties, Dorantes, like Cabeza de Vaca, was a soldier of fortune, his face already scarred from battle. The son of a Salamancan physician and himself a graduate of the University of Salamanca, Castillo—also a captain of infantry—stood a rung higher on the social scale than the Royal Treasurer and Captain Dorantes. Like them, though, he was eager to push his status up a notch or two as a principal in the Narváez colony.

When the wrecked rafts proved unusable, four Spaniards decided to continue overland to Pánuco, a Spanish settlement south of the Río de las Palmas that the Spaniards, despite everything, believed must be just ahead. Five other Spaniards who were quartered nearby on the coast, meanwhile, succumbed to cannibalism. Survivors lived off the dead until only one Spaniard remained. Understandably, the remaining fifteen Spaniards—a group that included the one secular priest—named their new domain the Isle of Misfortune.

Now ensued four years, from 1528 to 1532, of captivity and enslavement for the surviving Spaniards, who were divided into two groups, the Royal Treasurer and his men in one, and the survivors of the Dorantes and Castillo raft in the other. In time, only four men survived: Cabeza de Vaca, Dorantes, Castillo, and the black slave Estebanico. After being enslaved, Cabeza de Vaca lived for two years as a trader between coastal and inland Indians, keeping up contact whenever possible with Dorantes and Castillo, whom he urged to escape. These four years of struggle were comparable to Las Casas' four years at the Dominican Convent of Santo Domingo. The Royal Treasurer, however, wore no habit—by his own report, he went naked, although his trading business involved animal skins from which he might have fashioned a garment. Again and again throughout *The Narrative* Cabeza de Vaca stresses his nakedness. Perhaps nudity was not only a fact of his life in these years but also a perfect emblem (like the white robes of Las Casas) of his spiritual and psychological condition. Everything external had been stripped away, and Cabeza de Vaca had to rebuild his identity out of this New World with its indigenous peoples and the religion he found within himself as he, Castillo, Dorantes, and Estebanico embarked upon their extraordinary journey across the Borderlands.

Learning, describing, healing

The land taught the Royal Treasurer and his companions what they could eat: walnuts, prickly pears, fish, oysters from nature; beans, squash, corn from cultivation; venison and smaller animals from hunting. Cabeza de Vaca enthusiastically describes geography and weather, fauna and flora, including reports of great shaggy horned cattle in the interior, refracted first information regarding the American buffalo. Once freed from captivity, Cabeza de Vaca also delights in the people he encounters on his epic journey. He presents them from an anthropological perspective—how they organized their communities, how they attired themselves, what they ate, how they performed religious rites—and his observations constitute the foundation for centuries of subsequent scholarship. In stories of his enslavement or that of other Spaniards, he tells of cruel beatings, wanton murder, and treacherous negotiations as well as one instance of surprising empathy, the collective weeping on the Isle of Misfortune.

Early in *The Narrative*, he relates an incident that forecasts a profound connection to native peoples and will, it turns out, ensure the survival of him and his companions. One evening, the Royal Treasurer chronicles, some Indians approach the Spaniards, complaining of headaches. Alonso del Castillo, son of a physician, makes the sign of the cross over them and offers a prayer. Almost at once, the Indians exclaim, their pain is gone! Later, they return with gifts of prickly pears and venison. When news of their cure spreads, other Indians arrive that night seeking the same sign of the cross and blessing. Freed of their ailments, they also return with venison, so much that the Spaniards have a storage problem. The cured Indians not only feed the Spaniards but also brief them on the route ahead.

The next day, the Indians bring the Spaniards to their village to attend to even more sick. Herein occurs, in chapter 21, a sequence of events that both establishes a whole new relationship of Spaniard to Indian and raises *The Narrative*'s level of religious intensity. In one hut the Spaniards find an Indian who appeared to be dead—eyes rolled back, with no discernible pulse or movement—and was being mourned by relatives and tribesmen. Cabeza de Vaca nevertheless prays over the man, asking God that the sick Indian be cured in the name of our Lord Jesus Christ. That night, Cabeza de Vaca recounts, the Indians return to the Spaniards with the startling news "that the dead man whom I attended to in their presence had resuscitated, risen from his bed, walked about, eaten, and talked to them, and that everyone I had treated was well and in very good spirits. This caused great surprise and awe, and all over the land nothing else was spoken of. Everyone who heard about it came to us so that we might cure them and bless their children."

While with the Avavares in the region northwest of present-day Corpus Christi Bay for eight months, the Spaniards added exorcism to their repertoire. A demonic figure, the Avavares told them—*Mala Cosa* (Bad Thing), a short, bearded man—was wont to enter their huts and seize his intended victim.

> With a sharp knife made of flint [Cabeza de Vaca writes] as broad as a hand and two palms in length, he would then make a cut in that person's flank, thrust his hand through the gash, and take out the person's entrails. Then he would cut off a piece one palm long, three cuts in one of the person's arms, the second one at a place where people are usually bled, and twist the arm, but would reset it soon afterward. Then he would place his hands on the wounds, which, they told us, would close up at once. Many times he appeared among them while they were dancing, sometimes in the dress of a woman and other times as a man, and whenever he took a notion to do it he would seize a hut or lodge, take it up into the air, and come down with it again with a great crash. They also told us how, many a time, they set food before him, but he would never partake of it. When they asked him where he came from and where he had his home, he pointed to a rent in the earth and said his house was down below.

Initially, this story amused the Spaniards, but when victims of the Bad Thing showed them their wounds and scars, they became convinced that they were in the presence of demonic possession. "We told them", the Royal Treasurer writes, "he was a demon and explained as best we could that if they would believe in God, our Lord, and be Christians like ourselves, they would not have to fear that man, nor would he come and do these things to them, and they might be sure that as long as we were in this country he would not dare to appear again. This pleased them greatly and they lost much of their apprehension."

The third significant section of chapter 21 is the best known. Despite their previous successes, including the cure of a man believed to be dead as well as a confrontation with demonic possession, the Spaniards remained in quasi-bondage to the Indians and thus were frequently given work to do. The Spaniards wore little if any clothing. Subsequent report says they traveled completely naked, Cabeza de Vaca at least, although at one point he mentions trading an animal skin for food. Nakedness and wounds dominate this crucial passage in which the Royal Treasurer links himself to the Passion of Christ. "I have said already that we went naked in that land," Cabeza de Vaca begins this spiritually dynamic passage,

> and not being accustomed to it, we shed our skin twice a year, like snakes. Exposure to the sun and air covered our chests with great sores that made it very painful to carry big and heavy loads, the ropes of which cut into the flesh on our arms. The country is so rough and overgrown that often after we had gathered firewood in the forest and dragged it out, we would bleed freely from the thorns and spines that cut and slashed us wherever they touched us. Sometimes it happened that I was unable to carry or drag out the firewood after I had gathered with great loss of blood. In all that trouble my only relief or consolation was to remember the passion of our Savior, Jesus Christ, and the blood he shed for me, and to consider how much greater his sufferings had been from those thorns than I from the ones I was then enduring.[1]

With this outburst of Spanish Catholic piety—vivid, physical, Christocentric, at once psychologically realistic and otherworldly, a fusion of Ignatius of Loyola and El Greco—the Royal Treasurer and his companions emerge as confident figures in a landscape previously intimidating and oppressive. Cabeza de Vaca and Castillo, the physician's son, are considered healers, and the freed Spaniards move through the future Borderlands of New Spain, passed from one tribe to another as honored guests: Children of the Sun, the Indians call them. Indeed, the Spaniards become revered shamans as they march westward, escorted by admiring Indians. The one-time slaves are now triumphant figures revered by their onetime enslavers, whom they rarely address directly, leaving all negotiations to Estebanico.

In one instance, the Royal Treasurer is presented with an Indian who was shot in his back with an arrow years before and lived in debilitating pain. Drawing upon his experience as a soldier in Italy, Cabeza de Vaca cuts into the wounded Indian with a knife, probes, finds and removes an arrowhead lodged dangerously near his heart, and then stitches the chest closed with gut thread and a needle of deer bone. Fascinated, the Indians pass the arrowhead around for inspection and celebrate that night with village-wide dancing. The next morning, Cabeza de Vaca cuts the stitches. The Indian says he no longer feels any pain.

Detour to the north

An argument can be made that the Spaniards, as *The Narrative* presents them, are by now aware of the reconnaissance and pilgrimage they are making through the territory Narváez had hoped to rule as governor. From Florida to the Gulf of California, they measured out step by step, league by league, day by day, month by month, year by year, in their westward journey. Confidence and a sense of mission might have motivated them in the summer of 1535 when, leaving present-day Texas and moving south into Mexico, they encountered two Indian women carrying baskets of maize flour from the northeast and came across a copper bell from the same region, which further suggested developed Indian cultures. And so, making the transition from wanderers to explorers, the Spaniards deliberately veered northwest into the Land of Maize, as they called it, along a thousand-year-old trail that links present-day Nuevo León with the sedentary corn-growing cultures in or adjacent to what is now New Mexico and Arizona. Making a wide loop through the Land of Maize, they proceeded south down the western edge of Mexico within reporting distance of the South Sea (today's Gulf of California), on the other side of which the Californias fronted the Pacific.

In these regions the Royal Treasurer and his companions continued their healing ministry, moving from tribe to tribe through regions of agricultural development and further promise. When Castillo encountered an Indian boy wearing a Spanish belt buckle around his neck, they knew they were approaching the Spanish settlements of mid-Mexico. In April 1536, almost nine years since they had left Europe, Cabeza de Vaca and an advance party of Indians met four Spanish horsemen. The one African and three Spanish survivors of the Narváez expedition began the next phase of their lives.

A Christian commitment

For Cabeza de Vaca, that meant defending the Indians, for the newly met Spaniards were part of a slaving raid that was driving the local people into the mountains. Immediately, Cabeza de Vaca came to their protection, as he did later in Mexico City and back in Spain, when he petitioned for the governorship of La Florida, whose western regions he and his compatriots had trekked through and explored for so long. Yet before Cabeza de Vaca's petition could be heard, the royal court and the Council of the Indies assigned the governorship to Hernando de Soto, whose later exploring expedition of 1539–1543 introduced into North America the highest possible level of deceit, cruelty, murder, and rapine against indigenous peoples by Europeans and cost de Soto his own life in 1542. After three more years of patient lobbying, Cabeza de Vaca secured an appointment as governor of Río de la Plata, a province encompassing portions of present-day Argentina, Uruguay, and Paraguay. There, as Samuel Eliot Morison chronicles, he distinguished himself as an explorer and an administrator yet ran afoul of the local colonial establishment because of his enlightened policies toward the Guaraní people of the region.

A dedicated colonizer, Cabeza de Vaca in theory approved of the enslavement of bitter opponents to Spanish settlement. He disapproved, however, of Indian slavery and slave raids as the foundation of the local economy. Hence he opposed the system of encomienda, which fused land and forced Indian labor into one economic unit. And while he himself was no saint, as governor Cabeza de Vaca deplored the exploitative sexual culture of the capital city of Asunción, where many Spaniards, taking advantage of the liberality of the Guaraní people—for whom sexual services cemented diplomatic alliances—were living in haremic polygamy amid households

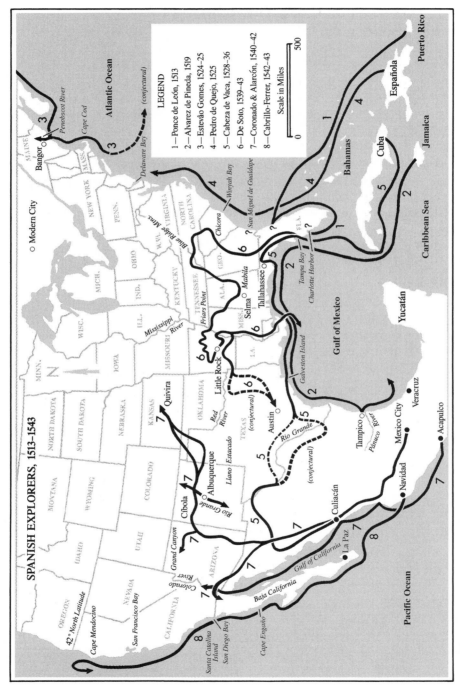

Map 5. Spanish Explorers, 1513–43. From David J. Weber, *The Spanish Frontier in North America* (New Haven: Yale University Press, 1992), 32. © *Yale University Press, used by permission.*

SPANISH EXPLORERS, 1513–1543

of up to sixty female Guaraní servants. With the mothers, daughters, and wives of native men, the Spaniards had by the 1550s created a population of nearly three thousand mestizo children, so many of whom were left to fend for themselves. Cabeza de Vaca considered such arrangements a form of slavery, no matter how they might suit the Guaraní way of life, as well as incompatible with Christian morals and culture, and as governor he did his best to oppose them. Deposed from office in the spring of 1544, he was sent back to Spain in chains (a sympathetic captain had them removed at sea), imprisoned, and later brought up on charges before the Council of the Indies. Convicted, he barely on appeal avoided exile to North Africa. Returning to his ancestral village of Jerez de la Frontera, Cabeza de Vaca lived until his late sixties, dying around 1557, and was accorded the dignity of being entombed in the Dominican monastery of Santo Domingo el Real beside his great-grandfather Pedro de Vera, conquistador of Gran Canaria.

Cabeza de Vaca had wanted to be a conquistador, and he became one, though of a different sort: a conquistador sensitive to place, languages, ways of life, and the fundamental humanity of the Indian peoples he encountered on his journey. He was not a writer, but he wrote the *Odyssey* of North American exploration. He was not a saint, but his Catholic faith sustained him and led him to defend indigenous peoples. He became a lay missionary on behalf of a cautious and respectful evangelization of the peoples of the southern tier of the North American continent, a naked John the Baptist living on prickly pears, walnuts, and gifts of venison and corn. An upstart and improbable Saint Paul, he foreshadowed the coming of the Church to this extension of La Florida. In repeated patterns of missions, presidios, and scant and struggling European and mestizo settlements, the Church would cross the Borderlands to California on the Pacific.

Seven cities

Arriving in Mexico City on Sunday, 23 July 1536, two days before the feast of Saint James, patron saint of pilgrimage, Cabeza de Vaca and his companions caused a sensation. The first viceroy of New Spain, Don Antonio de Mendoza, welcomed and housed Cabeza de Vaca in the viceregal palace, where he was waited on by Indian servants and witnessed the elaborate court ritual through which Mendoza was establishing a royal presence in the recently conquered province's capital city. A native of Granada of noble lineage and a knight of the Order of Santiago, Mendoza (then in his late forties) had served successively as a fighting general, the ambassador to Hungary, and the queen's chamberlain before his appointment in 1535 as viceroy and president of the Audiencia de Nueva España, the highest governing council in the Indies.

Cabeza de Vaca's descriptions of what he had seen in the north, as well as others of even more remote areas, inspired Viceroy Mendoza to commission an exploring expedition to these regions. Mendoza was especially intrigued by Cabeza de Vaca's report that Indians had informed him of flourishing cities farther north. Already rumors were circulating about wealthy cities there, whose grandeur equaled or even exceeded that of the Aztec capital city, Tenochtitlán, taken in 1521 by Hernán Cortés—whom Mendoza, a nobleman of higher rank, had bested as a candidate for appointment to the viceroyalty.

The possibility of seven great cities in the Indies had roots in an earlier tale of seven Portuguese bishops who, fleeing invasion by Muslim Moors, established the Seven Cities of Antilla westward beyond the Ocean Sea. Such stories were more than legends to the late medieval, early Renaissance Iberian imagination; hence the name Antilles given by the Spaniards to the island group they discovered in the Caribbean. The conquests of Mexico and Peru only tended to confirm these reports, alive as hearsay or imaginative fiction, as in the novel *Las sergas de Esplandián* (The deeds of Esplandián) by Garci Ordóñez de Montalvo, published in Seville in 1510 as a final installment of the *Amadís de Gaula* cycle. The novel was partially set in an island on the right hand of the Indies. Ruled by Queen Califia, the commonwealth of Amazon warriors was called California, a name that Cortés and his men would soon use to describe the peninsula—first thought to be an island—they were exploring to the west of Mexico across the waters of the Gulf of California.

Viceroy Mendoza initially wanted Cabeza de Vaca to command the expedition, but the Royal Treasurer had larger ambitions in mind, the governorship of Florida, and in the fall of 1536 he departed for Spain to lobby for this appointment. Mendoza next turned to Andrés Dorantes. Unlike Alonso del Castillo, who preferred being a gentleman encomendero in Mexico (a life the viceroy had arranged for both men—married to a wealthy widow and assigned a prosperous encomienda), Dorantes still harbored hopes of a great career and for a while seriously entertained heading the expedition. For some reason, however (too much of the good life, perhaps), Dorantes lost interest, and the viceroy, improbably but persistently, lobbied Dorantes for the services of his Moroccan slave, Estebanico, who had become a respected member of Dorantes' household. Estebanico knew the territory and had demonstrated diplomatic skills. Dorantes at first resisted—he refused the viceroy's payment of five hundred pesos for the Moor—but eventually Dorantes released Estebanico at no cost for the expedition. Estebanico most likely was delighted at the prospect of freedom, wealth, and upward mobility that few men of African descent experienced in this era.

Yet while Francisco Pizarro had recently set new standards for greed, violence, and treachery in his conquest of Peru, and Hernando de Soto would soon be doing the same in North America, the struggle for better behavior toward Indians had created progress. In Rome, Pope Paul III would soon issue the bull *Sublimis Deus* (published 29 May 1537), asserting the spiritual equality and brotherhood of all men by stating that "said Indians and all other people who may later be discovered by Christians are by no means to be deprived of their liberty or the possession of their property, even though they be outside the faith of Jesus Christ; and that they may and should, freely and legitimately, enjoy their liberty and the possession of their property; nor should they be in any way enslaved; should the contrary happen, it shall be null and of no effect."[2] At the insistence of Emperor Charles V, the pope later removed from the bull ecclesiastical penalties for mistreatment of Indians, to be leveled locally by missionaries on the scene. Bartolomé de Las Casas' lengthy treatise "The Only Method of Attracting All People to the True Faith", written earlier in the Dominican monastery of Santiago de Guatemala, had set the bar for *Sublimis Deus*, and the Dominican friar (who helped persuade the Vatican to issue the bull) would soon return from Rome to Guatemala to evangelize in the company of such ardent Dominican defenders of Indian rights as Fray Luis Cancer de Barbastio, soon to lose his life in La Florida.

A Franciscan reconnaissance

Given the momentum of the reform movement, it is not surprising that Viceroy Mendoza, Franciscan Juan de Zumárraga (the first bishop of Mexico), and Fray Antonio de Ciudad Rodrigo (the Franciscan provincial for Mexico), who were sensitive to the new direction Spanish policy was taking—culminating in the New Laws of 1542–1543, which outlawed Indian slavery—should choose an experienced missionary sympathetic to the Indians to lead the reconnaissance north. Born around 1495 in the city of Nice in the Duchy of Savoy, Fray Marcos de Niza, a Franciscan, transferred to Spain around 1530 as a volunteer for missionary work in the Indies. During three years in Peru and Ecuador, the French- and Spanish-speaking Savoyard served as *custodio* (superior) of Franciscans in the region and wrote a vivid description of conquistador cruelty there that Las Casas appended to his *Brevísima relación de la destrucción de las Indias*. It is also possible that Marcos de Niza met Las Casas in 1536 when the Franciscan friar was briefly in Guatemala. In any event, the venturesome Fray Marcos accepted the offer to head the reconnaissance. The very fact that a Franciscan priest was directing the effort, assisted by a Franciscan lay brother, Fray Onorato, signaled its peaceful intentions.

This reconnaissance—too small to be called an expedition—left Mexico City in late 1538 in the company of Don Francisco Vásquez de Coronado, the newly appointed governor of Nueva Galicia, the recently (1529–1530) subdued north-ernmost province of New Spain. Twenty-eight at the time of the group's depar-ture, Coronado had risen rapidly in the world, made eligible for promotion by birth, ability, marriage, connections, good looks, and performance. A Salamancan of noble lineage, Coronado (like so many conquistadors) had limited prospects in his homeland, since he and his brother Juan saw the entire family estate go to their older brother Gonzalo, save for the dowries paid to the local convent in which their two sisters became nuns. In 1535 Juan and Francisco migrated to the Indies in the entourage of Viceroy Mendoza, who fostered their careers, Juan's in Costa Rica and Francisco's in Mexico City, where the younger Coronado remained in the viceregal service. Within two years, the handsome, fair-haired young man—again, with the viceroy's assistance—made a brilliant marriage to Doña Beatriz de Estrada, daughter and heiress of the recently deceased wealthy treasurer of New Spain, Alonso de Estrada, widely believed to be the illegitimate son of the late King Ferdinand. Viceroy Mendoza assigned Coronado to successive challenging leader-ship roles, first as commander of a force sent north to repress an uprising, then as a member of the Mexico City Council, which positioned the nobleman for his instal-lation as governor of Nueva Galicia, following the death of its second governor, Diego Pérez de la Torre, in a battle against rebellious Indians.

Publicized by the *Relación* (1539) Fray Marcos dictated upon his return, the reconnaissance caused a sensation throughout both New Spain and Spain and had dramatic consequences. Its power arose from its immediate acceptance as a verifi-cation of all that Cabeza de Vaca and his companions had been saying since their arrival in Mexico City three years earlier and from further commentary by Fray Marcos after he returned from the north in late August 1539. (The Oxford geographer Richard Hakluyt published an English version from a 1556 Italian translation of the *Relación* in his famed *Voyages* [3 volumes, 1598–1600], thereby establishing Fray Marcos' report as a classic of its genre.) The problem was, *The Relación*'s essential revelation—that seven wealthy, culturally developed cities existed in the north—was not true. Fray Marcos was not a liar, John Gilmary Shea argues, but he did believe just about everything the Indians of the north told him. At best, the Savoyard friar was mistaken, edged into his conclusions—that the seven cities existed and that he had personally beheld one of them from a distance—by wishful thinking and the power of the Seven Cities myth. But mistaken he was, and his false report had both good and evil consequences. Viceroy Mendoza, for example, noted Fray Marcos' failure to reach the South Sea, as the Pacific was called. The viceroy had already strongly supported efforts to explore north by sea that by 1543 would establish the existence of the Gulf of California, the peninsular nature of Baja California, and the northward extension of the California coastline, thus alerting Crown and Council to the necessity of eventually creating new provinces in Las Californias. Yet just how far west that Pacific shoreline lay remained uncertain. Many, including the viceroy, then believed that the South Sea might extend as far east as present-day New Mexico. That issue was still to be explored. More dramatically, the report of Fray Marcos led Mendoza to envision, organize, and launch an *entrada* (a reconnaissance in force) that would advance New Spain northward to the Seven Cities described by Marcos, followed by fully financed and staffed efforts at evangelization, settlement, and, if necessary, conquest.

Seeking Cíbola

Like Cabeza de Vaca's *Narrative* of 1542, Fray Marcos' *Relación* of 1539 displays a representatively Spanish admixture of sacred and profane ambition, especially as the friar and his party approach the alleged city of Cíbola—in reality, Hawikúh—the first of six Zuñi pueblos just inside the western boundary of present-day New Mexico, south of Gallup. Describing the trek of his party up through western Mexico and the fiercely hot desert country of what is now western Arizona, Fray Marcos tends to emphasize the evangelical ambition behind the reconnaissance and the kindliness of the Indians his men encounter. He only obliquely notes Estebanico's frank delight in collecting gifts of turquoise from these Indians and securing the services of Indian porters to carry these treasures. (No mention is made of the young and comely Indian women the lusty Estebanico selects to service him sexually along the Turquoise Trail.) By the time the Marcos party entered New Mexico, Estebanico's retinue of porters, interpreters, and female company had reached the three hundred mark. Disapproval of Estebanico's traveling seraglio as well as Fray Marcos' respect for the Moor's diplomatic abilities led to his being sent ahead of the main party to function as herald and frontline negotiator, the same role he had played for Cabeza de Vaca, Castillo, and Dorantes. A number of Indian groups, in fact, recognized Estebanico from his previous passage with the Cabeza de Vaca party and thought well of the Moroccan. Approaching a village, Estebanico announced himself by dispatching a gourd rattle with bells and feathers that denoted peaceful intentions, which usually led to an invitation to parley. Once having seen the village in question, the Moor would mark the trail with small crosses and send back to Fray Marcos etchings of a hand, an arm, or a body to signal the size of the Indian settlement.

On Holy Thursday, 27 March 1539, a messenger from Estebanico carrying an etching of man-sized height reached Fray Marcos. Hurry on! went the Indian's message. Estebanico was hearing reports of a great country only thirty days away. Hope and expectation drove the Marcos party across the most difficult part of their journey, the uninhabited and scorching Arizona desert. On the other side of it, Fray Marcos encountered an irrigated pueblo of Indians dressed in cotton clothing, their ears, noses, and necks adorned with turquoise ornaments. Here he received word of *ciudades*, *reinos*, and *provincias* (cities, kingdoms, and provinces) inhabited by a people who kept sheep, spun wool, and lived in intricate residential complexes. Yet another account came from Estebanico, who was pushing on with his retinue, marking the trail with crosses, his two greyhounds roaming ahead of the advance party as canine scouts. The messenger reported that only fifteen days of travel stood between the Marcos party and a great pueblo (now being called Cíbola in the *Relación*) that Estebanico was approaching. By this point of the *Relación*, moreover, Fray Marcos had accumulated so many reports and interviews with Indian leaders on the trail—including details of daily life in the first of these seven alleged cities in the near distance—the reality of Cíbola seems firmly established in the friar's mind. For Fray Marcos de Niza, dictating his account back in Mexico City, all that he was telling had to be true!

Dreadful news

Twelve days later, on what Fray Marcos now describes as the trail to Cíbola, a young Indian—the son of a *principal* (leading man of the pueblo) who was traveling with Estebanico—arrived at the Marcos camp, traumatized and exhausted. Estebanico was dead! he announced, killed along with most of his party by the inhabitants of Cíbola, only one day's march away. As usual, the Moroccan had announced himself by sending ahead his gourd rattle decorated with bells and feathers, but the principal of the city had thrown the gourd to the ground and, telling Estebanico's messengers that he knew who these people were and did not like them, threatened death if they dared enter the city.

Estebanico, in turn, had laughed off his messengers' report. He had met such resistance before, the Moor related, and had turned such enemies into friends. When he approached the pueblo, however, Estebanico was stripped of his treasure by the principales of the settlement and confined with the other leaders of his party in a building outside the city. The next morning, the young Indian relating this tale to Fray Marcos managed to slip away and go upriver a short distance for a drink of water and thus witnessed the massacre of Estebanico and his retinue. Two more Indian escapees, wounded, exhausted, and weeping with shock and grief, stumbled into camp and confirmed the story.

Fray Marcos shows no sorrow whatsoever at the death of Estebanico, whose sexual behavior had caused the Franciscan such distress. Black, exotic, larger than life, striding across desert and mountain—with porters, houris, and bodyguards in attendance, his two greyhounds dancing circles around him as he marched—the

Moroccan Moor (nominally a Christian) belonged to another sphere entirely, more Arabic than Spanish, although he spoke each language fluently, along with the Indian languages he had learned in those years he had set the pace and concluded the agreements for Cabeza de Vaca, Castillo, and his master, Dorantes, who had grown to respect him. Born into slavery or thrust into it at an early age, Estebanico through sheer force of will had become so much more: a Moor from before the Reconquest, an emanation of the life force itself, assured, laughing at danger, sexually self-indulgent—yet few Spanish Catholics in the Indies in these early years could cast the first stone. Besides, Estebanico paid the ultimate price for his improvident satyriasis. Later reports traced the anger of the Zuñi principales to Estebanico's demands for women as well as treasure, made to a people who zealously protected their females. In any event, Estebanico now lay fallen in the field, pierced by multiple arrows, his head soon to be removed (or already removed, according to a later report) so as finally to slay the demon the Zuñi feared Estebanico might have been.

A glimpse from afar

A personal retainer of Fray Marcos soon informed the friar that Indians in his own party, relatives of those who had been killed, were planning to murder Marcos for leading them into such a disaster. Breaking into his trove of gifts intended for Cíbola, Marcos distributed the clothing and trade items to the principales of the Indians willing to continue on with him. "With those [principales] and with my own Indians and interpreters," he writes, "I continued on my way until [I was] within sight of Cíbola. It is situated in a plain, on the lower slope of a round hill. As a town it has a very handsome appearance, the best I have seen in this region. As it appeared to me from a hill where I positioned myself in order to view it, the houses are arranged in the way the Indians told me, all made of stone with their upper stories and flat roofs. The settlement is grander than the Ciudad de México. A few times I was tempted to go there myself, for I knew I was risking only my life, and I had rendered that to God."[3]

Discretion proved the better part of valor, especially since, as Fray Marcos points out, if he were to be killed, the authorities in Mexico City would never know what he had seen. "In my view, this [land] is the grandest and best of all [those that have been] discovered. When I told the *principales* I had with me how excellent Cíbola seemed to me, they told me that it was the least of the seven *ciudades* and that Totonteac is much grander and better than all the seven *ciudades*. And [they said] that [Totonteac] comprises so many buildings and people that it has no end. Considering the excellence of the *ciudad*, it seemed [appropriate] to me to call that land the Nuevo Reino de San Francisco."

Just before departing the scene, Fray Marcos reports, "I erected a large mound of stones there with the help of the Indians. On top of it I set a small, thin cross, since I did not have the equipment to make it bigger. I declared that the cross and mound were being erected in token of possession in the name of Don Antonio de Mendoza, viceroy and governor of Nueva España, [and] on behalf of the emperor, our lord, in accordance with the [viceroy's] directive. I declared [further] that [by] that act I was there taking possession of all the seven *ciudades* and the *reinos* of Totonteac, Acus, and Maratta. [I stated] that I was not going on to them in order to return to give a report of what had been seen and done." This ceremony completed, Fray Marcos and his diminished band retraced their journey through the *despoblado* (unsettled) desert regions of eastern Arizona, and on 2 September 1539 the party arrived in Mexico City for the friar to make his report to Viceroy Mendoza.

Entrada and conquest

Sunday, 22 February 1540, Compostela, the outpost capital of Nueva Galicia: Viceroy Mendoza is on hand to review a grand mustering of the soldiers, Indian auxiliaries and their wives and children, a half dozen Franciscan friars—led by Fray Marcos de Niza, now promoted to provincial of Franciscans in New Spain—and at least three wives of Spanish soldiers, all due to depart the following day on an entrada north to Cíbola under the command of Francisco Vásquez de Coronado, captain general of the expedition. For the past ninety days and more, members of the entrada have been moving north to Compostela in small groups to avoid alarming the indigenous peoples, who might feel under invasion and flee to the mountains if the entire expedition were to march as a single column.

From eyewitness accounts, a surviving muster roll, and subsequent scholarship, the muster, parade review, and oath taking of that dramatic day can be reimagined in all its bravado and optimism: Mendoza in viceregal finery, an entourage in attendance; Coronado in the gleaming armor and finery of a captain general; his staff officers and captains—chosen from the best officers of New Spain—equally armored and splendid as, surrounded by subalterns and flag bearers, they file past the viceroy and captain general to the accompaniment of drum and bugles at the head of 225 mounted soldiers, 62 soldiers on foot, and several hundred Indians attached to the expedition as armed auxiliaries, servants, hostlers for the thousand horses and lesser number of mules, and drovers and herdsmen for the sheep and cattle that would feed one and all in the wilderness. After the review and the Mass that followed, Viceroy Mendoza gave an inspiring address regarding the service each Spaniard was rendering God and the king by volunteering for the entrada, with some suggestion as well of the material rewards to come from the *repartimientos* and encomiendas of a new province in such a promising region. (The recovery of costs for the entrada, being primarily borne by Mendoza and Coronado and a few other Mexico City investors, must also have been on the viceroy's mind, although he did not mention it.) Following the viceroy's address, the entire entrada force, Spaniard by Spaniard, beginning with Coronado, took an oath promising allegiance to God and king and proper conduct. The next morning, the march to Cíbola commenced, north by northwest through northern Mexico and present-day Arizona, then eastward into present-day New Mexico—a total of six months since the expedition began its recruitments in central Mexico.

The Coronado expedition survives in history as a tour de force of geographical exploration. Penetrating the interior as far as modern-day central Kansas and Nebraska to the northeast, and to the northwest as far as the Grand Canyon, the Coronado expedition—like the concurrent explorations of de Soto by land and Juan Rodríguez Cabrillo by sea northward along the Pacific coast—resulted in new knowledge of the North American continent and established even further claims for Spain. As an entrada, however, an entrance into a new region, followed by the establishment of a colony, it met with total failure. First of all came the shock of the Seven Cities of Cíbola themselves, as Fray Marcos had designated the westernmost Zuñi pueblo of Hawikúh and the six others said to be further inland. Actually, there were only six Zuñi pueblos, Coronado reported back to the viceroy, and none of them bore any resemblance to the rich and gleaming city adorned with turquoise that Fray Marcos had described. The soldiers cursed Fray Marcos as an outright liar, and the disgraced Franciscan provincial, fearing for his safety, left the expedition and returned to Mexico.

Coronado endorsed the assessment of Fray Marcos as a liar. Still, while he admitted that the inhabitants of Hawikúh were not the European-like people Fray Marcos had claimed them to be, Coronado—as is evident in a lengthy letter to Mendoza dated 3 August 1540—is generally favorable in his descriptions of the Zuñi people of Hawikúh, which he renamed Granada in honor of Mendoza's birthplace, commenting appreciatively on their clothing, food, basic way of living, and zealous protection of women. Profit might be gained from this country, runs Coronado's implied argument, given the possibilities of gold and silver in its mountains and abundant animal life, including the great bison of the interior, which Coronado knows only by report and from the Zuñi use of their hides.

The problem was the Zuñi. Having been read the *Requerimiento*, a lengthy declaration outlining the history of Christianity and offering a peaceful takeover if the Zuñi submitted to God and king, the principales of Hawikúh replied that they had no interest in the Spanish offer. Worse, they followed up their rejection with a shower of arrows shot from the pueblo down on the Spaniards reading the *Requerimiento* on the flatland below. Reluctantly, as this harassment continued, Coronado decided to storm the pueblo, despite his commitment to a peaceful encounter (albeit on Spanish terms). The Zuñi defended themselves with arrows and stones thrown from the roof of the pueblo, and Coronado had to be removed from the melee with two facial wounds and an arrow in one foot—his life saved, he later reported, only when one of his captains, García López de Cárdenas, threw himself upon the fallen captain general as a shield. Once subdued, at the loss of a few Indian dead (the Spaniards suffered no fatalities), the Zuñi of Hawikúh proved agreeable enough, at least willing to parley, and the remaining five Zuñi pueblos would soon sue for peace.

Tewa and Quivira

Following the conquest of the Zuñi pueblos, the search for fabled cities continued in two new directions. Fray Marcos had described cities to the west, and so, despite the Franciscan's being blatantly wrong in the matter of Cíbola, Coronado dispatched a detachment west by northwest into northern Arizona. There they encountered the equally disappointing pueblos of the Hopi, who, like the Zuñi, briefly resisted the Spaniards. Another group, under the command of Cárdenas, who had saved Coronado in the taking of Hawikúh, reached the Grand Canyon but failed to find any cities worthy of conquest.

An Indian principal whom the Spaniards named Bigotes (Big Whiskers) arrived in Hawikúh from the Cicúique (Pecos) pueblo to the east and described a network of pueblos called Tewa along a great river. To the north and northeast of these pueblos, Bigotes related, wide and open plains were inhabited by woolly, humpbacked cattle. A detachment sent ahead under the command of Pedro de Alvarado discovered the sky-high pueblo of Ácoma atop a 380-foot rock, then pushed on to Tewa and its great river—the Río del Norte, Spaniards first called it, later the Río Grande—where they found a network of twelve Tewa pueblos north of present-day Albuquerque. As part of this advance guard, Alvarado took along hostages, including Bigotes, in case his report of pueblos to the east proved false; an aged Pecos leader, Cacique; and two captive Plains Indians acquired as guides by Alvarado at the Pecos pueblo while Alvarado was on reconnaissance, Ysopete and an Indian the Spaniards called El Turco (the Turk). As the Alvarado party moved eastward along the Canadian River, buffalo came into view. Shortly thereafter, the Turk began to describe in gesture and pidgin Pueblo a magnificent kingdom, Quivira, farther to the northeast. Quivira was rich in gold and silver, fertile and abundant. Bigotes knew about Quivira, the Turk insisted, and owned a gold brace-let from there. Running out of time, Alvarado returned to the Río Grande valley and sent a message back to Coronado, still in Zuñi country, detailing the advantages of the Tewa region. Encouraged by this news, Coronado began to move his force into the Río Grande valley, where he planned to spend the winter.

Hunger! At the siege of Hawikúh, Coronado reported to Mendoza, many of his soldiers were so weakened by hunger that they could barely fight. Frustration: no fabled cities, nothing to show for their time. Things now went from bad to worse. Hungry, snowbound, short on provisions, the Spaniards requisitioned the pueblo Alcanfor from the Tewa for their winter quarters, along with requisitions of turkeys, maize, beans, calabashes, and three hundred blankets. The requisition of a pueblo and full support for more than three hundred men for an entire winter was bound to cause resentment, which built upon bad feelings from an earlier incident—an accu-sation of rape in the pueblo of Arenal lodged against Juan de Villegas, the brother of a high official in Mexico, by the woman's husband. The aggrieved man could not identify Villegas from a lineup organized by Captain Cárdenas but recognized his horse, which he was watching at Villegas' request—shame heaped upon shame—when the sexual assault occurred. The Spaniards took no action in the matter, how-ever, given the political connections of the accused. And when Coronado arrived at Hawikúh ahead of his main party, he was told nothing of the rape.

The Tewa defend themselves

Collections of blankets, cloaks, and provisions commenced. Eyewitness accounts as to how these collections were carried out differ. Coronado urged patience and kindness. Yet an increasing number of incidents of arrogance and outright abuse by Spaniards and resistance from Tewa occurred. Resentment festered. Plotting against the Spaniards began in earnest. Early one morning, rebellion broke out. A Tewa raiding party killed a Mexican Indian hostler and kidnapped a drove of horses and mules from the Spaniard-occupied pueblo. The Tewa raiders then slaughtered the kidnapped animals as a gesture of defiance. Coronado called a council of war, which recommended military action. In one last effort to avoid bloodshed, Coronado sent Cárdenas to the Arenal pueblo and Rodrigo Maldonado to the Moho pueblo, each now barricaded with palisades into an armed camp. The captains met with war cries and showers of arrows. Informed of this continuing resistance, Coronado ordered sieges of the pueblos.

After a day and night of siege—according to the account written twenty years later by Pedro de Castañeda, a member of the expedition—Cárdenas broke into the lower floors of Arenal and started smudge fires to drive the Tewa from the pueblo. Overcome by smoke, Tewa on the pueblo roof surrendered to two Spaniards, Pablo de Melgosa and Diego López, by making the sign of the cross, which the Spaniards returned. This, the Indians believed, constituted surrender and pardon. When the Indians voluntarily proceeded to Cárdenas' tent, however, he knew nothing of what the Tewa understood to be their confirmed surrender and pardon. Citing Coronado's order that no rebellious Tewa be taken alive, Cárdenas gave orders that all two hundred of the surrendering Tewa be burned at the stake as an example to the other Tewa pueblos. Why Melgosa and López, who had received the surrender and granted the pardon—under the sign of the cross—did not speak out at this point remains a mystery, provided that Castañeda's account is accurate. As the burnings began, a number of Arenal Indians tried to break away and were either hacked to death or run down by Spaniards on horseback as they fled across open fields. Not a man survived, Castañeda reports, and the Spaniards were now even more hated by the Tewa as a people who did not keep their word.

All this occurred at the end of December 1540. The siege and destruction of the Moho pueblo, which had also fortified itself, now ensued. Twice, Coronado sent Captains Maldonado and Cárdenas to parley, but each effort met with trickery and resistance by the Moho principal, a man called Juan Alemán, "John the German", because of his resemblance to a well-known German soldier in Spanish service. Why should he parley with the Spaniards for a peaceful surrender, the Tewa principal asked, given the Spaniards' treachery at Arenal? Better to die fighting than to be burned at the stake or run down by Spanish horsemen and their dogs.

The siege of Moho lasted from early February to late March 1541 in conditions of bitter cold and resulted in numerous Spanish deaths from arrows tipped in rattlesnake venom. Coronado himself led the siege, which proceeded in the European manner, with the Spaniards assaulting the upper floors of the pueblo via ladders and the Tewa resisting them from above with stones and arrows. In mid-March the Moho defenders, suffering from a water shortage, surrendered their women and children in an effort to save their lives, although such a surrender could very well mean slavery. In late March the remaining Moho defenders, now desperate, tried an early-morning breakout but were ridden down and killed by Spaniards on horseback. A few made it across the freezing Río Grande and were subsequently taken into captivity. An even smaller number remained inside the pueblo, which the Spaniards assaulted and burned—against Coronado's wishes, he later claimed.

Another nearby Tewa pueblo, meanwhile, was also besieged, but the men escaped, leaving behind approximately a hundred women and children in the belief—not yet disproved—that the Spaniards would not slaughter them. Following this quasi-surrender, Coronado dispatched Captain Maldonado to destroy any other pueblo fortifications in the area. Maldonado did so, and in the process put a number of pueblos to the torch as well—not by his orders, Coronado again later insisted.

These assaults ended the Tiguex War or, more correctly, the destruction of the Tiguex pueblo kingdom. Together with the much less fatal attack on a Hopi pueblo in Arizona, the actions would earn the displeasure of the viceroy upon Coronado's return to Mexico City and bring him before the Audiencia of New Spain on charges of waging gratuitous violence against the people of Tiguex. Coronado would prevail against these charges, citing his efforts to parley and the recalcitrant ferocity of Tewa resistance. But again—and how persistently—had the well been poisoned by unnecessary violence in the matter of the evangelization of Indian peoples.

Still hoping to find that fabled city, even after all this disappointment, Coronado continued his journey into the interior at the head of a select detachment, the Chosen Thirty, moving north by northeast through present-day Texas and Oklahoma into Kansas, in search of Quivira. As the leader of a force that pushed the Spanish presence and subsequent claims into the heart of the North American continent, Coronado earned a permanent place in history. Quivira, however, turned out to be a nondescript Wichita Indian village on the Arkansas River. He had invented Quivira, the Turk confessed, at the request of the Indians from the Pecos pueblo, to lead the Spaniards away from pueblo country into the trackless prairies of the northeast, where they would perish.

Return to Quivira

With Fray Marcos de Niza's departure from Cíbola for Mexico City, three professed Franciscans had remained with the Coronado expedition—the priest Juan de Padilla and the lay brothers Luis de Escalona and Juan de la Cruz—as well as two *donados* (oblates or nonprofessed associates who wore the gray Franciscan habit), Lucas and Sebastián, Indians from the monastery at Zapotlán in Mexico. Also attached to the Franciscan contingent were laymen Andrés do Campo, a Portuguese soldier who was a gardener by profession, and two enslaved Africans: Cristóbal, a young man belonging to Juan de Jaramillo (a native of Extremadura serving as a horseman, who would later write an account of the expedition), and a second Sebastián, belonging to Melchior Pérez, son of the late *licenciado* Diego Pérez de la Torre, second governor of Nueva Galicia. This second Sebastián also had with him his wife and an unspecified number of children.

When Coronado decided to return to Mexico, the professed Franciscans, led by Fray Juan de Padilla, their superior, expressed a desire to remain in Tierra Nueva (New Land) as missionaries. Padilla hoped that a detachment of soldiers would be assigned to protect the Franciscans. Indeed, at one point, up to sixty soldiers and at least one soldier's wife and son (Francisca de Hozes, an intelligent, outspoken woman, who had brought her young son on the expedition) preferred to stay in Tierra Nueva and make a go of a settlement. Their petition, though, was vetoed by Coronado, who wanted all serving soldiers to go back to Mexico, where they were needed. Still, Coronado generously supported the Franciscans with supplies and escorts from Cíbola to their chosen destinations: Fray Luis de Escalona, Cristóbal, and the difficult-to-document Fray Juan de la Cruz to Pueblo country; and Fray Juan de Padilla, the Portuguese soldier Andrés do Campo, and the two Indian lay oblates, Lucas and Sebastián, along with a free black interpreter (also robed as an oblate, according to Shea), an unnamed mestizo, and several servants to Quivira. As lay brothers, Fray Luis and the elusive Fray Juan de la Cruz (whom some modern historians doubt existed) could baptize and catechize but not celebrate Mass, so they traveled light. Fray Juan de Padilla, by contrast, a priest, left on his seven-hundred-mile journey with pack mules carrying bread and wine and liturgical garments for Mass as well as other equipment, a horse, and a small herd of the sheep that had been with the expedition from its beginning. The enslaved black man Sebastián and his family presumably returned to the service of Melchior Pérez.

History records Fray Luis de Escalona as a saintly desert anchorite in his final days and Fray Juan de la Cruz as a shadowy specter, more legendary than real. Last seen at the Pecos pueblo by a party of soldiers who left him with a small flock of sheep, Fray Luis—according to one report, he lived in a hut or cave, surviving on tortillas, beans, and cactus fruit provided by locals—told the soldiers that he retained hopes for a successful mission but was losing the support of the older men, who might kill him. Whether they did will never be known, for at this point Fray Luis disappears. Fray Juan de la Cruz was rumored to have been done in by Indian arrows.

In contrast, Fray Juan de Padilla emerges in chronicles as full-bodied (a phrase used frequently by Herbert Eugene Bolton, archdeacon of Borderland historians)—manly, assertive, physically active, courageous, and very much a soldier despite his sandals, tonsure, robes, crucifix, and staff. He served with Cortés before becoming a Franciscan and was a respected counselor of Coronado throughout the expedition. Coronado sent this soldier-priest on nearly every scouting or reconnaissance mission he commissioned: with Pedro de Tovar to the Hopi country, with Hernando de Alvarado to Tiguex and to the plains farther to the northeast, with the Chosen Thirty pushing north through endless seas of grass in search of Quivira. While with Tovar in Hopi country, Padilla urged attack when a band of Hopi tried to block the way. After the horse-killing raid at Tewa, Padilla was a member of the council of war that recommended an aggressive response.

Yet he was a priest as well as a former soldier respected for his military bearing and skills. Before the troubles began, he had good relations with the Pecos pueblo and later with the Tewa. In Texas he proselytized among the Teya, whom he held in high esteem; and in Quivira he grew to admire the impressively tall Wichita, to whom he would soon return. One hopes, moreover, that he celebrated Mass in all these remote places, the first priest to do so. For Catholic historians of subsequent generations, the image of this Franciscan priest celebrating the central rite of Catholic Christianity at the core of the North American continent at such an early date—and planting crosses along the trails the Spaniards were pioneering—takes on symbolic value. It turns into a statement about the priority of Catholicism in the unfolding history of Christianity in what later became Canada and the United States. While appreciating Juan de Padilla's fusion of faith and soldierly fortitude, one speculates that this Franciscan must have experienced (as did another soldier-priest, Bartolomé de Las Casas) a grave disturbance of spirit as he witnessed—indeed, participated in as chaplain and counselor—the destruction wrought against the Indians of Tierra Nueva by the Coronado expedition. What a terrible record! Three hundred or more Indians killed, including those burned at the stake for the crime of defending their homeland; perhaps as many as two hundred women and children taken into captivity, some enslaved or forced into servitude; three or four pueblos razed and torched; fierce war dogs sicced upon Indian men as a means of interrogation. Is this why he had come into this New Land? Fray Juan de Padilla might very well have asked himself. Was this how the gospel of Jesus Christ should be preached?

A cruel execution

Take, for example, the strangulation of the Turk, the captive Plains Indian whom Padilla had interviewed first at the Pecos pueblo and later in Tiguex, where the Spaniards had brought the Turk—with an iron ring around his neck—and other hostages.

An intelligent, voluble young man, the Turk told a story similar to that of Fray Marcos de Niza. To the northeast, on the plains just beyond his homeland, lay Quivira, a great kingdom. There an astounding river flowed, its fish as large as horses. The chiefs and nobles of Quivira plied this river in large canoes driven by sails and forty oarsmen, a golden eagle on each prow. Quivirans dined off gold and silver service and wore gold and silver jewelry, such as the gold bracelet the Turk claimed to have presented to Bigotes, which he would be happy to retrieve if permitted to return to Cicúique without Bigotes.

Fearing that the Turk would provoke a revolt if released, Coronado refused permission, but he wanted to believe the Turk's story, and he turned to Fray Juan de Padilla for counsel. Padilla advised that the truth of the matter hinged on the gold bracelet the Turk allegedly gave Bigotes and volunteered to interview the chief. Confronted by Padilla, Bigotes denied receiving such a gift from the Turk. Coronado and his lieutenant Alvarado—and perhaps Padilla—thought Bigotes was lying. With Coronado's knowledge, Alvarado set the war dogs on the chief, who, despite the terror and bites on his arms and legs, persisted in his denial. The aged Cacique was also submitted to the same form of canine interrogation, but he remained adamant as well. There was no bracelet, and hence no Quivira. The Turk was lying.

Yet the Spaniards retained this hope for Quivira, which was why the Franciscan eventually found himself part of the Chosen Thirty selected by Coronado to help him find Quivira on the buffalo plains of present-day Kansas. When Quivira turned out to be an ordinary village of Wichita Indians, and the Turk confessed that he had fabricated the story to deflect the Spaniards' attention from his home territory and to escape there to his awaiting wife, Coronado approved of the young man's execution by garrote, provided it be done covertly, to avoid alarming the rest of the camp. This need for secrecy suggests that the Turk had by this time become a sympathetic figure to the Indian retainers on the march, perhaps even to Fray Juan de Padilla.

And so, a rope around his neck tightened by a garrote—most likely being twisted by Francisco Martín, a butcher from Mexico City—the Turk died secretly, in the dark of midnight. The young man was simply trying his desperate best to regain his freedom and return to his homeland: to feel once again his wife's embrace, to hunt buffalo, to grow in the esteem of his tribe, to live to old age, his children's children around him in a place undisturbed by Spanish conquest. Later scholars have surmised the Turk was probably a proto-Pawnee, and it remains doubtful that the Spaniards understood his hand signs. What is grimly ironic is that his story may have contained a grain of truth, if he was referring to the highly developed chiefdoms of the lower Mississippi valley, through which Hernando de Soto was now busy cutting such a violent swath.

To live in their own way, undisturbed: the same could be said of the peoples of the Hawikúh, Arenal, and Moho pueblos and the other places the Spaniards had besieged, pillaged, and torched. A tragedy had been played out, a conflict of cultures, an imposition of greed and ambition, that perhaps no evangelization—however well intended—could ever fully heal. Here was a wound that would have to be cauterized by further conflict and rebellion before even a begrudging acceptance could emerge.

Quivira

The Franciscans who remained behind believed there had to be a better way to settle in Tierra Nueva. Near the Pecos pueblo, Fray Luis de Escalona tried to be of service and to preach the gospel of Jesus Christ, saying prayers and baptizing dying infants when permitted. Fray Juan de la Cruz, serving in real life or in legend, proclaimed love and salvation. Others stayed as well: the resourceful black teenager Cristóbal, Fray Luis' assistant; the robed Indian oblates, Lucas and Sebastián; the unnamed interpreter of African descent, possibly a robed oblate as well; and Andrés do Campo, the Portuguese gardener turned soldier, a layman touched by evangelical zeal and an abiding interest in finding the real Quivira.

Fray Juan de Padilla, the full-bodied former soldier, had once believed the stories of Fray Marcos de Niza and the Turk. But what were they now looking for, this Franciscan priest and his small coterie of retainers? Certainly not power or wealth. Perhaps they were in search of redemption, their own as well as that of the peoples of the buffalo plains, and atonement for the violence against the Pueblo peoples. As a soldier with Cortés and a soldierly chaplain with Coronado, Padilla had seen death aplenty among Indians killed by Spaniards. Could he now—changed, reformed, by what he had experienced—bring to these peoples something else, something better?

Significantly, Padilla returned to the village that was supposed to have been Quivira—two or three days south of Tabás—where the Spaniards had erected a cross and where the Turk had been garroted. Padilla preached at Tabás for a while, and then—against the advice of the friendly people there, who warned him of hostile Indians to the east—he moved eastward into the territory of the Gaus, later known as the Kansas people, in the company of Andrés do Campo, Lucas and Sebastián, and a few other retainers. Herbert Eugene Bolton attributes this move east across the buffalo plains to Padilla's restlessness. Restlessness for exactly what remains a question. A conscious desire for martyrdom does not seem a possibility, since Padilla brought along his entourage, and it is too much to believe that each of them would choose to go to a collective doom. It was, more likely, a restlessness to redeem the mission of the expedition: to make an entrada into Tierra Nueva and to find and assimilate the reported wealth of Cíbola into the Spanish Empire, but also to make a religious connection with its indigenous people on behalf of Catholic Christianity, perhaps even moving beyond the obtuse and arrogant demands of the *Requerimiento*. Padilla, by this time more priest than soldier, might very well have nurtured such foolish hopes as he reached Quivira and Tabás and dreamed of even further redemptive efforts on the buffalo plains to the east.

Barely into his journey, Fray Juan de Padilla spied a group of Gaus warriors in the distance. From their numbers and dress, it was obvious that they were on the warpath. Immediately, he urged his party to flee. There was no need for all of them to be slaughtered. Do Campo escaped on his horse. Lucas and Sebastián fled on foot and hid in the high grass. Fray Juan de Padilla knelt quietly on the prairie, his head bowed in prayer. From their hiding place, the oblates watched (they would subsequently report) as the Gaus war party drew closer and took the Franciscan's life with an onslaught of arrows. With the permission of the Gaus warriors, Lucas and Sebastián later returned to bury the body of the murdered friar on the plains of Quivira.

3

Saint Augustine 1565

Evangelization falters amid violence, slavery, and revolt

The expedition that led to the founding of Saint Augustine, the oldest city in North America, was launched on 28 June 1565, the eve of the feast of Saints Peter and Paul, when fifteen hundred soldiers, sailors, and colonists set sail from Cádiz for Florida via Puerto Rico in one galleon and fourteen light caravels under the command of Pedro Menéndez de Avilés, the newly appointed *adelantado* (governor) of a territory Spain had unsuccessfully been attempting to settle since its discovery by Juan Ponce de León on Easter Sunday (Pascua Florida) 1513. Storms scattered the Menéndez armada as it departed the Canary Islands, but rather than tarry in Puerto Rico—which the fleet reached in increments throughout July and August—Menéndez sailed for Florida on 15 July with five vessels, five hundred soldiers, two hundred sailors, and one hundred colonists.

The reason for the adelantado's haste was the establishment of Fort Caroline a year earlier by French Huguenots at the mouth of the Saint Johns River, forty miles north of Saint Augustine's harbor. Fort Caroline represented an intolerable intrusion by French Protestants into territory claimed for Catholic Spain. Arriving at Cabo Cañaveral (Cape Canaveral) on 25 August, Menéndez's landing party learned from friendly Timucuan natives that the French encampment lay to the north. As he sailed northward along the coast, Menéndez discovered on 28 August the harbor he named in honor of Saint Augustine of Hippo, whose feast day it was, then continued toward the mouth of the Saint Johns River, where on the afternoon of 4 September he encountered four French galleons under the command of Captain General Jean Ribault. That night, around ten o'clock, following a thunderstorm, Menéndez sailed into the French flotilla and challenged its right to be there. Ribault challenged him back and then, under cover of darkness, slipped through the Spanish fleet and headed out to sea. Menéndez gave chase but was outrun by the French.

Heading north of the Saint Johns River, the adelantado hoped to blockade further access to Fort Caroline. Instead, the Spaniards met three more French vessels, cannons at the ready, sailing their way. The Spaniards now stood in danger of attack from two directions, should the four galleons they had been pursuing return. Deciding that he had been outmaneuvered, Menéndez broke contact and, sailing south, returned to the harbor of Saint Augustine.

As if to compensate for being outmaneuvered by the Huguenots, Menéndez orchestrated a lavish ceremony to signify the establishment of Saint Augustine as the first fortified harbor and civilian settlement on the northern coast of Florida, from which a prosperous crown colony would soon be developed. Entering the harbor on 6 September, Menéndez sent three companies of soldiers ashore under the command of two respected captains, with orders to scout the best site for a fort and build a preliminary fortification. Welcomed by the local Indians, the soldiers spent the next day digging ditches and constructing temporary ramparts.

That same day the fleet chaplain, Don Martín Francisco López de Mendoza Grajales, a secular priest, came ashore to supervise the erection of an altar for use on the next day, 8 September, the feast of the Nativity of Mary. The following morning, as shipboard cannons and artillery roared in salute and trumpets sounded, the flags of Aragón and Castile were unfurled on shore. Holding aloft a cross, a fully liturgically vested Grajales processed toward the landing party in the company of another secular priest, Don Pedro Menéndez de Áviles (a cousin of the governor), trailed by a line of soldiers as a Te Deum was collectively chanted. Advancing to the cross, Menéndez and each member of his party kissed it on bended knee. Chaplain Grajales then celebrated the solemn high Mass.

Regular and secular clergy

All this ceremony was intended to usher in a grand and assured enterprise, once the disquieting matter of the French enclave to the north was taken care of. Catholicism advanced into North America through three modes: exploration and conquest, missionary activity, and settlement. Conquistadors were quick to legitimate their enterprises utilizing the language of evangelization. Their basic goal, they claimed, was the conversion of native peoples. Added—in Spanish, no less!—to the Laws of Burgos in 1513 was the Requirement (*El Requerimiento*) to be read to native peoples at first encounter. The Requirement summarized the Old and New Testaments, the role of the papacy, and the nature of Catholic Spain; it was followed by a promise of good treatment if the people in question converted and became subjects of the Crown.

Bound by solemn vows and formed by communal discipline and the defining charisms of their orders, religious priests were well suited for the missionary life they dominated. The more settled colonial society became in the Caribbean, however, the more diocesan the ecclesiastical polity became, with a bishop based in an urban setting and diocesan or secular clergy ministering to the population. Even if a bishop were a member of a religious order before promotion to the episcopate (as many were in the early years of the Spanish Empire) and retained the habit of his order following episcopal consecration (as did Las Casas), he no longer belonged to his order in the strictest sense. He belonged, rather, to his diocese; indeed, he embodied it apostolically and administratively and hence held direct authority over his diocesan or secular clergy and to a lesser, but still important, degree over the religious-order clergy.

There was also a distinction between a parish and a mission. A parish served a stable population of Catholics and was located in a settlement. Served primarily by secular diocesan clergy, a parish possessed canonical status within its diocese. In the early years of the Spanish colonial system, pastors of parishes were salaried through the Crown, and in the case of parishes in important urban settlements, pastoral appointments might be passed upon by the Crown as well. As secular priests, diocesan clergy took no religious vows, although they promised obedience to their bishop and, upon being ordained to the preparatory rank of subdeacon, pledged to observe celibacy. Having sworn no vow of poverty, they could possess personal funds and property and in certain cases could receive compensation from church endowments following the importation of the benefice/endowment system from Spain. As was evident in Las Casas' years as a secular priest, such a priest could also hold and work land in his own name and even have slaves.

By contrast, a religious priest took solemn vows of poverty, chastity, and obedience to his superiors. Members of religious orders, however, were exempt from direct episcopal supervision, except when serving in diocesan parishes if a shortage of diocesan clergy occurred. In general terms, diocesan clergy were bound to a diocese, while religious clergy enjoyed a certain mobility within the frameworks of their orders and hence cultivated a missionary spirit.

Religious clergy reached the Indies early, starting with four Franciscans who accompanied Columbus' second voyage in 1493. Dominicans arrived in 1510, along with a handful of Mercedarians (Trinitarians), another order of mendicant friars, dedicated to the care of the sick and the ransoming of Christian captives. Regulars following the rule (*regula*) of a specific order constituted the majority of clergy in the initial years of the Spanish Empire in the Indies, their missionary spirit and sense of independence buoyed by a papal grant, the *Omnimoda* of 1522, which bestowed on religious orders a worldwide autonomy. Forty-six years later, however, a diocesan structure had emerged. An increasing number of secular clergy were available for service as well as bishops with a secular diocesan background. The orders, meanwhile, had grown into autonomous ecclesiastical polities, reporting to the Crown on a basis nearly equal to that of the bishops.

Something had to be done to regularize the situation. In 1568 King Philip II convened a special junta to reexamine the administration and protocols of ecclesiastical organization in the Indies. The junta recommended, and the king approved, a revocation of the *Omnimoda* of 1522 in favor of a more conventional diocesan structure, which placed religious-order priests under the jurisdiction of local bishops and regularized the role and support of the diocesan clergy.

As Don Martín Francisco López de Mendoza Grajales was assuming his duties as the first parish priest of Saint Augustine, the practices and regulations of diocesan organization in the New World were moving toward their final promulgation as the Laws of the Indies issued by the Council of the Indies in Seville, the governing body for the colonies. Established in 1511 by King Ferdinand, the Council of the Indies was composed of clergy and jurists, and it governed with exacting specificity the civil and ecclesiastical affairs of the colonies. The *Recopilación de Leyes de los Reynos de las Indies* spelled out the rights, privileges, and obligations of bishops and diocesan clergy. One law, for example, fixed the shares that bishops, cathedral canons, and parish clergy were to have in tithes collected for the Crown. Other regulations pertained to the construction and support of cathedrals and parish churches. Another law mandated that only secular priests were to be appointed confessors to nuns. Other laws forbade secular priests from deriving outside income as alcaldes (mayors), lawyers (notaries), traders, or owners of mines or boats used for pearl fishing. Law V of Title VIII stated that if secular clergy were established in a settlement, no religious orders should found convents there. All secular clergy, however, should make every effort to teach the Spanish language to local Indians and to cat-acheticize them in Spanish whenever possible.[1]

A next-to-impossible colony

A future diocesan structure, then, was implicit in the ministry of Martín Francisco López de Mendoza Grajales as chaplain to the garrison, parish priest, and vicar, as he soon became following the arrival in 1566 of five additional secular priests. A native of the province of Jerez de la Frontera, Grajales had received his chaplain's appointment from Menéndez and his priestly faculties (license to practice) from the bishop of Santiago de Cuba. In a very real way, Grajales represented the diocesan future of Florida, over which the bishop of Cuba held jurisdiction.

For more than half a century, Florida and its indigenous peoples had resisted settlement. Juan Ponce de León attempted a settlement in 1521, sailing that spring from Puerto Rico in two ships laden with soldiers, colonists, secular priests, and some Dominican friars to evangelize the Indians. Also on board was an impressive collection of horses, cattle, sheep, and pigs. Landing near present-day Charlotte Harbor on the Gulf of Mexico coast of the Florida peninsula that Spaniards still thought might be an island, the colonists built houses and a chapel and set about the Hispanicization of the area, just as they had previously done on Española (1496), Puerto Rico (1508), Jamaica (1509), and Cuba (1511). Prior to his departure, Ponce de León had written letters to Emperor Charles V and the cardinal of Tortosa (later Pope Adrian VI), declaring his intention to found a profitable Catholic colony as well as to convert the Indians, who, Ponce de León promised, would not be attacked, captured, or otherwise harmed, provided they saw the light and submitted to the Catholic Church and the king of Spain.

Ponce de León's new neighbors, the Timucuan, however, were not interested in either Catholicism or the king, having perhaps been visited by rogue Spanish slavers in times past or, at the least, been made aware of such slaving raids on other tribes. Conflict between Spaniards and Indians was immediate and continuous, and in an encounter in early July 1521, Ponce de León—veteran of Columbus' second voyage, pioneer conquistador and settler of Española, successful courtier in the court of Charles V, governor of Puerto Rico, veteran fighter in the war of elimination against the fierce Caribs, discoverer of Florida, and holder of an *asiento* (a royal patent for conquest and resettlement) from Charles V—was seriously wounded by an arrow shot by an anonymous Timucuan as Ponce de León led the last charge of his career. Dispirited, defeated, with their governor dying from his wound, the colonists abandoned their settlement and boarded ship for Havana. Ponce de León died either on the voyage, in a stopover in Veracruz, or in Havana itself. He was forty-seven.

A second effort at settlement

The next effort to establish a foothold in Florida was launched in June 1526 by Lucas Vázquez de Ayllón, a wealthy licentiate (judge) from Española. Ayllón backed into colonization when a ship he sponsored to reconnoiter the Florida coast turned slaver as its captain came under the influence of a slaving caravel owned by a rival

Española judge. The caravel was returning from an unsuccessful attempt to capture and enslave Caribs in the Bahamas. Reaching the coast of eastern Florida, the two captains discovered the mouth of a great river on 25 June 1521, the feast of Saint John the Baptist, and named it accordingly. As the Huguenots were to discover forty-three years later, the mouth of the Saint Johns River seemed promising for settlement. Ayllón's captain, Francisco Gordillo, claimed the territory for Ayllón. The other captain, Pedro de Quexos, claimed it for his owner, the judge Juan Ortiz de Matienzo. Contrary to Ayllón's orders, Gordillo joined Quexos in seizing some seventy natives, whom they brought back to Española as slaves. Horrified, Ayllón demanded that the Indians be released. A commission of inquiry headed by Diego Columbus granted Ayllón's request, which was later thwarted through delay and noncompliance.

The entire affair quickened in Ayllón an ambition to establish a settlement on the eastern coast of Florida that would be a model of profitability and proper Christian treatment of natives. To that end, Ayllón sailed for Spain in 1522, taking with him Francisco de Chicora, a young Indian seized as a slave in the 1521 expedition, who had been baptized, now spoke Spanish, and served in Ayllón's household. In Spain, Francisco dazzled court and council with descriptions of a lush land to the north of Winyah Bay (north of present-day Charleston), where he had been captured. The Land of Chicora the region was immediately named, a new Andalucía on the north Florida (South Carolina) coast, awaiting settlement and evangelization.

Buoyed by Francisco's reports, Charles V and the Council of the Indies granted Ayllón a cédula on 12 June 1523 authorizing him to explore the north Florida coast and, once a site was selected, to organize and finance a settlement. Ayllón was to take with him, the cédula stated, religious-order priests to evangelize the natives, whom the expedition was explicitly prohibited from enslaving. Ayllón was temporarily delayed when he was sent to Puerto Rico on judicial assignment. To fulfill his mandate and retain his asiento, Ayllón dispatched two caravels under the command of Pedro de Quexos in early 1525 to explore the coast and to leave stone crosses at various intervals, claiming the territory for Charles V. Quexos reconnoitered as far north as Chesapeake Bay, thus establishing a Spanish claim to present-day North Carolina and Virginia, which Pedro Menéndez de Avilés and the Society of Jesus would later attempt to consolidate. A challenge to Ayllón's asiento by Juan Ortiz de Matienzo, on charges that Ayllón had made fraudulent claims to exclusivity, delayed Ayllón's colonizing armada even further. At long last, in early June 1526, three large vessels—a caravel, a Breton, and a brigantine—sailed from Puerto de la Plata carrying six hundred colonists, sailors, soldiers, physicians, secular priests, three Dominicans, and one hundred horses. A heavily mortgaged Ayllón bore the brunt of the expenses.

To signify and implement his desire to do right by the Indians, Ayllón recruited as a member of his Dominican cadre the renowned Fray Antonio de Montesinos, the first priest in the Indies to denounce Indian slavery—in 1511, from the pulpit of the cathedral in Santo Domingo—and, along with Bartolomé de Las Casas, the continuing leader of the abolition movement. The Ayllón expedition did include, however, a number of black slaves (commonly held in Spain during that era) and several Indian interpreters who, like Francisco de Chicora, had been baptized and taken to Spain to perfect their Spanish. Surely, Lucas Vázquez de Ayllón, digging deeply into his pockets and leveraging his estates, had done everything in his power to ensure a successful colonization on the Florida coast.

When the flotilla made landfall near Winyah Bay in South Carolina, however, bad things began to happen. For one thing, Francisco de Chicora and the Indian interpreters—the avatars of the Christianized Indian the Dominicans hoped to foster—jumped ship and fled into the interior. So much for Christianity and the Indians' long exposure to Spanish culture in Española and Spain. Far from being another Andalucía, moreover, the fabled Land of Chicora proved to be a dry, sterile, underpopulated wasteland unsuitable for agriculture. Breaking into two parties, the expedition proceeded southward by land and sea until a more suitable site was chosen, on Sapelo Sound in present-day Georgia. There on 18 October 1526 the first Spanish settlement in the United States, San Miguel de Guadalupe, was hastily constituted.

It was late fall, however; hence no crops could be planted. The winter of 1526–1527 proved ferocious. Contaminated water sickened and killed numerous colonists, including Lucas Vázquez de Ayllón himself, who died in the arms of Fray Montesinos, his dreams come to naught on a deadly coast. Hostilities broke out with the neighboring Guales. Spaniards were killed. Insurrection erupted when one group imprisoned Francisco Gómez, the temporary administrator, and other alcaldes. Civil conflict ensued, abetted by a revolt by the black slaves. A semblance of order was eventually restored. But the cold, the hunger, the hostile Guales, and the violent factionalism destroyed hopes for a colony, and the decision was made to disband the enterprise and sail back to Española through hurricane-whipped seas. Of the original 600 settlers, only 150 made it home. Ayllón's body was lost at sea when one of the returning ships went down in a storm.

The de Soto expedition

Thus ended the second effort to colonize Florida and to begin a settled diocesan structure. The conquest and occupation of Mexico, Central America, and Peru, meanwhile, focused attention elsewhere; indeed, the 1527 expedition led by the veteran conquistador Pánfilo de Narváez, which accidentally brought Cabeza de Vaca and hundreds of others to Florida, was en route to western Mexico across the gulf before storms and navigational errors washed it ashore on Florida, which the stranded Spaniards fled as quickly as they could. Hernando de Soto, who prevailed over Cabeza de Vaca in securing an appointment from Emperor Charles V as adelantado of Cuba with the right to conquer Florida, was not interested in colonization or evangelization at all, although he paid the usual lip service to the sacred task of converting the Indian population. Narváez had brought along several secular priests and five Franciscans, all of whom were lost. De Soto's party evidently included up to twelve priests (eight secular and four religious) but only two women—hardly the makings of a colony. The seculars must have been employed as chaplains, for even if de Soto were to have established a settlement, there would been too few women, no children, and hence no parish for the seculars to administer.

The records of the de Soto expedition, John Gilmary Shea (the protohistorian of Catholicism in North America) laments, show little evidence of religious activity: no liturgical dedications, no missionary functions, only one Mass celebrated in the field, and the name of a sole priest, Juan de Gallegos (a Franciscan) documented.

Three Franciscans and one secular priest survived the campaign that sailed from Sanlúcar, Spain, in April 1538, saluted by trumpet and cannonade. Financed by de Soto and a group of Genoese bankers, the operation was the most formidable thus far to depart Spain for the Indies. Nearing forty, de Soto had made a fortune in the brutal conquest of Central America and Peru and was determined to become even richer and rise even higher in status as the conquistador of Florida and the as-of-yet-unknown regions to the north and northwest. De Soto, lured by rumor, alleged reports, the example of Mexico, and his own experiences (particularly in Peru), believed those areas contained realms of gold, jewels, and opulent Indian cities ready for the taking.

Sailing from Havana in early May 1539, the de Soto flotilla—570 men, 2 women, and 223 horses, mules, pigs, and war dogs in 9 ships—landed on the west coast of Florida, most likely near Tampa Bay, later that month. Once ashore, de Soto had the good luck to make contact with Juan Ortiz, a survivor of the Narváez expedition, who in his involuntary sojourn among the Indians had gone native and mastered the language and its variations spoken by the Apalachee and Muskogean peoples of the southeast.

Over the next three years, until his death from fever on the lower Mississippi in May 1542, Hernando de Soto and his men set new standards for exploration of the interior of the North American continent, trekking as far north and west as present-day Kansas. Desirous of great wealth, de Soto died in the wilderness owning five Indian slaves, three horses, and a herd of swine. Outstripping his record of reconnaissance involving eight American states was his record of cruelty to and wanton devastation of indigenous peoples, which totally contrasted with the pious pronouncements initially attached to his campaign as well as his own statements. Shea confesses his scandalized disappointment in the behavior of the de Soto party and ascribes full responsibility to its commander. "De Soto had been trained in a bad school; he had no respect for the lives or rights of the Indians"—a somewhat understated introduction to Shea's two accounts of the expedition, each based on the encyclopedic *Historia general y natural de las Indias* (1535) of Gonzalo Fernández de Oviedo. Shea does shy away from providing lurid descriptions of de Soto's path of destruction in his foundational essay "Ancient Florida" in the first volume of Justin Winsor's magisterial eight-volume *Narrative and Critical History of America* (1886) and the shorter version that appears in *The Catholic Church in Colonial Days* (1886). However, without indulging in gory detail, the historian David J. Weber in *The Spanish Frontier in North America* (1992) correctly assesses the de Soto expedition as a three-year assault by the Spaniards against some of the most highly developed Indian villages and cultures on the North American continent by a veteran of two previous conquests whose self-confessed favorite sport was hunting fleeing Indians from horseback and who had set sail from Spain with a supply of iron chains and collars as part of his Indian program.

Employing previously tested conquistador techniques, de Soto seized hostages, preferably chiefs and Indian guides, holding them captive until a region was plundered for food, pearls, and the ever-elusive gold and jewels, along with women enslaved for domestic service and sexual purposes, provided they "were not old nor the most ugly", as de Soto's secretary later noted. A number of these captive women were even baptized. Thus the Spaniards cut a murderous swath through

the Apalachee, Cofitachequi, Coosa, and Tuscaloosa peoples in the densely populated, agriculturally developed southeast as well as the equally advanced peoples
of the Mississippi region. Burning, looting, raping, torturing, mutilating, throwing
captive Indians to savage dogs as the Spaniards extracted wealth and sought ever
more prosperous cities to loot: here was Bartolomé de Las Casas' worst nightmare.
Mass murder and pillaging had become as true of North America as they had been
of Española, Puerto Rico, Cuba, Jamaica, Central America, Mexico, and Peru.
Such crimes against humanity constituted a blasphemous poisoning of the well at
the intersection of Spain and native America.

A doomed Dominican mission

How could well-intended clergy bridge, much less heal, this breach of trust born
of greed, rapine, and murder? How could they dare to preach the message of Jesus
Christ to the victims of such behavior or to those who had heard of it and escaped?
Las Casas and his fellow Dominicans had been asking these questions for three
decades, ever since Fray Antonio de Montesinos had mounted the pulpit in the
cathedral of Santo Domingo to denounce Indian slavery in 1511. Throughout these
years, led by Montesinos, the Order of Friars Preachers headed the antienslave-
ment campaign, which is what attracted Las Casas to the order. Had the Ayllón
expedition—which included Montesinos and two other Dominican friars—
succeeded, who knows what good beginning might have been made in Florida?
And had Cabeza de Vaca instead of de Soto been given command of the 1539
expedition, one can speculate that Cabeza de Vaca—who had lived for years among
the Indians as a captive, experienced a profound identification with the Passion of
Christ during his long ordeal, and became a religious healer in the name of Jesus—
might have tried to bring about better treatment of the indigenous peoples of Florida and beyond. History, however, has a way of remaining intractable even within
the shifting parameters of historical interpretation. In Florida, the Friars Preachers
and the missionaries of the other orders who followed them were forced to deal
with alienation and violence: the wake of the de Soto expedition, which included
eight seculars, two Dominicans, one Franciscan, and one Mercedarian who did not
seem to exercise any documented influence.

The 1537 papal bull *Sublimis Deus*—which declared that the Indian was a rational
human being to be treated with dignity and respect, not to be physically abused or
enslaved—obviously did not sway the de Soto expedition, especially since a year
later the bull was revised at the insistence of Emperor Charles V to revoke any
ecclesiastical penalties clergy might have imposed on conquistadors under its influence. Thus, while *Sublimis Deus* represented a theoretical victory, it lacked power
of enforcement. Nevertheless, the bull encouraged Las Casas, now a bishop, and
his fellow Dominicans in their struggle to end the de facto race war being waged
against the Indians. Fray Antonio de Montesinos, alas, was not on hand to savor
the theological and philosophical victory represented by *Sublimis Deus*, having died
some seven years earlier in Venezuela, an event that his community of profession
(the convent of Saint Stephen in Salamanca) entered into its register as a martyrdom. Still, Dominicans such as Fray Luis Cancer de Barbastro, a longtime colleague
of Las Casas in Guatemala and Mexico, felt a surge of hope. The definitions and

prohibitions advanced by Pope Paul III offered optimism that the treatment of Indians might improve and hope that the Order of Friars Preachers might be able to implement a more humane missionary practice. Dominicans had sought to do just that in Tuzulutlan, the Central American region known by the conquistadors as the Land of War, later renamed the Land of True Peace by Crown Prince Philip II (regent for his father, Emperor Charles V), in recognition of the Friars Preachers' success in bringing calm to that once violent region.

Late 1547 found Fray Cancer and Bishop Las Casas back in Spain—Cancer in Seville before the Council of the Indies and Las Casas before the royal court at Valladolid—advocating a daring, innovative scheme: a purely missionary expedition to Florida by Friars Preachers that was to include no soldiers or settlers, but only Dominicans and Indian interpreters, there for purposes of peaceful evangelization. Astonishingly, Cancer and Las Casas succeeded and were issued a royal cédula on 28 December 1547, instructing Don Antonio de Mendoza, the viceroy of Mexico, to supply the Dominicans with whatever they needed to carry out the enterprise. Even after the cédula was granted, however, the Council of the Indies resisted the directive. Juan López, an experienced navigator with knowledge of Florida, when asked to give expert testimony, was afraid that he would be assigned to the mission and testified against it. Also opposing the project was the Dominican provincial of Aragón to whom Cancer (chosen to lead the enterprise) appealed for volunteers; the provincial voiced reluctance to commit his friars to such a quixotic endeavor. Las Casas and Cancer persisted, however, and after further wrangling, the mission was authorized. Still, for all the hopefulness expressed by Las Casas and Cancer, it was a very small group—five priests (including Cancer) who were missionary veterans, a lay brother, and a baptized Florida Indian serving as interpreter, Magdalena—that set sail from Veracruz, Mexico, and arrived at the Florida coast on the eve of the feast of the Ascension.

Things went wrong immediately. Juan de Arana, the captain of the caravel, was supposed to continue the voyage to the Bay of Saint Helen on the eastern coast, but Arana refused to sail beyond the Tampa Bay region south of the western gulf panhandle through which de Soto had campaigned so murderously. Proceeding along the coast, the priests landed and encountered Indians they believed to be friendly. Father Diego de Peñalosa, Brother Fuentes (his first name lost to history), and an unnamed sailor decided to visit the natives' inland settlement, taking with them the interpreter Magdalena. The next morning Magdalena was on shore with a group of Indians to tell the Spaniards hovering offshore in a tender that the priest, brother, and sailor were traveling overland to Tampa Bay, where they would rendezvous with the expedition. At each point the Spaniards made contact with Indians on the shore from the tender, Magdalena provided the same answer: the Dominicans and the sailor were en route by land. Finally, following the last of these tender-to-shore contacts, the Spaniards returned to their caravel to find on board one Juan Muñoz, a veteran of the de Soto expedition, who had escaped by canoe after ten years of captivity. Father Peñalosa and Brother Fuentes, Muñoz told the Spaniards, were dead. They had been tortured and executed amid heathen orgies; he had seen their scalps. The sailor was being held as a slave.

As far as the already skittish Captain Arana was concerned, that was it! He would proceed no farther. Reluctantly, Father Gregorio de Beteta and Juan García agreed.

It seemed futile to continue with the mission, given the Indians' hostility. That left Father Cancer, the originator and superior of the enterprise. Would Muñoz serve as his interpreter if he went ashore? Cancer asked the escaped captive. Not surprisingly, Muñoz, declared he would not go.

At this juncture, one can only speculate about the turmoil seething within Fray Cancer, now alone in his desire to continue the grand mission for which he and Las Casas had argued so eloquently before court, council, and viceroy. The mission was failing. Where did that leave the dream of an evangelization based on rights and respect? Did the Dominican still hope to demonstrate what his order had for so long been arguing was the proper way to spread the word of Jesus Christ? Or, on a more human level, was the devout religious anxious to atone for his sense of failure—two Dominicans tortured and executed, two other veteran missionaries voting to regroup, the ship's captain in open revolt, the Christianized Indian interpreter turned traitor or compelled to do so—with his own death?

In any event, Fray Cancer spent all day Monday, 15 June 1549, quietly arranging the presents he would carry ashore the following day, writing letters to his superiors, and updating his diary. The next morning, sailors rowed him toward the beach, but they refused to land, fearing the rough surf. The next morning he had them try again. Fathers Beteta and García were in the tender with him. (More ambiguity. Why were they there? To prevent the martyrdom they suspected their colleague had in mind?) As they neared the shore, the priests beheld a war party armed with bows, arrows, and clubs. When the Spaniards were within shouting distance, the Indians demanded the return of the escaped slave. Muñoz yelled back at them defiantly.

"Silence, brother. Cease to anger them," Cancer cautioned.

"No people could be more enraged," cautioned Father Beteta. "For the love of God, wait. Do not land."

Fray Cancer leaped from the tender and, waist-deep in the water, waded ashore, his white Dominican habit billowing about him in the surf. Reaching the beach, Cancer knelt in the sand. Raising his arms heavenward, he bowed his head and prayed. The Indians waited until he had risen from prayer before they dragged him to a nearby mound and, as the priests and sailors watched from offshore, clubbed him to death.[2]

Another disaster

Perhaps somewhat paradoxically, the widely reported martyrdom of Fray Luis Cancer de Barbastro brought to the fore the Dominican point of view regarding a more humane treatment of native peoples. The enslavement of Indians was progressively weakened by the papal bull *Sublimis Deus* in 1538, the New Laws of 1542–1543 qualifying the encomienda system, the debates of 1550 in Valladolid between Las Casas and Juan Ginés de Sepúlveda, the Dominicans' continuing advocacy following Las Casas' death in 1566, and an outright condemnation in 1573 from both Spain and the papacy of the notion that Native Americans were a species of subrational human being. This final declaration, however, would prove an empty gesture, given the millions of Native Americans dead from enslavement and slaughter as well as the concurrent increase in the African slave trade. As many historians have pointed out, Native Americans suffered from various forms of forced labor in the mission system well into the nineteenth century, along with more cunning socially disguised techniques, including the retention of the medieval-like system of Spanish land monopoly and Indian peonage.

Still, the rising sentiment in favor of abolition made it easier to express missionary intent toward the unconverted peoples of Spanish North America and helped bring into office such figures as Don Luis de Velasco, the second viceroy of New Spain, who served from 1550 to 1564. A wealthy nobleman, Velasco had already distinguished himself as viceroy in the kingdom of Navarre. In New Spain, Velasco personally negotiated the emancipation of fifteen thousand Indian slaves and founded three towns and the Royal and Pontifical University of Mexico, as well as a number of hospitals and other public institutions. Velasco not only secured the slaves' freedom but remained vigilant in ensuring for them expanded rights and protection. In short, Velasco embodied the humanistic and humane ideals of a dawning golden age of Spanish culture and Counter-Reformation that coexisted with abuses of empire.

Perhaps no public figure better embodied the Counter-Reformational aspects of this golden age than Philip II, regent for his father, Emperor Charles V, toward the final years of his reign and king of Spain following the emperor's abdication in 1556. Assiduous, hardworking, and deeply Catholic, Philip lived a near-reclusive life in the Escorial, a monastery-palace administrative complex Philip had built for himself outside Madrid. The king's simple bedroom looked down on the altar and tabernacle of the chapel in which Hieronymite Hermits of Saint Jerome, an order long close to the Spanish monarchy, daily celebrated Mass and chanted the Divine Office.

Given his ardent Catholicity and authority over church affairs in the Indies, no wonder Philip listened closely when Don Ferdinand de Urango—the bishop of Santiago de Cuba, whose diocese included Florida—urgently urged the king to establish colonies in Florida, lest that region be colonized by others, including French Huguenot heretics. By the late 1550s, a religious war was on the horizon in the Caribbean, perhaps best symbolized by the illegal entry in 1562–1563 of Captain John Hawkins into the Caribbean slave trade. However reprehensible the Indian slavers of an earlier era were (from Philip's point of view, at least), Spaniards did not represent a threat to Spanish sovereignty. Hawkins, by contrast, was an English Protestant and presaged the entry of Protestant England into a shadow war of state-authorized piracy in the Caribbean that would last for nearly two centuries. Secretly condoned and rewarded by the English Crown, this shadow war fused geopolitical and religious implications. Neither French Huguenots (nor French Catholics, for that matter) nor English Protestants could be expected to set much store by Pope Alexander VI's awards of the New World to Spain and Portugal. Arriving in the Caribbean as slavers and pirates, Protestants could come as colonists as well, which posed a threat to Catholic Spain. By the mid-sixteenth century, Spaniards were generically classifying pirates as Lutherans (meaning Protestants), and soon pirates of every degree were upgrading themselves into crusaders against Catholicism.

Eager to establish a foothold in Florida after nearly half a century of trying, Philip II authorized Viceroy Velasco to mount yet one more colonizing enterprise, the third since Ponce de León's abortive attempt of 1521. Proceeding cautiously, the viceroy in September 1558 dispatched three vessels under the command of Guido de Labazares to explore the Florida coast for the best possible settlement sites. Upon his return, Labazares recommended Pensacola Bay on the gulf. Learning of French intentions to colonize on the eastern Florida coast, Philip II expanded the plan to include a settlement on Point Saint Helena on the border of present-day Georgia and South Carolina.

In his petition to the king, Bishop Urango had argued for multiple colonies. That meant men, women, and children in significant numbers, which meant town-ships, parish churches, and a secular diocesan clergy. Yet Alfonso de Montúfar, the archbishop of Mexico, who had seconded Urango's request through official channels, was a Dominican—further testimony to the ascendancy of the Order of Friars Preachers during this period—and wanted Friars Preachers on the expedition as well. On 30 September 1558 Viceroy Velasco informed the king that religious orders in Mexico universally opined that Dominicans be assigned jurisdiction on the forthcoming enterprise and that the king underwrite expenses for "ornaments, crosses, chalices, bells, and other things necessary for the service of the divine cult".[3]

The fleet being assembled by Viceroy Velasco in Veracruz on the gulf coast of Mexico, however, as well as its cadre of soldiers (a number of whom were veterans of the de Soto expedition), was more military than civilian in nature. Next to no mention survives of civilian colonists, not even their total number—as opposed to the precise enumeration of military units—and there is no reference to secular diocesan priests on board. By contrast, each of the six Dominicans on the voyage, under the direction of Vice Provincial Pedro de Feria (later the bishop of Chiapa), is mentioned by name. Here, in brief, was not a civilian colonizing venture, protected by soldiers, but a Dominican missionary effort backed by military force. The under-taking thus represented a fusion of old and new approaches to the Indian question as well as an effort to block French incursion.

Thirteen ships under the command of veteran conquistador Tristán Luna y Arellano—fifteen hundred soldiers, unnumbered colonists, six Dominican priests, and one lay brother—sailed from Veracruz on 11 June 1559, with Viceroy Velasco on hand to wish them Godspeed. The voyage to Florida occurred without incident, but disaster again awaited. After arriving at Pensacola Bay, instead of rapidly dis-embarking as planned, Luna accepted his pilots' advice and relocated to Santa Rosa Bay. There he rode at anchor for weeks while an exploring party ventured inland. On 19 September 1559, a hurricane struck the anchored ships. Seven were lost, taking with them most of the settlers and nearly all the provisions.

Relief arrived from Mexico, and the Spaniards went ashore to found the city of Santa María de Filipino, but Luna again delayed sailing to the Atlantic side of the peninsula. Instead, the Spaniards temporarily settled Santa Cruz on the Alabama River above Mobile Bay near the Indian town of Nanipacana, where they hoped to find provisions, but the Indians fled at their approach and took their stores with them. Stranded and near starvation, the Spaniards wasted even more time wintering at Santa Cruz before returning to Pensacola in the spring. Meanwhile, the vessel Luna sent to reconnoiter Point Saint Helena foundered in a storm. After two years, the expedition had accomplished little. The Dominicans were making no progress either, having converted only one local, and were increasingly being called upon to minister to the surviving Spaniards in the fever-ridden Pensacola settlement.

Map 6. Spanish Forts and Settlements in Florida. From David B. Quinn, *North America from Earliest Discovery to First Settlements: The Norse Voyages to 1612* (New York: Harper and Row, 1977), 266. © *David B. Quinn. Reprinted by permission of HarperCollins Publishers.*

Luna himself grew debilitated from fever and was intermittently delirious. Factionalism verging on mutiny broke out, and Luna condemned two soldiers to death, though the Dominicans successfully interceded on behalf of one of them. Dissension continued, and Luna sentenced to death his second in command and his immediate supporters. Yet one more time, the Dominicans intervened; Fray Domingo de la Anunciación brokered a reconciliation during Palm Sunday Mass.

A few days later, two vessels arrived from Mexico. In late June or early July 1560, a decision was made to abandon Santa María de Filipino on Pensacola Bay—which lost to Saint Augustine the title of the oldest continuously settled city in the United States—and to sail around the peninsula to the Atlantic side and establish the Point Saint Helena settlement, which both the king and the viceroy were urgently calling for. By this time, Tristán Luna y Arellano had been relieved of his command. His successor, Ángel de Villafañe, however, found Point Saint Helena unsuitable for settlement and in 1561 brought what remained of the expedition back to Mexico.

What had been achieved? Next to nothing. The Dominicans had committed eight priests and one lay brother to the effort. These were learned and able men, with a record of success in Mexico and the Caribbean. Fray Domingo de la Anunciación was said to have mastered all Mexican dialects. Fray Gregorio de Beteta, who arrived with Fray Juan de Contreras as part of the Villafañe relief, had turned down a bishopric to join the expedition. Fray Domingo de Salazar later became the first bishop of the Philippines. Fray Pedro Martín was appointed bishop of Chiapa. Fray Jaime de Santo Domingo became master of novices for the province of Mexico. Bartolomé Mateos, the lay brother, had been an artilleryman with Gonzalo Pizarro and had joined the order after experiencing the vanity of human wishes in the aftermath of Pizarro's failed revolt against the Crown. Yet when it was all over—shipwreck, hunger, forced marches, numerous efforts at contact and evangelization—the enterprise yielded only one conversion on the Atlantic coast, that of a younger brother of the cacique of Axacan, who returned with the Dominicans to Mexico. Following this failed attempt, King Philip was by 1562 expressing doubts that Florida was worth the cost of settlement, and the Dominicans were deciding to set aside thoughts of Florida and concentrate their energies elsewhere in the New World.

Coligny's efforts at colonization

Philip II, however, soon discovered that he did not have the luxury of taking Florida out of the picture. Even as the Luna expedition was struggling to establish a Spanish presence in Florida, Gaspard de Coligny, admiral of France and seigneur de Châtillon, was planning a French settlement on the north Florida coast. The French, Catholic and Protestant alike, had never been overly impressed by the papal bull *Inter Caetera* of 4 May 1493, in which Pope Alexander VI granted Spain near-exclusive rights to the New World. He would like to consult the will of Adam, King Francis I reportedly told a papal envoy in 1540, to see how the Father of Mankind had divided up the world.

The maritime explorations of Giovanni da Verrazzano in 1524—as far south as North Carolina and as far north as Maine—and those of Jacques Cartier in 1534 of the northern North American coast bolstered French resistance to Spanish claims. The sheer sweep of the Verrazzano reconnaissance prompted King Francis I, then on the verge of dispatching Cartier to the northern coast, to seek in 1533 a formal qualification from Pope Clement VII regarding the papal pronouncement of 1493. A de' Medici, grandson of Lorenzo the Magnificent and cousin of Pope Leo X (who had ignored Clement's illegitimacy to name him archbishop of Florence and cardinal), Clement had spent the previous decade whipsawed between Francis I and Emperor Charles V, who had conflicting designs on Italy. In this contest, Clement sought a via media but generally favored the French. In October 1533 Clement traveled to Marseilles to officiate at the marriage of his grandniece Caterina de' Medici (in French, Catherine de Médicis) to Francis I's second son, thereby setting in motion the eventual enthronement of a Medici as queen, later queen mother, of France. As might be expected, Clement's response to Francis I's query regarding the Papal Donation of 1493 was evasively conciliatory.

In 1562, a series of religious civil wars broke out in France that pitted Protestants against Catholics, nobles against the Crown. These Wars of Religion lasted until 1598, when the Edict of Nantes guaranteed religious freedom to Protestants. The wars included the infamous Saint Bartholomew's Day massacre of 1572—planned in part by Queen Mother Catherine de Médicis—in which Catholics killed hundreds of Huguenots who had come to Paris under a flag of truce to discuss peace. Slain that terrible day was Admiral Coligny, leader of the Huguenots. Coligny's death and the long ordeal of the Wars of Religion fulfilled the admiral's foreboding decades earlier that France was heading toward civil war and that cooperative colonies in the New World might provide a mode of reconciliation by partnering the Huguenot minority with Catholics in the service of the Crown.

In 1555, years before the outbreak of the Wars of Religion, Coligny tried to establish a Huguenot colony in Brazil and failed when it was expelled by the Portuguese. By 1561 the admiral was busy planning another endeavor, this time in the lands north of Spanish Florida.

Coligny's second attempt at a colony—five ships carrying 150 volunteers, the overwhelming majority Protestants but various Catholic sailors as well—left Le Havre-de-Grâce on 18 February 1562 under the command of Jean Ribault, an experienced sea captain, and the mariner-geographer René Goulaine de Laudonnière. Spotting the Florida coast at the later site of Saint Augustine, the Huguenot fleet sailed northward past Point Saint Helena (which the Luna expedition had failed to settle) to Port Royal Sound. On an island just south of the present-day United States Marine Corps base at Parris Island and three miles west of Beaufort, South Carolina, they established in May 1562 Charlesfort, named in honor of the young king Charles IX. It was the first French settlement and the first Protestant colony in North America. Like its Spanish predecessors to the south, Charlesfort proved a disaster due to hunger (no agriculture was established), dissension, mutiny, and murder. The situation was so desperate that Ribault and Laudonnière returned to France for more colonists, and the twenty-five colonists left behind followed suit in a homemade boat and were fortunate enough to be rescued on the high seas by an English ship.

Once again, Coligny renewed his effort. Another expedition was fitted out under the command of Laudonnière, which in late June 1564 established a second colony, Fort Caroline, on the Saint Johns River north of Saint Augustine in territory clearly claimed by Spain. Fort Caroline almost succumbed to the same woes as Charlesfort, even as two ships returned to France for more colonists. Luckily, the English slaver John Hawkins, a fellow Protestant, came to the rescue, followed shortly thereafter by the arrival of seven ships and six hundred colonists from France under the command of Ribault. The French fleet reached Fort Caroline on 28 August 1565, the same day that the Spanish armada under the command of Pedro Menéndez de Avilés made landfall off Florida.

A pitiless confrontation

Thus the stage was set for a confrontation between Spain and France regarding France's right to establish a colony—indeed, as it soon turned out, regarding the very survival of the French colonists. Historians invariably refer to Fort Caroline as a Huguenot colony; the leadership and majority of the colonists were Huguenots. Yet the year 1565 constituted an interval of peace between the first and second Wars of Religion. Admiral Coligny saw the colony as a means of reconciliation between Huguenots and Catholics on behalf of France. Catholics were among the venture's financial and political backers, who included Queen Mother Catherine de Médicis. Fort Caroline, then, can be considered a French as well as a Huguenot endeavor and was viewed as such by Spain. France, after all, had challenged the Papal Donation of 1493. The pope had no right to divvy up the world, the French believed. In the long run, force must determine who had the right to settle.

That Fort Caroline was sponsored, led, and peopled by Huguenots triply damned it in the eyes of Spain. First, the colony was French. Second, it was Protestant. Third, it fit into the context of the religious warfare increasingly characteristic of piracy, slave running, illegal trading, and boundary jumping in the Caribbean. Corsairs increasingly accepted the generic name Lutheran imposed upon them by Spaniards. Why be just a pirate on the Spanish Main or a mere Caribbean slave trader when you could be a champion of the New Religion, especially after Queen Elizabeth of England began to back your ventures, however discreetly?

Thus the Wars of Religion melded with anti-Spanish freebooting in the Caribbean and grew more fierce. In 1555 the pirate Jacques Sorie plundered and burned Havana, butchered civilians and military alike, and desecrated churches. In 1559 the corsairs Megander and John de la Roche pillaged the ships and settlements of Puerto Rico and Cartagena, Colombia, respectively, with comparable ferocity. The corsair Jacques Le Clerc, better known as Pie de Palo or Pegleg, sacked Havana a second time in 1564. On Saturday, 15 July 1570, a flotilla of five Huguenot privateers commanded by Sorie intercepted the Portuguese ship *Santiago* off the Canary Islands. On board were forty Jesuits and lay missionaries bound for Brazil. In France the third War of Religion was raging, and so Sorie, sparing all others on board, had the entire Jesuit group butchered. (The forty were beatified en masse by Pope Pius IX in 1854.) The Huguenots of Florida fit into this take-no-prisoners context. As Laudonnière would later admit in his autobiography, *Histoire notable* (1586), the Huguenots used Fort Caroline as a base for raiding Spanish ships, seizing six or seven and killing their crews, although two crewmen eluded capture and made it safely back to Fort Caroline.

Into this scenario entered the paradigmatic figure of Pedro Menéndez de Avilés, adelantado of Florida, having returned to the just-founded city of Saint Augustine after his encounter with the French ships at the mouth of the Saint Johns River. Despite his grand commission, his experience at sea, his title of admiral, his knighthood in the Order of Santiago, and his personal relationship to King Philip II (whom he had accompanied as captain of the royal ship and member of the entourage when Philip traveled to England in 1554 to marry Queen Mary Tudor), Menéndez, like so many conquistadors, had come up the hard way from a background of impoverished minor nobility. Born into a family of twenty children in 1519 in the seaport city of Avilés in Asturias, Menéndez went to sea at fourteen as a privateer against French shipping. He spent the next sixteen years in that quasi-piratical calling until, at the age of thirty, he was taken into imperial service by Emperor Charles V and named protector of the north coast of Spain. In 1554 Menéndez was promoted to captain general of the fleet that protected shipping between Spain and the Indies. As such, he made three voyages to the Caribbean, retaining his command despite growing opposition from the Casa de Contratación to Menéndez's alleged high-handed treatment of merchants and his refusal to encourage a culture of bribery. The Casa eventually prevailed. Menéndez was removed from office in 1563 and spent twenty months in confinement before being cleared of all charges. His son Juan, meanwhile, had been lost in a shipwreck off the Bermudas, although Menéndez never lost hope that his son had survived and found his way to the Florida coast.

Hence the fusion of religious, entrepreneurial, political, and personal goals behind Menéndez's asiento (contract) to lead an armada to Florida in March 1565: to block the southward advance of the Huguenots, set up a city served by diocesan priests in a parochial parish structure, evangelize the natives with the assistance of Franciscans and Jesuits, and find his lost son. A skilled and experienced sea and land captain, as well as a courtier of impeccable connections, Pedro Menéndez de Avilés impressed the Crown as having the ability to reverse the burden of failure attached to Spanish Florida and, at long last, to establish it as a Catholic commonwealth. As Francis Parkman points out, Menéndez was the de facto governor of North America, with authority over Spanish claims from Labrador to Mexico. Once Florida was consolidated by Menéndez, Spain could move north to the Chesapeake Bay (called Saint Mary's Bay by Spaniards) and then—according to the geography of the day—find a water connection to the north and secure a Spanish hold on the Gulf of Saint Lawrence and the seas of Newfoundland. From the Gulf of Saint Lawrence, a sea passage would be discovered that led to the Moluccas and other ports of the East Indies.

The Huguenot campaign

Such geopolitical ambitions help to explain why Menéndez moved precipitously against the Huguenots shortly after his arrival and in the process came close to being captured in his launch when the French ships outmaneuvered him off Saint Johns Bay—an escape Menéndez considered an outright miracle. With Saint Augustine dedicated and under construction, Menéndez boldly planned and carried out his counterattack: a forced march north to Fort Caroline, executed while Ribault was still at sea. A number of Menéndez's captains and the two secular priests on his staff argued against such an all-out campaign, fearing that Ribault would attack Saint Augustine in Menéndez's absence. Menéndez nonetheless persevered. On 16 September 1565, he led approximately five hundred soldiers out of Saint Augustine on a thirteen-day march through rain and difficult terrain that killed two soldiers from exhaustion, drove some to desertion, and brought others to mutinous muttering. On the morning of 30 September, the Spaniards attacked the sleeping Huguenot colony, scaling its palisades with ladders they had carried with them.

The slaughter of the surprised Huguenots was terrible. Men dazed from sleep were dispatched by sword or pike as they emerged from their cabins. Around fifty escaped amid the attack, unarmed in their nightshirts, and were killed in the nearby woods or on the banks of the Saint Johns River. Others were, at Menéndez's orders, hanged from trees surrounding the encampment. Women and children under the age of fifteen were spared, again per Menéndez, but the ten or so men apprehended the following day were executed.

When it was over, 132 Huguenots lay dead. Not one Spaniard lost his life. It was a massacre—an ethnic cleansing, in modern terminology—fully in the spirit of the Wars of Religion. Among the French (and widely accepted as fact to this day), word soon grew that Menéndez placed on each hanged man a label declaring, "I do not do this to Frenchmen, but to Heretics."[4] From one perspective, this allegation makes little sense. Fort Caroline was a French incursion on Spanish claims, and Menéndez destroyed it because it was French. Yet in the context of Caribbean piracy, in which anti-Spanish corsairs were considered Lutherans engaged in Wars of Religion, the report of such taunting signs was certainly compatible with the take-no-prisoners ethos of Spaniards and corsairs alike.

While at Fort Caroline, Menéndez sensed a major hurricane in the offing. Two days after the Spaniards left Fort Caroline, the hurricane struck. The French fleet was driven ashore and destroyed.

In Florida the following month, the death toll was on the verge of rising even higher when Menéndez—back from San Mateo, as he renamed Fort Caroline—learned from Indian informers that the French had lost their ships. Many men had drowned, but a remnant of 140 had made shore and were stranded on an inlet six leagues from Saint Augustine. Marching to the site with a small force, Menéndez commenced negotiations via a French sailor who swam back and forth across the estuary between the parties. They wanted to return to Fort Caroline, the French stated. Fort Caroline was no more, Menéndez told them. What religion are you? he asked. They were of the Reformed faith, the French answered. Then surrender or be put to the sword, Menéndez countered. A French officer crossed over in a Spanish boat in an effort to secure better terms. Leave us here, he requested, until French ships can rescue us. The officer promised a ransom of five thousand ducats. According to a report later given by the secular priest Solis de Meras, a brother-in-law of the governor, Menéndez replied that "if they wished to lay down their colors and their arms, and throw themselves on his mercy, they could do so, that he might do with them what God should give him the grace to do; or that they could do as they chose: for other truce or friendship could not be made with him." Menéndez later wrote in his official report to Philip II, "I replied that they might surrender me their arms and put themselves under my pleasure, that I might do with them what our Lord might ordain; and from this resolution I do not and will not depart, unless Our Lord God inspired me otherwise."[5]

The Huguenots must have seized upon Menéndez's ambiguous statement as a half-offer of mercy, for they began to send over their banners, weapons, and armor, to signal surrender. According to the Latinist and historian Bartolomé Barrientos, writing in Spain two years after the event, Menéndez was careful to keep the French ignorant of his ultimate intentions. Following the surrender of banners and weapons, the Spanish ferried the Huguenots across the estuary in groups of ten and escorted them behind a hill (out of sight of the French remaining on the other side of the water), where they bound their arms for what the prisoners were told would be a march back to Saint Augustine. When the entire party was assembled, sixteen Catholic Breton sailors were separated from the group and unbound. The remaining French—200, says Barrientos; 111, says John Gilmary Shea—were marched to a spot Menéndez had previously chosen and cut to the ground with pikes, swords, and daggers.

The slaughtered men, it turned out, were an advance party sent south by Ribault. Back in Saint Augustine, as Menéndez was writing a report to the king describing the massacre and his intentions to fortify Florida in four more places, he was informed that a second French party, led by Ribault, was stranded on the same inlet, unable to cross. Losing no time, Menéndez marched there with a column of 150 soldiers. When the Spaniards arrived, both sides went into battle formation. The French, however, were stranded on the opposite side of the river, and Ribault raised a flag of truce and crossed over in an Indian canoe provided by the Spanish to parley with Menéndez after learning of the fall of Fort Caroline and the massacre of his advance party. Menéndez received Ribault courteously, and Ribault made a ransom offer of 150,000 ducats for himself and his staff, as well as a second amount to be raised from the nobles in his group. Once again, Menéndez declined the offer and repeated the demand he had previously made of the advance party: unconditional surrender, with no promises.

The majority of the Huguenots, aware of the slaughter of their colleagues, refused Menéndez's offer. Ribault, however, and seventy-plus men accepted Menéndez's terms and were ferried to the Spanish encampment, where Ribault surrendered the banners of France, Admiral Coligny, and his own expedition, together with his personal armor and seal of office. Taken into custody, the Huguenots were bound, as had been the party before them. As he was being tied, Ribault intoned a hymn. "We are of the earth, and to earth we must return", Ribault concluded. He was not afraid to die. "Twenty years more or less is all but as a tale that is told." Another terrible butchery ensued.[6]

For Spain, a valuable goal had been accomplished: a French Protestant incursion into Spanish Catholic Florida had been thwarted. After reading Menéndez's report, the king sent his congratulations. Menéndez had done well; he had done what he had to. Bartolomé Barrientos elaborated upon that justification a short time later. The Lutherans, he argued, outnumbered the Spaniards by at least two to one. Spanish food stocks were low. Had Menéndez spared the Lutherans and taken them into captivity, starvation would have been inevitable. Then there was the possibility that the Lutherans, once released, would have second thoughts and resume their aggression. For Philip II, Menéndez, and Catholic apologists of the time—and those of a later era—the massacres constituted standard procedure in the War of Religion raging between Spain and Protestant corsairs in the Caribbean. In defense of this argument, John Gilmary Shea points to the fact that when, a month later, Menéndez captured a third group of 150 Huguenots on Cape Canaveral—some of Ribault's men who had previously refused to surrender—Menéndez (no longer under immediate threat) accepted their surrender with a promise that their lives would be spared and kept his word.

From the point of view of Huguenot France, however, the massacres represented unmitigated atrocities that reflected Spanish bigotry, cruelty, and duplicity. The artist Jacques Le Moyne de Morgues, a member of the Huguenot expedition who escaped, later claimed in his posthumously published *Brevis narratio* (1591) that Menéndez in the second slaughter had promised amnesty if the French would surrender, then reneged. Other French accounts related the horrors of the slaughter at Fort Caroline; the American historian Francis Parkman covered such reports at length in his *Pioneers of France in the New World* (1865), the inaugural volume of his magisterial history of French Canada. To his credit, Parkman—although he despised Menéndez as a corsair and bigot—acknowledges that no documentary evidence supports the allegation that those hanged at Fort Caroline were hanged for heresy, not for being French.

The Jesuit mission

Signed in Madrid by King Philip II on 20 March 1565, Menéndez's asiento called for him to take on his expedition two secular priests for the care of Spaniards and ten to twelve religious-order priests for missionary work among the Indians. In addition to these religious-order missionaries, Menéndez was to recruit four members of the Society of Jesus, which was founded in Paris in 1534 by the Basque nobleman Ignatius Loyola and six companions, approved by Rome in 1540, and further organized in 1550 through the adoption of a formal constitution. By the time of Menéndez's asiento, the dramatically growing Society of Jesus (one thousand members by the time of Ignatius' death in 1556 and thirty-five hundred members by 1600) was advancing on three major fronts: education, eventually earning the Jesuits the designation Schoolmasters of Europe; the reconversion of European regions lost to Islam and Protestantism; and foreign missions in Asia, Africa, India, and the New World. The Society's missionary character was evident in a fourth vow taken by senior professed members of the order—in addition to the traditional vows of poverty, chastity, and obedience—to accept any assignment extended by the pope, regardless of where the assignment might take them. The Jesuit rule did not require recitation of the Divine Office in choir or obligate a monastic form of community life; hence Jesuit missionaries could act on their own or in small groups. Within a hundred years of the order's founding, Jesuit missionaries had exported Catholic Christianity to the known world, including to all the Americas.

Even with an asiento signed by the king, however, Menéndez had to do a great deal of wheedling to secure staffing for the Florida enterprise from Francis Borgia, the third general of the order, and his Spanish provincials. Menéndez began to lobby Borgia while the former Duke of Gandía—a widower who had renounced his title, seen to the welfare of his eight children, and become a Jesuit—was serving as vicar general or acting head of the order, pending his election as the third father general on 2 July 1565. Yet even in his new position, Borgia encountered delays among the Jesuit provincials of Spain as an anxious Menéndez postponed his fleet's departure until the Jesuits arrived. But after a long wait, Menéndez sailed without them.

Once in Florida, Menéndez sought to be fair and respectful in his dealings with the Calusa people of southwestern Florida, where he first landed and had the satisfaction of rescuing twelve Spaniards, survivors of shipwrecks and long captives of the Calusa (who had a bad habit of drawing from their cadre of captives for human sacrifice in annual celebrations or when their gods otherwise required appeasement). Backed by thirty harquebusiers holding lighted fuses for instant firing, Menéndez negotiated the release of these captives with Calusa chief Carlos, who attended the parley supported by nearly three hundred bowmen. The Spaniards suspected treachery, but Menéndez refused his captains' advice to seize Carlos when he and his caciques were being entertained aboard Menéndez's flagship and hold him for ransom until the Calusa delivered all the gold from Spanish shipwrecks in their possession. Such action represented standard procedure among conquistadors, but Menéndez—at this point, at least—had come to convert, not to conquer, and kept his word guaranteeing Carlos and his men safe passage to and from his vessel.

In a return of hospitality, Carlos entertained Menéndez and twenty Spanish officers at an elaborate banquet in which Carlos, his wife, and his sister sat on an elevated platform surrounded by hundreds of revelers. Following feasting, ceremonial dancing, and an exchange of gifts, Carlos rose to address the Spaniards. His people, he informed Menéndez, regarded Menéndez as an elder brother, and to signify this new relationship he was offering his sister to Menéndez to take as his wife. Rising in reply, Menéndez thanked Chief Carlos but pointed out that Christians were permitted to marry only Christians. Menéndez thereupon briefly described basic Christian beliefs. At some point in these proceedings, Menéndez's captains urged the adelantado to accept Carlos' offer, lest the chief be insulted and turn ugly. A detachment of Spanish soldiers stood at the ready outside the compound, but they were surrounded by as many as a thousand Calusa. Menéndez accepted Carlos' offer. Take her and her retinue to your ship, Carlos urged. Teach them to be Christians. When they return, they will teach us.

In short order, Menéndez had Carlos' sister baptized and renamed Doña Antonia. With Carlos and his caciques present, a wedding ceremony was performed aboard Menéndez's flagship, followed by feasting and music from the ship's musicians and the retirement of the newlyweds to Menéndez's cabin. What occurred there is anyone's guess. The following morning, Menéndez had a great cross erected on shore and delivered another address, this time asking the Calusa to abstain from worshipping idols while Doña Antonia and her companions received further instruction in Christianity in Havana, prior to their return as catechists.

This early missionary effort by Menéndez has understandably bothered later Catholic historians. Was it a necessary improvisation, to keep peace with the Calusa and open up the possibility of a mass conversion? What form did the shipboard marriage take? A version of the Catholic ceremony would have been disturbing, if not blasphemous. One report describes the chief's sister as older and unattractive, as if suggesting the absence of sexuality in this impromptu union. But even if this were the case, could Menéndez have afforded to insult Chief Carlos, and Doña Antonia as well, by refusing to consummate the union, however illicit by Catholic standards?

Or was Menéndez—perhaps not consciously yet dramatically—suggesting a paradigm for the long-term Christianization and Hispanicization of Florida through a fusion of Spaniards and indigenous peoples? Instead of a merging through rapine, sexual bondage, or the haremic promiscuity Cabeza de Vaca encountered in Asunción, could there be a blending through marriage, children, families, and permanent settlements that nurtured the emergence of a mixed race Spanish and Catholic in culture and religion, with its own bishop and diocesan clergy, similar to the settlements developed in Iceland half a millennium earlier? Was not a simulacrum of marriage, however irregular by Catholic standards, a better pathway to Christianity than the conquest and annihilation of Caribbean native peoples? Did not Menéndez—a hardened corsair and privateer in his youth, a respected admiral in his middle years—speak to the Calusa the morning after his alleged nuptials as the adelantado of a province he was trying to create, linking it to the cross he had erected on the beach as he stood before the people he had promised the king to Christianize?

In the meantime, Menéndez dispatched several of the religious-order priests he had brought with him as missionaries to various Indian groups and continued to lobby Francis Borgia to send to Florida the twenty-four Jesuits King Philip II had requested. Two Jesuit priests and a lay brother arrived within the year, but one of the priests, Pedro Martínez, was murdered by Indians on an island off the mouth of the Saint Johns River when stranded ashore after a storm blew his ship—along with the other two Jesuits—back to Havana. Father Juan Rogel and Brother Francis de Villareal remained in Havana temporarily, studying the native language of south coastal Florida. When they returned to Florida, Menéndez sent them to the compound of the Calusa chief Carlos, whose sister Doña Antonia had also returned. Menéndez built a house for Doña Antonia and a chapel for the Jesuits.

Menéndez then returned to Spain to visit his family and see to his affairs at court, and when he returned in 1568 he brought with him ten Jesuits personally selected by Francis Borgia for the Florida mission. Rapidly deployed, the Jesuits showed the characteristic ambition of their order. Father Rogel's mission to the Calusa was expanded, and missions were begun with the peoples of Tocobaga, Tequesta, and (later) Guale (present-day Amelia Island, Georgia). Brother Domingo Agustín Baez prepared a grammar and a catechism for use in the region. Father Rogel and others advanced north into present-day South Carolina, whence Rogel fanned out from Santa Helena into the interior, where he established a chapel in the Indian settlement of Orista and began seriously studying the local language.

Yet for all the Jesuits' dedication and diligence, results were few, if any. On the island of Guale, the natives lost interest after the Jesuits ran out of the corn provided by Don Juan del Castillo, the bishop of Santiago de Cuba, to win the locals' goodwill. Brother Baez died of malaria, and his colleague and religious superior, Father Antonio Sedeño, returned to Santa Helena thoroughly discouraged. Likewise, Father Rogel grew discouraged at Orista, where the Indians refused to accept his demand that they cease appeasing the Evil One, whom they favorably considered a war god. Dispirited, Rogel demolished his chapel and returned to Santa Helena.

A year into their mission, the Jesuits found themselves reunited in Santa Helena ministering to near-starving soldiers and civilians, a role more fitting to the secular priests under the jurisdiction of Don López de Mendoza, the episcopal vicar and superior of diocesan clergy. After a short time at Santa Helena, Father Rogel returned to the Indian seminary school he and Brother Villareal had previously founded in Havana. When Father Sedeño and Brother Villareal returned to Santa Helena, they were stricken with malaria and put on a ship for evacuation to Havana. However, a storm drove the ship onto the coast, wrecking it, and the two sick Jesuits barely survived the long overland trek back to Saint Augustine.

Now ensued the final blow to the Jesuit mission. Paradoxically, this defeat represented the most ambitious effort on the part of both Menéndez and the Society of Jesus. Fundamental to Menéndez's plan for the consolidation of Spanish Florida was a fort and a mission on Chesapeake Bay, the northernmost reach of the Spanish claim. In 1566 Menéndez sent two Dominican friars to the bay; accompanying them to act as guide, intercessor, and interpreter was Don Luis Velasco, brother of the head chief of Ajacan, a district on the Chesapeake. Recruited in 1561— most likely as a captive in Villafañe's failed effort to establish a settlement on the Chesapeake—the young cacique had come under the protection of the Dominicans and the viceroy, whose name he was given at baptism. Raised in Mexico City as a hidalgo, Don Luis embodied the hopes of both the Dominicans and the pro-Indian Viceroy Velasco of connecting with the tribes of the Chesapeake region, along with the conversions to Catholic Christianity that would inevitably follow.

Unfortunately for the Dominican mission of 1566—which consisted of two friars, Don Luis, and thirty soldiers—the captain of the ship had no desire to proceed any farther north and (later claiming that storms deterred him) returned directly to Spain. There the young cacique was further feted, presented at court, and otherwise treated with respect. Having returned to Spain for a second visit, Menéndez personally recruited Don Luis as an auxiliary member of the Jesuit team he was taking back to Florida. The team was headed by Father Juan Bautista de Segura, the vice-provincial of Florida, and Father Luis de Quirós, a veteran of missionary work in southern Spain among Muslim Moors resisting Christianization. The group included three lay brothers—Pedro de Linares, Gabriel Gómez, and Sancho Zeballos—and three novices—Juan Bautista Méndez, Gabriel de Solís, and Cristóbal Redondo. The commitment of three brothers indicated the long-term ambitions of the Jesuit mission. Brothers were lay coadjutors with the practical skills required for long-term settlement (design, construction, pharmacology, military); they served also as sacristans, catechists, schoolmasters, and infirmarians. The presence of three novices further underscored hopes for the future. Now serving as catechists, these young men would eventually continue their studies in Havana and be ordained priests for a future Cuba-Florida Jesuit province. From this perspective, Don Luis Velasco was especially comforting in his favorable descriptions of his homeland and his assurances of the friendly reception the Jesuits would receive there.

By 10 September 1570 the Jesuit mission to the Chesapeake had entered Saint Mary's Bay, ascended the Potomac, and reached the shores of the Rappahannock in the vicinity of Don Luis' homeland. The Jesuits were thus adding present-day Virginia to Florida, Georgia, and South Carolina, the inventory of American states pioneered by Spain for Catholicism. Instead of the land of milk and honey promised by their guide, however, they found a sparse and bedraggled population reduced by war and starvation. They themselves were already short of food, having consumed two of the ship's four barrels of biscuits, and were thus facing a winter with insufficient bread. Furthermore, they had arrived too late to plant any winter food, though that point was moot, since they possessed no seed or agricultural implements. (Their ship's captain promised to return within the month with supplies.) Once again, Spaniards in Florida had failed to deal with the realities of survival.

To further complicate things, Father Segura sent the soldiers back with the crew. Only Jesuits and a few Indian retainers remained. When the relief vessel did not appear and winter set in, the Jesuits struggled to get by on roots and herbs. Don Luis Velasco slipped away to rejoin his people and ignored all entreaties to return. The Jesuits were alone in the wilderness, abandoned by their guide—who, the Jesuits soon discovered, had abandoned his Spanish dress and was living polygamously in an uncle's village. As in Menéndez's alleged marriage to Doña Antonia, the cultural paradigm involved in this situation reverberates with suggestions. For nearly a decade, Don Luis had willingly conformed to Spanish Catholic practice. He had received instruction from learned and devout Dominicans who were sensitive to his culture, been sponsored by the viceroy whose name he bore, been treated as a nobleman in Mexico and Spain, been received at court at the apex of Spanish power, and been befriended by the Society of Jesus and the governor of Florida. Yet none of this seems to have made a difference when, returning to his people, he was greeted with warmth and was welcomed back into the Indian way of life.

That way of life Don Luis seems to have fully embraced, including its warrior code. Not only did he resist the abjurations of Quirós, Solís, and Méndez, but he organized their assassination on 4 February 1571 as they sought to return to the Jesuit compound. Interestingly, from a psychological point of view, Don Luis wore a Jesuit cassock the next day when the Indians stripped and burned the bodies of the three Jesuits. And five days later, attired in a Jesuit cassock, Don Luis led a band of warriors to the Jesuit chapel and compound. Arriving at dawn on Candlemas Day, 9 February 1571, he called Father Segura from the chapel, where he was praying with the other Jesuits. Seeing Don Luis in his blood-stained cassock, Segura must have instantly known that his worst fears were true. Quirós, Solís, and Méndez were dead, and the rest of the Jesuit mission soon would be as well. Although later reports stated that Segura acted in complete innocence, surely he sensed his imminent fate when Don Luis asked for all the axes and machetes in the compound. The Indians would use them, Don Luis promised, to cut wood for fuel. Instead of heading into the woods, however, the Indians surrounded the chapel and the adjacent living quarters. Leaving a guard outside to kill anyone escaping, Don Luis and his band entered the chapel and hacked the Jesuits to death.

Don Luis personally dispatched Father Segura, chopping away at the missioner's fallen body. Only the Indian altar boy, Alonso, was left alive. Adding to the psychological and cultural complexity of the massacre, Don Luis burst into tears as he beheld the bloody corpses of the Jesuits. Declaring them martyrs, he heeded Alonso's urging and buried the bodies in a dignified fashion, each holding a missioner's crucifix. Don Luis later tried to have the boy—sole witness to the massacre—killed, but by that time the youngster had come under the protection of a powerful cacique and escaped.

Even before he learned of the massacre, taking into consideration the meager results of a five-year effort as well as the need to consolidate the Society in Cuba and Mexico, Francis Borgia decided to withdraw the Jesuits from Florida. Dated 20 March 1571, Borgia's letter of withdrawal to Menéndez basically constituted an indictment of the convertibility—for the time being, at least—of the indigenous people of Florida. Borgia wrote Menéndez:

> Since, therefore, those pagans are so badly disposed that they are said to prefer the devil and to go to hell with him rather than to our God, and say that he who talks against their god, cannot be good; and since it is evident, in our long experience in Florida, that we could count, so to say, with the fingers of our hand those who during this long period have been converted, and even they have turned back to darkness, and since, moreover, there is in this Company, as I wrote to your Excellency, and it is truly so, such a small personnel for the many enterprises which the Company has assumed; it is evident that for a time until God our Lord, little by little, stirs those pagans in the capacity of their souls, that not only is it not fitting to keep the Company in that land, but it must not be done; for even if there were many missionaries, we are always obliged by the Christian religion and our own Institute to seek the greater glory of God and the greater good for our neighbor, for as our Lord says: "If

they do not receive the sacred Gospel in one place, we should go from that land to another, shaking the dust from our feet."[7]

Further troubles

What an indictment of the Florida enterprise! Even the Society of Jesus—in the process of spreading Catholic Christianity across the known world, sensitive beyond other missionary orders to the cultural context of evangelization—was calling it quits, thus adding to Menéndez's mounting difficulties. One hundred Spaniards had died from starvation the first winter of the expedition, victims of faulty supply from Havana and nonexistent agriculture. Fugitive Huguenots were inciting Indians against the Spaniards, now confined to the fort settlements of Saint Augustine and San Mateo. While Menéndez had been at sea in the winter and early spring of 1566, seeking his lost son among the Tortugas and adjacent coast, San Mateo and Saint Augustine had come under Indian attack. Saint Augustine had been assailed with flaming arrows and seriously damaged by fire. Even Menéndez's personal banners had been lost.

Mutiny and desertion remained problems, and Menéndez was forced to allow a group of dissidents to return to Cuba. Eventually, a relief fleet arrived from Havana with supplies, but approximately five hundred Spaniards abandoned the enterprise in its first years. While Menéndez was in Spain in 1566–1567—among other things, arranging for the Jesuit mission—the French corsair Dominique de Gourgues made an alliance with the fiercely anti-Spaniard cacique Saturiba and attacked San Mateo, killing (the French claimed) one hundred twenty Spaniards and hanging fifteen survivors. An Indian cooking fish ignited the San Mateo powder magazine as the French were transferring the Spanish artillery to their ship. De Gourgues proceeded downstream to the mouth of the Saint Johns River, where he hanged an additional thirty or so Spanish prisoners under the sign "Not as to Spaniards, but as to Traitors, Robbers, and Murderers", in retaliation for the sign Menéndez allegedly used when he hanged the Huguenot prisoners at Fort Caroline.

Returning to Florida from Spain in 1572, Menéndez sailed to the Chesapeake Bay and unsuccessfully tried to capture Don Luis and his brother, who had fled into the interior. The Spaniards did manage to capture, however, eight Indians who had participated in the massacre of the Jesuits. One of them, another brother of Luis, was wearing a paten around his neck; another was found dressed in a chasuble. Menéndez had the eight captives hanged from the yardarm of his vessel. First, however, they were given a brief course in Christianity by Father Rogel, who had accompanied the expedition, and were baptized by the surviving Jesuit of the Florida mission.

4

Apalachee 1595

Friars and soldiers hold the Florida frontier

The establishment of mission networks in Florida at the turn of the sixteenth century involved theoretical as well as practical preparation. To this end, a Dominican and two Franciscans offered historical and theological justifications for the evangelizing efforts of their orders. The ideologies they created would remain relevant for the next two hundred years.

Dominican Francisco de la Cruz and Franciscan Gerónimo de Mendieta advanced separatist scenarios concerning the punishment of Spain for its sins. As a young friar, de la Cruz sat at the feet of Las Casas in the Dominican monastery in Valladolid and from him absorbed a conviction that Spain would be castigated for its crimes against the Indians. Assigned to Peru, de la Cruz pushed this denunciation further, preaching that Spain was the Babylon of the Apocalypse, destined for destruction, after which the Indies would become the seat of a millennial kingdom, with Indians as the new chosen race. Such pronouncements—in addition to certain opinions regarding the nature of angels that were judged heretical, his calls for a married clergy and licensed polygamy to facilitate the founding of a new mixed race, and the child he fathered with his mistress—earned de la Cruz a condemnation by the Inquisition to be burned at the stake in Lima in 1578.

Gerónimo de Mendieta of Mexico, by contrast, remained discreet in the notions he advanced in his *Historia eclesiástica indiana* as well as conformist in his personal life. Hence Mendieta died in his bed at the age of seventy-nine, and his ideas had more lasting influence, especially among his fellow Franciscans, although the *Historia* was not published until 1870. Like de la Cruz, Mendieta foresaw a millennium on the horizon, located in the New World and populated by faithful Creoles and refugees from Spain, Christianized Indians, and their Franciscan guardians. Mendieta deplored Philip II's policy of replacing Franciscans with secular clergy in New Spain, to the detriment of the Indian in favor of the colonist and the Creole. Franciscans and Indians, Mendieta argued—not secular priests and Indians—were destined to achieve the terrestrial paradise that was to come at the fulfillment of history. King Philip II and the Council of the Indies, however, proceeded with the scheme of diocesan organization based on a bishop and secular clergy. The Franciscans thus began to move their ministry northward, starting with La Florida, where an estimated seven hundred friars would serve in its mission system across two hundred years. Here in this remote province, Franciscans believed, might be achieved the visions and prophecies being advanced for a new generation by Peruvian Franciscan Gonzalo Tenorio.

Born a Creole of noble descent in 1602, and having been a professor of law at the University of San Marcos in Lima before entering the Franciscans, Tenorio served in the missions of Peru and Ecuador, taught theology, rose to provincial, and wrote a number of published theological treatises and an unpublished treatise of sixteen manuscript volumes that he never received royal permission to publish. Tenorio's visionary concept of the exalted role to be played by Spanish America in the unfolding drama of Christianity understandably encountered resistance from authorities in Spain. Tenorio anchored his prophetic scenario in Mariology. Born without sin through the mystery of her Immaculate Conception that saved her from original sin, Tenorio theorized, Mary embodied perfected humanity and was hence the prototype for the universal reign of Christ at the fulfillment of time. In that history of salvation, the Jews of the Old Testament had served as the chosen people. The people of Spain and the Spanish Indies were the chosen people of the New Testament.

In the era of the Primitive Church, Tenorio argued, the ancestors of the Indians of the Spanish Indies had rejected Christianity; otherwise, Christianity would have long since migrated to the Indies. It was now the Indians' destiny to be associated through conversion to Christianity with the salvation drama of Spain and the Spanish Indies. Whatever suffering this fate intertwined with Spain involved—including conquest and slavery—Indians, Tenorio asserted, were privileged to be playing a role in the eschatological destiny of the human race. A time of great trouble was forthcoming, to be followed by a struggle against the Antichrist. But after the defeat of the Antichrist, a third age would ensue, a millennial kingdom in which all mankind would accept the Risen Christ.

The doctrine of the Immaculate Conception (the belief that Mary was preserved from original sin) that Tenorio held in such high regard would be proclaimed a dogma of the Catholic Church in 1854. The *criollismo*, or aggressive creolism, however, of Tenorio's historical scheme—his prediction, for example, that the pope would be forced to take refuge in the New World when Catholic Europe failed—kept his sixteen-volume manuscript locked away in the archives of the Franciscan monastery of Nuestra Señora de Regla in Cádiz, Spain, where Tenorio had gone in vain in 1663 to defend his idea before the authorities.

Missions, Indians, Franciscans

The goal of Catholic missionary practice was the creation of a diocesan structure and a local secular clergy, no matter how long this effort took. Central to Franciscan missionary intent, however, was the strong influence of a philosophy and practice of continuing guardianship dated only by the millennium of a distant future. Such millenarianism lay beneath the surface, of course, and did not exist as canonically approved theory. Yet it had the force of residual subconscious thought anchored in the very nature of Franciscanism itself as a movement dating back to the Franciscan mysticism of the thirteenth century and expressed recently by figures such as Tenorio and Mendieta. Hence the migration of Franciscans north to La Florida and hence their restiveness with the supervision (if only nominal) of the episcopal vicar or a secular priest in Saint Augustine, or any other infringement on their prerogatives.

Spain's failure to establish a diocesan structure in Florida set the pattern for the Spanish Southwest. Hurricanes, shipwreck, starvation, and a hostile and obstinate native population capable of defending itself had made it impossible to colonize Florida as Spaniards had colonized Española, Puerto Rico, and Cuba. Nor were Spaniards able (despite adelantado Menéndez's ambiguous union with Doña Antonia) to bring into existence a new mixed people, as they were doing elsewhere. For three centuries—until the establishment of the Diocese of Both Californias in 1841—the Spanish Southwest would remain uncolonized land held by soldiers and missionary Franciscans, a vast region devoid of cities, bishops, and diocesan clergy. Few colonists migrated to the Borderlands from Spain or New Spain, and the various native peoples brought under the jurisdiction of the mission system rarely, if ever, advanced to the level of Hispanicization or Catholicity the system was allegedly intended to foster. Instead they were assembled into mission compounds whenever possible or otherwise supervised into a nominal compliance with Catholic Christianity, beneath which survived previous beliefs and observances in the age-old manner in which non-Christian people were abruptly subjected to Christian culture. In Sonora, Arizona, and Lower California, Jesuit missionaries pursued another model—that of economically self-sufficient Indian commonwealths protected from political or economic exploitation—but with the suppression of the Society in 1773, a less trustful, frequently harsh Franciscan model prevailed. Among the Franciscan missions, revolts were frequent, sometimes heroic in scale, and resistance characterized the intervals between rebellions.

Crisis, however, is another name for opportunity. In the failure of Florida as a colony and the intractability of its indigenous peoples, the Franciscans of New Spain saw a chance to enter Florida as missionaries. Arriving with Columbus in 1493 on his second voyage, Franciscans were the first order to exercise a ministry in the New World, and they played the major role in the evangelization of Mexico, Ecuador, and Bolivia. In 1522 the papacy issued grants of Omnimoda, conferring on religious orders in the Indies a universalized jurisdiction largely independent of diocesan organization. With few diocesan clergy on hand, religious-order Franciscans, Dominicans, Augustinians, and Mercedarians constituted the dominant clergy of the colonies and enjoyed a direct reporting relationship to the papacy. As diocesan organization emerged, however, this system of Omnimoda began to cause redundancy and conflict between the religious orders and the bishops and diocesan clergy, and in 1568 Philip II convened a junta to look into the matter. The Junta Magna regularized matters in favor of bishops and the growing number of diocesan clergy. Bishops, the junta decided, were to exercise primary jurisdiction. Religious orders were no longer to report directly to Rome and were to pay to the bishop one-quarter of their income.

In earlier years, religious orders had received men of mixed blood into membership on a limited basis, mainly as lay brothers but also as priests. Ordinations of educated Indians to the diocesan priesthood took place as well. By the late 1560s, however, resistance surfaced in Spain and the Indies against the ordination of mestizos, Indians, and mulattoes, which in turn led to a de-emphasis on their education. Brought to the Americas in 1570, the Inquisition began to enforce a number of royal and local prohibitions against the ordination of anyone lacking limpieza de sangre (purity of blood), soon to be aided in that effort by an unambiguous royal decree issued in December 1578.

Still, there were exceptions to these prohibitions motivated by a suspicion of submerged Muslim and Jewish loyalties following the expulsion of these groups from Spain. Three priests of mixed blood managed to become bishops (one each in Mexico, Honduras, and the Philippines), and in 1588, lobbied by Rome, Philip temporarily lifted the ban. In general, though, a pattern had been established in the Latin American Church that would last for centuries. Priests, diocesan and religious alike, were required to be Spaniards of pure blood or Creoles of unmixed Spanish descent. No mestizos, Indians, or mulattoes need apply.

Thus the Indies remained missionary territory, even after the Junta Magna of 1568 gave primacy to diocesan structures. In the seventeenth century alone, more than eleven thousand priests, secular and religious, left Spain and its European dependencies for Latin America and the Philippines. The secular priests on duty in Saint Augustine throughout the seventeenth century bore unmistakably Spanish names. A number of them—Sebastián Pérez de la Cerda, for example, on duty in 1674—held university degrees. Franciscans serving in Florida and the Borderlands were equally Spanish and included learned men, but their ranks had long since lost the passion for educating Indian boys that had characterized the apostolate in Mexico in the 1520s and 1530s. Now they were primarily missionaries, edged into that work by the growth of diocesan structures and clergy in Mexico and the Caribbean, and sent forth from missionary colleges to evangelize and hold the frontier as servants of the Crown protected by the military. Millennial dreams were not completely abandoned, evidenced by the speculations of Fray Gonzalo Tenorio. Yet La Florida had already destroyed dreams aplenty. Would it do the same to a residual Franciscan dream of preparing for the Kingdom of Heaven on earth? Was La Florida on the cutting edge of Christian history or a backwater, a failed experiment, testing the faith of the Friars Minor and forcing them to confront a more limited sense of themselves and their hopes for success?

Florida missions

Saint Augustine remained an urban enclave served by diocesan clergy. The sacking of the city by Francis Drake on 29 May 1586 and subsequent pillagings in the next century led to the construction of the Castillo de San Marcos, a stone fortress in High Renaissance style, the mother of all Spanish presidios in North America, which endures to this day. Warned of Drake's impending arrival, the three-hundred-plus inhabitants of the city fled into the hinterlands to avoid massacre. Drake plundered and burned the city to the ground before moving north to the ailing English colony at Roanoke. The diocesan pastor of Saint Augustine, Don Rodrigo García de Trujillo, a former naval chaplain, served until 1593, assisted for a time by another secular priest, Don Diego Escobar de Sambrana, his successor. Fray Francisco Marrón, the superior of Franciscans serving in Florida, ran the parish from 1594 to 1597 until another secular, Don Ricardo Artur, was appointed. Born in Ireland, Richard Arthur—the first of innumerable Irish-born secular priests to serve in North America in the centuries to come—had left his homeland to enlist in the Irish Brigade and Legion, who fought in the Spanish Netherlands, first for the Dutch and later for Spain, in the Dutch revolt against Spanish domination in the 1570s. Hispanicized as Ricardo Artur and ordained a priest, he arrived in Saint Augustine in June 1597 and was confirmed as pastor in February of the following year by Don Antonio Díaz de Salcedo, the bishop of Santiago de Cuba, who also appointed Artur episcopal vicar and ecclesiastical judge for La Florida. Artur thus became the bishop's representative in all matters ecclesiastical, including oversight of Franciscans, who chafed under such supervision. The year 1598 witnessed an important addition to the Saint Augustine infrastructure, the hospital Nuestra Señora de la Soledad (Our Lady of Solitude), the first hospital in North America (which stayed in operation for the next 150 years). Opened by 1605, a small Franciscan academy became the first school in the present-day United States.

The Franciscans, meanwhile, were steadily increasing their presence. This was no easy task. Florida had a way of thwarting the best of intentions. Thirteen friars arrived in September 1587, including the noted scholar Alonso Escobedo, who later composed the metrical narrative *La Florida* based on his and other Franciscans' missionary experiences. All but one of the thirteen arrivees of 1587 went into the field as missionaries. Yet by 1592 only three priests and two lay brothers remained on duty. The rest had failed to establish themselves.

A second beginning was made in September 1595 with the arrival of a group of missionaries under the able leadership of Fray Francisco Marrón. This time, each missionary was escorted to his station by no less than Governor Gonzalo Méndez de Canzo himself. In the presence of the Indians of a selected village, Canzo would kneel before the friar he was installing, kiss his hands, and then, rising, announce to the assembled natives that the Franciscan before whom he had just knelt represented God and the king. Thus a more stable chain of missions (*doctrinas*) and dependent stations (*visitas*) was established under the direction of its Franciscan doctrinero.

From the beginning, the Franciscan missions of Florida—wattle-and-daub walls between pine posts, roofed with palmetto thatching—did not display the architectural ambition of later missions in other regions, particularly those of Texas and Baja California. A chapel, an adjacent cabin for the friar, a nearby service building: the setup was as rudimentary as nearly everything else in this difficult province. What lonely lives these Franciscan missionaries must have endured, despite the consolations of their faith and their formation in the values of their order! In Europe, as well as in Mexico and the Caribbean islands, Franciscan convents were comfortable facilities, reinforced by a daily round of communal life and worship. But to volunteer for a remote mission on the edge of nowhere, living alone in a scratch-built friary and preaching to a frequently resistant congregation, was truly to pursue within the limitations of human frailty the vows and ascetic lifestyle of religious practice.

The life was lonely, uncomfortable, and dangerous, especially when it came to efforts to modify polygamy and other related sexual practices. In September 1597, historian Michael Gannon relates, in the Guale village of Tolomato on present-day Pease Creek in McIntosh County, Georgia, the warrior Juanillo, son of the local chief, was living with several women in addition to the one to whom he was married under the laws of Christianity and the Crown. The local Franciscan, Fray Pedro de Corpa, admonished Juanillo, but to no avail. In consultation with Fray Blas Rodríguez from the nearby mission of Tupinqui, Fray Corpa successfully lobbied to have Juanillo removed as heir to the chieftainship of Guale in favor of another candidate. Armed with a macana club, the aggrieved Juanillo entered Fray Corpa's hut when the priest was at prayer, killed him with a blow to his skull, and then mounted the Franciscan's severed head on a lance, which he planted prominently on the creekside embankment for all to see.

Seven villages joined the Juanillo Revolt, which took the lives of four more Franciscans and enslaved another priest temporarily before his rescue. A total of seventeen priests and brothers, Jesuits and Franciscans, had at that point given their lives on the Florida mission. Learning of these murders, the new king, Philip III, thought seriously of closing down the Florida enterprise entirely and sent Fernando de Valdés, son of the governor of Cuba, to Florida to investigate. Valdés found the Franciscans reluctant to terminate their mission. The surviving friar, Fray Francisco de Ávila, who had spent nine humiliating months as a captive of the Guales, pleaded canonical privilege and refused to identify the perpetrators of the revolt; he would not even discuss its details, fearing a military reprisal that would permanently embitter the Guale mission and end it entirely. Only years later, in Havana, under obedience to his superiors, did Ávila write down an account of the revolt and the martyrdom of his confreres. At Tupinqui, Ávila related, Fray Rodríguez, accosted in his chapel, had asked the Indian intruders permission to finish Mass, which he did as his soon-to-be executioners sat waiting on the chapel floor. On Guale Island, Fray Miguel de Aunon and lay brother Antonio de Badajoz, hearing of the approach of hostile Guales, completed Mass and Communion and waited patiently in prayer for their murderers.

Such willingly embraced martyrdom represented the highest form of witness, as evidenced in the later recovery of the slain Franciscans' bodies, hastily buried by faithful Guales, and their reinterment with great ceremony in Saint Augustine. The blood of such martyrs, the Franciscans believed, all but guaranteed the long-term success of their mission.

Indeed, it was already doing so, according to other reports Valdés received regarding concurrent Franciscan efforts untouched by the Juanillo Revolt. Fray Pedro Bermejo, for example, had Christianized nearly 200 Indians in three villages, who had helped him build an impressive stone chapel at Nombre de Dios; they flocked there on Sundays for high Mass and vespers, which they accompanied with singing. At San Juan del Puerto near the mouth of the Saint Johns River, Fray Francisco Pareja reported the conversion of 500 Indians in seven villages, as well as a large number under instruction. Farther north on the Atlantic coast, at San Pedro, Fray Baltazar López counted 384 converts and expressed hopes for a mission to the Guale to reclaim the 1,200 Indians who had followed Juanillo into revolt. Father López was prophetic in his hopefulness. When Governor Canzo visited the province of Guale in 1603, he was able to renegotiate peaceful relations as far north as Santa Elena. Later that same year, Canzo's successor, Pedro de Ybarra, authorized three new doctrinas in Guale and promised to send more Franciscans.

Patterns of mission experience

The indigenous peoples being gathered into mission communities on the Atlantic coast between Saint Augustine and Santa Elena—the Timucuan, the Guale, and the Cusabo—constituted three interrelated subgroups of Muskogeans. Like all such subgroups, they both resembled and differed from each other. The Timucuan were the most advanced in social organization. The language of the Guale, while

linguistically related to that of the Timucuan, varied enough to require an interpreter. Living north of the Guale in present-day South Carolina, the Cusabo barely
possessed an autonomous identity and were frequently considered by the Spaniards
as a subgroup of the more powerful Guale. When the Guale rose up in revolt under
Juanillo, the Cusabo joined in briefly but backed out just as quickly and aligned
themselves with the stronger Spaniards. A Guale grammar said to have been written by the Jesuit Domingo Agustín Baez during the Society of Jesus' short-lived
mission to these people reportedly was useful to Franciscan missionaries among the
Cusabo. This grammar has never surfaced, however, but if it were truly written and
published, it would have to be considered the first book written in North America.

All three peoples were organized as villages—pueblos, as the Spanish described
them—headed by a *cacique*, or chief. The Guale also supported federations of villages under a *mico* (head chief), to whom the villages paid tribute. Women could
hold either cacique or mico positions. In 1603, the overlord of Nombre de Dios—
one of four Indian provinces (the others being San Pedro, Río Dulce, and San
Sebastián)—was *casica* Doña María Vernal. Wedded to a Spanish soldier, Doña
María foreshadowed the married mothers of the mixed race that might have developed over time, had circumstances permitted such a fusion in La Florida, as eventually occurred elsewhere in the Borderlands. The name of another cacica, Doña
María Meléndez, likewise suggests marriage to a Spaniard. That same year the
Timucuan province of San Pedro was governed by *cacica y cabeza* (head chief) Doña
Ana, the young niece of the previous cacique. She presided as a secular ruler over
an architecturally ambitious mission church on a parity with that in Saint Augustine, dedicated on 10 March 1603, in partnership with the local Franciscan, Fray
Baltasar López. Like the upper-class women who facilitated the missionary labors
of Saint Paul, these women notables allied themselves with the Catholic cause and
facilitated the reconsolidation of the missions of La Florida in the aftermath of the
Juanillo Revolt.

The mission system established in 1633 across the gulf panhandle represented a
strategic as well as evangelical corridor that linked Saint Augustine to the agriculturally rich districts on the gulf between the Suwannee and Apalachicola Rivers.
The indigenous people of this region, the Apalachee, like the people of the Atlantic
coast, belonged to the Muskogean group. In contrast to the Timucuan, Guale, and
Cusabo, however, the Apalachee were skilled agriculturalists—maize, squash, and
beans grew easily in the fertile panhandle soil—in addition to being hunter-gatherers.
Apalachee, the province and the people, represented a crucial acquisition for Saint
Augustine, which suffered from poor soil and lagging agricultural productivity.

Moving through this area in earlier decades, Narváez and de Soto noted the
Apalachee's hostility and warlike abilities, which served them well, given the desperation of the shipwrecked Narváez expedition and the murderous, rapacious
intent of de Soto. By the early 1600s, however, the Apalachee had adjusted themselves to the Spanish presence, and in 1607 they requested that missionaries be sent
to them. That it took until 1633 for the Franciscans to arrive testifies to the delays
endemic to development in La Florida under Spain, but at long last the Franciscans
did arrive, supported by a government eager to exploit western Florida's agricultural
abundance. Within two decades, a mission network—centered on and protected
by Fort Saint Louis de Talimali, near present-day Tallahassee—was ministering to

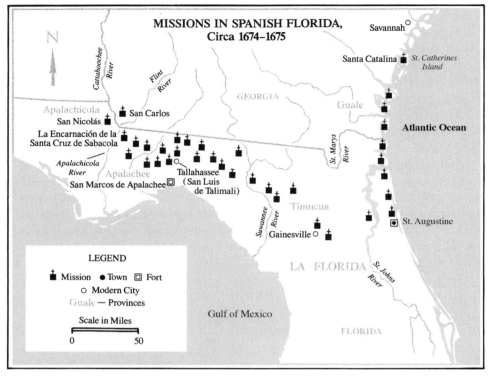

Map 7. Missions in Spanish Florida, circa 1674–75. From David J. Weber, *The Spanish Frontier in North America* (New Haven: Yale University Press, 1992), 101.   © *Yale University Press, used by permission.*

a Christianized population gathered into mission-centered communities named in honor of Catholic saints.

Fundamental and long-standing differences did not fade away, though, as evidenced by rebellions in 1638 and 1647. The Apalachee fiercely resented the system of forced labor used to transport local foodstuffs either by sea from the gulf or, even more deadly, overland to Saint Augustine on the backs of Apalachee carriers. They also were angered by the drafts of Apalachee men to work on the ongoing construction of the harbor fortress at Saint Augustine.

These rebellions, however, did not involve the entire Apalachee confederation, and they were as much against the Crown as against the Church; in the midst of one uprising, chiefs specifically stated that they were rebelling not against the Franciscans but against the forced-labor system. Still, given the unity of Church and Crown, plus the fact that the Franciscans were paid servants of the state, it is difficult to disentangle the two institutions when apportioning responsibility for a system of forced labor that lasted into the early eighteenth century. The mulish portage of food sacks and baskets across more than two hundred miles of difficult terrain, the hauling of great stones for the ramparts of the Castillo de San Marcos—such labor would be onerous to any race, but, as Las Casas and the Dominicans had pointed out constantly in times past, it was especially debilitating to indigenous people unaccustomed to such burdens. The unremitting pace of work broke their bodies, shortened or ended their lives, and led some despairing Apalachee mothers to say that they would prefer their sons dead—indeed, they would kill them themselves—rather than have them conscripted into forced labor.

By 1655, forty-plus Franciscan friars were ministering to perhaps as many as twenty-six thousand Christianized Indians in thirty-eight doctrinas in four missionary provinces: Timucua and Guale on the Atlantic coast, and Apalachee and, briefly, Apalachicola across the Florida panhandle. At the height of the program, however, the mission system showed its weakness when revolt broke out in 1656 in Timucua and Apalachee. The Franciscans must have mistreated the Indians, Governor Diego de Rebolledo claimed. Not true, the Franciscans replied. The rebellion was about forced labor, as the Indian leadership itself claimed. Of two hundred Indians on one forced march to Saint Augustine, only ten survived. The rest died of exhaustion and hunger.

Episcopal considerations

Saint Augustine, meanwhile, remained diocesan, staffed by secular clergy salaried by the Crown. Three to four priests saw to the spiritual needs of a garrison of three hundred soldiers, the parish church that served three hundred civilians, the hospital, dependent chapels, and as many as nine confraternities organized around various Catholic devotions. The development of traditional Catholic life was symbolized and rewarded in 1607 by a visit from the bishop of Cuba and Florida, Don Juan de la Cabezas de Altamirano, a Dominican of upper-class background who was the son of a judge. A graduate of the University of Salamanca, Altamirano had previously served as a professor of theology in Santo Domingo, followed by a stint in Rome representing Dominicans in the New World, prior to his consecration as bishop. It took courage for Altamirano to set sail for Florida. In 1604 he had been seized by the group of French pirates who had previously sacked Havana and burned its cathedral and was held prisoner until a sizable ransom was handed over.

The bishop made it safely to Saint Augustine, however—ironically, on a captured English pirate ship—and, landing on 15 March 1607, was greeted with ceremonies that surpassed those of the dedication of the city in 1565. The following week, Holy Week, Altamirano consecrated the sacred oil on Holy Thursday for use throughout the year, and on Holy Saturday he is said to have administered minor orders to twenty young men preparing for the priesthood. The exact nature of this ceremony remains unclear. Saint Augustine did not have the population or the seminary to prepare twenty young men for the diocesan priesthood. Were these men Franciscan candidates? This is also doubtful, since the Franciscans did not possess such manpower or training facilities either. Such a mass ordination to the priesthood (as some sources claim of the ceremony) would have constituted an epic chapter in La Florida development and would have long since been investigated. Thus the conferral of minor orders—porter, lector, exorcist, and acolyte—remains a possibility, although even this is problematic.

The following week, Altamirano set out for the Indian missions. Traveling to nearby Nombre de Dios, then northward to the Guale missions in Georgia, then southwest to two Timucuan missions in the vicinity of present-day Gainesville, the bishop confirmed a reported 2,633 Indians and Spaniards. As a Dominican and a confrere of Las Casas, Altamirano most likely was pleased by the Christianized Indian life he saw developing, although he did upbraid the Guale for attending church ceremonies in their accustomed breech clouts and other forms of near-nudity.

An alleged golden age

Various historians have described the time between the visit of Bishop Altamirano in 1607 and the second visit of a bishop of Cuba to La Florida—that of Don Gabriel Díaz Vara Calderón in 1674—as a golden age for Spanish Catholic Florida. Evidence indeed exists for such a positive assessment, most dramatically the seventy-nine doctrinas and visitas that extended two hundred miles north of Saint Augustine into present-day Royal Sound, South Carolina, and more than two hundred miles westward to the Chattahoochee River, where the current states of Florida, Georgia, and Alabama meet. During the seven decades of this alleged golden age, hundreds of Franciscans (grouped into provincial autonomy as members of the Provincia de Santa Elena de la Florida) staffed this system as priests and brothers of the Church and agents of the Crown dedicated to the Christianization of native peoples and the maintenance of the Spanish frontier. That frontier ran as far north as Chesapeake Bay and as far west as the Bay of Espíritu Santo, into which flowed the river of the same name, more enduringly known as the Mississippi.

As early as 1607, Bishop Altamirano expressed displeasure with the Franciscans' efforts to push aside secular clergy from parish and chaplaincy assignments in Saint Augustine. Returning to Cuba, Altamirano wrote King Philip III to inform him of this overreaching by the friars and of the Franciscans' general reluctance to respond to episcopal authority. Although his predecessor as bishop of Cuba had been a Franciscan, Altamirano informed the king, he had deliberately staffed Saint Augustine with secular clergy more amenable to royal and episcopal supervision. Conflict between regulars and seculars was commonplace. In more settled regions, the outcome of such rivalry usually favored the bishop and the seculars. In Florida and the Borderlands, however, where the possibility of a locally recruited diocesan clergy remained remote, Franciscans had the advantage in numbers and motivation. Historian Maynard Geiger describes the Franciscan mission to Florida as a conquest. Geiger lists more than seven hundred Franciscans on duty in Spanish Florida between 1528 and 1763. Seven hundred—versus a handful of diocesan clergy and no resident bishop. Seven hundred friars were committed to the Florida mission system not as a transitional frontier institution leading to diocesan organization (an agent of Crown and diocese-to-be) but as a realization of a heavenly kingdom on earth under Franciscan guardianship.

Bishop Calderón spent a full eight months in La Florida in 1674. Upon his return to Cuba, he wrote to Queen Mother Marie Anne that he was generally impressed with the culture and values of the 13,152 Christianized Indians he visited and confirmed on his journeys through the four mission provinces. Calderón's enumeration and naming of the missions in this letter formed the basis for the archaeological investigations of the Florida mission system in the twentieth century.

The Indians, the bishop reported, lived simply in reed huts that they heated with interior fires. Each village contained a large council house, which seated between two and three thousand people, where communal festivals were held. Their diet consisted of hominy porridge, pumpkins, beans, local fish and game, and water—no wine or rum—as well as a nonintoxicating beverage brewed from seacoastal weeds.

The Indians themselves, the bishop opined, "are weak and phlegmatic as regards work, though clever and quick to learn any art they see done, and great carpenters, as is evidenced in the construction of their wooden churches which are large and painstakingly wrought." Weapons consisted of bows and arrows and small hatchets. Echoing Altamirano's complaint about their clothing, Calderón noted, "They go naked with only the skin [of some animal] from the waist down, and, if anything more, a coat of serge without a lining, or a blanket. The women wear only a sort of tunic that wraps them from the neck to the feet, and which they make of the pearl-colored foliage of trees, which they call *guano* and which costs them nothing except to gather it. Four thousand and eighty-one women, whom I found in the villages naked from the waist up and from the knees down, I caused to be clothed in this grass like the others."

Regarding their practice of Catholicism, Calderón emphasized what he perceived to be their heartfelt dedication:

> As to their religion, they are not idolaters, and they embrace with devotion the mysteries of our holy faith. They attend Mass with regularity at 11 o'clock on the holy days they observe, namely, Sunday, and the festivals of Christmas, the Circumcision, Epiphany, the Purification of Our Lady, and the days of Saint Peter, Saint Paul and All Saints' Day, and before entering the church each one brings to the house of the priest as a contribution a log of wood. They do not talk in the church, and the women are separated from the men; the former on the side of the Epistle, the latter on the side of the Evangel [Gospel]. They are very devoted to the Virgin, and on Saturdays they attend when her Mass is sung. On Sundays they attend the *Rosario* and the *Salve* in the afternoon. They celebrate with rejoicing and devotion the Birth of Our Lord, all attending the midnight Mass with offerings of loaves, eggs, and other food. They subject themselves to extraordinary penances during Holy Week, and during the twenty-four hours of Holy Thursday and Friday, while our Lord is in the Urn of the Monument, they attend standing, praying the Rosary in complete silence, twenty-four men and twenty-four women and the same number of children of both sexes, with hourly changes. The children, both male and female, go to the church on work days, to a religious school where they are taught by a teacher whom they call *Athequi* of the church; [a person] whom the priests have for this service; as they have also a person deputized to report to them concerning all parishioners who live in evil.[1]

Here, indeed, would seem an evocation of the golden age of the Florida missions claimed by some historians. Yet even Bishop Calderón, so eager to provide good news to the queen mother (who had urged him to visit Florida in the first place), made certain qualifications. Saint Augustine, he noted, was too hot in the summer and too cold in the winter. Furthermore, it was located on infertile sand and was forced to import its food from Apalachee, two hundred miles away. Hurricanes frequently flooded the city. No local industry or trade existed; soldiers and friars had to rely on a yearly royal *situado* (subsidy) from Mexico City for support.

One of the key reasons Calderón made his visitation, moreover (although he did not divulge the information to the queen mother), was that earlier he had deputized one of his leading priests, Don Francisco de Sotolongo—the proprietary pastor of Saint Augustine under the European system of designated benefices, who was then living in Havana while the chaplain of the fort, Don Antonio Lorenzo de Padilla, fulfilled his duties—to return to Florida in his place. The Florida Franciscans, however, had vigorously objected to Sotolongo's appointment (fearing it would impart too much authority to a well-connected secular priest), forcing the bishop to replace him with two other clerics approved of by the Franciscans. John Gilmary Shea reports that when Calderón was in Saint Augustine, he conferred minor orders on seven young men of good family. Historian Michael V. Gannon, however, writing eighty years later, claims that Calderón ordained these young men as priests, the first to be ordained in the present-day United States. If so, the majority of them must have been Franciscans—at most, two were diocesan—for, as in the claims of ordinations by Altamirano in 1607, it is difficult to imagine so many diocesan clergy being ordained in such a sparsely settled outpost that was devoid of diocesan structures, much less a seminary of the simplest sort.

Also unmentioned in Calderón's report to the queen mother was the bishop's dissatisfaction, as reported by Shea, with the level of instruction in Christian doctrine being provided at the doctrina attached to the Franciscan Convent of Saint Francis that ministered to the Indian servants of the city. Calderón must have been shocked, if one is to judge from the edict he issued at high Mass the following Sunday. All Indian servants, he ordered, must be released from work on Sundays and holidays to receive religious instruction from Franciscans in the Timucuan, Apalachee, and Guale languages. Spaniards who resisted this obligation would be excommunicated.

More serious charges

Such resistance brings up the most pertinent qualifications to be made against the golden-age theory: forced labor and its repressive enforcement. In signaling their willingness to accept Christianity and the mission system, the caciques of La Florida were expressing a readiness to sacrifice some of their religious and priestly authority in exchange for an alignment—a modus vivendi—with the superior power of the Spaniards. What the caciques could not recognize at the time, however, was the crushing might of the Spanish system, in both economic and military terms, as manifested most brutally in levies of forced labor. With no agriculture and no economy outside the annual subsidy from New Spain—which was frequently reduced or overdue (besides, there was so little to purchase in the first place)—La Florida rested on the backs, literally and figuratively, of its Indian subjects. From this perspective, the appropriation of foodstuffs from Apalachee and the forced labor of its Indians constituted the internal economy of La Florida as a failed colony kept alive by government subsidy and the mission system.

The Franciscans themselves were dependent on Indian agriculture and hunting and gathering and in many instances helped to improve Indian agriculture through the introduction of wheat, oranges, grapes, figs, and other fruits. When crops failed or barely met the needs of the military at Saint Augustine or the other presidios, the friars, like their charges, went hungry. Thus developed a system of food offerings or food gifts connected to the exercise of priestly functions—Mass, baptism, marriage, funerals—by the Franciscans. Such a system of barter tithing was commonplace in the agricultural economies of New Spain and Spain itself, but in La Florida it was the major means of survival. Hence it possessed a corrupting influence born of dependency, and even desperation, in times of scarcity. Corporeal punishment crept into the system. In 1687 a mission inspector from Spain stated that he had heard reports of Indian youngsters being whipped by friars if they failed to bring foodstuffs to Sunday Mass.[2]

When Governor Juan Márquez Cabrera forbade whippings by friars, the Franciscans defended the punishments as a family matter. The friars, they argued, were chastising their children as dutiful fathers. Governor Cabrera's admonition contained a strong element of irony, even conscious hypocrisy, given the military's enforcement of the forced-labor system and the fierce suppression of the all-too-frequent Indian revolts. Since La Florida was totally dependent on Indian agriculture and forced labor, such revolts constituted a threat to the survival of the failing colony and were responded to accordingly. The Apalachee revolt of 1638 was punished by increased drafts of forced labor. The Apalachee revolt of 1647 resulted in the prompt execution—most likely by garrote—of twelve ringleaders and the sentencing of twenty-six others to hard labor on the fortifications of Saint Augustine. A decade later, eleven rebellious caciques were summarily garroted, one by one, when captured during the even more ambitious Apalachee rebellion of 1657. Infuriated, the Indians destroyed the missions in their territory. Six Franciscans, disgusted with military repression and fearing for their lives, fled their posts and, taking ship from the gulf coast to Havana, were lost at sea.

Nevertheless, the Franciscans did not abandon the Florida mission. Thirty-three replacement friars arrived in 1658, an impressive commitment of manpower for such a remote post. La Florida still embodied hopes, dreams, and metaphors for a millenarian realization of Kingdom Come on earth—distant yet compelling—an expectation at the core of the Franciscan movement since the thirteenth century. But La Florida had a way of wearing down the Franciscan presence and fervor. By the 1690s a staffing crisis was evident, and an increasing number of friars tended to be assigned to the less challenging life of the Convent of Saint Francis in Saint Augustine. Physical hardship and disease ruined the health or ended the lives of many missionaries. Isolation, difficulties in mastering languages, malnutrition, and hunger eroded energy and tempered ambition.

The extreme versions of Franciscan millenarianism (most notably, that of Gerónimo de Mendieta) considered the Indians of the New World not only a chosen people but also a race of noble savages, foreshadowing a favorite conception of the Enlightenment. Yet the realities of Indian life challenged this ideal, even in such a peripheral issue as sports. The Indians of La Florida played a village-wide game in which teams of men fought to maintain control of a ball and move it from one point to another. Beating, gouging, kicking, trampling, and occasional killing were the essence of the game, which had deep-rooted ceremonial and warfare-related significance. The friars opposed the game on humane and religious grounds. The military, by contrast, including the governor, was more tolerant of it, and this difference created a point of tension throughout the alleged golden age.

Noble savages, moreover, are by definition unbothered by sexual guilt or, at the least, freed from civilization and its discontents. A commitment to a life of celibacy was now being thrust into the free-flowing sexual ethos of native peoples. As the two visiting bishops indicated disapprovingly, Indians dressed minimally, even when attending Sunday Mass. Chiefs were accustomed to polygamy, and even men of lesser rank frequently took a second wife for breeding purposes or to replace a wife captured or exchanged into another village. The friars dutifully fought polygamy, discouraged women from going about bare breasted, and monitored feasts and celebrations, which offered dancing and temptations to sexual adventure. But they were men as well, living alone in the prime of life, and the sexual tendencies of their charges—while technically sinful and to be corrected—engendered environments that made the friars' vowed celibacy an especial trial (if not, now and then, a near occasion of sin).

The very organization and deployment of Franciscans as licensed and paid agents of the Crown under the ultimate supervision of a military governor clashed with the Franciscans' sense of themselves as an autonomous force. In the mid-seventeenth century, during the administration of Governor Diego de Rebolledo (1654–1658), the Franciscans complained to the Crown regarding government levies for forced labor, the granting of permission to play the ball games prohibited by the missionaries, the excessive punishments of rebellious caciques, and the discriminatory pricing of agricultural produce. In 1668 they sent their grievance to Madrid: Governor Francisco la Guerra y de la Vega was living openly—scandalously—with a woman not his wife. By the late 1680s, it was government members' turn to complain to the Crown, as Franciscan staffing, fervor, and behavior allegedly went into decline.

In 1687 Governor Diego de Quiroga squared off against Franciscan provincial Pedro de Luna over Luna's decision to assign eight Franciscans to Havana to hold professorial chairs and serve as confessors, while another was sent to Rome on special assignment. These men, the governor complained, had been licensed and paid to serve in La Florida. Their departure left eleven vacant posts in the missions. In 1691 charges grew more serious, centered on alleged incidents of Franciscan cruelty. Three hundred fifty to four hundred Indians had fled Mission Nuestra Señora de la Candalaria de la Tama due to whippings, it was charged, and were living in the woods and mountains or among the English in Carolina. The scarred backs of many Indians of Mission Santa Catalina in Timucua, the brief continued, bore witness to the practice of whipping in that doctrina. In 1697 the Council of the Indies, having received so many complaints, explicitly directed the governor to take steps to ensure the good treatment of Indians in the mission system.

Threat from the north

An even more dangerous threat was forthcoming. For more than one hundred years, hostile English ships—pirates and privateers alike—had plied the Caribbean in war against Spain, which in 1588 had led Spain to attempt unsuccessfully the invasion of England with a great armada in one of the most decisive battles of naval history. Prior to the defeat of the Spanish Armada, England had twice tried and failed to establish a colony on Roanoke Island off present-day North Carolina. In 1607 a beachhead was established at Jamestown, Virginia. In 1629 King Charles I formally asserted England's claim to the territory south of Virginia. Decades later, following civil war and the Protectorate, Charles II (restored to the English throne) initiated the settlement of this southern territory, Carolina, named in honor of his father; a proprietary colony was founded in 1670 at Albemarle Point. Ten years later, the Carolina colonists moved their settlement across the river to Oyster Point and named it Charles Town (later Charleston), in honor of the king. Charleston served as the capital of the colony of Carolina until its division into north and south in 1713.

In 1668, as if in an overture of things to come, an English pirate ship landed a force of one hundred men by night and sacked Saint Augustine, shooting down men, women, and children as they fled the city for the Castillo de San Marcos. As a result of this attack, more Indians were forced to work on the fortifications. An assault in 1670 by an English ship on Mission Santa Catalina on Saint Catherine's Island off Georgia prompted a retaliatory operation—three frigates and fourteen pirogues under the command of Juan Menéndez Márquez—against the newly established settlement of Charles Town, but a hurricane disabled the expedition.

The year 1680 witnessed more attacks on the missions by Yuchi, Creeks, and Cherokees in league with the English, which led almost immediately to the abandonment of Mission Santa Catalina by Guale Christians and, in time, to the abandonment of missions farther south by Christianized Yamasee, who both feared hostile Indian attacks and faced a growing disenchantment with mission life. In short order, this initial Yamasee flight developed into a wholesale desertion to the English on the part of the Guale tribes of the north. Worse, it became active warfare by the Yamasee against their former masters, as inaugurated in February 1685, when a group of fifty or so renegade Yamasee—thirty of them armed with guns supplied by the English—attacked the mission village of Santa Catalina de Afuyca, pillaged its church, killed ten men and eight women, and carried off twenty-two men and eight women (killing and scalping a woman who refused to march), to be sold into slavery. By 1686 the north coastal mission system of Guale stood virtually abandoned, its population of Christianized Indians having fled en masse to the south.

English-backed Yamasee raids on mission enclaves continued throughout the ensuing decade, weakening the periphery of La Florida through desertion and destruction that drove loyal Indians closer and closer to Saint Augustine, including those being forcibly drafted into labor gangs to work on its fortifications. The Castillo de San Marcos, whose construction started in 1672, was completed by 1700, thanks to Indian toil. A massive European-style bastion, the Castillo—first envisioned by Governor and Captain General Pedro Menéndez de Avilés in the founding era—asserted Spanish sovereignty over La Florida and the adjacent sea lanes that were essential for a safe, swift sail to Spain. Looking south to Saint Augustine and southwestward to French Louisiana, being established on the Mississippi, the aggressively Protestant, slave-hungry plantation owners of the Carolinas feared the French-Spanish alliance that was formed in 1700 when the dying Spanish king Charles II named as his heir Philip, Duke of Anjou, grandson of Louis XIV of France, to reign as Philip V of Spain and thereby bring into existence a threatening coalition of Catholic power. Their fears were justified. In 1701 western Europe swept into the War of the Spanish Succession (Queen Anne's War in North America), pitting the Catholic alliance of France, Spain, Bavaria, Portugal, and Savoy against the Protestant coalition of England, Holland, and the Protestant German states. Even before the war broke out, the Carolina governor

James Moore and the planters elected to the Carolina Commons—anti-Spaniard, anti-French, anti-Catholic plantation owners eager to increase their ownership of Indian and African slaves—were preparing for military action against La Florida and (eventually) Louisiana, lest the entire gulf region be sealed off from them or, even worse, lest a Spanish-French alliance march north to reclaim Carolina.

On 16 October 1702, five hundred to six hundred English militiamen and three hundred to six hundred Yamasee and other Indians embarked south on a two-pronged attack; the land force was under the command of Colonel Robert Daniel, and the sea crew was under the command of Governor Moore, who led a flotilla of fourteen vessels confiscated from private sources. Converging on Saint Augustine, the English marched into an abandoned city whose entire population had taken refuge in the Castillo. Moore sent Colonel Daniel and troops to Jamaica in several of the larger ships to acquire siege artillery and in the meantime had his men surround the Castillo, to try to starve its population into submission before the artillery arrived. After two months, the siege guns had not yet come, and the Castillo had not surrendered. Indeed, the Spaniards were launching sallies against the English, and the Carolina forces were losing their discipline and their will to continue—never more so than in late November, when two Spanish frigates (twenty-two and sixteen guns, respectively), accompanied by four troop transports, appeared offshore and landed soldiers on Anastasia Island, prompting Moore's Yamasee allies to take flight. Burning boats laden with booty, Moore withdrew from the field and marched his men to the mouth of the Saint Johns River, where another flotilla awaited to sail them north.

Before departing, Moore's men burned Saint Augustine to the ground. The English took special satisfaction in torching the parish church and its dependent hermitage of Nuestra Señora de la Leche, as well as the convent and chapel of the Franciscans, which included the friar's library of Greek and Latin Fathers and assorted theological works in Latin. On their march north, the English assaulted missions San José and San Francisco, killing any Christian Indians who resisted or otherwise proved inconvenient and taking another five hundred northward into slavery. For all practical purposes, La Florida now extended only forty miles northward to the Saint Johns River, and the missionary province of Guale was no more.

The failed siege of Saint Augustine cost Carolina 8,495 pounds and temporarily forced the colony to issue paper currency. Although some praised Moore for his orderly retreat and the few (only two) lives lost during the expedition, Moore's reputation suffered a significant setback, and he resigned the governorship. Within a year, however, Moore—anxious to regain his standing and once again to go a-slaving—was back in the field, this time with a subsidized force of fifty English militia and a thousand Lower Creeks. Moore's plan was to march westward into the Apalachee missionary province, causing as much havoc and taking as many slaves as possible—which Moore and his men proceeded to do with murderous efficiency. One hundred thirty-eight years previously, Pedro Menéndez de Avilés earned centuries of excoriation for his slaughterous suppression of the Huguenots. Fairness would seem to dictate a similar condemnation for Moore as his men and their Lower Creek allies hacked, burned, and tortured their way through the Apalachee province, destroying eight out of fourteen doctrinas as their contribution to an English victory in Queen Anne's War.

Moore's destruction of the village of Concepción de Ayubale on the morning of 25 January 1704 offers a paradigm of the entire campaign. The English and Lower Creeks attacked early that morning but were delayed by Apalachee archers long enough for Fray Ángel de Miranda to gather men, women, and children into the church enclosure and organize resistance. The English attacked the doors of the besieged church with axes but did not gain entrance. Fourteen were wounded. Later that afternoon, three attackers died when the church doors were set on fire and the church was successfully rushed. Twenty-four Indians were killed resisting the takeover. One hundred sixty people were taken captive. Learning of the attack, Captain Juan Ruíz Mexía led a relief force of thirty mounted Spaniards, two Franciscan friars, and four hundred Indians from the nearby village of San Luis to Ayubale. The English and Lower Creeks, however, held off the relief force until the Spaniards and Apalachee ran out of ammunition and either surrendered or fled.

Over the course of the next two days, at Ayubale and the nearby mission village of San Pedro y San Pablo de Patale, the English and their Lower Creek allies took their revenge for the local resistance. When Fray Miranda pleaded with Moore to stop the massacre at Ayubale, Moore replied that the Lower Creeks outnumbered his men and could not be controlled. In any event, whoever was responsible— or whoever was responsible for those who were responsible—effected a most thorough massacre. The three captured Franciscans (Fray Miranda, Fray Juan de Parga Araujo, and Fray Manuel de Mendoza) were tortured to death. That is, the latter two were beaten, burned, butchered, and beheaded; Fray Miranda's body was never found. Bodies of scalped and mutilated men, women, and children lay scattered about the ground or hung from the stakes on which they had been tortured. Colonel Moore returned to Carolina, so he reported, with more than four thousand Indians in captivity as slaves. More than a thousand had been killed. Another three hundred had been driven into exile. Within thirteen years, the English would reap the whirlwind, however, when their onetime ally the Yamasee formed a league of Native American groups and launched a two-year war that almost destroyed South Carolina by 1715. Seven percent of the colony's white population were killed in an expanded version of James Moore's 1702 campaign against the Apalachee mission system.[3]

Failure and paradigm

The Moore expedition did not immediately dislodge the Franciscan mission system of La Florida, but it did create a tipping point in the direction of its ultimate disappearance that was never reversed, even after caciques from 161 villages—Yamasee, Lower Creeks, and Apalachees—arrived in Saint Augustine in 1715 and requested a resumption of doctrinas in their villages. Only nineteen replacement friars, peninsulars from Spain, arrived between 1719 and 1722, and all but two soon returned to Cuba due to the hardships of mission life and the hostility and neglect they experienced from the colonial-born, colonial-trained Creoles who now controlled the order in La Florida. In 1735 the remaining Franciscan peninsulars separated themselves into an independent chapter. By 1759 only ten Franciscans remained on active duty in the mission system that for more than 150 years had held the Florida frontier for Spain, and these survivors had more or less urbanized themselves into an impressive new convent in Saint Augustine (built between 1724 and 1737) that allowed them to compete with the secular clergy for Sunday Mass attendance by the upper strata of the city.

It seemed that no chance of establishing a diocesan structure remained. Since 1690 the bishops of Cuba had been calling for the creation of an independent Florida diocese. The Council of the Indies, however, countered with the offer of an auxiliary bishop resident in Florida, an arrangement that King Philip V recommended to Pope Clement XI, who approved of the plan in May 1703. Dionisio Resino, a Creole secular priest who was a canon on the staff of the Havana cathedral and the oldest priest in Cuba, was appointed to the post. Still, the bishop of Cuba delayed, arguing that Florida required its own diocese. The matter was not resolved until the bishop died and a new bishop of Cuba replaced him, and the aged Resino was consecrated and sent to Florida. Bishop Resino arrived in Saint Augustine on 23 June 1709 after barely escaping capture by English warships. Appalled by what he encountered—a parish church in ruins, no episcopal residence, the mission system in disarray—Resino sailed back to Cuba three weeks later on the same ship that had brought him the Florida. Two years later, the prelate died in Havana.

Not until July 1735 did Florida receive a second auxiliary bishop, Francisco de San Buenaventura y Tejada, a Franciscan of the Recollect reform who had served as a professor of theology and guardian of the Recollect monastery of Seville. Tejada possessed the learning, temperament, administrative experience, and personal piety and asceticism of a devoted priest formed in his youth by a reformed wing of the Franciscan movement that even then was playing an important role in the evangelization of Canada and the Mississippi valley. Bishop Tejada served in Florida for ten years, until his transfer to Yucatán in 1745. During that time, he displayed the personal magnetism and energetic leadership that would later characterize his administration of the Sees of Yucatán and, eventually, Guadalajara, a posting that made him bishop of Texas as well. Tejada died in 1760, having earned a lasting reputation, John Gilmary Shea tells us, "as one of the holiest men who have adorned the Mexican hierarchy".[4] At long last, Florida had a bishop! A great bishop, in fact, the first Roman Catholic bishop to serve permanently in North America—albeit in a fading Spanish colony, once again coming under attack from England in 1740 during the War of Jenkins' Ear, which became part of the larger European War of the Austrian Succession. Tejada found Saint Augustine run-down and dispirited. He rebuilt the parish church, adding a stone sacristy, and staffed it with three seculars, whom he mentored. He opened a school and personally instructed the children of the city three days a week. He organized religious processions and conferred confirmation on Spaniards, Indians, and a growing population of people of African descent. He preached effectively, urged good behavior, and banned gambling from local taverns. When the English under the command of Governor James Oglethorpe laid siege, he rallied the people, leading them in an Ave Maria each time the ships fired on the city. In short, he functioned as a good bishop should, practicing what he preached and preaching through what he practiced.

As bishop, Tejada embodied a Diocese of Florida that might have been: had sufficient colonists arrived from Spain; had earlier settlement efforts been successful; had a permanent place for Christianized Indians been created, freed from forced labor; had a Creole and mixed-race population grown; had a secular clergy developed to match the Franciscan presence; had the region not suffered so much piracy, slavery, civil-religious conflict, and war; or, of equal importance, had there been more agriculture and trade and less interference from the Council of the Indies and the Casa de Contratación. For a short while, during the episcopal tenure of Tejada, things seemed hopeful. Even the Jesuits returned. Fathers Joseph Mary Monaco and Joseph Xavier de Alana arrived from Havana in July 1743 to evangelize southern Florida and the Keys. After great resistance and discouragement, they fostered the development of a community of Christianized Indians, fishing folk, which held together until the Americans forcibly removed them to the Indian Territory following the conclusion of the Seminole War in 1842, although they had not participated in the conflict.

Still, for all the hopefulness the charismatic Tejada emanated, his ten-year tenure constituted a twilight and lingering afterglow for Catholic Florida. His successor as bishop remained on site for a mere ten months, then returned to Cuba. The next bishop to visit Saint Augustine, Pedro Agustín Morell, the bishop of Santiago de Cuba (a Creole born in Veracruz, Mexico), did not come of his own free will. Taken prisoner by the English when they seized Havana in 1762 after a bitter siege, Bishop Morell was transported to Charleston on a British man-of-war, detained there for two weeks, and then repatriated to Saint Augustine, where he carried on his episcopal duties as best as he could manage. In April 1763 Morell went back to Cuba. By that time, Spain had ceded Florida to Great Britain in exchange for Havana. England divided Florida into two provinces. East and West Florida remained under British jurisdiction for twenty-one years until the second Treaty of Paris returned Florida to Spain.

PART TWO

The Spanish Borderlands

5

Ácoma 1599

New Mexico, anchor kingdom of the Borderlands, begins with a massacre

News of Fray Padilla's martyrdom reached Mexico City within the year. New Spain withdrew from Tierra Nueva until a Franciscan lay brother, Fray Agustín Rodríguez, and his company pushed north again with the viceroy's permission and in June 1581 reached the pueblos of the Río Grande valley. Much had happened in the thirty-eight years between Coronado's return to New Spain and Fray Rodríguez's reentry into Pueblo country. Disgraced, financially devastated, and in failing health, Coronado—who had ridden at the head of his soldiers as a youthful knight in sun-reflecting armor so few years before—returned to Mexico City to face charges of needless cruelty to Indians. He escaped the judgment of the courts, however, and lived quietly in retirement in Mexico City until his death in 1554. His chief lieutenant, García López de Cárdenas, also brought up on charges, was less fortunate. Cárdenas died in prison in Spain while appealing his conviction. Fray Marcos de Niza, whose *Relación* (1539) had set the entrada in motion, returned to New Spain under a cloud, but even in semidisgrace, the opinionated friar reemerged in 1541 to counsel severe measures against the rebellious Indians of Nueva Galicia. He later retired to the pleasant suburban township of Jalapa, where each month his friend Fray Juan de Zumárraga, the bishop (archbishop after 1547) of Mexico City, sent along an *arroba* of wine for his enjoyment. Niza died in Mexico City in March 1558, having outlived the martyred Padilla, the disgraced Coronado, the imprisoned Cárdenas, the disappointed Mendoza and Zumárraga, the garroted Turk, and the hundreds of other Pueblo Indians who had lost their lives as a result of the entrada inspired by the exaggerations of his *Relación*.

New Spain continued to advance into northern Mexico. Even as Coronado first ventured north, Viceroy Antonio de Mendoza was personally in the field in northwestern Nueva Galicia during the Mixtón War (1541–1542), leading the resistance against the Indians who were trying to drive the Spaniards from this area. The discovery of silver in central Nueva Galicia in 1546 precipitated the emergence of the mining settlement Zacatecas at the center of the otherwise unsettled Gran Chichimeca region. This development in turn set in motion forty years of further warfare, culminating by the mid-1580s in the stabilization of Gran Chichimeca into a northern frontier of settlements, mines, encomiendas, and presidios, linked to each other and to Mexico City by established roadways.

The rise of this region constituted a long and bloody ordeal, and no religious order played a more important role—or suffered the loss of so many personnel to hostile Chichimeca Indians—than the Franciscans. Paradoxically, however, the pacification and development of the Gran Chichimeca threatened the future of the friars in northern Mexico. With the peaceful settlement and evangelization of the Gran Chichimeca and the subsequent moving north of the frontier, a resident bishop and a diocesan structure served by diocesan priests would inevitably follow. The junta convened by Philip II in 1568 to examine the relationship between religious orders and diocesan bishops repealed the 1522 papal grant of *Omnimoda* through which religious-order priests in the Indies (such as the Franciscans) received their faculties directly from the pope. Diocesan bishops were placed in charge of all priests, diocesan and religious alike, and the growth of a diocesan clergy was to be encouraged. The Franciscans' awareness of their eventual displacement in Mexico was reinforced by a mystical millenarianism that was slowly gaining strength. It was the destiny of their order, Franciscans believed, to establish the Kingdom of Heaven among the indigenous peoples of the Indies; hence they must continue to move north into nonevangelized regions if they were to fulfill that mission. By the early sixteenth century, the Franciscan movement was divided between Observants, who favored a strict interpretation of the Franciscan way of life, and Conventuals, who followed a more monastic version of Franciscanism. (Pope Leo X had formalized the distinction in the papal bull *Omnipotens Deus* in June 1517.) In 1567 Pope Saint Pius V, a Dominican, ceded all Conventual provinces in Spain and Portugal to the Observants. The Observant movement then transformed into four variations: Discalced, Récollects, Reformed, and Capuchins, each observance represented in one way or another in the saga of New World evangelization. With thirty-five thousand friars worldwide, the Observant Franciscans constituted a solid majority of Franciscans in the Indies.

And so on 5 June 1581 three Observant Franciscans—the lay brother Fray Agustín Rodríguez, a native of Niebla, Spain, who organized the expedition; and the priests Fray Francisco López, the religious superior, an Andalusian, and Fray Juan de Santa María, a Catalan—accompanied by nine soldiers and sixteen Indian servants, set forth from the northern outpost town of Santa Bárbara in search of new opportunities for evangelization among the Pueblo Indians of New Mexico. Reaching the Río Grande valley, the friars and even the soldiers—as evident in declarations certain soldiers made in Mexico City upon their return—were delighted by the Zuñi and Tewa pueblos and the possibilities they presented for the peaceful evangelization King Philip II had called for in the Royal Ordinances of 1573, which outlawed gratuitous violence against indigenous peoples. Exhilarated by this new prospect for Franciscan preaching of the gospel, Fray Juan de Santa María decided to return at once to Mexico to ask for more missionaries. Within three days, he was killed on the trail by Pueblo Indians who, perhaps having heard of the Coronado expedition, believed that the friar was heading back for more soldiers. When the captain of the escort declared that it was time to return south, Friars López and Rodríguez, unaware of their colleague's murder, stated that they would remain on and found a mission at the Tewa pueblo of Puaray. They were likewise slain in short order, as an expedition discovered in November 1582.

The operation was organized, financed, and led by Antonio de Espejo, a wealthy merchant. While claiming to be on a rescue mission in the company of Franciscan friar Bernardino Beltrán in search of the three stranded missionaries (who were already murdered), Espejo was in reality searching for gold and silver deposits.

Further poisoning the well first poisoned nearly forty years earlier by the Coronado expedition, Espejo sacked the Puaray pueblo and executed sixteen captives. His actions constituted a direct defiance of the Royal Ordinances of 1573.

The ordinances, moreover, explicitly prohibited unauthorized private expeditions into New Mexico. Two such rogue incursions followed Espejo's return to Santa Bárbara in 1583, after Espejo had dictated a long narrative describing peaceful pueblos inhabited by well-fed and well-clothed natives who were light-skinned and friendly, a prosperous and promising landscape, abundant flora and fauna, gold and silver deposits that he had personally inspected, and reports of the near proximity of the Strait of Anián flowing westward to the South Sea. A troop of soldiers sent north by the viceroy arrested the leader of the first rogue expedition, Gaspar Castaño de Sosa, and brought him back to Mexico City in chains. Francisco Leyva de Bonilla, who led the second illegal foray, was murdered by one of his soldiers while on the plains of Kansas in search of Quivira.

Northern ambitions

The collection of documents chronicling the colonization of New Mexico by Juan de Oñate between 1598 and 1607—assembled, edited, and translated by George P. Hammond of the University of California–Berkeley and Acapito Rey of Indiana University for publication by the University of New Mexico Press in 1953—runs to 1,187 pages in two oversized volumes that testify both to the importance of New Mexico as the anchor province of the Spanish Borderlands and to the prodigious scholarship devoted to Borderland studies by American academics in the first half of the twentieth century. Furthermore, the dynamics of this colonizing effort parallel, encapsulate, and compress into a more narrow time frame the ambitions and assumptions behind the colonization of Florida. Like Pedro Menéndez de Avilés, Oñate held an appointment as adelantado and captain general of the region he was to colonize. Also like Menéndez, Oñate privately financed a colonizing expedition in the hope of greater rewards through mining and encomienda. In contrast to Menéndez, Oñate was born rich. His father, Cristóbal de Oñate, a Basque, had made a fortune as an encomendero of Nueva Galicia and the discoverer and developer of one of the richest silver mines of Zacatecas. Juan further improved the family's status by marrying Isabel Tolosa Cortés Moctezuma, the wealthy daughter of a Zacatecas mine owner, the great-granddaughter of the last Aztec emperor, and, on her mother's side, a granddaughter of Hernán Cortes, conqueror of Mexico. Oñate adored his wife—whose bloodlines bespoke a Mexico in the making—and her early death in the late 1580s reportedly turned his attention to New Mexico as a way of recovering from his grief.

Oñate envisioned New Mexico as more than a remote colony. After all, his father had helped bring about the settlement and development of Nueva Galicia and the pacification of the Gran Chichimeca precisely because the region's silver mines had attracted enough Spaniards to establish mining camps that evolved into mining towns. These towns motivated these settlers to defend their interests from marauding Chichimeca, which in turn led the viceroy to establish a network of garrisoned presidios for protection. If the accounts of Antonio Espejo and others were correct, and silver and gold lay to the north, Spaniards would flock to New Mexico. Espejo had also

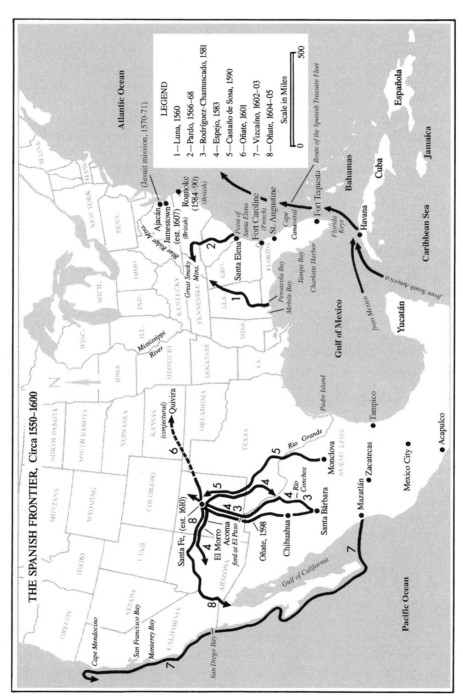

Map 8. The Spanish Frontier, circa 1550–1600. From David J. Weber, *The Spanish Frontier in North America* (New Haven: Yale University Press, 1992), 66. © *Yale University Press, used by permission.*

mentioned reports of the Strait of Anián on the northern edge of the region, which would link New Mexico to the Pacific. And reports of Quivira to the far northeast still lingered: that reputed kingdom and capital city not found by Coronado or de Soto, alas, or by Leyva de Bonilla on his recent rogue expedition, but persisting as a magical kingdom in the collective imagination of New Spain as a breathtaking possibility that could not be extinguished. Put all this together, Oñate speculated—silver, gold, settlements, encomiendas, maritime access to the Pacific (for which he had already secured rights to two voyages a year)—and you had the makings of more than a colony. You had the makings of a populated and prosperous viceroyalty extending from Florida to California, with Juan de Oñate enthroned as viceroy.

In his continental ambition, Oñate earns his reputation as the Last Conquistador. Despite his wealthy upbringing, moreover, Oñate had the experience and the ability to back such dreams as he entered his mid-forties, for his life on the far frontier of northern New Spain had been—and in a very real sense continued to be—one long campaign against the challenges of mining and the constant warfare being waged by the fiercely resistant Chichimeca. As an explorer, he would secure a place alongside Coronado and de Soto, trekking northeast through Texas into Oklahoma (again seeking Quivira) and then westward through Arizona in search of the Strait of Anián. He descended the Colorado River to the mouth of the Gulf of California, leaving upon his return an inscription brimming with a laconic sense of mission accomplished on El Morro, a sandstone promontory between the Ácoma and Zuñi pueblos: "There passed this way Adelantado Don Juan de Oñate, from the discovery of the South Sea, on the 16 April 1605."[1]

Evangelical aspirations

Oñate's undertaking involved as well the establishment of missions in Pueblo country by the ten Franciscans attached to the expedition. During the three-year period of preparation and authorization, numerous written declarations of nonviolent religious intent—required in light of the Royal Ordinances of 1573—were notarized, submitted, and filed. These declarations were made not only by Franciscans (which can be expected) but also by Juan de Oñate himself. Yet in his formal request and provisional contract submitted to Viceroy Luis de Velasco for the New Mexican governorship, dated 15 December 1595, Oñate fused discovery, pacification, and conversion as the mission he would accomplish for the Crown. When the Franciscan commissary general allocated five priests and one lay brother to the New Mexico mission, Oñate requested an increase to twelve, to staff the churches, chapels, and reductions (villages) of previously scattered Indians. Interestingly enough, the Franciscans successfully lobbied for the recall of Fray Diego Márquez, who represented the Inquisition, from the venture. In matters ecclesiastical, New Mexico would be a purely Franciscan jurisdiction. The Inquisition represented another line of authority entirely, linked to diocesan bishops and the royal Audiencia.

After interminable delay, the formal mustering, enrollment, and review of the Oñate expedition began at the northern mines of Todos Santos on 22 December 1597. Juan de Frías Salazar, a prominent mine owner from Pachuca, represented the new viceroy, Gaspar de Zúñiga Acevedo y Fonseca, the count of Monterey, as royal inspector. The mustering lasted eighteen days and created yet another lengthy document—itemizing men, equipment, cattle, and sheep—for later perusal by historians. Each male member was enrolled by name, birthplace, father's name, and personal characteristics, along with a description of his weapons and armor. Wives and children accompanied the expedition but were not formally enrolled. Oñate's contract with the viceroy called for 200 soldiers. He was able to muster only 129, but thanks to a loan from friends, he posted a bond guaranteeing further recruitment. Finally, on 21 January 1598, the mustering document was signed and notarized, and Oñate was free to depart.

Some weeks into the march north, Oñate sent a reconnaissance party ahead to reconnoiter a more direct route into Pueblo country than the one previously used via the Conchos River and the Río Grande. The group returned with a report of a shorter course directly through the northern sand dunes. Choosing this option, Oñate established the beginnings of a two-thousand-mile Camino Real that would eventually link Mexico City with the Taos pueblo in the northern Río Grande valley and thus establish New Mexico as the anchor province of the Spanish Borderlands.

First contact

The Oñate expedition began on a note of triumph. Riding out ahead of his main party in the company of two Franciscans and a small group of soldiers, Oñate in early July 1598 reached the pueblo Quigui, one of an eight-pueblo group inhabited by Cherechos Indians. Greeting the Spaniards was a gathering of pueblo captains, whom Oñate's official report named one by one in a lengthy roll call of captains and pueblos that evoked both the extensive pueblo culture of the region and the individuality of indigenous peoples as represented by their elected leaders. Once the captains assembled in the commodious kiva (communal worship space) of Quigui, Oñate addressed them personally through interpreters.

> He told them [reads the report] that he had been sent by the most powerful king and ruler in the world, Don Philip, king of Spain, who desired especially to serve God our Lord and to bring about the salvation of their souls, but wished also to have them as his subjects and to protect and bring justice to them, as he was doing for other natives of the East and West Indies. To this end he had sent the Spaniards from such distant lands to theirs, at enormous expense and great effort. Since, therefore, the governor had come with this purpose, as they could see, it was greatly to their advantage that, of their own free will and in their own names and in those of their pueblos and republics, as their captains, they render obedience and submission to the king, Don Philip, our lord, and become his subjects and vassals, as had the people of the kingdoms of Mexico, Tezcuco, Michoacán, Tlaxcala, Guatemala, and others. By doing so they would live in peace, justice, and orderliness, protected from their enemies and benefitted in their arts and trades and in their crops and cattle.

At the end of this meeting, the captains conferred with their advisors. Returning to Oñate, they declared their desire to pledge themselves as vassals of the king and were doing so of their own free will. Oñate thereupon asked them to proclaim their loyalty on bended knee, which they did. After they rose, the governor continued his address, this time in an explicitly religious direction.

The main reason the king had sent the Spaniards, Oñate informed them, was the salvation of their souls,

> because they should know that their bodies had also souls which did not die even though the bodies did. But if they were baptized and became good Christians, they would go to heaven to enjoy an eternal life of great bliss in the presence of God. If they did not become Christians, they would go to hell to suffer cruel and everlasting torment. He told them that this religion would be explained to them more at length by the most reverend father commissary and the friars, who were present, and who came in the name of his Holiness, the only universal pastor and head of the church, the Holy Father at Rome; they were sent likewise by the king our lord for the healing of the souls of the natives. Therefore, it was important that in spiritual matters and in things pertaining to their salvation they should acknowledge God and His vicar on earth and render obedience in His name to the father commissary. Having replied that they understood it and were pleased with all that had been said, the governor continued that since it was their desire to offer obedience to God and the king, they should fall on their knees, as a sign that it was indeed true and as proof of vassalage and submission, and kiss the hand of the father commissary, in the name of God, and that of his lordship, in the name of his majesty.

The captains then knelt before Fray Alonso Martínez, commissary of the expedition, kissed his hand, and again swore allegiance to the king and obedience to the governor and repeated that they were doing so of their own free will. The report of these proceedings was signed by Oñate, stamped with the seal of his office, and dated 7 July 1598 at the newly renamed pueblo of Santo Domingo. In the weeks that followed, the same ceremony was held at the pueblos of Piro, Acolocu, Cueloze, Ácoma, Zuñi, and Moqui in Hopi land.[2]

How spectacular, the winning to Catholicism of an entire people! Or so it seemed. Was this a stunning mass conversion, like the wholesale baptism of the Franks by Saint Remigius during the reign of Clovis and Clotilde? Or did it resemble the officially enacted conversion of Norse Icelanders in late 1000? Did New Mexico represent the beginning of a new, nonviolent relationship between Spaniards and a socially and culturally developed indigenous people? For a while, it might have appeared that way, as on 18 August 1598 the main group of Spanish colonists reached the pueblo of Piro—now renamed in honor of San Juan Bautista (Saint John the Baptist)—where they subsequently established a settlement and built a church, dedicated on 8 September, and as friars of the expedition fanned out into the pueblos of the region to begin their ministries.

Ácoma

Such optimism, if it existed, was short-lived. The Spaniards had no notion of the enduring power of Pueblo religion, with its intricate responses to unseen powers, and even when the Pueblo religion was explained, they considered it a form of devil worship to be extirpated. And while the Spaniards might have forgotten or put aside the memory of the lives lost and pueblos destroyed forty years earlier by Coronado, the attacks, burnings, and massacres were part of the pueblo dwellers' legacy that cautioned cunning when dealing with Spaniards. Then there was the simple factor of resentment. Lacking provisions, the Spaniards took what they needed from the Pueblo people—food, blankets, unpaid labor—with no reciprocity and few if any expressions of gratitude.

On one such foraging expedition—searching for supplies as the fierce New Mexican winter set in—Oñate's nephew and camp master Juan de Zaldívar approached Ácoma pueblo in early December 1598 at the head of thirty mounted soldiers. Set atop a stone *peñol* (level butte) that rose four hundred feet above the earth, the seventy-acre fortified residential complex was reached by narrow trails and footholds carved patiently from the rock over generations. Pueblo in the sky! Here was the Masada of Pueblo land, its people psychologically secure and independent in their strategic aerie. True, for whatever mixture of reasons, the Ácomans had recently promised fealty. Yet when Zaldívar and twelve of his men (ten soldiers and two servants) ascended to the pueblo—tricked into doing so after two days of negotiations by a promise of blankets, wood, water, and food in exchange for hatchets—they were attacked by a war party armed with bows, arrows, clubs, and stones. After a fierce fight, the Spaniards either were killed or were thrown or forced to leap from the pueblo. Three soldiers, slowed in their descent by winds that blew them against the butte wall, landed on the sand dunes below, seriously hurt but alive. Adding insult to injury, the war party pursued the fleeing Spanish survivors, killed one horse with arrows, and wounded another, all the while crying out in defiance that more of the same would greet them if they dared to return. The war party also dug up and took back to Ácoma a cache of hatchets, horseshoes, and other iron implements the Spaniards had hastily buried.

Hearing the news, Oñate spent that night weeping and praying in his tent. His dead nephew and soldiers (a tenth of his entire force), the treasonous insult to the Crown and to him personally as governor, the possibility of a general uprising among the Pueblos, the subsequent failure of the colony, his financial ruin: all these troubles bore down on Oñate throughout the long night. But during those hours emerged a resolve born of his family's experience in the remorseless campaigns of the Gran Chichimeca, in which neither Spaniard nor Indian gave or expected quarter. Was he not the descendant of conquistadors—the Last Conquistador, in fact, as history would remember him—ruthless when necessary, decimating with no regret, an attitude imported into the Indies after the seven centuries of the Reconquest?

Regarding the image of Oñate as the Last Conquistador, Oñate would be lauded in an epic poem by one of his trusted captains, Gaspar Pérez de Villagrá, a criollo born in Puebla (near Mexico City) who had gone to Salamanca to earn a bachelor of letters degree. After several years at the court of Philip II, Villagrá had returned to Mexico and joined the Oñate expedition, in which he invested seven thousand pesos of his own money, as chief of supply. Villagrá took quickly to soldiering and secured the confidence of Oñate, who soon promoted him to be one of his top captains. Villagrá modeled his *Historia de la Nueva México* (published in Alcalá, Spain, in 1610) on Virgil's *Aeneid*, with Oñate playing the role of Pius Aeneas as conquistador, bringing Spanish Catholic civilization to an otherwise benighted New Mexico—with swift and deadly violence when necessary. Oñate held somewhat the same view of himself.

By the morning after receiving word of the attack, Oñate was no longer weeping. Leaving his tent, he called for a council of war.

Punishment

Held at San Juan Bautista, now a Spanish settlement as well as a pueblo, the council of war was methodically managed. Oñate had no desire to run afoul of viceregal or royal laws relating to proper conduct in such a situation. Testimonies were transcribed as sworn documents, which were notarized and correctly submitted; they eventually made their way into the Archives of the Indies in Seville.

Proceedings began on 28 December 1598 with formal declarations by the surviving officers and soldiers of the Ácoma massacre, who reported what had happened and how they viewed the events from a military perspective. Those who testified agreed that the Zaldívar detachment had harmed no Indians en route to Ácoma and had tried to deal peacefully with the Ácoma captains upon arrival at the pueblo but had been met with deceit, evasion, and, finally, lethal violence. From a military standpoint, Ácoma was a near-impregnable fortress that, if left in hostile hands, could become a gathering point and stronghold for Indian resistance.

On 8 January 1599 Oñate took transcribed testimony from the Franciscans regarding requirements for a just war. Fray Martínez, the commissary, made the first statement. A just war, Martínez testified, required sovereignty on the part of the aggrieved. It could be waged to protect the innocent, to restore unjustly seized property, to punish transgressors against the laws of nature or the just laws of men, and to preserve the peace. A just war, however, could not be waged if its primary purpose were power, revenge, or greed. Nor could a just war be waged carelessly, indiscriminately, or against innocent parties. In his elaboration on these points, Martínez drew upon Scripture as well as the words of the Church Fathers and ancient philosophers: testimony to his personal learning and suggestive, perhaps, of the manuals and reference books the Franciscans might have brought with them on the expedition.

All four remaining friars endorsed the commissary's analysis, although one of them, Fray Juan Claros, added an important qualification. Any compulsion of heathens to obey the divine law, he argued, must be made only by admonition and persuasion. The Franciscans, in short, did not urge Oñate to wage war against Ácoma; but citing traditional Catholic theory, they did not try to prevent him from doing so, either. From Oñate's point of view, he could more than meet the requirements the friars had set forth. Rather than rushing headlong into retribution, he had examined the issue publicly and judiciously from a Catholic perspective.

Next on Oñate's agenda was the council of war itself, an open-air meeting with soldiers and colonists held on 10 January 1599 following high Mass. The result of this meeting was a consensus that the Indian leaders responsible for the deaths at Ácoma should be punished as quickly as possible; otherwise, the effort to colonize New Mexico would collapse in the face of a united Indian resistance led by the Ácoma pueblo. Following this meeting, Oñate drew up precise instructions for Vicente de Zaldívar Mendoza, sergeant major and lieutenant governor of the province, who had been chosen to lead the campaign after officers determined that Oñate could not risk his life in case he were needed to lead the colonists back to Mexico. In his directions, Oñate characterized the forthcoming campaign as a just war on behalf of the recovery of stolen goods and the future evangelization of the Pueblo people. At all times, Zaldívar Mendoza was to keep in mind this holy purpose—the survival of the Catholic faith in New Mexico—as he moved against the Ácoma pueblo. En route, he was to prevent harm to any Indians he encountered. Once at Ácoma, he was to arrange his soldiers in battle formation and then, speaking through interpreters, call upon the Ácomans three times to lay down their arms as befitted sworn vassals of the king. Zaldívar Mendoza should also demand the return of the bodies of the killed Spaniards as well as the horseshoes and other iron implements.

Now came a more draconian order. Zaldívar Mendoza was to demand that the people of Ácoma leave their pueblo, which would be razed to the ground, leaving no stone, then burned for good measure. Should the Indians refuse, a council of war might recommend storming the citadel, keeping in mind the need to preserve the army as protection for the colonists at San Juan Bautista. If the Indians resisted and Ácoma was taken by storm, the entire population was to be considered guilty of this resistance. The Spaniards were then authorized to execute those whom they judged to be the leaders—provided it be done publicly, to set an example—and to allow the rest to live, saying that they were being spared at the friars' request.

Obviously, the Ácomans could not accept such terms. Their alleged vassalage to the Spanish king and their acceptance of Christianity meant nothing to them. And even if the captains had been sincere as they knelt before Oñate or his representative, the shamans of Ácoma had managed to change the captains' minds after the Spaniards departed. Abandoning Ácoma, so long and lovingly created atop its skyborne mesa, seeing it razed and burned to the ground, constituted a willful cooperation in the destruction of their civilization, and hence a suicidal ending of themselves as a people. Forces had been set in motion for a fatal encounter that certainly would do little to foster a long-term evangelization of the Pueblo people that was anchored in peace and mutual respect.

Siege

What happened next became a nightmarish multiplication of horror on horror. The proceedings were so violent that at every stage, in the midst of battle, Zaldívar Mendoza justified himself by dictating to Juan Velarde—Oñate's secretary and secretary to the punitive expedition—his reasons for the steps he was taking.

In his first dispatch, Zaldívar Mendoza described how, while he was asking three times for peace, the Ácomans—some of them wearing chain mail and brandishing swords they had seized from the Spaniards—had hooted, hollered, and harassed the Spanish and challenged them with arrows, spears, and stones, daring them to fight. Withdrawing his men to a safe distance (so Zaldívar Mendoza dictated to Velarde on 22 January 1599), he had continued to try to negotiate throughout the long night as the Ácomans danced and shouted and went so far as to send out a reconnaissance party that attacked his party with arrows, killing two horses.

At this point, according to the second report, Zaldívar Mendoza, "in view of the imprudence and bold determination of the Indians to kill the Spaniards, ordered his men to give battle without quarter, as was authorized in his instructions". The first assault, notes Zaldívar Mendoza's third report, began at three o'clock in the afternoon on the feast of Saint Vincent and lasted until nightfall. By that time, the Spaniards had most likely reached the pueblo itself on the summit mesa. Zaldívar Mendoza ordered them into defensive positions. The next day, 23 January, the feast of San Ildefonso, so states dispatch number four, the fighting resumed in the early morning. Through his interpreter, Zaldívar Mendoza once more pleaded with the Ácomans to consider the number of their dead and to surrender. He, in turn, "would do justice to all who surrendered and placed themselves in his care". The Ácomans refused. The women and children wanted to die alongside their men, they replied, attacking Zaldívar Mendoza's interpreter with arrows and stones.

Zaldívar Mendoza's fifth and final battle brief details a scene of total terror. As the Spaniards penetrated even deeper into the pueblo, warriors fled into an underground network of kivas and tunnels beneath the complex. Other Indian men began to run from house to house, killing all inhabitants and then each other. "In view of this situation," reads this last documentation, "the lieutenant governor ordered the battle to proceed without quarter, setting fire to all of the houses and even the provisions. He ordered that all Indian women and children who could be found should be taken prisoner to save them from being killed by the Indian warriors. So they rounded up about five hundred of them, young and old, men and women. He sent them all to his excellency, Don Juan de Oñate, governor and captain general of these kingdoms and provinces."[3] Historian David Weber estimates that five hundred men and three hundred women and children died in the siege and destruction of Ácoma, and eighty men and five hundred women and children were taken back to San Juan Bautista as captives.

The next set of records in the Archives of the Indies relating to the destruction of Ácoma chronicles the February 1599 criminal trial of the Ácoman captives. The documents include the depositions of a number of eyewitnesses, both soldiers and servants, on the Spanish side. Captain Alonso Gómez Montesinos was sworn in as defense attorney for the accused. Testimony from military officers filled out the details of the night and early morning of the second day of fighting. With the coming of daylight, they testified, a group of Ácomans had approached the Spaniards with gifts of blankets and turkeys and asked for peace, but Zaldívar Mendoza had refused their offer. On day three, Indian prisoners taken by Zaldívar Mendoza had broken out of confinement and gone into the underground kivas and tunnels, whereupon Zaldívar Mendoza repeated the order of no quarter until resistance ceased and the captives were taken. Weber writes that the Spaniards participated in the killing of women and children, which is not mentioned in any of the survivors' testimonies. Did Zaldívar Mendoza and his captains lie under oath or otherwise collaborate to offer false testimony? In a final frenzy of despair, Ácoman men had killed their own families. However horrible, this tragedy can be imagined. But one can also imagine that, in the agitated fog of war, Spaniards were responsible for some of the deaths of women and children. The capture of five hundred women and children, however, argues against any charge of general massacre. Still, the hyperlegalism of the Spaniards' approach—based obsessively on a sworn vassalage and the friars' discussion of the theory of a just war—may be considered simply another instrument of aggression against an indigenous people. Too, it may have been a defensive move on Oñate's part when he realized that his peaceful entry into New Mexico—so favored by king and viceroy since the Royal Ordinance of 1573—was falling apart.

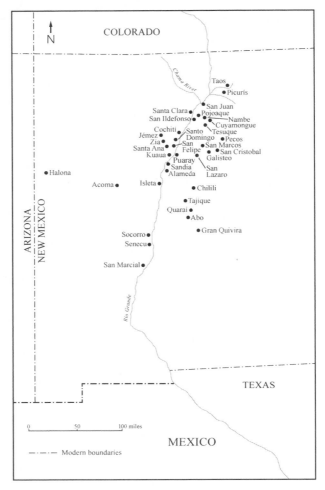

Map 9. The Pueblos in the Sixteenth Century.

His severity did not help matters. The punishments Oñate leveled against the surviving Ácomans, once all but the children under twelve were found guilty of treason, scared Pueblo country into submission, as intended, but their cruelty established a gap of fear and distrust between Spaniard and Indian that for the century to come no Franciscan could bridge. Every male over the age of twenty-five was to have one foot cut off, followed by twenty years of servitude. All males and females between twelve and twenty-five were sentenced to twenty years of servitude as well. These men and women, Oñate declared, "shall be distributed among my captains and soldiers in the manner which I will prescribe and who may hold and keep them as their slaves for the said term of twenty years and no more". Each of the two Hopi Indians who were in Ácoma during its resistance would lose his right hand and be sent back to Moqui as an example of Spanish justice.

"All of the children under twelve years of age," Oñate concluded, "I declare free and innocent of the grave offense for which I punish their parents. And because of my duty to aid, support, and protect both the boys and girls under twelve years

of age, I place the girls under the care of our father commissary, Fray Alonso
Martínez, in order that he, as a Christian and qualified person, may distribute them
in this kingdom or elsewhere in monasteries or other places where he thinks that
they may attain knowledge of God and the salvation of their souls. The boys under
twelve years of age I entrust to Vicente de Zaldívar Mendoza, my sergeant mayor,
in order that they may attain the same goal."[4]

A prophetic paradigm

The Ácoma massacre resulted from a chasm of religion and culture between Spaniard and Pueblo Indian that remained for centuries and expressed itself in a number
of mid- to late-seventeenth-century rebellions, including the largest Indian uprising in North American history, in 1680. In the massacre's immediate aftermath,
Juan de Oñate struggled to make economic sense of the New Mexican enterprise
he had financed. Reconnaissances to the northeast and east in search of Quivira
and its riches proved futile. An exploratory venture to the west, while it reached
the mouth of the Colorado River and made the first overland connection with
California by Europeans, failed to reach the South Sea (Pacific) ports through
which Oñate and his fellow investors had hoped to establish maritime trade with
New Spain and the Philippines. For New Mexico to pay for itself, it had to succeed in terms of encomienda, land, and labor. Yet what would be its product?
Ácoma had underscored the limits and dangers of a purely confiscatory economy.
Oñate had brought five hundred colonists and soldiers into New Mexico with no
means of support except for what could be seized from the pueblos. How long
could such an economy last?

The Franciscans must have been equally unhappy, facing the massacre of eight
hundred Indian men, women, and children; the cruel enslavement of eighty men,
with those over the age of twenty-five having lost a foot; the women and girls
sent into slavery, which often meant sexual servitude; and children under twelve
bound over to friars, soldiers, and colonists for what turned out to be a lifetime
of servitude for many of them. Even the friars who had argued on behalf of the
Ácoma venture as a just war must have had to admit to themselves—cultural differences notwithstanding—that this was not the way to begin the evangelization
of Pueblo country.

Franciscan ambitions for New Mexico were further intensified in the 1620s when
the Spanish mystic María de Jesús Coronel (also referred to as María de Ágreda), the
young abbess of the Immaculate Conception monastery of Poor Clare Franciscan
nuns in Ágreda, Spain, began having visions of herself mystically transported to
New Mexico as an evangelist. Around 1623 the Franciscan missionary Juan de Salas
reported to Fray Alonso de Benavides, the *custos* (guardian) of New Mexico, and his
fellow missionaries that the Indians of a pueblo to the east (later named Gran Quivira) had described the appearance of a young woman in Franciscan robes who had
instructed them in the doctrines of the faith. Fray de Salas' account soon became
accepted fact among seventeenth-century Spaniards, accustomed to treating visions
as true events. Such was the case with the reported presence of Saint James of
Santiago, who led the Spaniards up the steep pathways during the final assault on
Ácoma, or the Amazons who were alleged to govern California. Indeed, when Fray

de Benavides later visited María de Ágreda at her monastery in Burgos, she and her sisters separately confirmed the visitations.

It was all very Franciscan—the mysticism, the miraculous presence in New Mexico—and it tied in totally with the developing sense of religious and political aspirations for the remote borderland kingdom. Like many Franciscans of her era, Abbess María de Ágreda was devoted to promoting the yet-undefined doctrine of the Immaculate Conception that was at the core of much Franciscan thought regarding the role of the order in the Indies. As the paradigm of perfected humanity kept from all sin by divine fiat, Mary served as the teleological archetype of that goal of perfection in Christ toward which all history could be directed and Spain could be redeemed in the Indies by Franciscans and their Indian charges. The Abbess María got into trouble with the Inquisition, posthumously and temporarily, for expounding such ideas in her three-volume treatise, *The Mystical City of God and the Divine History of the Virgin Mother of God*, published in Madrid in 1670, five years after her death. The treatise was put on the Index of Forbidden Books in June 1681 but taken off three months later at the request of King Charles II, the abbess' longtime epistolary correspondent.

Like the reforming Carmelite mystic Teresa of Ávila in the previous century, María de Ágreda had great influence at court, which can be viewed as a Franciscan characteristic. Not only had the friars reversed the royal inclination to shut down the New Mexico colony—and in the process gained ecclesiastical control of the newly constituted royal colony—but also they had adopted as their influential patron and protector a Franciscan mystic of respected holiness and political clout, conferring on her as well the status of an actual, on-the-ground New Mexico missionary. Only the most pious Catholic historians have taken María de Ágreda's alleged flights to New Mexico literally, but even skeptical Catholic historians have not scoffed at this story as secular historians have. Of course, Poor Clare abbesses do not cross the Atlantic to evangelize the Pueblo people of New Mexico. Yet dreams and legends have their value. Spaniards of the early modern era—including playwright Félix Lope de Vega, poet Pedro Calderón de la Barca, and novelist Miguel de Cervantes—knew such visions could express, guide, direct, enliven, and justify personal and social ambitions.

For seven years following the massacre at Ácoma, Oñate struggled to make the colony successful. When in November 1601 he returned from the Quivira expedition to San Gabriel, the chief Spanish township of the province, Oñate discovered that the majority of the colonists had gone back to Mexico. The Franciscans defended this decision, arguing that the colonists could not continue to support themselves from the pueblos by force of arms and consider themselves good Catholics or good Spaniards, according to the Royal Ordinances of 1573. Furious, Oñate ordered the colonists to return under pain of death and sent Captain Gerónimo Márquez to Mexico City to justify Oñate's long absence from San Gabriel on the Quivira expedition (which took him into present-day Oklahoma) and to protest the encouragement certain captains and Franciscans had offered the colonists to desert the colony.

Strategically, the Franciscans had baptized a large number of Ácoman children and enslaved Ácoman women before the colonists' departure. The report of these and subsequent baptisms would soon provide them the leverage they needed to seize control of the colony. That opportunity came in 1607 when Oñate, who had failed to deliver significant profit to the crown, was forced to resign, and King Philip III was seriously considering closing down the entire New Mexican enterprise. By this time, however, the Franciscans were claiming seven thousand baptisms, with more pending. Here, then, was a tipping point in the king's decision making: the prospect that New Mexico, despite the disaster of Ácoma, could be Christianized as well as colonized in the spirit of the Royal Ordinances of 1573. Thanks to the Franciscans' skilled lobbying in Mexico City and Madrid, New Mexico was in 1609 reconstituted as a royal colony—a kingdom, in Spanish imperial parlance—and, after further negotiations, a new governor, Pedro de Peralta, was appointed. Oñate returned to Mexico City to face charges of incompetence, neglect, and needless cruelty. He was found guilty, fined six thousand Castilian ducats, and banished from Mexico City for four years. Several of Oñate's captains were similarly convicted and punished.

In this newly established kingdom, Franciscans would be the sole clergy, with religious affairs governed by a resident Franciscan custos; Fray Isidro Ordóñez arrived in 1612 as senior prelate. Thus the royal kingdom of New Mexico became a Franciscan kingdom as well, with the Franciscan custos exercising near-episcopal powers and the friars serving as both missionaries to the pueblos and parish clergy in Santa Fe, the newly established (1610) capital city.

The Inquisition

The Franciscans also controlled the Inquisition, the ecclesiastical tribunal responsible for adjudicating issues of faith and morals, which was now part of the governance structure of the kingdom. Founded by Ferdinand and Isabella in 1478 with the reluctant approval of Pope Sixtus IV—who viewed it as a usurpation of the power of the pope and bishops to judge in such matters—the Spanish Inquisition went into high gear following the conquest of Granada and the expulsion of Jews in 1492, tracking down heretics and secret Muslims and Jews. Interrogating through torture, the Inquisition had the authority to condemn to death by fire or strangulation those it found guilty, although its victims were turned over to the state for the implementation of such extreme penalties.

Pope Sixtus IV opposed the founding and expansion of the Spanish Inquisition and tried to bring it under the control of local bishops but failed. The Inquisition was thus acknowledged by the papacy as an instrument of the state staffed by clerical judges, with the pope having only the prerogative to approve or veto the appointment of the inquisitor general, who presided over the Supreme Council of the Inquisition. Under the inquisitor generalship of the Dominican Tomás de Torquemada from 1483 to 1498, the Spanish Inquisition entered history and folklore as a cruel and relentless tool for attempting to eradicate (unsuccessfully, as it turned out) ingrained Moorish and Jewish beliefs on the Iberian Peninsula by rooting out, arresting, torturing, and sentencing to death people convicted of following such traditions. With the coming of the Reformation, the Spanish Inquisition went into even higher gear in its efforts to prevent the incursion of Lutheranism (the generic Spanish term for Protestantism) into the Iberian Peninsula. Hundreds of victims—Jews, Muslims, suspected heretics, mystics, alleged witches, and other perceived enemies of church and state—were sent to the fire in autos-da-fé, public burnings intended to serve as a form of warning and instruction. The omnivorous and exacting investigations of the Spanish Inquisition caught up, temporarily, such ultra-Catholic figures as Ignatius of Loyola, the founder of the Jesuits, and Teresa of Ávila, the Carmelite mystic and reformer later proclaimed Doctor of the Church.

Brought to the Indies and headquartered in Mexico City and Lima, the Inquisition continued its work. In later centuries, the transcribed interrogations and reports of the Inquisition would prove a treasure trove for historians hungry for the details of private life. In the case of New Mexico, the archives of the Inquisition do not yield a record of squelched heresies or secret Jews (although historians later documented the presence of secret Jews there). Noted instead are clashes between Franciscans and governors over jurisdiction (one deposed governor of New Mexico, Bernardo López de Mendizábal, would die in an Inquisition prison, held there on charges of heresy, blasphemy, and secret Judaism) and reports of friars violating their vows of chastity, in a number of cases egregiously.

Ambiguities of an alleged golden age

Chroniclers of the Franciscan missions of the Borderlands—Florida, Georgia, New Mexico, Texas, Arizona, and the Californias—frequently cite golden ages of development. The growth of the mission system in New Mexico in the first three decades of the seventeenth century fits into this pattern. The Pueblo Indians were already in one place; no reduction or ingathering was necessary. Rather than an elaborate mission complex, only a church and friars' quarters had to be constructed near each pueblo. Thirty-two mission churches or dependent chapels were established. Six more, serving the Zuñis and allied tribes, extended westward into Arizona. The missions were pueblo-like in design, geometric and devoid of surface ornamentation. Internally, they featured a reredos and altar, a gathering space for congregants, and a choir loft, which was reached by a ladder. Joined to the church, arranged around a courtyard, were the friary and storage and service rooms. A cemetery was close by. Massive and unadorned, with narrow or small windows and walls up to nine feet thick, these mission complexes seemed fortresslike. Or did each merely reflect the architecture of the nearby pueblo, which was fortresslike as well?

The mission San Esteban del Rey was constructed atop Ácoma between 1629 and 1642 after that pueblo had been reestablished with a new population. For the altar and roof, the new Ácomans cut ponderosa pine on Mount Taylor forty miles away and carried the logs and other building materials up the steep trails to the pueblo. That Ácoma was resettled suggests one dimension of mission culture and society in New Mexico: despite all differences, common ground managed to be established. The Pueblo people, for one thing, admired the Spaniards' iron-based technology, not only their military weaponry—which they had experienced the hard way and feared—but also their construction and agricultural implements; they appreciated the expanded array of crops the friars introduced as well. The Franciscans, as historian John Gilmary Shea notes, taught the Indians to herd cattle and sheep; spin and weave cloth on improved wheels and looms; work as carpenters, wood-carvers, stonecutters, and masons; irrigate their fields; play musical instruments; and speak, read, and write Spanish. Spanish administration and military, meanwhile, curtailed warfare between various tribes and pueblos.

A more fundamental interface resulted in a growing number of Spanish-Indian mestizos, a significant part of the population by the end of the seventeenth century; they were joined by Hispanicized Indian colonists from Mexico and other colonists of African or African-Indian or African-Spanish descent. Throughout the Indies, a new population of mixed bloodlines was being created, and New Mexico was no exception. From a legal and demographic standpoint, it is difficult to sort out the percentages of marital and nonmarital, permanent and temporary, unions. The allied institutions of encomienda and slavery often included sexual servitude; the general shortage of Hispanic or Hispanicized Indian women in the kingdom intensified the problem. This is not to say that freely chosen unions were not possible across racial divides, especially among Spaniards and Hispanicized Indian women from Mexico. Hispanicized black men and Hispanicized Indian women formed comparable unions. Across two centuries, Spanish, Indian, and African bloodlines would further meld as upwardly mobile mestizos married into the higher levels of society, while the general population became increasingly more diversified.

Pueblo culture, moreover, provided women—even married women—leeway in the matter of sexual selection through temporary or new and permanent liaisons. Men who possessed strong personal magnetism as well as spiritual power were considered especially desirable, which helps explain the haremic entourage gathered around Estebanico the Moor during Fray Marcos de Niza's reconnaissance into Pueblo country. Governor Oñate was later denounced for multiple liaisons of this sort. Inquisition records show that the fusion of spiritual and political power in the individual friar (who now functioned as pueblo chief and head shaman) and Pueblo women's receptivity to such authority led a documented number of Franciscans to put aside vows of celibacy temporarily or semipermanently through concubinage or seduction under color of authority (or worse); some raised their mixed-blood children in the mission friary.

Pueblo culture also involved intricate and ritualized rhythms of sexual restraint (in hunting protocols, for example), indulgence (dances and communal celebrations followed by sexual activity), and practices (polygamy among high-ranking men, divorce, and temporary liaisons) that resisted the corrective action of observant missionaries. Such sexual patterns were easily misinterpreted by Spanish soldiers, especially in the early years of colonization, as promiscuous availability. Official testimony from the military regarding the first instance of violence at Ácoma, for example, suggested that everything was peaceful until a soldier named Martín de Vivero stole a turkey from an Ácoman woman, and she protested loudly, persistently, and in full view of others to Vivero's captain. Historian Ramón A. Gutiérrez, however, believes that the woman was protesting a form of sexual assault. A stolen turkey would not be considered serious enough to motivate the retributive violence that soon occurred. True, the turkey was considered a sacred bird, as one eyewitness testified, but it was still consumed as ordinary food. Complicating the matter further was the language barrier between the woman and the Spanish captain to whom she was hysterically complaining.

The contretemps becomes even more complex when put into the context of gift-giving, an important ritual among Pueblo people that signified trust and fealty up and down the social ladder. Perhaps a stolen turkey did represent a serious violation, given the reluctance of the Ácomans to provision the Spanish at sword point. But would it be enough to spur an entire pueblo into coordinated revolt? From the perspective of future Spaniard-Pueblo relations, this Ácoma incident—if it were a sexual assault—would certainly serve as a prophetic paradigm of a culture of sexual exploitation of Pueblo Indian women by Spaniards (including some missionaries) that, according to historians Cheryl Foote and Sandra Shackel, permanently destablized the social structure of seventeenth-century New Mexico.

Religion did the same. The pledges of conversion accorded to Governor Oñate by the chiefs and captains of the Río Grande valley pueblos throughout the spring and summer of 1598, forced and superficial as they were, affront our twenty-first-century concept of religious liberty. And yet, from the perspective of the early modern era and prior centuries of conversion to Christianity, politically motivated conversions did not preclude a long-term harmonization of religious culture. Religion and culture are dynamically interactive and difficult (if not impossible) to extricate from each other as social and existential forces in any but the most abstract of ways. Christianity was not above conversion by force, or via tribal or clan allegiances. Christian evangelists such as Saints Gregory the Illuminator, Remigius, Patrick, Augustine of Canterbury, Boniface, and the brothers Cyril and Methodius converted the Armenians, Franks, Irish, Saxons, Bavarians, and Moravians, respectively, by converting key leaders and tapping into clan and tribal sentiment. Thanks in great measure to Leif Ericsson, the Norse on Iceland voted themselves into Christianity. Olaf Haraldssön, the king of Norway from 1016 to 1029, personally converted to Christianity and proceeded to bring good parts of his country into the fold along with him the old-fashioned Viking way—at the point of a sword. In the thirteenth and fourteenth centuries, the Teutonic Knights introduced Christianity to the Baltic region in the same military manner.

But for such conversions to mature required time, even centuries, and an assimilative process as old and new beliefs and cultures meshed into Christian culture and dogmatic orthodoxy. Integrating non-Christian cultures was an intricate operation. Mediterranean classicism, for example, including its polytheistic pantheon, went through numerous refinements and reiterations across centuries until it emerged triumphantly as classical Christian humanism. The Italian Jesuit scholar Matteo Ricci spent twenty years studying Chinese culture before composing *The True Doctrine of God* (1595) in Chinese, along with a Chinese-language catechism and translation of the Ten Commandments. Ricci's fellow Jesuit Roberto de Nobili, meanwhile, mastered Sanskrit and became a Brahmin before embarking upon a missionary career in Goa as a writer, preacher, and evangelist reported to have brought around one hundred thousand converts into the Roman Catholic Church.

In the Indies, by contrast, Franciscan missionaries were in no mood for inter-religious, intercultural dialogue. Nowhere was this truer than with the Aztecs in Mexico. Branding Aztec religion as devil worship, Franciscans and civil authorities did their best to suppress its practice, raze its temples, and destroy its written record. The friars brought the same point of view to New Mexico. But just as Aztec beliefs and folkways (or Jewish or Islamic identities, for that matter, back in Spain) were submerged under outward conformity, the intricate Pueblo religion and its practices continued as a belief and value system beneath the surface of mission culture.

Still, the assimilative process might have worked had the friars not so violently tried to eradicate in a few short decades all vestiges of the previous religion. If the Franciscan missionaries in New Mexico had possessed the time, language skills, academic background, and philosophy of mission practice—and, above all else, if they had not already been convinced that the Pueblo people worshipped the devil—they might have made a connection to their New Mexican Indian constituency similar to that being made in the same era by the Jesuits Ricci and de Nobili in China and India (or between the Jesuits and the Guaraní and other indigenous people gathered into the Reductions of Paraguay). The Franciscans might have discovered subtle parallelisms on which they might have based their evangelization.

Unlike the Aztec religion, for example, with its fierce war gods and human sacrifice, Pueblo religion was irenic, communitarian, and in its worship practices sensitive to sacred objects and ceremonial dance. Its sense of the Katsina—the spirits of the dead subsumed into the heavens as cloud formations that subsequently functioned as potent rain spirits—paralleled Catholic teachings on the afterlife and the intercession of saints. The Snake Spirit who was the object of the rain campaign, however, was not assimilable, nor were the other polytheistic deities. Yet the Pueblo creation myth of how the Corn Mothers crawled upward through an opening in the earth to make it habitable for men offered a benevolent beginning for discussions of Genesis. Every phase and aspect of the highly communitarian life of the pueblo—birth, coming of age, marriage, death; hunting, harvest, selection for high office—was marked by ritual and ceremony, yet another Catholic trait. Prayer sticks suggested rosaries. The kiva—a subterranean chamber, rounded to resemble the earth, dominated by a fire altar and stone fetishes that suggested a connection to the larger creation and to the pueblo itself as a sacred and profane space—certainly bore similarities to the mission church. The Pueblo philosophy and practice of reciprocity based on a network of obligation and service that bound society into a communal whole could be linked to the Sermon on the Mount or, more doctrinally, to Saint Paul's discussion of the Church as the Mystical Body of the Risen Christ. In each instance, a parallelism did not have to be considered an equivalent; it could have been a grounding, a beginning, for ongoing catechesis.

Aside from the barrier of an alleged diabolism, however—formidable enough, to be sure!—the Franciscans were disconcerted by the overt sexuality of certain ceremonial dances and the general fluidity of pueblo sexual culture based on divorce, polygamy for high-ranking men, and a degree of sexual freedom and choice for females. The acceptance of *berdaches*, transvestite men who lived as women and had sexual unions, also appalled the friars, although Inquisition and related records studied by Gutiérrez reveal that some friars were homosexually active and, in some instances, sodomized recalcitrant Indians as a form of punishment.

As a rival clerical caste, the shamans of the pueblos were anathema to the Franciscans and vice versa. Pueblo religion resided in the shamans as guardians of unwritten tradition and memory-based practice. The shaman thus competed with the Franciscan attached to a pueblo, who knew that the shaman was doing his best to sustain traditional religious practice and undercut Franciscan authority.

And so the friars strove to prevent ceremonial dancing; to forbid reverence for the Katsina; to suppress the kivas and physically destroy them; to end the use of Katsina masks, prayer sticks, and related fetishes; to forbid initiation rites; to regularize

sexual behavior according to rigid norms; and—most importantly—to force shamans out of business. Such a campaign, as might be expected, drove pueblo religion
underground, sustained on the sly by faithful shamans.

In 1634 Fray Alonso de Benavides, the custos of the kingdom, presented a revision of a 1629 report to Pope Urban VIII on the missions of New Mexico in hopes
that the pope would establish a separate bishopric for the kingdom. New Mexico
had initially been under the jurisdiction of the Diocese of Guadalajara. In 1620 it
was placed under the jurisdiction of the newly established Diocese of Durango.
Neither diocese was able to send secular priests to the kingdom, however, and the
Franciscans served the entire population. As custos, Benavides served as episcopal
vicar, with the power to administer the sacrament of confirmation, act as chief
judge in the local religious tribunal, and represent the Inquisition. The establishment of a New Mexican diocese would provide a local bishop—Benavides himself
being the leading candidate—and thus keep New Mexico under Franciscan influence. Eager to impress the pope, Benavides described mission life as possessing the
regularity and observant spirit of a well-ordered monastery, with the pueblo as
the monastic dependency and the mission church its monks and chapel. As with a
monastery, the mission chapel had its own choir to accompany Mass in Latin and
to sing evening vespers in the local language according to the feast of the day, concluding with the Salve Regina, the eleventh-century hymn to Mary that ended the
monastic day throughout the Catholic world. Every aspect of the mission, Benavides reported—choral singing, housekeeping, and food service, as well as farming,
cattle raising, and dispute resolution—was minutely monitored by the resident friar
on behalf of the pueblos he supervised. Records indicated, Benavides claimed, that
eighty thousand Indians had been baptized by the Franciscans since their arrival.
That statistic, repeated by John Gilmary Shea, must be considered wildly inflated,
since the total population of the pueblos stood at eighty thousand in 1598, dropped
to seventeen thousand by 1620 (due to European diseases, against which the Indians
had little immunity), and climbed to sixty thousand by 1630 before dropping back
to forty thousand in 1638 due to a smallpox epidemic that killed twenty thousand.[5]

Rome, in any event, did not buy into Benavides's rosy summary. A separate diocese was not created. In late 1634, Benavides, then in Rome to present his report,
was authorized to return to New Mexico. The ambitious Franciscan lingered in
Spain and Portugal for two more years, however, until he was appointed auxiliary
bishop of the Diocese of Goa in India. Benavides died en route to his new post.

In contrast to Benavides' whitewashed presentation, what actually happened—
baptismal numbers notwithstanding—was a surface conformity to Catholicism and
an underground practice of the indigenous religion. Following the massacre at
Ácoma, the Pueblo people respected Spanish power and Spanish fury. They conformed. But they also learned to deceive. They met secretly with shamans in kivas
that had not yet been detected and destroyed, listened to the old myths, and chanted
the old prayers. John Gilmary Shea reports that the Pueblo people concealed prayer
sticks and other religious objects in the mission church in order to pray with them
during Mass or other times of required Catholic prayer.

The system of encomienda, meanwhile, imposed on the Pueblo Indians continuing and unremunerated obligations of labor and tribute. First of all, the
Indians—mainly women and youngsters, for Pueblo men considered such labor

unmanly—were recruited to build mission churches and adjacent buildings. Each pueblo, moreover, as well as the villages being formed by Hispanicized Indians brought in from Mexico, owed its resident Franciscan an acceptable level of support and a fixed percentage of tribute (corn, textiles, animal hides, lumber, and cut stone); it also owed labor to its encomendero, an established settler, who usually had a family, as well as to the Crown, as represented by the governor or his local agent. These biannual obligations of goods and labor handed over to a privileged few violated the system of reciprocity so crucial to indigenous culture and rankled the Pueblo people from the outset, starting with the Ácoma incident. Enslavement of indigenous populations was supposed to be a thing of the past, yet the Pueblo Indians were still expected to do the bulk of agricultural work for their encomenderos. At the same time, the number of household slaves increased throughout the century, beginning with the five hundred enslaved women and children from Ácoma.

Uprisings

By the mid-seventeenth century, the pueblos were reduced in population due to disease as well as outmigration by Pueblo people, who preferred life in villages of *genízaros* (Hispanicized Indians from Mexico) or among the migrant Apaches—now fast-moving marauders who had mastered the horse—to the constraints of mission life. Two generations had come of age under the friars' domination. Some, raised as Christians since childhood, accepted the system. Others did not. In 1632 the Zuñis killed two friars and were in turn invaded and subdued by the Spanish military. Rebellion broke out again in late December 1639 in the northern Tiwa pueblos of Taos and Picurís, two thousand miles north of Mexico City. For the previous two years, the Taos Indians had been complaining to Governor Luis de Rosas (who was no friend of the Franciscans) that the resident friar at Taos, Fray Nicolás Hidalgo, was a sexual predator of the worst sort—a sodomizer and castrator of children, a rampant rapist and adulterer, the father of numerous offspring, the murderer of one resistant husband—charges backed up by Inquisition records examined by Ramón A. Gutiérrez. The lurid charges against Hidalgo underscored a decline in the power and prestige of the mission friars among the Pueblo people by the mid-century, the natural result of dissatisfaction with Spanish dominion, civil and Franciscan alike.

Following investigation by the Inquisition, Fray Hidalgo was removed; but when his successor, Fray Pedro de Miranda, upbraided the Taos Indians for lying to the Inquisition about Hidalgo, a group of them killed Miranda and two soldier-settlers, destroyed the mission church and friary, and profaned the reserved Eucharist. Following this rampage, the rebels marched south to Picurís, whose resident friar was absent, and then continued on to Jemez, where they killed Fray Diego de San Lucas as he clung to a cross. The insurgents thereupon fled the region. In the aftermath of these and other killings at various pueblos, martyrdom became a strong possibility for Franciscans in New Mexico—forty-nine out of the hundred who served there in the seventeenth century met violent ends—as well as a fixed component of spirituality among the devout and observant Franciscans. Less observant, less devout friars were driven to open warfare against their charges, whom they considered sexual libertines and recidivist devil worshippers. In 1655 one such extremist, Fray Salvador de Guerra, went so far as to drench with burning turpentine an already beaten Hopi Indian by the name of Juan Cuna (who had been caught worshipping idols) to give him a foretaste of the hellfire that awaited him. A number of other Hopis received the same treatment, which Fray Guerra defended in recorded testimony and later confirmed when further investigated.

The Pueblo Revolt of 1680

Only recently has the Pueblo Revolt of 1680 begun to take its place alongside the near-contemporaneous King Philip's War (1675–1676) in New England as a signature Indian uprising of the colonial era, resulting in a devastating loss of human life and a long-term setback for frontier development. Like King Philip's War, the Pueblo Revolt signaled an effort by indigenous people to recover a way of life that was threatened but not yet vanquished. The revolt began with an open and defiant revival of the Katsina dance among the pueblos of the northern Río Grande valley: an act of rebellion that expressed a myriad of discontents as well as the long-term survival of a reenergized religion. Around this religious resurgence and enduring dissatisfaction with Spanish rule clustered a constellation of more recent causes. The 1670s opened with a drought, under way since 1665. The primary reason for the revival of the Katsina dance was to bring rain. In times past, Apaches had remained on friendly terms with the pueblos; in the early years of Spanish rule, Pueblo people discontented with encomienda and the mission system frequently sought refuge with these migrant tribes. By the late 1670s, however, drought and the mastery of horse warfare, as well as encroachments by Comanches into Apache territory, had transformed the Apaches into dedicated and effective marauders. Hence they were a source of annoyance but also an example of militancy for the Pueblo people. Incessant quarreling between Franciscans and civil authorities had weakened the prestige of both, as the Pueblos quickly learned how to play one side against the other. Furthermore, friars and military alike, along with a growing number of landed settlers with families, were proving to be an increasing burden under the encomienda system of forced tribute and labor.

Soldiers, settlers, and rogue friars were associated not only with forced labor and tribute but also with outright slavery, as well as a continuing epidemic of sexual exploitation in its many manifestations. The sexual intermingling of races, forced or freely chosen, created a growing population of mestizos of various combinations of Indian, African, and Spanish ancestry. These individuals of mixed bloodlines were enslaved, free, or in an in-between arrangement. The majority of free mestizos, along with genízaros, settled in Santa Fe or as farmers and sheepherders, thus forming the nucleus of an emergent population of civilian settlers.

Founded in or around 1610 (the exact date is uncertain) by Pedro de Peralta, Juan de Oñate's successor as governor and captain general, the Villa Santa Fe was intended to function as the civilian capital of the newly organized kingdom; the pueblo of Santo Domingo, slightly to the south, served as the ecclesiastical headquarters, where the Franciscan custos resided. Built with levied Indian labor, Santa Fe grew slowly, not as a well-planned city but rather as a mosaic of ranches and farms leading into a central plaza containing the governor's palace, with the nearby Chapel of San Miguel (1620) and Church of the Immaculate Conception (1626). By 1630 the community numbered 250 Spaniards, 700 Indians, and 50 mestizos.

Although growth was not rapid in the next half century, the population of those of mixed descent increased proportionally as mixed ancestry became more common. Some New Mexicans of mixed descent, however, either were born and raised in pueblos or moved to them in later life. Shaped by the discontents of their cultural backgrounds in various mixtures of bloodlines and influences, such mestizos frequently constituted an energized, subversive leadership in the pueblos.

As can be expected from a rebellion with such strong religious causes, historians have focused on Popé, a Tewa medicine man from the San Juan pueblo at the confluence of the Río Grande and the Chama Rivers in the northern valley. Other leaders have been identified, but they remain shadowy and of lesser rank. Popé possessed the charisma and organizational ability of Metacomet (English name: King Philip), the chief of the Wampanoag and leader of the Indian warriors in King Philip's War (1675–1676, in New England), and an indefinable something else that arose from his thwarted shamanism and his deep desire for revenge after being put to the lash. Even as he survives fragmentarily in the documents and restrained renditions by academic historians, Popé emanates a fierce hierophantic anger and will to power—the rebel as dictator, an Indian Robespierre, a New Mexican Emperor Jones awaiting a playwright—as he bestrides the stage in his years of authority.

In 1675 Governor Juan Francisco Treviño, alarmed by the growing restiveness of the pueblos, which he attributed to the persistence of the old religion, launched a campaign against medicine men and the practice of idolatry. Inaugurating his own reign of terror, Treviño ordered his soldiers to fan out into Pueblo country and arrest medicine men. Forty-seven were rounded up. Three were hanged; one committed suicide; the rest, including Popé of San Juan, were brought to Santa Fe, where they were flogged and imprisoned.

Then something thoroughly unexpected happened. A contingent of fully armed Tewa warriors traveled south to Santa Fe, invaded the governor's private apartment, and successfully demanded the release of the imprisoned medicine men. Popé relocated to the Taos pueblo at the northern extreme of Pueblo country. There, for the next five years, Popé grew in power as he planned a monumental revenge—region-wide revolt and massacre, the eradication of Christianity, a return to the old ways—for the arrest, flogging, and imprisonment of him and his fellow medicine men. All this was based on the lesson he learned in Santa Fe when the Tewa warriors had forced his release: the Spaniards were not all powerful. They could be bested, if a pueblo league were formed and a pueblo-wide uprising were organized. That meant unity, as well as the suppression of Christianized Indians or anyone skeptical of success. When Popé's son-in-law, the principal at San Juan, refused to join the movement, Popé had him assassinated. Fulfilling the friars' most negative opinions regarding Pueblo religion, Popé claimed to be in contact with the Evil One, who would take revenge on any pueblos who refused to join the conspiracy.

Other capable leaders emerged during the five years of preparation: Luis Tupatír of the Picurís pueblo, for example, whose name suggests partial Spanish descent, and Catití of Santo Domingo, the Franciscan headquarters in front of which Catití's forebears had pledged allegiance to king and church eight decades earlier. Catití threatened to behead anyone not in favor of the revolt. Only the Piro pueblos in the southern sector escaped recruitment.

Timing of the revolt was signaled by a knotted yucca cord sent to each pueblo, each knot representing an interval of days in a countdown to 13 August. The time-table was abbreviated, however, when Juan Ye, captain of the Pecos pueblo, alerted Governor Antonio de Otermín that a rebellion was pending. Violence broke out on 10 August 1680 and continued over a twenty-four-hour period until more than 401 settlers (out of a population of 2,800) and 21 Franciscans were massacred. The rebellion's fury was evident in the ritualistic murder of the friars. At the Jemez pueblo, the elderly Fray Juan de Jesús was paraded naked tied to the back of a great hog. Removed from the pig, Jesús was ridden like a horse by members of the crowd, who kicked at him repeatedly before he was dispatched by a sword through his heart.

In retaliation for the destruction of the kivas, Katsina masks, prayer sticks, and other religious objects throughout the decades, mission altars and crucifixes were destroyed, the Eucharist was profaned, and statues were smeared with excrement. Popé and other medicine-men leaders urged their people to destroy rosaries and medals, to wash away their baptisms through ritualistic bathing, and to abandon the wives they had married in Catholic ceremonies in favor of the new wives Popé would present them—principales and other leaders especially—for polyga-mous unions with as many women as they wanted. Even the gardens, orchards, and irrigated fields developed under Franciscan supervision were destroyed.

A cultural revolution was eradicating more than eighty years of missionary effort. Confessing to be shocked by the rapidity and totality of this violent repu-diation, John Gilmary Shea chronicles how one young Tano Indian named Fras-quillo, the most promising scholar in his pueblo—skilled in Spanish, Latin, and chant; a prospective priest in the eyes of his priest, Fray Simon de Jesús—immediately became a leader of the revolt, murdered his Franciscan mentor, and assumed the leadership of the Tano pueblos. Popé himself claimed absolute rule over the entire pueblo confederation.

In the meantime, refugees streamed from north and south into Santa Fe, where Governor Otermín gathered people and livestock into a defensive compound cen-tered on the governor's palace. After a nine-day siege, in which sallies by the Span-iards inflicted heavy casualties on the warriors, the besiegers allowed the Spaniards and their dependents, including numerous women and children, to pass through their lines and leave the country. Linking up with a second contingent of refugees under the command of his lieutenant governor, Otermín led a dispirited caravan out of New Mexico to the Spanish settlement of El Paso, the present-day city of Juárez on the Mexican side of the Río Grande, where a relief expedition led by Fray Francisco de Ayeta brought welcomed supplies. At El Paso, with the vice-roy's permission, on the right bank of the Río Grande in northern Nueva Vizcaya province, Otermín established a settlement of twenty-four hundred refugees and a government in exile.

Reconquest

It took sixteen years to reestablish Spanish authority in New Mexico. Urged on by Mexico City, Governor Otermín attempted a reconquest in late 1681 at the head of a column of 146 soldiers and 112 Indian allies. Moving up the Río Grande,

Otermín encountered a series of pueblos abandoned by their populations when news arrived of the approaching Spanish column. At the Isleta pueblo in midvalley, 1,500 Indians submitted to the Spaniards. North of Isleta, however, reconnaissance revealed solid resistance, and the woefully outnumbered Otermín returned to El Paso, accompanied by numerous Isleta Indians, who settled in the vicinity.

The next attempt at reconquest, mounted in 1688 by the new governor, General Domingo Jironza Petriz de Cruzate, an experienced campaigner, resulted in the slaughter of five hundred Indians at the pueblo of Zía—hardly the beginnings of reconciliation!—before Cruzate, like Otermín before him, found himself outnumbered and returned to El Paso. The destruction of Zía intensified a process of abandonment and relocation under way since Otermín's 1681 campaign. Rebel leader Popé had envisioned a confederacy of pueblos under his general jurisdiction, but Popé died shortly after the rebellion, and the pueblos resumed their autonomy and internecine warfare.

With the Spaniards gone from the scene, Apaches and Utes stepped up their raids, which also encouraged some pueblos to relocate. Frasquillo, the hoped-for seminarian turned rebel-chieftain, led four thousand of his people westward to the pueblos of the Moqui, where with the aid of his fifteen hundred warriors he established himself as king and reigned unconquered for thirty years from his fortified capital at the Oraybi pueblo, now and then discussing a possible return to Christianity.

Yet another governor, Diego de Vargas, appointed in June 1688, launched a four-year effort at reconquest in August 1692 that ultimately proved successful due to Vargas' military skills and bravery and to his repeated efforts at reconciliation and reconquest. On 16 September 1692 Vargas led a column of forty soldiers, fifty Indian allies, and three Franciscans into a near-deserted Villa Santa Fe. Mass was celebrated the next morning on the plaza, and one hundred Indian children were baptized. From there Vargas proceeded westward to the Pecos pueblo, then upriver to Taos, receiving submissions from thirteen reclaimed pueblos by mid-October and baptizing nearly a thousand children. Vargas continued to march west and reclaimed Jemez, Mejía, and the ever-symbolic Ácoma. Even farther west, he received the reluctant submissions—yet submissions nonetheless—of Zuñi and a number of Moqui pueblos.

Despite all this outward conformity, submissions did not run very deep. In Mexico City, however, an ecstatic Gaspar Melchor Baltasar de la Cerda Silva Sandoval y Mendoza, conde de Galve, the viceroy of New Spain, authorized and helped finance a full-scale recolonization of the recovered kingdom. In early October 1693, Vargas led an expedition of one hundred soldiers, eighteen Franciscans, seventy-plus families of settlers, a large party of Indian allies (eight hundred or so in the entire column), along with nine hundred head of livestock, two thousand horses, and one thousand mules, north from El Paso, headed for Santa Fe. At Pecos, friendly Indians informed Vargas that resistance to this massive new entrada was being planned among many of the pueblos, including Zuñi, Taos, and Ácoma. Hearing this news, some soldiers and settlers deserted the expedition and returned to El Paso.

Entering Santa Fe on 16 December 1693, the Spaniards were received with the usual gestures of submission—bended knees, prayers, pledges of allegiance to the king—but the chiefs in charge refused to surrender the city, forcing the

Spaniards to camp outside the city in bitter cold. Responding to colonists' complaints, Vargas demanded that the Indians turn over Santa Fe. Instead, the Indians shut all gates and prepared for a siege. Vargas begged them to surrender. They refused—blasphemously, Vargas later reported. After three days of violent fighting, the Indians surrendered, and the Spaniards entered the city. Putting aside his previous policies of reconciliation, Vargas had seventy warriors executed and four hundred women and children distributed to the colonists as slaves. As with the slaughter at Zía in 1688, these executions and enslavements further deepened an abyss of alienation between Pueblo people and their Spanish overlords. What good was the baptism of a thousand children in 1692 in the face of nearly six hundred men killed at Zía and Santa Fe in less than two years, along with the other unrecorded deaths of the reconquest, or the four hundred women and children sent into slavery, or the unnumbered others left as widows and orphans? And all this death and destruction was happening to a population in the process of dwindling from an all-time low of seventeen thousand. Was this the basis for further evangelization of the Pueblo people? Had nothing been learned during a century of occupation?

Vargas required nearly nine months, until August 1694, to reestablish Spanish authority over the pueblos of the Río Grande valley through a blend of military force, intimidation, and negotiation. Still, peace did not come. A decisive elite within the pueblos—Indian and, to a lesser extent, mestizo—would never be fully reconciled to either sacred or secular domination by New Spain and continued to resist the reconquest even as the pueblos' population, depleted by disease and desertion, plunged to fourteen thousand.

In any event, on 4 June 1696, another coordinated rebellion broke out, which eventually involved nineteen out of twenty-four pueblos. Twenty-one settlers and soldiers and five Franciscans lost their lives in yet another flare-up of desperate fury: desperate because the pueblo population was small and weak, and a strong Spanish garrison at Santa Fe was available to Vargas to launch a reconquest of the reconquest. By the end of 1696, Vargas was once again reporting the general pacification of the kingdom.

Reconciliation and refoundation

Still, despite the pueblos' enduring unwillingness to accept fully either New Spain or Catholicism, New Mexico in the eighteenth century did develop into a Catholic province, thanks to its Spanish, mestizo, and genízaro populations. It was a challenged outpost, to be sure. Drought, famine, and marauding Apaches, Utes, and Comanches saw to that; yet it managed to hold on and to anchor the Borderlands. Settlement consisted of four towns (Santa Cruz, Santa Fe, Cerrillos, and Bernalillo); sixteen missions (including Santo Domingo, where Catholic New Mexico first began and sustained its headquarters; Pecos, the ever faithful; and Taos, ground zero for rebellion); and numerous hamlets, ranchos, and outposts scattered throughout the Río Grande valley.

Once a solitary extension fifteen hundred to two thousand miles north from Mexico City, New Mexico by the mid-1700s stood as the key province of the Borderlands between the Gulf of Mexico and the Pacific Ocean, edging northward into the San Luis valley of present-day Colorado and westward into southern Arizona.

Via the Gulf of California, moreover, this vast region now had maritime access to the Pacific; established routes would in time connect it overland to Texas and the Californias. Unlike Florida, moreover, New Mexico had people—colonists, Spaniards, allied Indian people, enslaved Indians, people of African descent, and mestizos of every variety, many enslaved (too many) but mostly free—brought into the region in increasing numbers by Vargas and his immediate successors, with the backing of viceroys eager to fortify the northern boundaries of New Spain. These laymen and -women married, established households in towns and hamlets, and multiplied. In the peak years of resettlement, Vargas and the viceroy promised the Spaniards hidalgo (gentry) status, but many of mixed ancestry achieved this border-land nobility as well. In time, New Mexico became a quasi-feudal society presided over by leading families: lords of land, cattle, sheep, and dependent constituencies.

The kingdom was desert and mountain country, water-scarce in its western regions; yet the Río Grande valley enjoyed water and had already proven its ability to support eighty thousand people in the pueblo area. During the eighteenth century, agriculture grew more varied and productive; land barons ran herds of cattle managed by skilled vaqueros; and sheepherding flourished among lower-ranking folk. The sheepherders of New Mexico bespoke something ancient and civilized, suggestive of the Good Shepherd of Jewish and Christian Scripture.

Dangers abounded. In the late spring of 1780, smallpox carried off 31 people in the Villa of Albuquerque, founded in 1706. The next year, it killed 142 soldiers and settlers in Santa Fe. Apache, Comanche, and Ute raids added to the death toll. Life, in short, was simple, harsh, and frequently short. Yet the loathed system of encomienda did not appear in the reconquest, with the exception of one grant to Governor Vargas; free *paisanos* (mixed-race people of the region) and Indians could work for themselves or for wages or barter for compensation. The freeing of slaves, however, remained decades in the future.

Religious life improved during the eighteenth century. Supported by state stipends, Franciscans returned in numbers sufficient to restaff the pueblo missions. The relentless warfare against indigenous religious practices—reverence for Katsina ancestors, Katsina dances and ceremonial masks, gatherings in the kiva—was toned down, however, allowing a gradual process of syncretic accommodation to assert itself in the pueblos. But the pueblos withdrew more and more into themselves. By the end of the eighteenth century, up to a third of New Mexico's population were genízaros—free Indians, Hispanicized and Catholic, some of Pueblo descent—which in itself represented an achievement. Had this not been the stated goal of Spanish missionaries since the early 1500s: the creation of an acculturated indigenous population, Spanish in language and lifestyle, Catholic in religion?

6

San Fernando de Béxar 1718

Texas is organized as a buffer province

In late April 1718 two elements of a joint entrada—the one civil/military and the other Franciscan—were converging in south-central Texas on the San Antonio River at its intersection with the spring-fed waters of San Pedro Creek. Under the command of Don Martín de Alarcón, the governor of the frontier province of Coahuila and its borderlands to the northeast, the civil/military expedition consisted of thirty-five soldiers (six with families), seven civilian families, mule drivers (a number with their families as well), a carpenter, and a mason, for a total of seventy-two soldiers and settlers, along with 548 horses, a large herd of cattle, sheep, oxen, pack mules, and goats. Led by the veteran missionary Fray Antonio de San Buenaventura y Olivares, the Franciscan unit contained four priests, a lay brother, and Indian retainers. Olivares and Brother Pedro Maleta had left for Texas later than their main party but, traveling faster, arrived at the specified location before it and did not encounter the Alarcón party on the trail when the governor, misreading his instructions, temporarily changed his destination and chose another route.

On 1 May 1718 Alarcón, having at last arrived, formally conferred on the Franciscans title to a site on the east side of the river for the establishment of Mission San Antonio de Padua, named in honor of a canonized thirteenth-century Franciscan preacher. Two years later, the name was changed to San Antonio de Valero to pay tribute to the current viceroy, Don Baltasar de Zúñiga, the Duke of Arión and Marquis of Valero, who had authorized and partly financed the entrada. At the time, Mission San Antonio consisted of a *jacal*—a temporary structure of brush, dried mud, and straw—in which Olivares lived and celebrated Mass. Alarcón formally established the Presidio and Villa of San Fernando de Béxar, named in honor of the saintly medieval King Ferdinand of Castile, canonized in 1671, and the Duke of Béxar, the viceroy's brother, who had lost his life during the recent defense of Budapest against the Turks. The presidio and villa were located near Pedro Springs on the west side of the San Antonio River some two miles from the mission.

While yet mere brush huts and a log fortification, the mission, presidio, and villa founded during these five days signaled New Spain's deepening interest in the Borderlands. In contrast to New Mexico, Arizona, and Baja California, as well as Alta California after 1769, Texas was intended to be colonized both as a civil colony devoid of slaughter and encomienda and as an evangelical enterprise upgraded in the quality of its clergy, who were to receive prior preparation at newly established missionary colleges that offered advanced modes of training and intense spiritual formation.

Efforts at reform

The War of the Spanish Succession (1701–1714) confirmed a Bourbon, Philip V, on the throne of Spain, and with him came an opening to the Enlightenment through the reigns of four Bourbon kings. The charge was not enough to alter the nature of Spanish colonial society in any radical way, but it did lead Spain and its empire—along with the other nations of Catholic Europe—to higher levels of rationality and reform in civil and ecclesiastical administration and, in the case of the Spanish Empire, to a better approach to evangelical, civil, and military practice.

The popes of the eighteenth century demonstrate this uptake in Enlightenment values in their growing respect for and support of science and critical history, their improved relations with Protestant nations, their willingness to negotiate Church reform, and their concern for informed and benevolent missionary practice. Occupying the See of Peter from 1740 to 1758, Benedict XIV epitomized this Enlightenment papacy, free of personal scandal and confident in its relationship to secular culture. Benedict studied and wrote history and established chairs of chemistry, higher mathematics, and surgery. Voltaire dedicated a play in his honor. The English savant Horace Walpole described Benedict as "a priest without insolence or interest, a prince without favourites, a pope without nephews". Affable and engaging, ever curious, Benedict liked to stroll around archaeological sites in Rome with few or no attendants, chatting with people like a village priest making his rounds, emanating a benevolent attitude as well as an intensified hopefulness regarding the human prospect.[1]

In terms of missionary activity, the creation of the Sacred Congregation for the Propagation of the Faith by Pope Gregory XV on 6 January 1622, confirmed in June by the papal bull *Inscrutabili Divinae*, dramatized the entry of Enlightenment principles into the management of overseas Catholicism, by now a global phenomenon. Under development since the mid-sixteenth century, the Sacred Congregation consisted of thirteen advisory cardinals (one of them serving as prefect), two administrative prelates, and staff, headquartered in a palace on the Piazza di Spagna designed by Gian Lorenzo Bernini and donated to the Sacred Congregation by one of its founding prelates. Its charge: the regularization and reform of the Church's worldwide missionary effort, starting with an ambitious twenty-year review of missionary practice through surveys and reports from the field under the supervision of its founding administrative secretary, Francesco Ingoli, a zealous and talented priest and civil servant from Ravenna. Thus was inaugurated the ongoing creation of what by the eighteenth century was a unique archive and library of global cultures and patterns of missionary practice. Analyzing these reports as they slowly filtered into the palace on the Piazza di Spagna, the cardinals of the Sacred Congregation formulated their recommendations to Gregory XV and succeeding pontiffs. The program evolving at the Sacred Congregation through the seventeenth and eighteenth centuries involved a rising level of scholarship and education for future missionaries, including language training, as well as the creation of catechetical and related texts in local languages. (By the end of the eighteenth century, the Sacred Congregation's printing press possessed type fonts for forty-four Asian and African languages,

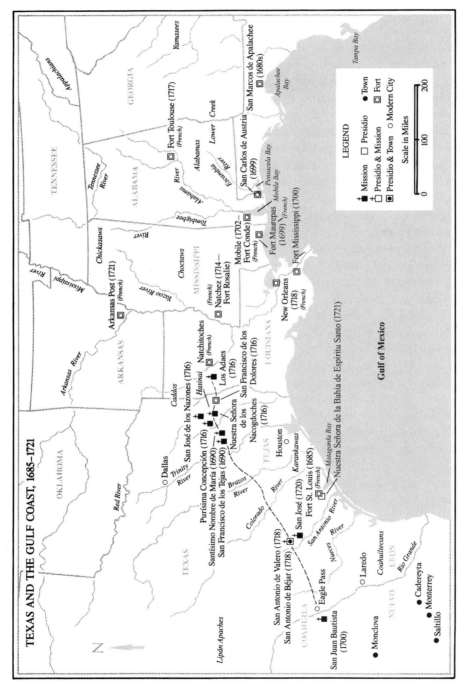

Map 10. Texas and the Gulf Coast, 1685–1721. From David J. Weber, *The Spanish Frontier in North America* (New Haven: Yale University Press, 1992), 150. © *Yale University Press, used by permission.*

which Napoleon seized and shipped back to France.) The Sacred Congregation also sought to bring the Church's worldwide missionary effort under its administrative supervision through the establishment of local jurisdictions called apostolic vicariates. These provisional dioceses were to be governed by prelates the Sacred Congregation would appoint from religious orders or from the growing ranks of secular missionary priests trained at its own Urban College seminary in Rome or emerging from the Société des Missions Étrangères de Paris (Paris Foreign Missions Society), an institute of French secular priests organized in 1663 and approved by the Holy See the following year. Such an exercise of authority on behalf of secular clergy, Europeans, and the local clergy the Sacred Congregation was charged to recruit and educate naturally met with opposition from entrenched missionary orders, although in Asia and French Canada, religious orders were eventually recruited into this Vatican-controlled system. Yet in the Spanish and Portuguese empires, the most dogged and effective opposition came not from religious orders but from the Crown and its viceregal entities, for the long-established system of *patronato real*—the church-state relationship of cooperation and interdependence—directly clashed with the Sacred Congregation's desire to establish a worldwide missionary culture under its jurisdiction. In Spain and Portugal and their empires, kings and viceroys shared with Rome the authority to create dioceses, nominate bishops, and employ and support religious-order missionaries as agents of the state. They could also entrust high civil offices to ecclesiastics; thus Cardinal Giulio Alberoni served as prime minister of Spain from 1716 to 1719, and nearly a dozen archbishops and bishops served as viceroy of New Spain between 1535 and 1821.

The Indian question

One of the earliest ambitions of the Sacred Congregation for the Propagation of the Faith was cultural: to speak, within the parameters of orthodoxy, to indigenous peoples in their own language in concepts and metaphors to which they could relate. The Sacred Congregation also stressed respect for racial identities and local ways of life, though again within the bounds of traditional Catholic beliefs and practices. In controversies over the Malabar and Chinese Rites that came to a head in the late seventeenth and early eighteenth centuries, such efforts at acculturation reached administrative limits, and Jesuit efforts to replace Latin with vernacular languages in liturgical ceremonies were rejected by Rome. Yet the Sacred Congregation held fast to its call for respect—and kindness—whenever possible.

The most powerful of all ameliorating influences in New Spain was the most faith oriented. Those devoted to Our Lady of Guadalupe held that in December 1531 the Virgin Mary appeared on a number of occasions to an elderly Indian named Juan Diego at Tepeyac, a hill northwest of Mexico City. The apparition instructed Juan Diego to fill his mantle with flowers for presentation to Fray Juan de Zumárraga, the bishop of Mexico. According to tradition, when Juan Diego emptied his mantle before the bishop, the image of Mary as a young Indian woman was imprinted on it.

Anchored in the doctrine and iconography of the Immaculate Conception, so beloved and historically significant among Franciscans in the Indies, devotion to Our Lady of Guadalupe—named in honor of the site of her shrine—emerged in the mid-sixteenth century, grew steadily in the seventeenth, and in the mid-eighteenth achieved iconic status. In 1746 the Most Holy Mary of Guadalupe was proclaimed the patroness of New Spain. In 1754 Pope Benedict XIV established 12 December as a feast day in her honor for the universal Church. Many scholars had grave reservations arising from the absence of compelling contemporary documentation regarding the life of Juan Diego and the apparition narrative. Putting aside these reservations, John Paul II on 30 July 2002 in the Basilica of Guadalupe proclaimed the canonization of Juan Diego.

Yet, in the course of this controversy, no scholar expressed doubts as to the significance and power of Our Lady of Guadalupe as a liberating, reconciling image. As the Vincentian historian Stafford Poole points out, criollos, the native-born Mexicans of Spanish ancestry, did the most to advance this devotion as an expression of criollismo. Having conquered the Indies by the sword, nearly destroying the indigenous peoples of the Caribbean through massacre and slavery, criollos were gradually developing a devotion to Mary, the Mother of God, depicted as a young Indian woman—a reflection of the countless Indian women whose lives had been destroyed by Spanish Catholic conquerors. Beneath the surface of history, the Guadalupe devotion represented an apology, a request for forgiveness and atonement, on the part of criollo New Spain.

The entradas of Coronado and Oñate had advanced into the Borderlands behind the image of Mary as La Conquistadora. Once arrived, Spaniards intimidated indigenous people with reenactments of recent victories over the Moors during the Reconquest. Appearances by La Conquistadora and Saint James of Santiago, the patron of a military order devoted to the expulsion of the Moors from the Iberian Peninsula, were widely reported in the aftermath of the attack on Ácoma, as if Ácoma were a reprise of the taking of Granada. The statue of La Conquistadora before which the Spaniards marched was later enshrined with great reverence in Santa Fe. The Virgin of Guadalupe offered a bold counterstatement. With the depiction of Mary, the Mother of God, as Indian, the conquerors were acknowledging that the indigenous peoples of the Indies had prevailed through their long genocidal agony and were now being assumed into the image of the new Eve, who represented perfected humanity and who had been celebrated by Catholics across the centuries as the Mystical Rose, the Tower of David, the Tower of Ivory, the House of Gold, the Ark of the Covenant, the Gate of Heaven, the Morning Star.

The missionary colleges

The three Franciscan apostolic missionary colleges founded during this era for northern New Spain and the Borderlands—the Colegio de Santa Cruz de Querétaro (1683), the Colegio de Propaganda Fide de Nuestra Señora de Guadalupe de Zacatecas (1707), and the Colegio de San Fernando in Mexico City (1734)—exemplified a subtle infusion of Enlightenment values into Franciscan piety and missionary practice. Fifteen such Franciscan missionary colleges were established in South, Central, and North America (Mexico) in the course of the eighteenth century. Guided by the program at the Urban College of Propaganda Fide in Rome, these colleges constituted a quasi-autonomous movement among Franciscans aimed at producing well-trained and highly motivated missionaries.

Rigorously selected at the local level, candidates were put through a one- to two-year program of spiritual formation and language instruction before being sent to serve in existing missions or to establish new missions guided and staffed by members of a particular college.

Thus, in addition to being members of their original Franciscan province, the Franciscan missionaries of eighteenth-century Texas were Querétarans, Zacatecans, or Fernandans in terms of their missionary training and practice, assignments, and community identification. College missionaries wore a distinctive light-gray Franciscan habit, in contrast to the darker blue-gray habits of noncollege Franciscans or the coffee-colored habits of strict-observance friars.

The *Libros de los Decretos* of the missionary college of Zacatecas—records kept between 1707 and 1828 of meetings, assignments, arrivals, departures, and ongoing issues—reveal the fused culture of a friary, an academy, an Oxbridge college, a lodge, a regimental mess, and a selective men's club. The college was democratically run by an elected president or guardian and his consultors or by meetings of the entire membership, called chapters. A commissary oversaw college operations and the organization and transportation of supplies for the missions. The day was carefully balanced among prayer, classes, study, chores, and recreation according to a monastic ritual adapted to the instructional purpose. Each friar had his own room. The communal refectory offered three meals a day, including hot chocolate at breakfast (served in cups and saucers imprinted with the college logo) and wine with dinner on feast days. On special occasions, cigars and perhaps a glass of brandy were available at evening recreation.

Preparation for the missions remained the college's central purpose, although some elderly or ill friars were in residence in retirement or in the college infirmary. Candidates for admission to the program were rigidly scrutinized as to intelligence, health, motivation, and prior performance in the order and were periodically reviewed by consultors as they underwent formation. Occasionally, a candidate voluntarily withdrew from the program and returned to his home province. In certain cases, a candidate might be asked to withdraw. Candidates for the lay brotherhood were equally scrutinized, albeit from the perspective of their present or future skill sets, since lay brothers were responsible for supplying missions—which involved arduous travel across vast distances—as well as on-site construction and maintenance. As was true of candidates for the priesthood, if they were already ordained, candidates for the brotherhood were required to be of legitimate birth (which in a few instances constituted a straight and narrow gate for a brother candidate to pass through, aided by friendly consultors).

Within shared Franciscan parameters and practices, missionary colleges maintained distinctive identities, styles, and revered worthies. The college of Zacatecas, for example, was anchored in the spirit and values of its founder, former Querétaran Fray Antonio Margil de Jesús, whose habit, broad-brimmed hat, rosary, and walking staff were preserved as relics and whose case for canonization was opened with the local bishop. He was declared Venerable—that is, showing a life of heroic virtue—by Pope Gregory XVI in 1836. The focus of the Zacatecans on Texas can also be traced to Margil, along with a regard for good architecture at the college and in the Texas missions.

Between 1717 and 1834, successive generations of Zacatecans prepared for and entered the service of the Texas missions. Thirty-one of them died while on assignment: older men died of natural causes, younger men were brought down by hardship and disease, and a few suffered martyrdom. The rest returned to retirement at their college or to easier assignments. How well the system worked remains an open question if considered from the perspective of numbers of converts. The success of the missionary colleges in comparison with earlier missionary efforts, however, is apparent in terms of outreach and behavior. Judging from the existing record, Querétarans, Zacatecans, and Fernandans appear to have conducted themselves with a high level of commitment and patience. They avoided scandal and produced a half dozen martyrs as well as a number of holy and enlightened missionaries, including Venerable Fray Antonio Margil de Jesús and Fray Junípero Serra, a Fernandan, founder of the missions of Alta California who was declared Venerable by Pope John Paul II in 1985, beatified in 1988, and canonized by Pope Francis in 2015.

The northward progress of diocesan creation in New Spain, moreover— Guadalajara (1548), Durango (1620), Linares (1777), Sonora (1779)—foretold a future of episcopal jurisdiction and diocesan clergy extending into the Borderlands, which also helped clarify the Franciscan mission. A suggestion of millenarianism— the notion that the Borderlands as a Franciscan protectorate would redeem Spain's past sins in the Indies—lingered, yet Texas, unlike New Mexico and the Jesuit missions on the Gulf of California, was civilian from its foundation and remained under the jurisdiction of the Diocese of Guadalajara; by midcentury it enjoyed the services of a few civilian-oriented secular clergy. In November 1759 Texas was graced by a visit from the bishop of Guadalajara, the saintly, energetic Francisco de San Buenaventura y Tejada, formerly the auxiliary bishop in Saint Augustine, Florida.

Tensions with the military persisted, especially over the issue of whether the Indians of Texas should be brought into reductions near the missions in order to be more completely instructed in Christianity, agriculture, and manual arts—the Franciscan preference—or the missionaries should take to the field, following the migratory cycles of the Indians and evangelizing them on the move. The military opposed reductions and favored the migratory option, fearing that the massing of large numbers of Indians close to undermanned presidios would prove dangerous in times of discontent or rebellion. The Pueblo Revolt of 1680 and the revolts that followed in the next decade remained as warnings. In addition (as usual), the proclivity of soldiers to exploit Indian women sexually caused further strain between the military and the friars. Franciscans also opposed conversion by force, which had been the case with the foundation of Mission San Antonio de Valero, when Governor Alarcón told a gathering of chiefs that if they did not bring their people to the newly established mission, he would search them out and put them to the sword. As a result of this threat, the local people fled the region, and the Franciscans remained seriously underemployed in the months that followed—instruction not given, fields unsown.

A founding encounter

From the founding of the eastern coastal settlement of Pánuco by Cortés in 1522, New Spain (Mexico) had steadily advanced northward up the central plateau. In 1579 the Kingdom of Nuevo León, which incorporated parts of Texas, was established north of Pánuco. In 1655 Spaniards crossed the Río Grande for the first time in the course of a military expedition against the Cacaxtles. In the early 1670s the Franciscans established missions on the Coahuila frontier west and northwest of Nuevo León. On one of his journeys during this period, Fray Manuel de la Cruz, a lay brother, crossed the Río Grande into Texas. By this time, lower Texas stood surrounded to its south and southwest by the developing frontier provinces of Nuevo Santander, Nuevo León, and Coahuila, also known as Nueva Estremadura (Texas was also known as Nuevas Filipinas, the new Philippines).

In April 1675 Don Antonio Balcárcel, the alcalde of Coahuila, commissioned a reconnaissance across the Río Grande into Texas. Ten soldiers, two Franciscans, and more than a hundred Indians were led by the veteran soldier Fernando del Bosque and the veteran Franciscan missionary Juan Larios, a Mexico-born criollo from the Franciscan province of Santiago de Jalisco, which was headquartered in Guadalajara. Their mission: to explore the regions to the north and to ascertain prospects for evangelization.

Coastal and inland present-day Texas had been crossed or explored numerous times since the early sixteenth century. Accounts of some of these expeditions have already appeared in this narrative. In his monumental six-volume history, *Our Catholic Heritage in Texas* (1936–1950), historian Carlos E. Castañeda spends nearly two-thirds of his first volume chronicling incursions into Texas before the 1680s, including the 1554 shipwreck on the Texas coast and subsequent evangelizing efforts of five Dominicans, only one of whom survived. The majority of entradas into Texas, however, were expeditions in search of Quivira, the Seven Cities of Cíbola, or mineral wealth, or forced marches following shipwreck. Yet the Franciscan friars on these campaigns did attempt evangelization and in certain instances paid for it with their lives.

By contrast, the Bosque-Larios expedition of 1675 and its subsequent report led to the founding of four missions in northern Coahuila to serve Indians south and north of the Río Grande. While camped at a place the Spaniards called San Ysidro, most likely on one of the branches of the Nueces River, Fray Larios celebrated a high Mass, the first such ceremony in Texas; Fernando del Bosque wrote of the joyous event in his diary. Following the Mass, Bosque details, numerous Indians asked to be baptized, but Fray Larios refused, telling them that "he could not baptize them until they knew their prayers." To console the disappointed Indians, however, Larios "baptized fifty-five infants, the Spaniards acting as their godfathers. They were instructed in the doctrine, and counted, and the people of the four chiefs (Xoman, Terrodan, Teaname, and Teimamar) were found to comprise four hundred and twenty-five warriors and seven hundred and forty-seven women, boys, and girls, of all ages, making in all eleven hundred and seventy-two persons." During that same visit, an Indian presented to Bosque a young Spanish captive, judged to be around twelve years of age, his face extensively tattooed. Through interpreters, Bosque learned that the youth (who knew no Spanish) had been captured by the Cavezas as a boy and brought into the interior, where he had been adopted and well treated by a Gueiquesal family, who were now willing to return him to his own people as a gesture of respect toward the Spaniards.

Bosque continues:

The Indian was asked if there were other Spanish boys among the Indians. He replied that all he knew was that at the time when they brought the boy the Cavezas brought another boy and a Spanish girl; that they killed the boy with arrows, having made him stand up for the purpose; that when the boy saw this he took a cross in his hands and began to say his prayers, and was praying till he died; that the Spanish girl they brought with them likewise, as a servant, and because during an expedition which the Cavezas made to rob and kill, they killed one of their companions, they captured and shot her with arrows until she died, leaving her lying where she fell; that two years later they passed by there and found her just as they had left her, the body being undecayed and the animals not having eaten it. In view of this they took it and carried it to a cave, where it now is; and that it has long hair; that he knows no more, and that this is the truth.[2]

"Stories of miraculous happenings of this particular sort were common in New Spain", historian Herbert Eugene Bolton notes of this diary entry. This is exactly the significance of these two events recorded by Bosque. First of all, Fray Larios' refusal to baptize the Indians until they had received instruction stands in marked contrast to the mass baptisms of the previous century in New Mexico. As an experienced missionary—touched, if ever so slightly, by Enlightenment values—Larios wanted to anchor Catholic Christianity in instruction and assent before conferring it on adults. In the case of infants and children, however, according to traditional Catholic practice, baptism was conferred before the age of reason without instruction, with adults serving as sponsors and godparents (a respected and lifelong responsibility in Spanish Catholic culture). That soldiers were willing to serve in this capacity represents an improvement in the military's attitude.

Significant as well in Bosque's narration is the Gueiquesal Indians' willingness to return the twelve-year-old captive Spanish boy who, they claimed, had become a beloved member of their tribe. However reluctant his sojourn, the boy emerges in Bosque's retelling as the first Spanish resident of the precolonized province. At the same time, he possesses a workable Indian identity in terms of language, family, and facial tattoo. His return to Christianity foreshadows the development of a Hispanicized Indian and mestizo culture in a Texas awaiting settlement and conversion. The martyrdom of the two other captives, as well as the report that the slain girl's corpse remained uncorrupted (a claim common in early Christian literature), encoded the enduring Catholicism of the Spanish people and the emergent Catholic destiny of Texas under Spanish jurisdiction.

Even more compellingly, the Bosque-Larios expedition reacquainted Spaniards with an impressive tribe, the Tejas people, who lived to the northeast on the Louisiana border. The Tejas were members of a highly developed Caddo confederacy that was centered in northeast Texas, northwest Louisiana, southwest Arkansas, and southeast Oklahoma. The social organization and material culture of the Caddo people impressed Spaniards and French from their first encounter. The Caddo combined village life and agriculture with bison hunting. They could be warlike when necessary, but their basic temperament—the result, in part, of the geographical range and material prosperity of their civilization—was irenic; indeed, the word *taysha* (friend or ally), heard and recorded by Spaniards as *tejas*, would give the tribe and future province their name. Over the years, the Tejas people emerged in the imagination of the Spaniards of New Spain as a partial fulfillment of their long-held belief in a culturally developed Middle Kingdom, a Quivira, in the region north of the Borderlands. The impressive Tejans were also friendly and thus were perceived as promising allies in New Spain's advance to the north. Such a hope pervades the diary of Fernando del Bosque from the encounter of 1675: a notion that the Tejas people might very well be instinctive Christians, and hence founding members of a future province.

Further favorable reports regarding the Tejas resulted from a second reconnaissance in 1683–1684, this time from New Mexico, led by Captain Juan Domínguez de Mendoza and Franciscan Nicolás López. A mere three years after the massive and murderous repudiation of the great Pueblo Revolt, Fray López, the custos of New Mexico, found himself being lobbied in the refugee capital of El Paso by delegations of Julimes, Conchos, and other tribes to the east (some of whom gave evidence of a collective memory of the Cabeza de Vaca party in its passage through southern Texas a century and a half previously) requesting that the Spaniards return; one delegation reported that some tribes were already scouting out sites for missions. The leader of one delegation, Juan Sabeata, a Jumano Indian chief, had already been baptized and promised further conversions should the Franciscans come to them.

After departing from El Paso on 1 December 1683, Fray López and two other Franciscans found that the Julimes—whom they encountered on the Texas side of the Río Grande—had already built a fair-sized church of reeds, complete with an altar. Based out of that church and a second one they found in readiness, the Franciscans immediately began evangelization among the Julimes and Jumanos. So encouraged by these developments that he did not even wait for viceregal authorization, Coahuila Governor Domingo Jironza Petriz Cruzate commissioned Captain Mendoza and Fray López to rejoin forces and push even deeper into Texas. Reaching the Colorado River (which they called the San Clemente) near its junction with the main branch of the Concho, Mendoza and López stayed for six weeks in a combined stronghold and chapel, hunting buffalo to a prodigal degree for hides, instructing and baptizing local Indians, and visiting with delegations from farther east, promising to return within the year.

On their return, Mendoza formally took possession of the north bank of the Río Grande and commissioned four local chiefs to act as representatives of the Crown, presenting them with the batons and other insignia of an Indian governor. Back in Mexico City, López and Mendoza prepared and in 1686 submitted a memorial of their reconnaissance in which they called for the establishment of missions and presidios in the regions they had visited, fortified, and claimed.

The French threat

Matters might have stalled at that point—the official response to the López-Mendoza report was tepid—had not dramatic news reached Mexico City. The famed French explorer Réne Robert Cavelier, sieur de La Salle, who in 1682 had descended the Mississippi to its mouth and claimed the entire Mississippi valley for France, had now (after lengthy negotiations in Quebec and Versailles) established Fort Saint Louis on Matagorda Bay on the gulf coast. With this news, Texas suddenly became strategically important as a buffer zone against French incursion. First, however, La Salle's colony had to be located and neutralized. Sea and land searches were dispatched. Internal dissension and the murder of La Salle by his own men, however, ended the French threat, although the news of La Salle's death was kept secret in

France until the summer of 1688, and a Spanish reconnaissance—the last of four led by the experienced soldier Alonso de León—at long last discovered the ruins of Fort Saint Louis on 22 April 1689.

Franciscan Damián Massanet was attached to this expedition. Following the discovery of the ruined French fort (which had been destroyed by Indians), the León-Massanet party headed into Tejas country in search of survivors, having received a letter written with red ochre to the effect that two survivors were living among the Tejas, one of whom signed off as "Jean de l'archevêque" (leading one Franciscan to suggest that an archbishop had been at Fort Saint Louis!). Two survivors were indeed found among the Tejas, Jean L'Archevêque and Jacques Grollet. The former turned out to be not an archbishop but one of the men who had plotted against and killed La Salle and La Salle's nephew. Arrested, L'Archevêque and Grollet were sent back to Mexico City for interrogation, then shipped to Spain for further debriefing and testimony. Released from custody in 1692, the pair returned to New Spain and resettled in New Mexico.

An early mission

While among the Tejas, Fray Massanet carried on conversations with a Tejas chief who was ratifyingly knowledgeable about Catholic Christianity. The chief had a clear notion of a Supreme Being and pointed to the sky when referring to him. Even more impressively, the Tejas chief possessed a small portable altar, decorated with four portraits of saints, and a cross as well, with a figure of Christ painted on it, before which he kept a sanctuary light burning night and day. Massanet immediately thought of the Franciscan-backed tradition of María de Ágreda, the Spanish Franciscan abbess reported to have miraculously evangelized the Indians of New Mexico as well as the Jumano and Tejas Indians of Texas a half century earlier. When questioned, the Tejas chief replied that, while he had never personally seen the Woman in Blue, his aged mother had. The very old men of the tribe, moreover, had passed down the story that a beautiful young woman wearing a robe similar to Massanet's and a blue cloak had visited the Tejas and instructed them in Christianity.

However one interprets this report—a skeptic might argue it was merely wishful thinking on Massanet's part or a pious fable that encoded a sense of Franciscan destiny—it added weight to the memorial that Fray Massanet submitted to the viceroy in Mexico City. A Tejas chief, Massanet reported, had formally requested the establishment of missions among his people. Once Viceroy Gaspar Melchor Baltasar de la Cerda Silva Sandoval y Mendoza, eighth count of Galve and lord of Salcedón and Tortola, assured himself that La Salle's colony no longer posed a threat, he readily agreed that missions and a presidio in eastern Texas (a geographical designation Fray Massanet was bringing into prominence) were a very good idea.

A good idea, perhaps—but in reality, it lasted less than three years. On Tuesday of Easter week, 28 March 1690, the Querétaran Franciscans who had accompanied Captain Alonso de León and Fray Damián Massanet on previous reconnaissances to east Texas departed Coahuila once again, this time with the intention of establishing a mission among the Tejas. Captain León again commanded the military escort. The Spanish were well received by the Tejas upon their arrival in late May, Fray

Massanet later wrote the viceroy, and after visiting with an important local chief (and discovering in the vicinity the remains of two quarreling Frenchmen who had shot each other with carbines) set out in search of a suitable mission site. León and Massanet discovered a peaceful spot near a brook surrounded by trees, identified in the early twentieth century by Herbert Eugene Bolton as a site northeast of the present city of Weches, Houston County, six or seven miles west of the Neches River in a valley through which runs San Pedro Creek. There the Spaniards constructed a log church and friary, dedicated as the Mission San Francisco de los Tejas on the feast of Corpus Christi, 1 June 1690, with a military salute, a Eucharistic procession, Mass, the hosting of a royal standard and banner of Our Lady of Guadalupe, and the singing of a Te Deum, followed by more musketry.

The establishment of San Francisco de los Tejas not only gave Texas its permanent name but also prompted the creation of Texas as an official province the following year, with Domingo de Terán de los Ríos named as governor of Coahuila and Texas. In May 1691 Terán, Fray Massanet, and five other Querétarans set forth for east Texas with the intentions of reconnoitering any continuing French presence infiltrating into Texas from Louisiana and founding a second mission. Arriving at Mission San Francisco de los Tejas on 2 August, the Spaniards found a disaster. Smallpox had devastated the surrounding villages, killing three thousand Tejas within a month, and carried off two of the four Franciscans on staff. Fray Antonio Bordoy remained in charge at San Francisco, doing what he could, while the other survivor, Fray Francisco Casañas, had left in search of a more healthful location. In October 1691 Casañas established a second mission, Santísimo Nombre de María, among the Neches in the southwestern part of present-day Cherokee County.

In a 1692 report to the viceroy, Fray Casañas was hopeful regarding the prospects of this second mission as the nucleus of a Spanish outpost in east Texas. However, sexual assaults by Terán's soldiers were rapidly alienating the Tejas. Discouraged, some Franciscans returned to Coahuila. The remaining few asked Fray Casañas to go to Mexico City and personally meet with the viceroy. The veteran missionary Fray Francisco Hidalgo remained at the mission as religious superior.

On 30 December 1692 Fray Casañas succeeded in obtaining a viceregal order regularizing Mission Santísimo Nombre de María, reasserting the importance of Mission San Francisco de los Tejas, and calling for the establishment of more missions. Throughout 1692 and 1693, however, the Querétarans still at the mission grew progressively discouraged by soldiers' sexual assaults of Indian women and the consequent growing hostility of the tribes in the region, as well as the influence of pro-French tribes farther east. The soldiers themselves grew fearful and in the spring of 1693 deserted their posts. The remaining Franciscans likewise returned to Coahuilla until the situation could be regularized through viceregal action.

Refoundation

The required renewal of formal commitment by the viceroy to the colonization and evangelization of Texas by New Spain took twenty-five years. The War of the Spanish Succession, first of all, made Spain and France allies against England, Holland, and the majority of German states (with the conspicuous exception of

Catholic Bavaria, who sided with Spain and France in an effort to keep the European Spanish empire intact and safeguard a Bourbon on the Spanish throne). Given this new alliance, the French presence in Louisiana no longer posed a threat.

Wars, however, cost money and command government attention. As Spain put its efforts (with mixed success) into the protection of its Atlantic, Caribbean, and gulf ports from English raiders, the development of Texas declined into the category of unfinished business, for which funds were no longer available. On the eastern Borderlands, moreover, the English settlers of the Carolinas and their Indian allies were in the process of destroying the mission systems of Florida and Georgia. Now was not the time to launch a major missionary effort into unsettled Texas.

Energized by apostolic zeal, however, Fray Francisco Hidalgo, the last Franciscan superior at Mission San Francisco de los Tejas, refused to give up. Throughout his middle years and into old age, Hidalgo continued to lobby government officials for the resumption of the Franciscan effort among the Tejas. Hidalgo got nowhere with this effort, neither in Mexico City nor with his missionary college of Santa Cruz de Querétaro. Without military protection and government support for suppliers and the maintenance of the friars, Querétarans reluctantly concluded, how could such an effort be mounted?

In January 1711 Fray Hidalgo went so far as to write to the governor of French Louisiana, Antoine de La Mothe Cadillac, requesting his help in establishing a mission among the Tejas. Sensing an opportunity—the opening of trade between Louisiana and northern New Spain overland through Texas—Cadillac issued passports and commissioned the resourceful young frontiersman Louis Juchereau de Saint Denis (then serving as governor of Biloxi) to lead an expedition across Texas to scout for possible mission sites, linking up with Fray Hidalgo if possible, while transporting ten thousand livres of merchandise from the public store for sale and trade in northern Mexico. Passing through east Texas with the help of friendly Tejas, and noting en route the suitability of the San Antonio River as a site for a future mission and presidio, Saint Denis and four Frenchmen were placed under friendly arrest upon their arrival at the presidio of San Juan Bautista in Coahuila and escorted to Mexico City. There they were personally interviewed by Viceroy Fernando de Alencastre Noroña y Silva, the first Duke of Linares and Marquis of Valdefuentes, and required to submit a formal memorandum regarding the purpose of their journey.

On 22 August 1715 the viceroy put the entire matter for deliberation and action before a general junta consisting of the Audiencia, assorted judges, treasury officers, and other high officials. The result: a decision to resume the Franciscan mission into Texas under the joint supervision of the apostolic colleges at Querétaro and Zacatecas. Fray Hidalgo had won! He was, in fact, named in junta instructions, along with Fray Antonio de San Buenaventura y Olivares, as being assigned to the refounding of Texas.

Other founders

In his own way, perhaps from sheer persistence (not to mention his chutzpah in writing Cadillac!), Fray Francisco Hidalgo was a noteworthy Franciscan, as was his confrere Antonio Olivares. Although archives contain stories of shocking behavior of Franciscan missionaries in the Borderlands, the incidents seem to be fewer than those reported of missionaries in Florida, Georgia, and New Mexico, especially in the horrendous matters of whippings and sexual abuse. From this perspective, one can argue that the Enlightenment-oriented apostolic college system for training Franciscan missionaries—so central to the establishment of the Texas missions— was sending higher-caliber, better trained, more spiritually formed missionaries into the field. A higher caliber of military and government officials at this point enters the Texas picture as well. As a colonial and evangelical venture touched by Enlightenment values and reformed clerical formation, Texas witnessed the grow- ing presence of Spaniards, lay and clerical, of more than ordinary valor and virtue.

Fray Antonio Margil de Jesús was one such notable figure. He spent the major part of his missionary career as preacher, evangelizer, explorer, road builder, founder of missions, architect, mason, carpenter, construction supervisor, college founder and administrator, confessor, spiritual director, and saintly inspiration within the param- eters of Querétaran responsibility around the Gulf of Mexico and the Caribbean Sea (embracing present-day Costa Rica, Nicaragua, Honduras, El Salvador, Guatemala, Mexico, Texas, and Louisiana) but did not enter the missionary fields of Texas and western Louisiana until the last decade of his life. Hence the record of Margil's ministry is diffused into Central American localities that did not become North American but remained part of Latin America. The Texas in which Margil labored was linked in every way to the gulf and Caribbean continuity of Spanish colo- nial settlements organized as New Spain and the separately established Kingdom of Guatemala that, in time, would evolve into six Spanish-speaking nations; Texas, a longtime province of Mexico, would win its bilingual, bicultural independence as a partially Spanish-speaking (and Catholic) seventh nation in 1836.

Born in Valencia, Spain, Margil entered the Franciscan order at sixteen and, following his ordination to the priesthood in 1682, volunteered for New Spain as part of the founding cadre of friars assigned to transform the friary at Querétaro, Mexico, into the first Colegio de Propaganda Fide in the Indies. Margil spent the years 1684 to 1697 as an energetic evangelist and mission builder in southern Mex- ico and Central America before being elected to the post of guardian of the college at Querétaro. Margil and his longtime confrere Fray Melchor López are credited for founding or restoring twenty missions in Costa Rica alone between 1689 and 1691. Returning from Costa Rica to evangelize in the frontier between Guatemala and eastern Chiapas—after helping establish a hospice (branch house) of his college in Santiago de los Caballeros (Antigua), the capital of Guatemala—Margil worked with Mercedarian friars to set up a mission and sub-mission in eastern Chiapas among Lacandon Indians long hostile to Christianization.

After four years at Querétaro—three as guardian and one as vicar, awaiting the arrival of the newly elected guardian—Margil returned to Santiago de los Cabal- leros to expand the existing hospice into a full-fledged, freestanding apostolic col- lege, the Colegio de Cristo Crucificado (of which he was elected guardian), a new Franciscan church, and a friary. Between 1702 and 1705 Margil labored in Nicara- gua, Costa Rica, and again in Guatemala before he was instructed to establish yet another missionary college for the Propagation of the Faith, this time in the town of Guadalupe near the city of Zacatecas, Mexico, where a hospice of Querétaro established in 1703 was being raised to independent collegial status. Since the friar first chosen to lead the Zacatecas foundation, Fray Pedro de la Concepción, was appointed bishop of Puerto Rico, Margil served two terms, 1707 to 1713, as the president of the new institution, soon to be involved as Querétaro's partner in the re-evangelization of Texas.

How does one evoke and summarize such a man, now on the verge of becoming a Texas founder? From the perspective of his previous thirty years in the missionary field, most obviously. Take into consideration his regard for Indians; his courage in the face of hostility; the direct and self-surrendering faith of a priest who signed his letters *La misma nada* (Nothingness itself), suggesting a mystical and very Spanish piety that was not harsh or self-punishingly ascetic (no reports of self-flagellation or hair shirts) but rather totally dependent on the Almighty ("Nothing is nothing and can do nothing. Not I, but God will govern this new College"); and—from a human and cultural perspective—a love of the trail, which he tackled like an athlete, setting records, such as five weeks from eastern Chiapas to Querétaro ("I take shortcuts, and God helps me").[3]

Margil's love of road building and construction indicates an engineering capacity, energetic and useful. His skills as an architect—judging from the ruins of the church of Antigua's Colegio de Cristo Crucificado, which he founded, or the Colegio de Nuestra Señora de Guadalupe near Zacatecas, begun in 1707 under his supervision (so an inscription on one wall tells us)—bespeak an accomplished Spanish colonial culture characterized by aesthetic dignity: the grace, balance, and historical reference of Catholic Mediterranean Europe reprised in New World circumstances. For all his religiosity, Fray Antonio Margil de Jesús impresses us also as being a civilized cleric, representing the best possibilities of Franciscan missionary culture touched by Enlightenment values in the era of apostolic colleges.

Achieving Texas

In April 1716 five Querétaran and four Zacatecan priests and three lay brothers set forth with an escort of twenty-five mounted soldiers (as well as the usual entourage of baggage handlers, herdsmen, cattle, goats, and sheep) to establish missions in east Texas. Captain Domingo Ramón commanded the entrada, with none other than Louis Juchereau de Saint Denis, now in the employ of New Spain, serving as guide and second in command at pay equal to that of Ramón. Among the friars was a white-haired Francisco Hidalgo, who had lobbied for such an expedition for nearly a quarter century. Unfortunately, Fray Antonio Margil de Jesús was ill at the time—some thought he was dying, and he was given the last sacraments—and could not join the entrada.

On 5 May the party stopped between the Río Grande and the San Antonio River to celebrate the marriage of a soldier, Lorenzo Mercado, and a Texas-born mestiza, Ana Guerra, under the protection of Captain Ramón's family: the first such marriage in Texas and a good omen for the future peopling of Spanish Texas. On 23 May the expedition crossed the Colorado River just below the present-day city of Austin. Four days later, the first buffalo was downed, its meat enjoyed the following day in a creekside barbecue. On 18 June, after encountering other friendly Indians en route, four Tejas buffalo hunters and two Tejas women traveling with them greeted the Spaniards.

The party camped near the Trinity River on 24 June while Saint Denis, who spoke some Tejas, and Ramón's son went out ahead to make contact with the main Tejas settlement. On 26 June Saint Denis brought into camp more than twenty-five Tejas chiefs and leaders, for whom the soldiers dismounted and stood at attention in single file. At the head of an entourage of Franciscans holding crucifixes and an image of Our Lady of Guadalupe, Ramón greeted the Indian delegation after they had filed past the military honor guard. Seated on blankets Ramón had set out, Tejas and Spaniards smoked and passed pipes of peace. The Tejas presented Ramón with a gift of tobacco. He, in turn, gave some of it back to them as a gift and, a young bull having previously been slaughtered, invited the Tejas to a feast.

On a second visit two days later, a Te Deum was sung, and a group of Tejas women set out a feast of corn, watermelons, tamales, and cooked beans for the Spanish and Tejas leadership. Ramón then distributed one hundred *varas* (about a hundred yards) of flannel cloth, along with blankets, hats, and tobacco, to his guests. William Penn and his Quakers could not have managed it better. As a matter of geography, time, attitude, and behavior, these days of visiting, eating, and gift giving were a long way from Ácoma.[4]

July 1716 found the Spaniards camped on the site chosen for the first of four missions. Time was spent scouting a site for a presidio, commissioning a local Tejas leadership, and breaking down the mission supplies into four components, one for each mission. On Sunday, 5 July, Fray Isidro Espinosa, president of the Querétaran contingent, formally installed Fray Francisco Hidalgo as minister of the newly reestablished San Francisco de los Tejas amid the usual ceremonies and military salutes. On 7 July similar exercises were held on behalf of Fray Gabriel Vergara, minister of the second mission, La Purísima Concepción, which lay nine leagues northeast of Mission San Francisco de los Tejas at a site near the Angelina River and the main village of the Hainai—a location, Captain Ramón later noted, watered by two brooks and already teeming with crops.

Next came the dedication on 9 July of the Zacatecan establishment, Nuestra Señora de Guadalupe, the easternmost of the four, nine leagues southeast of La Purísima Concepción, on the site of the present-day city of Nacogdoches. Captain Ramón presented this mission to no less than the president of the Zacatecan college himself, Fray Antonio Margil de Jesús, who had recovered from illness and with his usual celerity caught up with the expedition. Margil, in turn, the next day installed Zacatecans Fray Matías Sáenz de San Antonio, Frey Pedro de Santa María y Mendoza, and Fray Agustín Patrón as ministers at Nuestra Señora de Guadalupe.

Captain Ramón, meanwhile, having left on 9 July, was en route to the site of the fourth foundation, Mission San José de los Nazones, to which Fray Espinosa, the president of Querétaro, was also heading by alternative route in the company of Saint Denis, taking time to acquaint himself under the Frenchman's guidance with the people of the region. The date for the formal establishment of Mission San José de los Nazones is not clearly established, but it was most likely on 11 July 1716 that Fray Benito Sánchez, a Querétaran, was installed as minister of the fourth mission, set on a creek in an arroyo near the northern boundary of present-day Nacogdoches County. Having established four missions and pledged and installed a number of local Indian governments; having noted in his journal the three hundred Masses celebrated since the entrada began, the thirty-plus sermons preached, the ten or more large crosses planted on the trail, the feast days and days of obligation observed with special ceremonies, Captain Ramón returned to La Purísima Concepción, which he had chosen as temporary headquarters for the newly reestablished Spanish Texas, in a mood he describes as *gustoso* (exultant), about a job well done.

Continuing challenges

All was well in the newly reestablished Spanish Catholic province of Texas, Ramón and the Franciscans reported on 22 July 1716 to Viceroy Baltasar de Zúñiga, the Duke of Arión and Marquis of Valero, yet the situation remained challenging. How long, Ramón asked, could nine Franciscans in four missions protected by two dozen soldiers be expected to hold such a vast region so far (300 leagues, or 780 miles) from the nearest outpost of New Spain? Yes, the thousands of Indians surrounding them were now friendly, especially the respected Tejas, who might serve as a link to further alliances. Yet the enterprising French, accustomed to entering Texas from Louisiana via the trail that passed directly through La Purísima Concepción, might turn those Indians hostile, not to mention the already hostile Apaches, Younes, Chanes, and other tribes to the north. Saint Denis had informed Ramón that on a recent trek northeast he had noticed French guns, knives, hatchets, and assorted cloth and clothing among the Indians of the region.

The Franciscans, as might be expected, were more optimistic—not to mention cunning—in their assessment of the situation. Texas had every possibility, they argued, of becoming the Nuevas Filipinas that was first envisioned. By this comparison, the Franciscans meant the gold and silver mines that were rumored to be in Texas as well as the rich harvest of converts the Philippines had provided. But the Philippine comparison also implied more missions and missionaries and the funds to support them and to provide the indigenous peoples of the east Texas frontier with suitable gifts. Ramón agreed, and he used a colonial comparison as well. If the Texas enterprise were properly staffed and supported, he concluded, the Crown would someday enjoy a second New Spain in its possession.[5]

On 23 July 1716, a mere day after these reports were dated and signed for delivery to Mexico City, a report reached Ramón that four Frenchmen had established a camp among the Natchitoches. Without waiting for a reply from Mexico City, much less authorization and staffing (which could take years), Ramón, Fray Margil, and a few other Zacatecans set out to determine for themselves what was happening. Sure enough, crossing into Louisiana, they found two Frenchmen living among the Natchitoches in a well-built log cabin and stockade on a small island in the center of a river. Ten more Frenchmen, the intruders told the Spaniards, were expected to arrive soon. The French, in brief, were reinforcing their own western Louisiana frontier, albeit in disputed territory.

Making the best of the situation, Fray Margil and the Zacatecans insisted that the French raise a large cross on the property, which established it as a hospice or branch mission, however informally, of La Purísima Concepción. On their return, but still in Louisiana, the Spaniards stopped among the Ades people, some nine leagues away from the Natchitoches. Receiving a friendly reception, as well as a request for a mission, Ramón appointed the lead Ades chief as regional governor and, with all due solemnity and paperwork, presented Margil and the Zacatecans title and responsibility for Mission San Miguel de Linares, located on the banks of an arroyo a league from a lake, the site of present-day Robeline. Crossing into Texas, at a site halfway between the first four established missions and the just-founded San Miguel de Linares, Ramón and Margil spent time among another tribe, the Ais, who received them well. The Spaniards went through the by-now repetitive process: establishment of a local government, selection of a site, paperwork, and dedication of a third Zacatecan foundation. Fray Margil, liking its central location, chose Mission Dolores de los Ais as his headquarters.

Aguayo to the rescue

Founded on the banks of the San Antonio River in south-central Texas in late April 1718, Mission San Antonio de Valero and the civilian settlement of San Fernando de Béxar anchored the second cluster of missions to be established in the aftermath of the east Texas foundations. In late February 1720 Fray Margil founded Mission San José y San Miguel de Aguayo, named in honor of Saint Joseph, Saint Michael the Archangel, and the governor of Texas. Initially located seven and a half miles from San Antonio de Valero, this second mission was established as a full-service agricultural community with assigned land, water, and timber rights, as well as an authorized Indian government fully distinct from that of San Antonio de Valero. Two years later, in early 1722, the governor himself, José de Azlor y Virto de Vera, the Marquis of San Miguel de Aguayo, was on hand to found a third mission in the San Antonio group. Created by Aguayo at the insistence of Chief Juan Rodríguez, the convert Indian who had taken a Spanish name and guided the Spaniards into east Texas in 1716, San Francisco Xavier de Nájera lay on a plain one league south of San Antonio de Valero, into which the small (fifty-five families) community was later absorbed.

As governor and captain general of Coahuila and the province of Texas, since October 1719, however, Aguayo had more on his mind than repaying Rodríguez for his services. Propelled by background, temperament, and enlightened self-interest, this formidable figure was to devote his talents, fortune, and considerable energies for more than a decade to the recovery and civil settlement of the Borderland province under his jurisdiction.

A recent (1712) arrival to New Spain, Aguayo had distinguished himself as a soldier in Spain and Navarre and on the Coahuila frontier before his appointment as governor and captain general. Aguayo was an impeccably connected aristocrat; his wife was a direct descendant of a conquistador. The couple's estate, Hacienda de Patos, comprised nearly half the province of Coahuila. Given the realities of status, power, and wealth in New Spain, Aguayo was ideally suited for his assignment, which consisted of nothing less than the refounding of Spanish Texas. By 1718 war had broken out between Spain and a Quadruple Alliance (the Holy Roman Empire, France, England, and Holland) over Spanish claims to the French throne, Spanish designs on (and invasion of) Italy, and Spanish support of a Stuart restoration in Great Britain. All this was under the direction of the Spanish prime minister, the Italian-born Cardinal Giulio Alberoni, whose career had been advanced by King Philip V's second wife and queen, Princess Elizabeth Farnese of the Duchy of Parma.

In 1719, as a result of this war provoked by Spain, the French began to advance into eastern Texas, driving the Spanish Franciscans from their missions. Some of these missions were already in crisis. Supplies failed to reach Nuestra Señora de Guadalupe in 1717. Torrential rains destroyed crops, forcing the Indians to leave the mission in search of food and the Franciscans to submit to a steady diet of barbecued crow. In the summer of 1719 the friars of east Texas abandoned their missions to the invading French and sought refuge in San Antonio, where the Zacatecans built a temporary friary before Fray Margil—over the vehement objections of Fray Olivares, the minister of the Querétaran Mission San Antonio—built the nearby Zacatecan Mission San José y San Miguel.

Aside from this invasion of east Texas, Spaniards were equally concerned regarding French intentions to establish a port on the Gulf of Mexico, from which they could control the Texas coast. In response to this threat, in late February and early March 1721 Aguayo brought to San Antonio five hundred soldiers, many with their families, who intended to stay on as military or civilian settlers. Early in 1720 Fray Espinosa had convinced the viceroy in Mexico City that the well-being and success of the Texas missions depended on settlers with families—and soldiers with families as well, who would be committed to the progress of the province and not be inclined to exploit Indian women sexually. In addition to the stabilizing influence of families, Aguayo had further stabilized his soldiers by having two of them shot for desertion on the main plaza of the staging settlement of Monclova in Coahuila en route to Texas.

Organized into eight companies of mounted infantry, each flying a different religious banner, Aguayo's column of soldiers escorted six hundred carts of supplies and large herds of horses, cattle, sheep, and mules, guided by the requisite number of drovers and herdsmen. As impressive as Aguayo's battalion was, however, a full-scale military operation ended up not being necessary; with the successful negotiation of a peace treaty in Europe by the spring of 1721, armed resistance from the French was no longer expected. Aguayo's goal now became to reestablish the mission system in east Texas, strengthen the presidios in that region, and secure a mission and presidio on the gulf.

On 4 April 1721 the main body of Spanish soldiers reached San Antonio, the same day that the previously dispatched Captain Domingo Ramón, commander of the expedition into east Texas in 1716, successfully occupied the Bay of Espíritu Santo on the gulf. Throughout the next year, April 1721 to April 1722, Aguayo reinstalled the appropriate Franciscans in the missions established in east Texas during 1716 and 1717, negotiated new governments with local Indians, and regularized matters with the French who lived in the region. The latter involved dealing with Louis Juchereau de Saint Denis, now back in the service of France, regarding a very reluctant French withdrawal from their frontier settlement of Los Adaes in the vicinity of Mission San Miguel de Linares on the Louisiana side of the border, where Aguayo established a presidio. Although he was ill at the time and required a week in bed to recover, the governor was on hand on 10 April 1722 to install Fray Agustín Patrón, a Zacatecan, as minister to the newly established Mission Nuestra Señora del Espíritu Santo de Zúñiga on the lower San Antonio River. The ceremony was attended by Cocoma, Cujame, and Karankawa chiefs and people, with the chief of the Cocoma installed as governor of the nearby pueblo. All this took place under the protection of ninety soldiers commanded by Captain Ramón at the strategically located coastal Presidio of Nuestra Señora de Loreto at La Bahía.

As of late 1722 Governor Aguayo could take satisfaction in what he had accomplished. He had recovered the missions of east Texas; established two strategically placed presidios; moved the San Antonio presidio to a better site and reinforced its garrison; founded two missions at San Antonio; and brought a number of new settlers into the province. Now in bad health, Aguayo submitted his resignation to the viceroy and was replaced by Fernando Pérez de Almazán, whom Aguayo had nominated. Boldly, Almazán chose to move the capital of Texas to Los Adaes, where, with the large presidio garrison erected by Aguayo, he established a military frontier.

Canary Islanders

Regardless of what Aguayo had accomplished in Texas, he remained dissatisfied with the paucity of civilian settlement at San Fernando de Béxar and elsewhere throughout the province. Missions and presidios alone could not hold Texas for Spain. The region needed a flourishing civil population. In the spring of 1719, the Council of the Indies in Seville was wrestling with this problem, and on 27 March the council made a formal request to the king that His Majesty's government recruit up to two thousand families from the kingdom of Galicia and the Canary Islands for settlement on the Bay of Espíritu Santo as a buffer against the French. At first, nothing came of this bold proposal. Upon his return from Texas, however, Aguayo wrote the viceroy and king to the same effect, though he reduced his request to an initial recruitment of two hundred families. Aguayo recommended that civilian settlements also be founded at Los Adaes on the eastern frontier, at San Fernando de Béxar, and at some point between these two settlements. Of significance to the racial composition of such civil settlements, Aguayo additionally argued that two hundred families of Hispanicized Tlaxcaltecan Indians be recruited for Texas settlement to assist in the conversion and Hispanicization of the Texas tribes as tutors and exemplars. On 18 March 1723 the Crown reacted favorably to Aguayo's proposal. The Canary Islanders were experienced colonists. Already, the intendant of the islands was reporting, twenty-five families, weary of their hardscrabble life as farmers, were in the process of relocating to Puerto Rico, where they hoped to better their lot.

Yet ships between the Canary Islands and New Spain were few and far between. Following the immediate rejection of two thousand families as an unrealistic request, there remained some confusion about the number of families to be recruited: two hundred, as cited by the king, or four hundred, as cited by the Council of the Indies. Time passed as communications wended their leisurely way among the Crown, the council, the intendant of the Canary Islands, the viceroy, and those responsible for getting the colonists to Veracruz for overland travel to Texas. Melancholy and indolent, King Philip V worked slowly, when he worked at all. In 1724, in fact, he abdicated in order to pursue a life of religious contemplation but returned to the throne a year later at the death of his son and heir, Louis I, whom some believed had stood a chance of succeeding to the throne of France as well as that of Spain. Back in Texas, the new governor of the province, Brigadier General Pedro de

Rivera—who disliked Aguayo (perhaps out of jealousy)—lost no opportunity to oppose Aguayo's civilian option in favor of what he argued was a more effective and much less expensive program of a strengthened military occupation augmented over time by internal migration from New Spain.

In any event, not until 19 June 1730, after seven years of planning and negotiation, did a mere fifteen families of fifty-nine settlers arrive in Veracruz, where they rested for nearly two months before setting forth in early August on the long journey to San Fernando de Béxar. Governor Rivera, meanwhile, had persuaded the viceroy to write to the king—that same month the families departed Veracruz—to end the enfeebled Canary Island program. Thus, instead of the two thousand European colonists first proposed by Aguayo, fewer than sixty (fifty-five, by one estimate) Spanish men, women, and children were on hand as of March 1731 to populate the newly established civilian settlement of the Villa San Fernando de Béxar at San Antonio. The diminished count was a true setback for the development of Texas as a Spanish Catholic colony, given what might have been accomplished by two hundred European settlers, in association with an equal number of Hispanicized Indians, in three or four strategic locations.

Still, in terms of the social and ecclesiastical culture of Texas, a beachhead had been established by the two hundred or so civilians living in the vicinity since 1718 and the newly arriving isleños (islanders). Perhaps most important was the notion—the idea and the ideal—of a stabilizing civilian population with its own civilian elite. The viceroy of New Spain, Juan de Acuña y Bejarano, the Marquis of Casa Fuerte, had earlier conferred hidalgo status on the first Canary Island families and their descendants to arrive at the Villa San Fernando de Béxar; he had also authorized the establishment of an autonomous government for the civilian settlement. In short, the Villa San Fernando de Béxar and its leading families had full standing in the imperial scheme of things. The formal granting of hidalgo status represented a rare exception in the Borderlands and set up a provincial squirearchy that, had Aguayo's ambitious migration program been continued, would have further stabilized Texas as a colony.

Diocesan expectations

Concurrent with the mission program for the Indians, a diocesan culture might have developed more rapidly than among the missions, where progress toward a parish structure and diocesan clergy was proving slow, as testified to (among other symptoms) by the restless relocation of many mission sites. It would take a long time for a full-fledged Catholic culture to reach a point throughout the mission system at which mission lands would be distributed to a Hispanicized Indian population and the missions converted to parish churches staffed by diocesan clergy, as had happened in the more developed portions of the Indies. As part of the Diocese of Guadalajara, Texas had an effective bishop, the Right Reverend Fray Francisco de San Buenaventura y Tejada (now considered one of the great bishops of Mexican history). The Spanish-born reform Franciscan was formerly the auxiliary bishop of Havana, residing in Saint Augustine, Florida, from 1735 to 1745, and hence the first bishop to take up a permanent post in the Borderlands. As such had the demand proved pressing, Tejada might be fully expected to meet the needs of a developing lay Catholic population in Texas with parish and parish clergy, no matter how reluctantly his fellow Franciscans might relinquish their hold on the province. As it was, in November 1759 Tejada would pay one visit to Villa San Fernando de Béxar, where he functioned with his usual efficiency.

Nevertheless, despite its small civilian population, a lay-centered parish culture did develop at Villa San Fernando de Béxar. Upon the arrival of the Canary Islanders, a military barrack was converted into a chapel, and Bachelor José de la Garza was appointed parish priest. Although raising the necessary capital took a number of years, a subscription fund—to which King Philip V, the viceroy, the governor, the second parish priest, Juan Recio de León, and the congregation contributed— yielded sufficient money for the laying of a cornerstone for a permanent church on 11 May 1738. An architecturally ambitious structure of solid rock, designed as a Latin cross with transepts, dome, sacristy, and baptistery, the Church of San Fernando took eleven years to complete; yet the very fact of its construction represented a gesture toward the future. Located on Military Plaza across from the Governor's Palace (1749), the Church of San Fernando survived to be incorporated in 1873 into the Cathedral of San Fernando of the Diocese of San Antonio created by Rome the following year.

Still, nothing is perfect. Even as the Church of San Fernando was being financed, planned, and at long last constructed (the first contractor reneged on the contract), quarrels broke out between the Canary Island settlers, their parish priest, and the local Franciscans. In one contretemps, the settlers sided with the Franciscans against their parish priest, Bachelor Juan Recio de León, whom they accused of neglecting his duties and responsibilities, requesting that a Franciscan be assigned to the Church of San Fernando to see to their needs during the Lenten and Easter seasons of 1741. When a delegation of Canary Islanders called on León to discuss this alleged neglect, the affronted parish priest flew into a rage, threw the delegation out of his rectory, and called to his houseman, "Bring me my guns! Bring me my guns!" While León sulked in hostile alienation, the Canary Islanders brought in a Franciscan to finish out the Lenten and Easter seasons as they searched for a successor to their hot-tempered pastor.[6]

An earlier flare-up pitted the settlers against the friars. In 1731 three eastern missions—San Francisco de la Espada, La Purísima Concepción, and San Juan Capistrano—were relocated to the San Antonio region as part of an expansion and upgrading of the San Antonio network. The Canary Islanders wanted free access to this newly enlarged Indian labor pool. The governor approved, but the Franciscans resisted, and the matter went to the viceroy, who decided in favor of the Franciscans. Accusations by the settlers that the friars were dealing in unfair trade (profiting from the sale of agricultural goods produced by free Indian labor) were eventually proven to be false, but they created a rift between the Franciscans and the settlers that was slow to heal.

Despite these disputes, a regular parish life—and, by implication, a civil society— had been established, and a succession of diocesan parish priests served the Church of San Fernando. In 1839 its rector, Refugio de la Garza, was said to be the last living Roman Catholic priest in Texas.

In the course of his November 1759 visit to San Antonio de Béxar, however, Bishop Tejada was not pleased with the state of affairs he and his secretary, Doctor

Matías Juan de Arteaga, observed at the Church of San Fernando: no tabernacle for the reservation of the Blessed Sacrament, a lack of liturgical vessels and portraits of saints, holy oils not under lock and key, no door or window in the baptistery, a general atmosphere of neglect—and this in a parish church that served 582 parishioners! Tejada kept his counsel in the matter, since he had other business at hand—644 confirmations, as well as visits to missions San Antonio de Valero and La Purísima Concepción, where he noted his approval of Franciscan management in the mission registries—but, back in Guadalajara at the next regularly scheduled clergy conference, the resignation of the San Fernando incumbent, Juan Inigo Cardenas, was accepted and a more energetic parish priest, Bachelor Casimir López de Lara (who could preach in one or two Mexican Indian languages as well as Spanish), was appointed.

Bishop Tejada insisted that the Hispanicized Indians of San Antonio enjoy a full-service ministry alongside their Spanish counterparts. Tejada also mandated that Spanish settlers in greater San Antonio attend services not at the local missions (five had been founded in the area since 1731) but at the diocesan parish of San Fernando, which he instructed to establish a school and regularly scheduled catechetical instruction of children by the parish priest. Tejada was by no means anti-Franciscan. He had spent the better part of his priestly life as a Franciscan friar. He was, however, eager to introduce greater San Antonio's Spanish population of three thousand or so—settlers, soldiers, rancheros, and their families—to the diocesan culture that would, in time (if everything worked out), replace the mission system with canonically established parishes and diocesan priests. In fact, secular priests were already ministering at all the presidios but one (Los Adaes in Louisiana, which Franciscans served) and at the civilian settlements at La Bahía and Nacogdoches.

Midcentury expansion

Meanwhile, between 1740 and 1762, the mission system was being expanded into four new regional clusters. As historian Herbert Eugene Bolton underscored in his pivotal 1917 essay, "The Mission as a Frontier Institution in the Spanish-American Colonies", missions functioned simultaneously as evangelical institutions aimed at conversion, educational institutions aimed at Hispanicization, agencies of agricultural and industrial development, and agents of imperial expansion. Hence the mission functioned as an agent of frontier advancement with a built-in mechanism, secularization, to put itself into a new mode once its mission (as its very name indicated) was complete. Franciscans felt the paradox at the heart of the mission system, as evident in their frequent quarrels with the soldiers and military officials they depended upon for their safety and, in many cases, with the governor and captain general of the province or territory in which they were laboring. Nevertheless, however much they might find themselves at odds with the military and civilians, the Franciscans did function as salaried agents of the Crown committed to imperial expansion on the frontier. How else could Texas be held save by missions and presidios while a more developed society was in the making? That, at least, was the theory, and thus the mid-eighteenth-century Texas mission system expanded.

Each expansion between 1746 and 1762—with the exception of the foundation of Nuestra Señora de la Luz (1756) among the Orcoquiza Indians on the lower Trinity

River—as well as the last mission established in 1793, was added to a region already served by a mission, in an effort to maximize the Franciscan presence and hence further consolidate a frontier region. Espíritu Santo (1722), first established by the Zacatecans on the site of the French Fort Saint Louis on the gulf coast, was moved farther inland in 1726 and in 1749 moved again farther south to a location on the San Antonio River. In 1754 the Zacatecans established Nuestra Señora del Rosario near the present-day city of Goliad as the second of a lower Guadalupe and lower San Antonio grouping. Rosario was augmented by the Zacatecans in 1793 with the founding of Nuestra Señora del Refugio at the junction of the two rivers. The briefly existing Xavier grouping began with the founding in 1746 of the Querétaran Nuestra Señora de los Dolores del Río de San Xavier on the San Gabriel River (then called the San Xavier) nine miles north of present-day Rockdale in Milam County, central Texas. To this Querétaran cluster were added two more San Xavier River establishments, San Ildefonso (1749) and Nuestra Señora de la Candelaria (1749). In 1756, in an attempt to evangelize the Orcoquiza Indians, the Zacatecans established Nuestra Señora de la Luz on the lower Trinity River. An ill-fated entrance into Apache country on the San Sabá River in present-day Menard County, southwest Texas, was attempted jointly by the Querétarans and the Franciscans from the College of San Fernando in Mexico City with the founding of Santa Cruz de San Sabá (1757), San Lorenzo (1762), and Nuestra Señora de la Candelaria (1762).

Lest any of this give a false impression of triumphant expansion, it must be noted that, with the exception of the San Antonio group, many of these missions disappeared without a trace until Borderlands historian Herbert Eugene Bolton identified their sites in the early twentieth century. Some Texas missions, in fact, lasted only a few years before they were abandoned. The Franciscan effort in New Mexico, by contrast, left behind restorable structures. In Arizona and the Californias, Franciscans founded missions that are still in use as parish churches. As in Florida and Georgia, many mission structures in Texas have disappeared. Only the San Antonio group—San Antonio de Valero (the Alamo), San José y Miguel de Aguayo, La Purísima Concepción, San Juan Capistrano, San Francisco de la Espada, and the Church of San Antonio de Béxar—left behind either usable or restorable structures; an irrigation system still functions at San Francisco de la Espada. Set among promising but ultimately resistant tribes, the remaining frontier missions survive as notations on scholarly maps or, at best, archaeological sites under exploration or manuscripts in archives that offer case studies in continental ambitions destined to reach fruition under different flags.

With the exception of San Antonio de Valero, conversion rates, as judged by registered baptisms, remained low. Despite the welcomes the Franciscans had initially received, conversion rates at the three interior missions—San Francisco, La Purísima Concepcion, and San José—were so disappointing, and protecting the friars proved so difficult, that after ten years the three missions were moved to the San Antonio group in 1731 under the new name of San José y Miguel. The three missions on the San Xavier River were plagued by continuing hostility between the military and the friars over soldiers' sexual abuse of Indian women and related issues. Bad blood culminated on the night of 11 May 1752 when four soldiers and an apostate Indian named Andrés came to Mission Candelaria to arrest the soldier José Ceballos, who had taken refuge in the mission after presidio captain Felipe de

Rábago had appropriated his wife, for which—along with other charges involving dissolute behavior—the friars had upbraided Rábago. At the mission, Andrés shot and killed Fray Ganzábal with a bow and arrow and would have murdered a second friar had the Franciscan not dropped to the floor when wind through an open door extinguished all candles and the room went dark. When Rábago blamed the local Indians for the assassination, they fled the missions in fear of reprisals, and all but one of the Franciscans, fearing further murders by Rábago or an Indian uprising, likewise fled, in their case to San Antonio de Valero.

Rábago, meanwhile, still in authority (and ultimately cleared of any guilt by a viceregal court), continued to argue for the relocation of the few San Xavier neophytes to flourishing Mission San Antonio de Valero and the removal of the San Xavier missions to Apache country on the San Sabá and Concho Rivers, where they would be more strategically situated. Reluctantly, the friars agreed. The friars' repeated requests for permission to close down the system and move elsewhere went unanswered, and in the summer of 1755, not waiting for permission from the governor or the viceroy, the Querétarans—after ten years of struggle—terminated their San Xavier operation. Nor did the three jointly sponsored Querétaran-Franciscan missions on the San Sabá River do well evangelistically among their Apache and Comanche clientele.

Martyrdom remained a possibility for missionaries in the Borderlands, Spanish or French. In 1689 Karankawa Indians slaughtered three priests—the Abbé Chefdeville, a French Sulpician, and Flemish Franciscans Zénobe Membré and Maxim Le Clercq—as well as the surviving garrison of Fort Saint Louis. In 1749 Fray Francisco Xavier Silva, a Zacatecan, met his end along with eight soldiers at the hands of Natages as the Spaniards were journeying from San Antonio de Valero to San Juan Bautista on the Mexican side of the Río Grande. On 16 March 1758, at Mission Santa Cruz de San Sabá, two Franciscans, Alonso Giraldo de Terreros and José Santiesteban, lost their lives to a war party of Comanches and their allies. Terreros was shot to death while parleying at the gate; Santiesteban was beheaded in the mission church while praying before the altar. Eight soldiers were killed in the same assault, and a third friar, Miguel Molina, was seriously wounded. The mission was destroyed. Five years later, after sixty years in the field, the Querétarans withdrew from Texas entirely.

The Zacatecan missions were not faring much better, plagued as they were by tribes who refused to surrender their migratory lifestyle; by tribes breaking into open hostility (hostile tribes forced the closing of Mission Guadalupe at Nacogdoches in 1773); by low conversion rates, even in peaceful circumstances; and by quarrels with local presidios regarding misbehaving soldiers. Nuestra Señora del Rosario de los Cujanes (1754), for example, recorded a mere twenty-one baptisms—and only one baptized Indian in residence!—at the end of its first four years.

The Texas frontier changed dramatically after 1763. As a result of the Treaty of Paris, which ended the French and Indian Wars (1689–1763)—localized in North America as King William's War (1689–1697), Queen Anne's War (1702–1713), King George's War (1744–1748), and the eponymous French and Indian War (1754–1763)—Great Britain acquired French North America, and Spain lost Florida to Great Britain. One year before the Treaty of Paris, however, in the Treaty of Fontainebleau (1762), France secretly ceded Louisiana west of the Mississippi and the Isle of New Orleans to Spain, lest all Louisiana be acquired by Great Britain. Because of this Louisiana Cession, as it was called, New Spain no longer had to consider its eastern Texas frontier a buffer against French advancement. That frontier had now moved farther east, to the British province of East Florida. Still, the Borderlands of New Spain had not lost their vulnerability. Texas now stood fronted to the east-northeast by a triumphant Great Britain and to the north-northwest by hostile Comanches and Apaches. Texas remained a buffer province, only now its line of defense extended around a 350-degree perimeter that included Apache land to its west and, on its southern border, the gulf coast.

Presidios and civilian settlements now became increasingly important; missions became less so, especially since by the 1760s the Franciscans' failure to produce a stabilizing population of Hispanicized Indians had become apparent. Within the decade, the attention of the Franciscans would be focusing on replacing the expelled Jesuits in the missions of southern Arizona, evangelizing Upper California, and continuing to preach the gospel in the northern provinces of Mexico.

Securing New Orleans

In the first phase of reorganization and reconsolidation following the Treaty of Paris, King Carlos III and his ministers in Spain and New Spain debated whether they wanted to accept and govern Louisiana west of the Mississippi. Stretched to the limit by Texas, they reasoned, how could New Spain hope to govern such a vast new territory? Through inheritance from his mother, the Bourbon King Carlos III, the younger son of Philip V, had sat on the throne of Naples before ascending to the throne of Spain in 1759 upon the death of his older brother, Ferdinand V. When Carlos was king of Naples an English fleet had threatened to bombard the city of Naples in 1738 and thereby gained control of the kingdom. Could not the English, he reasoned, now based in the provinces of East and West Florida, move against Louisiana by land and sea? They could seize New Orleans as they had captured Naples when he reigned there or taken Havana in the recent war, or they could pour across the frontier by land, as they did from Carolina into Florida in the early 1700s.

As these and other points were being debated, the French settlers of New Orleans broke into open revolt in October 1768, forcing the Spanish governor and his wife to flee the city. Learning of this rebellion, Carlos III convened a junta of his senior advisors, who met and considered their options from January to March 1769. The result: a decision to mount an extraordinary display of military force— four thousand troops and fifty heavy cannons under the command of the seasoned Spanish soldier of Irish descent, Lieutenant General Alexander O'Reilly—instructed to sail for Cuba, then proceed from Havana to New Orleans (twenty-eight transports were required to move so many troops and so much artillery) and reestablish Spanish authority in New Orleans and, by extension, Louisiana.

Once anchored off New Orleans, O'Reilly received a delegation of French rebels with disarming courtesy. On 18 August 1769, however, the Spanish force landed with a dazzling display of military pomp. Six days later, O'Reilly rounded up the ringleaders of the revolt. Following a scrupulously enacted trial, six ringleaders were given lengthy prison sentences and had their property confiscated. Five more important ringleaders were sentenced to be hanged and left as corpses on the gallows as an example. No hangman could be found in the city, however, and so the leaders were executed by Spanish firing squads.

A reorganized perimeter

Step one—the decision to regain New Orleans and thereby hold western Louisiana—had been made. Now came step two: reorganization of the military defense of the Borderlands. On 7 August 1765 Carlos III wrote the marqués de Cruillas, viceroy of New Spain, that he was sending the marqués de Rubí, field marshal of the army, to New Spain. Rubí's assignment was to inspect every presidio in the Borderlands from California to Texas and then write a detailed report, including recommendations for the future protection of the frontier. Rubí made this tour of inspection in the company of his able assistant, Nicolás de Lafora, captain of engineers. The tour itself—twenty-three months, 7,600 miles, its maps drawn and daily events chronicled with precision and literary skill by Lafora—constitutes an epic gathering of military and topographical intelligence unprecedented in the history of New Spain and thoroughly in the spirit of Enlightenment values and reform being so deliberately fostered by Carlos III.

Returning to Mexico City on 23 February 1768, Lafora reviewed his maps and engineering reports, and Rubí dictated his recommendations. Although the men differed vastly in rank, their documents must be studied in tandem, for Lafora's eagle eye for detail reinforced Rubí's more sober official assessments. There were two Borderlands, Rubí and Lafora argued: the one claimed and imagined, and the other actually held. The one held was nominally secured by military garrisons in twenty-four presidios. Yet these presidios were ill chosen, their sites too often dictated by missions or other considerations, rather than by military logic and necessity. (A number of near-empty missions in Texas, the men noted, were still protected by presidios.) Many of these presidios, moreover, were poorly staffed and equipped. At Los Adaes, for example, on the far Texas frontier reaching into Louisiana, only twenty-five of the sixty-one soldiers were fit for service. When these men were lined up for inspection, Rubí was appalled. No one wore a complete uniform; numerous soldiers lacked shirts, hats, and shoes. Only two rifles were found to be serviceable, and a mere seven men possessed swords capable of passing inspection. Presidio families likewise lived in horrid poverty. Many, in fact, would not show themselves, they were so ashamed of their wretchedness.

The field marshal called for an overhaul of the entire system. Reduce the number of presidios to fifteen on line and two in support, he urged. Site them at strategic points along the thirtieth parallel from the Gulf of California to the mouth of the Guadalupe River in Texas at intervals of forty leagues (one hundred miles). In Texas, align them on a roadway linking San Fernando de Béxar with Santa Fe, crossed by a north–south roadway connecting Béxar with the presidio of La Bahía, which should be moved closer to the gulf. Recruit younger soldiers for defined periods of enlistment, followed by retirement and a land grant. Pay and supply them well. Eliminate corruption in the supply system.

If he could, Rubí admitted, he would move the San Antonio mission and civilian settlement back to the Mexican side of the Río Grande in an effort to tighten the Spanish line of defense; but the Crown had a half century of investment in these two settlements. The eastern frontier, however, was another matter. Its three settlements—the mission and settlement of Los Adaes, the mission at Nacogdoches, and the presidio at Orcoquisac—were separated from San Antonio by vast, empty, and indefensible distances. The missions of Los Adaes and Nacogdoches were forlorn places, staffed by a few Franciscans praying for Indian converts who never came. Orcoquisac was equally isolated and desolate. Here thirty-one forgotten soldiers and their families lived in abject poverty, forced to live off the wilderness for months at a time when supplies failed to arrive. Close these three useless outposts, Rubí concluded, and the king would save wasted money and lose nothing by way of protection or validated ownership.

The civilian equation

From an economic and military perspective, Rubí's recommendations made sense. Enacted by their acceptance and issuance as the Reglamento of 1772, they more or less guided future policy. Rubí, however, cannot be accused of an overfondness for civilian settlement. As noted, he would have argued for withdrawing Béxar back to the Mexican side of the Río Grande. From the point of view of the field marshal, moreover, the mission system itself—with the exception of the San Antonio missions—was less than impressive in its results, an opinion the Querétaran Franciscans seemed to share in the letter of withdrawal from Texas submitted by Fray Mariano de los Dolores, the guardian of the College of La Santa Cruz de Querétaro, on 6 February 1769. In his letter, though, Fray Mariano placed the primary blame for the failure of the Querétaro missions on a slack civil administration and rapacious military.

Rubí, however, provided a valuable insight (obliquely stated) when he included the success of the Church of San Fernando serving Villa San Fernando de Béxar—by now two distinct settlements—as a compelling reason why the missions and two civilian settlements could not be moved to the south, no matter what viceregal economy and military logic might dictate. Together with the five San Antonio missions, the people of San Fernando and Béxar had successfully brought Catholic Christianity to Texas.

Catholic people! Spaniards from Mexico and the Canary Islands, as well as a few European-born. The caste system gave precedence to full-blooded *españoles* (Spaniards), but it consisted as well of upwardly mobile mestizos, *coyotes* (Indian-mestizo), *mulatos* (Spanish-African), *lobos* (Indian-African), Hispanicized Indians, and various combinations thereof, all of whom tended to register their offspring as simply *español* as they intermarried and rose in prosperity. Catholic people of Béxar! Whatever their bloodlines, all 860 of them as of 1770 now constituted a parish. To house their long-serving pastor Pedro Fuentes, the parish authorized and paid for a rectory that was most likely the only two-story house in town.

As read and inventoried by historian Jesús de la Teja, the parish registry of Béxar reveals the life passages of these Catholic people: births (legitimate and illegitimate baptized equally), funerals (so many children!), marriages (and remarriages, for the frequently widowed), along with the usual round of Sunday and holy day services, Christmas, Holy Week, Corpus Christi, local devotions to Our Lady of Guadalupe and the Immaculate Conception, Candelaria, the patronal feasts of San Antonio and San Fernando, Rogation Days praying for rain, harvest, festivals, and observances in honor of local or visiting notables. Here flourished the Catholic observances keyed to the daily rhythms of life that the Franciscan missionaries sought to bring to the Native American peoples of Texas. Here was the Church—the *ecclesia* (ingathering), as the Greeks of the first century termed it—the community of believers.

The Franciscan missions cannot be dismissed as failures, despite the fact that they were only able to Catholicize the San Antonio region. They constituted, after all, an effort in the direction of a reformed approach to evangelization and left behind no record of slaughters or scandalous misbehavior. Indeed, one among them, Fray Antonio Margil de Jesús, was eventually declared Venerable, and three were recognized by the Church as martyrs, which the Church considers a form of de facto sanctity.

All the while, the laypeople of Béxar and San Fernando and their succession of diocesan pastors and secular priests, along with the families of soldiers in the far-flung presidios and their secular priest chaplains—José de la Garza (1731–1734) at Villa San Fernando, followed by the irascible Juan Recio de León (1734–1743), Juan Francisco de Espronceda (1743–1746), and Francisco Manuel Polanco, who was appointed in 1746 and served until the long tenure of Pedro Fuentes into the 1770s—kept alive ordinary Catholic practice in Texas.

During these years a Hispanic Catholic city took form. San Antonio may have been a far cry from Guadalajara or Antigua, but it was a city nevertheless, laid down with the ideals proposed by the Laws of the Indies—a grid of streets; a plaza with church and civic buildings; irrigation ditches to creek and river cooperatively dug; houses constructed of wood, stone, and adobe, with thatched annexes in the rear for cooking purposes. As in medieval cities, gardens were everywhere, and spiraling out from these gardens and from the presidio settlements were agricultural fields and, extending even farther, ranches.

No collectable art form seems to have developed, yet the missions and parish church of the San Antonio region—assertions of Spanish colonial values on the far frontier—achieved an architectural class of their own. Their strength and permanency of materials, their orchestration of European baroque chastened by frontier austerity, embodied San Antonio as a Catholic place. These domes and arcades, these friary gardens and cross-topped bell towers, these façades and cloisters represented Mediterranean Catholic values translated to a new place for a new people with new bloodlines. Strongly Indian in their ambience, the missions of New Mexico reprised pueblos. The San Antonio missions, by contrast, echoed Mexico at its Spanish Colonial highpoint. In so doing, they maintained a connection to Spain. In the next century one of these structures, the Alamo, would offer a mise-en-scène for a turning point in the history of Texas, but for the time being, missions, chapels, and parish churches made their statement. Here was Spain and New Spain. Here was Mexico. Later, after falling partially to ruin, these beautiful structures would be lovingly rebuilt. Reconstructed between 1768 and 1782, Mission San José y San Miguel de Aguayo has achieved national landmark status. Its Rose Window—at least the sculpting and perhaps the design—is reputed to have been the work of Pedro Huízar. Listed as a *mulato* of partial African descent in the 1779 census (so Jesús de la Teja tells us), Huízar was noted as an *español* in the census of 1793 and elevated to Don Pedro in the census of 1798: upward mobility for a carpenter and stoneworker turned surveyor in his later years, having on the way achieved distinction as a religious artist.[7]

A refusal to leave

Don Pedro Huízar had also become a *tejano*, along with 3,980 other Spanish-speaking residents of Texas, according to the census of 1804. At the recommendation of the marqués de Rubí, the Crown might mandate the abandonment of the eastern frontier, but the settlers at Los Adaes—led by a native of that settlement, Antonio Gil Ibarbo—did not want to leave. Even when they were forcibly marched to Béxar, some stayed behind (including members of Ibarbo's family), burying their iron tools in a secret cache for their return. In Béxar and Mexico City, Ibarbo lobbied nearly two years before receiving permission from the new viceroy, Fray Antonio María Bucareli—a professed Knight of Malta, lieutenant general of the army, and former governor of Cuba—to establish a settlement, Pilar de Bucareli, on the Trinity River at the intersection of the San Antonio and La Bahía roads. When Pilar de Bucareli for various reasons (Comanches, trade restrictions, scarce supplies, and flooding) proved unsustainable, Ibarbo moved the settlement in January and February 1770 to Nacogdoches, which by 1804 constituted one of the three remaining civil settlements of Texas (along with San Antonio and La Bahía). In authorizing the Ibarbo community's return to eastern Texas, Viceroy Bucareli was helping to end the mission era. Early in 1792 Fray Manuel Silva, the commissary and prefect of the missionary college at Zacatecas, presented a memorial in Mexico City proposing that all but two of the San Antonio missions, including Mission San Antonio de Valero, be secularized: their lands distributed, that is, to the mission Indians—now thoroughly Christianized and Hispanicized, with many of them married into local families—and the missions turned over to the Diocese of Monterrey (established by Rome in 1777), thereafter to be staffed by secular priests as parish churches. Fray Silva also recommended that the mission at Nacogdoches be secularized, its two Franciscans reassigned to missionary work and a secular priest appointed to the civilian settlement. After a year and a half of deliberation in viceregal and Franciscan circles, Fray Silva's recommendation was accepted, decreed, and duly promulgated in San Antonio by Governor Manuel Muñoz to Fray José Francisco López, the president of the Zacatecan missions, who speedily enacted the process of inventory, divestment, and distribution.

The mission era was not exactly ending, but it was entering a period of transition. As the Zacatecans were terminating their missions in San Antonio, other Zacatecans were planning a new mission—their last in Texas—Nuestra Señora del Refugio, near Matagorda Bay, among the Karankawa, a nonevangelized and decidedly hostile tribe on the gulf coast. Not until 1830 would the mission system formally come to an end, with the secularization of both Espíritu Santo and Refugio. Fray José Antonio Díaz de León, the last Zacatecan Franciscan missionary at Refugio, was assigned to a parish ministry in Nacogdoches, where, despite his age and limited English, he accomplished much good work. On an evening of May 1833, in a ceremony held in a private parlor, Fray Díaz baptized a newcomer to Texas by the name of Sam Houston.

Yet the friar received death threats from newcomers hostile to Mexicans in general and Mexican Catholic priests in particular. Fray Díaz took such menaces seriously and drew up a last will and testament. A mere two days later, an hour or so before daybreak, the last Franciscan in Texas was shot to death under uncertain circumstances while on the trail in the company of an American.

7

Loreto 1767

The Society of Jesus gains and loses its Pacific domain

On the evening of 24 June 1767, Carlos Francisco de Croix, the Marquis of Croix and viceroy of Mexico, held in his hands a sealed packet from King Carlos III. The viceroy must have been alerted to the importance of the parcel and to the date and time he was to open it, for in the room with him was the archbishop of Mexico and other high officials, including José de Gálvez, a special representative of the king. Opening the sealed packet, the viceroy found a second sealed envelope with a dire warning attached to it: upon pain of death, do not open until the evening of 24 June 1767! The threat certainly must have gotten the attention of the marquis and the others in the room. One can only imagine the silence as a secretary, or perhaps the viceroy himself, opened the sealed envelope, unfolded its document, and held it to better light. All Jesuits in New Spain, the page read, were to be taken into custody that very evening and removed to the port of Veracruz for deportation to the Papal States.

As startling as this news was, it represented not an abrupt decision but rather an escalation of an anti-Jesuit campaign already under way. In 1759 Portugal had expelled the Society from the homeland and colonies. France outlawed the Society in 1764 but did not expel members from France or its colonies. Now it was Spain's turn, with an expulsion of the thirty-four hundred Jesuits in Spain and its dependencies in Europe, Africa, and the Indies, together with the confiscation of all properties. Not since the suppression of the Knights Templar in 1312 had a powerful religious order been put to such a sweeping and violent end, and for many of the same reasons. Like the Knights Templar, the Society of Jesus had become a rich and influential transnational organization centered on a single administration in Rome; the Jesuits also bore a special loyalty to the papacy at a time when the Enlightenment monarchs, ministers of state, and Church hierarchies of Spain, France, and Portugal were seeking more localized control. Touched by the Enlightenment in its love of science and its optimism regarding human prospects, the Society of Jesus seemed anti-Enlightenment to its Enlightenment-oriented critics in its commitment to the papacy and the concept of a universal Church. Its autonomy, meanwhile, disquieted many bishops and diocesan clergy, while its wealth, reputation, and alleged behind-the-scenes influence evoked envy in other religious orders. In the New World, this supposed capacity for secret dealing inspired fears that the Society was favoring the rise of autonomous Indian commonwealths while concealing the riches it was gathering in the territories under its jurisdiction, defrauding church and state of tithes and other forms of legitimate income and growing wealthy from local gold

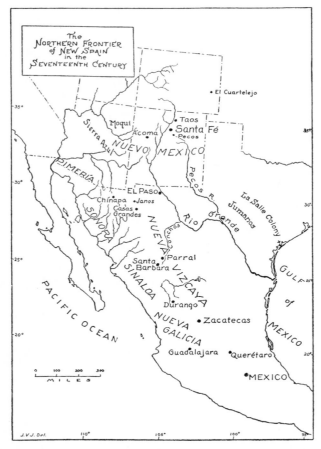

Map 11. The Northern Frontier of New Spain in the Seventeenth Century. From J. Manuel Espinosa, *Crusaders of the Rio Grande* (Chicago: Institute of Jesuit History, 1942), 7.   *Courtesy of Jesuit Archives, Central United States.*

and silver (and pearls, in the case of Lower California), as well as large bequests and other forms of support from affluent laity.

In New Spain, these charges and others—too many Jesuits were being assigned to Mexico, for example, and a suspicious number of major bequests were going to Lower California, which the Jesuits were running as an independent fiefdom— were further inflamed by an anonymous manifesto, *Sucinta relación*, that appeared in 1765, which was widely circulated and discussed. Father Francisco Ceballos, the provincial of New Spain from 1763 to 1766, did his best to dispute the claims in *Sucinta relación*. Galled by accusations of Jesuit pearl trafficking, Ceballos forbade Jesuits in Lower California from accepting pearls as payment of any kind and even from using pearls to decorate statues in mission churches. More dramatically, Provincial Ceballos turned down an astonishing bequest of 600,000 scudi from the estate of the recently deceased Doña Josefa de Arguelles y Miranda, lest it be seen as further proof of Jesuitical designs on bequests from the well-to-do. Even more dramatically, Ceballos in 1766 offered to withdraw the Jesuits from mission work entirely. That offer was uniformly rejected by the governors and bishops of the

Mexican provinces in which the Jesuits had been active for more than the past century and a half.

A troubled transition

Although ordered to be carried out immediately, the expulsion of the Jesuits from Lower California and the handing over of their missions to Franciscans from the College of San Fernando in Mexico City took a year, involved an impressive cast of characters, and resulted in the long-delayed entrada into Upper California. The official responsible for overseeing the removal, Captain Gaspar de Portolá, the newly appointed civil and military governor of California, completed his task with kindness and tact. A native of Catalonia and a thirty-year army veteran with combat experience and wounds from service in Italy and Portugal, Portolá had only recently (1763) arrived in New Spain and, promoted to captain of dragoons (mounted infantry), had been scheduled for duty against rebellious tribes in Sonora before being given the Lower California assignment. Meeting first with Fernando de Rivera y Moncada, the longtime captain of the presidio of Loreto, and later with Father Franz Benno Ducrue, the senior Jesuit (after Ducrue had traveled south to Loreto from his post at Guadalupe), Portolá delayed a formal reading of the expulsion order until Saturday, 26 December 1767, to avoid interfering with Christmas observances. Once assured of Captain Rivera's loyalty and compliance (Rivera, after all, had been living in Lower California since he was seventeen and had been promoted by the Jesuits to captain), as well as the Jesuits' full cooperation, Portolá disregarded instructions to confine Jesuits to their quarters and forbid them to say Mass as they awaited transportation to the mainland. Traveling about the region, Portolá was shocked to discover—and report back to Mexico City—that the fabulously rich mission system of popular account did not exist. Instead, many Jesuit missions were poor, and agriculture had been damaged by a recent plague of locusts, leaving neophytes and *gente de razón* (converts) on the verge of starvation. The poverty and general wretchedness of the mining camp at Santa Ana, one of the few civilian settlements in the Jesuit-controlled area, ran counter to the claim that the Jesuits were running a flourishing mining industry in Baja.

The Jesuits, meanwhile, were completing inventories of their missions with designated soldiers and civilian officials of Portolá's command and, inventories finished, converging on Loreto, which all seventeen reached by 2 February 1768. Last to arrive was Wenceslaus Linck, who had been granted a week's delay due to an outbreak of sickness at Mission San Francisco de Borja. The next day, following a Mass and departure ceremonies (which, once again, Portolá kindly permitted) conducted by Father Ducrue, the seventeen Jesuits processed down to the beach. They were leaving after dark, as Portolá decreed, to forestall any demonstrations, but a large crowd of Christianized Indians—converts from Lower California and immigrants from the Jesuit missions in Sonora across the gulf—turned out anyway, kneeling on the sand with outstretched hands, kissing the hands and feet of the departing missionaries. One by one, the Jesuits were carried piggyback through the surf to the waiting skiff that would take them to the two-masted bark *Nuestra Señora de la Concepción*, which would transport them to Mexico for further removal, under protective custody, to Mexico City and thence to Veracruz for deportation.

Pacific ambitions

The vast Pacific, so unknown in its extent, had kept its hold on the Spanish imagination since that restless and improvident conquistador Vasco Núñez de Balboa had, as the English poet John Keats would later imagine it (erroneously attributing the discovery to Hernán Cortés),

> stared at the Pacific—and all his men
> Looked at each other with a wild surmise—
> Silent, upon a peak in Darien.

Within seven years of that awesome moment, three Spanish ships under the command of the Portuguese navigator Ferdinand Magellan, having left Spain on 20 September 1519 with the express purpose of circumnavigating the globe, crossed that expanse of sea. The three-month voyage cost Magellan his life when his flotilla reached the Philippines in mid-March 1521 and he attempted to broker a local conflict. However, one of Magellan's ships, the *Victoria*, commanded by Juan Sebastián del Cano, returned to home port, Sanlúcar de Barrameda, on 6 September 1522, having completed the first circumnavigation of the globe.

The crossing of the Pacific by three Spanish ships so soon after its discovery and one ship's successful continuance of the voyage back to Spain attached the ocean to a narrative, a dream, an obsession, on the part of Spaniards in the Indies as well as their superiors in Spain. That dream eventually became a reality: the linkage of Mexico, the Borderlands, and the Californias into a trans-Pacific nexus of tribute, trade, and evangelization via the Manila galleons and a network of (predominantly Jesuit) Catholic missions and settlements running along an arc from northwestern Mexico up the Pacific coast, then across the Pacific to the Philippines and Portuguese Macao.

Hernán Cortés inaugurated this arc of connection. Following his conquest of the Aztec empire, Cortés spent time and treasure advancing north into the area of Mexico that fronted the Gulf of California (later to be known as the Sea of Cortés) and, after a number of attempts, founding a briefly held colony on the gulf coast of Lower California; before and after this brief settlement, he sent his men north to explore the Lower California shoreline. In 1539 one of Cortés' men, Francisco de Ulloa, established that Lower California was a peninsula, not an island. That recognition never fully cohered in the Spanish imagination or, indeed, convinced Dutch mapmakers, who continued to depict California as an island off western North America until King Ferdinand of Spain officially declared in 1747 that California was not an island and should not be depicted as such on maps. Historians trace this persistent belief that California was an island to a number of causes.

Nearly a quarter of a century before Cortés began to explore and colonize the peninsula, the novelist Garci Ordóñez de Montalvo described it in his *Las sergas de Esplandián* (1510) as an island on the right hand of the Indies off Cipango (Japan), inhabited by fierce black female warriors governed by Queen Califia. Since fact and fable blended so easily in the Spanish imagination of the sixteenth century, not only the name but also the island identity of Montalvo's Amazonian realm—rich in gold, pearls, and diamonds—clung to the peninsula in the years that followed.

Such a belief, linked to the comparably compelling stories of El Dorado, Quivira, and the Seven Cities of Cíbola, allowed conquistadors entering the southwestern region of lower North America to imagine that the Pacific Ocean (or South Sea, as it was then called) cut into the continent diagonally and thus created a shoreline that could be accessed directly from the southwest. Hence the interest of Coronado and his successors in connecting the South Sea with the west: an interest that brought Coronado to the southern tip of Upper California in 1540, followed by a similar visit by Juan de Oñate in 1604–1605.

Reconnaissance by sea

In any event, the name *California* referred to the landmass west across the water from Mexico by the annus mirabilis 1540, when the very able Antonio de Mendoza, the first viceroy of New Spain, authorized and set in motion three foundational efforts: Coronado's entrada into New Mexico; Hernando de Alarcón's commission to explore the lands north of the Gulf of California; and the first phases of commissioning the Portuguese-born navigator Juan Rodríguez Cabrillo to sail north along the western coast of California (as of yet undefined in its extent) until he reached the Strait of Anián, the Northwest Passage that allegedly linked the Atlantic and the Pacific across North America. Moving north by land, Alarcón and his men traveled two hundred miles up the Colorado River, and either his team or one led by another explorer, Melchor Díaz, crossed the river near present-day Yuma, Arizona, and—the first Europeans to do so—set foot in Upper California.

On 27 June 1542 two small ships, the *San Salvador* and the *Victoria*, under the command of Juan Rodríguez Cabrillo set sail from the port of La Navidad on the Mexican coast north of Acapulco and, rounding the tip of Lower California, headed north in search of harbors. On 28 September the expedition discovered and anchored in San Diego Bay, the first of three harbors to prove useful to Spanish California. On Christmas Eve, exploring the island of San Miguel in the Santa Barbara Channel, Cabrillo fell and broke his arm near the shoulder. He kept sailing north, however, until adverse winds drove him back to San Miguel Island, where on 3 January 1543 Cabrillo died from an infection of his wound. His chief pilot, Bartolomé Ferrer, after burying Cabrillo beneath an incised rock on the nearby island of Santa Rosa, honored Cabrillo's dying wish and continued the voyage north as far as latitude 42 degrees north, the current border between California and Oregon.

Although nearly three decades passed before it was accomplished, the next step in this Pacific advance by New Spain—the conquest of the Philippines from Mexico across the Pacific by conquistador Miguel López de Legazpi, followed by the establishment of a yearly Manila galleon between the Philippines and Acapulco, loaded with income and tribute—remains a singular achievement in the history of global trade. Even after a Manila galleon under the command of Francisco de Gali in 1584 discovered the eastward flow of the Japan Current to Cape Mendocino on the coast of Upper California, the trans-Pacific passage back to Mexico could take as long as two hundred days. Scurvy, dysentery, beriberi, vermin, shipboard accidents, and lightning strikes, however, took deadly tolls. What was needed, Pedro de

Moya y Contreras, the viceroy and archbishop of New Spain, decided, was a harbor in Upper California where Manila galleons could be resupplied and crews could rest and recover before continuing south.

No such harbor was known to exist, save for San Diego Bay, which was too far south. Encouraged by the viceroy-archbishop, the Portuguese merchant-adventurer Sebastián Rodríguez Cermeño, returning from the Philippines in the galleon *San Agustín* in November 1595, went in search of such a harbor but ran aground and was shipwrecked at Point Reyes, north of the yet-to-be-discovered San Francisco Bay. He and his crew of seventy were forced to creep down the coast and around the cape of Lower California to Acapulco in a jerry-rigged launch, the *San Buenaventura*, assembled from the wreckage of the *San Agustín*.

In 1602 the viceroyalty of New Spain made its third effort in sixty years to find and secure an Upper California harbor closer to Cape Mendocino: a three-vessel expedition under the command of Sebastián Vizcaíno, a merchant navigator with much experience in Mexico and the Philippines. Having reached and officially named the Bay of San Diego on 10 November 1602, Vizcaíno methodically explored the coast northward and on 16 December discovered a new harbor, which he named in honor of the viceroy, Gaspar de Zúñiga Acevedo y Fonseca, the count of Monterey. Sailing as far north as Cape Mendocino, Vizcaíno—like all before him—missed the great bay to the north of the Bay of Monterey, its entrance concealed by fog and the Farallon Islands and perhaps by the possibility that Angel Island, seen from a distance, masked the open entrance to the harbor. In his account of this reconnaissance, Fray Antonio de la Ascensión, one of three Carmelite friars on the expedition, described California as an island and sent his report and charts back to Spain on a ship captured by Dutch pirates. The friar's documents wound up in Amsterdam and in 1622 served as the basis for the depiction of California as an island—a depiction that remained in force for another hundred years. In his final report, moreover, the too-eager-to-please Vizcaíno exaggerated the extent, depth, and landing opportunities of the Bay of Monterey. This misrepresentation temporarily lulled the sponsors of Vizcaíno's reconnaissance into the belief that the Bay of Monterey constituted the best possibility for the northern port required for trans-Pacific connections via galleon from Asia and that this bay would soon be reached and settled.

Nova Albion

As with the Atlantic coast, a long-standing threat from England hovered over the question of who would dominate the Pacific coast of North America. In late 1577 the English freebooter Francis Drake organized an expedition intended to extend the geographical reach of the Caribbean-centered, religiously reinforced English campaign of pirating, sacking, looting, kidnapping, ransoming, and slave-trading on the sea lanes of the Spanish Main in the name of Reformation values. This undeclared war became even more ferocious—and more justified, as far as the English were concerned—after the rigorist Dominican reformer and former inquisitor general of Christendom, Pope Pius V, excommunicated Queen Elizabeth I on 25 February 1570. English Protestants charged that he thereby declared open season on her, making her a target of assassination by her Catholic subjects. Although English Catholics denied the claim, the excommunication had the reverse effect of declaring open season on them, ushering in more than forty years of savage persecution and recasting English freebooting in the Caribbean and Atlantic into something that approached a sacred—and quite profitable—crusade.

Drake organized a five-ship expedition that sailed from Plymouth on 15 November 1577 with an ambitious plan. Sack ports and seize galleons on the Pacific coast of South America. Sail north in search of the Northwest Passage, then cross the Pacific to the fabled Spice Islands of the Far East. Enter the Indian Ocean via the Strait of Malacca, the main shipping channel between the Pacific and Indian Oceans. Round Africa, then sail north to England via the Atlantic, having completed the second circumnavigation of the planet. By the spring of 1579 Drake had successfully freebooted in the Caribbean, navigated the Strait of Magellan, and sacked Valparaíso and other settlements on the Pacific coast. His flotilla, though, had been reduced to one ship, the *Golden Hinde*, whose timbers creaked from the strain of being a hundred-ton vessel carrying thirty tons of looted treasure. Having sailed north on his quest for the Northwest Passage, most likely as far as Washington State, Drake could go no farther without repair and resupply. He turned south, returning to a bay on a central California coastal peninsula he had noted on his voyage north. The bay was guarded by steep white cliffs that reminded him of the Channel Coast of England.

On 17 June 1579 the *Golden Hinde* entered Drakes Bay, as it is now called, on the Point Reyes Peninsula in Marin County, just north of the still-undiscovered Bay of San Francisco. Drake and his crew spent five weeks ashore, resting, repairing, and resupplying the *Golden Hinde*, and making contact with the Coast Miwok people of the region, who, guided by one of their legends, thought that the English were their ancestors returned from the dead. As later reported by Francis Fletcher, the chaplain on the *Golden Hinde*, in *Hakluyt's Voyages* (1598–1600), this sojourn was peaceful—unmarred by any violence or sexual abuse. Fletcher's narrative might have been a deliberately crafted fable. Then again, it might have been true or substantially so. Whether fable or fact, or something in between, Fletcher's account of mutual accord—as historian Arthur Quinn has so tellingly pointed out—offers a paradigm of the Peaceable Kingdom that would soon find expression in the Pocahontas episode in Captain John Smith's *True Relation* (1608) and, a little later, would serve as an icon of moral meaning for the English Quakers of Pennsylvania.

Fletcher also conducted the first Book of Common Prayer services in North America (a scene vividly depicted by Jan Henryk de Rosen and Antonio Sotomayor in a mural in San Francisco's Grace Cathedral), and his account of this service reinforces the solemnity and Reformational significance of his narrative. Even more significant in geopolitical terms, Fletcher describes Drake naming this region Nova Albion (New England), claiming it for England, and posting an engraved brass plate to this effect on a tree according to the rituals of exploration and discovery before finishing the refitting of the *Golden Hinde* and venturing west into the vast Pacific.

Northern aspirations

Drake's claim foreshadowed, underscored, and reinforced the long-term competition between Catholic Spain and Protestant England for North American hegemony—a conflict in which France and, to a lesser extent, Russia would also play their parts—and was understood as such by the Spanish. All this meant that the Spanish in North America must do as geography made clear: push north, then farther north, as much as possible. With vision and daring, Spaniards advanced northward by land and by sea, in reconnaissance and settlement. Amid the pedantic redundancies of imperial administration, a remarkable sequence of men energized, administered, and realized these continental ambitions. The roll call of these visionaries on behalf of Church and Crown included viceroys and public servants, mariners, soldiers, civilian settlers, Jesuit and Franciscan missionaries, Native American neophytes and Hispanicized converts, a cardinal prime minister in Spain, a Knight of Malta, and a reform-minded king.

On the Atlantic coast, the Spanish advance to the north reached, however briefly, Virginia and the Chesapeake. On the Pacific coast two centuries later, continental ambition created a Borderland cluster that included the northwestern Mexican provinces of Sinaloa and Sonora, southern Arizona, Lower California across the Gulf of California, and Upper California extending northward. It is essential to consider this Gulf of California–Pacific coast region geographically and administratively integrated. In terms of its mission systems, Jesuits pioneered development, followed after 1767 by Franciscans and Dominicans. Herbert Eugene Bolton and the historians of the Bancroft Library circle at the University of California–Berkeley devoted more than a half century to researching and chronicling this Jesuit epic in the western Borderlands as well as its abrupt termination. Jesuit Land, Bolton calls this Gulf of California and western Pacific region in *Rim of Christendom* (1936), his masterful biography of Eusebio Francisco Kino, one of its two most important founders, along with his Jesuit colleague and friend Juan María de Salvatierra. For the better part of two centuries, Jesuit missionaries—Black Robes, Indians called them, in reference to the black cassock worn by members of the Society of Jesus—advanced a well-organized mission system northward into the northwestern province of Sonora, southern Arizona, and the Lower California peninsula. The system was economically anchored in agriculture and cattle raising and characterized by serviceable, well-designed churches of local stone, some of which remain in use to this day.

Most significantly, the system—which flourished during this era alongside similar Jesuit efforts in New France and across the Pacific—was anchored in the philosophy and practice of cultural accommodation that was central to Jesuit spirituality and catechetics: a concern with and respect for culture as the starting point and continuing context for evangelization. In China and India, Jesuit missionaries Matteo Ricci and Roberto de Nobili spent years earning Mandarin and Brahmin status as a first step toward evangelization. In Japan, Jesuit missionaries unsuccessfully petitioned Rome for permission to celebrate Mass in Japanese. In South America, this philosophy of accommodation within the boundaries of orthodoxy was evident in the Reductions of Paraguay, in which Jesuit missionaries were creating Native American communities that were quasi-autonomous in terms of secular authority while remaining under the religious guidance and political protection of Jesuit advisors.

The driving force behind this missionary philosophy and practice was the central doctrine and mystery of the Incarnation. In the person of Jesus Christ, as Saint John writes in the opening lines of his Gospel, the Word became flesh and dwelt among us. Fully human, fully divine—as early Christianity, after some debate and outbreaks of violence, came to define Him—Christ was Himself shaped by and responsive to human culture in a way already evident in the Gospel narratives of the first century of the Christian Era. His Passion and death were on behalf of all mankind, in all its variety of cultures. The duty of the Christian missionary, therefore, was to seek out points of intersection between a non-Christian culture and the gospel message and to maximize these arts, codes, beliefs, and folkways. Here, then, was a missionary approach that did not automatically consider non-Christians as devil worshippers and hence members of a debased culture. Then there was the continuing issue of the sexual exploitation of Indian women. In the New World, the Jesuits were suspicious, for all the obvious reasons, of mixing Spanish and Indian settlements and of assigning single male soldiers to presidios in support of missions. Franciscans and Dominicans were equally cautious. Yet in Paraguay, Sonora, southern Arizona, and Lower California, the Jesuits—due to the remote locations of their missions and their own political heft and diplomacy in the Catholic capitals of Europe and the Indies—were more successful in developing their mission systems into enclave protectorates.

Kino, Salvatierra, and their Jesuit colleagues were orthodox Catholic priests, formed by long study and spiritual preparation and skilled in the arts and sciences as well as the practical arts. The northern Italians among them, as German in their origins and culture as they were Italian, were noticeably touched by Enlightenment values. Many, indeed, were research-oriented savants in addition to being missionaries in the service of the Spanish Borderlands, devoting their lives to the evangelization of Pimería Alta (Sonora and southern Arizona) and the Lower California peninsula and looking forward to spreading their system farther north into the Pacific shores of Upper California, the logical extension of their assigned missionary territory. Like Bartolomé de Las Casas, Juan de Padilla, Antonio Margil de Jesús, and Junípero Serra, Eusebio Francisco Kino and Juan María de Salvatierra have entered secular as well as ecclesiastical history because of the strategic and cultural importance of their accomplishments. Arizona and California, in fact, would one day select Kino and Serra to represent them, respectively, as Founders in the Hall of Statuary in the south wing of the national Capitol.

A remarkable Jesuit

Born in the Tyrolese town of Segno on the edge of the Dolomite Alps into the lesser nobility that played such a notable role in the development of the Indies, Kino was educated in Jesuit schools. To fulfill a vow made when he was seriously ill, he entered the upper German Province of the Society of Jesus at age twenty. As a Jesuit, Kino developed into an accomplished scientist and mathematician. The Duke of Bavaria offered him a professorship at Innsbruck following his ordination to the priesthood and the completion of his Jesuit studies. Kino, however, turned down this prestigious offer. He dreamed instead of following his hero, the pioneering Jesuit missionary Francis Xavier (whose name he adopted), to China. In pursuit of this goal, Kino requested a transfer to the Spanish Province but failed to secure an assignment to China, receiving instead a posting to New Spain, which he accepted, considering it as a back door to China via the Philippines. For a number of years, in a manner thoroughly consistent with Jesuit rapport with the upper classes, Kino maintained a lively correspondence with the Duchess of Aveiro, a

Portuguese patroness of the Jesuit mission to China, in hopes of having her support when he would at long last be assigned there.

Although he never reached China, Eusebio Kino never lost his psychological and imaginative orientation toward the Pacific, nor did he cease to project northward—poetically, imaginatively, theologically, and imperially—the Jesuit missionary effort in Pimería Alta and California. Toward the goal of advancing the Jesuit missionary system northward and with it expanding Christendom as religion, society, culture, and economy, Eusebio Francisco Kino marshaled and directed his formidable energies and talents. As a savant, Kino was attracted to exploration, mapmaking, astronomy, natural science, and—most dramatically—economic activity: agriculture, cattle raising, mining, manufacturing, trade, and commerce. He reveled in the work of the world, the big picture and the practical detail, nurturing human life as well as advancing the Borderlands northward, helping to make people's daily life peaceful and secure and hence establishing the proper conditions for the practice of religion and the well-being of the Church. To this grand end, Kino—a Padre on Horseback, as Bolton describes him—devoted three decades of exploration, cartography, mission foundation and development, agriculture, stock raising, negotiation, and peacemaking, along with ceaseless writing of memoranda, reports, letters, histories, and an early book (his first) on the significance of the great comet of 1680, which made him an instant semicelebrity in Mexico and won the approbation of the poet and playwright Sor Juana de la Cruz. A missionary's desire to save souls was at the root of all this. Ignatian spirituality, however, taught that souls were saved within a context of culture and economy, and Eusebio Kino wanted that context expanded west and north into the North American continent.

Along with Jesuit confreres Matías Goñi and Juan Bautista Copart, Kino participated in an effort to colonize Lower California between 1683 and 1685 under the command of Admiral Isidro Atondo y Antillón. Although this endeavor collapsed due to the perennial difficulties of such entradas—Indian hostility following repressive violence by Spaniards, plus the failure of local agriculture and scarce food supplies from the mainland—Kino did have opportunities to evangelize the indigenous people and make a few converts and to explore the peninsula, including expeditions to the north and westward to the Pacific coast. With the exception of certain southern sections, Kino found Lower California difficult terrain, ruggedly mountainous and arid. Only the discovery of pearl beds offered signs of economic opportunity.

Yet Lower California was so strategically placed for a Spanish advance to the north, and its people, if properly approached, had the makings of a Catholic population. And so while he was withdrawn from Lower California and assigned to Pimería Alta by his order, Kino kept California in mind during the ensuing years as he evangelized among the Pimas, based out of Mission Nuestra Señora de los Dolores, which he founded in the spring of 1687. Successive Jesuit missions into the north were established in the years to come on sites first explored and selected by the Padre on Horseback on one of his many journeys on behalf of exploration, evangelization, and negotiation arising out of the usual round of hostilities between the military and Indians as well as intra-Indian conflicts.

Within three years, colonists and the military were complaining to the viceroy in Mexico City, charging that Kino was overly protective of the Indians and took the side of rebellious groups. Upon his arrival, in point of fact, Kino insisted upon strictly observing the recent cédula from King Carlos II, which decreed that recent Indian converts were to be exempted for twenty years from enforced labor in the mines. Nor did the success of agriculture and cattle raising at Dolores in Sonora and other missions—all the work accomplished with free Indian labor—endear Kino to the settlers.

Jesuit California

To investigate these complaints, as well as to exercise the accustomed Jesuit practice of oversight and report, the Jesuit provincial dispatched Padre Juan María de Salvatierra to Pima land as *visitador*, an official visitor charged with making a formal report. A mere ten months older than Kino, Salvatierra was also a northern Italian, born in Milan to a Spanish father and an Italian mother. Entering the Society of Jesus in Genoa, Salvatierra requested a missionary assignment early in his Jesuit formation and was sent to Mexico in 1675 to finish his theology and tertian year (second novitiate) following ordination to the priesthood. Contemporary accounts of Salvatierra, along with a portrait of him painted in Mexico while he was serving as provincial, emphasize his muscular physique, his hawk-nosed, square-jawed visage, and his evident mien of command. Like Kino, Salvatierra would be professed in the Society—admitted, that is, to its inner ranks—and in time would serve in such key roles as master of novices, regional superior, and, later, provincial of the more than three hundred Jesuits in Mexico. At the time of his appointment as visitador to Sinaloa and Sonora, Salvatierra had been serving for nearly a decade as missionary and regional rector among the frequently restive Indians of the Chínipas range of the southeastern Sierra Madre Occidental, where two Jesuits had been martyred in 1632.

In the course of his visitation to Mission Dolores and its padre—a visit that included a two-hundred-mile horseback survey of further mission sites—the two Jesuits had ample opportunity to discuss the Jesuit missionary effort in the Province of New Spain. Kino did his best to familiarize Salvatierra with local efforts, present and future, and thereby won from the visitador a supportive report upon Salvatierra's return to Mexico City. Yet Kino also lobbied Salvatierra regarding prospects for a mission to Lower California, despite the failure of the Atondo venture. Salvatierra went back to Mexico City with a new friend and colleague in the Society, as well as a commitment to Kino that he would try to persuade the provincial to reconsider a renewed mission across the gulf to Lower California.

It took Salvatierra seven years of incessant lobbying (while serving as rector of the college at Guadalajara and then as master of novices at Tepotzotlán) to make his case successfully. Three provincials, the Audiencia of Guadalajara, a viceroy, and the king himself at one time or another turned him down. The Atondo entrada had cost the Crown 200,000 pesos, and the king and his advisors were in no mood for a repeat performance. During these years, Kino and Salvatierra kept up their hopes and their correspondence, and Kino began to envision the missions of Pimería Alta as sources of meat, wheat, beans, and corn for the proposed Lower California missions and worked to expand his farming and ranching operations accordingly. Kino even committed his talent and manpower to the design and construction of a small schooner on the gulf coast to carry provisions and other freight to the Lower California missions until they became self-sufficient. Reaching the top of El Naza-reno mountain in February 1694, Kino could see across the gulf to Lower Califor-nia, and this vista reinforced his belief in the geographical unity of the region as a premise for its unified development as a Catholic commonwealth.

After nearly seven years of unsuccessful preparation, lobbying, dreaming, and praying, Kino decided to bring matters to a head. In 1696 the indefatigable traveler made the arduous fifteen-hundred-mile journey by horseback south to Mexico City, where he joined Salvatierra in one last appeal to the viceroy and the Jesuit provincial, Juan de Palacios. At first, Kino and Salvatierra received the usual rejec-tion on the usual grounds—the region showed no signs of profitability, the Indians were hostile—but as they continued their campaign, two interventions turned the tide. In Rome, Tirso González, the father general of the Jesuits—a former mis-sionary and a longtime friend of Kino (when Kino and González were stationed together in Seville, Kino had designed and built a sundial for González)—opened the door to further negotiations. The Society of Jesus, the father general decreed, could commit to California if local authorities approved. After further lobbying by Salvatierra, who recruited his young novices as part of his persuasive effort, Juan de Palacios finally agreed. The Jesuits of New Spain would take on responsibility for California, Provincial Palacios decreed, provided that the necessary funds be raised from private sponsors.

A third Jesuit joined the California enterprise: Juan de Ugarte, a professor of philosophy at the Colegio Máximo in Mexico City. (Kino had returned to his post in Pima land.) Salvatierra and Ugarte raised the necessary funds from local nobility (the conde de Miravalla and the marqués de Buenavista), pious associations (the sodality of the Jesuit Church of San Pedro y San Pablo in Mexico City), and secular priests of personal wealth and high position. One such priest, Don Pedro Gil de la Sierpe, the royal treasurer of Acapulco, donated money and jewelry and promised four craft (a launch, a galliot, and two smaller boats) for use as supply ships for a total gift of 25,000 pesos. Don Juan Caballero y Ocio, a priest of Querétaro and commissary of the Inquisition, contributed 20,000 pesos at first request, followed by two further gifts. Thus were created the first installments on the Pious Fund of Cal-ifornias. Income from this fund would help support the Catholic Church in Lower and Upper California under Spanish, Mexican, and United States jurisdictions until the last payment was sent to the bishops of American California in 1967.

Funds in hand or pledged, Salvatierra and Ugarte approached Viceroy José Sarmiento y Valladares, conde de Moctezuma y Tula, seeking official permission for the enterprise. The previous viceroy, Don Juan de Ortega Cano Montáñez y Patiño, the former bishop of Michoacán, had been consistently opposed to the venture. His successor, however, was a layman whose wife, Doña María Andrea de Guzmán, was thoroughly in favor of the California undertaking and did not hesitate to share her opinion with her husband. Viceroy Valladares, in any event, approved of the project—on one startling condition. The Jesuits were to take responsibility for Lower California in all matters, sacred and secular, including its ongoing finan-cial support. Even soldiers stationed there would report to the Jesuits, who would pay their salaries. The regional rector of Lower California would function as the de facto governor of this clerically governed missionary province.

Thus the Jesuits now possessed, at least in theory, a reduction in the Northern Hemisphere paralleling that of Paraguay: an Indian commonwealth under Jesuit guidance and supervision, with colonization prohibited and only soldiers under Jesuit jurisdiction and their families allowed to settle. Lower California's lack of economic promise had just delivered to the Jesuits a clerical authority new to the Borderlands. The entire process of permission and funding, moreover, from top to bottom—the father general in Rome; the viceroy, his wife, and the nobility; rich, highly placed secular clergy; and the autonomous Jesuit jurisdictions—testified to the hierarchical nature of Spanish colonial society: its wealth, its piety, its institutions of high urbanism, its fusion of church and state. Educated, worldly wise, and accustomed to reception in the highest circles, Jesuits were at home in such a milieu, whether in Europe, North or South America, or Asia.

Yet, as the destruction of the Jesuit effort in Japan and the wholesale martyrdom of vast numbers of Japanese Catholics had already shown, the Crown that gaveth could become the state that taketh away. That authority was also evident in northern Europe during the Reformation and in the Indies, as so many missionaries had learned to their distress throughout the past three centuries. But the power of the Crown to take away was sixty years into the future, and not foreseen by members of the Society of Jesus, which—like New Spain—was in a golden age of achievement and influence. That prospect was certainly not on Salvatierra's mind as he set out for the west coast of Mexico to prepare for this unique entrada, stopping en route for courtesy calls on his benefactors and a farewell visit to his neophytes and Jesuit colleagues in Chínipas. There, a rebellion broke out among local Indians as he was departing for the coast, forcing his return (and suggesting, no doubt, the perils of missionary life) and delaying his arrival on the coast until 16 August. The good news: the galliot *Santa Elvira* and the launch *El Rosario* and their crews were waiting for him, as promised by Don Gil de la Sierpe. The bad news: Father Kino had been removed from the Lower California mission; indeed, he had been turned back when he was already on the trail to rendezvous with Salvatierra. Kino's regional rector and provincial insisted that Kino was needed at Mission Dolores and its affiliated missions. The governor of Nueva Vizcaya and other civil officials and settlers agreed, fearing that upper Sonora without Kino would be in danger of a destabilization that could spread to their province. All this persuaded the viceroy, who persuaded the king, who personally ordered his celebrity missionary-explorer to remain in place. Writing to the father general in Rome, Kino negotiated a compromise—half a year in Lower California, half a year in Pimería Alta. Despite being Kino's friend, His Paternity Gonzáles issued only a concession, not an outright directive, and hence left the matter to local discretion, which allowed the provincial of New Spain to shelve quietly Kino's request.

It had been agreed that Father Ugarte would remain behind in Mexico City as treasurer and manager of the Pious Fund. And so when Kino's orders were canceled and the fourth Jesuit assigned to the venture, Francisco María Pícolo, was delayed at his prior assignment, Salvatierra set sail for Lower California on 10 October 1697, the feast of Saint Francis Borgia, third general of the Society. Aboard the galliot and the launch were one Jesuit, a sea captain and six sailors, a military officer (Captain Sebastián Romero, a veteran of the Kino-Atondo expedition), six soldiers, and three Christianized Indians from Jesuit missions in northwestern Mexico. Loaded with provisions assiduously assembled by Salvatierra, the two ships also carried thirty head of cattle, ten sheep, four pigs, and one horse.

The work of a lifetime

Although Eusebio Kino never returned to Lower California, he devoted the rest of his life to creating an integrated mission system that included an imaginative projection of more Spanish Catholic provinces to the north. He served this grand goal through his own missionary labors, along with arduous and time-consuming explorations and equally demanding compositions of histories, memoranda, and reports. His pastoral responsibilities as a missionary involved founding more than a half dozen missions and developing them as self-sustaining farms and cattle ranches. All this effort advanced the Jesuit mission system into the northern regions of Pimería Alta, lands that would become part of the territory of Arizona in 1853 with the Gadsen Purchase: 29,640 square miles south of the Gila River and west of the Río Grande, which the United States purchased from Mexico for $10 million.

In 1700 Kino finished his opening of the northern edges of the Sonoran Desert with the foundation of Mission San Xavier del Bac (from *bacórdia*, the place near the spring), southwest of present-day Tucson. The new mission served as an anchor and Pima settlement for a network of affiliated missions and villages (San Cosme del Tucson, San Agustín del Oyaur, San Clemente, and Santa Catarina de Cuituabagum), testifying to the northern march of Catholicism into the Borderlands despite the recent setbacks in New Mexico. Yet Pimería Alta also experienced its revolts and pockets of continuing resistance. One uprising cost the life of Kino's young Jesuit colleague Francisco Xavier Saeta, a Sicilian recently arrived in America, who was martyred on 1 April 1695 at Mission Nuestra Señora de la Purísima Concepción de Caborca, one hundred miles east of Mission Dolores. The assassination of Father Saeta led to a punishing military action in reprisal, which Kino ultimately negotiated to a halt. Harassment from Apaches on the northeastern frontier remained an ever-present danger. Still, nothing on the scale of the great Pueblo Revolt of 1680 in New Mexico occurred. Kino's negotiating skills were nevertheless frequently called upon to keep the peace.

California on his mind

Kino advanced the Lower California cause on two fronts: development of mission farming and stock raising in an effort to create a surplus for shipment elsewhere and exploration of a route for a direct connection by land. If California were an island, as nearly everyone believed, such a land route would be impossible. Yet Kino and Salvatierra had their doubts regarding the island theory. On a previous expedition north, Kino had noticed that the body of water separating Sonora from California grew increasingly narrow the farther north he progressed, which suggested that the Sea of California (as it was then called) was tapering toward an end. On a subsequent exploration and evangelization to the north, Yuma Indians he met at the village of San Pedro on the Gila River just east of the Gila Range had given him blue abalone shells that, Kino reasoned, could not be found in the desert but must have been brought overland from Lower California. A second gift of twenty blue shells on a string attached to a cross further convinced him.

At this point, certain that a land route to California must exist, Kino ceased work on the launch he had been constructing to carry cattle and freight across the Sea of California to the Jesuit mission. If California were a peninsula, the Sea of California was a gulf, which meant that instead of being driven to port and shipped so expensively by sea, as was now the case, cattle and other supplies could be taken by land across the headlands above the gulf, then down to the missions on the other side. The two Jesuits agreed to explore such a route: Salvatierra would go northward up the Lower California coast turning east, and Kino would journey north and west across the Arizona desert, the country of the Papago, where he was evangelizing, then westward to the Gila River in the land of the Yuma.

Between 1694 and 1700 Kino made four expeditions into the north in search of the termination of the Gulf of California and a land route to Lower California. He never found one because it did not exist. The desert reaches, arroyos, and mountain ranges of the region did not allow for the kind of human, cattle, and freight passage Kino and Salvatierra envisioned. Yet Kino did establish that the Gulf of California ended at its northern edge, into which flowed the Colorado River. This discovery alone would have earned him a place in history.

On 24 September 1700 Kino, ten servants, and sixty horses and mules set forth on a thousand-mile round trip that would establish California's nonisland geography. By 7 October the party had reached the head of the gulf. Ascending a high hill, Kino peered through his telescope to the north and northwest and beheld the Colorado River in the far distance across an expanse of open country, no sea in sight. California was clearly not an island!

The next year, this time in the company of Salvatierra, Kino confirmed the findings of the previous year. In mainland Mexico on mission business, Salvatierra was eager to try to return to Lower California by land. The Jesuits failed to do so, of course, since such a route did not exist, but they did substantiate the peninsular nature of Lower California, especially through an observation at sunset from atop a peak—judged by Jesuit historian Peter Masten Dunne to be the Sierra Hornady— that revealed a continuous landmass.

In February 1702 Kino embarked upon a journey (the third in as many years) to the headlands above the gulf to reach the Colorado River, which he hoped to cross into California. Such a passage had been very much on Kino's mind before his departure, as evident in a visionary letter he wrote His Paternity Tirso González, the sympathetic father general of the Society in Rome who had so crucially backed Kino and Salvatierra's Lower California project. Along with his letter, Kino enclosed a map of the region. Soon, he promised the father general, not only would Pimería Alta be supplying cattle overland to the western missions, but also there would be cattle ranches established on the California side to the north. Why not, he suggested, call this area above latitude 30 degrees north Alta or Upper California? The map enclosed by Kino extended to latitude 32 degrees north.

Kino had already written a Latin treatise on Lower California entitled *Novae Carolinae* (the new Carolinas). He now planned to write a treatise on Alta California as well, tentatively entitled *Novae Philipinae seu California Superior* (the New Philippines or Upper California). Alta California, Kino continued, if made Catholic and

Spanish, would bring New Spain that much closer to China and Japan—and perhaps even to Europe, if "north of these our lands we may be able to find a shorter road to Europe, partly through these lands and partly by way of the North Sea."[1]

The sickness of Kino's Jesuit colleague on the expedition, Father Manuel González, ended this journey before Kino could cross the Colorado River into Alta California. Kino would never make the necessary treks north to explore Alta California and compose *Novae Philipinae*, and his Latin treatise on Lower California has been lost. Like Moses, Kino reached but did not enter the Promised Land. No matter: he had more work to do in Pimería Alta on behalf of the Jesuit mission system, which was now established in Lower California and would one day move even farther north. Although Kino's treatise on Lower California has not been found, his letter to the father general outlining his grand vision survives in the Jesuit archives in Rome.

Working in Mexican archives in the early 1900s, historian Herbert Eugene Bolton located, assembled, edited, and translated into English for publication Kino's previously undiscovered diary-history of the Jesuit missionary effort in Pimería Alta and California. The resulting publication, *Kino's Historical Memoir of Pimería Alta* (1919), issued in two volumes by the respected publisher Arthur H. Clark of Cleveland, launched Bolton into a prodigiously productive career as an editor and translator of crucial Borderlands documents and a biographer of major Borderlands personalities. In the course of his research, Bolton discovered a previously unknown manuscript, *Favores celestiales* (*Celestial Favors*), a title suggested to Kino by his longtime friend Tirso González, to whom the book is dedicated. Bolton included an English translation of *Favores celestiales* as the conclusion of Kino's historical memoir. Largely written in 1708, and finished and signed in 1710, a year before Kino's death, *Celestial Favors* carries the history of the California missions forward to 1707 and as such can be considered the founding document of California historiography.

Celestial Favors ends Kino's memoir—and life—on a note of triumphant, visionary optimism, directed at Church and Crown. The evangelization, settlement, and development of Pimería Alta and California, Kino argues, foreshadows a very real possibility: the creation to the north of future provinces, Spanish and Catholic, now barely dreamed of. The Seven Cities of Cíbola might not have materialized, but Spain had an opportunity to form seven new kingdoms in North America: Nueva Vizcaya, Nuevo México, California Baja, Nueva Navarra, California Alta, Gran Quivira, and Gran Teguayo or Nueva Borboña. Here was a chance, with Nueva Navarra, to establish a barrier against Apache and Comanche raiders from the north and eventually to absorb these regions as peaceful provinces; with Gran Teguayo, Spanish Catholic civilization could advance into the heart of the continent, bringing untold peoples into the Catholic faith and earning new treasure for the Crown.

These kingdoms, moreover, would connect with the southern advance of Catholic New France (thanks, in significant measure, to the exploration and evangelization of Kino's French Jesuit colleagues!), and from this linkage—building upon the two Catholic nations' dynastic unity since the assumption of the Spanish throne in 1700 by Philip V, grandson of the French Sun King, Louis XIV—new avenues of trade and commerce would open to the Atlantic. The Pacific-oriented kingdoms of North American Spain, meanwhile, would strengthen and facilitate connections to Asia as well as foster business and the transportation of imports and exports between western North America and the Far East. From such exploration, travel, shipping, and settlement, the North American continent would become progressively better known, and better maps could then be drawn. So many current maps, explorer-cartographer Kino complains, were either vague or wrong, or both. It was time to map the continent properly.

In terms of future sea travel, Manila galleons might land in a developed port at San Diego or the Bay of Todos Santos (present-day Ensenada) rather than Acapulco, thereby both lessening the perils of their long voyage and establishing a more direct connection to the Philippines, China, and other parts of Asia where Jesuits were also active. Kino does not explicitly mention these confreres, yet a sense of a linked missionary effort—joining the Jesuits of Canada, the Mississippi valley of New France, and the Far East in continuities of religion, culture, and development— pervades the visionary exhortation with which Kino concludes *Celestial Favors* and, within a few more years, his remarkable life and career as explorer and missionary.

Kino had found a cause worthy of his original desire for China: a universal Church that fostered the salvation of diverse peoples, east and west; and a Franco-Spanish Catholic hegemony in western and central North America—linked to similar hegemonies in the Philippines, China, Latin America, and the Caribbean—that served as the matrix and facilitator of this unity. All this, in turn, integrated into the collective unity of Catholic Europe. Such was the ultimate meaning of each and every mission planted in Pimería Alta and each and every mission being established in the rocky, arid landscapes of Lower California preparatory to an advance farther to the north.

Salvation history

In concluding this grand vision for continental and oceanic advancement, Kino invokes the primary motivation for his life's work: seeking the fundamental wealth of this New World in North America, "the innumerable souls ransomed by the most precious blood of our Redeemer, Jesus Christ". Here was the basis of his vocation as a missionary, the dream of his youth fulfilled! The doctrine of the Incarnation formed the foundation of Kino's spirituality and evangelization, and hence he perceived mankind as upgraded beyond measure by the Incarnation and sustained in that identity by the Risen Christ. This sensibility, this sense of the world transformed while remaining knowable on its own terms, motivated the Jesuit expertise in science as well as Scripture, theology, the humanities, and the professional and practical arts so widely evident since the establishment of the Society of Jesus in the mid-sixteenth century. In this context were nurtured Kino's skills in mathematics, natural sciences, cartography, and architecture along with his expertise in diplomacy, whether exercised to end an Indian revolt, to lobby within or beyond the Society of Jesus, or to seek the patronage of a wealthy duchess. His commitment to the writing of history also reflected that Jesuit understanding. Eusebio Kino was, in brief, a man of the Enlightenment, Jesuit-style. As a physiocrat and scientific farmer, he revered agriculture and delighted in the development of his missions as cattle ranches and flourishing farms. He ends *Celestial Favors* with a satisfied sizing up of his cattle and a walk through his mission garden. If multiplied like the loaves and fishes of the Gospel, Kino believed, farms and ranches such as these could feed a hemisphere so that its peoples, in peace and security, might be introduced to the message of salvation.

"The greater the means," writes Kino in the conclusion of his visionary tract, "the greater our obligation to seek the salvation of so many souls in the very fertile and pleasant lands and valleys of these new conquests and conversions. There are already very rich and abundant fields, plantings, and crops of wheat, maize, frijoles, chick-peas, beans, lentils, bastard chick-peas, etc. There are good gardens, and in them vineyards for wine for Masses, with cane-brakes of sweet cane for syrup and *panocha* [candy] and, with the favor of Heaven, before long for sugar."

At this point, Kino become Virgilian, echoing the *Georgics* in his enumeration of abundance:

> There are many Castilian fruit trees, fig-trees, quinces, oranges, pomegranates, peaches, apricots, pear-trees, apples, mulberries, pecans, prickly pears, etc., with all sorts of garden stuff, such as cabbages, melons, watermelons, white cabbage, lettuce, onions, leeks, garlic, anise, pepper, mustard, mint, Castilian roses, white lilies, etc., with very good timber for all kinds of building, such as pine, ash, cypress, walnut china-trees, mesquite, alders, poplar, willow tamarind, etc.
>
> Another temporal means which our Lord gives us for the promotion of these new conquests are the plentiful ranches which are already stocked with cattle, sheep, and goats, many droves of mares, horses, sumpters-mules as well as horse-pack animals necessary for transportation and commerce, with very rich and abundant pastures all the year, to raise very fat sheep, producing much tallow, suet, and soap, which already is made in abundance.

What a domestic catalogue for a colonial enterprise that, in the past—in Florida and the Borderlands of North America—had so often failed to provide for itself! What a grand vision of free labor and sustainability for an empire begun in slavery and exploitation!

At the same time, Kino is thoroughly attuned to the economic promise of the proposed new kingdoms in western North America. The climate is good, he argues, not too hot but not too cold, a climate comparable to the best of Mexico and the Mediterranean shores of Europe. And minerals are abundant, gold and silver, as evident in the mining camps being established on the northern frontier. The coastal regions show great promise in their salt beds ready for harvest and their waters teeming with oysters, shrimp, and varieties of savory fish.

But in place of slavery, that perennial curse of the Indies, Kino proposes an alliance with the indigenous peoples based on trade, commerce, free labor, and mutual defense. These peoples, Kino argues, are willing to work if properly treated, and the linguistic unity that extends far into the region will facilitate trade and commerce. Their material culture had already reached a high level, as evident in their "very good fabrics of cotton and of wool; also many nicely made baskets, like hampers, of different sizes, many colored macaw feathers, many deer and buffalo hides, and toward the sea coast much bezoar [an antidote against poison], and the efficacious *contrayerba* [a medicinal plant] and in many parts the important medicinal fruit called *jojoba* [a digestive]".

Defensive alliances could be achieved, Kino believes. In his personal experience, the peoples of Pimería Alta were "docile, affable, and very friendly, and at the same time warlike and valiant", and thus quite willing and able to defend themselves—and hence the entire province of Sonora—against Apaches and other marauding tribes.

Above all else, in the midst of every advantage Kino enumerates to his father general, stands the paramount and compelling fact that the peoples of Pimería Alta and beyond were open to evangelization. Unlike other Indian peoples, he points out, they did not have a fixed and hostile belief system; nor did they practice polygamy, which had proven such a barrier to evangelization. On the contrary, he argues, the peoples of Pimería Alta seemed to be characterized by an instinctive monotheism, which led them easily to "comprehend the teaching that God Most High is the All-Powerful and He who created the sun, the moon, and the stars, and all men, and all the world, and all its creatures". Although Kino does not explicitly mention the Pueblo Indians of New Mexico, he undoubtedly is alluding to the great Pueblo Revolt of 1680. Indeed, over the years, Kino continues—most recently during the stay of a Jesuit visitor—their leading men among the Indians of the region would descend upon the fathers, requesting that a priest be sent to them, which stood in such contrast to the hostility of the chiefs and shamans in other Indian cultures, or the belligerent aristocracies and bonzes of Japan and China. Kino does not propose that these future kingdoms remain Jesuit enclaves. His final reference is to the continuing support and approval of the Jesuit missions extended by both the bishop of Durango, Señor Doctor Don Ygnacio Dias de la Barrera, and the higher clergy of the diocese. Doctor Dias, in fact (that "most pious prince of the Church", Kino—ever the diplomat—calls the good bishop), not only has offered the Jesuits present and future material support but also has openly expressed his wish that Jesuit missionaries bear primary responsibility for the extension of his diocese into northern regions.

"These, then," Kino concludes, "are the opportune means which our Lord offers us to enable us to accomplish a great service for both Majesties and the eternal salvation of very many souls in all this most extensive North America." Like Moses surveying the land of Canaan from atop Mount Nebo, Eusebio Kino—a missionary of continental ambition—beheld a promised land, Spanish and Catholic, awaiting its future. Generations of Jesuit missionaries had helped bring this promising Pacific region to its next point of development: Now was the time to form fresh and peaceful alliances, to settle Catholic people in new regions alongside the native population. Missions and parish churches awaited establishment, from which the gospel might be proclaimed, Mass and marriages celebrated, children baptized, the departed laid to rest. Now was the time to plow, irrigate, plant, and harvest, lay out fruit trees and flowerbeds, raise cattle, tend to beans and cabbages, foster trade and commerce, explore, map. A Spanish and Catholic country awaited fulfillment, reformed in its practices and guided by prosperity, good order, Catholic and Enlightenment ideals faith, hope, and charity.[2]

Las Californias

Initial responsibility for the eventual evangelization of Upper California had been assigned to the Society of Jesus. That was the way that Eusebio Kino, Juan María de Salvatierra, and their fellow Jesuits had understood it in the late 1690s as they prepared for, and then launched, the mission system of Lower California. Las Californias, Lower and Upper, were perceived as a unity—the Pacific front, in missionary terms—with the Jesuit missions of northwestern Mexico and southern Arizona. For seventy years Jesuit missionaries had been laboring in Lower California in the expectation that one day they would advance their mission system into those northern reaches whose possibilities had been the lifetime dream of Eusebio Kino.

Lower California had been a difficult assignment: rocky and barren, pirate-ridden in its southern extremities, with freebooters lying in wait for a Manila galleon or pressing Indians into illegal diving for pearls. The usual barriers to the first stages of settlement and evangelization by Spaniards—no agriculture, no supplies, near starvation—almost ended the Lower California mission in its preliminary phases. Kino's plan to supply Lower California overland came to naught, and even when Salvatierra acquired a dedicated supply ship (after initially being supplied by the leaky *San José* and the launch *San Javier*), the Jesuits could never afford a serviceable ship of their own and nearly went broke when they tried to do so. In 1711, for example, Father Francisco Peralta, sent to the mainland to acquire a dedicated craft, paid for the renovation of the bark *Rosario*; when launched, it promptly sank. A second ship—which cost 22,000 scudi and took a year and a half to build—sprung a leak on its first storm-tossed voyage, was abandoned by its crew, and sank. One of the three Jesuits on board, Father Benito Grisi, newly assigned to Lower California, drowned alongside five other passengers and loyal crew. Another craft survived a mere two voyages before going down in the gulf. A fourth ship, the sloop *Nuestra Señora de Guadalupe*, the gift of Viceroy Fernando de Alencastre Noroña y Silva, the first Duke of Linares and Marquis of Valdefuentes, survived for several trips before sinking with a full cargo. Its successor foundered in the harbor of Acapulco, providing further testimony to the unseaworthiness of vessels serving the gulf or the incompetence of local captains and crews, or both.

Nevertheless, the first generation of Jesuit missionaries—Salvatierra, Francisco María Pícolo, Juan de Ugarte (who turned the management of the Pious Fund over to another Jesuit in 1700 and joined Salvatierra in the field the following March), Clemente Guillén, Francisco Peralta, Jaime Bravo, and the long-serving Portuguese layman Estevan Rodríguez (who was elected presidio captain by a free vote of his soldiers and served for forty-nine years)—prevailed over heroic difficulties. By the time of Salvatierra's death in 1717, they had established a network of five missions centered on Nuestra Señora de Loreto, whose restored church bore above its doorway the inscription *Madre y Cabeza de las Californias* (mother and head of the Californias). The 1720s saw six more missions established, beginning with Nuestra Señora del Pilar de la Paz, 150 miles south of Loreto; like Loreto, it eventually became the nucleus of a civilian settlement. Two of the three missions founded in the 1730s—San José del Cabo (1730), on the tip of the peninsula, and Santa Rosa (1733), named in honor of its sponsor, Doña Rosa de la Peña, but more commonly known as Todos Santos (All Saints), after its affiliated *ranchería* (encampment)— likewise stimulated the development of small civilian settlements on a peninsula destined to remain sparsely settled into the twentieth century. Santa Rosa/Todos Santos was the fourth mission in Lower California to receive foundational support from the mainland; Doña Rosa's brother-in-law, the Mexican philanthropist José de la Puente y Peña, the Marquis of Villapuente, had already donated 30,000 pesos toward the establishment of San José de Comondú (1708), La Purísima Concepción (1720), and Guadalupe (1720). These benefactions testified to the ability of the Jesuits of New Spain to attract support from elites.

Santa Rosa/Todos Santos served as the only mission on the Pacific coast. Spain would very much have liked the Jesuits to found a mission and future settlement on a Pacific coast harbor, but none existed, with the possible exception of Sebastián Vizcaíno Bay, which lay two-thirds up the peninsula. That vast indentation, though, was hardly protected—it was, in fact, open sea—and so throughout the Jesuit era the Pacific coast of the Californias remained unsettled between Santa Rosa/Todos Santos in Lower California and the Bay of San Diego in lower Upper California until the Franciscans founded Mission San Diego de Alcalá in 1769.

Hence a mission system was developed, pushed even farther north in the 1750s and 1760s with the founding of Santa Gertrudis (1752), San Borjo (1762), and Santa María (1767), at the base of the Sierra San Pedro Mártir range at the Peninsula's northern edge, which formed a natural barrier (for the time being) to further expansion northward. It was a remarkable achievement, seventeen missions in all. A number of them have been restored and remain in use to this day, and even those in ruins suggest an enduring presence.

Long-term assessments

How, finally, is this mission system to be assessed? Did the Jesuits achieve the confederation of Christianized, Hispanicized peoples intended by the spirit of their order and the political autonomy they had been granted and exercised for seventy years? Were any of the continental ambitions evoked by Eusebio Kino in the final chapters of *Celestial Favors* achieved? And how could they be achieved in purely Indian circumstances, as the Jesuits were insisting in their protected domain? How could Lower California fully develop and thereby establish New Spain on the Pacific without the infusion of new peoples, as had occurred in Texas and New Mexico, and the inevitable fusions of bloodlines and cultures?

In *Black Robes in Lower California* (1952), Peter Masten Dunne wrestles with the question of how amenable the indigenous peoples of Lower California were to the evangelization and Hispanicization process. As a Jesuit priest writing about Jesuit priests, Dunne has no trouble with the spiritual dimensions of the enterprise. As human beings with immortal souls, the Indians of Lower California were, according to Catholic belief, worthy of evangelization. They possessed souls to be saved, and the Jesuits would do their best to save them. Yet the Society of Jesus was also acting as an agent of the Crown in securing Lower California—and by implication, Upper California as well—for development. How suitable was Lower California for social, cultural, and economic development? Most of Lower California, Dunne admits, was rocky, barren, arid, and certainly resistant to extensive agriculture or cattle raising. Nor did it show promise in terms of potential harbors, save for one or two southern locations, which contained pearl beds. But pearl fishing alone could not develop an economy, and most of the pearl fishers operating in the region were operating illegally. Gold or silver might be discovered; but even if that were to occur, the Jesuits, protective of their de facto commonwealth, did not want a gold rush on their hands.

All these negatives weighted the human factor more heavily. Did the indigenous peoples of Lower California have the makings of a Christianized, Hispanicized, self-sufficient population, capable of maintaining developed communities and earning their keep in a future Spanish empire? From a contemporary perspective, such questions seem arrogant, mere justifications for takeovers of one sort or another. Yet history, while subject to interpretation, remains history. This was the challenge facing the indigenous peoples of Lower California, although it was a challenge being imposed on them. Once Salvatierra crossed the Gulf of California and established the first mission at Loreto, *alea iacta est*—the die was cast as far as the fate of the indigenous peoples of Lower California was concerned. Their Jesuit evangelizers wanted nothing more than for the Indians of California, once converted (and, to an appropriate degree, Hispanicized), to flourish as Catholic subjects of the Crown, their families intact, their women unviolated by predatory soldiers, their economies and governance structures remaining under their own control. The question now became: Would the Indians thrive, survive, or decline under Jesuit administration? Had they the strength, the culture, to grow and prevail in the circumstances being thrust upon them?

Initial contact

Reactions of the first generation of Jesuit missionaries to the native population were by and large positive, although the people of Lower California contrasted dramatically with the indigenous peoples of north-central Mexico and southern Arizona, the Pimería Alta of Kino's labors. Their social, cultural, and economic achievements differed even more radically from those of the Pueblo people of New Mexico or the Caddo people of east Texas. Men went naked, possessed the bow and arrow, and hunted what small game was available, but the Indians were always hungry. The majority of their day was spent foraging for food, so desperate that they would pick through deposits of human or animal excrement in search of undigested seeds. In the first years of evangelization, the Jesuits made contact with the ever-hungry locals by daily serving *pozole*, a cooked cornmeal porridge, followed by efforts to catechize. Soon, crowds of Indians gathered to be fed—dozens, then scores, then hundreds. Now and then, trouble ensued, especially when the locals were caught stealing. (In New Mexico, by contrast, hungry Spaniards had stolen from the Indians.) Flogging, administered by soldiers, was introduced as a form of punishment and remained in use for decades to come, although its frequency varied from tribe to tribe.

The southern Guaycura and Pericú proved the most resistant. Especially hostile were the Uchitíes at the tip of the peninsula. A mixed-race-group—Indian blended with African, Dutch, English, and Filipino bloodlines from the pirates, freebooters, pearl fishers, and deserting Manila galleon crews long operative in the region—the Uchitíes broke out in open rebellion in October 1734, following the establishment the previous year of Mission Santa Rosa at Todos Santos by the Jesuit missionary Sigismundo Taraval. Neither Taraval nor the Jesuit previously evangelizing the Uchitíes, Nicolás Tamaral, thought highly of the Uchitíes, given the persistent resistance to evangelization among their leaders and significant sectors of the population. Both Afro-Indian ringleaders of the revolt, Chicori and Botón, had special grievances. Chicori, the chief of Yeneca, a village near Mission San José del Cabo that refused to accept Christianity, kidnapped a Christian Indian woman from the mission, whom he claimed to be his wife, and refused to return her despite the intervention of Father Tamaral, which further infuriated the chief. Botón, a leader at Mission Santiago (1721), had been deposed and flogged for bad behavior and, fleeing to Yeneca, vowed vengeance against the mission priest, Lorenzo Carranco.

Eager to find and establish a port for Manila galleons en route to Acapulco and hence increase the value of Lower California to the Crown and the Society of Jesus (their ambition continental as well as evangelical), the Jesuits had entered the southern peninsula quickly and hugely—five missions in thirteen years. The goal of securing a stopover seemed on the way to fulfillment in early 1734 when a Manila galleon under the command of Vice Admiral Don Gerónimo Montero limped into the cove of San Bernabé and its sick and near-dying crew was ministered to by Father Tamaral and the neophytes of San José del Cabo with fresh water, meat, eggs, vegetables, fruit, and prickly pear (an effective antidote against scurvy). A recovered and very pleased Admiral Montero surveyed the cove before leaving and made a favorable report upon his return to Acapulco. A connection to the annual arrival of the Manila galleon would literally put Lower California on the map and ensure the continuing interest of the Crown and the viceroy in the Jesuit mission there—and, in turn, result in continuing support and influence for the order.

Resistance surfaces

That was the good news. The bad news: the conspiracy being fostered by Chicori and Botón was attracting new adherents, especially among leaders and shamans who had been urged or forced by the Jesuits to give up their polygamous way of life or who had been flogged or otherwise aggrieved. By late September 1734 the rebellion was ready for execution: attacks on all five missions in the region and the killing of all Jesuits, soldiers, and resisting neophytes. On 1 October Lorenzo Carranco was dragged from his house at Mission Santiago, shot with arrows, clubbed, and stoned until he expired. His weeping houseboy was bashed to death against a wall. Two days later at Mission San José del Cabo, Nicolás Tamaral was dragged from his house (like Carranco), beaten, and beheaded; his corpse was profaned and burned, and the mission church was looted. Sadly, some of Carranco's own neophytes joined in the mayhem. By the second week of October, forty-nine women and children at Todos Santos had been murdered, along with two Jesuits and one soldier, and four missions—La Paz, Santiago, Todos Santos, and San José—lay in ruins. Hundreds of loyal neophytes fled to the north.

Hearing of the outbreak, Estevan Rodríguez, captain of the presidio at Loreto, organized a force of twenty soldiers and a hundred faithful Indian allies from the north and headed south by ship to fortify the ruined mission at La Paz, where they held off two further attacks. In January 1735 rebellious Indians attacked a landing party from the Manila galleon *San Cristóbal* at the cove of San Bernabé, killing all thirteen sailors on the beach and destroying their launch. In the meantime, the ship's captain, Don Mateo Zumalde, unaware of the massacre, moved his galleon nine leagues (twenty-two and a half miles) west to escape contrary winds. Growing suspicious of offers of help on the way from San José del Cabo, Zumalde barely escaped a ruse advanced by a rebel leader named Gerónimo that would have brought a party of nearly one hundred Uchitíes and their allies to the beach, intent on attacking and seizing the *San Cristóbal* with a bravado befitting the partial descendants of Dutch and English pirates.

Meanwhile, the viceroy of New Spain and archbishop of Mexico, Juan Antonio de Vizarrón y Eguiarreta, allowed the Jesuits of New Spain to recruit, equip, and send to Lower California at their own expense a relief force of Christian Yaqui and Sinaloa Indian soldiers from the Jesuit missions of Mexico. The viceroy-archbishop stated, however, that he did not possess the authority to commit the Crown to a full-scale relief effort and would have to look into the matter. Behind this delay, Dunne points out, was a long-simmering feud between the viceroy-archbishop and the Jesuits for the Jesuits' refusal to pay ecclesiastical tithes to Vizarrón, the archbishop, as called for in the Laws of the Indies, on the grounds that they were canonically exempt from such payments. The viceroy-archbishop thoroughly disagreed and excommunicated the Jesuit lay brother who was serving as treasurer of the Province of New Spain when he refused to make the required payments; he then excommunicated both the rector of the Colegio Máximo and the provincial of New Spain himself, Father José Barba, the religious superior of more than three hundred Jesuits in Mexico. Barba sent to Madrid two Jesuits disguised as laymen who pled the Jesuit case for exemption. The Jesuits prevailed in the tithing fracas, and Viceroy Vizarrón eventually sent a relief force to Lower California. The entire dispute, however, underscored the fault lines that were developing between the Society of Jesus and sectors of the establishment of New Spain, lay and ecclesiastical and fusions thereof.

A renewed effort

Lower California was retaken, its missions were rebuilt, and a new generation of Jesuit missionaries began to arrive, part of a larger influx of European Jesuits into the Indies that had begun in the 1660s and was sustained into the mid-eighteenth century. In 1735 alone, nineteen priests, five scholastics, six brothers, and fifteen novices were assigned from Europe to New Spain and Lower California (along with a smaller number assigned to the Far East). Thus Lower California in the mid-eighteenth century saw the arrival of Germans (Johann Bischoff, George Retz, Franz Benno Ducrue, Franz Inama, Joseph Gasteiger, Lambert Hostell, and Franz Xavier Wagner), Bohemians (Wenceslaus Linck and Ignacio Tirsch), a Moravian (Antonio Tempis), an Italian (Miguel Barco), an Alsatian (Jakob Baegert), and a Scotsman (William Gordon). These were men of education and Enlightenment values who spent up to two years in Jesuit houses of transit (Cádiz and Genoa) awaiting departure and in further study (astronomy, mathematics, and practical and fine arts). Each carried one well-packed trunk of personal effects as well as compasses, telescopes, and other scientific instruments; a Bible, plus liturgical and scholarly books; and paper, pens, and ink. Some even brought watercolors to illustrate the flora and fauna of this new place (the forty-six watercolors completed by Father Ignacio Tirsch are now housed in the National Library of the Czech Republic). The presence of such missionaries corroborated and reinforced Eusebio Kino's vision, for all these men—all this talent and education, all this missionary and Enlightenment zeal—could not be intended solely for Lower California. Something larger and grander was in the offing. Here were astutely trained men fully capable of moving northward from Pimería Alta and Lower California (once it was consolidated) into Upper California, advancing evangelization, creating alliances, fostering new settlements, establishing Catholic societies and cultures along the Pacific coast and its hinterlands. And here were men capable of bending the rules on behalf of their Society, no doubt inciting suspicion and envy among other New World orders, among diocesan priests eager for assignments and livings, among great landowners and mine operators greedy for Indian labor denied them by the protection of the Society, among viceregal officials who resented Jesuit influence in Rome and Madrid, and with at least one viceroy-archbishop who fumed over too much Jesuit autonomy and too many unpaid tithes.

Realistic evolutions

The rebellion of 1734 and the slow recovery from it forced the Jesuits laboring in Lower California to be more realistic. That realism was compounded by the arrival of a more internationally oriented, less unambiguously and patriotically Spanish cadre of Jesuits from outside the Spanish Empire. The new arrivals were more touched by science and Enlightenment values, and they were trained to serve long years in a remote place among peoples of uncertain capacities and loyalties. By the third generation of missionaries, the crisis of 1734 had passed, and matters had improved. The natives, now neophytes or baptized Christians, were wearing clothes. Some missions provided their Indians with a sort of uniform, shirts and pants for men and blouses and long skirts for women. Still, doubts remained. The Alsatian Jakob Baegert, for example, edged into negativity in assessing his charges: their tendency to steal what could be stolen; plunder mission gardens; rustle, kill, butcher, and barbecue mission cattle; fake illnesses in order to be provided with roast chicken; lie to get out of unwanted marriages; and persist in sexual activity outside the bonds of matrimony, young people and elders alike. "In general," writes Baegert in his *Nachrichten von der Amerikanischen halbinsel Californien* (An account of the aboriginal inhabitants of the California peninsula, published in Mannheim in 1772), "it can be said about the Californians that they are stupid, dull, coarse, dirty, insolent, ungrateful, liars, lazy, slothful in the extreme, great gabblers and in their intelligence and actions children to their dying day. It can truthfully be said that they live in a fog of confusion, are improvident, thoughtless, and irresponsible. In nothing have they self-control and in everything they follow their natural instincts after the manner of brute beasts."[3] Still, Father Baegert labored seventeen years as a missionary in what he considered a barren, unpromising place, among a people with whom he obviously had difficulties. Those people, in their own private discourse, most likely had equally discourteous things to say about the Jesuits, who had come uninvited into their lives, changed their way of life, restricted their sexual practices, dazzled them with their wealth and display of their material culture but punished them when they helped themselves to some of it, and flogged or jailed them when they ran afoul of a bewildering array of restrictions. Baegert's candid utterance voiced the paradox of the Jesuit era in Lower California. In China, India, and Japan, European Jesuits had encountered high cultures commensurate

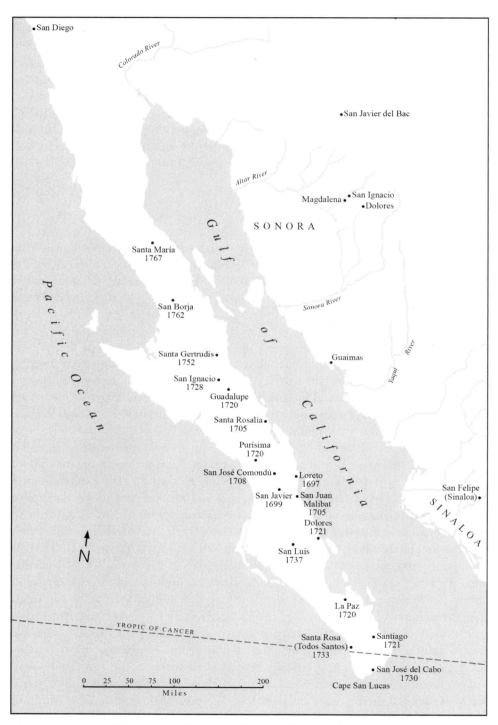

San Diego

Colorado River

San Javier del Bac

Altar River

Magdalena • • San Ignacio
• Dolores

Gulf SONORA

Santa María
1767

of

San Borja
1762

Sonora River

Santa Gertrudis •
1752

Guaimas

Yaqui River

San Ignacio •
1728

Guadalupe
1720

California

Pacific Ocean

Santa Rosalía •
1705

Purísima
1720

San José Comondú •
1708

• Loreto
1697

San Felipe
(Sinaloa) •

San Javier • San Juan
1699   Malibat
           1705
Dolores
1721

SINALOA

San Luis
1737

La Paz
1720

↑
N

TROPIC OF CANCER

Santa Rosa
(Todos Santos) •
1733

• Santiago
1721

0   25   50   75   100   200
    Miles

• San José del Cabo
1730
Cape San Lucas

Map 12. Jesuit Missions in Lower California, 1697–1768.

with their own training and advanced educations. In north-central and northwest Mexico and Pimería Alta, they had contended with indigenous people who, while capable of resistance and rebellion, likewise earned respect for their bravery, intelligence, social development, and material culture. In Lower California the Jesuits faced a more fundamental challenge from Indian communities who balked at what was being imposed on them. Unlike their Franciscan counterparts, Jesuits did not take refuge in visions of millenarian kingdoms. They preferred power, polity, results—and this preference, having made them enemies, would in 1767 end their role in Spanish Catholic America.

Suppression of the Society

Resettled in Europe—in many cases, after suffering from incarceration, shipwreck, hunger, and lack of medical attention—the Jesuits expelled from Mexico and Lower California, Central and South America, and the Caribbean now had a further shock: the suppression of their entire order following a long campaign by Spain, France, and Portugal in the brief *Dominus ac Redemptor Noster*, issued on 16 August 1773 and promulgated throughout Europe (except in Prussia and Russia, whose non-Catholic monarchs, the Lutheran Frederick the Great and the Russian Orthodox Catherine the Great, out of regard for their Jesuit advisors and teachers, refused to publish or otherwise acknowledge the papal directive). The record of Jesuit Lower California survived, however, in an outpouring of pre- and postsuppression histories and memoirs by Jesuits and former Jesuits, such as Miguel Venegas' three-volume *Noticia de la California* (1757); Jakob Baegert's *Nachrichten von der Amerikanischen halbinsel Californien* (1772); and Francisco Javier Clavigero's magisterial four-volume *Storia della California* (1789)—researched by the Jesuit scholar in the archives of Mexico City, Rome, Milan, and Venice, where it was belatedly published—today regarded as a foundational work of Mexican history.

And so the Jesuits said good-bye to the scene of their hopes and labors for seventy years. During a different time in the fortunes of their order, they established a foothold on the Pacific for Catholic Spain. Now, with the expulsion, to be followed within six years by the suppression, only memory and the writing of memoirs and history could offer consolation against all that had been lost. Even Father Baegert, Dunne tells us, softened and grew wistful as he remembered the people he had served to the best of his ability—and within the framework of a sense of superiority—for seventeen years. Despite his criticisms of place and people, Dunne writes, Baegert

> returned to comfortable Europe with a broken heart. He regaled his family and friends with stories of that far distant and mysterious land sitting on the rim of the world. He delighted and instructed those close to him with specimens of the flora and fauna of California, of varieties of cactus, of the bighorn sheep, of the beads and feathers used by the natives. Then four years later he published a book about it all, the oft-cited *Nachrichten*. But the wound to his spirit never healed. Like missionaries of every age and the world over, he had become attached to his people and although he knew no nostalgia on his departure from Europe, he did know it on his return, nostalgia for rock-ridden and cactus-studded Lower California, nostalgia for the degraded people for whose improvement, material and spiritual, he had devoted his days.[4]

PART THREE

Las Californias

8

San Blas 1768

New Spain launches an entrada into Alta California

As Eusebio Kino argued, the best entry into Alta (Upper) California was north from Sonora into Pimería Alta (southern Arizona) to the confluence of the Yuma and Colorado Rivers, across the Colorado River into the Colorado Desert, and then west by northwest to the Pacific coast. Such an approach, however, was temporarily impossible. The Jesuits' expulsion prompted disturbances in mining settlements across the northern frontier and the Jesuit-dominated northwest sector that kept José de Gálvez in the field for the better part of two years at the head of military and militia forces suppressing demonstrations and near revolts. Mixed-race miners resented oppressive local restrictions and taxes. Indians loyal to the Jesuit mission system joined militant Indian conspiracies that were hoping to regain tribal autonomy and reestablish prohibited religions and sexual practices. This wave of perturbations did not reprise the great Pueblo Revolt of 1680. It was not a well-organized rebellion that resulted in wholesale death. Indeed, it is difficult to track any significant bloodshed against Spaniards. The uprisings represented, rather, outbreaks of resistance by Indians and marginalized mixed-race peoples against a colonial scheme of things upset—and hence made vulnerable—by the wholesale arrest and deportation of the Jesuit missionaries, which had brought an abrupt end to the Jesuit-military partnership that had stabilized the region for the past century and a half.

Thus José de Gálvez, inspector general and intendant (executive) with plenipotentiary powers, journeyed across the northern frontier from east to west at the head of a column of well-armed dragoons and militia, suppressing rebellions, bringing to trial and executing hastily convicted ringleaders (in some cases mounting their heads on pikes above their homes or in other prominent places to warn about the consequences of civil disobedience), reorganizing local governance, and then moving on to other scenes of disorder that required a stabilizing presence. As a result of the first phase of Gálvez's campaign to restore order 3,000 people were brought to summary trial for hostile demonstrations, disorderly conduct, destruction of property, and the harboring of anti-Spanish attitudes. Eighty-five men were executed for more serious convictions; 73 were sentenced to the lash; 674 were sent to prison; and 117 were banished. Calm then reigned throughout the land, earning Gálvez a reputation as a pro-consul not to be trifled with. This enforcer of order and orthodoxy would be fearfully remembered even by later generations, up to the time of the early nineteenth-century revolution against Spanish rule by criollos and mestizos tired of second- and third-class status as well as alienated Indians who still dreamed of restoring autonomy in their own republics.

With the most restive of the northern provinces pacified, Gálvez turned his attention to the Californias, Baja (Lower) and Alta (Upper). Lower California had to be reorganized as a civil society. Since it was no longer a Jesuit fiefdom, Upper California needed to be occupied as far north as the Bay of Monterey, which was to serve as a harbor for returning Manila galleons. Another presidio should be established farther to the north, given the possibilities of a Russian advance southward down the Pacific coast. Indeed, on the second day of Gálvez's return journey to San Blas, a courier sent by Viceroy Carlos Francisco de Croix brought him a message from no less a personage than the marqués de Grimaldi, the minister of state in Madrid, urging decisive action in the settlement of Upper California. As evidence of the need for expediency, Grimaldi included a report that three hundred Russian soldiers, advancing south, were said to have been killed in a pitched battle with Indians. The account was not true, of course, but it suggested court circles' preoccupation with a Russian advance. And regarding Gálvez's fixation on the Bay of Monterey, one must remember how fulsomely Vizcaíno had exaggerated that harbor's capacities following his reconnaissance of the Upper California coast in 1602–1603. Monterey Bay, Gálvez believed, could be the site for a mission, a presidio, a settlement, and harbor facilities that—like the recently established harbor settlement of San Blas on the Gulf of California coast—could service Manila galleons and anchor the long-deferred colonization of Upper California.

Educated and experienced in law and administration before his rise in court circles, José de Gálvez had arrived in New Spain in 1765 as a reformer of civil government and administrative procedures and—to his great stress!—had edged into the grisly business of pacification only out of necessity. By contrast, the reorganization of Lower California, the enhancement of its civil sector, and the organization of an entrada into Upper California activated and fulfilled Gálvez's administrative talents and continental ambitions. Arriving in San Blas in the spring of 1768, Gálvez spent a busy two weeks taking care of a few local matters and organizing the Alta California project. Two newly constructed brigantines, the *San Carlos* and the *San Antonio* (the two best vessels on the Gulf of California coast), were assigned to the expedition, and maritime matters were put under the supervision of a junta composed of Miguel Costansó, an engineer and cosmographer; Manuel Rivero Cordero, *comandante de la marina*; mathematician Antonio Faveau y Quesada; Vicente Vila, a pilot in the Royal Navy; and Gálvez. (Faveau was on hand not only to help with maps and navigation, but also in anticipation of the arrival in Lower California of a French-Spanish scientific expedition tracking a transit of Venus.) The junta proposed a seaborne expedition of men and supplies to the Bay of San Diego, where it would rendezvous with two land columns advancing north from upper Lower California. A second ship would arrive with further provisions. From San Diego, a rested and resupplied land column could then advance north to the Bay of Monterey.

Clerical competition

In Franciscan circles, meanwhile, three organizations—the Province of Jalisco, the Apostolic College of Santa Cruz at Querétaro, and the Apostolic College of San Fernando in Mexico City—were lobbying to replace the Society of Jesus in Lower California and be given responsibility for advancing north. Well connected in the capital, the Fernandinos were initially given the assignment, and two talented friars, Francisco Palóu and Juan Ignacio Gastón, were assigned to accompany Governor Portolá to Lower California to make preliminary preparations for the transfer. While Palóu and Gastón were waiting in San Blas for a second attempt to cross the gulf, however—the first having been thwarted by a storm—the provincial of the Province of Jalisco persuaded the commissary of all Franciscans in New Spain, Fray Manuel Nájera, to lobby Viceroy Croix to cancel the first order and give the assignment to Jalisco. Responding to this reversal, Fray Junípero Serra, the assigned leader of the Fernandino mission, sent Palóu, his lead assistant and second in command, and another friar, Miguel de la Campa y Cos, to plead with Visitador General José de Gálvez to restore California to the College of San Fernando. Gálvez assented.

Technically, Gálvez outranked the viceroy, who was rankled by this upstart bureaucrat running the show, but the viceroy agreed to reverse his reversal, and despite the fact that Jaliscan friars were at that point assuming responsibility for two of the Lower California missions, Franciscans from the Apostolic College of San Fernando were assigned to the mission and departed for Lower California. An alliance formed among Gálvez, Portolá, Serra and Palóu, and Loreto presidio captain Fernando de Rivera y Moncada (whom Portolá had come to accept as a loyal servant of the new administration). These able men now organized and led the last great entrada in the history of the Borderlands, reaching as far north as the soon-to-be-discovered Bay of San Francisco.

Gálvez and his entourage arrived in Lower California on 5 July 1768 after a stormy forty-day passage across the gulf. Their flotilla of small ships (a bilander, a packet, and a barque) was driven as far south as Mazatlán, thus allowing the Spaniards to discover a group of small islands and for Gálvez to claim them for Spain. For the next three months, the inspector general awaited the arrival of the previously engaged *San Antonio* and the *San Carlos*. Based in the royal mining camp of Santa Ana (a settlement that had been exempt from Jesuit jurisdiction), Gálvez threw himself with characteristic energy into the final stages of the transfer of the fifteen missions—temporarily controlled by soldier commissaries—to Franciscans from the Apostolic College of San Fernando, on duty since April. Inspecting the southern missions, Gálvez found them in decline and restored full authority to the friars. In an effort to serve the 7,149 Indian residents of the missions better, Gálvez ordered Dolores and San Luis Gonzaga closed and their 800 inhabitants relocated to Todos Santos and Santiago. In the north, Gálvez ordered the Indians of the faltering Guadalupe and Santa Gertrudis to relocate to the flourishing San José de Comondú and La Purísima Concepción. By creating these denser settlements, Gálvez sought not only to alleviate hunger (an ever-present problem in Lower California) but also to establish the beginnings of pueblos or Indian settlements with limited self-governance under Franciscan jurisdiction.

Appalled by the rudimentary nature of non-Indian settlement in Lower California, Gálvez also attempted to found a colony at Cape San Lucas on the tip of the peninsula and to improve the rough settlements at La Paz and the mining camp at Santa Ana—unsuccessfully, as it turned out. Lower California would never prove an easy place for civilian settlement. Yet these endeavors by Gálvez, along with his efforts then and later in Sinaloa to introduce secular clergy and a diocesan structure, testify to his vision of the Californias as a postmissionary Catholic society.

According to his biographer, Herbert Ingram Priestley, Gálvez, although primarily concerned with civil and administrative matters, must be accorded the major credit for the organization of the missionary enterprise as well. While the Franciscans did found a new mission—San Fernando de Velicatá, in the northern sector of Lower California—the friars favored a more gradual, mission-by-mission advance into Upper California, as opposed to Gálvez's ordered leapfrog north to San Diego across hostile mountain and desert terrain, leaving the rest of northern Lower California to later development. Quite correctly, Priestley admits, the friars felt that there was not enough military and financial support to accomplish successfully such an entrada, which was to be followed almost immediately by the establishment of a chain of missions between San Diego and Monterey. The vision and iron will of Gálvez, Priestley argues, were the forces behind Junípero Serra's commitment to the project. Prior to the inspector general's arrival, Serra had no idea that such a bold advance north was in the offing or that Gálvez had chosen him to lead its evangelical effort as father president. Indeed, Priestley believes, Gálvez made Serra a convert to the cause, and Serra in turn convinced the Apostolic College of San Fernando to undertake the Alta California mission.[1]

War, madness, recovery

His work done in Lower California, Gálvez returned to Sinaloa and Sonora, where protracted guerrilla warfare by Seris, Pimas, and Sibubapas was turning the region into a wasteland of abandoned mines and missions and destroyed or abandoned haciendas. In 1768 rebel Indians killed seventy-five Spaniards, mestizos, and loyal Indians in the area. The tribes' willingness to take up arms against New Spain surfaced as early as 1751–1752, when nine villages of Pimas and Seris revolted and maintained their independence through force of arms for nearly twenty years. In Madrid, King Carlos III—as a matter of humanity, Enlightenment values, and expense—favored negotiation over full-scale suppression. Gálvez offered amnesty, but ringleaders of the rebellion thwarted his efforts. He next tried threats. "Let them see if they can find a place within the womb of earth wherein to hide themselves from the immense power of God and the King, who will convert them into ashes", Gálvez thundered.[2]

Ignoring the preferences of the Crown, Gálvez took to the field at the head of his troops. A revolt by Charay Indians in Nueva Vizcaya was soon put down. Seizing their goods, destroying their homes, and sowing their village sites with salt, Gálvez beheaded twenty leaders of the rebellion and had their heads posted on pikes at the entrances to their villages. Seventeen others were sentenced to two hundred lashes, which frequently constituted a de facto death sentence. Gálvez's secretary, Juan Manuel Viniegra, later claimed that Gálvez had promised the Charay leaders amnesty but had them seized and tried when they took him at his word and returned to their villages. By this time, Viniegra had come to believe that Gálvez was insane. Another member of Gálvez's staff, Eusebio Ventura Beleña, a civil and canon lawyer, agreed with Viniegra's assessment.

By August 1769, it was clear that something was very wrong with the inspector general. In previous campaigns in central and north-central Mexico, he had shown signs of instability during executions, when he would fervently exhort those who were about to die to accept the justice of their fate as preparation for a happy death. Two years later, his behavior was far worse. First came a month-long collapse, which Gálvez described as a walk in the shadow of death. Allegedly recovered, he suffered a relapse in mid-October while at the presidio of San Buenavista. This time, the symptoms were mental as well as physical. On 13 October he took to his bed. The next night, he called for his colleague Francisco de Armona at two in the morning. Saint Francis of Assisi had consulted with him, Gálvez told Armona, and the saint had described the officers of the current expedition as incompetents. Gálvez would replace the current army with six hundred apes from Guatemala, put them in uniform, and take to the field against rebels! The following day, he got up and went to the barracks to spend time with the enlisted men. He was on their side, he said. He would give them substantial raises and put to death any officers who did not comply with this decree.

Gálvez's secretaries brought him back to his room and kept him there. The surgeon bled Gálvez three times, to little avail. His staff then moved him to the mission of Ures in Sonora, where he spent the next forty days bedridden and psychotic. By December he appeared to have recovered. On 3 February 1770, when the weather cleared, Gálvez resumed his journey south to Mexico City but soon suffered a third relapse and was confined to quarters by his staff through mid-March, ranting as before, declaring himself the king of Prussia, the king of Sweden, the bishop of Puebla, even the Eternal Father Himself!

By the time Gálvez reached Mexico City in late May or early June, he was claiming a full recovery. Woe betide the staff members—administrative secretaries Juan Manuel Viniegra and Juan Antonio de Argüello, plus civil servant Miguel José de Azanza—who had taken care of him during his illnesses and reported on him to Mexico City during these psychotic episodes! By order of the viceroy, they were jailed and commanded to retract their written statements. They refused and were kept in prison until November. Viniegra and Argüello were sent back to Spain under a cloud, and Azanza was allowed to bury himself in obscurity in Havana.

Thanks to the intervention of Francisco Antonio de Lorenzana, the all-powerful archbishop of Toledo (elevated to cardinal in 1789)—who had been archbishop of Mexico at the time of Gálvez's episodes and hence knew the full story—Viniegra was restored to his career and appointed a treasury official in the viceroyalty of Peru. (We have no record of what happened to Argüello.) Azanza was also eventually restored to the royal service. On 31 May 1798 Azanza, now the Duke of Santa Fe, returned to Mexico City as viceroy, making his official entry (with delicious irony) at Tepotzotlán, where thirty years earlier he had been imprisoned.

Recalled to Spain in 1772 as a member of the Council of the Indies (and named minister general of the Indies in 1775), Gálvez—after some persuasion—made a formal statement that, in his opinion, Viniegra and Argüello were worthy of reinstatement to royal service. Gálvez left behind in New Spain an impressive record of administrative reforms in the spirit of the Enlightenment-oriented policies of Carlos III. In Spain he continued on this same course. As minister general of the Indies and councilor of state, Gálvez ended the rigid mercantilism of colonial trade in favor of a program of restricted free trade. He finalized the sweeping reorganization of colonies into administrative intendancies (based on the French model) that he had inaugurated while inspector general in New Spain. Gálvez ended his career as Marquis of Sonora, which was ironic: it was in Sonora and Sinaloa that, loyal to the Crown, he had put down rebellion and, with the horror of it all, gone mad.

Guilt and expiation

Did the organization of the Sacred Expedition, performed so speedily and efficiently by Gálvez, represent an effort to atone for arresting and deporting 678 Jesuits from New Spain and suppressing the disturbances that followed? Priestley argues that Gálvez's major motivation in restructuring Baja California and organizing the Alta California venture was the maximization of royal income. Yet the acquisition of new lands and tithes for the Crown did not preclude the extension of Spanish Catholic Christianity. The two had gone hand in hand—often with tragic results— since the establishment of empire in the Indies. Eusebio Kino knew this, and so did José de Gálvez. Still, the expulsion of a large and respected religious order from its ministry and material achievements must have weighed on the consciences of those who brought it about. Supervising the matter in Lower California, Governor Portolá might have behaved humanely. However—as recorded by Alberto Francisco Pradeau in his pioneering *La expulsión de los jesuitas de las provincias de Sonora, Ostimuri y Sinaloa en 1767* (1959)—on the mainland, especially in the northern frontier provinces, local officials charged with the roundup, arrest, imprisonment, and transportation of Jesuits found ample opportunities both to pay back the Jesuits for their long-standing protection of Indians against enforced labor and to appropriate Jesuit property.

On 9 June 1768 the royal ship *El Príncipe* anchored off Loreto filled with Jesuits under orders of arrest and deportation. Portolá supplied the ship with food and water but, afraid of upsetting the local Indians, forbade any landing of sick Jesuits and demanded that Miguel del Pino, the captain of *El Príncipe*, depart immediately. Pino refused and instead moved the ship to Puerto Escondido some fifteen miles from Loreto and disembarked the sickest of his Jesuit passengers. There they remained for a month, visited by Portolá, who worried about scarce food and water, and by Junípero Serra. The Franciscan superior joined Portolá in urging Pino to leave as quickly as possible, which was finally managed on 15 July 1768. Landing in San Blas, the Jesuits marched overland to Guadalajara for further processing. Historian Harry Crosby describes this forced trek as a death march. Twenty Jesuits died en route. Crosby bases his account on Pradeau's *La expulsión* and on letters by Portolá and Pino now housed in the Mexican General National Archive in Mexico City.

Francisco Palóu does not mention this episode in either *Relación histórica de la vida y apostólicas tareas del venerable padre Fray Junípero Serra* (1787) or his monumental diary-history, *Noticias de la Nueva California* (first published in 1857). Nor is it referenced in such otherwise comprehensive tomes as the four-volume *Writings of Junípero Serra* (1955), in Spanish with English translations, edited by Franciscan historian Antonine Tibesar; the equally monumental two-volume *Life and Times of Fray Junípero Serra* (1959) by Franciscan Maynard Geiger (both works about Serra are publications of the Academy of American Franciscan History); or Jesuit historian Peter Masten Dunne's *Black Robes in Lower California* (1952–1968). For eighteenth-century and present-day historians alike, the roundup, arrest, and expulsion of the

678 Jesuits in New Spain—educators and missionaries, the majority of whom were ordained priests, astutely trained members of a learned order with a record of more than two hundred years of dedicated service in the Indies—was perhaps too painful to chronicle, especially by historians belonging to the two orders involved. After all, it was a Conventual Franciscan, Lorenzo Ganganelli, who, as Pope Clement XIV—succumbing to political pressure from Spain, France, and Portugal—suppressed the Society of Jesus. The pope went into paranoia and depression for the remaining year of his life, fearing assassination in this world and punishment in the next for his suppression of the Society.

The Sacred Expedition

But all this was to occur soon, in 1773 and 1774. As 1768 edged into 1769, it was time to bypass the Lower California peninsula by ship or march through it by land, reach the Bay of San Diego, establish a base camp, and then advance north to the Bay of Monterey and there establish a mission, presidio, and harbor settlement.

The seaborne component of the Sacred Expedition consisted of three packets constructed at San Blas. Under the command of Vicente Vila, a member of the San Blas organizing team, the *San Carlos*—blessed before departure by Father Serra—left La Paz on 9 January 1769. Formerly known also as *El Príncipe*, the *San Antonio* sailed from Cabo San Lucas on 15 February under the command of Juan Pérez, a skilled pilot with long experience in the Philippines. The *San José* sailed from Loreto on 16 June. The packets were scheduled to arrive at staged intervals in San Diego, where they would rendezvous with the land parties. They would then make subsequent trips to San Blas and return for resupply as well as move parts of the expedition farther north to Monterey.

Two overland parties, meanwhile, would trek from Velicatá north to San Diego, one under the command of Fernando de Rivera y Moncada, the longtime captain of the presidio at Loreto, and the other commanded by Governor Portolá. The Rivera party—twenty-five soldiers, naval pilot and land navigator José Cañizares, Franciscan Juan Crespí (the official historian of the expedition and scout for future mission sites), three muleteers, and forty-four Christianized Indians from Lower California—departed Velicatá on Good Friday, 24 March. The Portolá party, in which Junípero Serra traveled in his capacity as father president—nine or ten soldiers under the command of the energetic Sergeant José Francisco Ortega, six muleteers, two servants, and forty-two Christianized Indians from Lower California—left on 15 May, following the trail blazed by the Rivera group. Like Crespí, Cañizares kept a meticulous account of the journey, while the diversely talented Crespí assisted Cañizares in taking elevations of the sun and calculating latitudes.

Although Rivera had previously led a reconnaissance to the north, a week after departure his crew entered terra incognita, and local languages became incomprehensible. By 12 or 13 April, as the Rivera party ventured into the territory of the Paipai, an improvised sign language offered the only means of communication. Ten days or so later, however, the Spaniards reached the homeland of the southern Kumeyaay, whose language proved less of a challenge and remained the lingua franca, more or less, until they reached San Diego. Words were acquired from locals encountered en route.

On the trail, the Lower Californian Indians were expected to forage for themselves. Early on, a number of them died, and Rivera had to assure his Indians that they were not being punished for marching into other people's territory. Still, more died—from exhaustion and hunger—and others began to return south to their homeland. Altogether, thirty of the forty-four Lower Californians in the Rivera party died or deserted. Portolá's group lost a similar number.

On 2 May Rivera reached the Bay of La Ensenada de Todos Santos and camped that night on level land that is today the center of the city of Ensenada. Although the Spaniards could not have realized it at the time—they may well have been distracted by groups of local Indians appearing at a distance, the men gesturing with bows and arrows as if to suggest an imminent attack—they were within two weeks of their destination. On 9 May the Rivera party encountered a Kumeyaay encampment. Captain Rivera approached the camp in the company of one soldier and left gifts of ribbons and cloth on the ground at a proper distance. The next day, in the course of further friendly contact, an Indian took hold of Crespí's gray habit and indicated that there was a man dressed the same way, along with other Spaniards, on the bay to the north.

The *San Antonio* reached San Diego on 11 April after two months at sea. Delayed by storms, the *San Carlos* limped in on 29 April after a horrendous voyage of four months, its crew and soldiers dangerously debilitated by scurvy. The Rivera party followed on 14 May. The Portolá party followed on 1 July after a comparatively easy trek of forty-seven days. Bothered by an ulcerous leg en route, Serra had directed a muleteer to apply the same poultice used to treat a similarly afflicted mule. The poultice worked wonders, and Serra—as was his wont on previous missionary assignments—walked all the way to San Diego. Portolá and his mule train brought badly needed provisions. Due late summer or early fall, the *San José* was to bring in more supplies.

On to Monterey

Portolá felt confident enough to order the *San Antonio* back to Mexico for supplies and reinforcements, leaving the empty *San Carlos* anchored on the bay, and to organize and launch within two weeks of his arrival at San Diego a reconnaissance north and a second base camp at Monterey, the stated objective of the Sacred Expedition. Selected from the ablest and fittest of the 126 men who had made it to San Diego, this second Portolá party represented a distinguished distillation of personnel. It included such capable officers as Captain Rivera; Lieutenant Pedro Fages, the commander of the Free Company of Catalan Volunteers; Lieutenant Miguel Costansó of the Royal Corps of Engineers; the multitalented Sergeant José Francisco Ortega, the senior noncommissioned officer in a contingent of twenty-seven soldiers; and six Catalan volunteers. Juan Crespí joined the party as historian and chaplain, along with Fray Francisco Gómez, who had arrived on the *San Antonio*. Seven muleteers (to manage twenty-five mules); a labor force of fifteen Lower California neophytes; Portolá's servant, Ignacio; and an unnamed servant for Rivera completed the force.

The sheer size and staffing of this reconnaissance north underscored how fixedly Inspector General Gálvez—energized by the tales of Vizcaíno and his Carmelite chaplain, Antonio de la Ascensión—had established in the minds of the Sacred

Expedition leadership the importance of Monterey as the best site for the first Spanish port on the Pacific coast of North America. Monterey, in Gálvez's opinion, was the culmination of the entire enterprise, and Portolá had every intention of fulfilling his mandate from the inspector general. Two days before Junípero Serra dedicated Mission San Diego de Alcalá in honor of the fifteenth-century Didacus of Alcalá, a Franciscan lay brother commonly known as Diego, Portolá rode out of this first Spanish camp at the head of a formidable column, with Sergeant Ortega and soldiers riding ahead as scouts and a caballada of spare mules and horses constituting the final element. From San Diego northward up the coast to the Los Angeles River, the march (frequently in sight of the sea) was easy enough. With few incidents, the Portolá party proceeded through present-day San Diego and Orange Counties, camped near the Santa Ana River, moved on through the San Gabriel Valley to the Los Angeles plain and river, turned up Sepulveda Canyon to the San Fernando Valley, continued north through the Santa Clara Valley and Ventura County, and then skirted the Santa Barbara Channel, where white beaches and mirage-like islands appeared in the distance. Friendly Indians at various points along the way provided food and directions. Each day began with Mass and ended with the singing of the Salve Regina. As it progressed north, the Portolá party, following the liturgical calendar, conferred on geographical features saints' names that have endured to this day. This procession, like Serra's dedication of Mission San Diego, was part of the founding of Alta California as a Catholic place.

When the expedition passed Morro Bay, however, and reached the Santa Lucia Mountains flanking the south of the impassible Big Sur region, the Spaniards were forced to pick their way painfully through rugged terrain—suitable, Crespí noted, to deer and mountain goats, not men, especially those already weakened by scurvy. On 15 September the expedition turned inland, entered the Salinas Valley, proceeded north, and then followed the Salinas River to the sea.

The latitude reported by Costansó indicated that Monterey Bay was nearby. Astonishingly, the Spaniards failed to find it. No Bay of Monterey, after coming all this way! Classic accounts blame the exaggerations of Vizcaíno and his chaplain for this failure—which is to say, Portolá and his men could not believe that what they were seeing was the great harbor described nearly 170 years earlier. Fog has also been cited as a contributing factor: the kind of dense Pacific-coast fog that prevented as well any sighting of the entrance to San Francisco Bay to the north. In 2001, however, the husband-and-wife team of Robert Senkewicz and Rose Marie Beebe of Santa Clara University gave a convincing account of why and how the Spaniards failed to find such a major geographical feature.

The Portolá party, Senkewicz and Beebe tell us, was using as its gazetteer a 1734 navigational guide prepared by José González Cabrera Bueno, a Manila galleon pilot, who in turn had based his account on that of Fray Antonio de la Ascensión. The Carmelite friar had described an entrance to the bay from the south. The Portolá party, however, approached inland along the Salinas River, which they mistakenly thought was the Carmel River noted by Fray Antonio and pilot Bueno. The Spaniards thus reached the shore north of Point Pinos via a route skirting present-day Castroville and Salinas River State Beach. They grew confused. Their guidebook recounted passing the mouth of the Carmel River, rounding Point Pinos, and then beholding the bay extending (in the shape of a fishhook, Robert Louis

Stevenson would later describe it) from Point Pinos to Santa Cruz. From their vantage point, however, the Spaniards could not see Santa Cruz in the distance (here, fog might very well have been a factor). Nor did the inlets at the mouths of the Salinas and Carmel Rivers resemble the harbor described in the literature; their Carmel River (low at that time of year) impressed them as little more than a creek. So they pushed north through the redwoods of the Santa Cruz peninsula in search of the bay their guide extolled.

On 23 October the Portolá party reached Half Moon Bay. From there Portolá sent Sergeant Ortega and a few soldiers into the hills ahead as scouts. At the top of one crest, the scouting party could see forty miles across open water north-northwest to the Farallon Islands and Point Reyes, known to be the entrance to Cermeño's (Drakes) Bay. Moving farther north, the Ortega party mounted a high ridge (Sweeney Ridge, outside present-day Pacifica), and there in the distance the soldiers espied a vast inlet or estuary that Crespí would later describe as large enough to offer anchorage to all the ships of Spain—indeed, all the navies of Europe.

The Spaniards further explored the southern shore of this great estuary, and they also saw far away the connecting San Pablo Bay, but hostile natives blocked their advance, and they thus failed to discover the entrance to this inland sea. On Saturday, 11 November, following Mass, Portolá held a council in camp. Provisions were running short, he said. Those showing symptoms of scurvy were growing weaker. Some men had fallen sick, having eaten raw acorns. The *San José* was nowhere in sight. Crespí tells us that Portolá was eager to continue with the advance, but in deference to his officers and the two Franciscans, he assented to their wish to return south and make one more effort to find the Bay of Monterey before returning to San Diego. The matter-of-factness of Crespí's reporting of this decision—expressing no exultation about the farthest northern advance of Spaniards on the Pacific coast of North America, no pride or joy regarding the vast inland sea just discovered, only a persistent anxiety about having missed the Bay of Monterey—testifies to the men's fatigue after so many months on the trail as well as the fixation on Monterey instilled in the Sacred Expedition by Gálvez.

Starvation, attack, novena

Back in San Diego, meanwhile (to which the Portolá party, having failed in its second attempt to discover Vizcaíno's harbor, returned on 24 January 1770), conditions had gone from bad to worse. Only half of the Sacred Expedition had reached San Diego in the first place, and many of those who arrived by sea continued to die from scurvy and malnutrition. Lost at sea, the *San José* would never arrive, and the *San Carlos*, having delayed as long as possible at anchor in San Diego Bay, had returned to home port for resupply. Camp discipline grew lax, which meant further disease from sewage and related waste, which in turn meant more deaths. The expedition's surgeon, Pedro Prat, suffered a nervous breakdown trying to cope with the increasing disaster.

Upon his return, Captain Rivera established what camp discipline he could. The experienced officer had latrines dug and segregated the sick into an improvised infirmary, but matters steadily deteriorated due to scurvy, starvation, and lack of sanitation, and were exacerbated by local Indians' thievery and one Indian attack on 15 August, the Feast of the Assumption. In the assault, José María Vergerano, a young servant attached to Serra and the Franciscans, bled to death in Serra's arms from an arrow lodged in his neck. Three other expedition members were wounded.

The return of the Portolá party to San Diego meant no second settlement in Monterey and more mouths to feed. In early March, Portolá informed Serra that he would return to Lower California if no relief ship arrived by 19 March, the feast of Saint Joseph. The previous month the four Franciscans—Serra, Crespí, Gómez, and Fernando Parrón—had signaled their intention to remain in San Diego, no matter what Portolá decided to do; yet the friars realized how slim their chances of survival would be with no military protection, no labor force, and no supplies. On 12 February, Rivera, twenty soldiers, three muleteers, and the fifth friar on the expedition, Juan Vizcaíno (wounded in the Indian attack of 15 August), had left for Lower California in hopes of returning with cattle and provisions. Serra, meanwhile, negotiated a compromise with Vicente Vila, the captain of the *San Carlos*, who promised to remain at anchor as long as he could, even if Portolá left, but should all else fail, he and the friars would have to return to San Blas. Informed by Portolá of Captain Vila's decision, Serra proposed a novena, nine days of Mass and prayers in honor of Saint Joseph. Portolá agreed, and the novena began. On the ninth and final day of the novena, 19 March, the feast of Saint Joseph, around three o'clock in the afternoon, following the celebration of a high Mass that morning and an exhortatory sermon from Serra, the *San Antonio* appeared on the horizon. The ship sailed on, however, its destination being Monterey, where the main party was expected to land. Four days later, however, under the command of Juan Pérez, the *San Antonio* reentered San Diego Bay. The Sacred Expedition was saved!

Junípero Serra

While thoroughly documented, the providential arrival of the *San Antonio* reads like a passage from a miracle-filled life of a medieval saint. The comparison is appropriate, for Junípero Serra, as historian James Sandos of the University of Redlands has argued, was in and of his time as missionary administrator and—in terms of piety, temperament, philosophy, and social and ascetical practice—equally outside of his time as well. From Palóu (1787) to Maynard Geiger (1959), Franciscan biographers of Serra have noted his achievements in a density of detail that justifies Serra's reputation as an action hero of Catholic history. The four volumes of Serra's own writings, published between 1955 and 1966, nearly all of which deal with practical matters of his missionary years, further corroborate this impression of heroic devotion to duty as Serra saw and embraced that duty, with next to no regard for personal comfort. Popular Catholic piety, such as that evidenced in Agnes Repplier's influential biography (1933), has treated Serra as a de facto saint—popularly canonized, if you will, as in the early Church, or like Saint Francis of Assisi, who was officially canonized a mere two years after his death. Serra's cause for canonization, by contrast, was initiated in 1934 by the Diocese of Monterey-Fresno. It was under investigation by the Congregation for the Causes of Saints for nearly half a century. In 1986 Serra was declared Venerable. A declaration of Blessed followed in 1988. In January 2015 Pope Francis unilaterally— and somewhat surprising—declared his intent to canonize Serra within the year, which he did eight months later. The cause for this delay before canonization may very well be the controversy surrounding the California mission system itself, as well as the chiaroscuro of Serra's personality and missionary practice. In times past, however, Catholics and non-Catholics alike had little trouble regarding Serra as a founder, as evident in the selection of Serra in 1931 as one of two statues representing California in the Hall of Statuary of the Capitol in Washington, D.C.

Born and raised a Catholic, Sandos intuitively grasps the texture and coloration of Serra's religiosity. As an academically trained Latin Americanist and Borderlands scholar, however, Sandos is neither a basher nor a booster of Serra (both categories of which have more than enough members). Sandos' *Converting California: Indians and Franciscans in the Missions* (2004) encourages us to place Serra in social, cultural, and psychological context—which is difficult to do in such a man of action—in an effort to find the multidimensional man behind the statue, the saint, the founder, or the ogre, depending on one's point of view. For one thing, Sandos urges us to see Serra as an outsider faced with an insider's challenge to found Spain's last colony in the New World. At the same time, he was hostile to civil settlement, viewing Alta California as the Franciscans' final opportunity to realize their deepest hopes for their order in the Indies: the establishment of a Franciscan protectorate for Christianized Indians as a fulfillment of history and a millenarian model of Kingdom Come.

Spanish was not Serra's first language. He had to acquire Spanish through the Mallorquí dialect used in Petra and through Mallorcan, the local variety of Catalan spoken on Majorca. Serra was probably introduced to Spanish when, at the age of fifteen, he entered the household of a priest canon of the cathedral at Palma and embarked upon the study of philosophy at the Franciscan Convento San Francisco, most likely in preparation for the diocesan priesthood. Given his brilliance (and perhaps his parents' wishes), the young man had the opportunity for a distinguished career as a diocesan ecclesiastic. Instead, Serra chose to join the Franciscans, although an outsider element surfaced. Serra's paternal grandmother was named Duana Abraham, which suggested Jewish ancestry, not unknown on Majorca; as Sandos points out (briefly, in a footnote), the name Serra itself appears a number of times in the Inquisition record of the island. Still, after a short delay, Serra was admitted as a novice at the Convento de Jesús just outside Palma and was professed the next year under the name Junípero, who had been an early and close companion to Francis of Assisi. Fray Junípero, as he now was, showed academic promise throughout his courses in philosophy (1731–1734) and theology (1734–1737) at the Convento San Francisco, an institution that served Franciscan and diocesan candidates for the priesthood as well as laymen.

Following his ordination in December 1738 and his election to a lectorate of philosophy, Serra served a year as librarian and choir director at his home friary before returning to the Convento San Francisco as an instructor in philosophy. His influence on two of his Franciscan students there, Francisco Palóu and Juan Crespí, lasted a lifetime.

Majorcan and Scotist influences

While on the staff of the Convento San Francisco, Serra worked on a doctorate in theology, which he received from the Lullian University in Palma in 1742. In

January 1744 Serra was appointed primary professor to the Scotistic chair of theology at the Lullian University, engaged in teaching the thought of the venerated Franciscan medieval philosopher and theologian John Duns Scotus. Although his influence on Serra is not documented, Raymond Lull, born around 1235, the founder and namesake of the university, epitomized the idiosyncratic insider/outsider nature of Catalan/Majorcan culture. A Palma-born poet, mystic, linguist, philosopher, missionary, and martyr, Lull began his distinctive career as a page in the service of the Infante Jaime II, who in 1276 became king of a briefly existing (1276–1344) autonomous Kingdom of Majorca. Formed by the troubadour tradition (like Dante and Petrarch), Lull loved one woman as an unattainable ideal, whom he celebrated in poetry, but married another, the long-suffering Blanca Picany, who bore his children and saw him through a midlife crisis. When his courtly ideal died unexpectedly, Lull experienced a personal crisis followed by a religious conversion. Remaining a layman, and most likely becoming a Franciscan tertiary, he devoted the rest of his life to prayer, mysticism, philosophy, Arabic studies, and missionary work among the Muslims of North Africa.

The Moors governed Majorca from 902 to 1114, bringing to the island that irenic coresidence of Christian and Jewish communities under Muslim domination characteristic of the medieval Muslim world. Thus Lull mastered Arabic as a living as well as a literary language, which he taught to prospective missionaries and in which he wrote a number of treatises. Although Lull thought and wrote primarily in the tradition of Augustinian Platonism beloved by Franciscans, Sufi influences can be detected in his *Book of the Lover and the Beloved*; Lull's grandly schemed and multilayered *Ars veritatis inventive* (The art of conversion) is a treatise on Christianity and the kabbalah that he wrote in Latin and rewrote in Arabic, based in part on religious assumptions shared by Christians, Jews, and Muslims. Hundreds of years before the founding of the Propagation of the Faith, Lull devoted considerable effort to persuading various popes and hierarchs to establish missionary colleges and was stoned to death at the age of eighty while preaching to Muslims in North Africa.

John Duns Scotus—so named in honor of Duns, Scotland, his birthplace—the thirteenth-century Franciscan philosopher and theologian, was to Serra and all Franciscans what Thomas Aquinas was to the Order of Preachers: the brightest star in the firmament, the glory of the order in terms of Scholastic thought, and the guide to intellectual formation for generations to come. An Oxford and University of Paris don in a golden age of Scholasticism who was known as the Subtle Doctor because of the intricacies of his thought, Duns Scotus followed a line of succession—Scripture, Augustinian theology, Neoplatonism, the mysticism of Saint Francis of Assisi, and the illuminist teachings of the Franciscan cardinal Bonaventure, saint and Doctor of the Church—that formed the intellectual and devotional tradition in which Serra came of age and was named professor. While philosophically anchored in existence and rational analysis, the tradition at the same time prized the innate capacity of the human mind to grasp intuitively the existence and abiding love of God and to respond with assent, choice, and love in return. More recently, this Scotist tradition was reinforced by the 1639 publication in Lyon of Duns Scotus' *Opera omnia* in twelve volumes, edited by the Salamanca-educated, Rome-based Irish Franciscan Luke Wadding, a giant of Counter-Reformational scholarship and Church reform.

Serra abandoned academic life in 1749 in favor of a missionary assignment in New Spain. He left behind no treatise on Duns Scotus or any other academic writings of significance. Yet Serra's commitment to his Franciscan identity, the record of his life, the four volumes of his correspondence, and the reports of his preaching suggest an obvious connection between the Subtle Doctor and the professor turned missionary. Scotus taught the univocity of being: reality is one and universal, finite and infinite simultaneously. The finite possesses an innate drive toward the infinite. Nature aspires upward, as do men. The Infinite with a capital *I*, meaning God, is Infinite Being and Infinite Love. Hence, from the Franciscan perspective—in terms of evangelization—all men, including the Indians of California, were capable of grasping and assenting to the Supreme Being presented to them as Infinite Being and Infinite Love as made manifest in Jesus Christ, God's loving gift of Himself to the human race.

In *Converting California*, Sandos criticizes Serra and the Franciscans for baptizing the Indians of Alta California too quickly, then treating such baptisms as true conversions. Sandos considers this the essential flaw of the mission system in California: its lack (although Sandos does not define it as such) of cross-cultural reference and patient instruction. The Scotist Franciscan tradition fostered an end run around culture driven both by a desire to compile conversions as a sign of success and by a belief in the innate human capacity to grasp the Infinite as Being and Love and Jesus Christ as messenger of this truth.

Duns Scotus was an early and important defender of the doctrine of the Immaculate Conception: the preservation of Mary from original sin, and hence her existence as the epitome of perfected humanity, a belief eventually recognized (in 1854) as accepted Catholic doctrine. As already suggested, this belief played a decisive role in the evolution of Franciscan missionary practice in the Borderlands. For Franciscans of the Scotist persuasion, Mary stood at the end of time as the model toward whom history was tending. The goal of the Franciscan missionaries in the Borderlands, therefore, was to prepare for that era and, in the course of doing so, help atone for the sins of Spain against the Indians through the creation of stabilized Catholic communities of baptized Indians under Franciscan guardianship.

Another figure of major influence on Franciscan missionaries, María de Ágreda, the Franciscan abbess and mystic, likewise advanced the doctrine of the Immaculate Conception. Her *Mystical City of God and the Divine History of the Virgin Mother of God* (1670) so vigorously (and perhaps so clumsily) argued the cause that, taken together with its equally energetic espousal of private revelations, it earned for the book a short time on the Index of Forbidden Books and, for its author, accusations of Jewish ancestry. Serra loved *The Mystical City* and took its three volumes (along with a violin) with him when he hiked into the Sierra Gorda from Mexico City on his first missionary assignment. Theologians of the Sorbonne were disturbed by intimations of the kabbalah and of Sufi that lurked within *The Mystical City*, reverberations reminiscent of Raymond Lull's *Book of the Lover and the Beloved* nearly four hundred years earlier. The expulsion of the Jews and the defeat of the Moors in 1492, as well as the subsequent scrutiny and harsh penalties of the Inquisition, could never fully drive the influences of Iberian Jewish and Islamic mysticism from the Spanish Catholic mystical tradition. Despite Catholic Spain's obsession with *limpieza de sangre* (pure blood) and orthodoxy, and despite its loathing of heresy, three faiths of the Book had coexisted for so long on the Iberian Peninsula that temperaments, approaches, and literary forms had overlapped. Evident as well—in Teresa of Ávila, mystic reformer and Doctor of the Church; and (less definitely) Bartolomé de Las Casas, Protector of the Indians; and (allegedly) Junípero Serra himself—was a thread of Jewish bloodlines.

Ascetic preoccupations

The issue of religiosity brings us to the perplexing question of Serra's ferocious asceticism, which seems to be a medieval throwback for a late-eighteenth-century member of a missionary college purportedly touched with Enlightenment values. By the fourth century, the monasticism of the Egyptian desert (and a good dose of residual Manichaeism, with its conviction that the flesh was intrinsically evil) had introduced athletic asceticism into Christianity—prolonged fasting, hair shirts, self-flagellation, and other deliberate mortifications—and such practices ebbed and flowed over the next thousand years. In the Middle Ages, the Franciscan movement split into opposing camps in part because of differing opinions regarding the need or value of self-inflicted physical punishment. Ignatius of Loyola, a Basque nobleman and former soldier, remained ambivalent to its usefulness and once admonished a fasting Jesuit novice to eat his dinner. One can never imagine Eusebio Kino endangering his health through excessive fasting or self-flagellation. Life on the trail was tough enough. Extreme ascesis, moreover, was never part of the culture of diocesan clergy, either before or after the Council of Trent.

Junípero Serra, by contrast, a throwback in so many ways—he rejected the Copernican theory, for example, in favor of a terracentric scheme in which angelic intelligences moved the planets—wholeheartedly embraced the physical self-chastisement of an earlier era. His enthusiasm seemed particularly evident following the crisis of the late 1740s that led him to resign his professorship and request a missionary assignment. Arriving in Veracruz, Serra insisted upon walking the entire 250 miles to Mexico City and in the process acquired an ulcerated leg from either a snake bite or scratched insect bites that would give him no end of pain in the years to come, especially since he persisted in walking to his next destination. Assigned to the preaching circuit as a home missionary (Serra held the rank of preacher within the order), he practiced an uberemotive style of delivery, which included self-flagellation in the pulpit and beating his chest with a stone to express remorse for sin. The latter caused damage to his chest, another lifelong ailment.

No documentation contains statements from Serra concerning the whys and wherefores of all this self-punishment. Was the crisis that brought about his career change the motivation? The onetime librarian, choir director, and professor who had been housed in beautiful surroundings, following a leisurely schedule of teaching and contemplation, was now storming the gates of heaven as the heroic missionary. Or were his self-injuries, in part, a reaction against the opulence of upper-class Mexico City: the clothing, the jewelry, the lavish meals, the pearl-bedecked women being served hot chocolate as they sat together in church, gossiping during services? How better for Serra to counter such self-indulgence than by flagellating himself in the pulpit? He once got so carried away, one story claims, that an unknown man grabbed the whip from Serra and began to flagellate himself as a more worthy candidate for punishment—and died as a result. Or was Serra trying to root out, through pain, the unacknowledged (but there, beneath the surface) suspicion of Jewishness in a man whose grandmother's last name was Abraham, yet who served as the Inquisition commissary for the Sierra Gorda missionary region?

The first two missions

The *San Antonio* having arrived and the Sacred Expedition having been saved, Serra and his Franciscan colleagues got to work on the development of Mission San Diego on its first of two sites. This was Serra's second California mission; upon departing Lower California, he had established Mission San Fernando at Velicatá while en route to San Diego and left behind Padre Miguel de la Campa y Cos to develop it. While serving among the Pames people in the Sierra Gorda between 1750 and 1758 (as regional president from 1751 to 1754), Serra built—working personally on the construction site as a jack-of-all-trades—the impressive Church of Santiago at Jalpan. To help carry large beams, the five-foot-two Serra made himself the same height as the Pames laborers by bunching up his Franciscan habit between his shoulder and the wood. Missionaries under Serra's supervision built churches that are still in use at four other locations. Unlike his Zacatecan counterpart, Fray Antonio Margil, Serra did not design churches, but his taste was shaped by the superb Franciscan architecture of Spain and Spanish colonial Mexico, as evident in the friaries and colleges of Majorca and Mexico. In Mexico, Serra showed a passion for building that would initiate in California the construction of twenty-one missions, a number of which survive as icons of regional identity.

Since Monterey was the final and most important destination of the Sacred Expedition, as planned by Gálvez, it quickly became the site of the second Alta California mission. Given the confusion and frustration of the 1769 Portolá reconnaissance, which failed to identify Monterey Bay, it is gratifying to note that—after a difficult voyage during which adverse winds blew his ship as far south as Lower California, then north to the Farallones—Captain Juan Pérez navigated the *San Antonio* easily into Monterey Bay on 1 June 1770; on board were Serra, engineer Costansó, and ailing physician Pedro Prat, who was suffering from a nervous breakdown. At Monterey the *San Antonio* passengers met up with an overland expedition under the command of Portolá that included the talented and ever energetic Fray Juan Crespí, Lieutenant Pedro Fages, twelve Catalan volunteers, seven "leatherjackets" (criollo soldiers, so called because of their breastplates of hardened leather), two muleteers, five Lower California neophytes, and Ignacio, Portolá's faithful servant. The Portolá party had arrived a week earlier and made camp on Carmel Bay at the mouth of the Carmel River. That Sunday, the Feast of Pentecost, 3 June 1770, Serra and Crespí celebrated high Mass under the great oak tree under which Fray Antonio de la Ascensión and the other Carmelite chaplains of the Vizcaíno expedition in 1602 had celebrated the first Mass in Alta California.

It was a memorable day, the true founding of Alta California as a Spanish colony in terms of formal ceremonies. Nine days later, Serra reported on it in great detail to Fray Juan Andrés, the father guardian of the Apostolic College of San Fernando. "The day came", wrote Serra of the day in which he once and for all entered North American history.

A little chapel and altar were erected in that little valley, and under the same live-oak, close to the beach, where, it is said, Mass was celebrated at the beginning of the last century. Two processions from different directions converged at the same time on the spot, one from the sea, and one from the land expedition; we singing the divine praises in the launch, and the men on land, in their hearts.

Our arrival was greeted by the joyful sound of the bells suspended from the branches of the oak tree. Everything being in readiness, and having put on alb and stole, and kneeling down with all the men before the altar, I intoned the hymn Veni, Creator Spiritus, at the conclusion of which, and after invoking the help of the Holy Spirit on everything we were about to perform, I blessed the salt and the water. Then we all made our way to a gigantic cross which was all in readiness and lying on the ground. With everyone lending a hand we set it in an upright position. I sang the prayers for its blessing. We set it in the ground and then, with all the tenderness of our hearts, we venerated it. I sprinkled with holy water all the fields around. And thus, after raising aloft the standard of the King of Heaven, we unfurled the flag of our Catholic Monarch likewise. As we raised each one of them, we shouted at the top of our voices: "Long live the Faith! Long live the King!" All the time the bells were ringing, and our rifles were being fired, and from the boat came the thunder of the big guns.

Then we buried at the foot of the cross a dead sailor, a calker, the only one to die during this second expedition.

With that ceremony over, I began the high Mass, with a sermon after the Gospel; and, as long as the Mass lasted, it was accompanied with many salvos of cannon. After taking off my chasuble after Mass, all together we sang in Spanish the Salve Regina, in harmony, in front of the wonderful painting of Our Lady, which was on the altar. The Most Illustrious Inspector General had given us the picture for this celebration, but with the obligation of returning it to him afterward, as I will do when the boat sails.

As a conclusion to the liturgical celebration, standing up I intoned the Te Deum Laudamus; we sang it slowly, and solemnly, right to the end, with the responses and prayers to the Most Holy Trinity, to Our Lady, to the Most Holy Saint Joseph, patron of the expedition, to San Carlos, patron of this port, presidio and mission, and finally the prayer of thanksgiving.

May God be thanked for all things! Meantime, having put off my vestments, and while I was making my thanksgiving after the Mass of the day, the officers proceeded to the act of taking formal possession of that country in the name of His Catholic Majesty, unfurling and waving once more the royal flag, pulling grass, moving stones and other formalities according to law—all accompanied with cheers, ringing of bells, cannonades, etc. In addition there was a banquet served afterward to all of us gathered together on the beach; later a walk at sunset along the ocean concluded the celebration, when the men of the land expedition returned to their Carmel, and we to the boat.[3]

The lyricism and detail of Serra's description suggest his deep Catholic faith and commitment to evangelization. Serra displays his skills as a writer, so evident in the reports that would pour forth from his pen over the next fifteen years. Evident as well is the survival (amid his asceticism) of a poeticism—engaged, emotional, occasionally sensuous—that made him such a skilled preacher and such an enthusiastic appreciator of roses and wildflowers. In the rest of this long letter, which functions as a prophetic text for the next fifteen years of mission founding, Serra talks of money—the 700 pesos the Crown owed the college for missionary services in Alta California; and supplies—candles for Mass, inner tunics (long johns) for the cold, blankets imprinted with the name of each mission (soon to be three, Serra promises), and clothes for the local male Indians, who tended to go naked. And more chocolate, Serra adds, "which till now we have not run short of, thank God, and thanks to the good offices of the Most Illustrious Inspector General [Gálvez]". Roses, wildflowers, and chocolate! Hot chocolate, as served in the apostolic colleges. How do these fit in with Serra's fierce asceticism? Perhaps they signaled that he had not completely succeeded in flagellating a Majorcan joy in life, an appreciation of natural beauty and small pleasures, into submission. "It is a truly delightful spot," Serra writes of Carmel, "which thanks to a plentiful supply both of land and water, gives promise of abundant harvests."[4]

On a darker but very human note, Serra confesses to a fear of being alone on a far shore amid soldiers and savages (his term), given that Crespí was scheduled to return south to establish a third mission, San Buenaventura, on the Santa Barbara Channel. "If at any time I am called upon to mention what I find hard, it is this: I find it hard—a sinner like me—to be left all alone, with the nearest priest more than eighty leagues away, and in between nothing but savages and rough roads." He preferred, Serra writes, to have a minimum of two priests per mission or, failing that, for missions to be established a reasonable distance from each other. In any event, a good beginning had been made—to the glory of God, the king, and the college— with the establishment of Missions San Diego de Alcalá, in honor of a humble lay brother, and San Carlos Borromeo, in honor of the nephew of a pope and cardinal archbishop of Milan. "I wish to congratulate Your Reverence sincerely," Serra concludes this pivotal report, "because, during the time of your administration, our Institute has been made greater by the foundation of these missions. The increase, counting Velicatá, is already three; and before long it may possibly include four more. If I have helped in some small measure, it was done in the name of Your Reverence and of our holy College; and there is no reason why my name should be mentioned except for the blunders I may have committed in doing the work that Your Reverence commissioned me to undertake."[5] To the college, then, and not to Serra would go all the credit. In the drama that was unfolding, Serra claims the role of San Diego, the humble lay brother promoted into high office. For the next fifteen years, however, he would make his headquarters in a mission named for a prince of the Church.

The Serra years

What an impressive record achieved by Serra: nine missions in fifteen years, ten if San Fernando de Velicatá in Lower California is counted, and fifteen if the record of his Sierra Gorda ministry is included in the total. The Alta California missions founded by Serra extended from San Diego to San Francisco and hence marked the boundaries of Alta California under Spanish governance. José de Gálvez favored a simple Franciscan jurisdiction for the two Californias, to be organized and staffed by the College of San Fernando; but the Dominicans, anxious not to be shut out of the Californias entirely, appealed to the Crown in October 1771 and were granted Lower California. Established by a concordat signed on 7 April 1772 by Fray Rafael Verger, the guardian of the College of San Fernando, and Fray Juan Pedro de Iriarte, the Dominican vicar general for Lower California, the boundary between the two jurisdictions remains as the border between American and Mexican California.

Starting from the recently founded San Fernando de Velicatá, the Dominicans advanced the existing Lower California mission system by eight solidly built stone structures—six of them named for Dominican saints—as far north as Descanso Bay south of San Diego. The expansion of the Alta California Franciscan system north of San Francisco Bay in 1817 (San Rafael Arcángel) and 1823 (San Francisco Solano) completed a string of missions that extended along the Pacific coast of the Californias for six hundred miles. Dominican ambition had more than Lower California in mind, and for the first years of his tenure as father president, Serra feared that the Crown might assign Alta California to the Dominicans as well.

In Alta California, the last of the Borderland provinces to be established, the fundamental paradox and resulting tensions of continental ambition through mission settlement quickly surfaced. The Crown believed that it was employing the Franciscans to secure a foothold on Alta California, which was true. The Franciscans were paid servants of the Crown. The second half of the formula was more problematic. In time, the missions were supposed to produce a Hispanicized population. Together with newcomers into the province, these Hispanicized Indians would become the people of the country. The missions would then be absorbed into a diocesan structure, their lands distributed to the Hispanicized Indians or sold off to settlers, and become parish churches under diocesan clergy serving an established civil population. This scenario, however, ran counter to the Franciscan ambition to establish a social order based on an enduring guardianship keyed to final times. The Franciscans' protectionist point of view inevitably had to clash with the civil/military order within which the missionaries exercised their calling. Who exactly was in charge and of what? The partnership was always uneasy, given the key roles played by the missionaries in preparing for a civil order they did not believe in and the civil/military officials who believed that they were on hand not only to protect the missionaries but also to ensure the proper evolution of the colony into a civil Catholic province of New Spain. Put this continuing tension into the context of day-to-day conflicts—solidiers' sexual abuse of Indian women, Franciscans' resistance against the enforced labor of Indian neophytes, the right of sanctuary for those fleeing secular authorities, the appropriation of mission cattle and agricultural produce for support of the civil sector, the property disputes resulting from locating civil settlements too near the missions—and a condition of chronic disequilibrium was established.

While serving as president of the missions of Sierra Gorda, Serra quarreled with Colonel José de Escandón, the regional military commander, who favored pro-settler policies aimed toward the establishment of a civil order. Escandón also advocated the development of self-governing Indian pueblos versus the Franciscan program of Indian guardianship under the missions. As father president of the Alta California missions, Serra butted heads with one military commander and three governors. Serra got along rather well with Portolá, the first commander, during the organization and execution of the Sacred Expedition and the founding of San Diego and Monterey. By contrast, he and Pedro Fages—Portolá's successor between 1770 and 1774 and governor in his own right from 1782 to 1791—quarreled continually over an array of issues, large and small. A career officer from Catalonia who had been serving in New Spain only since 1767, Fages commanded a unit of elite Catalan volunteers as well as the criollo leatherjackets. He opposed Serra's program of rapid expansion on the grounds that Alta California did not contain enough soldiers to provide these missions with proper security. Fages believed, moreover, that military considerations should always take precedence over the Franciscan program of mission development. He thus argued that mules could be appropriated from Mission San Diego to construct a presidio or—even more threatening to the Franciscans—Indians could be put to work. Serra, naturally, opposed such efforts. Furthermore, the Franciscans were outraged by various soldiers' sexual behavior, which made a mockery of friars' attempts to introduce monogamy and marriage into Indian life. Worse, at the recently established Mission San Gabriel Arcángel (1771), soldiers rode about in posses, plundering Indian encampments and lassoing Indian women like cattle and raping them. In one horrible incident, a notorious San Diego soldier named Camacho raped and murdered an Indian girl and otherwise terrorized the local Indians.

In late 1772 Serra made the long, arduous journey back to Mexico City to present these and other grievances to Viceroy Bucareli. Serra almost died en route, once in Guadalajara and again in Querétaro, from recurrent fever. In Mexico City, Serra met with the viceroy at the viceregal palace on a number of occasions in March 1773. From one perspective, there could be no greater contrast than that between Antonio María de Bucareli y Ursúa, the Marquis of Vallehermoso and count of Jerena, lieutenant general and former governor of Cuba, who had popes and cardinals in his family tree, and the farmer's son from Majorca. Yet each man was a religious under vows: Serra a Franciscan, Bucareli a professed Knight of Malta. Like Serra, Bucareli was intensely attuned to the evangelical significance of the Alta California venture. Assuming the office of viceroy on 22 September 1771, the aristocratic soldier-monk inherited responsibility for Alta California—thus far a money pit for the Crown—along with another brainchild of José de Gálvez, the poorly sited naval base and shipyard at San Blas on the Gulf of California coast of Mexico, which Bucareli was in the process of reorganizing concurrently with Serra's visit. Thus, when Serra spoke of the evangelization of the Indians of Alta California being endangered by Lieutenant Fages' intransigence and inability to control his troops, Bucareli listened. He fully grasped the strategic importance of New Spain's fragile hold on the Pacific coast and realized that it would take decades to settle a civilian population in the region; therefore, the Franciscan missions (as Gálvez had planned) represented the best way for New Spain to hold Alta California in the meantime. As a professed religious brother, the viceroy likewise respected Serra's evangelical arguments on their own terms and asked the father president to draw up a *representación* (summary statement with recommendations) of how Serra thought things should be run in Alta California. In the thirty-two-point representación he submitted to Bucareli, Serra called for the removal of Fages, the promotion of Sergeant José Francisco Ortega to lieutenant, and the granting of authority to missionaries to expel aberrant soldiers from the system and return them under arrest to Mexico to face charges.

Serra returned to Alta California with a new *reglamento* (civil code), based on his thirty-two requests, although Ortega, while promoted, was not named governor, as Serra had also requested, but was assigned to the San Diego garrison. To serve as military commander, and hence the de facto governor, Bucareli appointed the veteran captain Fernando de Rivera y Moncada. The Crown seriously qualified missionary authority over soldiers; thus, despite Serra's seemingly triumphant return to Alta California, the stage was set for three more years of turmoil, for the veteran Rivera—an older officer with a prickly disposition—would prove even more resistant than Fages had been to the Franciscans' efforts to exercise authority over the military.

Although each man tried to be civil to the other, a disaffinity of temperament existed between Rivera and Serra, which was perhaps traceable to prior difficulties during the Sacred Expedition. On one occasion, Serra and Rivera half-admitted such troubles and tried to laugh them away—unsuccessfully, as it turned out. Rivera and Serra fought over food rations for servants and soldiers. They quarreled when Serra resisted Rivera's request to have Rivera's good friend Fray Fermín Francisco de Lasuén assigned as a full-time chaplain to the Monterey presidio (which, with the arrival of a few wives and children, constituted a settlement). The post, Serra argued, belonged to a diocesan priest, but since no secular clergy were available in Alta California (and would not be until the arrival of Bishop García Diego in 1842), Serra eventually—and very reluctantly—temporarily approved, pending Lasuén's assignment in 1775 to found Mission San Juan Capistrano (1776).

Another problematic issue was the matter of mission guards. Serra was advancing an ambitious program of establishing missions within reachable distance to each other, anchored on earlier foundations. Thus San Antonio de Padua (1771) stood as a spur from San Carlos Borromeo (1770); San Gabriel Arcángel (1771) was projected from San Diego de Alcalá (1769), as were San Juan Capistrano (1776) and San Buenaventura (1782). San Francisco de Asís (1776) engendered Santa Clara de Asís (1777). Misreading Viceroy Bucareli's terrible handwriting, Serra believed that he would be authorized thirteen, as opposed to three, soldiers per mission. Rivera begrudged him two and, taking up a clear and legible copy of Bucareli's instruction written out by the viceroy's secretary, gleefully pointed out Serra's misreading of the number.

Haughty and defensive, and at times emotionally on edge to a point of imbalance, Rivera nitpicked and delayed each new mission during his tenure. In opposing the founding of a mission and presidio at San Francisco, Rivera went so far as to be rude to his fellow captain, Juan Bautista de Anza, a highly regarded (and noble) officer operating on direct orders from the viceroy. Rivera also granted land from Mission San Carlos property to one Manuel Burrón, a soldier who requested retirement from the army and enrollment as a colonist. This granting of 140 square varas—on which Burrón had already planted corn—was no minor matter, for it foreshadowed (by sixty years) the mission system's secularization and the distribution of mission lands by civil authorities according to the Laws of the Indies, whose *recopilación* (summary) Rivera cited in his grant, although no one in Monterey had a copy on hand.

Matters came to a head following a more significant crisis: an attack on Mission San Diego an hour after midnight on 5 November 1775 by some eight hundred Kumeyaay (called Diegueño by Spaniards) warriors, prophetic of an even larger revolt to come in July 1781 by the related Quechans (called Yumans by Spaniards) farther south. The Kumeyaay of the San Diego region consisted of two groups, Ipai and Tipai, both of whom were hostile to Spaniards and the mission program from the beginning. Grazing Spanish cattle, horses, and mules destroyed Kumeyaay farmlands, for one thing, and when the Indians killed the animals, soldiers retaliated viciously. Friars Luis Jayme and Vicente Fuster were unable to develop agriculture at their mission to support a resident population of baptized neophytes, so Indians who did accept baptism were sent back to their rancherías, which removed them from Franciscan influence. In August 1774 Jayme relocated his mission five miles east to create a semblance of distance from the presidio as well as to take advantage of a more agriculturally promising site. An even more serious problem was soldiers' treatment of women. As noted earlier, the sexual exploitation of Indian females—girls as well as women—was epidemic among the soldiers of the San Diego presidio, including the notorious Camacho, most conspicuously, for whom rape was a way of life. In one terrible incident, two soldiers attacked two underage girls, and one of them died as a result. Sandos considers this pattern of sexual violence central motive for the November 1775 uprising. As Geiger points out, a whipping recently administered to baptized Indians for attending a forbidden dance at a nearby ranchería added to the Kumayaay's resentment.

Such a large-scale conspiracy, whatever its immediate causes, had to be rooted in the Kumeyaay's wholesale rejection of the Spaniards—who they were, how they behaved, what they stood for. In short, the insurrection organized by the shamans of the region as well as an apostate named Carlos and fellow conspirators was fairly sophisticated. In the weeks before the actual attack, Indians in increasing numbers visited the mission on a friendly basis; the Spaniards thus became accustomed to more numerous Indians in the vicinity. By the night of 4 November 1775, eight hundred or so warriors were in the area, and at one o'clock, they struck. Plans called for two attacks, the one on the presidio to signal the other on the mission to begin. Only the attack on the mission materialized. When it was over, a desecrated church stood looted of its vestments and sacred vessels, the mission complex was reduced to ashes, two Spaniards lay dead, and various soldiers and one Franciscan were suffering from serious wounds.

One of the two dead Spaniards was Father Luis Jayme, a thirty-five-year-old Majorcan from Serra's home monastery (the Convento de Jesús, outside Palma) and, like Serra, a former philosophy professor turned missionary. Awakened by the attack, Jayme rose from his cot, put on his habit, and walked out to a group of warring Indians, greeting them with the customary "Amar a Dios, hijos" (Love God, my children), to which the Indians replied with a dozen or more arrows into his body. Stripping Jayme of his habit—whether he was alive or dead at the time is not chronicled—they clubbed and stoned his head and face beyond recognition. Father Fuster fainted when he first saw Jayme's battered body and was never the same following the attack, which involved baptized Indians as well as the unbaptized. Who, Fuster asked himself and perhaps others, could be trusted? How could evangelization continue under such circumstances? Serra transferred the traumatized priest to Mission San Gabriel.

But before he was transferred, Fuster—a loyal and devout priest despite his post-traumatic stress—unintentionally created one more point of conflict between Serra and Rivera. Carlos, a key organizer of the insurrection, after having been in hiding for five months following the attack, on the night of 27 March 1776 sneaked into the San Diego presidio warehouse, then converted into a temporary chapel, and claimed sanctuary—the right of an accused to claim refuge in a church—which Fuster granted. Claiming that the warehouse was a church only when Mass was being said there, the outraged Rivera entered the makeshift chapel with soldiers and placed Carlos under arrest. Hearing of this, Serra excommunicated Rivera, not only because Rivera had violated sanctuary but also because Viceroy Bucareli had decreed that a policy of amnesty was the best way to recover from the San Diego revolt. Excommunication proved a trump card for Serra. Rivera returned Carlos to Fuster on 18 May, and the excommunication was lifted.

"Thanks be to God", Serra reportedly said when informed of Jayme's death. "Now that the terrain has been watered by blood, the conversions of the San Diego Indians will take place."[6] Serra was mistaken. Fuster proved more correct. Although Mission San Diego was rebuilt, it never equaled the other Southern California missions founded during Serra's tenure as father president—San Gabriel, San Juan Capistrano, and San Buenaventura—in terms of converts, agriculture, or other aspects of mission culture, including architecture. Its irrigation system, however, built between 1807 and 1816—a dam six miles upriver that shunted water through cement flumes across or through steep gorges—foreshadowed the development of semiarid Southern California through water engineering.

9

The Bay of San Francisco 1776

New Spain secures a strategic harbor on the Pacific coast

Between 17 and 27 June 1776, sixteen soldiers, seven male colonists, and their wives and children marched under the command of Lieutenant José Joaquín Moraga north from Monterey to San Francisco Bay. Two Franciscans and a half dozen muleteers and vaqueros driving more than two hundred cattle and a pack train of supplies for the journey were also part of the expedition to establish a presidio and a mission on the peninsula jutting into San Francisco Bay and a second mission and civil settlement near the Guadalupe River, which ran into the bay on its southwestern shore. The soldiers and their families were nearing the conclusion of a heroic overland trek of fifteen hundred miles that had begun ten months earlier under the command of Lieutenant Colonel Juan Bautista de Anza. Having started from the presidio of Tubac in Pimería Alta (southern Arizona), they had crossed the Colorado Desert into Upper California and gone through the Mojave Desert country to Mission San Gabriel Arcángel in Southern California, where they had rested before continuing north to Mission San Carlos Borromeo and the presidio at Monterey.

Miraculously, no one was lost on this epic journey. In fact, three women gave birth en route; even now one was causing a three-day delay as she brought another colonist into the world. Moraga was following the trail he and Anza had reconnoitered two years earlier on the first of two reconnaissances. The trail proceeded north through the Salinas valley over the Gabilán Range to the San Benito valley, moved northwest through the Gilroy valley into the Coastal Range via Coyote Pass, continued northward up the coast to Santa Clara, passed Palo Alto (named in honor of the high redwood beneath which the first Anza party had rested), and then moved into the northern headlands of the San Francisco peninsula.

The Indians they met en route seemed friendly. In Gilroy valley the Moraga party encountered a herd of elk and shot three without leaving the road. Butchering and barbecuing the elk, the Spaniards feasted on their savory meat (better than the best beef, in the lieutenant's opinion) while marveling at the size and antlers of these previously unknown sources of venison.

The two Franciscans on the journey, Francisco Palóu and Pedro Benito Cambón, were perhaps disconcerted by the Indians' nakedness; yet they made no mention of it in later reports. The nudity or near nudity of the Indians only reinforced in these veteran missionaries—zealous and well-trained members of the Apostolic College of San Fernando in Mexico City—the importance of the work before them: the conversion and Hispanicization of these new peoples in this previously unsettled (and most northern) portion of New Spain. A lector in philosophy and a skilled preacher, administrator, and historian, Francisco Palóu to this day enjoys a reputation as one of the most talented, energetic, accomplished, and upright Franciscans to serve in the Borderlands during more than two centuries of evangelization. Palóu already had traveled north from Monterey to San Francisco Bay twice, the winter of 1774 and the fall of 1775, as a member of the reconnaissance parties scouting sites for a presidio, mission, and pueblo on San Francisco Bay, which were intended to establish a defense perimeter against Russian incursion from the north as well as to Catholicize and Hispanicize the indigenous inhabitants of Upper California.

Born in 1723 in Palma, Majorca, Palóu entered the Franciscan order at the age of sixteen and distinguished himself as a student of philosophy and theology before turning away from an academic career at twenty-seven to join his professor and life-long friend Fray Junípero Serra and eighteen other friars as volunteers for missionary work in New Spain. At fifty-three—after a quarter century in the missions of the Sierra Gorda of northern Querétaro in central Mexico, followed by assignments in Baja and Alta California as missionary and administrator—Palóu was eager for the biggest challenge of his priestly service: the establishment of the sixth and most northern mission in the Alta California system. That challenge would lead to the writing of a foundational history, *Noticias de Nueva California*, as well as a biography of its first president, Junípero Serra.

Palóu's confrere, the thirty-eight-year-old Pedro Benito Cambón, another Spanish-born (from the province of Galicia) volunteer for the College of San Fernando, had worked closely with Palóu in Baja California prior to the surrender of that missionary field to the Dominicans. Transferred to Alta California in 1771, Cambón helped found Mission San Gabriel Arcángel, the fourth installation in what would be (by 1823) a twenty-one-mission system. While at San Gabriel, Cambón had fought against soldiers' sexual exploitation of Indian women before he finally left in disgust for a brief assignment in Baja California, supervising the transfer of Franciscan property to the north. In July 1775 Serra selected Palóu and Cambón for the San Francisco venture, assigning them to Mission San Carlos Borromeo in the interim.

Under the steady guidance of thirty-five-year-old Lieutenant Moraga—a veteran of frontier service chosen by Anza as his second in command for his intelligence, military record, and writing abilities—the settlement party reached the San Francisco peninsula on 27 June. Moraga established a camp of tents and brush shelters near a lagoon previously named by Anza in honor of Nuestra Señora de los Dolores (Our Lady of Sorrows) and chosen by his chaplain, Fray Pedro Font, as the location for the proposed San Francisco mission. On 29 June, the feast of Saints Peter and Paul, the friars celebrated Mass in a bower of branches designed to serve as the settlement's first chapel.

The Spaniards were forced to wait a month both for the arrival of the supply ship *San Carlos*, thrown off course from Monterey by adverse winds, and for the return of the mule train sent back to Monterey for further supplies. Lieutenant Moraga and his men spent the month cutting logs and gathering materials for construction as well as exploring the areas adjacent to the site Anza had previously indicated for the presidio. Refining Anza's general directions, Moraga selected a site on the crest of an open field that rose from the shoreline on the peninsula's northwestern edge and that was watered by two springs Moraga found at a nearby white cliff (present-day

Fort Point) overlooking the entrance to the great bay. The previous August, naval lieutenant Juan Manuel de Ayala and his sailing master, José Cañizares, had sailed the *San Carlos* and its pilot boat through *la boca* (the mouth) and into the bay, the first Europeans to do so.

Ignoring Governor Fernando de Rivera y Moncada's directive to build the presidio before building the mission (Rivera openly and rudely opposed the venture), Moraga directed his men to work on the presidio and the mission simultaneously. Following the arrival of the *San Carlos* on 18 August, captain Fernando Quirós proved accommodating and lent his sailors and two ship's carpenters to construction efforts. By mid-September, a rudimentary presidio—the commander's residence and headquarters, a warehouse, and cabins for soldiers and their families—stood complete in log-cabin splendor.

The two Franciscans, meanwhile, with the help of six soldiers, three servants, a civilian settler, and sailors and carpenters from the *San Carlos*, were assembling a log church, friary, and service building at the mission site adjacent to the lagoon. On 17 September 1776, the newly completed Presidio of San Francisco was dedicated with appropriate ceremonies. On hand for the event were four Franciscans—Palóu and Cambón, joined by Fray José Nocedal, the chaplain of the *San Carlos*, and Fray Tomás de la Peña Saravia, assigned from Monterey to establish a second mission on the south bay—along with nearly everyone connected to the expedition, with the exception of a few sailors left on board the *San Carlos*. A solemn high Mass commenced the observances, followed by the reading of the relevant documents by Moraga. The gathering then processed into the chapel for the singing of the Te Deum while soldiers shot their muskets in salute, the chapel bell was rung, and the *San Carlos* fired its swivel guns. Two beeves were barbecued for the ensuing festive picnic.

On 8 October 1776 the Mission of San Francisco de Asís (more commonly known as Mission Dolores, in honor of the name Anza gave to the nearby lagoon) was dedicated in ceremonies that likewise included musket salvos, swivel-gun firings from the *San Carlos*, fireworks, and a beef barbecue. Presidio and mission in operation, the *San Carlos* set sail for its home port, San Blas, on the Gulf of California coast of central Mexico.

During the next three months, soldiers, settlers, and Franciscans prepared for phase two of the occupation of this northernmost outpost of the Spanish Empire in the Americas: the founding of a second mission and the first civilian pueblo in Alta California. The same able team remained in charge, with the addition of Fray Tomás de la Peña, the designated minister for the proposed Mission Santa Clara de Asís, named in honor of the founder of the first Franciscan sisterhood. At age thirty-three, Peña resembled most Ferdinandians: he was a Spanish-born (from the province of Cantabria) volunteer, a qualified preacher, and an experienced missionary, including a stint as chaplain and diarist on the *Santiago*, commanded by Juan Pérez, on its coastal reconnaissance to the far north during the summer of 1774. Following the dedication of Mission Dolores, Peña returned to Monterey in late November to link up with settlers, soldiers, and families assigned to the south bay pueblo; the settlement party was under the command of Governor Rivera. Rivera selected locations on the shore of the Guadalupe River for Mission Santa Clara and the Pueblo de San José de Guadalupe, the first civil settlement in Alta California. The Franciscans would have protested that the sites were too close to each other, in violation of Laws of the Indies statutes requiring strict separation of missions and pueblos. Rivera, however, was not one to argue with, and the pueblo of San José was duly established. The settlement would later be linked to the Mission Santa Clara by a tree-lined *alameda* (pathway) after Peña relocated it farther away from the floodplain of the Guadalupe River.

Southern Arizona

Thus was brought to a degree of success New Spain's northward advance out of Pimería Alta that had been the lifelong and prophetic hope of Eusebio Kino eighty years earlier. From the perspective of Kino, Juan María de Salvatierra, and their fellow Jesuit missionaries, northwestern Mexico, Pimería Alta, and Baja and Alta California constituted a geographical region that called for further unity through missionary and civil development, with Pimería Alta serving as the gateway to the Californias. Throughout the eighteenth century, however, Jesuits concentrated their development efforts on southern Arizona and Baja California.

Founded by Kino in 1700 and named in honor of the famed Jesuit missionary to Asia, San Xavier del Bac represented for sixty-seven years the northernmost advance of the Society of Jesus into the Sonoran Desert. From the beginning, San Xavier del Bac proved a challenging outpost. Its first resident priest, Francisco Gonzalo, who arrived in 1701, fled Indian hostility and died within the year. The mission struggled on in marginal circumstances and was seldom visited until 1720, when ten additional Jesuits were assigned to northwestern Mexico. In 1727 Don Benedict Crespo, the bishop of Durango, made a personal visit to the area (an impressive feat for a prelate) and upon his return successfully lobbied the Crown for more Jesuit missionaries for his diocese. Three other Jesuits arrived in the region in 1732. One of them, Philip Segesser von Brunegg, a Swiss, joined the crusty, independent-minded Father Joseph Agustín de Campos in making service visits to San Xavier del Bac from Mission San Ignacio to the south. Another Swiss Jesuit, Kaspar Stiger, spent three miserable years at San Xavier del Bac before being reassigned to San Ignacio in 1736, when Campos was removed from that mission for insubordination. Once again, San Xavier del Bac received only sporadic care, and the mission program languished.

The Northern Pimas of the San Xavier del Bac area, Jesuit Joseph de Torres Perea reported in 1744, were indifferent or hostile to Christianity. Most refused baptism, and even those who accepted baptism knew little about their new religion and preferred to live indiscriminately with pagans rather than regrouping into Christian rancherías. San Xavier del Bac was an unlucky place, Father Carlos Rojas reported in 1748, yet the Society refused to close it down. In 1751 another Jesuit, Franz Bauer, divided his time between San Ignacio and San Xavier del Bac.

In late November of that year, the Pima Revolt of 1751 flared up. As in previous rebellions in the Spanish Borderlands, a fundamental cultural disjunction between an Indian way of life, thought, and belief and an enforced evangelization constituted the root cause of the uprising. In 1709 Kino had written optimistically about the evangelization of the Northern Pimas. The reality turned out to be less positive. The Jesuit approach favored the concentration and stabilization of Indians into pueblos associated with a particular mission, as well as the creation of an Indian-administered economy and a limited level of self-governance, all under Jesuit guidance and control. Cultural barriers nonetheless remained formidable. Pimas stubbornly resisted living in mission-affiliated pueblos, and even when such arrangements were established, the farther north the mission, the more likely the Indians were to come and go as they pleased, joining their nation communities for hunting or seed-gathering expeditions according to long-established cycles. Nor did the Jesuit orientation toward inculturation—so evident in China, Japan, and India, and among the Guaraní of Paraguay—seem to carry much weight as no-nonsense European Jesuit missionaries confronted naked or near-naked Northern Pimas determined to follow their own practices regarding walkabouts, sexual and marriage practices, and sacred dances. As in Lower California, where a similar disjunction occurred, whippings and confinement in stocks emerged as punishments for transgressions. One Jesuit, Ignacio Xavier Keller of Mission Santa María de Suamca, seems to have been notably harsh—and hence particularly hated.

As even the Apaches recognized, Northern Pimas were excellent warriors. In 1749 the viceroyalty recruited Northern Pimas as an auxiliary force in a campaign against rebellious Seri Indians on the Gulf of California. Led by Luis Oacpicagigua, a baptized Northern Pima from Mission Santa Gertrudis on the headwaters of the Altar River, the Northern Pimas performed with distinction: in fact, they out-performed Spanish units in some battles, for which they were rewarded and their baptized chiefs officially honored. From this experience the warriors, especially the chiefs, gained self-confidence on the field of battle as well as an awareness that Spaniards were not almighty. Returning to their homelands, Northern Pimas, again the chiefs especially, found it galling still to be treated as errant children by Jesuit missionaries; particularly troublesome were Ignacio Xavier Keller and Tomás Tello, of La Purísima Concepción at Caborca (another Altar River mission), who, among other offenses, put a pregnant woman in the stocks.

Thus a revolt was organized among baptized Northern Pimas, now apostates, and unbaptized auxiliaries. Luis Oacpicagigua was chosen as leader. The rebellion broke out in late November 1751. Its first phases were familiar. Four mission churches were trashed, sacred vessels and vestments taken. Nearly one hundred Spaniards were killed, including two Jesuits, Tello of La Purísima Concepción and Henry Ruhen, then working among the Papagos of Papaguería to the west, who also joined the uprising. In the aftermath of this bloodletting, Lieutenant Colonel Diego Ortiz Parrilla, the governor of Sonora and an experienced Apache fighter, entered Pimería Alta at the head of a large force. In one pitched battle, facing a well-organized army of more than two thousand rebels under the command of their captain general Oacpicagigua, Parrilla realized that negotiation was the better part of valor. Among the Northern Pimas' demands was the removal of Father Keller from Pimería Alta. Parrilla agreed. By the spring of 1752, the rebellion was over. As in their campaign against the Seri, the Northern Pimas returned to their home districts in a state of intensified self-assurance.

The founding of Tubac

In terms of the resettlement and continuing Christianization of Pimería Alta, two new developments directly resulted from the Revolt of 1751. In the spring of 1752

Governor Parrilla received permission to establish a presidio at Tubac near the Santa Cruz River just south of San Xavier del Bac. Also authorized was the resettlement at the ranchería of San José de Tucson, eighteen leagues (forty-six miles) from the new presidio, of Indians displaced by the revolt. A measure of stable density was thus created along the axis of Tubac, San Xavier del Bac, and San José de Tucson. As it grew among relocated Indians and soldiers' families, this density fostered the development of a Spanish Catholic culture that by the end of the eighteenth century would find expression in a glorious new mission church at San Xavier del Bac and an impressive parish community and church at Tucson.

But first came one more outbreak of violence, in October 1756, provoked by the efforts of Jesuit Alonso Ignacio Benito Espinosa, a recent arrival from Spain, to take control of the traditional harvest festival by summarily banning its rituals, which included intoxication, necromancy, and ceremonial dancing. The uprisings at San Xavier del Bac and Tucson were quickly put down by the soldiers from the Tubac presidio and a larger force under the command of Sonoran governor Juan Antonio de Mendoza. Violence reignited, however, in Tucson in May 1757, forcing the Jesuit resident there, Bernhard Middendorff (a recently arrived German) to flee for his life to San Xavier del Bac. The good news: missionaries Espinosa and Middendorff grew in patience and wisdom in the following years, which were not easy for either of them as they coped with Apache raids and the extremely slow pace of Catholic development among the Pimas.

Still, despite their heightened understanding and tolerance, and despite their hard labor on behalf of their charges toward spiritual (conversion) and economic (agriculture and cattle raising) goals, Espinosa, Middendorff, and other European Jesuits of their generation in upper Sonora and Pimería Alta would always have trouble with the Pima tendency to vanish into the desert in search of birds, sparse game, seeds, or ripe cactus fruit; and to resist the strict requirements of marriage as explained by the fathers or otherwise to regulate their sexual activity. Nevertheless, a process of familiarization was under way. The Revolt of 1751 arose from the Northern Pima's increased understanding of themselves in terms of comparison with the Spaniards, and that act of comparison was in itself a form of cultural dialogue. Besides, for the Jesuits, the worst was yet to come. In 1767 an order for their arrest and deportation would come from a most unexpected quarter: the Crown itself, His Catholic Majesty Carlos III, whose northern New World frontier the Society of Jesus had been doing its best to Hispanicize.

From Tubac to Alta California

In 1762 the Spanish military encouraged the Piman Sobaipuri of the San Pedro River region, known to be excellent warriors, to relocate west to the Tucson area as a way of consolidating a defensive line against Apache incursions from the northeast. The relocation of the Sobaipuri proved a mistake in the short run. Apache raids increased once the Sobaipuri were gone from the southwestern border of Apache land. Yet in the long run the move ensured the biological survival of the Sobaipuri and added to the population density of the Tucson region. Following his extensive tour in 1766–1767 of the Borderland defenses, the marqués de Rubí recommended further such consolidations along with a realignment of northern frontier presidios into a defensive perimeter against the Apaches. The Crown approved Rubí's recommendations and in 1772 issued a reglamento calling for such a realignment, which necessitated the relocation of Tubac farther north. In August 1775 Lieutenant Colonel Hugo Oconor, a Hispanicized Irish infantry officer and former governor of Texas—known to his soldiers as El Capitán Colorado because of his red hair—having been appointed inspector of military presidios, recommended to Viceroy Bucareli the relocation of Tubac to Tucson eighteen leagues (forty-six miles) to the north, which was accomplished in October and November 1776, leaving Tubac a sparsely fortified settlement.

Two formidable Spaniards—army officer Juan Bautista de Anza and Franciscan friar Francisco Garcés, both men of ability and continental ambitions—now enter the story of the effort to link upper Sonora, Pimería Alta, and Alta California via an overland route across two deserts. In so doing, Anza and Garcés blazed a trail that in time would develop into a well-traveled route connecting Mexico, southern Arizona, and Southern California.

Within the range of Borderland personalities, no greater contrast existed than that between the stately frontier soldier Anza, who followed orders and said little, and the talkative friar known to make his own assignments. Born in 1735 on the Arizona border, the son and grandson of renowned Indian fighters, Anza entered the army in 1755 as a lieutenant following the death of his father at the hands of marauding Apaches and spent the first phase of his career fighting these formidable opponents as well as the Seris and the rebellious Sibubapas and Suaquis (Lower Pimas). During the campaigns, Anza captured or killed many Indians—some twenty-nine Apaches dispatched by his own hand, he reports—in the direct and unsparing manner of Borderland warfare. The fact that Anza kept an exact count of the Apaches he personally eliminated in the first five years of his army career suggests a form of retribution for the killing of his father. By 1767 Anza, now thirty-two and promoted to captain, was serving as commander of Tubac and was arguably the most experienced and respected officer on the Arizona frontier.[1]

Francisco Tomás Hermeneglido Garcés, by contrast, was a *peninsular*, born in Aragón in 1738 to a family blessed with two highly secular priest relatives, an uncle serving as chaplain to a count and an older brother well placed as a parish rector, who raised Garcés in his household. At fifteen, however, Garcés rejected a diocesan career and opted for the Franciscans and the Indies. Sailing to New Spain in 1763 following his ordination, he entered the College of the Holy Cross in Querétaro to prepare for a missionary ministry on the frontier. Garcés possessed a streak of naïveté along with an almost childlike garrulousness that now and then surfaced spontaneously as part of his genial optimism and direct intelligence, earning him the nickname Children's Priest among fellow Franciscans at Querétaro. When Garcés finished the course at Holy Cross, he was assigned to the boondocks of boondocks, which is to say, San Xavier del Bac.

Garcés was delighted. En route to San Xavier del Bac in the summer of 1768, he stopped off at Tubac. Anza was away on campaign, but Garcés enjoyed the hospitality of Anza's wife and family—and no doubt charmed them all—before continuing his journey. "The graciousness of your wife and family", he wrote Anza on 29 July 1768, "reflects your own good manners and education." Garcés also informed Anza that he was more than pleased with the character and behavior of the two soldiers assigned to San Xavier, which he admitted he found a challenge—the remoteness, the flies and mosquitoes, the general poverty of the region—as had the Jesuits of an earlier era. He had made good contacts in Tucson as well, he reported. The Pima people living there had voluntarily built him a hut and said that they wanted him all to themselves.[2]

Within two months of his arrival, Garcés took off on the first of many missionary journeys. Guided by four unbaptized Indians from the region, he reconnoitered westward across the Sonoran Desert, through the lands of the Papagos, as far as the Gila River, preaching through an interpreter. After two months, Garcés returned from his trek suffering from exhaustion and chills. While he was recovering at another location, Apaches raided San Xavier del Bac, killing its Indian governor and seizing as hostages the two soldiers on duty. Yet within seven months, the peripatetic friar was back on the road, this time eastward into the San Pedro River valley. Again he fell ill; and twice more, in April and July 1769, Apaches struck San Xavier.

What motivated Garcés to undertake these extensive journeys? Nothing less than the desire to make an on-the-ground assessment of the challenges facing Franciscans in southern Arizona and how best to plan for such inevitabilities. Jovial and accommodating by temperament, Garcés grew cautious when appraising Franciscan prospects in the region. A vivid writer, he sent in effective reports from the field, peppering military and Franciscan authorities with the lessons he had learned from his peregrinations. Upon his initial arrival at San Xavier del Bac, for example, Garcés had with characteristic optimism predicted an easy future for the evangelization of the region by Franciscans living solely and peaceably among the people, as he had reported the Pimas of Tucson wanted him to do. Now he reversed his point of view. More soldiers were needed, he urged, especially at Tucson; and assigning a single Franciscan to a post was unwise. At minimum, friars should come in pairs and be given authority over the Indians at each mission and not be expected to guide their development through Indian governors.

Garcés' argument for a stronger partnership between mission and presidio further aligned him with Anza at Tubac. Early in 1770, Sobaipuri refugees who had settled in Tucson from the San Pedro River valley planned to remove themselves to the Gila River. Faced with the loss of possible Christians, Garcés sought the assistance of Anza, who immediately understood that the Sobaipuri's departure would weaken Tuscon's defenses. Arriving in Tucson in late April at the head of a force of sixty, Anza persuaded the Sobaipuri, already on the trail, to return. Furthermore, Anza initiated the process of transforming Tucson from a ranchería of scattered brush huts into a permanent settlement, beginning with the construction of protective ramparts and a church for Garcés. All this was accomplished without violence, as Tucson Indians voluntarily labored in exchange for the promise of regular food supplies through Garcés, who promptly provided wheat from San Xavier del Bac and a farm he had started at Tucson.

Thus Garcés and Anza embarked upon a mutually beneficial partnership. With one crisis over, and a pattern of sustainable settlement established, Garcés on 8 August 1771 set out on yet another reconnaissance, this time reaching the Colorado

River. Once returned in October, no one since Eusebio Kino seventy years earlier remotely approached Garcés in his knowledge of the desert between Tubac and the entrance by land into Alta California or, as Anza would soon describe it, from Sonora to the South Sea.

A bold proposal

On 2 May 1772 Anza wrote to Viceroy Bucareli proposing such an expedition. In his letter, Anza requested the help of Garcés and twenty to twenty-five soldiers from Tubac. When Junípero Serra, in Mexico City on official business since February 1772, heard of Anza's proposal, he enthusiastically endorsed it in a memorandum he submitted to Bucareli the following month; and Bucareli, already attuned to the viability of the project, cited Serra's endorsement in his own report to the Council of the Indies. The viceroy also consulted Miguel Costansó, the engineering officer who had accompanied Portolá to New California three years earlier. Yes, Costansó replied in writing. The 180-league journey from Tubac to San Diego, as he calculated it, would be difficult—desert, mountains, more desert, more mountains—but Indians were doing it, as Costansó had discovered when he found that the Indians of Southern California possessed New Mexican artifacts. Without such a link, Costansó continued, both Lower and Upper California would remain isolated, given the difficulties of a sea voyage from San Blas or the march north from Baja. At this point in his official reply, Costansó expressed an officer's concern for the welfare of the troops stationed in Alta California, condemned to "perpetual and involuntary celibacy", if Sonora and the Pacific coast were not more closely connected. Women, children, and family life had to be brought overland to this remote new colony.[3]

Serra, one must remember, was in Mexico City precisely to complain about the soldiers' predatory sexual behavior. Serra's solution was to have soldiers marry Christianized young women from the mission system. Bucareli and other viceregal officials surely comprehended that such a solution—if it could be realized—would take time; decades might pass before the mission system in Alta California would be capable of graduating young Indian women sufficiently Hispanicized for cross-cultural Catholic marriages based on mutual respect. Concubinage was out of the question as a norm for a Spanish Catholic colony. Alta California required a civilian population if it were to maintain its Catholicity and achieve social stability—and a population of that sort and size could be introduced only via a new overland route. Alta California had to be Mexicanized. The mestizo people of Sinaloa and lower Sonora—a culture now reentering Pimería Alta, via the married soldiers of Tubac, after its expulsion in the Pima Revolt of 1751—would stabilize the mission system.

The first Anza expedition

It took Viceroy Bucareli the following year and a half to shepherd the Sonora–California expedition through the approvals process in Mexico City and Madrid—among the first of his many achievements as viceroy on behalf of empire and religion—but by January 1774 personnel were assembling at Tubac for the first of two phases of a two-year epic of exploration and colonization. The effort was unprecedented, then and thereafter, in North American history, unless one makes reference to the Lewis and Clark expedition three decades later. Lewis and Clark, however, as historian Herbert Eugene Bolton points out, were not required, upon returning to Missouri, to organize and return within months to the mouth of the Columbia River, escorting 240 civilian settlers.

The initiator of the expedition, Captain Anza, arrived with twenty soldiers volunteering for the campaign. (One brought along a violin.) Garcés, by now a legendary explorer, was joined by Fray Juan Díaz, another experienced missionary, chosen for his writing ability to serve as diarist-historian. The veteran scout Juan Bautista Valdés, whom Bolton describes as the Kit Carson of the expedition, had traveled the length of California from San Diego to San Francisco four times with Portolá in 1769–1770. Another guide, Sebastián Tarabal, was a Christianized Baja California Indian who, tiring of life at Mission San Gabriel, had left with his wife and relative in an effort to go home but instead got lost in Yuma country and nearly died, along with his wife and relative, before being rescued by the famed Yuma *cofot* (chief) known to Spaniards as Salvador Palma. Chief Palma promptly turned Tarabal over to Anza, who, rather than ordering the whipping Tarabal expected as a runaway, hired him on the spot for the expedition back to Alta California. A carpenter, two servants, and five muleteers completed the party. The muleteers would handle thirty-five mules loaded with baggage and provisions—including tobacco for gifts to Indians, as recommended by Garcés—as well as drive the sixty-five cattle to be consumed en route. A resupply of saddle horses and mules rounded out the animal train.

The two Franciscans celebrated Mass on the morning of 8 January 1774 for the entire company. A bugle sounded at around one in the afternoon, and the caravan set forth from Tubac amid the cheers and waving handkerchiefs of stay-behind soldiers, wives, and children.

The Bolton canon

These details, as fact and coloration, come directly from Herbert Eugene Bolton's *Outpost of Empire* (1939), initially published as the first volume of *Anza's California Expeditions* (five volumes, 1930), edited by Bolton for the University of California Press and later reissued as a separate volume at the direction of the legendary publisher Alfred A. Knopf, among whose many publishing interests was the history of the western United States. Explicit recognition is necessary because—as in the case of *Rim of Christendom* (1936), Bolton's biography of Eusebio Kino—no event or detail of landscape, no point of interpretation or contention, in the matter of Anza's California expeditions can be referred to or re-presented in any way without reference to the Bolton canon. For inclusion in *Anza's California Expeditions*, Bolton translated and edited the diaries and finished narratives of the first and second expeditions of Anza, Díaz, Garcés, Palóu, Font, Fray Tomás Eixarch (a missionary who joined the second Anza expedition en route), and Lieutenant José Joaquin Moraga (second in command on the second expedition) as well as the personal and official correspondence of Anza, Bucareli, and Minister for the Indies José de Gálvez relating to the expeditions and their aftermath.

Bolton meticulously traveled by horseback, mule, station wagon, and foot every inch previously traveled by Kino and Anza, guiding himself by relevant Spanish narratives and taking innumerable photographs. At the Bancroft Library of the University of California–Berkeley, Bolton trained two generations of Spanish Borderland historians, lay scholars of all shades of belief and nonbelief as well as a handful of Jesuits. He was also a close friend of San Francisco archbishop Edward J. Hanna and was invited to give formal testimony in hearings concerning the canonization of Junípero Serra.

What drove Bolton, a lifelong Methodist, to devote his life to excavating the history of the Spanish Catholic Borderlands—including his native Texas—with such prodigious research and writing remains a chapter in the frequently mysterious subject of why historians, publishers, and patrons are drawn to particular subjects. (Why a wealthy Jewish San Francisco lawyer, Sidney M. Ehrman, should have subsidized the printing costs of these publications for the University of California Press is another mystery.) Bolton's five-volume edition of *Anza's California Expeditions*, in any event, constitutes an epic presentation of the literature of fact so central to the record of exploration in North America, whether in Spanish, French, or English. As prepared and interpreted by Bolton, the diaries and reports of *Anza's California Expeditions* fuse history and literature, fact and imaginative possibilities, along with the prophetic warnings, ironies, and reversals so frequently encountered in the literature of travel and exploration. In the introductory volume to *Anza's California Expeditions*, Bolton does what the historical scholars of the nineteenth century and his early-twentieth-century generation did so well. (Washington Irving, William Hinckling Prescott, George Bancroft, Francis Parkman, and Samuel Eliot Morison come to mind.) Master the documentary record. Master the bibliography. Master the geography. Tell the story in a straightforward manner. And do not be afraid, now and then, to offer personal commentary, however value laden. Otherwise, why would anyone be doing all this work in the first place?

The expedition unfolds

Following its departure from Tubac, the Anza party retraced Kino's footsteps, recently retraced by Garcés, north and west through Papago land (the vast deserts of southern Arizona) to the Colorado River. The Spaniards crossed that mighty river with the help of the friendly Chief Palma. Once across, they trekked through the Colorado and Mojave Deserts north and west into Alta California, crossed the southern Sierra Nevada, and, ten weeks into the journey, left the barren desert behind in favor of the panorama they beheld on Tuesday, 15 March, from the height Anza named the Royal Pass of San Carlos, 227 leagues (635 miles) from Tubac. "From it", Anza writes in his diary of this first view of Southern California, "are seen most beautiful green and flower-strewn prairies, and snow-covered mountains with pines, oaks, and other trees which grow in cold countries." These prairies impressed the Spaniards as "suitable for seasonal crops and the planting of fruit trees" and gave evidence of "pastures sufficient for maintaining cattle". The later development of Riverside, San Bernardino, Orange, and Los Angeles Counties as centers of cattle raising, agriculture, and citrus growing would bear out the truth of his statement; but for the time being, the perennial obstacles to Spanish colonization—delayed planting, scarcity, near starvation—proved the order of the day, as the Anza party discovered on 11 April when it reached the recently established Mission San Gabriel Arcángel and found the priests and soldiers living on three maize tortillas a day.[4]

At this point, Garcés split off from the main party to explore south to Mission San Diego, where, the Spaniards had learned, Junípero Serra, returning from his discussions with Viceroy Bucareli in Mexico City, had recently arrived on the supply ship *Nueva Galicia*. Garcés and Serra must have spent time together in San Diego, but these two legendary figures—friars of different colleges, San Fernando and Holy Cross Queretaro; men of equal energy but vastly different temperaments—make no mention of each other in their respective writings. Anza, meanwhile, had departed north to Monterey at an impressive pace, trekking four hundred miles in nine days. From Monterey, Anza continued north to San Francisco Bay to survey sites for a presidio, mission, and settlement. In the course of doing all this reconnaissance work, Anza and his men completed a comprehensive exploration, inventory, and description of the geography of the promising region later developed as the American states of Arizona and California.

Returning to San Gabriel to find Anza already gone, Garcés was not about to waste an opportunity for further exploration. To follow Anza up to San Francisco would be to travel, from Garcés' perspective, a well-worn highway. Among the desert Indians on the outer edges of Yuma country, Garcés had previously seen blankets from the Moqui (Hopi) pueblos of northern Arizona. If a blanket could move from Moqui to Yuma and beyond, Garcés reasoned, and if the Moqui pueblos stood parallel to the pueblos of the upper Río Grande valley of New Mexico, was there not the possibility of a direct east–west connection from Alta California to Santa Fe? Such a route would link the mission systems of New Mexico, Sonora (northern Mexico), southern Arizona, and Alta California into a network that could in time be supplemented by development on sites he and Fray Díaz had surveyed on their way out, in addition to other locations yet to be inventoried. What a prospect! A chain of missions extending from Santa Fe to San Francisco Bay! And what about the reports Garcés had heard of a great lake to the north? Was this lake connected to the San Francisco (San Joaquin) River just discovered? (Bolton suggests Garcés was referring to either the Great Salt Lake or Lake Tahoe.) With these and other geographical questions on his mind, Garcés backtracked into Yuma country on a quest to mark a shorter return trail for the main party, which he did, saving nineteen leagues (forty-nine miles). He also reclaimed for the Anza party, after some difficulty, the cache of supplies Anza had left behind under the supervision of Chief Palma to ensure its availability upon the main party's return to Tubac. Meanwhile, Valdés, who had accompanied Garcés back to Yuma, proceeded at a rapid pace to Mexico City with the diaries of the expedition, Anza's formal report to Viceroy Bucareli, and a memorandum from Garcés. Valdés reached Mexico City in early June.

Upper Sonora, Bucareli learned, was now linked overland to the Pacific; and a new ally, the Yuma, led by the ever-friendly Chief Palma, stood strategically centered at the confluence of the Gila and Colorado Rivers. The next step: secure San Francisco with the proposed settlements, which is precisely what Bucareli asked

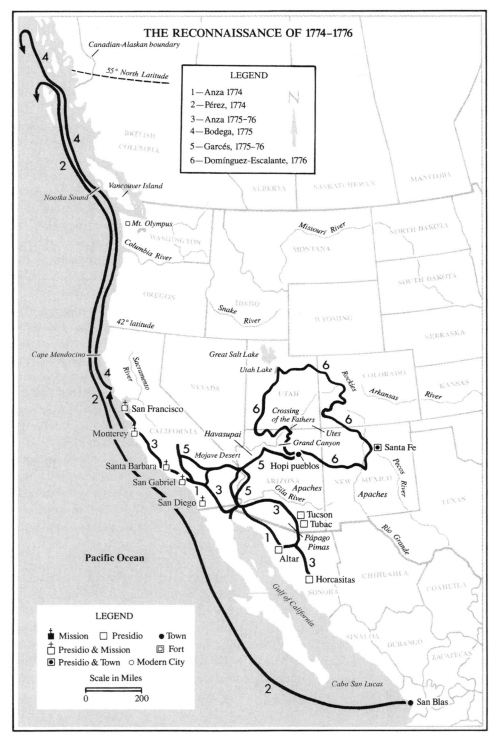

Map 13. The Reconnaissance of 1774–76. From David J. Weber, *The Spanish Frontier in North America* (New Haven: Yale University Press, 1992), 250.   © *Yale University Press, used by permission.*

Anza to do when Anza presented himself to the viceroy on 13 November 1774 and was promoted on the spot to lieutenant colonel.

The second expedition

Anza already had a settlement program in mind, which he now discussed with the viceroy. Recruiting for San Francisco, Anza advised, should be carried on in Sinaloa and Sonora among people already accustomed to frontier living who wanted a second (or third) start in life. Men thus recruited should be married with children and should receive a crash course in military training from experienced corporals before departure to enable them to act as a paramilitary force. Ten experienced soldiers from Tubac who had already been to California should be added to this second, colonizing expedition. Because of the continuing threat from Apaches, equally qualified men should replace these ten soldiers at Tubac. Colonists should be well provisioned for the journey and promised land once a pueblo was established on San Francisco Bay. Ample gifts for Indians encountered en route should also be provided. The viceroy should explicitly require the *hacendados* (ranchers) of Sinaloa and Sonora to supply the expedition with the sturdy horses and mules required for the fifteen-hundred-mile journey.

Regarding the development of Sonora and Alta California by New Spain, Anza's second expedition answered certain fundamental questions. Was this vast region to experience civil growth as well as the evangelization of its indigenous peoples through the mission system? Would pueblos (civilian townships) and haciendas (ranches) emerge alongside the missions and presidios? Would the Sonora and California frontiers over time become Mexicanized, creating a society of supportive criollos of mixed bloodlines and Hispanicized Indians attached to parish churches served by secular clergy governed by a diocesan bishop—or would the Franciscan protectorate last indefinitely?

To Bucareli and Anza, the answer was obvious. New Spain must be advanced north in all its social complexity if the Spanish Empire were to strengthen and maintain its fragile hold on the North American southwest. Thus the second expedition and founding of the San Francisco colony—as related in the diaries and histories Bolton gathered of the Spaniards who played major roles—serves as an epic prologue to the intermittent efforts of New Spain and the more consistent efforts of an independent Mexico to develop Alta California as a civilian settlement.

Anza spent the first eight months of 1775 in Sonora organizing the colonizing expedition and recruiting families from some of the oldest cities in Mexico—Culiacán, Fuerte, Mocorito, and Sinaloa, all with mid-sixteenth-century origins—as if to bring to San Francisco families already accustomed to urban living as well as eager to make a fresh beginning. When these settlers were recruited and assembled, Anza marched them 400 miles northward to Horcasitas. There Anza learned that Apaches had raided Tubac and made off with 500 of the horses and pack animals he had planned to use for the expedition, thus forcing a hasty purchase of new animals, many of them of lesser quality. Next up: a march of 250 miles from Horcasitas to Tubac for the settlement party, grown to 172 people, accompanied by a mule train of 140 loaded mules, 450 saddle horses, and other mules driven in two herds. At Tubac, reached on 15 October 1775, 63 more soldiers, settlers, wives, and children joined the colonists. The second Anza expedition now stood at 240 men, women, and children. It included three Franciscans: Garcés and Tomás Eixarch, both scheduled to remain as missionaries with the Yuma at the junction of the Gila and Colorado Rivers, and the talented and energetic Pedro Font, serving as navigator of latitudes, diarist, and chaplain. The military contingent comprised two officers, Anza and José Moraga, the senior noncommissioned officer Sergeant Pablo Grijalva, eight veterans from the presidio at Sonora, twenty newly enlisted recruits scheduled to remain in California, and ten Tubac soldiers serving as escorts and scheduled to return. More than 1,000 head of stock—695 horses and mules, plus 355 cattle—were to be driven in the rear van of the expedition behind a 140-mule train loaded with provisions.[5]

At 11:00 A.M., Monday, 23 October 1775, the second Anza expedition left Tubac on its thousand-mile journey. Late that afternoon, a soldier's wife went into labor and at nine that evening was delivered of a healthy (lusty, Anza describes him) boy. Unable to pass the afterbirth, however, the woman went into serious decline, made her confession and was anointed, and died. Thus was underscored on its very first day the civilian nature of the expedition. Catholic laypeople, including women and children in abundance, were bringing a more complete Church to California.

But first, another thousand miles lay ahead of this more complete Church in the making. As if to underscore the undertaking's Catholicity, a layman, Anza, and a priest, Fray Pedro Font, played out and recorded highly representative roles. A married man (how subtly did Anza's wife, Doña Ana Regina Serrano, seek to delay her husband's departure from Horcasitas!) and a father, Anza showed a special rapport with women. The battle-scarred Apache fighter evinced surprising sensitivity to the needs of women on the trail, three of whom gave birth in the desert wilderness. When the journey was over, his mission completed, Anza prepared to leave Monterey and return to Mexico City. Crossing barriers of gender, military rank, and social class, these women—toughened by their fifteen-hundred mile trek and expecting little from their frontier lives—gathered in the presidio plaza and, in an almost operatic scene, as Anza records it, said good-bye to the chivalric officer who, like Moses, had led them through the desert, seen them through danger with no loss of life, and treated them respectfully.

"This day has been the saddest one experienced by this presidio since its founding", Anza wrote in his diary on the evening of Sunday, 14 April 1776, his genuine emotion evident in every line.

> When I mounted my horse in the plaza, the people whom I have led from their fatherlands, to which I am returning, remembering the good or bad treatment which they have experienced at my hands while they have been under my orders, most of them, especially the feminine sex, came to me sobbing with tears, which they declared they were shedding more because of my departure than of their exile, filling me with compassion. They showered me with embraces, best wishes, and praises which I do not merit. But in remembrance of them, and of the gratitude which I feel to all, and the affection which I have had for them ever since I recruited them, and in eulogy of their faithfulness, for up to now I have not seen a single sign of desertion in anyone of those whom I brought to remain in this exile, I may be permitted to record this praise of a people who, as time goes on, will be very useful to the monarchy in

whose service they have voluntarily left their relatives and their fatherland, which is all they have to lose.

Here, then, was Anza's primary point of connection to the ultimate importance of the colonizing expedition: the bringing to California of women, wives and mothers and female children, the wives and mothers of the next generation. Indeed, Anza himself, a practical medic in the manner of military on the frontier, supervised the three births on the journey.[6]

The official historian of the second expedition, the Catalonia-born Fray Pedro Font, provides a fitting contrast to the layman Anza. Bucareli and Anza selected Font because of his reputation as a cartographer and writer as well as an accomplished preacher. Font did not disappoint in any of these expectations. Bucareli provided Font with an up-to-date astronomical guardant for the measuring of latitude and longitude by the stars, which Font supplemented with a less-than-adequate compass borrowed from San Xavier del Bac and, for the return journey, an astrolabe and graphometer borrowed from the Franciscans at Monterey. Throughout the journey, Font made exacting—and largely accurate, Bolton assures us—measurements of latitude and trackings of direction. As cartographer, he produced an important series of early maps of the San Francisco Bay region, including a precise rendering of the mouth of the bay (*la boca*) and the opposite coastlands (*contra costa*). Safely returned to Horcasitas, Font prepared his *Short Diary* for submission to Bucareli, finishing it on 23 June 1776. Throughout the next year, drawing on his notes, he expanded this document fivefold. Completed on 11 May 1777, Font's *Complete Diary* and accompanying maps remained in manuscript until Bolton published his English translation 153 years later in the fourth volume of *Anza's California Expeditions*.

Bolton describes the *Complete Diary* as "one of the best in all Western Hemisphere history", which is saying a lot, given four centuries of frontier journalizing in Spanish, English, French, and other languages. One suspects that Bolton, like Samuel Eliot Morison (another on-the-ground historian anchored in primary sources and a personal retracing of geography), was most impressed with the scientific rigor of Font's approach: his exacting latitudes and directions, and the precision with which he described and measured the Casa Grande on the Gila River, that mysterious ruin on the Sonoran Desert, popularly thought to be Moctezuma's palace, built around 1350 B.C. by architecturally accomplished Native American ancients.[7]

Font represented a blend of the Franciscan tradition and Enlightenment thought. The Enlightenment's effect on his mind and imagination is evident in his omnivorous appetite for exact detail: how a mule was packed or a river forded, the heat of the sun, the welcomed morning dew on grass as the desert was left behind. Font was a Catalan, formed by the literary Franciscanism of his region. Hence a streak of poetry now and then shines amid his precise observations. Yet unlike the Majorcans Serra, Palóu, and Crespí—all of whom were members of the virtually all-European College of San Fernando—Font joined the largely criollo College of the Holy Cross at Querétaro. He was thus a peninsular among criollos, which perhaps accounts for his occasional tendency to criticize or second-guess decisions made by the Mexican-born Anza. Or was this merely a recurrance of the tension between Franciscan and soldier apparent throughout Borderland history? Font, in any event, was aware of his dignity and position as a priest and did not hesitate to disagree with Anza on a number of practical matters.

Although Font was a Franciscan, he was no Friar Tuck making merry with Robin Hood and his men in Sherwood Forest, or even a sympathetic parish priest at a church festival. Among other points of contention, Font disapproved of Anza's tendency to distribute *aguardiente* (brandy) on certain occasions, which led to revelry and dancing among the colonists. Font resented the evident drunkenness, and drunkenness was a sin; hence the lieutenant colonel was fostering sin, and Font openly told him so one night on the trail when Anza allowed the settlers a barrel or two of aguardiente. Anza said nothing in reply. As a soldier, he knew human nature from a different perspective. A break from the hard routine, with some brandy and dancing—provided that security was maintained and things did not get out of hand—was no sin, whatever the friar might claim.

Font held the formal rank of preacher in his college. Through his vivid discoursing on the fifteen-hundred-mile trek—sermons he remembered with satisfaction as he recreated them from notes for the *Complete Diary*—Font deployed moral exhortation and scriptural analogy to theologize the second expedition. Upon the departure from Horcasitas, Font placed the journeying party under the protection of Our Lady of Guadalupe, the Archangel Michael, and Saint Francis of Assisi as he received the stigmata (five wounds) of Christ. The expedition would need fortitude and courage (Michael), Font preached, endurance of pain (Francis), and intercession (Our Lady of Guadalupe). When the party passed safely through Apache territory, Font expressed gratitude for the protection of these heavenly intercessors, especially the Virgin of Guadalupe.

Yet Font could be as admonitory as he was encouraging. On the Sunday before leaving Tubac, Font preached from the Gospel of that day the text "Nolite timere pusillus grex" in the Vulgate (Lk 12:32; Fear not, little flock), comparing the colonists to the children of Israel as they departed Egypt for the Promised Land. This analogy was at once a source of encouragement and a cautionary tale. The children of Israel, Font pointed out, had sinned en route and otherwise disobeyed Moses, which in the expedition's case translated to a lack of discipline on the trail or mistreatment of the Indians en route. "I reminded them", Font later remembered, "of the punishment which God might mete out to them if they mistreated the heathen on the way or scandalized them by their conduct, as He did with the Israelites who committed such excesses, or if they murmured at the commander of the expedition or his orders as they did at their leader Moses, failing to render him due obedience."[8]

In December 1775, in the dead of winter, the expedition became separated into three groups in the Sierra Madre, partly because of command decisions by Anza with which Font took issue and partly because of mistakes in provisioning that Font believed Anza had made in Tubac. Once the three parties reunited, the settlers, with Anza's concurrence, gave themselves a celebratory fandango. When the sole widow listed on the manifest, Señora Feliciana Arballo, sang a few risqué verses before the fire, her newly acquired suitor grew jealous and began to berate her loudly. Hearing this, Anza dashed from his tent and told the gentleman to leave the lady alone. Font took it upon himself to intervene. "Leave him alone, sir," the friar admonished. "He is doing just right." Anza disagreed. "I cannot permit such excesses," he replied, "when I am present."

One marvels at Font's prudery over off-color words as well as his boldness in publicly confronting the commander of the expedition. In any event, the Saturday-night celebration went on into the early morning hours, and the next morning at Mass Font scolded the settlers for partying when they should have been praying. "Instead of thanking God for having arrived with their lives, and not having died from such hardship, as the animals did," Font preached with puritanical choler and an excess of rhetoric, "it appeared that they were making such festivities in honor of the Devil." Anza was at the Mass, Font notes. "I do not think that the commander liked this very well, for he did not speak to me once during the whole morning."[9]

No wonder! Font's skills as a scientist and a writer offset his priggishness, of course, but such lack of sympathy for laypeople does underscore the eventual need for diocesan clergy if and when Alta California were settled by lay Catholics, rather than remaining a Franciscan protectorate in which the friar served as the father guardian of his Indian children. It is difficult to imagine an experienced parish priest getting apoplectic over a celebration of surviving a great peril in the mountains in the midst of a harsh winter.

Anza came to love the people he was leading through the wilderness. He knew when to indulge them and when to punish them. Having reached California, for example, Anza sentenced a few temporary deserters to physical punishment, not the lash but blows deftly administered by a corporal expert in such matters. Font showed little patience with human foibles, but he sincerely made every effort to care for his temporary flock. On the afternoon of Christmas Eve, for example, Font ministered to a frightened Señora Gertrudis Linares as she endured the pains of a difficult childbirth. "She was very fearful of dying," Font recalls, "but having consoled her and encouraged her as best I could I returned to my tent, and at half past eleven at night she very happily and quickly gave birth to a boy." The next morning, Christmas Day, Font solemnly baptized Salvador Ygnacio Linares, the third and last infant born on the expedition. Yet he bypassed the opportunity to link the birth of Salvador Ygnacio to the birth of Christ, as any seasoned parish priest would have done, and instead used the occasion to denounce Christmas Eve revelry with quotations from the Latin Vulgate and the fifth-century Pope Saint Leo the Great as well as to complain about the settlers' lack of confessions.[10]

Font's dilemma

At times in the *Complete Diary*, Font wrestles with his own doubts and demons. Sick for much of the journey, his mouth riddled with sores, Font—even when reworking his notes in retrospect—does not manage to conceal a note of dyspepsia surfacing now and then in his account. Underlying his words is an ambivalence to the whole enterprise, especially its missionary dimension. Could these Native Americans ever truly be transformed into a self-sufficient Catholicized population? Although Font describes the Papagos and Yuma of southern Arizona and the Quechan and Cahuilla on the western side of the Colorado River with an amplitude of near-anthropological detail, he does so without affection and sometimes with an edge of contempt. Not for Font was the *embrazo* (embrace) of Garcés, literally and figuratively: Garcés willingly sat with tribal elders by the hour, enjoying a smoke of tobacco, laughing, talking, sharing stories, or quietly staring into the fire. All this was preparation, when the opportunity presented itself, for the moment he could break out his illustrative banner—Mary and the Child Jesus on one side, the condemned in hellfire on the other—and launch into a rip-roaring sermon.

Such rapport in the service of evangelization was nearly impossible for Font. An accomplished, highly educated member of his order who had been slated for a life of prayer, writing, and teaching in the developed Franciscan culture of Catalonia, Font volunteered for the missions of northern Sonora and the Borderlands. Still, like certain Jesuit missionaries from Mitteleuropa in Lower California thirty years earlier, he tended to make value-laden evaluations of indigenous people. "In my opinion," Font writes of the Cahuilla people encountered in the mountains bordering the Colorado Desert of southeastern Southern California, "these are among the most unhappy people in the world. Their habitation is among the arid and bleak rocks of these sierras. The clothing of the men is nothing at all, and the women wear some tattered capes made of mescal fiber. Their food consists of tasteless roots, grass seeds, and scrubby mescal, of all of which there is very little, and so their dinner is a fast. Their arms are a bow and a few bad arrows. In fine, they are so savage, wild, and dirty, disheveled, ugly, small, and timid, that only because they have the human form is it possible to believe that they belong to mankind."[11]

Here is surfacing the temptation to consider Indians less than human, a sentiment officially repudiated but now being reprised and intensified in Baja and Alta California due the hardscrabble lifestyle of so many of the indigenous people. Arising at the same time may have been the questions: Was this what I surrendered Catalonia for? Why am I here? Such pondering must have troubled the missionary during moments of seemingly unbridgeable cultural disconnect.

Font works through these difficulties in a meditation he inserts in the *Complete Diary* on Monday, 4 December 1775, in the course of a lengthy description of the Yuma. Anchoring himself in the ninth chapter of John, Font repeats the question the disciples asked of Jesus regarding a beggar born blind: "Rabbi, quis peccavit, hic aut parentes ejus, ut caecus nasceretur?" (Jn 9:2; "Rabbi, who sinned, this man or his parents, that he was born blind?") The Gospel narrative continues with Jesus' answer: "It was not that this man sinned, or his parents, but that the works of God might be made manifest in him. We must work the works of him who sent me, while it is day; night comes, when no one can work. As long as I am in the world, I am the light of the world" (3–5).

The blind man and his parents were innocent, as the indigenous people were innocent of what Font considered their inferior (barely human) condition. In John's account, Jesus anointed the blind man's eyes with spittle, which was believed to have medicinal value in the ancient world, and instructed him to wash himself in the pool of Silóam. The man did this and returned with his sight restored, telling people that Jesus had healed him. Just as Jesus discerned in the blind man an opportunity for ministry, so did Font eventually regard the Indians of California. The adverse circumstances of the indigenous people he was encountering in southeastern California—chronic starvation, lack of clothing or shelter, and even the promiscuity and polygamy that he found especially disturbing—were not their fault, nor did their condition imply a subrational nature. However degraded they might seem to him, Font came to realize, these people were fully human, and evangelization could help them gain faith, reason, and culture.

Arrival and settlement

According to the Laws of the Indies, civil settlements, parish churches, a diocesan bishop, and secular clergy were scheduled to replace the Franciscan protectorate. Despite this inevitability—or was it in part because of it?—the Franciscans of Alta California in general resisted civil settlement. Many military also balked at the establishment of a third sector in society alongside missions and presidios. Arriving at Mission San Gabriel on 4 January 1776, Anza encountered open hostility to a settlement in San Francisco on the part of the aging governor, Captain Fernando de Rivera y Moncada, then en route to San Diego to quell the revolt that in November 1775 had resulted in the death of Fray Luis Jayme. Rivera had explored the San Francisco peninsula in 1774, considered it unsuitable for settlement, and advised Anza to leave his civilian colonists at San Gabriel under his supervision. Anza refused. He outranked Rivera, for one thing, and was operating under the direct orders of Viceroy Bucareli. In the months that followed, Rivera grew choleric to the point of imbalance regarding the San Francisco venture.

The progress of the Anza party north from San Gabriel through the Los Angeles plain, along the Santa Barbara Channel to San Luis Obispo, inland into the Salinas valley, and then north and west to Monterey (where Anza arrived on Sunday, 11 March 1776) brings to mind not only present and future mission sites but also the civilian settlements—San Gabriel, San Fernando, Ventura, Santa Barbara, San Luis Obispo, Paso Robles, Salinas, and Monterey, among others—that would in time develop in these places. The arrival at Monterey prompted Font to deliver an ambitious farewell sermon before a congregation that included seven Franciscans (one of them being Serra), as well as soldiers and colonists, to the text "Simile est regnun caelorum sagenae missae in mare, et ex omni genere piscium congreganti" (Mt 13:47; [T]he kingdom of heaven is like a net which was thrown into the sea and gathered fish of every kind). The colonizing expedition was the net, Font suggested, and the colonists were the fish of every sort, taken from the sea of Sinaloa and safely brought to this place. Momentarily putting aside prior disagreements, Font went out of his way to praise Anza for his "patience, prudence, and good conduct" and broke into tears at the conclusion of his sermon, when he charged all to do well in this new world and to "have patience in the trials which the future promises to you, and by those trials prove worthy to live in the grace of God, so that when we die we may meet in heaven".[12]

Leaving his settlers behind at Monterey under the protection of Father Serra and Lieutenant Moraga, Anza departed Monterey on 22 March 1776 for a seventeen-day reconnaissance of the San Francisco Bay Area that, as presented in Font's *Complete Diary*, not only references the sites selected for a mission and presidio on San Francisco Bay but also evokes the locations that would in time support an array of civilian settlements in the American era. Font scientifically measures the height of the Palo Alto redwood that would lend its name to the American township. Lake Merced on the edge of present-day San Francisco is duly noted as—passing through the later Lakeshore, Parkside, Sunset, Golden Gate Park, and Richmond districts of the eventual city—the Spaniards make their way to a campsite on the shore of Mountain Lake Park adjacent to the future presidio. With appropriate ceremony, Anza raises a cross on Fort Point, which overlooks the strait leading into the mouth of the estuary, later (1846) named the Golden Gate. From this height, looking out to the ocean, Font notes, the Spaniards "saw the spouting of whales, a shoal of dolphins or tunny fish, sea otter, and sea lions".[13]

Moving south down the peninsula, then eastward and north through present-day Alameda and Contra Costa Counties, Font chronicles the sites that would in time become Oakland and Berkeley. The reconnaissance party next explored the Carquinez Strait, trying to ascertain whether it was the previously reported San Francisco River. Anza and his men then traveled south and east to Mount Hamilton before turning south once again and returning to Monterey, having successfully brought Catholic laity to San Francisco and served the continental ambitions of New Spain.

Santa Barbara 1842

Secularization brings a bishop to the Californias

On 11 January 1842 at eleven A.M., the Right Reverend Francisco García Diego y Moreno, the first bishop of the Diocese of Both Californias, arrived at Santa Barbara on the sloop *Guipuzcoana*, having sailed there from San Diego, where he had spent the first months of his episcopacy. A friendly crowd of townspeople, Franciscan friars from the mission, and soldiers from the presidio greeted the bishop as he disembarked at wharfside with an entourage appropriate to his episcopal status: two Franciscan friars, six diocesan seminarians, his niece Doña Josefita Gómez, her elderly duenna, and two servants who exercised between them the functions of sacristan, valet, houseman, and gardener. Soldiers marching in formation and artillery salutes accompanied the bishop's party as it made its way through an ornamental arch en route to a magnificent midday meal at the home of Don José Antonio Aguirre, the owner of the *Guipuzcoana*, and his new bride, Rosario Estudillo.

After the meal, the bishop proceeded to Mission Santa Barbara by carriage. Nearing the mission, the carriage halted near a roadside bower, where the prelate donned pontifical vestments before proceeding once again by carriage, now being drawn by townspeople, who had detached its horses. Wearing the mitre of his office and carrying a crosier, García Diego y Moreno entered the most architecturally ambitious of the twenty-one California missions. Blessing the congregation as he processed down its lengthy central aisle to the episcopal throne awaiting him at the altar, the bishop sat enthroned as a well-trained orchestra and choir of Chumash Indians performed a Te Deum and other hymns and compositions chosen for the ceremony.

Months earlier, San Diego had proven equally welcoming of the bishop, albeit on a smaller scale. Don Juan Bandini, a Peruvian-born rancher, trader, and politician, provided quarters, and the presidio chapel offered the bishop a venue for Masses, preaching, and the ordination to minor orders of the seminarians the bishop brought with him as the nucleus of a diocesan clergy. But San Diego, chosen by Mexico City and Rome as a midpoint between Baja and Alta California, was a mere village of 125 residents and hence inadequate to serve as the seat of an episcopal see. Thus—following his welcome at Santa Barbara and with the eventual permission of Church and secular authorities—García Diego y Moreno relocated his episcopal seat to Santa Barbara, where he took up temporary residence (until an official residence could be built) at the Franciscan friary adjacent to the mission.

Now fifty-seven, García Diego y Moreno had spent his missionary career as a Franciscan connected to the Apostolic College of Our Lady of Guadalupe at Zacatecas. His tenure at Zacatecas had recently included a brief tour of duty in Alta California from 1833 to 1836. Based out of Mission Santa Clara, García Diego y Moreno had supervised the transfer of the missions of the northern region from the Fernandinos to the Zacatecans as an aging population of Spanish-born Fernandinos, royalist in political sentiment and never fully reconciled to an independent republican Mexico, passed on or retired to Spain.

Like many Zacatecans, García Diego y Moreno was a criollo. Born in 1785 to wealthy parents in the city of Lagos in the province of Jalisco, he received the first three years of his education for the priesthood in a diocesan seminary before transferring to the Franciscans. A friar's robes, however, did not extract García Diego y Moreno from the upper-class criollo caste soon to govern an independent Mexico. His apostolic college promoted him to important posts—representative, master of novices, lector in philosophy, counselor, commissary prefect of missions—and his boyhood friend Anastasio Bustamente, now president of Mexico, in 1840 requested of Rome the creation of a Diocese of Both Californias and cited Fray García Diego y Moreno as his preference to be its first bishop. Rome agreed, and President Bustamente personally administered the required constitutional oath to the bishop-elect. On 4 October 1840 the abbot-bishop of the Basilica of our Lady of Guadalupe in Mexico City consecrated García Diego y Moreno to the fullness of the priesthood.

The elite social background of García Diego y Moreno underscores the Church's relatively easy transition into the new republican order. Like everything else in Mexico, the episcopacy would remain in the control of upper-class Spaniards. Class identification, in fact, would soon contribute to the new bishop's unpopularity among certain middle- and Baja-class Santa Barbarans who saw in this well-born prelate yet another Spanish-oriented protector of Indian versus local interests.

Such open hostility, however, would take a few more years to surface as the crusade to secularize the missions of Alta California gained momentum. In the meanwhile, the new bishop did his best to establish his diocese. All twenty-one priests then serving in the Californias were members of religious orders: five Dominicans in Baja California and sixteen Franciscans in the north. On 29 June 1842 García Diego y Moreno ordained one of his seminarians, Miguel Gómez, to the priesthood, the first such ordination to be held in the Californias. Two more ordinations followed in October 1843. The bishop assigned two of these secular priests—the first to serve in California—to replace the Franciscans at Mission San Luis Obispo and Mission San Buenaventura, the first two canonically authorized parishes in the diocese. In 1846 García Diego y Moreno ordained three more priests, bringing the number of secular clergy of California to six, the number of seminarians he had brought with him to California four years earlier.

As a former seminary professor, the bishop was fully capable of supervising the studies of these six seminarians, now the first generation of a future diocesan clergy, yet García Diego y Moreno had a more formal arrangement in mind. The Council of Trent (1545–1563) had called for the creation of diocesan seminaries in each diocese if at all possible. Shortly after his arrival in Santa Barbara, García Diego y Moreno announced plans for not only a cathedral, seminary, and episcopal residence, as might be expected, but also—with his niece in mind—a school for girls, most likely under the leadership of Doña Concepción Argüello.

In 1807, following the death in Siberia of her Russian fiancé, Nikolai Petrovich Rezanov, the founder of the Russian-American Company, Concepción had entered religious life as a Franciscan tertiary, since there were no convents in California. She devoted the rest of her life to charitable works and service to the Church. In 1842 Concepción was living as a respected retainer in the household of the wealthy de la Guerra family, and it was in the Casa de la Guerra near the presidio that Captain George Simpson, the general superintendent of the Hudson Bay Company, was received by García Diego y Moreno in January in a handsomely appointed room. The bishop sat in a throne-like chair draped in purple velvet as Concepción Argüello served the two gentlemen fruit, wine, brandy, and cigars. In his journal entry about the visit, Simpson claims that not until he described to Concepción the specifics of her fiancé's death from pneumonia did she know how Rezanov had died and thus ended her hopes for marriage.

In 1851, at the age of fifty-nine, Concepción Argüello entered the Dominican convent then being established in Monterey and became the first nun to be professed in California. As Sister Maria Dominica, she helped open the first Catholic girls' school in California, in the city of Benicia on the northeastern edge of San Francisco Bay. For the time being, however, that school, as well as the cathedral, seminary, and episcopal residence planned for the new diocese, consisted only of the stones Bishop García Diego y Moreno began to have assembled in impressive piles at selected sites throughout Santa Barbara.

Civil settlement

The second Anza expedition of 1775–1776 not only resulted in the founding of the pueblo of San Jose, but also stimulated civil settlement at Monterey, Santa Barbara, and Los Angeles in Alta California and Tucson in Pimería Alta. Of these population centers, only San Jose (1777) and Los Angeles (1781) enjoyed official pueblo or civic status in the Spanish colonial era ending in 1821, although the emergence of Monterey as regional capital represented a comparable upgrade. In the presidio-centered settlements of Monterey and Santa Barbara, military families made up the core civilian population, along with civilian employees of the military—carpenters, muleteers, vaqueros, herdsmen, drovers, servants—and their families of mixed ancestry. The numbers were pitifully small, given the settlers' importance in holding a vast region for the empire and standing in dramatic contrast to the seven-million-plus population of Mexico itself. By 1820, the last year of imperial rule, Alta California had more than 21,000 indigenous people living in twenty missions (twenty-one after 1823) and approximately 3,200 mestizos and Spaniards in its civil population. Southern Arizona had a civil population of 1,000 by 1800. Still, as meager as these numbers might seem, every Catholic colonist, including Catholic Indian immigrants from Mexico and Baja California, played a role in establishing the beginnings of civil Catholic settlement, which in turn would bring into being a diocesan-based Church.

In 1694, en route to the Gila River, Eusebio Kino was the first European to visit the Northern Pima ranchería of Schookson (Black Place Near the Mountain). Kino returned to Schookson in 1697 and 1698. By 1699 he was identifying Schookson as San Cosme de Tucson when on tour of the region with his Jesuit superior. Kino also gave saints' names to two other rancherías in the area, San Xavier del Bac and San Agustín del Oyaur. In this well-watered oasis, Bolton tells us—the Bac-Tucson valley, as it came to be called—some two to three thousand Pimas lived and flourished within a dozen miles of each other, raising maize, beans, calabashes, melons, and cotton in irrigated fields. Here Kino envisioned a cluster of missions similar to the one he had established farther south, and in 1700 he founded the Mission of San Xavier del Bac nine miles south of Tucson. Jesuits ministered at this site (intermittently, due to shortages of personnel) for sixty-seven years.

In 1775 Hugo Oconor, the inspector of frontier posts, moved the garrison of Tubac to San Agustín del Tucson, as the settlement was now designated. Under the command of Captain Don Pedro de Allande y Saabedra—a career officer from Navarre and a veteran of campaigns against Portugal, the Moors of North Africa, and the Seri on the Gulf of California's coast—the garrison of the Tucson presidio played the lead role in the ongoing war with the ever-active, ever-resourceful Apaches, who on the first day of May 1782 launched a surprise attack on the presidio itself. Ten years later, after numerous campaigns, a stable peace was at long last negotiated with the western Apaches. For the remaining twenty-eight years of Spanish colonial rule, Tucson grew as a population center of soldiers, civilians, Christianized Indians, and their families under the pastoral care of Franciscans and the jurisdiction of the bishop of Sonora, Sinaloa, and the Californias.

Meanwhile, the nearby San Xavier del Bac (Franciscan since 1767), in addition to its associated Native American settlements, enjoyed as of 1801 six civilian families—Spanish, coyote, mestizo, mulatto, and baptized Yuma youngsters being raised halfway between adopted children and indentured household servants—as well as ten single individuals of a similar mixed ancestry. The 1801 census lists the considerable population of the Native American ranchería of San Agustín del Tucson—sixty-five families and thirty-four single individuals—by first name, age, gender, marital status (married man, married woman, widow, widower, bachelor, spinster, boy child, girl child), and tribal origin (mainly Papago, followed by Pima and a few Gileño). These enumerations do not differ from those used for non-Indians, which suggests a growing Hispanicization of indigenous peoples. By 1804 Tucson and San Xavier del Bac were reporting a total population of 1,015 soldiers, settlers, and Indians.

Franciscan resistance

Tucson had come into being with next to no controversy between soldiers and Franciscans. Indeed, Fray Garcés was one of the signatories, along with Hugo Oconor, calling for the relocation of the presidio from Tubac to Tucson. A thousand miles to the northwest, by contrast, the founding of San Jose in 1777 and Los Angeles in 1781 involved an ongoing controversy between Governor Felipe de Neve and Junípero Serra. As father president of the Alta California missions, Serra got along with Gaspar de Portolá, the commander of the Sacred Expedition. The excitable father president, however, eager to assert the prerogatives of the Franciscan protectorate, quarreled bitterly with two of Portolá's successors, Pedro Fages and Fernando de Rivera y Moncada. Rivera was particularly piqued because, as the longtime captain of the presidio at Loreto, he had enjoyed good relations with his Jesuit colleagues prior to their banishment. But in 1776, the experienced captain who had led the first contingent of the Sacred Expedition into Alta California in 1769 found himself excommunicated by Serra for violating the right of sanctuary in having the rebel leader Carlos arrested in the chapel of the San Diego presidio.

Traveling all the way to Mexico City to make his case to Viceroy Bucareli, Serra succeeded in having Rivera transferred back to Loreto as lieutenant governor. Rivera's successor, however, Felipe de Neve, proved a much more effective foil to Serra than the aging, hot-tempered Rivera. He proved especially adept when, after two years of governing from Loreto (1775–1777), Neve moved his headquarters to Monterey, just a few miles from Mission San Carlos Borromeo at Carmel, where Serra resided. Neve was an aristocrat, born in 1724 in Bailén, the province of Jaén, to Andalusian nobility. Enlisting as a cadet at the age of twenty, he fought with distinction for twenty years as a cavalry officer in continental wars—Flanders, Italy, Portugal—before accepting an assignment to New Spain in 1764 in the entourage of José de Gálvez in hopes of further promotion. In 1774, after a decade of service that included suppressing the civilian uprising to protest the expulsion of the Jesuits as well as administering the resources of the former Jesuit college, Neve achieved promotion to colonel, followed by appointment as governor of the Californias.

Considering these aspects alone—birth, career, and political connections— Neve was a governor whom Serra, a Majorcan farmer's son, would find difficult to intimidate. Neve possessed an ideological edge as well. Like most high-ranking officers being promoted in the reign of Carlos III, Neve was a man of the Enlightenment. Hence, like the king and the ruling class of New Spain, Neve was a Catholic—yet oriented toward court-nominated bishops and secular clergy and hostile to the semiautonomous prerogatives of the religious orders, one of which he had helped suppress in Michoacán. As governor, Neve favored the development of civilian settlements, the employment of secular priests as military chaplains and parish clergy, and the secularization of mission properties, including distribution of land to neophytes and sale to colonists. In the interim, before these reforms could be initiated, Neve supported the establishment of limited self-governance for mission Indians through the appointment in each mission of Indian officials variously called governor, captain, or alcalde; such was the practice in the other Borderland provinces as a transition to the creation of self-governing pueblos of Hispanicized Indians.

Serra would have none of this. To his way of thinking—and that of his Franciscan colleagues as well—Alta California was first and foremost a mission system, not a civilian settlement. The mission Indians were children and the Franciscans their protective parents, involved in and responsible for each detail of their lives, including employment and the brokering of marriages. Presidios might very well be necessary, but soldiers had turned out to be sexual marauders of Indian women, a menace that, while somewhat abated, continued. Nor did the Franciscans relish pastoral responsibility for soldiers, colonists, and their families, as evident in Fray Font's continual complaining and admonishments on the second Anza expedition. Franciscans, after all, had chosen the cloister in some measure to get away from the world, its pleasures and distractions, and not to live in the world as secular priests. As Font presented them in his *Complete Diary*, civilians were overfond of alcohol and given to dancing and singing salacious songs. They fell easily into sin but neglected confession, profaned Christmas with fandangos, and in other practices failed in Christian observance. In the missions, by contrast, a semiutopian, protected way of life prevailed and might be maintained, leading—at some very distant, unspecified date—to the creation of a Hispanicized Indian Catholic population.

Controversies continue

In 1777, when the site for the pueblo of San Jose was chosen—the first of two pueblos and one presidio to be founded under Neve's authority—Serra complained that it was too close to Mission Santa Clara, and hence in violation of the Laws of the Indies. The pueblo site was adjusted, in part, to avoid flooding from the Guadalupe River, but it still lay too near the mission for Franciscan comfort, despite the alameda that soon grew up between the two.

Neve was thrilled with the success of San Jose, especially its agricultural and cattle-raising productivity, which soon allowed it to provision itself, Mission Santa Clara, Mission Dolores, and the presidio of San Francisco without shipping supplies all the way from San Blas, around the tip of the Baja California peninsula, and northward up the California coast. Was this not a model, Neve asked, for the development of Alta California?

In 1779 Governor Neve wrote a reglamento, or civil code, for the governance of Alta California that remained in use throughout the Spanish colonial era. As might be expected in a work from Neve, the reglamento was largely oriented toward the authorizing, recruiting, financing, and provisioning of civil settlements during their first phases. Each settler was to be provided with irrigated land outside the pueblo for cultivation, farm animals, and equipment, as well as a lot for a home in the pueblo; the lots were to be laid out around a public square, according to the provisions of the Laws of the Indies. The Crown would finance the construction of each house, but once occupied, the house would belong to the settler and his heirs. The governor would initially appoint officials for each pueblo, but in the next phase of development the township would nominate its own officials for approval by the governor. Each able-bodied male settler would be provided with a saddle, shield, lance, and shotgun and would be expected to train for, and participate in, a local militia.

Each of the eight missions thus far founded, charged Title 15 of the reglamento, would be allowed for the time being to maintain its staffing of two priests, but upon the death or departure of one of these priests, staffing should drop to one, except in those cases in which a second priest was needed to serve as chaplain of a nearby presidio if no secular priest were available. Clearly, the reglamento was not a mission-friendly code. Serra found the requirement that each mission allow for the appointment of an Indian alcalde especially threatening. On Palm Sunday, 29 March 1779, he and Neve had a confrontation on the issue when Serra arrived at the Monterey presidio to celebrate Mass. Serra was so upset by the encounter, he wrote to Fray Lasuén the next day, he could barely regain his composure for the Mass. He spent the day in wretched distraction and had trouble sleeping that night until he cried out, "What is the meaning of it all, O Lord?" To this query, he heard a voice within him say, "Be prudent as serpents and simple as doves," Christ's advice to His twelve apostles regarding the time they would set forth to spread the gospel (see Mt 10:16). By this, Serra meant that the Franciscans would go along to get along, but that they would prevent the alcalde requirement from usurping their authority by appointing Indians who had already earned their trust. The Franciscan superior of the mission, furthermore, would be the only one to receive and to read out the diploma making such an appointment. This would ensure the impression that the office was coming from the Franciscans and not from another—perhaps adversarial—authority.

Adding insult to injury, Neve also argued that the missions founded by Serra were doctrinas, that is, catechetical centers under the authority of the bishop of Sinaloa, Sonora, and the Californias, as opposed to autonomous establishments. This claim rankled Serra and led to a controversy about Serra's authorization to confer the sacrament of confirmation, a function usually reserved to a bishop but allowed to a ranking priest in missionary territories. Serra was administering confirmation at Carmel in August 1779 when Neve—basing his actions on a royal cédula of November 1777 requiring viceregal review and *pase* (permission) for important ecclesiastical decisions and exemptions—demanded that Serra show him the brief granting him the privilege to confer confirmation. He had only a copy of the brief, Serra replied; the original was deposited at the College of San Fernando in Mexico City. He would have to see the original brief, Neve countered, if he were to affix his own approval to Serra's continuing to confer confirmation. Such was the intent, as Neve interpreted it, of the cédula of 1777. An exchange of letters ensued, with each side making its case. Serra sent along a letter from Viceroy Bucareli congratulating Serra on receiving the privilege of confirmation. Neve replied that this letter did not constitute official documentation of the cédula.

Neve obviously was eager to strip Serra of a privilege—administering confirmation—that enhanced both his status and that of the Franciscan protectorate through the granting of an episcopal privilege. Serra, on his part, correctly perceived Neve's wish to lessen the ecclesiastical authority of the Franciscans not only among mission Indians but also among soldiers, settlers, and families who desired the sacrament of confirmation. Serra and the College of San Fernando considered the mission system of Alta California a near-autonomous entity under Franciscan jurisdiction; Neve considered Alta California part of the Diocese of Guadalajara. On 25 September 1779 Neve suspended Serra's right to confer confirmation. Prudently, Serra refrained from administering confirmation for Neve's remaining two-plus years in office.

Serra's withdrawal from the field on the confirmation front, however, did not bring peace to the valley, given the ongoing dispute between the Franciscans of Mission Santa Clara and the civilian colonists of San Jose regarding rights to agricultural lands that both parties claimed. This controversy broke out almost immediately after the founding of the mission in January and the founding of the pueblo in November 1777. The Franciscans resented the establishment of a civilian pueblo

a mere three-quarters league (two miles) from their mission. The conflict continued in one form or another throughout the next twenty years, and (like many such
chronic controversies) it ended in compromise. In the meanwhile, when the quarrels heated up, Neve and Serra squared off against each other, with Neve arguing a
pro-settler interpretation of the relevant statutes of the Laws of the Indies and Serra
advancing counterarguments.

Reorganization

During this time, Serra was also laboring under the burden of a widespread report
that Bishop Antonio de los Reyes of Sinaloa, Sonora, and the Californias—although
himself a former Franciscan missionary in Sonora—was seriously considering
replacing the Franciscans with Dominicans in Alta California so that all California missions would be supervised by one order and one provincial, as opposed to
the Dominican provincial and the administrations of three Franciscan apostolic
colleges now in place. Bishop Reyes additionally wanted to reorganize the overlapping Franciscan administrative entities—three colleges, three provinces—into
four custodies (subsections). The colleges would be relegated to education and
training, while the custodies would administer Franciscan missionary efforts in
the provinces.

First proposed by José de Gálvez in the late 1760s and implemented by royal
decree on 22 August 1776, the Provincias Internas reorganization was central to
Carlos III's efforts to reform and strengthen the North American frontier of the
empire. Under this scheme, the provinces of Nueva Vizcaya, Coahuila, Sinaloa,
Sonora, New Mexico, Texas, and the Californias were administratively detached
from the viceroyalty of New Spain and reorganized as a unified frontier zone under
military jurisdiction called a commandancy general, headquartered in the city of
Arizpe in Sonora. The concept of a military frontier zone dated to Roman and
medieval times. For the pro-Enlightenment Bourbon monarch of Spain, the commandancy general—to which he appointed Teodoro de Croix, the nephew of Carlos Francisco de Croix, the viceroy of New Spain from 1766 to 1771—represented
an effort to unify and make more efficient frontier defense and administration. For
Bishop Reyes, the Provincias Internas program suggested a comparable simplifi-
cation of overlapping constituencies and the creation of a unified, all-Dominican
custody of San Gabriel in the Californias. For Serra, the commandancy general
meant the loss of a reporting relationship to his friend and fellow religious, Viceroy
Bucareli, and, more traumatically, the loss of a brave start and a decade of hard work
for the Franciscans of Alta California.

Ironically, despite the fact that Bishop Reyes continued to press the matter of
assigning Alta California to the Order of Preachers, causing Serra such stress, the
proposal received little if any support. Even Serra's longtime adversary Felipe de
Neve, the general in chief of the Interior Provinces since 1782, opposed it. On
29 December 1783 Neve wrote to Bishop Reyes praising the work of the Ferdi-
nandino Franciscans in Alta California and opposing any proposal to replace them
with Dominicans. Even more gratifying: just prior to his death in Carmel on 28
August 1784, Serra learned that the now-exalted Governor Neve had reversed his

postponement of building a mission on the Santa Barbara Channel, the tenth in the system, until the Santa Barbara presidio could be better staffed. Thus Serra died with the future of a tenth mission assured from a most unexpected source.

The founding of Los Angeles

The Franciscans would now have their Queen of Missions at Santa Barbara, and civilian Alta California—again, in large measure due to Neve—would have its Queen of Pueblos, the civil settlement El Pueblo de Nuestra Señora la Reina de los Ángeles del Río de Porciúncula, founded on 4 September 1781. Twelve years earlier, on 2 August 1769, the Portolá expedition had made camp on a bare plain near a river the Spaniards named the Porciúncula in honor of the village two miles outside Assisi where Saint Francis began his ministry in 1208, received Saint Clare in 1212, maintained his headquarters for the rest of his life, and died in 1226. Fray Juan Crespí liked the place immediately, despite the three earthquakes that shook the region that day. "It has good land for planting all kinds of grain and seeds," Crespí noted in his diary, "and is the most suitable site of all that we have seen for a mission, for it has all the requisites for a large settlement." The next day, the Spaniards followed the river westward through grassy fields ablaze in wild grapevines and blooming flowers and stayed that evening near a marshy fen running with water and oily pitch. Pushing on the next day, they reached low hills near the ocean. On 5 August they passed through a steep canyon into another great valley, which they named the Valley of Santa Catalina de Bononia de los Encinos, where they made camp. Thus was completed in rapid order a survey of a region: fertile plain, river, springs and creeks, tar pit, more plains, low mountains, the Pacific in the distance, a canyon leading to another valley of equal magnitude. In conjunction with all this exploration came friendly greetings from the Tongva people, starting with the village of Yang-na at the bend of the river. The abundant water, the rich and loamy soil, and the rolling fields of grass and wildflowers suggested to Crespí the possibilities of ambitious settlement.

In 1780 Governor Neve glimpsed these same possibilities and moved his headquarters for a year to Mission San Gabriel to be on site for the founding of a civil settlement that, according to his plan, would serve as a source of food supply for a proposed presidio on the Santa Barbara Channel. Appointed *comisionado* (commissioner) of the new community, a young officer by the name of José Darío Argüello surveyed and subdivided Neve's simple plan for an urban development around a central plaza. Neve had already commissioned his lieutenant governor, Fernando Rivera, to proceed to Mexico across the Gulf of California from his headquarters at Loreto and recruit settlers for the proposed pueblo, to be laid out and supplied in strict accordance with the Laws of the Indies.

Traveling along the Mexican coast as far south as Mazatlán, Rivera—despite his seventy years, which is rather old for a serving officer—fulfilled his task admirably, recruiting a cadre of forty-one soldiers and their families and forty-four civilians (twenty-three adults and twenty-one children) willing to pull up stakes and found a pueblo a thousand miles to the north. Rivera sent the civilians by ship to Baja California, then northward into Alta California by the trail he had blazed in 1769. The soldiers and their families, meanwhile, proceeded overland under Rivera's command via the Anza trail. Smallpox delayed the Baja California group, forcing it to advance in two increments. Rivera himself remained behind at Yuma with a small detachment of soldiers to allow a collection of exhausted cattle, mules, burros, and horses to regain their strength.

Despite the difficulties, thirty-two settlers were on hand on 4 September 1781 for the dedication of the pueblo of Los Angeles. Their bloodlines—African, Indian, and various Caucasian mixtures, with African and Indian predominating—embodied the racial eclecticism of the Mexican frontier. To these simple, hardscrabble people, Alta California and the new pueblo of Los Angeles represented the chance for a better life.

A proposed Yuma commonwealth

When Anza returned to Mexico City from his second, colonizing expedition, he brought with him Salvador Palma, the chief of the Yuma, and three other leaders of the tribe. Palma's assistance had proven crucial to both Anza expeditions, and the powerful chief had personally expressed to Anza his desire to become a Christian and to have missions established among his people. On 11 November 1776 Chief Palma submitted a memorandum to Viceroy Bucareli. Prepared by the viceroy's secretariat under the direction of Juan de Lazaga, counselor to the viceroy, with Anza's assistance, the memorandum nevertheless must be considered a sincere reflection of Palma's beliefs and hopes, given his record of service to Anza as well as his earlier efforts to obtain the services of Franciscan missionaries for the Quechan. On a previous visit to Sonora, moreover, Palma had been deeply impressed by the role Hispanicized Indians and mestizos played in the larger society. As *kwoxot* (head chief) of the Quechan, Palma wanted such a role for his own people, who were already a settled nation based on agriculture.

Palma's memorandum requested missionaries and baptism and offered the viceroy the opportunity for a grand alliance. "My country", Palma promised, "is abundant in wheat, maize, beans, cotton, tobacco, watermelons, calabashes, and cantaloupes, and is capable, as I see it, of producing many other products, with which the settlements would be able to sustain themselves in plenty. My people number more than three thousand, with whom I obligate myself to defend the missionaries and Spaniards from every insult. I believe that my neighbors will follow my example; and, in case of necessity, I have no doubt I could draw into a general alliance in the services of his Majesty the Galchedunes, Jamajá, or Soyopas, Pimas, Opas, Cocomaricopas, Cajuenes, Jaliquamas, Cucupas, Comeiás, Pápagos, and part of the Apaches who live on the opposite bank of the Colorado River and who do not communicate with those of this other bank, some because of enmity, and others for the fear which my victories have inspired in them."

At this point, Palma—speaking, of course, for Anza, the uncited coauthor of this text, as well as for himself—proposed an alliance between New Spain and the Quechan and their allies: the creation, in effect, of a friendly buffer Indian confederation centered on the intersection of the Yuma and Colorado Rivers that linked the northern Sonoran Desert and Alta California. "This alliance," he continued, "together with the establishments in my country, would not only keep the roads secure for the Spaniards, and keep free mutual communication between California and Sonora, San Francisco and New Mexico, because they will be situated in the center of these provinces, but also aided by the arms of the Spaniards, we could serve to advantage in the pacification of the neighboring kingdoms."[1]

What an attractive offer—and how strategically presented by Anza via Chief Palma: the establishment of a Yuma buffer state in Pimería Alta (Arizona), providing a corridor of protection into Alta California and opening negotiations for a confederation of surrounding tribes, even the Apaches! Such an alliance would benefit Chief Palma, reinforcing his authority through an impressive association with New Spain, and would foster the Quechan's dominance over traditional enemies. From Bucareli and the Crown's point of view, the Quechan alliance would stabilize the Gila and Colorado River region at a crucial time of overland colonization.

For some time Bucareli had been hoping for the discovery of a direct route between Santa Fe and Monterey that would link the entire Southwest. Early in 1776 Fray Francisco Garcés tried but failed to blaze such a trail by way of the San Joaquin Valley of Alta California. Garcés nearly reached New Mexico but was stopped by hostile Hopi in Pimería Alta. However, a letter Garcés wrote from the Hopi village of Oraibi was carried by a friendly Indian to the Zuni pueblo, the most westerly of the New Mexican settlements, and then on to Santa Fe. There it was read by Fray Silvestre Vélez de Escalante, who by chance was in the New Mexican capital trying to organize his own east-to-west connection from Santa Fe to Monterey.

Garcés' letter encouraged Escalante in his own efforts to fulfill Viceroy Bucareli's call for a Santa Fe–Monterey connection. Escalante also failed to find a direct route in the expedition he undertook between late July and early August 1776 in the company of Franciscan friar Francisco Atanasio Domínguez, soldier-cartographer Bernardo Miera y Pacheco, interpreter Andrés Muñiz, and five others. Each attempt involved epic, history-making explorations: Garcés came within reach of a hand-delivered letter to Santa Fe, and Escalante achieved the latitude of Monterey, but in Utah. Thus Viceroy Bucareli still had no assurance that a direct Santa Fe–Monterey connection was possible, and this uncertainty turned his attention to the trail broken by Anza, which had to be protected.

No wonder, then, that Bucareli treated Palma as a ruling prince. The viceroy ordered for the chief a blue uniform topped off with a scarlet vest trimmed in gold braid. Palma, Bolton notes, was treated like Benjamin Franklin in Paris: he was invited to receptions, feted on Court Days at the viceregal palace, and presented by Bucareli with a rod of office on King Carlos' birthday. "The faces of those faithful heathen", Bucareli wrote José de Gálvez, minister for the Indies, on 26 November 1776 regarding this presentation, "reflected the internal contentment which they breathed, and this was greatly augmented when they saw the love with which I received them, giving to Palma another cane, the benevolence which I showed them, and the appreciation for them manifested by the brilliant concourse of people who were present that day in this palace."[2]

When the time came for Chief Palma and his three retainers to be baptized (after having received instruction), the ceremony was held at the cathedral of Mexico City. A cathedral canon, the licenciado Don Agustín de Echeverría y Orcolaga, presided over the ceremony. Anza stood at the baptismal font as godfather.

In Madrid, hearing of these developments from Gálvez, a very pleased Carlos III appointed Anza governor of New Mexico.

The Yuma uprising

Chief Palma and his men, Catholics all, returned to their home territory at the junction of the Yuma and Colorado Rivers. For this new order to work, full-fledged missions protected by a presidio should have been established at this crucial midway point between Tucson and Alta California. The Franciscans had, in fact, been envisioning a chain of missions extending across the Southwest—from Santa Fe to Tucson, from Tucson to the Colorado River, and from the Colorado River into coastal Southern California. Teodoro de Croix, however, the first general in chief of the Interior Provinces, was eager to establish an outpost at Yuma but lacked the resources for two missions and a presidio. Croix, moreover, was hostile to the mission system itself (an Enlightenment trait in officers promoted by Carlos III) as well as distracted by ongoing Apache raids and yet another uprising by the Seris. Croix resisted Franciscan calls for missions and a presidio at Yuma in favor of two fortified villages, La Purísima Concepción and San Pedro y San Pablo de Bicuñer, established by mid-January 1780. The four Franciscans assigned there, including Francisco Garcés, were to attend to the spiritual needs of the settlers and to evangelize the Yuma when possible—but without a residential program for neophytes or the military protection of a garrisoned presidio.

These arrangements led to a catastrophe that mocked the hopes of four short years earlier, when Chief Palma had proposed a Yuma-Spaniard alliance and, wearing his specially designed uniform, stood before the baptismal font. The Quechan resented the appropriation of ranchería farmland by the Spaniards, who showed little regard for Indian water rights. Spanish cattle trampled planted fields, a problem compounded when the Los Angeles settlement party under the command of Fernando Rivera quartered 257 exhausted livestock near the ranchería. Even worse, when conflicts arose and Quechans had allegedly been offenders, the Spaniards locked them in stocks or submitted them to public whippings.

Ill will concerning these abuses was compounded by disjunctions of religion and culture. Palma and his associates had seen Mexico City in all its glory; they had been feted, outfitted, and commissioned by the viceroy himself. The Quechan leaders had sincerely requested baptism en route to Hispanicization; they had submitted a memorandum (which, being illiterate, they had signed with crosses) requesting an alliance. Quechans knew nothing of such matters. In contrast to the buildings of Mexico City, they lived in huts and lean-tos. Their ancient way of life was based on the flooding of the Colorado River and the planting of its alluvial soil; their religion offered its own stories of how the world came to be; they had their own dances and ceremonies, their own sexual protocols and practices. Who were these Spaniards to put them in stocks for punishment or trample crops with their cattle? Who were they to forbid their dances, tell them that their stories were not true, take their women from them? Anti-Spaniard sentiment thus grew and eroded Palma's influence. Among the Quechan, Palma's power as kwoxot was negotiable; it depended on the consent of the governed. And even he, who had brought the Spaniards to their homeland, could see how matters had taken a wrong turn.

On the morning of 17 July 1781, two groups of Quechan and Mohave warriors launched an attack on the two Spanish settlements. In the hours and days that followed, the Indians massacred thirteen male soldiers and settlers, including Captain Rivera and his party, but in general spared women and children, whom they took as prisoners. Having guided a group of women and children from La Purísima Concepción to a hidden place near the river, Franciscans Juan Barrenche and Francisco Garcés took refuge at the ranchería of a baptized Quechan woman who was not participating in the rebellion and had sent her husband out to find the priests.

Four years later, a survivor of the massacre, María Ana Montielo—whose husband, the ensign commanding La Purísima Concepción, had been clubbed to death before her eyes—wrote a letter to the Franciscan superior in Sonora regarding what happened next, as she had heard the story from another Spanish woman captive. Days into the massacre, on 21 July, Fathers Barrenche and Garcés sat in their safe house drinking their morning chocolate, served to them by their Quechan hosts. A group of rebels approached the ranchería. "Stop drinking that and come outside", the rebel leader hollered. "We're going to kill you." To this, Garcés replied, "We'd like to finish our chocolate first." The rebel leader answered, "Just leave it." Barrenche and Garcés stepped outside and were immediately clubbed to death. The Quechan woman who had given the two friars refuge recovered and buried their bodies.[3]

Thus with panache and more than a little sangfroid ended the life of one of the great pathfinders and missionaries of his era and that of his equally brave and devoted confrere. Garcés had devoted his life to evangelization and trailblazing. Now both aspects of his lifetime effort, religion and access through the Borderlands, had come to an impasse. In the ensuing decades, the Quechan consistently resisted Christianity and remained hostile. For the next forty years, to the detriment of civil settlement, the Anza trail—the sole entry by land into Alta California via Pimería Alta—remained impassible. For the remaining four decades of governance by New Spain, the civil settlements of San Jose and Los Angeles and the presidio settlements of San Diego, Santa Barbara, Monterey, and San Francisco continued to be small and isolated places, unable to compete with the mission system as sources and models for development.

The Lasuén years

Junípero Serra died at Mission San Carlos Borromeo on 28 August 1784 at the age of seventy. On 6 February 1785 the College of San Fernando appointed Fray Fermín Francisco de Lasuén father president of the missions of Alta California, and the interim president, Francisco Palóu, left for Mexico, where he spent the last four years of his life writing his history and serving as college guardian. The appointment of Lasuén possessed a gentle irony. In his first years in Alta California, Lasuén was discontented with his assignment as a third priest at San Gabriel and requested to be sent back to Mexico. His second assignment, as chaplain to the presidio at Monterey, caused Lasuén no end of grief due to Serra's opposition to a Franciscan holding this position, which was traditionally assigned to a secular priest. Lasuén likewise struggled with his third assignment, San Diego, where he served from 1777 to 1785, sent there by Serra under a vow of obedience when no other Franciscan volunteered for the difficult and dangerous posting.

During those eight years at San Diego, Lasuén did his best to improve relations with the recently rebellious Kumeyaay, first cousin to the Quechan and equally restive. Three years after the 1775 uprising, another conspiracy was under way among the Kumeyaay and was thwarted only when a local headman warned Lasuén, who in turn warned presidio commander José Francisco Ortega, who then sent soldiers to arrest the ringleaders. Four were shot, the rest flogged, and the bows and arrows of a larger group were destroyed. All this tumult did not foster Bucareli and Serra's option for an irenic settlement of Indian-Spanish difficulties.

The poor soil and lack of nearby water did not help matters, for with the meager agriculture that Lasuén found in San Diego, the mission could not afford to support a large population of neophytes, who remained living among their nonneophyte and generally hostile brethren. The only way to tell baptized from unbaptized Indians, Lasuén observed, was that baptized Kumeyaay wore clothing while the unbaptized were naked. To improve the agriculture, Lasuén in 1779 built a diversion dam on a nearby creek, which helped somewhat, but the dam had no storage capacity and was useless during the frequent dry spells. Nevertheless, Lasuén did manage to improve San Diego's production of wheat, corn, barley, and peas as well as its holdings in cattle, sheep, goats, and horses, which foreshadowed his later success as an agriculturalist while serving as father president.

Serra appreciated Lasuén's efforts at San Diego, and as Serra entered old age—and realized that Palóu did not have the makings of an effective administrator—he began to view Lasuén as not only the most able friar in the system but also his successor. Similar in that they were both Franciscan missionaries from the College of San Fernando as well as outsiders—Serra a Majorcan, Lasuén a Basque—the first and second father presidents had their differences. Serra was a trained theologian who sought power. Lasuén was an intuitive, empathetic nonacademic who valued applied intelligence and peaceful solutions. Serra often quarreled with the military. Lasuén avoided arguments whenever possible. Serra never doubted himself or his calling. Lasuén at times expressed fears that he lacked sufficient apostolic ambition for the missionary calling and in his early years in Alta California dreamed of returning to a more sheltered version of Franciscan life. Still, he observed his vows and prized the vow of obedience that kept him in Alta California during those initial years of doubt. Like Serra, Lasuén was traditional in thinking, pre-Enlightenment in orientation, and royalist in his politics. Serra fasted and practiced a near-medieval asceticism. Lasuén left behind no suggestion of self-inflicted suffering or a proclivity to fast. Indeed, Lasuén appreciated the pleasure of the table (he grew stout in his later years) and was adept at entertaining Spanish naval officers (twenty-one at dinner, Lasuén noted of an especially enjoyable evening at Mission San Carlos) as well as celebrity visitors, such as the French admiral the comte de Lapérouse (1786), the Italian scientist Alejandro Malaspina (1791), and the British naval captain George Vancouver (1792, 1793, 1794). These were men of Enlightenment value, engaged in momentous voyages of scientific exploration and discovery. While each had reservations regarding the mission system (Lapérouse in particular), they were nevertheless charmed—and properly entertained!—by its amiable father president.

The Russian and British threats

Evident since the 1740s in Crown and viceregal circles was a growing apprehension of Russian designs on the Pacific north coast that began with the explorations of Vitus Bering between 1728 and 1741. In 1759 the Spanish Franciscan Fray José Torrubia, a veteran missionary in Mexico and the Philippines, writing in Italian, issued a geopolitically alarmist *I Moscoviti Nella California* (The Russians in California), which warned of the inevitable Russian drive south along the California coast toward Mexico. The highest levels of the Spanish military urged action to secure Spain's fragile hold on Alta California and extend Spanish jurisdiction farther north. In August 1775, under orders from Viceroy Bucareli, the schooner *Sonora*, commanded by Juan Francisco de la Bodega y Quadra, reconnoitered the Alaskan coast between latitudes 55 and 58 degrees 30 minutes north in search of that ever-elusive strait Spaniards had for so long mistakenly believed united the Atlantic and Pacific Oceans. Not finding it, Bodega sailed into a calm bay on the southern Alaska panhandle on the western side of present-day Prince of Wales Island at 55 degrees 14 minutes north latitude, which he named Puerto de Bucareli. Bodega was thereupon laid up with a fever (which later led to false charges that the Spaniards had introduced smallpox into the local Indian population), and so second officer Francisco Antonio Mourelle led a landing party ashore and, with the usual ceremony, claimed the entire northern Pacific region for King Carlos III. For fifteen years Spain's claims to the northern coast of North America remained uncontested. Spain sent a number of expeditions to the region during this period as a way of keeping its claim current.

The British, meanwhile, also became active in the area. Captain James Cook commanded a Royal Navy expedition in 1778, and Captain James Hanna arrived from China in the merchant ship *Harmon* in 1785 and returned the next year in the merchant ship *Sea Otter*. Although Cook did not take formal possession of the region, the fact that he was leading an official Royal Navy expedition provided the pretext for a British claim building upon the long-neglected, but now valuable, claim of Francis Drake to Nova Albion in 1579.

In the spring and summer of 1789, a crisis developed. Under viceregal instruction, naval captain Esteban José Martínez on 5 May sailed the warship *Princesa* and the perennially useful supply ship *San Carlos* into Nootka Sound on the western coast of Vancouver Island with orders to take formal possession of the harbor, fortify it, and establish a colony. Martínez found two American ships, the *Columbia Rediviva* and the *Lady Washington*, and one British ship, the *Iphigenia*, in the harbor. Martínez expelled the English ship.

On 8 June, however, a British-owned vessel, the *Northwest America*, sailing under Portuguese registration, arrived. Martínez seized this ship—in payment, he claimed, for supplies he had provided the *Iphigenia* before expelling it—and renamed it the *Santa Gertrudis la Magna*. On 24 June, in front of a gathering of English and American detainees as well as Spaniards, Martínez took formal possession of Nootka Sound and the entire northwest coast of North America for Spain.

Nine days later, two more British ships, the *Princess Royal* and the *Argonaut*, arrived within hours of each other. Martínez expelled the *Princess Royal*; seizing the *Argonaut*, he put its Chinese crew to work building Fort San Miguel, which he armed with ten cannons. When the *Princess Royal* returned briefly on 12 July and dropped anchor outside the harbor, Martínez ordered it seized as well. He then ordered the *Argonaut* and the *Princess Royal* to sail to San Blas, using Spanish crews. The English captains and crews were placed under arrest.

Clearly an international incident was heading toward a more serious conflict. Fortunately, Spain and Great Britain negotiated an agreement—the first Nootka Sound Convention—which opened the northwestern coast to both Spanish and British trade and arranged for the return of or indemnity payment for the seized British ships. When Spain and Britain entered a war against France as allies, an even stronger Second Convention was drawn up in January 1794, establishing a joint-use agreement between Spain and England that precluded the participation of any other nation in the development of this northern region.

Renewed importance of Alta California

The Nootka Sound crisis reinforced a self-evident principle. Claiming a territory was not enough. For a country to sustain its claim, it had to settle, occupy, and develop. No one realized this more intensely than Diego de Borica, governor of the Californias from 1794 to 1800. A Basque native like Lasuén, Borica had arrived in New Spain in 1763 as a lowly cadet. Twenty years later, Borica had risen to lieutenant colonel and Knight of the Order of Santiago following distinguished service that included stints as inspector of presidios for the Internal Provinces and, from 1789 to 1791, personal representative of the viceroy for Indian affairs in Nueva Vizcaya. In 1792 Borica successfully petitioned the Crown for the governorship of the Californias. By late 1794, Borica was serving in office in Monterey and was soon promoted to full colonel. The assignment to California of a governor of Borica's stature (a knight and a politically connected soldier-diplomat of high rank) expressed the Crown's renewed interest in Alta California following the Nootka controversy. In terms of actual settlement on the North American coast, Alta California stood as Spain's sole property that was clearly claimed, settled, and developed—and this only in the fragile form of thirteen missions, four sparsely garrisoned presidios (San Diego, Monterey, San Francisco, and Santa Barbara), and two even more sparsely populated civil settlements at San Jose and Los Angeles. Borica inaugurated a three-fold program of intensified occupation: better presidios, a third civil settlement, and five new missions. In short, Borica, not the Franciscan order, was directing the program now that the state-supported mission system had become, post–Nootka Convention, the primary assertion of Spanish sovereignty in Alta California.

Fortunately for military-Franciscan accord, Lasuén had little objection to Borica's expansion program, provided that the new missions be correctly sited and supported. Unlike previous tensions between Serra and Governors Fages, Rivera, and Neve, which could and did take on a personal edge, the relationship between Lasuén and Borica was cordial. The genial Lasuén held his fellow Basque in high regard, and Borica—like everyone else in or visiting Alta California during these years—found much to admire in the affable, roly-poly father president.

Founded by Borica in 1797 on the southern edge of the Santa Cruz peninsula on Monterey Bay, Villa Branciforte (named in honor of the current viceroy) was a disaster. Borica intended that the community be a township for retired soldiers and their families, but retiring leatherjackets preferred land grants, and so, sadly, the villa later became a place for the resettlement of those found guilty of minor crimes. This program failed as well, and by 1815 Branciforte supported a mere fifty-three residents. By contrast, the four missions established in 1797 at the direction of Governor Borica—San José, San Juan Bautista, San Miguel Arcángel, and San Fernando Rey de España—thrived, as did San Luis Rey de Francia, founded in 1798.

Lasuén passed away at Mission San Carlos on 26 June 1803 after eighteen years in office and was interred before the altar on the Gospel side of the mission church. From every perspective—missions (nine to eighteen), missionaries (eighteen to forty), baptisms (6,736 to 37,976)—the mission system in Alta California flourished during Lasuén's tenure, historian Maynard Geiger points out. The system became so extensive and productive that the College of San Fernando established a new position, commissary prefect, to share authority with the father president, particularly in economic and administrative matters. Thus Serra and Lasuén's successors as father president, while continuing to serve as regent in spiritual concerns, never exercised as much power as their first two predecessors.

San Xavier del Bac

Iconic missions—Florida, Georgia, Texas, Arizona, and even the deeply troubled system in New Mexico—seem to have had a golden age. In certain instances, a single mission embodies this golden age in overall achievement, including architecture, and survives as an icon of religious and regional identity. Better known as the Alamo, San Antonio de Padua stands as the primary image of Texas heritage, given its importance in the war of independence. In the case of San Xavier del Bac, no less an Arizonan than the late U.S. Senator Barry Goldwater has argued that San Xavier del Bac shares parity with the Grand Canyon as a regional symbol.

For its architecture alone, San Xavier del Bac would rank as an important American structure. Two Franciscans deserve credit for this achievement. In 1776 Fray Juan Bautista Belderrain, a missionary with previous construction experience, joined Fray Francisco Garcés at San Xavier del Bac, by then the site of the largest ranchería of baptized Indians in Pimería Alta. In 1783, after Garcés' martyrdom, Belderrain began to build what can only be described as a monumental church. Belderrain worked on this structure for the remaining six years of his life. In 1790 Fray Juan Bautista Llorens arrived at San Xavier del Bac and brought to completion what Belderrain had started: a harmonious, two-steepled, cross-shaped and domed structure of stucco-covered brick, its altar backed by an impressive hand-carved reredos and its entrance surmounted by a perfect Churrigueresque portal.

The entire San Xavier del Bac complex, church and adjacent buildings, rises from a parched plain nine miles south of Tucson against the desert sky, a Spanish Colonial daydream of Mediterranean Europe. This northernmost Sonora mission emerged out of a collective, near-anonymous effort in the manner of a medieval cathedral, built by Papago and peaceful Apaches (yes, peaceful Apaches!) in testimony to a religion that—all things considered—came to them in peaceful circumstances during the Jesuit era. The Franciscan era that followed continued this general mood of goodwill with the assignment of such friendly, accommodating figures as Garcés, Belderrain, and Llorens.

To search for an equivalent to San Xavier del Bac in Alta California is to cite a number of contenders. Depending on the aspect—strategic site, successful relationship with Indians, agricultural productivity, architecture—nominees vary considerably. As the mission of the capital settlement at Monterey and the headquarters of the father president, Mission San Carlos Borromeo del Río Carmelo (1770) leads any such list. Here the most important decisions were made and the most important visitors entertained. Here relations with Ohlone (Castañoan) and Esselen peoples remained reasonably positive, especially in comparison with San Diego de Alcalá (1769). Designed by master mason Manuel Ruiz and dedicated in 1797, the seventh mission church and the last to be built—strongly Moorish in its tower and graced by a star-shaped window on its façade—was nearly lost to the elements in the mid-nineteenth century but was restored in the 1930s as the cathedral parish of the Diocese of Monterey.

Located on the eastern entrance to the Los Angeles plain, San Gabriel Arcángel (1771) long served as the official entry point into Southern California. Of all the twenty-one missions, San Gabriel possesses the most distinctive architecture. Its side wall serves simultaneously as its façade. The stairway and main entrance are on one side, and nine high, narrow windows in geometric sequence alternate with capped Moorish buttresses; the church's designer, Fray Antonio Cruzado, intended that these features reflect the cathedral of Córdoba in his native city of Alcaracejos. Agriculturally, San Gabriel led all missions in productivity. Its vineyards introduced wine making to California. Like San Diego, however, it had a troubled relationship with the local Tongva (Gabrielino) people, its beginnings marked by a comparable uprising that was foiled only at the last minute.

San Luis Obispo (1772), San Francisco de Asís, or Mission Dolores (1776), and San Juan Capistrano (1776) likewise remain in use today as flourishing parish churches, with primary schools attached. In 1918 Mission Dolores was supplemented with a Spanish Colonial basilica as a companion structure. Set in their city centers, the original San Luis Obispo and a restored San Juan Capistrano anchor their respective squares as integrated components of the urban fabric. (A rebuilt Santa Clara de Asís serves the same centralizing function on the campus of the Jesuit-founded Santa Clara University and is used as the university chapel.) Completed in 1805, the Church of San Juan Capistrano—shaped in a cross, with a vaulted ceiling that supported seven domes, a 120-foot-tall bell tower at its entrance, and four great bells in its belfry—equaled San Xavier del Bac in architectural achievement. In December 1812, however, crowded with Mass goers, it was destroyed by an earthquake with significant loss of life. The collapse of its massive stone and concrete walls and ceiling left only the remnants of the sanctuary standing, a Piranesian ruin before its time.

The missions on the Santa Barbara Channel—San Buenaventura (1782), Santa Barbara (1786), La Purísima Concepción (1787), and Santa Inés (1804)—were favorably sited in terms of population density, maritime access, water resources, and agricultural promise. Agriculture flourished at San Buenaventura and La Purísima Concepción; San Buenaventura in time developed a profitable business supplying ships anchored offshore with produce and other provisions. The major earthquake of 21 December 1812 damaged the serviceable architecture of these missions. La Purísima Concepción—the only mission laid out not in a quadrangle but linearly—suffered additional harm from flooding.

The indigenous people of the region, the Chumash, however, had a highly developed maritime culture and over the years resisted leaving their intricate lodge-centered and seagoing ways for dormitory life at a mission, although enough were recruited to keep the system in operation and to develop highly skilled choral singers and musicians. In any case, in February 1824 a serious uprising occurred in Santa Inés and La Purísima Concepción that involved the seizure of La Purísima Concepción and its fortification, plus armed resistance for a month against military counterattack. Sixteen Indians were killed in the siege and many wounded. Seventeen Indian leaders were tried and condemned to death. Eighteen others were imprisoned.

Architecture offered little compensation to mission Indians disaffected with their lives. Still, these buildings would endure (some of them barely) to become icons of regional identity. The fourth Mission Santa Barbara church (1820), for example—built by Fray Antonio Ripoll in the aftermath of the 1812 earthquake and chosen by Bishop García Diego y Moreno in 1842 as his procathedral—quickly earned the title Queen of the Missions. To guide his design, Ripoll drew upon plates from an edition of the designs of the Roman Augustan architect M. Vitruvius Polion published in Madrid in 1787. Set on a knoll with a commanding view of the channel, solidly constructed of sandstone blocks fixed together with limestone cement, its façade adorned with purely decorative Ionic columns, the Santa Barbara mission church remains in use as an active parish to this day, its adjacent friary and seminary buildings serving as a provincial headquarters and educational center.

Farther south, the architecturally and agriculturally ambitious San Fernando Rey de España (1797), in the eponymously named San Fernando valley, and San Luis Rey de Francia (1798), north of San Diego in the present-day city of Oceanside—missions named for canonized medieval kings of Spain and France—radiate a similar mood of recovery and renewal on the part of the Spanish royalist Franciscan effort in Alta California. That period was soon to be followed by a time of twilight splendor as the Spanish Empire went into decline and Mexico launched its decade-long effort to achieve political independence. Each of these penultimate missions are grand in design, intricate in irrigation and agriculture, and—again, like so many missions—destined to be restored and used into the twenty-first century.

A noticeable achievement

During the presidency of Lasuén, Antonio Peyrí, yet another Catalonian, cofounded Mission San Luis Rey in 1798 and then built it into the largest and one of the two most agriculturally productive (the other being La Purísima Concepción) of the twenty-one missions. Peyrí remained on duty until 1831, well into the Mexican era. In contrast to many Spanish-born royalist missionaries, who returned to Spain, Peyrí took the oath of allegiance to Mexico in 1826 and became an enthusiastic citizen of the new republic, whose oath *Dios y libertad* (God and liberty) he adopted as his own. Peyrí became a good friend of the able Mexican governor José María de Echeandía, in office from 1825 to 1831, the year that Peyrí turned San Luis Rey over to Fray José Antonio Anzar, a Mexican-born member of the criollo-dominated apostolic College of Our Lady of Guadalupe, Zacatecas.

Both San Luis Rey and San Fernando Rey enjoyed impressive physical plants at the height of their prosperity; San Luis Rey covered six acres, while San Fernando

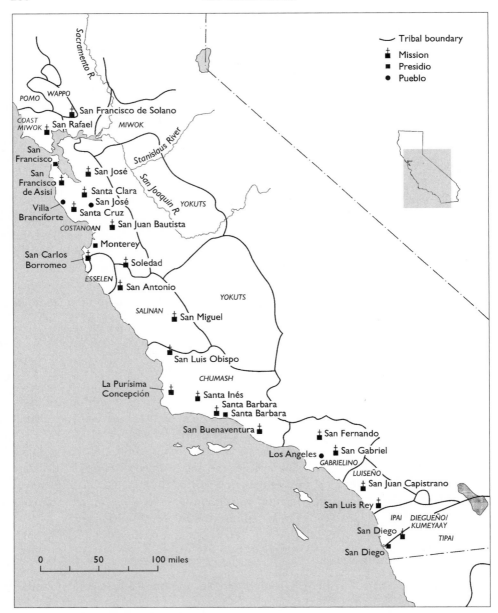

Map 14. California Spanish/Mexican Settlements in the Mission Zone, circa 1823. From James A. Sandos, *Converting California* (New Haven and London: Yale University Press, 2004), 2.   © *Yale University Press, used by permission.*

Rey was smaller and understated. Each complex contained main buildings fronted by boldly arched arcades as their defining feature. In contrast to the unpretentious San Fernando Rey church, at San Luis Rey master mason José Antonio Ramírez designed for Peyrí a twin-towered (only one was built in 1815) cruciform structure in the style of San Juan Capistrano. An ambitious dome rose over the transept, from which hung a great octagonal lantern that held 144 panes of glass. In addition to the standard main altar, reredos, crucifix, statuary, and baptismal font, side altars stood at each end of the transept; even more unusual was the mortuary chapel, entered from the nave, which featured a raised balcony for families of the deceased to gather and observe burial services.

This care for architecture suggested Peyrí's high degree of culture anchored in Spanish Catholic Europe and Spanish colonial Mexico. Peyrí was noted for his benevolence toward his Indian charges. San Luis Rey experienced no uprisings, and when Peyrí left his mission by ship, numerous neophytes reportedly accompanied him to the beach as a sign of farewell.

Far from wanting the Franciscan protectorate to remain in place indefinitely, Peyrí anticipated an era of secularization, parish churches, and a diocesan clergy of inclusive bloodlines. When he left Alta California in 1831, Peyrí took two young Indian men, Pablo Tac and Agapito Amamix, with him back to Spain, then sent them on to train for the diocesan priesthood at the Propaganda College in Rome. What a change of prospect for these gentlemen—Mexico, Catalonia, Italy, Rome, the baroque grandeur of their seminary! Yet they experienced the diseases of Europe as well, so deadly to their untested immune systems. Both of these promising young men died before reaching the priesthood and never returned to Alta California as diocesan pastors.

Throughout his career, Peyrí was strategically located on the southern coast of Alta California, with its growing rancho culture—the huge herds of longhorn cattle, the hide and tallow trade with the United States, and an increasing number of European visitors under the more liberal and visitor-friendly Mexican regime. French merchant captain Auguste Duhaut-Cilly visited Peyrí in 1827, followed in 1829 by Americans James Ohio Pattie, a fur trapper and trader, and Alfred Robinson, a representative of the Boston trading firm of Bryant, Sturgis, and Company. Each reported favorably on the accomplished friar's demeanor, his graciousness as host, and the success of his operation. Alexander Forbes, a British merchant who later became vice consul at Tepic, Mexico, met Peyrí while Peyrí was en route to Spain and left a laudatory assessment of him as well as a full-page frontispiece portrait in Forbes' influential *History of Alta and Baja California* (1839), as if to evoke Peyrí as the best living representative of the Franciscan ascendancy now passing into history. Now that the mission era was ending, Forbes wanted Alta California transferred to the British-run California Company (modeled on the Hudson's Bay Company in Canada) as a way for Mexico to pay off its outstanding debt to Great Britain.

Friars in transition

One hundred forty-two Franciscan friars served in Alta California between 1769 and 1848. A few found their way into history. In 1969 Franciscan historian Maynard Geiger published a biographical dictionary of all 142 missionaries: ordinary men, on the whole, called to an unusual life. These Catalans, Majorcans, and Spaniards might have spent their lives in the developed Franciscan culture of their homeland, but they opted instead for a missionary ministry on the other side of the planet. Their ten-year obligation completed, many renewed their contract. Some achieved a dignified and comfortable retirement at the College of San Fernando. Others died on duty or, refusing to take an oath to the new government, went into exile following the Mexican Revolution. Educated in their Franciscan provinces in Spain and at San Fernando in Mexico City, they were in the main practical, pious, and intelligent, though not intellectual, skilled in agriculture, cattle raising, and related manual arts. They loved to build and they built well. The twenty-one surviving missions prove this.

Few left personal records behind. Only Peyrí of San Luis Rey wrote a formal autobiography. Palóu, Crespí, and Font, however, were skilled diarists and historians, and Serra was an equally skilled writer of letters that blend personal sentiment and administrative directions. Gerónimo Boscana of San Juan Capistrano penned a pioneering ethnological treatise. Translated into English and published in 1846 after Boscana's death, *Chinigchinich* (named for a local divinity) endures as a founding text for anthropological studies on the Pacific coast. Narciso Durán of Missions San José and Santa Barbara, an experienced choirmaster, devised a system for teaching Gregorian chant and other modes of liturgical music to neophytes that brought the musical culture of both missions to impressive levels. Historian James Sandos views the extraordinary achievement of mission Indians as musicians and singers as the most successful point of cultural contact between Franciscans and neophytes. Such perfection possesses a certain poignancy as Sandos presents it, given the dysfunctions that otherwise characterized the relationship between friar and Indian.

In addition to the achievers, Geiger chronicles the misfits who were eager to return to Mexico before their obligated ten-year tour of duty was complete; those broken in health and spirit after trying their best, repatriated as well before their time; and the sexually truant, most likely criminally so in many cases and at the least scandalous and hypocritical, in light of Franciscan efforts to introduce a sacramental concept of monogamy into Indian life. The most notorious offenders seemed to surface at the end of the mission era.

¡Viva Mexico!

The transition in 1823 from a Spanish royalist jurisdiction dominated by European-born *peninsulares* to a Mexican republican jurisdiction dominated by criollos and mestizos constituted for many friars a traumatic change of polity and value. From 1821 to 1823 Mexican independence briefly took the form of the semiroyalist dictatorship of Agustín de Iturbide, who assumed the title of emperor and reigned from a power base of upper-class laity and clergy of European descent. In 1823, however, a criollo-dominated republic was formed, which represented a tectonic shift of major proportions. In Alta California this change was expressed in part by the falling off of missionary personnel from the royalist-dominated Peninsular College of San Fernando through death, retirement, or refusal to take a republican oath and the growing presence of republican criollo Franciscans from the College of Our Lady of Guadalupe at Zacatecas. Between 1769 and 1823, missionaries in Alta California functioned in a culture of strict formation, screening, and control. The Mexican republic, however, created new hegemonies, hierarchies, and controls in criollo Franciscan culture as well as the secular sphere. Observant Franciscans remained true to their vows, but they became more independent. Increased association with republican laymen contributed to this shift, as did a concurrent dissatisfaction with the mission system itself: its restrictions, its lack of success in its primary goal—the creation of a Hispanicized Indian laity—its hostility to the new political order. In Mexico, low-ranking secular clergy had played an important role in the revolutionary process. In Alta California, a number of friars began to show a similar capacity for independent action. The young Catalan friar José Altimira, for example, although royalist in political sentiment, was discontented with the foggy and damp location of Mission Dolores and in March 1823 appealed directly to the legislature in Monterey—rather than to his Franciscan superiors—in an attempt to move Mission Dolores across the bay to Sonoma. With the support of the legislature and Governor Luis Antonio Argüello, Altimira did exactly that, to the dismay of Father President José Señán, then residing at San Buenaventura. After much wrangling, Altimira achieved a compromise. Mission Dolores remained where it was, and the name of the new mission in Sonoma so boldly established by the young friar was changed from San Francisco de Asís (Dolores) to San Francisco Solano (1823): the only mission founded during the Mexican era.

Going rogue

Altimira went against the norm out of evangelical zeal. After fifty years, results in San Francisco were meager. Why not make a new beginning? The restless young friar was backed in his effort by lay friends and local lay officials eager to secure a new foothold in the North Bay. Yet Altimira remained an observant friar. For other friars in this era, however, going rogue involved a drift in the direction of a lay-centered macho camaraderie that included hunting, drinking, gambling, and sexual adventurism. The Suárez del Real brothers, Fray Antonio de la Concepción and Fray José María del Refugio, offer dramatic cases. Both Antonio (born in 1794) and José (born a few years before or after that) entered the Franciscan Order at the College of Guadalupe, Zacatecas, and were ordained and sent as missionaries to Alta California when the Zacatecans were assigned to the area. In fact, the brothers arrived together by ship at Monterey on 13 January 1833 as part of a group of Zacatecan friars under the leadership of Fray Francisco García Diego y Moreno, the future bishop of the Californias. However sincerely the Suárez del Real brothers began their lives as Franciscans (or were they inserted into the order by other forces with no consideration of their suitability?), Mexican California proved an environment for each of them to go rogue. Within a decade, Fray Antonio, named in religion for the doctrine of the Immaculate Conception so central to Franciscan devotion, had become a misbehaving friar out of Boccaccio's *Decameron*. French naval officer Cyrille Laplace describes him as an insolent, swaggering bandit-priest, his stained gray habit tucked up into the cord around his waist, a broad-brimmed hat slanted bravo-style atop his head, and a blunderbuss shotgun slung across his back. In the years to come, Fray Antonio lived riotously at Monterey, where he had replaced his brother. Basing himself in a house in town, for which he had tried to trade a crumbling Mission San Carlos Borromeo, Antonio drank and gambled in taverns and was known to have little regard for his vow of celibacy.

    Meanwhile, José María—a less disheveled figure than his brother but also a boozer: a drinking buddy, in fact, of former governor Juan Bautista Alvarado, himself a known carouser—was denounced by diocesan priest Doroteo Ambris in a letter to Rome on 16 July 1859 for his long record of living openly with women and fathering children. Ambris charged that when José replaced another errant Zacatecan friar (whose full name was Jesús María y José Guadalupe de la Trinidad Vázquez del Mercado) at Mission Santa Clara, he assumed possession of Mercado's children and mistress, who proceeded to bear Real's children as well. Even more horrible, rumor (which was never proved) had it that Fray José poisoned the Reverend José de los Santos, a secular priest brought to California and ordained by Bishop García Diego y Moreno, on the night Father Santos arrived at Mission Santa Clara to replace him. In any event, Santos was found dead in his bed on the morning of the very day, 26 March 1846, he was scheduled to celebrate his first Mass as diocesan pastor.

Despite this misbehavior, the brothers Suárez del Real remained on active duty as priests. Returning to Mexico after providing for at least two of the women in his life and their children with homes in Monterey, José left the Franciscans, was incardinated as a secular priest into the Diocese of Sonora, and served as a pastor in San José del Cabo and, later, Mazatlán. Fray Antonio remained in the Franciscans. Indeed, he must have experienced a metanoia of some sort upon his return to Mexico, for he was elected novice master at Zacatecas. During 1850, in the course of courageously ministering to cholera victims, the onetime rogue friar died and was buried with full honors in the vault of his college church.

Such characters as Vázquez del Mercado at Santa Clara and the Suárez del Real brothers and at least two others—Blas Ordaz of Santa Inés and San Buenaventura, the last Fernandino to die in California (1850), who fathered at least three children; and the tumultuous, disruptive Zacatecan José Lorenzo de la Concepción Quijas, a hard-drinking onetime muleteer and trader of Ecuadoran Indian descent—embody the decline and confusion of a Franciscan protectorate long past its ascendancy. Even at the height of the system, as Geiger documents, human weakness asserted itself. Fray Mariano Rubí, for example, contracted syphilis, grew unstable, and was sent back to Mexico for treatment of his *morbo gálico* in 1793. Both he and his contemporary Fray Bartolomé Gilí, dispatched home in 1794, showed signs of disorderliness verging on mental instability even before their departure for the California missions. Fray Tomás de la Peña, a colleague of Serra and the founder of Mission Santa Clara, was sent back to the College of San Fernando in 1794 in a depressed and demented state. His condition must have been a form of mission fatigue, for Peña recovered and remained active at the college until his death in February 1806.

A slope of decline

During the final years of the Franciscan system, friars' rebelliousness and misbehavior became more chronic and open as a seventy-year hegemony, now clearly a failure, lost support and went into decline. For the half century of domination from New Spain, James Sandos points out, the missionaries, supported by the Crown, remained overreliant on baptismal statistics as indicators of success, as opposed to the number of Hispanicized Indians living on their own, which seemed never to happen. As Indians died or ran away, they were replenished with replacements from the field in a repetitive process that maintained statistics of Indians living in the system—7,700 by 1790, up to 21,000 by 1820, down to 16,800 by 1832—without, unfortunately, graduating into Christianized/Hispanicized self-sufficiency. The numerous Indian rebellions already cited, including the most recent Chumash uprising of 1824, bespeak continuing areas of abuse against those Indians in residence: sexual assault by soldiers, corporal punishment, the dictatorial authority of the Franciscan-approved Indian alcaldes, prohibitions against dancing and related ceremonies, the rigid separation of young men and women at a time of developing sexual expression in their indigenous cultures.

The Franciscans saw themselves as the fathers of their Indian children. But what happened when a father was abusive? A group of Indians at Mission Santa Cruz, outraged by Fray Andrés Quintana's particularly cruel whipping of an Indian named Donato with a leather and wire whip that cut into the victim's buttocks, plotted Quintana's murder. On the night of 12 October 1812, Quintana was lured to a nearby orchard with a false request for confession. There he was surrounded, taunted, tortured, and strangled, his habit pressed against his face to stifle his cries. Either during the torture or after the strangulation, the Indians removed one of Quintana's testicles. Thinking he was dead, the assassins returned Quintana to his bed. When he showed signs of revival, they strangled him further, this time successfully, and removed his other testicle. Quintana's residence was looted. Released from confinement in their dormitories, meanwhile, the young men and women of the mission repaired to the same orchard and indulged in the sexual behavior the mission system prohibited.

The ruse worked. His body unexamined, Quintana was buried, following a hasty and negligent ruling of natural death. Two years later, however, careless talk by one of the women conspirators led to the exhumation of Quintana's body, further investigation, and the arrest of the conspirators. The assassins were sentenced to a *novenario*, nine successive days of fifty lashes per day, followed by years of hard labor on public works in San Diego. Only one conspirator survived his sentence to return to his homeland. Sixty-five years after the murder, researchers from the Bancroft Library uncovered the story and took transcripts from Lorenzo Asisara, an Indian born in Mission Santa Cruz, for later corroboration from other sources.[4]

The sentence of hard labor leveled against Quintana's killers raises the issue of labor in general. Wasn't the mission system of Alta California a thinly disguised form of encomienda—that is, a land grant, with the right to Indian labor? Weren't the missions—vast agricultural and livestock enterprises, worked by coerced labor—de facto plantations, traceable in their lineage to the latifundia of ancient Rome? On a practical level, the missions provisioned the military, and the military held the territory for the Crown. But so did the missions. At their acme, they represented the most socially complex and economically successful Spanish settlements on the Pacific coast, proof positive to the other European powers represented by visiting naval expeditions that Spain was there to stay.

The indigenous people working in the missions did not negotiate their labor. They were merely moved into the system. In time, as skill levels increased, occupations such as musician, chorister, artisan, and vaquero achieved status, stability, and some rights of negotiation. None, however, achieved the power of the Indian alcalde or foreman specially chosen for his loyalty to the system, as Serra himself had initially decreed when Governor Fages called for the creation of Indian captaincies. Indians trapped in the system by and large adapted to it—in part, Sandos suggests, by mimetic double-dealing and double-speak similar to those employed by Africans in bondage on the other side of the continent. Certainly some level of accommodation must have been established at least by 1820, when twenty-one thousand indigenous people were living in the missions; at a high count of four hundred, there were not enough soldiers in Alta California to keep such a population under control if a large-scale rebellion had developed. Escapes, however, were frequent, as were refusals to return from reluctantly granted furloughs. The military was constantly organizing roundups of the escaped or too-long-absent, and the regions in central California beyond military reach were steadily filling up with people from the coast who preferred freedom and their traditional way of life.

A healthier way of life, one might add. As difficult and dangerous as aboriginal life might be, mission life was more so, as evident in the population decline of the indigenous peoples of Alta California in the Spanish and Mexican eras—a reduction by half, it has been argued—as well as the equally compelling testimony of mission burial grounds. Diseases against which Indians had no immunity constituted the major threat. Introduced by infected soldiers, Indians from Mexico and Baja California, and settlers, syphilis spread like wildfire through the coastal population, with soldiers doing most of the damage. The entire mission era, Sandos points out, occurred within one of the four phases of a long-term syphilis epidemic and caused chronic debilitation, especially to women, and a high death rate.[5] Aside from sexual contact, syphilis spread through nonvenereal practices. Indians sucked wounds to clean them. Bloodletting via cuts from sharp flint stones, followed by sucking, constituted a common cure for tumors or related ills. Ear piercing and ritual scarification were widespread. Indian women served as wet nurses for infected settlers. Indian children slept in the same bed as their infected parents. Unwashed clothes, bedclothes, and blankets were shared among the infected and noninfected alike. Thus the contagion spread.

The birth rate plummeted as spontaneous abortion as well as serious birth defects reached epidemic levels, adding to the population decline. By 1806, one-third of the children under five were succumbing to measles. In 1820, mission president Fray Mariano Payeras admitted in a report to the College of San Fernando that non-neophyte Indians were living longer than mission residents. Payeras also pointed out, however, that the establishment of missions on the coast was complete. Since four thousand or so unbaptized Indians were living in the interior, he noted, a mission or two and a presidio should be established there. Such a development would bring more Indians into the system—replacing, one presumes, those being given a de facto death sentence in the existing system.

Secularization of the mission system

During the Spanish era, the non-Indian population of Alta California had remained small. By 1820, it had barely passed 3,000. But under Mexico's more liberal immigration and land-grant policies, the civil population began to grow. By 1830 it had reached 4,200; by 1840, it was at 8,000, one in eight of them non-Mexican foreigners. The count included native-born Californios, Mexican immigrants, South Americans, continental Europeans, English, and an increasing number of citizens of the United States. Land-grant ranchos, more than two hundred of which were established during the Mexican era, began to equal, then replace, the cattle holdings of the missions. Large families filled the haciendas of these ranchos, and a population of hard-riding vaqueros of various bloodlines—among the best horsemen ever to ride the ranges of North America—managed the great herds of longhorn cattle, whose hides and tallow the rancheros sold to the California representatives of the Boston-based trading firm of Bryant, Sturgis and Company for shipment to the United States.

Monterey acquired a school and a printing press. A fusion of American-style two-story wood-framed construction and a second-story veranda with walls of local adobe brick, pioneered in the early 1830s by Thomas Oliver Larkin of Massachusetts, created a new style of architecture, Monterey Colonial, which brought new levels of domestic comfort to civilian life. Californios provisioned these homes with furniture and decorative items shipped around Cape Horn from New England or arriving from China or the Hawaiian Islands. Raised in such circumstances, and educated in the Monterey school established by the English merchant William Hartnell, a generation of native-born Californios was coming of age. Their ranks included Mariano Guadalupe Vallejo (born in 1808) and Juan Bautista Alvarado (born in 1809), both of whom were destined to play major roles in the future of the province.

Leading Californios such as the de la Guerra family of Santa Barbara and the Bandini family of San Diego and Los Angeles, led by patriarchs of education and property, wanted Alta California to be developed as a civil society and not remain partially governed as an ecclesiastical preserve. The Bandinis (father José was born in 1771, and son Juan was born in 1800), émigrés from Peru, arrived in 1822 with Mexican independence and thrived in a variety of enterprises. Building upon a first draft of a manifesto written two years earlier by his father, Juan Bandini issued a call in 1830 for the secular development of Alta California that in its comprehensive advocacy of investment and free trade, local governance, the transformation of the missions into Indian pueblos, and a selective sale of mission lands to non-Indians epitomized the point of view of the rising generation.

A mere twenty-four aged Franciscans, Bandini argued, were exercising absolute authority over a significant portion of the region's resources as well as the twenty-one thousand Indians on mission rolls. Moreover, because of venereal disease and poor living conditions in the missions, these Indians had become lethargic, reproducing well below replacement level and dying in high numbers. The best hope for the development of California was in its entrepreneurial émigrés (such as the Bandinis, he might as well have added), who should be encouraged to reform California's antiquated institutions.

Mexico agreed. As early as 1813, in fact, there had been calls for the secularization of the mission system. Lieutenant Colonel José María Echeandía, the first governor appointed under the newly adopted republican constitution, arrived in Alta California in 1824 with a mandate for secularization and took steps in that direction. However, he was distracted by the North–South political conflict and a soldiers' revolt (1829) in Monterey over outstanding wages, followed by a coup and a countercoup, and the appointment of a new governor from Mexico.

Significantly, the Franciscan who as bishop of the Californias would in the next decade be in charge of the transition to a diocesan polity, Francisco García Diego y Moreno, played an important role in keeping alive the Franciscan presence. He was the leader of a band of Zacatecans who arrived in January 1833 at Monterey, whence they fanned out to relieve the departing Fernandinos in the northern missions. Diplomatically, García Diego y Moreno resisted Governor José Figueroa's query as to which missions under his jurisdiction were prepared for secularization by saying that none of them were. The mission Indians in question, García Diego argued, were not ready for self-government. A brigadier general of mestizo descent, Figueroa was not impressed. Not ready, he queried, after more than a half century of evangelization and tutelage? Was the good friar asking for another fifty years for the Franciscan protectorate?

Figueroa's hand was immeasurably strengthened when on 17 August 1833 the Mexican Congress passed the Secularization Act, to which García Diego y Moreno advised a measured acquiescence. Throughout the next year and a half, Figueroa—an enlightened liberal and a genuinely impressive reformer—devised schemes for secularization while García Diego y Moreno (who got along personally with the governor) and Fray Narciso Durán, commissary prefect of the Fernandinos, drew up plans for a diocesan structure to fill the void and protect the interests of Indians when secularization inevitably occurred.

A beleaguered diocese

All this planning and negotiation led nine years later (nothing moved fast in these matters) to the arrival of His Excellency the Right Reverend Francisco García Diego y Moreno, bishop of the Californias, and his entourage of chaplains, seminarians, niece, and duenna at Santa Barbara on 11 January 1842 and the festivities that followed. The bloom was soon off the rose, however, as García Diego y Moreno began to encounter serious challenges to his secularization efforts and building program.

First of all, Mexican president López María de Santa Ana confiscated the Pious Fund established by the viceroyalty in the late 1690s for the support of the California missons. For the four years of his episcopacy, García Diego y Moreno received no money from Mexico, not even his salary. He tried tithing—he even issued a pastoral letter to this effect—but to no avail. The civilian population, rich and poor alike, was not accustomed to supporting the Church out of its own pocket. Even the seminary García Diego y Moreno was able to establish in May 1844 at Mission Santa Inés (1804) depended on a grant of land from Governor Manuel Micheltorena.

Soon, the inability or reluctance of laypeople to pay tithes developed into a personalized animosity against the bishop, who was now considered a champion of Indian over settler interests or, just as bad, a representative of the Mexican central government against local control. In one notorious incident, a bull attacked and overturned the carriage in which the bishop and his secretary were riding on the outskirts of Santa Barbara. Bystanders did nothing; they did not even pull the bishop from his carriage or give him a ride back to the mission. Greeted so enthusiastically upon his arrival at Santa Barbara just a few short years earlier, the Right Reverend Diego y Moreno walked home after he and his secretary extricated themselves from the wreckage.

Equally distressing was the hostility the bishop began to experience from his fellow Franciscans at the friary adjacent to the Santa Barbara mission where he was living pending the construction of an episcopal residence (which was never built). Opposed to the bishop's secularization program—which had already resulted in the loss of Missions San Luis Obispo and San Buenaventura to diocesan clergy—the Franciscans resented the bishop's presence in the friary and allegedly assigned him to a small, airless room and otherwise made him feel unwelcome.

Francisco García Diego y Moreno died at midnight, 30 April 1846. Three weeks prior to the bishop's death, the assembly in Monterey on 4 April 1846 voted to sell all remaining missions, with the exception of Santa Barbara and Santa Inés. Pío de Jesús Pico, the last Mexican governor of California, concurred in the decision. Before he died, Bishop García Diego y Moreno specified that he be buried not in the friars' vault in front of the altar of Mission Santa Barbara but, appropriate to his status, separately on the epistle side of the sanctuary, marked by an entablature. Following García Diego y Moreno's death, an extraordinarily able and devout friar, José María de Jesús González Rubio, the bishop's secretary and personal choice as vicar general to succeed him, guided the Church into the American era.

PART FOUR

New France

I

Port-Royal 1606

Humanism inspires the foundation of New France

On 16 November 1606, following a reconnaissance southward to present-day
Cape Cod, an exploring party under the command of Jean de Biencourt, sieur de
Poutrincourt and lieutenant governor of Acadia, returned to the French habitation
of Port-Royal on the Bay of Fundy, present-day Nova Scotia, in a barque with a
damaged rudder. The expedition had ended badly on the morning of 15 October
when a large party of Cape Cod Indians, provoked by what they considered aggressive behavior, attacked a group of Frenchmen sleeping on the beach, killing two
and mortally wounding two others. A retaliatory attack led by Poutrincourt subsequently cost more French lives. Off Nantucket Sound, the two shallops under tow
surged into the barque's rudder, which the cranky but skilled pilot Pierre Champdoré was barely able to put back into operation.

When the returning French anchored off Port-Royal on the forenoon of 16
November, a landing party boarded one shallop and rowed toward the settlement:
a group of solid structures arranged around an open square, surrounded by a drainage moat and protected at its corners by stockades, firing platforms, and cannon
in a rough-and-ready rustic reprise of a French walled town. In the approaching
shallop sat a half-dozen men destined one day to serve as entries in the *Dictionary
of Canadian Biography* as founders of Canada, starting with the lieutenant governor
himself. Poutrincourt was the aristocratic deputy of an even more highly placed
aristocrat back in France, Pierre Du Gua, sieur de Monts, who held a vast grant in
Acadia from King Henri IV. On 25 February 1606, with the approval of de Monts,
Henri IV had granted Poutrincourt the seigneury of Port-Royal, with the requirement that he establish a colony there, which Poutrincourt was now in the process
of doing.

Charles, the teenaged son of Poutrincourt—hence the heir apparent of the
lands coming into view—was sitting in the shallop as well, along with another
well-born young man, Robert du Pont, son of François Gravé, sieur du Pont, a
nobly born naval captain turned fur trader, who held a monopoly from de Monts.
The pilot Champdoré was also on board. Like many others in the course of the next
century and a half, Champdoré would rise to baronial (sieur) status in the feudal
system of land tenure introduced into New France. So, too, would others in the
shallop eventually do well. The apothecary Louis Hébert, a cousin of Poutrincourt,
for example, would bring his family to New France and prosper in Quebec as an
agriculturalist, property owner, and community leader.

Two other men in the shallop, the surgeon Estienne (no last name has surfaced)
and master carpenter Daniel Hay, occupied a solid middle ground in regard to social

279

status, given the recurring need for medical attention in a hostile frontier environment and the ability of a master carpenter to design and supervise the construction
of habitable and fortified environments capable of withstanding an Indian attack or
six months of Canadian winter. Poutrincourt's valet, a second Estienne, was also
aboard, seeing to the dress and other needs of his master. The appearance of this
second Estienne's name in the record testifies to the importance of a well-placed
manservant during this era.

Surgeon Estienne had three wounded men under his care in the shallop: Robert Potgravé, son of the expedition navigator, minus three fingers from a musket
accident; locksmith Jean du Val, who would survive his wounds and later achieve
the distinction of becoming the first Frenchman to be executed in New France (for
conspiracy to mutiny); and an unnamed crewman wounded on Cape Cod, soon to
die in Port-Royal.

Last to be mentioned but first in terms of historical importance was Poutrincourt's
second in command, Samuel Champlain, a native of the walled city of Brouage,
on the Bay of Biscay. A soldier, mariner, explorer, geographer, courtier, promoter,
publicist, and journalizer, Champlain had already done enough to earn the place in
history he would even more fully secure across three decades of service as the
chief architect, promoter, and military protector of New France in its formative
years. With his personal philosophy regarding religion, Indian dignity and rights,
and cultural and social values for the colony, along with his valor and rectitude,
this tolerant and humanistic Catholic convert from Protestantism would place his
stamp on New France as a better place for French and Indians alike: a colony that
was prosperous, equitable, humane, and Catholic, yet accommodating other points
of view. In his grand nineteenth-century narrative, the Unitarian Francis Parkman
acknowledges (sometimes begrudgingly) these qualities and goals of Champlain.
In another biography, Harvard historian Samuel Eliot Morison testifies—as one
sailor to another—to Champlain's achievements as a maritime, coastal, and riverine
explorer. Most recently, Brandeis historian David Hackett Fischer openly states in
his masterly and encyclopedic *Champlain's Dream* (2008) that he is fighting against
the revisionist skepticism of contemporary history in his exhaustive documentation,
lengthy narrative, and spirited defense of Champlain as exemplary founder and
Roman Catholic layman.

A surprise event

But wait! Just as the shallop approaches the landing dock of Port-Royal, bugles and
cannonfire break out. A flotilla of canoes emerges from cover to greet the returning
party. In the lead craft is a Frenchman theatrically crowned and costumed as Neptune, god of the sea, in flowing robes and holding a three-pronged trident. Canoes
carrying six Frenchmen attired as Neptune's Tritons and four Frenchmen wearing
Native American dress accompany Neptune's vessel. The shallop and the canoes
meet offshore, within hearing distance of an audience of Frenchmen and Indians
gathered onshore. Among the French spectators—some of whom have speaking
parts in the proceedings about to unfold—is Jean Rallvau, the able secretary and
confidant of Governor de Monts, as well as Eustache Boullé, Champlain's future
brother-in-law. The revered sagamore Membertou, reputed to be one hundred

years old, sits in a place of honor among the Algonquian-speaking people subsequently known as the Mi'kmaq, members of a larger Souriquois Confederacy.

Thereupon begins a masque, a play-pageant with music and song that was then popular in court circles. Its author and director, lawyer-poet Marc Lescarbot, whom Poutrincourt had left in charge of Port-Royal during his absence, has entitled the masque *Le Théâtre de Neptune en la Nouvelle-France*. Upon his return to Europe, he will publish it as part of his anthology *Les Muses de la Nouvelle-France* (1609). The characters of *The Theater of Neptune* speak in rhymed alexandrine couplets, the heroic poetic mode of the period, which have six beats in each line. For comic relief, the Fifth Triton recites his satirical lines in a broad Gascon dialect.

Grandly attired, Neptune—most likely played by the author—opens the masque with a welcome home to Poutrincourt, whom he addresses as Sagamos, a classicized version of sagamore, the Algonquian term for captain or chief. He rules the sea, Neptune informs Poutrincourt, and thoroughly approves of current French efforts to cross the water to this new place and here establish a colony. Though ten thousand crossings of the sea prove necessary, Neptune continues, he swears by his scepter that he will always be on hand to protect the French as they pursue this grand project of settlement. "Go, then, with happiness," Neptune urges them,

> And follow on your way
> Wherever fortune leads you, since I foresee the day
> When a prosperous domain you will prepare for France
> In this fair new world, and the future will enhance
> The glory of de Monts, so too, your name shall ring
> Immortal in the reign of Henri—your great king.

The six Tritons—with the exception of the gasconading Fifth—chime in to amplify Neptune's sentiments. The sea winds, promises the First Triton, will favor the French. As will the weather, vows the Second. Your laws will be established and obeyed, pledges the Third. History itself, swears the Fourth, will record and promulgate the record of French achievement. Let us not get too serious, chimes in Triton Number Five. Neptune likes to kiss a pretty girl, and—suggests this Triton—there will be pretty girls for the French to kiss in this new place, along with high ambitions to pursue. The Sixth Triton ends the waterborne salutations of the Tritons with a hymn of praise for King Henri IV, who has sponsored this expedition, which is inaugurating the French empire abroad, as well as offering a promise of future evangelization and a prayer for success.

Neptune and his attendant Tritons move their canoes away from the shallop, and canoes bearing four Frenchmen dressed as Indians approach. Holding aloft a haunch of venison, the First Indian vows assistance in the hunt and loyalty to the sacred fleur-de-lis being unfurled in their lands, with its promise of fair government for all on behalf of a common good. Raising a bow and arrow, the Second Indian pledges alliance and protection. Offering scarves and bracelets made by women, the Third Indian notes Indian women's approval of the arrival of the French and their promise of continuing support. Concluding the presentation, the Fourth Indian displays a fishing spear and offers to help fish the rocky coast. The coastal waters, he states, are as important a source of food as forest animals snared in the hunt, as he himself has learned through long and hard experience.

At this, read Lescarbot's stage directions, the sieur de Poutrincourt thanks Neptune and his troupe of Tritons and Indians. The shallop pulls alongside the loading dock, and its party disembarks to the accompaniment of a four-part song:

> Give us your pledge, great God Neptune,
> Against wild ocean arrogance.
> And grant us all, as your high boon,
> That we may meet again in France.

The lyrics suggest the interdependence of the colony and the European homeland. Another cannonade is fired; it echoed, Lescarbot later tells us, for fifteen minutes across the bay and into the hills. The gate of the Port-Royal habitation, meanwhile, has been decorated in colorful bunting and signs draped with greenery proclaiming the king's motto, *Duo protegit unus* (One protects two); the coat of arms of the sieur de Monts above a line from the *Aeneid* (book I, line 99), "Dabit Deus his quoque finem" (To these [toils] also God shall give an end); and the arms of Poutrincourt above a line from Ovid's *Metamorphoses* (XIV, line 113), "Invia virtuti nulla est via" (To valor, no way is pathless). At this point, a Merry Companion bids the party to enter the habitation through this decorated gate and enjoy good wine and a joyful feast.

> Come, then, chefs, cooks, and boys—all you who make good cheer.
> Scullions and pastry cooks, let soup and roast appear.
> Ransack the kitchen shelves, fill every pot and pan,
> And draw his own good portion for every eager man!
> I see the men are thirsty, SICUT TERRA, SINE AQUA.
> Come, hurry, boy, and pour for each his beaded measure.
> Bestir yourselves, be brisk. Are the ducks on the spit?
> What fowl have lost their heads? The goose, who cares
>   For it?
> Hither have sailed to us a band of comrades rare;
> Let portions and their hunger be matched with equal care.
> Enter within, messires, your welcome gaily seize,
> Let each man drain his cup! Let each man strongly sneeze!
> That never a frosty humor his person may contain
> And only sweetest vapors may crowd his merry brain.

And so, the masque completed, the Frenchmen of Port-Royal, including those still in costume, entered the dining hall of the habitation to enjoy good wine and a bountiful, well-prepared meal.[1]

Masqued intentions

What is going on here, aside from Gallic fancifulness and panache? A year before the establishment of Jamestown, on the edge of the same North American wilderness that would reduce the English settlement to murder and cannibalism, are

Frenchmen conducting themselves as if they were on a spring picnic in rural France? Two winters earlier, Frenchmen had succumbed to scurvy or related ailments in the first Acadian settlement on Sainte-Croix Island, forcing the move to Port-Royal. Yet here were Frenchmen glorying in an abundance of meat, fish, produce, and wine. Just weeks before, Indians of Cape Cod had killed Frenchmen. Yet here were Frenchmen dressed as Indians reciting alexandrine verses that promised concord, loyalty, and support, and Lescarbot was predicting empire and Christianization.

Answers to such paradoxical questions must be speculative. Still, they may throw light on the historical experience of Roman Catholic New France from its first years of exploration and settlement into the postconquest era. Even an improvised masque produced on the border of an unsettled frontier can possess an alchemy of intuition, analysis, and prediction. Marc Lescarbot was trying to please his patron, obviously, but he was also trying to convey the opinions he shared with others of his background and education concerning what they hoped to accomplish in New France. Such perspectives involved—as was ever true in this era of exploration and settlement—an amalgam of economic and religious motivation, and in Lescarbot's case an element of artistic and professional advancement was added to the mix. Acquisition, empire, profits from the fur trade: *The Theater of Neptune* expresses each of these ambitions. Odder still, a promise of evangelization is made through this unusual vehicle, albeit the Christianity in question is generic rather than aggressively Catholic. Henri IV's motto (One protects two) posted over the entrance to the habitation even more pointedly reinforces this notion of accommodation in a realm ruled by a Protestant prince who had accepted Catholicism while guaranteeing the rights of Huguenots. Nor are the Indians objects of exploitation and conquest. They are, instead, partners of the French and future Christians and subjects of the Crown. All these issues, then, appear in *The Theater of Neptune*, although the masque most often is cited by historians only in passing as an eccentric folly, not to be taken seriously as text or production. Ignored as well, or only cursorily noted, is the importance of its author as the founding father of French Canadian history. Marc Lescarbot wrote during a brief interval of Catholic-Protestant détente, which makes his work relevant to any understanding of New France in its early years and prophetic of the Catholic-Protestant détente eventually reached following conquest by Great Britain in 1759.

Past failures

As of 16 November 1606, the day in which the sieur de Poutrincourt was welcomed back to Port-Royal, the French reconnaissance of the Americas, north and south, had been promising. As early as 1504 the French ship *L'Espoir*, financed by merchants from Honfleur and commanded by Binot Palmier de Gonneville, was blown off course in an effort to circumnavigate Africa and compete in the spice trade. Gonneville and his men spent six months on the coast of Brazil amid friendly Indians and returned to France with valuable cargo of hardwood that was, alas, hijacked by pirates off the Channel Islands. Despite this setback, the report of Gonneville's initial success—as well as the exotic presence in France of the son of a Brazilian chief voluntarily sent by his father to learn the French manner of warfare, a young man now baptized and married to Gonneville's daughter—piqued

French interest in the Americas. King Francis I, for one thing, refused to accept the right of the papacy to divide the New World between Spain and Portugal, and he commissioned the famed Italian navigator Giovanni da Verrazzano to undertake a reconnaissance of the North American coast in 1524, followed by a reconnaissance of the West Indies and Brazil. During the second phase of the expedition, the great navigator was killed and cannibalized by Caribs, most likely on the island of Guadeloupe in the Lesser Antilles.

Financed by the Norman merchant prince Jean Ango and other haut bourgeois investors from Normandy, French ships were operating extensive—and illegal, from the Portuguese point of view—hardwood logging operations on the Brazilian coastline by the mid-1520s. An aggrieved Portuguese government then retaliated with an expeditionary force under the command of Cristóvão Jacques. Capturing three French ships at Bahia, Jacques had some three hundred French sailors and loggers either hanged or shot under brutal circumstances—buried up to their necks in sand, then used for target practice. This savaging of one Catholic people by another thereby put the Caribs' killing and eating of Verrazzano into mitigating perspective.

Despite this violent dissuasion, neither France nor its key merchants lost interest in Brazil. In 1555 King Henri II commissioned a full-scale colonizing expedition— three ships, with six hundred men—under the command of Nicolas Durand, chevalier de Villegagnon. Villegagnon had distinguished himself in the Order of Malta, then an important naval force, and risen to commander of war galleys. No one, it would seem, could be more Catholic than this professed monk-warrior who, among other exploits, had evaded an English fleet to extricate Mary Stuart from Scotland so that she could wed the dauphin and thereby strengthen the pro-Catholic Scots-French alliance. And yet, while commanding the provisional French colony that was half Catholic, half Huguenot on an island in the magnificent harbor of Rio de Janeiro (a settlement called France Antarctique because it was below the Tropic of Capricorn, and hence Antarctic in the Northern European terminology of the era), Villegagnon went over—temporarily, as it turned out—to the Calvinist camp. Not every historian, however, accepts such a full-blown conversion by Villegagnon, who did his best while governor to temper religious divisiveness, to the point of banishing from the colony various overly contentious Calvinist clergy. In any event, Villegagnon rejoined the Catholics before returning to France in 1559, a year before Portuguese forces ruthlessly destroyed France Antarctique, slaying the majority of its residents and scattering the rest into the interior.

It took two attempts for the Huguenots to establish Fort Caroline in Florida. Three hundred Huguenots were hanged or otherwise slaughtered when Pedro Menéndez de Avilés suppressed this colony. Huguenot efforts in Canada were even less successful, although they did not involve such a woeful loss of life. Although Jacques Cartier scouted out and identified sites for possible settlement, including the eventual location for Quebec on the Saint Lawrence River, the two expeditions led by Cartier in 1534 and 1535–1536, were primarily voyages of reconnaissance in search of mineral wealth and the Northwest Passage to Asia, still believed to be just over the horizon across a relatively narrow continent. In 1542 Cartier joined a third expedition, this one with a colonizing attempt, led by Jean-François de La Rocque, sieur de Roberval, in command of three ships. Sailing up the Saint Lawrence, the Roberval-Cartier party established a settlement on Cape Rouge near the

Quebec site, where the French briefly believed they had discovered diamonds and gold (in reality, quartz and iron pyrite) and spent a horrific scurvy-ridden winter of 1542–1543 that severely depleted manpower and convinced Roberval and Cartier to abandon the settlement in the spring and return to France.

Renewed efforts

Following a fifty-six-year hiatus—increasingly consumed in seven to nine outbreaks of devastating civil war based on religion (historians differ on the exact count)— France and its new king, Henri IV, a Protestant turned Catholic for the sake of peace, tried once again to establish a colony in Canada. This time the chosen site was Sable Island, off the Grand Banks, where cod fishing had remained profitable to assorted French, Basque, and Portuguese entrepreneurs throughout the troubled sixteenth century. Financed in part by Henri IV and led in 1599 by the marquise de La Roche, who had already profited from the fishing trade as an investor, the Sable Island colony—its members recruited from jail cells, some of them awaiting execution—was precariously set on little more than a sandbank and almost immediately abandoned by its leader. Over the next three years, Sable Island degenerated into a nightmare of mutiny, murder, and starvation, which reduced the colony to eleven survivors grateful for a passing Spanish ship that offered to return them to Europe.

Champlain's 1600–1601 effort at Tadoussac—a site that would eventually emerge in importance as port of entry to the Saint Lawrence River and valley—also was unsuccessful. In part, the settlement failed, Champlain believed, because it was located too near the mouth of the river, and hence beleaguered by arctic winds sweeping unhampered from the north, rather than midway into the valley, where it would have been protected by the mountain ranges lining the Saint Lawrence. More important, persistent Catholic-Huguenot tensions divided the colony. Its two leaders—Pierre de Chauvin, sieur de Tonnetuit, and Pierre Du Gua, sieur de Monts—were Huguenots and insisted that only Huguenot ministers accompany the expedition. The sixteen settlers, however, were Catholic. When both Tonnetuit and de Monts departed for France before winter to carry on further negotiations with investors and the Crown, the colony fell into religious quarreling, general laxity, and ineptitude, followed by scurvy and starvation, forcing the five survivors to take refuge with friendly local Indians.

In early 1604—back in the court and mercantile circles, from which affairs in New France would be minutely managed for the next century—the ever resilient de Monts organized Huguenot and Catholic investors in Rouen, Saint-Malo, La Rochelle, and Saint-Jean-de-Luz for an even grander venture, once again with the help of Champlain, who had also returned to France. (All in all, Champlain would cross the Atlantic twenty-seven times between 1599 and 1633.) This time around, a top crew was recruited, beginning with Champlain's appointment as chief military commander, explorer, and diplomat to Indian tribes. He was assisted by Mathieu Da Costa, a Portuguese sailor of African descent, perhaps from the Cape Verde Islands, who had spent time (for an unspecified reason) in Acadia and had mastered the local dialect of Algonquian. De Monts also enlisted a cadre of craftsmen in the trades required for the construction of an ambitious habitation (including a snug prefabricated cabin for his own use, shipped across the Atlantic for reassembly in

New France), as well as a number of men skilled in hunting, fishing, and agriculture. Also signing on were various gentleman-adventurers bearing the honorific *sieur*, including Jean de Biencourt, sieur de Poutrincourt, an accomplished soldier and classicist from Picardy, who said he was seriously considering reestablishing himself and his family in New France and therefore was eager to travel there in an organized way to scout out prospects.

Of prophetic importance, the Huguenot de Monts recruited two secular priests to minister to the Catholic half of his constabulary: not the sailors, who generally were Protestant and, dressed in the bright colors of their seaman's garb, antiphonally chanted psalms as they tended to the rigging, nor the middle-ranked managers, who were Huguenots as well, but certainly most of the craftsmen, workers, and soldiers—if not, alas, their wives and children. The recruitment of women to New France would remain a problem for the next seventy years and would never be fully solved. Since these religious men were secular priests, they were oriented primarily toward a ministry among Frenchmen rather than missionary work among Indians. Nicholas Aubry came from a respectable Parisian family; Champlain records the other priest only as *le curé* (the curate), meaning that he did not come from a family of rank but was nevertheless ordained. He may have possessed a greater common touch than Aubry, whose well-positioned family fussed about his departing on the expedition in lieu of establishing himself in an ecclesiastical position commensurate with their standing. Young and hot-tempered and wearing a sword, Aubry is believed to be the priest who argued violently with the Huguenot pastor assigned to the expedition. Their confrontation reached the point of fisticuffs, Champlain reports, which qualifies the ecumenical nature of the venture. Searching for his lost sword, Aubry became separated from the main party on the Bay of Saint Mary and spent sixteen days in the wilderness, barely surviving on wild berries and sorrel before being rescued.

The trauma of this experience seems to have taken the edge off Aubry's desire to remain in Acadia, and he returned to France within the year. Still, he and the unnamed curé of Port-Royal (who most likely succumbed to scurvy that first winter) did bring to French Canada in its formative phase the model of secular clergy serving as pastors to French laity, in contrast to the religious-order priests, Franciscan Recollects and Jesuits, who would later arrive as missionaries. By the end of the seventeenth century, though, secular priests associated with the Society of Saint-Sulpice, the Paris Foreign Missions Society, and the Seminary of Quebec would be serving as frontier missionaries as well.

The winter of 1604–1605 proved disastrous for the second de Monts expedition. Champlain wanted to locate the settlement on a site named Port-Royal on the present-day Annapolis Basin of the Bay of Fundy but was overruled by de Monts in favor of a wooded five-acre tract on an inland bay on the Saint John River where three rivers converged. De Monts liked the fact that the Isle Sainte-Croix (Island of the Holy Cross), as he named it, was a natural fortress guarded on three sides by granite cliffs. The locale also showed signs of mineral wealth (or so de Monts thought) and, he believed, represented a shortcut into the Saint Lawrence valley. The brutal Canadian winter, however, negated just about every advantage de Monts had hoped for. For one thing, the estuary froze with ice thick enough to block boats but too thin to cross, which curtailed fishing and hunting. Water casks froze as well, and the French were forced to live off salted meat and melted snow. Thirty-five of the seventy-nine colonists died of scurvy.

By late March a mere eleven settlers remained in good health, and de Monts, having learned his lesson, moved the survivors south to Port-Royal, which had a milder climate, access to winter fishing, inland hunting, early spring forest greenery to be harvested for an antiscurvy tea, and, most important, friendly Mi'kmaq Indians of the powerful Souriquois Confederacy. Astonishingly, given the devastation of the French by scurvy that first winter, the settlers constructed an impressive fortified habitation before the onset of winter 1605–1606. Irrigated gardens were planted as a defense against scurvy: an early crop for the fall and storage for winter, another crop as early as possible in the spring to assist recovery, and, if possible, a third planting and harvest before winter returned.

In mid-fall 1605, de Monts (and Poutrincourt) returned to France to lobby Henri IV and investors for continuing support at a time when the attention of the king and investors alike was turning to Brazil. To promote interest in Canada and its inhabitants, de Monts brought back for presentation to the king a moose calf, a caribou, a muskrat, a hummingbird colony, Mi'kmaq weapons and wampum, and—most impressive of all—a thirty-foot birch-bark canoe stained red, which the sailors of de Monts' flagship the *Don de Dieu* (Gift of God) paddled at great speed up the Seine to the Louvre, to the delight of Henri IV and his four-year-old son.

Humanists in New France

When Poutrincourt had previously left with de Monts for Canada, he had placed his friend and lawyer Marc Lescarbot in charge of his affairs. A classicist and musician as well as a military man, Poutrincourt was turning to a like-minded attorney, humanist, historian, musicologist, and versifier who belonged to a class of academic advisors and publicists rising in importance as the Renaissance, Reformation, and Catholic Reform (Counter-Reformation) matured into the Early Modern era. As the sixteenth century wore on, this genre of intellectual advisor, originally clerical in origin, became increasingly lay and lawyerly in both Catholic and Protestant circles, and by the mid- to late seventeenth century such figures in France bifurcated into a legal nobility of the robe and a smaller but equally influential cadre of skilled civil servants attached to the Crown.

Poutrincourt was the fourth son of a noble family from Picardy with a three-century record of royal attachments and military service. Ardently Roman Catholic, Poutrincourt lost two brothers in the French wars of religion, in which he also fought. His sister Jeanne was appointed lady-in-waiting to Mary Stuart, later queen of France and still later Mary, Queen of Scots, the iconic rallying point (whether Mary wished it or not) for Roman Catholic resistance to Queen Elizabeth I and the Protestant cause. Following Henri's reconciliation in 1594 with the Catholic League in the last of the religious wars, accompanied by his conversion to Catholicism, Poutrincourt became an ardent supporter of the king, who returned the favor by appointing him a royal chevalier, a gentleman of the chamber, and governor of Méry-sur-Seine in Champagne.

Poutrincourt was also something of an idealist and a dreamer. Few nobility, even those in his financially challenged circumstances, would think—much less take the first practical step of going there for a personal preview—of moving with his wife and children to New France in pursuit (however vaguely defined) of a better way of being French. Poutrincourt's love of music, moreover, which he composed as well as appreciated, testified to an aesthetic sense that also linked him to Lescarbot, whom Poutrincourt might have helped with *The Theater of Neptune*.

Upon his return to France, de Monts was successful in raising royal approval and private-sector support for continuing efforts in Acadia, the Gulf of Saint Lawrence, and the Saint Lawrence River and valley, to be organized and managed as fur and fishing monopolies reporting to de Monts. For the immediate future, de Monts planned to remain in France as lobbyist, fund-raiser, and executive director of the fledgling monopoly. He thus appointed the experienced sea captain François Gravé, sieur du Pont (known in maritime circles as Point-Gravé), as supervisor of commercial operations—which included responsibility for suppressing unauthorized fishing and fur trading by nonmembers of the monopoly. De Monts also named Poutrincourt as lieutenant governor based in Port-Royal. Poutrincourt, in turn, recruited Lescarbot to accompany him to North America and to explore possibilities for his own career.

Lescarbot was ready for such a life-changing decision. He was, after all, single, ambitious, and—so he would soon be versifying—thoroughly disenchanted with his situation in France. Born around 1570 to a haut bourgeois family in the city of Vervins in the Thiérache region on the frontier between France and the Spanish Netherlands, Lescarbot received a solid secondary education in Vervins and, thanks to the sponsorship of Monsignor Valentin Duglas, the Catholic bishop of Laon, went on for further study at the College of Laon and the University of Paris. In the course of this extensive learning, Lescarbot mastered Latin, Greek, Hebrew, ancient and modern literatures, and civil and canon law. With his bachelor of law degree in hand by 1598, and eager for a public and legal career, Lescarbot served as a junior attaché in the negotiations between Spain and France presided over by papal legate Allesandro de' Medici, the cardinal archbishop of Florence; the exchange led to the Treaty of Vervins in settlement of a long-standing border dispute. At a critical moment, when talks were on the verge of collapse, Lescarbot stepped in with a Latin oration in defense of peace, which he gave in the presence of the papal legate, that helped prompt a resumption of discussion. The youthful attaché followed this up with a second oration at the signing of the treaty and composed a commemorative inscription in Latin as well as celebratory poems in French, published as *Poèmes de la Paix*.

All this represented a minor but heady experience for an ambitious young lawyer called to the bar in 1599 by the Parlement of Paris, where he maintained his residence and practice while finding time to translate from the Latin three treatises indicative of his developing interest in religion and history: monographs on Church reunion and the history of Russia by historian and Vatican librarian Caesar Cardinal Baronius and a manual for parish practice by Charles Cardinal Borromeo, the reforming archbishop of Milan. In the spirit of the era's polymathic culture of humanism, Lescarbot also studied medicine, moved in scholarly and publishing circles, and kept in touch with his native region through visits and correspondence. At the same time, he developed his legal practice, including his work for Poutrincourt and, presumably, a number of other well-placed clients he met through Poutrincourt and associated connections.

Lescarbot would later intimate that one to three adverse decisions handed down by judges he believed to be corrupt motivated his decision to sail with Poutrincourt for New France. (The *Jonas* left La Rochelle in May 1606 and reached Port-Royal at the end of July after a long, difficult voyage.) Historians have unanimously accepted Lescarbot at his word, precisely because there seems little reason not to. An examination of Lescarbot's extensive writings, however—whether written at the time or later revised and attached to his three-volume *Histoire de la Nouvelle-France* (History of New France), published in Paris in 1609 and reissued in two successive and expanded editions (1611–1612, 1617–1618), earning for Lescarbot comparison to Richard Hakluyt and his work in England—reveals the complex nexus of social, economic, imaginative, and religious ambitions Lescarbot shared with his patron Poutrincourt and Poutrincourt's chief executive officer, Samuel Champlain, destined to remain in memory and historical scholarship as the founder of New France. Like Poutrincourt, whose patrimony was brought to the brink of ruin by the religious wars, and like Champlain, a self-made man with first-rate connections, Lescarbot saw an opportunity both to upgrade his finances at Port-Royal by sharing in profits promised by the fur trade and to acquire an estate in Acadia (if he decided to settle there) and thereby add a *sieur* to his currently unadorned name. Yet, like his fellow humanists Poutrincourt and Champlain, Lescarbot also saw in the North American continent the chance for a new France that had put aside old quarrels in favor of a fresh beginning.

Lay French humanists of this era—even such an ardent Catholic as Poutrincourt—were weary of the half century of internecine slaughter France had endured from successive civil wars that pitted Catholics and Calvinists against each other. For educated humanists, Catholic and Protestant alike, Henry of Navarre had saved France by converting to Catholicism, which he declared the official religion of France, while at the same time granting to Huguenots through the 1598 Edict of Nantes liberty of conscience, full civil rights, and continuing governance of the provinces and two hundred cities in which they constituted the majority. While the edict remained in effect (for the next thirty years), France contained two states, Catholic and Calvinist, within one realm, which was officially Catholic; lay humanists approved of that détente.

Humanism adhered to a moral and imaginative republic of intellect, learning, and toleration. Humanism sought truth and value through reason within the context of a universalized religious impulse. Prior to the Reformation, humanists had almost invariably belonged to the party of reform, even when they were clerics, especially in northern Europe. The greatest humanist of the early sixteenth century, Desiderius Erasmus, while an ordained Augustinian canon, left his monastery for further study in Paris and never returned, spending the rest of his life in declericalized circumstances as an editor, translator, commentator, and Cambridge University professor poised midway between Catholicism, which he never left, and the rising Reform he never officially joined but that nevertheless claimed him as one of its own. The scholarly model and habit of mind established by Erasmus and others in the first decades of the sixteenth century was anchored in a commitment to Scripture and the classics, read in the original languages whenever possible, with special regard for the Hebrew Bible and the Greek New Testament. Humanism favored a simplified version of Catholic Christianity focused on the Gospels and the writings of the Church Fathers, with a strong emphasis on Saint Augustine; and a significantly lay-centered lifestyle accompanied by a renewed regard for marriage as spiritually equal (if not superior) to the enforced celibacy of the clergy. Pervading all this was an irenic ecumenism or, at the least, a preference for peace over war. Among French humanists as the century wore on, humanism involved a sense that France was eating itself alive through internecine slaughter.

Humanism gained strength during the reign of Henri IV between 1589 and 1610. Henri welcomed both Catholics and Huguenots into his inner circle. The early Canadian venture followed this model. De Monts was a Huguenot married to a Catholic; Champlain, a Huguenot converted to Catholicism, married a Huguenot who likewise converted. Money for de Monts' early ventures came from Huguenot investors, a fact that did not seem to bother the devout Catholic Poutrincourt. In later years, Poutrincourt would continue de Monts' effort to bring secular Catholic clergy to Acadia when a preference for secular clergy over Jesuits began to characterize French Catholic humanism in its twilight years of ascendancy.

Lescarbot as humanist

Within this context, Marc Lescarbot can be seen as a French Catholic humanist of a reforming ecumenical point of view. None of his writings contain anti-Protestant sentiments. Indeed, Lescarbot used the Geneva Bible for his citations rather than the Catholic versions he might have had recourse to. His Catholic connections were impeccable; Monsignor Duglas' decision to finance Lescarbot for higher studies in theology, philosophy, Scripture, and civil and canon law might well have been with an eye to his future ordination for the Diocese of Laon. Along with this early ecclesiastical patronage and his quasi-ecclesiastical role at the negotiations prior to the Treaty of Vervins, the writings of Lescarbot prior to his departure for New France—especially his translations of Baronius and Borromeo—suggest the interests of a scholar for whom a career in the Church remained a possibility. Openly pious in his writings, Lescarbot remained single until he was fifty or so, and while at Port-Royal he provided Sunday-morning religious instruction to the men, to which the local Mi'kmaq leadership was invited. Lescarbot serves as an early example of the *dévot*: a single, educated, devoted Catholic layman, or a pious widow of means, both of which were emerging as significant figures in the seventeenth-century Catholic Reform in France and New France alike, most noticeably in the founding of Montreal.

Any consideration of the writings from Lescarbot's one-year sojourn in Port-Royal involves a contrast with the contemporaneous writings of Samuel Champlain, which Lescarbot would later appropriate as an openly acknowledged source. Champlain was not university educated; indeed, the documentation of his secondary education is uncertain. He was, however, an able presenter of vivid real-time experience in straightforward prose, and since he was so central to the establishment of New France, the record Champlain created—like the life he lived—remains foundational. Champlain lived history, acted history, made history, was history.

Lescarbot, in comparison, perceived history through a lens of labyrinthine learning. His prose arises from a deliberate and self-conscious assembly of sources and achieves its effect through comparison, contrast, metaphor, and imaginative refraction. While Champlain worked to create a record that cumulatively became a first draft of history, Lescarbot wrote as a man of letters: a scholar in search of history, but also a writer seeking aesthetic pattern as well as corroboration of his humanist point of view. Master of existential event, Champlain cannot be imagined writing a masque with music as a gloss on New France. Lescarbot, by contrast, could not experience New France without recourse to alexandrine reflection. Still, Champlain was destined to grow more reflective—and more Catholic—over the years. Lescarbot, meanwhile, would struggle as a historian to reconcile the record of what actually happened with what he had hoped New France might have become: a humanistic utopia, a place of healing and good humor and reconciliation, a masque with music, a peaceable kingdom, a foretaste of paradise.

Farewell to France

Dated 26 May 1606, on the eve of his departure for North America, Lescarbot's poem "Adieu à la France" presents a first draft of his humanist agenda. France is praised as the mother country, beautiful in its natural and human environment, to which Lescarbot hopes he will one day return in triumph. The ocean voyage will have its dangers, but the goal of the journey makes it worth the risk.

> Nous allons sous l'espoir d'une bonne fortune
> Combattans la fueur du tempesteux Nepturen
> Pour parvenier aux liux où d'une ample moisson
> Se présente aux Chrestiens une belle saison.

Fortune and a good harvest await those Christians making the voyage across the stormy Atlantic, as well as honor, glory, the gratitude of the nation, and everlasting fame.

> A ceux-là qui poussez de sainte intention
> Auront le bel object de cette ambition
> Les peoples à jamais béniront l'enterprise
> Des autheurs d'un tel bien: & d'une plume apprise
> A graver dans l'airain de l'immortalité
> J'en laisserai mémoire à la postérité.

Harvest, sacred intention, blessing of future generations: the language echoes both the Hebraic and the classical. The settlement of New France is at once an Exodus and an *Aeneid*.

   Under the guidance of de Monts and Poutrincourt—a Huguenot and a Catholic, equally beloved by the king—the venture will prosper. The younger Poutrincourt will serve as a second Aeneas to lighten the burden of the aging de Monts.

> De rendre à l'Eternel une agreable offrande,
> Lui vouant toi, tes biens, ta vie, & tes enfans,
> Que tu vas exposer à la merci des vents,
> Et d'un pole voguant jusques à l'autre pole
> Pour son nom exalter & sa saincte parole.

While both de Monts and Poutrincourt are necessary, Poutrincourt speaks to the soul of the poet, inspiring in him a devout love and an ambition to serve this holy enterprise. For that is what New France represents for Poutrincourt: an expansion of French empire taken up as a sacred cause, to which Poutrincourt has dedicated his family and fortune, risking all, so that the name and holy word of the Eternal will be exalted.

De Monts shares his high intent, Lescarbot concludes; and their success will inspire posterity to carry on the sacred task. Lescarbot ends with a prayer:

> Gran Dieu, sois noster Guide en ce douteux voyage
> Puis que tu nous y as enflamé le courage;
> Lasche de tes thrésors un favorable vent
> Qui pousse notre barque en peu d'heures au Pouant,
> Et fay que là pussions arrivez par ta grace
> Jetter le fondement d'une Chrestienne race.

Having inspired this expedition and instilled courage in its participants, Almighty God will send favorable winds their way and, following the crossing, will aid them in projecting forward the foundations of a Christian race.

The identity of the Christian race being projected forward by Huguenots and Catholics in New France seems to be primarily the French people. While the evangelization of the Indian can be inferred, Lescarbot does not state this objective as directly in the poem as he does in a letter of farewell to his mother written at the same time. The primary goal of the venture, Lescarbot tells his mother, connecting this ambition explicitly to Poutrincourt, "is to establish the Christian faith and the name of François among barbarian people who are destitute of the knowledge of God".[2]

Writing in "Adieu á la France" of the entire expedition, a joint venture between Catholics and Huguenots, Lescarbot emphasizes the transition to a second and new France of Christian French people from a realm officially Catholic but tolerant of Protestantism. Even when he is trying to please his Catholic mother and therefore stresses Poutrincourt's desire to evangelize the Indians of New France, Lescarbot keeps his references generically Christian. Through his evocation of Poutrincourt's intent to bring his wife and children to New France, moreover, Lescarbot suggests a society based in a generically Christian laity in partnership with a Christianized Indian population.

The Indian issue

In an effort to win his Catholic mother's support in his decision to go to New France, Lescarbot refers to the indigenous people of Acadia as barbarians with no knowledge of God. On the whole, however, the humanists of the first generation in New France—and, for that matter, successive generations—tend not to use disparaging terms when speaking of Indians but, rather, make every effort to admire the native peoples they encounter. Even French humanists, though, take issue with the Indian habit of torturing captives to death in hideously cruel ways. Their improvident feast-or-famine economies and their toleration of uncleanliness also provoke criticism. Yet these and other issues do not prevent French humanist writers, most notably Champlain and Lescarbot, from recognizing the fundamental and frequently admirable humanity of *Des Sauvages* (1603), as Champlain designated them in the title of his first book. David Hackett Fischer argues that the word simply means "people of the forest" in old French and early English—from the Latin *silva* (forest)—and hence does not connote barbaric ferocity.

Champlain chronicles an intricate array of tribes, subtribes, confederacies, and language groups that requires Fischer five closely printed pages in an appendix to enumerate. Champlain knew these peoples, as individuals and as groups, through personal contact and a kind of participatory anthropology. As a humanist, he depicted them—even his enemies—as human beings conditioned by environment and culture but fully capable of good or bad behavior. Lescarbot shares this humanist view of Indians, although his experience with them was limited to a year's stay at Port-Royal, at the end of which de Monts lost his monopoly, and Poutrincourt, Lescarbot, and others returned to France, leaving behind a skeleton crew.

Back in France, Poutrincourt secured for de Monts a one-year extension of monopoly running through 1608. While Poutrincourt was busy lobbying, Lescarbot plunged himself into composing an epic poem, *La défaite des sauvages Armouchiquois* (1607), and the first edition of his *Histoire de la Nouvelle-France* (1609), two pioneering assessments of the Native Americans of the region. In these works, Lescarbot employs a generic fourfold division for the tribes the French encountered in their colonizing efforts: the Armouchiquois, the Indians of present-day Maine and Massachusetts as far south as Cape Cod; the Souriquois, the Indians of Acadia, present-day Nova Scotia; the Floridians, the Indians encountered by Huguenot colonists of that region; and the Brazilians, the Indian contacts in South America. A fifth Indian category, the Virginians, is only sketchily discussed and may suggest the peoples of northern Spanish Florida, which at the time extended as far north as the Chesapeake. Although Lescarbot was not as experienced an observer as Champlain, he did his best to research his subject through personal contact and interviews while he was on the scene. His notation for Souriquois music and his description of their folklore, dances, and burial practices have earned him a place in the history of anthropology in Canada. For his knowledge of the Armouchiquois, Lescarbot relied on the testimony of Poutrincourt, Champlain, and other veterans of the two expeditions the French had made southward along the coast. He referenced the published reports of René Goulaine de Laudonnière regarding the Indians of Florida and those of Jean de Léry for the Indians of Brazil. As important as such sources were, Lescarbot had more than reportage in mind. Trained in Greek, Hebrew, and Latin literatures, Lescarbot had comparative ambitions: to align Native Americans with ancient Israelites and the peoples of the classical world as revealed in the Hebrew Bible and a profusion of extensively quoted Greek and Latin sources. *The Defeat of the Armouchiquois Savages*—in which Lescarbot snatches a French victory, or at least a draw, from the jaws of defeat—is modeled on the classical epic and thereby demands as a literary genre that the French face a worthy opponent. The second and final book of the first edition of his *History of New France* (book 4 in later, expanded editions) serves as an anthropology of Indian life measured against biblical and classical manners, mores, and folkways as described, among others, by the Hebrew Bible, Herodotus, Diodorus, Theophrastus, Pliny, Plutarch, Tacitus, Suetonius, Petronius, Virgil, Ovid, and Apollinarius.

Despite the brevity of his stay, Lescarbot's inventory of Indian life is remarkably complete. It includes creation stories, religious beliefs and practices, hierarchy and social organization, language usage (what do the Souriquois mean when they say, "Ho! ho! ho!"?), sexuality and marriage (as well as polygamy, divorce, and the sexual freedom enjoyed by younger women prior to marriage), family life, diet (no bread and no wine, Lescarbot laments), music (he provides notations), ceremonial dances (he approves and admires), canoes and snowshoes (he marvels), tobacco usage (he considers it a substitute for alcohol), sweat lodges (of special interest to this student of medicine), and funerary practices (he devotes his longest consideration to them): Lescarbot earns his subsequently bestowed honorific as anthropologist in his discussion of these topics. Regarding warfare, he admires their skills as archers. At the Cape Cod battle, an Indian arrow pierced a Frenchman and the little dog he was carrying in a makeshift backpack, killing both and affixing them to each other. On the one hand, Lescarbot notes, Indians could be gluttonous, thievish, and unclean. On the other hand, they possessed a code of manners and revered their elders. Most disturbing, they went to war primarily for revenge; they tortured their prisoners, ate them, and flayed their skins as trophies of victory for use as cloaks in ceremonial dances. Yet, they showed mercy to their enemies' women and children—in dramatic contrast to French practices.

From the perspective of contemporary anthropology, Lescarbot's cascade of classical and biblical comparisons as his major matrix of reference creates more questions than it answers. From the perspective of early seventeenth-century humanism, however, Lescarbot achieves something very important: the perception of Native Americans as fully recognizable in their humanity as are the Egyptians, Greeks, Romans, Germans, Gauls, Scythians, Moabites, and Israelites described in his sources. Lescarbot's attitude stands in contrast to an earlier, albeit not universal, opinion among Spaniards that Indians were not fully human, or at the least were seriously deficient and should be treated accordingly. Early in his discussion, Lescarbot explicitly cites the Spanish genocide of Indians in the first decades of dominion in the Indies: treatment centered on an avaricious lust for gold that Lescarbot compares to a parallel tendency in ancient Rome, quoting the *Satyricon* of Petronius Arbiter to that effect as well as Ecclesiasticus (the book of Sirach), the same biblical text that inspired Bartolomé de Las Casas to amend his life and devote himself to Indian liberations.

Lescarbot's treatise went almost immediately into German and English editions, suggesting that Lescarbot was striking a chord among Protestant and Catholic humanists alike. Pierre Erondelle, a Huguenot humanist émigré living in London, produced the English translation. Lescarbot was not calling for evangelization or annihilation or some combination thereof. Nor was he particularly aggressive in the matter of conquest and colonization. He was urging, rather, the recognition on the world's stage of a humanity shared by Indians: a recognition based on experience and scholarship.

In subsequent editions of the *History*, Lescarbot—responding, like Champlain, to the growing influence of the Catholic Revival—would expand references to the evangelization of Indians as central to the mission of New France. As of 1609, however, such an appeal would have to have been made to Huguenots and Catholics alike, given the precarious balance of French society in religious matters. The Huguenot humanist Pierre Erondelle, moreover, could see the value of Lescarbot's first take on the Indian question for the continental ambitions of English Protestants in North America. Such sentiments were soon to be further reinforced in England by Captain John Smith through his account of Pocahontas.

Establishing the narrative

Had Samuel Champlain been only a man of action and never written more than was necessary, today we might perceive Lescarbot's *History of New France* as a foundational chronicle. As it is, Champlain's published narratives, edited and enhanced by twentieth-century scholarship, vividly document the founding years of New France. A man of action, a leader, a soldier and explorer, with his mind uncluttered by the literary scholarship, intimidations, and pedantries of university education in the late sixteenth century, Champlain wrote from personal experience and entrepreneurial necessity. He was a visionary publicist, true, but he personally earned every word he wrote. Lescarbot, by contrast, a man of law and letters tempted merely once to cross the Atlantic, produced his *History of New France* as literary art shaped by the needs and preoccupations of its time. Lescarbot developed his history rapidly and in good order at a time when the French experience in Canada was resuming after a hiatus of six decades. Coming so early, 1609, and revised and expanded over the next decade, the *History of New France* proved immediately useful and remained useful well into the century and eventually earned Lescarbot a royal pension. Taken at its most basic—as a digest of narratives—Lescarbot's *History of New France* earned and remains worthy of the Hakluyt comparison first advanced by Canadian historian H. P. Biggar in 1901. An even more generous assessment was made by the eighteenth-century Jesuit historian Pierre-François-Xavier de Charlevoix, who considered Lescarbot the father of historiography for New France, praise re-echoed ("the best of the historians of New France") by Geoffrey Atkinson in *Le nouveaux horizons de la Renaissance française* (1935).

What qualities were these historians praising? Primacy of place, for one thing: the fact that Lescarbot got there first with a history. Narrative verve, for another. Lescarbot has an eye for telling incident and detail, and his style grows in strength and suppleness with each edition. But most of all, Lescarbot deserves laud because he first touches upon the grand themes of the French experience in North America: religion, culture, place, biology, the physical texture and satisfactions of human experience, and that particular capacity for camaraderie so distinctively French that the word has never required translation.

Regarding religion, Lescarbot comes across as—like France at the time—officially Catholic but not unilaterally so. This theme of mutual acceptance between Catholic and Huguenot became especially relevant when a year following the publication of Lescarbot's history a Catholic fanatic assassinated Henri IV, around whom a religiously divided France was rebuilding itself, thus putting the stability of the realm again in danger. Lescarbot considered a Huguenot investment crucial to the success of New France. When delayed with Poutrincourt in the Huguenot city of La Rochelle awaiting spring tides high enough to afford passageway for the 150-ton *Jonas*, Lescarbot was dismayed to learn that, while the Huguenot pastors

of the city prayed from their pulpits for the expedition's safety and the conversion of the Indians of New France, the Catholics of the city seemed indifferent.
Indeed, Poutrincourt informed Lescarbot, when he returned from the first de Monts
expedition, he spoke in court of the Indian souls to be won in New France. "How
many?" a high-ranking Catholic ecclesiastic had asked. Some 150,000, Poutrincourt
had replied, making a wild guess. "Is that all?" the prelate had scoffed, pointing out
the decidedly larger population of France. The local Catholic vicar at La Rochelle,
moreover, refused to recommend to Poutrincourt a secular priest who might want
to join the expedition as chaplain. Nor would the vicar supply the expedition with
Viaticum (consecrated hosts) for the voyage, as was done in ancient times (so the
scholarly Lescarbot informed him) when Christians traveled without clergy. And so
no Mass or Eucharist was available to Catholics on the long voyage out, and, once
in Port-Royal, Lescarbot the layman served as Sunday-morning catechist and leader
of prayer services.[3]

On matters of geography and environment, Lescarbot presents the dangers (the
Atlantic crossing), the challenges (the six months of winter), the possibility of finding the Northwest Passage to Asia (perhaps the Saint Lawrence River reaches the
Pacific, he speculates), and the economic opportunities offered by fish, fur, and
timber. Lescarbot favors the system of royally granted monopolies and laments that
Frenchmen are increasingly joining Portuguese and Basque entrepreneurs in unauthorized activity. Mining sets off his ire because he associates it with the Spaniards'
decimation of Indians by forced labor, whereas the fur trade remains controlled at
its source by the various Indian nations acting in partnership with the French to
whom they sell their furs.

In history and poetry alike, Lescarbot expresses poetic environmentalism vis-
à-vis this new place. He inventories and celebrates its birds, fishes, animals, and
wildflowers. The hogs brought over by the French, he informs us, have increased
and multiplied. The beaver especially attracts his attention and gains his respect, not
simply for its fur but because of its sleek appearance and engineering skills and, it
must be admitted, the savory taste of its tail when roasted.

Frequent references to edibility imply more than a Gallic love of a well-
provisioned table. As a student of medicine, Lescarbot was intrigued by issues of
nutrition, and in 1602 he had translated a pamphlet concerning the alleged three-
decade fast of a religious mystic. Lescarbot provides ample discussion of starvation
and scurvy in his *History*, beginning with the scurvy that devastated the Cartier
expeditions in the 1530s and the recent outbreak of the disease in the first de Monts
expedition, which killed thirty-six and brought the venture to the verge of collapse. With his usual reference to classical sources, Lescarbot cites ancient opinions
regarding starvation and scurvy; from more contemporary evidence, he speculates
on scurvy's causes and particularly its cures, paying special attention to fresh meat,
the Indians' solution, as well as the herbal (pine needle) tea mentioned by Cartier,
another Indian remedy. Interspersed with such discussions—and running counter
to them—are comments about Lescarbot's esteem for the fertility of the soil of Acadia and his own work at helping to raise wheat and produce at Port-Royal. Such
efforts were successful at first without fertilization, and they proved even more successful when a second crop was irrigated with the aid of a newly constructed water
wheel and fertilized with fish bones, seashells, and hog dung.

For all its classical and biblical references, then, and its humanistic high-mindedness, Lescarbot's *History of New France* remains remarkably focused on New France in terms of its environment, flora, and fauna, as well as on the Indian peoples who first learned to survive and thrive there and the handful of Frenchmen now learning to do likewise. To be French Canadian would soon mean to be Catholic, almost exclusively so. It would also mean—after a French-derived population began to be born in New France—to be in close connection with a part of the North American continent that nurtured them, making them tall and strong, a region they could never wrestle into submission but could nurture in turn that would challenge them to become not simply French men and women but a new people.

A circle of friends

Camaraderie constituted an early building block of this new identity, and, over time, a capacity for group practice and communal celebration would influence the evolution of the distinctive texture and practice of Catholicism in New France. Here was a people who learned to be happy in the forest together and to worship God accordingly. Moments of friendship and good cheer appear frequently in Lescarbot's writing, beginning most conspicuously with *The Theater of Neptune*. Some of these delights are not explicitly shared with others—the enjoyment of birds and flowers, for example—but as winter ensues and the French remain confined together in the habitation, pleasures become more communal. Even before winter, Lescarbot tells us, from late July to late August, the colony enjoyed a midsummer semiholiday, thanks to a hogshead of the good wine de Monts left behind when he departed for France. Work did not cease, for the French still had to struggle to survive, but they enjoyed long-lit summer evenings together after pleasant days of exploring the countryside's resources. Then came the masque and all the shared pleasure of rehearsing for it, followed by the unusually mild winter of 1606–1607, which allowed the French to revel in an outdoor songfest on the shores of the nearby Equille River. Later that month, a group of French tramped out to inspect the settlement's wheat fields some two leagues (five miles) from the habitation and savored a picnic lunch there in the sunshine.

Like Champlain—whose journals, David Hackett Fischer tells us, constitute a gastronomical tour of frontier Canada—Marc Lescarbot had a high regard for the pleasures of the table: not simply well-prepared food and drink but the camaraderie and conversation of a lively dinner party. Winter-driven scurvy had nearly destroyed previous French efforts to establish a foothold in Canada, but since then, Champlain had organized a cadre of hunters and fishermen to keep the settlement supplied with fresh meat and fish, augmented by whatever could be shipped across the Atlantic (such as good wine) or grown and cellared in the summer and fall, such as onions, turnips, and other sturdy root vegetables.

Ever resourceful, Champlain organized these providers and the upper echelons of Port-Royal into an *Ordre de Bon Temps* (Order of Good Times), more commonly known in subsequent English translations as the Order of Good Cheer: a hunting and dining society designed to keep scurvy at bay in the settlement and the more well-to-do amused through the long winter. The order was symbolized by a chain and medal that with due ceremony was placed around the neck of a chief steward charged with supervising the hunting, fishing, cooking, and preparing for the day's main meal as well as leftovers for breakfast and a light third repast. Once the meal was ready and the leadership of the colony gathered at table in the dining area, the chief steward led a procession of members of the order carrying pitchers of wine and platters of meats, fowl, fish, bread, and vegetables while musicians played fanfares and the assembled company cheered. A similar but less ambitious parade ushered in the dessert. At the conclusion of the meal, the chief steward removed his chain of office and ceremoniously settled it around the neck of the next in line for these duties.

The dinners were excellent, Lescarbot tells us. The meat equaled any sold by butchers in Paris on the rue aux Ours. The fact that the duties of chief steward passed to an individual every fortnight testifies to the limited number—fourteen or fifteen—of members of the order in this rigidly stratified society. Still, the order fed the entire settlement, and Mi'kmaq sagamores such as Membertou and his associates were invited to sit at table as honored guests, while their extended families sat on the sidelines, eating bread and enjoying the proceedings.

Port-Royal as prophetic paradigm

Camaraderie and cheer in the midst of winter on the edge of the North American continent in the presence of its indigenous peoples: Marc Lescarbot remembered these times upon his return to France and included them in his history. The journals he used as sources contained tales of disasters and failures aplenty. His own memoirs, however, which he liberally utilized in his narrative, reflected optimism and good humor. Lescarbot's commitment to French culture speaks for itself. Who else would welcome back a badly mauled reconnaissance party with a costumed and fully produced masque with music? Or spend the evening hours in his room composing poetry? Or embark upon the *History of New France* when that history had barely begun? Only a devoted Frenchman, is the answer, committed to the development of New France as a colony playing a reconciling role through humanism—through the Muses, as Lescarbot puts it—as well as through commerce and conversion. In chronicling Huguenot efforts at colonization in Florida, Brazil, and Acadia (cooperatively, with Catholics), Lescarbot once and for all ensured that the contribution of Calvinist France would be permanently placed in the historiography of New France.

12

Quebec 1615

The Counter-Reformation and Catholic Revival take hold in New France

In early June 1615, four Franciscan Recollect friars, having sailed on 24 April from Honfleur in the company of Samuel Champlain, were making their way up the Saint Lawrence to begin their ministries as missionaries to the Huron. Recollect superior Denis Jamet arrived at Quebec on 8 June, joining Fray Jean Dolbeau, who had arrived six days earlier, but Jamet remained there less than a day before continuing up the river toward Huron country, so eager was he to launch the Recollect ministry among these people. Later that month, at Rivière des Prairies, Fray Joseph Le Caron joined Jamet, and on 24 June the two priests celebrated the first Masses to be offered on the Island of Montreal. Shortly thereafter, Le Caron went on with Champlain into Huron country, where on 12 August he celebrated Mass for the first time in that region. Jamet thereupon returned downstream to Quebec, where he planned to establish Recollect headquarters for what he hoped would develop into a growing ministry of his order among the Huron and other native peoples.

Jamet rendezvoused at Quebec with Fray Dolbeau and the talented and versatile lay brother Pacifique Duplessis, who had trained as an apothecary in his youth. Dolbeau and Duplessis were already busy building rooms and a chapel for Recollect use. As superior, Jamet filed his first report from the field to Cardinal François de Joyeuse, the archbishop of Narbonne, a prelate of a ducal family influential in court circles; Jamet described the country and its people and called for further support. In December, Dolbeau left Quebec to establish a mission among the Montagnais at the harbor settlement of Tadoussac at the mouth of the Saint Lawrence. Although New France contained only four Recollects, their ministry extended along the length of the Saint Lawrence valley from Tadoussac to the Island of Montreal. Failing eyesight forced Dolbeau to return to Quebec in the spring of 1616, but he was eventually replaced by Fray Paul Huet, who arrived from France in July 1617 and briefly remained at Tadoussac before becoming the first priest to serve at Trois-Rivières (Three Rivers) on the Saint Lawrence River between Quebec and Montreal.

Obviously more Recollects would be required if this reformed branch of Franciscans were to serve as the core clerical cadre for the evangelization of the indigenous peoples of the Saint Lawrence valley and the Huron country beyond, as Champlain hoped. Indeed, Champlain had personally recruited the Recollects for this mission when, having returned to France in 1614, he appeared before the cardinals and bishops gathered in Paris for a meeting of the Estates General and stated his case, not simply for Recollects but for the launching of a grand crusade to evangelize all the indigenous peoples of French North America. Papal nuncio Roberto Ubaldini supported Champlain's cause. In Rouen in late March 1615, at a meeting of Huguenot investors in the company Champlain was organizing to control the fur trade along the Saint Lawrence River and its tributaries, Champlain introduced the Recollect father selected for the mission. The enterprise was sponsored by Henri de Bourbon, prince of Condé and duc d'Enghien, who was a cousin of the young King Louis XIII and the newly appointed viceroy of New France. As in the case of Spain, continental and missionary ambitions were driving each other.

The Huguenot factor

Between 1604 and 1632, the years of Champlain's entrepreneurship in New France, Champlain participated in four trading companies: two ventures controlled by the Huguenot Pierre Du Gua, sieur de Monts (1604–1608); the company Champlain organized, with strong Huguenot support, for the prince of Condé (1614–1627); and the subsequent partnership between this company and the Huguenot merchants William de Caën and Caën's nephew Émery (1621–1627). All four of these companies depended on Huguenot investment. In addition, Champlain took part in the Company of New France, also known as the Company of One Hundred Associates, organized in 1627 under the authority of Cardinal Richelieu on behalf of the Crown and limited to Catholics.

Champlain was born (around 1570) and raised a Huguenot in the strongly Huguenot city of Brouage in the province of Saintonge, a port city on the Gulf of Saintonge fronting a mainly Huguenot region of port cities dominated by the Huguenot stronghold of La Rochelle. The circumstances of Champlain's conversion to Catholicism are unknown, but it can be surmised that his conversion, like that of his mentor Henri IV, fit into a pattern of détente ending (for the time being) a half century of brutal civil strife. Champlain's wife, Hélène Boullé, had strong Huguenot connections as well; like Champlain, she may have been born a Huguenot prior to her father's conversion to Catholicism. Once Catholic, Champlain was sincerely so: he remained steadfast in his religious practice throughout his lifetime. In his last years, he was especially close to the Jesuits, especially Paul Le Jeune, himself a convert from Calvinism. Samuel Champlain, in short, shows every sign of converting to Catholicism as a matter of state, convenience, and personal preference. The convenience of his conversion cannot be held against him without violating an understanding of such a conversion, led by the king himself, in the name of peace and proper Christianity in late-sixteenth- and early-seventeenth-century France.

A necessary distinction

While sincerely Catholic, Champlain never became anti-Huguenot, which at the least would have constituted a psychological oxymoron for an entrepreneur supported by Huguenot investment. At this point, a distinction must be made between the Catholic Revival and the Counter-Reformation. The Catholic Revival—so evident in such first-generation pioneers of New France as Poutrincourt, Lescarbot, and Champlain—was anchored in the reform-minded Christian humanism of Erasmus and his generation. As such, it advocated a reformed Catholicism. Once Henri IV restored the peace by his own conversion and the Edict of Nantes, which guaranteed religious freedom within a framework of officially established Catholicism, Catholic humanists of this persuasion had little trouble cooperating with Huguenots in continental ambitions relating to New France. The Counter-Reformation, by contrast, came late to France and never took hold as fully as its supporters (the Jesuits especially) would have wished. The Counter-Reformation advocated the militant re-Catholicization of Christian Europe, including the reconversion of territories and governments lost to Protestantism during the Reformation. The Counter-Reformation favored an organizationally reformed Roman Catholic Church standardized in her doctrine and practices and governed by an authoritative papacy. Centered in Italy and Spain, and served by Jesuits, Capuchins, and other reformed orders, the Counter-Reformation considered itself on crusade on behalf of a re-Romanized, re-Catholicized Europe. As a matter of either temperament or policy, toleration was not part of its program.

The conflict in France between the Catholic Revival and the Counter-Reformation continued through the seventeenth century and reached its most intense point during the 1650s in the controversies between mathematician-philosopher Blaise Pascal and the Jesuits as argued by Pascal in his *Provincial Letters* (1656–1657), initially written in defense of the Jansenist-leaning theologian Antoine Arnauld, then under threat of censure from the Counter-Reformation-oriented theologians of the Sorbonne. As evidenced in his defense of Catholic eucharistic doctrine against the eucharistic teachings of Calvinism, Arnauld in general remained within the Catholic camp. Yet the anchorage of Jansenist theology in the thought of Saint Augustine regarding grace and redemption, as well as its commitment to the strong tradition of Gallicanism in the French church, which favored local control and a national church over Roman authority, suggest enduring linkages to Calvinist theories equally acceptable to French humanists of the Catholic persuasion in the late-sixteenth and early-seventeenth centuries.

Jesuits in Acadia

By the time Champlain was trying to recruit Recollects to New France in 1614–1615, tensions between the Catholic Revival and the Counter-Reformation had played themselves out in Acadia. Regaining control of his Acadian properties, along with a monopoly on its fish and fur trade, Jean de Biencourt, sieur de Poutrincourt, sailed to Port-Royal in 1610 on the well-provisioned *Grâce de Dieu* in the company of his eldest son, Charles, artisans and workers, and a secular priest from the diocese of Langres by the name of Jessé Fléché. Unlike Nicholas Aubry, the sword-bearing secular priest of the first Poutrincourt effort, who had been intent on riches and adventure, Fléché had been recruited by Poutrincourt for a more formally religious purpose: the launching of an evangelization attempt aimed at the Mi'kmaq people of the Souriquois Confederacy living in the vicinity of Port-Royal, including their aged sagamore Membertou, last seen enjoying the hospitality of the French at the performance of Lescarbot's *Theater of Neptune* maritime masque in October 1606 and at one or another of the festive dinners prepared by Champlain's Order of Good Cheer in the winter of 1606–1607.

During the years Poutrincourt spent negotiating his return to Acadia, highly placed supporters of the Society of Jesus had incessantly lobbied him to take Jesuit missionaries with him. Most notable in this regard was a circle of noble women attached to the pious young widow Antoinette de Pons, the marquise de Guercheville and a lady-in-waiting to the queen, reputed to be the most beautiful woman in France and certainly among the wealthiest. Poutrincourt resisted such lobbying, however. Henri IV was still alive at the time, and he had expelled the Society from France in 1594, although the king had relented and readmitted it in 1603, provided that only Jesuits who were native-born Frenchmen be allowed to return and that they swear allegiance to the Crown. The Society of Jesus was reestablished in France and prospered. As of 1610, in fact, Henri IV had a Jesuit confessor, Pierre Coton, who must have taken a diplomatic view of the king's sexual omnivorousness (or been patient with his transgressions), given Henri IV's energetic ambitions in such matters, which on at least one occasion had been unsuccessfully directed toward the marquise de Guercheville, who resisted—indeed, outwitted!—the king with an admixture of piety and tact.

Henri IV's expulsion of the Jesuits and, paradoxically, his readmission of the Society, as well as his subsequent dependence on and affectionate friendship with his Jesuit confessor, underscore the reasons for Poutrincourt's resistance to having Jesuits assigned to Acadia. The Society was simply too powerful. Even when it experienced reversal, it came back stronger than ever.

A lingering anti-Semitism lurked within this critique. The Jesuits themselves had been divided in the 1570s on the delicate matter of Old versus New Christians when Old Christian Jesuits of the Spanish and Portuguese provinces protested the prevalence and preeminence of New Christians, conversos of Jewish descent, in the Society of Jesus. Between the pogroms of the late fourteenth century and the wholesale expulsion of 1492, a significant number of Iberian Jews converted to Christianity either willingly (a few) or under various degrees of pressure (the majority). Many descendants of these New Christians, as they were called—mainly men and women of urban, educated backgrounds—entered clerical and/or religious life and, given their backgrounds and talents, rose to prominence in the ecclesiastical state, including the hierarchy. In no religious order was this more the case than in the Society of Jesus. Even before the Society was founded and officially recognized in 1540, Ignatius of Loyola found a ready welcome among New Christians eager for renewal and reform. Loyola himself ran afoul of the Inquisition and was imprisoned when the vicar general of the university town of Alcalá grew suspicious of his association with reform-minded converso students loyal to the reform program of Erasmus and thought that Loyola was a secret Jew. In the order's early years, between the mid-1530s and the 1570s, many New Christians joined the Society of Jesus, and a number of them, personally recruited and promoted by Ignatius, attained prominent positions. Alfonso de Polanco, for example, Ignatius' longtime executive secretary and, later, an assistant general of the Society, was a New Christian, as was Diego Laínez, a founding member of the order and Ignatius' successor as father general. Other notable Jesuits of Jewish ancestry included the historian Pedro de Ribadeneyra, Ignatius' first biographer; Jerónimo Nadal, Ignatius' plenipotentiary emissary; the philosopher Francisco Suárez; and the papal diplomat Francisco de Toledo Herrera, the first Jesuit to be promoted to the College of Cardinals.

This presence of Iberian New Christians in an order rapidly growing in numbers, prominence, and power did not go unnoticed. Critical of the number of New Christians being promoted during the tenure of its third father general, Francis Borgia, an Old Christian duke by birth, His Most Catholic Majesty King Philip II described the Jesuits as "a synagogue of Hebrews" and the Society as a synagogue in disguise, up to no good. When Borgia died in 1572, his next two successors sided with Old Christian Iberians and approved a series of regulations expelling nonprofessed New Christians from the Society and prohibiting the future admittance of candidates with such a background, no matter how talented they might be. However breached in their observance, these regulations remained on the books until 1946.

This attempted ethnic cleansing of the Jesuits, however, did not satisfy critics. The transnationalism of the Society, for one thing, threatened developing nation-states. The order's loyalty to the papacy, reinforced by a solemn vow administered to an inner circle of elite members, threatened localism in the Church, including the prerogative of kings to nominate bishops. Its affinity with the aristocracy, whose children the Jesuits educated in their network of colleges or personally tutored, drew a criticism born of envy along with charges that Jesuits were too lenient with their aristocratic clients in the confessional. Pascal's pet peeve was the Jesuits' alleged adherence to probabilism, a theory allowing a morally uncertain course of action to be embarked upon, even in cases when more certain outcomes or probabilities were apparent. Pascal considered probabilism an open door to sanctioned bad behavior, both public and private.

This background (and more) explains why it took the marquise de Guercheville and her allies nearly four years to negotiate the approval of the queen regent, the father general and French provincial of the Society, the pope, and the archbishop of Rouen—who held nominal ecclesiastical jurisdiction over New France—for a Jesuit mission to Acadia. No one resisted such an assignment more vigorously than the sieur de Poutrincourt. As a French humanist of irenic and ecumenical inclinations, and accustomed to working in partnership with Huguenot investors, Poutrincourt had reason to fear the Counter-Reformational Jesuits, whose stated goal was the reconversion of Protestant territories, including the Huguenot regions of France. Poutrincourt also resented that the Society of Jesus had negotiated a percentage of the profits from Poutrincourt's trading company toward the upkeep of its mission and its missionaries in Acadia in an agreement that he believed constituted a de facto partnership. In contrast to the Jesuits, the secular priest Jessé Fléché was a contract employee of the trading company who reported to Poutrincourt and not to a Rome-dominated, transnational Society of Jesus.

Fléché, moreover, was fully capable of evangelizing the Mi'kmaq, Poutrincourt argued. With Poutrincourt's encouragement, that is exactly what Fléché—an outgoing, genial cleric known to the Mi'kmaq as the Patriarch—proceeded to do: to baptize a number of Mi'kmaq, including the great and aged Membertou, after minimal instruction and to have them take as their baptismal names the names of the king and queen mother, prominent royalty, and other highly placed nobility in France. Membertou, for example, was named Henri in honor of the recently assassinated king, while Membertou's son was named after Henri's son Louis XIII, Membertou's wife Marie in honor of the queen regent, her daughter Marguerite after the queen regent's daughter, the sagamore's second son Paul after the pope, and so forth. As soon as these baptisms were accomplished, Poutrincourt dispatched a letter to Queen Regent Marie de Médicis outlining this triumph of evangelization and calling for further assistance from the Crown. Poutrincourt's son Charles immediately took the letter back to France on the *Grâce de Dieu*, and in rapid order Poutrincourt's friend and lawyer Marc Lescarbot read it and produced a pamphlet praising the documented success and directly calling upon the queen regent to launch an expanded evangelizing effort led by Poutrincourt. Such a campaign, Lescarbot suggested, would also serve the French expansion into North America along the Saint Lawrence River already under way under the leadership of Poutrincourt's deputy, Samuel Champlain, recently returned from a successful military sortie on behalf of Indian allies of the French. Ironically, Lescarbot ended his call for evangelization with an evocation of Champlain and his Indian cohorts coming back from Iroquois (Mohawk) country with fifty scalps held aloft in triumph, along with more peaceful references: the recent conversion of 140 Souriquois (Membertou, Lescarbot noted, recently raised a large cross over his village) as well as the possibility of discovering the Northwest Passage across the continent to Asia. All this was to be realized by Poutrincourt, Champlain, and devoted priests such as Jessé Fléché and other presumably secular or amenable religious, who would be sent over by the queen regent to labor alongside the trading company headed by Poutrincourt. Needless to say, no Jesuits need apply! Lescarbot almost said as much, given the ambition of his pamphlet to offset the efforts of the marquise de Guercheville and her associates to have the Society of Jesus sent to New France. Like many of his fellow humanists, Lescarbot had no love for the Society and in 1614 would be briefly imprisoned on charges of writing an anonymous anti-Jesuit pamphlet.

Persuaded by the marquise de Guercheville and her friends, and by the Jesuits themselves, who informed the queen regent that her late husband the king had previously promised the Society an assignment to New France, the queen regent authorized a Jesuit mission. Jesuit Pierre Biard, formerly a professor of theology at the College of Lyon, had already been assigned and had been waiting for two years for matters to be finalized. In September 1610 a second Jesuit, Enemond Massé, an associate of Pierre Coton, confessor to Henri IV, and himself the confessor of the marquise de Guercheville, was also assigned to the Acadian mission. Reaching Dieppe in late October 1610, whence they expected to take passage for Acadia on the *Grâce de Dieu*, still under the command of Poutrincourt's son Charles—who now held the grand title *Vice Admiral en la Mer du Ponant* (Vice Admiral of the Sea of the Setting Sun)—the Jesuits ran into a serious delay when the two leading investors refused to fund the rerigging of the *Grâce de Dieu* if the ship were to be used to transport Jesuits. Any other Catholic order was fine, the Huguenot merchants declared, but they would not support members of an order dedicated to an ongoing anti-Protestant campaign! Historians debate whether this prohibition was fully sincere: courageously made, that is, on grounds of religious aggrievement, to the point of defying the queen regent, who ordered the Huguenots to receive the Jesuits aboard ship, which they refused to do. Or was this refusal a calculated stratagem? What the merchants may have been hoping for actually occurred, when the marquise de Guercheville raised the 4,000 livres necessary to purchase the cargo scheduled for the *Grâce de Dieu* and pay for the rerigging. Finding herself involved in an anti-Jesuit enterprise as well as being owed 3,800 livres by hostile investors, the marquise de Guercheville assigned ownership of this debt to the Jesuits. She also assigned to them the management of the extensive property rights on the Atlantic coast she had negotiated with the friendly Huguenot Pierre Du Gua, sieur de Monts. The Jesuits thus became limited partners in a Huguenot-dominated company.

Even prior to departure on 26 January 1611 on its four-month voyage to New France, however, this venture seemed doomed to failure for the Jesuits despite (or because of?) the concessions the marquise de Guercheville had negotiated on their behalf. Not only were the financial arrangements heavily tilted in favor of Poutrincourt and his investors, but also—and more fundamentally—the two Jesuits inevitably faced hostility when they reached Port-Royal. Its official monopoly not-withstanding, Poutrincourt's company was losing out to illegal Huguenot traders operating out of La Rochelle and Saint-Malo. Sagging revenues and inadequate supply forced Poutrincourt to return to France to seek further investment, leaving his son in charge. Poutrincourt took the priest Fléché with him back to France for public relations purposes. (Fléché never returned to toil in the Acadian vineyard in which he allegedly had had such success.) Once again, the marquise de Guercheville came to the rescue and assigned 3,000 livres to Jesuit lay brother Gilbert Du Thet to refinance the venture. Du Thet spent some 1,200 livres outfitting a return expedition. He and Jesuit Father Jacques Quentin sailed with the company and arrived at Port-Royal on 26 January 1612.

At Port-Royal, matters went from bad to worse. When Du Thet questioned the bookkeeping of company agent Simon Imbert, the agent accused him of making remarks on the voyage from France in favor of the regicide of Henri IV by right-wing Catholic extremist François Ravaillac. Investigating the matter, Charles de Biencourt cleared Du Thet. Hard feelings continued to grow, however, building upon the bookkeeping dispute, the charges against Du Thet, and the Jesuits' refusal to baptize Indians at the rate that Jessé Fléché—for propaganda purposes—was call-ing for back in France, insisting instead on a long period of instruction before doing so. Such teaching required the Jesuits' mastery of the local language, with which Father Biard in particular had difficulty, causing even further delay. Biard also refused to allow Membertou to be buried with a Catholic ceremony because his ancestral burial site was not consecrated ground.

When Biard and Du Thet secretly boarded a departing ship to return to France to report on the state of affairs in Port-Royal, Biencourt had them forcibly removed and placed under arrest. Biard, in turn, issued a sentence of excommunication. An uneasy peace was eventually reached, but as an evangelical effort, the Jesuit mission to Acadia was in shambles. The Jesuits withdrew from active ministry and said their Masses in private.

When Du Thet reached France in October 1612, he informed the marquise of how the Jesuits were faring. (Biencourt had refused to allow the Jesuits to post letters to their patron.) The marquise broke off all dealings with Poutrincourt and financed—for the third time!—another iteration of the project: the separate Jesuit mission (and future trading company) of Saint-Sauveur, initially planned for a site near present-day Bangor, Maine, but relocated to the coast opposite Mount Desert Island when the pilot of the *Jonas* refused to voyage into unknown waters.

Again, matters went from bad to worse. While building was under way, an English reconnaissance expedition commanded by Captain Samuel Argall, a member of the Council of Virginia, happened upon the anchored *Jonas* and its crew on shore. When the English *Treasurer* bore down on the *Jonas*, Du Thet, taking the place of the absent gunner, manned the ship's cannon and fired one round in its direction. Du Thet missed, but an English sharpshooter did not, and the intrepid Jesuit fell mortally wounded. Landing, the English torched the French fortress under construction as an incursion into English territory. Captain Argall allowed Father Massé to leave with a group of Frenchmen, but he took Fathers Biard and Quentin and six other prisoners back to Virginia with him after sacking the French settlements at Saint Croix and Port-Royal and, upon his return from this sortie, further destroying Saint-Sauveur. In Virginia, the Jesuits barely escaped hanging. From there—after numerous misadventures—they were eventually returned to England and released into French custody.

The Recollect years

Thus, rather ignominiously, ended the first Jesuit venture into New France. Witnessing this debacle, Samuel Champlain went to work recruiting the Recollects, who arrived in Quebec in 1615. Had the Jesuit mission been successful, a large, powerful, and decidedly anti-Protestant order would have gained a foothold in New France and risen to control religious practice earlier than actually happened, at midcentury. As it was, the Catholic temperament of New France—despite the fall of Poutrincourt, Port-Royal, and all they stood for—remained oriented toward the more accommodating ecumenical Catholic Revival, which paralleled the prevailing mood in France itself. While the Jesuits embodied the centralizing, re-Romanizing energies of the Counter-Reformation, the Recollects arose from an earlier tradition of decentralized reform that fostered prayer, contemplation, and asceticism as well as missionary outreach. Wealthy, well-connected, and highly educated, Jesuits saw themselves acting on a world stage. Recollects had no such ambitions. By definition, they were a more modest order.

Sixteen Recollect priests and six lay brothers served in New France between 1615 and 1629, when English privateers seized Quebec and expelled all Catholic clergy. Recollects served both as missionaries and as parish clergy—celebrating Mass, hearing confessions, baptizing, witnessing marriages, catechizing children, and presiding at funerals—in a colony devoid of diocesan organization. Recollect priest Nicolas Viel arrived in 1623 and was murdered two years later by Indians he trusted. Viel sailed to New France in the company of the Recollect best remembered by history: the lay brother explorer, missionary, historian, and anthropologist Gabriel Sagard, who previously had served in Paris as private secretary to Recollect provincial Polycarpe Du Fay. Sagard had wanted to join the first Recollect levy in 1614 but had to wait until 1623, when he was released by his provincial to accompany Father Viel to Quebec. The two newly arrived Recollects took up residence a mile and a half inland at a site on the banks of the Saint Charles, a small tributary, where, with the help of hired artisans, Father Jamet had supervised the construction of Notre-Dame-des-Anges (Our Lady of the Angels), a serviceable priory of wood and stone. On the adjacent farm, the Recollects were pioneering agriculture, poultry (chickens, ducks, and geese) and egg production, pig raising, and livestock development, beginning with two donkeys delivered from France that initially terrorized local Indians with their truculent braying.

All this Sagard would later describe in detail and with good humor. Here at Notre-Dame-des-Anges he might have stayed, a friar farmer in a gray robe and wooden-soled sandals, serving the development of the colony. But Sagard had missionary and exploratory ambitions. While in Paris, he had studied a manuscript dictionary of the Huron language prepared and brought back to France by Recollect missionary Joseph Le Caron in 1616 when he temporarily returned to recruit more missionaries.

On 16 July 1623 Sagard left Notre-Dame-des-Anges and joined a group of French traders heading up the Saint Lawrence to acquire furs from the Huron at Cap-de-la-Victoire at the mouth of the Rivières des Iroquois, soon to be renamed the Rivière Richelieu. By 20 August, after an arduous journey later reported in full detail, Gabriel Sagard was standing on the shores of a vast inland sea to the east (Lake Huron), named the Lake of the Attigouautan by Champlain in honor of the Bear Clan of the Huron in the summer of 1615, when Champlain was on campaign against the Onondaga of the Iroquois League and hoping at the same time to find a water route across the continent.

Sagard spent the better part of a year in this region, initially on his own and then later joined by Fathers Viel and Le Caron. The three Recollects built a convent in the lodge style of the Huron near the village of Carhagouha. During his time at Carhagouha, Sagard continued to study the Huron language, marveling at its flexibility and capacity for rapid development, such that Huron barely two generations apart had trouble understanding each other. As with Notre-Dame-des-Anges, this Recollect convent on the shores of Lake Huron might have proven Sagard's destiny. Those ten months, in fact, constituted an idyll of sorts, filled with hope for a growing connection between the Huron and the Recollects.

True, Sagard admitted, the Huron could be thievish and promiscuous, but the nearby French traders (to whom the friars also ministered as best they could)—lying about all day, getting drunk when they had the chance, consorting with Indian women at every opportunity—were hardly models of Christian probity. And, true, the Huron cruelly tortured their prisoners. But note, Sagard urged, that the Hurons loved their children and treated their elders with respect. They were a good-looking people, moreover, tall and muscular (Champlain noted the same), and were at their most attractive when displaying their gifts for hunting, fishing, canoeing, and singing communally. Most important, some of them seemed genuinely interested in Christianity. Given proper support from France, the Recollects might very well achieve a Catholic Huronia.

Married life and family formation

As the Recollects were achieving this fragile but ultimately prophetic connection with the Huron, another development of religious importance was under way: the beginnings of married family life among the French in Quebec as exemplified by Louis and Marie Hébert. Apothecary Louis Hébert, the son of a Paris apothecary in the service of Queen Catherine de Médicis, was connected by marriage to the Sieur de Poutrincourt, who had married the niece of Hébert's wife, Marie Rollet. This distant connection by marriage helps explain Hébert's presence in Port-Royal in 1606–1607. Like his patron Poutrincourt, Hébert dreamed of establishing his family in New France. For Hébert, this involved a hope of rising beyond his social position as an apothecary—the first rung in the medical practice of that era and well into the nineteenth century—through the acquisition of land and, eventually, a fiefdom and title of *sieur*.

Aside from being an adept healer and brave campaigner, Hébert won Champlain's and Lescarbot's praises for his skills as an agriculturalist in his first one-year tenure at Port-Royal. In the fall of 1602, Hébert accompanied Poutrincourt back to France on the *Jonas*, intending to help his wife's nephew-in-law win a second monopoly. In 1610 Hébert returned to Port-Royal with his patron. The English destruction of Port-Royal in November 1613 forced Hébert to return to Paris, where he rejoined his wife, two daughters, and a son at the family home and garden.

Four years later, persuaded this time by Champlain—who promised Hébert a salary of 200 crowns a year for his services as an apothecary in addition to land grants for agricultural development—the entire Hébert family emigrated to Quebec. Even before they set sail, however, investors cut in half the salary and grants Champlain had promised. But the apothecary, now in his early forties, refused to renounce his chance for a better life in New France and went ahead with his plans.

Settled in Quebec, Hébert established a medical practice, planted grain and vegetables, built a home of wood and stone on the edge of a high cliff (the first private household in Quebec), and raised cattle in a field on an even higher promontory, later designated the Plains of Abraham. Treating Europeans and Indians alike in his medical practice—indeed, insisting on the dignity and worth of Indian people—setting a model of sustained agriculture, establishing his family in a well-built house that presaged a future city: it is difficult to exaggerate the importance of Louis Hébert, his wife, and their children as pioneers and prototypes of Quebec in its initial phases of development when almost everything done rightly or wrongly possessed prophetic value.

Given their Catholic faith and shared interest in agricultural development, the Héberts formed a strong attachment to the Recollects. In 1618 the legendary Father Le Caron witnessed the marriage of Anne, the eldest Hébert daughter, to Etienne Jonquet. Tragically, Anne died the following year in childbirth. Although documentation remains inconclusive, the child is thought to have survived. A pattern of migration, marriage, and family had thus been established. The Héberts had entered a third generation, foreshadowing a future people, the Quebecois. Anne's younger sister Guillemette would soon marry and bear ten children. By the time of her death in 1684, she would have more than 250 descendants.

Another kind of union

In the summer of 1620, a very different but equally prophetic married couple, Samuel and Hélène Champlain, took up residence in the citadel of Quebec. Although such marriages were common among nobility and haute bourgeoisie, and their marriage contract (again, as was often the case) called for a two-year delay before cohabitation, there is something disquieting from a contemporary point of view regarding the marriage in December 1610 of Samuel Champlain, age forty or so, and Hélène Boullé, age twelve, at the Church of Saint-Germain-l'Auxerrois in Paris. Even for the year 1610, twelve seems shockingly young. This particular child bride, in any event, was "bitterly unhappy" with the marriage, "in a fury about her fate", according to biographer David Hackett Fischer, who usually finds no fault with Champlain. For his part, Champlain showed indifference to "the child who was forced to marry him against her will".[1]

This arranged marriage was obviously valuable to Champlain, as it linked him with a recently Huguenot haut bourgeois family of wealth and court connections. Nicolas Boullé, Champlain's father-in-law, had served Henri IV as a key civil servant in matters both financial and administrative and had married one of his daughters to an equally important civil servant on the staff of the prince of Condé. That Champlain held the title of royal geographer and had enjoyed a personal relationship with the late Henri IV—he had such ease of access, in fact, that there was (and remains) a suspicion that Henri IV was Champlain's biological father—and was himself a civil servant of sorts in Canadian affairs perhaps helped make Champlain acceptable as a son-in-law. He had also served alongside two of Hélène's brothers: Nicolas in Brittany in the mid-1590s and her younger brother Eustache more recently in Acadia and the Saint Lawrence valley. Nicolas Boullé paid Champlain a generous dowry of 6,000 livres—4,500 of it up front—rendering Champlain a wealthy man.

Since Champlain rarely mentions his personal life in his extensive writings, little is known of it beyond what is revealed in a surviving documentation of betrothal, marriage, property arrangements, and bequests. And yet the Quebec sojourn of Hélène Boullé de Champlain from 1620 to 1624 resonates to this day alongside the parallel experiences of the Hébert family with a power that edges into foundational myth. Because this imaginative resonance lies outside documentation, professional historians are reluctant to pay it much heed. Writers of a more literary orientation, however, exhibit less caution. Even David Hackett Fischer, the master academic biographer of Champlain, cannot resist edging into speculation.

First and foremost, Fischer notes that the Champlains had no children, which leads to the possibility that the marriage was never consummated. Such a theory makes sense in psychological terms—disparity in their ages, Hélène's lack of initial consent—and can be supplemented with a religious factor. Their relationship may have been unconsummated on a mutually voluntary basis. Such marriages had a place—a restricted place, to be sure—among privileged dévots of the upper classes during the Catholic Revival of the seventeenth century. Pious widows of means, who had enjoyed a special status since apostolic times, frequently remained single. Furthermore, young women of established families, especially younger daughters, often entered convents due to family pressure. Some entered willingly. Throughout her life, Hélène Boullé, a convert to Catholicism, openly expressed her desire to become a nun. It is not inconceivable, then, that Champlain honored her wishes and voluntarily assented to a platonic relationship.

Hélène Boullé de Champlain arrived in Quebec in the summer of 1620 as a somewhat reluctant sojourner, a married woman of means attended by maids and retainers, the wife of the most important man in the colony. Yet she was a dévot as well, living a nun's life fifteen years before her husband's death. A mix of privilege,

personal beauty, and nunlike service to others in a society woefully scarce of French
women animates the frequently romanticized narratives of Hélène Champlain, in
which she is cast as a gracious presence, bringing comfort and support to Indian residents in and near the settlement; her acts of mercy prefigured those of the Ursuline
and Hospitaller Sisters who would soon arrive. In these stories—most likely based
in fact—the First Lady of Quebec shows a special regard for Indian girls. Attaching
a small hand mirror to her cincture, she would hold it before their eyes, telling them
(and their parents) to look into the mirror, which they loved doing, to see who was
in her heart.

Madame Champlain certainly stood in complementary contrast to the robust
and conjugally fulfilled presence of Marie Rollet Hébert, busy with her family,
her farm, her stone home on the hill. The contrast was even greater in the years
to come with the Héberts' daughter Guillemette, married in 1618 to Guillaume
Couillard in a ceremony presided over by Recollect Father Le Caron. Guillemette
bore ten children; and to this exuberant, overflowing household she and her husband added Oliver Le Jeune, a black boy brought to Quebec by the English as a
slave from Madagascar, then released to the French. Two Indian girls also joined the
Couillard household, Charité and Espérance (Charity and Hope), children Champlain had adopted and unsuccessfully tried to take back to France following the
seizure of Quebec by the English in 1629. Guillemette Hébert Couillard was as
devotedly and efficaciously Catholic as Madame Champlain. As wife and mother,
she served as a precursor to the 770 or so *filles du roi* (daughters of the king) from
greater Paris, Normandy, and other central-western regions who, between 1663
and 1673, accepted royal dowries and passage to North America in order to marry
men—of their free will, it was insisted!—and raise up for France and the Church a
new Catholic people.

Richelieu, Razilly, and the Malta perspective

The France to which Samuel and Hélène Champlain returned on the first day of
October 1624 was entering the first of two decades in which the king's first minister, Armand Jean du Plessis Cardinal de Richelieu (1585–1652), exercised supreme
political authority. Ever since Alexandre Dumas presented Richelieu in *The Three
Musketeers* (1844) as a sinister, largely offstage presence, historians, biographers,
novelists, playwrights, directors, and actors alike have felt challenged to capture
the compelling paradoxes and legendary career of this all-powerful Prince of the
Church. Richelieu had been en route to a military career when his older brother
entered a Carthusian monastery and voluntarily took himself out of the running to
be named bishop of Luçon, forcing the younger Armand to abandon his military
hopes, take holy orders, and, at the age of twenty-two, be consecrated bishop of
Luçon, a diocese bequeathed to his family by King Henry III. As bishop, Richelieu proved himself an orthodox and reforming prelate. He rebuilt his cathedral,
founded a seminary, and wrote instructional manuals. As first minister, he devoted
himself with equal fervor to the creation of absolute monarchy as the highest
embodiment of the state and to the primacy of France as a European power. An
aristocrat born to lesser but influential nobility, the cardinal brought the higher
nobility to heel, sending some of their most illustrious leaders to the scaffold when

they rebelled against the king. Tolerant of the Huguenots' right to religious practice, he nevertheless took to the field as military commander when the Huguenot
nobility rose up against the monarchy and laid siege to their fortress city of La
Rochelle. Resplendent in his scarlet robes of office, Richelieu defied the Vatican
when it was to the advantage of France and, even more dramatically, fought wars
alongside Protestant powers—the Dutch, the Danes, the Swedes—when it suited
French purposes.

   Richelieu lived simply, yet he was obsessed with money and grew rich in office.
He lavished those funds on his beloved niece, who ran his household and for whom
he secured promotion into the higher nobility as the duchesse d'Aiguillon. Perhaps
the only person truly close to him other than his niece was his advisor and confidant,
François Leclerc du Tremblay, a Capuchin Franciscan friar known as Father Joseph
of Paris following his entrance into the order or, more informally, as the *éminence
grise* (gray eminence) to Richelieu's *éminence rouge* (scarlet eminence) because of the
contrasting colors of their robes and their shared exercise of Richelieu's power as
cardinal (His Eminence) and first minister of state. Like Richelieu, Father Joseph
was of noble descent and a student at the University of Paris heading for a military
career before he entered the Capuchins, the most extensive and powerful order of
reformed Franciscans in France at the time, so named because of the long pointed
hood (*capuche*) attached to their habit, which they believed reflected the *cappuccino*
worn by Saint Francis of Assisi.

   New France remained of tertiary importance to Richelieu, given the great game
he was playing on behalf of France as an absolute monarchy internally and as a
power in Europe. Still, he was the ranking ecclesiastic in France; some suspected he
wanted to create an autonomous Gallican patriarchy with himself as patriarch. Furthermore, he never left his military identity behind, having gained firsthand experience in war leading troops against Huguenot rebels. In addition, he possessed an
understanding of sea power and established France in this field as well, to the point
of being remembered in years to come as founder of the French navy. He also,
finally, was an impossible snob regarding nobility of descent, a characteristic he
shared with his era. Money, investment, and profit; the exercise of royal authority;
the need for military power on land and sea; a dawning recognition of the vast-
ness of North America beyond Quebec, and hence continental ambitions; and a
sense of an overseas empire being assembled by France in Canada, the Caribbean,
Brazil, and North Africa: all this and more led Richelieu to concentrate, however
briefly, on New France. As of October 1626, moreover, the cardinal held the additional title of grand master chief and general superintendent of the navigation and
commerce of France along with his earlier appointment as president of the Royal
Council and first minister of state.

   To clarify his thinking, Richelieu sought out the chevalier Isaac de Razilly,
Knight of Malta, and requested an *aide-mémoire* (administrative memorandum) on
the present condition and future prospects of French efforts at overseas trade and
settlement. In turning to Razilly, Richelieu was availing himself of one of his
own: a member of the nobility, first of all, and an experienced naval captain with
an outstanding combat record as a squadron commodore in the recent seizure
of La Rochelle, blocking English intervention by sea and hence preventing any
form of resupply. An explosion aboard his flagship had cost Razilly an eye, yet the

black eye patch he wore as a result, like the eight-pointed Cross of Malta on his tunic, only added to his air of distinction. Like Richelieu, Razilly had entered the Church as a young man, in his case in the Order of Malta, and remained a professed knight under vows in this military brotherhood throughout his life. Razilly's 1626 aide-mémoire for Richelieu constituted nothing less than a founding text for an overseas French imperium written by a naval captain who was also a member of an order whose European estates, priories, hospitals, and maritime bases constituted an empire of long standing. If all this were not enough, Razilly had a personal background in empire-building: in Brazil, where he and his brothers had in 1612 helped the Capuchins establish a mission on the Amazon and, following the failure of that venture, in New France, where Razilly had come to know and admire Champlain.

The Crown, the chevalier de Razilly advised Richelieu, should establish trading settlements in Africa (Guinea and Senegal), South Asia, the East Indies, and South America, plus an even more ambitious populated colony in New France. State-sanctioned companies assisted by naval support and protected by military garrisons should be formed to administer commercial operations. In the case of New France, a state-sponsored company capitalized at 300,000 livres would be required. Some four thousand colonists would be necessary to hold this region against English invasion. Given the friendship between Razilly and Champlain, it is not far-fetched to discern Champlain's vision—as well as that of Razilly, inspired by the Order of Malta—in this influential document. Foreign trade, both men were arguing, was not a sideshow but the main event when it came to royal revenues. The king of Spain, Razilly pointed out, who once had languished on the revenues of a few orange and lemon groves in his home kingdom, now enjoyed the limitless revenues of overseas empire. Trade, moreover, led to settlement, and settlement made possible the evangelization of indigenous peoples.

Acting on Razilly's memorandum, Richelieu in 1627 canceled the monopoly of the Huguenot merchants William de Caën and his nephew Émery and organized in its place the Company of New France, also known as the Company of One Hundred Associates, and, purchasing the title from the duc de Montmorency and his nephew the duc de Ventadour, abolished the office of viceroy of New France. On behalf of his young king, the cardinal now ruled absolutely in both France and New France.

The Counter-Reformation takes hold

In these and other developments, the 1620s witnessed a resurfacing of animosity between Catholics and Huguenots, followed by open rebellion. Thus ended the fragile détente animated by mutual self-interest and a shared Christian humanism that had run as a shallow but persistent subterranean stream during the first two decades of New France. Henri IV embodied the polarities and contradictions not only of the Wars of Religion but also of the uneasy peace he brought to France. His Edict of Nantes (1593) had allowed for Huguenot hegemony in some two hundred towns, along with the survival of a restive Huguenot nobility, a rising bourgeoisie of merchants and investors with pan-European ties, and an equally rising artisan class: Protestant culture, in short, formed by Calvinist theology, Presbyterian polity, and capitalist entrepreneurialism. Protestant values must have played a role in Henri IV's pioneering efforts to modernize the royal administration, promote agriculture and public works, and lay down the tentative beginnings of overseas trade now being reformulated by Razilly and retaken up by Richelieu. The success of the Huguenot regions also inflamed far-right members of the Catholic League, and one such zealot, François Ravaillac, stabbed Henri IV to death when the king's carriage became stalled in a traffic jam on the rue de la Ferronnerie during coronation ceremonies for Marie de Médicis.

Richelieu rose to power thanks to the queen regent, and he was not noticeably anti-Huguenot in his early years of authority, although he did compose a defense of Catholicism and a catechism during a two-year exile from the royal court. That ended in 1619 when, due in part to Father Joseph's efforts, he was recalled to court and reinstated in the favor of the queen regent. Richelieu helped reconcile the regent with her son Louis XIII, and for this and other services he was created cardinal in 1622 and named president of the Council of Ministers two years later. When the Huguenot nobility rebelled in 1621, protesting the enforced introduction of Catholicism in the city of Béarn, Richelieu directed a two-year campaign against a Huguenot league and, upon victory, left the Edict of Nantes in place but revoked the Huguenots' permission to maintain self-governing fortified towns, with the exception of Montauban and La Rochelle. When the Protestant nobility rose up again in 1624 and yet once more in 1627, Richelieu the soldier—splendid in gleaming armor and scarlet cloak—personally led the suppression of the rebellions, stripping Montauban and La Rochelle of their autonomy.

All this ferment occurred as the cardinal was formulating plans for overseas commerce, fortified trading centers, naval development, and the civilian settlement of New France. The newly established Company of New France was limited to Catholic investors, which shifted the center of investment in French North America from the Huguenot cities and a dispersed Huguenot elite to Catholic Paris and the cardinal's trusted associates. Richelieu also set a policy that Huguenots could not invest in New France, nor could they go there to trade or settle. Huguenots were thus excluded from a newly strengthened seigneurial system. The Counter-Reformation was arriving in France and New France alike.

The return of the Jesuits

The Recollects, meanwhile, were facing the fact that their order of reformed Franciscans did not possess the financial resources or the manpower necessary to meet the challenges of New France. Between 1615 and 1625, only sixteen Recollects arrived for service. By 1629 their count totaled twenty-two, sixteen priests and six lay brothers. But what was this number in so vast a region? As the Recollects were pondering this question, a highly placed Jesuit by the name of Philibert Noyrot was influencing the outcome of this Recollect debate.

Jesuits made a specialty of serving as confessors and spiritual directors to the noble and wealthy or to others strategically placed in the stratified society of the early modern era. In 1624 Noyrot assumed such a position in the household of the triply titled Henri de Lévis, duc de Ventadour, prince de Maubuisson, and comte de la Voulte. Father Noyrot's task most likely involved more spiritual direction than confession of sins, for the twenty-seven-year-old Ventadour (a veteran of recent campaigns against the Huguenots) showed strong signs of a Counter-Reformational piety that would eventually lead him to the priesthood. Ventadour's wife, the heiress Marie Liesse de Luxembourg, evinced a similar faith and inclination to the life of a religious under vows. The couple agreed not to consummate their marriage and to devote their lives to prayer and good works. Marie was eight and her future husband twenty-three when they were engaged; she was twelve and he twenty-seven on their wedding day. Aside from a shared piety, the two may have experienced a somewhat incestuous barrier to their relationship. Ventadour's mother had raised Marie in the Ventadour household following the death of Marie's parents, and so she was like a younger sister to her much older husband. Hence the duc and his wife were dévots of the most intense sort: upper-class laity pursuing lives of Counter-Reformational devotion and ascetical practice.

As confessor and spiritual director of the religiously ardent young nobleman, Father Noyrot had every opportunity to influence the thoughts and actions of this gentleman en route to the priesthood. Thus, regarding the desire of the Society of Jesus to return to New France, matters soon fell into place. With Cardinal Richelieu increasingly in charge of all matters of state, including New France, the viceroy of New France, Henri II duc de Montmorency, the governor of Languedoc, decided (with Richelieu's encouragement) to refocus his energies on governing his province and to cede the viceroyalty to his nephew Ventadour for a consideration of 100,000 livres. As viceroy-to-be before Richelieu purchased and abolished the office, Ventadour requested that the Recollects obtain the assistance of the Society of Jesus in New France. This finagling was quickly settled during Noyrot's first year as Ventadour's confessor, and in April 1625 five Jesuits—the priests Charles Lalemant, superior; Enemond Massé, veteran of the failed effort in Acadia; and the stalwart Norman nobleman Jean de Brébeuf; and two temporal coadjutors, lay brothers François Charton and Gilbert Burel—sailed from Dieppe for Quebec. They arrived there in June, and the Recollects offered them shelter in their nearby stone convent on the banks of the Saint Charles River until they were able to establish themselves. The next year, in July 1626, Noyrot himself arrived, bringing with him an impressive force of twenty artisans and assorted workmen for the construction of a Jesuit chapel, residence, and college.

In the year between the arrival of Lalemant's party and the arrival of Noyrot and his workmen, the superior and his two priestly colleagues had become convinced—by what might be termed a Counter-Reformational point of view—that the two-decade-long alignment of Catholic and Huguenot interests in New France was no longer viable. Even as their ship reached Quebec on 15 June 1625, the Jesuits were initially refused permission to land by the Huguenot acting governor of the settlement, Émery de Caën, standing in for Champlain (who was then in France), on the trumped-up claim that he had received no official word of their arrival. Only by the intervention of the Recollects, who enjoyed official status in the Huguenot-controlled Caën company and the Catholic company directed by Montmorency and Champlain, was the issue resolved, and Émery de Caën released the Jesuits into Recollect custody at the Recollect convent of Saint Charles until the matter could be clarified. That September, Montmorency officially granted the Jesuits a tract of land, where they began to develop a farm, a residence, and a chapel.

A reconnaissance to Huron country

Nor did Lalemant neglect the missionary future. Four months following the arrival of the Jesuits in Quebec, Lalemant sent Jean de Brébeuf on a five-month trek into the interior in the company of a group of Montagnais living near the settlement. Traveling by canoe, portage, and snowshoes, Brébeuf underwent an ordeal of physical hardship, enduring constant exhaustion, execrable food, and surly traveling companions who spoke in an impenetrable tongue; yet he experienced as well moments of beauty and imaginative release amid rivers and forests while an autumn of varied color and bright skies crowded with birds in migration yielded to snow-shrouded trees and the empty iron-gray firmament of winter. These challenging months constituted an apprenticeship, a sort of military-style basic training, for the priest. Despite great height and physique inherited from his Norman ancestors who had long ago accompanied William the Conqueror into battle, Brébeuf had suffered a period of incapacitating illness prior to his ordination that required a three-year assignment as steward at the Collège of Rouen to allow him to recover before embarking upon the missionary assignment to New France that was his preference. On behalf of the Jesuits' return to New France, Brébeuf and other younger French Jesuits inspired by Pierre Coton, confessor to Henri IV, formed a league of prayer, pledging themselves—these talented, well-educated junior members of the Society, who might have remained in France in teaching or pastoral assignments—to the hardships of a missionary career.

No sooner had Brébeuf returned in March 1626 than Lalemant sent him and a newly arrived Jesuit named Anne de Noüe on a second, even more arduous expedition into Huron country in the company of Recollect Bonaventure de la Roche-d'Aillon, another new arrival. Like Brébeuf, Noüe was of noble birth and in his youth had served as a page in the court of Henri IV (where he was admired for his good looks), followed by a promotion to officer of the Privy Chamber, a rarefied and privileged position. Noüe wintered with Brébeuf in Huron country but returned in the spring to Quebec, where he lived among the Montagnais and unsuccessfully tried to learn their language and adjust to their way of life. Brébeuf, by contrast, remained among the Huron and thrived. In July 1626, having progressed in his language studies, he embarked upon an 800-mile reconnaissance by canoe and portage across the rivers and lakes of Huron country and beyond that to the Great Lakes. Brébeuf's journey constituted a prologue to four decades of missionary-driven exploration by French Jesuits in North America.

A disruption of previous accord

In the meantime, Jesuit superior Lalemant was painfully experiencing the breakdown of the Catholic-Huguenot détente among the French, both in Canada and in the homeland. The rift was part of a pan-European pattern; as the Thirty Years' War raged in Europe, Huguenot resistance to Catholic royalism resurfaced in France itself, and competition between Catholic France and Protestant England—on the continent and in North America alike—edged into open warfare. For the Jesuits, tensions began on the voyage to New France as the Huguenot crews of the Caën company ships sang psalms while they worked or held aggressively Calvinist services on Sundays on the main deck. Then came Émery de Caën's attempt to prevent the Jesuits from landing in Quebec. Once ashore, the Jesuits had to contend with the persistent underground circulation of the virulently anti-Jesuit publication *Anti-Coton*, which accused Father Pierre Coton, former confessor to Henri IV and now provincial of French Jesuits, of helping to organize the king's assassination in 1610 as well as other nefarious activities on behalf of the Catholic League. A product of mixed Huguenot, Catholic, and humanist influences himself, Samuel Champlain had previously defended the Huguenot sailors' right to sing Protestant hymns as they worked ships on the Saint Lawrence. Yet even the usually tolerant Champlain found the *Anti-Coton* polemic disruptive and ordered it burned. His order was to no avail: such a pamphlet had a life beyond its physical survival. Suspicions and animosities ran high. Marc Lescarbot, the founding historian of New France and the epitome of a humanist accommodation between Catholic and Calvinist regarding the development of New France (as well as the friend and colleague of the anti-Jesuit sieur de Poutrincourt), was suspected of being the secret author of *Anti-Coton* and spent a brief stint behind bars as a result.

Lalemant was also disturbed by the failure of the Huguenot Caëns to support at least five Recollects, as called for in their contract, or to take any interest in the long-term growth of the colony beyond their preoccupation with making money in the fur trade. The Caëns, for their part, most likely viewed the future Quebec as a Catholic-dominated enterprise, so why bother? Perhaps even more troubling—precisely because it was dominated by Catholics—the Montmorency company seemed likewise obsessed with an immediate return on investment from the fur trade and appeared comparably indifferent to colonization and religious outreach.

At this point, the Jesuit superior decided upon a course of action. As soon as Father Noyrot arrived at Quebec with his workmen, Lalemant ordered him—after first seeking and receiving permission from Provincial Coton in Paris, of course—to return to France and use his excellent connections at court to lobby for a reorganization of the Canadian enterprise, including a revocation of the Edict of Nantes in terms of New France. Such a move would end Huguenot participation as investors, shippers, and on-the-ground participants in the fur trade.

Noyrot obtained a personal interview with Richelieu, who, swayed by the chevalier de Razilly's aide-mémoire and his own restiveness with the Huguenot nobility, was organizing the Company of New France to be limited to Catholic investors, and to whose monopoly contract was now added a prohibition of Huguenot involvement, including immigration to New France.

War and surrender

The Scots Calvinists currently occupying Port-Royal were neither impressed nor fazed by the cardinal's keep-out sign and remained determined to create Nova Scotia (New Scotland) on the North Atlantic coast. In 1621 Sir William Alexander, later Earl of Stirling, obtained a charter from King James VI of Scotland, concurrently sitting as King James I of England, to settle a Scottish colony on the Gaspé Peninsula northward into Acadia, despite claims and prior settlement by France in the region. After a first failed effort, the king, at Sir William's urging, added hereditary baronetcies to lands granted under charter, titles similar to the hereditary knighthoods he had created in 1611 to encourage English and Scots settlement in Ulster province, Northern Ireland. While few Scots were willing to pay Sir William the required sum—1,000 marks or 670 English pounds—to acquire *Sir* and a tract three by ten miles on the Atlantic coast, enough Scots had arrived by 1626 to seize control of Port-Royal. The Scots Calvinists' official hold on Port-Royal, along with the two further settlements they subsequently established, lasted only until 1632, when it was ended by treaty between France and England; yet for some six years Nova Scotia in its first phase (aside from leaving behind a remnant of Scots settlers and a regional name that would eventually prevail) asserted the possibility of an Ulster-style Protestant ascendancy in this previously French Catholic region, as well as a French-style importation of a titled British Protestant gentry into North America. Had a class of titled hereditary landowners been established in Nova Scotia and extended to the English colonies to the south, the American Revolution—had it happened at all—might have been less decisively republican.

In 1625, in an effort to create peace between France and England, Richelieu negotiated the marriage of Henrietta, sister of Louis XIII, to the young King Charles I. Instead of peace, however, a war broke out between the two realms that ended, temporarily, France's continental ambitions in North America as well as the Counter-Reformation brought there by the Jesuits. Richelieu delayed paying Henrietta's dowry, for one thing, given English support of the Huguenots, while in England, the new queen's entourage was so openly and aggressively Catholic that the ardently Anglican Charles sent most of her retainers back to France, with the exception of a few personal attendants.

Maritime conflict between the two nations escalated, with each nation seizing the shipping of the other on charges of smuggling or related offenses. In 1627 the Huguenot citadel of La Rochelle went into open rebellion, and an English fleet tried to come to its aid as the undeclared war between the two nations became official. With the encouragement and assistance of Nova Scotia founder Sir William Alexander, now secretary of state for Scotland, Charles I issued letters of marque against French shipping to New France to the large and influential Kirke family, which consisted of patriarch Jarvis Kirke, a longtime Dieppe-based merchant, and his five sons, one of whom, Sir David Kirke, would rise to governor of the English colony on Newfoundland. The letters of marque granted by Charles I, together with English efforts to relieve La Rochelle by sea, constituted a final attempt by Huguenot France to free itself from a Catholic crown. Flying the English flag, the armada assembled by the Kirkes comprised a large number of French Huguenot sailors, including its vice admiral, Jacques Michel.

At great effort and expense, the Company of New France assembled a flotilla of four ships carrying two hundred settlers and supplies. On 28 April 1628 the flotilla sailed from Dieppe for Quebec under the command of Claude Roquemont de Brison—a founder of the Company of New France and a member of Richelieu's inner circle—as part of a larger armada of fourteen ships bound for Newfoundland, where French, Portuguese, Basque, and English fishing vessels uneasily shared the North Atlantic waters. Two Jesuits, Paul Ragueneau and Charles Lalemant, sailed with the convoy. Jesuit Father Noyrot sailed in a separately chartered vessel. The previous year, Lalemant had returned to France to secure protected shipping for Jesuit supplies (the Caëns had already seized one shipment organized by Noyrot before it could be loaded from the docks at Honfleur) and to assist in arranging for this first wave of expanded settlement under the newly established and very Catholic Company of New France.

A colony lost and found

In Quebec, Champlain and his small band of settlers—fifty-five or so permanent residents, with a higher population during the trading season—eagerly awaited the newcomers' arrival and the supplies that would boost the French colony and the Recollect and Jesuit missions. This reinforcement, however, was not to appear. The English defeated the French convoy under the command of Roquemont in a fifteen-hour gun battle on the lower Saint Lawrence, and an English raiding party came up the river to the very palisades of Quebec and demanded surrender. Champlain refused, the raiding party left, and the ensuing winter of 1628–1629 plunged the colony into a long ordeal, bringing the settlers to the edge of starvation.

On 19 July 1629 the English force under the command of the Kirke brothers reappeared outside Quebec and again demanded surrender. This time, Champlain had no choice, although he insisted on dictating the terms of surrender. He also expressed his belief that if France and England were no longer at war, as was rumored, the English conquest of Quebec was illegal. (The war was over, and the conquest was illegal, but negotiations would last four years.) One of Champlain's conditions was safe passage back to France for Recollects and Jesuits. Outspoken even in defeat, Champlain denounced the Huguenots serving under the Kirkes, including his former subordinate Etienne Brulé, as traitors to France as well as blasphemers against true Christianity. Kirke's Huguenot vice admiral Jacques Michel took such offense at Champlain's remarks that he flew into a rage and died from stroke. Truly, the years of Catholic-Huguenot détente in French Canada had ended. Continental ambitions were transforming Quebec into a Protestant citadel.

But only temporarily. In March 1632 the Treaty of Saint Germain-en-Laye restored Acadia and the Saint Lawrence valley to France. Richelieu wanted the chevalier de Razilly to assume the governorship of the newly returned territories; but the experienced monk-warrior deferred in favor of Champlain, whom Razilly believed to be more qualified. The chevalier accepted a subordinate role in Acadia while Champlain returned to Quebec as lieutenant governor to Richelieu.

Richelieu gave the Society of Jesus exclusive control of missionary efforts in Huronia and elsewhere in the Saint Lawrence valley. Small contingents of Recollects and Capuchins were allowed to remain in ministry in Acadia, which did little to assuage the Recollects' sense of betrayal over their exclusion from the missionary territory they had pioneered. In recompense and protest, Gabriel Sagard brilliantly documented this Recollect effort in *Le grand voyage du pays des Hurons* (1632). Four years later, Sagard expanded his account into the more ambitious four-part *L'histoire du Canada*. Sagard opened the narrative with a chronicle of Recollect missionary efforts in the Holy Land, India, Tartary, Slavonia, Bulgaria, and China. He then traced Recollect efforts in Canada up to the year of surrender to the English. Sagard put the Recollect mission at the center of the entire evangelical enterprise, where— correctly, one can easily argue—he believed it belonged. The trading companies, Sagard complained, in which Huguenots heavily invested, had thwarted Recollect efforts in New France. Why banish the Recollects—who had shown such success in so many other mission fields—from the regions they had dramatically explored and evangelized?

With the publication of *Le grand voyage* and *L'histoire du Canada*, along with the pioneering *Dictionnaire de la langue huronne* (1636), based on an earlier work by Recollect Joseph Le Caron, with whom Sagard had sojourned in Huronia, Sagard disappears from the record. Did he grow tired of his job as amanuensis to the provincial, resign from the Recollects, and return to lay life? Or, filled with continuing zeal, did Sagard find another, more exacting outlet for his religiosity? No answer has surfaced as to the next great journey upon which this influential missionary embarked.

Restoring Acadia

The chevalier de Razilly, meanwhile, was leading an effort to restore and expand the French hold on Acadia on behalf of a newly formed Razilly-Condonnier company. In partnership with the Company of New France, Razilly and a group of investors operating as the Razilly-Condonnier trading company financed a colonizing expedition of more than three hundred settlers, including fifteen families and six Capuchin friars, who reached Acadia on 8 September 1632. The following three years—prior to Razilly's unexpected death in his late forties—witnessed a whirlwind of activity fully justifying Richelieu's and Champlain's confidence in the chevalier's leadership skills. Razilly's success further consolidated the link between New France and the Order of Malta. First up on the agenda was the construction of a habitation and associated structures at the port of La Hève: homes for families, dormitories for unmarried workmen, a chapel and residence for the Capuchins, and a hastily constructed Fort Sainte-Marie-de-Grâce for protection. Next: the retaking of Port-Royal from the English. The garrison commander surrendered peacefully upon being guaranteed safe passage home. Razilly later launched a similarly successful campaign against New Englanders occupying Fort Pentagouet on the Penobscot River and Bay in present-day Maine. Distributing settlers into strategically placed clusters, Razilly encouraged the development of farming, fishing, timbering, and fur trading. An experienced sea captain, he established Fort Sainte-Françoise to protect the port of Canseau and later put down a rebellion and seizure of the fort by Mi'kmaqs. Amid all these operations, the chevalier continued negotiations with the cardinal to request that the king finance five ships in Acadia to promote trade and defend against piracy. By the time of his death, Razilly had brought Acadia safely back into the French fold and in the process had helped launch a distinctive regional culture that would later be exported to yet another French province, Louisiana, on the southern shores of North America.

Death of the founder

As far as the reinvigoration of Catholicism in New France was concerned, the transformative event was the Jesuits' return to Quebec in 1632 under the leadership of Father Paul Le Jeune, a convert from Calvinism. Le Jeune formed a close friendship with Champlain, another former Huguenot, and most likely absorbed from him aspects of the comprehensive program of development that Le Jeune would advocate during his tenure as founding superior of the Society of Jesus in New France. Conversely, Le Jeune's influence as well as that of Champlain's Jesuit confessor, Charles Lalemant, is evident in the warm glow of Champlain's religiosity in these lion-in-winter years: his daily prayers and devotion to the Mass and other sacraments; his dining late each afternoon in Fort Saint Louis atop Quebec while *The Lives of the Saints* was read aloud, as if Champlain were himself a professed religious in cloister; his cherished conversations with Le Jeune on Canadian development and Catholic faith; his construction of the stone chapel Notre-Dame-de-la-Récouvrance on a high cliff overlooking the settlement, commemorating the recovery of New France by the French. As usual, Madame Champlain was absent from what by now had become a household characterized by a near-monastic observance; but such had been the case nearly all the years of their married life.

When the time came to make his will, Champlain's piety in these last years and his continuing plans for New France were evident in bequests to Notre-Dame-de-la-Récouvrance and the Society of Jesus as well as marriage dowries and cash gifts to families residing in the Saint Lawrence valley. To his wife, he left properties in France and his personal papers, which were subsequently lost. On Christmas Day 1635, a month following the death of his friend and covisionary, the chevalier Isaac de Razilly, in the Quebec he had founded twenty-seven years earlier, Samuel Champlain, after an illness of two and a half months, passed into eternity and history as Father Lalemant prayed at his bedside. In the midst of his final illness, Le Jeune later recorded, Champlain remained eager for the continuing development of New France and the conversion to Catholic Christianity of its indigenous peoples.

Three years after Champlain's death, his widow entered the Ursuline Convent of Faubourg Saint-Jacques in Paris as Sister Hélène de Saint-Agustin. While still a novice, she left Saint-Jacques to found a new Ursuline convent under strict rules of cloister in the city of Meaux. Her brother Eustache, a professional soldier who had long served with her late husband in New France, ended his days in Italy as a priest in the Order of Minims, a rigorously ascetic congregation inspired by Counter-Reformational ideals.

13

Ville-Marie (Montreal) 1642

Dévots found a city on the far frontier

Mid-May 1642 found Champlain's successor, the chevalier Charles Huault de Montmagny, Knight of Malta, sailing upriver by pinnace and barque in the company of Madame Marie-Madeleine de Chauvigny de La Peltrie, secular foundress of the Ursulines of Quebec, and her colleague and companion Mademoiselle Jeanne Mance, newly arrived from France. Since Champlain had served only as commandant in New France, reporting to Richelieu, who held the governorship, Montmagny was the first fully constituted resident governor of the colony. Others in the party included military officer Paul de Chomedey, sieur de Maisonneuve; Pierre de Puiseaux, sieur de Montrénault, a seventy-five-year-old veteran of the country and a landowner; Jesuit superior Barthélemy Vimont; and forty sailors, artisans, laborers, and soldiers, most of them recent arrivals from France.

The goal of this expedition was nothing less than the founding of a settlement on the Island of Mont Réal (Royal Mountain) at the navigable head of the Saint Lawrence River, just below the great rapids that prevented any further sailing upriver. Jacques Cartier had sojourned on the island in 1535, and Champlain had scouted it out for a settlement in 1611, but Mont Réal had remained little more than an occasional gathering place for the following thirty years as French settlement advanced up the Saint Lawrence through such developing places as Tadoussac (1600), Quebec (1608), and Trois-Rivières (1634), Champlain's final foundation. Puiseaux had settled in the area previously and, approaching retirement, was now prepared to donate his ownership rights in exchange for yet-to-be-determined land or cash or both, which was why he was accompanying the colonizing party.

On 18 May 1642 the members of the expedition dropped anchor off the Island of Montreal and went ashore. Father Vimont celebrated Mass on an improvised altar decorated with wildflowers by Madame de La Peltrie and Mademoiselle Mance. Following Mass, the Blessed Sacrament was left on the altar in a small monstrance as a sign that New France and its Catholic culture had begun a permanent sojourn in this hitherto-unsettled place. "Look, gentlemen," an early account has Father Vimont saying in his sermon that morning (did the good father forget the two ladies present?), "what you see is but a grain of mustard seed, but it is sown by hands so pious and so moved by the spirit of faith and piety that Heaven must doubtless have vast designs since it uses such workmen, and I have no doubt that this seed will grow into a great tree, one day to achieve wonders, to be multiplied and to spread to all parts."[1]

The colonists spent the spring and summer erecting a fortified settlement under the direction of the sieur de Maisonneuve, who commanded twenty soldiers and a comparable number of artisans and laborers now that the chevalier de Montmagny had returned to Quebec. Maisonneuve and his soldiers explored the immediate region and appropriated whatever supplies donor Puiseaux had previously left behind in his brief time as seigneur of the Island of Montreal. Madamoiselle Mance remained on as nurse and cofounder and, to the happiness of everyone, Sulpician historian François Dollier de Casson tells us, Madame de La Peltrie and the elderly Puiseaux remained on as well. As of yet, Dollier quickly adds, the settlement was undiscovered by hostile Iroquois.

In the fall, good news reached the outpost via Monsieur Pierre Legardeur de Repentigny, commander of the merchant fleet serving New France. On 2 February that year, Repentigny reported, the feast of the Presentation of Jesus in the Temple, at a ceremony held in the Cathedral of Notre-Dame in Paris, a gathering of influential and wealthy laity and clergy collectively known as the Société Notre-Dame de Montréal had reaffirmed its commitment to fostering the development of the French Catholic settlement now being established on the headwaters of the Saint Lawrence. The society, Repentigny continued, had presented him with 40,000 livres for supplies for the colony, which the experienced sea captain was delivering, along with several cannons for defense and a skilled carpenter and other workmen recruited by the society. A donor who refused to be identified, moreover, had pledged fifty to sixty thousand crowns for a hospital to be constructed in Montreal at a later date, to be staffed by Hospitaller Sisters of Saint Joseph, whose passage would be sponsored from France.

Reasons for support

How did this happen? Why was the Society of Our Lady of Montreal, so prestigious in its lay and clerical membership (even Anne of Austria, the queen regent, was a supporter), pledging to support a settlement on the far western frontier of New France, where the fierce and implacably hostile Iroquois operated freely?

First of all, the Jesuits were expanding their mission to New France and publishing vivid reports of their efforts there. Printed in France in book form each year until 1673, these *Jesuit Relations*, as they are cumulatively titled, were selected and edited letters and reports from the field that Jesuit missionaries in Canada were required to submit to the provincial in France. As such, they constituted an immediate source of inspiration. Over time, they accrued into an archive of history monumental in scope and ambition, documenting more than half a century of exploration, evangelization, and environmental and ethnographic reportage.

Second, spirituality among laity was gaining strength and becoming part of the Canadian venture. Women—including upper-class women of wealth as well as sisterhoods—were increasingly involved in religious affairs. Along with the upswing of an intensely Christocentric spirituality and a retheologizing and reform of the priesthood to which this lay movement was synergistically attached, the rise of dévots—lay men and women of education and means in pursuit of religious perfection—was a dramatic development of Catholic practice in seventeenth-century France. While the dévot movement remained coeducational, women

Ruins of Garðar on Erik's Fjord, Igaliku, Greenland. Erik the Red established an Eastern Settlement that would last for more than four hundred years. *© Cindy Hopkins/Alamy.*

Cape Spear, Newfoundland. Christianized Scandinavians attempted a settlement that did not last.
© Robert A. Metcalfe/Shutterstock.com.

ABOVE Theodor de Bry, *Group of Indigenous Men, Women, and Children Taken by Armed Westerners*, 1594. Forced into hard labor, the indigenous peoples of the Caribbean were threatened with extinction. *Rijksmuseum, Amsterdam, RP-P-BI-5272.*

LEFT *Bartolomé de Las Casas*, sixteenth century. The Dominican Bartolomé de Las Casas argued on behalf of the full humanity and fundamental rights of these abused peoples. *Biblioteca Capitular y Colombina de Sevilla. De Agostini Picture Library/Bridgeman Images.*

Trekking from Florida to Mexico City with three companions, Cabeza de Vaca experienced a pilgrimage of distance, duration, healing, and spiritual growth. *Photo by MPI/Hulton Fine Art Collection/Getty Images.*

The ruins of Mission Gran Quivira, New Mexico. The Kingdom of Quivira entered the consciousness of Spaniards as a distant dream of a fabled city awaiting conquest and evangelization. *© Efrain Padro/ Alamy.*

ABOVE W. Langdon Kihn, *Spanish Explorers Entering Hawikuh.* The brutal siege and conquest of the Tewa pueblos of New Mexico in 1540 cast a shadow across subsequent efforts to evangelize.
W. Langdon Kihn/National Geographic Creative.

LEFT Bartolomé Esteban Murillo, *Immaculate Conception of the Venerable Ones, or of Soult,* ca. 1678. Devotion to Mary as the perfected paradigm of humanity motivated Franciscan missionaries as they sought to atone for atrocities against indigenous peoples.
Prado, Madrid, Spain/Bridgeman Images.

The reconstructed Mission San Luis de Apalachee in Tallahassee, Florida, recalls an era that would end under English attacks from the Carolinas. *Courtesy of Mission San Luis, Florida Department of State.*

Theodor de Bry, *Timucua Indian Village, Food Transportation by Canoe.* The indigenous peoples of Florida—including the Timucua of the coast and the Apalachee of the panhandle—fiercely resisted encomienda, the Spanish system of forced labor. *© PRISMA ARCHIVO/Alamy.*

Castillo de San Marcos, Saint Augustine, Florida, was constructed under the encomienda system.
Victor R. Boswell Jr./National Geographic Creative.

Ácoma, New Mexico. The siege, massacre, and cruel punishment at Ácoma fueled an animosity between Spaniard and Indian that in time would result in the largest Indian uprising in North America.
© Josemaria Toscano/Shutterstock.com.

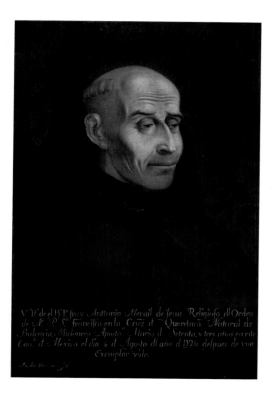

ABOVE Nicolas Enriquez, *Portrait of Fray Antonio Margil*, ca. 1770. The Texas pioneer Fray Antonio Margil de Jesús excelled as an explorer, a road builder, an architect, a mason, a carpenter—and a saintly missionary. *Collection Our Lady of the Lake University of San Antonio. Photo Peggy Tenison/ Courtesy of the San Antonio Museum of Art.*

ABOVE RIGHT Julian Martinez, *Eusebio Francisco Kino*, Wesley Bolin Memorial Plaza, Phoenix, Arizona. The Arizona pioneer and Jesuit missionary Eusebio Francisco Kino diversely excelled as an astronomer, an explorer, an agriculturalist, a horseman, a cattle rancher, a chronicler—and a tireless evangelizer. *Photo © Dennis MacDonald/Alamy.*

RIGHT Juan Miralles, *Antonio María de Bucareli*, 1962. Fray Antonio María de Bucareli, Knight of Malta and viceroy of New Spain, sponsored an entrada into Alta California and a maritime exploration of the Pacific coast. *Fray Junípero Serra Museum, Petra, Mallorca, Balearic Islands, Spain. © age fotostock/Alamy.*

Developed across a century, Mission San Xavier del Bac near Tucson, Arizona, remains an architectural jewel of the mission system extending from Florida to Southern California. © *Andrzej Gibasiewicz/Shutterstock.com.*

Alfredo Ramos Martínez, *Fray Junípero Serra*, ca. 1931. Fray Junípero Serra left a promising academic career on Majorca to labor in the missions of northern Mexico and Alta California. *California Historical Society/Gift of Albert M. Bender/ Bridgeman Images. © The Alfredo Ramos Martinez Research Project, reproduced by permission.*

Arthur F. Mathews, *Discovery of the Bay of San Francisco by Portola*, 1896. Spanish soldiers under the command of Gaspar de Portolá, governor of the Californias, chanced upon a great bay that would soon support the northernmost outpost of New Spain. *John H. Garzoli of Garzoli Gallery, San Rafael, California.*

Ferdinand Deppe, *San Gabriel Mission*, ca. 1832. Modeled on the cathedral of Córdoba, Spain, Mission San Gabriel Arcángel stood strategically on the edge of the San Gabriel Valley nine miles east of the enduring pueblo of Los Angeles. *Collection Laguna Art Museum. Gift of Nancy Dustin Wall Moure.*

After more than two centuries of use, San Gabriel and a number of other Alta California missions remain to this day active parish churches. *© Ken Wolter/Shutterstock.com.*

Hugues Pommier, *The Venerable Marie of the Incarnation*. Marie de l'Incarnation brought the Ursulines to Quebec, where she devoted her life to teaching Native American and French girls and young women, documenting her times in brilliant letters, and keeping an exacting schedule of cloistered prayer. *Musée des Ursulines de Québec, Collection Monastère des Ursulines de Québec.*

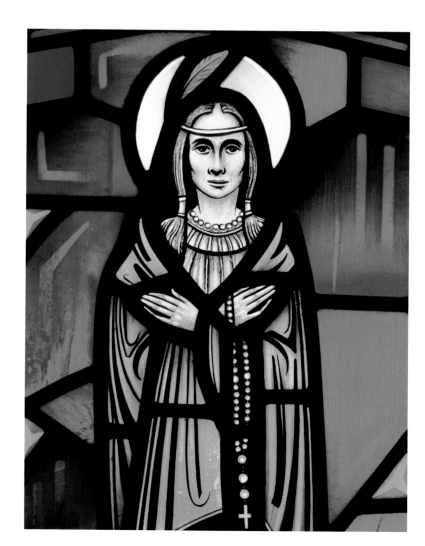

Iroquois convert Kateri Tekakwitha, Lily of the Mohawks, pursued a celibate life of prayer and good works, combining a spirituality of Christian belief and Iroquois courage. © *Nancy Bauer/ Shutterstock.com.*

Monseigneur de Montmorency-Laval, Bishop of Canada. As vicar apostolic and, later, diocesan bishop of Quebec, François-Xavier de Montmorency-Laval brought Roman Catholicism in New France to new levels of spirituality, culture, and governance.
Société des Missions Etrangères, Paris, France/Bridgeman Images.

Philippe de Champaigne, *Armand Jean du Plessis, Cardinal de Richelieu.* Cardinal Richelieu reorganized the Company of One Hundred Associates (also known as the Company of New France) into an exclusively Catholic enterprise, thus ending a previous Catholic-Huguenot entente cordiale in Canadian development. *La Sorbonne, Paris, France/Archives Charmet/ Bridgeman Images.*

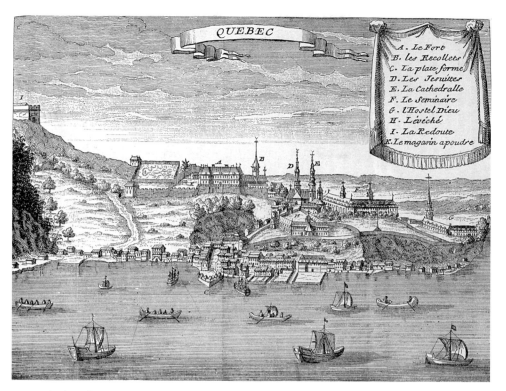

Quebec, after Bacqueville de la Potherie, from *Narrative and Critical History of America*, volume 4, 1886. In short order, Quebec developed into a strategically sited urban center for religion, governance, education, hospital care, and commerce.   *Private Collection/Bridgeman Images.*

Richard Short, *A View of the Bishop's House with the Ruins as They Appear in Going Down the Hill from the Upper to the Lower Town [Quebec]*, 1761. Constructed in the 1690s, the episcopal palace of Quebec remained in use for nearly two hundred years as a center of church and (after 1830) civil governance.   *Library and Archives Canada, Acc. No. 1989-283-11, Richard Short Collection.*

LEFT Claude François (Brother Luke), *Jean Talon*, ca. 1671. Sent to Canada in 1665 as *intendant* (inspector general and chief administrator), Jean Talon promoted marriage and family life through a *filles du roi* program that brought thousands of dowry-less young women to New France for purposes of marriage. *Collection Monastère des Augustines de l'Hôtel-Dieu de Québec. Photo: Jessy Bernier-Perspective Photo.*

BELOW From June to late September 1673, in an epic voyage of discovery and evangelization, explorer Louis Jolliet and Jesuit missionary Jacques Marquette led a canoe sortie southward down the Mississippi until reaching the Arkansas. *Bridgeman Images.*

Trade between Mexican Indians and the French at the Port of Mississippi, ca. 1720. The founding and development of New Orleans in the early eighteenth century connected Louisiana to Gulf of Mexico trade and established a leading North American port.   *The Historic New Orleans Collection/Bridgeman Images.*

Ursuline Convent, New Orleans, Louisiana. As they had in Quebec, Ursuline nuns from France established in New Orleans a convent and school that reinforced the French culture of the city.
Library of Congress, Prints and Photographs Division, photo by Carol M. Highsmith (LC-DIG-highsm-12641).

LEFT Daniel Mytens, *George Calvert, 1st Baron Baltimore*. George Calvert, first Baron Baltimore, spent years and treasure in an effort to found a Catholic colony in North America. *Private Collection/ Peter Newark American Pictures/Bridgeman Images.*

BELOW Emanuel Gottlieb Leutze, *Founding of the Colony of Maryland*. On 25 March 1634, on Saint Clement's Island, George Calvert's dream of a Catholic colony was realized with the raising of a cross, the celebration of Mass by Jesuit Andrew White, and the formal founding of the proprietary colony of Maryland. *Private Collection/Bridgeman Images.*

Saint Mary's Chapel and other buildings were recreated in 1934 by the state of
Maryland to commemorate the three hundredth anniversary of the founding of Saint
Mary's City as the capital of the colony. *Pubdog/Wikimedia Commons/Public Domain.*

Louis S. Glanzman, *Margaret Brent before Maryland Assemblymen*, 1976. Landowner Margaret Brent served
as Lord Baltimore's attorney and business agent. Following the destruction of Catholic properties in
Saint Mary's County during the English Civil War, she and her brother relocated to Virginia, where they
became the nucleus of a small but influential Catholic circle. *Louis S. Glanzman/National Geographic Creative.*

Founded by Jesuits in 1733, Saint Joseph's Church ministered to the small but influential Roman Catholic community of Philadelphia. Two blocks from Independence Hall, Saint Joseph's remains in service to this day.

Samuel Richards, *Evangeline Discovering Her Affianced in the Hospital*, ca. 1887–1889. Henry Wadsworth Longfellow's narrative poem *Evangeline* (1847) tells the story of a betrothed couple separated from each other when the English expelled the French Acadians from Nova Scotia. Having become a nursing sister in the Catholic hospice of Philadelphia, Evangeline is reunited with her dying fiancé.   *Detroit Institute of Arts, USA/Gift of Mr. Bela Hubbard/Bridgeman Images.*

John Wollaston, *Mrs. Charles Carroll of Annapolis*, ca. 1753–1754. Elizabeth Brooke, a member of a distinguished Roman Catholic family and the mother of Charles Carroll of Carrollton, remained an enigma until the full story of her life was revealed. Here was a woman who suffered, endured, and in the final years of her life prevailed. *Detroit Institute of Arts, USA/Founders Society Purchase, Mr. and Mrs. Walter Buhl Ford II Fund/Bridgeman Images.*

Joshua Reynolds, *Charles Carroll of Carrollton*, ca. 1763. Charles Carroll of Carrollton spent his formative years in Europe in the study of humanities, philosophy, and law. Painted while Carroll was a student at the Inner Temple of London, this signature portrait by Joshua Reynolds calls to mind a generation of Catholic Marylanders forced to seek education abroad. *Yale Center for British Art, Paul Mellon Collection, USA/Bridgeman Images.*

Joshua Reynolds, *Henry, 8th Lord Arundell of Wardour*, ca. 1764–1767. Following the suppression of the Society of Jesus, the English Catholic peer Henry, eighth Lord Arundell, wanted his Saint Omer's classmate John Carroll to remain at Wardour Castle as chaplain and fellow crusader for Catholic emancipation.

The Dayton Art Institute, Dayton, Ohio, USA/Gift of Mr. and Mrs. Harry S. Price, Jr./Bridgeman Images.

Gilbert Stuart, *Bishop John Carroll*, ca. 1804. But John Carroll chose to return to Maryland, where another destiny awaited him. *Booth Family Center for Special Collections, Georgetown University. Gift of Pacificus Ord.*

constituted the dominant presence, especially when dévots were operating in concert with a sisterhood as patrons and benefactors. Politically, dévots were conservative, favoring the governance of France through regional and local aristocracies and opposing Richelieu's efforts to centralize through a strong monarchy. Midcentury, during the regency of Anne of Austria and the prime ministership of Cardinal Mazarin, dévot sentiment pervaded the two uprisings of the antimonarchical Fronde movement on behalf of Parlement (1648–1649) and the nobility (1650). The rise of Louis XIV as absolute monarch redirected the dévot movement into nonpolitical channels. Dévot sentiment, however, remained influential in France—even with the monarchy—as a moral and spiritual force.

Third, New France continued to enjoy the support of Richelieu; his niece and heir, the duchesse d'Aiguillon; Richelieu's successor, the soldier-diplomat Jules Cardinal Mazarin; and Anne of Austria, the queen regent Mazarin so assiduously served and to whom, many believed, he was secretly married. Although a cardinal, Mazarin never took major orders and hence technically remained a layman or, at the most, a minor cleric; yet as cardinal he was expected to observe celibacy.

Under the guidance of the Company of New France, also known as the Company of One Hundred Associates, money could be made in Canada. Hence continental ambitions intensified as *coureurs de bois* (rangers of the forest), whether licensed or not, penetrated farther and farther into the interior in pursuit of furs and frontier freedom and returned to tell the tale. A number of subsidiary companies were making an appearance along with such unsanctioned ventures. Even the Jesuit missions were being supported by proceeds from the fur trade.

A religious order, finally, was in charge of New France. In the aide-mémoire the chevalier Isaac de Razilly drafted for Richelieu in 1626, recommending the overseas expansion of France as a commercial power, Razilly suggested that the order to which he belonged, the Knights of Malta, be given jurisdiction over local constabularies and the protection of the sea lanes. Responding favorably to the idea of an aristocratic order of knights under religious vows governing a French and Catholic overseas network, Richelieu kept Razilly's recommendation in mind. Just before Champlain's death, Richelieu gave religious jurisdiction over the Saint Lawrence valley to the Society of Jesus. Following Champlain's death, Richelieu conferred the secular governorship of the Saint Lawrence valley and beyond to the chevalier Charles Huault de Montmagny and through the chevalier to the Order of Malta in which he was a professed Knight of Justice under vows of poverty, chastity, and obedience. As Marcel Trudel has pointed out (and as David Hackett Fischer acknowledges), from 1636 onward, chevaliers of the Order of Malta exercised Richelieu's authority in New France.[2]

Governance by Malta

The chevalier Huault de Montmagny and his lieutenant, Achille de Bréhaut de L'Isle, also a Knight of Malta, reached Quebec on 11 June 1636. Stepping ashore, the two knights—operatically resplendent in their red vests and black capes adorned with the eight-pointed white Cross of Malta—were greeted by yet another Knight of Malta in religious habit, the chevalier Marc-Antoine Bras-de-Fer de Chateaufort, who had been serving as interim governor since Champlain's death. The three knights were greeted with the fanfare the small colony could muster. En route to the church, they knelt briefly before a roadside cross and offered prayers of thanksgiving for their safe arrival. At the church, following the singing of a Te Deum, Bras-de-Fer de Chateaufort handed over the keys of Fort Saint-Louis to the new governor, who would guide the embattled colony for the ensuing twelve years. The presence of Cardinal Richelieu and the Counter-Reformation could be felt in this simple ceremony. The cardinal had made up his mind that New France was to be governed by soldier-monks characterized by orthodoxy, aristocracy, military competence, and Catholic ambition.

At age fifty-three, a Jesuit-educated nobleman from a landed family and a naval officer with combat experience fighting Turks and pirates in the Mediterranean, Montmagny possessed such traits in abundance. While no Samuel Champlain (who could be?), he would acquit himself honorably in office. Following a tour of the colony, Montmagny drew up a regional plan of defense that involved posting the chevaliers Bréhaut de L'Isle and Bras-de-Fer de Chateaufort in field positions—Bréhaut de L'Isle was sent to the border settlement of Trois-Rivières to organize its defenses against the Iroquois—and rebuilding Fort Saint-Louis in stone. Montmagny also laid out the central streets of Quebec, with the help of surveyor Jean Bourdon, signaling its future as a city, naming streets in honor of Saint Louis, Saint Anne, and Mount Carmel, and presided over years of serious construction as a Quebec of wood began to yield to a Quebec of stone structures in the Norman style.

This half monk, as Francis Parkman called him, lived simply and piously in Fort Saint-Louis, first of all on the heights built by Champlain and then, after 1647, at the Château Saint-Louis built by Montmagny within the fort at its highest point. Constructed of stone, flanked by sturdy Norman towers, and featuring a balcony supported by three buttresses, the Château Saint-Louis emanated an ambience of France recreated in North America that became increasingly characteristic of Quebec during the chevalier Montmagny's term. A surviving stone panel carved with the eight-pointed Cross of Malta suggests that Montmagny intended the château to function eventually as a full-fledged priory of his order. In any event, the governor lived there in quasi-monastic austerity during his years in office. His furniture was simple and solid. A crucifix and a tapestry depicting the achievements of his order adorned the walls of the main hall. A prie-dieu remained on hand for daily prayer. Montmagny lived in community with other Knights of Malta when possible and enjoyed the company of the Jesuits with whom he shared jurisdiction over the developing colony.

Montmagny's official relations with the Jesuits—a number of whom were also of noble birth—remained excellent. In France, Jesuit colleges were famous for student productions of serious theater. Thanks to Jesuit approval, Montmagny sponsored amateur productions at the château by young officers (perhaps Jesuit-educated) of comedies and the tragedy The Cid by Corneille. As a sign of their good relations, the Jesuits presented the governor with a horse, the first to be seen in the colony. Indians considered it a kind of moose.

Montmagny's piety was self-evident. Across the social divides of the era, he did his best to make connections with the people of Quebec. On Sunday mornings he stood in line with the public to approach the Communion rail, and he walked in religious processions, taking his turn alongside baptized Indians as a pole bearer of the canopy held over the priest bearing the Eucharist. Most dramatically, when the Company of New France ran into serious difficulties (which ended up being terminal), the chevalier negotiated the right of *habitants* (locals) to form their own trading company, the Communauté des Habitants, as a profit-sharing subsidiary. Thus the Communauté des Habitants became part of the governance structure of the colony, which brought Montmagny into an even closer relationship with the people of the Saint Lawrence valley. Although Montmagny disapproved of the founding of Ville-Marie—it was too far upriver, he believed, too vulnerable to Iroquois attack—he eventually gave reluctant approval, perhaps due in great measure to its aristocratic and Jesuit backing. When war with the Iroquois did break out in 1641, Montmagny became more opposed to the Ville-Marie project than ever. Nevertheless, he accompanied the founding caravan upriver, then returned to Quebec as quickly as possible to put the colony on a wartime footing.

A Jesuit hegemony

Between 1611 and 1613 the Jesuits failed to establish themselves in Acadia. During the early 1630s, Recollect Franciscans also made an unsuccessful attempt in the area. From 1639 on, however, Capuchin Franciscans became an important presence in Acadia, with thirty-seven Capuchin priests and twenty lay brothers serving there between 1639 and 1656. The Jesuits returned to Quebec in 1625 and grew in power and authority following England's restoration of the colony to France in 1632. Thus the two most influential religious orders in France (a Jesuit served as confessor to the king, and a Capuchin was Richelieu's closest advisor) shared semi-sovereignties in New France as well. The unexpected death of the chevalier de Razilly in 1635 deprived Acadia of the governor it needed to continue its development on a stable trajectory. Instead, Razilly's brother Claude de Rasilly (who spelled his name differently) inherited the governorship, and he in turn appointed his cousin Charles de Menou d'Aulnay as his representative. D'Aulnay and Charles de Saint-Étienne de La Tour, a trader who had briefly served as governor before the arrival of the chevalier de Razilly in 1632, spent the next two decades in a violent contest for dominance. This civil strife delayed development of the colony and prevented the full flowering of the Capuchin mission, as the friars were forced to negotiate continually between warring forces.

This, the Jesuits resolved, would not happen to their mission. They would stay close to power and keep their finances in order. In considering the development of Catholic institutions in Quebec, the city and the colony, from the restoration of 1632 onward, the skills of the Jesuits as secular agents and their dedication as missionaries are equally noteworthy. As pragmatists, Jesuits realized that support for their mission to New France must be acquired not only from the wealthy in France but also from participation profits in the fur trade in Quebec colony. Indeed, their early Acadian adventure failed, in part, due to quarrels with traders when such shares in profits were not forthcoming. Following their return to Quebec, the Jesuits took great satisfaction in Richelieu's establishment of the all-Catholic Company of One Hundred Associates, which held a monopoly in the New France fur trade and from which Jesuit missionaries received a percentage of the proceeds. The Jesuits also linked the evangelization of the Indians to an increase in the fur trade, since the traders acquiring furs for the company procured them from Native Americans or, in some instances, from Frenchmen who lived and trapped with the indigenous people, speaking their language, absorbing their skills, and forming families. So dedicated were the Jesuits to the expansion and ongoing success of the fur trade that, when French rule was reestablished in 1632, they had no objection to the possibility of William de Caën being named governor rather than Samuel Champlain, given Caën's ability to raise money and secure ships. Caën was a Calvinist, the Jesuits admitted, but he was a moderate Calvinist. Besides, he had suffered great losses three years earlier when the English had seized the colony.[3] Such practicality was part of the Jesuit ethos from the beginning: a conviction that the world must be dealt with on its own terms, provided that the terms were not intrinsically sinful, if the world were to be made a more Christian place.

Yet these particular Jesuits were Frenchmen as well, many of them from noble or haut bourgeois families, and while they believed that Native Americans were fully human, with souls to be saved, they admitted to experiencing cultural shock now and then. For example, a Parisian of good family, Father Charles Lalemant, superior of the Jesuits who arrived in Quebec in 1625, had earlier enjoyed an elegant, yet rigorous academic education. Following a novitiate at Rouen, philosophy and theology at La Flèche, and a final year of tertianship in Paris under the renowned Jesuit Antoine Le Gaudier, Lalemant embarked on a career as a teacher of logic and physics at the Collège de Bourges and, later, as principal of the boarding school at the Collège de Clermont, two well-appointed Jesuit schools for the nobility and wealthier classes. Imagine, then, Lalemant's thoroughly human reaction to the lifestyle of his Indian charges in Quebec colony, which he documented in a letter to his brother Jérôme, also a Jesuit priest, dated 1 August 1626 and published in Paris the following year as a prelude to the *Jesuit Relations* series.

"As to the customs of the Savages," Lalemant writes,

it is enough to say that they are altogether savage. From morning until night they have no other thought than to fill their stomachs. They come to see us only to ask for something to eat; and if you do not give it to them they show their dissatisfaction. They are real beggars, if there ever were any, and yet as proud as they can be. They consider the French less intelligent than they. Vices of the flesh are very common among them. One of them will marry several women, and will leave them when he pleases, and take others. There is one here who married his own daughter, but all the other Savages were indignant at him for it. As to cleanliness among them, that never enters into the question; they are very dirty about their eating, and in their cabins they are covered with vermin, which they eat when they catch them. It is a custom of this Tribe to kill their fathers and mothers when they are so old that they can walk no longer, thinking that they are thus doing them a good service; for otherwise, they would be compelled to die of hunger, as they have become unable to follow the others when they change their location. When I had it explained to one of them one day that the same thing would be done for him when he became old, he answered that he certainly expected it.

Their method of making war against their enemies is generally through treachery, watching to find them alone; and, if they are not strong enough to make prisoners of those whom they encounter, they shoot them with their arrows, then cut off their heads, which they bring back to show their people. But, if they can take them to their cabins as prisoners, they subject them to unparalleled cruelties, killing them by inches; and, strange to say, during all these tortures, the victims sing constantly, considering it a dishonor if he cries out or complains. After the victim is dead, they eat him, and no one is so insignificant that he does not get his share.[4]

Putting aside the question of whether such barbarities—with the exception of cannibalism, perhaps—occurred in the Thirty Years' War raging in Europe, or whether Frenchmen were models of chastity, one can almost feel Lalemant's visceral disdain for the indigenous people of Quebec. Still, despite their repulsive lifestyle, he continued, these people did believe that "there is a One who made all, but they do not render him any homage." The more sedentary tribes reported to be living farther into the interior, he added, might have a more promising culture. The point is, the Jesuits cannot be considered naïve regarding the cultural disjunctions involved in the task of evangelization they had set for themselves.

The Jesuits were willing to assume that task, although within the decade following Lalemant's letter, their thinking would move in the direction of colonization of young men from France, reinforced by intermarriage with Indian women, as opposed to the self-sufficient Christian communities they had created in Japan or the self-sufficient reductions they were establishing among the Guaraní of Paraguay. An able-bodied young man, Champlain's good friend Father Paul Le Jeune would be arguing via *Jesuit Relations* by 1636, that he could make his way in New France, even if he had to begin his career there as a contract laborer, paid with half the land he personally cleared in a year. Should four such workers form a cooperative, they could clear twenty-four arpents a year, enough to support thirty-six persons, and become men of property. (An arpent represented .84 acre.) "There are so many strong and robust peasants in France who have no bread to put in their mouths", Le Jeune argued. "Is it possible that they are so afraid of losing sight of the village steeple, as they say, that they would rather languish in their misery and poverty, than to place themselves some day at their ease among the inhabitants of New France, where with the blessings of the earth they will far more easily find those of heaven and of the soul?"[5] To educate Indian girls to become wives for such colonists and raise up a mighty race of mixed ancestry, the Jesuits helped arrange the arrival of Ursuline nuns in 1639 to establish a convent and boarding school in Quebec City.

Mission to Huronia

By that time the Jesuits were deeply involved in what at first appeared promising but later seemed increasingly problematic: the evangelization of the Huron people north of Lake Ontario and the transformation of Huronia into a Native American Catholic society. Hereupon ensued an epic of treks, language study, preaching, patience, and suffering by Frenchmen of ancestry and education that for Francis Parkman, writing *The Jesuits in North America in the Seventeenth Century* (1867), constituted an exercise of vision and will pushing the limits of human frailty.

A thirty-two-year-old Norman nobleman, the near-giant Jean de Brébeuf, inaugurated the evangelization of Huronia with a three-year (1626–1629) sojourn among the Bear People, one of the five families (Bear People, Cord Makers, Rock People, Deer People, and Swamp People) of the Huron Confederacy. During this

time, Brébeuf acquired the Huron language and learned to regard the Huron people and way of life with understanding and some sympathy, although his efforts at
evangelization came to naught. No matter: Brébeuf accomplished a useful reconnaissance on behalf of a future endeavor, interrupted when the English took Quebec and Brébeuf and his Jesuit colleagues returned to France to wait out Protestant
England's occupation of the colony. Brébeuf returned to Quebec in 1633 and the
following year reentered Huronia, this time in the company of two other Jesuits,
Antoine Daniel and Ambroise Davost. Returning to Ihonatiria, the Huron village
where he had lived, Brébeuf and his colleagues founded their first mission, Saint-
Joseph; they remained there for three years.

Between 1634 and 1649, the Jesuits made a brave and sustained effort to evangelize the Huron, centered after 1639 in the mission and fortified post of Sainte-
Marie-aux-Hurons on the Wye River. This core mission soon developed into a
twenty-building complex: church, hospital, Jesuit house, farm buildings, and cabins
for French workers and Huron converts. To this headquarters was attached a network of ancillary missions throughout Huronia whose litany of names began with
Mary the Mother of God, celebrated in her Immaculate Conception (Mission La
Conception) and two other mission Saint Marys as well, and, after referencing the
angelic order (Saint Michael the Archangel), proceeded through Christian history
from Scripture (Saint John the Baptist, Saint Joseph, Saint Mary Magdalene) to
the great French king (Saint Louis) to Saint Ignatius of Loyola, founder of their
Society—as if such a roll call, invoking the Catholic past, might in and of itself constitute an invocation and prayer on behalf of the Catholic Huronia the Jesuits hoped
to bring into existence. Two priests were assigned to each mission and were, in
turn, brought back to Sainte-Marie-aux-Hurons for half-year or quarterly periods
of rest, retreat, and spiritual direction according to Jesuit requirements.

To these missionaries, as they embarked from France, Brébeuf sent religious and
practical advice, which his superior, Paul Le Jeune (based in Quebec), included as
a separate chapter in his *Relation of What Occurred in New France in the Year 1637*,
published in 1638 as part of the increasingly influential *Jesuit Relations* series. First
of all—and most profound in religious terms—Brébeuf advised, "You must have
sincere affection for the Savages—looking upon them as ransomed by the blood
of the Son of God, and as our brethren with whom we are to pass the rest of our
lives." Brébeuf then gets down to practical notes animated by the Jesuit ethos of
inculturation: take people for what they are, on their own terms, whenever possible, in all things save ignorance and sin. Eat their *sagamité* (boiled cornmeal or other
cereal), he urges, as prepared and served. The food may be dirty, half-cooked, and
tasteless, but eat it anyway, all of it. "As to the other numerous things which may be
unpleasant, they must be endured for the love of God, without saying anything or
appearing to notice them." When you get into an Indian canoe, take off your shoes
and stockings and hike up your cassock. Do not splash water into the canoe. That
constitutes a major misstep. And do not try to talk with the men paddling the canoe,
no matter how long the journey or how much you want to learn the language. You
will annoy them as they negotiate the waters. "Silence is a good equipment at such
a time." Always be cheerful, and have gifts to distribute—fishhooks, pocketknives,
plain or colored glass beads. Volunteer to paddle and when on portage, carry something, if only a kettle. The Indians appreciate this courtesy. Never offer a slight or

prove troublesome. "It is almost incredible how they observe and remember even the slightest fault." Finally, empty yourself, forget about your accomplishments, the respect you enjoy in France. Thus Brébeuf advises his fellow Jesuits—well-educated men prepared for teaching careers in well-appointed colleges and seminaries or preaching assignments in developed French cities, living in civilized Jesuit houses among men of comparable formation and academic achievement.

Brébeuf does not, however, mention the Native American traits that so disturbed Charles Lalemant: promiscuity, thievery, a lack of hygiene, and, particularly, the cruel torture and cannibalistic devouring of captured prisoners. Instead, he ends with psychological and theological considerations. The last and more important lesson he wishes to impart, Brébeuf writes, "was easy enough to learn, but very difficult to put into practice; for, leaving a highly civilized community, you fall into the hands of barbarous people who care little for your Philosophy or your Theology. All the fine qualities which might make you loved and respected in France are like pearls trampled under the feet of swine, or rather of mules, which utterly despise you when they see that you are not as good pack animals as they are. If you go naked and carry the load of a horse upon your back, as they do, then you would be wise according to their doctrine, and would be recognized as a great man, otherwise not. Jesus Christ is our true greatness; it is He alone and His cross that should be sought in running after these people, for, if you strive for anything else, you will find naught but bodily and spiritual affliction. But having found Jesus Christ in His Cross, you have found the roses in the thorns, sweetness in bitterness, all in nothing."[6]

The urban apostolate

The Jesuit presence through the 1640s in Huronia and the Tobacco and Neutral Nations to the southwest of Huronia—eighteen priests, four coadjutor brothers, twenty-three *donnés* (long-term volunteers), eight soldiers, and eleven paid employees—represented a major investment on the part of the Society of Jesus. As laymen living under a simple promise of service to the Society, the donnés did not have to be paid beyond room and board. Soldiers and workmen, however, were on the payroll. The large numbers of donnés in Huronia and Quebec reprised in a different format Jesuit practice in Japan, where the Society had been active since the 1550s. There the Jesuits had created a class of Japanese catechists whom they trained and dressed in black cassocks similar to their own, leaving these nonclerical figures behind to catechize and further develop the nascent Christian communities the missionaries had evangelized. The donnés of New France, by contrast, were skilled and semiskilled artisans and workers, bound to the Society by an oath of service and responsible primarily for construction, agriculture, and related enterprises.

In the case of Japan, Jesuits—beginning with Francis Xavier in 1549—had entered a populous, highly advanced society into which over time they made major inroads, to the point that the feudal elite of the country feared a wholesale conversion of the population, followed by an invasion from Europe. Starting in 1596, the shogunate launched a persecution that would all but eliminate the Christian community, drive its remnants underground, and keep Japan largely isolated from the West until the mid-nineteenth century.

Catholic Japan, once gained and now in the process of being lost, was on the Jesuits' minds as they launched their Canadian venture. In Japan, the Jesuits had encountered a developed feudal society with people settled in villages and towns, plus a handful of more ambitious settlements, such as Edo (the nucleus of modern Tokyo) and the imperial capital of Kyoto. Indeed, European Jesuits found a civilization fully equivalent—and in certain cases, palpably superior—to that of their home countries. Moreover, Japan's agricultural economy, as well as its sophisticated language (once mastered) and rigid social system, so like those of Europe, meant that the Jesuits did not feel obliged to reinvent the country, only to convert it.

One of the attractions of Huronia in terms of evangelization was that the Huron were semisedentary agriculturalists, living as hunter-gatherers for only part of the year. The Huron, as Brébeuf first reported, built large houses clustered in villages and grew crops of corn, squash, and beans, in contrast to the aggressively nomadic ways of the Montagnais and Algonquians. As in Japan, stability linked to an agricultural economy suggested an evangelization keyed to social structures supportive of Roman Catholic civilization. Hence, in addition to encouraging Native Americans of New France to stay put, clean up, remain monogamous, stop torturing and eating their enemies, and come to a rudimentary understanding and acceptance of Catholic Christianity, the Jesuits internalized an agenda of social and institutional development centered on Quebec City, the Saint Lawrence valley, Huronia, and—as it would soon turn out—Ville-Marie on the Island of Montreal. Such a goal involved establishing Huronia as a Christian Indian commonwealth along with comparable efforts to settle the Montagnais and Algonquians into a less nomadic lifestyle and to prepare young Indian women to become the Catholic wives of European men and mothers of a new Catholic people, as was already happening in the regions controlled by Spain. This enterprise meant schools, seminaries, cities and towns, and the creation of stable Indian communities and economic cooperatives, as well as an influx of upstanding young French men as colonists.

In this effort, the Jesuits enjoyed the consistent support of the governor of New France and, through him, the powerful Order of Malta. Another Knight of Malta, the chevalier Noël Brûlart de Sillery, a onetime ambassador to Rome and Madrid and a minister of state during the regency of Marie de Médicis, in 1637 obtained title from the Company of One Hundred Associates to a tract of land four miles upriver from Quebec (although he never left France), which he donated to the Jesuits for a mission. Sillery sent over to Canada the skilled artisans and workmen required to build (in stone as well as wood) the palisaded village and mission station—chapel, hospital, priests' house, and residences—that soon attracted a stable Christian Indian population of Algonquians and Montagnais. Under the name Sillery, the settlement served as the paradigmatic headquarters for the Jesuit mission to the indigenous peoples of Canada.

Jesuit relations

As a dévot, the chevalier de Sillery exemplified the tsunami of fervid piety sweeping the upper classes of Catholic France and maintaining its momentum for the rest of the seventeenth century. Indeed, Sillery was on the verge of entering the priesthood when he made his gift. The vehicle of imaginative and emotional connection between French dévots and New France was the *Jesuit Relations*, inaugurated by Father Paul Le Jeune with the publication of his *Brève relation du voyage de la Nouvelle France* (1632) and his *Relation de ce qui s'est passé en la Nouvelle France en l'année 1633* (1634), each bound in duodecimo volumes by the Parisian press of Sebastien Cramoisy on the rue Saint-Jacques at the Sign of the Storks.

In 1858 the Canadian government issued a well-edited edition of the *Relations* in three stout octavo volumes that was used by Francis Parkman in researching *The Jesuits in North America in the Seventeenth Century*. New York City collector James Lenox, meanwhile, was busy assembling a complete collection of the Cramoisy volumes, a major feat given the scarcity of surviving copies, and two New York City–based Irish Catholic historians—Dr. E. B. O'Callaghan, editor of *The Documentary History of New York* (1851) and the pioneering historian of American Catholicism, John Gilmary Shea, at work on his *History of the Catholic Missions among the Indian Tribes of the United States* (1854)—were discovering the value of the *Relations* as a source for New York history. Between 1857 and 1866 Shea produced limited editions of twenty-five Cramoisy volumes. During the 1860s and 1870s French Canadian Jesuit scholars Felix Martin and August de Carayon and Abbés C. H. Laverdière and Henri Casgrain edited and published further versions of Jesuit letters and journals from the seventeenth century. Then, in a heroic feat of American publishing, the Burrows Brothers Company of Cleveland, Ohio, sponsored and published between 1896 and 1901 a monumental seventy-three-volume edition under the general editorship of Reuben Gold Thwaites, secretary of the State Historical Society of Wisconsin. Heavily annotated and copiously illustrated with portraits, maps, and title pages of the Cramoisy and other editions, the Thwaites volumes offered face-to-face French texts and English-translations and thus entered into English-language historiography a vast and compelling record of North American continental ambitions.

The dévots of the 1630s and 1640s encountered the *Relations* not as a cumulative epic of reportage and documentation but as individual advances on a work in progress: a Roman Catholic parallel to the contemporaneous and highly documented and reflective Puritan errand into the wilderness. These Catholic evangelists were of equal learning and dedication and being single men with no prospects of marriage and family, were willing to live among Indians and share the hardships of their life, down to the day-to-day danger, physical challenge, and discomfort. As the *Jesuit Relations* series progressed, its grand theme—the winning of a continent and its indigenous people for Catholic France—emerged as the grand cause of a devout generation, a growing number of dévots and nuns who wished to join the crusade as patrons or missionaries.

In this process of outreach, Le Jeune's *Relation* of 1636, building on his *Relations* of 1634 and 1635, played a key role. Overall, Le Jeune would write fifteen of the original forty-one volumes. He was a skilled writer, with a novelist's eye for detail, and—working at it deliberately—he got better and better at the genre with each volume, coming to sense intuitively the proper balance of narrative and reflection, dialogue and incident, and, in an account of a drunken onetime Christian Indian (the Apostate, Le Jeune calls him) on a destructive rampage, grotesque comedy and terror.

Le Jeune, in short, had the instincts and ability of a born writer. As superior of the Jesuits of Quebec from 1632 to 1639, moreover, he was privy to letters and

firsthand reports from Paris. He was thus aware of the buzz his *Relations* were creating in France. Like any born writer, Le Jeune loved an audience, especially one
of wealthy, highly placed dévots and members of the various sisterhoods. Growing
numbers of such readers were supporting the goal of the Society of Jesus and Le
Jeune's own life: the creation of New France as a prosperous mixed-race Catholic
commonwealth. The *Relations* helped connect the Jesuits to the state as well. In Le
Jeune's 1636 *Relations* he aligned himself boldly with the French establishment, in
France and New France alike—beginning with Cardinal Richelieu himself, first
minister and head of the Company of One Hundred—and the directors of the
company, Catholics all. In honor of his son, a Jesuit, benefactor Nicholas Rohault,
the marquise de Gamache, in 1626 had presented the Society 16,000 écus of gold
and an annuity of 3,000 livres to maintain a boarding school and seminary in Quebec City for Indian boys. Opening in 1636, the school operated for five years,
after which time the Gamache endowment was used to support the Jesuit college
founded in Quebec City in 1635 as well as the Indian settlement of Sillery.

Recruiting sisterhoods

Next up on the Jesuit agenda: a hospital and a boarding school for Indian girls.
Those projects required nursing and teaching nuns willing to serve in Quebec and
the funds necessary to send them there and finance their efforts. In this regard, Le
Jeune reported, the contemplative nuns of France and the teaching and hospital
sisters were aflame with a desire to support the Canadian venture. The contemplative Benedictine nuns attached to the Church of Saint-Pierre de Montmartre in
Paris, he noted, were praying day and night for the Canadian missions. Carmelite,
Ursuline, Visitation, and Notre Dame nuns were proving equally prayerful—one
fire, as Le Jeune put it. The Hospitaller nuns were insisting that some of them
be dispatched to New France within the next year. To these remarks, Le Jeune
attached a series of quotes extracted from letters he had received from various
convents. "You must know," writes one Ursuline, "that New France is beginning
to enter the minds of a great many people, which makes me think that God is
looking upon it with a favorable eye. Ah, would you say, my Reverend Father, if
his divine Majesty were so to shape events that we would soon have the courage
and the means to go to you? I will tell you that if such be the will of God, there
is nothing in this world that can prevent me, even if I were to be engulfed in the
waves on the voyage."[7]
     Thus it came to pass the very next year, on 4 May 1639, that after much nego-
tiation six nuns, patroness Madame de La Peltrie, and Jesuits Barthélemy Vimont
(assigned to replace Le Jeune as Jesuit superior in Canada) and Joseph-Antoine
Poncet de La Rivière sailed from Dieppe on the *Saint Joseph*, flagship of a three-
ship flotilla (Jesuits Pierre-Joseph-Marie Chaumonot and Claude Jager were on
the other ships). On 15 July the flotilla reached Tadoussac, and from there the
nuns proceeded by small craft to Quebec (living on salted codfish, Parkman tells
us), arriving on 1 August. Three of the nuns—Marie de l'Incarnation, Marie de
Saint Joseph, and Cécile de Sainte Croix—were cloistered teaching sisters from the
Ursuline convent at Dieppe. The remaining three—Mothers Marie de Saint Ignace,
Marie de Saint Bonaventure de Jésus, and Anne de Saint Bernard—were nursing

sisters, members of the Augustinian Canonesses of the Mercy of Jesus attached to the Hôtel-Dieu (hospital) at Dieppe. Once arrived in Quebec, the Hospitallers were housed in a newly completed company storehouse near Fort Saint-Louis on the cliff and the Ursulines in a small house on the quay until convents and a hospital could be built. The nuns immediately got to work acquiring a rudimentary knowledge of Algonquian from Le Jeune. Almost simultaneously, an epidemic of smallpox broke out, and the Hospitallers and the Ursulines threw themselves into the arduous, dangerous, and frequently unpleasant task of caring for stricken Indians and Frenchmen alike.

A pioneering dévot

The nuns' work was being financed by the duchesse d'Aiguillon (the Hospitaller Sisters) and Madame de La Peltrie (the Ursulines). No one would expect a duchesse—especially a duchesse who was the beloved niece and de facto hostess and eventual heir of the most powerful churchman and minister of the Crown in France—to accompany the Hospitaller Sisters she had sponsored to ends-of-the-earth New France. Madame de La Peltrie, by contrast, was another matter. Of the nobility, a Chauvigny, she had wanted to enter the convent as a girl, but at seventeen, at the insistence of her father, the sieur d'Alençon et de Vaubougon, she had married the chevalier de Gruel, seigneur de La Peltrie. The five-year marriage was happy enough, although the couple did lose their one child, a daughter, in infancy.

At twenty-two, then, Madame de La Peltrie found herself a widow, childless, and once again yearning for the cloister. Reading Le Jeune's *Jesuit Relations* of 1635, she became dedicated to the cause of converting the Indians of New France. Brought close to death by a sudden illness, she vowed to Saint Joseph that, should she recover, she would devote herself to the education of Indian girls in Canada. She recovered, and to head off her father's insistence that she remarry, she contracted on her own a marriage in name only to another well-born dévot, Jean de Bernières de Louvigny, who had similar inclinations toward a life of celibate asceticism. The death of her father and a successful defense in court of her right to administer her inheritance left Madame de La Peltrie a unique figure in that era: a woman of wealth and independence who, thanks to her marriage in name only, was free to design for herself a distinctive role in the service of religion.

Following the advice of the eminent priest Monsieur Vincent de Paul—the founder of two religious institutes, the Congregation of the Mission and the Daughters of Charity—and the Jesuit Joseph-Antoine Poncet de La Rivière, whom she and her accommodating second husband consulted in Paris, Madame de La Peltrie went to Tours to discuss her Canadian project with the sisters of the Ursuline convent. There she met Mother Marie de l'Incarnation, who had also been advocating an Ursuline mission to Quebec. The two women made plans for a convent and school for Indian girls in Quebec. To support such a foundation, Madame de La Peltrie bequeathed property yielding 900 livres annually and resolved to accompany the Ursulines herself as secular foundress and auxiliary. When a ship proved unavailable, de La Peltrie chartered and provisioned the *Saint Joseph* at a cost of 8,000 livres. To the party of three Ursulines and herself was added Charlotte Barré, nineteen, as

companion to Madame de La Peltrie and, in time, as Mother Saint Ignace, the first
nun to be professed in Canada.

Madame de La Peltrie was driven, a somewhat skeptical Francis Parkman tells
us, by "that restless longing for *éclat*, which, with some women, is a ruling passion.
When, in company with Bernières, she passed from Alençon to Tours, and from
Tours to Paris, an object of attention to nuns, priests, and prelates—when the Queen
herself summoned her to an interview—it may be that the profound contentment
of soul ascribed to her had its origin in sources not exclusively of the spirit."[8] All
this might merely be Parkman's way of saying that Madame de La Peltrie and the
Ursulines were devout French women of the privileged classes, and hence concerned for panache in even the most sacred of circumstances. Parkman does admit,
however, that for all her self-regarding theatricality, de La Peltrie chose well, beginning with Anne de Saint Bernard, then moving on to Marie de l'Incarnation—who
would turn out to be one of the most formidable Catholic sisters in North American history—and, finally, Cécile de Sainte Croix and Charlotte Barré, a mainstay
of the Quebec Ursulines in later years. In Quebec, moreover, de La Peltrie—who
did not lose her éclat and lived in her own home, once it was built—made herself
useful to Hospitallers and Ursulines for tasks great and small with little regard for
her rank. Having lost her own daughter in infancy, she was particularly fond of the
Indian girls at the Ursuline convent, whom she hugged and kissed and cooed over
and who followed her about in groups when she visited them.

And then came her eighteen months' sojourn upriver in Ville-Marie, the last
and uttermost civilian settlement in New France, soon to be revealed as a dangerous place. Arriving there, where no woman in her right mind (whatever her class
background) had a right to be, she assisted with her usual verve Jeanne Mance, a
woman of lesser rank who possessed a style of her own, in decorating a makeshift
altar with wildflowers for the first Mass to be celebrated in this new and faraway
colony, as if the two of them were on holiday and helping out at a local parish in
the French countryside.

Shared visions of a city

Who was this Jeanne Mance, and what religious devotion had brought her to
Ville-Marie? And the young but combat-tested Paul de Chomedey, sieur de
Maisonneuve—the refined, lute-playing officer in such contrast to the *miles glorio-
sus*, the braggart soldier one might have expected—now in charge of this errand
of fifty-some men and two women into the wilderness: how had he arrived here?
The answer to these questions presents a representative interaction of forces great
and small: wealthy *dévots*; the *Jesuit Relations*; the Catholic Revival flourishing in
France; the influence of assorted Jesuit advisors; the guidance of the ever-present
Monsieur Vincent de Paul and one of the many young priests he advised, Jean-
Jacques Olier, who, like his mentor, was to dedicate himself to parish work and the
education of diocesan priests; and the Society of Our Lady of Montreal. All these
elements coalesced to advance the enterprise of creating a city in the wilderness,
Ville-Marie on the Island of Montreal.

In its repeated appeals for more French involvement in New France, as well as
in its recurrent use of direct address, Le Jeune's *Relation of What Occurred in New*

France in the Year 1636 exercised a mesmerizing effect on its readers, many of whom were already caught up in a Great Awakening of Catholic fervor. "New France", Le Jeune lyricized, "is truly a region where one learns perfectly to seek God alone, to desire God alone, to have sincere intentions toward God, and to trust to and rely solely upon his divine and paternal Providence; and it is a rich heart treasury, impossible to estimate. To live in New France means truly to live in the bosom of God and to breathe only the air of his Divine guidance; the sweetness of the air can be realized only by actually breathing."[9]

Given the pervasive power of the Catholic Revival on the imagination and emotions of religious men and women, it is not too surprising that so many protagonists in the founding of Montreal became involved due to an intersection of personal crisis and visionary dream: sickness in Madame de La Peltrie's case, for example, and a prolonged sense of spiritual abandonment in the case of Marie de l'Incarnation. Around the same time, very similar (devout Catholics) and dissimilar people (a priest, a tax collector, and a thirty-year-old provincial nurse) were likewise facing serious challenges for which a dream vision of Canada calling would provide an answer.

In 1636 Jean-Jacques Olier was a twenty-eight-year-old priest three years into his priesthood but undecided about the exact nature of his ministry. The son of a well-connected judicial administrator, and thus tied to the nobility of the robe, Olier had proven a brilliant student in classics at Lyon under the tutelage of the Jesuits, philosophy at the Collège d'Harcourt at the University of Paris, and theology and patristics at the Sorbonne, where he defended his theses in faultless Latin and Greek. The bishop and court preacher Francis de Sales had encouraged Olier to take holy orders and predicted his great service to the Church. As Bishop de Sales and others recognized, Olier was an outstanding candidate for higher office in the Church. Tonsured a cleric at the age of twelve (when de Sales made these predictions), the Abbé Olier became progressively wealthier through his teenage years as his father, now a counselor to the king, secured lucrative benefices for his son—the Benedictine priory of Clisson, the abbey of the Canons Regular of Saint Augustine at Pébrac, the priory of Saint Mary Magdalene at Provence— allowing Olier the honor of wearing a prelate's cassock as well as enjoying a sizable income as honorary abbot of one or another institution. The privileged young abbé enjoyed the friendship and company of other wealthy young abbés en route to high office in the Church, who shared his love of socializing in upper-register Parisian circles. Jean-Jacques Olier, in short, was the perfect product of the ecclesiastical system as it then existed, in which the Crown controlled benefices and routinely made appointments to the hierarchy from the nobility. Cardinal Richelieu had come up this way, and soon it would be Olier's turn.

Following his studies at the Sorbonne, Olier went to Rome to add Hebrew and a smattering of other ancient languages to his repertoire. Once he was there, however, his eyesight began to fail, and he feared he might be going blind. Deeply distressed, he made a pilgrimage to the Shrine of Our Lady at Loreto, where he experienced a profound change of mind and heart and, rejecting his worldly ways, considered entering a Carthusian monastery in southern Italy. His father's death in 1631, however, recalled him to Paris. There he embarked upon a self-assigned mission of preaching to the poor of the city, standing on the streets of the needier districts, to which he commuted by carriage, two footmen in attendance as, in his abbé's purple-piped cassock, he expounded Christian doctrine.

To a contemporary way of thinking, this has its ironic side; yet Olier was only reflecting his class and perhaps some of that éclat noted by Parkman of Madame de La Peltrie. Olier was still considering joining the Carthusians, but while thinking the matter over at his country estate of Verneuil, he had the first of a series of dream visions in which the pope Saint Gregory the Great and Saint Ambrose, the bishop of Milan, were seated in the company of a group of robed Carthusians and a third seat, intended for a simple parish priest, stood empty. That was his seat, he decided. He would become a secular priest, not a Carthusian.

Making the several retreats required prior to ordination to the subdiaconate, diaconate, and, on 21 May 1633, Trinity Sunday, the priesthood, at the church of the Collège des Bons-Enfants (the Holy Innocents), later renamed Saint Lazare, Olier was affected by the retreat master, the charismatic peasant priest Monsieur Vincent de Paul, himself a secular priest. Opposites attract. Monsieur Vincent recruited the Abbé Olier, first to one of his campaigns—preaching missions to the rural poor—and then to a related and concurrent interest, the reform of the secular diocesan priesthood.

Already guided by two future saints, Francis de Sales and Vincent de Paul, Monsieur Olier now met yet another master of the spiritual life, Charles de Condren, superior general of the French Oratory, a community of contemplative and teaching secular priests established in Paris in 1605. It was modeled on the Oratory of Rome, which arose in the 1560s and, after some tribulation, was authorized by Pope Gregory XIII in 1575 as a community of secular priests living in common without taking vows.

Thus Jean-Jacques Olier came under the influence of a line of theological thought and reform that would guide his life and, quite soon, help found Montreal, then govern it. In due course, Olier was recognized as a founder of the city, although he never set foot in New France. Francis de Sales and Vincent de Paul were secular priests. The founder of the Roman Oratory, Philip Neri, was a secular priest, as were the founder of the French Oratory, Pierre de Bérulle (later cardinal), and his successor, Charles de Condren. These priests, joined by Jean-Jacques Olier and another disciple of de Condren, John Eudes, sustained a high regard for the secular priesthood, as reflective of the priesthood of Jesus Christ, which they in their various writings developed into a full, compelling theology of priestly identity and service. According to this line of thought, while the religious orders educated their candidates for the priesthood, the preparation of secular priests remained haphazard despite the decrees of the Council of Trent (1545–1563) that each bishop establish a seminary in his diocese, if at all possible, where future secular clergy could be prepared by an educated and dedicated faculty.

Praying at either the Cathedral of Notre-Dame or the ancient Church of Saint-Germain-des-Prés (accounts vary) on 2 February 1636, the feast of the Presentation of Jesus in the Temple, Olier knelt quietly as the Office of the day was being chanted from the altar. The liturgical text "lumen ad revelationem gentium" (a light for revelation to the Gentiles; Lk 2:32) was being sung, so Olier later recalled, and intuitively he knew two things: one, he would play a role in the upgrading of priestly education by forming a society of secular priests devoted to that purpose;

and, two, he and this society would help found a city in New France under the protection of Mary.

A similar dream vision

A year earlier, according to one account, or five to six years earlier, according to another, at either the Cathedral of Notre-Dame in Paris or his home parish in La Flèche, Jérôme Le Royer de la Dauversière—a middle-aged layman and dévot, the father of six, a civil servant who served as tax collector for the town of La Flèche in Anjou—had a similar revelation. As he knelt in prayer following Communion on Christmas Day, Dauversière beheld in his mind's eye the Island of Montreal in far-off Canada, although, he subsequently claimed, he had no previous knowledge of this place. For that island, so his dream vision continued, he would found a Hôtel-Dieu and an order of nursing sisters to serve there. Upon inquiry, Dauversière was surprised to learn that the Island of Montreal was by all reports empty and would for the time being not be in need of a hospital or nursing sisters.

Nature and grace are interactive. One can therefore consider the natural circumstances behind these revelations. Samuel Champlain and, most recently and eloquently, his good friend Paul Le Jeune had written of the Island of Montreal, and among dévots the settlement and evangelization of New France was, as we have seen, a persistent concern. Growing up in La Flèche, Dauversière, whose father was recently incorporated into the minor nobility, had attended the Jesuit-staffed Collège de La Flèche, founded in 1604 by Henri IV. The philosopher René Descartes was one of his classmates, but so were future Jesuit missionaries to Canada. These schoolboy acquaintanceships, as well as the *Jesuit Relations*, might have played some role in Dauversière's dream vision. So may have brief associations with Jesuit missionaries Enemond Massé and Charles Lalemant.

Whatever Dauversière's psychological state might have been at the time, Olier was still in crisis as he wrestled with the prospect of accepting the bishopric he knew would soon be coming his way or rejecting it and bitterly disappointing his status-conscious mother in favor of, say, a missionary ministry at home or abroad. Over the course of his lifetime, Olier would be offered and turn down a number of appointments to the Church hierarchy as well as opportunities to go to Indochina or Persia as a missionary bishop.

The fable-like aura of the founding of Montreal continues when we learn that, for guidance on his inspired mission, Dauversière in 1639 turned to his fellow dévot Marie Rousseau, a Parisian with multiple connections in Church circles and a reputation as a clairvoyant. Rousseau immediately informed Dauversière that the Abbé Olier had similar ambitions for New France. Pierre Chevrier, the baron de Faucamp, another ardent dévot and a friend of both men, made a comparable connection and—in a less hagiographical version of the story—introduced the two. Shortly thereafter, runs another and more pious version of the encounter, Olier and Dauversière met in the suburb of Mendon, where each had gone to consult the royal chancellor Pierre Séguier (a cousin of the well-connected Olier) on various matters, in Dauversière's case in an effort to create further interest in the Montreal venture.

Seeing each other in the gallery at the entrance to the chancellor's château, each man—so the official story goes—instantly recognized the other as a proponent of a Montreal foundation and embraced as friends and comrades in a noble cause. On that day or the next, Olier celebrated Mass in the château chapel, Dauversière received Communion, and the two of them spent two to three hours walking together in the adjacent gardens, planning the enterprise. It would be a city on the Island of Montreal, they decided, named Ville-Marie in honor of Mary. Recruitment of colonists, individuals capable of keeping spiritual ambitions alive in the midst of economic activity would be key. Their first responsibility would be to fortify the settlement against attack, followed by developing it as a self-sustaining community through the clearing of land and the planting of crops. In time, a community of priests would be formed to evangelize the Indians of the region, along with two communities of nuns: teaching sisters for a school and hospital sisters for the care of the sick. In France, meanwhile, a support society should be set up as quickly as possible to raise funds for the first phases of settlement. The society would take full responsibility for all costs. No funds would be asked of the Crown, the Church, or the Company of One Hundred Associates. At the conclusion of their meeting, Olier (a man of significant personal wealth throughout his life) presented Dauversière with a draft for one hundred louis d'or, saying, "There, sir, is some money to begin the work of God at Montreal. I want to have a part in it."

The following year, 1640, the Society of Our Lady of Montreal was formed in Paris. In addition to Olier, Dauversière, and Marie Rousseau, founding members included Claude Leglay, Pierre Chevrier, and Jean Baptiste Gaston, the baron de Renty. Educated at the Jesuit Collège de Navarre in Paris and a would-be Carthusian in his youth, the baron de Renty was now married at his father's request for dynastic reasons. But he dedicated himself to piety and good works as a member of the Company of the Blessed Sacrament, an association of lay dévots and clerics (Olier and Dauversière were members) devoted to prayer and charities.

Two crucial recruits

In their long conversation in the gardens of Chancellor Séguier's château, Dauversière and Olier had discussed, among other topics, the need to acquire development rights to the Island of Montreal from Jean de Lauson, intendant for Dauphiné, who held the rights; essential as well was a military man of birth and piety to serve as on-site governor of Ville-Marie. Through Jesuit Charles Lalemant, recently returned to France and serving as the Paris-based procurator of the Canadian missions, Dauversière heard of a young, experienced—and pious!—army officer of noble lineage by the name of Paul de Chomedey, sieur de Maisonneuve, who was temporarily between assignments. Having grown up on the family estate in Champagne, Maisonneuve had joined the army at thirteen (he was now in his late twenties) and was by disposition and long practice a well-mannered, clean-living dévot, despite the temptations of his career. (Like another military man, Cardinal Richelieu, Maisonneuve enjoyed playing the lute.) Offered the governorship of the proposed colony by Olier and Dauversière, Maisonneuve accepted, over the objections of his father, to whom his son reportedly quoted Matthew 19:29: "And every one who has left houses or brothers or sisters or father or mother or children or lands, for my name's sake, will receive a hundredfold and inherit eternal life."

Equally important as Maisonneuve's appointment was the entrance of Jeanne Mance into the ranks of Montreal founders. Born in 1606 into a large family (six boys and six girls) from the administrative middle class, Mance acquired nursing skills in Langres during the Thirty Years' War as a member of a society of hospital volunteers established by Sebastien Zamet, bishop of that beleaguered frontier town. Pious since childhood, when she was reputed to have taken a vow to remain single, Mance had avoided both marriage and the cloister in favor of an unusual role for a daughter of the bourgeoisie: a single female dévot living at home and devoting herself to prayer and good works as she awaited the grand cause—most likely connected to hospitals and nursing—that would define her life.

That revelation came in April 1640 through her cousin Nicolas Dolbeau, chaplain of Sainte-Chapelle in Paris and tutor to the young duc de Richelieu, nephew of the duchesse d'Aiguillon (excellent appointments for a secular priest of middle-class origins). Nicolas' younger brother Jean, a Jesuit, had just left for New France, which Nicolas and his cousin discussed, along with the prior departure of Madame de La Peltrie, the Ursulines, and the Augustinian Hospitallers, under the sponsorship of the duchesse d'Aiguillon. From these conversations Jeanne Mance found the grand cause she was looking for: New France and a ministry there relating to hospital service. This sudden revelation of purpose galvanized previously unrecognized abilities in the dévot. In short order, on 1 May 1640, with the approval of her spiritual director, she was en route to Paris, where in the year that followed she assembled a circle of clerical and dévot subscribers for the Montreal venture. Even a short outline of her campaign from connection to connection, ascending higher and higher up the social ladder, constitutes a who's who of dévot support for New France. To begin her drive, Mademoiselle Mance called on Father Charles Lalemant, procurator of the Canadian missions, who introduced her to his fellow Jesuit Jean-Baptiste Saint-Jure. Arranging their meeting took a little time, given Saint-Jure's busy schedule as spiritual director to a cadre of elite dévots, but the good father's acceptance of Jeanne Mance into his spiritual care led to introductions to such well-placed dévots as Charlotte-Marguerite de Montmorency, princesse de Condé, the wife of Chancellor Pierre Séguier; the duchesse d'Aiguillon; the marquise de Liancourt; Louise de Marillac, a widow soon to cofound the nursing Sisters of Charity in partnership with Vincent de Paul; and Marie Rousseau, the celebrated clairvoyant. Finally, the queen herself, the devout Anne of Austria, expressed a desire to meet this dynamic daughter of the provinces, aflame with evangelical ambition for New France. Father Rapine de Boisvert, provincial of the Recollects, introduced Mance to his cousin the widow Angélique Faure de Bullion, daughter of Guichard Faure de Berlise, secretary and master in ordinary to the king; and to her dear friend Madeleine Brûlart de Sillery, sister of the Knight of Malta who had donated his Quebec lands to the Jesuits.

On Mance's fourth visit to the Hôtel de Bullion, Madame de Bullion informed her that she, Madame de Bullion, shared Mademoiselle Mance's desire to found a hospital in New France, provided that Mademoiselle Mance would take charge of the project—and how much, incidentally, had the duchesse d'Aiguillon donated for the hospital scheduled for Quebec? She would find out, Jeanne Mance replied. After a few discreet enquiries, she had the answer. With the help of her uncle the cardinal, the duchesse had given 22,000 livres, later raised to 40,500. Jeanne Mance

obtained the consent of her spiritual director, Father Saint-Jure, to accept the assignment of organizing the hospital in New France to be built and staffed thanks to the
largesse of Madame de Bullion, who in turn now promised to finance the venture,
provided that Jeanne Mance never reveal the identity of her patroness.

Departure and foundation

Thus in April 1641, eleven months after her first trip to Paris, Jeanne Mance was
back in Langres saying good-bye to friends and relatives prior to setting off to La
Rochelle to arrange her departure for Canada with major support promised for the
founding of a hospital in the wilderness. The situation was—and remains—barely
believable, but true! A pious middle-class woman from the provinces takes upper-
register Paris by storm in eleven short months and leaves for New France with the
best wishes and financial support of the queen regent and dévot Paris. Every protag-
onist related to the founding of Montreal seems to be a socially prominent dévot, a
Jesuit, a prominent prelate or secular priest, a teaching or nursing sister, a founder
of a religious order, or some combination thereof.

But there is even more to the story. On her second day in La Rochelle, visiting the Jesuit church in the city, Jeanne Mance met Jérôme Le Royer de la Dauversière, tax collector of La Flèche. As in the case of Dauversière's meeting with
the Abbé Olier at Mendon two years earlier, these two dévots instantly recognized
each other as partners in the same enterprise. Describing the plans of the Society
of Our Lady of Montreal and learning of Jeanne Mance's own hopes, Dauversière,
acting on behalf of the society, offered her the role of bursar (business manager)
of the proposed Montreal hospital if she would agree to join the already endowed
venture to which he was connected and for which money, material, and volunteers
had been accruing for the past eighteen months. Yes, she would, Mance replied,
provided that her spiritual director (and Madame de Bullion, whom she did not
name) approved. Receiving Mance's letter of query, Father Saint-Jure approved, as
did Madame de Bullion, contacted more discreetly following Saint-Jure's approval.
Perhaps at the instruction of Madame de Bullion, Jeanne Mance—now fully an
equal among equals in this grand venture—requested that Dauversière write up a
full description of the plans of the Society of Our Lady of Montreal (which Mance
had joined) and provide her with multiple copies of the text, which she would have
delivered into the hands of more possible supporters, along with an invitation to
join the Society.

Initially, difficulties arose regarding Mance's passage to New France as the sole
unaccompanied female on a transatlantic voyage, but when a number of soldiers'
wives decided to accompany their husbands to Canada, decorum was reestablished.
On 9 May 1641 the expedition set sail in two ships. Mance's ship experienced an
easy passage, and she arrived at Quebec on 8 August. Maisonneuve's ship, by contrast, was sent back to La Rochelle three times because of coastal storms, and he did
not arrive at Quebec until 20 September.

By 17 May 1642, however, the two founders were on the Island of Montreal
before a flower-bedecked altar: the young captain Paul de Chomedey, sieur de
Maisonneuve, standing in front of his soldiers and artisans; and Jeanne Mance, the
nurse dévot, standing on her own behalf, but also representing two absent founders.

There in spirit were the Abbé Jean-Jacques Olier, whose connection to the city he would never visit would soon grow in importance and who in the meanwhile had begun his life's work as seminary educator and pastor of Saint-Sulpice in Paris; and Jérôme Le Royer de la Dauversière, who remained at home in La Flèche with his wife and six children, planning the organization of the society of Hospitaller Sisters he would one day send to Ville-Marie. Also in the group before the altar were Father Barthélemy Vimont, who had put the Society of Jesus solidly behind the project, celebrating Mass and preaching; Governor Charles Huault de Montmagny, Knight of Malta, who still believed the settlement was too far upriver; the aged Pierre de Puiseaux, major donor of land on the island, doing his best to look generous; and Madame Marie-Madeleine de Chauvigny de La Peltrie, bringing her usual éclat to the founding of this improbable city on the edge of unexplored wilderness and representing all those privileged and devout women of Paris, including the queen, who had aligned themselves behind the founding of Ville-Marie.

14

Saint-Ignace 1649

Iroquois destroy Huronia and threaten the survival of New France

In the *Jesuit Relations* issued between 1646 and 1650, Paul Ragueneau, since 1645 the superior of Jesuits in Huronia, chronicled the destruction of Huronia as a Jesuit mission that ended the existence of the Huron as an autonomous confederation and came close to wiping them from the face of the earth. As a survivor of this debacle, Ragueneau compiled his reports from personal observation and from the testimony of other survivors. "It is no longer from the country of the Hurons", Ragueneau wrote in his report for 1649–1650 to Claude de Lingendes, provincial of the Society of Jesus in France,

> that I send to your Reverence the Relation of what has happened therein. The poor infant Church—which was seen, a year ago, bathed in its own blood, trodden down by the cruelty of the Iroquois, the enemies of God's name and of the Faith—has since then undergone yet greater sufferings. The larger number of our good Neophytes, with some of their Pastors, have followed through fire and flame the steps of their predecessors, and now bear them company in Heaven. A terrible famine, prevalent everywhere, has wrought desolation. We count over three thousand baptized during the past year; but the dead outnumber those who survive the ruin of their native Land. Reduced thus to extremity, we found ourselves at last compelled to relinquish a position that was no longer tenable, that we might, at least, save those who remained. It was on the tenth day of last June that we took our departure from this land of Promise, which was to us a Paradise, and in which death would have been to us a thousand times more sweet than life will be in any place where we could dwell.[1]

Central to this story of destruction, genocide, and exile were the events of mid-March 1649. Already the Jesuits of Huronia were aware of the dangers they faced from marauding Iroquois armed with muskets provided by Dutch traders based out of Fort Orange (Albany) in upstate New York who were eager to enlist the Iroquois as roving pirates of the fur caches of other tribes as they were being stored or brought to market by canoe on the Richelieu, Ottawa, and Saint Lawrence Rivers. By 1643 an estimated three hundred muskets were in Iroquois hands, transforming the Iroquois—the Mohawks and Senecas especially—into a formidable guerilla border army on behalf of New Holland against Huronia as a frontier outpost of New France, with an increasing capacity to operate down the Saint Lawrence River as far as Ville-Marie, Trois-Riviéres, and Quebec. On 18 October 1646 donné Jean Lalande and the renowned missionary and explorer Isaac Jogues—among the first Frenchmen to reach Lake Superior, preaching there with plans to move even farther west to the headwaters of the Mississippi and evangelize the Sioux—became the first two Jesuits of the French missions to be murdered in the line of duty. Jogues was returning against all advice to Mohawk country in upstate New York, where in 1642 he had been cruelly tortured and held captive for thirteen months. He and Lalande were tortured and decapitated at the Mohawk village of Ossernenon (Auriesville, New York) near Lake George. Claiming that they were sorcerers who had brought sickness and agricultural blight to their land, the Mohawks displayed their severed heads on the palisades and threw their bodies into the Mohawk River.

On 4 July 1648—taking advantage of the fact that most Huron of warrior age were off hunting, scouting, or engaging in the fur trade—Iroquois raiders descended upon the villages of Saint-Joseph and Saint-Michel in the early morning hours as Jesuit missionary Antoine Daniel was saying Mass for a congregation of women, children, and the elderly. As the Iroquois destroyed the villages, Daniel comforted his congregation, who remained within the chapel, and baptized a number of neophytes. Urging his flock to flee, Daniel thereupon walked boldly from the chapel to confront the Iroquois marauders busy with massacre. Pausing for a moment to admire Daniel's bravery, the Iroquois riddled the Jesuit with arrows and one musket ball to the chest. The Iroquois took seven hundred Huron captives, the majority of them—again, women, children, and the elderly—burned to death in their cabins prior to departure or slain en route.

Eight months later, before sunrise on 16 March 1649, the advance guard of an Iroquois raiding party one thousand strong mounted a surprise attack on Saint-Ignace. Once again, most able-bodied men were away, this time out hunting or, ironically, patrolling for Iroquois. Although the Iroquois were twice repulsed, the palisaded village fell to the third attack, and nearly all of its inhabitants, including women and children, were slaughtered in retaliation for their resistance.

Four kilometers away, at the palisaded village of Saint-Louis, a handful of refugees from Saint-Ignace managed to reach temporary safety and sound the alert. Eight Huron warriors were on hand at Saint-Louis to meet the forthcoming attack. The Iroquois arrived at sunrise, but, lacking the element of surprise, they lost thirty warriors and many wounded on their first strike. Nor were the Iroquois able to scale the palisades on subsequent tries. Finally forced to cut their way through at ground level with hatchets, the Iroquois commenced their second massacre of the morning.

During the assault, the two Jesuits stationed at Saint-Louis—the veteran missioner Jean de Brébeuf, fifty-six, and Gabriel Lalemant, thirty-six, only two years in New France and a mere eight months of that on mission in Huronia—were tending the wounded and baptizing the dying. Although they had an opportunity to escape, the two priests voluntarily remained with their flock and were captured. Taken by their captors back to Saint-Ignace, the two Jesuits endured a pornography of torture that to this day sickens the reader and defies belief: the gouging of eyes, the tearing away of lips and tongues and scalp, the pouring of burning resin over lacerated skin, the burning and stripping of flesh to the bone, the cannibalism of flesh torn from the still-living men and devoured derisively. The infamy was witnessed by other captives and confirmed four days later in an examination of the two corpses by Jesuit donné Christophe Regnault.

Compounding the hideousness of this torture was the fact that the Indians most active as tormentors were not Iroquois but apostate Huron who had fled Huronia and defected to the traditional enemy of the Huron Confederacy. Making explicit references to Catholic rites, they poured boiling water over their victims in a mock baptism and hung about their necks rosaries of red-hot tomahawk heads.

The robust and athletic Jean de Brébeuf—Échon, the Huron called him, meaning a man who on portage or the trail carried his fair share of the load—took three hours to die. Not once, tradition has it, did Brébeuf answer his tormentors. Finally, as if his torturers were growing tired of their gruesome play, he was dispatched with a tomahawk blow to his skull, from which much flesh had already been stripped. In contrast to the sturdy outdoorsman Brébeuf, his colleague Gabriel Lalemant was a refined Parisian, the cherished youngest of six children born to dévot parents, the nephew of two famed Jesuit uncles (Jérôme and Charles Lalemant), and the brother of a cloistered Carmelite nun. Although "no one could be more frail and delicate", as Marie de l'Incarnation observed, Lalemant had nevertheless volunteered for missionary duty in New France, winning the love and respect of his colleagues. Yet this sensitive man lasted fifteen hours at the stake, from six at night until nine the next morning. In addition to baptizing him with scalding water and wreathing his neck with the rosary of red-hot tomahawk blades, the torturing apostate Huron gouged out one of his eyes (some sources claim both) when Lalemant lifted them to heaven, poured hot coals down his throat to end his praying, and slit the flesh of his thighs to form crosses.

The genocide continues

Having finished their ghastly task of torturing the two Black Robes, the Iroquois (joined, presumably, by their apostate Huron allies) returned to the task of decimating the Huron people. The populations of the villages and mission stations they had already taken—Saint-Joseph, Saint-Michel, Saint-Ignace, Saint-Louis—were exterminated. From a Catholic perspective, each death—each mother or child tomahawked, or burned alive, and each Huron warrior felled while resisting—was as great a loss as that of each of the four martyred Jesuit missionaries. When Lalemant's sister, the Carmelite nun, heard of his death, she dropped to her knees and intoned a Magnificat, a song of praise, that her brother, having died for the faith, was now with God; and his widowed mother forsook the world to become, like her daughter, a cloistered nun. These lost and lovely Huron people, especially the loving mothers and innocent children, hacked or burned to death in the forests of New France, stand alongside canonized saints in history and theological discourse alike.

The destruction of Huronia did not cease until one last terrible massacre following fierce fighting at Saint-Marie. Huron warriors from La Conception and Saint-Madeleine arrived as a relief force, held two hundred attacking Iroquois at bay, and drove them back to Saint-Louis, which the Huron then carried, taking thirty Iroquois prisoners. The main force of invading Iroquois, however, soon reached Saint-Louis. It cost them about a hundred lives, but by 18 March 1649 the forests of Huronia emanated an eerie silence, and Saint-Louis was in ruins, its Huron defenders dead or in captivity. Time to end this expedition and to leave Huronia, the Iroquois decided. As it was, they could barely carry all the furs they had seized. The stronger of the Huron captives gathered at Saint-Ignace survived as packers of pirated furs back to the Iroquois homeland. The remaining women, children, and elderly were either hacked to death on the spot or tied to the posts of cabins set afire. Their cries could be heard as the Iroquois and their Huron pack train headed into the forest.

The Huron of the destroyed villages of Saint-Jean-Baptiste and Saint-Michel had survived by joining the Senecas of the Iroquois Confederacy as a captive people, perhaps in bondage but still alive, and Catholic in their new location. The Bear People, who had so welcomed Brébeuf in 1626, fled to the Tobacco Nation. The Neutrals, the Eries, and the Algonquians took in other remnants of the once for-midable Huron Nation. Even then, the danger from the Iroquois continued, as the Huron Bear People of the village of Saint-Jean on the shores of Georgian Bay dis-covered when Iroquois pillaged it in December 1649; and two more missionaries, Charles Garnier and Noël Chabanel, joined the ranks of murdered Jesuits.

The grandson of a Catholic commandant hanged for refusing to turn Protestant when his city fell to the Huguenot prince de Condé, Garnier possessed Gabriel Lalemant's likeability but escaped his long torture, being felled by musket fire and then killed by tomahawk when, despite his wounds, he tried to continue minister-ing to dying victims. Noël Chabanel had suffered from depression since his arrival in Huronia due to his inability to learn Huron, which was rather embarrassing for a former professor of rhetoric and poetry in the Jesuit colleges at Rodez and Tou-louse. And if this were not enough, Chabanel—were he forced to admit it—did not really like the Huron or Tobacco People. He found them impossibly dirty and loathed the gross food they served. Only martyrdom, Chabanel decided, could sal-vage his thus-far-disastrous missionary career. His depression lifted sometime after 21 June 1647, when he first had this insight and vowed to remain with the Huron mission for the rest of his life. Martyrdom eluded Chabanel when he was transferred from Saint-Ignace a month before it fell to the Iroquois, but he got his wish at last in December 1649 when, en route to Saint-Jean to assist Father Garnier (whose death at that point was not known), he was tomahawked by his boatman, an apostate Huron, and thrown into the Nottawasaga River.

In all Huronia, only the flagship village of Sainte-Marie-aux-Hurons survived and was receiving refugees. The Jesuits moved the entire population of Saint-Marie by ship and raft to a safer location on the Ile Saint-Joseph on Georgian Bay. Some ten thousand Huron, Huron chiefs informed the Jesuits, had been killed. The rest had scattered westward. If the remaining Huron were to survive massacre and famine, the chiefs opined, they must resettle in Quebec. The next year, under the direction of Father Paul Ragueneau, the remaining three hundred baptized Huron retraced the route that Jean de Brébeuf had pioneered a quarter century earlier, passing through a once-populated Huronia that had become a no-man's-land save for patrols of savage Iroquois, and settled on the Island of Orleans in the Saint Lawrence River near Quebec. There, for the time being, they thought they would be safe.

The Iroquois attack Montreal

Ville-Marie on the Island of Montreal, the fleeing Huron decided, was too dan-gerous a place to stop for long, and so they stayed there a mere two days before continuing on to Quebec. The Huron made the right decision. In times past, they had cooperated with Iroquois attacking this settlement. The theologized urbanism of Ville-Marie/Montreal, moreover—at once the most frontier and the most self-consciously Catholic civil settlement in New France—confers on it a distinctive identity in the history of continental ambitions on the part of Roman Catholic nations in North America prior to the American Revolution. Montreal sprang from a clarity of idea and purpose, reinforced by its primary founders' religious sentiment that literally willed a Catholic city into being far ahead of what might have been the normal course of events. Thus Francis Parkman, while generally respectful of the religiosity of the first generation of settlers at Ville-Marie, cannot help but distance himself from their belief that a rising of the Saint Lawrence threatening to flood the newly founded colony into oblivion ceased on Christmas Day and receded inches from destroying the powder magazine, which the settlers took as a miracle. To commemorate this miracle, they constructed a large cross in thanks-giving that the Maisonneuve, with great difficulty, carried to the top of Mont Réal for permanent emplacement, followed by a Mass at which "Madame de La Peltrie, always romantic and always devout, received the sacrament on the mountain-top, a spectacle to the virgin world outstretched below."[2]

Along with Madame de La Peltrie, there was the less improbable but still mysterious presence of Jeanne Mance. These women crossed the sea (a perilous voyage), went upriver to Quebec, and, finally, proceeded to this place on the edge of Mohawk territory, where—piling improbability upon improbability—they had constructed a fully supplied hospital on higher ground outside the fort. The sixty-by-twenty-four-foot building contained two wards, a kitchen, and chambers for Mademoiselle Mance and staff yet to arrive, all furnished with cots, linen, and medicine. A small stone oratory chapel stood adjacent to the structure, and to support the nutritional needs of future patients, two oxen, three cows, and twenty sheep were shipped over from France, to pasture on four arpents of land. "Here Mademoiselle Mance took up her abode," Parkman notes, "and waited the day when wounds or disease should bring patients to her empty wards."[3]

Not until June 1643, however, did Mohawks even learn of the existence of Ville-Marie—and this from a group of sixty Huron bringing furs downriver by canoe. In an effort to distract the Mohawks from seizing their furs, the Huron suggested that they attack Ville-Marie for a quick victory. Forty Iroquois proceeded to ambush six Frenchmen cutting timber outside the fort. They killed three and took three prisoners for future torture. Following a victory feast that night, the Iroquois rose up in stealth and slaughtered most of the sleeping Huron, who thought they were among friends. A few surviving Huron made it safely to Ville-Marie and, claiming an unprovoked attack, were given sanctuary.

Once aware of Ville-Marie, the Iroquois grew persistent in their efforts at ambush, forcing the French into a life confined behind the palisades, going beyond the fort only on occasion to farm (to the detriment of the crops they had been cultivating) or to cut wood for the long winter. Maisonneuve kept the colony on constant alert. In July 1643 Governor-General Montmagny returned with good news from Paris. The king had authorized the Society of Our Lady of Montreal to complete Ville-Marie as an official fort, complete with artillery. His Majesty had also made a gift of the 350-ton ship *La Notre-Dame* to the society for the colony's use. Madame de Bullion, moreover, was donating an additional 12,000 livres for the hospital.

In September 1643 forty new recruits arrived from France under the command of military engineer Louis d'Ailleboust, who was accompanied by his wife and sister-in-law, an unusual trio of nobly born dévots who belonged to the Society of Our Lady of Montréal and volunteered for Canada following Madame d'Ailleboust's recovery from a near-fatal illness. Ville-Marie now had four pious nobility in residence, with Louis d'Ailleboust a welcomed partner to Maisonneuve in matters of military defense and engineering as well as further agricultural development. Also in residence were a half dozen or more French women of all classes, including several soldiers' wives—already mothers or soon to become mothers—plus a number of baptized Indian mothers and children living nearby. This population foreshadowed the civilian future of the settlement. Arriving as well from France were sentry dogs to be employed scenting out Iroquois hiding in ambush. Madame de La Peltrie's sentry dog, Pilote, proved especially adept at this crucial service, although Madame herself and Monseigneur Pierre de Puiseaux, now in his late seventies, soon thereafter returned to Quebec after eighteen months in the new settlement, thus depriving Ville-Marie of two of its most unusual inhabitants.

The Iroquois, meanwhile, continued to harass the settlement, and the soldiers grew restive with their confinement, due to Maisonneuve's belief that they were not skilled enough to confront the Iroquois in open battle. When the barking of Pilote and other sentry dogs gave warning on 30 March 1644 of a band of more than one hundred Iroquois in the vicinity, the soldiers confronted Maisonneuve, and he finally relented. Taking to the field, Maisonneuve positioned his men behind trees on the approach to the fort. When the Iroquois arrived, the French began firing, but the Iroquois—dexterous in their snowshoes—outmaneuvered the immobile French, killing two and fatally wounding a third. Maisonneuve gave the order to withdraw, which his men did with alacrity, leaving their captain to hold down the rear of their retreat on his own, armed with two pistols. Attacked by the chief of the Iroquois, Maisonneuve fired once and missed. The Iroquois then wrestled with Maisonneuve before he managed a second shot that killed the chief. The Iroquois warriors thereupon broke off their attack to recover the body of their fallen leader.

The rising influence of Ville-Marie

From that point on, Maisonneuve enjoyed the full confidence of his men as well as the support of Anne of Austria, the queen regent. At the urging of influential members of the Society of Our Lady of Montreal, she sent a letter dated 13 February 1644 appointing him governor of the island and seigneur of Montreal and thus, in effect, making the Montreal settlement an entity independent of Quebec, the Company of One Hundred Associates, and the Society of Jesus. The Jesuits, moreover, were balking at the prospect of a lay-dominated colony not only conducting its own affairs, financed and politically supported by influential nobility in France, but also ambitiously evangelizing Indians. Two competing Catholic polities were coming into conflict: a Jesuit-dominated missionary culture (the Recollects having been banned) allied to a Capuchin presence in Acadia and a lay-dominated Ville-Marie that by 1647 was, through the sponsoring Society of Our Lady of Montreal in Paris, asking for the appointment of secular priests to Ville-Marie and the establishment of a diocese in Canada.

Jean-Jacques Olier had by this time come into his own as pastor of the parish of Saint-Sulpice in the faubourg Saint-Germain of Paris and the founder of an influential group of reforming seminary professors. It was unusual for a priest of noble rank such as Olier to turn down a bishopric and even more unusual for a nobleman to assume the direction of a large urban parish. But Saint-Sulpice was not an ordinary parish. It was huge, for one thing, embracing a good portion of Paris and reputed to be the largest single parish in the Church. Second, the appointment of its pastor by long custom came directly from the pope, thereby freeing its pastor from local ecclesiastical authorities' excessive interference. Thus Olier, while saying *nolo episcopari* to the offer of a mitre, had in effect gained jurisdiction over a near-autonomous diocese within the Archdiocese of Paris. Nearly eighty secular priests were associated in one way or another with the multiple parish ministries of Saint-Sulpice.

To this parish, Olier attached a seminary program dedicated to the reinvigoration and reprofessionalization of the secular diocesan priesthood. Olier staffed this seminary with members of an institute of secular priests he also founded, the Company (or Gentlemen) of Saint-Sulpice: men such as himself, from established families and academic backgrounds, and similarly committed to a theologically intensified concept of the priesthood, exercised on its own terms as the priesthood of Jesus Christ, sufficient unto itself, and not requiring membership in a religious order but remaining supportive of the hierarchy and diocesan organizational structures.

Thus as early as May 1645, with the consent of Cardinal Mazarin, the Society of Our Lady of Montreal came close to having Thomas Legauffre, a Sulpician abbé, named bishop in New France, but Legauffre had a stroke and died while he was on religious retreat mulling over the offer; and the Jesuits, who had initially approved of the appointment, on second thought opposed it, and the prospect of a bishop for New France went into remission.

Attacks continue

War with the Iroquois resumed in October 1646. Following the murders of Jesuit Isaac Jogues and donné Jean Lalande, Mohawk Iroquois intermittently ambushed or besieged Ville-Marie over the next four years, but their main objective was the destruction of Huronia, accomplished by 1650. Still, Ville-Marie settlers kept losing their lives to Iroquois fury. On 6 May 1651 Iroquois killed two men and carried off a young wife, Katherine Mercier Boudart, whom they tortured horribly, cutting off her nose, ears, and breasts and burning her at the stake in revenge for the eight warriors they had lost on the raid. Four days later, forty Iroquois once again struck Ville-Marie but were driven off. A month later a third raid approached, but this time the French intercepted the Iroquois at some distance from the settlement. A second detachment of French came to the aid of the interceptors, and thirty Iroquois were killed in the battle that followed, with the French suffering one fatality and three wounded. The training and organization being provided by Maisonneuve and d'Ailleboust was paying off. Despite the Iroquois effort, Ville-Marie would not succumb to attack and massacre, as even more failed Iroquois attacks proved on 26 July 1651 (a major raid of some sixty Iroquois), followed by smaller attacks on 13 and 16 August, with the French successfully defending themselves and losing only one settler to the Iroquois and one to friendly cannonfire from the fort. To buy themselves safety, Huron who had taken refuge in Ville-Marie directed invading war parties to the very settlement that had offered the Huron refuge.

Maisonneuve made two voyages to France in these years, leaving the ever-competent d'Ailleboust in command from 1645 to the summer of 1647. When Maisonneuve returned, he had important news for his colleague: per an agreement between the Company of One Hundred Associates and the Society of Our Lady of Montreal, d'Ailleboust was to replace Montmagny as governor of New France. After eleven years of service, the Knight of Malta wanted to retire. The council of the king had originally wanted Maisonneuve to serve, but that selfless soldier had declined the appointment in favor of his colleague. D'Ailleboust was to return to France as soon as possible to receive his commission.

The next year, on 8 September 1648, Jeanne Mance returned alone to France on behalf of Ville-Marie, testimony to her standing as an equal to Maisonneuve and d'Ailleboust in the leadership of the colony. While there, Mance secured from Madame de Bullion promises of continuing support and yet another gift, this time to purchase two hundred acres from the seigneurial domain for the hospital. From the Society of Our Lady of Montreal Mance attained a formal declaration, dated 21 March 1650, stating that the Associates of the Society, meaning Maisonneuve and d'Ailleboust, held equal status with members of the society in France as far as ownership of the seigneurial domain of Ville-Marie was concerned, thus strengthening even further the autonomy of the Montreal colony. Mance also helped to head off an effort by the pro-Jesuit duc and duchesse de Liancourt to persuade the Society of Our Lady of Montreal to shift its support from the Montreal plan to the embattled Jesuit mission to the Huron. How exactly all this was accomplished by an unmarried middle-class dévot nurse serving as the matron of a hospital on the edge of a dangerous wilderness—who would soon be returning to her post there—remains an intriguing question. Suffice it to say that Jeanne Mance must have possessed extraordinary self-assurance and negotiating skills in addition to her persuasive religious commitment.

Population grows

Mance returned to a Ville-Marie on the verge of significant development, as Maisonneuve inaugurated a program of land grants of forty acres (in the safe vicinity of the fort) to artisans who, at the conclusion of their contracts, wished to remain as permanent settlers. Thus, as Huronia was falling, the land immediately surrounding Ville-Marie began to spring up with small but well-crafted, well-defended homes, each with a bedroom, a kitchen warmed by a fieldstone fireplace (where cooking was done in a single pot), a granary under the roof, and small windows covered with oiled paper, and surrounded by fields of wheat and Indian corn and smaller patches of onions, carrots, and pumpkins. Heads of households retained rights to their property as well as rights to hunt and fish. In 1650 Louis Prudhomme established a brewery for the colony thirty-eight years before the Jesuits opened a brewery in Quebec.

Life nevertheless remained dangerous for Montreal habitants as long as Iroquois roamed the forests, which remained the case for the rest of the century, even after the Onondaga branch of the Iroquois concluded a separate peace treaty with

Ville-Marie in June 1652. Hence the joy in October 1653 when, after much tribulation and delay, 105 new male recruits arrived in Ville-Marie on five-year contracts to the colony. To fortify the permanent population further, Maisonneuve began the very next year to launch a new and expanded recruitment program. He would, Maisonneuve announced, annul the five-year contract of any new recruit who declared his intention to remain, thus freeing him to become a self-assigned wage earner, as well as offer him a land grant and a bounty from money loaned by Jeanne Mance from the hospital fund recently augmented by Madame de Bullion, provided that the recruit pledge himself by binding contract to remain permanently in the colony. Forty recruits accepted Maisonneuve's offer in 1654, ten more in 1655.

Despite the dangers of living at Ville-Marie, ten marriages had taken place in the settlement between 1642 and 1653. Fourteen more were solemnized in 1654. Grooms were young, brides even younger, and families large. Charles Le Moyne, twenty-eight, for example, the colony's lead interpreter, married Catherine Thierry, fourteen, on 28 May 1654 with Maisonneuve and Mance standing as witnesses. In recognition of Le Moyne's service to the colony, Maisonneuve granted the couple eighty acres, the largest grant thus far, with hunting and fishing rights and a building site for their home on prize land near the hospital. The couple had eleven children, seven of whom would have outstanding military careers in the years to come.

Two competing models

Two competing ecclesiastical models had by now developed along the Saint Lawrence River: Montreal, dominated by prominent laity in France and New France alike and connected to the secular clergy via Father Olier and the Sulpician movement; and Quebec, dominated by the Society of Jesus, given in 1632 exclusive jurisdiction in ecclesiastical matters in the region by Cardinal Richelieu, who in that same year also barred the Recollects from returning to Quebec when the colony reverted to French jurisdiction. Richelieu had, in fact, made the Jesuits part of the governance structure and fur-trading economy of Quebec. Governor-General Montmagny's initial suspicion of the Montreal venture was more than a matter of believing that the Island of Montreal was too far upriver, and hence unsafe and perhaps indefensible. Montmagny resented the quasi-autonomy of Ville-Marie. Indeed, he had arrested and briefly imprisoned an employee of Ville-Maria, shipmaster Jean Gorry, for firing his ship's cannon to honor the feast of Saint Paul (after whom Maisonneuve was named) without the governor's permission.

Both Montreal and Quebec were Catholic and committed to evangelizing the indigenous populations. Yet when the laity of Ville-Marie embarked on such a mission, it disquieted the Jesuits, since the conversion of Native Americans and the reform of certain aspects of their lifestyles to conform with Catholic practice was the Society's primary reason for being in Canada in the first place. Secular or diocesan clergy, by contrast, were expected to remain celibate and obey their bishops, but they could own private property. Their primary duty—and this was especially true among clergy of lower ranks—was the spiritual care of laypeople in a parish setting. The higher clergy in this era came from the nobility and only rarely were members of religious orders. As already suggested, the Catholic Revival in France during the first half of the seventeenth century was very much concerned with the theology and reformed practice of the secular parish priesthood. As of yet, the presence of secular priests in New France had been minimal. Before the rise of Ville-Marie, Canada did not contain enough French families to support a parish structure. New France was missionary territory. The aim of the Frenchmen there was to acquire furs, and the aim of the Jesuits was to convert Indians and transform them into acceptable Catholics in belief and lifestyle.

Hence the Jesuits established the mission settlement of Sillery and founded their first school in Quebec, initially a school for young Indians. The Ursuline Sisters were committed to work there as well, at first to educate Indian girls into becoming young Catholic women to marry young Catholic Frenchmen—or young Catholic Indian men, for that matter—and create a Frenchified Catholic population for Canada. Thus the disappointment of the Jesuits when the Indian boys they sent to their school in Quebec failed to learn, ran away, or, in one ghastly instance of two youngsters, broke into the larder and ate themselves to death. And thus the disappointment of the Ursulines when their charges likewise ran away to rejoin their people or otherwise proved reluctant—despite Madame de La Peltrie's hugs, coos, and kisses or the patient tutelage of the sisters—to transform into nice French girls or even nice Frenchified Indian girls. Not all Indians, of course. Records show that a number of Native Americans—older women, mainly, and a handful of chiefs or sachems—authentically converted to Catholic Christianity and became religious leaders of their people. And a mixed population did develop over time with its unique version of French Catholic culture, but this blending happened mainly in less developed regions and on its own terms.

Think, then, how the Jesuits must have responded as their mission to Huronia came increasingly under stress: as conversion rates remained low and Huron shamans convinced the people that the Jesuits were sorcerers who had brought disease and cursed their crops; as the Huron refused to conform their sexual practices to Catholic teachings; as they continued to torture captives; as they maintained their faith in fetishes and ritual practices based in prior beliefs; as they in so many other ways resisted evangelization. Jesuit missionaries did have an orientation toward inculturalization. Their successes in China, India, and Japan proved that. But those societies, especially that of Japan, were comparable to the Jesuits' own. The same could not be said of Huronia. The Huron practiced a culture and way of life in another mode entirely, or so it seemed in the early years of evangelization. Jesuits such as Jean de Brébeuf and others, however, managed to master their language—particularly Brébeuf, who compiled a dictionary and became adept at using Huron metaphor in formal oratory—and to overlook as much as possible what they considered chronic deficiencies, such as sexual promiscuity, the torturing of prisoners, ritualized cannibalism, eating orgies, and deficient hygiene. Still, a formidable cultural barrier remained.

Yet a vision beckoned, a Catholic-friendly Huronia, nurturing a growing number of Catholic Christian Huron gathered into villages under Jesuit care. The theology of such an ambition was self-apparent. Each Huron, the Jesuits believed, possessed an immortal and rational soul and was therefore redeemable through instruction, conversion, baptism, and the other sacraments. True, the Huron religion, as practiced by various shamans, had diabolical elements (seventeenth-century French Catholics had a special sensitivity to diabolical possession), but the Huron religion did admit the concept of a single all-powerful Creator, and the Huron language possessed concepts and metaphors that could be used to convey Catholic truth.

And so the Jesuit missionaries toiled on despite relatively meager results. Cultural intractability—especially in sexual matters, the torturing of prisoners, and ritual cannibalism—disease, and Iroquois antagonism each played a role in impeding evangelization. Historians hostile to the Jesuit effort (although not Francis Parkman) frequently blame the fall of Huronia on the fact that it was Christianized and hence grew weak and unable to resist the Iroquois. Not so. For one thing, epidemics—smallpox and dysentery in 1634, malignant influenza in 1636, and smallpox again in 1639—reduced the Huron population by two-thirds, from an estimated thirty thousand to twelve thousand, and outbreaks of agricultural blight made it difficult for even those few to survive. Cleverly, Huron shamans attributed these epidemics—which originated in New England and were brought to the Saint Lawrence valley by visiting Indians who passed them on to the Huron trading with the French—to the Jesuits, and the resulting hostility helped to destroy the Jesuit mission to Huronia.

A growing obsession with martyrdom

At this point, with physical harm and expulsion being threatened against them, a growing sense of violent death, perceived as martyrdom, entered the collective consciousness of the Jesuit missionaries to Huronia. "We are probably about to pour out our blood and to make the sacrifice of our lives", Brébeuf wrote his Jesuit superior, Barthélemy Vimont, in Quebec from Ossossané village (La Conception) on 28 October 1637. To that end, in the event that and the other four Jesuits in the region were slain, Brébeuf had instructed a convert named Peter to lead the neophytes to safety and save the sacred articles in the chapel as well as his manuscript Huron dictionary and other writings on the language. "Whatever the end may be," Brébeuf concluded, "our only worry is about the unhappy moral condition of the savages, whose wickedness thus closes on themselves the gates of salvation."[4]

Brébeuf and his colleagues were not killed—at least not then—but they were persecuted even more intensely: their chapels attacked, their crosses torn down, they themselves threatened with death upon entering Huron villages. This intimidation climaxed in April 1640 with the beatings of three priests, Brébeuf included, which led to the closing of the latest Jesuit mission, Saint-Joseph II at Téanostaiaé. Under the direction of regional superior Jérôme Lalemant, Brébeuf and Father Pierre-Joseph-Marie Chaumonot then spent the next five months trying to establish a mission in the southwest but met with equal hostility. As they returned, Brébeuf fell on the ice, breaking his clavicle, and was forced to crawl on his hands and knees to negotiate difficult terrain after refusing the offer of a pack sled for the remaining thirty-six miles. The collarbone was never set properly and remained a constant source of pain. Temporarily unfit for field duty, Brébeuf was reassigned to Sillery just outside Quebec, where he spent the next three years as procurator (supply officer) for the Huron missions.

By 1644 the Society of Jesus in both France and New France had a new hero in its midst, Isaac Jogues, a missionary who had come as close to martyrdom as one could and live to tell the tale. A former professor of literature at the Jesuit college at Rouen, Jogues had arrived in Canada in June 1636 on the same ship as Governor-General Montmagny and joined Brébeuf and the other Jesuits laboring among the Huron. Over the next six years, Jogues evangelized as far west and north as Sault Sainte-Marie, the eastern outlet of Lake Superior, one thousand miles inland, and was investigating the possibility of evangelizing the Sioux who lived on the headwaters of the Mississippi on the western side of this greatest of the Great Lakes. Returning from a visit to Quebec on mission business, Jogues was kidnapped by Mohawks near Trois Rivières on 3 August 1642 and held in slavery for thirteen months at the village of Ossernenon on the Mohawk River, some forty miles north of present-day Albany. Jogues had initially escaped the Mohawk attack on his convoy but, watching from a hiding place as a group of Catholic and catechumen Indians were being rounded up, he recognized his duty. "It must be, I said in my heart," Jogues later stated, "that my body suffer the fire of earth, in order to deliver these poor souls from the flames of Hell; it [my body] must die a transient death in order to procure for them an eternal life." Leaving his safe site, Jogues surrendered to the Mohawks.

What followed during the next thirteen days as the Mohawks returned to their home base—cuttings, beatings, torture by fire, the removal of fingernails, the biting and chewing away of fingers, whippings when naked with thornbush branches, all repeated with variations once they entered Mohawk territory, including three days and three nights staked out on the ground in the shape of a Saint Andrew's Cross, beaten and tortured all the while ("such was our entrance into Babylon", Jogues describes it)—was climaxed by the tomahawking to death of Jogues' colleague, the donné René Goupil, a medically trained infirmarian assigned to Sillery and the Hôtel-Dieu in Quebec. Goupil's offense: making the sign of the cross on a child's forehead. Dying with the name Jesus on his lips, Goupil was described by Jogues as a true and blessed martyr.[5]

On the verge of being burned to death after thirteen months of slavery (during which time he managed to baptize more than sixty Mohawk children), Jogues was rescued by Dutch traders from Fort Orange (Albany), taken to New Amsterdam (New York), and repatriated by ship to Brittany, where—emaciated and semicrippled from his ordeal—he presented himself to the porter of the nearest Jesuit college, who at first thought he was a beggar. Soon, Jogues found himself a celebrity, received by the queen regent and by Pope Urban VIII, who authorized him to celebrate Mass despite his chewed-down finger stubs. Jogues returned to Canada at his own request in the spring of 1644 and was posted to Montreal.

A mystic in search of martyrdom

Jean de Brébeuf, meanwhile, had spent the same two years at Sillery, purchasing and shipping supplies to the Huron missions and supervising the reception and sale of the furs allocated to the Jesuits in support of their activities. Once before, from 1622 to 1625, prior to being chosen for New France, Brébeuf had held a similar position when he served as steward of the Jesuit Collège de Rouen. There and at Sillery he proved himself to be an excellent administrator. War with the Iroquois was openly raging, and Brébeuf saw convoys of supplies he had painstakingly assembled for Huronia seized by Mohawk brigands. The examples of René Goupil and Isaac Jogues could not help but have a profound effect on a brilliant and brave missionary temporarily in rear-echelon service, especially since that individual was in the process of linking his long-developing mysticism to a concept of martyrdom as the next necessary step in the fused challenge of his spiritual development and continuing usefulness in a failing enterprise. Mysticism, a sense of personal and professional failure, martyrdom as solution: here was coalescing in Brébeuf and some of his colleagues a theologized and psychologized response to a growing sense of doom connected to Huronia.

Ignatius of Loyola did not envision the Society of Jesus as an order that fostered the development of contemplative mystics or religious for whom a life of prayer was their primary goal. While Jesuits were encouraged to pray, they were primarily called to evangelical action in conjunction with prayer. The fundamental document of Jesuit formation, *The Spiritual Exercises of Saint Ignatius*, offered a concretized scenario aimed at instilling in each Jesuit a commitment to discernment, choice, and action anchored in an existentialized visualization of the life of Jesus Christ. Prayer as an end in itself belonged to such monastic orders as the Benedictines, Carthusians, and Cistercians. Canon law allowed Jesuits seeking such a contemplative life to leave the Society of Jesus for another order if they sincerely felt called to do so.

The psychological basis for such a prayerful life was an emptying of self. As a young Jesuit in formation, Brébeuf showed a natural tendency to downplay himself. He begged his superiors to allow him to become a lay brother and not a priest, which, after consideration, they refused to do. As a scholastic assigned to teach a class of unruly youngsters in grammar school, he suffered a psychological collapse and was put semipermanently on the unassigned sick list and allowed to study theology as a private student. Thus the Jesuit whom the Indians called Échon, the man who pulls his own load, and who encouraged his fellow missionaries to pull their full load as well, began his Jesuit life as a self-described lay brother on the sick list. The young scholastic incapable of pounding basic grammar into restive boys becomes not only a missionary who never loses his calm when facing a mob but also a pioneer linguist and compiler of dictionaries of a language as impenetrable as the Canadian forest and a writer of clean and pungent French. Brébeuf is today ranked among the founders of Canadian literature in testimony to his anthropological and environmental works.

In addition to his Jesuit vows, Brébeuf took a private vow: to seek perfection—not because he wanted to glory in his own goodness, but because he found himself so imperfect. A hair shirt and pointed iron cinctures around his legs as well as self-scourging (up to twice a day) and fasts were part of this program. Key, too, was humility in all things—in Jesuit matters and also before the Huron. This Norman nobleman, this physical giant, was capable of standing impassively before howling Hurons spitting in his face, striking him with fists and clubs, tearing his cassock off his back. All the while, in season and out, Brébeuf practiced contemplative prayer and meditation, filling his notebook with visualizations of Christ, Mary, angels, and saints. As often occurred in seventeenth-century France, he experienced the presence of fallen angels, devils who assaulted him with temptations of spirit and flesh, as if he were Saint Antony in the Egyptian desert.

At some point in 1640 or so, Brébeuf wrote a vow of martyrdom. "Jesus, my God and Savior," he wrote, "what can I give Thee in return of all Thou hast given to me? I will take from Thy hand the chalice of suffering, and will invoke Thy name. I therefore vow in the presence of the Eternal Father and the Holy Ghost, and of Thy most holy Mother, and her chaste spouse, Saint Joseph; before the Angels, Apostles and Martyrs, and my blessed Fathers Ignatius and Francis Xavier, never to miss the grace of martyrdom, if, out of Thy mercy, Thou dost offer it some day to Thy unworthy servant. I bind myself in such fashion, that it will not be lawful for me, where I am free to avoid the occasion of dying and shedding my blood for Thee, except insofar as I judge that it is for Thy glory that I should do otherwise. And when I am about to receive the stroke of death, I bind myself to accept it from Thy hand with pleasure and joy of heart."[6]

The postapostolic Christian Church wrestled with the concept of martyrdom. What was its nature, and what was it for? The Greek word *martus* means "witness"; and that concept ultimately prevailed. Martyrdom was the willing election of a Christian to bear witness to the faith, no matter what the consequences, even unto death. "Martyrem non facit poena, sed causa", argued Saint Augustine in one of his letters: "Physical pain does not make a martyr, but the reason [for it does]." Martyrdom, in brief, was a form of theological witness. Other causalities and consequences might be attached to martyrdom—war, politics, racial or cultural animosity, economic competition, robbery, personal hatred—but the act of religious witness had to be central for martyrdom and to earn for the martyr in question a designation bespeaking the highest form of Christian witness. "It is the constant teaching of the Church", writes Dominican theologian Thomas Gilby in the *New Catholic Encyclopedia* (1967) regarding martyrdom, "that such an intensity of love is expressed as to justify the sinner, baptized or unbaptized, and bring to him the forgiveness of all his sins, removing all guilt and stain, pardoning all debt of temporal punishment, and adorning him with a special crown, or aureole."[7]

Writing in the late fourth and early fifth centuries, Saint Augustine tried to put into perspective the role played by martyrdom in the growth of postapostolic Christianity and to tamp down the cult of martyrs that had grown up. Augustine, writes the Redemptorist theologian Francis Xavier Murphy, "changed the emphasis on the sufferings and tortures suffered by the martyrs to a reconsideration of the martyr. He considered him to be one who professed his faith in Christ by the perfection of his virtues and the living of a life in full conformity with the spiritual teachings of the Church." During the very century of Jesuit evangelization in New France, some scholars were revising downward the number of martyrs in the early Church.[8]

During his years as procurator in Sillery, Brébeuf had ample opportunity to view the dangers and scarce results of the Huronia enterprise, despite the commitment of eighteen Jesuits and donnés. As a sometime chaplain to the Ursulines, moreover, he both ministered and was ministered to in that the cloistered sisters reflected his own contemplative inclinations, especially Mother Marie de l'Incarnation, his fellow mystic in missionary service. In the previous ten years or so, Brébeuf had increasingly seen himself as flawed and sinful, as his penances and writings reveal. He also experienced a growing sense of spiritual aridity, described by the tenth-century Spanish Carmelite John of the Cross as the dark night of the soul. So then: Brébeuf was sinful (in his own eyes, at least); God was absent (to him, at least); and Huronia was a failure. The answer: death. Death as atonement for sin. Death as martyrdom. Death as a sacrifice, repaying Jesus Christ for His death on the Cross. A martyr's death that just might leverage a more promising future.

Brébeuf was not unique in fashioning for himself such a scenario. "Yes, my Jesus, my love!" Gabriel Lalemant, Brébeuf's future companion at the stake in Mission Saint-Ignace, was entering in his journal at the time, "let Thy Blood, which was poured out for the savages as for us, be applied efficaciously for their salvation. Let me cooperate with Thy grace and be immolated for them. Thy name must be adored; Thy kingdom must be extended throughout the world, and my life must be devoted to withdrawing from the hands of Satan, Thine enemy, those poor souls who have cost Thee Thy life and Thy Blood."[9] In New France, a theory of deliberately chosen, bloody, real-time martyrdom was being developed by Jesuit missionaries as a means of reviving a failed evangelization and giving meaning to Jesuit lives that otherwise felt wasted in the face of Huron indifference and Iroquois rage.

No Jesuit personified this embrace of martyrdom better than Isaac Jogues, who went to Sillery following his return to Canada. He and Brébeuf paid a visit to Mother Marie Guenet de Saint-Ignace, superior of a small detachment of Hospitaller Sisters from Quebec who ran an infirmary for Indians. Mother Saint-Ignace and Brébeuf felt themselves in the presence of a living saint. In May 1646, two years after returning from France, at the request of Governor-General Montmagny and under orders from his superior, Jérôme Lalemant, Jogues traveled in civilian clothes (so as not to inflame resistance among the Mohawks) as a member of an official party on a diplomatic mission to renegotiate a continuation of the treaty between the French and the Mohawks. Jogues was chosen for the mission because of his hard-won knowledge of the language, homeland, and folkways of the Mohawks. The Mohawks respected him, moreover, due to his stoicism under torture. As Jogues revealed in a letter to Lalemant, he was initially terrified of returning to the scene of his torture and captivity. "Ibo et non redibo", Jogues wrote another friend. "I shall go and I shall not return." Distressed by the chilly reception they received, and on the advice of several semifriendly Mohawks, the French left stealthily and swiftly, and Jogues did manage to make it back. Almost immediately, however, he requested permission to act as a missionary to the Iroquois, and after some resistance Father Jérôme Lalemant granted his request.

By then, martyrdom was in the air. The Jesuit mission planned for the village of Ossernenon in Mohawk country was to be named the Mission of the Martyrs. There Jogues had been horrifically tortured in August 1642; and there, following a beating on the shore of Lake George, he was once again taken captive, despite the peace treaty. A few days later, on 18 October 1646, Jogues and his assistant, the young donné Jean Lalande, were tomahawked to death, their heads displayed on the palisades and their decapitated bodies thrown into the Mohawk River. Hearing of this, Jogues' fellow Jesuit missionaries offered a Mass of Thanksgiving.

By this time, Jean de Brébeuf was equally eager to die what he believed to be a martyr's death and thus become a living sacrifice. "O my God," Brébeuf wrote in his diary, "why art Thou not known? Why is this barbarous country not converted? Why is not sin abolished? Why art Thou not loved? O my God! If all the cruel torments which the captives can endure in this country should fall on me, I accept them with my whole heart; I alone am willing to suffer all the pains that the martyrs have undergone."[10] Soon, tied to a stake at Mission Saint-Ignace, Jean de Brébeuf and Gabriel Lalemant would be granted their desire for bloody immolation.

A diplomatic alternative

Contemporary analysis adds layers of anthropological and economic insight to the tragic story of the collapse of Catholic Huronia. In their eagerness to win converts and save souls, the Jesuits tended to underestimate the cultural barriers that existed between the French and the Huron and Iroquois, especially once the Mohawks were armed and paid by the Dutch for pirated furs. Add to this their ruthlessness when on the warpath, and you have in the Iroquois a rage against the French and their Indian allies of genocidal intensity.

Then there was the question of the contest among Spain, France, and England for control of North America. As Francis Parkman points out in the final chapter of what he considered a saga of Jesuit failure, the Huronia venture and other Jesuit missionary efforts represented case studies in continental ambition. Had Huronia succeeded, Parkman argues, other pro-French Catholicized tribal homelands might have extended eastward and southward as a barrier to the English colonies of the East Coast.

As Parkman speculates, "Savages tamed—not civilized, for that was scarcely possible—would have been distributed in communities through the valleys of the Great Lakes and the Mississippi, ruled by priests in the interest of Catholicity and of France. Their habits of agriculture would have been developed, and their instincts of mutual slaughter repressed. The swift decline of the Indian population would have been arrested; and it would have been made, through the fur-trade, a source of prosperity to New France."

France, in short, would have blocked the westward advance of the English colonies by creating a network of allied Indian tribal commonwealths. "Unmolested by Indian enemies," Parkman continues, "and fed by a rich commerce, she [France] would have put forth a vigorous growth. True to her far-reaching and adventurous genius, she would have occupied the West with traders, settlers, and garrisons, and cut up the virgin wilderness into fiefs, while as yet the colonies of England were but a weak and broken line along the shore of the Atlantic; and when at last the great conflict came, England and Liberty would have been confronted, not by a depleted antagonist, still feeble from the exhaustion of a starved and persecuted infancy, but by an athletic champion of the principles of Richelieu and Loyola."[11]

What if another proposal were entertained, Jesuit missionary Gabriel Druillettes might have replied to Parkman had they been contemporaries, one linking New France and New England in a common pact of defense against the Iroquois? What if priest and Puritan, as you posit it, joined forces to promote a common defense of Christianity and—of related importance—a trade agreement fostering cooperative continental ambitions in North America?

Born in 1610 in central France but educated as a Jesuit in Toulouse in southwestern France, Druillettes arrived in Canada in 1643, following ordination and tertianship. Like other Jesuits of his generation, Druillettes was a skilled and tireless explorer and a devoted missionary. Unlike many of his confreres, however, Druillettes was neither an intellectual nor a former professor of a prestigious Jesuit college. He was, rather, an intelligent, good-humored, gentle, and practical man, devoid of guilt or mystical aspiration. Also unlike many of his confreres, Druillettes truly liked and got along with Indians. Perhaps this was because Druillettes was not assigned to Huronia but began his missionary career as chaplain to a group of roving Christian Montagnais hunters. Sharing the life of the trail with these friendly companions (whose language he had mastered in record time at Sillery), Druillettes not only learned to trek, portage, snowshoe, and eat or fast like an Indian, but also came to appreciate the Montagnais way of life. For one thing, the Montagnais whom Druillettes was accompanying did not wantonly kill or torture other Indians and did their best to observe the proprieties of the sixth, ninth, and other commandments. Only the smoke of their lodges bothered Druillettes, to the point that he started to lose his eyesight. A kind old woman tried to help him by scraping his cornea with a rusty knife—searingly painful, dangerous, and to no practical effect. Asking the Montagnais to gather around him one morning, Druillettes from memory celebrated Mass in honor of the Virgin Mary. Midway through the Mass, his blindness ceased and he found himself bathed in glorious light.[12]

So Druillettes told the story. Though more likely a recovery from a temporary condition due to smoke and snow, the event was remembered as a miracle and reported in *Jesuit Relations* as a wondrous rite of induction. The prayers of his beloved Montagnais companions had brought the dazzling white winter light of Canada back to the young priest's eyes, and he would never forget how the Montagnais as a Catholic community had prayed for him as he celebrated Mass and brought about his astonishing recovery. He would spend the rest of his life as an intercessor on their behalf, and they in turn would forever regard him as a man touched by the miraculous.

Not that he lost his sense of realism. At the best of times, Indian life was difficult, as Druillettes discovered again and again on subsequent treks; and when the Montagnais went to war to defend themselves against the Iroquois, he accompanied them as chaplain. In 1646 the Abenakis of the Kennebec River basin (present-day Maine) requested his presence. Traveling there, he learned Abenaki in three months and assisted the Capuchin friars working in the region. He also made friends with the agent in charge of the English trading post of Augusta, twenty-four-year-old John Winslow, who was the younger brother of Edward Winslow, a leader of Plymouth Colony.

Druillettes was temporarily back in Quebec in 1649–1650, awaiting Capuchin permission to resume his ministry in the Kennebec River basin territory assigned to them, permission the Capuchin superior initially resisted but later granted. Druillettes therefore was at Jesuit headquarters as things were falling apart in Huronia. When he received permission from the Capuchins to return to the Abenakis, the new Jesuit superior, Jérôme Lalemant, wrote to the French provincial that Druillettes' success among these people (their patriarch, they called him) represented a new and valued opening for the Society, now that the Huron mission had collapsed. Arriving in Kennebec on 1 September 1650 in the company of donné Jean Guerin, Druillettes was this time—like Isaac Jogues in 1646—on a diplomatic as well as a pastoral mission. Massachusetts Bay Colony was requesting permission to trade in French territory and was prepared to grant reciprocity to the French. Beleaguered by the Iroquois, the Abenakis were requesting English protection. With the approval of Governor d'Ailleboust and his advisors, Druillettes was asked to travel south to Massachusetts in the company of the chief of the Christian Indians at Sillery; the two of them, acting as representatives of Quebec and the Abenakis, were to suggest to the English a joint alliance against the Iroquois in return for the reciprocity-of-trade agreement. Once Druillettes was at the trading post at Augusta, his friend John Winslow secured passage for him on an English vessel departing from Merrymeeting Bay for Boston. Forced ashore by storms at Cape Ann, Druillettes reached Boston in December after making his way south by foot and shore-hugging boat.

Two separate yet complementary themes—one overt, the other more subtle—characterized this first phase of Druillettes' mission to Massachusetts. First of all, as Parkman gleefully notes, Druillettes as a Jesuit embodied the Puritans' worst nightmare: the very agent of the Antichrist, to be (by a law passed in 1647) arrested and deported if arriving in New England on any purpose save an authorized diplomatic mission and, if returning, and not on a diplomatic mission, to be arrested and executed forthwith. From this perspective, it is remarkable how graciously Druillettes was treated by the Puritan worthies who granted him an interview. The Jesuit was, after all, making a bold proposal, even if its boldest implications remained beneath the surface.

Forget—for the time being, at least—Druillettes was urging, English-French and Protestant-Catholic rivalries. The Iroquois posed the single greatest threat to the creation of a Christianized Indian population and to the desire of French and English people to live safely in North America. In contrast to so many of his Jesuit colleagues, Druillettes was not exhorting martyrdom as the answer. He was recommending armed resistance. Joined together in an anti-Iroquois defense league, the English and French colonies could put thousands of well-armed, well-trained fighting men in the field and contain the Iroquois threat to Christian civilization in northeastern North America.

The defense of Christian civilization! That was what Druillettes was talking about. The concept included Protestants and Catholics alike as well as the realities of trade, profit, and war when required for defense. As a Jesuit, Druillettes believed in miracles; indeed, his eyesight had been restored by one. He believed in martyrdom, when necessary. But he also believed in self-defense. And as far as evangelization was concerned, he must have looked beyond the Protestant-Catholic divide to a more ecumenical and irenic consideration of Scripture, basic doctrine, and the need for baptism as a mandatory rite of initiation if one is to judge how famously he got along with the noted Puritan minister John Eliot. Eliot was a Cambridge University graduate, the chief compiler of the Bay Psalm Book (1640), the translator of the Bible into Algonquin (1661–1663), and the author of the *Indian Primer* (1669), which to this day remains a primary sourcebook regarding the Indians of Massachusetts. Eliot put Druillettes up at his home in Roxbury and invited him to spend the winter as his guest. What interesting conversations they must have had as they sat together before a blazing fireplace on long winter evenings.

Once back in Quebec, Druillettes was almost immediately dispatched on a second mission to New England, this time to New Haven in the company of leading citizen Jean-Paul Godefroy, an experienced trader and military/naval strategist, again to argue Quebec's case before the commissioners of the four English colonies meeting there. On all fronts, on each journey, Druillettes met with English refusal to join the French in an anti-Iroquois league. Druillettes returned to his missionary duties.

His habit of mind, however, remained unchanged. Like the Jesuit Eusebio Kino on the Mexican frontier in the next generation, Druillettes continued to pursue not martyrdom in the line of duty (although he would come close to death on a number of future missions) but, rather, a life of action, prayer, and acceptance as he returned to his missionary efforts in Maine. He later advanced a grandiose plan of expansion westward from Montreal into the lands of the Chippewa, Ottawa, Potawatomi, and Sauk on Lakes Huron, Superior, and Michigan, preaching there the Word of God in a spirit of friendship and respect. By 1670 Druillettes was evangelizing at Sault Sainte-Marie, where those three Great Lakes intersect, preaching among the Chippewa and Ottawa and filling his reports to his superiors with good news of Indian peoples heeding him, with a number of them converting in their own manner to Christianity and the practice of the Catholic faith. Retiring to Quebec at age seventy, Druillettes enjoyed a brief retirement before passing peacefully in his bed.

An envoy named Simon

For two of the years of Druillettes' fruitful ministry in Sault Sainte-Marie, 1675–1676, the English colonies were fighting for their survival against the Mohawks and their allies in the bloody and debilitating King Philip's War. The Mohawks continued their war against the white man in New England, who had turned down Druillettes' proposal, just as they had kept waging war against the French and their Indian allies.

Perhaps the most audacious and paradigmatic instance of Mohawk daring and cruelty occurred earlier, on the night of 19 May 1656, when three hundred Mohawk warriors paddled their canoes silently past Quebec and secretly landed on the Island of Orleans, where four hundred or so Christian Huron had found refuge. The Mohawk mission: to kidnap Huron women and younger males as a population replenishment for a warrior force that was hovering at just over two thousand. A thousand of these warriors were younger Huron, Algonquian, and other tribal captives turned by adoption and adaptation into Mohawks. (The fiercest Mohawk warrior, the French had come to believe, was a turned Huron.) Taking up ambush positions, the Mohawk raiding party waited until the Huron women—who, according to Indian custom, did all the fieldwork—fanned out into the farmlands adjacent to the settlement for a morning of work. Pouncing on the women, the Mohawks quickly dispatched their four male guardians, took eighty younger women and girls into custody, and loaded them aboard canoes. At midday, to their collective horror, the citizens of Quebec, looking down from rocky heights to the Saint Lawrence below, beheld a flotilla of Mohawk canoes filing upriver. As the canoes passed the citadel, the paddling Mohawk warriors jeered and gestured in defiance. The captive Huron women were forced to sing and chant joyous songs of repatriation, and a few—at risk of overturning the vessels—were compelled to stand up and dance with comparable defiance and feigned joy.

This spectacle, so humiliating to the hapless French, reveals the fierce biological battle being waged by the Mohawks against the French. Adopted into the tribe, these Christian Huron women would soon replenish the Mohawks with male offspring who would grow into warriors in an endless war that had as its goal the extinction of the French. Enter onto the scene another Jesuit missionary, Simon Le Moyne, who (like Gabriel Druillettes) believed that negotiation—not self-activated martyrdom—represented the best way to end this intractable conflict. A product of elite Jesuit training (philosophy at the Collège de Clermont in Paris, theology at La Flèche), Le Moyne almost died in June 1638 traveling to his assignment in Huronia when his Huron guides deserted him in the wilderness. He and a young French hunter survived for fifteen harrowing days before being rescued by another Jesuit missioner. Surviving the downfall of Huronia, Le Moyne, a master of Indian language (like Druillettes), was (again, like Druillettes) recruited into diplomacy and between 1654 and 1662 made six harrowing forays into Iroquois country on behalf of the governor and of his Jesuit superiors.

At first, things looked promising. In 1655, to the surprise of the French, the Onondaga Iroquois requested a Jesuit mission. What a breakthrough! Peace at last! On 30 March 1656 two Jesuits set out as an advance guard. Six weeks later, on 17 May 1656—a mere two days before the Mohawk raid on the Island of Orleans— four priests, two brothers, an unspecified number of donnés, and fifty French workmen departed Quebec for Onondaga country without encountering the invading but evasive Mohawks en route. Reaching the Onondaga settlement of Ganentaa in upstate New York, the French completed in record time a Jesuit residence for the proposed Sainte-Marie de Ganentaa lead mission for the evangelization of the Onondaga Iroquois. Then, through intelligence gathered from friendly Indian sources, came the bad news. The whole affair was a ruse to lure the French into an impending massacre. Some historians believe that the initial Onondaga request might have been sincere but soured when the Onondagas found themselves outperformed by the French as fur trappers and traders. In any event, rather than be martyred in hopes of a better day, the French managed a stealthy withdrawal on 20 March 1658 and by 23 April were safely back at Montreal.

Like Druillettes, Le Moyne enjoyed friendly contact with Protestants and Protestant clergy, in his case Pastor Jan Megapolensis. During the third of his six diplomatic missions to the Mohawks, from 27 August 1657 to 21 May 1658, Le Moyne traveled to New Amsterdam ostensibly and belatedly to thank the Dutch for rescuing Isaac Jogues and securing him passage back to Europe. There Le Moyne met Pastor Megapolensis, and the two struck up a relationship based on mutual respect as they debated the papacy, ecumenical councils, and notions of orthodoxy and heresy. Le Moyne later followed up these discussions with handwritten letters to the pastor.

Slowly, although he did not secure breakthroughs in these missions to the Mohawks, Le Moyne built up respect for himself among the murderous marauders of the forest, who were made even fiercer by their resentment of the Onondagas' separate dealings with the French. In the summer of 1657 the French allowed more than a hundred Onondaga warriors to come to Quebec and negotiate the repatriation of fifty or so Christian members of the Cord Makers family of the Huron. The meeting proved a disaster. Encountering resistance from a young woman to whom he was making advances, an Onondaga chief tomahawked her to death, which was followed by the killing of seven Huron men in front of their wives and children. Only the fifty-some Onondaga warriors taken as hostages in Quebec prevented a wholesale massacre of the remaining Huron and their French escorts.

Still, Le Moyne persisted in patience and optimism and returned to evangelization in upstate New York. By 1661 Le Moyne had come under the protection of the renowned Onondaga chieftain Garakontié. Although he himself was not a Christian, Garakontié respected Le Moyne—a linguist, a sagacious diplomat and advisor, a Frenchman who showed respect for the Onondaga way of life—built him a chapel, and invited the Jesuit to stay as a guest in his lodging whenever he required long-term shelter. By the time Le Moyne passed peacefully away on 24 November 1665, four of the five Iroquois tribes were in the process of seeking peace with the French.

The uses of martyrdom

Following the recovery of the bodies of Jean de Brébeuf and Gabriel Lalemant, Father Paul Ragueneau—superior of the Huron mission (1645–1650), soon to be appointed superior of all Jesuits in Canada (1650–1653)—had them buried beneath the altar of the chapel of Sainte-Marie Mission, as befitted two saints and martyrs. In the 1649 *Jesuit Relations*, moreover, Ragueneau stated that, while the Church possessed the final authority to decide in such matters, in his opinion, Brébeuf and Lalemant had met the canonical requirements for martyrdom, and hence sainthood, and would in time be so recognized.

When Sainte-Marie was abandoned, Brother Christophe Regnault relates in his later *Récit veritable* (True testimony), the bodies of Brébeuf and Lalemant were disinterred, the residual flesh was removed by soaking in lye and then burning or reburying (accounts differ) the bones, which were brought back to Quebec for reburial in the Jesuit chapel; Brébeuf's skull was deposited in the nuns' chapel at the Hôtel-Dieu, where he had served as chaplain. In 1652 Ragueneau—who had also found and preserved Brébeuf's and Lalemant's personal papers—assembled a "Manuscrit de 1652" (still preserved in the archives of the Jesuit Collège Sainte-Marie in Montreal) in which he laid down the case, through documentation and argument, for a canonical declaration that not only Brébeuf and Lalemant but also the other four Jesuits and two donnés who had met violent deaths in the destruction of Huronia were martyrs (and thus saints), explicitly dying for the faith. These deaths, especially those of Brébeuf and Lalemant, were chronicled in *Jesuit Relations* and subsequent publications. But no coherent, persistent cult of the murdered Jesuits developed in the late seventeenth or eighteenth century prior to the suppression of the Society of Jesus. Indeed, the situation ironically resembled that of early postapostolic Christianity, when martyrs were acknowledged and respected but martyrdom was not made into a self-referencing cult. The conquest of Quebec and its acquisition by Great Britain through the Treaty of Paris in 1763 saved the Quebec Jesuits from expulsion when France expelled the Society of Jesus in December 1764, and the British government refused to recognize either this order or the subsequent suppression of the Society of Jesus as a whole by Pope Clement XIV in 1773. As of 16 March 1800, however, with the death of Father Jean-Joseph Cazot, there were no Jesuits in Quebec until 1842.

The narrative of the North American Martyrs, as they came to be called, was recovered with the rise of French Canadian historiography in such figures as the Abbés Jean-Baptiste-Antoine Ferland and Étienne-Michel Faillon of Quebec and the Americans Edmund B. O'Callaghan, John Gilmary Shea, Francis Parkman, and Reuben Gold Thwaites. Parkman termed it a noble failure; O'Callaghan and Thwaites referred to it as a tour de force of documentation. The romantic conservative Catholic historians Ferland, Faillon, Shea, and their successors deemed it a cult to be recovered as an inspirational and usable past. In 1912, following a half century of such pious reassertion, the hierarchies of Canada and the United States requested that the Vatican open the cause of the North American martyrs, who were beatified in 1925 and canonized in 1930.

15

The Abbey of Saint-Germain-des-Prés 1658

*The secret consecration of a vicar apostolic for Quebec
brings Roman Catholicism to new maturity*

On 8 December 1658, in a secret Mass of Consecration held in the Notre-Dame Chapel of the Abbey of Saint-Germain-des-Prés in Paris, Celio Piccolomini, papal nuncio to France, raised the Abbé François-Xavier de Montmorency-Laval to the fullness of the priesthood, anointing him as titular bishop of Petraea, a defunct diocese in the Middle East, and vicar apostolic (missionary bishop) in New France. The consecration was held covertly because powerful personages in the French Church—supporters of the Sulpician Gabriel de Thubières de Levy de Queylus, among others; François II de Harlay de Champvallon, the archbishop of Rouen, who considered New France under his authority; and other Gallican-oriented bishops resentful of Roman authority—opposed Laval's appointment by the Sacred Congregation for the Propagation of the Faith in Rome as an unwarranted intrusion into French affairs. But the thirty-five-year-old Laval—a secular priest of noble descent, a graduate of the elite Jesuit colleges of La Flèche and Clermont, a licentiate in canon law from the University of Paris, a cathedral canon and former archdeacon of the Diocese of Évreux, and a dévot of unquestioned piety—was the Jesuits' candidate, and the Jesuits had secured the support of young King Louis XIV and Anne of Austria, the Queen Mother, and their support prevailed.

Despite the intrigue surrounding his selection and consecration, the administratively experienced but still young priest kneeling before the papal nuncio for the ancient ceremony of episcopal anointing was fully qualified for higher office in the Church according to criteria for appointment to the hierarchy—noble birth; an early tonsure for clericalization; academic distinction; political and social connections; wealth, either inherited or from benefices; and piety (which was not always required)—operative in France at the time.

The Montmorencys dated back to the first generation of Frankish nobility to accept Christianity along with King Clovis in 496. Over the ensuing centuries, the family had provided France with six constables—including Mathieu de Montmorency (1174–1230), the Great Constable of France, who added his wife's name Laval to his own—along with twelve marshals, four admirals, several cardinals, and other assorted notables. As bishop, in reference to his fifth-century ancestor, Laval placed the family motto on his coat of arms: *Dieu ayde au premier baron chrestien* (God aid the first Christian baron).

Destined for the Church, François de Laval was tonsured as a cleric at the age of eight. Entering the primary school of the elite Jesuit college at La Flèche, he went on to spend the years 1631–1641 in literary and philosophical studies. In 1637, when he was fourteen, his uncle, François de Péricard, bishop of Évreux, named him canon (chapter member) of his cathedral, a benefice carrying with it a stipend that allowed Laval to continue his education at the equally elite Jesuit Collège de Clermont in Paris. Although Laval's family had selected him for a clerical career, by his teens that had become his choice as well, due in part to the influence of the Jesuits at La Flèche, who sponsored his early admission to the Congrégation de la Sainte Vierge (the Society of the Holy Virgin), a spiritual honor society under the direction of the respected Jesuit confessor and spiritual director Jean Bagot. From Bagot Laval heard reports of the Jesuit mission in Canada, which led to vague thoughts of one day becoming a missionary himself.

Although formed by Ignatian spirituality, Laval was already a member of the secular clergy and was encouraged by his Jesuit teachers to continue on that path. While he was studying theology at Clermont, however, Laval's pathway to the priesthood was interrupted when his two older brothers lost their lives (in 1644 and 1645) while on active military service, leaving the young Laval—whose father had died in 1636—the head of his financially stressed family. His mother advised Laval, still only in minor orders, to leave the ecclesiastical state and make a good marriage to a woman from a wealthy family. Even Laval's uncle, the bishop of Évreux, agreed with this solution. The twenty-two-year-old abbé, however, was committed to a priestly career.

He did not, however, abandon his family. Taking the name Abbé de Montigny to signify his leadership of his family's estate, Laval took a leave of absence from Clermont and spent a number of months in the market town of Montigny-sur-Avre in the department of Eure-et-Loir successfully reorganizing the Montigny farming operations, business interests, and general finances. The young abbé had a head for administration as well as for theology. He was also a dévot of the first order at the high point of the Catholic Revival. At Clermont, Laval had furthered his spiritual development and interest in overseas missions as a member of a dévot society of upper-class ecclesiastics and laymen called the Bons Amis (Good Friends), directed once again by Father Bagot, who was now stationed in Paris. Returning to Clermont, Laval resumed his studies and was ordained to the priesthood in May 1647. He spent the following year continuing the reorganization of his patrimony, teaching abandoned children, and caring for the indigent sick. In December 1648 Laval was named archdeacon (chief operating officer) of his home diocese of Évreux and hence found himself at age twenty-five responsible for the oversight of 155 parishes and four chapels as well as other administrative matters: good training, in short, for a future bishop.

During the years Laval served as archdeacon of Évreux, 1649–1654, forces were in motion on a number of fronts that would eventually bring him to the Chapel of the Holy Virgin in the Abbey of Saint-Germain-des-Prés for consecration as bishop and vicar apostolic. In the first phase of Roman Catholic evangelization of Asia and the Indies, the Vatican allowed Spain and Portugal to exercise exclusive rights over matters relating to evangelization. By the early seventeenth century, however, Rome had grown restive with these privileges, and in 1622 Pope Gregory XV established the Sacra Congregatio de Propaganda Fide (Sacred Congregation for the

Propagation of the Faith) to return to Rome authority over evangelizing efforts. Portugal and Spain, however, were holding on to their rights in these concerns as best they could. France, meanwhile, was sponsoring the evangelization endeavors of religious orders, especially those of the Jesuits, in North America, the Caribbean, and southwest Asia.

By the early 1650s, the French Jesuit Alexandre de Rhodes was announcing that Catholic efforts at evangelization in these places had reached a point of crisis and transformation. A veteran missionary in Goa, the Moluccas, Cochin China, and Tonkin—where he persuaded the Vietnamese to adopt Latin script (the first Asian people to do so)—Rhodes had originally tried to enter Japan but had been denied entry to that nation, which had eradicated its Christians and closed its doors to further efforts at introducing Christianity. Only recently, before his temporary stay in Paris, Rhodes had been arrested and exiled from Cochin China when he tried to return there from Macao. The problem, Rhodes began to argue with such influential Jesuits as Jean Bagot and his Bons Amis circle of mission-oriented dévots, was the lack of any means of creating a local secular clergy in overseas places. Religious-order priests could introduce the faith and nurture its development through its initial phases, but they were foreigners and could go only so far in crossing cultural barriers. What was required was a local clergy, anchored in the culture in all aspects not contrary to faith or morals, capable of caring for and deepening the faith of a flock once it had been evangelized. Such a clergy, moreover, would be less likely to arouse suspicion and thus be sentenced to expulsion, if not death. To train and ordain said clergy, vicars apostolic would be necessary: missionary bishops with a secular diocesan background authorized by the Sacred Congregation for the Propagation of the Faith in Rome and dedicated to the creation of a local secular clergy who would build the Catholic community from within.

In 1652, with the personal permission of the pro-missionary Pope Innocent X, who was in the process of strengthening the authority of the Sacred Congregation, Rhodes was actually searching for suitable candidates for three French appointments as vicars apostolic to Tonkin and Indochina. Through the influence of Bagot and the Bons Amis circle, three candidates—François Pallu, Bernard Picques, and François de Laval—were chosen and their files forwarded to Rome, where the three men went to be interviewed. There they languished for fifteen months, as Portugal opposed the naming of French bishops to Portuguese territories and even the cardinals and staff of the Sacred Congregation began to suspect the proposal was a Jesuit ploy to retain control of missionary territories, given the candidates' close Jesuit associations. By 1654 the proposal seemed dead in the water.

The whole experience—his nomination, followed by controversy and delay—deepened the spiritual side of Laval. He realized that sooner or later important missionary work might be expected of him and he ought to prepare himself for it. As a secular priest, Laval had every right to retain his wealth; but now the Abbé de Montigny had a more ascetical path in mind, and in 1654 he renounced his rights of primogeniture and all his titles to the seigneury of Montigny and Montbeaudry in favor of his brother Jean-Louis. Laval's brother Henri became a Benedictine monk at the Monastery of La Croix-Saint-Lauffroy, where he rose to prior. His sister, Anne-Charlotte, took the veil with the Nuns of the Blessed Sacrament and rose to superior as well. Laval resigned as archdeacon of Évreux, refusing the pension that was offered. At thirty-one, he was beginning life all over again as a freelance abbé living off a modest benefice.

A time for preparation

Where to go? What to choose? Alexandre de Rhodes would soon (in 1655) be off to Persia for a brilliant five last years of missionary and diplomatic effort. In 1660 the shah himself would attend Rhodes' funeral. Laval, by contrast, remained on the home front as he sought to develop his prayer life and service to the sick and the poor in the spirit of Vincent de Paul. The venue he chose for this period of his life was a community of laymen and clerics gathered around the mystic and dévot activist Jean de Bernières-Louvigny, a layman who lived in a hermitage in the outer courtyard of the Ursuline convent at Caen, where his sister was foundress and superior.

Born in 1602 to a noble Norman family, Bernières-Louvigny belonged to the Compagnie du Saint-Sacrement (Company of the Holy Sacrament), a private association of lay dévots and clerics that was established in 1630 and flourished until it went into decline after Cardinal Mazarin persuaded Parlement in 1660 to outlaw its secret meetings. In some fifty chapters throughout France, the Company brought together laity and clergy under the dual leadership of a layman director and an ordained spiritual director. Meeting on Thursdays for spiritual direction and prayer before the Blessed Sacrament, members of the Company devoted themselves to social action on a number of fronts as well as growth in personal holiness. By 1666, the movement had all but disappeared, but for more than three decades it constituted a force for social and ecclesiastical reform, Catholic Revival piety, good works among the sick and the poor, and defense of Catholic orthodoxy. Among its members, aside from Jean de Bernières-Louvigny, were such Catholic Revival luminaries as Vincent de Paul, John Eudes, Jean-Jacques Olier, Charles de Condren, Jacques-Bénigne Bossuet, and François de Laval.

Bound by private vows of poverty and celibacy, Bernières-Louvigny, while remaining a layman, acquired a reputation as one of the great mystics and spiritual directors of mid-seventeenth-century France, then in the throes of an era of intense Catholic Revival. Bernières-Louvigny did not publish in his lifetime. His influence came from personal charisma. The posthumous publication of his notes and letters, moreover, earned him in 1689 a place in the Index of Forbidden Books on charges of quietism: excessive passivity in the face of God's will, to the point of teaching that all things must be abandoned, even the desire for salvation, in a great quiet of contemplation and acceptance. Supporters of Bernières-Louvigny believed that the controversial passages cited in the condemnation were emendations by another writer and did not represent the fullness of Bernières-Louvigny's thought. However that might be, the Abbé Laval, influenced by Bernières-Louvigny's spirituality, devoted himself to good works—ministering to the poor, reforming a monastery, acting as a spiritual director and legal defender of three separate sisterhoods during a period of residence in the Diocese of Bayeux—as well as a practice of silence and acceptance of God's will regarding the future.

It took seven long years for Laval to be nominated for appointment as a vicar apostolic, receive episcopal consecration, and negotiate further obstacles. Such were the complexities of ecclesiastical politics in the mid-seventeenth century. The

Sacred Congregation for the Propagation of the Faith consumed nearly two years as it grew increasingly fearful of a possible—indeed, probable—Jesuit dominance over the three proposed missionary bishops and delayed their appointments. In addition, as early as 1645, the Paris-based Society of Our Lady of Montreal had been arguing for the appointment of a vicar apostolic for Canada from the ranks of their own movement. In January 1657 the group put forward a strong candidate, the Abbé Gabriel de Thubières de Levy de Queylus, a talented and pioneering Sulpician. Since the Sulpicians were closely allied to the secular diocesan clergy and the Abbé Queylus was an exemplary candidate—learned, upright, and wealthy—the Assembly of Clergy quickly ratified his nomination.

The Jesuits, however, countered with the nomination of François de Laval, who, while a member of the secular clergy, had graduated from their schools and remained close to the Society of Jesus. In 1651 the Jesuits had requested the establishment of a Jesuit-dominated diocese in Quebec, with Jesuit clergy and a Jesuit bishop; but the idea had gone nowhere.

François II de Harlay de Champvallon, the archbishop of Rouen, meanwhile, considered all New France as territory under his jurisdiction and, once Laval was nominated for Quebec, successfully inspired the withdrawal of the offer by three sitting French bishops to consecrate him bishop. Following Laval's secret consecration by the apostolic delegate at Saint-Germain-des-Prés, the French hierarchy—affronted by Rome's overreaching in this matter—went into overdrive in their opposition, which consumed another four months of negotiation before Laval could take his oath of loyalty to the king and set sail on 3 April 1659 for New France, his appointment in order and an annual stipend of 1,000 livres pledged by the Queen Mother.

A remote, sparsely settled vicariate

French settlement had barely reached two thousand when Laval arrived in Quebec on 16 June 1659. Quebec proper and its adjacent seigneuries supported nearly twelve hundred French inhabitants; Trois-Rivières (Three Rivers) and its adjacent seigneuries contained a few hundred more; the Island of Montreal held the remainder. For more than a half century, the clergy of New France—Recollect Franciscans, Jesuits, and Capuchin Franciscans—had been religious-order missionaries, with secular or diocesan priests few and far between. Thus priests of religious orders saw to the spiritual needs of habitants, soldiers, sailors, artisans under contract, the occasional coureur de bois, and colonial officials as assignments ancillary to their missionary work. After arriving in Quebec in 1639, the Ursulines and the Augustinian Hospitallers of the Mercy of Jesus ministered more to Native Americans than to French habitants in the first few decades, yet they had formally acknowledged themselves to be under the authority of the archbishop of Rouen as a condition for their ministries, an action that canonically foreshadowed their growing service to French habitants.

Ville-Marie organizes

All this domination by religious orders throws into relief the distinctive nature of Ville-Marie (Montreal). Initially, Jesuits saw to the settlement's spiritual needs and, indeed, established a house there, mainly oriented to missionary outreach. The dévots behind Ville-Marie, however, wanted a diocese in New France and a secular clergy responsible for parishes and thus supported the candidacy of the Abbé Queylus. At the insistence of Maisonneuve and Jeanne Mance, Father Olier agreed to send four Sulpicians to Montreal as parish priests and founders of a seminary as the first step toward creating a diocese. Queylus was appointed superior of the group, which included the Abbés Gabriel Souart and Dominique Galinier as well as deacon Antoine d'Allet. En route to Canada, Queylus obtained papers from the archbishop of Rouen, who was still nominally in charge of New France, naming him vicar general with authority over Church affairs in New France.

The Abbé Queylus was an able man, and had his candidacy prevailed, he likely would have performed well as a bishop. Born in 1612 to a seigneurial family in Rouergne, tonsured at eleven, and presented at the Abbey of Loc-Dieu, a secular priest of private wealth with a doctorate in sacred theology, Queylus came from a background similar to Laval's, although his family was not as venerable in its descent. At age thirty-three, the abbé joined the Sulpicians and helped found and direct five regional seminaries and in addition served as superior at Saint-Sulpice. He also spent six years as a missionary to Huguenots. Choosing Souart, Galinier, and the deacon d'Allet to accompany him (d'Allet would be ordained to the priesthood at a later date, when New France had a bishop in residence), Queylus led his pioneering band of Sulpicians across the North Atlantic and up the Saint Lawrence River into what they believed to be a diocesan future for Ville-Marie. The Sulpicians landed in Quebec on 29 July 1657 and were courteously received by the Jesuits, who acknowledged Queylus' authority, since the Jesuits themselves had in 1649 acknowledged the authority of the archbishop of Rouen over New France. The Abbé Queylus, in turn—with a panache that boded well for his impending episcopacy—confirmed Jesuit Joseph-Antoine Poncet de la Rivière as *curé* (parish priest) of Quebec. Arriving upriver at Ville-Marie in the first week of August, the four Sulpicians were warmly welcomed and housed in the hospital until a residence could be built for them. Continuing in his role as vicar general of New France, Queylus confirmed Souart as curé of the parish of Ville-Marie, which had previously been served by a Jesuit, and thereby raised Ville-Marie to the level of a canonically established parish under the care of a secular priest.

Quarreling with the Jesuits

This era of good feeling between Queylus and the Jesuits ended abruptly, however. Within months, the Sulpician vicar general, affronted by the Jesuit superior Father Jean de Quen's replacement of Father Poncet as curé of Quebec without consulting him, returned to Quebec and named himself parish priest. The quarrel reflected the battle in France regarding Laval's consecration as vicar apostolic, which in turn reflected the Jesuits' stubborn holding on to their established authority in the face of an impending era of habitant growth and a secular clergy. The Abbé Queylus not only attacked the Jesuits from his newly occupied pulpit but also went to court in an (unsuccessful) effort to evict them in his favor from their residence on the grounds that it was a parish structure. (It was not. The Jesuits had paid the Communanté des Habitants 6,000 livres to build it.) Hearing eventually of the dispute, the archbishop of Rouen ordered a compromise. The Abbé Quey-lus was to serve as vicar general of the Island of Montreal. Father de Quen was to exercise this function in Quebec and the rest of New France.

Thus New France was temporarily but symbolically divided into two ecclesiastical enclaves: Sulpician and secular in greater Montreal, which included Three Rivers, and Jesuit in Quebec and elsewhere in the Saint Lawrence valley. When Laval arrived in Quebec on 16 June 1659, he was understandably nettled when the Ursuline and Hospitaller Sisters and certain settlers scrupulously inquired whether the archbishop of Rouen still held final authority in New France, with Laval merely serving locally, or was Laval now the final authority in a newly established apostolic vicariate? It took Queylus two months, moreover, to make the ten-day journey down to Quebec and pay his respects to Laval, who had by then firmly established his authority.

No, the abbé promised Laval, he would no longer claim or seek further authorization from the archbishop of Rouen. Yet when a letter from Rouen arrived mistakenly authorizing Queylus to continue to function as vicar general on behalf of the archbishop of Rouen, the abbé immediately sought to have Laval recognize Sulpician autonomy in Montreal. A letter from the king arrived shortly thereafter, however, reversing the initial decision to allow Montreal to report to Rouen. Admitting temporary defeat, Queylus sailed for France on 22 October 1659. Once there, though, he traveled secretly in the autumn of 1660 to Rome, where—skilled negotiator that he was—he lobbied for and (avoiding the Sacred Congregation) procured from another source, the datary responsible for announcing official appointments, a bull that declared Ville-Marie a parish independent of the vicar apostolic. Returning to Paris, Queylus acquired from the still-aggrieved archbishop of Rouen his own appointment as parish priest of an autonomous Montreal.

Queylus then sailed secretly for Quebec, where he arrived incognito on 3 August 1661 and shortly thereafter submitted his paperwork to an astonished Laval, who refused to confirm the abbé as parish priest of Montreal until he could verify the appointment with Rome and the king. Laval also produced a canonically correct letter forbidding Queylus from going to Montreal until the matter was resolved. The abbé nonetheless slipped away by canoe to Montreal and ignored Laval's further demand to return to Quebec or be suspended from his priestly functions. The king, meanwhile, had learned of Queylus' clandestine departure from France and sent a directive with the new governor, Pierre Dubois Davaugour, ordering Queylus to return to France. On 22 October 1661 a twice-defeated abbé left New France for the second time in as many years, having crossed the Atlantic six times since 1657 in an effort to secure for Montreal an ecclesiastical autonomy dominated by the Society of Our Lady of Montreal and the Compagnie des Prêtres de Saint-Sulpice (Company of Priests of Saint-Sulpice).

For the time being, at least, the Abbé Queylus had blotted his copybook. (He would return to Montreal, however, in 1668 to do what he did best, found a seminary.) The contretemps between Queylus and Laval might today seem like an *opéra bouffe* by Rossini, with its two capable abbés of privileged backgrounds competing for royal patronage. Larger issues, though, were at stake. While not yet possessing the momentum it would gain in the eighteenth century, Gallicanism—the belief that the Church in France should be run primarily by the French—was developing by the mid- to late-seventeenth century. From this perspective, the Society of Our Lady of Montreal, the Sulpicians, and the Abbé Queylus were oriented toward the French authority of the archbishop of Rouen, while Laval represented the Rome-oriented, Rome-dependent Society of Jesus and the Vatican-based Sacred Congregation for the Propagation of the Faith. In short order, Laval's episcopal authority would be anchored in one vast Diocese of Quebec, embracing Canada, the Mississippi valley, Louisiana, and New Orleans.

Jesuit educated and Jesuit friendly, Laval was nevertheless a secular priest committed, like the Sulpicians, to a reformed and upgraded seminary education and to the system of parish priests, appointed by the local bishop from a secular clergy, formally charged with caring for the spiritual welfare of the existing Catholic community. Like the Sulpicians, Laval was committed to the seminary not only as a place for priestly formation but also as a continuing source of clerical community and support. Between 1658 and 1663, he was an early proponent of the establishment of the Société des Missions Étrangères de Paris (the Paris Foreign Missions Society), an association of secular clergy trained and educated in a separate seminary on the rue du Bac. Functioning as the anchor and matrix of the society, the Foreign Missions Seminary educated candidates for the priesthood, assigned them to posts abroad, supported them in their ministry, and in other ways served as their lifelong community. Laval would soon be exporting such a program to Quebec.

The rise of Ville-Marie

Laval was a product of the dévot culture that had led to the formation of both the Society of Our Lady of Montreal and the Company of Priests of Saint-Sulpice and, while friendly to the Jesuits, was in no way hostile to either organization. That was a good thing, for in 1662 the Society of Our Lady of Montreal—its members aging, its coffers depleted—transferred ownership of Ville-Marie and the Island of Montreal to the Gentlemen of Saint-Sulpice, which meant that a major portion of Laval's vicariate (a diocese after 1674) was now owned by an influential association of secular priests functioning as seigneurs and parish clergy.

In the mid- and late 1650s, Maisonneuve and Jeanne Mance returned to France on diplomatic and fund-raising business. Maisonneuve, as might be expected, had a diverse agenda: defense, more immigrants, urban development, the confirmation of seigneurial titles. Jeanne Mance traveled in the autumn of 1657 with Marguerite Bourgeoys, a close friend who had arrived with the recruits of 1653. Their mission was to recruit Hospitaller and teaching sisters and to obtain further funding from Madame de Bullion. For nearly twenty years, Jeanne Mance had lived as a woman alone in the wilderness, or at least without women of her kind. Now she had the company of Marguerite Bourgeoys, a middle-class dévot in her late thirties, a woman of energy and talent who, while attracted to a life of prayer, had for various reasons not entered the cloister. In fact, she had a more active form of religious life in mind: a noncloistered secular sisterhood, as she described it, dedicated to teaching girls and young women from all ranks of society.

Mance and Bourgeoys, then, arrived in France with recruitment in mind: Mance for the hospital and Bourgeoys for the educational work she had already inaugurated in a one-room schoolhouse. Each woman faced considerable challenges. The

Abbé Queylus had brought two Augustinian canonesses up from the Hôtel-Dieu to run the hospital in Ville-Marie, contrary to the plans of Mance, Olier, and Dauversière, who wished to staff the hospital with nursing sisters from the congregation Dauversière planned to found in La Flèche. Queylus, however, preferred the presence of an established Parisian congregation that dated back to medieval times rather than that of a new congregation to be founded in the provinces. In any event, Mance was determined to staff the hospital according to the original plan she and Dauversière had devised eighteen years earlier.

For her part, Marguerite Bourgeoys believed that the increasing number of women and children in Ville-Marie demanded an expanded educational ministry. Born in 1620 at Troyes in Champagne into a bourgeois family (her father was a master candlemaker and coiner in the local mint), Bourgeoys had at the age of twenty joined the auxiliary community of teachers associated with the convent of the Congrégation de Notre-Dame in Troyes. Founded in 1598 by Peter Fourier, a Jesuit-educated Canon Regular of Saint Augustine and reforming educator, and Mademoiselle Alix Le Clerc, one of Fourier's dévot parishioners, the Canonesses Regular of Saint Augustine of the Congregation of Our Lady were devoted to the education of girls and young women of the less-privileged classes. Receiving papal approval in 1616, the congregation grew rapidly. Since the canonesses were cloistered, however, and could teach only within the confines of their convent, each Notre-Dame convent also maintained an auxiliary community of young women teachers who, while not nuns, lived communally as they ran various educational programs (including vocational education) in conjunction with the cloistered nuns. The cloistered director of the auxiliary community of Troyes was Louise de Chomedey, the sister of Paul de Chomedey, sieur de Maisonneuve, the founding governor of Ville-Marie. From her, Marguerite Bourgeoys first learned of Canada. When Maisonneuve passed through Troyes in 1652, both Mother Louise and Marguerite Bourgeoys volunteered for Ville-Marie, but Maisonneuve turned down his sister on the basis that Ville-Marie could not at present support a cloistered convent. He did, however, accept the more adaptable Marguerite Bourgeoys, who arrived in Ville-Marie the following year.

With no children to teach, Marguerite Bourgeoys spent the next five years in Ville-Marie doing various volunteer services for the community. She was not a nun but a laywoman, yet the people of Ville-Marie accepted her—as they accepted Maisonneuve and Jeanne Mance—as a person set apart by personal religious vows. Among the offices she held was sacristan at the hospital chapel, dedicated to Saint Joseph, and in this capacity she joined Maisonneuve in scouting a site for what every Catholic French town featured: a shrine to Mary. To Marguerite Bourgeoys' way of thinking, the life of Mary, Mother of Jesus, as set forth in the Scriptures, represented a model for the kind of noncloistered but consecrated life Bourgeoys was pursuing. Thus in time was achieved the stone chapel of Notre-Dame-de-Bon-Secours (Our Lady of Good Comfort), a title of special relevance to a colony still fighting for its survival against the Iroquois.

In May 1660, a hunting and trading party of seventeen Montrealers in their twenties under the leadership of twenty-five-year-old Adam Dollard des Ormeaux was killed or captured and tortured to death by Onondaga Iroquois who besieged the Frenchmen's hastily constructed palisaded encampment at Long Sault Rapids on the Ottawa River. The massacre was cherished in the memory of Montreal as a Battle of Marathon, in which the young men knowingly sacrificed themselves, like ancient Spartans, to hinder invasion. Historians later qualified this conception, viewing it more as a tragic stumbling into each other by Onondaga and French. Still, the loss of seventeen men in their twenties came as yet another trauma for a settlement subjected to Iroquois terror throughout the past eighteen years and as such possessed mythic resonance. These men were to be the biological fathers of the French Canadian Catholic people struggling to be born in a North American wilderness. Just as each married or marriageable young woman who arrived in Ville-Marie in these years made a difference, so, too, did each young man, each husband or future husband, each present or future father. All this potential was now lost forever in the case of the Dollard party.

Already, as of April 1658, there were enough Indian and French children in Ville-Marie for Maisonneuve to grant Marguerite Bourgeoys the thirty-six-by-eighteen-foot stone stable near the hospital for use as a schoolroom. The building on the edge of the common had been vacant since 1652, when cowherd Antoine Roos had been killed by roving Iroquois. There Marguerite Bourgeoys began to teach the children of Montreal—few in number, true, but encouraging enough a beginning to motivate her to accompany Jeanne Mance to France to recruit teachers from the Notre-Dame auxiliaries at Troyes. Which she did: Edmée Châtel, daughter of a notary; Marie Raisin, daughter of a master tailor; and Anne Hiou, an orphan under the guardianship of her uncle, the procurator for the Hospitallers at La Flèche. These women in their early twenties shocked their parents or guardians with their willingness to travel halfway around the world to teach French and Indian children in a dangerous place when France contained plenty of children to teach. Tears, arguments, resistance—but the three young women prevailed, as did Catherine Crolo, a strong-bodied, hardworking auxiliary to the auxiliaries, whom Marguerite Bourgeoys respected from her earlier days at Troyes. Once the congregation was established in Ville-Marie, lay sister Catherine Crolo would run the farm, do the laundry, and bake the bread, living long and usefully past eighty, with a reputation for holiness. Also in the party was Marguerite Maclin, an orphan under Dauversière's guardianship, entrusted to Marguerite Bourgeoys until Mademoiselle Maclin could be suitably married in Ville-Marie. She in fact married twice; as a widow with two children, she remarried and brought ten more children into the world, living on in good health to age ninety-five.

Reaching La Flèche, Jeanne Mance was delighted to learn that three members of the Institute des Hospitalières de Saint Joseph de La Flèche (Institute of Hospitaller Sisters of Saint Joseph of La Flèche)—Mothers Judith Moreau de Brésoles, Catherine Macé, and Marie Maillet—had already volunteered for Ville-Marie. These Hospitallers were slightly older, in their mid- to late thirties, than the teachers recruited by Marguerite Bourgeoys. Judith de Brésoles, the designated superior, was a skilled pharmacist who earned from the Indians of Ville-Marie the title "The Sun That Gives Light" due to her healing skills with native plants. At thirty-five, Mother Maillet had been living comfortably on her income before joining the Hospitallers, which suggests that she came from a more privileged background than did the teaching sisters. So improbable was the notion of such accomplished women leaving La Flèche for Ville-Marie, and so hostile were locals to the Montreal recruiters, a rumor spread that the Hospitallers were being abducted, and a crowd with drawn swords tried to bar their way, enraged by the departure of both the Hospitallers and a group of young women who had agreed to accompany them either as future nuns or as future wives and mothers. The contretemps, which so revealed the finality of immigration to New France for ordinary people, was resolved, however; in September 1659 the women converged on La Rochelle for departure to Canada. Dauversière was on hand to wave good-bye from the dock.

Dauversière died two years later—broke and, in Parkman's opinion, a deluded visionary—yet the city he and Father Olier had dreamt of founding was indeed established and flourishes to this day. Mother Macé's brother, the Paris-based Sulpician René Macé, agreed to act as the procurator for the Hospitaller Sisters of Saint Joseph and their hospital in Montreal; with the ease and familiarity with donated funds characteristic of the Sulpicians, Monsieur Macé kept the hospital well financed and supplied in the years to come. A vanguard of French women—nurses, teachers, and future wives and mothers—was sailing for Ville-Marie under Catholic auspices: a vanguard because within the decade the Crown would put itself behind this great work of helping to bring young women to New France. Women, it seemed, were crucial for New France's emergence from frontier to colony. Until this time, there had never been enough of them, but now they would be coming in larger numbers, despite the dangers of crossing, despite the murderous Iroquois, despite the long winters, the lack of amenities, and the loss of home.

A half-century agenda

The episcopal service of François-Xavier de Montmorency-Laval divides itself into three phases: vicar apostolic, first bishop of Quebec, and Monseigneur L'Ancien, technically retired but still serving as an episcopal presence (1689–1708). As vicar apostolic (1659–1674), the titular bishop of Petraea, Laval established his presence as missionary bishop in residence and—this was much more difficult—in charge, despite uncertain lines of authority. During these years, he toured his vast vicariate, insisted on the primacy of his office, fought the brandy trade, negotiated an increasingly Gallican environment, and lobbied for the creation of a diocese. He founded a seminary for the education, financial support, and community of secular clergy modeled on the seminary program of the Paris Foreign Missions Society. As first bishop of Quebec (1674–1688), Laval continued to oppose the brandy trade but made an overall peace with the Gallican dimension of Church governance in France while firmly establishing the role and authority of himself in that culture. He furthered the development of his seminary and secular clergy, whom he sought to support through a system of fixed tithes. He tried—but failed—to establish authority in his diocese over the four separate sisterhoods, which he wanted to consolidate. He settled his disagreements with the Abbé Queylus and the Sulpicians of Montreal, remained on excellent terms with the Jesuits (who had brought him to power in the first place), and dealt with the rebellious return of the Recollects. He created parishes, built churches and shrines, founded a trade school for boys, and obtained the required authorizations to establish a chapter of cathedral canons, which rounded out the diocesan culture of Quebec and put it on a par with diocesan organization in France. Of equal importance, he fostered the development of devotions—to Saint Anne, the mother of Mary; to Saint Joseph, the foster father of Jesus; to the Holy Family in its totality—which he thought promoted family values in a society bringing itself into being, doubling its population every twenty-seven years, through marriage and family life.

Vicar apostolic

As vicar apostolic, Laval was essentially a missionary bishop—appointed by the Sacred Congregation for the Propagation of the Faith in Rome, with the concurrent nomination of the king—charged with developing his vicariate into a diocese. Clergy in the Saint Lawrence valley consisted of seventeen Jesuits, four Sulpicians, and six secular priests. In addition, there were two small sisterhoods and a handful of Jesuit donnés. The Jesuits were the first to offer Laval hospitality, followed by the Hospitaller Sisters. When an epidemic, brought to Quebec by an arriving French ship, broke out in the autumn of 1659, the bishop worked as a volunteer chaplain and hospital attendant, administering the sacraments, caring for the sick, and making beds, just as he had once done at the Caen community.

Laval lived at the Hôtel-Dieu for three months and then moved into a small home owned by Madame de La Peltrie, on grounds adjacent to the Ursuline convent, and paid rent of 200 livres a year. In observance of canon law, the home was separated from the convent by a stone wall. "He lives there like a holy man and an apostle," noted Mother Marie de l'Incarnation, "his life is so exemplary that he commands the admiration of the country. He gives everything away and lives like a pauper, and one may well say that he has the very spirit of poverty. He practices this poverty in his house, in his manner of living, and in the matter of furniture and servants; for he has but one gardener, whom he lends to poor people when they have need of him, and a valet who formerly served M. de Bernières."[1]

Yet within three months of his arrival, this humble servant of the people set up an ecclesiastical court for which he claimed final responsibility for judging all matters pertaining to religious affairs in New France. The gesture was bold, even defiant, on behalf of episcopal autonomy in an environment in which the governor exercised sole authority over secular and religious affairs and had his prie-dieu set before all others in a place of unambiguous precedence when at Mass or other church gatherings. No more! Laval declared. From now on, the bishop's prie-dieu would hold the place of honor at Mass, and in processions or related church events the bishop would lead the people. Thus Laval placed the governor's prie-dieu in a subordinate position at Mass and at solemn high Masses had him incensed not by the deacon, as previously, but by the thurifer, the lowest-ranking person on the altar. Even worse, the thurifer incensed the governor only after this lowly acolyte had finished incensing the choir, thus lowering the governor to a single step above the entire congregation, who were the last to be incensed. When the governor was absent from Quebec, moreover, Laval had him removed as honorary warden of the parish church.

The governor, Pierre de Voyer d'Argenson—chevalier, Seigneur de Chastre, and vicomte de Mouzay, of a lineage almost as old as the bishop's—was not amused. Two can play that game, he decided. For the Corpus Christi procession, the governor ordered his soldiers not to remove their headdress when the bishop stopped to bless them with the gold monstrance carrying the Eucharist. Laval thwarted this scheme by bypassing the governor and his soldiers entirely. Caught in the middle of this quarrel, the Jesuits stopped inviting both men to dinner. Historians have been tempted to dismiss this dispute as a trivial matter of personal pique between two aristocrats. That it might very well have been—in part. But the bishop and the governor knew that the discord had deeper implications in the context of the drama of an emergent Gallican ascendancy in which Laval was involved. In France, as in Spain, the Crown held an almost exclusive responsibility and authority for evangelization of indigenous people. Laval had been approved of and sent by the king. Yet he had been vetted and confirmed, after much delay, by the Sacred Congregation for the Propagation of the Faith in Rome on behalf of a papacy that was reinvolving itself in missionary activity. As vicar apostolic, Laval was obligated to pope and king in equal measure.

But how much authority could he carve out for the Church when he was not, strictly speaking, bishop of Quebec? And what did he risk by opposing d'Argenson's claim to primacy of position when in the Gallican culture of France the king had to authorize a diocese for Quebec and name Laval to it? In any event, Laval seemed to have won round one. After a mere three years in office, d'Argenson returned to France. Subsequent governors, however, would resume the battle.

As early as his chaplaincy and Hospitaller efforts during the two epidemics of 1659, the bishop got to know his Native American constituents personally. The French appreciated a pontifical solemn high Mass, Laval learned, because the rite was familiar to them. For the Indians, however, this ceremony—the bishop in mitre and liturgical regalia, a vested deacon and subdeacon on the altar, together with a master of ceremonies and a thurifer holding a thurible of fragrant burning incense, the Latin chants and choral hymns—possessed an element of sensuous enchantment; and Laval knew the value of celebrating such a Mass on their behalf.

In 1660, with his Indian constituents in mind, Laval made an extensive tour of his vicariate, taking his turn as oarsman as his canoe negotiated the Saint Lawrence and its tributaries. To a certain extent, he was on pilgrimage into the past, present, and future of the evangelization of Native Americans in New France. These people—the Mi'kmaqs of the Gaspé Peninsula and the gulf region, and the Abenakis and Algonquians, on either side of the Saint Lawrence River between Tadoussac and Montreal—had been the first to hear of Catholic Christianity a half century earlier. Many of them had received the new religion, and even those who had not had learned to live in peace with the French. A healthy man in his mid-thirties, Laval bore up under the rigors of portage and trek, ate Indian food, sat at campfires and listened to speeches, exchanged presents, and slept in Indian lodges or outside under bearskins on cold, starry nights. He celebrated Mass, preached through interpreters, heard the laughter of their children, and learned to respect their elders' dignity. Attired in episcopal regalia, he administered the sacrament of confirmation to hundreds of Native Americans and a smaller number of French alike.

Laval also discovered a lifetime cause fighting the brandy trade. It was wrong for traders to use brandy or other forms of alcohol as currency when purchasing furs. He heard too many disturbing reports of how otherwise peaceable Native Americans reacted to intoxication and even more disturbing accounts of the influence alcohol had on already hostile Native Americans. When the rampages, domestic violence, promiscuity, sexual attacks, paybacks for grievances, and various other violations of the social order were over, Indians blamed alcohol for producing a sort of dream life in which what was dreamed—however bad—must be done by the dreamer, no matter the consequences in the nondream world to which the drinker returned when the alcohol wore off. Dutch and French traders, however, recognized how much the Indians prized brandy, despite its pitfalls, and how available and portable a form of currency it offered them. Prohibition against trading spirits for furs went back to Champlain's time, and in 1657, two years before Laval's arrival, the king's council had reaffirmed this long-standing policy. Yet in the opinion of Laval and others, the prohibition was being increasingly violated.

On 5 May 1660 Laval issued a decree declaring that violators of this prohibition would be excommunicated—an escalated penalty in a society in which church and state were so interdependent—and the following year he excommunicated one Pierre Aigron for trafficking in spirits. The excommunication had its desired effect. Within a week of the excommunication, Aigron, a mariner turned fur trader, was doing public penance and petitioning for readmission to Holy Mother Church. When, however, the new governor, Baron Pierre Dubois Davaugour—a brusque and plainspoken soldier of distinction—came out in favor of the trade, it resumed with all its previous force and in fact spiraled. Laval, thoroughly committed to ending the traffic, sailed for France to seek a judgment from the theological faculty of the Sorbonne and to lobby the king and his royal council. As he hoped, the theologians of the Sorbonne responded in Laval's favor. Yes, they decided, given the effects of alcohol on Native Americans, a bishop could prohibit such a trade under pain of excommunication and could exercise this option against any violator. The king and his council, moreover, repeated their support of the prohibition, and for the five years following Laval's return from France in 1663, the trade receded, temporarily.

A fateful year

The year 1663 was truly an annus mirabilis in the social, political, and religious development of New France. First of all, the Great Earthquake struck on the night of 3 February 1663. "The weather was very calm and serene," Mother Marie de l'Incarnation wrote her son, Claude, a Benedictine monk in France,

> when a sound of terrifying rumbling was heard in the distance, as if a great many carriages were speeding wildly over the cobblestones. This noise had scarcely caught the attention than there was heard under the earth and on the earth and from all sides what seemed a horrifying confusion of waves and billows. There was a sound like hail on the roofs, in the granaries, and in the room. It seemed as if the marble of which the foundation of the country is almost entirely composed and our houses are built were about to open and break into pieces to gulp us down. Thick dust flew from all sides. Doors opened of themselves. Others, which were open, closed. The bells of all our churches and chimes of our clocks pealed quite alone, and steeples and houses shook like trees in the wind—all this in a horrible confusion of overturning furniture, falling stones, parting floors, and splitting walls. Amidst all this the domestic animals were heard howling. Some ran out of their houses; others ran in. In a word, we were all so frightened we believed it was the even of Judgment, since all the portents were to be seen.[2]

This religious interpretation of the quake, so natural for the era, as well as the cooperative attitude of yet another governor, the chevalier Augustin Saffray de Mézy, not only helped keep a lid on the brandy trade but also signaled a temporary cessation of church-state conflict in the colony. Laval played a key role in Mézy's appointment. Mézy had come under the influence of Laval's mentor, Jean de Bernières-Louvigny of the Hermitage, when Mézy, an army officer of noble Norman descent, was posted to Caen. Repenting his past life, Mézy grew religious in the style of his class and became a semidévot.

The appointment of a governor general for New France had become a matter of increased importance. On 24 February 1663 the barely surviving Company of New France, under pressure from the king's first minister, Jean–Baptiste Colbert, returned to the Crown its assets and contract to govern New France, which then became a royal colony. As minister and advisor to the king and the second-most powerful man in France, Colbert was intent upon creating an efficiently run overseas empire that would strengthen France as a commercial power in competition with England and the Netherlands. To assist in this effort, New France would henceforth be governed by a sovereign council consisting of the governor, the bishop or senior ecclesiastic in the country at the time, and five councilors chosen by the governor and bishop, one of whom would serve as attorney general for the province. Thus Laval, so recently in conflict with the secular sector, now found his authority nearly coequal to that of the governor. Laval was also encouraged by the king's promise that he would ask Rome to upgrade Quebec to a diocese and that he would nominate Laval to the pope as its first bishop. Laval was, moreover, given primary responsibility for recommending the first man to serve as royal governor, and he recommended Mézy, who accepted a three-year term on condition that the Crown liquidate his debts.

Laval and Mézy sailed together for New France in mid-June 1663. (Also on board was Colbert's agent, Louis Gaudais, charged with filing confidential reports back to Colbert from Quebec regarding all aspects of the new governance structure, including the performances of the bishop and the governor.) Sixty of the 219 indentured workers and prospective settlers aboard perished during a terrible crossing that took four months. The death rate suggests poor selection, overloading, underprovisioning, an epidemic, or combinations thereof. Still, the arrival of new recruits was encouraging, as was the falloff in Iroquois raids, which was due to an outbreak of smallpox among the Five Nations as well as wars with neighboring rivals.

A seminary and the secular clergy

From 1663 into the early 1700s, historian W.J. Eccles emphasizes, New France was governed as a royalist welfare state controlled and subsidized from Versailles on behalf of the emergence of France as a European power served by a profitable overseas empire. In founding a seminary in October 1663 and modeling it on the overseas-oriented seminary of the Paris Foreign Missions Society, to which the Quebec institute became formally affiliated in January 1665, Laval was further developing his diocese-in-the-making along congruent lines. The seminary of the Paris Foreign Missions Society was, first of all, an academy for training secular priests for service in the overseas missions of a French empire in its first phase of development. After 1665 it had a branch office in Quebec. Laval had an affinity for group identities, with his history as a member of the Bons Amis as a student, a member of the cathedral chapter at Évreux, and, later, a resident of the Hermitage at Caen. He admired the community spirit of the Sulpicians (indeed, in 1668 he would welcome the Abbé Queylus back to Canada and appoint him vicar general of Montreal), and as a pioneering vicar apostolic missionary, originally slated for an assignment to the Far East, he had himself played a minor role in the creation of the Paris Foreign Missions Society. Upon his arrival in Quebec, he had lived communally with the Jesuits at their college and returned there for the winter of 1661–1662 before his departure for France.

As the former archdeacon of the Diocese of Évreux, Laval was familiar with the details of how secular parish priests could and should be managed. As vicar apostolic, he was charged with the task of building up a cadre of parish clergy for Canada. He began this phase of his assignment in 1659 by recruiting three secular priests and a deacon to accompany him to Quebec. One of these priests, the Abbé Charles de Lauson, had served as acting governor of New France in 1656 when his father resigned as governor and returned to France. When his young wife died in childbirth that same year, Lauson resigned and, putting his infant daughter temporarily with a good family, returned to France to study for the priesthood. Taking advantage of the Abbé Lauson's prior business and administrative experience, Laval named him judge of his newly established ecclesiastical court and vicar general of Quebec.

Within the year, Laval ordained the twenty-five-year-old deacon, Henri de Bernières, to the priesthood, the first ordination in Canada. Bernières was the nephew of Jean de Bernières-Louvigny, Laval's spiritual mentor at the Hermitage at Caen, and thus the nephew by marriage of Madame de La Peltrie, whom Bernières-Louvigny had married in name only to prevent a forced remarriage of the young widow. Bernières-Louvigny also served as Laval's representative in the matter of the two benefices he still held in France. The young priest Henri de Bernières was like a younger brother to Laval, who trusted him completely. When the Abbé Jean Torcapel, whom Laval had assigned to create a fully functioning parish for Quebec City, decided to return to France in the autumn of 1660, Laval named Bernières in his place. Over the next two years, in addition to ministering in Quebec City and acting as Laval's secretary, Bernières supervised the building of a presbytery, which served as Laval's residence following his return from France in the summer of 1663.

Laval returned with a royal charter authorizing him to build and operate a seminary for the theological education and pastoral training of a diocesan clergy for the Quebec colony. He named Bernières to serve as founding director. Laval had more than a teaching institution in mind. With a French population of barely three thousand, his vicariate could not support, then or in the foreseeable future, a network of tithe-supported, financially independent parishes staffed by secular priests holding canonical right as permanent pastors. A communal organization was more appropriate to a missionary situation, Laval believed. Not only would the seminary educate the secular priests of Quebec, Laval decided, but also it would offer them lifetime support from education to retirement and would supervise their assignments as well. This was the Paris Foreign Missions Society seminary model, to which the Quebec seminary would become formally affiliated. Canada, in short, would be served in the same manner as Southeast Asia and the Chinese mainland: by secular-priest missionaries joined in community through seminary affiliation, whose support would come from the Crown and from donors, benefices, and properties owned in France and tithes paid locally by habitants.

Promulgated by decree in October 1663, these tithes, approved by the king, called for a payment of one-thirteenth of annual income. Habitants, however, had grown accustomed over the decades to receiving religious services for free from Recollects, Jesuits, and, lately in Montreal, Sulpicians: that is, from priests with their own sources of support. Now they were expected to pay for a clergy devoted exclusively to their interests. The one-thirteenth levy was resisted, especially after Laval made the mistake of reducing it to one-twentieth for the parish of Quebec City. Governor Mézy, whom Laval had been opposing regarding appointments to the sovereign council, supported the lower figure, and Laval relented, setting the tithe at one-twentieth for the entire province and postponing its payment for two years, which turned into five years when resistance persisted. In August 1667, under a new governor, a figure of one twenty-sixth for twenty years and one-twentieth after that became official and began to gain traction.

Laval, meanwhile, was busy arranging financing for his seminary scheme from the Crown and from other official French sources and private donors. To the seminary he gave his personal property, the seigneuries he held, and the proceeds he derived from the Abbey of Montigny, which he held from the king. He had only one condition: a priest of the seminary must say one low Mass daily for the repose of his soul and for the souls of the departed priests of the Paris Foreign Missions Society seminary. Over time, Laval also secured for the support of the seminary such local properties as the Isle-aux-Coudres and beach and shore sections on the Saint Lawrence and Saint Charles Rivers as well as the Beaupré. For the rest of his life, Laval lived simply as a member of the seminary community, eating his meals at a common table alongside his priests, sharing with them the duties of the household. He spent part of each summer at the Saint Joachim trade school he founded in the nearby countryside.

The first seminary structure was built of wood on a sixteen-acre site Laval purchased from Guillemette Hébert Couillard, the widow of Guillaume Couillard, both of whom were offspring of founders of New France. He also purchased and altered a neighboring stone building for use as a *petit séminaire*, a preparatory school for boys and younger men interested in one day qualifying for entrance into the seminary. The professors at the nearby Jesuit college also served as needed as seminary faculty in the humanities, sciences, philosophy, theology, and Scripture. In 1679 Laval laid the foundations for a substantial stone edifice to replace the original wooden structure. It was ready for use by the end of 1680. Thus, concurrent with the religiously affiliated Harvard (1636) and William and Mary (1694) in the English colonies to the south, New France was supporting an Ursuline boarding school for girls (1637), a Jesuit school for boys (1635), a Jesuit classical college (1655), a trade school (1688), and a divinity school (1663).

A mystic and missionary of Quebec

The census of 1681 lists twenty-five priests attached to the Quebec seminary, with twenty seminarians in residence. The Jesuit college was staffed with eight priests, seven brothers, and four donnés. The Recollect monastery at Quebec (the Recollects returned to Quebec in 1670) housed seven friars and three donnés. One of the donnés was a married man who worked for the friars in various capacities. Altogether, some forty-seven priests and friars were housed in Quebec City. Also in residence were twenty-two choir sisters and seven lay sisters living and working at the Ursuline convent. The Hôtel-Dieu held nineteen professed canonesses and nine lay sisters. Those numbers meant that approximately 12 percent of the total population of Quebec of 1,345 residents were clergy or religious engaged directly and indirectly in full-time pastoral, educational, or hospital service. More than half of these, fifty-seven in all, were Ursuline or Hospitaller Sisters. By 1681, Quebec had become a citadel of Roman Catholic missionary outreach significantly female in its staffing—and missionary, moreover, despite the strict enforcement of cloister in the aftermath of the Council of Trent. The Ursulines began in Brescia, Italy, in the mid-1530s as a society of single women devoted to the teaching of girls but who remained in their homes and did not become nuns. In 1572 these teachers adopted community life and simple vows. In 1612 Pope Paul V allowed the Paris community to take solemn vows, adhere to strict enclosure, and follow a modified Rule of Saint Augustine that called for a blend of choral worship and teaching. As in the case of the Benedictines, Ursuline monasteries were autonomous, but from 1612 onward Paris provided the dominant model for the Ursuline mission and way of life.

Besides the foundress of the order, Angela Merici (1474–1540), who was canonized in 1807, the best-known figure in the entire Ursuline movement remains the Quebec-based mystic, teacher, mother superior, and letter writer Marie Guyart (1599–1672), known in religion as Marie de l'Incarnation, canonized on 3 April 2014. In reference to her prayer life and posthumously published religious writings, the noted court preacher Jacques Bossuet called Guyart the Saint Teresa of Ávila of New France. In reference to her epistolary career, she also might have been described as the Madame de Sévigne of Quebec; like her contemporary Sévigne, whose more than fifteen hundred letters have earned a permanent place in French literature, Marie de l'Incarnation was an avid letter writer, and the surviving hundreds of letters she wrote during her thirty-five years in Quebec have helped ensure her position in secular French literature, the literature of mystical theology, and the history of New France between 1637 and 1672. At once gossipy and high-minded, these letters encapsulate both her times and the interior life of a hyperintelligent, pervasively competent woman on the margins of seventeenth-century France, who dramatically embodied the full range of devotionalism, dissonances, and subconscious suppressions of the Catholic Revival. As was true of her contemporaries Olier, Dauversière, and Mance, dream visions played a crucial role in Marie Guyart's self-identification. She had her first such experience, she later recalled, at the age of seven when she dreamt that she was playing with a friend in a country school yard. Suddenly, the heavens opened and Jesus Christ appeared. " 'Look!' I cried to my companion," she recalled in *The Relation of 1654* she provided to her son, Dom Claude Martin, a Benedictine monk of the Congregation of Saint Maur and prior of Marmoutier Abbey, " 'There's our Lord and he is coming to me!' It seemed to me that he had chosen me rather than her because she had been guilty of some imperfection, although she was, nevertheless, a good girl. However, there was a secret involved which I did not know then. As this most adorable Majesty approached me, my heart felt on fire with love for him and I started to open my arms to embrace him. Then he, the most beautiful of all the children of men, took me in his arms and with a look full of indescribable sweetness and charm kissed me with great love and asked me, 'Will you be mine?' I answered, 'Yes!' Then when he heard my answer, we saw him return to heaven."[3]

The eroticism of this passage, with its presentation of Christ as lover-spouse emerging from the heavens, would be disturbing if it were seen as truly and exclusively describing a childhood memory. But it was not. It was, rather, the wording of a cloistered nun in her fifty-fifth year who had been using such language for decades, having acquired it earlier in her life from Catholic Revival influences. Most vivid of those was the theology of Pierre de Bérulle, as preached, perhaps, in her hometown of Tours by the Oratorian revivalist Clément Metézeau, a devoted disciple of Bérulle, who along with Bérulle advocated a close and personal relationship to the Risen Christ as the God-man Word Incarnate. To Bérulle and Oratorian spirituality as well must be linked Marie's devotion to the Sacred Heart of Jesus as the physical manifestation of His divine love and a devotion to the Blood of Christ as the physical embodiment of His redemptive suffering. At the height of the Iroquois War, Marie, like many of the Jesuit missionaries she admired, would link that concept to one of redemptive martyrdom.

A daughter of the artisan class (her father was a wholesale baker, and her mother came from a branch of an established family that had proven downwardly mobile), Marie, prayerful and contemplative by nature, had wanted to join the local Benedictine monastery where a distant relative of her mother was serving as abbess. Marie's father, however, married her off at the age of seventeen to silk maker Claude Martin. Marie was tall and handsome, good-humored and lively, and had loved reading romances prior to her marriage, even though she considered entering a convent. In the brief two years of her marriage, she became a daily churchgoer and a reader of the Psalms and pious books as well as an excellent supervisor of the workers in her husband's shop. Much later in life she would obliquely suggest to her son that the physical aspects of the married state had not made a lasting impression on her. There remained from the relationship, moreover, two points of sorrow and grievance, the first when her husband was falsely accused of a malfeasance by his mother-in-law and the other when he died and ensnared Marie in lawsuits that left her a broke young widow with a son to raise. Placing her son with a wet nurse, she moved back to her father's house, rejected a number of marriage offers, and then moved with her son into her sister's household, where she spent the next ten years as a chargé d'affaires for her brother-in-law's successful freight drayage business. Waiting for her son to reach an age sufficient for her to enter a convent, she attended daily Mass and read Teresa of Ávila, John of the Cross, and the more practically oriented *Introduction to the Devout Life* (1609) by Francis de Sales.

At this point, on 24 March 1620, she precisely notes in *The Relation of 1654*, she experienced the second great revelation of her life, this time in front of the chapel of the Feuillant Fathers (reformed Cistercian) in Tours. It was a sensation of sinfulness, her own, and redemption through Christ's shedding of blood on Calvary. "Suddenly," she remembered, "I was brought stock-still, both inwardly and outwardly. Even my thoughts were abruptly brushed aside. Then, in an instant, my inner eyes were opened and all the faults, sins, and imperfections that I had committed since my birth were shown to me in the most vivid details: so clear and distinct were they that no human certainty could have expressed them thus. At the same moment I saw myself immersed in the blood of the Son of God, shed because of the sins which had been shown to me; and furthermore, realizing that it was for my salvation that this Precious Blood had been shed. I think I would have died of terror had God's goodness not maintained me, so frightful and shocking is the sight of sin, no matter how slight."[4] Recovering her composure, she entered the chapel and went to confession to Dom François de Saint-Bernard, who became her spiritual director until her entrance into the Ursuline monastery at Tours in 1631. At first, she volunteered to enter as a lay sister but was appointed to the choir, despite her lack of a dowry required for such an appointment, and was named mistress of novices within two years.

The removal of Mother Marie de l'Incarnation to Canada began in the winter of 1633 after a period of spiritual bleakness frequently experienced by mystics. Marie was then under the spiritual direction of Jesuit Georges de la Haye just as the Jesuit mission to Canada was being restored. In contrast to the lack of imagery in her experience outside the Feuillant chapel, dream vision number three, as it might be called, was vividly narrational and visual. Walking in the company of a laywoman, Marie and a companion ascended a rugged trail until they came to "a small church of white marble, constructed in a pretty, ancient style. On top of the pinnacle was a chair in which the Blessed Virgin was seated, holding her little Jesus in her lap with her arms around him. The place was very elevated and beneath it lay a great, vast country, full of mountains and valleys and thick fog which covered everything except a tiny house which was the church for this country, and which alone was freed from the mists. The Blessed Virgin, Mother of God, gazed at this country which aroused as much compassion as fear."[5]

The place, of course, was Canada, and the secular woman was soon to come into her life as Madame de La Peltrie. Within four years Madame de La Peltrie, her companion Charlotte Barré, and three Ursulines—Mothers Marie de l'Incarnation, Marie de Saint Joseph from Tours, and Cécile de Sainte Croix from Dieppe—and three Hospitaller Sisters from Dieppe—Mothers Marie de Saint Ignace, Anne de Saint Bernard, and Marie de Saint Bonaventure de Jesus—were moving upriver to Quebec on a pinnacle filled with salted cod.

Missing sisters

These six women, accompanied by their patron and foundress (and her companion), were pioneering a new genre of religious, the missionary sister. They did this, moreover, under cloistered circumstances, although the Hospitaller Sisters by definition pursued a more public ministry. Arriving eighteen years before Laval, they brought a new level of ecclesiastical culture to Quebec. Sponsored by the duchesse d'Aiguillon, the niece of Cardinal Richelieu, the most powerful prelate in the kingdom, the Canonesses Regular of Saint Augustine of the Mercy of Jesus belonged to a tradition of hospital nuns that dated back to the eleventh century. As befitted such an established order, and backed by such a powerful patron, the canonesses had their own advance agent and chaplain waiting for them when they arrived in

Quebec, the Abbé Jean Le Sueur. The first secular priest to practice in the colony, Le Sueur was a schoolteacher and chaplain on the estate of Jean Bourdon just outside Quebec City. Prior to the hospital sisters' arrival, Le Sueur acquired property near Sillery, where he supervised the construction of a hospital and residence. Throughout the next eleven years the Abbé Le Sueur served as hospital chaplain, continued his ministry as an unpaid parish priest, farmed his own land grant, and directed choral music for local liturgies.

While a recently established order, the Ursulines also followed the Rule of Saint Augustine and, as solemnly professed choir nuns, chanted the Divine Office (liturgical hours), thus bringing monasticism as well as teaching to the Saint Lawrence valley. By November 1642 a stone-built convent monastery with a schoolroom and boarding dormitory was ready atop the upper heights, and on a cold morning Mother Marie and five Ursulines (more sisters had arrived from France) and a file of Indian students followed Jesuit Barthélemy Vimont up the hill singing a Te Deum of thanks as they took possession of a building that was not yet paid for. Nor could it be paid for, Jean de Bernières-Louvigny—Madame de La Peltrie's husband, who served as procurator for the Ursulines in France and manager of Madame de La Peltrie's money—informed the Ursulines. Not right now, anyway. Madame de La Peltrie's sojourn at Montreal had thrown Ursuline finances into turmoil. A shortfall was threatening the very sustainability of the Ursuline mission. Madame de La Peltrie returned to Quebec. Mother Marie, utilizing her phenomenal letter-writing skill, found more donors in Paris, and the workmen who had built the convent monastery were paid. The finances of the monastery, however, remained precarious. For the next thirty years Marie de l'Incarnation pursued her multitrack existence as mystic, teacher, linguist, mother superior, fund-raiser, advisor to the colony's ruling elite, and tireless writer of letters chronicling the life and times of Quebec, without leaving the Ursuline cloister high atop the city.

A challenged pedagogy

For Roman Catholics in search of a usable North American past, it is encouraging to consider this Ursuline monastery—its sisters chanting the Divine Office in choir day by day, its classrooms of Indian and French students, its polished floors and orderliness, its gardens and playgrounds vibrant with the sounds of children playing—in such a remote place as Quebec. Consider as well the heightened contemplative life of not only Marie de l'Incarnation but also other Ursulines during the early decades. Here is the prototype of countless schools, boarding schools, and orphanages that for three and a half centuries to come would constitute the gift of Catholic education, taken at its best. In addition, recall the teaching efforts of the Ursulines on behalf of female Indian children: the Mi'kmaq, Abenaki, Algonquian, Huron, and even Iroquois girls brought there by their Christian or Christian-friendly fathers as boarders or day students, scrubbed down upon arrival with soap and water to remove repeated applications of bear grease, hugged and kissed and cooed over by Madame de La Peltrie, who personally fashioned for them little-girl dresses in the French style. The school's original intent, later modified, was to expose these girls to French values as much as possible so that when they came of age they could marry Frenchmen or Christian Indians and exercise a long-term influence on domestic life. To that end, Marie de l'Incarnation and her fellow Ursulines mastered seemingly impenetrable Indian languages while instructing their charges in French. Marie herself learned Algonkinian, the language of the Montagnais, and Huron and wrote several dictionaries—French-Algonquian, Algonquian-French, Iroquois—as well as a catechism in Huron. She knew and loved her students and did her best to understand them, which over time included comprehending how their respective cultures prevented these youngsters from ever being completely transformed into nice little French girls.

Early letters by Mother Marie de l'Incarnation describing her students appeared in the *Jesuit Relations* and thus helped promote interest in the Canadian mission. She detailed their willingness to pray the Rosary, attend daily Mass, and slip into the nuns' choir stalls to sing parts of the Divine Office—the Ave Maris Stella, the Gloria Patri—with them in Latin, helping the sisters hold their choir books. For recreation, they loved dancing together in their native fashion, although they once told Mother Marie that they would not dance on Fridays, having been informed that Jesus died on that day. Three of them had already made their First Communion.

In the glow of these early years, Mother Marie de l'Incarnation and her fellow Ursulines maintained that the youngsters could absorb enough of the French religion, language, and lifestyle to enable them to become the wives and mothers of a new *métis* (mixed) race, at once Indian and French, that would populate the colony. Yet as much as they loved the dresses made by Madame de La Peltrie, the sisters' teaching, the prayers, the singing, the good sagamité (sometimes boiled with plums as a special treat), and the warm, soft beds of the sleeping room, these children of the forest could not fully adjust to the cloister or the French way of life, for they loved the forest as well, more deeply than they loved the sisters. After a while at the school they would spontaneously leave, returning to their homes and their people to resume lives in a culture in which they were also cherished and given a certain wild freedom they could never completely forsake.

And so, in time, as Natalie Zemon Davis of Princeton has underscored, Mother Marie de l'Incarnation came to another conclusion. These wonderful Indian girls were being prepared as Christian emissaries to their own people, as a leaven that would work from within. They would become the wives and mothers of Indian peoples arrived at Christianity or en route to it, due in part to the presence within the tribes of strong females educated by Ursulines and functioning in cultures in which women exercised leadership in many matters, including questions of war and peace. Thus this inveterate writer began to chronicle in her letters a different kind of Indian female: the older woman who carried Christian values and practice back to her people. One Huron woman, a former student at the school, who was taken into captivity at the age of thirteen or fourteen by the Iroquois and married into that people, maintained her prayer life and taught others how to pray as she grew into a female leader of her community. A Huron girl lived with the Hospitaller Sisters, as their interpreter; reading, writing, and speaking French with astonishing fluency, she served as a bridge between the two cultures. The Huron Celine Gannendaris was so knowledgeable of the faith that she served as a catechist when non-Christian Indians came to Quebec asking for instruction.

Thus in the years following *annus horribilis* 1650, when the first Ursuline convent burned down and the Iroquois devastated Huronia, French girls from the growing habitant population increasingly began to form part of the Ursuline student body (thirty boarders and perhaps an equal number of day students as of October 1669), sitting in class alongside Indian and métis girls from Catholic families in an even more commodious stone convent—worthy of France itself—surrounded by walled orchards and gardens. The Ursuline community now numbered twenty-two religious (fifteen choir nuns, four lay sisters, and three novices), including several Canadian-born women, all living in a monastery convent designed to serve as a fortress of last resort in case of an Iroquois attack on Quebec City.

Advising the great

During this time, it was customary in Catholic Europe—especially in Italy, Spain, Portugal, and France—for mother superiors of Marie de l'Incarnation's stature to serve as advisors to clerical and lay leaders. Thus Teresa of Ávila advised Philip II and other officials. And so to the Ursuline cloister atop Quebec City came Jesuits, secular priests, Bishop Laval himself on a number of occasions, North American leaders, habitant leaders, construction chiefs, donors, potential donors, vendors, parents of students, governors, intendants, members of the sovereign council, and at least one de facto viceroy (marquise Alexandre de Prouville de Tracy, lieutenant general of America) to sit in the visitors' parlor and discuss matters with Mother Marie, who sat behind a grille that partially obscured her features but did not diminish her presence.

Concerning certain policies, Bishop Laval was not always friendly as the two formidable figures negotiated through the grille that separated them. Laval, after all, considered himself the father superior of the Ursulines, who, one must remember, had questioned the scope of his authority upon his arrival in Quebec. When the Ursulines from Tours and those from Quebec drew up a lengthy constitution creating the autonomous Ursulines of Quebec, Laval wanted the document reduced to five or six pages. He also directed the Ursulines to sing only late-afternoon vespers and early-evening compline in choir, thus saving time for other work, and to cease their practice of singing hymns during Mass, which he believed distracted from the priest at the altar. Later, fearing the proliferation of religious orders in sparsely settled Quebec, Laval urged the Ursulines to merge with the newly formed Notre-Dame Sisters of Montreal. Mother Marie was not in favor of any of these proposals. The constitution for the autonomous Ursulines of Quebec was shortened, which was most likely a good thing; but Laval's other suggestions were resisted.

From these sessions with the great, the near great, and the ordinary, Mother Marie gathered the news and gossip of the colony, which she transformed into detailed letters to her son, Dom Claude Martin. These letters function today as foundational literature for French Canada and hold an honorable place in the history and literature of France itself. How human! How poignant, even. Here was the son she never held or kissed as a boy (so he tells us) lest (so she later told him) he grow too attached to a mother only waiting to enter a convent when her son reached a certain age. And when he learned as a boy of eleven or twelve that she was entering, he ran away for three days, sending her into a paroxysm of anxiety, and when she finally entered the convent he wept in despair and, a little later, organized a troop of schoolboys to stand outside the convent with him as he cried,

"Give me back my mother! Give me back my mother!" The trouble with her son filled her with dread and made her first years as an Ursuline an emotional wasteland. His aunt and her husband raised him after that, followed by an education with the Jesuits at their college at Rennes. He applied to the Society but was turned down. He did not have the temperament, perhaps, for such a quasi-military organization and became a Benedictine instead, entering the Congregation of Saint Maur, which was devoted to patristic, historical, and literary studies. This life suited him, and he became an editor and published scholar as well as rising to the rank of prior, the chief executive officer reporting to the abbot.

Dom Claude also became his mother's primary correspondent. Many of their letters have been lost, but those that survive reveal Marie de l'Incarnation reaching out to her son, seeking reconciliation. Or perhaps half reconciliation would be more accurate, for her central point on this matter was that what she did in enter-ing the convent and leaving him behind had been the making of him—indeed, his salvation—given his present status as a Benedictine monk and scholar. He, in turn, seems to have come to terms with being the abandoned son of a living saint who resembled the early Christian saints he studied and wrote about. He may even have forgiven her for writing that her greatest wish for him (as for herself) was that he be granted the gift of martyrdom: as if he had not already paid his dues in the suffering department!

In any event, Dom Claude prompted from his mother some of her most incan-descently mystical letters and motivated her to write *The Relation of 1654*, an import-ant contribution to the literature of mystical experience. Good scholar that he was, he wrote his mother's biography and edited her letters following her death on 30 April 1672. In the biography he presents Marie Guyart as a saint from the begin-ning and Mother Marie de l'Incarnation as a majestic figure who in old age still showed the vigor of her younger years. She was a missionary, Laval wrote Dom Claude in a letter intended to be used in the biography's preface. "Her ardour for saving souls and especially for the conversion of the Indians was so great and so far-reaching, that it seemed as if she bore them all in her heart, and we do not doubt that she contributed greatly by her prayers to obtaining from God the blessings which He has showered on this newborn Church."[6]

A diocese at last

In 1662 King Louis XIV promised Laval a Canadian diocese with himself as found-ing bishop. With the authority of a diocesan bishop, Laval believed, he could fight the resurgent brandy trade more effectively and be in a better position to put the Church in Quebec on a self-sustaining basis through tithing. While a missionary vicariate might be appropriate to a Church staffed by religious-order missionaries, the French population of Quebec was growing through immigration and live births, and it was becoming increasingly awkward to serve and govern a French population (which was entitled to local parishes and parish priests who were devoted to their interests) through a missionary-oriented apostolic vicariate structure.

It took twelve years to bring the Diocese of Quebec into being and to have Laval confirmed as its first bishop. Diplomatic difficulties between Rome and Versailles caused delay, as did the desire of the independent-minded, Gallican-oriented French

Crown and hierarchy to monitor and have input into the Rome-driven process. The cardinals in Rome, moreover, bowing to Gallican pressure, proposed that the Diocese of Quebec be a subordinate diocese to the Archdiocese of Rouen, which reflected the wishes of its former archbishop, François II de Harlay de Champvallon, now archbishop of Paris. Worldly and ambitious, and wanting to succeed Cardinal Mazarin as first minister of state, François II had succeeded his uncle François I as archbishop of Rouen in 1651, despite Vincent de Paul's objections to the political aspirations and dubious private life of the wealthy and socially prominent young abbé. Louis XIV brought François II to Paris in 1671, appointing him archbishop of Paris, raising that office to a ducal peerage, and making François II a trusted advisor and director of affairs for the religious-order clergy of the kingdom. As archbishop of Paris, Harlay de Champvallon in 1684 performed the secret morganatic marriage between the king and the formidable Françoise d'Aubigné, marquise de Maintenon. As of the 1660s, however, despite his rise to power, the archbishop was still smarting over his loss of control of New France to Laval and thus had issues with the notion of an independent Quebec diocese.

Laval opposed the subordination of Quebec to Rouen, but for the time being the archbishop of Paris had the king's ear, and there the matter stalled. Besides, Quebec could not yet pay its bills either to Rome (Peter's Pence) or to the king or maintain a full operation in Canada as a diocese was expected to do, nor could Laval close this gap with private funds. Laval dropped his opposition to the Rouen ascendancy in 1669, the same year that Louis XIV and Colbert, in order to reactivate negotiations with Rome, dropped it as well.

That left the money issue on the table. Could a freestanding Diocese of Quebec afford itself and pay its bills? The question remained open. In 1671 Laval sailed for France to resolve the matter once and for all, vowing not to return to Quebec until a diocese was established, even if that meant not returning at all. He remained in France four years, lobbying Versailles, besieging Rome with letters and memoranda, raising money from old and new donors—and he finally prevailed. Rome and Versailles relinquished their financial requirements. The bulls were sent to Versailles in October 1674. By the end of May 1675, having taken his oath of loyalty to the king, Laval sailed for New France as the first bishop of the newly established Diocese of Quebec.

Diocesan development

For the first year or so following the creation of the Diocese of Quebec, Archbishop François II de Harlay de Champvallon used his considerable influence to have Laval's diocese placed in subordination to Champvallon's Archdiocese of Paris. Rome resisted, and Harlay de Champvallon failed in this last attempt to get Quebec back, but his prolonged effort motivated Laval to develop the administrative structure and autonomy of his diocese throughout the remaining thirteen years of his appointment. By way of prologue to this endeavor, he toured his diocese in the summer of 1681, accompanied by his trusted vicar general, the Abbé Louis Ango Des Maizerets. A noble Norman with an independent income and, like Laval, both a graduate of the Jesuit colleges at La Flèche and Clermont and a member of the Jesuit-sponsored society Bons Amis, Ango Des Maizerets associated with Laval later

as well at the Hermitage at Caen. Recruited by his friend Laval, he had sailed with
him for Canada in May 1663 on that terrible four-month voyage during which so
many died, and Ango Des Maizerets came close to succumbing to scurvy. He never
fully recovered his health after that ordeal, and Laval himself was nearly sixty—a
venerable age in that era—but the bishop and his vicar set off in their birch-bark
canoes in the summer heat (although presumably neither of them took a turn at
the oar, as Laval had done in his younger years) and visited his diocese up along the
Saint Lawrence River as far as Montreal. This upriver region's growing population
demanded the establishment of parishes, staffed by seminary priests and supported
by colony-wide tithing, although this very arrangement was coming under attack
by the current governor general, Louis de Buade, the Comte de Frontenac, who
was arguing for a conventional parish system of permanent pastors with lifetime
tenure, supported by local parish revenues. For the time being, the point remained
moot, for only Quebec and Montreal could afford permanent parishes. In 1678
Laval had joined the parish of Notre-Dame of Montreal with the seminary of Ville-
Marie, all of which (including a nearby chapel, Notre-Dame de Bonsecours) fell
under the guardianship of the Company of Priests of Saint-Sulpice, who held seigneurial rights to the Island of Montreal and were not short of revenues.

Frontenac had launched his anti-seminary, anti-tithing campaign while Laval was
still in France lobbying for a diocese and also openly opposed Laval regarding the
brandy trade, which had regained its momentum during Laval's absence. Supporters
of the brandy trade went so far as to obtain a declaration by the theologians of the
University of Toulouse—to counter Laval's declaration from the Sorbonne—that
the bishop of Quebec had no canonical right to declare the sale of alcohol to Indians
a mortal sin, much less a mortal sin that only he could forgive.

To press counterarguments concerning tithes, the role of the seminary, and the
brandy trade, Laval decided that the Diocese of Quebec needed a permanent representative and procurator in France, and to that post he appointed yet another
Norman aristocrat with a connection to the Hermitage at Caen, the Abbé Jean
Dudouyt. Ever since the abbé had arrived in 1663, Laval had trusted Dudouyt's
administrative abilities and advice in matters great and small. In 1671 he made him
vicar general for Quebec and shortly thereafter ecclesiastical superior of the Hôtel-
Dieu. Here was the perfect man to represent the diocese in Paris and Versailles.
Leaving for France in the autumn of 1676, Dudouyt took up residence in the seminary of the Paris Foreign Missions Society and represented the Diocese of Quebec
and conducted its financial business until his death at age sixty in 1688.

The Abbé Dudouyt, however, could not block the lobbying of such powerful
figures as Colbert, Frontenac, the intendant Jacques Duchesneau, and all the others
who considered the brandy trade essential to the economic well-being of New
France. Seeking a resolution, Louis XIV directed Frontenac to survey twenty leading habitants about the matter; the habitants were chosen by the sovereign council
at a time when Laval no longer held coequal authority with the governor general
but sat, rather, as one of seven. And then, putting Laval's case at even further disadvantage, the king asked his confessor, the Jesuit François de La Chaise, and his
trusted advisor, Laval's longtime nemesis François II de Harlay de Champvallon, to
review the twenty opinions and report back to him with a recommendation. Issued
on 24 May 1679, the resulting ordinance—as might be expected from this panel of

two—was a divided recommendation. Liquor could be sold to Indians, but only in French settlements. Traders could not use alcohol as a medium of exchange. In one sense, Laval had only half won, yet that half included a prohibition against wholesale drunkenness in the field (if it could be enforced, that is), which offered some consolation.

The Gallican factor

Laval would reach retirement before he lost his other great campaign on behalf of a tithe-supported, seminary-administered parish system. The fault lines beneath this issue were created by the Gallican-versus-ultramontane, king-versus-pope, conflict at the heart of the French Church during this era. As historian W.J. Eccles points out, Louis XIV of France held more authority over the Roman Catholic Church in France than Henry VIII ever held over the Church of England following his break with Rome. In France, church and state had reached a point of interdependence that only a violent revolution more than one hundred years into the next century could sever. The king nominated bishops to Rome, and they took an oath of loyalty to him once their appointment was approved. The king also distributed ecclesiastical benefices—income from flourishing abbeys—thereby creating a corps of titular abbés as well as the on-site abbots of these establishments, who also required royal approval. The two renowned first ministers of the century, Richelieu and Mazarin, had been cardinals, and the hierarchy came almost exclusively from the landed nobility. Thus bishops, abbés at every level of Church administration or royal service, secular priests of the parish clergy, and abbots and monks of the ancient monasteries under the control of the Crown had a royalist and Gallican orientation, as did the ancient and great monasteries for women.

The papacy, meanwhile, was in a process of recovery born of the Counter-Reformation. Interestingly enough, a number of pontiffs during this period—Gregory XV (1621–1623), Urban VIII (1623–1644), and Clement IX (1691–1700)—were Jesuit-educated. Since their beginnings in the 1540s, the Jesuits had been pro-papal and on the cutting edge of the Counter-Reformation; solemnly professed members of the Society of Jesus, in fact, took a fourth vow to go anywhere and assume any mission the pope might assign them. The French Jesuits of the seventeenth century, then, were ultramontane—favoring the other side of the Alps, meaning Rome—as well as global in their orientation as missionaries. Since Jesuits did not enter the hierarchy, however, the Society existed in an uneasy and sometimes interrupted peace with the French hierarchy, given the success of Jesuit colleges in France and the tendency of French kings to have Jesuit confessors. The clerics of the French Catholic Revival—Sulpicians, Oratorians, Vincentians, and Eudists—tended to steer a middle course between cismontane Gallicanism (this side of the Alps, meaning France) and the ultramontane Jesuits.

Enter Jean-Baptiste Colbert, first minister, minister of marine with oversight of the colonies, economic planner, civil servant extraordinaire. As the son of a draper from Rheims, Colbert had defied the odds in rising to his position; and if there were no Huguenots in his background, he nevertheless had a thorough distrust of the Catholic clergy. There were too many of them, Colbert believed. They were overly privileged, did next to no true work, created no real wealth, consumed

40 percent of the nation's assets, and refused the obligations of marriage and family life. Of the clergy, the Jesuits were the worst offenders, Colbert opined, because they were the most successful at self-aggrandizement and subterfuge. At the apex, then, of the administration of New France in the years that Laval was developing the Diocese of Quebec, he was dealing with an anticlerical first minister and a governor-general who shared his attitudes. Indeed, upon his arrival in Quebec in 1672, while Laval was in France, Frontenac reignited the incense and church-warden battles fought by Laval and Governor d'Argenson thirteen years earlier, this time against Laval's vicar general, the Abbé Henri de Bernières, whom Frontenac harassed on matters of protocol in a number of other ways as well.

Frontenac was faced with three well-organized bodies of Catholic clergy: Jesuits, Sulpicians, and seminary priests. Frontenac accused priests from these groups of being puritanical, intolerant, acquisitive, oppressive of the laity, and, even worse— here he specifically named the Jesuits in at least one memorandum he sent to Colbert—desirous of setting up an Inquisition in New France and using the confessional to pry into people's lives in an untoward manner. In matters of sexual behavior, W.J. Eccles suggests, Frontenac was perhaps more accustomed to the relatively relaxed ways of the court. But as Eccles also notes, New France lacked females. An earlier campaign to educate Indian women to become wives of Frenchmen had failed to gain momentum; and so, given human nature, it should not be denied that married habitant women, whose husbands were away from home in the fur trade for up to a year or more, should pursue other relationships, or that young bachelors, whether ranging the wilderness or idling on the home front, should avail themselves of the accommodating attitudes of non-Christian younger Indian women.

The return of the Recollects

In any event, seeking a kinder, gentler clergy, Colbert allowed the Recollects to return to Canada. In the spring of 1670, Father Gabriel de La Ribourde brought the gray-robed reformed Franciscans back to Canada, where they had ministered from 1615 to 1629. The Recollects took up residence at Notre-Dame-des-Anges, a friary they built just outside Quebec City, to which they were virtually quarantined by Laval, despite La Ribourde's effort to secure permission for them to extend their operation to Three Rivers and Montreal. Arriving in 1678, La Ribourde's successor, Valentin Leroux, held a title—provincial commissioner for Canada and guardian of the convent in Quebec—that revealed the Recollects' ambition for growth. Working diligently, Leroux secured ecclesiastical and civil permission for Recollect expansion to Three Rivers and Montreal. He also had a chapel constructed in Quebec City and arranged to transfer to its vault the Recollects and laymen buried in the cemetery at Notre-Dame-des-Anges. Of equal importance in terms of the rebranding of the Recollect enterprise in Canada, Potentien Ozon, the superior of Notre-Dame-des-Anges, received two native-born Canadians, Joseph Denys and Didace Pelletier, into the order.

A member of one of the colony's leading families, Denys was professed in 1678 by Father Leroux and sent for theological studies to France, where he was ordained to the priesthood prior to his return to Canada in 1682. Master carpenter Didace Pelletier, a graduate of the Saint-Joachim school for arts and crafts founded by

Laval in 1668, entered as a lay brother. In 1683 Father Denys and Brother Pelletier accepted a call to the seigneury of Ile Percée, an important fishing station, to develop further the Recollect ministry carried on there for the previous ten years by Father Exupère Dethunes on behalf of a small permanent settlement and a fluctuating population of fishermen.

In 1681 the Recollects resumed their advance on Quebec City with plans to construct a hospice in the upper city. Located half a league outside the city, the Recollects argued, Notre-Dame-des-Anges was too far from Quebec for friars to commute back there following their ministry as chaplains to Fort Saint-Louis in the upper city or for Recollects to travel into the city for medical care. Not mentioned to Laval but documented in an internal report most likely written by Recollect superior Dethunes was the fact that an increasing number of colonists, dissatisfied with the secular clergy's strictness, were coming secretly to the Recollects for confession. Because the hospice was already covered by royal and local governmental approval, Laval reluctantly gave his assent to the project on one condition: the proposed hospice could not ever be turned into a Recollect convent and chapel open to the public. Recollect provincial commissioner Leroux, however, went ahead and built a chapel topped by a belfry, which Laval considered a sign that the Recollects were establishing not a private chapel for the benefit of friars staying overnight in the city but a church that would soon welcome the public. Not so, the Recollects replied. The bell turret was intended to support a lantern for nighttime safety and a small bell for the use of the resident friars.

The quarrel escalated in the months to come, with Frontenac backing the Recollects. Each side appealed to the king. The Recollects charged Laval with antipathy toward them as evidenced not only in the bell-tower controversy but also in Laval's refusal to grant them permission to expand their ministry in his diocese. Indeed, affronted by the Recollect resistance, Laval suspended permission for a number of Recollects to function as priests in his diocese. Disgusted by this treatment, up to five Recollects, including the new provincial commissioner, Henri Le Roy, returned to France. To counter charges that he was on the warpath against Recollects in general (which probably was the case, as Laval feared the rise of exempt religious orders in his diocese), the bishop invited Recollect Adrian Ladan to preach the Advent sermons at the cathedral. Ladan then had the temerity to use one of his sermons to criticize those who did not abide by the decisions of the intendant and the governor-general, as the Recollects believed was the case with the bishop regarding the bell tower. As usual, the royal decision, when it arrived on 10 April 1684, split the difference. The Recollects were not to open a public chapel in Quebec, but the bishop was to remove his restrictions on a Recollect ministry to the habitants.

Parishes and a cathedral chapter

To emphasize the importance of the secular clergy and to comply with royal directives, Laval reversed his position vis-à-vis permanent parishes. Between 1659 and 1678 he had created no permanent parishes on the grounds that, one, the parish he created for Quebec in 1664 was noncanonical because as vicar apostolic he did not have the power to create parishes and, two, no settlement had sufficient funds to support a parish, even though he now had the authority as bishop of Quebec to create one. In 1679 alone, however, Laval created seven parishes. They would not operate on his missionary-oriented seminary plan; in May 1679 the king signed an edict declaring that New France, now that it was a diocese, would be served by permanent parishes served by curés with lifetime tenure supported by local revenues, as was the case in France. Laval took this reversal of his longtime plan with good grace, and in its aftermath he created six new parishes in 1684. Yet some of these thirteen parishes, despite the royal decree, for years continued to remain dependent on seminary support. Thus Laval's seminary plan remained in place, which perhaps helped account for his equanimity when the royal decree favoring permanent parishes arrived.

A diocese required a cathedral, to which was attached a chapter of canons that basically functioned as a board of advisors to the bishop; it also met certain liturgical requirements connected to the cathedral's role as the seat of the bishop and the worship center of the diocese. (One of these obligations, the daily chanting of the Divine Office, had in most European cathedrals long since been assigned to deputies.) Designed in 1645 and completed in 1647 as the parish church of the city, Notre-Dame-de-Québec was specified as Laval's cathedral in 1674. In 1684 Laval established a chapter of canons for Notre-Dame-de-Québec, to which he appointed priests who had helped him establish the institutions of the diocese. Longtime aide Henri de Bernières was named dean of the chapter. Laval also appointed to the cathedral chapter Charles de Lauson, former acting governor of the colony, longtime vicar general, and ecclesiastical superior of the Hôtel-Dieu; Joachim Fornel, judge of the ecclesiastical court; Louis Ango Des Maizerets, longtime superior of the seminary; and Jean Dudouyt, longtime business manager of the vicariate, who was named precentor (master of ceremonies) in absentia, since he was in France at the time, representing the Diocese of Quebec at Versailles. In terms of seventeenth-century French Catholic culture and society (and Laval was a man of his times), the promotion to canonical status of such accomplished abbés—men of family, university education, and distinguished priestly service— constituted a statement by Laval that Quebec was indeed a diocese in every sense of the term: fully developed in its institutions, people, and clergy, and properly governed by a bishop and a cathedral chapter.

By 1688, the year Laval retired, sheer statistics bore out the truth of this assertion. The Diocese of Quebec enjoyed the services of 102 priests (36 Jesuits, 33 seculars, 19 Sulpicians, and 14 Recollects), 13 of whom were Canadian born, and 97 nuns, 50 of them born in New France. There were thirty-five canonically established parishes and a number of chapels and stations in more remote areas. Jesuits, Recollects, Sulpicians, and Paris Foreign Missions Society seminary priests were ministering to existing Catholic Indian communities as well as continuing the work of Indian evangelization. Both greater Quebec and Montreal contained fully staffed hospitals. A divinity school, a Jesuit college, a minor seminary, two schools for girls, and an arts and crafts trade school for boys were flourishing. Local devotions for a family-oriented population, which was doubling itself every twenty-seven years, centered on the Holy Family of Jesus, as revealed in the Gospels: Mary, his Mother; Joseph, his foster father; his grandmother Anne and grandfather Joachim; and his first cousin John the Baptist. Reflecting the shrines of Europe with their stories of intercessions and miracles was the shrine of Sainte-Anne de Beaupré on the shore of the Saint Lawrence River; where Breton sailors were said to have been miraculously saved from drowning in 1658, a chapel had been built in 1662 to commemorate the event, and miracles were said to continue there.

Local saints

The Diocese of Quebec even possessed its own roll call of saints, already acknowledged or soon to be recognized as such in the early years of the ensuing century. Marie de l'Incarnation headed the list, especially following the publication of her biography, spiritual writings, and selected letters as edited by her son. Mother Marie herself was convinced of the sanctity of her Ursuline colleague Marie de Savonnières de La Troche, known in religion as Mother Marie de Saint Joseph, who had sailed from France with her in 1639.

A talented teacher noted for her fine singing voice, her playing of the viol, and her encouragement of Indian girls to enjoy their native dances during recreational periods, Mother Marie de Saint Joseph was the kind of early childhood educator that children love, girls especially; and (as in the case of Madame de La Peltrie) the Indian girls at the Ursuline school in Quebec adored this young nun, and she returned their affection. Entering the Ursuline convent school at Tours as a girl of nine and the Ursuline order itself at the age of fourteen, Marie de Saint Joseph was the youngest member of the community and was treated as such, with marked affection, by Ursuline colleagues old enough to be her mother. Indian adults who came into contact with her called her the Smiling or Laughing Nun because of her serene temperament and amiable disposition. Her parents, who were members of Anjou nobility, had bitterly opposed her decision to go to Canada, and following the fire in 1650 that destroyed the Ursuline convent, they made every effort to have her return to France. Suffering from tuberculosis, which was later compounded by dropsy and gangrene, Marie de Saint Joseph died a painful death on 4 April 1652, attended by Marie de l'Incarnation and Madame de La Peltrie. Miracles were immediately attributed to her. Life in New France at times seemed unrelentingly difficult for habitants and Ursulines alike, and remembrances of this sweet young woman contained some of the ambiance of a reimagined France— like a fairy tale, perhaps, or the figure of a female saint in a stained-glass window mellow with afternoon sunlight. Such images were comforting amid the realities of a long, long winter or, God forbid, the threat of an Iroquois attack. Here was the only Ursuline capable of communicating through kindness with a French girl returned from long captivity among the Iroquois, who remained beyond the reach of everyone at the convent school until this young nun befriended her and guided her return to European life. In any event, the tales and reports of miracles were innocent enough.

According to one story, on the very night of her death, Mother Marie de Saint Joseph appeared in a dream to an elderly and ailing lay sister who had taken care of her as a child boarder at Tours and said, "Dear Sister Elizabeth, you have a journey to take." The elderly sister died in full serenity within the month. Marie de l'Incarnation wrote and published a brief biography of the saintly young nun, and the reports of miracles due to her intercession continued.[7]

Another popularly recognized saint, the native-born Recollect lay brother and master carpenter Didace Pelletier, was also characterized by innocence, simplicity, and amiability. Brother Didace's promoter after his death was Father Denys, in whose company Didace had worked for years of missionary labor, including a stint of service in Newfoundland, where Didace assisted Denys in various ways and built chapels and a church. Before dying of pneumonia in 1699 while stationed in Three Rivers, Didace was already associated with miracles as a result of having done the woodwork for the second shrine of Sainte-Anne de Beaupré, a stone structure seven leagues from Quebec. Following his death, Brother Didace became a source of miracles in his own right: twenty-two of them by the mid-eighteenth century, as reported in a dossier prepared for submission to Rome on behalf of opening his cause for canonization. As for Laval, he was too contentious, too insistent regarding his prerogatives—so Marie de l'Incarnation suggested—to enjoy the popular acclaim accorded such peaceful (and less administratively burdened) souls as Brother Didace and Mother Marie de Saint Joseph. Yet time would erase the memory of inevitable difficulties, and both he and Marie de l'Incarnation would one day be canonized.

Choosing a successor

Laval was past sixty in 1684, when he finished setting up his cathedral chapter, and so he embarked on the final task facing him in establishing Quebec as a full-fledged diocese: the choice, appointment, and installation of a successor. Having sailed for Europe in the autumn of that year, Laval secured the nomination of the very able Abbé Jean-Baptiste de la Croix de Chevrières de Saint-Vallier, a thirty-one-year-old priest who shared Laval's background: noble birth, private money, a Jesuit education, a licentiate in theology (from the Seminary of Saint-Sulpice), court connections (he was appointed almoner in ordinary to the king at age twenty-three, thanks to family ties), piety, and service to the sick, the imprisoned, and the rural poor. To all this Saint-Vallier added distinguished service as a combat chaplain tending the wounded and dying while on campaign with the king in Flanders. Like Laval, Saint-Vallier had rejected offers of the more commodious sees of Tours and Marseilles in favor of a missionary career. Appointed to Quebec in 1684, Saint-Vallier spent eighteen months in Canada as Laval's vicar general (Laval himself remained in France) and was said to have visited every parish between Acadia and Montreal to acquaint himself with his future diocese. Upon his return to France in 1687, the Abbé Saint-Vallier wrote and published *État present de l'Église de la colonie de la Nouvelle-France*, a glowing account of the people and clergy of the Diocese of Quebec.

The senior clergy of France, however, had serious doubts about whether this aristocratic, autocratic abbé was the right choice for a frontier diocese. True, Saint-Vallier was good in the field. He proved that during his tour of the diocese. And he was reform minded, but only if he dictated the terms of reform. Furthermore, he lavishly spent money, his own and the diocese's, and left the seminary 10,000 livres in debt. Laval relayed to Saint-Vallier the opinion of his senior clergy that Quebec and he did not constitute a good fit and communicated their request that he withdraw his nomination. Saint-Vallier refused. Matters eventually settled down, and Saint-Vallier was consecrated bishop in the Church of Saint-Sulpice on 25 January 1688.

Freed from office, Laval returned to Quebec and lived nearly another two decades as Monseigneur L'Ancien, supporting his successor Saint-Vallier, even when that successor dismantled his most cherished program for parish clergy. During his successor's absences in Europe, moreover, while Laval stayed away from governance and policy matters, he filled in at liturgies and processions to maintain an episcopal presence. Moving to his beloved seminary, where he came under the care of Jesuit donné Hubert Houssart, Monseigneur L'Ancien pursued on a full-time basis the life of prayer and pastoral service that had been his mode of life at the Hermitage of Caen a half century earlier.

16

New Orleans 1722

A Jesuit savant reconnoiters French North America

On 10 January 1722 Pierre-François-Xavier de Charlevoix, the eminent Jesuit historian and geographer, found himself in the recently established city of New Orleans upstream from where the Mississippi River enters the Gulf of Mexico. A professor of classics and philosophy at the Jesuit Collège Louis-le-Grand in Paris as well as a historical geographer, the forty-year-old Charlevoix was on personal assignment from the regent Philippe, duc d'Orléans (after whom the new city was named), to investigate the perennially rumored existence of a great sea on the western boundary of the North American continent that would provide access to Asia. This was the Pacific, of course, but not until the explorations of Lewis and Clark (1803–1806) would the full western extent of the North American continent and the best route across it to the Pacific (ascend the Missouri River, cross the Continental Divide, and descend the Snake and Columbia Rivers) be known to geographers. As of 1722, there was still the possibility, so the regent (and many others) believed, that New France—having reached south to the Gulf of Mexico—could veer west and achieve a connection via the Pacific to Asia.

Should such a continental ambition be realized, New Orleans—strategically located as a future port on the gulf—might become important to future Asian trade as well. In 1719 Charlevoix had already provided useful services to the government regarding the border of Acadian territories ceded by France to Great Britain in the Treaty of Utrecht (1713), which ended the War of the Spanish Succession. (Yield only the Nova Scotian peninsula, Charlevoix had urged.) A mere year later, the polymathic Jesuit embarked for Canada to explore possible riverine pathways to the rumored ocean to the west. In retrospect, Charlevoix' journey can be considered a semiceremonial recapitulation of a century of French exploratory and missionary effort as well as an on-the-ground research trek preparatory to the report he would make to the regent upon his return and the travel journal and history he would publish.

Westward from Montreal, Charlevoix trekked and canoed across the Great Lakes region, then moved southward down the east side of Lake Michigan to Fort Saint-Joseph on the Saint Joseph River and from there to the Illinois River and the Mississippi. He proceeded down that great river to the mouth of the Missouri, where at Cahokia Mission (East Saint Louis) he rested in the company of two seminary priests he had taught between 1705 and 1709 while teaching as a regent at the Jesuit college in Quebec prior to returning to France to study theology and receive ordination. Continuing down the Mississippi, Charlevoix spent the Christmas season among the Natchez, studying these distinctive and formidable Indians for inclusion

397

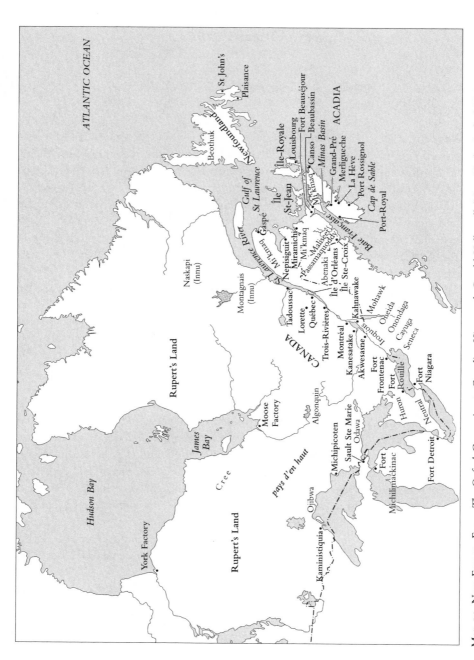

Map 15. New France. From *The Oxford Companion to Canadian History*, ed. Gerald Hallowell (New York: Oxford University Press, 2004), 686. © 2006 Oxford University Press Canada, used by permission.

in his journal, then followed the final stretch of the Mississippi to New Orleans, where he arrived after another two weeks of travel.

In 1720, as part of the speculative euphoria created by Scots investor John Law, then serving as controller general of finances for the French Crown, the Paris newspaper *Le Mercure de France* published a fulsome description of New Orleans as a city of eight hundred well-built homes and five parishes. Not so, Charlevoix points out in letter 31 of his *Journal*, organized as thirty-six letters addressed to the highly placed Duchesse de Lesdiguières and published in 1744 as part of his long-awaited *Histoire et description générale de la Nouvelle France*. The New Orleans he encountered consisted of an assortment of haphazardly placed cabins along with two or three houses that would provide no ornament for an average French village and an unimpressive warehouse, half of it set apart for divine worship until this makeshift chapel could be moved to a separate tent. Still, despite this poverty of outward aspect, Charlevoix continues, it was deeply pleasurable "to see this future capital of an immense and beautiful country increasing insensibly, and to be able, not with a sigh like Virgil's hero, when speaking of his native country consumed by the flames, *et campus ubi Troja fuit* [the field where Troy has been] but full of the best grounded hopes to say, that this wild and desert place, at present almost entirely covered over with canes and trees, shall one day, and perhaps that day is not very far off, become the capital of a large and rich colony."

Why believe this? Why have such faith in the future of this new settlement? In answering these queries, attributed to his interlocutor, the duchesse, Charlevoix launched into a rhapsodic riff approaching booster overdrive—yet sincerely felt for all its exaggeration. Location, location, location was Charlevoix' answer. His hopes for New Orleans, he informed the duchesse, "are founded on the situation of this city on the banks of a navigable river, at the distance of thirty-three leagues from the sea, from which a vessel may come up in twenty-four hours; on the fertility of its soil; on the mildness and wholesomeness of the climate, in thirty degrees north latitude; on the industry of the inhabitants; on its neighbourhood to Mexico, the Havana, the finest islands of America, and lastly, to the English colonies. Can there be any thing more requisite to render a city flourishing? Rome and Paris had not such considerable beginnings, were not built under such happy auspices, and their founders met not with those advantages on the Seine and the Tiber, which we have found on the Mississippi, in comparison of which, these two rivers are no more than brooks."[1]

Amid this Virgilian evocation of the assured destiny of New Orleans as port city— expectations more than fulfilled by the city's long reign as the second-busiest port in North America—Charlevoix was also forced to chronicle what Virgil describes in the *Aeneid* as "Tantae molis erat Romanam condere gentem" (of such a burden was it to found the Roman people). Rome, Charlevoix realized, was not built in a day. Nor was French Canada. Nor would be this new Carthage on the Gulf.

Quebec enters the eighteenth century

The offspring of a family of minor nobility that had provided the town of Saint-Quentin in the Aisne department of Picardy in northern France with generations of legal officers, aldermen, and mayors, Pierre-François-Xavier de Charlevoix entered the Jesuits in 1698 before turning sixteen, having begun his education at the Collège des Bons-Enfants in his native Saint-Quentin. Following a two-year novitiate and a year of rhetoric, he was posted for four years as a student of philosophy and dormitory prefect to the Collège Louis-le-Grand in Paris, where one of his charges was a precocious youngster by the name of François-Marie Arouet Voltaire, who later remembered Charlevoix as talkative but likable. In retrospect, the connection, however slight, possesses a prophetic resonance. While moving far beyond traditional Catholicism, Voltaire maintained good relations with his boyhood teachers, to the point of having a live-in Jesuit as part of his household entourage during his long exile in Switzerland, a learned and companionable cleric who was available for card games and philosophical conversation in the evening. Charlevoix, for his part, was a Jesuit in whom the spirit of the Enlightenment flourished. Sincerely religious, a lifelong Jesuit professed and observant in the four vows that brought him into the upper strata of the Society of Jesus, he displayed no signs of seeking martyrdom in a foreign land. He was, rather, a man of reason, scientific observation, reflection, and writing: an even-tempered polymathic scholar dependent on information and research, a respected counselor who relished his connections to the well-placed and renowned, a man of lively social life and good conversation, a tireless and meticulous professor at an elite college, an editor of a prestigious journal, a historian of the Society, and a councilor to the Crown. Charlevoix, in short, was a Jesuit destined to die at an advanced age in his bed, recognized and respected for his achievements.

Charlevoix was twenty-three and an ordained deacon when he sailed for New France following the completion of his philosophy course in order to spend the next four years as a regent (a teaching seminarian) assigned to the Jesuit college in Quebec, where he arrived on 7 September 1705. Also living at the Jesuit college that year was Monseigneur L'Ancien, the retired Bishop Laval, temporarily displaced from his room at the seminary by a serious fire. Seminary students took their courses at the Jesuit college, which made Charlevoix a contributor to the grand goal of Laval's career, the creation of a diocesan clergy, and given Charlevoix' innate friendliness, he might have occasionally conversed with the aged bishop, now in the final years of his life. Since his retirement in 1688, Laval had been living quietly at the seminary. Devoted to seminary students, whom he counseled, Monseigneur L'Ancien also functioned as a simple parish priest, usually being the first to open the parish church of Notre-Dame-de-Québec early each day, even in the midst of winter. While his strength lasted, Laval rose every morning to say Mass for the parish, hear confessions, take his meals at the common table of the seminary, read much, and pray even more. Charlevoix was on hand for Monseigneur L'Ancien's funeral when, having contracted a chilblain in his heel on an especially cold morning during Holy Week 1708, he grew ill, continued to weaken, and then died at half past seven on the morning of 6 May 1708. Crowds filed past his body as it lay in state in the cathedral parish church, touching their rosaries and prayer books to his remains, cutting off snippets of his vestments to keep as relics.

A troubled succession

The administration of Laval's successor Saint-Vallier did not begin auspiciously when the young prelate, consecrated bishop at Saint-Sulpice on 25 January 1688, arrived in Quebec on 31 July of that year. Nor did Saint-Vallier's tenure, which ended with his death in 1717—a tenure marked by long absences in Europe—improve much over time. After all, three of the leading clergy of the diocese—the Abbés Bernières, Ango Des Maizerets, and Charles de Glandelet—had openly requested that Saint-Vallier not be appointed. These three clergy, moreover, constituted the operating core of the seminary as Laval had organized it along the lines of the seminary of the Paris Foreign Missions Society, that is, an organization of secular priests. Almost immediately, Saint-Vallier ordered that this arrangement end. The seminary, he decreed, was a seminary, nothing more.

The three abbés refused to implement this decree. Not content with mere resistance, moreover, they charged that Saint-Vallier's vicar general, the Abbé André-Louis de Merlac, whom Saint-Vallier had brought with him from France, was a Jansenist: a follower of the rigorist theories of faith, grace, morals, and salvation advanced by theologian Cornelius Otto Jansen in his treatise *Augustinus* (1640) on the theology of Saint Augustine. The Sorbonne in 1649 and Innocent X in 1653 had condemned this book as heretical, yet it remained a strong force among a sector of upper-class, religious-right French Catholics, most notably the mathematician and philosopher Blaise Pascal. Saint-Vallier returned to France in the spring of 1691 and successfully pleaded his case to the king. Returning to Quebec, he ended the seminary system and implemented a conventional arrangement of fixed parishes and permanent pastors.

During the next two years, 1693–1694, Saint-Vallier managed to quarrel with his cathedral chapter, the seminary, the Jesuits, the Recollects, the Hospitaller Sisters of the Hôtel-Dieu of Quebec, and the nuns of the Congrégation de Notre-Dame in Montreal. When Governor-General Frontenac wished to sponsor a production of Molière's *Tartuffe* (1644), a comedy satirizing religious hypocrisy, Saint-Vallier considered the production a personal insult and convinced the sovereign council to cancel the production as an occasion of mortal sin.

Frontenac was not amused. Nor were the bishop's other adversaries, and by December 1694 Saint-Vallier was back in France dealing with a request from the king that he resign his diocese. Throughout the next three years, the embattled prelate successfully defended his position. Had he not founded a new general hospital for the poor of Quebec, he argued, financing much of it with his own money? Had he not installed the Jesuits and Recollects in Montreal, where he also sponsored the creation of a community of Hospitaller Brothers? He had visited Newfoundland and Acadia, and stood solidly behind Governor Frontenac in 1690 when an English fleet under Sir William Phips was threatening Quebec. As usual, the king appointed a committee to look into the matter, but its eminent members—among them the bishops François Fénelon and Jacques Bossuet; François de La Chaise, the Jesuit confessor to Louis XIV; and the king's morganatic wife, the pious and brilliant marquise de Maintenon—could or would not come to a decision against Saint-Vallier. When Saint-Vallier defended himself one last time before the king, promising to moderate his zeal and be prudent in his future dealings, Louis XIV relented, and Saint-Vallier returned to his diocese in the summer of 1697. Once there, he reconciled with the abbés of the seminary, fostered the establishment of a new Ursuline ministry in Three Rivers, and (temporarily) kept a low profile in the impressive episcopal palace designer-builder

Claude Baillif had been constructing for the Diocese of Quebec during Saint-Vallier's absence in France.

Built of cut stone, the seventy-two-foot-long building with its attached sixty-foot-long chapel was as fine as any episcopal residence in France and set new standards for design and construction in all of North America. Saint-Vallier intended it that way. Personally, he was not given to luxurious living; indeed, in the course of earlier quarrels, he had upbraided his cathedral canons for being overly concerned with bourgeois comforts, as this upper-class semi-ascetic prelate snobbishly phrased it. Yet when it came to the bishop's palace, Saint-Vallier wanted this grand two-story edifice and its adjacent gardens—set on the heights of Quebec City overlooking the Saint Lawrence—to assert in no uncertain terms not simply the Catholicity of New France but the diocesan structure and the episcopal governance of that Catholicity, made manifest for all to see. The ambitious building remained in use for the next 186 years as a church and (after 1830) a government complex.

Daughters of the king

The mixed church-state usage of this building was appropriate. Louis XIV and his ministers Colbert and Jean Talon had done as much as any clergy to ensure the Catholicity of Quebec by making certain that a Catholic population would be in place. With sly Yankee Unitarian humor, historian Francis Parkman notes the difficulties of peopling New France in the seventeenth century, given what seems to him an overwhelming number of celibate clergy, nuns, and dévots in the colony. Parkman also might have mentioned the scarcity of French women of child-bearing age in the first half of that century when one went to Canada to fish for cod and trade for furs, then returned to France for domesticity. In contrast to the majority of English colonies to the south, Quebec only slowly began to attract families and, even more slowly, single women looking to marry and to make a home in the colony. Thus is conferred true founders' status on Champlain's good friend, Paris apothecary Louis Hébert and his wife, Marie Rollet, who emigrated to Quebec in 1617 with their three children and Marie's brother, built a home, and started to cultivate seven acres on the heights of the future city. Hébert suffered a fatal fall from scaffolding in 1627 but not before seeing two of his daughters, homeschooled by their mother, marry and start families of their own. After England returned Quebec to France ship's surgeon turned fur trader Robert Giffard organized a colonizing effort that in 1634 brought to Canada forty-three colonists, including six families with children, the first of some fifty families Giffard (now Seigneur Giffard) would bring between 1634 and 1663 to properties he controlled in Canada. On 11 June 1636 a composite clan of minor (and impoverished) Norman nobility, the Le Gardeur and Le Neuf families—forty-five people in all—arrived in Quebec under the sponsorship of prominent trader and public servant Jean-Paul Godefroy. Quebec could now develop its own resident nobility for military careers and public service and marriages within a rising elite. Eleven of the fifteen children of Charles Le Gardeur de Tilly, for example, either became officers or married into the officer corps and saw naval or army service in Canada, the Caribbean, French Africa, or Europe.

The Society of Our Lady of Montreal did what it could to recruit artisans' families to Ville-Marie. The first census of Montreal, completed in 1666, reveals 760 residents, including an impressive number of artisan families. Tailor Nicolas Hubert, for example, age 55, is listed as living with his wife, 40; four sons, 12, 9, 3, and 1; a daughter, 7; and one household servant, 17, recently recruited from France. The Urbain Tessier household lists Tessier himself, 42; his wife, Marie, 30; sons, 15, 11, 4, 3, and 7 weeks; daughters, 9 and 7; and two servant recruits, 18 and 25. Crafts cited in the census include carpenter, joiner, mason, locksmith, tailor, baker, shoemaker, hatter, and butcher. Also listed are a large number of younger single men who have indicated a desire to become habitants of the country. The roll call of female offspring in Ville-Marie and environs, however, shows the majority of them to be children, which meant they were a decade or more from marriageable age, even given the young ages at which women married during this era.

For young men to become stable and productive householders, an influx of young women from France was required. First Minister Colbert understood this, despite his fear of depopulating France. Sent to Canada in 1665 as part of the reorganization of the Quebec colony, Jean Talon responded to the challenge more enthusiastically. As an intendant (an office created by Richelieu), Talon functioned as the senior civil servant and public administrator in Quebec, exercising authority in such matters as police, justice, finance, civil administration, economic and social development, and supply. A graduate of the Jesuit Collège de Clermont, Talon had entered public administration as a logistics manager for the army, risen to the intendancy of the province of Hainault, and won the respect of Mazarin. Colbert sent him to Canada as part of a new scheme in which the governor-general would exercise military and diplomatic authority, the intendant would serve as inspector general and chief administrator in civil affairs, and the sovereign council—consisting of the governor, the bishop, and five councilors from the regions—would function as legislature and high court.

In the course of his two terms as intendant, 1665–1668 and 1670–1672, Talon addressed numerous challenges, with varying degrees of success, in an effort to bring the Quebec colony to a new level of administration and development. He promoted agriculture, livestock development, shipbuilding, the lumber industry, and the growth of hemp, and in addition he built the first brewery in Quebec as a way to encourage the planting and harvesting of wheat. Through it all, he remained amiable and won the admiration of Colbert and the king, who personally persuaded him to accept a second term.

Talon surveyed the human prospect with equal attention. New France's population was undeveloped and woefully lacked marriageable females. As a consequence, bachelors were dissatisfied and falling into bad habits, with too many of them fleeing into the forest and taking up an Indian way of life as coureurs de bois. When the Carignan-Salières regiment finished its tour of duty against the Iroquois in 1667, the shortage problem was compounded, for many soldiers and officers of the regiment expressed a desire to remain on as settlers, provided they could find suitable wives without needing to make a round trip to France and back.

Talon responded to this challenge with three programs. First, over the next seven years he imported as many as one thousand marriageable young women to Quebec: *filles du roi* (daughters of the king), they were called. Second, he rewarded those who married with land grants and financial subsidies and paid bonuses for large families as well. Third, he fined or otherwise penalized young men who refused to marry or parents with single children remaining at home into their twenties. Historians have been critical of Talon for these penalties, which they see as violations of civil liberties. Many also have objected to what they consider the enforced immigration of these young women and the requirement that they marry virtual strangers. A smaller number of observers—much smaller, fortunately—have questioned the respectability of the young women who arrived.

This canard began with Louis-Armand de Lom d'Arce de Lahontan, whose *Nouveaux voyages dans l'Amérique septentrionale* and its sequel, *Mémoires de septentrionale* (published together at The Hague in January 1703), along with a third volume titled *Supplément aux voyages* that appeared shortly thereafter, were the most read accounts of New France to appear in the eighteenth century. Lahontan spent ten years in Canada, from the age of seventeen to twenty-seven, and never returned. An army officer by profession, he observed and wrote in a lively manner and frequently adopted a persona of witty detachment from what he was reporting, with the notable exception of the frontier combat he experienced, when he dropped his ironic posing. A lifelong bachelor, Lahontan had no interest in marriage or family life. At a time when he was very broke, which was most of the time, he turned down an advantageous marriage Frontenac arranged for him with the governor's eighteen-year-old goddaughter. Nor was Lahontan a believing Christian, much less a supporter of Catholic family life. His one-page spoof of the arrival of the filles du roi in Quebec, with its suggestions of a flesh market—written when he knew that he would never return to Canada—has had a lingering effect to this day.

While it was true that the Crown did have some Paris prostitutes deported to French-held islands in the Caribbean, the recruitment of the filles du roi was rigidly controlled by Church and Crown. Two types of young women—village girls and second or third daughters of farmers; and (a much smaller number) orphans and foundlings in the care of the Church—dominated the ranks of the filles du roi. Middle-class young women and widows who expected to marry within their class when they arrived in Canada had for some time enjoyed access to other sources of support for emigration, including family connections, and hence were nearly nonexistent in the program. Thus the filles du roi for the most part were farm or village girls, the majority of them from the Ile-de-France and the province of Normandy, with the provinces of Aunis, Champagne, Poitou, Anjou, Beauce, Maine, and Orléanais also represented. Stipulations included that the young women be reasonably attractive and capable of bearing children as well as performing farmwork and enduring the hardships of frontier life. A good reputation was crucial; the women had to be recommended by the curés of their parishes or, in the cases of the orphans and foundlings, the nuns conducting such institutions.

Filles du roi also had to be brave. These young women showed their willingness to take a chance on a dangerous trans-Atlantic crossing to meet and marry a young man (likewise vetted by church and state) and start life on a farm of their own, with land and money coming directly from the king via his intendant Monsieur Talon or his representative. What were their prospects in France, after all? With no dowry, no inheritance, no marriage, they would have toiled away a lifetime as the Cinderella servants of older sisters or brothers or elderly parents. Staying in France meant never to have their own trousseau, their own furniture and pots and pans, their own home and new name; never to hold a child of their own in their arms or, if such a child were to be born to them while unmarried, to have entered next to the child's name "father unknown" in the baptismal registry.

In Quebec, lay sisters of the Ursuline convent would meet and greet the daughters of the king as they departed their vessel and escort them to the convent on the heights of the city, where they would be taken care of by the sisters and through appropriate venues introduced under supervision to young men who had expressed interest. Marriage followed four stages: mutual selection, official registration, published banns, and the marriage ceremony itself. The state paid all the bills. Since selection was mutual, a young woman did not have to marry a particular young man or lose her status as a daughter of the king. Even after the engagement was officially registered and the banns of marriage were announced, a young woman could withdraw from the contract, and a number of them did, choosing a different husband at another time. Even remaining single was an option, although not a preferred one, provided that the daughter of the king be taken into an established family.

Over the millennia, most of the human race has handled marriage and pro-creation in a similar manner, and it is not for moderns to preclude the possibilities of contentment or downright happiness in such arrangements (at a time when arranged marriages remained the norm in all classes). Suffice it to say that families were formed, farms established, grants of money and livestock made, children born. Parishes were canonically founded, priests assigned, and parish churches built. In reasonably short order—by the mid-eighteenth century—a North American French Catholic people had come into existence alongside the First Peoples, métis, and Acadians of Canada.

Domestic life

These new people lived in stone and wood houses—Norman in inspiration around Quebec, Breton around Montreal—adapted over time to furnish protection against six months of brutal winter (the most ferocious winter on the planet, some climatologists claim) through an integration of stone, wood, plastering, and roughcast made from a clay base. Cellars were sunk into the earth four feet or more, their floors fortified against the cold by mixing earth with straw and pounding it solid. Homes averaged from fifty to sixty feet in length and twenty to thirty feet in width and featured thick walls, narrow windows, and slanted roofs. The closer the home to Montreal and Iroquois country, the more fortresslike the domicile.

The home's entrance opened into a large central room dominated by a hearth and chimneypiece from which hung pots and pans and other cooking utensils, and nearby stood a table and rush-covered chairs or benches. Against one wall in this same room—to conserve heat—a curtained bed featured a featherbed mattress, pillows, woolen blankets, and sheets. Also in evidence were two other work areas: a spinning wheel and loom in one corner for the mistress of the house, and a tool table and workbench for her husband in another area, which held as well a rack for thawing out tools used on winter days. Other rooms included a sleeping alcove for older children, storerooms for provisions, and a latrine cabinet for the worst of winter days, kept from becoming offensive through near-instant freezing. Thus for half the year a Canadian family worked, cooked, ate, and socialized in a communal space, and at night parents slept snugly in their curtained bed within hearing distance of their sleeping infants and children. Family life was close, especially in winter, and observers have speculated that the repair tasks, communal prayers, and storytelling on long winter evenings played a strong role in shaping the composite character of the French Canadian people in terms of their self-sufficiency, love of song and story, and capacity for independent thought.

Breakfast was light, comprising only bread (dipped in brandy for those going outside to work) or porridge. The main meal, though, taken at noon, featured a notable array of venison, birds, and local fish (as well as bacon, frozen through the winter and considered a luxury) in addition to seasonal green vegetables (including asparagus, plus an abundance of cabbage in wintertime) and dishes composed of locally grown corn (roasted, mashed, or made into cakes or sagamité in the Indian style), barley, peas, lentils, and beans. Dessert consisted of fruit (in winter, preserved through crystallization in molasses); strawberry, raspberry, or blackberry jam on bread or served with cheese; or a glass of sugared milk. Supper was a reprise of leftover dishes from the noonday meal. Recipes were basic; but in time—with the importation and availability of pepper, cloves, nutmeg, cinnamon, vinegar, salt, brown sugar, and molasses—they grew more sophisticated. By the eighteenth century, rum and other imported liquors joined the abundance of wine imported since the establishment of New France and the locally produced beer available since the mid-seventeenth century. As roads began to link cities and townships, a tavern culture developed. An evergreen branch prominently displayed outside a tavern entrance during winter meant that specially prepared warming drinks were offered.

Habitants who farmed worked long, hard hours, but they did so in the knowledge that they were to a significant degree working for themselves. In Canada, the seigneurial system was more of a squirearchy of the recently arrived rather than a nobility of ancient, fixed privilege and financial entitlement. A habitant owned his farm on one or another seigneurial jurisdiction and paid the local sieur a minimal fee or presentation in kind—in effect, a sort of property tax. His seigneur, moreover, was most likely a farmer as well; it was not uncommon for the more recently ennobled sieurs and their spouses to labor side by side with their habitants in the fields.

The size of habitant families has been exaggerated, the norm being six as opposed to ten or twelve, although families of ten to a dozen children were not unknown and received cash awards during the Talon intendancy. Despite typecasting, a daughter of the king or her daughters when they were grown and married were not considered breeding machines. The fille du roi's rate of reproduction barely exceeded that of her counterpart in rural France. But more of her children survived, and they grew stronger and taller. She worked hard, true, but so did her husband, with sunrise to sunset the sanctioned workday of them both. She and her husband lived longer and in better health, furthermore, once the Iroquois wars abated, and by the very nature of their shared frontier life enjoyed a noticeable degree of partnership. Various historians who dismiss claims of women leading happy lives during this era have focused on derogatory statements or instances of abuse; yet unless such negative examples are proven to be of statistical significance, they cannot be referred to as proofs. Statistically, very few—next to none, in fact—daughters of the king requested a return to France, as was their right.

Transformations

Thus men and women built French Canada together, and in turn French Canada over time transformed them into a new people. Although they remained French in their bloodlines (just as the English colonists to the south remained English), the sheer scale of French Canada and the environmental and lifestyle challenges it presented involved changes. They grew taller and lived longer, for one thing, and became more independent in their outlook on life. As already suggested, the exact standing, psychological and sociological, of colonial women in the seventeenth-century Americas remains a topic for ongoing research. In the cases of the self-documenting Marie de l'Incarnation or such highly documented figures as Jean Mance or Marguerite Bourgeoys, detailed records survive. How Canada affected the relatively undocumented filles du roi is more difficult to ascertain. Because the majority of them spoke the mainstream French of Paris or Normandy, French survived in Canada as a written and spoken language, thus keeping French Canada an integrated part of French culture. Genealogists document filles du roi and their descendants with exactitude and near reverence as mothers of the race, founders of the commonwealth, tracing their descendants down to recent times. To descend from a fille du roi remains a mark of distinction.

Historians of Roman Catholicism in North America owe the daughters of the king and the men they married proper acknowledgment, for the families they created were gathered into parishes that could not exist without them, and these parishes constituted the Church in French Canada in terms of earthly organization and spiritual realities. Furthermore, the model of diocesan organization put into operation in seventeenth-century Canada—as complete in its array of institutions and services as those of any smaller rural diocese in France—provided the Catholic citizens of the new American republic to the south, when it came into being, a model for their own ecclesiastical organization and culture, along with many of its most notable clergy.

French Canada came of age in an era of intense Christocentric theology and devotionalism, which, like the good French of Paris and Normandy, established a continuity of orthodox religious practice. True, the diocesan clergy of late seventeenth-century Canada, including Laval and Saint-Vallier, now and then revealed a rigorist streak, which drove penitents to more-lenient Recollect confessions. Yet the more extreme rigorism of theologically sophisticated Jansenism never took hold among the lay faithful, who relished life when they found it enjoyable and endured it when they found it painful, who were sorry for their sins, and who otherwise trusted in the promise of redemption. Even the Hospitaller Sisters of Quebec, encountering the crypto-Jansenism of their chaplain and religious superior André-Louis de Merlac, whom Saint-Vallier had brought with him from France in 1688, rejected the young abbé as their chaplain and documented for Saint-Vallier some of Merlac's suspicious teachings. The sisters forced the reluctant bishop to remove Merlac from office, and the abbé returned to France.

The devil in New France

One of the continuing certainties of seventeenth-century French Catholicism was the existence of devils and the participation of these fallen angels in tempting and tormenting the righteous. A sense of the devil as an actor in human affairs gained renewed intensity in the Middle Ages and survived into the early modern era. Spanish missionaries brought this demonology to the New World and equated an active diabolism with indigenous religions. Ignatius of Loyola placed a tempting Satan—the Prince of Darkness, the great fallen angel Lucifer (Light Bearer)—at the center of the struggle between good and evil in the world and the need for the individual Christian to align himself with the correct side of that contest. Spanish Jesuits, historian Peter Goddard argues, adhered to this formulation into and throughout the seventeenth century (as did Spanish clergy in general, he might have added). French Jesuits, however, Goddard states, began to detach themselves psychologically from this belief in the early seventeenth century, given their patron Henri IV's distaste for claims of diabolical possession. By the mid-seventeenth century, moreover, an increasingly influential Cartesianism—which postulated an epistemological distinction between the perceptions of spiritual and empirical phenomena—was swaying the intelligentsia of France, Jesuits included. Thus, while diabolism was never denied as a factor in spiritual affairs, it was by mid-century rarely postulated as an exclusive factor, even in something as horrendous as the Iroquois destruction of Catholic Huronia.

That being noted, however, the devil remained a frequent explanation in matters of sexual stress among clergy or avowed religious. In 1633 in the city of Loudun, as an example, in what developed into a classic case of its kind, mass hysteria of a sexual nature broke out among the nuns of the local Ursuline convent involving claims by the convent superior, Mother Joan of the Angels, of diabolical possession. The outbreak resulted in the trial, condemnation, and burning at the stake of the convent chaplain, Urbain Grandier, on charges of being in league with devils, who assisted him in his efforts to seduce the sisters. Twentieth- and twenty-first-century explanations of the Loudun incident, as well as presentations of the event in fiction, opera, and film, are justifiably Freudian. A handsome, magnetic priest with a prior conviction (which was mysteriously voided) for sexual misbehavior seduces Joan of the Angels and her community into mass hysteria. Even the Jesuits of the era suspected other than demonic causes at work; they blamed political intrigue. Grandier was suspected of writing an anonymous pamphlet against Richelieu, and to make matters worse, the cardinal had a relative in this particular convent. When one of their fellow Jesuits, Jean-Joseph Surin, charged with exorcising Joan of the Angels and her sisters, claimed that the exorcised demon had now gained possession of him, Surin's fellow Jesuits considered it a case not of demonic possession but of mental derangement.

One of the earliest candidates for popular, possibly even canonical, canonization in seventeenth-century Quebec was Mother Catherine de Saint-Augustin of the Hôtel-Dieu, who died in 1668 at the age of thirty-six. According to the posthumous testimony of her private journal, Mother Catherine endured a lifelong conflict with demons tempting her against faith and her calling as a Hospitaller Sister. In 1671 the veteran Jesuit missionary Paul Ragueneau published a biography of

Mother Catherine based on this journal that in effect allows the late nun to tell her own story. A precocious, well-born little girl of three, so the biography informs us, advised by her Jesuit spiritual director, resolves to find God through suffering and humiliation. An ear infection leading to bone decay gives her an opportunity for this when physicians treat her case—before it is miraculously cured—by pouring red-hot ashes into the infected ear. At age ten, this child pledges herself to a life of service and purity of heart. Shortly thereafter, however, she evolves into a spirited preteen aware of her growing femininity and attractiveness. She reads romantic novels, sings love songs, and adores being popular. At the age of twelve and a half, she experiences a reconversion, however tentative, and considers joining her sister at the convent of Hospitaller Sisters at Bayeux. Still, she remains in love with the world and her place in it, and when she finally applies to the Hospitaller Sisters, she insists that she is not entering as a regular novice but merely as someone who is testing the religious life.

Mother Catherine remained in the convent at Bayeux and took vows before she was sixteen. Moreover, she volunteered for Canada and arrived in Quebec in 1648, when the Iroquois depredations were putting New France's sustainability into question. At the Hôtel-Dieu she prospered and rose in rank as time passed— senior Hospitaller in 1663, mistress of novices in 1665—but in the meantime she endured a secret burden: attacks by demons that left her depressed and in a state of psychological dissociation from herself, on the edge of despair, tempted to be damned forthwith. "My Saviour and My All!" she prays. "If the demons' sojourn in my body is pleasing in your sight, I am willing that they should stay there as long as you wish; provided that sin does not creep in with them, I fear nothing, and I hope that you will grant me grace to love you for all eternity, even though I were in the depths of hell."[2]

At this point, the biography gets truly interesting. In answer to her prayers, Mother Catherine relates, God sends her apparitions of the late Jesuit martyr Jean de Brébeuf, another native of Bayeux, who counsels and consoles her in the last years of her life. She had never met Brébeuf before his death in 1649, but there he is, guiding and comforting her in her affliction like a loving father, which is how she addresses him. From Brébeuf she comes to understand that the pain resulting from her conflict with demons is on behalf of her country. She is suffering to atone for the sins of Canada!

Clinical observation would first take into consideration that Mother Catherine was suffering from a progressively worsening case of tuberculosis and that since childhood she showed signs of a latent schizophrenia, or at the least a clearly defined opposition of personality types: by turns ascetic and worldly, virginal and sexually restless. While relevant from a contemporary perspective, clinical psychology cannot uncover the full texture of the experience of a believing seventeenth-century French nursing sister struggling to maintain her equilibrium in the face of declining health and psychological horrors that were as real to her as Quebec itself and struggling as well to render these sufferings of use by offering them up in expiation for the sins of Canada.

Or is the exact nature of these sins not the main point? Was the main point that a Hospitaller Sister experiencing private torment played out her role in life as best she could—and saw in that role her gift to Canada, to which she had chosen as a young novice to dedicate her life? Like the Jesuit Brébeuf, who mysteriously guided and comforted her, she loved and revered her Catholic faith and loved the North American place in which she continued to serve with good humor and efficiency as long as she could, despite the demons besetting her. Her suffering was not wasted. She was a patriot and a founder of Canada, claims her contemporary biographer, Ursuline historian Marie-Emmanuel Chabot. "Lively and wide awake," Chabot writes, "this delightful young Norman girl hurled herself into paradise at a heroic pace. She must be depicted above all as a missionary on foreign soil, as a nurse, as an enterprising woman who died with a Te Deum on her lips. In that way she will emerge gloriously from the shadows, reassuring both theologians and psychiatrists."[3]

A tale of one city

Following his arrival at Quebec on 23 September 1720, Charlevoix spent a busy fall and winter with the Jesuit community, writing his final report on the Acadian border dispute between France and England, refamiliarizing himself with Quebec, taking notes regarding the city and its history, and, as usual, enjoying the pleasures of research and social life. Rising from the Saint Lawrence River to the summit of its rocky acropolis, the Quebec that Charlevoix encountered—at once a sacred place and a 7,000-strong outpost of empire—took 110 years of French effort to achieve. From a distance, it possessed an almost magical quality, like Toledo as seen by El Greco or the Church of Mont Saint-Michel rising from its tidal site. Charlevoix reads Quebec as a historical text, a record of institutions struggled for and achieved. Yet present and future Canada is also on his mind. While the city of 1720–1722 is the prism through which he recaptures the past, Quebec is also a symbol of a larger possibility: a continent-wide, continent-deep French Catholic North America.

Charlevoix begins his description with an evocation of the Saint Lawrence, the great navigable river running downward to the sea through an equally great valley, fed by other rivers en route, the same way the Mississippi runs down its valley, fed by other rivers, until it flows into the gulf. He approaches the city by water, conjuring the First Peoples of the region by reviewing the Algonquian names for the city—Quebio, Quebec, or Quelibec—which mean the narrowing of a great strait. With its founder Champlain in mind, he disembarks in Lower Town and, entering a square from the quay, encounters the recent past in Notre-Dame des Victoires. Formerly the Church of L'Enfant Jesu, it was renamed Notre-Dame de la Victoire to commemorate the defeat in 1690 of an invading naval and land force from Massachusetts under the command of the Maine-born, self-made colonial Sir William Phips; the church's name was later pluralized to commemorate another English defeat when, in 1711, in the course of the War of the Spanish Succession, a massive invasion force under the command of Sir Hovenden Walker—seventy ships, including fifteen men-of-war, and twelve thousand troops—intent on seizing French Canada, became enveloped in fog off the Bay of Seven Islands in the Gulf of Saint Lawrence and (thanks to bad piloting) was driven upon the rocks by a fierce storm, resulting in the loss of multiple ships and fifteen hundred men.

Ascending into Upper Town via a steep pathway into which steps had been cut, Charlevoix encounters the ecclesiastical history of the city through its surviving buildings: the cathedral, the church of the Recollects, the bishop's palace, the seminary, the Ursuline convent and school, the Jesuit college where he had taught as a seminarian, the Hôtel-Dieu, and the Hôpital-Général. The cathedral disappointed him. It seemed hardly equal, he writes, to a parish church in a small town in France, although it served a diocese as large as ancient Rome. Ironically, given Laval's opposition to the Recollects' establishing themselves in Quebec, Charlevoix has high praise for the church of the Recollects. It was, in fact, worthy of Versailles! The adjacent seminary was also impressive.

Bishop Saint-Vallier was still alive, but he did not live in the grand palace he had constructed for himself. That building was being used as a home for single male artisans and elderly men in need of shelter. Saint-Vallier resided in a single austere room at the Hôpital-Général, which he had financed with his own funds, where he served as chaplain in addition to governing his far-flung diocese. Time and suffering, including five years under detention in England when his ship was captured in 1704 during the War of the Spanish Succession, had transformed the aristocratic and slender young bishop of 1688 into a sixty-eight-year-old prelate, haggard and flabby jowled, who looked even older than his years. Once resented for his imperiousness, Saint-Vallier was now respected as a wise, holy, and efficient prelate in the quiet and service-oriented manner of his predecessor.

Augustinian Hospitaller Sisters of the Mercy of Jesus conducted the Hôpital-Général and the Hôtel-Dieu alike, although the Hôpital-Général sisters wore a silver cross on their gray habit and were canonically incorporated as a separate community as a result of a division among the sisters in 1692 about whether to staff Saint-Vallier's new establishment. Marie Forestier (Mère Marie de Saint Bonaventure de Jésus), the last survivor of the original three Hospitaller Sisters of Dieppe who arrived in Quebec in 1639, had died in 1698, leaving behind notebooks that chronicled the early years of the Hôtel-Dieu. These notebooks came into the possession of Jeanne-Françoise Juchereau de la Ferté (Mère Jeanne-Françoise de Saint Ignace), the third Hôtel-Dieu sister to bear the name de Saint Ignace following the death in 1646 of Marie Guenet, one of the original three, and the death in 1657 of Marie-Françoise Giffard, the first native-born Canadian to enter the order. Giffard was also the aunt of the Quebec-born Jeanne-Françoise Juchereau. On her deathbed, Giffard told her six-and-a-half-year-old niece that she would one day replace her aunt at the Hôtel-Dieu. Overcoming the strong opposition of her mother, Juchereau took the white veil of a novice as the third de Saint Ignace in succession.

She was a notable one at that, for Juchereau embodied the transition under way for Canadian-born members of the women's religious orders in New France. When she was only twenty-three, Bishop Laval named her trustee for alms for the poor. At thirty, she became mistress of novices, followed by election to superior at age thirty-three; she served twenty-four years in that office during the influenza epidemics of 1688, 1703, and 1711. As mother superior, Juchereau opposed Saint-Vallier on the Hôpital-Général project, but when the matter was finally decided in his favor, she helped the two communities reconcile. Bedridden from 1713 until her death in 1723, Juchereau refashioned the notebooks of Mère Marie de Saint Bonaventure de Jésus into a sustained narrative, dictating her contributions to her collaborator, Marie-Andrée Regnard Duplessis (Mère Marie-Andrée de Sainte Hélène), a Paris-born Quebec-raised beauty, the last European-born Hospitaller Sister to serve in Quebec. Mother Duplessis had put off entering the monastery until the age of twenty (which was regarded as mature during this era), after considering a number of marriage offers, and would lead the Hôtel-Dieu for three terms as superior, interspersed by three terms as assistant superior before her death in 1760.

Although Mothers Juchereau and Duplessis' *Les annals de l'Hôtel-Dieu de Quebec, 1636–1716* was not published until 1752, the impulse behind the writing of this history paralleled Charlevoix' response to Quebec. After eighty years of institutional development, the Catholic culture of Quebec—and, by extension, that of the Saint Lawrence valley as far west as Montreal—had come of age. More remained to be done, but as of the dawn of the eighteenth century there was a rich past to document, as the cleric Cotton Mather of Boston had accomplished in his *Magnalia Christi Americana* (1702), which chronicled the translation of a Christian society to North America. From this perspective, *Les annals de l'Hôtel-Dieu de Quebec, 1636–1716* constituted a down payment on a historiography that Charlevoix would himself in good time advance to a new level.

Lest Charlevoix' inventory of Quebec seem preoccupied with religion, it must be noted how agreeable he found the colonial city's social life. First of all, Charlevoix opines, Quebec had the tone of a capital. A governor general, an intendant, military officers, and other government officials and their wives were in residence, along with an ecclesiastical establishment of a bishop, upper clergy, Jesuits, and Recollects. The city possessed a certain esprit, a zest for life, among all classes. Each resident realized his obligation to make the most of things. "They accordingly do," he notes of the circles in which he socialized that winter, "every one contributing all in his power to make life agreeable and cheerful. They play at cards, or go abroad on parties of pleasure in the summer-time in clashes or canoes, in winter, in sledges upon the snow, or on skates upon the ice. Hunting is a great exercise amongst them, and there are a number of gentlemen who have no other way of providing handsomely for their subsistence. The current news consist of a very few articles, and those of Europe arrive all at once, though they supply matter of discourse for great part of the year. They reason like politicians on what is past, and form conjectures on what is likely to happen; the science and fine arts have also their part, so that the conversation never flags for want of matter."

Not only did residents of Quebec have much to talk about, Charlevoix continues, but also they spoke freely and well. "The Canadians," he notes, "that is to say, the Creoles of Canada, draw in with their native breath an air of freedom, which renders them very agreeable in the commerce of life, and nowhere in the world is our language spoken in greater purity. There is not the smallest foreign accent remarked in their pronunciation."

In addition, Charlevoix observes, citizens of Quebec were a well-bred, well-dressed, fine-looking people "of advantageous stature, and both sexes have the finest complexion in the world. A gay and sprightly behavior, with great sweetness of manners are common to all of them; and the least rusticity, either in language or behavior, is utterly unknown even in the remotest and most distant parts."[4]

A second city

The citizens of Three Rivers were included in these generic compliments. Leaving Quebec by horse-drawn sled in early March 1721, Charlevoix spent a few days at

Three Rivers en route to Montreal. A trading post founded in 1635 near the site where the Saint Maurice River discharged into the Saint Lawrence through three separate mouths, Three Rivers did not enjoy the vibrant social life of Quebec City. The fort had grown into a no-nonsense commercial settlement of between seven hundred and eight hundred residents oriented toward the fur trade. In the description of his two-day journey from Quebec to Three Rivers, Charlevoix focuses on the beaver, to which he devotes all of letter 5, as well as on details of the natural environment. Even Charlevoix' treatment of Three Rivers in his *History* is somewhat cursory.

Still, Charlevoix finds much to admire at Three Rivers, particularly the siting of the town: nestled into a sandy declivity against the Saint Lawrence River, surrounded by cultivated fields, with "the noblest forest in the universe" rolling upward into the far distance. Three Rivers, he notes, played an important role in the economy of New France and was staffed accordingly with well-paid government and company officials who could afford well-built homes. The Recollects maintained a fine convent and parish church, and the Ursulines a convent and a school. Bishop Saint-Vallier had recently established a hospital. The local fishing was excellent, Charlevoix remarks, and hunting bear, moose, elk, and caribou put venison on the table. Ever the classicist as well as the natural historian, he devotes two full pages to the production and enjoyment of maple syrup, a process he finds fascinating and redolent with Virgilian associations. "Et dura quercus sudabunt roscida Mella", he quotes from the *Georgics*. Thanks to maple syrup, Canada was enjoying its own golden age while the sturdy oak yielded honey.

The men of Three Rivers were by and large coureurs de bois turned interpreters and trading clerks, men such as Jean Nicollet. Having arrived in the colony in 1618 as a young man, Nicollet spent years in the forests of the far frontier, living with the Algonquian and Huron, mastering their languages, and pushing as far west as Green Bay, Wisconsin, carrying a Chinese robe with him in hopes of reaching the Pacific and encountering Asians on that distant coast. Moving even farther west, almost reaching the Mississippi, Nicollet became the first European to reach these midcontinental places. He was a religious man, a friend of the Jesuits in general and an especially close friend of Jean de Brébeuf following Nicollet's return to Three Rivers as a trading clerk for the Company of One Hundred Associates. In 1637 Nicollet married a granddaughter of Louis Hébert. Transferred to Quebec, he was sailing upstream from Quebec on the Saint Lawrence in 1642 to rescue a captured Indian ally of the Iroquois when his shallop overturned in a sudden storm and Nicollet—a veteran of endless treks across open water who had never learned to swim—drowned. The interior development of the man was revealed in the inventory of the books in his library: classics, history, travel, *The Lives of the Saints* in folio, and numerous manuals of devotion.[5]

A representative man

Three Rivers was also home to Pierre Boucher—soldier, statesman, naturalist, and utopian seigneur—who four years before Charlevoix' visit died in the manor house of his seigneury, Boucherville, at the age of ninety-five, eighty-two of those years having been spent in New France. In terms of his worldly achievement and lifetime of high Catholic purpose (Boucher was as devoutly Catholic as Nicollet), Boucher embodied, expressed, and served New France throughout eight decades of a remarkable life. He arrived in Canada at the age of thirteen in the company of his parents and three siblings as part of the Robert Giffard colonizing party of 1634. Gaspard Boucher, Pierre's father, a carpenter, became an employee of the Jesuits at their farm at Notre-Dame-des-Anges. The move was fortunate, for young Pierre received an education from the Jesuits, both at Notre-Dame-des-Anges and at Téanostaiaé (Saint-Joseph II) Mission in Huronia, where he spent four years as an assistant to such notable missionaries as Charles Lalemant, Jacques Duteux, the legendary Jean de Brébeuf, and Pierre-Joseph-Marie Chaumonot. Like many teenaged male colonists in New France, Boucher became enamored of the Indian way of life. He mastered the Huron and Algonquian languages and became proficient in the woodcraft, hunting, fishing, trekking, and military skills of these First Peoples as well as absorbing from them an intimate, highly specified knowledge of landforms, rivers, lakes, forests, flora, and fauna, the terminology for which he learned in three languages. At this point, the governor of the colony, Charles Huault de Montmagny, hearing of this extraordinary young man from his Jesuit advisors, brought Boucher to Quebec to serve as his aide-de-camp, interpreter, and guide, with the rank of sergeant.

What an extraordinary *cursus honorum* for a young man barely out of his teens, especially given the class distinctions and barriers of the era! Within eight short years, this carpenter's son had received a dual-track formation—French, Catholic, and Jesuit on the one hand; Native American and Canadian on the other—as well as the highest possible political and social connection in the colony as aide-de-camp to the aristocratic governor, whom he now accompanied on his official rounds. Boucher thus was a member of the founding party of Ville-Marie on the Island of Montreal in May 1642 and fought side by side with Montmagny the following August against an Iroquois raiding party at the mouth of the Richelieu River, admiring (and learning from) Montmagny's Knight of Malta panache under fire and his negotiating skills following battle. Canada itself—the place, the environment, the First Peoples—New France, the French Catholic colony, and the Order of Malta had coalesced to prepare young Boucher for a lifetime of leadership.

That leadership began in 1644, when Pierre Boucher was appointed clerk and interpreter at Three Rivers, where his parents joined him on a land grant of twenty-four acres he received in March 1646. All this by age twenty-four! Three years later, having absorbed from the Jesuits and from his own experience in Huronia the belief that French men and Christianized Indian women could create a new Canadian people, Boucher in 1649 married Marie Ouebadinskoue (Marie-Madeleine Chrestienne), a Huron girl educated by the Ursulines of Quebec. Within the year, tragically, Marie and her infant son were lost in childbirth. Still, the marriage, as brief as it was, underscored Pierre Boucher's powerful identification with his teachers and mentors among the Huron and Algonquian peoples.

This connection had its ironies, given that the colony of Quebec found itself in a life-or-death struggle against invading Iroquois that brought Three Rivers—indeed, the entire colony—to the brink of extinction, through either massacre or wholesale evacuation back to France. During these years, Pierre Boucher the soldier, rising in rank, was constantly in leadership roles and harm's way. As captain of Three

Rivers, he set up a fortified stockaded retreat to which he gathered the residents of the town each evening. Boucher organized the able-bodied men of Three Rivers into a militia trained in maneuvers and the use of firearms. Daytime work could be performed only under the tightest of restrictions. When the acting governor of the Three Rivers regions, tired of the continuing attacks and losses, organized an offensive sortie, Boucher advised against it and kept his men in a defensive position at Three Rivers. On 19 August 1652 twenty-two settlers and soldiers, including the acting governor, were massacred in the wood outside Three Rivers in a devastating defeat that almost spelled the beginning of the end for the colony. Shortly thereafter, Boucher became acting governor of a town that on 23 August 1653 found itself besieged by six hundred Iroquois. Under Boucher's command were forty old and young men. The settlers prevailed. The Iroquois lifted the siege and withdrew. Had Three Rivers fallen, Governor Jean de Lauson told Boucher, all Quebec would have been lost to an invading force.

By then Pierre Boucher had remarried, in 1652. His second wife, Jeanne Crevier, was French, born in Rouen but raised in Canada. In the course of their long marriage, the couple would have fifteen children. The early death of Marie Ouebadinskoue, Boucher's first wife, left her a somewhat shadowy figure. No one can know what she might have become. Jeanne Crevier Boucher, by contrast—wife, mother, a civic leader alongside her husband—developed into a seigneurial presence beloved by family and community, a grand lady at ease with high-born and habitant alike.

Savior of the town, happily married father of a large family, landowner, church warden, judge in civil and criminal cases, member of the sovereign council in Quebec (elected by his peers): Three Rivers would seem to be Pierre Boucher's destiny. Yet he was restless. He had the instincts and idealism of a founder, which in Boucher's case meant the founding of a community that displayed the potential not simply of New France the colony, anchored in the fur trade and other forms of wealth-seeking (including the liquor business that so bothered him), but of French Canada. Canada, Boucher believed, should grow into its best possible self as a new society, born and reborn in North America, pervaded by an amalgam of Catholic, French, Christian Indian, and métis value. Canada! Not merely a European outpost, but Canada—a fusion of Europe, France, Native America, social and economic cooperation, Catholic belief and values, and a transformative attachment to place. He would do his best to make this happen by demonstrating that it could be done.

Initially, Boucher inaugurated this Canadian experiment on the two hundred acres he owned at Cap-de-la-Madeleine, where he gathered like-minded settlers and organized them into a seigneury designed for high ideals and self-protection, the latter of which kept them safe from the renewed Iroquois attacks of 1658 and 1659. He could pursue this project on his own authority when in 1661, thanks to Governor Davaugour, letters of nobility for Boucher arrived from France. In recognition of his military service, he was now Sieur Boucher and could thus leverage the seigneurial system to his utopian purposes.

But before that, Davaugour and the Jesuits had a mission for him: a voyage to France in the fall of 1661 with dispatches and audiences with the king, Colbert, and the prince of Condé on behalf of the beleaguered colony. A skilled playwright or film director might very well reenvision the scenes that followed during the next two years as Pierre Boucher—recently ennobled, true, but a man of thoroughly

Canadian formation—enjoyed Paris, renewed his friendship with Jesuit Paul Le Jeune (Champlain's good friend in times past and the founder of *Jesuit Relations*), and, finally, found himself in conversation with Louis XIV. The Sun King listened to Boucher's arguments and (perhaps sensing the sheer authenticity of the man) promised, as Boucher later retold the story, to take New France under his personal protection. These promises were further elaborated in subsequent conversations with Colbert and the prince of Condé.

Many factors, including an earthquake, coalesced to motivate and facilitate the transition of New France into a royal colony in 1663: the Iroquois, most of all, who made the loss of the colony a real possibility; the inefficiency of company governance; Colbert's master plan for the reform and renewal of France; a growing interest in overseas empire; and the king's personal interest in and commitment to the Canadian venture. Thus were fused absolute monarchy and the administrative clout and efficiency of Colbert, minister of marine and first minister. In this scenario, Pierre Boucher's interview with Louis XIV, Colbert, and the prince of Condé is relevant. Here at Versailles, lobbying for New France, was a new kind of Frenchman— a Canadian. (In decades to come, Benjamin Franklin would have a similar effect on the French on behalf of the rebellious English colonies.) Two specific results can be unambiguously attached to Boucher's lobbying efforts: a foundational book and military assistance that saved the colony and gave it twenty years of peace.

To keep the French interested in Canada, Pierre Boucher wrote a book entitled *Histoire véritable et naturelle des moeurs et productions du pays de la Nouvelle France vulgairement dite le Canada* (A true and natural history of the customs and products of the country of New France commonly called Canada), which appeared in 1664 as a slender volume of fifteen short chapters from bookseller-publisher Florentin Lambert on the rue Saint-Jacques in Paris. Environmental historian Lynn Berry has written a pertinent, appreciative essay on this important book, which Pierre Boucher's descendant Edward Louis Montizambert translated as *Canada in the Seventeenth Century* (1883). Berry argues, quite plausibly, that the drama of Boucher encountering France after a twenty-seven-year absence sharpened his perception of Canada through a simple process of comparison and contrast. The eventful mission of 1661–1662 hybridized Boucher, Berry claims, like the French plants and animals now flourishing in Canada. This process of hybridization built on Boucher's time in Huronia as a teenager, his mastery of Indian languages, his marriage to an Indian woman, his extensive practice of forest warfare against the Iroquois, and other events throughout twenty-seven years of Canadian life. Experiencing the distance to France via a long sea voyage across the Atlantic, encountering the urbanity of Paris and the magnificence of Versailles, Boucher came to appreciate the achievement of France as a two-millennial creation. Being interviewed by the Sun King at Versailles, and meeting and planning with Colbert and the prince of Condé and other officials, he experienced the grandeur of the state. All this was well and good—and a bit overwhelming. Yet the mountains of Canada, the forests of Canada, the rivers of Canada, the flora and fauna of Canada: *Canada* trumped anything he was seeing in France. And so in his *History* Pierre Boucher evokes Canada as here—not there, overseas, but *here*, in its own autonomous and promising environment—challenging and demanding hard work and commitment from anyone wishing to settle in the place, yet worthy of distinction.

Altogether, Berry points out, Boucher presents by name and discrete description 44 birds, 24 land and 3 marine mammals, 25 fish, 28 trees and shrubs, and 22 edible plants: 146 species accurately detailed. The list evokes Adam in the Garden of Eden, naming animals and plants. It is the masterwork of a Canadian taking inventory of nature in a territory new to Frenchmen, using Indian names when necessary or most appropriate, which was often. Berry notes that the poet Marc Lescarbot, the Recollect missionary Gabriel Sagard, the writers of the *Jesuit Relations*, and even Samuel Champlain remain Frenchmen describing Canada for other Frenchmen as another place. Pierre Boucher, by contrast, writes from here and for here, for a Canada that would develop in partnership with France, provided that it was settled by properly motivated people—and protected from the Iroquois.

War and peace

Central to Boucher's *History* is this call for protection, for a skilled militia (regular, well-trained, and well-equipped troops) and an experienced general willing to take advice from seasoned Canadian Indian fighters. Enter the marquise Alexandre de Prouville de Tracy, lieutenant general of America. If Pierre Boucher embodied the Frenchman reborn in North America as a Canadian, the marquise de Tracy epitomized the grand Frenchman in the service of New France as overseas empire. Overly tall, massive to the point of corpulence (Marie de l'Incarnation wrote that he was the largest human being she had ever seen in her life), and afflicted with gout, Tracy had risen from obscure origins to high positions—regimental commander, commissary general, ambassador with plenipotentiary powers, king's counselor, a marquisate rank in the nobility—as a combat-tested officer of light cavalry, an expert in maneuvers and logistics, and a skilled negotiator. Tracy, then in his early sixties, was also something of a dévot, given to long hours of prayer. While in Quebec, he frequently called on Marie de l'Incarnation, who became his trusted counselor and epistolary booster. Tracy's assignment from the king as lieutenant general of America (a position equivalent to viceroy, although another noble technically held that title) was to secure overseas French interests by driving the Dutch from French-claimed islands in the West Indies and subduing the Iroquois in New France.

Tracy's mission, Colbert wrote Bishop Laval on 18 March 1664, was "to destroy utterly these barbarians, whose numbers are already diminished, according to the latest accounts that we have of them, both as a result of the losses that they have suffered in warring against their enemies and because of a sort of contagious malady which has carried off a good number of them".[6] To that end, the king was committing the elite Carignan-Salières infantry regiment—raised by the prince de Carignan and commanded by Henry de Chapelas, sieur de Salières—which had recently fought with distinction against the Turks. Four companies were dispatched at once to Quebec, four more companies were assigned immediately to Tracy, and another eight would depart for Quebec while Tracy was in the West Indies.

Tracy set sail from La Rochelle on 26 February 1664 in command of four infantry companies and 650 settlers for the West Indies. By late April 1665 Martinique, Tortuga, Guadeloupe, Grenada, and Marie Galante had been pacified or reclaimed, or both, and Tracy and his troops set sail for Quebec, where they arrived on 30

June. The reception they received was appropriately operatic. Tracy and his aide-de-camp followed an entourage of twenty-four uniformed guards from quayside to the Church of the Immaculate Conception. Behind them marched more guards and staff officers in dress uniforms. The bells of Quebec rang forth, and the population of the city cheered their progress to the church, where a fully vested Bishop Laval and attendant clergy greeted Tracy and his staff officers, whom they escorted to the altar for the singing of a Te Deum. The marquise refused the use of a prie-dieu and knelt on the stone floor with the rest of the congregation.

Over the next fourteen months, the French prepared for a massive invasion of the Iroquois homeland. Forts Saint-Louis, Sainte-Thérèse, Saint-Jean, and Sainte-Anne were constructed and manned on the Richelieu River, as was Fort Lamothe on an island in Lake Champlain, to serve as a defensive perimeter and as advance camps for the invasion. In January 1666 Governor Rémy de Courcelle led a reconnaissance force of four hundred to five hundred men on snowshoes into the Iroquois homeland. Militarily, it was a disaster. Courcelle got lost, failed to make contact with the enemy, and suffered the deaths of some sixty men to the cold; yet the Courcelle column did reach as far south as Corleav (Schenectady, New York), which meant that for the first time a major French military force had penetrated the Iroquois homeland. A half year of inconclusive negotiations ensued: feigned negotiations, the French determined, when a Mohawk force ambushed a French detachment and Tracy's nephew was killed and a number of French soldiers were taken prisoner, including one of Tracy's cousins. The marquise arrested and imprisoned the Iroquois delegation in Quebec at the time, refortified Montreal, and sent a raid into Mohawk country to free the French prisoners, who were released before any important fighting occurred.

On 1 September 1666 Intendant Talon submitted a long and persuasive memoir to Tracy. The lieutenant general, Talon respectfully argued, had spent more than a year trying to bring the Iroquois to meaningful negotiations; yet even as they negotiated, the Iroquois continued their hostilities. It was now time to move against the Iroquois in force. Tracy agreed. Advance forts had been built, along with a fleet of flat-bottomed boats. Some thirteen hundred regular soldiers and militia were available. Sending Courcelle ahead with an advance party of four hundred, Tracy staged a departure from Quebec of six hundred splendidly uniformed Carignan-Salières regulars, an equal number of militia, and one hundred Huron and Algonquian allies. This leave-taking was even more operatic than Tracy's first arrival. Among other displays—confessions heard, blessings given by Laval and clergy, a dozen Huguenots received back into the fold, bells pealing, drumming and military music from the Carignan-Salières regimental band—Tracy paraded his men past the Iroquois delegation led by a mixed-blood chief (who had a Dutch father and a Mohawk mother) whom the French called the Flemish Bastard. The Iroquois wept, it was reported, as they beheld this huge force marching into their homeland.

Theater of this magnitude had the desired effect. The Mohawks, who were the target of this invasion, fled before the French, deserting their villages. A disease-depleted Mohawk nation could not stand up to the force of efficient regulars who had bested the Turks in open battle or to colonials and their Indian allies whose guerilla tactics matched their own. The invasion went riverine, as troops moved by flat-boat flotilla and march sixty leagues beyond the perimeter of the newly constructed forts on the Richelieu River, then deployed deeper into Mohawk country, which the French again found deserted. Burning villages and crops, and seizing furs and other goods, the French raised a cross and a post bearing the arms of Louis XIV, for whom they claimed the territory. With winter on the horizon, they revised their plans to invade the nearby Oneida and instead headed back to Quebec, barely escaping the full ravages of the season.

For his reentry into Quebec, Tracy staged yet another triumphal procession. Once again, the marquise provided the Iroquois delegation with a good view of the parade, followed by the hanging of a particularly hostile Iroquois delegate named Agariata. After this instructive ceremony, Tracy sent representatives back to each of the Five Nations, asking them to query their people about future intentions vis-à-vis their relationship with the people of New France.

The Iroquois remained at peace with the French for the next two decades. This interval allowed for the administrative consolidation of New France and the first phases of the creation of a French Canadian identity. Intendant Talon, who facilitated these developments, would have preferred—so he wrote Colbert—to have decimated the Iroquois and sent the survivors to the galleys. But Talon was a Frenchman, a civil servant of empire, and not a habitant, a Canadian, as many of the discharged soldiers of the Carignan-Salières regiment were now seriously considering becoming, if the king and Talon could provide them with wives.

The marquise de Tracy was likewise a Frenchman in the service of empire: a Frenchman on a heroic scale, both physically and in what he had accomplished for the Crown in the West Indies and Canada. Moreover, he loved Quebec. It spoke to the dévot in his character. An attack of gout had forced him onto a stretcher for two days during the recent campaign. (Alas for the poor stretcher bearers!) A man of his age and infirmities might have attempted to prolong his assignment in this pleasant place. But even greater assignments beckoned, and the marquise departed Canada on 28 August 1667 as a founder, despite the brevity of his sojourn. Mother Marie de l'Incarnation praised him for setting an example of virtue and dedication to religion and good works. Besides freeing the colony from Iroquois attacks, the marquise de Tracy left behind a number of gifts and bequests: 2,500 livres for a chapel for the Ursulines, 500 livres for a chapel for the Jesuits, scholarships for Indian students, and a painting over the main altar at Sainte-Anne de Beaupré, where he went on pilgrimage. During his Quebec sojourn, Tracy attended daily Mass whenever possible, prayed frequently, appeared conspicuously at solemn ceremonies to reinforce unities of church and state, helped settle the tithing issue, presided over the previously fractious meetings of the sovereign council, and, without fanfare, tended personally to the needs of the sick at the Hôtel-Dieu. The king sent one of his best ships, the *Saint-Sébastien*, to bring him home. Monsieur de Tracy, noted the annalist of the Hôtel-Dieu, "took ship to return to France, after charming all Canada by his manners, his solicitude, and his benefactions".[7]

Boucherville

But what about those who remained behind? How were these Canadians in the making to live? What kind of society should they create? Sieur Pierre Boucher, among others, had for some time been asking such questions. By now Boucher had risen to the highest levels of influence among permanent residents of the colony as a member of the sovereign council and a friend of both Talon and the marquise de Tracy, with whom he had recently campaigned as a militia officer in the grand invasion of 1666. His eldest daughter had made a brilliant marriage to the highly respected officer René Gaultier de Varennes. Yet Boucher, in his mid-forties, was unhappy with the values and ambitions of a colony dominated by the fur trade and its abuses. That discontent became personal when his mother-in-law and two brothers-in-law were implicated in trading brandy for beaver pelts with Indians.

There had to be a better way, a better Canada, guided by Catholic and seigneurial values. And so Boucher persuaded Governor-General Courcelle and the marquise de Tracy to permit him to resign as governor of Three Rivers and to grant him a seigneury in the Iles-Percées in Indian country under the jurisdiction of Montreal. Settling there in the company of like-minded families, in the words of the manifesto he drew up, Boucher hoped "to live a more cloistered life freed from the cares of a world which serves only to busy us with its trivialities and thus to sever us more finally from God, and also to enable me to work out my salvation and that of my family".[8]

Boucher's intent, in short, was to establish a model community within the seigneurial system—a reprise, if you will, of the Robert Giffard colony that had brought his own family to New France thirty-two years earlier. Recruiting thirty-seven carefully chosen habitants and recently discharged veterans of the Carignan-Salières regiment, Boucher led his model colony into the wilderness. Following a three- to four-year trial period, Boucher gathered his colonists in his manor house and admitted them as freeholders in the seigneury, now called Boucherville. Being a freeholder meant full ownership at a nominal rent: one sou per year per acre, two live capons per year for each acre under cultivation, and six pennies per year in quit-rent fees, all due each 1 October, the feast of Saint Rémi.

Boucherville was not a wealth-sharing cooperative. Each freeholder managed his own property and took his living from it. Yet cooperation in civil matters, as well as mutual assistance of other kinds, was expected. As sieur of the seigneury, Boucher appointed a judge, a notary and scrivener, a fiscal procurator, a teacher for the children, and a former sergeant in the Carignan-Salières regiment as captain of the village. Boucher also set aside property for a parish church and presbytery, which were eventually built and staffed. In time, the manor house and the parish church embodied the conjoined values of church and state. The Bouchers lived as simply as their freeholders. No servants were necessary in their large family. Sieur Boucher and his sons worked their own fields, and his daughters helped in household management and light fieldwork. The boys and girls of the seigneury were educated equally.

Crosses and a roadside shrine; the thrice-daily pealing of the Angelus after the church was built; communal and family observance on Sundays, feast days, and holy days of obligation, Advent, the Christmas season, Lent, and Eastertide; baptisms, weddings, and funerals: signs of Catholicity at Boucherville consolidated into a shared symbolic system. Here at Boucherville laypeople were achieving Catholic Canada; and here at Boucherville, at the age of ninety-five—having written his memoirs, in which he saluted his late wife and each of his fifteen children separately

by name, attaching a thumbnail sketch of their personalities and temperaments—
Pierre Boucher on 19 April 1714 passed from the life he had lived with such high
achievement and Canadian Catholic purpose.

Montreal as Sulpician enterprise

The seigneury of Boucherville fell under the jurisdiction of Montreal. Charlevoix
reached Montreal on 14 March 1721. Since 1663 the seigneurs of Montreal had been
the Gentlemen of Saint-Sulpice. For Boucherville as a model Catholic community to have as its seigneurs an elite community of Roman Catholic priests devoted
to seminary education, professionalization, and spiritual formation of the Roman
Catholic diocesan priesthood was more than a happy coincidence. At the core of
Sulpician Montreal there survived a comparable strain of utopianism in what was
otherwise a flourishing fur-trading mart and border town between Laurentian Canada and the Great Lakes frontier.

As he had in Quebec and Three Rivers, Charlevoix admired the site. The Island
of Montreal measured ten by four leagues and was dominated by two summits,
against which, half a league from the shore, was the city, as populous as Quebec.
North of the island, separated from it by rapids, was a second island. (In these waters
Recollect Nicolas Viel had drowned in 1625 when returning from Huronia.) The
fact that the Sulpicians held seigneurial rights over the entire island, Charlevoix
believed, had helped Montreal (the name Ville-Marie, he noted, had long since
fallen into disuse) develop into well-planned upper and lower towns of handsome
houses, streets, and well-placed squares. As in Quebec, the lower town contained
quays, warehouses, the hospital, the arsenal and square for military drill, and merchants' homes. In the upper town was the new (1710) seminary building where the
Sulpicians resided in community (no students were enrolled there yet) and from
which they served the nearby parish church of Notre-Dame and other churches
and chapels in the region. Close by was a convent for Notre-Dame sisters. The
governor and other officials also lived in the high town. Off to one side of the high
town, near a small stream, stood the general hospital; further on the outskirts were
a Recollect convent and a Jesuit church and residence.

Two matrices of values and identity characterized Montreal: frontier fur-trading
town and dévot utopia. In his *Journal* entries for 1721, Charlevoix concentrates
on the fur-history aspect, graphically describing the effects of fur trader–provided
brandy on local Christianized Indians. "Even in the very streets of Montreal,"
Charlevoix writes, "are seen the most shocking spectacles, the never-failing effects
of the drunkenness of these barbarians; husbands, wives, fathers, mothers, children,
brothers and sisters, seizing one another by the throats, tearing of one another by
the ears, and worrying one another with their teeth like so many enraged wolves.
The air resounded during the night with their cries and howlings, much more horrible than those with which wild beasts affright the woods." That allegedly Catholic traders were providing this brandy to recently converted Indians, Charlevoix
laments, made such displays as scandalous as they were horrid.[9]

As condemnable as the abuse represented by the brandy trade was—blasphemous
even when exercised by Catholic traders against converted Indians—one must
ask: Is this all Charlevoix can manage to say regarding the third Laurentian city on

his itinerary? Did Charlevoix harbor ill will toward the Sulpicians (about whom he says next to nothing), leading him to pass over Montreal's rich religious heritage and record instead the horrendous scene of Indian drunkenness? Charlevoix gives Montreal a mere two and a half paragraphs before proceeding to mention the coureurs de bois, whom he censures as greedy libertines, and then comments at great length regarding the seals, sea lions, and porpoises that make it all the way up the Saint Lawrence from the Atlantic Ocean. Noting Charlevoix' relatively thin coverage of the founding of Ville-Marie in his *History*, John Gilmary Shea attributes it to a lack of sources, since Sulpicians did not submit regularly published reports that paralleled the *Jesuit Relations*. In his translation and editing of the *History*, Shea fills in the story in volume 2 with two pages of "Notes on Montreal". Neither too much nor too little should be made of these omissions. Yet while the Sulpicians were a small community and not a religious order on the scale of the Jesuits, they were, like the Jesuits, a wealthy and politically influential priestly fraternity that was Paris oriented, enrolling many nobly born and beneficed abbés. Sulpicians, moreover, enjoyed the strong support of the French hierarchy, taught in their best seminaries, and shared their Gallican orientation favoring home rule for the French Church. The Abbé Queylus, a Sulpician—and thus a diocesan priest subject to the hierarchy—had been the French hierarchy's overwhelming choice to serve as the first resident bishop in New France.

When the Society of Our Lady of Montreal yielded its seigneurial rights to the Gentlemen of Saint-Sulpice in 1663, the Sulpicians were more than capable of equaling the Jesuits of Quebec as the region's dominant clergy. As Canadian classics professor Wayne Hankey has convincingly analyzed, the Sulpicians inherited from the reform movement launched in the early 1600s by Pierre de Bérulle an orientation toward a close alliance between church and state. In this Bérullean formula, the Church was willing to cooperate with the state for the sake of political peace, but she remained confident of her identity as the senior member of the relationship. Hence the paradox of Montreal: a fur-trading frontier town under the lordship of a seminary in Paris with a branch seminary in Montreal responsible for local welfare.

Hence also the vitality of Montreal as a center of Sulpician ministry and a nursery of consecrated religious life. In September 1659 Mother Judith Moreau de Brésoles, a pharmacist, brought the Hospitaller Sisters of Saint Joseph—she and two colleagues, Mothers Catherine Macé and Marie Maillet, arrived—to Montreal, where they assumed the management of the Hôtel-Dieu from its founder, Jeanne Mance. Opposed to the expansion of religious orders, Laval disapproved. The Hospitaller Sisters of Quebec, he argued, should be assigned this task. Backed by the Sulpicians, the Hospitaller Sisters of Saint Joseph persisted and kept the Montreal assignment. In 1669 three more sisters—Andrée de Ronceray, Renée Le Jumeau, and Renée Babonneau—arrived from France; and two years later, the first Canadian-born sister, Marie Morin (whose elder brother Germain was the first Canadian-born priest), entered the community. Mother Macé served as superior from 1663 to 1681; her brother René Macé, a Sulpician based in Paris, served as procurator for the Montreal community and succeeded in ensuring a steady flow of royal and benefactor support for the Hôtel-Dieu.

Living on until 1730 and serving a number of terms as depositary (business manager) and superior, Mother Morin both participated in and recorded as annalist

the building of an expanded hospital, begun in 1689, as well as its long and painful rebuilding when it burned down in 1695 three months after it opened. Since
Jérôme Le Royer de la Dauversière, receiver of taxes at La Flèche and stay-at-home
cofounder of the Hôtel-Dieu with Jeanne Mance, had so mismanaged the endowment provided by Madame de Bullion, the Hospitaller Sisters were perennially
short of funds, but gifts from Bishop Saint-Vallier and Governor-General Frontenac
enabled reconstruction. This building, in turn, burned down in 1721 in a general
conflagration that destroyed much of the lower town.

Another two new religious orders

During the second rebuilding, the Hospitaller Sisters of Saint Joseph were housed
at a farm owned by yet another local religious congregation, the Brothers Hospitallers of the Cross and Saint Joseph, where the sisters worked in the fields to
support themselves. Wealthy Montreal merchant François Charon de La Barré
and three colleagues formed the brotherhood in 1688 under the name Brothers
of Charity as staffing for an almshouse proposed for elderly men with no means
of support. In June 1694 the first resident—a forty-year-old mentally retarded
indigent—was admitted to the newly completed three-story, twenty-four-room
stone structure with a slate roof, flanked by two thirty-foot wings, built just outside the city on nine acres donated by the Sulpicians. Constructed with donations
from Charon and his associates, the hospice hospital was at the time perhaps the
most impressive building of its kind in North America. In 1691 one of the four
founders, Jean Le Ber du Chesne, was killed in an Iroquois attack; another, Jean
Fredin, returned to France in 1700. Charon and Pierre Le Ber (Jean's brother)
nonetheless reported for duty to the almshouse as Brothers Hospitallers and
recruited other men to the cause. In October 1694 Bishop Saint-Vallier authorized the brothers to live as a diocesan religious community under his sponsorship.
Letters patent from Louis XIV, meanwhile, expanded the almshouse's mission to
receive orphaned children and to educate them in crafts, which added teaching
to the brothers' program at the institution now called the Hôpital Général of
Montreal. On 17 May 1707 six brothers—attired in the clerical frock-coat with
cross they had adopted as their habit—pronounced simple provisional vows of
religion as a diocesan community following the Rule of Saint Augustine generally
employed by service orders of this kind.

At this point, however, the Crown began to oppose the formation of new religious orders in France or its possessions. Charon spent time in France seeking to
reverse this policy—or to have the Brothers Hospitallers attached to the Gentlemen
of Saint-Sulpice—and recruiting teachers for the diocesan brotherhood he served as
superior and the Hôpital Général to which he had devoted his financial resources.
Charon died at sea in 1719 returning from France with six newly recruited teachers.
At the time of his death, the membership of the brotherhood stood at twenty-seven.
The new superior appointed by Saint-Vallier, though, while pious, was incompe-
tent, and the Brothers Hospitallers of the Cross and Saint Joseph went into decline.
By 1747, when it was disestablished as a religious community after fifty-nine years
of existence, four elderly Brothers Hospitallers and four old men were living in the
run-down Hôpital-Général.

The Congrégation de Notre-Dame de Montreal, by contrast, was flourishing. For the first five years of her apostolate in Montreal, starting in 1653, teacher Marguerite Bourgeoys spent her time doing good works in the community. On 30 April 1658 she opened a one-room school in a converted stable. Later that same year she returned to France to recruit teachers and brought back to Canada three young middle-class women eager to help her form a teaching association and one young peasant woman who hoped one day to become a lay sister. For the next eight to nine years, the women devoted themselves to teaching and to helping newly arrived filles du roi begin their Canadian lives. Already the colony regarded the women as nuns and called each one Sister. In 1670 Bourgeoys traveled to France to seek letters patent from the king allowing her community to organize as a religious congregation. Alone and nearly broke, Bourgeoys managed an audience with Louis XIV, aided by a favorable letter from Intendant Talon to Colbert praising the women's work in Montreal and elsewhere as teachers and mentors for local children and filles du roi. Marguerite Bourgeoys returned to Montreal with three of her nieces and the king's and Laval's approval to form a secular community of pious women committed to teaching and taking as their model Mary's life of service and devotion to her Son, Jesus.

But not yet a religious order! A boarding school in Montreal for upper-class girls, yes. Five literacy and domestic arts academies for habitant and Indian girls, yes. A school in the parish of Sainte-Famille on the Ile d'Orléans. A school for the poor girls of Lower Town, Quebec. Service in the Hôpital-Général, Quebec. Yes to each of these. But a royally and canonically authorized order, no! Not yet. Worse, Bishop Saint-Vallier wanted the Notre-Dame Sisters to join the Ursulines, which meant cloister, which the Notre-Dame Sisters loathed. Even worse, perhaps, the bishop threatened to impose on the women a rule of life that he would personally write. But finally, with the help of the superior of the Sulpicians in Paris, royal and canonical permission was obtained for a community of noncloistered secular sisters, a category Bourgeoys herself devised. On 1 July 1698 the women of the Congrégation de Notre-Dame de Montréal took simple vows. Marguerite Bourgeoys became Sister Marguerite of the Blessed Sacrament for the remaining two years of her life. In the years to come, the Montreal-based religious community thrived.

The Sulpician ethos

At the time of Charlevoix' visit to Montreal, the Compagnie des Prêtres de Saint-Sulpice had approximately a dozen members. The seminary, completed in 1687, stood as an austere and assured example of French Regime classicism graced by equally formal gardens. Architecture and landscaping perfectly expressed the ethos of the Gentlemen of Saint-Sulpice: French, royalist, mildly Gallican, elite, and so identified with their grand seminary in Paris that their Montreal residence was designated the seminary even though students would not be instructed there for another 120-plus years.

Although Canadian-born candidates were not accepted into the company until after the Conquest (1760) and the Treaty of Paris (1763), the first Sulpician to serve in Canada was the French-born secular priest Guillaume Vignal, an abbé serving as chaplain to the Ursulines of Quebec who returned to France in the late 1650s to join Saint-Sulpice. In September 1659 Vignal went to Ville-Marie to join Sulpicians Gabriel de Queylus, Dominique Galinier, Gabriel Souart, Jacques Le Maistre, and Antoine d'Allet in developing a Sulpician seminary that would serve the needs of New France once the Abbé de Queylus was raised to the episcopacy, which never happened. Furthermore, Ville-Marie proved a dangerous place. When Le Maistre, the bursar of the seminary, was assassinated by Iroquois in August 1661, Vignal replaced him. Two months later, out with a group of workmen collecting stones and wood for the seminary, Vignal met the same horrible fate, his body roasted and devoured by the Iroquois. Le Maistre and Vignal would not be the last Sulpicians to die at the hands of hostile Iroquois or other Indians. Unlike the Jesuits, however, the Sulpicians never made a cult of martyrdom, nor did they publicize their missionary efforts, which would prove considerable. Instead they maintained a strict code of silence, perhaps a reflection of their dévot spirituality. Admixed with that piety was an aristocratic aloofness apparent in such well-born Sulpician missionaries as the Abbé François de Salignac de la Mothe-Fénelon, the older half brother of the famous literary archbishop of Cambrai, and the abbé's cousin, the Abbé François-Saturnin Lascaris d'Urfé. In the autumn of 1687 the Abbé d'Urfé barely escaped with his life when the Iroquois, resuming their depredations after a twenty-year hiatus, attacked and massacred the parish of Saint-Louis just outside Ville-Marie, where the abbé was serving as parish priest.

Voilà un homme!

The most representative and accomplished Montreal Sulpician of the late seventeenth century, however, came not from the nobility but from the military gentry. The Abbé François Dollier de Casson as a youth served as a captain of cavalry in Flanders, where he was cited in dispatches and won the esteem of his commanding general, the Marshal de Turenne. Born in 1636 in Lower Brittany in the diocese of Nantes, Dollier originally intended to pursue a military career until, reconsidering his life, he decided in 1657 to resign from the army and enter the seminary of Saint-Sulpice. Following his ordination as a priest of the Diocese of Nantes, Dollier applied to the Company of the Priests of Saint-Sulpice, was accepted, and in 1666 was posted to Canada, where approximately fourteen Sulpicians were serving. Appropriately, the former cavalry captain sailed for Quebec as a chaplain with the Carignan-Salières regiment, which he accompanied as one of two Sulpician chaplains on its invasion of the Mohawk homeland in 1666. During this campaign, Dollier tells us, he grew so weak from hunger that, despite his efforts, he did not have the strength to rescue a drowning young donné.

Regardless of a bad knee damaged on campaign and the botched bleeding by surgeons that followed, Dollier was then dispatched overland to Fort Sainte-Anne on an island on the north end of Lake Champlain, where he served as chaplain to a garrison of sixty, forty of whom were debilitated by scurvy. The commanding officer at Sainte-Anne sent Dollier on a forced-march mission to Montreal for supplies. Ever the resourceful military man as well as chaplain, Dollier returned with several sleighs loaded with salt pork, onions, poultry, purslane spinach, and Touraine prunes. When the commanding officer complained that the provisions were inadequate, an affronted Dollier said that he personally would not consume anything from the cache. He had the supplies stored in his room and daily doled out rations to scurvy victims through the remaining months of winter. Eleven soldiers nevertheless died, and the rest were repatriated to Montreal by sleigh as they recovered.

Next, at the direction of his Sulpician superior Queylus, Dollier and a second Sulpician, deacon René Bréhaut de Galinée, an accomplished geographer, spent a year—July 1669 to June 1670—on the north shore of Lake Erie on an epic reconnaissance for missionary opportunities. The two Sulpicians and the seven laymen in their entourage held a ceremony in which they took formal possession of Lake Erie on behalf of the king. Dollier loved the grandeur of lake and mountain forest, experiencing the landscape as a source of spiritual growth. Both he and Galinée noted in their narratives that Dollier would have been content to spend the rest of his life as a missionary in the region. Indeed, upon his return, he accepted yet another overland assignment in 1671, this one drawing upon his military background: a secret and rapid reconnaissance to Lake Ontario to scout out sites for frontier forts.

Loving the camaraderie of the regiment, the congeniality of an officers' mess or a Sulpician common room, as well as the shared hardships of the trail, Dollier fit the description of a man's man. At the same time, he was close to his two sisters, one the mother superior at the Benedictine convent at Le Calvaire in Angers and the other married to a country nobleman, the baron de Bossac. Dollier, in short, was a parish priest turned Sulpician who loved people as any good curé should—just as he loved his pipe and tobacco (a habit he acquired in Canada), a good meal, and a glass or two of something in the evening.

Tall and strong (he could carry two men at a time when needed), an experienced former officer from a military family, and by 1671 the most traveled Sulpician in New France, the Abbé Dollier was a natural leader as well as a seasoned campaigner. His leadership abilities were appreciated by Tracy, Frontenac, Courcelle, his parishioners at Three Rivers (where he served briefly as parish priest), and his fellow Sulpicians, most notably his superior Queylus in New France and the Abbé Louis Tronson, superior of the Company of Saint-Sulpice. Thus when the Abbé Queylus returned to France in the autumn of 1671, it did not surprise anyone that the Abbé Tronson appointed Dollier superior of the seminary of Saint-Sulpice in Montreal—and hence of all fifteen Sulpicians living in Canada—and seigneur of the island. What might not have been as well known (or expected) was that Dollier prepared himself for this new role as Sulpician superior and secular seigneur of Montreal by writing a pioneering history of Montreal and fragments of a memoir of his life in Canada.

Written between the autumn of 1672 and the summer of 1673, Dollier's history remained in manuscript in the Mazarine Library in Paris until 1844 before it was discovered, edited, and published in French in 1868 and 1871 and in 1928 in an elegant bilingual edition (which included a life of the author) translated and edited by Ralph Flenley. The work instantly vaulted Dollier into the founders' ranks of Canadian historiography. Dollier as historian is first on the scene in Ville-Marie; he based his account on interviews with surviving principals from the foundation of the outpost in 1642 as well as on issues of the *Jesuit Relations* and other manuscripts subsequently lost. The history is lively and straightforward, its information occasionally wrong and its author sometimes too eager to see the hand of Providence in everything (how could that not be, given his calling?). Yet Dollier's *History* establishes a record of events and a portrayal of founding personalities that has remained authoritative in the historiography of Montreal since the book was published.

Dollier's autobiographical addenda, presented in the third person, display both a mild irony when Dollier is depicting himself and a restrained, charitable anecdotalism that bolsters his narrative with detail and color. Something of a soldier's humor, for example, pervades Dollier's account of a woman who remarried before her first husband had been buried or the slightly risqué story of how another woman, confronted by an Iroquois bent upon scalping her, grabbed him by his private parts and twisted until her assailant fled in agony, but who then, upon being embraced shortly thereafter by a Montrealer eager to show his joy at her survival, boxed his ears as punishment for what she interpreted to be a covert act of seduction.

Dollier—now Sieur Dollier the seigneur as well as Monsieur Dollier the Sulpician priest—used the research and writing of this history as a way to clear his mind and focus his energies for the challenges ahead. The project also inspired him with examples of past achievements and providential intercessions. Now that the founders were deceased (the last of them, Jeanne Mance, died in 1673) and such second-wave figures as Talon, Tracy, and Courcelle had returned to France, it was Dollier's turn to work in cooperation with the local governor and other civil officials to bring the thousand-people settlement of Ville-Marie (the name survives for another thirty years) to its next phase of development. Although rich in spiritual traditions, thanks to its founding by the Society of Our Lady of Montreal, Ville-Marie remained an earth-bound frontier town living off the fur trade. Hundreds of coureurs de bois operated out of Ville-Marie or at least flocked into town for the annual fur-trading fair that filled the settlement with wholesale merchants and Indians, their canoes lined up on the riverbank, with racks of fur for buying and selling on display in impromptu villages of birch-bark tents. A quasi-barbaric splendor pervaded such scenes, which could turn violent and ugly, especially when Indians were paid in brandy for their furs. Dollier fought against that practice throughout his thirty-plus years as seigneur more or less without the support of secular officials, starting at the top with Governor-General Frontenac, a part-time fur trader himself who took a live-and-let-live attitude toward the brandy trade.

Dollier's status as seigneur came from his position as superior of the Sulpician seminary. His first responsibility to Ville-Marie, therefore, was pastoral: to supervise the community life of his eight to twelve fellow Sulpicians and their work as missionaries (including one Sulpician who served in Acadia) or as curés in local parishes; to maintain the Bay of Quinté mission on the island, paying particular attention to the education of the Indian children living there; and to serve as vicar general for the bishop in the Montreal region. As vicar general, Dollier used the available resources of land and money to assist the Hospitaller Sisters of Saint Joseph, the congregation of Notre-Dame, and the Brothers Hospitallers of the Cross and Saint Joseph, as well as the Jesuits, plus the Recollects when they later sought to establish themselves on the island. For the people of Ville-Marie, he built a parish church that remained in use until 1829 and a parish school. For the Sulpicians, he built the impressive seminary completed in 1687.

As a former military officer, Dollier loved the planning and engineering responsibilities of his office. As early as 1672 he laid out and named for saints the streets of the present and future city and over the years made certain that this foundational city plan was enforced. He began, but on three attempts failed, to deliver plans for a canal that would bypass the rapids at the headwaters of the island, allowing a direct connection by water to the western regions. Such a bold and premature venture was beyond the financial or engineering capacities of his seigneury, but Dollier's advocacy of it—like George Washington's promotion of the Potomac Canal—suggested the perspective of the military engineer that endured in the priestly seigneur. Dollier did succeed in having a number of water-driven grain mills constructed that remained in use for decades.

A priestly point of view most likely encouraged Dollier to remove himself and his fellow Sulpicians from the judicial functions of the seigneury. One could not sit in judgment in both the courtroom and the confessional. Besides, as Montreal grew in population (nearly six thousand by 1700) and complexity, the need for a professionally prepared judiciary became apparent. Initially, Dollier remained in the judicial process by retaining the seigneurial right to nominate a royal judge, but in 1693 he surrendered to the Crown all authority in civil and criminal cases except at the seminary itself and its farm at Saint-Gabriel, where the Sulpician seigneur continued to judge.

In general, Dollier's relations with Frontenac and other royal officials remained on an even keel, although they got off to a rocky start when the civil governor of Montreal, François-Marie Perrot, threw judge Jean-Baptiste Migeon de Branssat into jail after a quarrel, filing no charges, simply to teach him a lesson. Dollier persuaded the governor to release the judge, and peace was restored—temporarily. On 25 March 1674 the Sulpician missionary François de Salignac de la Mothe-Fénelon preached an Easter Day sermon in which the outspoken nobleman criticized in a barely disguised manner the equally outspoken and noble Frontenac for overstepping his authority. The sermon set in motion a chain of events that resulted in the Abbé Fénelon's being recalled to France after arguing his case before the sovereign council and, when not feeling backed by his confreres, resigning from the Sulpicians.

Sadly, Dollier was on the same ship that carried Fénelon back to France in the autumn of 1674. That February, Dollier had fallen through a patch of thin ice and had been trapped in freezing cold water for several hours before being rescued. Dollier's recovery from the accident was slow, and Sulpician superior Louis Tronson ordered him back to the easier climate of France to recuperate. He was absent for four years, two of them spent pleasantly with his sister (who had earlier guaranteed Dollier an annuity of 1,200 livres a year) and her husband, the baron de Bossac, at their chateau. While he was regaining his strength, Dollier tutored their son, his nephew. Returning to Canada in 1678, Dollier continued and amplified his role as designated peacemaker for the colony, beginning with negotiating a reconciliation between a quarreling Governor Frontenac and Intendant Jacques Duchesneau.

In 1694 another prie-dieu affair erupted when the governor of Montreal, Louis Hector de Callières, claimed prie-dieu preference over Saint-Vallier at religious services during the bishop's visit to Montreal, and a furious Saint-Vallier, who had already written a letter admonishing Montrealers for excessive drinking, put the parish church of Montreal under interdict and took his case to the sovereign council. Dollier backed Saint-Vallier as a matter of principle—in church, before the altar in a liturgical ceremony, no one, not even the governor, outranked the bishop—yet he also managed to restore peace between the quarreling parties. He so won Saint-Vallier's respect that the bishop appointed him vicar general of the entire diocese if and when Saint-Vallier were absent in Europe. Sulpician Dollier was now the highest-ranking priest in the diocese.

As influential as he might be on the local level, however, matters of war and peace on a regional scale were beyond Dollier's influence. Personally, and as a priest, he was devoted to the Indian people, having initially intended to be a missionary. He was known to use his own money to provide dowries for Christianized Indian girls who were marrying Frenchmen. As seigneur and Sulpician superior, he sponsored scholarships for Indians to local schools and took pride in Montreal's pioneering outreach to the Iroquois; the mission on the Bay of Quinté on Lake Ontario's north shore was established in 1668 by Sulpicians Fénelon and Claude Trouvé and conducted there for twelve years before being moved to the Island of Montreal. Indians in turn acknowledged Dollier as an obvious chief in terms of both his fair-mindedness and his strength. "*Voilà un homme!*" a local chief said of the Sulpician seigneur. "There is a man!"

17

Natchez 1729

The Mississippi valley and Louisiana are explored and evangelized

Fascinated by the Natchez, Charlevoix spent most of letter 30 describing this ferocious, self-contained people, ruled over by a chief called the Great Sun and his
nearest female relative, the mother of the son who would succeed him. Charlevoix
was especially intrigued by the Natchez practice of an accelerated form of suttee in
which a hundred or more men, women, and children were sacrificed to accompany
a male or female chief to the grave. (The best a solitary and defenseless missionary
might manage, Charlevoix obliquely suggests, was to baptize these victims prior to
their executions.) He was also struck by the sexual culture of the Natchez people.
He notes in the *Journal*:

> I know no nation on the continent where the sex is more disorderly than in this. They
> are even forced by the grand chief and his subalterns to prostitute themselves to all
> comers, and a woman is not the less esteemed for being public. Though polygamy is
> permitted and the number of wives which a man may have is unlimited, yet everyone,
> for the most part contents himself with one, whom he may divorce at pleasure; but
> this, however, is a liberty never used by any but the chiefs. The women are tolerably
> well-looked for savages, and neat enough in their dress, and every thing belonging to
> them. The daughters of a noble family are allowed to marry none but private men;
> but they have a right to turn away their husband when they think proper, and marry
> another, provided there is no alliance between them. If their husbands are unfaithful
> to them, they may cause them to be put to death, but are not subject to the same
> law themselves: on the contrary, they may entertain as many gallants as they please,
> without the husband's daring to take it amiss, this being a privilege attached to the
> blood of the sun.[1]

Not surprisingly, the Natchez had resisted evangelization.
   The only man to attempt to evangelize the Natchez was the seminary priest
Jean-François Buisson de Saint-Cosme, a veteran of missionary work among the
Illinois and Tamaroa. Along with his seminary colleagues, Saint-Cosme had moved
south to the lower Mississippi when the efforts of the seminary missioners came into
conflict with Jesuit jurisdiction over this region. Saint-Cosme spent the years 1700
to 1706 among the Natchez but accomplished next to nothing. "An ecclesiastic of
Canada", Charlevoix noted of Saint-Cosme in his *Journal*, "was sent to the Natchez,
where he resided a sufficient time, but made no proselites [*sic*], though he so far
gained the good graces of the woman-chief, that out of respect to him, she called
one of her sons by his name. This missionary being obliged to make a voyage to the

Mobile, was killed on his way thither by some Indians, who probably had no other motive for this cruel action, but to plunder his baggage, as had before happened to another priest, on the side of the Arkansas."[2]

Jean-François Buisson de Saint-Cosme: murdered in the line of duty by Chitimacha Indians who wanted his gear. Thus Saint-Cosme would seem to have passed into history, a nearly forgotten seminary priest sent by his parents to the Petit Séminaire (minor seminary) of Quebec when he was a boy of eight, moving from there to the seminary and ordination in his early twenties, as did his younger brother Michael; Saint-Cosme's two sisters became nuns, and his prosperous and pious parents ultimately gave their wealth to the seminary and served as administrators of the seminary farm on the Ile Jésus.

In her entry on Saint-Cosme in the *Dictionary of Canadian Biography*, however, historian Céline Dupré notes the presence in the Bibliothèque Nationale in Paris of an unsigned document discovered following Saint-Cosme's death alleging that the seminary priest had been the lover of the female Great Sun of the Natchez, who bore him a son named Saint-Cosme. Charlevoix' claim—that the female Great Sun so warmly admired Saint-Cosme in a chaste way that, while rejecting his religion, she named her son and heir after him—strains credibility, not only in the matter of human nature but also in the matter of Natchez sexual practice and the life-or-death power the female Great Sun held over the Canadian priest, not to mention how attracted she might have been to a young man who had spent his lifetime in required celibacy.

As wise as he was, Charlevoix shows a certain naïveté in his acceptance of this story of virtuous attribution as well as in his assertion in the same *Journal* passage that French couples in Louisiana had no right to start living together as man and wife without a marriage ceremony before a priest, despite the near-total lack of clergy in the region. This was not the sin of concubinage, as Charlevoix querulously suggests. Canon law recognized that the sacrament of marriage was administered by a couple to each other, with a priest serving as witness, and if no priestly witnesses were available, a couple might pledge their troth to each other, move in together, and let nature take its course until a priest showed up and formally blessed their union.

In any event, twenty-two years after the death of his namesake and/or alleged father, Saint-Cosme II, now himself the Great Sun of the Natchez people, planned and executed on Monday, 28 November 1729, a surprise attack on Fort Rosalie and its adjacent settlement. As Saint-Cosme II sat under the tobacco shed of the Compagnie d'Occident (Company of the West), which held trading rights in the area, the Natchez massacred seventy or up to twice that number (sources vary) French soldiers and civilians, including the commandant of the fort, whose head was laid at the feet of the Great Sun. Looting followed the massacre, and then came a few days of brandy drinking, singing, dancing, and mutilation of French bodies.

Despite initial promises of loyalty to the French, the Yazoo soon joined the uprising, attacking the local military post and killing eighteen men, including a priest. Shortly thereafter, the Yazoo attacked Jesuit Stephen Doutreleau and five other travelers en route on the Mississippi from Illinois country to New Orleans. The Yazoo quietly attended Mass with the party, then began their assault when the Kyrie Eleison was pronounced. One Frenchman was killed, three fled, and Doutreleau—dressed in a chasuble and holding a chalice and paten—nevertheless managed to swim out to his boat and, despite being shot in the jaw, negotiate the river to New Orleans.

The Revocation of the Edict of Nantes

If the American Revolution is included, the century 1685–1785 is characterized by a nearly uninterrupted sequence of wars in Western Europe and North America. While the dynastic, imperial, social, and economic causes behind these wars are multiple, religion also played a role. Issued by Henri IV in 1598, the Edict of Nantes ended a century of religiously based civil war in France by granting the Huguenots what was in effect a state within the state. Taking to the field in the late 1620s, Cardinal Richelieu reduced by siege and conquest the political autonomy of the Huguenot regions. Mazarin did his best to further this effort. The Huguenot ascendancy, meanwhile, having tried and failed to maintain its autonomy through revolt, continued to internationalize itself through expatriation and global business. Still, approximately one million Huguenots remained in France as of the rise of Louis XIV. Their ongoing autonomy in religious matters as well as the increasing internationalization of their enterprises—now operating out of Protestant England and the Netherlands—rankled the absolutist, centralizing ambitions of the Sun King, his ministers, and the Roman Catholic leadership. Starting in the 1660s, Huguenots were gradually excluded from the professions, down to and including bookseller. A Catholic who converted to Protestantism risked being sent to the galleys for life. A Huguenot child over the age of seven who wished to become a Catholic could be removed from his family so as to receive additional instruction. In 1685, after two decades of intensifying harassment, Louis XIV declared that since the majority of Protestants had become Catholics, the Edict of Nantes was no longer necessary and was therefore revoked. All Protestant ministers were to leave France within fifteen days. The Huguenot people themselves, however, were to remain in France but would be allowed to practice their religion in private.

The promise of private privilege was a ruse. The true goal of the Revocation was forced conversion. The Revocation, in effect, returned France to a state of religious war, only this time the Huguenots were in no condition to resist the power of an aggressively Catholicizing government and its cruel campaign of intimidation, terror, torture, murder, the burning of villages, the closing of seaports, the sending of young and old men alike to the galleys, and the execution of ministers brave enough to remain at their posts. (Even saintly Pope Innocent XI, while approving the Revocation, condemned the ruthless manner of its enforcement.) An estimated one million Protestants fled France, the majority of them middle-class citizens and professional and business elites, many of whom settled in England or its American colonies.

England, meanwhile, was experiencing an upheaval in the opposite direction. Restored to the English and Scottish thrones in 1660, Charles II—married to a Catholic, attracted to Catholicism, dying a Catholic—pursued pro-Catholic policies at home and abroad, including a secret Treaty of Dover (1670) with Louis XIV, promising to bring England back into the Catholic fold (led off by Charles's own conversion) and to join France in an alliance against the Dutch. Such covert dealings could have earned Charles II the same fate from Parliament received by his father, Charles I, beheaded for treason in 1649. As it was, the alleged Popish Plot fabricated by Anglican priest Titus Oates in 1678 whipped anti-Catholicism to a high level of frenzy, and Charles moderated his course; yet the king managed to defeat efforts by Parliament to bar his brother James, Duke of York, a Roman Catholic convert, from being named his successor. James succeeded to the throne in 1685, and his Catholic second wife gave birth to an heir to the throne, Prince Charles, yet another Catholic. These developments, together with James' egregiously pro-Catholic policies, led to the Glorious Revolution of 1688, in which a joint Tory and Whig leadership put James II's Protestant son-in-law and Protestant (although Catholic convent–educated) daughter, William and Mary of Orange, on the thrones of England and Scotland.

An era of massacres

Thus the French-English rivalry for dominance in North America, charged from the beginning with religious meaning, became even more formally the two-sided, Catholic-versus-Protestant crusade that Francis Parkman considers to be its fundamental dynamic. France led the Catholic cause, and England emerged as the champion of Protestantism. Wars of religion are unusually cruel, and these wars—named for King William and Queen Anne—involved in their North American versions an onslaught of massacres by each side.

Already, as of 1688, when war broke out between England and France following the removal of James II from the English throne, Joseph-Antoine Lefebvre de La Barre, a governor-general of New France, had made a bad situation even worse. Since he owned shares in a trading company, La Barre informed the Iroquois that French fur traders on the Illinois River lacking a passport personally signed by him were there illegally (and in the service of a rival trading company headed by René-Robert Cavelier, sieur de La Salle) and the Iroquois could seize their furs. Before La Barre's proclamation, the Iroquois had been steadily eroding the peace imposed on them two decades earlier by the marquise de Tracy. La Barre's permission to seize furs from a rival French company—criminal, perhaps treasonous by modern standards, given his rule as governor-general—inflamed the Seneca Iroquois, who began to pillage any and all French traders. The Seneca even attacked Fort Saint-Louis, the largest French settlement in the region. Of the five Iroquois tribes, the Seneca were the largest and farthest west; hence they were never disciplined by French military action and remained eager to take on the foreign troops.

With both Canada and his private interests coming under threat, La Barre—keen to teach the Seneca the same lesson the marquise de Tracy had taught the Mohawks in the mid-1660s—requested a regiment of regulars to be sent from France. Instead, he received only three companies. Louis-Armand de Lom D'Arce de Lahontan, a young officer in this contingent, would later earn fame as a chronicler of La Barre's weak-willed and inconclusive 1684 incursion into the Seneca homeland with a force of regulars, militia, and Indian allies. La Barre kept his forces encamped at Fort Frontenac on Lake Ontario while he negotiated a sham treaty. The Seneca ceded next to nothing in return for La Barre's calling off the invasion.

Learning of the debacle, Louis XIV, on the advice of Colbert's son, Jean-Baptiste Antoine Colbert, marquise de Seignelay, who had succeeded his late father as minister of marine, replaced La Barre with the battle-hardened brigadier Jacques-René Brisay, marquise de Denonville, with orders to resubdue the Iroquois. Sixty of the five hundred regulars sailing with Denonville, however, died of typhus and scurvy on the voyage. Another eighty were incapacitated. Upon arriving in New France, Denonville found Quebec in the midst of a devastating influenza epidemic, which also took its toll on his soldiers. Yet the energetic brigadier—in much the same manner as his military predecessor the marquise de Tracy twenty years earlier—immediately seized control of the situation. He reorganized the colony's defenses (including fortifying Montreal) and reformed the civil administration. Most important, Denonville spent nearly three years building up military resources, and in June 1687 he led a force—832 regulars, 900 militia, and 400 Indian allies—on a punitive expedition against the Seneca. These Iroquois fled into the forest, as the Mohawks had twenty years earlier, leaving the French with a pyrrhic victory of destroyed villages and food supplies as well as a claim on the Seneca homeland (present-day Ontario and New York).

On the diplomatic front, French-Iroquois relations were going from bad to catastrophic. On orders of the minister of marine, Denonville (reluctantly, it must be noted) sent to France for service in the galleys thirty-six of the fifty-eight male Iroquois prisoners being held in Quebec as hostages for bargaining. Broken promises and a condemnation of men to the galleys: this affront to the Iroquois—instead of intimidating them, as the minister of marine intended—galvanized the Five Nations to launch an all-out campaign. The hundred-man garrison Denonville had left at the fort he had established at the mouth of the Niagara River remained trapped behind the palisades by constant siege. Eighty-nine men died of scurvy or related causes. Raids on Fort Frontenac cost Denonville another hundred men. Unable to reinforce Fort Frontenac, Denonville ordered it blown up and abandoned. On the home front, influenza continued to take a heavy toll. Out of a population of eleven thousand, fourteen hundred Quebecois lost their lives.

When the Iroquois learned from the English at Albany that King William's War had broken out in Europe—hearing this news before it reached Quebec—a force of fifteen hundred Five Nations warriors secretly converged on the village of Lachine a few miles above Montreal. At daybreak on 5 August 1689, they unleashed what must be called an Iroquois Fury: the massacre of sixty men, women, and children amid scenes of horrible torture—some of which they inflicted on the shore closest to Montreal so that Montrealers could better observe it—including, it was later reported, forcing a mother to turn the spit on which one of her children was roasting. Copious draughts of brandy fueled this Iroquois Fury, which lasted more than a day. The *Walpurgisnacht* of booze-driven savagery was far worse than anything Bishop Laval might have imagined as he campaigned against the brandy trade.

Five months later, during an expedition into New York organized by a recently returned Frontenac—now beginning his second term as governor-general—a French Fury was exacted against Schenectady in retaliation for Lachine. Albany had been the original target of the invasion, but when it was learned that up to five hundred troops were garrisoned there, the French and their Indian allies advanced westward into Mohawk country. On the night of 17 January 1690, a detachment of French and Indians infiltrated the palisades of the sleeping village of Schenectady and slaughtered sixty residents, including ten women and twelve children. Some of the children, the English reported, were thrown alive into burning cabins.

Cross-cultural mayhem

And so it continued. On the morning of 28 March 1690, French and Indian forces entered the slumbering town of Salmon Falls near present-day Portsmouth, New Hampshire, killed thirty, set the community afire, and carried off fifty-four women and children as prisoners, who were fortunate to have escaped death. Not fortunate were the women and children of Fort Loyal near present-day Portland, Maine. Receiving the surrender of the fort in late May 1690 after fierce fighting, René Robineau de Portneuf, commander of a force of fifty French and sixty Abenakis, promised safe conduct to the nearest English settlement for all surrendering English, soldiers and civilians alike. When the English exited the fort, however, the Abenakis fell upon the English, an attack the French managed to bring under partial control following significant slaughter.

King William's War ended in 1697, and Frontenac negotiated a tentative peace with the Iroquois in 1701. Yet as barbaric as the Iroquois could be, the less populous French depended on friendly Indians as military allies, and these auxiliaries, even when Christianized, had long practiced torture and massacre as a way of life, to which they could (and did) frequently revert. In becoming Canadians, the French—especially young men of fighting age and most particularly the coureurs de bois—had assimilated Indian ways to one degree or another, including Indian warfare and prisoner practices. While it is perhaps not surprising that coureurs de bois and other far-frontier, multigenerational French residents of Canada adopted these methods, Indian prisoners were at times tortured and killed in the settlements. In this regard, no one imitated the Iroquois more enthusiastically than the polished courtier Frontenac, who offered bounties for Iroquois or English scalps, allowed prisoners to be tortured to death (after publicly honoring them with gifts), and joined Iroquois delegations and other Indians in their war whoops and dances as a sign of respect and for his own enjoyment.

Still, these massacres were more than a reflection of cross-cultural influences. While Lachine was labeled an Iroquois barbarity, the massacres for which the French bore responsibility seem not to have provoked much self-scrutiny on the part of the French, as they would have eighty years earlier in the time of Champlain and Lescarbot, both of them eager to find in Canada an escape from the murderous religious conflict that had kept France in a state of civil war for more than a half century. The Revocation of the Edict of Nantes renewed that civil war and made it even more deadly because it was now being implemented by militarily efficient nation-states willing to give and take sizable casualties. Thus while France could devastate the Palatinate and send one hundred thousand people into flight, it could also in 1693 leave twenty thousand of its own subjects dead on the battlefield to win the battle of Neerwinden. From this perspective, a hundred-plus English civilians killed in the forests of North America perhaps pales in comparison, especially when put into the context of the fierce, nearly seven-decade guerilla war waged by the Iroquois that had come close to driving the French from the Saint Lawrence valley.

And so in the second year of Queen Anne's War—which represented a renewal of the previous conflict of 1688 to 1697—under orders from yet another aristocratic soldier serving as governor-general, Philippe Rigaud, marquise de Vaudreuil, a party of fifty French and two hundred Abenaki and Caughnawaga allies under the command of the Canadian-born Hertel de Rouville (accompanied by his four brothers) left Montreal on snowshoes and, following a three-hundred-mile forced march, on 27 February 1704 approached the fortified village of Deerfield on the extreme northwestern frontier of Massachusetts. Taking up concealed positions outside the village, the invaders waited until dawn of the next day to launch their attack.

In *A Half-Century of Conflict* (1892), Francis Parkman devotes a full chapter to this massacre and the subsequent captivity of its survivors based on contemporary documents and two hundred years of antiquarian inquiry. The first half of Parkman's narrative presents in horrific meticulousness the massacre and the residents' efforts at resistance. The name and the age of each tomahawked man, woman, child, and infant are given, along with specific circumstances of death, in the laconic but lurid detail Parkman derived from his sources. As a result, Parkman's version of the Deerfield massacre equals the more diversely chronicled Lachine as a repellent case study in frontier mayhem. The raid and massacre at Lachine lasted a night and a day. The Deerfield massacre, by contrast, was interrupted in its second hour when a relief party—alerted by gunfire, screams, and fires—arrived from nearby settlements, and the main body of attackers fled into the snowbound forest with 111 prisoners, leaving behind between 47 and 53 dead villagers and a remnant of looters, who were quickly driven from the scene. Summary executions on the trail, however, continued the Deerfield massacre. Prisoners unable to maintain the pace, especially older men and women, were tomahawked along with the infants they were carrying, as were boys and girls who for one reason or another—being too heavy to carry, for example—proved inconvenient to their Indian captors.

When Rouville's expedition and its surviving prisoners reached the French outpost of Chambly, twelve to fifteen miles outside Montreal, the focus of Parkman's narrative shifts to the religious dynamics connected to the massacre. Deerfield's resident pastor, John Williams, would later give a complete account of his experiences in *The Redeemed Captive Returning to Zion* (1707). His son would write an *Account of the Captivity of Stephen Williams, Written by Himself* (not published until 1837), as an appendix to his *Biographical Memoir of the Rev. John Williams*. A Harvard graduate, learned and devout, married and the father of eight children, John Williams embodies a paradigm of New England virtue who in his rectitude and sufferings—three of his children were murdered, and his wife died of exhaustion on the trail—reprises the battle between Protestant New England (liberty) and Catholic New France (authoritarianism) that structures the content and the outcome of Parkman's grand narrative.

Williams' impromptu sermons and prayers while on forced march establish the theological context of Parkman's story. With the arrival of the captives at Chambly outside Montreal, the theological drama becomes explicit as Williams endures a year-long effort to convert him to Catholicism. In Montreal a Sulpician temporarily converts Williams' son Samuel through a regime of whippings, instruction, and a forced sign of the cross before prayer. Samuel later recants; yet a number of survivors, particularly children kept from their parents, do convert. A smaller number are Indianized, including Williams' daughter Eunice, who is baptized a Catholic and later marries a Caughnawaga chief. In 1740 Eunice returns to Deerfield with her husband for a brief reunion with relatives. They visit again the following year and are treated kindly. Only once, however, does Eunice consent to dress in English clothes, which make her feel uncomfortable.

Conversion of adults through argument and of children through instruction, forced observance, cultural assimilation, and kindness remains the program once the Deerfield captives reach Canada. Williams himself notes specific instances of benevolence on the trail. Children—who only recently were being tomahawked on the trail by Indian allies—now become precious adoptees and future Canadian Catholics, many of whom Parkman chronicles in their marriages and offspring. Freedom French, for example, was the daughter of a blacksmith who served as Deerfield town clerk and a church deacon. Freedom's mother and infant sibling were tomahawked en route to Canada; her father and two surviving siblings were in time repatriated to New England. Freedom is converted and baptized as Marie Françoise and marries a Canadian. In 1806 Marie Françoise's direct descendant Joseph Octave Plessis, himself the son of a blacksmith (a calling that must have run in the family), became the eleventh Roman Catholic bishop of Quebec (the first archbishop after 1820). In fact, Plessis was the first post-Conquest bishop to win official recognition by the English government, which also named him to the legislative council of Quebec because of his rallying of French Canadians to the English cause during the War of 1812.

Such resolutions, however, were for the future. For the time being, as Queen Anne's War continued, so, too, continued a series of murderous raids into New England, albeit on a smaller scale, by French Canadian militia and their Indian allies. Massacre on a larger scale made one last horrible appearance in 1708. This time Indian allies were not to blame. The invading force—again under the command of Hertel de Rouville—that approached the eastern Massachusetts town of Haverhill on the Merrimac River in the early morning hours of Sunday, 29 August 1708, was largely French, having failed to rendezvous with its Indian allies. The French, moreover, were explicitly on a religiously motivated crusade, as Rouville informed his men when he led them in prayer just before dawn prior to the attack. The ensuing massacre left fifty English dead, including town pastor John Rolfe and his wife and one of their three children. Again, as in Deerfield, various townspeople heroically resisted. Rouville's brother was killed in the fighting, and the French once more fled before a relief party of English militia.

The battling imperial aspirations of France and Great Britain were causing death and havoc on the continent. The border warfare between Canada and New England was part of this scenario. The numbers were smaller, but the motivations remained the same. As Francis Parkman points out, these border massacres of the late seventeenth and early eighteenth centuries were drawing a line in the sand. Each side of the conflict had been pulled into a crusade on behalf of religion and continental ambition that, given the prejudice, hatred, and bitterness of each party, only one side could win.

Renewed missionary effort

French Canada had inextricably tied itself to Native America in order to prevail in this contest or to have the chance to extend its continental ambitions westward across the Great Lakes and southward through the interior of the continent. By the late 1660s, when dreams of North American empire began to coalesce, France's hold on the portions of the North American continent it claimed remained tenuous in terms of population, 3,215 as of 1666—538 separate families, 2,034 men, 1,181 women, according to the census taken that year on orders from Intendant Jean Talon—most of it aligned along the Saint Lawrence River. In an earlier era, contemplating the paucity of French people in New France, the Jesuits and the Ursulines had turned to intermarriage with Native Americans as the answer. This process remained in operation, especially in frontier regions, but not on the scale that was once expected. The filles du roi program had helped boost the French Canadian population, doubling it every twenty-seven years, but the numbers were still small in comparison with the amount of people needed to occupy and hold a continent. Thus rearose a missionary dream—primarily among Jesuits but in other clerical organizations as well—of holding vast territories on behalf of New France through the creation of a network of affiliated communities, of Christianized Indian tribes and/or language groupings. New France, in short, could extend itself through conversion and thereby serve evangelical and strategic aspirations at the same time. Saving souls was serving France and vice versa.

The fall of Huronia represented a depressing failure to create among the Huron a Canadian counterpart to the Jesuit reductions of Paraguay, where as of 1627 some 30,000 formerly nomadic Christianized Guaraní lived in fourteen flourishing commonwealths (reductions) under the protection of Spanish and Portuguese Jesuits. Only the Huron mission of Notre-Dame-de-Lorette, founded by Jesuit Pierre-Joseph-Marie Chaumonot in 1674, three leagues outside Quebec, approached this reductionist ideal, but Notre-Dame-de-Lorette never enrolled more than 300 Huron (and only 146 at the time of the census of 1685) and survived as a pale shadow of what the Jesuits had intended for Huronia.

The Quebec college

Still, another Jesuit ambition, education, was gaining momentum in these years, thanks to the steady growth of the college they had founded in Quebec in 1635. Almost from its foundation in the 1540s, the Society of Jesus had aggressively supported an educational apostolate in Europe and its missionary territories. The more complex the culture, the more developed became the local Jesuit college to serve its needs. By 1700, Jesuit colleges were enrolling 250,000 students worldwide. Initially planned for Native American students, the Quebec college was slow to start when young men recruited from local tribes proved disinterested in this kind of education (in contrast to the Jesuit college in Goa, India, which was in rapid order requiring a faculty of 120 Jesuit professors). Three decades later, however, Bishop Laval assigned to the Quebec college responsibility for instruction in classics, philosophy, and theology for students in residence at the seminary, and the college progressed appreciably as a center for the preparation of young men for either lay or clerical careers through an integrated sequence of late primary, secondary, and collegiate-level instruction. As remained true of Jesuit education through the late twentieth century, Latin and Greek, mathematics, grammar and rhetoric, and philosophy and theology dominated the curriculum. With the urging of Intendant

Talon, who was eager to encourage more practical subjects, instruction in higher mathematics, astronomy, hydrography, and navigation was initiated with the help of royal funding. Over the years, a number of distinguished laymen with French degrees held chairs in these subjects. According to Bishop Saint-Vallier, by the end of the seventeenth century, graduates of the Quebec college could hold their own with graduates of comparable institutions in France.

At the Quebec college, Charlevoix did his regency teaching between 1705 and 1709 before returning to France for theological study. Because the Jesuit residence at the college also served as a rest-and-recovery center for missionaries either temporarily returned from the field or in retirement, the young scholastic had an opportunity to meet some of the famed missionaries who would one day find a place in his *History*. These veterans—some of whom for years slept in birch-bark cabins and subsisted on sagamité and beans—gathered at table on Sunday evenings or feast days to enjoy (so travel writer Louis-Armend de Lom d'Arce de Lahontan tells us following a 1684 visit) a well-prepared meal of produce grown at the Jesuit farm at Sillery or the college's own vegetable garden and orchard, accompanied by claret and white wine shipped from France, the white chilled to proper temperature in the college icehouse.

Returning to Quebec in 1720, Charlevoix noted that the college complex, now passing the half-century mark, needed repair. Fifty-plus years earlier, Charlevoix declared, when Quebec was merely a collection of huts and hovels, the stone-built college and adjacent church had represented a much-praised step forward in the built environment, but now Quebec itself was a city of stone, and many buildings outclassed the college architecturally. The college courtyard, for one thing, Charlevoix complained, was as run-down as a stable, and in winter the wooden floorboards of the church chapel, having separated over time, let in the kind of icy drafts that had finished off Bishop Laval.

Charlevoix' observations from 1720 were not published until 1744. By that time, the Jesuit college at Quebec had been rebuilt by Jesuits who must have agreed with Charlevoix' opinions; for in the 1740s the fathers redesigned the college as an ambitious four-story stone structure fronted by gardens and an athletic field and backing into a grove on Esplanade Hill cited in maps of the era as the Jesuit Woods. An impressive chapel extended at an angle from the northwest corner of the college complex, which opened onto the marketplace and the adjacent cathedral.

The Great Lakes region

Leaving Montreal in mid-March 1721, Charlevoix spent the next three and a half months traveling through the Pays d'en Haut (Upper Country), which encircled the Great Lakes Huron, Superior, Erie, and Michigan. The vast midcontinental region of twenty-three tribal nations had been under the ecclesiastical leadership of its vicar general, the Jesuit missionary Claude Allouez, from 1663 until his death in August 1689 while evangelizing among the Miamis of the Lake Michigan region. From this edge of New France's western reach comes Charlevoix' most frequently quoted *Journal* description of Canadians—their great height and physical strength; their resilience and independent spirit; their skills as canoeists, trekkers, hunters, and fishermen—after the frontier had helped clarify in his mind the Canadian identity.

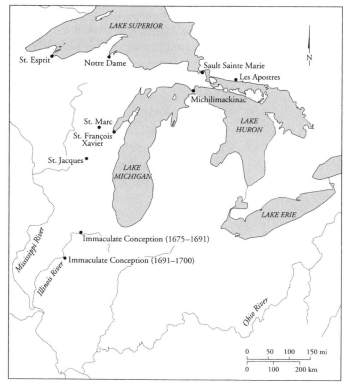

Map 16. *Pays d'en Haut* and Illinois Country, 1650–99. From Tracy Neal Leavelle, *The Catholic Calumet* (University of Pennsylvania Press, 2011), 53. *Reprinted with permission of the University of Pennsylvania Press.*

When Charlevoix turned to chronicling the exploration and evangelization of the Pays d'en Haut, the Illinois country, the Mississippi valley, and Louisiana (as he would do upon returning to France), the sheer physicality of what these missionaries accomplished—the sweep and grandeur of the continental ambitions they achieved, the settlements that could trace their origins to their campfires, the languages they mastered, the gospel they preached, the Native Americans they converted and baptized—provided much to ponder and appreciate.

Claude Allouez arrived in Quebec on 11 July 1658, following the completion of his Jesuit training at Toulouse and Rodez. After two years of study of the Huron and Algonquian languages, he was posted to Three Rivers as Jesuit superior. In 1663 Bishop Laval named him vicar general of the huge Great Lakes region briefly evangelized in 1661 by Jesuit René Ménard before his death (murder and robbery, most likely) on the Beaulieu rapids of the Wisconsin River. October 1665 found Allouez, despite much difficulty, evangelizing on La Pointe du Saint-Esprit on the southwestern edge of Lake Superior, present-day Wisconsin, within reach of Ottawa refugees to the east, Huron refugees to the south, and the legendary Sioux to the west; also within visiting distance were Pottawatomies, Sacs, Foxes, and an eclectic grouping of eight other tribes who used Chippewa as their lingua franca. At Saint-Esprit, Allouez built a birch-bark chapel and opened a mission. From there the intrepid vicar general made journeys of evangelical outreach that put him in contact with the once-Catholic Nipissings, whom he re-Catholicized, as well as a band of Sioux wandering eastward and Kilistinons speaking a form of Montagnais of the lower Saint Lawrence, testifying even further to the well-traveled, diverse population of the western Great Lakes region. In the summer of 1667, Allouez traveled with a trading flotilla to Quebec—where he stayed for two whole days of consultation with Bishop Laval and his Jesuit superiors—and then returned to his far-distant vicariate in the company of Jesuit Louis Nicolas, carrying a pastoral letter from Laval in which he urged French traders in the area to behave well.

The following summer Allouez and Nicolas were joined by two more Jesuits, Father Jacques Marquette and Brother Louis Le Boesme. Four Jesuits now covered mission stations at Sault Sainte-Marie on the straits between Lakes Huron and Superior and La Pointe du Saint-Esprit on the western edge of Lake Superior. Allouez traveled to Quebec the next year to argue, successfully, for the establishment of missions at Green Bay and other sites. The Jesuits founded a full-fledged Ottawa mission, sending the veteran missionary Claude Dablon out to Sault Sainte-Marie to serve as superior of a western missionary region. Dablon assigned Marquette to La Pointe du Saint-Esprit, where, in preparation for a mission farther south, Marquette began to study the language of the Illinois.

In November 1669 the energetic Allouez and two French traders traveled by canoe to Green Bay, Wisconsin, on the western arm of Lake Michigan at the mouth of the Fox River, where some six hundred Potawatomies and Winnebagoes were passing the winter. Based out of Green Bay, Allouez evangelized throughout the area. Surviving on corn, acorns, and fish until May, he established Mission Saint Mark among the Foxes and began a study of two exotic regional languages, the Algonquian of the Menomonees and the Dakota-related Winnebago. By summer, back at Green Bay, he was working on a translation of the Lord's Prayer and the Hail Mary, along with a brief catechism, in these newly acquired tongues.

The Ottawa Mission, as the Jesuits designated this effort, grew steadily in preparation for its extension into the Illinois homeland. Veteran missionaries Gabriel Druillettes and Henry Nouvel arrived in 1671. A little later, Louis André joined the team and continued Allouez' work among Sacs, Potawatomies, Winnebagoes, and Menomonees at Green Bay, building the ambitious Church of Saint Francis Xavier in 1673. Druillettes evangelized among Chippewa, Kiskakon, and Mississauga. Marquette was reassigned to Saint Ignatius Mission at the onomatopoetically engaging Michilimackinac on the southern tip of Michigan's Upper Peninsula, where the waters of Lakes Michigan and Huron meet. There, Huron refugees began to converge from east and west; the stockade they eventually built resembled a small reduction. Allouez, meanwhile, a tireless evangelizer from whose original contacts so much of the Ottawa Mission originated, was building on his earlier visits with the Miamis on the southern shores of Lake Michigan, dividing his time between Mission Saint Joseph in the Miami homeland and Green Bay, where Jesuit missionary Anthony Silvy would also be assigned in 1675.

Exploring the Mississippi

Inextricably connected to French Catholic plans to advance evangelization and continental ambitions southward from the Great Lakes into Illinois country and beyond was the necessity to discover, inventory, and map the riverine waterways of the interior. River navigation offered the most convenient means of travel through these vast regions, especially in the minds of the French, whose very survival in New France had been determined by the Saint Lawrence. Under various names and through indefinite reports, such grand rivers as the Mississippi, Illinois, Iowa, Ohio, Missouri, and Arkansas (as they would later be named) were vaguely known or suspected to exist. What dazzling prospects! A pathway southward to the Gulf of Mexico. A river running east and northeast in the direction of Lakes Erie and Ontario that connected to the Saint Lawrence and the Atlantic. Or a river flowing west to the Pacific. What avenues for trade, settlement, and evangelization! While eastward and westward river systems connecting to the Atlantic and the Pacific did not exist, large and small rivers did converge on the great river whose lower reaches were discovered by the de Soto expedition in 1541 and then not exactly forgotten, but not precisely remembered, either, since a deceased de Soto was lowered into the river's depths or buried on its shoreline. The Mississippi survived, then, as a trace memory. The French even had an Indian name for it, *Mitchi* (great) *sipi* (water), and renamed it in honor of Minister of Marine Colbert.

Technocrats and planners Colbert and Talon, however, wanted more than vague reports or Indian names, especially now that on 4 June 1671 a delegation headed by Simon-François Daumont de Saint-Lusson had taken formal possession of the Ottawa and Illinois country for Louis XIV before a gathering of the leadership of fourteen Indian nations at Sault Sainte-Marie. And so in 1672 Intendant Talon devised a plan to send an exploring party in search of this mighty river to determine whether it existed and, if it did, whether it ran south, east, or west.

To lead this exploration, Talon (just before he returned to France) turned to the twenty-six-year-old Canadian-born fur trader and hydrographer Louis Jolliet, who had been part of the Saint-Lusson delegation at Sault Sainte-Marie the previous year. Frontenac confirmed the nomination, for he (along with everyone else) wanted to prosper in the fur trade. Among other reasons, Frontenac was eager to make political and commercial alliances with the up-and-coming generation of Canadian-born noblesse and aspiring noblesse who were making their mark in the colony. A variously accomplished young Canadian, Jolliet had originally intended to become a priest and had entered Laval's new seminary, where he pursued studies in classics and philosophy, winning praise for his proficiency in Latin debate. At the same time, he studied music and became an accomplished organist. Although he took tonsure and minor orders, Jolliet decided that the continent and not the Church would constitute the content and commitment of his career. To that end, assisted by a small burse from Laval, he spent a brief period of study in France (most likely hydrography—the study of seas, rivers, and lakes—as well as mapmaking and navigation) and then returned to Canada and entered the fur trade. He continued, however, to volunteer as cathedral organist when back in Quebec from one or another of his far-ranging business trips.

While Talon and Frontenac were long on assignments, the royal treasury was short of funds. Jolliet thus formed a combination of scientific society and investment circle to finance a minimal expedition—seven men, including Father Marquette of Michilimackinac, in two canoes—to explore and trade and, in Marquette's case, evangelize in territories unknown. The enterprise encapsulated and forwarded New France's commercial, religious, and continental ambitions of the past sixty-eight years.

Jolliet and Marquette had met each other at Sault Sainte-Marie. The Jesuit missionary, at thirty-five a mere seven or eight years older than Jolliet, was overjoyed when the exploring party reached Michilimackinac on 8 December 1672 and Jolliet presented him with a letter from his superior Claude Dablon to join the expedition. That is exactly what Marquette had been hoping to do for the past few years, ever since he first heard Illinois Indians discussing the great river to the south. From the day he entered the Society of Jesus at the age of seventeen, Marquette had wanted to become a missionary; indeed, while still a young seminarian, he wrote a letter to the father general in Rome to that effect, following it up seven years later with a request to skip the required course in theology and be sent at once to the foreign missions. The Society insisted, however, that Marquette receive at least one year of academic theology before ordination and language study in Canada, where he took his final vows in 1671 and was fluent in six Indian languages by 1673.

And so began the great exploration and discovery, for it was both: an exploration of where the mighty river was and discovery—at the insistence of Talon, Frontenac, and anyone at all interested in the fur trade—of whether this magnificent waterway emptied into the South Sea (the Pacific), thus creating a direct trade route to the Far East. From Michilimackinac the Jolliet-Marquette party canoed westward across the north shore of Lake Michigan, then along the west shore of Green Bay to Mission Saint-François-Xavier near present-day De Pere, Wisconsin. They then ventured down the Fox River to the Mascouten village, followed by a brief portage to the Rivière Meskousing (Wisconsin), which they entered for a journey of 118 miles for a total of 500 miles before the two canoes carrying the seven Frenchmen entered the great river and paddled southward into present-day Iowa, past herds of bison grazing serenely along shorelines of rolling prairies golden from the summer sun.

At the juncture of the Mississippi and Iowa Rivers, spying a pathway, the French landed their canoes and followed it to a village of Peoria Indians and thereby made their first contact with the Illinois people. A delegation greeted them. The Illinois were wearing cloth garments, which meant they had had prior contact, if only second- or thirdhand, with the French. The Indians offered the French calumets (ceremonial pipes, adorned in feathers) for smoking, then conducted them to their village for speeches on both sides, gift giving (a calumet and a young captive slave taken in a recent skirmish), and a feast. The French ate the fish, the buffalo, and the sagamité but turned down the roasted dog.

This auspicious beginning augured well for short-term prospects for trade and evangelization and long-term prospects for integration into New France. The idyll continued as the party passed the mouth of the Missouri and Ouabouskigou (Ohio) Rivers—the Ohio being 1,200 miles from Michilimackinac—and the Indians remained friendly. The farther south the French paddled from the Ohio, however, the more the landscape changed and the Indians began to run the gamut from unfriendly to hostile. Worse, Marquette's six languages ran out, and the French could no longer communicate with the increasingly inhospitable people on shore.

Thus they reached the intersection of the Arkansas River and the Mississippi some 450 miles south of the Ohio at the present-day boundary between Arkansas and Louisiana. Fearing Indian hostility or capture by Spaniards, Marquette somehow crossed the language barrier during a visit to the Quapaw village on the right bank of the Mississippi, where they were resting, and learned that the French were a mere fifty leagues from the sea (the Gulf of Mexico), which was actually more than 700 miles away. Satisfied that they had achieved their mission's goal—to explore the Mississippi as far as the Great Sea—and ever more afraid of the antagonistic Indians on the riverbanks, the French in mid-July 1673 turned their canoes upriver and retraced their route to the intersection with the Illinois River, portaged to the Chicago River, followed the western shore of Lake Michigan to present-day Sturgeon Bay, Wisconsin, portaged to Green Bay, and reached Mission Saint-François-Xavier at the southern end of the bay in mid-October.

Jolliet returned to a commercial career, married, rose in influence, and devoted significant time and energy to explorations of the Hudson Bay and Labrador, where he formed positive contacts with Eskimo residents, whom he described with precision and sympathy. Jolliet also raised a large family, acquired land, and continued his work as a hydrographer and mapmaker, teaching these subjects intermittently at the Jesuit college in Quebec.

Marquette, by contrast, suffered a breakdown in health on the journey of discovery, but by 1675 he believed that he had recovered sufficiently to return, as he had promised, to the Kaskaskia people in Illinois territory. Although dying, Marquette nevertheless managed to reach the Illinois River. There, on the shores of that river, on Holy Thursday 1675, Marquette preached to a circle of five hundred Illinois chiefs and elders and the fifteen hundred young braves standing behind them. Like so much of Marquette's ministry, the scene was larger than life, redolent of promise for a future of affiliated Catholic Indian commonwealths. Returning to Saint Ignatius Mission by canoe shortly after Easter, Marquette collapsed en route. Carried ashore, the veteran missionary and explorer expired at the mouth of the river that now bears his name.

La Salle completes the task

Seven years later, on 9 April 1682, René-Robert Cavelier, sieur de La Salle, having descended the great river to its mouth—thus proving its direct connection to the sea—took possession for Louis XIV of all lands watered by the Mississippi and its tributaries. In honor of the king, La Salle named this region Louisiana. Rouen born, a longtime Jesuit seminarian, an astute student of physics and mathematics as well as the usual ecclesiastical subjects, La Salle (like Marquette) had initially requested a missionary assignment. After nine years in the Society of Jesus, however, La Salle immigrated to Montreal, where his brother was serving as a Sulpician. He devoted the remainder of his life to exploration and (likewise like Jolliet, with the backing of Frontenac) entrepreneurship in the fur trade. What Jolliet might have been expected to do—explore and trade in the west and the south rather than the north—became La Salle's lifelong obsession. Mercurial, occasionally paranoid, tireless in his projects, and resilient in defeat, La Salle left a string of fortified trading posts in his wake—Fort Miami on the Saint Joseph River, Fort Crèvecoeur near Lake Peoria, Fort Saint-Louis on the Illinois River, a smaller trading post on the site of present-day Chicago—that, along with his completion of the exploration of the Mississippi, set the stage for inland development.

La Salle envisioned Louisiana as a colony separate from Quebec, with himself at the helm, and to that end he traveled to France and successfully received an appointment as governor of Louisiana and the string of forts he had created in the Illinois country. Through various mishaps and betrayals, however, the colonizing expedition La Salle led from France in 1684 was forced to land in present-day Matagorda Bay, Texas, under reduced circumstances instead of the four-hundred-strong settlement at the mouth of the Mississippi that had been planned. Mutiny broke out, and La Salle was assassinated by one of his own men. Despite this debacle, a riverine pathway from Montreal to the Gulf of Mexico now stood revealed, and the inland empire dreamt of, reconnoitered, and settled by La Salle lay open to continental ambition.

Evolutions in missionary approach

A half century after these momentous discoveries and sacred and secular foundations, Pierre-François-Xavier de Charlevoix was retracing a landscape of missionary and secular enterprise in search of answers to remaining riverine questions. Was there a river that flowed westward from the interior of the continent to the Pacific, and how far was the Pacific from the Great Lakes region and the midcontinent between Montreal and New Orleans claimed by France? These were Enlightenment as well as commercial and geopolitical questions, and Charlevoix was a philosophe of Enlightenment inclinations that were increasingly evident in French society and in the Society of Jesus and other Roman Catholic missionary groups. An earlier generation of missionaries might have considered the devil himself—Satan, Lucifer, Beelzebub, one or another of the fallen angels—to be at work in Native American religions. An Enlightenment generation, by contrast, might speculate as to what fragments of rationality and truth could be found in the indigenous religions. Cannibalism, promiscuity, theft, gourmandizing, and other offenses against the Ten Commandments remained unacceptable; and missionaries sought to bring massacre and the torturing of captives under control, a difficult task in a society dependent on recently Christianized Indian allies. There also emerged a tendency to view First Nations culture in a positive light and to put the best possible (Christian) interpretation on Native American religious practices.

In 1724 the French Jesuit philosophe Joseph-François Lafitau, a former missionary among the Iroquois of Sault Saint-Louis, published an encyclopedic study entitled *Moeurs des savages Américains comparés aux moeurs des premiers temps* (Customs of the American Indians compared with the customs of primitive times) in an attempt, Lafitau wrote in his preface, to dispel the notion—found even among some missionaries and honest men—that Native Americans lacked religion, law, social controls, and government. Not true, Lafitau argued, then went on to bolster his case with two volumes of comparative analysis of Native American and early societies, blending Enlightenment belief in the intrinsic rationality of all human beings with Augustinian and Thomistic insights into the natural capacity of human beings, created in the image and likeness of God, to sustain within themselves the imprint of that first creation and hence to develop religious sensibilities that could be brought to perfection by Christianity. Such attitudes differed radically from the earlier era's theory that Indian religion was a creation of the devil. Lafitau and Charlevoix belonged to the same Enlightenment-oriented Jesuit circles, and so it is no surprise that Lafitau influenced Charlevoix' hopefulness regarding prospects for a Catholicized and francophone Indian North America.

A half century before Lafitau published his monumental study, in fact, Jesuit missionaries such as Claude Allouez, Louis André, and their colleagues in the Great Lakes and Illinois region were moving toward this same Enlightenment ideal. As Creighton historian Tracy Neal Leavelle argues so compellingly in *The Catholic Calumet: Colonial Conversions in French and Indian North America* (2012), the missionary encounter was by the 1660s becoming a two-way dialogue, and nowhere was this more evident than in the matter of translations of the Credo, the Our Father, and the Hail Mary by Jesuit missionaries at once skilled and precise in their theology and adept in the Indian languages they mastered. The very fact that these languages could carry the essential meaning of scriptural and theologized concepts proved the wisdom of the Jesuit practice of mastering a language as early and as completely as possible. These languages also allowed Jesuit missionaries, as Leavelle demonstrates, to anchor and re-present orthodoxy within a context of Indian color, flavor, social psychology, and ambient value.

The Iroquois mission

That Lafitau, a former missionary among the Iroquois—the fiercest and most long-standing enemies of the French—could present such an ambitious work of cultural reconciliation within a Catholic context speaks for itself. Merely as a concept, the evangelization of the Five Nations (outside the few Neutrals in their midst) demanded from each side strong doses of faith, hope, charity, and forgiveness.

Despite their small numbers, the priests of Saint-Sulpice pioneered the Iroquois ministry, starting with the year-long reconnaissance through Iroquois and Ottawa country from July 1669 to June 1670 led by Sulpician François Dollier de Casson. Then serving as parish priest at Three Rivers, Dollier was convinced that a great opportunity for evangelization awaited the Montreal-based Gentlemen of Saint-Sulpice as missionaries to the recently subdued Iroquois and the Ottawa farther west and convinced his Sulpician superior, the Abbé Queylus, to authorize a civil and religious reconnaissance into these regions. Others had been there before, Dollier argued, but it was time for a fresh assessment in the wake of the recent treaty with the Iroquois. Thus twenty-two Europeans and a handful of Algonquian interpreters departed Montreal on 6 July 1669 bent upon reconnoitering this enormous area newly opened to French enterprise, sacred and secular, by what turned out to be a nearly twenty-year peace. The party included Dollier and the Sulpician deacon René Bréhaut de Galinée, who had some background as a geographer, and René-Robert Cavelier, sieur de La Salle, who falsely claimed competence in the Iroquois language.

When the party reached Lake Ontario in early August, however, La Salle admitted his ignorance. Fortunately, Iroquois returning homeward offered to guide the Sulpicians and La Salle as far south as present-day Hamilton, New York. There, La Salle, feigning illness, left the party to return to Montreal. In three canoes, the two Sulpicians and seven retainers reached the north shore of

Lake Erie, where they waited—and where on 23 March 1670 Dollier and Galinée raised a cross and claimed the region for Louis XIV. The next day they continued their journey southward. Storms, the loss of two canoes (and the fortunate recovery of another), and the loss of Galinée's journals and Dollier's portable altar and eucharistic wafers and wine for daily Mass ended the reconnaissance, and the Sulpician party returned to Montreal via the Detroit River, Lake Huron, Michilimackinac, and Georgian Bay, reaching Montreal on 18 June 1670. By then, Sulpicians François de Salignac de la Mothe-Fénelon and Claude Trouvé had established a mission among the Iroquois on the Bay of Quinté on Lake Ontario, where Trouvé served for the next twelve years.

A Mohawk saint

In the late 1660s and early 1670s, meanwhile, Christianized Mohawks were migrating into the Montreal area, seeking a close—but not too close—relationship with the French. On the banks of the Saint Lawrence opposite Montreal, the Mohawks built a traditional Iroquois village called Kahnawake, where they survived on farming, fishing, and hunting. Kahnawake was a Christian Catholic community in terms of basic beliefs and practices—no polygamy, no divorce, no premarital sex, every effort made to combat drunkenness—but its residents, as historian Allan Greer of the University of Toronto points out, made every effort to remain as independent and as Iroquois as possible within the adjustments demanded by their new religion.

To serve the Kahnawake community, the Jesuits established the nearby Mission Sault Saint-Louis, and while the *Jesuit Relations* ceased publication in 1673, one of the Jesuits assigned to the mission, Claude Chauchetière, describes life there in great detail in a surviving letter dated 14 October 1682 that editor Reuben Gold Thwaites included in volume 62 of *Jesuit Relations* published years later. Chauchetière outlines the daily routine of the Catholic Mohawks of Kahnawake in generally idyllic terms and obliquely introduces an unnamed young female Mohawk convert of exemplary piety. Following her death at age twenty-four, the young woman's Jesuit confessor, Pierre Cholenec, wrote her biography— Catherine Tekakwitha was her name. By the time Charlevoix was writing his *History* a half century later, Catherine Tekakwitha had become such an important part of the evangelization story of New France that Charlevoix included a full chapter on her life based on Cholenec's account.

Through religious faith and practice, Tekakwitha and her small group of consecrated Catholic Mohawk women bridged the abyss of hatred and violence that separated the cultures on either side of the Saint Lawrence. Cholenec's biography of Catherine Tekakwitha is almost medieval in its account of the young woman's Cinderella childhood and adolescence as an orphan born in 1656 and raised in the household of her uncle and aunt following the death of her parents, a pagan Mohawk chief and a Christian Algonquian, and her younger brother in the great smallpox epidemic of the early 1660s. Catherine survived but was left with facial scars and impaired eyesight. Shy and reclusive, she kept to her household tasks but listened attentively to the conversation and teachings of the Jesuit missionaries who visited the household in the Mohawk settlement of Ossernenon (present-day Auriesville, New York). In a sense, she converted herself through careful listening and was then further instructed and baptized by Jesuit missionary Jacques de Lamberville. She also preserved her chastity and on one occasion dramatically avoided marriage by walking out of an arranged meeting with a prospective bridegroom. A leading family's resentment for this act prompted her move to the Christian Iroquois mission of Sault Saint-Louis.

At this point, the medieval French dimension of the Catherine Tekakwitha story—pious young orphan works hard, loves God, becomes a Christian, retains her chastity—took on a more Iroquois dimension. Catherine and a group of other religiously inclined Mohawk women, married and single alike, formed a spiritual warrior sisterhood that emphasized, in an Iroquois sort of way, the endurance of self-inflicted suffering—hair shirts, iron rings with sharp points worn as belts (*ceintures de fer*), lying naked in a snowstorm (not Catherine, but a pregnant married woman), or standing in ice water while praying the Rosary—to share in the sufferings of Jesus Christ and to follow the example of European saints who did likewise in atonement for sin. In his letter, Father Chauchetière reported on these practices with a sense of tension verging on open disapproval. The Native American dévots were clearly Iroquoian in their ability to bear pain publicly as a sign of religious commitment. The lot of an Iroquois woman was never easy. This new religion, these women believed, should not be easy, either.

The example of the Hospitaller Sisters of Saint Joseph at Montreal provided Catherine (and perhaps the others as well) a more measured model of religious life. Still, key to Catherine's religiosity was her older female Mohawk mentor in the Catholic faith, Anastasia Tegonhatsihongo. Tegonhatsihongo helped introduce the neophyte to a modality of Christianity that was at once positively Iroquois and Roman Catholic in spirit, which flowered in Catherine Tekakwitha as—like Thérèse of Lisieux in a later era—she grew in spiritual maturity during her brief life of twenty-four years. In death, this Lily of the Mohawks, as Catherine became known, was soon revered for her contemplative character, her devotion to the Eucharist, and her rapport with nature as touched by divinity, as expressed by her delight in birds and trees and the wildflowers she gathered for the altar. In a process as old as Christianity itself, what was local and particular and Iroquois in Catherine's instinctive spirituality not only survived but thrived as it was subsumed into her new religion, and her Jesuit mentors, grateful for this cross-cultural connection, transcribed the record of her life and promoted her memory as a Roman Catholic saint.

Enter the Recollects

Like Frontenac, René-Robert Cavelier de La Salle was no fan of the Jesuits, having left the Society of Jesus after a nine-year and increasingly unhappy membership; and like Frontenac, La Salle turned to Recollect Franciscans as his order of choice for Quebec. The Capuchin Franciscans of Acadia, the single largest order in New France at the time, were a power unto themselves on the coast. The Gentlemen of Saint-Sulpice, by contrast, never totaled more than sixteen or so in Canada during the seventeenth century. Nonetheless, the aristocratic, wealthy, and well-connected Sulpicians were literally and spiritually the seigneurs of Montreal and hence masters of their own destiny. Members of the Paris Foreign Missions Society likewise were few in number, although they enjoyed a strong connection to Bishop Laval (one of their founders) and his seminary in Quebec, to which their society was affiliated. The Recollects, however, were neither as numerous or politically connected as the Capuchins and Jesuits, nor as rich and entitled as the Sulpicians, nor as episcopally sponsored as the Paris Foreign Missions Society and secular clergy. The Recollects were therefore eager to expand their horizons. Recollects had served as the pioneer clergy of New France, and their expulsion by the British in 1629, followed by Richelieu's refusal to allow them to return, had represented a blow to both their self-esteem and their chances for political influence. When that ban was lifted in 1670, the Recollects joyfully returned to the colony of Quebec, in which the king and his ministers were taking renewed interest, now that it was governed directly by the Crown. Back in Quebec, the Recollects, while never formally challenging Bishop Laval and the Jesuits, oriented themselves to the governor general, the intendant, and regional officials, serving them and habitants as sympathetic confessors and colorful preachers. Between 1670 and 1678 the Recollects were confined to their convent at Notre-Dame-des-Anges outside Quebec. In 1678, however, they received permission to establish a chapel in the city proper. Over time, the Recollects gained parishes and chaplaincies in garrisons, an assignment traditionally restricted to secular priests. In short, the Recollects practiced a sort of freelance Franciscanism, an alternative Catholicism that remained orthodox yet was more popular and accepting—call it a clerical bohemianism—that existed in tension with the authority of the bishop, the diocesan clergy, and the Jesuits. At the same time, these Franciscans were sensitive to power, especially civil power, which constituted their source of protection against the diocese and the Society of Jesus.

Into this context must be placed the most enigmatic, idiosyncratic, talented, and rebellious priest to function (however briefly) in New France during the seventeenth century. Belgian by birth, a butcher's son, French by education in a French grammar school and as a member of the French Recollects, which he joined at seventeen, Louis Hennepin after ordination embarked upon a career as a wandering cleric. His chosen way of life had characterized such diverse figures as Erasmus and Rabelais during the Renaissance but had become increasingly rare following the reforms inaugurated by the Council of Trent. Once ordained, Hennepin studied Flemish, living in his sister's home in Ghent, then went on a self-assigned pilgrimage to Rome to share his desire for a missionary career with the proper authorities, who sent him back to his province via a tour of sanctuaries and monasteries in Italy and Germany. Assigned to a peripatetic ministry as a preacher along the Calais coast, Hennepin by his own admission used to frequent local taverns to overhear sailors' stories of the distant ports of call he so sorely wished to visit. Between 1672 and 1674 he served as a Hospitaller and chaplain in Maastricht during the French invasion of the Netherlands. Late May 1675 found him at sea in the company of four other Flemish Recollects the king was sending to New France, having accidentally acquired their services through his conquest of Flanders. (Also on board was another enigmatic wanderer, René-Robert Cavelier, sieur de La Salle, returning from a trip of self-promotion to France.) Hennepin spent the following year as an itinerant preacher along the Saint Lawrence, and then, in the spring of 1676, he achieved his goal: an assignment as one of two missionaries to serve Fort Frontenac on the eastern end of Lake Ontario (present-day

Kingston, Ontario), where Hennepin and his confrere Luc Buisset built a mission and began ministering to the Iroquois.

Hennepin, however, was not to spend the rest of his career—or even much of it—as an apostle to the Iroquois or any other Indian tribe. His sojourn at Fort Frontenac lasted less than two years. That brief period was time enough, however, for the Recollect friar to come into further contact with La Salle, seigneur since 1675 of the former Fort Cataracoui, which La Salle renamed Fort Frontenac in honor of the governor-general who had helped him secure this grant and with whom he was partnering in the fur trade. Returning in 1678 from yet another successful lobbying effort in France, La Salle secured permission from the Crown to establish trading posts at the entrance to Lake Erie and the southern edge of Lake Michigan where it discharged into the Illinois River and to explore western North America between New France, Florida, and Mexico.

Through the Recollect provincial, La Salle recruited Hennepin and the two Recollects stationed at Fort Frontenac, Gabriel de La Ribourde and Zénobe Membré, to the expedition. Hennepin joined the advance element—sixteen men in a ten-ton brigantine under the command of the sieur Dominique La Motte de Lucière—which reached the Niagara River on 6 December 1678 (Hennepin intoned a Te Deum of thanksgiving) and the Lewiston Mountain Ridge (Hennepin carved his name on a rock) and from there climbed up Queenstown Heights until on 8 December Niagara Falls came into view. In his *Description de la Louisiane* (1683), Hennepin describes the falls as "the most beautiful and altogether the most terrifying waterfall in the universe", as if the very power of the North American continent were being unleashed in cataracts of thunder. Champlain had depicted the falls on his map of 1632. The Jesuits Jérôme Lalemant and Paul Ragueneau mentioned the falls in the *Relations* of 1641 and 1648, respectively. But now the newcomer Recollect Louis Hennepin, who had for so long dreamt of beholding marvels in distant lands, and his companions were the first recorded Europeans to behold Niagara Falls in all its awesome splendor and to found a fortified house on the Niagara River above the falls. As Francis Parkman notes in his account of the discovery, whoever controlled the Niagara River controlled the entrance into the four Great Lakes above, and hence controlled a significant portion of the North American continent.

To that end, while Hennepin returned to Fort Frontenac to bring back the two Recollects waiting there, the French constructed a forty-five-ton bark—the *Griffon*, named in honor of Frontenac's coat of arms—in an inlet to the Niagara River. On 7 August 1679 thirty men and the three Recollect friars sailed into Lake Erie. Moving through Lake Erie and Lake Huron, La Salle guided the *Griffon* into the strait between Lakes Huron and Michigan, went ashore briefly at Saint Ignatius Mission at Michilimackinac, and then crossed Lake Michigan to Green Bay, where he traded for enough furs to fill the *Griffon*, which he sent back to Michilimackinac before proceeding south with fourteen men, including Hennepin and La Ribourde. On 1 November La Salle arrived at the mouth of the Saint Joseph River, where he built another fortified station, and then ascended the river and portaged to the Kankakee, which led to the Illinois. In early January 1680 the expedition reached the Illinois Indian village of Pimitoui near present-day Peoria. While La Salle busied himself with constructing yet another installation, Fort Crèvecoeur, Hennepin tells us that La Salle dispatched him and two companions as an advance guard toward the Mississippi, while La Salle returned to Michilimackinac to search for the *Griffon*, which was now missing.

At this point in his narrative of these events, Hennepin makes the claim that has since compromised his reputation: namely, that between 29 February and 25 March 1680 he and his two companions, Michel Accault and Antoine Auguel, descended the Mississippi to its mouth and then paddled upstream to the Illinois River, where they were captured by a canoe convoy of Sioux. Impossible, Parkman and others have pointed out, based on time-distance analysis. No one could make that journey in a mere thirty days. Hennepin was mistaken, delusional, lying, or a combination thereof due to his obsession with La Salle. Following La Salle's death in 1687, Hennepin updated each new edition of the several editions of his best-selling *Description de la Louisiane* to expand his own role in the expedition. The other sequences of Hennepin's narrative, Parkman argues in his *La Salle and the Discovery of the Great West* (1869), pass muster. The discovery of Niagara Falls, the voyages across the Great Lakes, the capture by Sioux, the subsequent descent by the Sioux war party down the Mississippi to Saint Anthony Falls in present-day Minneapolis, his half year of captivity among the Sioux as a member of the household of Chief Ouasi-coudé and his six wives: all this actually occurred, Parkman admits, although Hennepin was characteristically prone to exaggeration (regarding the estimated height of Niagara Falls, for example). But Hennepin increasingly gave himself equal billing with La Salle in subsequent years and editions, as if to dramatize himself as the great explorer he had always wanted to be.

Parkman also notes a lack of evangelical ambition in Hennepin's depiction of his life among the Sioux. Parkman, though, does not mention that reaching the Sioux, evangelizing this near-mythical people on the far western frontier, had long been an ambition of the French missionary effort. But Hennepin was Flemish, not French, and in the years to come, having returned to Europe, he would with Belgian flexibility unsuccessfully promote vague colonizing projects with French, Dutch, and English interests alike. Even with that said, however, Hennepin's harsh opinion of the Native American cannot help but shock the modern reader, especially when placed in the context of Catholic missionary outreach touched by Enlightenment value. Did Hennepin's experience among the Sioux cause this negative attitiude? Or the assassination by Kickapoos of his colleague Gabriel de La Ribourde as that elderly Recollect, thinking he was among friends, sat beneath the trees reading his breviary? For conversion to occur on a significant scale, Hennepin argues in his second of three books, *Nouvelle découverte d'un très grand pays* (A new discovery of a vast country), published in Utrecht in 1697, Native Americans—for whom Hennepin confesses outright contempt—would have to be forcibly concentrated and brought into closer contact with a more Europeanized North America, to become more densely populated through immigration. This, Hennepin maintains, had always been the Recollect position. "Our ancient missionary Recollects of Canada," he writes, "and those that succeeded them in that work, have always given it for their opinion, and I now own 'tis mine, that the way to succeed in converting the Barbarians, is to endeavor to make them men before we go about to make them Christians."

No talk here of shared humanity or common ground offered by the Native American concept of a Creator, a Great Manitou beyond the lesser manitous, a concept bridging cultures through the basics of natural theology. "We must all of us own," he argues, "that almost all the savages in general have no belief of a Deity, and that they are incapable of the common and ordinary arguments and reasonings that the rest of mankind are led by upon this subject; so dark and stupid are their understandings." Later in the course of this diatribe, Hennepin links the religion of the Indian shaman, such as it is, to diabolism. With relish, he catalogues the alleged stupidity and barbarism of Native Americans in a rant worthy of the contemporarily overused term *racist*. Not one aspect of Indian culture earns his praise. "Hence, 'tis manifest", he continues, "that the office of missionary is very troublesome and laborious amongst these numerous nations, and it must be granted that 'tis necessary to spend many years, and undergo a great deal of pains to civilize people so extremely stupid and barbarous." Detention, concentration, agriculturalization, and quasi-Europeanization must precede Christianization, Hennepin opines. "They should be fixed, enticed to clear the ground, and cultivate it, and work at several trades, as the Europeans do; and then we should see them reform their barbarous customs, and become more civilized, as well toward one another as us."[3]

The Mississippi valley

In the late seventeenth and first half of the eighteenth centuries, the presence of Roman Catholic people in the Great Lakes, Mississippi valley, and lower Louisiana, as encountered by Charlevoix in 1721–1722, grew so dramatically that a contemporary reader must turn to John Gilmary Shea's *The Catholic Church in Colonial Days* (1886) as a Baedeker's guide to whom and what Charlevoix found and recorded in his *Journal* (1744). Also of value are the annotations of Louise Phelps Kellogg for the Caxton Club edition of the *Journal* (2 volumes, 1923). From such a survey, augmented by subsequent scholarship, a scenario emerges even more clearly of how the religious and continental ambitions of French Catholic Canada pioneered a region that with the Louisiana Purchase of 30 April 1803 doubled the size of the fledgling American republic and became its heartland.

In contrast to Hennepin, Charlevoix has a respectful interest in the Indian societies he encounters, even when he considers some of their practices barbaric, such as the Seneca's torturing prisoners to death. Indeed, Charlevoix seems fascinated with the warfare operations of the Seneca; he includes in his *Journal* an almost clinical presentation of their torturing and execution methods. Exhaustive as well are his efforts to compile a natural history of the flora, fauna, and geography of the regions through which he is passing. He references other writers frequently, as when he beholds Niagara Falls for the first time and, after a brief statement of approval, discusses Lahontan's and Hennepin's erroneous measurements. While its volume of data constitutes the value of Charlevoix' *Journal* as an Enlightenment encounter with the midcontinent, sheer information frequently overwhelms the narrative, thus putting the *Journal* at a disadvantage when compared with the swiftly moving accounts of Lahontan and Hennepin, however biased and off base these writers can become. Still, Charlevoix was a savant, loving information for its own sake. His exhaustive notes on the coastlines, distances, and latitudes of the Great Lakes, for example—handed over to hydrographer Jacques-Nicolas Bellin—resulted in new and more complete maps of the region.

From Niagara Falls to Detroit (founded in 1701) to Michilimackinac—where he sojourned through July 1721 and made every effort to verify inconclusive reports of a great river that flowed to the west and emptied into the South Sea (the Pacific)—to Fort Saint Joseph on the Saint Joseph River (present-day Niles, Michigan), where he spent time with the Miami: as Charlevoix traveled southward, he never once left the boundaries of the Jesuit vicariate established by Bishop Saint-Vallier in 1690 with the appointment of Jesuit missionary Jacques Gravier as vicar general of this midcontinental region. At the Cahokia mission on the Mississippi at the mouth of the Missouri River (present-day East Saint Louis), however, which he reached in early October, enjoying en route the sight of great buffalo herds on the shoreline, Charlevoix met two of his former students from the Quebec college, the Abbés Dominique-Antoine-René Thaumur de La Source and Jean-Paul Mercier, two seminary (secular) priests assigned to the mission. When this seminary mission to the Tamaroa was first proposed in 1698, the Jesuits went into open and acrimonious opposition. The Quebec seminary was affiliated with the seminary of the Paris Foreign Missions Society, and in China a great rivalry had broken out between the Jesuits and the Foreign Missions Society over questions of rites and jurisdiction. The Jesuits saw no conflict between Catholic Christianity and Confucianism or reverence paid to ancestors, which the Foreign Missions Society priests considered idolatrous. Even more threatening, the Jesuits feared that the Paris seminary, backed as it was by a Gallican-oriented hierarchy, wanted to replace the Society of Jesus entirely in China and elsewhere in the Far East. It now appeared to the Jesuits of New France that the seminaries of Paris and Quebec were planning a similar move against the hegemony the Jesuits enjoyed over the Mississippi valley.

When Bishop Saint-Vallier approved of the entrance of seminary priests and three of them, including the Abbé Saint-Cosme, located themselves among the Tamaroa, the Canadian Jesuits took their cause to Rome and Versailles, but Saint-Vallier held fast to his decision, sailing to France in 1700 to lobby successfully on behalf of his policies. One small mission on the Mississippi had taken on global implications. In their fierce opposition to Saint-Vallier, the Jesuits branded him a scoundrel, a hater of the Society of Jesus, and a heretical Jansenist. The latter was evident in the catechism and liturgical guidebook he wrote for the diocese, which—seizing upon certain printer's errors in these books—the Jesuit superior in Quebec charged, included traces of Arianism (the Son was not coequal with the Father) and Pelagianism (an overreliance on human effort toward salvation), along with touches of Lutheranism and Calvinism. An outraged Saint-Vallier appealed to the Sorbonne and won a judgment against these charges. He also corrected the typos in question in new editions.

The Jesuits went equally into alert when Antoine de La Mothe, sieur de Cadillac, commandant of Detroit, and seigneur for the projected settlement, announced what can with some justification be described as the Hennepin plan: the consolidation at Detroit of Christianized Huron and Ottawas from Michilimackinac, Miamis from the Saint Joseph River, and other western Indian converts and their organization into settlements and defensive militia units, with missionaries teaching the young men and Ursulines teaching the young women, many of whom would marry French husbands. Cadillac, Shea tells us, considered himself a Moses leading these Catholicized Indians into a new Franco-Indian way of life. Beholding what

NEW FRANCE

they considered a threat to their plan for a network of Catholicized tribal enclaves under their guidance, the Jesuits opposed the plan and went into a posture of passive resistance.

Cadillac, however, was a persuasive proponent of consolidation, which remained voluntary, and within a few years—to the distress of the Jesuits—many Christianized Huron, Ottawas, and Miamis relocated to Detroit, an area then and thereafter under the care of the Recollects. By 1703 only the Jesuit mission at Green Bay remained in full operation. Meanwhile, the Fox nation went on the warpath, further destabilizing the situation. Recovery of the Jesuit mission began within the next five years, but by that time the Recollects had firmly established themselves at Detroit and elsewhere in the areas around Lakes Erie and Huron, while seminary and Foreign Missions Society priests (and, later, Capuchin Franciscans) established themselves in the Illinois country and Louisiana on the lower Mississippi. The Jesuits remained, but not as the exclusive agents of missionary outreach intended to save souls as well as create Indian alliances that would block English incursions into the trans-Appalachian west.

Taking and holding Louisiana

But what about Louisiana on the lower Mississippi? La Salle's failure in 1637 to found a colony at the mouth of the Mississippi left a void in French claims to the region. To address this problem, the minister of marine dispatched the renowned soldier and naval captain Pierre Le Moyne d'Iberville, the first (and thus far the only) Canadian-born officer to be invested as a Knight of Saint Louis, France's highest military honor. Born and raised in the frontier outpost of Ville-Marie, one of eleven sons and two daughters of a wealthy fur trader, the Indian-language linguist and frontier warrior Charles Le Moyne, Pierre Le Moyne d'Iberville epitomized the coming of age of a late seventeenth-century generation of self-made Canadian-born seigneurs adept in business, governance, and a military prowess that was half-French, half-Indian in its ruthlessness and skilled assurance of command on land or sea.

In 1686, at age twenty-five, Iberville joined two of his brothers as leaders of a company to drive the English from the drainage basin of Hudson Bay. In 1690 he joined Frontenac's war against English border settlements. In 1695 he commanded the campaign against English settlements on the Atlantic coast. Next up, in 1696–1697: a campaign to drive the English from Labrador. In each campaign, Iberville showed courage and tactical panache as well as a habit of trading on his own account in salted cod or furs whenever possible. Militarily, he exhibited the pitiless take-no-prisoners attitude developed by Canadians across seventy-five years of brutal warfare with the Iroquois and other Indian enemies.

Iberville's record for ruthlessness speaks for itself. In the attack on Corlear (Schenectady, New York) on 19 February 1690, made in retaliation for the Iroquois raid on Lachine, Iberville was second in command. Sixty inhabitants were massacred. At Fort York, Hudson's Bay, during the winter of 1694–1695, Iberville expelled his English prisoners into the wilderness, where they died of cold, starvation, or scurvy. In Newfoundland, 1696, with the resumption of the Atlantic campaign under Iberville's command, thirty-six settlements were destroyed, two hundred people killed, and seven hundred English taken prisoner. In each instance Iberville found time and opportunity to do his own business, for that also is a characteristic of the Canadian nobility, raised since childhood on fur trade and fishing.

Take this society, church and state, to Louisiana, the minister of marine commissioned Iberville in 1697 following his return from yet another expedition to Hudson's Bay. Reclaim the province Jolliet, Marquette, and La Salle claimed for France! Iberville left the port of Brest in late October 1698 in command of an exploratory expedition of four vessels and a garrison (as opposed to settlement) force. On 2 March 1699 the French flotilla was driven by a storm into the Birdfoot subdelta of the Mississippi. When local Indians shared with him objects presented to them by La Salle, Iberville declared himself satisfied that he had indeed reached the mouth of the great river. He built a temporary fort on Biloxi Bay (present-day Ocean Springs, Mississippi), garrisoned it with eighty-one men, and returned to France to recruit further support from the minister of marine and be invested with his knighthood of Saint Louis. Iberville went back to the gulf in October 1699 with the best support the minister of marine could manage: a second exploratory expedition. Establishing Fort Mississippi forty miles upstream from Biloxi, Iberville set about negotiating the support of local tribes while acquiring nine thousand pelts from trappers now trading in Louisiana rather than Montreal after hearing of the new fort and trading post on Biloxi Bay.

Iberville was reprising on the lower Mississippi the founding of Quebec on the Saint Lawrence. When the merchants of Montreal learned that Iberville—one of their own!—had sold nine thousand pelts in New York on his second return to France, they launched an anti-Louisiana lobbying campaign, building on Colbert's small-but-strong-colony agenda for Quebec. Could such a vast and decentralized empire be managed? they asked. The merchants had a point. Despite Iberville's third expedition to the gulf (where he arrived in late 1701) and the founding of a trading and naval station, Fort Louis (present-day Mobile, Alabama), progress was slow and immigration virtually nonexistent. Hence Indian alliances remained key if France were to hold Louisiana for future settlement, and thus Iberville—assisted in this regard by La Salle's loyal lieutenant, Henri Tony, who enjoyed excellent Indian contacts—aligned himself with the attempt to station at least one missionary priest with each large or influential tribe in the region. In 1702 Iberville was called to service in the West Indies, where in typical fashion he would lay waste to the English-held island of Nevis, the garden island of the Caribbean. (He had not been forced to resort to similar tactics during his assignment to Louisiana.) The deputy governor, Iberville's able younger brother Jean-Baptiste Le Moyne, sieur de Bienville, continued to support Iberville's one-tribe-one-priest program in the ongoing effort to hold Louisiana following the Treaty of Ryswick (1697), which ended the War of the Grand Alliance and left Louisiana in French possession.

Thus the Louisiana mission experienced an eclectic mix of clergy in the years leading up to the founding of New Orleans in 1718 as the slow progress of civil settlement necessitated an Indian-oriented, missionary-driven policy of containment. Seminary and Foreign Missions Society priests expanded their ministry to the Cahokias and other tribes on the lower Mississippi and in September 1704 opened the first canonically erected parish in the western country, the Church of the Immaculate Conception at Fort Louis, under the pastorate of Foreign Missions

Society priest Albert Davion, one of the three pioneers of the Tamaroa mission and
a veteran of missionary outreach to the Tonica, Ounspik, and Yazoo on the lower
Mississippi. By this time, seminary priest François Jolliet de Montigny was ministering to the Taensa, a tribe allied to the Natchez, to whom the ill-fated Abbé de
Saint-Cosme would soon be ministering.

New Orleans gets under way

As peace drew near on another prolonged conflict between France and England—
the War of the Spanish Succession (1701–1714), ended by the Treaty of Utrecht—a
thoroughly broke Louis XIV, forced to sell even the silverware at Versailles to
finance this latest struggle, granted wealthy financier Antoine Crozat a fifteen-
year monopoly on rights to commercial activities in Louisiana. Crozat had already
proven himself as a commercial developer in the French West Indies, and the
Crown hoped that he could do the same for lower and upper Louisiana—promote
immigration from France and the importation of slaves from the West Indies, as
well as the fur trade and agriculture—while the Crown bore the costs of defense
and day-to-day government. Halfway through his fifteen-year monopoly, Crozat,
finding the venture unprofitable, bowed out in favor of Scots speculator John Law's
newly formed Company of Louisiana. To assist this new effort, the minister of
marine appointed Jean-Baptiste Le Moyne, sieur de Bienville, as permanent governor (his older brother Pierre Le Moyne d'Iberville had died in Havana in 1706), a
post he would ably hold for forty years.

In 1717 Bienville began to plan a new city, New Orleans, named in honor of
the regent, the duc d'Orléans, to be developed on an island on the east bank of the
Mississippi, 107 miles from its mouth. The city was laid out by engineer Pierre Le
Blond de la Tour as a parallelogram, divided into streets and squares. Buoyed by
the boom of the John Law years, a fleet of seven vessels full of immigrants landed
in 1718, which is usually given as the founding year of the city, followed by eleven
more ships the next year. In 1719 more than five hundred slaves from the Guinea
coast arrived, thereby establishing a major difference between Louisiana and Quebec, whose economy was not dependent on African slave labor.

To this fledgling city Charlevoix, nearing the end of his research, came in early
January 1722 and reported on New Orleans with a mixture of accuracy and boost-
erism in the thirty-first letter of his *Journal*. From New Orleans Charlevoix began a
year-long process of return to France, where he arrived on 26 December 1722 and
twenty-five days later made the first of two official reports to the minister of marine.

Charlevoix' ancillary reports on the needs of the Church in the Illinois country
and Louisiana also furthered a momentum already under way. On 16 May 1722 a
declaration by the council of the Company of the West, successor to the Company
of Louisiana, announced Bishop Saint-Vallier's approval of the creation of two
vicariates on the Mississippi: the first, north of the Ohio down to Natchez, was to
be administered by the Society of Jesus and the priests of the Quebec and Foreign
Missions Society seminaries; the second, for the French settlements developing on
or near the mouth of the Mississippi, was to be administered directly from Paris by
auxiliary bishop Louis-François Duplessis de Mornay, a Capuchin Franciscan, who
for the time being would remain in Paris. Thus was created another differentiating

distinction for Louisiana. Capuchins—the largest and most popular religious order in France—took up a New Orleans–based, government- and company-supported ministry in Louisiana reporting directly to a Capuchin bishop in Paris. This structure meant that Church affairs in Louisiana would boast a high level of autonomy—independence from Quebec, for all practical purposes—as the Capuchins expanded into Mobile and other nearby settlements.

Not that secular priests or priests of other orders were restricted from a New Orleans ministry. Far from it. Jesuits and Ursulines, who were so important to the development of Catholicism in early Quebec, made their appearance in the city in 1727. As in Quebec one hundred years earlier, family creation and education formed the core of their ministry. Wives and young women of marriageable age were slow to arrive in Louisiana in these early years, and (as Intendant Talon had done on behalf of Quebec) Bienville returned to France in 1724 and began to arrange a recruitment program. That meant nuns were needed to supervise the marriage program, set up a school for girls, and conduct a hospital. In France to recruit missionaries, Jesuit vicar general Nicholas Ignatius de Beaubois successfully added to his portfolio the recruitment of Ursulines from Rouen: seven professed nuns under the direction of Mother Mary Tranchepain of Saint Augustine, a convert from Calvinism whom the Company of the West agreed to send to New Orleans, along with four servants. It took an arduous six and a half months, from 2 January to 23 July 1727, for the Ursulines to reach the mouth of the Mississippi, which they ascended via pirogue and a sloop in the company of their Jesuit escorts. Arriving in New Orleans on 6 August, the nuns established themselves in a large house vacated on their behalf by Governor Bienville, where they lived for the next seven years. On 17 July 1734 the Ursulines moved to a superb new convent (which still stands, the first and oldest convent in the present-day United States) in an elaborate public ceremony led by Governor Bienville and other government officials, followed by a vested priest holding the Blessed Sacrament in a gold monstrance beneath a portable canopy. Behind them came a procession of orphans and day scholars bearing lit tapers—including several little girls dressed as angels and a young lady of twelve costumed as Saint Ursula—and a throng of supportive citizens. Bells rang, and the military provided fife-and-drum accompaniment as the procession entered the chapel of the new structure. The following month, under the supervision of head infirmarian Mother Saint Xavier Hébert, a new hospital—financed by the Crown and the company on behalf of the military but also serving as a general hospital for the city—was inaugurated with appropriate ceremony. A separate school building was later added to this complex.

Thus within twelve years of Charlevoix' visit, the motley collection of shacks that had so disappointed him had become a well-planned town graced—thanks to the Ursulines and company and Crown support—by a well-run hospital, a boarding school for girls, an academy for day scholars, an orphanage, and a school program for the African children who were becoming increasingly more numerous. Louisiana's reliance on black slavery introduced a relationship between Catholicism and African people, slave and free, that would grow in complexity in a religious community that up until the Civil War was predominately southern in population and considered Baltimore its primal see.

The massacre at Fort Rosalie on 28 November 1729 did not put New Orleans in immediate danger. Paradoxically, the massacre served to unify the tribes of

Louisiana and the Mississippi valley who were mobilized by the French against the Natchez and their allies among the Chickasaw. This campaign was administered out of New Orleans as well as fought in the field, and it added to the city's importance. In 1731 Louisiana reverted to the status of a crown colony. The following year, it was administratively separated into upper and lower provinces. During this period, New Orleans continued to develop as capital city of the colony, as Bienville officially declared it in 1722. More than a hundred years would pass before any Great Lakes, midcontinental, or gulf city achieved such urbanism. Thus the great chief Chicagou of the Michigamea Illinois, having visited Versailles in 1725 to pay his respects to young King Louis XV, found it appropriate five years later to journey downriver to New Orleans to pay comparable respects to French officials in His Majesty's Louisiana capital.

History accomplished

Perhaps Chief Chicagou had an opportunity to meet with Charlevoix during his Versailles visit, for the intrepid Jesuit was back in Paris as of early 1723, as busy as ever, this time writing a biography of Marie de l'Incarnation, which he finished in 1723 for a 1724 publication. The report that Charlevoix made to the minister of marine in 1723 was tentative and erroneous. Charlevoix stated that the western sea in question most likely existed between 40 and 50 degrees latitude and that the Sioux lived nearby. (Charlevoix went so far as to volunteer to serve as a missionary to the Sioux if no other Jesuits were available.) Also, near the headwaters of the Missouri, Charlevoix went on, rivers flowing westward to the Pacific could most likely be found. He was wrong on each point, as would eventually be disclosed. In one sense, he did not have much to show for two and a half years of arduous travel. But no matter. Charlevoix was a geographer, but even more, he was a variously learned man of letters interested in natural history, the history of his order, and the history of New France. He was a tireless editor as well. Thus Charlevoix took up his pen to write the Marie de l'Incarnation biography, followed by a two-volume *Histoire de l'isle espagnole* (1730–1731). He then expanded into two volumes his shorter history of the Jesuits in Japan (1736) and began to gather material for a three-volume history of the Jesuits in Paraguay (1756). In the midst of all this, he edited for twenty years the respected Jesuit monthly *Mémoires pour servir à l'histoire des sciences et des beaux-arts* (Reflections serving the history of science and fine arts), more commonly known as the *Journal de Trévoux*.

All the while, one can presume, he was also working intermittently on the journal of his 1720–1722 journey to New France as well as a six-volume history of the colony. In this regard, the *Journal*, cast in the form of letters to a highborn lady (as was common in that era)—in this case, thirty-six missives to the duchesse de Lesdiguières, the niece of Madame de Montespan—and the *History*, dedicated to the duc de Penthière, suggest that the highly sociable Jesuit was maintaining his high-level social and professional contacts. Indeed, the minister of marine personally granted Charlevoix permission to keep archival documents for his history of New France in his room at the Collège Louis-le-Grand, where he did his writing. In 1742 the Society of Jesus appointed Charlevoix procurator (business agent) in Paris for the Jesuit missions and Ursuline convents in New France and Louisiana.

Charlevoix became busier than ever (he held this post until 1749), for the procuracy was 40,000 livres in debt, and Charlevoix was now responsible for raising or borrowing not only current operating funds but also funds to retire the debt.

This new role, however demanding, might have focused his energies on bringing to completion and publication in 1744 the long-delayed *Histoire et description générale de la Nouvelle France, avec le Journal historique d'un voyage fait par ordre du roi dans l'Amérique septentrionale*, nine volumes in all: six volumes for the *History* and three for the *Journal*. As procurator for Jesuits in New France, Charlevoix stood authenticated as the outstanding authority regarding the natural and human history of matters Canadian. The resources of five Paris printers were needed to produce these volumes, prized to this day as history and natural history on a grand scale as well as fine examples of eighteenth-century typography and engraving. Voltaire praised the work of his former dormitory proctor. The Encyclopedists quoted or referred to these volumes. The poet Chateaubriand paraphrased from the *Journal* shamelessly when he required exotic settings for his Indian romances *Atala* (1801) and *Les Natchez* (1826) set among the Indians of Louisiana, or to anchor his own travel narratives in solid fact. Finding in these volumes the first comprehensive history of Catholicism in North America based on archival documents, John Gilmary Shea translated, critically annotated, and published these volumes between 1866 and 1872 as a form of parallel statement and running commentary on the concurrent volumes of Francis Parkman. Shea's translation was reprinted in 1900, 1902, and 1962. The *Journal* first appeared in English in 1761. In 1923 the Caxton Club of Chicago issued a sumptuous two-volume edition edited, translated, and annotated by Louise Phelps Kellogg.

Contemporary historians can occasionally correct Charlevoix, but they can never replace him, just as Francis Parkman can never be replaced. Charlevoix lacks Parkman's grandeur of style and did not enjoy the range of sources available by the mid-nineteenth century. But each writer—Charlevoix the Jesuit philosophe and Parkman the energetic blend of Federalist, Romantic, and Unitarian sentiment—approached the subject of New France with epic intent as well as reliance on sources and personal observation. Parkman wrote one hundred years after this story was profoundly transformed by British conquest. Charlevoix, by contrast, believed that his tale, as extensive as it might be, was but a prologue to a continuing future. As in the cases of the western sea and west-seeking rivers, he was mistaken. New France had recently fallen to Great Britain by the time death interrupted Charlevoix' retirement at the Collège de La Flèche on February 1761 in his seventy-ninth year. Two years earlier, the Society of Jesus had been banished from Portugal and its overseas territories. France and Spain would banish the Society in 1764 and 1767, respectively. In 1773 Pope Clement XIV, a Conventual Franciscan, bowing to pressure from France, Spain, Portugal, and many Italian states, would suppress the Society. Yet the Society of Jesus would eventually be restored, and Quebec and Louisiana would retain their Catholic heritage, and the Roman Catholic peoples of an English-speaking republic not yet founded would lean heavily on French Catholic traditions when it came time to organize themselves as a community of faith.

PART FIVE

British North America

18

The River Boyne 1689

A king and a peer lose their colonies

Between 1664 and 1688 two English colonies in North America had Roman Catholic proprietors. Held as of 1688 by Charles Calvert, third Baron Baltimore, the proprietorship of Maryland dated back to a grant made in 1632 by King Charles I to Cecilius Calvert, the second baron of that title. In 1674, following the conclusion of the third and final Anglo-Dutch war via the Treaty of Westminster, the grant of the proprietorship of New York first made by King Charles II in 1664 to his brother, James, the Duke of York, then serving as lord high admiral, was officially confirmed, as was the name change of the colony from New Netherland to New York, which at the time included New Jersey across the Hudson. In 1685 the Duke of York succeeded his brother as king of England, Scotland, and Ireland; and New York was raised to an even higher level of proprietorship, that of a royal colony.

Owned and governed by Roman Catholics, neither colony possessed a Catholic majority—far from it. With a population by 1671 of four to five thousand Catholics out of an estimated twenty thousand residents, Maryland contained a respectable number of adherents to the proprietors' faith. The city of New York, by contrast, showed a mere nine Roman Catholics in residence as of June 1696, when a special census was taken, and one can easily suspect a comparable scarcity on Long Island and in the upstate communities. Both colonies enjoyed formally issued guarantees of religious liberty: Maryland's Toleration Act, issued on 21 April 1649, which simply confirmed the practice of the colony since its first settlement in March 1634; and the Charter of Liberties issued by New York on 30 October 1683 under the auspices of its Catholic governor, Thomas Dongan. Made by English Roman Catholics in power, such guarantees of religious liberty were obviously in enlightened self-interest. To issue religious liberty to all trinitarian Christian persuasions, the Catholic minority was ensuring liberty for itself as well.

In the years immediately prior to James II's ascension to the throne, the Whig Protestant establishment in Parliament had done its best to pass Acts of Exclusion to keep the Duke of York, a Catholic convert, from being named heir to the throne, but his brother, King Charles II—the son of a Catholic queen and himself a discreet Catholic sympathizer received into the Church on his deathbed—outmaneuvered the opposition. When King James II's Catholic wife, Mary of Modena, gave birth to a Catholic son and heir, James Francis Edward Stuart, on 10 June 1688, efforts were made to depose James II from the throne by military action and replace him with Mary, his daughter by his first wife, who had been raised as a Protestant at the insistence of Charles II. Mary was now married to William, the Protestant Prince of Orange in the Netherlands. Invited by the Whig leadership, with some Tory support, William raised an army and a fleet, which landed at Torbay on the English Channel on 5 November 1688. King James planned a London-based defense, but bad health (acute nosebleeds) and the abandonment of his cause by key supporters—among them Lord John Churchill, first Duke of Marlborough, the greatest general of his era, along with Marlborough's influential wife, Sarah, and (unkindest cut of all) the king's younger daughter, Anne, a Protestant eager to join her Protestant sister and brother-in-law—eroded James' power, and on 11 December he fled for France, where he had already sent his Catholic wife and son for safety.

In March 1689, in an attempt to retake his throne, James landed in Ireland and joined a force gathering at Cork under the command of the Earl of Tyrconnell. James hoped to use the conquest of Ireland as a springboard to control England and Scotland. The plan of the rebel chieftain Tyrconnell, however, was to restore James to the throne of an independent Ireland governed by a Catholic king and a Dublin-based parliament that would return to the Irish people the two-thirds and more of their country granted to English landowners and Scots settlers in a process begun by Elizabeth, furthered by James I, and intensified during the Puritan protectorate. The repression of Catholicism that accompanied this ethnic cleansing and misappropriation of land had continued through the religiously laissez-faire era of Charles II following his restoration to the throne in 1660, despite Charles' promise to Louis XIV in the secret Treaty of Dover (1670) that he would eventually declare himself a Catholic, restore full rights to his Catholic subjects, and in the interim not go to war with France.

The suppression of Catholic Ireland increased in the aftermath of the disclosure in 1678 by Titus Oates, an Anglican priest, and his coconspirator Israel Tonge of the fabricated Popish Plot to assassinate the king. The furor created an anti-Catholic hysteria that prompted Charles II to send his Catholic brother to a low-profile refuge in France until the trouble abated. Whig leader Anthony Ashley Cooper, first Earl of Shaftesbury and coproprietor of the Carolinas, led the anti-Catholic frenzy and personally orchestrated the arrest on 6 December 1679 of Oliver Plunkett, archbishop of Armagh and primate of Catholic Ireland, when Plunkett, defying a decree that denied Catholics admission into Dublin, entered that city in disguise to visit his dying uncle Patrick Plunkett, bishop of Ardagh and Meath. Brought to London for a trumped-up trial on bogus charges of plotting an Irish Catholic uprising, Plunkett—the last Catholic cleric to be so executed by the Crown—was hanged, drawn, and quartered at the longtime execution grounds at Tyburn Tree gallows on Edgware Road on the outskirts of the city, where in Elizabeth's era some four hundred English Catholic priests, religious, and a smaller number of laymen had met the same grisly fate.

In mid-June 1689 William of Orange landed in Carrickfergus, County Antrim, with a sizable force, and by late June the Irish and French army of James and the English and Dutch army of William had positioned themselves on opposite banks of the river Boyne near its entry into the Irish Sea near Drogheda, County Louth. On 1 July the two armies clashed, and a defeated James again fled to France.

In the aftermath of James' defeat on the battlefield at the river Boyne, his policy of religious toleration for England, Scotland, Ireland, and British colonies in North America was defeated as well. Five weeks before the Battle of the Boyne, Parliament passed a restrictive Toleration Act on 24 May 1689 excluding "Roman Catholics, Unitarians, Jews, and all who have no religious creed" from the grants of religious toleration made by James during his brief reign. Prior to his departure for New York, the new royal governor Henry Sloughter was instructed "to permit a liberty of conscience to all Parsons (except Papists) so they may be contented with a quiet and peaceful enjoyment of it, not giving offense or scandal to the government".[1]

Shortly after assuming the throne, William and Mary removed Charles Calvert, third Lord Baltimore, as proprietor of Maryland, and on 22 November 1689 the Maryland assembly excluded Papists from holding any military or civil office. Two years later, the new royal governor, Lionel Copley, banned Catholics from practicing law. In a parallel decree, the newly established royal government effectively banned Catholics in Britain from holding civil or military office by demanding that they take all Oaths of Allegiance laid down by Parliament, including the Act of Supremacy, which declared the ruling sovereign to be the head of the Church. William and Mary, in fact, expanded the Oath of Allegiance, decreed by James I in 1606, to read as a direct rejection of Catholicism. "I do swear," it now stated, "that I do from my heart abhor, detest and abjure as impious and heretical, that damnable doctrine and position that princes excommunicated or deprived by the pope or any authority of the see of Rome may be deposed or murdered by their subjects or any other whatsoever; and I do declare that no foreign prince, person, prelate, state or potentate hath or ought to have any power, jurisdiction, superiority, preeminence or authority, ecclesiastical or spiritual, within this realm, so help me God." In the years that immediately followed, various English colonies—Pennsylvania, New York, Massachusetts Bay, Virginia, and New Jersey—passed similar legislation.[2]

Legends and voyages

The statutory demise of separate but equal participation of Catholic settlers in the colonies of British North America curtailed a relationship that began in legend. Around 1170, the tale ran, a Welsh prince by the name of Madog ab Owain Gwynedd, seeking to escape internecine warfare in north Wales, set sail for North America with his family and dependents. The Welsh explored the interior of the continent and over time intermarried with Native Americans to create a hybrid Welsh-Indian civilization. Elizabethan England revived the legend to offset the claims of Spain. Scholars from the Elizabethan era on addressed the story's veracity, most of them treating the legend as containing some measure of truth. In 1806 the poet Robert Southey made the Madog tale the subject of a long narrative poem. The legend lost credibility in recent times, though a few scholars, mainly Americans, were willing to probe its possibilities in a serious manner. After all, as with the legend of Saint Brendan the Navigator, the story of Madog and his Welsh settlers established an imaginative connection between the British Isles and North America—a connection serving religious and continental ambitions—that, even if unverifiable, bolstered a dream of North American destiny and possession.

Basque and Azorean Portuguese sailors fishing in the North Atlantic off Newfoundland and Labrador in the late fifteenth century, by contrast, who went ashore to salt their catch, were real and Catholic, though anonymous in the historical record. Also real and Catholic, in addition to being well known in his time—and hence historically documented—was the Genoa-born Venetian mariner Giovanni Caboto (John Cabot). Having failed to gain support for his project in Spain or Portugal, Cabot returned to England in late 1495 to place a proposal before His Catholic Majesty Henry VII. Like Columbus, he would sail westward but at higher latitudes. Reaching North America, he would head directly to Cipango (Japan) and Cathay (East Asia) via the open sea route that undoubtedly existed in those higher latitudes north by northwest above the Island of Brasil that was now beginning to appear on North American charts, thanks to reports from Portuguese and English fishing fleets based out of the Azores and Bristol.

Under patents from Henry VII, John Cabot made two voyages. The first was in 1497 in one small ship, the *Matthew*, with a crew of twenty. The *Matthew* made landfall off either Cape Breton Island or Newfoundland on 24 June. Cabot went ashore and, encountering no residents, claimed these and related lands in the northern latitudes for Henry VII. He then made a sailing reconnaissance of the region that lasted a month. By December, Cabot was back in London, describing his discoveries to an enthralled king and reiterating, with a few refinements, his belief that a maritime passage to Cipango and Cathay awaited discovery at some point southwest of his recent landfall.

Cabot's second expedition—five ships, one fitted out by the king and four financed by merchants of Bristol—represented a much more ambitious enterprise. The flotilla carried provisions for a year and—for the planned trading post once the Far East was reached—a significant amount of exchangeable merchandise. No pious language regarding any intent to bring Christianity to the Far East has survived in the scanty record of this second venture, which historians must piece together from secondhand reports. This was a business undertaking: a stretch of continental ambitions to the breaking point, for nothing like it had ever been attempted before. Yet at least two priests were on board, an otherwise unidentified Friar Buil and an elegantly presented Milanese secular cleric by the name of Giovanni Antonio de Carbonariis, who might have performed administrative functions along with his priestly duties.

The second Cabot expedition sailed from Bristol in early May 1498 and met sundry disasters at sea. Some adventurers made it back to England. (How many is unclear.) Certainly John Cabot's son Sebastian returned, living to tell stories in later life of sailing through Hudson Strait on a subsequent voyage in 1508–1509 to the mouth of Hudson Bay, which he took to be the opening of the Northwest Passage across the top of North America to Cipango and Cathay. His father, however, went down with his second ship under uncertain circumstances. No matter whether the Northwest Passage sought by Cabot and his son on behalf of the king and the merchants of Bristol existed, the second Cabot expedition pushed too far ahead of the maritime charts to make it safely home. Yet thanks to John Cabot, a still Catholic England's claim to North America stood on firmer ground than the legendary journey of Madog.

A century of persecution

More than 120 years after John Cabot's failure to return from North America, practicing and self-identifying Roman Catholics constituted an estimated 4 to 5 percent of the English population, most of it in the north. With the exception of the Highland clans, who by and large had remained Catholic, Scotland had become predominately Calvinist Presbyterian. Although Irish peasantry and old nobility continued to be Catholic, Ireland was entering a hundred-year era of English Protestant colonization that would leave the country's Catholic population landless and persecuted. While the Reformation in England involved deep and dynamic forces within Western Christianity that had been gradually gathering strength since the Middle Ages, dynastic and economic considerations tied to the rise of nation-states offer a shorthand approach to narrating the process by which the state ended the thousand-year connection of English Christianity to continental Catholic practice and the papacy.

In 1534 Henry VIII made himself head of the Church of England, began to enrich himself and his supporters with confiscated monastic lands, flirted with Lutheranism, and tolerated some reforms but in the long run did his best to maintain a Catholic-style (albeit schismatic), state-sponsored Church. In 1547 Henry was succeeded by Edward VI, his ten-year-old son by his third wife, Jane Seymour. A strongly Protestant Privy Council headed by Edward Seymour, Duke of Somerset, brother of Jane Seymour and Lord Protector of his nephew, launched a campaign of Protestantization. Upon Edward's early death in 1553, his Catholic older half sister, Mary Tudor, the daughter of Henry VIII and his first wife, Catherine of Aragon, succeeded to the throne. Despite her Catholicism, the half-Spaniard Mary had outwardly conformed to the Henrician and Edwardian reforms and, after a period of humiliation, had been named the sickly Edward's successor. As queen, Mary initially tried to make peace with a now Protestantized Church of England while maintaining her Catholic identity, but a number of hostile Protestant plots, together with an unpopular marriage to King Philip II of Spain, drove her in the direction of a vigorous Catholic restoration, which included the installation of Reginald Cardinal Pole—a Plantagenet on his mother's side—as archbishop of Canterbury and the burning at the stake for heresy of a number of prominent Anglican bishops and dozens of other divines. All this mayhem was recorded in Latin by John Foxe, a pro-Calvinist Oxford don in exile on the Continent. First appearing in English in 1563, *Foxe's Book of Martyrs* helped seal the long-term victory of the Protestant cause among the English and earned for Mary an enduring reputation as Bloody Mary, arch persecutor of English Protestantism.

In 1554 Queen Mary briefly confined her younger sister, Elizabeth, to the Tower as an alleged accomplice of Sir Thomas Wyatt's plot and subsequent uprising against Mary. Released when Wyatt swore to her innocence as he faced the gallows, Elizabeth was readmitted to court. Despite its prior declaration of Elizabeth's illegitimacy, Parliament had made her third in line to the throne after her half siblings, Edward and Mary. Princess Elizabeth kept a low profile, living in semiretirement at Hatfield House in London and continuing her studies under her secretary and private tutor, the accomplished humanist and diplomat Roger Ascham, author of the educational classic *The Scholemaster* (1570).

Ascending the throne in 1558 upon the death of her half sister, Elizabeth I, the daughter of Henry VIII and his second wife, Anne Boleyn, ruled in two distinct phases regarding religious matters. In the first phase of her reign, 1558–1570, Elizabeth strove to bring religious peace to the realm. Albeit Protestant in upbringing and inclination, she had conformed as a Catholic during her sister's reign. Throughout her life, Elizabeth preferred a celibate clergy, favored a Catholic style of worship, and kept the composer William Byrd on the staff of the Chapel Royal despite his open Catholicism.

In 1570, however, the expatriate Catholic lobby on the Continent persuaded the tireless Dominican heretic hunter Pope Pius V, formerly grand inquisitor of the Roman Church before his election to the papacy, to issue on 25 February the papal bull *Regnans in Excelsis*, excommunicating Elizabeth I and releasing her subjects from loyalty to her. It was the last such condemnation and deposition in papal history. In terms of realpolitik, there was no need for *Regnans in Excelsis*. The Holy Roman Emperor and the kings of France and Spain were dismayed by its destabilizing presumption. To Elizabeth I, the ukase constituted a declaration of open season on her, either through coup d'état or assassination or a combination thereof. Would not the supporters of Mary Stuart, Queen of Scots, her once and future Catholic rival for the throne, now imprisoned in Scotland on Elizabeth's order, see *Regnans in Excelsis* as a call for Elizabeth's deposition by assassination? When Spain was threatening invasion in 1587, Elizabeth I ordered the execution of her cousin Mary, lest she become a rallying point for an uprising of Catholics.

Elizabeth I turned to the established Church of England, for which she served as supreme governor, to bolster her cause. She also began openly and aggressively to oppose Roman Catholicism at home and abroad. Catholic gentry—called recusants because they recused themselves from conforming to the Thirty-Nine Articles of Anglican church belief and practice—were heavily fined or imprisoned, and a number suspected of political plotting were executed. Catholic priests in England faced arrest, expulsion, and, increasingly—especially if the priest in question had entered England secretly and was operating undercover—a gruesome death at Tyburn. An estimated 26 percent of missionaries arriving in England at the height of the Elizabethan persecutions were apprehended and executed. Only half of these, moreover, had managed to stay in the field more than five years. Outlaws on the run, priests lived and worked in disguise, using other names and identities, moving from Catholic house to Catholic house for clandestine meetings, and hiding from pursuivants (priest hunters) in claustrophobic recesses beneath floors or behind walls or cabinets, many of which were designed and built by Jesuit lay brother Nicholas Owen before his own arrest and torture in the 1590s.

Between the issuance of *Regnans in Excelsis* in 1570 and Elizabeth's death in 1603, the practice of Roman Catholicism was all but eliminated in England through state suppression. Although rebellion brewed in Scotland and Ireland and on the Continent among expatriates, the majority of English Catholic martyrs did their best to die without a condemnation of the monarch, reflecting the spirit and intent of *Regnans in Excelsis*. Still, the memory of Catholicism did not fade from the consciousness of English people. As Hilaire Belloc has convincingly argued in his biographical studies of Charles II and James I, Catholicism remained a living memory among the general population of England into and through the seventeenth century. Otherwise, why should anti-Catholicism function as such a powerful and persistent counterforce?

The Gunpowder Plot

By the early seventeenth century, with the ascension to the throne in 1603 of the Stuart James I of England/James VI of Scotland (now styled king of Great Britain), the persecution of Catholics diminished but did not let up entirely. The Protestant-raised son of Mary, Queen of Scots, James I was not anti-Catholic. However, he initially promised English Catholics more leniency than he was prepared to deliver, and as a result a group of thirteen Catholic gentry entered into a terrorist conspiracy to store barrels of gunpowder beneath the House of Lords and blow up Parliament on 5 November 1605, when the king would be present. Managing this explosion was the task of one Guy Fawkes, an English-born veteran of the Spanish army with demolition experience. With king and Parliament out of the way and London in a panic, the conspirators planned to join up with a hoped-for Catholic uprising in the Midlands, march on London, seize the government, and place a Catholic monarch on the throne. The scheme was more than a little far-fetched, and its secrecy was shaky. One conspirator vaguely brought up the matter when confessing to Father Henry Garnet, superior of the English Jesuits, giving Garnet permission to break the seal of the confessional if the pope or comparable religious authority needed to be informed. Another conspirator most likely wrote the letter that tipped off the Privy Council. Having informed the king of the plot, Robert Cecil, first Earl of Salisbury, stage-managed its investigation, the arrest of perpetrators—including a cunningly, if falsely, implicated Father Garnet—and their subsequent torture, trial, and public executions (two were mysteriously disposed of). The pseudo-judicial melodrama played a role in inspiring the porter's scene and the central drama of Shakespeare's *Macbeth*. More important, it associated the struggling English Catholic community with something it had no part in and, worse, something it had for a hundred years done everything it could to avoid: treasonous intent, the killing of kings, plots against the state.

The Gunpowder Plot led to reinforced prohibitions against participation by Catholics in public life: no appointments to government, no eligibility for Parliament, no army or navy commissions, no admittance to university or election to fellowships, no membership in bench or bar. Catholic nobility and gentry were confined to a quiet life on large and small estates, attended to by Catholic servants and staff, with a resident house chaplain saying Mass each morning (vespers and compline on Sundays) and the woman of the house leading prayers and Rosary recitation each evening. Those wishing an education, a military career, or admission to a convent or monastery would have to seek it on the Continent.

A Catholic colony in North America?

In this context—loyalty in the secular sphere to a religiously persecuting and career-restrictive state—the notion of an English Catholic colony in North America surfaced. Colonization was tentatively organized on at least two occasions, argued against by a powerful Jesuit, and finally launched on a bipartisan basis of toleration by a converted Irish peer. In 1568 Sir Thomas Gerard of the Bryn, a Catholic squire from Lancaster who had spent time in confinement for recusancy, volunteered to Sir Henry Sidney, Lord Deputy of Ireland, to establish an English Catholic colony in Antrim, Ireland, featuring a four-hundred-man military constabulary as part of the English colonization of that beautiful but benighted island. The Crown decided the effort would be too expensive and would give too much autonomy to Catholic soldiers.

In 1582 Sir Thomas Gerard entered into conversation with Sir George Peckham of Buckinghamshire, another Catholic, recently released from prison for harboring priests, regarding the possibility of joining Sir Humphrey Gilbert, the half brother of Sir Walter Raleigh, in founding a colony in Florida in which Catholic gentry could either work with their tenants or merely invest as a means of raising funds to pay recusant fines. Gilbert, however, was lost at sea in 1583 while on a voyage of reconnaissance. Between 1603 and 1609 another Catholic, Thomas, first Baron Arundell of Wardour (who was also a count of the Holy Roman Empire for his services against the Turks), was involved in a number of discussions regarding the establishment of a colony in Maine of English Catholics and Irish soldiers recently discharged from the Spanish army; as in Gerard's first proposal, these men would function as a military buffer, a county palatine with broad powers on the northern edge of a still unsettled New England. The proposal led to a voyage of reconnaissance at Arundell's expense between March and June 1605 that scouted the Maine coast from Cape Cod north, but when its captain George Waymouth brought the *Archangell* back to England that July, he found that Lord Arundell had departed for a Spanish military command in the Spanish Netherlands. The Gunpowder Plot erupted in October, and plans for Catholic colonies in North America disappeared from view.

The state of affairs was perfectly fine with Father Robert Parsons, organizer in 1580 of the first Jesuit mission to England. For the past twenty-five years, Parsons had been rector of the English College in Rome and advisor to the Jesuit general on English matters, which made him the most influential English cleric after William Cardinal Allen, founder and longtime rector of the English College at Douai, France, where a generation of secular priests was trained for undercover duty in England at the height of the Elizabethan persecution. Fourteen years apart in age, Allen and Parsons were Oxford men, each of them subsequently elected to college fellowships. An Oriel fellow from 1550 to 1556, when he was concurrently elected principal of Saint Mary's Hall, Allen—still a layman but holding the office of university proctor in 1556 and 1557—played an enthusiastic role in the Counter-Reformational re-Catholicization of Oxford under way during the reign of Queen Mary. Under the supervision of Reginald Cardinal Pole, a university visitor, Protestant dons were purged and Catholic scholars such as the distinguished Spanish theologians Bartolomé Carranza and Pedro de Soto were recruited from the Continent. Young men from Catholic families were welcomed back to the university, many of whom returned to England in later life as undercover missionaries.

Elizabeth's ascension to the throne ended Allen's Oxford career, and, resigning from Saint Mary's Hall in 1560, he emigrated to the Low Countries to continue his writing career as a Catholic apologist and to prepare for the secular priesthood at the University of Mechelen in the Spanish Netherlands. Following one brief return to England—the last visit in his lifetime, during which he was scandalized by the growing laxity of the recusant community—Allen was ordained and in 1567 resumed his administrative academic career as rector of the English College at Douai (the college moved temporarily to Rheims in 1578), which he fashioned into the leading continental seminary training English Catholic secular priests for undercover ministries in England.

A decade and more later, serving as an Oxford don—fellow of Balliol (1569), lecturer in rhetoric (1571), college bursar (1572), and dean of the college (1573)—the outspokenly Catholic Robert Parsons (among other things, he refused to take the Oath of Supremacy upon graduation) antagonized many of his colleagues at the now largely re-Protestantized Oxford. Under pressure, he resigned from Balliol in 1574. Initially, Parsons planned to study medicine at Padua, but the experience of making a retreat at Louvain according to the Spiritual Exercises of Saint Ignatius while delayed en route to Italy led him to agonize for the next thirteen months while a medical student over whether to join the Society of Jesus. Admitted in July 1575, Parsons made rapid progress in the Society and at the Roman College it staffed. In three short years, he was ordained and was thereupon assigned as master of second-year novices at the Roman College (the present-day Gregorian University) and in 1579 as assistant to the rector at the English College, then under Jesuit supervision.

Thus two clerics—the secular priest Allen at Douai-Rheims, created cardinal-priest in 1587; the Jesuit Parsons in Rome, England (briefly on mission), the Low Countries, Spain (where he lived from 1589 to 1590), and then back to Rome as rector of the English College until his death in 1610—in constant contact and collaboration with each other, each hoping for a Catholic restoration with the help of Spain, constituted the intellectual and diplomatic leadership of English Catholicism in exile. Allen turned Douai-Rheims into a center of pro-Catholic scholarship and propaganda. The first English Catholic Bible was produced there in 1582 and lasted for three centuries of use. Some 471 priests were known to have been trained at Douai-Rheims for service in Elizabethan England. One hundred sixteen were executed. Seventeen died in jail. Disguised as an army captain, Parsons entered England in June 1580 as Jesuit superior. His onetime Oxford colleague Edmund Campion, now a Jesuit, arrived separately. Parsons played a cautious game and warned Campion to do likewise. Ignoring Parsons' advice, Campion compromised his security and was captured, tortured, and executed. Parsons fled to the Continent and endured a lifetime of criticism for not embracing the martyrdom he was so devotedly organizing for others.

Although they each avoided the assassination threat against the monarch implied in *Regnans in Excelsis*, Allen and Parsons tirelessly advocated a political response—namely, a regime change by military means via an invasion of England by Spain—to the Elizabethan persecution that reached such intensity in the 1580s. The cancellation of the Spanish Armada in 1576 and its defeat in 1588 left Allen, Parsons, and other exilic Catholic supporters of Spanish intervention stranded on the far side of an embarrassing diplomatic and military disaster linked to disloyalty to a finer idea of England and the queen. How disconcerting to loyal English Catholics, to say the least, that Allen had written a string of pamphlets leading up to the Armada of 1588, defending the deposing power of the pope, describing Elizabeth as a bastard who deserved deposition, and calling for the training of expatriate English Catholic men as a military force comparable to the missionaries, ready to assist in the deposition of Elizabeth when the time was right.

Becoming a permanent minority

The defeat of the Armada in 1588 can be considered a tipping point. Convinced of the loyalty of her England-based Catholic subjects, who had rallied to her cause,

Elizabeth decelerated her crusade of anti-Catholic persecution, and the English Catholic gentry began the process of settling into a minority status devoid of dreams of restoration. Their only hope: to be left alone. As cardinal-priest, Allen spent his last year in Rome living simply in a house on the Via Monserrato beside the English College, serving as cardinal librarian of the Church and a member of a committee charged with the revision of the Vulgate. He died in 1594. Two years later, Parsons became rector of the English College in Rome, a post he held until his death in 1610. (Parsons was entombed alongside Allen before the high altar of the English College.) Prohibited by mandate of the Society of Jesus to engage in direct political activity, Parsons involved himself—unsuccessfully—in efforts to encourage the conversion of James VI of Scotland, heir apparent to the English throne, and to moderate—again, unsuccessfully—the controversy in which a faction of secular missionaries appealed to Rome regarding the appointment of George Blackwell as archpriest (superior) of secular priests in England. These Appellants, as they were called, were in general pro–Oath of Allegiance and anti-Jesuit, especially anti-Parsons: another sign of a stabilizing and accommodated minority status among English Catholics, especially when Archpriest Blackwell, whose contested appointment was upheld by Rome, himself took the Oath of Allegiance on 7 July 1607.

In the aftermath of the Gunpowder Plot, Parsons maintained his controversial verve in the years that remained to him by writing spirited oppositions to the notion that recusancy was a form of treason. The vigor, pungency, and clarity of these pamphlets would later earn the approval of Jonathan Swift. Yet these writings were nonrestorationist. They sought, rather, to defend English Catholics as good English subjects, loyal to king and country, but loyal to Roman Catholicism as well—this, coming from a longtime rigorist Jesuit who had backed the Spanish Armada, the removal of Elizabeth from the throne, and, following the installation of a Catholic monarch, the launching from a revived Catholic England of an evangelical crusade to reclaim northern countries lost to Protestantism. Yet at age sixty—past all dreams and plots on behalf of the restoration he had so desired—Parsons was now in favor of having the surviving English Catholic remnant accept its minority status and in time win its way back into respectability.

To that end, writing from Rome on 18 March 1605, in one of his penultimate interventions in English affairs, Parsons responded to a plan proposed to him by a certain Mr. Winslade (first name unknown). Supported by continental Catholic princes and by English Catholic gentry willing to sell some of their lands to help finance the venture, ran the Winslade plan, one thousand English Catholics of the poorer but worthy sort—farmers, laborers, and craftsmen, guided by an appropriate number of gentry—would gather at an unnamed continental port prior to sailing to North America, where at an undesignated site they would establish an English Catholic colony and evangelize the indigenous peoples of the region. Parsons appreciated "the good and godly endes" of the plan and those behind it, he replied, but for the following reasons, it was impossible.

First and most important, the king would never allow it. Second, the Catholic gentry was in no mood to uproot itself, sell its lands, and depart England; and their dependents, even the poor, would not see how the scheme would improve their lot in life. Third—and here Parsons zeroes in on a key issue regarding the political loyalty of the Catholic gentry—Catholics would never join a colonization venture backed by foreign princes or, indeed, deal with foreign princes on such matters, lest they come under ridicule or, worse, provoke a return to restrictions against travel abroad by Catholics, which would cut off the supply of young English men going to the Continent to study for the priesthood. Even worse, such a scheme could very well resurrect the prior penalties for priests entering England. Fifth, who would pay for all this (a repeated concern), and what continental prince would allow a thousand unsupervised foreigners to encamp at one of his ports? Sixth, Spain claims the regions in the Indies, even those the Spaniards have as of yet failed to settle. Parsons is here most likely referring to the coast of North America as far north of Florida as the Chesapeake region that Spanish Jesuits had abandoned in the early 1570s after losing so many men to Native American hostility. And remember—Parsons' last caveat—how the Spaniards dealt with the Huguenots who tried to settle Florida!

At this point, finishing his seventh reason—a repeat of financial and diplomatic objections—the old Parsons surfaces, the Jesuit he had once been who sought a missionary life in faroff places before the matter of England claimed him for a lifetime: the prospect of evangelizing the peoples of the New World "liketh me soe well, and in soe high a degree, as for that onely I would desire my self to goe in the jorney, shuttinge my eyes to all other difficulties, if it were possible to obtayne it; but yet, for that wee doe not dele here for ourselves onely but for others also, wee moste looke to all other necessary circumstances, wheof the first and of moste importance are in my opinion that the matter be broken in England and Spaine, wherein for many reasons I may not be the breaker; but, if those two were once optayned, I would then be willing to do in Rome what lieth in me; and this is all that I canne say in this matter."

Seven months later, the Gunpowder Plot was revealed. In his prosecution of Father Garnet, attorney general Sir Edward Coke denounced the pope, Spaniards, Garnet, the Jesuits, and a certain Mr. Wysdale (Coke misspelled Winslade's name) as organizers of yet another plot against the realm. Winslade's seaborne venture was, Coke suggested, a prelude to invasion.[3]

Avalon

Born around 1580 in Yorkshire to minor Catholic gentry, George Calvert spent his early childhood as a Catholic. When his mother, Alice Crosland Calvert, was threatened with imprisonment for recusancy, George's father, Leonard, conformed to the Church of England to protect his wife and subsequently placed his promising son George under the care of an Anglican tutor. Having graduated from Trinity College in Oxford and Lincoln's Inn in London, George Calvert toured Europe, then joined the staff of principal Secretary of State Sir Robert Cecil (later first Earl of Salisbury) as one of Cecil's private secretaries and was in time sent out on short-term assignments in England and Ireland. King James I liked the company of bright, good-looking young men and invited Calvert to assist him in writing theological defenses of Anglicanism against the efforts of Dutch theologian Jacobus Arminius to purge Anglicanism of its Calvinist leanings. As a Scotsman, James revered Calvin, but given Calvert's background, it is somewhat ironic to find him helping his king take up the Calvinist cause. From 1609 to 1624 George Calvert served in Parliament. In 1619 he was knighted and named one of two principal secretaries of state, the position held by Cecil when he had first hired Calvert.

George Calvert, in the meanwhile, had invested in the Virginia Company and in the East India Company at a boom time for these aristocratic enterprises. In 1620 he acquired stock options in the Newfoundland Company, which he later exercised, most likely in partnership with family and close friends as joint investors. Two prominent Catholic families, the Arundells and the Howards, also joined the Newfoundland Company. Sir William Vaughan—an Oxford- and University of Vienna–trained legal scholar and social philosopher, then living in Wales—had purchased property in Newfoundland from the company in 1616. The dreamy and visionary Vaughan intended to develop the land as the assertively Anglican colony of Avalon, the city of Welsh mythology from which King Arthur would one day return to restore the lost glories of Camelot, which for Vaughan meant a profitable colony of Welsh people bringing Anglican Christianity to the region. Vaughan outlined his utopian vision in *The Golden Fleece* (1626) and other titles, establishing an imaginative and moral connection between colonial development and Protestant piety. The colony he actually financed (but did not visit) in 1617, however, failed within three years. A second venture launched in 1621 or 1622 struggled on obscurely, and so *The Golden Fleece* gained its popularity as a dream vision of a utopian colony of Avalon on the Atlantic.

In 1620 Sir George Calvert purchased from Sir William Vaughan a substantial tract on the Avalon Peninsula of Newfoundland. Fifty miles south of Saint John's, the lot included the harbor called Ferryland, its name a corruption of the Portuguese *farilham* (steep rock, reef, or small island). In 1621 Calvert provisioned and dispatched the experienced sea captain Edward Wynne, a non-Catholic Welshman like Vaughan, to establish a settlement of twelve colonists at Ferryland. The next year, twenty more settlers arrived: a surgeon, skilled artisans (carpenter, quarryman, stone mason, cooper, husbandman, fisherman), and seven women (two wives, one widow, two girls, a maid, and one woman of unidentified status). With this second group came an adventurous Anglican cleric by the name of Richard James, who would later earn a place in history as librarian and archivist to the famed book collector and antiquarian Sir Robert Cotton.

Things went well for the colony. Sturdy buildings rose. Crops were planted. Timber cutting was initiated. A quarry, a forge, and a salt-making operation were established. Captain Wynne sent Calvert optimistic letters. Encouraged, Calvert made plans to lobby for the expansion of his holding into a full-fledged proprietary province. On 7 April 1623 a charter for a colony called the Province of Avalon in Newfoundland was drawn up for royal approval, granting George Calvert and his heirs proprietary rights to the said Province of Avalon, a colony in Newfoundland endowed with palatine (viceregal) powers to make laws, raise forces, and grant titles. The previous year, Calvert's wife, Anne Mynne, had died, leaving him with ten children to support, educate, endow with dowries, and otherwise see into adulthood.

In the midst of all this, moreover, Calvert was doing his best as a principal secretary of state to effect a reconciliation between Spain and England through the marriage of Charles, Prince of Wales, and the Infanta María of Spain. Catholic gentry favored the policy as a means of decelerating the implacable hostility of the Protestant ascendancy to Catholic Spain and its empire. Negotiations for the Spanish Match nearly collapsed in 1624 after a disastrous visit to Spain by the Prince of Wales and royal favorite George Villiers, first Duke of Buckingham, who returned to England advocating war, not marriage, with Spain, and (despite the fact that he was married to the daughter of the Earl of Rutland, a Roman Catholic) reviving hostility to Catholicism in its Spanish and English varieties, to the delight of Parliament. The next year, following an expedition to France that two centuries later novelist Alexandre Dumas would make the stuff of great fiction, Buckingham—with the approval of Cardinal Richelieu—negotiated a match between Prince Charles and Princess Henrietta Maria, sister of King Louis XIII of France.

At some point, Sir George Calvert reverted to the Catholicism of his boyhood. Or should one say that he returned to his mother's faith? His mother's steadfast recusancy could have been one factor, but Calvert also may have been swayed by his aristocratic Catholic business partners in the Avalon venture. According to the proposed charter of the Province of Avalon, Catholics could settle in the colony freely, without taking the Oath of Supremacy (which declared the monarch the head of the Church of England), and Calvert deliberately used the name Avalon to suggest an earlier pre-Reformation Christianity. Some historians cite the effect of Don Diego Sarmiento de Acuña, Count Gondomar, the Spanish ambassador to England with whom Calvert was closely dealing in the matter of the Spanish Match, which had as a codicil the abolition of all fines and penal measures against English Roman Catholics; others note that Calvert's son and heir, Cecil, was married to the Catholic Anne Arundell, daughter of Lord Arundell of Wardour. A strong influence might very well have been the Discalced Carmelite priest Father Simon Stock of Saint Mary, the name in religion of Thomas Doughty, a graduate of the English College in Rome who joined the Carmelites following his ordination, entered England as a missionary in 1615, and eventually acquired diplomatic immunity as the chaplain to Count Gondomar and a conduit to Rome and to Catholic authorities on the Continent. Father Simon was the first to report Calvert's conversion to Vatican authorities at the Sacred Congregation for the Propagation of the Faith and to receive an acknowledgment on 16 March 1625, indicating a 1624 conversion date.

The mood of the times might also have affected Calvert's decision. The Prince of Wales would soon be king. He had a Catholic wife, who maintained her private chaplains and chapel and urged her husband to suspend the penalties being leveled against Roman Catholics. Charles himself was High Church and was anointed king in a High Church ceremony reprising pre-Reformation ritual. A close advisor to the young king was Bishop William Laud, a High Churchman so Anglo-Catholic in his outlook that Rome would eventually have hopes of reconciling with the Church of England, and there was talk of offering him an appointment as cardinal. As chancellor of Oxford (1629) and archbishop of Canterbury (1633), Laud enforced a rigid Anglo-Catholic discipline and opposed the growing presence of Puritans to the point of active persecution. The Caroline era—from Charles' ascension to the throne in 1625 to the outbreak of civil war in 1642 and the execution of the king in 1649—witnessed a bold return of piety and religious practice among High Church Anglicans that blended Catholic thought and values with a distinctively English sensibility anchored in Scripture, the Anglican Book of Common Prayer, cooperative communities, and married life.

Promotion to peerage

Making his Catholicism known, George Calvert resigned as secretary of state in 1625. The king nevertheless briefly kept him on the Privy Council and on 16 February 1625 raised him to the Irish peerage as Baron of Baltimore in County Longford. Sometime before September 1625 Calvert remarried. His second wife, Joan, was reputed to have been in service—perhaps as a kitchen maid—before her elevation to Lady Baltimore. Was this information merely a canard from the anti-Catholic camp? (Another charge was that the couple was not married at all but simply living together.) Or did the widower quite understandably come to appreciate a young Catholic woman in his household service and throw snobbery to the wind? He was, after all, only minor gentry in origin, and the marriage might have happened well before his elevation to the peerage. Calvert also might have been sincerely and honorably attracted to Joan, who, following their marriage, bore him two more children.

Whatever prestige his Irish peerage conferred, Calvert needed more money than his Irish property alone could generate. Besides, he had money—his own and others'—invested in the Virginia Company and in the Newfoundland properties he now owned. In short, Lord Baltimore was too leveraged to retreat into a quiet country life, although he did take up residence on his Irish estate. Having received reports from Captain Wynne as to the progress and promise of the settlement Calvert owned at Ferryland, he naturally turned to development of the Province of Avalon on Newfoundland, for which the final charter was still pending. To carry out bigger plans for Avalon, Calvert engaged the services of the veteran soldier Sir Arthur Aston of Fulham in Middlesex, a fellow Catholic, to sail to Newfoundland with fifteen more settlers (all Catholics) and replace Wynne as governor. The retention of Aston itself made a statement, for in 1621 Sir Arthur had commanded a force of eight thousand English volunteers fighting in Russia on behalf of Poland, a feat that, in contrast to the more modest achievements of Captain Edward Wynne, underscored the growing scope of Calvert's continental ambitions to establish an armed palatinate. Ashton made one voyage to Ferryland in the spring of 1625 but delayed returning when his ship came under a wartime ban that prohibited overseas travel. Transferring his sword to the Duke of Buckingham, then fighting in France, Ashton was killed on 29 October 1627 while on active duty.

Father Simon Stock of Saint Mary might have recommended the battle-tested Sir Arthur to Calvert, for the Discalced Carmelite friar had his own continental ambitions on behalf of his order: a foothold in Newfoundland, first of all, followed by a missionary assignment in British North America, and then a Carmelite presence in China, the Philippines, and the Indies. Each of these Asian places was to be reached via the Northwest Passage, still to be discovered but believed in nevertheless. The possibility of its presence underscored the importance of Newfoundland as a gateway to North America and Asia, where Jesuits, Recollects, Capuchins, and Dominicans were already at work and where the much smaller Discalced Carmelite order might come into its own. Father Simon advanced these ideas to the Sacred

Congregation in Rome and to Calvert. Father Bede (John Hiccocks), however, the Carmelite vice provincial for England, countered Father Simon's letters with more realistic approaches, echoing Parsons' letter of 1605. Protestant England, Father Bede argued, would never allow an explicitly Catholic colony in Newfoundland, and even if it did, there were not enough English-speaking Carmelites available to staff Father Simon's grandiose schemes. When Father Bede's prediction came true, and the only Carmelite available for assignment turned out to be Father Simon Stock of Saint Mary himself, Father Simon pleaded the importance of his current work in England as well as the impossibility of one priest achieving so great a task. He thus remained on the home front, serving until 1633 as chaplain to the Spanish embassy and, following that, residing as house chaplain with the Roper family (descendants of Sir Thomas More) at their estate at Canterbury—a much more conventional recusancy pattern of clerical employment.

Newfoundland in 1627

The ongoing war with France had severely restricted shipping, but by April 1627 Calvert had secured the necessary permissions for a voyage of inspection to his colony. Personal on-the-ground testimony would be necessary if Calvert were to continue to persuade the merchants of Bristol and other investors to maintain their financial support. Calvert took two secular priests with him on this inaugural voyage, Thomas Longville and Anthony Pole. Both were converts. Longville came from an aristocratic background and was a graduate of the Jesuit-staffed Saint Omer's College in France (founded by Parsons in 1593) and the English College in Rome. The middle-class Pole, who sailed under the alias Smith, also graduated from Saint Omer's and had studied for the priesthood at the English College at Valladolid, Spain (another Parsons foundation, established in 1589). During this era, numerous English secular priests who had been ordained on the Continent were entering the Society of Jesus following ordination. Longville, however, loathed the Jesuits, as later events would reveal. Pole had spent some time as a Jesuit after his ordination but left the Society to enter England as Father Smith, a secular priest. Arrested and imprisoned, he was released along with other imprisoned seculars as a goodwill gesture connected to the marriage of King Charles I and Henrietta Maria. Calvert spent the summer of 1627 in Ferryland and its vicinity, assessing prospects, and when he returned to England in the fall, Longville went back with him. Pole remained in Ferryland and thus became the first Roman Catholic priest to serve in British North America. Given Pole's later career, however, it is not surprising that this distinction did not earn him a conspicuous place in Catholic history.

Whether it was because Calvert liked what he saw in Newfoundland or because he was at the time too invested to consider other options or because he genuinely wished to establish a Catholic colony, Calvert, the very next year, resolved to embark upon a second and ostensibly permanent (or, at the least, semipermanent) sojourn. By June 1628 he was back at Ferryland, this time in the company of his wife and their young children, his daughters from his first marriage and their husbands, Sir Robert Talbot and William Peasley, forty-odd colonists (including Yorkshire recusants), and a secular priest by the name of Hacket, most likely an alias for one Anthony Whitehair. An Anglican minister named Erasmus Stourton was already on hand, having been sent out with Calvert the previous year as the officially designated preacher to the Colony of Ferryland.

Educated at Saint John's College, Cambridge, Stourton belonged to the anti-Catholic Calvinist wing of Anglicanism and was appalled by the open illegal celebration of Sunday Mass at Ferryland as well as by other Catholic observances. Stourton protested these matters to Calvert, who sent him back to England, where Stourton swore out a deposition and otherwise made trouble for a year or two. Stourton went so far as to claim that Calvert had allowed a child to be baptized into the Church of Rome against the father's wishes. In time, Stourton settled into a comfortable post as chaplain to Christopher Villiers, Earl of Anglesey, brother to the all-powerful Duke of Buckingham, and concurrently rector at Walesby, Lincolnshire. The fact is, however, that Stourton had the law on his side, had anyone in high places wished to take up the matter. (Informed of the charges, King Charles sent the matter to the Privy Council, which did nothing.) However inconclusive, this contretemps underscored the vulnerability of Calvert's efforts to establish a North American colony with a strong Catholic presence unless the Catholics of that colony had at least the tacit permission of Protestant England to participate in governance and to practice their religion with some degree of openness.

During his time at Ferryland, Calvert and his son Leonard from his first marriage captured six French fishing craft and returned them to England as prizes. Yet sickness and the long, cruel winter (mid-October to mid-May, as he described it) were eroding his confidence in a Newfoundland future. Crops did not grow in winter. Half the settlers had come down with scurvy. Nine died. He himself was unwell. When spring came, Calvert began to repatriate family members back to England. Writing to the king on 19 August 1629, he confessed defeat as well as thoughts of death and requested a palatinate in the better climate of Virginia, where he could grow tobacco.

Not waiting for the king's reply, Calvert and his wife and their two children and a number of colonists equally defeated by Newfoundland set sail for Virginia, where they arrived in October. How far negotiations advanced there with Governor John Pott and his councilors soon proved beside the point; for Calvert as a Catholic refused to take conjoined Oaths of Supremacy and Allegiance (the pair apparently insisted upon; allegiance alone he might have handled), and so Calvert sailed for England in total defeat and humiliation. Calvert left his wife and children behind temporarily under the protection of his friend John Harvey, now governor of Virginia. On their return voyage, Lady Baltimore and her children were lost at sea.

Calvert reached London safely, where the king's return letter finally reached him. "Men of your condition and breeding are fitter for other employments than the framing of new plantations," Charles wrote, "which commonly have rugged and laborious beginnings, and require much greater means in managing them than usually the power of one private subject can react to."[4]

A continuing struggle

Taking up residence at Lincoln's Inn Fields, George Calvert was not through trying to gain a Great Seal for another proprietorship. His damaged reputation brought his oldest son, Cecil, increasingly to the forefront in advancing his father's petition for a Virginia colony. The first Lord Baltimore, for one thing, upon his return had married for a third time, in this instance a maid of one of his daughters. The marriage did not work out, and Calvert caused a scandal in Catholic circles when he sought to annul the marriage on the basis of canon law. His first wife, he argued, had been his third wife's godmother, and this spiritual relationship made his third marriage null and void in the eyes of the Church. Lord Baltimore was not alone in his marital misadventures. The secular priest Anthony Pole (Smith) had illegally reentered England under a new alias (Gascoyne) and was being hunted by pursuivants. Pole escaped to France in 1631 and later was rumored to be functioning as a freelance priest. In the ecumenical spirit of the Edict of Nantes (or was he still trying to recover from the memory of those terrible Newfoundland winters?), Pole reportedly had bigamous unions with two women, one Catholic and the other Huguenot.

The archpriest controversy

The English Catholic front, meanwhile, was in a state of ecclesiastical turmoil that had implications for George Calvert's efforts to win a Virginia proprietorship. Ever since the Elizabethan persecutions, the secular clergy and the Jesuits had been competing for control of the English mission. As long as Cardinal Allen remained alive, the English mission enjoyed a titular head, a secular priest, of high ecclesiastical rank. Indeed, in 1587 Allen's Jesuit counterpart, Robert Parsons, had engineered Allen's promotion to cardinal to create a symbol of détente between seculars and Jesuits. George Blackwell's appointment as archpriest was intended to provide secular clergy with a comparable organization. The appointment of an archpriest was a Jesuit idea. Archpriest Blackwell was specifically instructed to cooperate with the Society of Jesus in the regulation of the English mission.

Already in charge of the English College in Rome, Jesuits of the English Province grew increasingly powerful as resident chaplains in the homes of wealthy and influential recusants and as seminary educators at Rome and at the English-language seminaries Parsons had established at Valladolid and Seville. A noticeable drift of ordained English seculars into the Society developed, and a steady supply of young Englishmen from established families was entering from Saint Omer. A differing attitude regarding the Oath of Allegiance was also developing. A number of secular priests expressed willingness to take this oath as early as the late Elizabethan era. Archpriest Blackwell urged calm and loyalty to the Crown in the aftermath of the Gunpowder Plot and himself took the oath on 7 July 1607. Taking the oath implied a rejection of papal authority to depose monarchs, as had been all but openly called for by Pius V in *Regnans in Excelsis*. The secular priests of England, meanwhile, were more and more emphasizing their loyalty to the Crown as English subjects. Thus began a cisalpine English Catholicism, which stressed a this-side-of-the-Alps loyalty to the Church along with a qualified independence from Roman control. The Jesuits, by contrast, belonged to an order expressly attached to ultramontane (beyond the Alps) papal authority; indeed, a professed elite within the Society took a vow of obedience to the papacy.

In 1621 the third and last archpriest of England, William Harrison, died. Rome, feeling more confident of a settled order in the British Isles, established a missionary vicariate there and authorized the episcopal consecration of the veteran Midlands missioner and, later, Paris-based academic William Bishop as titular bishop of the defunct see of Chalcedon in Greece and vicar apostolic of Britain. Consecrated in Paris on 4 June 1623, the soon-to-be-seventy Bishop left for England, where he exercised a brief ministry before succumbing to age and ailments.

Bishop was elderly and genial. His successor, Richard Smith—in his early forties upon his consecration in Paris in November 1624 as titular bishop of Chalcedon and second vicar apostolic to Britain—was a hard-charging academic, controversialist, and longtime member of Cardinal Richelieu's household. Richelieu, in fact, had successfully pressed Smith's case in Rome when the English secular clergy voiced favor of another candidate. Reaching England in April 1628, Smith chose to govern both clergy and laity aggressively, as if he were a duly constituted bishop and not merely a papal representative in missionary territory. Thus he treated the secular clergy as if he were their bishop and expected the Jesuits, whom he hated, and a smaller number of Benedictines to respect his authority as well. With even more arrogance, Smith tried to exercise control over the English recusant nobility and upper gentry who had formed the support system of the clergy, regulars and seculars alike, since the 1570s.

No one liked Richard Smith. Seculars wanted to be governed by a chapter of senior secular missionaries (the Old Brotherhood) established by the aged William Bishop in his brief but benevolent time in office. Jesuits and Benedictines were affronted by Smith's unauthorized intrusion into their sovereignty as exempt orders. The recusant gentry resented Smith's sheer effrontery in putting himself in charge of the upper strata of recusants; they also took umbrage at his campaign against Church Papists, that is, Catholics who attended Anglican services or otherwise publicly conformed in order to avoid harassment. George Calvert entered the resulting pamphlet war connected to the resistance against Smith with his *Answers of a Catholike Lay Gentleman* (1631), in which he spiritedly defended the Jesuit side of the argument. By that time, however, Bishop Smith had long since (1629) taken refuge in the French embassy before returning to France in 1631, resigning his office, and resuming his career as a prolific writer of polemical theology and a retainer to Richelieu, who provided Smith with a home in Paris and a steady income. Calvert, in short, was cheering on the Jesuit victors in this battle for authority. He was thus aligning himself with a rich and powerful transnational order over a localized secular clergy dependent on recusant gentry for support. Calvert had spent between 20,000 and 30,000 pounds sterling on his Newfoundland venture. How much of this remained as outstanding debt? Could he handle such a debt on his own? Would it ruin him and his family? And how did he propose to finance the Virginia colony for which he and his son Cecil were now petitioning the king? Lord Baltimore needed partners—the English Province of the Society of Jesus, for example.

At some point in 1629 George Calvert and perhaps his son Cecil met with Richard Blount, provincial of the English Jesuits, and several of his councilors, including Father Andrew White. Blount had his needs. If the English Jesuits lost their battle for independence from Bishop Smith, they would be looking for opportunities in British North America comparable to French Jesuit interests in New France. What venture could be better than Lord Baltimore's proposed colony?

Particularly noteworthy was his lordship's promise that in this colony the Statutes of Mortmain would not apply, which is to say, grants of property could legally be made to ecclesiastical entities such as the English Province of the Society of Jesus. Basically, Lord Baltimore was proposing a continuation in the new colony of the lay-dominated Catholic culture of recusant England. As proprietor, he or his successor would build the churches and exercise patronage. Supported by their own farms, Jesuits would serve as chaplains to the laity and missionaries to the Indians. The arrangement, in short, would be thoroughly reflective of Catholic England in the Caroline era. They had a deal. The English Province of the Society of Jesus had become, in effect, cosponsors of the enterprise.

Cecil sees it through

George Calvert, first Lord Baltimore, died on 13 April 1632. His finances were a mystery (as they largely remain to this day). Sadly, Calvert seems to have died on the verge of a second start. Within ten and a half months, his son Cecil snatched hopes for victory from the jaws of defeat as two ships, the *Ark* and the *Dove*, carried some 140 gentlemen adventurer-investors (as they were called) and settlers (mainly indentured servants) across the Atlantic. In June 1632 the Crown had carved from Virginia a proprietary and palatine colony, east of the Potomac River and split by Chesapeake Bay, and granted it to Cecil Calvert, second Lord Baltimore, and his heirs in perpetuity.

Like his father, Cecil (frequently given as Cecilius) Calvert was an Oxford graduate married into a prominent recusant family, the Arundells of Wardour. Planning to visit his colony eventually, perhaps even remain there, Cecil Calvert stayed in England for the time being to protect his charter from attacks and to handle the first phases of business operations, including, presumably, the gradual liquidation of existing debt. As governor, Cecil's younger brother Leonard would run things in the new colony. Leonard, twenty-four, had been to Newfoundland with his father and was familiar with the challenges of colony building. He had also played a key role in capturing the six French prizes off Newfoundland and could be depended on as a military leader if necessary.

The new colony was called Maryland in honor of both the French-born queen of England (whom Sir George Calvert had once sought to block with the Spanish Match) and Mary, the Mother of Jesus, which covertly suggested Catholic devotion. From the beginning, though, Cecil Calvert insisted upon the colony's inclusive and tolerant nature. His notable pamphlet entitled *Objections Answered* (1633) put him in the forefront of a recently developing English Catholic movement for religious tolerance. That same year, in November 1633, Cecil wrote out instructions for his governor brother. All trinitarian Christians—Anglicans, Puritans, Separatists, and Catholics—would be equally welcomed in the colony, Cecil Calvert wrote, and guaranteed the right to practice their religion free of harassment. Despite the romanticism that later surrounded Maryland in American Catholic circles, Maryland was not intended to be a recusant utopia. Instead, it reflected the emergent cisalpine accommodation of English Catholicism, as suggested by the second Lord Baltimore in his *Instructions to the Colonists* (1633) amid paragraphs of practical advice. Tolerate and hope to be tolerated. Pledge loyalty to the Crown. Take the Oath of Allegiance. Look to lay leadership. Give no offense to Protestant colonists.

The *Ark* and the *Dove*

Early voyages of settlement to North America—the *Mayflower* with its English dissenters in 1620, the *Saint Catherine* full of Sephardic Jews en route from Curaçao to New Amsterdam in 1654—remain mythical. Bringing the first English Roman Catholic settlers to the Atlantic seaboard of what in time would become the United States, the *Ark* and the *Dove* are no exceptions to this endowment of prophetic resonance by later members of the communities being thus introduced to what was hoped to be a new and better life. Fortunately, the *Ark* and its pinnace (tender) the *Dove* were ships fully up to the legend. At 350 tons, with a beam of 125 feet and an overall length of 170 feet from bowsprit to aft, the three-masted *Ark*—commanded by veteran mariner Richard Lowe—transported the majority of its 130 colonists and crew of 20, including a ship's physician, safely (if not comfortably for those in steerage) across the Atlantic. While much smaller, the two-masted, 50-ton pinnace *Dove* was a resilient sailer, as its performance on this particular journey would soon prove. Three dangers—storms, pirates, and anti-Catholic opposition—confronted the expedition. Against the storms (two of them, each ferocious) stood the shipshape condition of the *Ark* and the *Dove*, the skills of the ships' commanders and crews (for whom Lord Baltimore had secured a Privy Council promise that they would not be impressed at sea into the Royal Navy), the provisions on hand for the four-month voyage and the first year in Maryland (including a chicken coop and an ample supply of wine and beer), and prayers and Masses of good luck celebrated by the Jesuit Fathers Andrew White and John Gravener (alias Altham), who were accompanied by Jesuit brother Thomas Gervase. Against pirates, a major menace in this era (between 1609 and 1616 Algerian pirates alone had captured 466 British ships), the *Ark* carried nine cannons and hardy crew members who did not want to be killed or spend the rest of their lives in captivity. Hostility to the venture, however, was another matter and at times almost terminated the project. Even after Cecil Calvert received the Great Seal of England for his proprietorship, harassment continued. Half of 1633 was consumed by enforced delays. Even as the *Ark* and the *Dove* sought to leave England in mid-October, Secretary of State Sir John Coke had the ships delayed to ensure that all colonists aboard had taken the Oath of Allegiance. (The Oath of Supremacy was not required.) Picking up a few more passengers on the Isle of Wight—the three Jesuits were kept out of sight, lest they be arrested for illegal residence in England—the *Ark* and the *Dove* headed out into the open sea on Saturday, 22 November 1633.

Father White wrote an account of the voyage, which is notable for its description of the two storms. Subsequent scholarship has filled in the details. Striking almost immediately, the first storm separated the *Dove* from the *Ark* for the remainder of the Atlantic crossing. The second storm split the mainsail of the *Ark*. Not until the two ships reached the fortified English port town of Barbados were they reunited. A rebellion of indentured servants was in progress, and lest the *Ark* and the *Dove* be seized by the insurgents, the ships set off as quickly as possible for the Virginia coast via Martinique, Nevis, and Saint Christopher, fortunately avoiding the five Spanish men-of-war known to be operating in these waters.

By late February 1634 the *Ark* and the *Dove* had reached the coast of Virginia. Fearing a hostile reception, Lord Baltimore had instructed his brother Leonard to avoid landing at Jamestown, but once arrived, the young governor saw no alternative but to consult Virginians regarding the region and the best possibilities for settlement. Unlike at Ferryland, no prior reconnaissance had been carried out. Fortunately, Governor Harvey was an old friend of the first Lord Baltimore and proved helpful, despite a few Virginians' claims that the Indians of the region were armed and antagonistic due to reports of an imminent raid by Spanish slavers; Father White dismissed the statements as an effort to discourage the colonists. One friendly Virginian, Captain Henry Fleet, a military man and fur trader, volunteered to sail with the newcomers and help them find a suitable landing site on the Maryland grant. As the *Ark* and the *Dove* sailed north along the coast, White reports, Piscataway bowmen gathered onshore to watch the great canoes pass and by night ignited huge bonfires to announce the ships' impending arrival to those to the north. On 3 March the expedition entered Chesapeake Bay at the mouth of the Potomac ("the sweetest and greatest river I have seen," White enthuses, "so that the Thames is but a little finger to it"), then proceeded upriver to an island-like outcropping into the Potomac called Saint Clement's Island. Dropping anchor, the soon-to-be colonists went ashore in a shallop to reconnoiter. The shallop was also loaded with a large supply of linen, including underclothes, which were lost when the shallop overturned—a fitting symbol, perhaps, of the prosaic but distressing difficulties of founding a colony!

Saint Clement's was a pleasant place. The ground, White notes, was abundant with berries, nuts, and salad herbs, but at only four hundred acres it was far too small for a first settlement, although it would make a good location for a fort, with its commanding entrance to the upper Potomac. Nevertheless, the Catholic English settlers landed on Saint Clement's Island on 25 March 1634, the feast of the Annunciation of the Angel Gabriel to Mary, and following the celebration of Mass on a makeshift, flower-bedecked altar, they raised a large wooden cross fashioned from a single tree and, chanting the appropriate litanies, took possession of the region in the name of God, the king, and the proprietor: a scene later rendered iconic for American Catholics in Emanuel Leutze's dramatic depiction of 1861. After the ceremony, Governor Calvert and Captain Fleet sailed further upriver in the *Dove* for an interview with the Piscataway's head chief (emperor), a boy for whom his regent and councilors did the negotiating as some five hundred armed but friendly warriors stood by and monitored the proceedings.[5]

To the colonists' good fortune, they had walked into a balance of power created by Virginians over the past twelve years since that terrible Friday, 22 March 1622, in the course of the Second Anglo-Powhatan War, when a Pamunkey-Powhatan alliance slaughtered 330 English colonists along the James River, one-fourth of the total population of Virginia. Building a network of offensive and defensive alliances with the Susquehannock (also called the Conestoga by the English) to the north, the Patawomeck of the Potomac River, and the Accomack and Accohannock of the Eastern Shore, fur traders and militia leaders such as Henry Fleet and William Claiborne stabilized the region and taught the Indians the value of enduring ties. Thus

the Yaocomaco, Piscataway, and Patuxent beheld in the newly arriving Marylanders the possibilities of a similar alliance with strong and well-armed English allies,
in their case against the Virginia-allied Susquehannock and the even more feared
Iroquois Seneca from the Lake Erie region.

Leonard Calvert returned from his negotiations with an introduction to the
Yaocomaco below Saint Clement's, from whom Calvert purchased a thirty-mile
riverfront tract along the east bank of the lower Potomac. Running into the tract's
interior was a tributary, first named the Saint George's River by Calvert. Six miles
upstream, the colonists found the best location for a settlement, a site previously
occupied by a Yaocomaco village on a bluff overlooking the tributary. The Yaocomaco had chosen well. Yaocomaco, as the village was called, was directly served
by the Saint George's River and stood midway between the Potomac and the
Patuxent. The surrounding forests were devoid of underbrush. Over the centuries,
the Yaocomaco had cleared these forests, which now offered an almost parklike
setting (a carriage, White noted, could be driven between the trees) of white and
red oak, chestnut, poplar, and sweet gum along tributary riverbanks and creeks,
and pine groves down along the Potomac. Crested over the millennia by sedi-
ment and silt washed down from the mountains of Virginia, the soil of these
terraces, which stood forty to fifty feet above the Saint George's River, was—as
the Yaocomaco had discovered long ago—the most fertile in the lower Potomac
region. The Marylanders called this first settlement Saint Mary's in honor of the
Mother of Jesus and later changed the name of the river connecting it to the Potomac to Saint Mary's as well.

A manorial frontier

In contrast to the early experiences of the Spaniards in Florida or the English in
Jamestown, Saint Mary's did not begin with a Starving Time. The Marylanders had
brought along a year's supplies, and the Yaocomaco, who voluntarily vacated their
village, turned over to the English their cleared fields, which—again, in contrast
to Spanish and English initial neglect of agriculture—the Marylanders immediately
planted. Fish and game were abundant. Locally, the Susquehannock to the north
remained bellicose and carried out a number of raids in the early years of the colony, but the threat from this quarter receded after a concerted English counterof-
fensive in 1642. Yet the Marylanders were never forced to face anything resembling
the horrendous slaughter of the Second Anglo-Powhatan War in Virginia or the
century-long hostility from the Iroquois endured by the French. As in Spanish and
French settlements, European women were notable by their absence in Maryland
for most of the seventeenth century. Unlike in these other Catholic cultures, however, a métis population did not develop to any appreciable degree, given the coastal
nature of Maryland settlement patterns and the tobacco economy, the absence of a
far-ranging fur trade that pushed young men inland, and the outmigration of Native
Americans from the area.

In terms of religious practice, the minority status of Catholics in Maryland proved
an important difference. New Spain and New France were Catholic colonies of
Catholic realms. Following the Huguenots' uprising in the 1620s, Richelieu did his
best to squelch their initial participation in New France. Yet for all the sentiment

that Maryland has inspired in Catholic America, Maryland was a colony authorized by a Protestant state on behalf of Roman Catholic entrepreneurs. The alleged
Catholic ascendancy in Maryland was tenuous and problematic. From the beginning, Catholics knew who was in charge. One of the earliest colonists to receive
legal chastisement was William Lewis, a lay Catholic overseer on a Jesuit plantation
justifiably fined for criticizing the Protestantism of two indentured servants (the
majority of whom were Protestants) and forbidding them to own or to read Protestant books.

Still, in an aristocratic age, Catholic Spain and France and Protestant Britain had
aristocracy in common: aristocracy anchored in land, descent, and title. Spain and
France organized the governance of New Spain and New France along aristocratic
models, although the French Canadian seigneury did not match the elevated status
of the Spanish establishment. To aristocracy and to retainers and clients of aristocrats
Roman Catholicism owed its survival in England. Catholics in Scotland and Ireland
took refuge in parallel structures of clanship whenever possible, as in the Highlands
or the clan-like attachments of the Irish Catholic peasantry. Thus it is not surprising
that the first and second Lords Baltimore tried to export to Maryland the manor as
an institution and lords of the manor as administrators of governance. For this New
World gentry, Cecil Calvert targeted Catholic second sons from established families, men capable of investing in the expedition and paying for the transportation of
indentured servants. As second sons, these men would not in the normal course of
things succeed to lands or titles.

For such services, Baltimore established a scheme of land grants: two thousand
acres for every five able-bodied indentured servants brought to the colony, plus
one hundred acres for every servant beyond five. Grants exceeding one thousand
(later three thousand) acres were eligible for manorial status on the same basis that
manorial status brought in England: the right to hold court, sit on the governor's
council, enjoy a title, and tax tenants' share in profits from trade. While Protestant
candidates for this New World gentry were equally welcomed, Cecil Calvert initially attracted only Catholic adventurer-investors—and not second or third sons
from the great English Catholic families at that. The Calvert family and the Jesuits
remained the major investors in the enterprise. Lord Baltimore's younger brothers,
Leonard the governor and George, who also settled in Maryland, were investors,
as were Baltimore's wife, Lady Anne Arundell, and his brothers-in-law, Sir Robert
Talbot, William Peasley, and Ralph Eure. The Jesuits invested heavily and between
1633 and 1639 paid for the transportation of fifty or so servants to the colony. Yet
whatever the level of their investment, the English Catholic gentry who did join
the first expedition—Thomas Cornwaleys, Thomas Greene, Edward and Frederick
Winter, Henry Wiseman, Jerome Hawley, Richard Gerard, and John Saunders
of the first migration; subsequently joined by James Neale, Giles Brent, Thomas
Gerard, and John Langford—constituted a connection, however fragile, between
recusant England and Maryland.

Of this group, Thomas Cornwaleys was the most prominent (second only to Governor Leonard Calvert) and the most documented—and hence most remembered—
as planter, soldier, councilor, and legislator. Cornwaleys came from a family of
overseas investors and Irish colonizers. His grandfather Sir Charles Cornwaleys had
served in Ireland with George Calvert and sat in Parliament with him. A devout

Catholic, Thomas Cornwaleys accepted the ecumenical nature of Maryland but also believed, as he wrote Lord Baltimore, that Maryland offered Catholics an opportunity to exercise matters of conscience and religious preference in a safe venue.

Economic development

Over time Thomas Cornwaleys surpassed the Jesuits as the second-largest investor in the colony after the Calverts. To his initial investment in the joint-stock company, the *Dove*, and the transportation of twelve servants, Cornwaleys imported another forty-five servants in the years that followed to run his flourishing tobacco, retail trade, milling, agricultural, and related enterprises. The other manorial investors, Catholics all, comparably improved their status through migration to Maryland, risk taking, and hard work. No longer were they pushed to the sidelines of English life by their status as Catholics and second sons. Now they were planters, judges, businessmen, councilors, legislators, and officers commanding militia forces. They had chanced everything, and now everything was slowly coming back to them. Like the French to the north, the manorial elite turned to the fur trade; beaver pelts were harvested locally and brought in from the interior at a greater volume by indigenous people and English fur traders. While the fur trade dominated the economy, the manorial elite and the Jesuits dominated the fur trade in Maryland. To that end, a supply ship arrived in Saint Mary's City in December 1634 laden with what has been described as a king's ransom in trade goods—cloth, combs, kettles, axes, hoes, knives, bells—financed by Lord Baltimore. While the fur trade flourished, manorial Maryland remained vigorous. Operation of the fur trade required armed pinnaces and shallops, storage facilities, shipping docks, and indentured servants and crews to run these facilities, and in the early years that meant manorial investors such as Thomas Cornwaleys, who was second only to Governor Calvert in Maryland's fur trade. The Jesuits operated in the trade through their designated factors, one of whom, the Afro-Portuguese mulatto Mathias de Sousa, enjoyed access to the fierce Susquehannock, who went openly on the warpath in the early 1640s, disrupting trade. In terms of the fur trade, Marylanders remained middlemen. Indigenous people gathered the product, set the cost, and sold the skins while Marylanders did their best to master the Algonquian and Iroquoian dialects that constituted the lingua franca of the business. Thus beaver pelts joined such other Indian derivatives as corn, tobacco, and beadwork (*roanoke* and *peake*) as the currency of Maryland, and Indian words and names entered the English vocabulary.

By 1642 the sixteen private manors of Saint Mary's County totaled thirty-one thousand acres, which represented 83.1 percent of all lands thus far granted by the proprietor. The possession of these holdings, together with their relative wealth, enabled the sixteen lords of the manor to dominate the cultivation of tobacco and corn for export in a society in which the rest of the population were either indentured servants or freemen who had completed their four-year obligation and were now hardscrabble tenant farmers in small-scale operations. The cultivation of corn for export to New England and tobacco for export to England developed alongside the fur trade as key start-ups in the Maryland economy. Indian corn was easy to farm. It grew in most places and could be planted from March through May and had a short growing season. What was not consumed could be immediately sold to

New England, as the manorial owners of the *Dove* quickly learned and responded to when they sent their seaworthy pinnace to Boston in August 1634 filled with this new high-calorie staple (for corn pone and hominy) of the English North American diet. Tobacco was a more difficult crop. It required careful planting in a cleared and fertile field, constant hoeing against weeds, topping and trimming, deworming, and meticulous cutting of leaves at harvest, followed by curing, stripping cured leaves from stalks, and painstakingly packing leaves into barrels for shipment. Tobacco also devoured soil nutrients, and so new fields had to be constantly surveyed, cleared of trees, broken with broad hoes, watered, and planted.

Diversified agriculture required equipment and servants. Vegetable gardens, fruit trees, livestock, poultry, and animal products (milk, butter, cheese, eggs, and meat) hence first appeared on manorial properties. Milk cows and cattle brought over from England or acquired from Virginia were expensive to purchase but, once bought, flourished on weeds and grasses of forestlands long ago cleared by the Yaocomaco. Fertile and plentiful, swine thrived on acorns and chestnuts of the forest and thus supplemented cattle on the manors. Pork also edged its way into the diet of freeholders and servants. Chickens from England and local turkeys, geese, and peafowl were available.

Once again, Thomas Cornwaleys of Manor Cross offers a case in point. Cornwaleys had the staff—plowman, blacksmith, cow keeper, and even a dairymaid—to pursue diversified husbandry. Manor Cross—its fine home and furniture; its kitchen and bake house; its servants' dormitory; its smith forge and storehouses; its barn teeming with wheat, oats, barley, and Indian corn—could by the early 1640s pass for a farm in Old England and thereby suggested a future in which Maryland would evolve an English demeanor of stately homes and parklike fields.

Indentured servants

The indentured servants these gentlemen adventurer-investors brought to the New World were poor at a time when poor was very poor indeed by contemporary standards of support, consumption, health, and longevity. From these indentured servants, Irish or English Catholics and Protestants, and from internal migration came the next phase of Maryland development, bringing the population of the colony to four thousand by 1660; twenty thousand by 1680; and thirty-four thousand by 1700. The very fact that in-migration from Virginia did not boost the population higher testifies to the ravages of disease in the early decades and the chronic shortage of women eligible for "copulative matrimony", in the era's quaint but promising phrase.

Regarding disease, Maryland required of its early immigrants a dangerous period of Seasoning (another vivid localism). The riverine environment created mosquito-ridden marshes, which led to malaria on epidemic levels. Dysentery was a natural result of poor diet and food poisoning. Weakened survivors of these twinned ills, malaria and diarrhea, then became vulnerable to imported diseases such as smallpox, diphtheria, yellow fever, and influenza. Health statistics improved as the population moved into higher and drier regions, but in the colony's initial stages, a late teenager (the average age was seventeen) who arrived in Maryland and survived had an average of another twenty-three years of life. A comparable male in New England could expect another forty-five years. One out of every five males in Maryland would not reach thirty. Seven out of ten would not reach fifty.

As in New France before the filles du roi program, eligible women from the homeland were extremely scarce in the early decades and remained so in later years. Even the females who were present could not marry during their four years of indentured servitude. Freed Marylanders could easily rent or eventually buy land. Securing a wife, however, was another matter. Men lived alone for years—or for life—or ran their farms in partnership with another man; such a partner was called a mate, anticipating a term later used in Australia, another female-scarce colony. Men who did manage to marry thus tended to marry later in what was already an abbreviated life span and to marry an older woman, for widows hardly remained widows for long. This situation has been characterized as serial polyandry: the marriages of increasingly older men to increasingly older widows past their peak childbearing years. The result was smaller families in which roughly half the children born died before the age of twenty and the rest stood a strong chance of being orphaned before reaching maturity.

Still, indentured servants and, later, free in-migrants continued to arrive and, whenever possible, enter the local economy as tobacco and corn growers. At the very least, a freed servant could get a short-term lease on property from the proprietor or manor lord. That was enough to get started. By 1642, thanks to abundant land and ongoing credit, up to 25 percent of former servants and migrants from Virginia held their properties outright as freeholders and had become yeoman planters in their own right. Maryland remained hierarchical. It was, after all, a proprietorship. Yet society was leveling within its seventeenth-century parameters as new men came to the fore to replace the dominance of the initial few gentlemen adventurer-investors. Yeoman farmers, one should note, could not afford separate quarters for indentured servants. Their servants, rather, lived in their homes; they ate with them, worked alongside them in the fields, and became in many instances the psychological and emotional equivalent of family.

A Protestant colony

Through the 1670s, a restrained style of life prevailed in Maryland, reflective of the Puritan ascendancy following the victory of Parliament in the English Civil War that had broken out in 1642, the establishment of a Puritan-oriented Commonwealth in 1653, and the in-migration into Maryland of Puritans from nearby colonies. This plain style asserted the fact that Maryland was demographically a Protestant colony—nearly 90 percent of its population was Protestant—within the legal framework of a protectorate held by a Protector who was a Roman Catholic and a pro-monarch Cavalier in the Civil War. That Protector now was forced to spend the better part of a decade renegotiating his status with a newly victorious Parliament and Oliver Cromwell, Lord Protector of the Commonwealth. The protectorate of Maryland had never been an easy or stable role for either of the Lords Baltimore. George Calvert had died seeking it. Cecil Calvert held it at a disadvantage and came close to losing it on a number of occasions.

No sooner had the colony been established than Captain William Claiborne refused to vacate the fur-trading settlement he had founded on Kent Island, the largest island in Chesapeake Bay, granted to Claiborne in 1631 when Maryland was still part of Virginia. Offered an opportunity to swear allegiance to Baltimore, Claiborne refused on legal and religious grounds and went into armed resistance. Worse, incensed that his representative was forced to swear on a Latin Bible when testifying in Saint Mary's on behalf of Claiborne's case, Claiborne sent two forti-fied trading wherries to attack Saint Mary's. Two sloops commanded by Thomas Cornwaleys met them on the water, and in the ensuing battle, five of Claiborne's men were killed. Three weeks later, Cornwaleys successfully reattacked Claiborne's vessels. Claiborne turned his attention to Virginia, where he deposed the governor, had himself declared governor, and began talking of invading Maryland before he himself was deposed. In January 1637 Maryland governor Leonard Calvert invaded Kent Island, seized approximately ten thousand pounds' worth of furs and trading goods, and offered all settlers there amnesty if they would swear allegiance to his brother, which they did.

A Virginian of enormous prestige—the son of a prominent merchant family from Kent, a Cambridge graduate, a military leader in the mold of Captain John Smith, a man capable of having a governor of Virginia removed and himself installed in his place—William Claiborne embodied the heroic energies and political connect-edness of Anglican Virginia in its years of establishment. His open defiance of the Roman Catholicism of the proprietor and his brother the governor was exactly the kind of attention Lord Baltimore feared during the founding time of his colony, when a low profile in religious matters was essential. In years to come, Claiborne would return to do further damage.

Imagine Baltimore's shock when the next threat to the détente of discretion he had negotiated with the Privy Council and the Crown came not from Claiborne or other Protestants but from the English Province of the Society of Jesus. Even before the Middle Ages, once the Church, in any of her organizational formats—diocese, monastery, parish, college, hospital—acquired property, that property remained for all time to come in ecclesiastical ownership. It could not be sold. This concept of nonalienation of ecclesiastical property was in legal terms described as *mortmain* (dead hand), suggesting its irrevocability, and was dealt with as early as the Magna Carta. Church property was acquired steadily and hence the vast monastic lands that Henry VIII and a Protestantizing nobility beheld as offering an unprecedented opportunity for seizure in the ongoing land grab that, along with Henry's divorce and remarriage, was at the core of the Henrician Reformation. In the century and a half that followed, England passed Statutes of Mortmain forbidding the acquisition of property by the Church of England or any corporate religious body claiming mortmain. Yet on the Continent, Roman Catholic canon law continued to enforce this privilege of acquisition of property by ecclesiastical entities under conditions of nonalienation, forbidding resale.

In his early discussions with the Jesuits regarding the Maryland venture, the first Lord Baltimore had suggested that the Jesuits might be able to acquire prop-erty under mortmain in the proposed colony. His son Cecil, however, did not formally extend this privilege, nor did he offer to support the Jesuits once they arrived in Maryland. They would have to pay their own way, going to Maryland as adventurer-investors on the same footing as any other gentleman in this category. Individual Jesuits using aliases or their lay designees could hold property, but not the English Province of the Society of Jesus as a corporation. On this basis, the Jesuits of Maryland prospered as farmers and fur traders in support of their ministry. Rather early on, however—and secretly!—Andrew White received a gift of land on behalf of the Jesuits from the Patuxent chief Kittamaquund.

In the summer of 1637, Jesuit priest Thomas Copley arrived in Maryland and joined Fathers Andrew White, John Gravener, and perhaps Timothy Hayes at Saint Mary's City. If there were such a thing as recusant credentials, Thomas Copley would have easily made the A-list. He was from Old Catholic nobility, for one thing. Margaret Giggs, his grandmother on his mother's side, was a close friend of the Thomas More family. (She appears next to More's daughter Margaret Roper in Holbein's well-known portrait of the More family.) More sent her his blessing from the Tower following his arrest. Later, as a young woman, disguised as a milkmaid, she smuggled food to the imprisoned Carthusian monks of the London Charterhouse prior to their execution. Born in Madrid in 1594 following the expatriation of his father to Spain and his marriage there to Magdalen Prideaux, another well-born Catholic exile, Copley returned to England with his family at the age of nine and was raised there, but since he was unable as a Catholic to enter university, he returned in 1611 to the Low Countries (his sisters Mary and Helen had already entered the convent of Saint Monica there) to enroll at the University of Louvain. In his late teens he entered the nearby Jesuit novitiate on Mont César (Andrew White was already a novice there), followed by further philosophical and theological studies at Louvain. Ordained to the priesthood, Copley distinguished himself as an underground missionary in England—underground for only a while. Copley soon found himself in court circles, perhaps via some form of service to King Charles' Catholic queen, Henrietta Maria, as evident on 5 December 1663 when no less than the king himself issued Copley a signed warrant of safe conduct allowing him to travel unmolested throughout the kingdom in pursuit of his occupation.

Thomas Copley, in short, had standing and influence derived from nobility, recusant lineage, and connections with friends in high places; and so when Copley, in response to the restrictions of mortmain being advanced by Lord Baltimore, began to articulate his vision for Maryland, the Catholic founding elite of the colony listened closely. Maryland, Copley argued, was a refuge for Catholics, and hence a confessional commonwealth. Hence it fell under the jurisdiction of the canon law of the universal Church, which meant the Jesuits could receive property as a corporate body and hold such property as inalienable Church property under protection of mortmain! Furthermore, the Jesuits wished to exercise Catholicism more publicly in the colony. They had already begun to proselytize among indentured servants and had converted a number of them. They wanted a public chapel at Saint Mary's with an open celebration of Mass and the sacraments. The Calverts had guaranteed private worship only. Regarding Indians, the Jesuits wanted something resembling the *ascenciones* (mission communities) of Paraguay or the monopoly they would later achieve on the Baja California peninsula: districts under Jesuit control, that is, on which evangelized Indians might be settled, and a clerically driven mission system tailored to the Counter-Reformational ethos and strong missionary impulse at the core identity of the Society. The Jesuits had brought along such key Catholic figures as Thomas Cornwaleys to support such a scheme, which was blatantly at odds with the founding charter negotiated by the Calverts.

Lord Baltimore must have become enraged when news of these claims reached him. Here he was, the Catholic proprietor of a colony allegedly open to all bona fide Christians, and yet it was rumored that the decidedly anti-Jesuit William Laud, archbishop of Canterbury, was on the verge of requesting that the Privy Council cancel the Baltimore proprietorship because of the Jesuits openly operating there. And now one of these very Jesuits was arguing for the identity of Maryland as a Catholic refuge operating under Catholic canon law, with the Society of Jesus functioning as its established clergy! Add to this the fact that the Jesuits were challenging Baltimore's proprietorship of all Maryland property in perpetuity by arguing for a mortmain permit for Jesuit ownership of properties acquired by the Society. Worse, various leading Catholic investors, such as Thomas Cornwaleys, were coming around to the Jesuit point of view! Contacting the Sacred Congregation of Propagation in Rome and the apostolic delegate in Brussels, Baltimore asked that a list of suitable secular priests willing to undertake the Maryland mission be drawn up as replacements for the Jesuits. Only two seculars were sent over, however, and once there, they sided with the Jesuits. All in all, it took five years of negotiation and counter-negotiation for Baltimore—who at one point threatened to demand the return of all Jesuit properties—to bring the Jesuits around to his position. As part of the solution, the Jesuits could keep the property they had already acquired as adventurer-investors. If they obtained new properties, however, such properties could be held only by lay trustees and would not be considered ecclesiastical properties covered by mortmain. Finally, the Jesuits were to secure no new property from Indians either by gift or by purchase.

Fortunately for Lord Baltimore, this rift with the Jesuits—and, more particularly, Thomas Copley's description of Maryland as a colony under Roman Catholic auspices and law—occurred as the English establishment was facing its greatest crisis since the Spanish Armada. Otherwise, Archbishop Laud might have launched his attack on Baltimore's proprietorship. Had Cecil Calvert—Catholic peer and proprietor, man of business and entrepreneur—been able to migrate to Maryland and govern (as William Penn would later do in the proprietary colony of Pennsylvania), he might have been able to reconcile the contradictions at the core of his colony as a place of religious refuge for Catholics as well as a source of upward mobility and an economic engine for all. The instability of the Maryland formula, however, kept him in London, lest he be outmaneuvered in his proprietorship and his colony taken from him. The situation in Maryland, moreover, reflected the political, economic, and, above all else, religious instability of the realm itself, now engaged in civil war by the time Baltimore settled with the Society of Jesus.

The Plundering Time

Enter—or, rather, reenter—William Claiborne. Enter also another adventurer of comparably strong anti-Maryland, anti-Catholic instincts, the mariner and sometime pirate Richard Ingle. Their collaboration would bring the Maryland experiment to a halt, send founders into exile, banish Jesuits, and force Lord Baltimore's proprietorship into various levels of political limbo until 1657. While in England in 1637 and 1638 to argue his case, Claiborne suffered two defeats: the seizure of Kent Island by Maryland governor Leonard Calvert and a declaration by the Commissioners of

Plantation in April 1638 that Kent Island was legally within the bounds and limits of Lord Baltimore's Maryland grant. Claiborne returned to Virginia, where he recouped his fortune and position in society and was appointed major general of militia. The civil war offered Claiborne an opportunity for payback.

His partner in revenge, Richard Ingle—the name of whose ship, *Reformation*, underscored his sharing of Claiborne's anti-Catholic attitudes—had likewise experienced difficulties when he entered the *Reformation* in the tobacco trade in 1642. In the course of two sojourns to Maryland, Ingle had been charged with treason (speaking against the king) and piracy (seizing furs with failure to pay)—charges he beat in court—and, lastly, departing for England after failing to pay customs and other dues, for which his goods in Maryland were sequestered. The English Civil War, which broke out in the same year, offered Ingle the chance to return to the colony whose Catholic establishment, the governor and governor's council, had caused him so much grief. Ingle's intention was to bring the civil war to Maryland. He would succeed beyond his wildest dreams.

With letters of marque from the lord high admiral under authority of Parliament in hand, Ingle set sail for Maryland in the *Reformation*. (Ironically, Governor Calvert was in England at approximately the same time, obtaining letters of marque from the king on behalf of the Cavalier cause.) Arriving in Virginia in the fall of 1644, Ingle began to organize with Claiborne a joint invasion of Maryland on behalf of Parliament. He had already promised the crew of the *Reformation* a sixth of all goods plundered. Sailing the *Reformation* to Saint Mary's, where he arrived in early January 1645, Ingle secretly started recruiting important Protestant planters to his plan. The Plundering Time being organized would replicate the English Civil War on a small but deadly scale. It would disrupt the government and send Governor Calvert fleeing to Virginia for safety, depopulate (by killing or fleeing) the Western Shore of Maryland by five-sixths, burn manorial Maryland to the ground, destroy the Jesuit presence, come close to costing Lord Baltimore his proprietorship, and end once and for all any notion that Maryland constituted, if only subliminally, the Roman Catholic refuge some of its early investors had hoped it would be.

At the port of Saint Mary's, Ingle seized a Dutch ship loading tobacco: plundering prize number one. He also captured there Giles Brent, the Catholic manorial lord who, as acting governor (Leonard Calvert being in England) had unsuccessfully pressed charges of treason against Ingle before a total of four hung juries. (Brent owed Ingle money, but conflict of interest was not a very strong category in the seventeenth century.) Plundering prize number two was thus a special source of psychological satisfaction, as Ingle evened a score against an enemy. Sailing up Inigoes Creek, Ingle seized Manor Cross, Thomas Cornwaleys' fortified manor. Cornwaleys was away, but Ingle captured his overseer, Cuthbert Fenwick, who under pressure arranged for the surrender of the manor house. From Manor Cross, Ingle launched attacks on the lay and Jesuit manors on the Western Shore. Manor after manor was looted and then burned to the ground. Eventually, even Manor Cross, the finest manor house in the colony, was looted and burned, despite the fact that Thomas Cornwaleys had been a passenger on the *Reformation* in 1642, a business partner of Ingle, and the man who had come to his assistance when he was facing charges. Capturing the five Jesuits in Maryland, as well as John Lewger, the Catholic secretary to the governor's council, Ingle put them in chains. As his movement grew from an influx of Protestant freemen (including three members of the colonial assembly), Ingle shifted his headquarters to Fort Thomas, Governor Calvert's former house, as if to suggest a new and permanent change in government, which seemed more than possible once Governor Calvert had fled to Virginia.

In mid-April 1645 Ingle departed for England. Also on board the *Reformation* were Giles Brent, John Lewger, and the five Jesuits. The depth of Ingle's anti-Catholicism was revealed when, sailing past Susquehannock country, Ingle put ashore three of the Jesuits, John Cooper, Bernard Hartwell, and Roger Rigby. The Susquehannock hated Marylanders, doubly so since Marylanders had recently mounted an expedition into their homeland. Murderously, Ingle was dropping off the Jesuits in an environment in which they had next to no chance of survival. None of the three were ever seen or heard from again.

Giles Brent, John Lewger, Andrew White, and Thomas Copley reached England in chains: they were proof positive, Ingle argued, that Maryland represented a Catholic conspiracy and Lord Baltimore should lose his charter. Parliament initially listened to Ingle and appointed a committee to look into the matter. Lord Baltimore's proprietorship seemed to be hanging by a thread. But the parliamentary committee took no action. Brent and Lewger were ordered released. When Fathers White and Copley were brought to court, White argued that he could not be charged with being a Jesuit entering England illegally because he had not come voluntarily. Thomas Copley argued the same, but with the added proviso that he had been born in Spain and hence was not subject to the law forbidding English Jesuits from entering England. Each Jesuit was acquitted and ordered to leave the country. White remained in England and was briefly imprisoned. Released, he left for the Continent, never to return. Copley went back to Maryland and revived the Jesuit presence there.

Even more humiliating than these defeats, the admiralty court refused to grant Ingle prize money for the Dutch ship he had captured, since England and the Netherlands were not formally at war with each other at the time of capture. Ingle continued to press his case against Lord Baltimore, but a remotivated proprietor was fighting back. When Leonard Calvert died in June 1647 as the result of snakebite, Baltimore replaced his interim Catholic successor, Thomas Greene, with William Stone, a Protestant tobacco merchant from Virginia, disregarding Stone's previous cooperation with Claiborne and Ingle. Baltimore also reconstituted the governor's council, seating three Protestants and two Catholics. Of equal boldness, he ordered the recruitment of Puritan settlers from Virginia who had—in one of the most unusual acts of counterdefinition of the English Civil War era—served Leonard Calvert as mercenaries during the Plundering Time, despite Ingle's effort to cast the Plundering Time as a Protestant crusade.

Within a short time, the majority population of the newly reconstituted Maryland comprised Puritans from Virginia. To appease Puritans in power in England and Maryland, Baltimore encouraged the Maryland general assembly to pass on 21 April 1649 a Toleration Act that guaranteed freedom of worship to all trinitarian Christians. Nontrinitarians would be punished by death and forfeiture of all goods to the lord proprieter and his heirs: an amendment insisted upon by the Puritan-Protestant majority of the general assembly and wisely let stand by Lord Baltimore. First-time offenders against the religious peace would be subject to fines. Chronic offenders would be publicly whipped and their goods confiscated.

Oliver Cromwell was impressed by this Toleration Act, for it accorded with his own best instincts, as it did with those of Lord Baltimore himself, who had promised such policies—minus the nontrinitarian clause—in 1633 when arguing his case before the Privy Council. In any event, Baltimore clearly intended the Maryland Toleration Act to counter Ingle's smears and to appease the rising Puritan tide while reasserting Catholic rights alongside everyone else's. Still, Baltimore was also insisting upon an oath of loyalty to himself as proprietor, and that troubled Puritans, just as the Oath of Supremacy had recently troubled Roman Catholics.

The renewed crisis of the 1650s

And so for the third time William Claiborne reenters the scene, more determined than ever to remove the Calverts from their hereditary proprietorship. By the mid-1650s, Claiborne was more powerful than ever, and he now expressed concern regarding colonial matters. The colonies, Claiborne argued, had grown up haphazardly under differing schemes of organization. England should set in place systematic governance for its North American colonies as a prelude to empire. On the one hand, Claiborne's intelligence and continental ambition are admirable. On the other hand, Claiborne, as usual, had some old scores to settle. As the first step of this program to systematize colonial governance, Claiborne angled a commission from Parliament to bring all the plantations of the Chesapeake into conformity with the new parliamentary scheme. In partnership with Richard Bennett—the very man who had previously sided with Governor Leonard Calvert and led Calvert's Puritan mercenaries but who now saw the possibility of a Puritanized Maryland and Virginia by a Puritanized Parliament—Claiborne restructured the government of Virginia. Bennett assumed the governorship in the name of Parliament; Claiborne was named secretary. The two then organized and led an armed invasion into Maryland in the early spring of 1655. Their excuse: Maryland governor William Stone, a Protestant, sensing the rise of the more tolerant and inclusively minded Oliver Cromwell against the more hard-line Puritanizers of Parliament, had reduced the number of Puritans on the governor's council.

Bennett and Claiborne were, in effect, leading a Virginia-based Puritan coup d'état against the Calvert proprietorship. Seizing Saint Mary's, Bennett and Claiborne removed Stone and his council from office, appointed a ten-man Puritan-dominated committee to govern the colony, and repealed the Toleration Act. When deposed Governor Stone, under instructions from Baltimore, tried to regain the government by force, his men, landing on the shores of the Severn River near Annapolis in late March 1655, were decimated by crossfire from ambushing Puritan militia. In the course of the battle, four of Stone's men—Thomas Hatton (deposed Governor Stone's Protestant secretary), William Eltonhead and William Lewis (both of whom were Catholic), and a third soldier—surrendered on a guarantee of safe conduct. Instead, they were summarily shot by the Puritans in a breach of faith that underscored the era's intense religious hatred, even toward Hatton, a Protestant who had remained faithful to the proprietor. Lord Baltimore subsequently supported the widows and orphans of the executed loyalists.

Although not apparent at the time, these unjustified executions would prove a tipping point. Two years earlier, Oliver Cromwell had dissolved the Long

Parliament by military intervention on 20 April 1653 and on 12 December had assumed supreme authority as Lord Protector. Bennett and Claiborne's authority, in short, had lapsed with the dissolution of Parliament, and so each side of the controversy—Puritan invaders and Catholic proprietor—had to argue its case for two ensuing years before a newly established Council of State. Having deprived the Puritan party of its parliamentary power and having long since (in 1650) repealed the Act of Uniformity, which demanded one religious polity throughout England, the Lord Protector and his Council of State—so Lord Baltimore correctly surmised—were in no mood to cancel the Calvert charter and retroactively authorize a Puritan coup d'état. Instead, the Lord Protector ordered a return to the status quo ante in Maryland and authorized Baltimore to appoint a new governor and council. In addition, the ailing Cromwell ordered Baltimore and Bennett to come to an agreement. By late November 1657 they reached a compromise. Baltimore retained his proprietorship. The Toleration Act of 1649 was restored. Deposed governor William Stone and William Fuller, the leader of the Puritan militia, would sit together on a five-man council (a structure similar to that of the Council of State of the Commonwealth), governing the colony in partnership with a governor appointed by Baltimore.

An idyllic interlude

For the next quarter of a century, Maryland Catholics enjoyed a modified reflection of the religious toleration, the peace and quiet, that recusant England would have long since been happy to settle for. Minority status and a low population of Catholics prevented the rise of an ecclesiastical culture like that of Quebec Province or Spanish Florida. However, Saint Mary's City, in the simple manner of Pierre Boucher's seigneury outside Montreal, did manage to materialize the spiritual and imaginative possibilities of Maryland as Catholic place and sanctuary.

Like his father, Cecil Calvert spent most of his working life in London. The Calvert family likewise knew and appreciated the city of York in their home county as well as the elegantly developed provincial townships of that region. Almost as a matter of course, Cecil Calvert had hopes for an urban center in Saint Mary's County, Maryland. In his initial instructions, he directed that row houses be built on well-defined streets, with vegetable and flower gardens planted behind each home. A rude compliance with these orders was perhaps evident in the rows of timber cottages adjacent to the palisaded Saint Mary's Fort where the Maryland Assembly met in the first three years. In the beginning, Mass was celebrated in a large, oval Indian lodge, twenty feet long and ten feet high. Between 1634 and 1638, however, construction began on a brick chapel shaped like a cross. The Catholic and Protestant communities shared this chapel until a Protestant chapel was erected in 1642. Streets in these early years were little more than pathways, and an old Indian trail served as the main pedestrian entry into the settlement.

With time, Saint Mary's might have matured into the urban hub envisioned by Cecil Calvert. Instead, properties were dispersed throughout Saint Mary's County during the manorial era. Centralized settlement did not suit tobacco growing, which required easy access to water landings for shipping purposes. Designated "hundreds", three administrative units organized around manors grew up on the shores of Saint Mary's River, Saint Michael's Hundred and Saint Mary's Hundred on the eastern bank and Saint George's Hundred on the western; their population totaled 270. By 1642 Saint Clement's Hundred on the Wicomico River numbered 60 inhabitants, and Mattapanient Hundred, of 30 to 40 residents, had taken root on the Patuxent River five miles north of the original fort. Over the years, these hundreds and the manors they contained increased in population.

Like everyone else, the Jesuits dispersed. Early on, when numerous Indians lived in the region, the missionary impulse—as well as a desire to acquire land to support their ministry—ran strong in Maryland Jesuits. First of all, the Jesuits were entitled to twenty-eight thousand acres of land for having transported some sixty indentured servants to the colony. Only four thousand acres, however (Saint Thomas Manor), were immediately granted to individual Jesuits under their lay aliases. Jesuits under aliases also purchased from Richard Gerard another five thousand acres on the tip of the Western Shore, which they developed as Saint Inigoes Manor; its legal title was later transferred to laymen under personal trust at the insistence of Lord Baltimore. As with their other North American properties, the Jesuits developed Saint Inigoes—named in honor of Saint Ignatius of Loyola—into a prosperous plantation, which featured a Jesuit residence, servants' quarters, barns, stables, assorted service buildings (carpenter's shop, mill, weavers' workshop, cabin-sized meat locker, windmill, and henhouse), apple and peach orchards, vegetable gardens, grazing fields, and a direct pathway to a brick chapel (built between 1634 and 1638). Although the Jesuits exempted themselves from the judicial and political obligations of manorial ownership, Saint Inigoes Manor set standards for development in the early years of the colony. Coadjutor brothers and indentured servants probably provided most of the labor, since Jesuit priests were eager to evangelize the neighboring tribes as soon as Governor Calvert—once he deemed it safe, following a colonist's murder by local Indians—gave them permission to do so.

Father Andrew White was especially active as a missionary to local Indians, moving in 1638 to Mattaponi, home of the Patuxent. Father John Gravener evangelized on Kent Island. As a sign of goodwill, the Patuxent chief Macqmacomen in 1639 gave White a tract of Mattaponi land, on which the Jesuits developed a second plantation similar to Saint Inigoes. White then moved north to evangelize among the Piscataway. Achieving fluency in Algonquian, White composed a catechism in that language and in the summer of 1640 baptized the head chief Kittamaquund and his wife into the Church and solemnized their marriage. Despite these notable conversions and the success of their plantations, however, neither White nor any other Jesuit was exempt from the diseases of the Seasoning every Marylander had to endure. Illness forced White to abandon his mission to the Piscataway. Two Jesuits died of yellow fever. Ferdinand Poulton, the Jesuit superior, was accidentally shot to death. Several Jesuit servants were killed when the Susquehannock raided Mattaponi in 1642.

While very small enclaves emerged at Newton and upriver at Port Tobacco, Saint Mary's City remained the sparsely settled capital of a sparsely settled colony until the 1670s. During the English Civil War and commonwealth years, Cecil Calvert had expended his major energies regarding Maryland on protecting his right to the proprietorship. But in 1666 the Catholic-friendly Charles II—married to a Catholic queen, Catherine of Braganza of Portugal, and the brother of a Catholic

Map 17. Chesapeake Colonies.

convert, James, the Duke of York—was restored to the throne, and new ambition for his colony took hold of Cecil Calvert.

Already, Cecil in 1661 had sent his eldest son, Charles, to Maryland to serve as governor. On the voyage over, the recently widowed Charles spent time in the company of Jane Lowe Sewall, widow of the late Henry Sewall of Maryland, and the two were married following their arrival. Charles Calvert spent twenty-three vigorous years in Maryland as governor, from 1661 to 1684, the last nine of them as lord proprietor as well as governor, following the death of his father. (Cecil Calvert died in London on 30 November 1675.) The presence in Maryland of the proprietor's son—then the proprietor himself, third Lord Baltimore in the Irish peerage—brought cachet and coherence to the colony in general and to Saint Mary's City in particular. The city was formally incorporated in 1667 by letters patent, with all the privileges and immunities attached to this official designation, including the right to hold Saturday market days. Streets were formally laid out, starting with Middle Street in 1672 as well as two connecting roads to the outside world. In 1676 Lord Proprietor Charles Calvert, third Lord Baltimore, financed the construction of a statehouse from which the colony was administered. Saint Mary's City now had thirty buildings (and double that number by the end of the century)—homes, shops, warehouses, merchants' offices, a school, a market house, a mill, a jail, and the proprietary mansion—not as grand, perhaps, as a comparable English township, but fine enough for an emergent township in a reemergent colony. Besides, as Bernard Bailyn has pointed out, with the exception of a few outstanding buildings, the scale of the built environment in frontier colonial British North America was smaller than that of England.

The architecture of Saint Mary's City—if one is to judge from surviving buildings elsewhere in the area or from twentieth-century renderings of archaeological evidence—was striking, with a paleo-modern style of harmonious proportions, simplicity, fenestration, and sheltering rooflines. The people living and working in these structures, moreover, had begun to form a community that had made the transition from frontier to province. Philip Calvert and his nephew William Calvert of the proprietor's family lived on adjoining lots; Philip served as the first mayor of Saint Mary's City under its new charter and later at various times as governor, chancellor, and deputy governor. Maryland attorney general Charles Carroll the Settler, an emigrant from Ireland, whose sixty thousand acres made him the largest landowner in the colony, leased a house in Saint Mary's on Saint Inigoes Creek, where he lived when court was in session. A graduate of Douai and a member of the English bar, Carroll would be blessed with a grandson, Charles Carroll of Carrollton, who would follow in his grandfather's footsteps in achieving an education in France and the London Inns of Court.

Like Charles Carroll the Settler, Colonel John Addison, a relative of the English essayist Joseph Addison, brought a note of learning to Saint Mary's City. Acting governor Thomas Notley (the proprietor was in England and Ireland in 1676), another accomplished gentleman, owned a brick hunting lodge outside the city that he wryly named Bachelor's Hope. Providing Saint Mary's with conviviality and club life, Dutchman Garrett Van Sweringen kept a tavern on Aldermanbery as well as fifty acres on Saint Inigoes Creek. Van Sweringen also owned a second tavern, Smith's Town House, located in the first statehouse, and a nearby coffeehouse. Robert Gelley's tavern, Gelley's Ordinary, was temporarily closed by the mayor and aldermen because lawyers, jurymen, suitors, and others congregated there and thus disrupted or delayed the orderly conduct of the provincial courts. Clerk of council John Llewellyn was sued in 1686 for a debt worth 7,760 pounds of tobacco (a means of exchange in the Chesapeake colonies) that he had accumulated in one short month, February 1685, for punch and passado, which Llewellyn consumed by the bowl or half bowl and by the bottle.

Chapel and town plan

The residual Catholicity of Saint Mary's City was most directly expressed by its brick chapel (Saint Maries Chappell), finished in its third or fourth version in 1667 on the eastern side of the twenty-five-acre Chapel Land section of the larger, four-hundred-acre Chapel Freehold purchased between 1640 and 1641 by Jesuits Ferdinand Poulton and Thomas Copley and layman Cuthbert Fenwick. During Cecil Calvert's quarrel with the Jesuits over land ownership, the proprietor purchased the chapel in 1644 and briefly installed two secular priests there, but when the dispute was settled in 1646, the seculars returned to England and the Jesuits resumed responsibility for chapel services. The 1667 structure was a most impressive building. Excavations of that structure have revealed brick foundations three feet thick and four feet high in support of a Latin cross–shaped structure measuring fifty-five feet in length from nave to chancel and fifty-seven feet in width across the two transepts.

The chapel anchored the southeast end of the city. Representing a less spiritual aspect of Saint Mary's was the small but stout brick jailhouse on Gallows Greene.

A pillory threatened in front of the jail, and behind it was a ducking pool for less serious offenders. On the upper northwestern extremity of the town, on a bluff overlooking the Saint Mary's River, stood the third Lord Baltimore's imposing red-brick statehouse. The third such seat of government in the history of the colony, the three-story, forty-five-foot-long statehouse was also built as a cross and featured a veranda overlooking the river and adjoining structures for servants and supporting services. While hastily built and requiring serious repairs within six years (although it did stand until 1829), the statehouse—dominated within by a grandiose high-ceilinged Assembly Room, forty-one by twenty-six feet—dramatically asserted the survival and stability of proprietary Maryland after so many decades of conflict and uncertainty. For a brief time, the statehouse ranked among the most impressive buildings in the English colonies, and in the early 1930s it was reconstructed according to archaeological and comparative architectural evidence as part of Maryland's tercentennial celebration and furnished with copies of late seventeenth-century furniture.

In 1988 archaeology came to the aid of Henry M. Miller, archaeologist and historian of town planning. For years, historians of planning considered the Saint Mary's City layout irregular, in contrast to the systematic plans of Spanish colonial cities (as determined by the Laws of the Indies) or to the baroque regularity of grid, circle, and radial roadways in the schemes for Annapolis (ca. 1718) and Williamsburg (ca. 1722), both devised by Francis Nicholson (who served as governor, successively, of Maryland and Virginia). From this perspective, Saint Mary's City—like colonial New Amsterdam, Boston, and Quebec—grew according to topography and serendipities of ownership, as opposed to the grid-dominated townships of New Haven, Charleston, and Philadelphia, which reprised regularized plans that dated back to Roman times.

Not so, argued Miller, the director of research for Historic Saint Mary's City, the nonprofit foundation responsible for curation of the site. Baroque town planning, Miller writes in the journal *Historical Archaeology*, made statements of cultural and social value. Saint Mary's City possessed a regularized plan, and it was finalized in 1676 by the construction of the third statehouse. The chapel and the statehouse faced each other across a large meadow at opposite extremes of the property. Each building was located at the lower right base of two triangles formed by roads and streets. The top points of these two road-lined triangles met at the town center at right angles to each other. Thus church and state spaces were separate from each other yet connected at the town center. As rudimentary and unfinished as the plan of Saint Mary's City might have been, a statement was being made. Not for Maryland would there be the emplacement of church and governor's palace across from each other on an open central plaza as called for by the Laws of the Indies, nor the centrality of the town church on the village green, as became common in the Puritan villages of New England. According to the Toleration Act of 1649, church and state in proprietary Maryland were separate but convergent entities.

19

Annapolis 1704

Catholic settlement spreads through the Chesapeake region

John Coode, the leader of the 1689 seizure of the Maryland government, served briefly in England as an Anglican priest. Turned out of his parish for unknown reasons, Coode migrated to Maryland. Falling seriously ill as part of the Seasoning process, he recovered but was imprisoned for refusing to pay his physician. Coode married Susannah, the widowed daughter of Catholic manorial lord Thomas Gerard. Through inheritance from his father-in-law and from his own efforts, Coode became a wealthy landowner. At the time, Catholics, many of them related to the Calverts by blood or marriage, dominated the governor's council. Between 1666 and 1689, only eight Protestants managed to find a seat on the council alongside the nineteen Catholics who served. The development of Saint Mary's City as a town with more than a suggestion of Calvert and Catholic hegemony offended Coode and other prominent Protestants. A Protestant revolution was brewing in Maryland as well as in England.

When news of the Glorious Revolution reached Maryland, Coode helped form the Protestant Association that issued a manifesto calling for loyalty to the new monarchs. In 1689 the Protestant Association organized a march on Saint Mary's City and seized the government. In fear for their lives, Jesuit Nicholas Gurlick and two English Franciscan priests assisting at Saint Mary's City fled to Virginia. Two other Jesuits, Francis Pennington and John Matthews, went into hiding. As chief of government, Coode demanded the immediate recognition of the new monarchs, the revocation of the Calvert charter, and the establishment of Anglicanism as the official religion of Maryland.

The Calvert charter was withdrawn in 1689 and would not be fully restored until Benedict Leonard Calvert, fourth Lord Baltimore, conformed to the Church of England in 1713. The first three governors under this new regime—Lionel Copley, Francis Nicholson, and Nehemiah Blakiston—were Protestantizers but allowed Catholics a measure of influence and the private practice of their religion. The fourth governor, however—John Seymour, an outspoken Coldstream Guards officer—favored a return to penalizing Catholics. When Seymour and his council learned that the Jesuits who had returned to Saint Inigoes were offering Mass in public in the chapel in Saint Mary's City, Jesuits Robert Brooke and William Hunter were summoned to Annapolis for a hearing. The two priests asked former attorney general Charles Carroll the Settler to represent them.

Held on 11 September 1704, this hearing remains replete with historical resonance. First of all, it was held in Annapolis, which signified the new order of
things. Anglican Annapolis was now sitting in judgment on Catholic Saint Mary's
City and the prior Catholic hegemony, embodied by the two Jesuits who stood
before the governor and his advisors. William Hunter, the Jesuit superior, was a
Yorkshire man, like many early Marylanders. Robert Brooke, by contrast, was the
first native-born Marylander to enter the Society of Jesus and be educated and
ordained on the continent. (Professed in 1702 of the four vows as a Jesuit while
serving in Maryland, where he arrived in 1696, Brooke was chosen superior in
1710 and died at fifty-one.) Charles Carroll the Settler equally exemplified genera-
tional development. The first of his family to settle in Maryland—in October 1688,
the same year he was named attorney general—Carroll had previously received an
elite education on the Continent at the University of Douai and at Inner Temple, London, and was at the time of the Annapolis hearing the wealthiest man in
Maryland. Carroll was told, however, that he could not speak on behalf of the
two priests charged with consecrating a new chapel and offering Mass publicly,
contrary to the penal laws of England.

Only a bishop was empowered to consecrate a cathedral, Hunter replied when
the question was put to him, and there were no bishops in Maryland. Yes, he had
said Mass in the great brick chapel, Brooke answered when cross-examined, but so
had many Jesuits before him, going back for nearly seventy years. How could such
time-sanctioned usage be constituted an offense? The governor's council, however,
was not concerned with niceties of law. The priests were before them for the sake
of spectacle and public reprimand. Governor Seymour delivered the reprimand—a
rambling diatribe full of insults and anti-Jesuit invective—as if the governor were
back on duty with the Coldstream Guards, dressing down two misbehaving rankers.
Transcribed into the official record, Seymour's tirade survives in the Archives of
Maryland and has been quoted at length in a number of histories as a tour de force
of judicial distemper. He would send the two priests back to England in chains
for trial and punishment, Seymour threatened, should they ever offend again. He
thereupon ordered the sheriff to shut down the chapel in Saint Mary's City. Had
the Jesuits worn swords, Seymour might have broken them across his knee as a
symbol of disfranchisement from the regiment; for the governor was staging a scene
in which Catholic Marylanders—no matter how well educated or how rich—were
being drummed out of the colony. "Pray take notice," Seymour concluded, "that I
am an English Protestant gentleman, and can never equivocate."[1]

The following month, on 3 October 1704, the House of Delegates and the
council passed and Governor Seymour signed "An Act to prevent the growth of
Popery within this Province", which matched the governor's earlier tirade in anni-
hilating intent. Should any Popish bishop or priest or Jesuit, the act thundered,

> baptize any child or children other than such who have Popish parents, or shall say
> Mass or exercise the function of a Popish bishop or priest within this province, or shall
> endeavor to persuade any of her majesty's liege people to embrace and be reconciled
> to the Church of Rome and shall be thereof legally convicted, shall forfeit the sum of
> fifty pounds sterling for every such offense ... and shall also suffer six months' impris-
> onment of his or their body or bodies without bail or mainprise. ... If a Popish bishop,

priest or Jesuit after such conviction aforesaid shall say Mass or exercise any other part
of the office or function of a Popish bishop or priest within this province, or if any
Papist or person making profession of the Popish religion shall keep school ... such
person or persons ... shall upon such conviction be transported out of this province to
the Kingdom of England together with his conviction, in order to his suffering such
pains and penalties as are provided by the statute made in the 11th and 12th year of
the reign of his late Majesty, King William the Third, entitled an Act for the further
prevention of the growth of Popery.[2]

The act, however, proved too harsh for an ameliorating Queen Anne, and sitting in
council on 3 January 1706 she ordered it indefinitely suspended. Seymour and the
legislature, meanwhile, realizing that they had gone too far, had already suspended
the measure for eighteen months, which upon appeal from Catholics was extended
by a year until the queen's suspension made the matter moot. The Act against Popery was finally and fully repealed in 1718, and from that time forward the one and
only privilege Catholic Marylanders enjoyed (in addition to a continuing right to
pay taxes) was a right to gather privately for religious worship. Catholic proprietorship and hegemony were now officially things of the past; and the Maryland present
was highly circumscribed as far as Catholics were concerned. What to do? Where
to go? A number of prosperous Maryland Catholics contemplated relocating to the
West Indies. Charles Carroll the Settler seriously began to consider cashing out and
moving to French Louisiana. Maryland was starting to feel like Ireland all over again.

Crossing the Chesapeake

Jesuit Thomas Mansell (alias Harding), by contrast, was thinking of merely moving across the Chesapeake to the Eastern Shore and relocating on the northwestern edge of the Delmarva Peninsula between Chesapeake and Delaware Bays. An
Oxfordshire man, Mansell had studied at Saint Omer's College in France and then
entered the Society of Jesus at age eighteen. Assigned to Maryland in 1700 following his ordination, Mansell, like Robert Brooke, was professed in the four vows in
Maryland and, again like Brooke, was eventually named superior of the Maryland
mission. With hostility running so high in western Maryland, Mansell reasoned, a
move to the sparsely settled Eastern Shore looked promising.

Authorized by his superiors, Mansell began a search for property in Cecil County
on the northern tip of the Eastern Shore. He was already familiar with the area from
his previous ministering in the upper bay region between 1700 and 1704. After some
hunting, Mansell settled upon a 300-acre tract near the junction of the Great and
Little Bohemia Rivers and opened negotiations with its owners, the sisters Marian
and Margaret O'Daniell. Margaret O'Daniell was deathly ill at the time, and when
she died, Marian sold the land to Mansell, who used his alias, Harding, on the bill
of sale. Mansell subsequently purchased a second property, Worsell Manor, from
Catholic landowner James Heath. A total of 488 acres was authorized for transfer on
10 July 1706 as witnessed by Henry Darnall, keeper of the Great Seal of Maryland.
Over time the tract was expanded to 1,700 acres through further purchases.

Mansell built a simple log cabin and named the mission Saint Xaverius in honor
of Saint Francis Xavier, a founding member of the Society of Jesus and a pioneering

missionary in India and Japan. The log cabin functioned as chapel and residence and would later be replaced with a more finished wooden structure. Around 1729 (five years after Mansell's death), the Jesuits built a permanent red-brick church and manor house on the property. Each iteration of the chapel was adorned by the same five-foot wrought-iron cross (now in the Georgetown University Archives) brought over on the *Ark* and the *Dove*. Nearby, Bohemia Landing provided a pier and warehouse for shipping and storing needs. A roadway called the Delaware Path connected Saint Xaverius to the Chesapeake and Delaware Bays. Old Bohemia, as the mission complex was called, served a scattered congregation in the Maryland counties on the Eastern Shore, the three counties of Delaware, and southern Pennsylvania and was consistently staffed by the Jesuits as a center of pastoral service throughout the Chesapeake. In 1745 or 1746 Jesuit Thomas Poulton, a graduate of Saint Omer's College and a former prefect (headmaster) there, founded an academy at Little Bohemia to educate the sons of Maryland Catholic gentry prior to their crossing the Atlantic for further study.

To list the counties of the Eastern Shore in order, north to south, and to indicate the number of Catholics living in each county by the mid-eighteenth century is to suggest the fragility of Catholic settlement in this part of the colony: Cecil (49), Kent (40), Queen Anne's (179), Caroline (one family), Talbot (90), Dorchester (79), Somerset (81), and none recorded for Wicomico, Worcester, Accomack, and Northampton. However small they might be, these Catholic communities on the Eastern Shore conjoined the classes of British North America—indentured servant, yeoman planter, artisan, professional, and upper-register land baron (who was increasingly dependent on black slavery as the eighteenth century wore on)—into a society anchored in shared religious practice. The stratification of the manor era was long gone, yet large landowners such as Richard Bennett III of Queen Anne's County, James Heath of Cecil County, former surveyor general of the Eastern Shore Henry Sewall, and other Catholics of comparable wealth provided local leadership and offered their red-brick manors as gathering places for the Catholic community to worship. In the aftermath of the Protestant Revolution, for example, the Heath family maintained a fully equipped (but secret) chapel at their estate, Mount Harmon, on the Sassafras River. The most prominent of these men and the largest landowner on the Eastern Shore—5,791 acres by 1720—was Charles Carroll the Settler, who had married the daughter of Henry Darnall, proprietary agent, whom he succeeded in that post as well as serving as attorney general until Catholics were banned from public office.

In 1715 Charles, third Lord Baltimore, died in February. His son and heir, Benedict, fourth Lord Baltimore, an Anglican, died two months later. Benedict's son and heir, Charles, fifth Lord Baltimore, was only sixteen, and Lord Francis Guilford was chosen to act on Charles' behalf until the young baron reached maturity. Maryland Catholics were now receiving good news. Charles' mother, Lady Charlotte, had remained Catholic. The fifth Lord Baltimore, while an Anglican like his father, had many Catholic friends and relatives. Lord Guilford, the acting proprietor, was a Stuart-friendly, Catholic-friendly sympathizer who would convert to Catholicism in 1728. This good news was, however, simultaneously bad news; for the Protestant establishment of Maryland read these signs as a warning that the Catholic cause might make a comeback.

Indeed, a Catholic restoration seemed a possibility, briefly, when in December 1715 James II's son James Francis Edward Stuart, the Old Pretender—who in 1708 had tried a similar invasion—crossed over to Scotland for the second time to join a rebellion in his name being led by the Scots peer John Erskine, sixth Earl of Mar, who had been secretary of state for Scotland until King George I dismissed him in 1714. The rebellion was crushed by the army commanded by John Campbell, second Duke of Argyll, and the chevalier de Saint George (the Old Pretender's French title) fled back to France and, later, Rome. Two shiploads of eighty Scots and a number of Irish Catholics were deported to Maryland the next year, their services as indentured servants being auctioned off upon arrival. The presence of another eighty-odd Catholic indentured servants—proven rebels with military experience, some now in service to Catholic families—further heightened Protestant anxieties regarding a Catholic uprising in Maryland or, at the least, their political recovery.

In 1718 the Maryland Assembly finalized twenty-nine years of anti-Catholic legislation with an act that disfranchised Catholics from voting or holding office in Maryland if they refused to take the same oaths demanded of all officeholders in the colony. Should any suspected Catholic or Papist sympathizer attempt to vote, local judges and sheriffs were authorized to examine the suspected voter in question and demand that he take all the required oaths or, if he refused, to set aside any vote the voter under suspicion might have cast.[3]

Led by Charles Carroll the Settler, the Catholic leadership openly opposed this measure, and by 1720 the more moderate wing of the Protestant establishment was showing signs of sympathy. Affronted, Governor John Hart, an avid anti-Catholic, summoned the Catholic leadership of the colony—Charles Carroll, James Carroll, William FitzRedmond, Richard Bennett III, Henry Wharton, Nicholas Sewall, Charles Digges, Clement Hill, Henry Darnall II, Benjamin Hall, and the Jesuit Peter Atwood—to appear before the assembly on 12 April 1729 and argue their case against exclusion. Eleven years earlier, in 1718, Father Atwood had published *Liberty and Property: or, the Beauty of Maryland Displayed, Being a Brief and Candid Search and Inquiry into Her Character, Fundamental Laws and Constitution by a Lover of His Country*. Written in response to the flare-up of anti-Catholicism in the aftermath of the Old Pretender and Earl of Mar's rebellion of 1715–1716, Atwood had declared that all Christians by the very nature of Maryland's founding charter possessed the right to practice their faith freely, participate equally in public life, and acquire and hold property on an equal basis. Atwood most likely would have made an effective argument along these lines; but the Catholic leaders feared another display of abuse and refused to appear. The decision was perhaps wise, for the previous year five thousand Spanish troops had sailed for Scotland on behalf of the Old Pretender, who was then living in Madrid, landed a much smaller force following a serious storm at sea, and, along with their Highlander allies, once again met defeat at the hands of British troops.

The exclusionary act of 1718, unchallenged, remained on the books for the next half century, profoundly altering the nature of Catholic Maryland. Maryland Catholics were designated strangers in their own land, their disfranchisement equal to that of counterparts in the homeland. And so, as in the case of Great Britain, the Catholic community of Maryland became more defined, encapsulated, and politically marginalized—and, paradoxically, wealthier and looking more to Catholic Europe for higher education.

The Jesuit factor

The conversion of the proprietor to Anglicanism and the death of Charles Carroll the Settler in 1720 brought an end to the lay-led resistance of the early 1700s. Jesuits of the English Province, an increasing number of them Maryland born, now constituted the institutional locus of Catholic identity as British North America became, in Catholic terms, a permanent missionary territory under the jurisdiction of an English vicar apostolic and the pastoral care of up to nineteen Jesuit priests assisted by four temporal coadjutors. These Jesuits primarily reported to their own provincial but also were under the jurisdiction of Bonaventura Gifford, titular bishop of Madaura and vicar apostolic of the London District. An aristocratic Douai- and Sorbonne-educated secular priest missionary and academic, Gifford had formerly served as chaplain to James II, who made him president of Magdalen College, Oxford. Dr. Gifford served briefly at Magdalen until his ejection and two-year imprisonment in Newgate Prison following the Glorious Revolution. After Gifford's death in 1734, he was succeeded by his coadjutor, the Right Reverend Benjamin Petre, a member of a titled and influential recusant family. As his coadjutor with right of succession, Petre lobbied Rome for the appointment in 1741 of the Douai professor and veteran English secular priest Richard Challoner, who succeeded Petre in 1758.

Each of these prelates had spent his youth in great Catholic houses. The aristocratic prelates Gifford and Petre, however, and Challoner came from very different backgrounds. Challoner's widowed mother served as housekeeper to Lady Anastasia Holman at Warkworth Manor. Under the influence and tutelage of secular priest and house chaplain John Gotter, a widely published apologist and missionary and himself a former Presbyterian, young Challoner converted from Presbyterianism to Catholicism and shortly thereafter (1705) entered the English College at Douai, where he was ordained a secular priest (1716) and pursued an academic career until returning to England in 1730 as a missionary. Had Challoner been only an academic and a writer, he would be remembered for a score of devotional biographical and historical works that poured from his pen across the years—to this day, *Challoner's Garden of the Soul* (1740) remains a devotional classic—along with translations of *The Confessions of Saint Augustine* and *The Imitation of Christ* and a revision of the Douai-Rheims English translation of the Bible that remained in widespread use well into the twentieth century.

While Challoner was tireless when it came to traveling throughout his vicariate and preaching to the poor, journeying to British North America was out of the question, given the few Catholics there and the area's pervasive anti-Catholicism as well as the expense, time, and danger involved in crossing the Atlantic. Nor for the same reasons could Challoner establish a secular clergy in parishes in North America or any other format that required an open and stable ministry financed by tithing, as Bishop Laval was able to establish in Quebec. British North America was missionary territory in the extreme, and the English Jesuits were skilled missioners, eager to serve the fragile but developing Catholic communities of the Chesapeake and beyond, and in time to evangelize among the tribes of the interior. Several English Franciscans and an occasional secular served in the North American colonies during this era, but English and a few German Jesuits attached to the English Province functioned as the established clergy of Catholic British North America and hence constituted the visible face of the Church in terms of celebrating Mass, administering the sacraments, preaching, counseling, founding churches whenever and wherever possible (mostly in Pennsylvania), and discreetly proselytizing.

In covering this vast territory centered on the Chesapeake, Jesuits became weariless travelers by horseback, living for weeks at a time out of their saddlebags, in which they carried vestments, a Mass book and breviary, and chalices that could be disassembled into three pieces for easier packing. In the course of their ministries, these Jesuits kept meticulous records of marriages, baptisms, and funerals; and they preached from well-prepared, written sermons keyed to scriptural passages from the liturgical calendar, points of Christian doctrine, and pastoral encouragements. Uniquely for clergy, these Jesuits were also self-supporting. As gentlemen adventurer-investors, they had acquired properties—Mattapany, Newton, Saint Inigoes, Saint Thomas Manor, Cedar Point, White Marsh, Old Bohemia—which they farmed themselves as well as leased to tenants. In the founding era, indentured servants, many of them Irish Catholic, provided Jesuit farmers with the bulk of their labor force. Once their term of service was over, these former servants could become tenant farmers in their own right, sometimes on Jesuit properties. In the aftermath of the Glorious Revolution, however, resistance to the importation of Irish Catholic indentured servants grew in Maryland and South Carolina. By 1715 more African slaves than indentured servants were annually entering Maryland, including slaves acquired by Jesuits. By 1720 an estimated twenty-five thousand African slaves lived in the colony. Until the Jesuits of Maryland sold the last of their slaves in 1838, they lived and ministered with the contradiction of slavery at the core of their communal identity. The Jesuits shared this contradiction with their fellow Catholics in New France, the Mississippi valley, the Spanish Borderlands, and Louisiana. As of the eighteenth century, official Catholic teaching had never openly condemned this institution so at odds with gospel values; nor, as historian and federal judge John T. Noonan Jr. documents in *A Church That Can and Cannot Change* (2005), would the Church do so in no uncertain terms until the late twentieth century.

The Jesuits tried to treat their African servants (the Jesuits avoided the term *slaves*) humanely in terms of housing, clothing, diet, workloads, days off, and spiritual welfare. Considering their slaves to be members of the Jesuit community, they promoted marriage and home life and refused to break up families, purchasing new slaves if necessary to keep families together. Almost all Jesuit slaves became Catholics, and the Jesuit registries record their births, baptisms, marriages, and funerals. Names such as Mary, Rose, Delia, Prudence, Isaak, Patrick, Molly, Jonathan, Betsy, Neal, Joseph, Dilly, and Barney appear in the Saint Xaverius register at various stages of their journey through life. These entries are sometimes augmented with notations of treatment they received when sick: a gallon of molasses for Ralph, a half gallon of honey for Rachel. Most slaves did fieldwork. A few, however, were trained in skilled trades. None of this care erases the disquieting fact that Jesuits owned other human beings, on whom they depended for the ongoing support of their American ministry.[4]

Delaware beginnings

Despite their propinquity, the three counties of the Delmarva Peninsula facing Delaware Bay and New Jersey—New Castle, Kent, and Sussex—were not extensions of Maryland. Named in his own honor by Thomas West, Baron de la Warr, governor of Virginia, when he first explored the region in 1610, Delaware has a distinctive colorful history. The colony that began as New Sweden in 1638 was surrendered to the Dutch in 1655, seized on behalf of the Duke of York in 1664, restored to Dutch ownership in 1673, and returned to the Duke of York in 1674 before passing, finally, into the jurisdiction of William Penn's proprietary colony of Pennsylvania in 1682. In 1704 Penn allowed the three lower counties to convene a separate assembly. Thus Delaware became a semiautonomous extension of Pennsylvania until September 1776, when it drafted its first constitution as an independent state.

What Catholic life Delaware enjoyed in the colonial era came from Irish and, later, German immigrants moving south from Philadelphia. By 1730 an estimated 9,000 Catholics lived in the Three Lower Counties, as they were called. Between 1729 and 1735, some 3,667 Irish immigrants moved through the port of New Castle. The town of Canterbury below Dover was popularly known as Irish Hill. In the 1630s Catholic immigrants to Maryland had arrived in groups from similar regions and brought priests with them. The Irish immigrants into Delaware were more diverse; many shipped up from the West Indies, while others were uprooted by the disasters and dislocations of foreign wars and the continuing colonization of Ireland itself. There is no record of any priests arriving with or ministering to them. Jesuits riding in from Old Bohemia or sailing down from Philadelphia assumed this ministry. By 1734 nineteen Jesuits were on missions in Maryland, Pennsylvania, and the Pennsylvania annex of Delaware. Starting in 1730, Cornelius Hollahan, an Irish Catholic farmer and blacksmith, and his wife, Margaret Kelly, and their five children made their home at Mount Cuba, New Castle County, available for Sunday Mass; they continued the practice when they moved to Coffee Run in the same county. Other families followed suit, and Catholic communities served by Maryland Jesuits grew up around these home-based centers of worship at Lewes, Laurel, Dover, Appoquinimink (Odessa), New Castle, Mount Cuba, and Coffee Run, where in 1790 Saint Mary's Chapel, the first permanent Catholic church in Delaware, was constructed. The Jesuits also established mission stations south of Dover and at Cuba Rock to support this Delaware ministry.

A Virginia paradox

In terms of Catholic settlement on the Chesapeake, no greater contrast exists than that between Delaware and Virginia. Throughout the eighteenth century, the Three Lower Counties of Delaware filled up with Irish Catholic immigrants, while Virginia remained with one sole identifiable Catholic family, the Brents. As far back as 1570, Spanish Jesuits had tried and failed to evangelize the Native Americans of Virginia. Appalled by the Indian massacre of two Jesuit priests, three temporal coadjutor brothers, and three novice brothers, Francis Borgia, general of the Jesuits, withdrew the Society from the Chesapeake. Established by the English in 1607, two years after the Gunpowder Plot, the pioneering settlement of Jamestown set the tone for an official policy of anti-Catholicism in Virginia that persisted throughout the colonial era and beyond. A few Irish laborers were brought to Virginia in the early 1620s. Undocumented estimates of up to two hundred Catholics in the colony have been advanced. If true, these Catholics must have been of the most anonymous sort, perhaps indentured servants, who left no record whatsoever of their Catholicism.

The Brents were of decidedly aristocratic descent. The family patriarch, Richard Brent, Lord of Admington and Lark Stoke, traced his ancestry back to Ode Brent, a Norman knight who arrived in England with William the Conqueror. Matriarch Elizabeth Reed, the daughter of Edward Reed, Lord of Tusburie and Witten, traced her ancestry back to William the Conqueror himself. The Brents were a Church of England family whose forebears had become wealthy from monastic lands seized during the reign of Henry VIII. Acquired by ancestors in 1553, the Brent manor of Admington had once belonged to Winchcombe Abbey.

In 1619, however, a family crisis occurred. Catherine Brent, the couple's third daughter among thirteen children, converted to Catholicism and informed her parents that she wished to become a nun. A likely candidate for facilitating the-not-yet-twenty-year-old Catherine's conversion is Dom Laurence Lodowick, a Benedictine monk active as a missionary in the area, who later became house chaplain to the Brents. In any event, the entire Brent family—parents and remaining twelve children—converted to Catholicism in short order. Catherine's sisters Elizabeth and Eleanor joined her in entering the English Benedictine Abbey of Our Lady of Consolation at Cambrai in the Low Countries, directed there by Dom Laurence. As Dame Christina Brent OSB, Catherine served as abbess of Cambrai from 1641 to 1645 and from 1674 to 1681, the year of her death, winning praise in the annals of her order for her unpretentious sincerity and devotion to the poor. In 1652 her younger sister Elizabeth and a small group of nuns from Cambrai founded the English Benedictine Convent of Our Lady of Good Hope in Paris.

Brent sons Giles and Fulke and their unmarried sisters Margaret and Mary decided upon an equally dramatic alternative: emigration to Maryland. By becoming Catholic, the senior Brents had endangered the family's assets. By 1644 two-thirds of the family estates had been sequestered for recusancy fines, and much of the rest would be lost to the same fines during the parliamentary era. The Brents had also seriously curtailed their children's prospects. Emigration to Maryland offered another option. The four Brent siblings arrived in Maryland on 22 November 1638 and were immediately absorbed into the elite of the colony. Leonard Calvert named Fulke and Giles Brent to the governor's council and Giles to serve as treasurer of the colony; he also appointed Giles as acting governor in 1643–1644 when Calvert returned to England on colony business and there married Anne, the younger sister of the Maryland Brents. Giles acquired a manor on Kent Island in Chesapeake Bay. Around 1644, in a highly unusual move—intermarriage with Indians was not then characteristic in Maryland—Giles married the eldest daughter of the Tayac (emperor) of the Piscataway in hopes of inheriting, via his wife, the emperor's extensive landholdings. A distant male relative, however, succeeded the Tayac upon his death and kept control of the property.

In the meantime, Margaret Brent had become the most influential woman in Maryland. Armed with letters from Lord Baltimore authorizing the Brent sisters to receive the same privileges as the original settlers, Margaret and Mary Brent acquired seven hundred acres in Saint Mary's County on the basis of the nine servants the sisters had brought to the colony. Margaret Brent later added another thousand acres to her Sisters Freehold tract by subsidizing more transported immigrants, and she continued to expand Sisters Freehold throughout the decade. When Calvert returned in August 1646 from Virginia, forced there by the Claiborne rebellion, Margaret Brent raised volunteers for Calvert's campaign to regain the government. Before Calvert went back to England again in 1647, he named Margaret Brent as his executrix, and the provincial court appointed her attorney for the proprietor Lord Baltimore. In this capacity, Margaret Brent attended assembly meetings. She soon demanded two full votes in that body—one for Lord Baltimore, whom she represented, and another for herself as a landowner—but her request was rejected because of her gender.

Her brother Giles, meanwhile, having been taken to England in chains along with Father Andrew White by William Claiborne to face charges before Parliament, prevailed over the charges and was freed. At this point, a quarrel developed between Giles Brent and the Calverts regarding money, property, and power; and Brent, returning to Maryland in an aggrieved mood, began to look to Virginia for further opportunities. Virginia, despite its assertive Anglicanism, was not terra incognita to Marylanders. Maryland had been carved from Virginia, with which it shared the tidewater region and the grand Potomac pathway. Virginia and Maryland, Puritan writer John Hammond argued in a 1656 pamphlet, were the Leah and Rachel of the colonies: the two daughters of Laban for whom Jacob toiled seven years each, first for Leah the elder and less favored sister, and then seven more years for Rachel. The two colonies, in short, were conjoined at the center of the Chesapeake story, and each had its attractions. For Giles Brent, Virginia meant more land and freedom from Calvert domination. To that end, he moved his plantation around 1650 to an unsettled portion of land on Aquia Creek in Stafford County, Virginia, in the Northern Neck Peninsula created by the Rappahannock and Potomac Rivers facing Charles County, Maryland, across the Potomac. Margaret and Mary soon joined their brother there, and in the early 1650s the Brents acquired patents for the estates they had settled and developed.

In 1642 Virginia passed laws prohibiting the practice of Catholicism in the colony, laws that were stated and restated at near-regular intervals through the mid-seventeenth century. Yet the Brents were left alone regarding their religious practice, as were the small number of less conspicuous Catholics who may (or may not) have been in the colony. The history of Virginia in this period yields strongly worded anti-Catholic laws but little, if any, evidence of systematic persecution. Catholics lower on the social order were too unimportant to bother with (and many of them were probably connected to the Brent estates), and the aristocratic Brents were too socially acceptable (within limits) to make a vulgar fuss about their religion. Certainly silent on the subject was Virginia governor Sir William Berkeley, a member in his youth of the circle surrounding the ardently Catholic Queen Henrietta Maria,

Charles I's wife, and whose brother, Sir John Berkeley, was a personal friend of the Catholic convert Duke of York. As Lord Lieutenant of Ireland (viceroy) from 1670 to 1672, Sir John favored the Catholic party and supported public Catholic worship to the point of lending his official plate for use at Mass.

The Brents' estates stood at the northern edge of a colony still confined to its southern coastal regions. From the north, Virginia faced a continuing threat of hostile Indian action, and if the Brents wanted to hold the frontier for the colony, with Giles Brent serving as lieutenant colonel and captain of the militia, then well and good for the colony: so the Anglican establishment agreed. As long as the Virginia frontier lasted, the Brents kept their Catholicism to themselves and never proselytized as they stood watch on the northern boundary. In later years, Margaret Brent was especially remembered for how devoted she was to the welfare of her dependents and how energetically she presided over festivals and harvest celebrations with relatives and family. Catholic feast days were included in this calendar of observances, and now and then an English Jesuit or Franciscan discreetly crossed the Potomac to say Mass and administer the sacraments. Margaret Brent never married. Various recent writers have described her as a proto-feminist, given her request for voting rights in the Maryland Assembly, but there was something mother superior–like as well in her air of quiet command and resourcefulness, her ability to get to the problem at hand and solve it, a trait suggestive of the grand Lady Abbess she might have become had she gone to Europe with the rest of her sisters and entered a convent.

Between 1671 and 1672, Margaret and Giles Brent died within a year of each other. For the next hundred years and more, the Brent family flourished in Virginia and maintained its Catholicism. When the half-Indian Giles Brent II died at age twenty-seven, leadership of the clan passed to Giles Brent's nephew George Brent of Woodstock and his wife, Marianna (the daughter of Sir John Peyton), to George Brent's sisters Margaret and Mary, and to the brother of Giles Brent II's mistreated wife, who had secured a judicial separation on grounds of cruelty. George Brent of Woodstock flourished as a Stafford County landowner and lawyer in partnership with William Fitzhugh, an Anglican. George Brent also served as captain of a militia unit, the Stafford Rangers. After an initial reluctance to ride under the command of a Papist, the men of the Stafford Rangers accepted his leadership in a campaign against the Seneca. Two governors, Thomas, Lord Culpeper, second Baron of Thoresway, and Francis Howard, fifth Baron of Effingham, privately depended on George Brent for advice on legal matters, and Brent served two years (1686–1687) as attorney general of Virginia. James II's suspension of penal laws in April 1687 brought George Brent into further prominence, however briefly. Brent acquired a quarter interest in a syndicate that purchased thirty thousand acres from Lord Culpeper, proprietor of the Northern Neck, which in the aftermath of the revocation of the Edict of Nantes the syndicate hoped to settle with Huguenot refugees.

The Glorious Revolution brought a backlash to the Brents: Anglican cleric John Waugh charged that George Brent was part of a conspiracy to seize control of Stafford County with the help of Seneca Iroquois and Maryland Catholics. Abetted by rumor, this claim riled up the Protestant farmers of the region, as might be expected, and Brent had to take temporary refuge in the home of his Anglican law partner, Fitzhugh. Yet when the general and county courts looked into the matter, it proved unsubstantial, and the Reverend Waugh was forced to apologize to the court for spreading falsities. Two feeble efforts to disbar Brent were made between 1691 and 1699 (the year of his death), but they went nowhere. George Brent of Woodstock continued to acquire and develop land and to practice law; indeed, in a tableau vivant of reconciliation, one of Brent's clients in 1691 was none other than the Reverend John Waugh.

Prior to the Glorious Revolution, a Roman Catholic priest by the name of Father Edmonds was brought into court in the town of Norfolk in southern Virginia and questioned about whether he had performed a wedding ceremony for John Brock- well and Mary Bustian, a widow. Yes, he had, Edmonds replied. He was serving as chaplain to two Catholic households in Norfolk, the home of Mrs. Charles Egerton and the home of Captain Robert Jordan, and was entitled to exercise his ministry according to the proclamation of liberty of conscience recently issued by His Maj- esty King James II. The court let the matter drop. Father Edmonds does not appear on either the Jesuit or the Franciscan registries of the era, historian Gerald Fogarty admits, but he may have been a Jesuit operating under an alias. In any event, it was documented that by 1687 the town of Norfolk had a Catholic presence.

The Glorious Revolution temporarily ended the general laissez-faire stance of Virginians but did not unleash anything comparable to the anti-Catholic campaign in Maryland that followed John Coode's coup d'état and assumption of power. While in office, Coode complained by letter to the president of the Virginia Coun- cil that an English Franciscan priest named Basil Hobart had fled Maryland and was now practicing his Papistry at the estate of his Papish patrons, the Brents of Stafford County. The Virginia authorities did not act on the information, and thus Father Hobart most likely became the first documented Catholic priest to serve in Virginia since the Jesuits' failed missionary effort of 1570.

A New York interlude

Between 1642 and 1709 Jesuits from New France attempted to bring Catholicism into upstate New York via their ministry to the Iroquois and into present-day Maine through similar ministries carried on by Jesuits, Recollects, and Capuchins. As proprietor of New York (1674–1688), the Duke of York introduced a top- down Catholicism into the colony's governance, but despite the vigorous perfor- mance of Catholic governor Thomas Dongan between 1682 and 1688, Catholicism never took firm hold. Dongan came from an ancient Irish family and was both the younger brother of a baronet and the nephew of the first Earl of Limerick, to whose title he succeeded. He pursued a military career in an Irish regiment in the service of France, attained the rank of colonel, and then rose to major general in the English army following the Restoration, when he served as lieutenant governor of Tan- giers, an English protectorate. As governor of New York, Dongan proved energetic and effective. He regularized the borders of New York, granted civic charters to New York City and Albany, established postal service in the province, and, most dramatically, traveled upstate with Lord Howard, governor of Virginia, to receive a pledge of loyalty to Great Sachem Charles II by the leaders of the Iroquois Con- federacy that allied British North America, once and for all, with this formidable political and military power.

With equal drama, Dongan jump-started his governorship on 30 October 1683 by issuing a Charter of Liberties that guaranteed a representative assembly, no taxation without representation, an independent judicial system, and freedom of religious practice. "No person or persons," read this act of toleration for Christians (the Sephardic community of New York had long since established its right to be left in peace), "which profess faith in God by Jesus Christ shall at any time be anyways molested, punished, disquieted, or called in question for any difference of opinion or matter of religious concernment, who do not actually disturb the civil peace of the province; but that all and every such person or persons may, from time to time and at all times, freely have and fully enjoy his or their judgments or consciences in matters of religion throughout all the province; they behaving themselves peaceably and quietly, and not using this liberty to licentiousness nor to the civil injury or outward disturbance of others."[5]

With a Catholic king at his back, however, Thomas Dongan found it difficult to keep the low profile suggested by this edict of toleration. Like the Calverts, Dongan favored the appointment of Catholics to his governor's council. He even brought five English Jesuits—Fathers Thomas Harvey, Henry Harriman, and Charles Gage and two temporal coadjutors—with him to New York, where the Jesuits opened a school on the King's Farm property later leased to Trinity Church. The Jesuits also served a small chapel in Fort James, south of the Bowling Green. A chapel bell openly summoned the few but influential Catholic New Yorkers to the first Masses ever celebrated in that city, and on weekdays their sons trudged off to the first Jesuit secondary school in British North America.

All this and more had long since stuck in the craw of German-born New Yorker Jacob Leisler, himself a clergyman's son. Leisler had arrived in New Amsterdam as a twenty-year-old soldier of the Dutch West India Company, married a wealthy Dutch widow—on behalf of whose estate he successfully took her relatives to court—and in time built a formidable trading company active in the Dutch East Indies, Amsterdam, London, and New York. Leisler loathed the Dutch oligarchs of New York who had stood in his way when he was a young man and were now cozying up to the English as well as the established Dutch Reformed clergy who served them; these ministers, Leisler believed, were abandoning old-time Calvinism in favor of accommodating themselves to Anglicanism whenever possible. Leisler also hated Roman Catholics, who were far too conspicuous in the governance of the colony. Witness the Jesuit school and chapel and the two Jesuit chaplains to Dongan when he was governor. Now former governor Dongan, Leisler fumed, was out there on his Long Island estate celebrating the birth of a Catholic Prince of Wales. And so, like John Coode in Maryland, Jacob Leisler organized a rebellion in New York in support of William and Mary and had himself installed as governor. Before Leisler's hot temper and diplomatic indiscretions led to his arrest and execution, the revolt he led asserted unambiguously how shallow the hold of Roman Catholicism had been on downstate New York. A June 1696 survey conducted by Mayor William Merritt showed a mere nine New Yorkers openly identifying themselves as Roman Catholics: distinguished gentlemen, true—including Major Anthony Brockholes, acting governor before the arrival of Thomas Dongan, who was forced to flee to New Jersey during the Leisler rebellion—but certainly not a cadre capable of the vast plots of Reconquest evoked by Jacob Leisler a few years earlier.

William Penn's Holy Experiment

It took a number of years for Quaker William Penn, the founder and proprietor of Pennsylvania, to become convinced that Roman Catholics could handle the civil responsibilities of toleration. In numerous writings in the first half of his career, the prolific Penn defended the rights of all Christians to liberty of conscience. No Christian, Penn argued, should be persecuted for what he believed. Still, from the 1660s into the early 1680s, Penn expressed serious doubts as to whether Roman Catholics could remain loyal to non-Catholic heads of state, given the overwhelming authority exercised by the papacy, an institution Penn excoriated with blistering and vehement Whore of Babylon invective. Part of Penn's sensitivities and contradictions on this issue stemmed from the fact that many Protestants considered Quakers—who, like the recusants, refused to take oaths—Papists in disguise and Penn himself a secret Jesuit on the payroll of Rome!

With the naming of the Catholic Duke of York as heir apparent to the throne, however, Penn found himself in the position of being forced by his own arguments either to regard the duke and his brother the king (who named the duke heir to the throne) as tools of the pope, and hence subverters of the realm (by Penn's previous definition), or to reconsider the matter. Cynics might claim that Charles II began to buy off Penn's distrust of Catholics by granting Penn the southern half of his brother's proprietary colony of New York as a Quaker refuge in 1681, but such cynics would have to acknowledge that Penn adhered to his misgivings about Roman Catholics' civil loyalty and obedience up until he departed in 1682 for his colony, where he remained for two years, organizing governance and making initial land allotments in his Holy Experiment.

While in Pennsylvania, Penn had continuing oppositional encounters with Lord Baltimore and Governor Dongan regarding the southern and northern borders of his colony. Yet both Catholic officials treated him courteously amid difficult negotiations, and Penn was impressed by their professionalism as public servants. Returning to England in 1684, Penn made a grant of land in Bucks County to John Tatham (alias Gray), whom some historians believe was formerly a Benedictine monk, now married with a family, as well as grants of land to other Catholics, such as George Nixon of County Wexford, Ireland, and Frenchman Peter Dubuc. Tatham and Dubuc eventually rose to become among the wealthiest and most influential leaders of the colony. By this time, English Jesuit Thomas Harvey, first brought to New York by Governor Dongan, was offering Mass in Philadelphia for its nascent Catholic community. By the late 1680s, Penn—still in England—was deliberately involving Catholics in the governance of the colony and sending messages to government officials via John Tatham.

Penn had quieted his suspicions concerning Catholics' ability to remain loyal to non-Catholic states and was pointing to Holland and a number of German states as examples; in the spring of 1687, he also supported as a step in the right direction King James II's Declaration of Indulgence, which pardoned Catholic and Protestant dissenters imprisoned under prior penal laws. Unfortunately, the king was at the same time playing into the hands of his Protestant Whig opposition by appointing an inordinate number of Catholics to high positions in government, the military, and universities. These appointments would soon galvanize resistance and cost

James II his throne and, in the aftermath of this removal, earn for William Penn temporary charges of high treason for allegedly supporting the return of James to the throne.

In terms of its attitudes toward Catholics, then, colonial Pennsylvania presents a paradox. Catholics would be allowed to practice their faith with some degree of openness. Still, in the aftermath of the Glorious Revolution, they would not be permitted to vote or hold office. The provisions of this prohibition, moreover, given in the statutory statement by the Pennsylvania Assembly in 1705, displayed an intensity of theologized contempt. A prospective officeholder, the statute demanded, must swear that "I do from my heart abhor, detest and abjure as impious and heretical that damnable doctrine that Princes excommunicated or deprived by the Pope, or any authority of the See of Rome, may be deposed or murdered by their subjects or any other whatsoever." The statement underscores the persistent insult of Pius V's *Regnans in Excelsis* (1570) against Elizabeth and the recent efforts of James II to regain his throne at the Battle of the Boyne as well as the continuing Jacobite menace.

With politics taken care of, the statute got down to theological brass tacks with a reprise of the Reformation agenda requiring that the candidate for office must "solemnly and sincerely in the presence of God, profess, testify, and declare": "I do believe that in the sacrament of the Lord's Supper, there is not any transubstantiation of the elements of bread and wine into the body and blood of Christ, at or before the consecration thereof by any person whatsoever, and that the invocation or adoration of the Virgin Mary or any other saint, and the sacrifice of the Mass, as they are used in the Church of Rome, are superstitious and idolatrous."

Finally—in case the candidate for office harbored undeclared sympathies or hankerings Romeward or had learned any tricks of mental reservation from the Jesuits—he must "solemnly in the presence of God, profess, testify and declare": "I do make this declaration and every part thereof in the plain and ordinary sense of the words now read to me as they are commonly understood by English Protestants without any dispensation already granted me for this purpose by the Pope, or any person or authority, or without thinking that I am or may be acquitted before God or man, or any person or authority should dispense with or assume the same and declare the same null and void from the beginning."[6]

Yet despite the rabid nature of this oath, of all the thirteen original colonies, Pennsylvania would prove the most accommodating to Catholics—regardless of a strain of anti-Catholicism that now and then erupted, especially in times of perceived threat to the colony from Catholic France or when Anglican or Presbyterian leaders grew anxious about their diminishing numbers amid polyglot Pennsylvania's varieties of religious practice and were looking for someone to blame. But the Quakers of Pennsylvania did not participate in the flare-ups of anti-Catholicism that accompanied the invasion of Scotland in the spring of 1745 by the Young Pretender, Bonnie Prince Charlie, an effort brought to naught by British bayonets on Culloden Moor. Had England not prevailed against the Young Pretender, his Catholic continental backers, and the Highland clans rising up in support of the Jacobite cause, preached Methodist evangelist George Whitefield on 24 August 1745 in Philadelphia, "how soon would whole swarms of monks, Dominicans and friars, like so many locusts, have overspread and plagued the nations; with what winged speed would foreign titular bishops have posted over, in order to take possession of their respective sees? How quickly would our universities have been filled with youths who have been sent abroad by their Popish parents, in order to drink in all the superstitions of the church of Rome."[7]

Even Philadelphia printer and philosopher Benjamin Franklin—not yet transformed into a pro-Catholic Francophile by diplomatic service in France—warned his fellow Philadelphians in the aftermath of the invasion stopped at Culloden Moor that "we have a number of the same religion with those who of late encouraged the French to invade the Mother-country." An even bigger threat to Philadelphia, Franklin argued in the pamphlet *Plain Truth on the Present State of the City of Philadelphia* (1747), was the success of French Jesuit missionaries among the Iroquois. The Six Nations posed the gravest danger to Pennsylvania, Franklin pointed out, and must one day be confronted on the field of battle by the children of those who at the Battle of the Boyne "made so glorious a stand for our religion and liberties, when invaded by a powerful French army, joined by Irish Catholics, under a bigoted Popish King".[8]

Franklin's reference to Irish Catholics highlights another cause for anxiety among non-Quaker Protestants: the increasing immigration of Germans and Northern Irish into the colony. Only a small percentage of these Germans and Northern Irish were Catholic, but that was not known at the time, nor was it the issue. The issue was Anglican and Presbyterian Philadelphia's fear that Catholic Europe was on the rise. Pennsylvania was growing in an uncontrolled manner, and a Franco-Iroquois alliance loomed ominously on the frontier. French priests accompanied the Indian forces that composed the bulk of the French military presence there. By the mid-1750s Father Denis Baron, a Recollect, was serving as chaplain at Fort Duquesne, and Father Gabriel Anheuser, a Franciscan, had recently been ministering in Presque Isle (Erie) and Fort Le Boeuf (Waterford). Baron and other priests also were tending to the spiritual needs of French, Irish, English, German, and Indian residents in the area. Fort Duquesne, in short, was an armed French Catholic community on the frontier of an English Protestant province. Fought on a worldwide basis in Europe, North America, and India between Great Britain, Prussia, and Hanover against six European powers, the Seven Years' War (1756–1763)—known as the French and Indian War in North America—brought fears of a Catholic takeover to a fever pitch as Fort Duquesne began to serve as a staging area for Indian raids into Virginia and Carolina and for patrols in force into western Pennsylvania. Quakers nevertheless stood by their promise of toleration. Long after Catholics were suppressed in Maryland and driven from New York, they were allowed the open (but discreet) practice of their religion in Quaker Pennsylvania. When times got bad, Quakers prevented the burning of a Catholic church in Philadelphia and helped rebuild in Lancaster a chapel they had failed to save.

Rural beginnings

The story of Roman Catholicism in southeastern Pennsylvania opens with the mild irony that the first Catholic community began in a region under dispute between Pennsylvania and Maryland until a boundary was temporarily agreed upon in 1739 and not finalized until the Mason-Dixon Line was established in 1767, leaving

Pennsylvania and Maryland on opposite sides (north and south) of the most significant boundary in American history. In 1727 Lord Baltimore granted ten thousand acres to Irish immigrant planter John Digges in the Conewago Valley (present-day Adams County), west of the Susquehanna River, on the banks of Conewago and Plum Creeks. On his father's side, John Digges was from minor Irish gentry that traced itself back to Sir Dudley Digges, who had been killed in the service of Charles I during the English Civil War. Digges' mother was a Carroll, an aunt of Charles Carroll of Carrollton. The Diggeses were also related to the Neales and the Lillys.

Fertile, forested, and well-watered, Digges' Choice, as the property was called, promised much in the matter of future settlement. When the boundaries of Digges' Choice were resurveyed and regularized in April 1743, they were found to contain only 6,822 acres, and a supplemental grant of 3,679 acres was added, bringing Digges' Choice to a total of 10,501 acres. In 1731 John Digges moved his wife and seven children, several slaves, and a few white workers to 400 acres of the property, where he previously had a plantation house constructed. Thus Digges Quarters, Conewago, came into being. Around the same time, Colonel Robert Owings relocated his family to an adjacent property. The Samuel Lilly family, meanwhile, was en route from England (a son was born at sea in December 1730), and by 1731 Samuel Lilly had secured a grant in the Conewago Valley preparatory to moving his family there. As these properties were being acquired and developed, German and Irish squatters were settling west of the Susquehanna, and English and Irish freemen and their families were moving north from Maryland. When the temporary boundary between Pennsylvania and Maryland was agreed upon in 1739, the Penns purchased rights to 130,000 acres of Indian lands west of the Susquehanna and granted patents to many of these squatters, although land disputes—two of them to the point of bloodshed—continued to surface in the years to come. By November 1745, John Digges had sold a total of 1,360 acres to eleven families in parcels ranging from 50 to 200 acres. Digges continued to sell off parcels until his death in 1770.

At some time around 1730, Joseph Greaton—a London-born Jesuit based out of Old Bohemia Mission who was soon to be based in Philadelphia, a missionary given to dressing as a Quaker as he made his rounds by horseback so as not to attract attention—celebrated Mass and administered the sacraments at one or another Mass House (as private homes used for worship were called) in the Conewago valley, most likely the Owings home on Owings' Spring. The region emerged as a center of Catholicism in southern Pennsylvania—an area that included Goshenhoppen (Bally), Frederick, and Lancaster east of the Susquehanna; York and Conewago Township west of the river. Father Greaton served Catholics in northwestern Virginia as well. Hundreds of miles of trails linked these places where Catholics were living. The circuit was ridden by two generations of Jesuits, both English and German, who served an ever-developing network of Catholic homes, farms, townships, and mission stations, which led in time to the construction of chapels with attached cemeteries and school programs, including the first church to bear the Sacred Heart designation in the present-day United States. Conewago Township's wooden structure was followed in 1787 by a two-and-a-half-story stone structure that was raised to the dignity of minor basilica in 1962.

Who were these Catholics being ministered to by Father Greaton through the 1730s until more priestly help arrived? Most were English and Irish from Maryland, freemen looking for better opportunities, and Irish forcibly removed or otherwise deracinated from Ireland, who landed in increasing numbers in the port of Philadelphia and fanned south into Delaware and eastward into southern Pennsylvania. Many arriving Irish were impoverished redemptioners under the control of shipowners and their agents who, following the arrival of a ship, would auction off the services of an individual redemptioner for three to four years as an indentured servant, thus allowing the immigrant in question to redeem the cost of his passage and twenty-shilling landing fee. This redemptioner phenomenon had a dark underside in terms of English efforts to clear the Irish countryside of peasantry and rural townsfolk. An unknown number of Irish were either kidnapped (a word that came into the English language in the 1680s as a result of this program) or lured into transportation on false premises, which constituted the first steps in a program of de facto enslavement—an effort aided by the connivance of government officials. Shipowners and their agents made a profit akin to slave trading when they auctioned the persons and services of the men and women, boys and girls, whom they had transported. Unlike African slaves, however, redemptioners, even when working under grueling conditions in the West Indies or British colonies of North America, could look forward to an end of their servitude after three or four years—if they survived.

Not all redemptioners, however, were Irish, and not all were peasants. Scots, English, and Scots-Irish redemptioners included immigrants from the artisan class. Numerous redemptioners came from the Palatinate, the historic and agriculturally rich Rhineland region centered on Mannheim, Speyer, and Heidelberg. The people of the Palatinate endured the horrors of the Thirty Years' War (1618–1648), followed by ensuing invasions and counterinvasions in the interminable conflicts, great and small, that filled the second half of the seventeenth and early eighteenth centuries. In 1708 widespread blight devastated agriculture, and famine ensued. Hence Palatinate Germans migrated in the early years of the eighteenth century to New York along the Hudson and to southern Pennsylvania between the Delaware and the Susquehanna, two river-rich colonies that resembled the Rhineland in many respects, with Pennsylvania already well known for its tolerance and receptivity to newcomers. Another contingent of Palatines immigrated to the recently founded city of New Orleans and other sectors of French Louisiana. There, in the Mississippi, they encountered the mother of all Rhine River equivalents.

Those who landed in Louisiana found themselves in a Catholic colony. Palatinate Catholics immigrating to New York and New Jersey on the Hudson entered a decidedly anti-Catholic environment. Palatinate Catholics who became Pennsylvania Dutch—the name soon attached to this group—enjoyed religious freedom but faced a language barrier in the practice of their religion. The colony contained no German-speaking priests in the first four decades of the eighteenth century. Indeed, there was only one priest, period, the English Father Greaton, now based out of Philadelphia. While Greaton did his best to meet the spiritual needs of the German speakers in his scattered flock, he was no linguist and made little progress beyond basic communication, and his language skills were thoroughly inadequate for confession, counseling, or instruction. In 1741 Greaton was assigned a second Jesuit missioner, Henry Neale, from a well-known

Maryland Catholic family. Neale joined Greaton in Philadelphia and began to do his own rides on the rural circuit, financed by a bequest to Bishop Challoner from the convert Sir John James, second Baronet of Chrishall, Essex, for the support of two Catholic priests in Pennsylvania. In writing to Sir John from Philadelphia on 25 April 1741 regarding the bequest (4,000 pounds sterling, providing an annual payment of the interest), Neale touched upon his hopes for an expanded mission to German Catholics. "My heart has yearn'd," Neale wrote the generous baronet, "when I've met with some poor Germans desirous of performing their Duties, but whom I have not been able to assist for want of Language. I hope in a short time I shall be able to give you a more ample acct. of many particulars, being as yet almost a stranger in these parts. In ye interim my best wishes, and constant Prayers attend you."[9]

Neale, however, would not serve long on the rural route. His Paternity Francis Retz, father general of the Society of Jesus, a German speaker from Prague, was already in negotiations with the provincials of the Upper and Lower Rhine Provinces regarding the release of Fathers Theodore Schneider and Wilhelm Wappeler to the English Province for assignment to Pennsylvania. Himself a native of the Palatinate, Schneider had originally desired a missionary career and to that end had qualified in medicine in addition to his Jesuit course of studies. After a period as professor of philosophy and apologetics at the Jesuit college in Liège, Belgium, Schneider was named rector of the Jesuit house of studies at Heidelberg and served a term, 1738–1739, as *rector magnificus* of the university. The appointment of so diversely qualified a Jesuit to Pennsylvania—a priest, a physician, an academic of distinction—underscored the commitment of the Society of Jesus to the Pennsylvania mission in general and to the German community of the colony in particular. A Westphalian by birth, Wappeler possessed the quiet confidence and pastoral instincts of a perfect companion to superstar Schneider, if one judges from Wappeler's concurrent accomplishments on the Pennsylvania circuit.

After an initial assignment, most likely to Philadelphia, Schneider in mid-1741 established his headquarters at Goshenhoppen, thirteen miles from present-day Pottstown, where, with the help of local Mennonites, he built a cabin and Saint Paul's Chapel on land held in the name of English Jesuits Greaton and Neale, since nonnaturalized residents could not hold property in their own names in Pennsylvania. Schneider's precisely dated and place-located registers of Masses, sermons, baptisms, marriages, and funerals throughout twenty-three years of circuit riding (before his death on 10 July 1764) suggest a missionary who virtually lived on horseback to cover so much territory in Pennsylvania and New Jersey. Whether to pass the time in snowbound cabins or to avoid importing blatantly Catholic books past hostile customs—or perhaps simply to appreciate the meditation the task offered—Schneider meticulously copied in his own clear hand and had bound two complete Latin *Roman Missals* containing the prayers and Scripture readings of the liturgical year; the volumes are preserved in the archives of Georgetown University.

Arriving in the predominately German community of Conewago in mid-1741, Wappeler likewise built a cabin and a chapel dedicated to the Sacred Heart of Jesus, a Jesuit devotion that emphasizes the Incarnation, and in rapid order established a presence in Lancaster, where he built a chapel dedicated to Saint John

Nepomucene, the patron saint of Bohemia. From Conewago and Lancaster, Wappeler extended his ministry to points west and north. So pleased was Father General Retz with Wappeler's work that on 2 February 1744 he promoted Wappeler to the fourth vow of a professed Jesuit. Broken in health, Wappeler in 1748 was ordered back to Europe, where he recovered and, remaining attached to the English Province, was named prefect of Saint Omer's College and later served as a missionary in the Yorkshire District. Father Neale's death in 1748 and Wappeler's departure for Europe left Father Robert Harding, a newly arrived English Jesuit from Nottinghamshire, temporarily in charge in Philadelphia, with Father Schneider remaining as the only priest assigned to the German community. In 1752, however, Father Matthias Sittensberger (anglicized as Manners) arrived at Conewago and later added western Maryland, Virginia, and Delaware to his circuit riding. In 1764 Manners was named superior at Old Bohemia.

The year 1752 also witnessed the arrival of a diversely talented and likeable German Jesuit by the name of Ferdinand Steinmeyer (anglicized as Farmer), who in the course of his thirty-four-year ministry would serve Catholics in three states and become a fixed and respected figure in the Philadelphia establishment. A native of Weissenstein in Württemberg, born in 1720, Farmer studied philosophy and physics before joining the Jesuits at the age of twenty-three and volunteering for the missions. Initially scheduled for China, Farmer was diverted to the English Province and an assignment in 1752 to Lancaster, Pennsylvania, followed six years later by a transfer to Saint Joseph's Church in Philadelphia. While based in Lancaster, Farmer founded the mission of Saint Mary of the Assumption at Donegal (present-day Elizabethtown), eighteen miles from Lancaster, from which Farmer began to ride circuit on the trails previously blazed by Schneider. Altogether, Farmer was serving 394 Catholics in southern Pennsylvania as of 1757 before his transfer to Philadelphia. Once settled in his new assignment, Farmer surveyed existing records and followed up on leads with house calls in an effort to reactivate religious practice among Philadelphia Catholics. Within a year, Farmer had contacted numerous families and performed 78 baptisms: installments on the 2,089 documented baptisms Farmer would perform prior to the American Revolution. From Philadelphia, Farmer ministered southward into southeastern Pennsylvania and Delaware and joined Father Schneider in attempts to evangelize New Jersey and keep alive, if only intermittently, a Catholic presence in New York. In July 1764 Farmer preached the funeral oration for the departed priest-physician Schneider before Schneider's burial beneath a marble tombstone in front of the altar.

With Schneider gone, Farmer resumed on his own the demanding (and, in New York, dangerous) New Jersey and New York circuits, leaving Father Harding, his colleague at Saint Joseph's and Saint Mary's Churches in Philadelphia for fourteen years, to run the two chapels in his absence. In September 1772 Harding died and was replaced by the English-born (Lancaster County) Robert Molyneux, a sedentary man of some girth and scholarly interests who would one day serve a term as president of Georgetown College. Meanwhile, Farmer found time to continue his studies in mathematics and astronomy and as a result of his written observations on the transit of Venus on 6 June 1761 was elected to the American Philosophical Society in 1768. More honors were to follow.

Quasi-Quaker New Jersey

Father Schneider pioneered the New Jersey circuit, but Father Farmer brought it to a whole new level. Farmer documented his efforts in New Jersey but refused to record his forays into New York prior to the American Revolution. As far as Catholics were concerned, New York was a dark and unfriendly place, while New Jersey, despite various anti-Catholic laws, enjoyed an underlying Quakerism that dated back to the first Quaker settlement in West Jersey in 1675. Some 1,400 Quakers had immigrated to East Jersey, still part of New York, by 1681. In 1682 William Penn and eleven associates purchased East Jersey from its English proprietors and began to petition the Duke of York for a grant of self-governance. Limited self-government had already been granted to West Jersey in 1681 by its chief proprietor, Edward Byllynge, and for a few years East and West Jersey limped along as quasi-Quaker colonies, although Penn withdrew from the scene to devote himself to the development of the more explicitly Quaker colony of Pennsylvania, also originally part of New York, as East and West Jersey remained until 1738. The small Catholic population of late seventeenth-century East Jersey centered on Woodbridge and Elizabethtown and was visited by the New York–based Jesuits Harvey and Gage during the Dongan administration. In 1696 Major Anthony Brockholes of New York City purchased a five-hundred-acre estate in Patterson and, moving there, became the leading (yet low-profile) Catholic in the region. In the first half of the eighteenth century, the Catholic population, while remaining small, gained strength from a limited Irish, Palatinate, and Acadian augmentation.

Father Farmer's detailed registers document the extraordinary range and reach of his pastoral efforts in Pennsylvania and New Jersey while based in Philadelphia. In early 1758 he ministers at the home of Thomas Willcox at Ivy Mills, eighteen miles outside the city. March 1758 finds him at the home of Matthew Geiger in Salem County, New Jersey. June finds him back there again; indeed, by 1761 the private homes in Ivy Mills and Salem County, New Jersey, have become virtual mission stations for Catholics in these two regions. In 1762 Farmer establishes yet another station, this time at the home of Thomas McGuire in Chester County, Pennsylvania. For the year following Father Schneider's death, until the arrival in July 1765 of Father John Baptist de Ritter, Farmer takes care of Goshenhoppen as well. The year 1764 sees Haycock Run, Bucks County, Pennsylvania, added to Farmer's circuit; the following year, missions at Pikesland in Chester County, Pennsylvania, and Ringwood in Passaic County, New Jersey, are added. Between 1766 and 1774, New Jersey stopovers are noted in Farmer's registers for Basconridge, Pilesgrove, Burlington, Cohansey, Long Pond, Springfield, Middleton, and Sandy Run.

At Burlington, Farmer could encounter reminders of a prior Catholic presence in New Jersey, for William Penn's friend John Tatham had moved from Bensalem, Bucks County, around 1685, and Daniel Coxe, the Catholic physician to the late King Charles II, had lived there as well. Tatham's House, as it was subsequently known, was one of the finest homes in New Jersey and had once been intended to serve as the official residence of the first Anglican bishop scheduled for, but never appointed to, North America. In 1690 Tatham had been elected governor of West Jersey, but the assembly would not confirm him because, as a Catholic, he refused to take the required oaths. Tatham also assembled a private library that was among the largest of its kind in North America; it contained a plethora of classic Catholic titles as well as a collection of liturgical vessels. Farmer's registers, finally, record a spiraling densification of baptisms and marriages, suggesting growth in the areas' Catholic populations and the rise of an information network within what must be considered Father Farmer's four-colony ministry, if New York is included.

Whether Father Farmer ministered to Francis Furgler, the hermit of Burlington, New Jersey, is not recorded. If contact between the two occurred, it would possess an almost novelistic resonance. Furgler, who spoke a sort of pidgin Dutch (or German), had arrived in Burlington sometime in the early 1750s, reportedly from Canada or the Mississippi valley, and established himself as a hermit in a nearby forest, where for twenty-five years he lived a solitary life in a hollowed tree trunk reconfigured as a small hut. Local annals suggest that Furgler was doing penance for a sin committed long ago. In any event, when he was found dead in his hermit's cell in January 1778, a crucifix and a brass emblem of a fish (the early symbol of Christianity) lay within reach alongside his body. Mental illness—or the life of a hermit reprising an anchorite of the early Church? The local Quaker community believed the latter and offered the penniless hermit burial in their cemetery at Mount Holly.

Hostile New York

In 1741 the city of New York had ten thousand residents. Two thousand of them were black slaves. Such a juxtaposition of free whites of all classes living amid such a high number of enslaved black people created an imbalance that was destabilizing on a number of fronts. Wealthy slave owners feared a slave revolt, such as the Stone Rebellion in South Carolina that broke out on 9 September 1739 and cost sixty-five lives, twenty-one of them white. On the other end of the social scale, free white workers worried about being driven from the labor market by slaves. Marginal free whites, by contrast, subconsciously identified themselves with slaves as an oppressed class. New York City of 1741, in short, was beset by all the anxiety-producing forces endemic to a society in which one master white class kept two underclasses, one black and the other white, in submission.

The outbreak of war with Spain in 1740—a war that soon expanded into a conflict with Prussia and France and emptied the city of New York of the bulk of its resident military garrison for service in the West Indies—deprived the troubled community of its police force beyond a dozen or so civilian constables, which increased anxieties immeasurably. Add to this another intensification of feeling among the populace—a revival preached to thousands, indoors and out, by Methodist evangelist George Whitefield in November 1740—and the volatility factor rises even higher as Protestant New York (two thousand of them one evening alone, crowded into First Presbyterian Church to hear Whitefield) found itself brought to new heights of evangelical emotion.

Thus, when eight mysterious fires broke out between March and April 1741—four of them on a single day, 6 April—an already unstable city became convinced that a slave revolt was in the offing. In the ensuing panic, some 154 slaves were rounded up and incarcerated as Daniel Horsmanden, city recorder and justice on the supreme court, headed a specially convened grand jury to investigate the fires and the conspiracy (so Horsmanden was already convinced) behind them. Under

Horsmanden's guidance, the grand jury focused on a tavern run by John Hughson on the lower East River waterfront known to cater to slaves, free blacks, poor whites, soldiers, prostitutes, and the occasional young gentleman out slumming. Hughson had two prior run-ins with the law for fencing stolen goods and entertaining slaves. Living at the tavern, in addition to Hughson and his wife, daughter, and mother-in-law, were boarder Margaret Kerry, more commonly known as Peggy, a beautiful young Irish woman from Newfoundland who had recently borne a child to a well-placed slave named Caesar (who paid room and board for her and the child), and the Hughsons' indentured servant, sixteen-year-old Mary Burton, whom the grand jury enticed to testify by offering her freedom from indenture.

When Mary Burton's initial testimony proved inadequate—she refused to answer questions regarding the fires—she was briefly jailed for contempt of court. In the weeks that followed, she spun a narrative before the grand jury that moved from fact—a burglary, a fencing operation, a slave gang called the Geneva Club in honor of a shipment of Dutch gin (Geneva) it had once hijacked—to increasingly vivid accounts of talk by slaves in late-night sessions at the Hughson tavern to burn down the city, then govern it through two slave paramilitary organizations, the Long Bridge Boys and Smith's Fly Boys. By the time Mary Burton finished her testimony, nearly half the male slaves of New York over the age of sixteen were in jail or otherwise in custody. Caesar, the leader of the Geneva Club, and his aide-de-camp, Prince, were arrested, tried, and hanged.

Who was directing this conspiracy? When war broke out with Spain in 1740, an answer would soon come forth. Why, Catholic priests, of course! Yet another Papist plot was under way! Or so claimed General James Oglethorpe, governor of Georgia, in a letter to Lieutenant Governor George Clark of New York sent shortly after the War of Austrian Succession broke out. It had come to his attention, wrote Oglethorpe, that Catholic priests disguised as physicians, dancing masters, and other such occupations were working on behalf of Spain to sabotage the arsenals and magazines of the cities of British North America to prevent resupply of the British fleet now operating in the West Indies. Oglethorpe's warning struck a chord with Governor Clark, Justice Horsmanden, and the grand jury, all on the lookout for a leader of what had now become a Spain-driven slave conspiracy.

To their misfortune, five enslaved Spanish-speaking black men had recently been forced into New York. The five were immediately arrested and brought before the grand jury, where Mary Burton, who knew no Spanish, testified that she had heard these men, who knew no English, devising their plot. They were not slaves, the Afro-Spaniards argued. They were free Spaniards of color with surnames—Antonio de Bendito, Antonio de la Cruz, Pablo Ventura Ángel, Juan de la Silva, Agustín Gutiérrez—unjustly captured and sold into slavery, and they demanded repatriation. The court rejected their plea. Such a case, the court pointed out, should have been presented earlier to the Court of Admiralty. Juan de la Silva, who knew some English, was sentenced to hanging; the others were to be transported to the Spanish West Indies.

In regard to undercover priests, suspicious physicians proved in short supply, but a local dancing master by the name of John Corry was taken into custody. Suspicion likewise fell on a recently arrived gentleman living at the Fighting Cocks Tavern, a private tutor in Latin and Greek named John Ury, a small, pale, quiet man who was known to light candles and pray before a table in his room. No evidence of Ury's being a Roman Catholic priest, regular or secular, has ever surfaced. He may have belonged to a small group of Anglican bishops and clergy who in 1688 refused to take an oath of loyalty to William and Mary and in the decades that followed maintained a semischismatic relationship to the Church of England. Arrested, imprisoned, indicted, and brought before the grand jury, Ury fell victim to the fictitious testimony of Mary Burton and a growing number of testifiers—including several Irish-born soldiers—who hoped to survive in dangerous times by pleasing Horsmanden and the grand jury.

In the course of her testimony, Mary Burton was at her fanciful best, relating how Ury would conspire with slaves late into the night at Hughson's tavern to burn the city and kill white people. To this list of conspirators Mary Burton now added her mistress, Sarah Hughson, and Peggy Kerry, the late Caesar's Irish Catholic mistress and the mother of his child. Ury's trial before the bewigged and scarlet-robed justices of the supreme court involved presentations and statements regarding Ury's status as a Roman Catholic priest as well as a conspirator, hence making him doubly guilty and certainly corroborating Governor Oglethorpe's warning. Key testimony came from Joseph Hildreth, a rival schoolmaster, who testified that Ury had discussed with him the wafers and wine used in the worship Ury conducted Sunday evenings in his room. Such Communion would be compatible with non-juring Anglicanism, but it provided the prosecution ample opportunity to associate Ury's alleged worship style with the Roman Catholic Mass and the hated doctrine of transubstantiation. The jury took a mere fifteen minutes to find Ury guilty as charged. When passing sentence, the chief justice used the occasion to castigate the doctrines and political machinations of the Church of Rome before sentencing Ury to death by hanging.

At separate trials, John and Sarah Hughson and Peggy Kerry were likewise sentenced to hang and were executed, along with Juan de la Silva. Dressed neatly in white, his eyes fixed upon a crucifix that he frequently pressed to his lips, protesting his innocence to the last, Juan de la Silva met death with a quiet dignity and more than a suggestion of being martyred for his race and his faith on 15 August 1741, the feast of the Assumption. Altogether, while the hysteria lasted, eighteen other black men would be hanged and thirteen others burned to death. Seventy-two more were banished to British colonies in the West Indies or the Portuguese island of Madeira. John Ury conducted himself with equal dignity on 29 August 1741 as he mounted the scaffold, accompanied by his friend Joseph Webb, a carpenter, who had courageously testified in Ury's defense. Before being hanged, Ury handed Webb a written statement affirming his innocence and the orthodoxy of his Protestant faith. With Juan de la Silva and Peggy Kerry gone, there were now officially no Catholics left in New York.

Resistance in Maine

Reporting to Rome on the English colonies in 1763, Richard Challoner, vicar apostolic of London, noted that two colonies, Maryland (with twelve priests and sixteen thousand laity) and Pennsylvania (with six priests and eight thousand laity), constituted the Catholic presence in British North America. The other eleven colonies, by contrast, had no priests and only a scattered number of Catholics. So differing in so many ways, the British colonies of New England and the coastal British colonies below the Mason-Dixon Line were aggressively Reformational in their founding values and identities, and free of Catholics.

The future (1820) state of Maine in northeastern Massachusetts shared uncertain borders with New France, for while the Treaty of Utrecht (1713) that ended the War of the Spanish Succession yielded parts of Acadia to England, the exact boundary was not specified. The English believed that their Acadian domain extended to the Saint George River and included the homeland of the Abenaki, a loose confederation of Algonquian tribes, who were largely Catholic and pro-French. While willing to trade with the men of Massachusetts, the Abenaki preferred to maintain an affiliation with New France. In this regard, they were strongly encouraged over the years by the French Jesuit missionary Sébastien Rale, who had been evangelizing among them since 1694.

In many ways, Sébastien Rale was a typical Jesuit missionary: devout, ascetic, scandal-free, learned (the manuscript of the Abenaki dictionary he prepared is preserved at the Houghton Library at Harvard), diligent, and tireless. But Rale was a political leader as well, committed to the continuing alliance between the Abenaki and New France as the best means—no, the only means!—of preserving the cause to which he and his fellow Jesuits had dedicated their lives: the Catholicism of the resilient and entrepreneurial Abenaki. Rale was seeking to assist the Abenaki in holding on to their territory and their religion against the northern advance of an aggressively Protestant British North American network, spearheaded by the most bitterly anti-Catholic, anti-French, and economically forceful colony in the system, Massachusetts.

For some time now, Massachusetts had been engaged in a murderous border war with New France, as epitomized by the French-Indian attack on Deerfield on 29 February 1704 and the massacre that followed. Depending on who is writing the history—whether French Jesuit Pierre-François-Xavier de Charlevoix, say, or Thomas Hutchinson, the last royal governor of Massachusetts—Sébastien Rale is either a dedicated priest and Franco-Abenaki patriot or a duplicitous troublemaker. In June 1700—perhaps with Father Rale in mind, and certainly with French Jesuits in general in mind—the Massachusetts Council drew up and the House passed into law a bill against Jesuits and Popish priests whose preamble read, "Whereas divers Jesuits, priests and Popish missionaries have of late come, and for some time have had their residence in the remote parts of this province, and others of his Majesty's territories near adjacent, who by their subtle insinuations industriously labor to debauch, seduce and withdraw the Indians from their due obedience unto his Majesty, and to excite and stir them up to sedition, rebellions and open hostility against his Majestie's government, for the prevention whereof, be it enacted" that after 10 September 1700 any priest apprehended in Massachusetts territory would suffer perpetual imprisonment or, if he escaped and was recaptured, death.[10]

With the outbreak of the War of the Spanish Succession, Father Rale urged neutrality, but the Abenaki joined in a larger Franco-Indian attack on the village of Wells. The French government both blamed Rale for this attack and chastised him for being too neutral and briefly recalled him from his mission. The English also blamed him, and in the winter of 1705 they sent an expedition to Norridgewock, near the Kennebec River, where he was ministering, to capture him. Rale escaped, but the English burned his church and sacked the village.

And so it continued for the next nineteen years, with Rale energizing resistance to any accommodation with Massachusetts in an effort to preserve the Abenaki as French allies and Catholics. Finally, on 23 August 1724, after two previous attacks that Rale escaped, a Massachusetts force raided Norridgewock once again and he was killed: walking alone out to negotiate with the English, according to the French; killed in a cabin as he was directing musket fire, according to the English. Captain Johnson Harmon, commander of the raid, brought twenty-seven Indian scalps as well as Rale's back to Boston for financial payment. Harmon was also given a bonus of one hundred pounds for ridding the colony of the troublesome priest. "My children", Thomas Hutchinson generously quotes Rale as saying, "are cheated, driven from their lands and their religion; shall I not counsel and defend them? [The English] shall sooner take away my life than hinder me."[11]

Hutchinson seems especially generous given the continuing hostility of Massachusetts to anything Catholic. In January 1751, Judge Paul Dudley of Roxbury left a bequest to Harvard College to endow a lecture to be given every fourth year "for the detecting & convicting & exposing the Idolatry of the Romish Church, Their Tyranny, Usurpations, Damnable Heresies, fatal Errors, abominable Superstitions, & other crying Wickednesses in their high Places; And Finally that the Church of Rome is that mystical Babylon, That Man of Sin, That apostate Church spoke of, in the New Testament."[12]

20

London 1763

Catholic Maryland seeks education abroad while
Philadelphia prefigures an American Catholic future

At intervals between March and November 1763, Charles Carroll of Carrollton, a twenty-six-year-old student of law at the Inner Temple, sat for his portrait in an upholstered armchair at the studio of Joshua Reynolds at 47 Leicester Square, London. Lifted eighteen inches off the floor on a dais, the chair could be rotated on its wheels, which allowed Reynolds to experiment with various positions before deciding upon a final angle of approach for the three-quarter-view, life-size oval portrait. Reynolds chose a quarter turn to the left and a full-front gaze focused to the right, illuminating the right side of his subject's face and slightly shadowing the left. The overall effect is of Carroll emerging from a darkened background, against which played the coloration of his dark blue eyes, russet-brown hair and eyebrows, and high-colored features edging into the white lace stock at his throat (a facial coloration destined to grow pale over time due to Reynolds's faulty mixing of paint), his purple jacket with gold frogging dominating the rest of the portrait. The young man is self-assured, as befits the grandson and son of the two wealthiest Maryland planters in their successive eras—Charles Carroll the Settler, who had passed in 1720, and his son Charles Carroll of Annapolis, very much alive and commissioning the twenty-five-guinea portrait of his son now being created by the most noted portraitist of mid- to late-eighteenth-century Britain.

A certain studied politeness is evident in young Carroll. His testing, skeptical look suggests that here was no wealthy playboy from the colonies but, rather, a man of protracted education in the Jesuit *ratio studiorum* at Saint Omer's College in French Flanders, classics and humanities at Rheims, philosophy at the College of Louis-le-Grand, Paris (where he earned the equivalent of a master's), Roman and civil law at Bourges and Paris, and English common law at the Inner Temple, where he was currently embarked upon a five-year course of study. Here we behold a young American aristocrat possessed of manners and a gentlemanly demeanor who was interested in travel, horse racing, outdoor sports, fencing, dancing, drawing, and Italian lessons—but not cards, which he said he hated, although the expense sheets he regularly submitted to his father documented modest losses in what he considered a boring pastime. He took pleasure, too, in evenings at the theater and even later hours with fellow students at the Crown and Anchor Tavern on Arundel Street, where Samuel Johnson held forth and actor David Garrick, poet Oliver Goldsmith, parliamentarian Edmund Burke (with whom Carroll enjoyed dinner *en famille* that year), Joshua Reynolds himself, and a young James Boswell listened appreciatively as the Great Cham of London offered his resonant opinions.

Young Charles Carroll of Carrollton was also interested in women: his late mother, of course, to whose memory he remained devoted; young women to dance and fall in love with and perhaps to marry; Catholic grand dames and their virtuous daughters in recusant country homes; and the women of London as well—actresses, opera dancers, and the demimondaines of various social backgrounds about whom his father (who had studied in the Inns of Court as a young man as well) seemed constantly to be warning him in their regular exchange of letters, which began with the salutation "Dear Charley" on his part and "Dearest Papa" on the part of his son. So central are these letters to understanding their relationship that the designation "Charley" seems most appropriate when discussing issues that arose during the seventeen years in which these letters constituted the sole form of communication between father and son, save for Charles Carroll of Annapolis' visit to France in 1657.

Like the Carrolls before him in Ireland and Maryland, Charles Carroll of Carrollton was a Roman Catholic. His cousin John had joined the Jesuits upon graduation from Saint Omer's, but Charles was not overly pious. One might call him tribally Catholic, although his Catholicity lay far from that of Irish chieftains in the previous millennium, for whom Catholicism encapsulated mystery, held the world together, made sense of human experience, and taught loyalty to one's own. The perils of libertinage constituted a commonplace of eighteenth-century discourse, as evident in *The Harlot's Progress* (1732) and *The Rake's Progress* (1735), narrative engravings by William Hogarth; and Samuel Richardson's cautionary novels *Pamela; or, Virtue Rewarded* (1740) and *Clarissa Harlowe* (1747–1748). Even such sexually explicit novels as John Cleland's *Fanny Hill; or, Memoirs of a Woman of Pleasure* (1748–1749), the *Memoirs of a Coxcomb* (1751), and *The Surprises of Love* (1751) attempted either to reclaim or to castigate their protagonists by the conclusion of their storyline despite the erotic pyrotechnics preceding redemption or punishment. James Boswell, Samuel Johnson's famed biographer, an acquaintance of Carroll, struggled throughout these years from an addiction to prostitutes that forced him on a number of occasions to take the all-too-painful mercury cure. Among the most noted libertines of the period was Frederick Calvert, sixth Baron Baltimore, the young (four years younger than Charles Carroll of Carrollton) proprietor of Maryland, who reportedly maintained a harem in Constantinople and figured as the defendant in one of the most notorious rape trials of the era, in the course of which he barely avoided a conviction and mandatory death sentence. At the conclusion of the trial, Baltimore fled to the more accommodating environment of Venice, where he reestablished his ecumenical seraglio from Constantinople days and otherwise amused himself until dying in Naples in September 1771 at age forty from various excesses.

An age of libertinage, in short, required constant guidance from a concerned father. And yet, for all his warnings to his son to avoid the fleshpots of Egypt, Charles Carroll of Annapolis had a history, perhaps one that dated from his own years as a student. For all his admonitions regarding virtue, Charles Carroll of Annapolis had not until recently married his son's mother; their common-law marriage, which lasted until 1757, rendered his son illegitimate for his first twenty years and not fully legitimized until Maryland law was changed much later. Charles Carroll of

Annapolis delayed marriage for two decades until he felt satisfied that his son was worthy to serve as his heir and he did not have to risk that his fortune in land and slaves would fall to another man following his early death (which did not occur) and the remarriage of his wife. Furthermore, that son and heir was only eleven when he and his cousin John were sent to Saint Omer's College in French Flanders, after which his cousin the Jesuit priest headed toward a life of English and continental assignments, and Charles never saw his mother again.

Was this, then, the source of the gravitas in young Charles Carroll's gaze that Joshua Reynolds captured so subtly in the portrait now hanging in the Center for British Art at Yale University? He had endured a long exile as he met his father's onerous demands for a rigorous education in the humanities, philosophy, and comparative law—and yet he would be barred from a public career in Maryland because of his religion. His mother's long apprenticeship, moreover, paralleled his own, and he would learn of her death before his apprenticeship was over, and he was able to follow the Reynolds portrait back to Maryland.

A recusant reprise

In the aftermath of the Glorious Revolution, Catholics' life in Maryland was comparable to recusant life in England, with the all-important exception that Maryland Catholics depended on African slavery to support their estates, while English recusant gentry relied on a long-standing local English Catholic tenantry. To cite anti-Catholicism as a monolithic dynamic that forced Maryland Catholics into the shadows following the 1689 seizure of government by the Protestant Association is to ignore two decades, 1690–1710, of Maryland Catholics' resistance to surrendering their religious liberty. At a similar time of political upheaval, they argued, Catholics had passed the Toleration Act of 1649, which guaranteed religious freedom to trinitarian Christians and passively extended its benefits to the few Jews in the colony. A group of Catholics and various Protestant sympathizers had enough faith in the new order of things—William of Orange, after all, had been an ally of Catholic Spain while governing in the Netherlands and was known to be an open champion of liberty of conscience—to send an official delegation to sound out the monarch, via the Lords of Trade responsible for colonial affairs, concerning the continuation of religious freedom in Maryland, where, since the Toleration Act of 1649, Catholics had been enjoying the most freedom granted Catholics in either Britain or its New World empire. In December 1691 Don Manuel Coloma, the Spanish ambassador to the English court (the highest-ranking ambassador at the court now that England and France were at war), joined this effort with a brief but important memorandum of appeal in diplomatic French to the king, requesting full freedom of religious practice for Maryland Catholics. None of these petitions received a formal response, but no full-fledged systematic repression of Catholics in Maryland was launched once Maryland became a royal colony in 1690 and John Coode, the leader of the Protestant Association, was replaced as governor.

By 1694, after Jesuits and Franciscans returned from Virginia—to which they had fled in 1689 and where Virginia authorities had refused to act on Coode's repeated requests to arrest and return them—Mass was again openly celebrated in Saint Mary's City at the great brick chapel, which remained open for the following decade. The first three royal governors—Lionel Copley, Francis Nicholson, and Nehemiah Blakiston—showed little interest in suppressing Catholics, who were conspicuous among the elite of the colony. These governors were, however, thoroughly committed to launching the next notable development in the religious history of Maryland: its assimilation into the Church of England. Anglicanism was destined to win out in Maryland just as it had won out in the Elizabethan era, although not, fortunately, with the same violence. Anglicanism barely existed in seventeenth-century Maryland. Clergy were few, and several of them displayed behavior that was less than edifying. After some delay, however, the Glorious Revolution ushered in a growing effort, which gained momentum during Queen Anne's reign, to Anglicanize the colony—that is, to bring church and state into the closest possible unity. The first declaration of Anglican establishment came almost routinely in 1692 as part of the reorganization of Maryland as a royal colony. In 1702 a locally enacted Establishment Act further defined the Church of England as the officially established church of the colony, with the governor given the power to assign clerical compensation. There was talk of requesting a suffragan bishop, but the governor, legislature, and local vestries preferred to maintain a strong lay control over ecclesiastical matters, not wanting to introduce into the colony a bishop who would be second only to the governor in prestige and authority, and a close second at that. Unfortunately for Catholics and Quakers, however, proponents of Anglicanization saw these two dissenting groups as the major obstacles to the goal of making the Church of England supreme in the colony. Two developments—open worship at Saint Mary's City and reports of Jesuits proselytizing—compounded the ill will toward Catholics already evident in the Glorious Revolution of 1688 and the coup d'état of the Protestant Association the following year. Strangely enough, for a number of years Whig Protestant Anglicanizers had perceived Catholics and Quakers—so different from each other in beliefs and polity—as a conjoined threat; William Penn, suspected of being a secret Jesuit, was imprisoned following the Glorious Revolution as a Stuart Catholic sympathizer.

Both Catholics and Quakers could be marginalized by something as easy to administer as an oath to the monarch (or joint monarchs) as supreme head of the church in the realm, which neither Catholic nor Quaker would take. Long after the lurid and insulting anti-Catholic rants of the first wave of Catholic proscription had been rejected or toned down and redrafted by the Crown, the simple matter of an oath kept Catholics from voting or holding office in the colony. Removed from public life like their recusant counterparts in England, Catholic Marylanders had a tendency to withdraw into their own class, marry other Catholics (in many cases, cousins, just outside the boundaries of consanguinity), live as country gentlemen on their estates, and grow very rich as lords of acreage, slaves, and tobacco. Thus Maryland Catholics of the manorial class were increasingly dependent on their lands and slaves for their status in secular society.

A slave-based economy

De facto slavery, albeit on a small scale, had been part of the Maryland experience from the beginning. Jesuit Andrew White, for example, owned two mulatto servants, Matthias and Francisco. In his instructions of 1635, Cecil Calvert, second

Lord Baltimore, had envisioned short-term indentured servants as the colony's labor force, but these servants, once their term of service was completed, almost universally migrated into the lower reaches of the agricultural class. Gradually, African servants *durante vita* (while life lasts)—Negro slaves (a term just coming into use)—became increasingly crucial to the workforce and hence increasingly valuable, as bills of sale from the era prove. In 1664 Maryland passed an act formally expanding and defining the future lifetime slavery of Africans and their offspring, whether either parent was free black or free white. Enslaved children born before 1664 would have to serve until age thirty; those born after would serve for life. A small number of blacks sued for and won their freedom on the basis of authenticated oral contracts of term-limited indenture, and the very fact that they could sue under the common law showed that Maryland's legal system was still evolving. Yet despite subsequent laws forbidding cruelty, slavery based on race, with all its injustice and horrors, had come to Maryland as a primary institution. And upon this institution was founded the prosperity into which Catholic Maryland retreated.

Anglican Maryland

The Church of England, meanwhile, continued to take hold as a defining element of Maryland identity. By 1722, four years after the final disfranchisement of Catholics from public life, thirty-two Anglican ministers—English-born clerics, a number of whom held Oxbridge degrees—were active in parish life throughout the colony, ministering in well-designed and solidly built churches to an increasingly native-born population for whom Maryland had always been Anglican. By the 1760s, forty-three Anglican parish churches were in service, with various ones connected to smaller and more conveniently located chapels of ease. Fault lines existed in the system. Local vestries controlled parish resources, but the appointment of clergy was controlled by the governor during the royalist period and by the proprietor following the restoration of the proprietorship in 1715 (the proprietor by that time was himself Anglican), and tensions developed between elite vestrymen accustomed to running things and educated clergy who held their appointments from the bishop of London. Thus a measure of anticlericalism was built into this half-congregational, half-proprietary balance of power, which in certain cases erupted into bitter struggles in which vestrymen, in an effort to drive a local vicar from office, castigated him on charges of drunkenness, neglect of duties, simony, fornication, or combinations thereof.

Despite these occasional setbacks, Anglicanism progressed as Maryland (whose population reached 41,000 in 1755) and the Chesapeake developed into the most prosperous region in British North America, thanks to a continuing demand for tobacco at home and in England and a growing export trade, domestic and overseas, in grains and cereals. In his Hudibrastic romp of a satire, "The Sot Weed Factor", published in London in 1708, Maryland poet Ebenezer Cooke with rollicking good humor evoked Maryland as seen through the eyes of an English tobacco buyer as a crude, rude den of drunkenness, double-dealing, idle frolicking, and sexual debauchery among illiterate, ill-bred, hard-drinking, lower-class tobacco farmers and their sluttish wives. The verse was bawdy good fun, but it contained some truth, as all good satire does. It thus provided a point of reference for a growing Maryland elite struggling to define itself in the decades to come as gentlemen of English descent who maintained connections to England through credit, trade, fashions of dress and furniture, subscriptions to magazines and the creation of private libraries, and proper speech and good manners—a way of life that replicated as closely as possible country life among the gentry of the mother country. Their success was evident in their well-designed homes of brick and stone (whose interior arrangements were guided by architectural handbooks imported from England) with adjacent gardens and orchards; a full and hearty cuisine (far more diverse in its offerings of fish, shellfish, and wild game than a comparable English table in the provinces), and ample drink (wine, beer, rum, and port). Like English gentlemen in search of grouse or pheasant, they roamed the country-side hunting wild turkeys that could reach forty pounds when dressed and roasted. As might be expected, given the Anglophilia in vogue, fox hunting with hounds and livery and horse racing ranked high in the annual cycle of events. Marylanders founded racing clubs on a county-by-county basis, such as the famed South River Club of Anne Arundel County. Between 1730 and 1770, more than one hundred thoroughbred mares and stallions were imported from England for racing and breeding purposes.

Club, musical, and literary life took hold in Annapolis (the dominant city until the final years of the eighteenth century), where a printing shop, a newspaper, and a bookstore were in operation by the mid-1730s. Musical programs and theater works found appreciative audiences. In the summer of 1752 a traveling troupe staged John Gay's *The Beggar's Opera* and David Garrick's *The Lying Valet* before moving on to performances in Williamsburg, Upper Marlborough, Port Tobacco, and Chestertown. Beginning in the mid-1740s, the Tuesday Club of Annapolis met weekly for drinks, dinner, and learned discussion. Among the founders of the club were the eminent Edinburgh-trained physician Alexander Hamilton and Anglican cleric Henry Addison, a graduate of Queen's College, Oxford. Avoiding pomposity, Tuesday Club members loved to cross swords with their rival, the Baltimore Bards, in producing humorous printed exchanges.

The Catholic elite

Although for some time a clerically dominated historiography has preferred to focus on Jesuit achievement and the injustices perpetrated against lay Catholics, one must recognize that the Maryland Catholic elite desired the same good life that their Anglican counterparts had: they wanted the English genteel status; the sense of caste anchored in family and estate; the connection to overseas universities; the festive gatherings; the dances, horse races, and fox hunts; the dynastic wealth and evident social achievement. The displaced Catholic elite was as ambitious and worldly-minded as the Anglican elite now running the colony. Only they wanted to keep their Catholicism as well. With an intensity that matched that of their Anglican colleagues, Maryland Catholics pursued slave- and land-based prosperity and the benefits it brought. After all, was not the achievement of wealth, education, and breeding a counterbalance (or perhaps even revenge) for the disfranchisement they were enduring—no right to worship publicly, teach school, or proselytize; no right to vote or hold office—in the colony they had founded?

Property, Catholics believed, had constituted the foundation of religious liberty from the beginning, despite the penal laws in force when the colony's charter was granted. Charles and Cecil Calvert, first and second Lords Baltimore, designed the colony as an ecumenical society based on property rights, with religion considered a private matter. No effort was made to establish Catholicism beyond the granting of property to individual Jesuits as gentlemen adventurers, who then earned their living as planters. Nor was any Catholic polity organized; the Jesuits willingly functioned as self-supporting clergy. Similar conditions prevailed among Protestants in the founding generation. The Toleration Act of 1649 merely restated and reinforced this arrangement at a time of crisis following a Puritan coup d'état. In the aftermath of the Glorious Revolution, Governor John Seymour launched a second anti-Catholic crusade. To counter Seymour, Charles Carroll the Settler and his supporters, anchoring themselves in the elegant arguments developed by Jesuit Peter Atwood, again appealed to the colony's original charter, which enshrined religion as a private matter and guaranteed freedom of conscience. Even more important, they stressed, were the origin and support of these rights and freedoms (particularly in the matter of property) not only in the Maryland charter but also in ancient English value, usage, and common law that no governmental action, whether in England or Maryland itself, could ever abrogate.

As was the case throughout British North America, growing tensions between Catholic France and Protestant England, exacerbated by the renewed threat of a Stuart coup d'état, reenergized anti-Catholicism in Maryland. In 1744 the governor's council ordered all Catholics dismissed from the militia. Sure enough—and bad luck for Maryland's Catholics—Bonnie Prince Charlie did invade Scotland the following year, and the lower house of the Maryland Assembly tried to pass several bills suppressing Catholics even further. The efforts were unsuccessful because the upper house of the assembly, which was dominated by property owners, felt uneasy about the confiscatory intent of these laws; they attacked property rights, which the Protestant elite, like the Catholic elite, considered the bedrock of the Maryland experiment.

Up to this point, the Maryland Catholic elite had pursued wealth both as a means of self-protection and compensation for loss of political rights and as a way to connect with the equally independent-minded Anglican establishment alongside whom they were getting rich and acquiring transatlantic business ties, a growing anglophilic civility, and a taste for the good life. The Catholic elite had learned to partner with the Protestant elite in commercial enterprises, to manage mixed marriages with them (provided that children be raised Catholic), and in a number of instances to agree to raise Protestant children from prior marriages in their Protestant faith in a religiously mixed household. Elites, in short, had long since found personal and property interests stronger than confessional barriers.

Richard Bennett III, the richest man in Maryland in his time and hence among the most influential, bore out the reality of Anglican-Catholic interface. Bennett's Puritan grandfather had governed Maryland on behalf of Cromwell and Parliament, and his maternal grandfather was the Maryland Catholic James Neale, who had served Charles II and James, Duke of York, as English ambassador to Spain and Portugal in the late 1650s. Richard Bennett's mother, Henrietta Maria Bennett, was widowed following the birth of Richard (in 1667) and his brother. Remarrying Philemon Lloyd, an Anglican, Henrietta raised her two Bennett sons as Catholics and her ten Lloyd stepchildren as Protestants in the same Eastern Shore, Talbot County, household. As a young man, Bennett enjoyed friendship and business partnerships with Catholics and Protestants alike. A substantial inheritance from his Puritan grandfather launched his career as a shipper, merchant, and moneylender. When his mother died in 1697, Bennett became the codirector of the family's extensive land, slave, and commercial interests along with his Anglican brother-in-law. Bennett's mother also left money to her Catholic niece Elizabeth Rousby, the daughter of an Anglican father and a Catholic mother. She and Richard Bennett III were married in 1700 and set up their home in the grand Sayer House that Elizabeth inherited as well.

Aside from its ecumenical implications, Richard Bennett III's rise in the world underscored a self-evident fact of upper-class life in Maryland. Very few outsiders were able to break into the self-encapsulated, self-perpetuating elite of Maryland. By the eighteenth century, among an almost exclusively native-born elite, Protestant and Catholic alike, money from one generation passed to and was expanded upon by the next. Bennett III's experience reflected that of Charles Carroll the Settler, who set up his son Charles Carroll of Annapolis, who set up—after an unusual and cruel trial period, according to his son's mother—his son Charles Carroll of Carrollton.

Suffice it to say that merchant, planter, shipper, and moneylender Richard Bennett III grew rich, richer, and then even richer as the eighteenth century unfolded. By 1748, the year before his death at the age of eighty-two, Bennett was most likely the wealthiest man in North America; a contemporary estimated his worth at 150,000 pounds sterling. Equally impressive was Bennett's political influence in the colony despite the fact that he could neither vote nor hold elective office. Maintaining two Eastern Shore chapels, one at Sayer House and the other at Doncaster Town, the accommodating, moderate Bennett III rivaled the more insular and assertive Charles Carroll the Settler as the de facto (and certainly most effective) spokesman and lobbyist for the Catholic community, especially following the invasion of Scotland in 1715 and Maryland governor John Hart's subsequent hostility to Catholics. Hart's departure from office in 1720 and the appointment of Thomas Brooke—a former Catholic, now an Anglican, who had three brothers serving as Jesuits—as acting governor ushered in nearly twenty-five years of relative peace in the valley for Maryland Catholics, until the uprising of 1745. In 1731 Lord Baltimore named Bennett rent-roll keeper of the Western and Eastern Shores, an appointed position outside the voting franchise system. In 1732 Baltimore named him to the official commission adjudicating the boundary between Maryland and Pennsylvania.

Following the death of his wife in April 1740, Bennett recovered from a serious depression and spent his final years doing business and doing good. Childless, he and Elizabeth had raised two children as their own. One of them, Robert Knatchbull, went to Saint Omer's in Flanders, where the young man entered the Jesuits; the other, Ann Rousby, married Bennett's nephew. As a widower (his household was now run by his cousin Ann Brooke), Bennett continued to sponsor scholarships to Saint Omer's and dowries for the daughters of relatives and friends, to maintain a chapel in his private residence, and—reportedly—to foster his slaves' instruction in the Catholic faith.

Slavery and Catholicism

That Bennett remained active in the slave trade along with his many other commercial and philanthropic activities underscores the reality of who was doing the work to keep Bennett's 47,197 acres profitable as well as the fundamental contradiction of Catholic wealth anchored in race-based enslavement. New France, too, supported slavery during this era. As missionaries and laymen advanced westward into the Great Lakes region and southward into the upper and lower Mississippi valley, friendly Indians frequently gave them enslaved Indian captives as presents. The rising economies and urbanism of Quebec and Montreal, meanwhile, fostered the introduction of African slavery into these communities, especially in domestic service. Transfer to French ownership most likely led to improved treatment for Indian captives. Yet urban slavery in Quebec and Montreal had an ominous dimension that could—and did—erupt into violence. On the night of 10 April 1734, forty-six buildings burned to the ground in Montreal. A twenty-nine-year-old Portuguese-born black slave named Angélique was blamed for the fires. Angélique was arrested, tortured, convicted, paraded through the city, and hanged, and her corpse was burned in a prologue to the even more extensive repressions in New York City a decade later.

Still, as repugnant as this state of affairs might be, New France did not depend extensively on an institutionalized slave-based economy, while Maryland in no uncertain terms did. Christian elites, Anglican and Catholic alike, thus faced the question of their responsibility for the physical, social, psychological, and spiritual welfare of those people they continued to enslave. The Jesuits, as has already been suggested, were acutely aware of this duty, given the obligations of their profession. "Charity to Negroes", Jesuit superior George Hunter told planters attending a religious retreat at Port Tobacco on 20 December 1749, "is due from all, particularly their masters. As they [slaves] are members of Jesus Christ redeemed by his precious blood, they are to be dealt with in a charitable, Christian, paternal manner."[1] The English-born Jesuit Joseph Mosley, who was active on the Eastern Shore between 1765 and 1787, was especially dedicated to this ministry, if one is to judge from the 235 baptisms of slaves Mosley logged in his register and the fact that 60 percent of the recorded marriages he performed in the presence of witnesses were for slaves. Mosley also documented the administering of extreme unction for dying slaves although services for the dying and funerals were appreciably fewer than the baptisms and the marriages noted.

Richard Bennett's attention to the spiritual care of his slaves while continuing to profit from the slave trade illustrates the contradictions and incongruities inherent in the system. Ignatius Digges of Prince George's County insisted that before he would allow his daughter Molly to marry a Protestant, his future son-in-law would have to guarantee that Molly's slaves be allowed to attend Mass on Sundays and holy days. The leading historian regarding this topic, Beatriz Betancourt Hardy of the Maryland Historical Society, has speculated that on such issues as saints, sacraments, crucifixes, relics, incense, holy water, sacred oils, holy days (when no labor should be performed), the pageantry of the Mass, and other aspects of religious practice, Catholicism had affinities with West African religion that slaves could easily grasp as transition points to Christianity. Strong kinship ties formed another point of connection. Sixty-eight percent of the slaves baptized in Saint Mary's County between 1760 and 1776 were sponsored by known white godparents, and records show occasions when a white person and a Catholic slave jointly served a baptized slave as godparents and thereby established cross-racial ties of spiritual kinship.

Energized by the Society for the Propagation of the Gospel, founded in 1701, the Church of England launched a parallel effort to promote the spiritual welfare of slaves. In 1723 Edmund Gibson, the Anglican bishop of London, conducted a survey of the spiritual care of slaves by the twenty-three Anglican ministers in Maryland. Nineteen replied. Disappointed by what he learned, Gibson in 1727 initiated a campaign of pastoral letters, circulated in England and the North American colonies, calling for more evangelical outreach to slaves. Of all the colonies, the ministers of Virginia—the most Anglican of the Anglican colonies—responded the most effectively to the bishop's call. But when baptized Virginia slaves began to demand their freedom on the basis of their Christianity, the outreach program quickly lost momentum. Nonetheless, it affected law in Maryland, where the legislature passed a series of regulations prohibiting maiming or any cruel forms of punishment against slaves and offering freedom to any slave so mistreated.

Philadelphia story

Less than twenty miles north of the revised Maryland-Pennsylvania border, Philadelphia was developing into the leading city of British North America. This emergence included the rise of an urban Catholic community that dramatically contrasted with the rich, slaveholding Catholic community of Maryland just a few miles south of the Mason-Dixon Line. In 1701 Proprietor William Penn conferred an official city charter on the village of Philadelphia, whose population of 2,500 resided in five hundred brick houses between the Schuylkill and Delaware Rivers. A few Catholics had previously lived in the settlement: George Nixon of County Wexford, Ireland, arrived in 1688; John Tatham, a friend of Penn, arrived in 1685. Tatham later relocated to Burlington, New Jersey, taking with him his impressive library of Catholica and collection of liturgical art and vessels. Upon his death in 1693, the wealthy French Philadelphian Peter Dubuc left 100 pounds sterling to the poor of the town and 50 pounds sterling to a certain Father Smith of Talbot County, Maryland. Smith was later identified as Father Thomas Harvey (alias Thomas Barton), one of the two English Jesuit chaplains on the staff of governor Thomas Dongan and, under the alias John Smith, a prominent New York figure. Leisler's rebellion drove Harvey from the city, and he relocated his ministry and his alias to Maryland and Pennsylvania.

In 1707 one Lionel Brittin and several others were received into the Church at a public Mass most likely celebrated by one of the Jesuits from Old Bohemia Mission. In a letter dated 10 January 1708 to the Society for the Propagation of the Gospel in London, the Reverend John Talbot, the Anglican minister of Saint Mary's Church in Burlington, New Jersey, protested the open celebration of Catholic worship in Philadelphia, which he declared was the direct result of the leniency of William Penn, who at the time was imprisoned for debt in Fleet Street Jail. Despite his temporary vulnerability, however, neither Proprietor Penn nor Governor James Logan restricted Catholic practices, and for the next twelve years Jesuits from Old Bohemia regularly ministered to a small but active Catholic community in Philadelphia.

Throughout the 1720s Jesuit missioner Joseph Greaton served southeastern Pennsylvania and nearby areas. A native of London, born in 1679, Greaton converted to Catholicism at the age of fifteen. Educated at Saint Omer's and the Jesuit seminary at Valladolid, Greaton served for a decade in the Low Country before being assigned to the Maryland mission in 1720. Based in Anne Arundell County, Greaton rode a circuit that included northern Maryland, southeastern Pennsylvania, and Philadelphia. In 1729 he permanently relocated his ministry to Philadelphia and there waited out border negotiations to determine whether the growing city (11,500 residents by 1730) would belong to Pennsylvania or Maryland. By 1732 Greaton was confident that Pennsylvania would be the winner of Philadelphia, which pleased the Catholic community of the city, given the Quakers' accommodating policies.

Perhaps as early as 1729 Greaton had purchased, via a friendly intermediary, a lot on the south side of Walnut Street, east of Fourth, on the outskirts of the city near the Quaker almshouse. There in 1733 and 1734 Greaton built an eighteen-by-twenty-eight-foot chapel served by an adjacent rectory. At some point during construction, the lieutenant governor and his council grew anxious. Was such a public Roman Catholic chapel, they asked, contrary to the laws of England? No, the council concluded after deliberation. In 1706 Queen Anne had officially approved William Penn's law that guaranteed liberty of conscience and public practice in matters of religion, and this decision by the last Stuart monarch had contravened previous restrictions on Catholic worship issued by William and Mary. Sometime between late 1733 and early 1734, Greaton celebrated an inaugural Mass for thirty-seven or so congregants in what was the de facto (though not yet canonically established) first urban parish church in British North America. As such, Saint Joseph's prefigured the urban future of Roman Catholicism in English-speaking North America prior to the United States' expansion into the Louisiana Territory and the Spanish Borderlands.

Like Philadelphia itself, Saint Joseph's Church continued to increase in population and physical plant. A pulpit and organ were acquired before 1742. By 1757 the congregation had grown to the point that the old house-like chapel was torn down and replaced by a more explicitly ecclesiastical structure that measured forty-six by fifty feet. (Expanded in 1821, this second church served until 1839, when an even more impressive building took its place.) Above the altar of this 1757 structure hung a Madonna by Benjamin West. The church had two entrances, one on Walnut Street and the other on Willing's Alley (the small lane opened in 1746 when Thomas Willing needed a passageway to Fourth Street from his new mansion on Third). In 1763 Saint Mary's, a chapel of ease, was built on the nearby burial ground of Saint Joseph's Church for more sparsely attended weekday Masses. Palatinate Germans, who were followed by Irish, dominated the congregation, which included a smaller number of Catholic gentry as well. When Catholic Seneca Iroquois were in town for negotiation purposes, they were also known to attend.

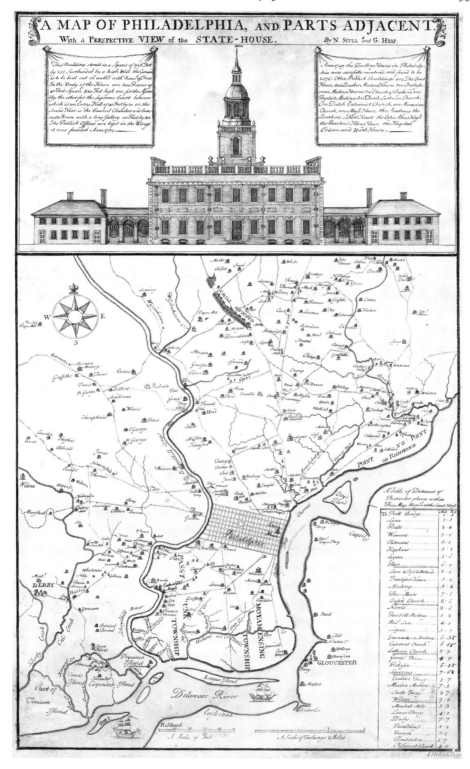

Map 18. *A Map of Philadelphia and Parts Adjacent: With a Perspective View of the State-House* (Nicolas Scull, George Heap, and L. Hebert, 1752). Library of Congress, Geography and Map Division.

When the British expelled the neutral French from Acadia in late July 1755, some 454 of these Catholic Acadians arrived by troop transport vessels in Philadelphia in late November and were temporarily confined to their ships by governor Robert Morris, who feared they would form a fifth column if they were immediately released. Quarantined in early December to the city's pest house on Province Island, at the mouth of the Schuylkill, the Acadians languished there until February 1756, when they were released on the condition that no more than one family settle in each town throughout the colony, an offer they refused. Not until that spring were the Acadians released as a group and allowed to settle as a group in a scrappy neighborhood near Saint Joseph's Church. There they resisted efforts to place their children as indentured servants, a common British colonial treatment of impoverished immigrants. When the Acadians appealed to British military commander John Campbell, Earl of Loudoun, protesting this practice, the general rejected their petition because it was written in French. Loudoun confined five Acadian leaders for several months on a British prison ship before their release, when he was recalled to London. In Longfellow's perennially popular narrative poem *Evangeline* (1847), his heroine, separated from her fiancé, Gabriel, tries unsuccessfully for a number of years to locate him before going to Philadelphia, drawn there by an accepting, democratic Quaker ethos that reminds her of her homeland, "where all men were equal, and all were brothers and sisters". As a nurse in the Quaker almshouse near Saint Joseph's Church, an aging and lonely Evangeline becomes an angel of mercy to the sick and dying who find refuge there. In time, one of these dying men is a prematurely aged and dying Gabriel, broken and beaten down by long exile and suffering. Gabriel and Evangeline recognize each other. He dies in her arms, knowing her at the last but unable to speak. Evangeline thanks God for this last reunion, however brief. Gabriel is buried in Saint Joseph's churchyard, where the saintly Evangeline herself is eventually laid to rest.

Fiction, a mere tale—true. But the narrative emphasized to a later generation the growing centrality of Saint Joseph's and Saint Mary's as Philadelphia landmarks. Being a Catholic landmark had its downside, however, at times of anti-Spanish or anti-French sentiment—in 1740 (war with Spain) and 1755 (Braddock's defeat)—as mobs converged on Saint Joseph's, intent on burning it to the ground. Fortunately, Quaker authorities intervened and prevented such actions.

When in 1750 Father Greaton retired as the Jesuit in charge of Saint Joseph's and took up residence at Bohemia Manor, he was succeeded by Father Robert Harding, who served until his death in 1772. Far from serving near-anonymously behind an alias, however, as Jesuits were forced to do in earlier years, Harding became a respected fixture in the city: a subscriber to the Pennsylvania Hospital in 1755, an elected member of the American Philosophical Society as of 1768, and in 1772 a founding member of the Society of the Sons of Saint George, an organization that helped Englishmen in distress. When Harding died on 1 September 1772, his funeral was attended by many of the city's leading citizens, and as a special recognition he was entombed near the high altar of an expanded Saint Mary's, which was now the leading Catholic church in a city of 33,482.

Jesuits based in Maryland ministered to Catholic aristocrats and their dependents in a slave-based economy. The Jesuits of Saint Joseph's and Saint Mary's in Philadelphia, by contrast, had for their congregants German and Irish working people, a small group of artisans, and a sprinkling of professionals. The entire city, as historian Sam Bass Warner Jr. notes in his classic *The Private City* (1968), was pervaded by a hardworking, democratic, and entrepreneurial ethos. Slavery was not unknown. In 1775, the city registered six hundred slaves along with nine hundred indentured servants and more than two hundred hired servants living with their employers. But slavery was not the distinguishing characteristic of Philadelphia—far from it. The distinguishing characteristic, according to Warner, was private life, in most cases linked to family, and a desire among immigrants to define oneself through occupation and, if possible, family-oriented enterprises. People were proud to define themselves by their calling (Benjamin Franklin remained Benjamin Franklin Printer long after he had become much more), and shopkeepers preferred to live over their stores in a city in which housing was at a premium and the line between spaces for living and working was blurred. Thus in spatialization and community life Philadelphia resembled the late medieval German cities so admired by Lewis Mumford. Workers lived near each other in places where they did their work together. Shopkeepers grouped into retail zones and resided alongside their wares. The gentry had its own district. Public buildings such as the Pennsylvania State House (1748) on Chestnut and the hospital (1756) on Pine marked the central city. Yet density was great, and the Delaware and Schuylkill Rivers demarcated spatial identity in the manner of medieval European city walls. William Penn had long ago made provisions for urban open space, where people could rest for a moment and enjoy the pageantry and flow of street life. Philadelphia coalesced in fact and identity as one place, one city, a whole greater than the sum of its parts. In such an environment, parish life flourished, as the Great Meeting House (1696) on the corner of Second and High, Saint Michael's Lutheran (1743) at the corner of Fifth and Appletree Alley, and Christ Church Episcopal (1744) on Second near Mulberry asserted on a grand scale. Saint Joseph's and Saint Mary's were much smaller edifices, but they also assembled a *plenum mundi* for whom these structures and communities and the liturgies, sacraments, and instruction they offered constituted Roman Catholicism as a faith, a way of life, to be lived day by day, week by week.

An alienation of identity

Despite the penal laws enacted in the early eighteenth century, Maryland Catholics, especially large landowners, remained loyal to the proprietor (who was now an Anglican in London) and adjusted to Anglican control of the colony. For Catholics, this era of good feeling—as epitomized by the life, times, and personal involvements of Richard Bennett III—depended in significant measure on an Anglican accommodation that could not last forever, given residual antagonisms, the stresses of war between Protestant Britain and Catholic Spain (1739), and the even larger, longer, and more consequential French and Indian War (1754–1763). That conflict built on four previous contests—King William's War (1689–1697), Queen Anne's War (1702–1713), the War of Jenkins' Ear (1739–1748), and King George's War (1744–1748)—that pitted Catholic France against Protestant England for control of the North American continent. An early tremor suggestive of fault lines came in 1751 when physician Charles Carroll, a convert to Anglicanism, sought to cover his embezzlements from the estate of James Carroll by having its two heirs, Jesuit priests, banned from inheritance on the basis of English penal laws that forbade Catholic priests from owning or inheriting property. Dr. Carroll was a member of the lower house of the assembly, which passed a bill in his favor. Twelve prominent Catholics, however, prevailed on the upper house—men of property, some of whom were connected by marriage with the Catholic elite—to void the bill. Did this near negation of Catholic property rights suggest dangers ahead, the Catholic elite asked itself, should confiscatory antagonism return to a colony whose population was only 10 percent Catholic and that 10 percent disfranchised from public life?

That is exactly what happened after the devastating defeat of General Edward Braddock's forces by the French and their Indian allies at the Battle of the Wilderness (9 July 1755) near Fort Duquesne, a defeat so total that it unleashed valid fears of an imminent Iroquois and French invasion of the Pennsylvania, Virginia, and Maryland frontiers. Following this disaster, not only did the assembly and governor's council ban Catholics from serving in the Maryland militia, but also Catholics were forced to pay a double tax for militia support. These actions were taken by a government in which Catholics could not participate and were approved by a proprietor on whom they depended for fair treatment as a disfranchised minority. The tax itself, a mere shilling per one hundred acres annually, was not so onerous. It was, however, vulgar in its evident desire to offer insult. In the aftermath of its passage, Charles Carroll of Annapolis (like his father, Charles Carroll the Settler, before him) began to doubt seriously whether a Catholic could ever feel secure in the Maryland that had revealed its distrust of English Catholics' loyalty to the Crown. (Carroll would soon liquidate his Maryland assets and seek from France a grant of land in Louisiana, where he would relocate his family and his slaves.)

Such talk, coming from the richest man in the colony, underscored the instability that Maryland demanded its Catholics psychologically negotiate. Partly as a result of these efforts made by a hostile government, the practice of Catholicism intensified within the private realm to which it was confined. By the 1760s the colony contained fifty or more house-chapels, staffed by up to a dozen Jesuits riding circuit from a half dozen mission stations. Served by a learned, well-trained clergy, Maryland Catholics enjoyed all aspects of Catholic worship and sacrament—Mass, baptism, marriage, last rites, funeral services, burial in consecrated ground—as well as confession, vespers, compline, benediction, sermons, religious instruction, hymn singing, and church fellowship. They did so without a church building, of course, since that would be public and hence in violation of the law. Still, gatherings of white and black Catholics (slaves were expected to stand to the side or in the rear of congregations) reached such densities that Masses were held outdoors when the weather allowed.

As a sure sign of the colony's Catholicity, Marylanders began to develop clergy and religious from their own ranks. By the late eighteenth century, forty-nine native Marylanders had become ordained priests, forty-three of them Jesuits; twenty-three returned to Maryland for local service. Thirty-three young women had become nuns. In 1790 three of these nuns, Discalced Carmelites, returned to Maryland to establish at Port Tobacco the first convent in what was now the United States. Thus a connection with Catholic Europe was formed, for British North America had no seminaries or convents, no bishops, no cathedrals, no novitiates, no monasteries. For English Catholics (which Marylanders remained), Catholic Europe meant the

Low Lands, especially French-speaking Flanders, the independent diocesan city of Liège (present-day Belgium), and France itself as represented by Douai, Bourges, Rheims, and Paris. To these places Catholic England had expatriated itself in the mid- to late-sixteenth century, as well as to Spain and Portugal, and there founded colleges, seminaries, monasteries, convents, and novitiates.

For Catholic Marylanders of the wealthier classes, Catholic Europe began to emerge as a second homeland. They began to send their offspring, boys and young men especially, to the same schools and colleges that the children of the recusant gentry of England attended so that these young Marylanders might gain the intellectual and cultural edge required to survive in their home colony as a disfranchised minority.

The Jesuits of the English Province had done their best to set up primary and secondary education in British North America, but anything resembling the grand Jesuit college in Quebec was beyond their reach as missionaries to a small minority under restrictive penal laws. Ralph Crouch, a former Jesuit temporal coadjutor, conducted a school at Newton Manor from 1640 to 1659. Readmitted to the Society, Crouch returned to Europe, finished his novitiate, and served at Liège for the remainder of his life. The Newton Manor school reopened in 1681 under the direction of scholastic Thomas Hathersal and was closed by the Maryland Assembly in 1704. The two Jesuits Governor Dongan brought to New York in 1682 opened the New York Latin School at the intersection of present-day Broadway and Wall Streets, but it was out of operation by 1690.

In 1745 or 1746 Jesuit Thomas Poulton, a former prefect at Saint Omer's College, opened the most ambitious of these briefly existing schools, Bohemia Academy at Little Bohemia, also known as Bohemia Manor, in remote Cecil County on the northeastern corner of the Eastern Shore. Founded by the energetic Father Robert Parsons in 1592, Saint Omer's provided Father Poulton with a fine model, for Saint Omer's was the leading English-language humanities college of its type, offering the present-day equivalent of secondary education and two years of collegiate studies for young men en route to either lay or clerical careers. Like Saint Omer's, Bohemia Academy offered instruction guided by the *ratio studiorum*, a course of studies adopted by the Society in 1599 as a sequenced code of liberal education for Jesuit colleges. The school's newly constructed building housed between twenty and forty students; three Jesuit tutors and one layman served as staff; fees totaled forty pounds per annum for the Latin course and thirty per year for the English course. Only the wealthy could afford such an expensive education, but that was precisely the point. Bohemia Academy was intended as an entry to further education at Saint Omer's for a Maryland Catholic elite in the process of reasserting its relationship to Catholic Europe. Early enrollees included young Charles Carroll of Carrollton; his distant cousins, the brothers Daniel and John (who later became the first archbishop of Baltimore); Leonard Neale (who followed as the second archbishop); and Robert Brent of Virginia. Other young men bearing such well-known Maryland family names as Brooke, Digges, Fenwick, Sewall, and Spalding also appear on the register.

With such support, Bohemia Academy should have lasted for decades. It survived the death of Father Poulton in January 1749 by a mere five or six years. First of all, the school violated the law of 1704 that forbade Catholics to conduct schools—which was why Father Poulton had located it in the middle of a

1,700-acre wilderness. Learning of the academy, however, Anglican vicar Hugh Jones, the rector of Saint Stephen's parish on Sassafras Island, embarked upon a crusade to have the lower house of the assembly close the illegal institution. He recruited to his cause many Protestant residents of Cecil County and at least one other prominent Anglican minister, the Reverend Nicholas Hyland of North Elk parish, near Bohemia. Once again, Catholics prevailed in the upper house of the assembly, but only at the cost of constant lobbying. The school was illegal, so how much longer could it be defended? Thus Bohemia Academy closed its doors, most likely in 1755 or 1756.

Saint Omer's in Flanders

By this time, the distant cousins John and Charles Carroll had long since embarked with Robert Brent of Virginia in July 1748 for Saint Omer's. The two Carroll boys, thirteen and eleven, were in the vanguard of a dramatic increase in Maryland Catholic students (thirty-five boys before 1750 and another forty-seven by 1773; seven girls before 1750 and another twenty-nine by 1773), which reflected the imaginative and psychological repossession of English Catholic Europe under way in the colony. By 1760, in fact, Jesuit procurators (business agents) in London, Paris, Saint Omer's, and Bruges had developed efficient protocols for paying invoices involved in conveying Maryland students to Europe, managing their expenses while they were there, and organizing voyages home. A small number of young women who made the journey wished to attend school. A larger number wanted to try out or enter life as religious at various monasteries and convents. Brother Thomas Spalding CFX has compiled a list (which he declares is incomplete) of thirty-five or so Maryland women who entered religious orders in Europe between 1684 and 1788. The list comprises a who's who of surnames of the Maryland elite. The young women entered such congregations as the Carmelites of Antwerp, Liège, and Hoogstraten; the Dominicans of Brussels; the Canonesses Regular of the Holy Sepulcher at Liège; the Poor Clares of Rouen and Aire; the Benedictines of Paris, Cambrai, and Brussels; and the Augustine Canonesses at Bruges. Entrance as choir nuns to such established convents required a dowry, but not as large a sum as a marriage dowry in Maryland, and no division of property was required if a daughter left for Europe, never to be seen again by her parents. As it was, only wealthy women could become nuns, and among the wealthy of Maryland (as was the case in recusant England), every Catholic family of note in this era seemed to produce at least one female religious.

Young men entering European schools had more than forty institutions to choose from. Saint Omer's, however, was overwhelmingly the prep school and college of choice for Marylanders. Charles Carroll the Settler had sent his three sons there. (Sadly, his son Henry drowned on the voyage home.) John Carroll's older brother Daniel had recently completed a full six-year course. Although Saint Omer's was not a seminary, since it welcomed lay and preclerical students alike, it did maintain a rigid schedule: up at five, in bed at nine in the spartan dormitories. It also required a uniform: a white doublet of sturdy canvas, knee breeches, and worsted stockings. The school offered a full schedule of classes and recitations; organized walks, games (ninepins, trap ball, and handball), and a lively calendar of theatrical performances (a specialty of Jesuit colleges); and various personal privileges (permission, for example, for senior scholars to leave the dormitory for more private accommodations). Institutional food was enlivened by special treats on religious holidays.

John and Charles Carroll were friendly but not close. Differences in age and temperament were involved, as well as differences in wealth and social standing (Charles was sensitive about his illegitimacy, despite his elite status). Religious commitment was also a factor. Charles Carroll was a Catholic as a matter of inheritance and social identity. He developed a taste for Voltaire upon leaving Saint Omer's. John Carroll was discreetly prayerful and pious and by the conclusion of his course at Saint Omer's had decided to join the Jesuits, which he did in 1753, entering the novitiate at Watten, seven miles from Saint Omer's, and taking his first vows two years later. Seven other young men joined John Carroll in the onetime abbey turned novitiate (presented to the Society in 1625), including fellow Marylander Robert Cole, for two years of spiritual training under the renowned novice master Father Henry Corbie, who in July 1756 would be named provincial of the English Province. Putting on his black Jesuit cassock for the first time, John Carroll later recalled, had provided him with the thrill of envisioning his future life as a Jesuit priest and teacher, for which he would now begin to prepare across sixteen years of advanced humanities study at Watten, philosophical studies at the Jesuit College in Liège, a regent teaching philosophy at Liège, theological studies at Liège, ordination to the priesthood, a year as instructor at the Jesuit College in Bruges, and tertianship and final vows as a Jesuit.

In an earlier era, John Carroll could have looked forward to a long and productive career of teaching in the English Jesuit colleges on the Continent. Most likely, he never would have seen Maryland again. Instead, he would have lived out the Maryland dream of Catholic Europe for the rest of his life. Yet the signs of the times portended another scenario. Hostility toward the Society of Jesus had existed since its establishment in the 1540s. But the Bourbon monarchies of Portugal (1758) and Spain (1767) had banished the Society from their empires, and the regional parlements of France began a similar process of suppression and confiscation, district by district, urged on by Louis XV and his onetime mistress and continuing confidante, Jeanne Antoinette Poisson Le Normant d'Étiolles, marquise de Pompadour. When the Paris Parlement issued an ultimatum of expulsion on 6 August 1762, the faculty of Saint Omer's, sensing the impending end of their institution in Flanders, organized a surreptitious departure from the college by groups of students who carried as little luggage as if they were going hiking. By 17 August the entire student body had safely removed itself to Bruges, where it operated in an ancient château for the next eleven years.

Student of philosophy

Charles Carroll of Carrollton, meanwhile, left Saint Omer's after four years for a first collegiate year at humanities-focused Rheims as a student of Latin and Greek poetry along with history, geography, and heraldry. Living in the English dormitory, he read widely in the college's exquisite 118,000-volume library. By the fall of 1755, he was ready for two years of philosophical studies at the Jesuit College of Louis-le-Grand in Paris. At Saint Omer's and Rheims, Charles had been under the benevolent watch of the Irish-born Anthony Carroll, a cousin then in the final stages of his Jesuit training. Anthony Carroll was now a priest, ordained at Liège in 1754, and away on mission in England; and so young Charles enjoyed less supervision once he moved into the English students' residence at L'Hôtel de Saint-Louis Rue in the district Saint-Antoine, where the London-born Father Edward Galloway served as master and tutor. Charles Carroll later opined that Saint Omer's, with its rigorous schedule and course of studies, was at its best as a place of preparation for young men intending to go on to the priesthood. His two years in Paris freed him from the constraints of Saint Omer's and introduced him to a more open environment. The College of Louis-le-Grand was the flagship school of philosophy for French Jesuits, where the faculty strove to harmonize Enlightenment ways of thinking with the wisdom of traditional philosophy from Aristotle through Aquinas.

Because Charles Carroll of Carrollton would within the decade become a noted intellectual figure in British North America, it is important to note the nature of his philosophical and political studies at the College of Louis-le-Grand. In year one, Carroll began his philosophical studies with logic, the art and science of thinking consistently. At the same time, he started a systematic review of great philosophers and Newtonian mathematics, followed by Newtonian physics in year two. Year two also witnessed further excursions into metaphysics, epistemology, ethics, and political philosophy, along with an examination of seventeenth- and eighteenth-century thought as represented in John Locke and the recently deceased (1755) political philosopher Charles-Louis de Secondat, baron de la Brède et de Montesquieu.

Such a comprehensive program would have been hard to come by in the colonies outside of a few institutions that Carroll, as a Catholic, could not have attended. As young Carroll would be demonstrating some fifteen years hence, he had developed a taste for philosophical analysis presented in an accessible format. Knowing his Aristotle, Carroll could sympathize easily with John Locke's empiricism, rejection of innate ideas, and advocacy of limited government anchored in natural law. The Thomism taught at Louis-le-Grand, moreover, was presented through the flexible, liberalizing interpretations of the great Jesuit commentator Francisco Suárez (1548–1617), who emphasized human freedom, personal choice, and limited government.

In Montesquieu's *De l'esprit des lois* (*The Spirit of the Laws*), first published in 1748, Carroll encountered a political philosopher and sociologist of critical importance to his future line of thought. A lifelong Catholic (entombed as of 1755 in the Church of Saint Sulpice), Montesquieu nevertheless nurtured the deistic and anticlerical tendencies of the era and had a taste for empirical investigation and comparative analysis as necessary requirements for political philosophy. How Montesquieu's *Spirit of the Laws* ever got on the Index of Forbidden Books during the generally open-minded pontificate of Benedict XIV is either baffling, suggestive of continuing tensions between Rome and the Enlightenment, or merely proof that Church authorities and the Sorbonne correctly grasped the revolutionary implications of Montesquieu's expansion of natural law as the basis for political organization to include not simply the law of nature as a philosophical concept, but the entire, empirically verified interactivity of environment, culture, race, demographics, and history that rendered a specific people suitable for either a monarchical, republican, or despotic form of government.

Political structures, Montesquieu argued, are not God-given, divinely ordained organizations that offered an immutable near-transcendent identity, but are empirical solutions to natural conditions that should remain as limited as possible in their powers, which in turn should be clearly differentiated according to executive, legislative, and judicial functions. A limited monarchy was best for France, Montesquieu opined, and perhaps it was the limitations he placed on monarchy, even for France (Montesquieu very much admired the hard-earned English relationship between Parliament and the Crown), that got ·The Spirit of the Laws on the Index.

But Montesquieu had good company on the Index. Another Charley Carroll favorite, the still very much alive François-Marie d'Arouet, or Voltaire, was also a favorite of his father. From Voltaire, both Carrolls, father and son, absorbed a taste for controversy and rational argument, as well as a humanism anchored in a deep respect for an individual's right to pursue happiness in private terms. It did Charles Carroll of Carrollton, a Roman Catholic, a world of good to encounter such thinkers as the Oratorian-educated Montesquieu and the Jesuit-educated Voltaire in noncanonical circumstances. These creative protagonists of philosophical and scientific inquiry—advancing into strange seas of thought, alone, as Wordsworth put it—helped Carroll to learn how to think independently. As an American, Charley Carroll had to learn to think for himself if he was ever to be able to think for his country. For the past eight years the Jesuits had helped him sharpen his capacity for independent thought, but now it was time—so Papa informed him—to professionalize his capacity for thought through legal study.

Coming to terms with Dearest Papa

On 10 August 1757 Charley Carroll enjoyed a Paris reunion with his Dearest Papa, whom he had not seen in nine years. First up on the agenda (thanks to a schedule change arranged by Father Anthony Carroll), Charles Carroll of Annapolis witnessed his son's oral examination for a degree and the presentation of the degree itself, which the proud father quickly framed and sent back to Maryland for display. Amid visits to Notre Dame, the Louvre, the Tuileries Gardens, assorted theaters, restaurants, and tailoring establishments, they took pleasure in the city that had fostered Charley's growth as a self-reliant intellectual. As subsequent letters reveal, they also had time to get to know each other and to talk. They talked about Maryland: leaving Maryland, that is, for Louisiana; aside from seeing Charley, that was one reason Papa was in France: to confer with Pierre de La Rue, l'Abbé de l'Isle-Dieu and vicar of Louisiana since 1734, and the colony's former intendant, Sébastien-François-Ange Le Normant de Mézy, regarding a possible grant of land on the Arkansas River. The second topic of conversation was the need for Charley to go on to study law, now that he had successfully completed the first phase of his education.

Most likely not on the agenda was the topic of his parents' recent marriage. On 15 February 1757 German Jesuit Matthias Manners (Sittensberger) of the Conewago mission presided over the marriage of Charles Carroll of Annapolis and Elizabeth Brooke. Father Manners issued a written statement testifying to the marriage, which Charles Carroll of Annapolis had gathered into a folio that also included the marriage articles he had Elizabeth Brooke sign, basically promising her one hundred pounds a year if he should predecease her. "To be delivered to my son", the documents read, but no time of delivery has ever surfaced, and the folio collection disappeared until it was discovered in a descendant's trunk in 1885. As of the Carrolls' reunion in the summer of 1757, Charley's mother had signed her letters—as she signed everything—Elizabeth Brooke. Not until 30 November 1757 did she sign a letter to her son as Elizabeth Carroll.

Charley Carroll had grown up in the knowledge that he was on probation. How else, historian Pauline Maier asks, does one explain Charley's long-standing and infinitely patient desire to please and his father's equally persistent desire (as the letters between them show) to lecture his son ceaselessly on a handful of topics, led off by the dangers posed by the unsupervised keeping company with young women, even those of good families? Struggling with the incongruity of a member of a leading Maryland Catholic family living for twenty years in a common-law marriage following an out-of-wedlock birth—thus disfranchising herself from family and respectability in the social sphere and keeping her from the sacraments of her religion—Maier makes a further speculation. There was obviously a pregnancy, she argues, but no proof of a common-law marriage exists. No more pregnancies occurred, for one thing, and Charles Carroll of Annapolis showed not a scintilla of chivalry toward a woman of good family whom he impregnated out of wedlock. Nor did he display the sense of obligation and loving-kindness of an alleged gentleman toward a woman who had put her life in his hands by bearing his child in such difficult circumstances and who was then forced to audition for respectability for the next twenty years, the determining point being the suitability of Charley Carroll as his father's heir. Maier thus speculates that Elizabeth Brooke ran the household of Charles Carroll of Annapolis and served as his hostess. Single female relatives frequently functioned in that role for patriarchal figures during this era. But a decision might have been made to live platonically. Maier suggests that this might have been the senior Charles Carroll's decision. It certainly fits in with his self-absorbed character, especially if—as intimated in his advice to Charley to avoid the unsupervised company of women of any social standing—he considered Elizabeth Brooke's pregnancy to have been not completely his fault. Or the decision might have been Miss Brooke's as well or perhaps even primarily her decision: not to live as a wife when not a wife and thus forfeit her peace of mind as far as her religion was concerned.

In any event, no record shows that Papa and Charley addressed the issue directly during their time in Paris that summer of 1757. From the letters that passed back and forth in the years to come, the outline of what they talked about was refracted and restated according to the epistolary culture established between them. Charley did display resistance to his father's Louisiana proposal, which contained the unstated scenario of Charley's continuing to prove himself to his father. Maryland, Papa argued, offered Charley no possibility for a public career, which was also a way of saying that it had offered Carroll Senior no opportunity, either, and Charley was to make up for that failure by living in a place in which he could enjoy a public career. He was not interested in a public career, Charley replied. He wished to be a farmer and a private scholar. That would be enough. No, Papa countered. On the contrary, the restrictions of Maryland would not guarantee such a private life for a Roman Catholic. A Roman Catholic must know the law if he was to flourish in Maryland as a farmer, a merchant, a moneylender. And were the Carrolls to reestablish themselves in Catholic Louisiana, formation in the law would be more important than ever, since a public career would then be possible.

Charley accepted his father's decision. He would study the law. Still, Charles Carroll of Annapolis did not liquidate assets, pack up, and leave for Louisiana, although he would continue to complain in letters to Charley that Maryland was no place for a Roman Catholic. Dutifully, Charley planned to spend the academic year 1758–1759 as a student of Roman and civil law at Bourges, then move to London to pursue a five-year course in English common law at the Inner Temple, one of the four Inns of Court that offered legal instruction and controlled admission to the bar. While at Bourges, Charley kept a servant, dressed well, played badminton and tennis, improved his riding skills, lost money at cards, went to dances, and indulged in Bavarian crèmes. On a summer hiking trip, Charley met and became enchanted by a certain Miss Alcock, the pretty and charming daughter of an English button manufacturer at La Charitá, a small town thirty-six miles from Bourges. Indeed, he might even have proposed to her after an evening of dancing; but the young woman laughed the proposal away—if, indeed, Charley ever voiced what he wrote to his father were the intentions of another young man enamored of Miss Alcock. When Charley's tutor at Bourges died unexpectedly in mid-course, Charley returned to Paris to finish his year of Roman and civil law at the College of Louis-le-Grand before going to London and taking up his course of studies at the Inner Temple.

London calling

In his essay on the Joshua Reynolds portrait, historian Fintan Cullen expands on the earlier observations of art historian T. H. Breen that the Reynolds portrait offers proof positive that Charles Carroll thoroughly enjoyed "playing at being English" during his London sojourn.[2] With his father's concurrence, Charley chose as artist the rising portraitist of upper-class England, already known in Maryland for his depiction of Sylvanus Groves, the London-based factor for a leading Maryland planter. The Carrolls could have chosen the American-born Benjamin West, who was then working in London, or the English painter Robert Edge Pine, who specialized in painting Americans. Yet Breen argues that the Carrolls wanted an English aesthetic— an elegant, assured, soft-colored daydream of aristocracy—in dramatic contrast to the hyperrealism of American portraiture at the time, which emphasized canny competence and bourgeois well-being: men, in brief, who looked like Charley's father. During the period he was being painted by Reynolds, Carroll was assisting a London researcher working on a genealogy for Carroll Senior, who hoped to discover—as in all such Irish genealogies—a king or two in the family tree. Joshua Reynolds, for sure, was discovering and devising a young English aristocrat for his canvas. Indeed, the recommendation for Reynolds to do the portrait might very well have come from aristocratic friends of the Carroll family, particularly Judge Daines Barrington, the younger brother of William Wildman, second Viscount Barrington. Between 1755 and 1774, Lord Barrington served terms as secretary of war. His four sons had been painted by Reynolds. In time, Reynolds would also paint the first Viscount Barrington and his sons Samuel (an admiral), John (a major general), and Shute (a bishop). Young Carroll, in short, came well recommended to Reynolds from connections that also help explain Carroll Senior's bitterness over being a militia-excluded, double-taxed political nonentity in his home colony.

Visits to the country houses of Catholic families helped establish in Charley Carroll's mind the attractions of life as a gentleman farmer. Absent from Maryland since he was eleven, Carroll had no adult experience of such an existence. In the spring of 1760, Charley made a direct and memorable connection with the recusant way of life when Lord Charles Arundell invited him for a sojourn at Wardour Castle. Destroyed as a royalist stronghold during the English Civil War, Wardour Castle had been partially rebuilt and continued to house the ennobled Catholic family that 130 years earlier had invested in the Newfoundland and Maryland enterprises of George Calvert, first Lord Baltimore. In 1628 Lord Thomas Arundell's daughter Anne had married George Calvert's oldest son, Cecil, later second Lord Baltimore; and Anne Arundel County was named in her honor. In 1760 Jesuit John Jenison, a younger classical scholar and antiquarian, was serving as chaplain at Wardour Castle, and he and Charley enjoyed long discussions of classics and recusant history as they toured Dorset and Somerset and visited the Roman ruins at Bath. Lord Arundell and the young Marylander equally appreciated each other's company. As a Catholic Marylander and Saint Omer's old boy with classical and antiquarian interests, Carroll fit in easily with the Arundells and the other recusant families he stayed with during his London years. His visits to the Russell family were so frequent and attentive, in fact, that one of the Russell daughters mistakenly began to believe Carroll was courting her. With the rural Catholic gentry—their homes that contained libraries and chapels, their social and familial interconnections— Carroll beheld a way of life he could export to Maryland. The difference, of course, was that slave labor would be needed to make it possible.

His own Wardour Castle or Russell House was within his reach back in Maryland, provided that money was available. Carroll Senior had named him heir, but his father could live another twenty or more years. And if he did not finish his law course at the Inner Temple, as he was contemplating, who knew what his father's response might be? Papa had tipped his hand as to how much he wanted his son to practice law when, to his son's shock, he had suggested that, for a financial consideration (read bribe), Charley might be admitted to the bar despite his religion—a suggestion made but once and somewhat obliquely, and quickly rejected by Charley.

Thus began the search for a Catholic heiress—perhaps not from Maryland, as his father suggested, but English nevertheless, and upright—whose fortune would put Charley's future on a more solid footing than if it rested on his father's goodwill. During his last full year in London, Charles Carroll was driven by an almost obsessive interest in an English heiress made wealthy on the island of Saint Croix in the West Indies: seventeen-year-old Louisa Baker, a boarding student at the Ursuline convent in Paris. Alerted to her existence by a letter from an old Carroll family friend—Father Alexander Crookshanks, the procurator for the Jesuit mission in England and Scotland, and hence a man sensitive to net worth in this life as well as the next—young Carroll threw himself into a six-month effort with Louisa's parents. Her father, John Baker, was a retired Saint Croix planter of Irish descent who had settled the family in Twickenham outside of London and maintained a country home in Grove Place, near Southampton; her mother, Mary Ryan Baker, was the daughter of an Irish Catholic expatriate turned West Indian planter. Carroll doggedly pursued the couple, asking to be introduced formally to their daughter and given permission to inaugurate a courtship.

There is no evidence that Charles Carroll the younger ever met Louisa Baker, although he most likely caught a glimpse of her as she walked in a line of Ursuline students. Nor would the Ursulines have allowed Carroll to call on Louisa without parental permission and strict supervision. No such visit was documented. Even for a young man, an obsession with a phantom young lady seemed odd. Perhaps Carroll's behavior was subconsciously motivated by two considerations: Elizabeth Carroll's death and her son's desire to come home to Maryland after nearly nineteen years with a visible achievement that would also give him a measure of financial independence from his father. Taken from his beautiful and loving mother when he was eleven and kept from her for the next thirteen years, Charley Carroll was ignorant of her last illness and death. Indeed, he wrote her a letter from London on 31 March 1761, nineteen days after her passing, in which he discussed women, love, and marriage. "For my own part," Carroll wrote, "I cannot conceive how my heart remains still unsubdued. No Lady at least can boast an entire conquest: I can give no other reason for this Phoenomenon, but that no one ever thought it worth her while: But shou'd some fair witty maid captivate my heart I might often attem[pt to] shake off my fetters, for even now I am frighted at the clincking of matrimonial chains; those are never to be broke."[3] Now Charley had found such a fair witty maid who had captivated his heart (possibly after a single brief sighting), and he was laying siege to her and to her father's fortune in order to bring her home in triumph as a posthumous gift to the memory of his mother, whose twenty-year ordeal as a Catholic woman precluded from the sacramental status of wife her son must have found painful to contemplate.

As usual, Charley turned to Papa for help in this matter, informing him of the John Baker family and his desire to inaugurate a courtship of their daughter, Louisa. And again, as in every aspect of his son's life, Carroll Senior assumed control, beginning with the securing of an assets and credit report obtained through his Irish friend Nicholas Tuite, who had long been involved in Saint Croix affairs and now divided his time between Saint Croix, London, and Bath. John Baker, Tuite stated, had an estimated net worth of 50,000 pounds, from which he was realizing an income of 3,500 pounds a year. Also, the family had four brothers from Baker's first marriage. Carroll Senior's own net worth was nearly 90,000 pounds. Nevertheless he, too, saw the advantage of Charley's bringing home a genteel, upper-class, wealthy Irish Catholic wife, who brought with her a sizable dowry (on which Charles senior agreed to pay 8 percent interest) and the promise of an eventual inheritance that would expand the Carroll empire into the Caribbean.

John Baker knew of and respected the Carroll fortune, and in January 1764 Charley was invited to Grove Place for a long visit (although Louisa Baker was still not in view). During the course of this stay, Charley became painfully aware of Mary Ryan Baker's objection to the prospect of her only daughter marrying and moving to Maryland. One suspects that, in addition to her love for Louisa, Mary Ryan Baker had had enough of life in the slave-based economy of Saint Croix— with which she could easily equate Maryland—and appreciated her present English life among her circle of retired Irish Catholic planters and their wives, with Louisa attending the finest Catholic boarding school for young ladies in France. When Charley returned for another visit in March, he found John Baker reluctant to discuss the detailed and generous marriage proposal Carroll Senior had prepared.

Baker instead noted that Louisa was much too young for marriage, and perhaps she and Charley could meet when she next came to London, just before Charley's departure for Maryland, and the two of them could correspond for a few years until Louisa reached an age suitable for Charley to return to England and pay court. Clearly, John Baker had been listening to his wife.

The shock of this shift brought Charley back to his senses, or so he thought. In the last letter he wrote his father prior to sailing for Virginia on the *Randolph*, Carroll thanked him for his help in the negotiations. "I am much obliged to you for letting me settle at the rate of 8 per Ct.", he wrote, getting down to the business aspects of the matter before expressing any personal opinions. "But that affair is entirely broken off nor do I choose to renew it, tho' I had sometime ago a very fair opening: but the young lady has been bread up with very high notions not at all answerable to her fortune; a domestick wife not so fond of show and parade, who is not above the business of her family, will best suit me: the mother is a vain empty woman who knows but the daughter may take after her? I do not chuse to run the risk."[4] The ideal woman, the real woman—who was not showy or vain or empty, nor above taking an interest in her husband's business (which was yet unfound)— awaited him in Maryland.

Yet this never-realized love might have helped Charley Carroll open his heart now that his mother was gone. He would have given to Louisa Baker everything his mother was given only at the end: respectability, full and unconditional approval, vows of marriage, the name Carroll. Leaving for Maryland one year short of completing his Inner Temple program, Carroll turned to Louisa Baker as a symbol of the fact that he had not completely failed during these years spent in France and England: this pageant of shadows, this dream-dance of Catholic Europe; this enjoyment of the stately achievement of Georgian London, and the dignity and peacefulness of the recusant countryside. He never met Louisa, but she meant all this to him as he prepared to return home in partial defeat. He said he would forget her. But as he was preparing to marry another, he described his Maryland fiancée as the most superior woman he had ever met, even in comparison to Louisa. To another friend he wrote of his betrothed, "A greater commendation I cannot make of the young lady than by pronouncing her no ways inferior to Louisa." As if this were not enough, he inquired of another friend, "How is Louisa? There [was] once more musick in that name than in the sweetest lines of Pope: but now I can pronounce it as indifferently as Nancy, Betsy, or any other common name—if I ask a few questions, I hope you will not think that I am not quite as indifferent as I pretend to be—but I protest it is mere curiosity or mere good will that prompts enquiry after her—is she still single? Does she intend to alter her state, or to remain single—if she thinks of matrimony, my only wish is that she may meet with a man deserving of her."[5]

He named his third daughter Louisa, and she became the first Carroll in the long Carroll genealogy to bear this name, which was given to one of his granddaughters as well. Like the Sir Joshua Reynolds portrait hanging in Carrollton, the memory of Louisa Baker recalled a time of youth and hope in the life of Charles Carroll of Carrollton and the lives of the other young Catholic Marylanders abroad during these years as they searched for a sustaining connection to Catholic Europe, recusant England, and a British identity they believed to be their birthright.

Envoy

John Carroll returns to Maryland

John Carroll remained in Europe a decade longer than his younger cousin. As a Jesuit (a member of the English Province), vowed to personal poverty, he had already renounced all claims to his father's property in Maryland in favor of his older brother, Daniel, and his four sisters. Headed toward a career in teaching and academic administration, he most likely would have been assigned to the faculty of one of the eight Jesuit colleges on the Continent that catered to English-speaking students, followed by semiretirement as chaplain to a great Catholic house in England. Ordained in 1769 and professed in 1771, Carroll seemed to be on the verge of a life of European and English service typical of numerous Jesuits whose entries are comprised by the two-volume *Collectanea of the Society of Jesus in England* (1882). Compiled by Brother Henry Foley, this biographical dictionary contains the alphabetized and comprehensive accounts of Jesuit priests and brothers going back to the establishment of the English Province in 1623.

Yet providence and politics had other plans, not simply for John Carroll but for the entire Society of Jesus. Even as Carroll was going through the *cursus honorum* of Jesuit formation, the Society was being suppressed throughout western Europe. As a scholastic teaching at Saint Omer's, he had assisted faculty and students who were fleeing to Bruges. Enlightenment-oriented Catholic regimes, led by the Bourbon royal families of Portugal, Spain, and France, as well as several Italian states and their ministers, had declared war on the Society of Jesus as (among other charges) a state within the state, a church within the Church, a covert business enterprise, a disturber of the ecclesiastical peace. Yet the greatest objection of all was to the Society's fidelity to the papacy at a time when many European governments wanted an increased authority over religious affairs. Seeking the right to name bishops and to exert greater control over diocesan clergy, they wanted, in short, autonomy for national Catholic churches linked to the state rather than the centralized model that developed during the Counter-Reformation, thanks in great measure to the overnight globalization of the Society of Jesus.

With the election as pope on 6 July 1758 of one of their students, the Venetian Carlo della Torre di Rezzonico (Clement XIII), the Jesuits hoped for a reprieve from persecution. The exact opposite occurred. Clement XIII appointed the fiercely pro-Jesuit Luigi Tonigiano as his secretary of state. Throughout the next ten years, Clement XIII and Tonigiano waged a bitterly fought defense of the Society but time after time went down in defeat as government upon government—Portugal (1758), France (1762), Naples and Sicily (1767), Parma (1768), and Spain (1769)—ignored Clement XIII's diplomacy and pleadings in the papal bull *Apostolicum Pascendi Minis* (12 January 1765), which defended and reaffirmed support for the Society. Finally, in January 1769, Clement XIII received a joint request from these powers that the

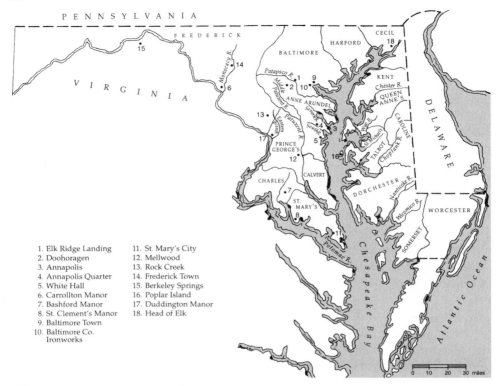

1. Elk Ridge Landing
2. Doohoragen
3. Annapolis
4. Annapolis Quarter
5. White Hall
6. Carrollton Manor
7. Bashford Manor
8. St. Clement's Manor
9. Baltimore Town
10. Baltimore Co. Ironworks
11. St. Mary's City
12. Mellwood
13. Rock Creek
14. Frederick Town
15. Berkeley Springs
16. Poplar Island
17. Duddington Manor
18. Head of Elk

Map 19. The Carrolls' Maryland World, 1765–82. From Ronald Hoffman, *Princes of Ireland, Planters of Maryland: A Carroll Saga, 1500–1782* (University of North Carolina Press, 2000), 188–89.   © *University of North Carolina Press, used by permission.*

Society be universally dissolved. The pope scheduled a consistory for February to turn down this request but died of a stroke the day before it was scheduled to meet.

In the summer of 1771, while serving on the faculty at Bruges, Carroll was sent on a special mission reflective of the close connection the English recusant nobility enjoyed with the Society. Lord Charles Stourton, a prominent recusant nobleman, requested of the English Province that Carroll be temporarily detached from his other duties in order to act as guide and tutor for his son Charles Philip, age nineteen, on a Grand Tour of western and central Europe that would formally complete the young man's education. Since Stourton was connected to the Howard and Petre families, his request was coming from the center of the recusant establishment that had sustained Catholicism—and the Society of Jesus—in England since the Elizabethan era. Indeed, the Duke of Norfolk, a Howard, Earl Marshal of England, was technically the senior peer of the realm, although his role had been in abeyance since the Reformation.

Thus Father Carroll was duly dispatched with Charles Philip on a protracted coach tour—Lorraine, Alsace, the Rhineland, the Palatinate, Swabia, Bavaria, Austria, the Tyrol, the Italian peninsula—that lasted from the summer of 1771 into the fall of 1772. At each important city—Strasbourg, Baden-Baden, Speyer, Heidelberg, Mannheim, Worms, Augsburg, Cologne, Munich, Trent, Verona, Mantua, Modena, Bologna, and, finally, Rome—Carroll and his young charge would pause for study sojourns, visits to cathedrals, conversations with local scholars, and other related exercises. The journal Carroll kept of this study tour does not constitute a rhapsodic record of personal discovery like the chronicles Americans wrote in a later era as they encountered the surviving fabric of the European past. Carroll's account, rather, is observant, precise, and dispassionate, touching upon matters of government and economies in an analytical, Enlightenment-oriented approach.

While frequently interesting in an antiquarian sort of way, the Europe Carroll was observing and presenting in his journal constituted a mosaic of overlapping jurisdictions, enmeshed in feudal ties and obligations. Swabia, like much of Germany, was overcontrolled and overtaxed by its nobility. Living under an oppressive feudal system, the people of Swabia seemed downtrodden, tired, and dirty. The province contained only two classes, nobility and peasant. "The generality of the inhabitants", Carroll observes, "are under so slavish a dependence, and they are so much accustomed to consider their lords as beings of a superior class, that it is very probably much the greatest part never conceive an idea of the original equality, or of the common rights of mankind."[1] One might argue that the slavery of Carroll's native Maryland clouds his right to such a critique, however accurate it may be. Still, the journal reveals a surprising point of view in this and other passages: an Enlightenment-driven predilection toward a society that balances equality and social stratification as well as fairness for all in governance.

Even the Papal States receive mild criticism. Carroll prefers that the papal government be more modernizing and reform minded, yet he does praise its benevolence, the contentment of the area's independent-minded populace, and the thriving vitality of its cities—such a contrast, he notes, to what he observed in Swabia and elsewhere on the other side of the Alps. Still, he cautions, it would be a mistake to judge that papal tyranny had replaced Roman liberty in Rome and its regions as of 1772. The grandeur that was imperial Rome, Carroll argues, was created amid tyranny. The Papal States were perhaps not as efficient as they should be, but their rule was mild in comparison to the tyranny of the ancient imperial city.

To experience John Carroll's far different reaction to Rome as papal court, however, one must leave the journal of his travels—for he says nothing of this matter there—and have recourse to the four letters Carroll wrote to Father Thomas Ellerker, a Jesuit colleague and friend at Liège. Not available to the public until Peter Guilday's biography of Carroll appeared in 1992, these letters might have kept Carroll out of the hierarchy had they been circulated at the time; for, in contrast to the journal's reserved tone and physiocratic generalizing, these four letters—aggrieved, emotional, detailed, gossipy—read like notes for a novel Stendhal never wrote dealing with the papal court during the chiaroscurist finale of Jesuit suppression.

On 19 May 1769, after a stormy conclave, the college of cardinals elected Lorenzo Ganganelli, a Conventual Franciscan of modest background (his father was a village doctor) who had risen through the ranks of his order and was created cardinal in 1759. As a curial cardinal, Ganganelli began to drift into anti-Jesuit territory. During the conclave, the anti-Jesuit, pro-Bourbon cardinals tried to force Ganganelli to sign a promise to suppress the Jesuits if elected. Since at the time Ganganelli was the only friar in the college of cardinals, and hence a professed religious under vows, he seemed to the anti-Jesuit lobby the best candidate to be the pontiff who would have the standing to put the Jesuits out of business. Ganganelli, however, refused to sign such an explicit statement. He did, however, sign a document certifying that he believed a pope had the power to suppress the Society of Jesus, provided that it be done according to canon law.

Taking the name Clement XIV, Ganganelli reversed the pro-Jesuit policies of his predecessor, made peace with the Marquis of Pombal, the prime minister of Portugal, raised Pombal's brother Paulo de Carvalho to cardinal (despite the fact that Portugal and the Vatican had been diplomatically estranged for the past decade), and confirmed all of Pombal's nominees for bishoprics. For four years, Ganganelli—reserved, hesitant, and lacking self-confidence despite his rise in the Church—delayed a final decision regarding the Society of Jesus against an onslaught of pressure by the Bourbon states. By the time John Carroll reached Rome in January 1772, Ganganelli was running low in resistance and thus, as Carroll puts it in a letter dated 23 January 1772 to Ellerker, "Our catastrophe is near at hand if we must trust to present appearances and the talk of Rome." The pro-Jesuit cardinals in the curia, Carroll reports, "now look upon the determination of our fate as entirely certain". Carroll thereupon launches into a detailed report of anti-Jesuit lobbying in Vatican circles.

In his 22 October 1772 letter to Ellerker, Carroll describes how he is remaining incognito while in Rome and not staying at Jesuit houses. His purpose, one supposes, was to protect his tutee, Charles Philip Stourton, from harm from anti-Jesuit demonstrations. For Jesuits, at least, Rome had become a dangerous place. Only recently, Carroll writes, when alumni sent a petition to the pope in support of the Jesuit-staffed Irish College, Cardinal Marefaschi "foamed with wrath" and violently insisted that the pope suppress the school. By this point, Carroll is edging into a postsuppression point of view, as he speculates how Jesuits in Spain and Latin America will find support as secular priests and requests that Ellerker say hello for him to his Jesuit colleagues at Liège, whose future must have seemed to him increasingly uncertain.

Carroll's 3 February 1773 letter to Ellerker contains news of more gloom and doom. It is all but over, he suggests, echoing the latest round of talk among clerics. The Jesuits will be disestablished in their present format, but the final form of disestablishment is unclear. Expulsion from Rome? Possibly. Reduction of status to congregations of priests governed by local bishops? Even more probable. Jesuit vineyards in southern Italy are being examined for transfer to the now Jesuit-free Irish College. The redoubtable Cardinal Marefaschi is heading a panel of prelates looking into the matter. Writings against the Sacred Heart devotion are multiplying.

Letter 4, 23 June 1773, is dominated by reports of various hostile actions against Jesuits—including the hunting down of illegal printing presses in his diocese—by Henry Cardinal York, the bishop of Frascati. Cardinal York was the grandson of James II and the second son of James Francis Edward Stuart, the Old Pretender, and was known to resolute Stuart supporters as Henry IX, King of Great Britain, France, and Ireland. The strong anti-Jesuit animus of such a cardinal, a prince of the realm as well as the Church, represented a depressing disconnect for English Jesuits. Even for Jesuits loyal to the House of Hanover, as they all were, it was dispiriting to have the grandson of the last Catholic king of England so hostile to a Society awash in the blood of martyrs from the penal era.[2]

In the summer of 1773 John Carroll bade good-bye to his tutee, Charles Philip, and returned to the college at Bruges. On 16 August 1773 Clement XIV published the brief *Dominus ac Redemptor Noster*, suppressing the Society of Jesus for the welfare and peace of the Church. Although the brief—a less authoritative declaration than a papal bull, which perhaps testified to the pontiff's tortuously divided conscience—made no charges of criminal behavior against the Society of Jesus, Jesuit Father General Laurence Ricci and his advisors were arrested and imprisoned in Castel Sant'Angelo, where Ricci died during the long trial that followed. Found not guilty of any offense by their judges, his companions were released by the next pope, Pius VI.

At the time of the suppression, 274 Jesuits belonged to the English Province, 135 of whom were serving on the Continent or on the Maryland-Pennsylvania mission. Ordained Jesuits were now secular priests under the authority of vicar apostolic Bishop Challoner of London, who required them—in England, the Continent, and Maryland-Pennsylvania alike—to sign an Act of Submission acknowledging their new status. This new status included John Carroll and the other Jesuits removed from Bruges by Austrian commissioners on the evening of 14 October 1773, who were briefly detained and then allowed to join their colleagues at Liège, where secularized English former Jesuits had set up a Liège Academy.

At this point, the Saint Omer's old-boy network kicked in. One of John Carroll's classmates at Saint Omer's was Henry, eighth Lord Arundell of Wardour and Count of the Holy Roman Empire. Henry's late father, Charles, the seventh Lord Arundell, had been supportive of Charley Carroll during his time at London than more a decade ago. His son now extended similar support to John Carroll, his temporarily unemployed priestly classmate. As his full-length portrait by Sir Joshua Reynolds illustrates, Henry was a man of style and attitude. Reynolds' portrait shows Arundell defiantly wearing the robes of a peer of the realm despite the fact that his Catholicism prevented him from taking his seat in the House of Lords. As was frequently the case with Arundells, Henry had married an heiress and thereby restored—once again!—the fortunes of the family, in decline since the English Civil War, following the destruction of Wardour Castle. Six foot six inches tall, a sportsman, a skilled agriculturalist, a connoisseur of Italian art, and a peer unembarrassedly Catholic, Arundell in the late 1760s commissioned architect James Paine to design a grand new Wardour Castle in the Palladian style, its Corinthian front facing south across parklands to the ruins of Wardour Castle against a backdrop of rising uplands. With the assistance of Jesuit Father John Thorpe, his teacher and advisor at Saint Omer's (who was now stationed in Rome and acting as an art agent for former pupils developing their estates), Arundell created in the west wing a chapel designed by Italian architect Giacomo Quarenghi and embellished by paintings and statuary acquired from Italy under advice from Father Thorpe. From the Roman workshop of Giacomo Quirenza, Thorpe commissioned a grand main altar in marble and obtained for it a circular tabernacle and six candlesticks of great height. When completed, the chapel at Wardour Castle stood as the most impressive Roman Catholic worship space in all England. Technically a private oratory, the chapel represented the fused result of recusant reverence for the Mass, a baron's faith and taste, the Saint Omer's old-boy network as sustained by Father Thorpe, and an heiress wife's money. In the 1940s Wardour Castle and its chapel served as inspiration for Brideshead, the seat of the Marchmain family in Evelyn Waugh's iconic novel *Brideshead Revisited* (1945).

In November 1773, Lord Arundell offered John Carroll a permanent appointment as chaplain. For an unemployed secular priest nearing forty, a Marylander living as an Englishman for the past twenty-five years, the chaplaincy was an attractive offer from a number of perspectives. It would put Carroll at the center of the English Catholic world at a time of stability edging into transition. In 1778 the first Catholic Relief Act marked the beginning of a long journey toward emancipation—not until 1829 would there be a full Emancipation Act—given reinforcement that same year when King George III and Queen Charlotte paid a two-day visit to Thorndon Hall in Essex, the home of Lord and Lady Petre, the leading Catholic peers in England at the time, now that the Duke of Norfolk preferred the life of a scholarly recluse. The royal visit cost Lord and Lady Petre 1,000 pounds, but paying that price was better than settling similar amounts of money in recusant fines.

Yet the fine home, the chapel, the ministry to the Arundells, their staff, their tenants, the nearby villages, the opportunity to play a role in an emergent English Catholic society, the leisure for scholarship and writing, and perhaps promotion to the episcopacy as a regional vicar apostolic (given Carroll's first-rate connections to the Catholic establishment) could not fill the void at the center of John Carroll's life now that he was no longer what he had been since entering the Jesuit novitiate. And besides, his aged mother, now a widow, needed him at home. Hearing that the former Jesuits in Maryland and Pennsylvania had decided to remain and continue to serve in British North America helped clarify Carroll's mind. He would restart his priestly life in the homeland he had left as a young man, where Carrolls aplenty could help him adjust to a new ministry. Despite his twenty years abroad, the Englishness and languages and polish he had acquired, he remained a Marylander. His Jesuit days were over, yet there remained much good work to do.

ACKNOWLEDGMENTS

I began my life as a Catholic under the guidance and care of the Dominican Sisters of Mission San Jose who conducted the Albertinium School in Ukiah, California, where I was raised as a child. I continued this journey of faith with the same congregation at Saint Boniface School in San Francisco. Franciscan Fathers conducted the adjacent parish church. In the years that followed, Jesuits and Sulpicians furthered my education at Saint Ignatius High School, San Francisco; Saint Joseph's High School and College, Mountain View; and the University of San Francisco. As a graduate student at Harvard in the 1960s, following my completion of military service, I studied religion as a social and cultural force under the guidance of Professor Alan Heimert, master of Eliot House, a preeminent historian of religion in colonial America.

For the past twenty-seven years, I have been privileged to be a member of the faculty of the University of Southern California. A sabbatical from USC enabled me to write *Continental Ambitions*, researched intermittently over the years as I completed the eight volumes of my Americans and the California Dream series. While at USC, I have enjoyed the resources of the Doheny Library and the generous array of journals made available to students and faculty via electronic retrieval.

In the course of preparing this volume, I have been privileged to have access to the ambitious American Catholic history collection of the Gleeson Library of the University of San Francisco and the continuing support of Dean Tyrone Cannon, university librarian; Associate Dean Shawn Calhoun; and such supportive librarians and staff members as Kelci Baughman-McDowell, Joseph Campi, Janet Carmona, Caitlin Collins, Matthew Collins, Patrick Dunagan, Bryan Duran, Kimberly Fisher, Joe Garity, John Hawk, Colette Hayes, Fabiola Hernandez-Soto, Ian Jacoby, Erika Johnson, Andres Lyon, Vicki Rosen, and Maren Salomon. At the Gleeson Library, I had access to a collection that was inaugurated in the aftermath of the earthquake and fire of April 1906 and continued down the century under the astute and energetic attention of Jesuit and lay faculty and learned librarians in acquisitions and collection development. In this regard, I must make mention of the late William J. Monihan SJ, longtime university librarian and ardent bookman, who—building upon the efforts of such scholars of Catholic history as Peter Masten Dunne SJ, John B. McGloin SJ, Robert Ignatius Burns SJ, and Monsignor John Tracy Ellis—continued the development of the Gleeson Library as a repository for American Catholic imprints.

To edit this manuscript as it developed, I enjoyed the assistance of Wilsted and Taylor Publishing Services. In this regard, I am grateful to Christine Taylor, LeRoy Wilsted, Nancy Evans, and Lynn Meinhardt, along with the exacting and devoted editing of Melody Lacina. I am grateful to the provost's university professor research fund at USC for the support of these services.

The Dan Murphy Foundation generously underwrote illustrations and maps for this volume.

I owe a debt of gratitude to Father Joseph Fessio SJ, founder and editor-in-chief of Ignatius Press for his continuing support of this project. I am equally grateful to Senior Editor Vivian Dudro and the staff of Ignatius Press for their dedicated professionalism.

I also wish to acknowledge the personal encouragement extended to me during this project by Cyriaque Beurtheret, Dana and Mary Gioia, Christopher Gray, Karin Huebner, Thomas F. Jordan, Gilbert Lee, Thomas McLaughlin MD, and Van Gordon Sauter and Kathleen Brown.

For the past forty years, I have enjoyed the friendship and the guidance, in matters Catholic and historical, of historian and jurist John T. Noonan Jr., who encouraged me to embark on this series following the completion of my Americans and the California Dream volumes. Also over the years I have received the professional support of the Sandra Dijkstra Literary Agency and the friendship of Bram and Sandra Dijkstra.

Throughout the preparation of this book, I have relied upon the editorial and research assistance and intellectual companionship of Sheila Starr, whose life I have been privileged to share for these past fifty-six years.

San Francisco and Los Angeles
5 May 2016

NOTES

Preface

[1] John Gilmary Shea, "Preliminary Remarks", in *The Catholic Church in Colonial Days* (New York: John G. Shea, 1886), 9–15.

Prologue: Garðar

[1] Samuel Eliot Morison, *The European Discovery of America: The Northern Voyages A.D. 500–1600* (New York: Oxford University Press, 1971), 18.

[2] William Hovgaard, *The Voyages of the Norsemen to America* (New York: American-Scandinavian Foundation, 1914), 91.

[3] Ibid., 96–99.

1. Santo Domingo

[1] Henry Raup Wagner in collaboration with Helen Rand Parish, *The Life and Writings of Bartolomé de Las Casas* (Albuquerque: University of New Mexico Press, 1967), 8–9.

[2] Ibid., 9–10.

[3] Bartolomé de Las Casas, "Very Brief Account of the Destruction of the Indies", trans. Francis Augustus MacNutt, Appendix 1 in MacNutt, *Bartholomew de Las Casas: His Life, Apostolate, and Writings* (New York: G. B. Putnam's Sons, 1909), 324–25. Las Casas provides a more extended description of the massacre in his *Historia de las Indias*. See also *New Iberian World: A Documentary History of the Discovery and Settlement of Latin America to the Early Seventeenth Century*, edited and with commentaries by John H. Parry and Robert G. Keith with the assistance of Michael Jimenez, 5 vols. (New York: Times Books, 1984), 2:268–71.

[4] Manuel Giménez Fernández, "A Biographical Sketch", in *Bartolomé de Las Casas in History: Toward an Understanding of the Man and His Work*, edited by Juan Friede and Benjamin Keen (DeKalb, Ill.: Northern Illinois University Press, 1971), 72–73.

[5] MacNutt, *Las Casas*, 330, quoting Las Casas's *Brevísima relación*.

[6] Ibid., 330–31.

[7] Sir 34:18–22; and *The New Oxford Annotated Bible with the Apocrypha, Revised Standard Version*, ed. Herbert G. May and Bruce M. Metzger (Oxford: Oxford University Press, 1977), 173.

[8] MacNutt, *Las Casas*, 73.

[9] Ibid., 105–6.

[10] Parry and Keith, *New Iberian World*, 2:409–10.

[11] MacNutt, *Las Casas*, 159, citing the *Historia*.

[12] Parry and Keith, 2:557–62, quoting Las Casas, *Historia de las Indias*, editors' translation.

2. Quivira

[1] Álvar Núñez Cabeza de Vaca, "How We Cured Several Sick People", in *Chronicle of the Narváez Expedition*, translated by Fanny Bandelier, revised and annotated by Harold Augenbraum (New York: Penguin Books, 2002), 56–63.

[2] Msgr. John Tracy Ellis, *Documents of American Catholic History* (Chicago: Regnery, 1967), 1:7–8.

[3] "Narrative Account by Fray Marcos de Niza, 26 August 1539", in *Documents of the Coronado Expedition, 1539–1542*, edited, translated, and annotated by Richard Flint and Shirley Cushing Flint (Dallas: Southern Methodist University Press, 2005), 75–76.

3. Saint Augustine

[1] James A. Robertson, "Notes on Early Church Government in Spanish Florida", *Catholic Historical Review* 17, no. 2 (July 1931): 162–64.

[2] John Gilmary Shea, "Ancient Florida", in *Narrative and Critical History of America*, edited by Justin Winsor, 8 vols. (Boston: Houghton, Mifflin, 1887–1889), 2:254–56; and V. Francis O'Daniel, *Dominicans in Early Florida* (New York: United States Catholic Historical Society, 1930), 30–69.

[3] Msgr. John Tracy Ellis, *Documents of American Catholic History* (Chicago: Regnery, 1967), 1:11–12.

[4] Shea, "Ancient Florida", 2:272.

[5] Ibid., 2:272–75.

[6] Ibid., 2:277.

[7] Ellis, *Documents*, 1:14–15.

4. Apalachee

[1] Msgr. John Tracy Ellis, *Documents of American Catholic History* (Chicago: Regnery, 1967), 1:18–22.

[2] Robert Allen Matter, "Mission Life in Seventeenth-Century Florida", *Catholic Historical Review* 67, no. 3 (July 1981): 401–20.

[3] Mark F. Boyd, Hale G. Smith, and John W. Griffin, *Here They Once Stood: The Tragic End of the Apalachee Missions* (Gainesville, Fla.: University of Florida Press, 1951), 13.

[4] John Gilmary Shea, *The Catholic Church in Colonial Days* (New York: John G. Shea, 1886), 474.

5. Acoma

[1] David J. Weber, *The Spanish Frontier in North America* (New Haven, Conn.: Yale University Press, 1992), 82.

[2] "Act of Obedience and Vassalage by the Indians of Santo Domingo", in *Don Juan de Oñate: Colonizer of New Mexico, 1595–1628*, translated and edited by George P. Hammond and Agapito Rey, 2 vols. (Albuquerque: University of New Mexico Press, 1953), 1:338.

[3] Ibid., 1:462.

[4] Ibid., 1:477–78.

[5] Ramón A. Gutiérrez, *When Jesus Came, the Corn Mothers Went Away: Marriage, Sexuality, and Power in New Mexico, 1500–1846* (Stanford, Cal.: Stanford University Press, 1991), 92.

6. San Fernando de Béxar

[1] J. N. D. Kelly, *The Oxford Dictionary of Popes* (Oxford: Oxford University Press, 1986), 296–98.

[2] "Diary of Fernando del Bosque, 1675", in *Spanish Exploration in the Southwest, 1542–1706*, edited by Herbert Eugene Bolton (New York: Charles Scribner's Sons, 1925), 301–302. See also Msgr. John Tracy Ellis, *Documents of American Catholic History* (Chicago: Regnery, 1967), 1:23–24.

[3] *Nothingness Itself: Selected Writings of Venerable Fray Antonio Margil, 1690–1724*, collected and translated by Benedict Leutenegger OFM, and edited and annotated by Marion A. Habig OFM (Chicago: Franciscan Herald Press, 1976), xv.

[4] Carlos E. Castañeda, *Our Catholic Heritage in Texas, 1539–1936*, 7 vols. (Austin: Von Boeckmann-Jones, 1936–1950), 2:55–58.

[5] Ibid., 2:63–66.

[6] Ibid., 3:91–92.

[7] Jesús F. de la Teja, *San Antonio de Béxar: A Community on New Spain's Northern Frontier* (Albuquerque: University of New Mexico Press, 1995), 28.

7. Loreto

[1] Kino to Thirso González, 2 February 1702, in Herbert Eugene Bolton, *Rim of Christendom: Eusebio Francisco Kino, Pacific Coast Pioneer* (New York: Macmillan, 1936, reissued 1960), 477–78.

[2] *Kino's Historical Memoir of Pimería Alta*, translated, edited, and annotated by Herbert Eugene Bolton, 2 vols. (Cleveland: Arthur H. Clark, 1919), 2:265–73. See also Bolton, *Rim of Christendom*, 574–79.

[3] Quoted in Peter Masten Dunne SJ, *Black Robes in Lower California* (Berkeley: University of California Press, 1968), 22.

[4] Ibid., 352–53.

8. San Blas

[1] Herbert Ingram Priestley, *José de Gálvez, Visitor-General of New Spain, 1765–1771* (Berkeley: University of California Press, 1916), 249–55.

[2] Ibid., 274.

[3] Serra to Fray Juan Andrés, Monterey, 12 June 1770, in *Writings of Junípero Serra*, edited by Antonine Tibesar OFM, 4 vols. (Washington, D.C.: Academy of American Franciscan History, 1955), 1:169–71.

[4] Ibid., 1:171.

[5] Ibid., 1:171–75.

[6] Maynard J. Geiger OFM, *The Life and Times of Fray Junípero Serra OFM*, 2 vols. (Washington, D.C.: Academy of American Franciscan History, 1959), 2:68.

9. The Bay of San Francisco

[1] Personal Services Report, 1 September 1767, in Kieran McCarty, *Desert Documentary: The Spanish Years, 1767–1821* (Tucson: Arizona Historical Society, 1976), 5–7.

[2] Garcés to Anza, 29 July 1768, in ibid., 8–10.

[3] Herbert Eugene Bolton, *Outpost of Empire: The Story of the Founding of San Francisco* (New York: Alfred A. Knopf, 1939), 34–35.

[4] "Anza's Complete Diary", in *Anza's California Expeditions*, edited by Herbert Eugene Bolton, 5 vols. (Berkeley: University of California Press, 1930), 2:89.

[5] Bolton, *Outpost*, 160–61.

[6] "Anza's Complete Diary", Sunday, 14 April 1776, in *Anza's California Expeditions*, 3:155.

[7] Bolton, preface to *Font's Complete Diary*, in ibid., 4:vi.

[8] *Font's Complete Diary*, in ibid., 4:20–21.

[9] Ibid., 4:139.

[10] Ibid., 4:151.

[11] Ibid., 4:144–45.

[12] Ibid., 4:299.

[13] Ibid., 332–41.

10. Santa Barbara

[1] Palma to Bucareli, Mexico, 11 November 1776, in *Anza's California Expeditions*, edited by Herbert Eugene Bolton, 5 vols. (Berkeley: University of California Press, 1930), 5:375.

[2] Bucareli to Gálvez, Mexico, 26 November 1776, in ibid., 5:396.

[3] María Ana Montielo to Father Francisco Antonio Barbastro, 21 December 1785 (Civezza Collection, Antonianum Library, Rome), in Kieran McCarty, *Desert Documentary: The Spanish Years, 1767–1821* (Tucson: Arizona Historical Society, 1976), 335–40.

[4] Lorenzo Asisara, "The Killing of Fr. Andrés Quintana at Mission Santa Cruz", in *Lands of Promise and Despair: Chronicles of Early California, 1535–1846*, edited by Rose Marie Beebe and Robert M. Senkewicz (Santa Clara, Cal.: Santa Clara University, 2001), 284–92.

[5] James A. Sandos, *Converting California: Indians and Franciscans in the Missions* (New Haven, Conn.: Yale University Press, 2004), 115–16.

11. Port-Royal

[1] Marc Lescarbot, *The Theater of Neptune in New France* [1606], French text with an introduction and English translation by Harriette Taber Richardson (Boston: Riverside Press, 1927), passim.

[2] Translation supplied privately by Dr. Cyriaque Beurtheret.

[3] *The Works of Samuel de Champlain*, ed. H.P. Biggar, 6 vols. (Toronto: Champlain Society, 1922), 3:289–295. See also Biggar, "The French Hakluyt: Marc Lescarbot of Vervins", *American Historical Review* 6, no. 4 (July 1901): 671–92.

12. Quebec

[1] David Hackett Fischer, *Champlain's Dream* (New York: Simon and Schuster, 2008), 288.

13. Ville-Marie (Montreal)

[1] *A History of Montreal, 1640–1672, From the French of Dollier de Casson*, edited and translated by Ralph Flenley (London: J.M. Dent and Sons, 1928), 99.

[2] David Hackett Fischer, *Champlain's Dream* (New York: Simon and Schuster, 2008), 520, citing Marcel Trudel's *Histoire de la Nouvelle-France*, 3 vols. (Montreal: Beauchemin, 1963–1979), 3:142–43.

[3] W.J. Eccles, *Canadian Society during the French Regime* (Montreal: Harvest House, 1968), 21.

[4] Jerome Lalemant SJ, Letter of 1 August 1626, published in Paris in 1627 as a prelude to the *Jesuit Relations* series. Subsequent references to this series will be to *The Jesuit Relations and Allied Documents*, edited by Reuben Gold Thwaites, 73 vols. (Cleveland: Burrows Brothers, 1896–1901).

[5] Paul Le Jeune SJ, *Jesuit Relations* for 1636 (1637), quoted by Eccles in *Canadian Society during the French Regime*, 25–27.

[6] Jean de Brébeuf, "Instructions for the Fathers of Our Society Who Shall Be Sent to the Hurons", in *The Jesuit Relations*, 12:117–123; and Msgr. John Tracy Ellis, *Documents of American Catholic History* (Chicago: Regnery, 1967), 1:49–51.

[7] *The Jesuit Relations*, 8:236–39.

[8] Francis Parkman, *The Jesuits in North America in the Seventeenth Century* [1867], edited by David Levin (New York: Library of America, 1983), 521–22.

[9] *The Jesuit Relations*, 7:169.

14. Saint-Ignace

[1] Edna Kenton, *The Indians of North America*, 2 vols. (New York: Harcourt, Brace, 1927), 2:23–24.

[2] Francis Parkman, *The Jesuits in North America in the Seventeenth Century* [1867], edited by David Levin (New York: Library of America, 1983), 584–85.

[3] Ibid., 586–87.

[4] Thomas Joseph Campbell SJ, *Pioneer Priests in North America, 1642–1710*, 3 vols. (New York: Fordham University Press, 1908), 2:118–19.

[5] Msgr. John Tracy Ellis, *Documents of American Catholic History* (Chicago: Regnery, 1967), 1:25–27, extracting "How Father Jogues Was Taken by the Iroquois, and What He Suffered on His First Entrance into Their Country", by Jérôme Lalemant SJ, in *The Jesuit Relations and Allied Documents*, edited by Reuben Gold Thwaites, 73 vols. (Cleveland: Burrows Brothers, 1896–1901), 31:17–119.

[6] Campbell, *Pioneer Priests*, 2:156–57.

[7] Thomas Gilby OP, "Theology of Martyrdom", in *New Catholic Encyclopedia* (Washington, D.C.: Catholic University of America, 2003), 9:314–15.

[8] Francis Xavier Murphy CSSR, "Martyr", in ibid., 9:312–14.

[9] Campbell, *Pioneer Priests*, 2:177.

[10] Ibid., 2:156.

[11] Parkman, *Jesuits*, 711–12.

[12] *The Jesuit Relations*, 27:215–19.

15. The Abbey of Saint-Germain-des-Prés

[1] A. Leblond de Brumath, *Bishop Laval* (Toronto: Morang, 1910), 34.

[2] Marie de l'Incarnation to son Claude, 20 August 1663, in *Word from New France: The Selected Letters of Marie de l'Incarnation*, translated and edited by Joyce Marshal (Toronto: Oxford University Press, 1967), 288–89.

[3] *The Relation of 1654*, in *Marie of the Incarnation: Selected Writings*, translated by Irene Mahoney OSU (New York: Paulist Press, 1989), 41–42.

[4] Ibid., 49.

[5] Ibid., 109.

[6] Marie-Emmanuel Chabot OSU, "Guyart, Marie, dite Marie de l'Incarnation" in *Dictionary of Canadian Biography*, vol. 1, University of Toronto/Université Laval, 2003–, accessed 30 September 2014, http://www.biographi.ca/en/bio/guyart_marie_1E.html.

[7] Agnes Repplier, *Mère Marie of the Ursulines: A Study in Adventure* (New York: Literary Guild of America, 1931), 137.

16. New Orleans

[1] *Charlevoix's Louisiana: Selections from the History and Journal*, ed. Charles E. O'Neill (Baton Rouge: Louisiana State University Press, 1977), 155–56, quoting L. P. Kellogg's translation of the *Journal*, 2:257–58.

[2] Marie-Emmanuel Chabot OSU, "Simon de Longpré, Marie-Catherine de, *dite* de Saint-Augustin", quoting 1671 biography of Mother Catherine by Paul Ragueneau SJ, in *Dictionary of Canadian Biography*, vol. 1, University of Toronto/Université Laval, 2003–, accessed 31 August 2015, http://www.biographi.ca/en/bio/simon_de_longpre_marie_catherine_de_1E.html.

[3] Ibid.

[4] *Journal of a Voyage to North America, Translated from the French of Pierre François Xavier de Charlevoix*, translated and edited with a historical introduction, notes, and index by Louise Phelps Kellogg, 2 vols. (Chicago: Caxton Club, 1923), 1:103–17.

[5] Thomas Joseph Campbell SJ, *Pioneer Priests in North America, 1642–1710*, 3 vols. (New York: Fordham University Press, 1908), 2:152–64.

[6] Léopold Lamontagne, "Prouville de Tracy, Alexandre de", in *Dictionary of Canadian Biography*, vol. 1, University of Toronto/Université Laval, 2003–, accessed 31 August, 2015, http://www.biographi.ca/en/bio/prouville_de_tracy_alexandre_de_1E.html.

[7] Ibid.

[8] Raymond Douville and Jacques Casanova, *Daily Life in Early Canada*, trans. Carola Congreve (New York: Macmillan, 1967), 22–23.

[9] Charlevoix, *Journal*, 1:205–6.

17. Natchez

[1] *Charlevoix's Louisiana: Selections from the History and Journal*, ed. Charles E. O'Neill (Baton Rouge: Louisiana State University Press, 1977), 146, quoting *Journal of a Voyage to North America, Translated from the French of Pierre François Xavier de Charlevoix*, translated and edited with a historical introduction, notes, and index by Louise Phelps Kellogg, 2 vols. (Chicago: Caxton Club, 1923), 2:248.

[2] Ibid., 157–58, quoting L. P. Kellogg's translation of the *Journal*, 2:259–60.

[3] Msgr. John Tracy Ellis, *Documents of American Catholic History* (Chicago: Regnery, 1967), 1:77–84, presenting Louis Hennepin's *New Discovery of a Vast Country in America*, edited by Reuben Gold Thwaites, 2 vols. (Chicago: A. C. McClurg, 1903), 2:457–74.

18. The River Boyne

[1] Francis Xavier Curran SJ, *Catholics in Colonial Law* (Chicago: Loyola University Press, 1963), 60–65.

[2] Ibid., 65–78.

³ Thomas Hughes SJ, *History of the Society of Jesus in North America, Colonial and Federal*, 4 vols. (London: Longmans, Green, 1907–1917), vol. 1, Text, 153–55; vol. 1, Documents, 2–5.

⁴ Thomas M. Coakley, "George Calvert and Newfoundland", *Maryland Historical Magazine* 71 (Spring 1976): 16.

⁵ Andrew White SJ, "A Briefe Relation of the Voyage Unto Maryland" [1634], in *Narratives of Early Maryland, 1633–1684*, edited by Clayton Colman Hall (New York: C. Scribner's Sons, 1910, repr., New York: Barnes and Noble: 1946 and 1959), 39–42.

19. Annapolis

¹ Edwin Warfield Beitzell, *The Jesuit Missions of St. Mary's County, Maryland*, 2nd ed. (Abell, Md.: St. Mary's County Bicentennial Commission, 1976), 51.

² Francis Xavier Curran SJ, *Catholics in Colonial Law* (Chicago: Loyola University Press, 1963), 82.

³ Ibid., 96–97.

⁴ Joseph S. Rossi SJ, "Jesuits, Slaves and Scholars at 'Old Bohemia' 1704–1756, as Found in the *Woodstock Letters*", *U.S. Catholic Historian* 26 (Spring 2008): 5–8.

⁵ John Gilmary Shea, *The Catholic Church in Colonial Days* (New York: John G. Shea, 1886), 91–92.

⁶ Joseph J. Casino, "Anti-Popery in Colonial Pennsylvania", *Pennsylvania Magazine of History and Biography* 105 (July 1981): 288–89, quoting *The Statutes at Large of Pennsylvania from 1682 to 1800*, edited by James T. Mitchell and Harry Flanders, 2 vols. (Harrisburg: State of Pennsylvania, 1896), 2:219–20.

⁷ Casino, "Anti-Popery", 297, quoting George Whitefield, *Works* (London: Edward and Charles Dilly, 1771), 5:82, 84.

⁸ Casino, "Anti-Popery", 298, quoting Benjamin Franklin's *Plain Truth on the Present State of the City of Philadelphia* (1747).

⁹ Lambert Schrott OSB, *Pioneer German Catholics in the American Colonies, 1734–1784* (New York: United States Catholic Historical Society, 1933), 37–38.

¹⁰ Robert H. Lord, John E. Sexton, and Edward T. Harrington, *History of the Archdiocese of Boston in the Various Stages of Its Development, 1604 to 1943*, 3 vols. (New York: Sheed and Ward, 1944), 1:74–75.

¹¹ Ibid., 133, quoting Thomas Hutchinson, *History of the Colony of Massachusetts Bay*, 3 vols. (Boston: T. and J. Fleet, 1764–1828), 2:198.

¹² Ibid., 181, quoting the will of Judge Paul Dudley, Roxbury, Massachusetts, January 1, 1750–1751.

20. London

¹ Beatriz Betancourt Hardy, "The Papists ... Have Shewn a Laudable Care and Concern", *Maryland Historical Magazine* 98 (Spring 2003): 10, quoting from Hunter's retreat notes.

² Fintan Cullen, "Charles Carroll of Carrollton: Painting the Portrait of an Irish-American Aristocrat", *Eighteenth-Century Ireland* 25 (2010): 156; quoting T. H. Breen, "The Meaning of 'Likeness': Portrait-Painting in an Eighteenth-Century Consumer Society", in *The Portrait in Eighteenth-Century America*, edited by Ellen G. Miles (Newark, Del.: University of Delaware Press, 1993), 54.

³ Charles Carroll of Carrollton to Elizabeth Carroll, 31 March 1761, in *Dear Papa, Dear Charley*, edited by Ronald Hoffman, Sally D. Mason, and Eleanor S. Darcy (Chapel Hill, N.C.: University of North Carolina Press, 2001), 203.

⁴ Charles Carroll of Carrollton to Charles Carroll of Annapolis, 26 July 1767, in *Dear Papa, Dear Charley*, 364.

⁵ Charles Carroll of Carrollton to William Graves, 16 January 1768, in *Dear Papa, Dear Charley*, 182; Charles Carroll of Carrollton to friend Christopher [last name unknown], 17 September 1766, in Kate Mason Rowland, *The Life of Charles Carroll of Carrollton, 1737–1832, With His Correspondence and Public Papers*, 2 vols. (New York: G. P. Putnam's Sons, 1898), 179; and Charles

Carroll to Esther Bird, 6 October 1766, in Ronald Hoffman in collaboration with Sally D. Mason, *Princes of Ireland, Planters of Maryland* (Chapel Hill, N.C.: University of North Carolina Press, 2000), 197.

Envoy

[1] John Carroll, "Journal of European Tour", *The John Carroll Papers*, edited by Thomas O'Brien Hanley SJ, 3 vols. (Notre Dame, Ind.: University of Notre Dame Press, 1976), 1:19.

[2] Carroll's letters to Thomas Ellerker SJ are presented in their entirety in Peter Guilday, *The Life and Times of John Carroll, Archbishop of Baltimore, 1735–1815* (New York: Encyclopedia Press, 1922), 36–42; and *The John Carroll Papers*, 1:26–31.

ESSAY ON SOURCES

Continental Ambitions is a work of synthesis, narrative, and interpretation. Each chapter depends on edited transcripts of primary documents cited in the text itself. Over the past century, a treasure trove of superbly edited, translated, and annotated original documents relating to Roman Catholic exploration and settlement in North America has become available. Many of these editions are bilingual and thus offer further color, context, and insights to readers familiar with Spanish and French.

I have made every effort, moreover, to consult influential secondary sources, many of which are classics in their field. If a secondary reference is especially commanding throughout a chapter or a section of a chapter, I make full and complete acknowledgment; indeed, it is impossible to discuss any of the subjects I have taken up in these twenty chapters without the guidance of experts. In a number of instances in this essay, I have described my first encounters with these books. As a professional librarian, I love books in both their intellectual and their physical presence. As a student of the late Alan Heimert, Powell M. Cabot Professor of American Literature at Harvard University, I absorbed from Professor Heimert (who in turn had absorbed this from Professor Perry Miller) a conviction that public discourse in the form of the published literature of an era constitutes an invaluable source for the historian.

Regarding John Gilmary Shea, see Monsignor Peter Guilday, *John Gilmary Shea: Father of American Catholic History, 1824–1892* (1926), from the United States Catholic Historical Society. Monsignors John Tracy Ellis and Robert Trisco's *Guide to American Catholic History* (2nd edition, revised and enlarged, 1982) and *The Catholic Periodical and Literature Index*, edited by Dana Cernainau (1994), both issued by the Catholic Library Association, proved invaluable, as did Edward R. Vollmar SJ, *The Catholic Church in America: An Historical Bibliography* (2nd edition, 1963), from the Scarecrow Press. As a faculty member at the University of Southern California, I enjoyed access through JStor to a multiplicity of titles. I have also built my bibliography through such recent references as *The Encyclopedia of American Catholic History*, edited by Michael Glazier and Thomas J. Shelley (1997), from the Liturgical Press, along with the two classic reference tools I am fortunate to own: *The Catholic Encyclopedia* (15 volumes and index, 1913), from the Encyclopedia Press, Knights of Columbus edition; and the *New Catholic Encyclopedia* (14 volumes and index, 1967), from McGraw-Hill. Written by the finest scholars of their era, these three encyclopedias are magisterial and authoritative in their content and bibliographical references and are fully acknowledged as guiding my inquiries and interpretations in every instance. Also useful in this regard for content, interpretation, and bibliographical reference is the equally magisterial *Oxford Dictionary of the Christian Church*, edited by F. L. Cross, 2nd edition, edited by F. L. Cross and E. A. Livingstone (1983); and

J. N. D. Kelly's *Oxford Dictionary of Popes* (1986). Invaluable for the interpretation of Catholic doctrine and moral teachings is the *Catechism of the Catholic Church* (2nd edition, 1997), from the Libreria Editrice Vaticana. Also of value for brief and concise reference is *The HarperCollins Encyclopedia of Catholicism*, Richard P. McBrien, general editor (1995), from HarperSanFrancisco.

More than forty years ago, I was fortunate to acquire from the Starr Bookshop in Cambridge, Massachusetts, John Gilmary Shea's four-volume history of the Catholic Church in the United States under the titles *The Catholic Church in Colonial Days* (1886), *Life and Times of the Most Rev. John Carroll* (1888), *History of the Catholic Church in the United States, 1808–1843* (1890), and *History of the Catholic Church in the United States, 1844–1866* (1892). Across four decades, I have lived with, read, and cherished these volumes, and I have used *The Catholic Church in Colonial Days* as guide and inspiration for *Continental Ambitions*. I have also read, meditated upon, and used for bibliographical reference a number of histories of American Catholicism, many of them classics. With its pioneering treatment of the relevance of Catholic political theory to the American Constitution and its exhaustive treatment of Catholic intellectual and literary life in the nineteenth and early twentieth centuries, Theodore Maynard's *Story of American Catholicism* (1941) has accompanied me as long as the Shea volumes and remains a comparable source of inspiration. In terms of content, interpretation, and reference, I have also profited immeasurably from John Tracy Ellis' *Documents of American Catholic History* (volumes 1 and 2, 1967; volume 3, 1987) and have made every effort in my narrative to quote from these selections. Ellis' *American Catholicism* (1956), *Perspectives in American Catholicism* (1963), and *Catholics in Colonial America* (1965) have guided my understanding and enlarged my bibliography as well. Sydney E. Ahlstrom, *A Religious History of the American People* (1972), from Yale University Press, has also proven of continuing value.

Continental Ambitions is a selective and narrative history that does not seek to be comprehensive. Nevertheless, I have guided my research and understanding of American Catholic history through the reading and assimilation of such respected and eminently useful histories as Francis Xavier Curran SJ, *Major Trends in American Church History* (1946); Theodore Roemer OFM Cap, *The Catholic Church in the United States* (1950); Peter J. Rahill, *The Catholic in America: From Colonial Times to the Present Day* (1961); Newman C. Eberhardt CM, *Survey of American Church History* (1964); Thomas Timothy McAvoy CSC, *A History of the Catholic Church in the United States* (1969); Philip Gleason, *Catholicism in America* (1970); James Hennesey SJ, *American Catholics: A History of the Roman Catholic Community in the United States*, foreword by John Tracy Ellis (1981); James Hennesey SJ, *Catholics in the Promised Land of the Saints* (1981); Jay P. Dolan, *The American Catholic Experience: A History from Colonial Times to the Present* (1985); Charles R. Morris, *American Catholic: The Saints and Sinners Who Built America's Most Powerful Church* (1997); *Building the Church in America: Studies in Honor of Monsignor Robert F. Trisco on the Occasion of His Seventieth Birthday*, edited by Joseph C. Linck and Raymond J. Kupke (1999), from the Catholic University of America Press; James T. Fisher, *Communion of Immigrants: A History of Catholics in America* (2002); Patrick W. Carey, *Catholics in America: A History* (2004); and James M. O'Toole, *The Faithful: A History of Catholics in America* (2008). See also Jay P. Dolan's *In Search of an American Catholicism: A History of Religion and Culture in Tension* (2002). Four collections of essays have also broadened my understanding and added to my bibliography: *The Catholic Church, USA,* edited by Louis J. Putz CSC (1956); *Essays in the American Catholic Tradition,* edited by P. Albert Duhamel (1960); *Catholics in America, 1776–1976,* edited by Robert Trisco, foreword by the Most Reverend Edward A. McCarthy (1976); and *An American Church: Essays on the Americanization of the Catholic Church,* edited by David J. Alvarez (1979).

Regarding the history and physical details of representative American Catholic churches, I have consulted Francis Beauchesne Thornton, *Catholic Shrines in the United States and Canada* (1954), and *Famous American Churches and Shrines: Catholic Edition,* edited by Walter T. Murphy (1968). See also Edward F. Rines, *Old Historic Churches of America* (1936).

Prologue: Garðar

For background to voyages of exploration and settlement in the early modern era, see *West and By North: North America Seen through the Eyes of Its Seafaring Discoverers,* edited, annotated, and introduced by Louis B. Wright and Elaine W. Fowler (1971); Samuel Eliot Morison, *The European Discovery of America: The Northern Voyages, A.D. 500–1600* (1971); Samuel Eliot Morison, *The European Discovery of America: The Southern Voyages, A.D. 1492–1616* (1974); and David B. Quinn, *North America from Earliest Discovery to First Settlements: The Norse Voyages to 1612* (1977). See also William H. Babcock, *Legendary Islands of the Atlantic: A Study in Medieval Geography* (1922).

The Latin text of *The Voyage of Saint Brendan Abbot* is presented and annotated in *Sancti Brendani Abbatis: From Early Latin Manuscripts,* edited and with introduction and notes by Carl Selmer (1959, reprinted 1989). For the best English version, see *The Voyage of Saint Brendan: Journey to the Promised Land,* translated and with an introduction by John J. O'Meara (1978). For English translations of the versions of *The Voyage* in other medieval languages, see *The Voyage of Saint Brendan: Representative Versions of the Legend in English Translation,* edited by W. R. J. Barron and Glyn S. Burgess (2002). Regarding Celtic monasticism, see Kathleen Hughes, "The Church in Irish Society, 400–800", in the first volume of *A New History of Ireland,* edited by Dáibhí O Cróinín (9 volumes, 2005). See also Máire and Liam de Paor, *Early Christian Ireland* (1958); and Thomas Cahill, *How the Irish Saved Civilization: The Untold Story of Ireland's Heroic Role from the Fall of Rome to the Rise of Medieval Europe* (1995).

For texts, translations, annotations, and interpretations of the Norse sagas, the following have proved invaluable: *The Finding of Wineland the Good: The History of the Icelandic Discovery of America,* edited and translated from the earliest records by Arthur Middleton Reeves (1895); *The Norse Discovery of America,* translations and deductions by Arthur Middleton Reeves, North Ludlow Beamish, and the Hon. Rasmus B. Anderson (1907); G. M. Gathorne-Hardy, *The Norse Discoverers of America: The Wineland Sagas* [1921], with a new preface by the author and a new introduction by Gwyn Jones (1970); and Edward F. Gray, *Leif Eriksson, Discoverer of America, A.D. 1003* (1930).

Regarding medieval Iceland, see Jesse L. Byock, *Medieval Iceland: Society, Sagas, and Power* (1998), especially chapter 7, "Integration of the Church". See also Byock's expanded version of this study, *Viking Age Iceland* (2001), especially chapter 16, "A Peaceful Conversion", and chapter 18, "Bishops and Secular Authority: The Later Church".

Regarding the Norse in Greenland, see Finn Gad, *The History of Greenland* (3 volumes, 1971–1982), volume 1 (1971), *Earliest Times to 1700*, translated from the Danish by Ernst Dupont. Of special relevance are chapter 4, "The Norse Settlers from 1100–1400", and chapter 5, "The Fifteenth Century". See also Vilhjalmur Stefansson, *Greenland* (1942).

The Norse discovery and temporary settlement of North America has engendered an extensive literature. For a discussion of nineteenth-century scholarship, see *Narrative and Critical History of America*, edited by Justin Winsor (8 volumes, 1886–1889), volume 1, *Aboriginal America*, chapter 2, "Pre-Columbian Explorations". Of special value to this chapter are William Hovgaard, *The Voyages of the Norsemen to America* (1914); Edward Reman, *The Norse Discoveries and Explorations in America* (1949); Farley Mowat, *Westviking: The Ancient Norse in Greenland and North America* (1965); Frederick J. Pohl, *The Viking Settlements of North America* (1972); and Kirsten A. Seaver, *The Frozen Echo: Greenland and the Exploration of North America, ca. A.D. 1000–1500* (1996), from Stanford University Press.

1. Santo Domingo

For the nonspecialist in search of critical and annotated editions of primary sources relating to the early discovery and settlement of Latin America, the magnificent *New Iberian World: A Documentary History of the Discovery and Settlement of Latin America to the Early Seventeenth Century*, edited and with commentaries by John H. Parry and Robert G. Keith with the assistance of Michael Jimenez (5 volumes, 1984), from Times Books, constitutes an archive and history of inestimable value.

Regarding Columbus as navigator and maritime entrepreneur, see Samuel Eliot Morison, *Admiral of the Ocean Sea: A Life of Christopher Columbus* (2 volumes, 1942). For more noir insights into Columbus as slaveholder, see Laurence Bergreen, *Columbus: The Four Voyages* (2011). For an early revisionist view of Columbus and slavery, see Edward T. Stone, "Columbus and Genocide", *American Heritage* 26 (October 1975). For a comprehensive overview of Caribbean history, see Franklin W. Knight, *The Caribbean: The Genesis of a Fragmented Nationalism* (3rd edition, 2011). For an accessible compendium of statistics, see Jan Rogozinski, *A Brief History of the Caribbean: From Arawak and Carib to the Present* (revised edition, 2000). Regarding the theory and practice of empire by Spain, see John H. Parry, *The Spanish Theory of Empire in the Sixteenth Century* (1940, reprinted 1969), and Parry's *Spanish Seaborne Empire* (1966). See also Lewis Hanke, *Spanish Viceroys in America* (1972).

I began my reintroduction to Bartolomé de Las Casas with Francis Augustus MacNutt's dated but still engaging and informative *Bartholomew de Las Casas: His Life, Apostolate, and Writings* (1909). I continued my investigations through the extraordinary collection of essays in *Bartolomé de Las Casas in History: Toward an Understanding of the Man and His Work*, edited by Juan Friede and Benjamin Keen (1971), from Northern Illinois University Press. Also consulted and of particular importance to an understanding of Las Casas as writer are Lewis Hanke, *Bartolomé de Las Casas, Historian: An Essay in Spanish Historiography* (1952); and Henry Raup

Wagner with the collaboration of Helen Rand Parish, *The Life and Writings of Bartolomé de Las Casas* (1967). See also Lewis Hanke, *Aristotle and the American Indians: A Study in Race Prejudice in the Modern World* (1959) and *All Mankind Is One: A Study of the Disputation between Bartolomé de Las Casas and Juan Gin* (1974). In terms of critical annotated and translated primary sources related to this chapter, chapters 22 and 26 of *New Iberian World* are especially rich in documents concerning Dominican resistance to genocide and the efforts of Las Casas to establish model colonies. For the scope of genocide in these early years of empire, see also *The Native Population of the Americas in 1492*, edited by William M. Denevan (1976); and Russell Thornton, *American Indian Holocaust and Survival: Population History Since 1492* (ca. 1987).

2. Quivira

Regarding *La relación* (1542) of Cabeza de Vaca, I have consulted the following translations: *The Journey of Álvar Núñez Cabeza de Vaca and His Companions from Florida to the Pacific, 1528–1536, Translated from His Own Narrative by Fanny Bandelier*, edited and with an introduction by Adolph F. Bandelier (1922); *The Account: Álvar Núñez Cabeza de Vaca's Relación*, an annotated translation by Martin A. Favata and José B. Fernández (1993); and Álvar Núñez Cabeza de Vaca, *Chronicle of the Narváez Expedition*, translated by Fanny Bandelier, revised and annotated by Harold Augenbraum, with an introduction by Ilan Stavans (2002), from Penguin Books, which has been used for quotations in this chapter. The most authoritative account of Cabeza de Vaca and his companions is Andrés Reséndez, *A Land So Strange: The Epic Journey of Cabeza de Vaca: The Extraordinary Tale of a Shipwrecked Spaniard Who Walked across America in the Sixteenth Century* (ca. 2007). Regarding Cabeza de Vaca's subsequent career in South America, see David A. Howard, *Conquistador in Chains: Cabeza de Vaca and the Indians of the Americas* (1997).

Essential to this chapter is yet another tour de force of translation and annotation, the bilingual *Documents of the Coronado Expedition, 1539–1542*, edited, translated, and annotated by Richard Flint and Shirley Cushing Flint (2005), from Southern Methodist University Press. Document 6 presents an annotated Spanish/English version of Fray Marcos de Niza's narrative account of 26 August 1539, which is presented as well in Fanny Bandelier's 1922 edition of *The Journey of Álvar Núñez*. See also Cleve Hallenbeck, *The Journey of Fray Marcos de Niza* (1949, reprinted 1973). The earlier *Narratives of the Coronado Expedition, 1540–1542*, translated and edited by George P. Hammond and Agapito Rey (1940), also contains the Fray Marco de Niza account and dozens of other primary sources. Also of importance, as well as a delight to read, is *The Journey of Coronado, 1540–1542, from the City of Mexico to the Grand Canyon of the Colorado and the Buffalo Plains of Texas, Kansas, and Nebraska, as Told by Himself and His Followers*, translated and edited with an introduction by George Parker Winship (1904). Winship also wrote and edited the pioneering scholarly compendium *The Coronado Expedition, 1540–1542* (1896), reprinted from the fourteenth *Annual Report of the Bureau of Ethnology*, issued by the U.S. Government Printing Office, which includes important documents in Spanish and English as well as early maps and ethnological photographs. Herbert E. Bolton's *Coronado on the Turquoise Trail, Knight of Pueblos and Plains* (1949), from the University of New Mexico Press, is the authoritative biography. See also the briefer but more ambitiously interpretive study, A. Grove Day, *Coronado's Quest: The Discovery of the Southwestern States* (1940), from the University of California Press. Gilberto Espinosa translated Gaspar Pérez de Villagrá's *Historia de la Nueva México* (1610) for the Quivira Society as *History of New Mexico*, with editorial notes by F. W. Hodge (1933). Regarding Juan de Padilla and his Franciscan colleagues, see Angelico Chavez, *Coronado's Friars* (1968).

3. Saint Augustine

The Spanish Frontier in North America (1992) by the admired historian David J. Weber, from Yale University Press, as narrative interpretation and source of bibliographical reference has guided my inquiry and presentation of this subject in this and subsquent chapters. Also of importance in this regard are Herbert E. Bolton, *The Spanish Borderlands: A Chronicle of Old Florida and the Southwest* (1921); and John Francis Bannon, *The Spanish Borderlands Frontier, 1513–1821* (1970). Of great value to Borderlands study is the collection of documents presented in *Spanish Exploration in the Southwest, 1542–1706*, edited by Herbert Eugene Bolton (1925), in the *Original Narratives of Early American History* series from Charles Scribner's Sons.

At this point as well, my narrative having reached the mainland, John Gilmary Shea's *The Catholic Church in Colonial Days*, the first volume of his *History of the Catholic Church in the United States* (4 volumes, 1886–1892), guides this and all subsequent chapters. Praised by Samuel Eliot Morison in his *European Discovery of America: The Northern Voyages, A.D. 500–1600*, Shea's essay "Ancient Florida" in *Spanish Exploration and Settlements in America from the Fifteenth to the Seventeenth Century*, the second volume of the *Narrative and Critical History of America*, edited by Justin Winsor (8 volumes, 1887–1889), has proven a rich source of incident and detail for this and the following chapter. Shea began his career with *Catholic Missions among the Indian Tribes of the United States* (1854), which also now becomes a guide to this subject.

Another continuing guide in the matter of the changing designations for indigenous peoples is Alvin M. Josephy Jr., *The Indian Heritage of America* (1968). Also of importance to this and the next chapter are John R. Swanton, *The Indians of the Southeastern United States* (1946, reprinted 1979), from the Smithsonian Institution Press; Charles Hudson, *The Southeastern Indians* (1976), from the University of Tennessee Press; James Leitch Wright, *The Only Land They Knew: The Tragic Story of the American Indians in the Old South* (1981); and Henry F. Dobyns, *Their Number Become Thinned: Native American Population Dynamics in Eastern North America* (ca. 1983).

Robert H. Fuson, *Juan Ponce de León and the Spanish Discovery of Puerto Rico and Florida* (2000), is a concise guide to the subject; its geographical discussion is especially strong. See also Edward W. Lawson, *The Discovery of Florida and Its Discoverer Juan Ponce de León* (1946). Regarding the conquest of Florida by Pedro Menéndez de Avilés, see Eugene Lyon, *The Enterprise of Florida: Pedro Menéndez de Avilés and the Spanish Conquest of 1565–1568* (1976). See also the two contemporary accounts in Spanish facsimile and English translation: Gonzalo Solís de Merás, *Pedro Menéndez de Avilés Memorial*, translated and with notes by Jeanette Thurber Connor, with an introduction by Lyle N. McAlister (1964); and

Bartolomé Barrientos, *Pedro Menéndez de Avilés, Founder of Florida*, translated and with an introduction by Anthony Kerrigan (1965). Francis Parkman chronicled the Huguenots' efforts to establish a colony in Florida in part 1 of *Pioneers of France in the New World* (1865). A contemporary presentation is Charles E. Bennett, *Laudonnière and Fort Caroline* (1964), from the University of Florida Press. See also the statement by the Huguenot leader Jean Ribaut [*sic*], *The Whole and True Discouerye of Terra Florida: A Facsimile Reproduction*, with an introduction by David L. Dowd (1964). Regarding the depth and intensity of Spanish claims to Florida, see Paul E. Hoffman, "Diplomacy and the Papal Donation, 1493–1585", *The Americas* 30 (October 1973): 151–83. See also Henry Harrisse's dated but bibliographically delightful *The Diplomatic History of America: Its First Chapter, 1452–1494* (1897), published in London and dedicated to Colonel John Hay, then serving as ambassador to the Court of Saint James.

Regarding the founding of Saint Augustine, see the scarce but detailed William W. Dewhurst, *The History of Saint Augustine, Florida* (1885). See also the contemporary anthology *America's Ancient City: Spanish St. Augustine, 1565–1763*, edited and with an introduction by Kathleen A. Deagan (1991), number 25 in the Spanish Borderlands Source Books series from Garland Publishers.

Concerning the Dominican mission to Florida, see V. Francis O'Daniel, *Dominicans in Early Florida* (1930). Regarding the short-lived Jesuit mission to Florida and the Chesapeake, see Clifford Merle Lewis and Albert J. Loomie, *The Spanish Jesuit Mission in Virginia, 1570–1572* (1953).

4. Apalachee

Regarding the history of missions and missionary effort in greater Florida in the seventeenth century, four Catholic-oriented monographs proved of great use. In its admixture of scholarship and pious argument, Michael Kenny SJ, *The Romance of the Floridas: The Finding and the Founding*, with a foreword by James A. Robertson (1934), from Bruce Publishing, epitomizes Catholic scholarship in the interwar period. A year later, John Tate Lanning's *Spanish Missions of Georgia*, with illustrations by Willis Physioc (1935), from the University of North Carolina Press, represents a level of exacting scholarship that won the praise of John Tracy Ellis and Robert Trisco. Following the war, Michael V. Gannon, *The Cross in the Sand: The Early Catholic Church in Florida, 1513–1870* (1965), a masterly narrative from the University of Florida Press, carries from that pre–Vatican II era the imprimatur of Joseph P. Hurley, archbishop of Saint Augustine, under whose jurisdiction Gannon was then serving as a diocesan priest. See also John H. Hann, *Apalachee: The Land between the Rivers* (1988).

Regarding the archaeology of the Spanish and Georgia missions, see Mark F. Boyd, Hale G. Smith, and John W. Griffin, *Here They Once Stood: The Tragic End of the Apalachee Missions* (1951), also from the University of Florida Press, which includes translations of important primary documents. See also John H. Hann, "Guide to Spanish Florida Missions and Vistas", *Americas* 46, no. 4 (April 1990): 417–513; Cristobal Figuero y del Campo, *Franciscan Missions in Florida* (1994); and Bonnie G. McEwan, "The Spiritual Conquest of La Florida", *American Anthropologist*, n.s., 103, no. 3 (September 2001): 633–44, a study of mission burial practices.

John Leddy Phelan, *The Millennial Kingdom of the Franciscans in the New World* (2nd edition, revised, 1970), from the University of California Press, is in a class by itself in terms of scholarship and interpretation and constitutes, in my opinion, one of the half dozen or so most important studies of relevance to the Franciscan enterprise in the Borderlands by excavating and explicating the millennial agenda of Franciscan missionaries during this period. My understanding and presentation of the Franciscan experience in this book has been guided by Phelan's landmark study. I pay tribute as well to the useful aid of Antonine Severin Tibesar OFM, "Church in Latin America", in *New Catholic Encyclopedia,* 8:440–51; and the twenty-three essays gathered into *From La Florida to La California: Franciscan Evangelization in the Spanish Borderlands,* edited by Timothy J. Johnson and Gert Melville (2013), from the Academy of American Franciscan History.

The eminent Franciscan historian Maynard Geiger OFM began his career with a PhD thesis, *The Franciscan Conquest of Florida, 1573–1618* (1937), published by the Catholic University of America Press. Geiger went on to produce the *Biographical Dictionary of the Franciscans in Spanish Florida and Cuba, 1528–1841* (1940), which briefly annotates more than 750 Franciscans over two centuries. Martyrdom is a major theme of Franciscan historiography. In this regard, see Geiger's translation and biographical introduction with notes of Bishop Luis Gerónimo de Oré's *The Martyrs of Florida, 1513–1616* (1936). See also *The Martyrs of the United States of America and Related Essays by John Mark Gannon,* edited by James M. Powers (1957), a collection of short accounts of 116 clerics and laymen who suffered violent deaths for their faith.

The alleged golden age of the Spanish missions in La Florida is disputed in two articles that were highly useful to this chapter: Charles W. Spellman, "The 'Golden Age' of the Florida Missions, 1632–1674", *Catholic Historical Review* 51, no. 3 (October 1965): 354–72; and Robert Allen Matter, "Mission Life in Seventeenth-Century Florida", *Catholic Historical Review* 67, no. 3 (July 1981): 401–20. For further discussion, see Robert Allen Matter, *Pre-Seminole Florida: Spanish Soldiers, Friars, and Indian Missions, 1513–1763* (1990), a reprint of a 1972 study; and John H. Hann and Bonnie G. McEwan, *The Apalachee Indians and Mission San Luis* (1998).

The conduct of ecclesiastical polity as set forth in the Laws of the Indies is examined by James A. Robertson in "Notes on Early Church Government in Spanish Florida", *Catholic Historical Review* 17, no. 2 (July 1931): 151–74. Bishop Calderón's 1675 letter to Queen Mariana of Spain describing his visit to the missions of Spanish Florida was first translated by Lucy Wenhold in 1936 and published that year in *Smithsonian Miscellaneous Collections* 95, no. 16; it is reproduced by John Tracy Ellis in *Documents of American Catholic History* and further discussed by Peter A. Cowdrey Jr., in *OAH Magazine of History* 14, no. 4 (Summer 2000): 40–43.

Regarding the 1702 English invasion of Florida from Carolina, see Charles W. Arnade, *The Siege of St. Augustine in 1702* (1959). For a more comprehensive treatment, see James Leitch Wright, *Anglo-Spanish Rivalry in North America* (1971), from the University of Georgia Press. For a gossipy and detailed insight into ecclesiastical politics in the waning years of Spanish Florida, see Robert Kapitzke, "The 'Calamities of Florida': Father Solana, Governor Palacio y Valenzuela, and the Desertions of 1758", *Florida Historical Quarterly* 72, no. 1 (July 1993): 1–18. For Florida under English occupation, see Charles Loch Mowat, *East Florida as a British Province,*

1763–1784 (1964). For an overall evaluation of the near-impossible challenges facing Spain's development of La Florida, see Charles W. Arnade, "The Failure of Spanish Florida", *Americas* 16, no. 3 (January 1960): 271–81.

5. Ácoma

The Bancroft *History of Arizona and New Mexico, 1530–1888* (1899), volume 17 of *The Works of Hubert Howe Bancroft*, provides a solid account of the early histories of these two regions. Marc Simmons' *New Mexico: A Bicentennial History* (1977) provides a thoughtful introduction to New Mexican history. Charles Fletcher Lummis helped introduce the history of New Mexico to a larger American audience in *The Spanish Pioneers* (ca. 1893).

France V. Scholes is the commanding scholar in the field of church-state relations in New Mexico. Of direct relevance to this chapter are Scholes' *Church and State in New Mexico, 1616–1650* (1937) and *Troublesome Times in New Mexico, 1659–1670* (1942), both from the University of New Mexico Press. Regarding Scholes himself, see Richard E. Greenleaf, "France V. Scholes: Historian of New Spain", *Americas* 27, no. 3 (January 1971): 223–27; see also Greenleaf's "France Vinton Scholes (1897–1979): A Personal Memoir", *Hispanic American Historical Review* 60, no. 1 (February 1980): 90–94.

A heroic compilation of the primary documents relating to the colonization of New Mexico by Juan de Oñate, together with magisterial interpretation and footnotes, is available in the foundational publication from the University of New Mexico Press, *Don Juan de Oñate: Colonizer of New Mexico, 1595–1628*, translated and edited by George P. Hammond and Agapito Rey (2 volumes, 1953). See also Marc Simmons, *The Last Conquistador: Juan de Oñate and the Settling of the Far Southwest* (1991). Regarding Ácoma itself, see Ward Alan Minge, *Ácoma, Pueblo in the Sky* (ca. 1991). See also Philip Wayne Powell, *Soldiers, Indians, and Silver: The Northward Advance of New Spain, 1550–1600* (1952); and Max L. Moorhead, *The Presidio: Bastion of the Spanish Borderlands* (1975). Concerning the citing and construction of presidios, see Janet R. Fireman, *The Spanish Royal Corps of Engineers in the Western Borderlands: Instrument of Bourbon Reform, 1764–1815* (1977).

Regarding the architectural background of the missions of New Mexico, see George Kubler, *The Religious Architecture of New Mexico* (4th edition, 1973). For documentation and discussion of the missions themselves, see Cleve Hallenbeck, *Spanish Missions of the Old Southwest* (1926); and Edgar L. Hewett and Reginald G. Fisher, *Mission Monuments of New Mexico* (1943). For two contemporary descriptions of life in the New Mexican missions, see *Fray Alonso de Benavides' Revised Memorial of 1634: With Numerous Supplementary Documents Elaborately Annotated, Edited and Translated by Frederick Webb Hodge, George P. Hammond, and Agapito Rey* (1945), from the University of New Mexico Press; and Fray Francisco Atanasio Domínguez, *The Missions of New Mexico, 1776*, translated and annotated by Eleanor B. Adams and Fray Angelico Chavez, with drawings by Horace T. Pierce (ca. 1956), also from the University of New Mexico Press.

Regarding the pueblo culture of New Mexico, see Alfonso Ortiz, *The Tewa World: Space, Time, Being, and Becoming in a Pueblo Society* (1969), from the University of Chicago Press; and John L. Kessell, *Kiva, Cross, and Crown: The Pecos Indians and*

New Mexico, 1540–1840 (1978). For an exhaustive chronicle of the disconnects and dysfunctions leading up to the Great Pueblo Revolt of 1680, see Ramón A. Gutiérrez, *When Jesus Came, the Corn Mothers Went Away: Marriage, Sexuality, and Power in New Mexico, 1500–1846* (1991), from Stanford University Press. See also Henry Warner Bowden, "Spanish Missions, Cultural Conflict, and the Pueblo Revolt of 1680", *Church History* 44, no.2 (June 1975): 217–28; and H. Allen Anderson, "The *Encomienda* in New Mexico, 1598–1680", *New Mexico Historical Review* 60 (October 1985): 353–77. See also the essay by Cheryl J. Foote and Sandra K. Schackel, "Indian Women of New Mexico, 1535–1680", in *New Mexico Women: Intercultural Perspectives*, edited by Joan M. Jensen and Darlis A. Miller (1986); and John L. Kessell, *Pueblos, Spaniards, and the Kingdom of New Mexico* (ca. 2008). Regarding the revolt itself, see Andrew L. Knaut, *The Pueblo Revolt of 1680: Conquest and Resistance in Seventeenth-Century New Mexico* (1995). See also the study guide *What Caused the Pueblo Revolt of 1680?*, readings selected and introduced by David J. Weber (1999), from the Historians at Work series from Bedford/St. Martin's.

Regarding the 1692 effort at reconquest, see *First Expedition of Vargas into New Mexico, 1692*, translated and with introduction and notes by J. Manuel Espinosa (1940), from the University of New Mexico Press; and *Crusaders of the Río Grande: The Story of Don Diego de Vargas and the Reconquest and Refounding of New Mexico* (1942), from the Institute of Jesuit History in Chicago. See also *Remote Beyond Compare: Letters of Don Diego de Vargas to His Family from New Spain and New Mexico, 1675–1706* (1989). Regarding the revolt of 1696, see *The Pueblo Indian Revolt of 1696 and the Franciscan Missions in New Mexico: Letters of the Missionaries and Related Documents*, translated, edited, and with an introduction by J. Manuel Espinosa (ca. 1988), from the University of Oklahoma Press.

Regarding the people of New Mexico and the other Borderland regions, see Oakah L. Jones Jr., *Los Paisanos: Spanish Settlers on the Northern Frontier of New Spain* (1996), from the University of Oklahoma Press. Of great value is the well-researched and lavishly illustrated *Spanish West* (2nd edition, revised, 1979), from the editors of Time-Life Books. For the Roman Catholic ambience of these people, see Angelico Chavez, *My Penitente Land: Reflections on Spanish New Mexico* (1974). Regarding the art of Spanish Catholic New Mexico, see José Espinosa, *Saints in the Valleys: Christian Sacred Images in the History, Life, and Folk Art of Spanish New Mexico* (revised edition, 1967), from the University of New Mexico Press.

6. San Fernando de Béxar

Carlos E. Castañeda's *Our Catholic Heritage in Texas, 1539–1936*, edited by Paul J. Foik CSC and prepared under the auspices of the Knights of Columbus of Texas (7 volumes, 1936–1950), is a heroic achievement by the renowned scholar and librarian at the University of Texas and worthy of the great state founded and anchored in the Catholic tradition. Enthusiastically and without reservation, I acknowledge the content and guidance of *The Finding of Texas, 1519–1693; The Winning of Texas, 1693–1731; The Missions at Work, 1731–1761; The Passing of the Missions, 1762–1782;* and *The End of the Spanish Regime, 1780–1810*, volumes 1–5. The Bancroft *History of the North Mexican States and Texas* (2 volumes, 1886), especially volume 1, which covers 1531–1800 of *The Works of Hubert Howe Bancroft*, is invaluable as guide and reference (as are all Bancroft volumes). See also Herbert Eugene Bolton, *Texas in the Middle Eighteenth Century: Studies in Spanish Colonial History and Administration* (1915), from the University of California Press. For the larger background regarding the need to create Texas as a buffer province, see Henry Folmer, *Franco-Spanish Rivalry in North America, 1524–1763* (1953). To gain further insight into Franco-Spanish relations during this era, see the gossipy and delightful Simon Harcourt-Smith, *Cardinal of Spain: The Life and Strange Career of Alberoni* (1944).

For a general survey of the Texas missions, see Thomas P. O'Rourke CSB, *The Franciscan Missions in Texas (1690–1793)* (1927). Regarding the dynamic figure at the center of the Texas missions, see Eduardo Enrique Rios, *Life of Fray Antonio Margil OFM*, translated and revised by Benedict Leutenegger OFM (1959), from the Academy of American Franciscan History; and *Nothingness Itself: Selected Writings of Venerable Fray Antonio Margil, 1690–1724*, collected and translated by Benedict Leutenegger OFM, and edited and annotated by Marion A. Habig OFM (ca. 1976). For the life and times of the Zacatecan Franciscans, plus biographical sketches of 121 fathers and brothers, see *The Zacatecan Missionaries in Texas, 1716–1834: Excerpts from the Libros de los Decretos of the Missionary College of Zacatecas, 1707–1828*, translated by Benedict Leutenegger OFM, which contains as well *A Biographical Dictionary* by Marion Habig OFM (August 1973), from the Texas Historical Survey Committee, Office of the State Archeologist Reports. See also these studies by the prolific Father Habig OFM: *Heroes of the Cross: The Franciscan Martyrs of North America* (1939); *The Alamo Chain of Missions* (1968); and *San Antonio's Mission San José: State and National Historic Site, 1720–1968* (1968).

Of special value to the Native American background of this chapter is John R. Swanton's *Source Material on the History and Ethnology of the Caddo Indians* (1942), from the Bureau of American Ethnology of the Smithsonian Institution. Regarding settlement patterns in early Texas, see D. W. Meinig, *Imperial Texas: An Interpretive Essay in Cultural Geography* (1969). For more information about the emergence of a Hispanic Catholic laity, see Jesús F. de la Teja, *San Antonio de Béxar: A Community on New Spain's Northern Frontier* (1995); and *Tejano Origins in Eighteenth-Century San Antonio*, edited by Gerald E. Poyo and Gilberto M. Hinojosa, and illustrated by José Cisneros (1991). Concerning the importance of religion to these Tejanos, see Timothy M. Matovina, *Tejano Religion and Ethnicity: San Antonio, 1821–1860* (1995). Regarding the importance of Our Lady of Guadalupe in this period, see Timothy Matovina, *Guadalupe and Her Faithful: Latino Catholics in San Antonio, From Colonial Origins to the Present* (2005). The undisputed historian of the Guadalupe devotion is Stafford Poole CM. See Poole's *Our Lady of Guadalupe: The Origins and Sources of a Mexican National Symbol, 1531–1797* (1997) and *The Guadalupan Controversies in Mexico* (2006).

7. Loreto

For general background on the epic saga of Jesuits in the New World, see *Jesuit Encounters in the New World: Jesuit Chroniclers, Geographers, Educators, and Missionaries in the Americas, 1549–1767*, edited by Joseph A. Gagliano and Charles E. Ronan SJ (1997), from the Jesuit Historical Institute in Rome. The story of the Jesuit mission to Alta Pimería (southern Arizona) and Lower California as related in this chapter incorporates three themes—the Spanish and English exploration of the northern Pacific coast; the missionary practice and explorations of Eusebio Francisco Kino; and the seventy-year Jesuit tenure in Lower California—each of which focuses on the northern ambitions of New Spain. Warren L. Cook, *Flood Tide of Empire: Spain and the Pacific Northwest, 1543–1819* (1973), from Yale University Press, is the authoritative study of this grand theme. I hereby acknowledge my debt and gratitude to this classic monograph, the seminal product of a lifetime of committed research by Professor Cook. See also Maurice G. Holmes, *From New Spain by Sea to the Californias, 1519–1668* (1963); and W. Michael Mathes, *Vizcaíno and Spanish Expansion in the Pacific Ocean, 1580–1630* (1968). See also Jim McDowell, *José Narváez: The Forgotten Explorer* (1998). Regarding the Nootka crisis, see Derek Pethick, *The Nootka Connection: Europe and the Northwest Coast, 1790–1795* (1980).

Regarding the reconnaissance of the Pacific coast by Francis Drake and the background on the Nova Albion claim, I am indebted to the thoughtful study by my University of San Francisco and Danforth Fellowship friend and colleague, the late Professor Arthur Quinn of UC–Berkeley, whose *Broken Shore: The Marin Peninsula, a Perspective on History* (1981) remains a classic of global and local historiography. See also Raymond Aker and Edward Von der Porten, *Discovering Francis Drake's California Harbor* (2010), a publication of the Drake Navigators Guild. Concerning the Cabrillo explorations, see Henry R. Wagner, *Juan Rodríguez Cabrillo* (1941), from the California Historical Society; and Harry Kelsey, *Juan Rodríguez Cabrillo* (1986), from the Huntington Library. New Spain's revival of the northern reconnaissance in the mid-1770s must be understood within the context of the viceregency of a leading figure in the history of that office. For such a perspective, see Bernard E. Bobb, *The Viceregency of Antonio María Bucareli in New Spain, 1771–1779* (1962), from the University of Texas Press.

This chapter depends as well on Herbert Eugene Bolton, *Rim of Christendom: Eusebio Francisco Kino, Pacific Coast Pioneer* (1936, reissued 1960), along with Bolton's edition of *Kino's Historical Memoir of Pimería Alta* (2 volumes, 1919). For the background, interpretation, and bibliography of Bolton's majestic oeuvre, see Albert L. Hurtado, *Herbert Eugene Bolton, Historian of the American Borderlands* (2012), from the University of California Press. See also Lewis Hanke, *Do the Americas Have a Common History? A Critique of the Bolton Theory* (1964).

What Bolton began was carried on by, among others, the renowned Jesuit historian Charles W. Polzer of the University of Arizona. Among Father Polzer's twelve monographs are *A Kino Guide* (1968), *Rules and Precepts of the Jesuit Missions of Northwestern New Spain* (ca. 1976), and *Kino: A Legacy: His Life, His Works, His Missions, His Monuments* (1998). On behalf of the Jesuit Historical Institute in Rome and Saint Louis University, Jesuit historian Ernest J. Burrus has edited *Kino Reports to Headquarters* (1954) and *Kino Writes to the Duchess* (1965). In addition, Father Burrus has written the influential *Kino and Manje: Explorers of Sonora and Arizona: Their Vision of the Future: A Study of Their Expeditions and Plans* (1971), also from the Jesuit Historical Institute, and translated and edited *Kino's Plan for the Development of Pimería, Arizona, and Upper California: A Report to the Mexican Viceroy* (1971). See also John Augustine Donohue SJ, *After Kino: Jesuit Missions in Northwestern New Spain, 1711–1767* (1969), also from the Jesuit Historical Institute. For a sense of

Kino in the context of New World travel and exploration by Jesuits, see Gagliano and Ronan's *Jesuit Encounters in the New World.*

My narrative and interpretation of the Jesuit saga in Lower California is based on Peter Masten Dunne SJ, *Black Robes in Lower California* (1968), from the University of California Press; and the anthology *Lands of Promise and Despair: Chronicles of Early California, 1535–1846*, edited by Rose Marie Beebe and Robert M. Senkewicz (2001), from Santa Clara University and Heyday Books. I am indebted to these two seminal studies for interpretation and multiple colorful details. Regarding the formidable Father Baegert, see Johann Jakob Baegert SJ, *Observations in Lower California*, translated and with an introduction and notes by M. M. Brandenburg and Carl L. Baumann (1979), from the University of California Press. I am fortunate to have in my personal library a gift from my friend the late Episcopal clergyman Canon Frederick Alexander McDonald—Captain George Shelvocke's *A Voyage Round the World by the Way of the Great South Sea: Performed in a Private Expedition during the War, Which Broke Out with Spain, in the Year 1718* (2nd edition, revised and republished by George Shelvocke, Esq., London, 1757), which chronicles a visit to the missions of Lower California.

8. San Blas

Regarding the general history of California through the 1840s of relevance to this section, I have guided myself, as usual, by two superb general surveys: Richard B. Rice, William A. Bullough, and Richard J. Orsi, *The Elusive Eden: A New History of California* (3rd edition, 2002); and James J. Rawls and Walton Bean, *California: An Interpretive History* (10th edition, 2012); both are outstanding surveys from McGraw-Hill. On occasion I have also had recourse to the early volumes of my own *Americans and the California Dream* series from Oxford University Press, as well as *California: A History* (2005), a Modern Library Chronicles book from Random House.

Regarding the crucial role played by José de Gálvez in the reorganization of the Borderlands, the suppression of various rebellions, the expulsion of the Jesuits, the organization of the Sacred Expedition, and related topics, see Herbert Ingram Priestley, *José de Gálvez, Visitor-General of New Spain, 1765–1771* (1916). Concerning the route taken by the Sacred Expedition, see Harry W. Crosby, *Gateway to Alta California: The Expedition to San Diego, 1769* (2003). See also Ignacio del Río Chávez, "Utopia in Baja California: The Dreams of José de Gálvez", translated by Arturo Jiménez-Vera, published in *The Journal of San Diego History* 18 (Fall 1972). Written by Fray Francisco Palóu, *Noticias de la Nueva California* is the classic contemporary account of the Sacred Expedition and the first fifteen years of the Franciscan mission to Alta California. Crucial to the entire Las Californias section of this volume, therefore, is *Historical Memoirs of New California by Fray Francisco Palóu, OFM*, translated from the manuscript in the archives of Mexico and edited by Herbert Eugene Bolton (4 volumes, 1926).

Likewise do all biographical treatments of Junípero Serra begin with Palóu's pioneering biography. In this regard, *Palóu's Life of Fray Junípero Serra,* translated and annotated by Maynard J. Geiger OFM (1955), from the Academy of American Franciscan History, has proven invaluable. Equally invaluable is Father Geiger's

Life and Times of Fray Junípero Serra OFM (2 volumes, 1959), from the Academy of American Franciscan History, and his *Franciscan Missionaries in Hispanic California, 1769–1848: A Biographical Dictionary* (1969), from the Huntington Library. Crucial to the understanding of Serra as an administrator is the bilingual edition of the *Writings of Junípero Serra*, edited by Antonine Tibesar OFM (4 volumes, 1955), from the Academy of American Franciscan History. Testimony to the continuing interest in Serra as a founder of California are more recent volumes: Steven W. Hackel, *Junípero Serra, California's Founding Father* (2013); Gregory Orfalea, *Journey to the Sun: Junípero Serra's Dream and the Founding of California* (2014); and Rosemarie Beebe and Robert M. Senkewicz, *Junípero Serra, California, Indians, and the Transformation of a Missionary* (2015), from the University of Oklahoma Press in cooperation with the Academy of American Franciscan History.

As acknowledged in the text, my personal interpretation of Serra in relationship to his Majorcan background and the influence of the Duns Scotus tradition has been strongly influenced by the masterful *Converting California: Indians and Franciscans in the Missions* (2004) by James A. Sandos, Farquhar Professor of the Southwest at the University of Redlands, from Yale University Press, a work of masterful scholarship and analysis that has coalesced for me a lifetime of scattered exposure to the subject. Worthy of note is another pioneering study, Steven W. Hackel's *Children of Coyote, Missionaries of St. Francis: Indian-Spanish Relations in Colonial California, 1769–1850* (2005), from the University of North Carolina Press. See also the readings and commentary in Beebe and Senkewicz, *Lands of Promise and Despair*, as well as their *"To Toil in That Vineyard of the Lord": Contemporary Scholarship on Junípero Serra* (2010), from the Academy of American Franciscan History. Of relevance as well is Henry Warner Bowden's *American Indians and Christian Missions: Studies in Cultural Conflict* (1981), from the University of Chicago Press.

Regarding the transition of Lower California to the Dominicans and their stewardship of the region, see Peveril Meigs III, *The Dominican Mission Frontier of Lower California* (1935), from the University of California Press.

Regarding the Indians of California, I have been guided by Alfred Kroeber, *Handbook of the Indians of California* (1925); Sherburne Friend Cook, *The Population of the California Indians, 1769–1970* (ca. 1976); Malcolm Margolin, *The Ohlone Way: Indian Life in the San Francisco–Monterey Bay Area* (1978); and James Rawls, *Indians of California: The Changing Image* (1984).

The early history of Spanish Alta California, its missions and settlements, has engendered an extensive bibliography. As usual, one can cite the Bancroft volumes as a primary source of reference. In this regard, see the *History of California* (7 volumes, 1886) written by Henry Lebbeus Oak for *The Works of Hubert Howe Bancroft*. James D. Hart, *A Companion to California* (new edition, revised and expanded, 1987), from the University of California Press, provides a standard source of reference. Of comparable importance to this volume is Monsignor Francis J. Weber, *Encyclopedia of California's Catholic Heritage, 1769–1999* (2001). Other early and enduring studies of value to me over the years and to this book include Irving Berdine Richman, *California under Spain and Mexico, 1535–1847* (1911); Charles Edward Chapman, *The Founding of Spanish California* (1916) and *A History of California: The Spanish Period* (1921); and Robert Glass Cleland, *From Wilderness to Empire: A History of California, 1542–1900* (1944). See also Iris H. W. Engstrand, "The Legal Heritage of Spanish California", *Southern California Quarterly* 75, nos. 3–4 (Fall/Winter 1993): 205–36; and the essays in *Contested Eden: California before the Gold Rush*, edited by Ramón A. Gutiérrez and Richard J. Orsi (1997), from the California Historical Society and the University of California Press.

Regarding visitors to Mexico or Alta California, or both, during this era, see—among so many who could be cited—Pedro Alonso O'Crouley, *A Description of the Kingdom of New Spain, 1774*, translated and edited by Seán Galvin (1972), from John Howell Books in San Francisco, designed and printed by Alfred and Lawton Kennedy; *Monterey in 1786: The Journal of Jean-François de La Pérouse*, with an introduction and commentary by Malcolm Margolin (1989); and Auguste Duhaut-Cilly, *A Voyage to California, the Sandwich Islands and Around the World in the Years 1826–1829*, translated and edited by August Frugé and Neal Harlow (1999), from the University of California Press.

As architectural survivors from the Spanish and Mexican eras, the missions of California have inspired a comprehensive literature at various levels of scholarship. See Kurt Baer, *Architecture of the California Missions* (1958), from the University of California Press; Rexford Newcomb, *The Franciscan Mission Architecture of Alta California* (1973); *The California Missions: A Pictorial History* (2nd edition, 1981), from Sunset Books; *California Missions*, with text by Becky Prunty and photography by Londie Garcia Padelsky (2005); and *The California Missions: History, Art, and Preservation* (2009), from Getty Publications. Also informative are Thomas Case, "San Diego and His Biographers", *Journal of San Diego History* 29 (Fall 1983); and the articles in *Mission San Fernando, Rey De España, 1797–1997: A Bicentennial Tribute*, edited by Doyce B. Nunis Jr. (1997), from the Historical Society of Southern California. See also *The Twenty-One Missions of California: Reproductions from Paintings by Edwin Deakin* (2009), from the Santa Barbara Mission Archive Library.

9. The Bay of San Francisco

In *Anza's California Expeditions* (5 volumes, 1930), from the University of California Press, Herbert Eugene Bolton translates, edits, and annotates the diaries and correspondence relevant to the settlement of San Francisco. Volume 1, *An Outpost of Empire*, was republished by Alfred A. Knopf in 1939 as *Outpost of Empire: The Story of the Founding of San Francisco*. See also Bolton's edition of Crespí's diaries in *Fray Juan Crespí: Missionary Explorer on the Pacific Coast, 1769–1774* (1927). See also Zoeth Skinner Eldredge, *The Beginnings of San Francisco* (2 volumes, 1912). My presentation of the Arizona background to the San Francisco settlement derives from the pioneering historian Zephyrin Engelhardt OFM, *The Franciscans in Arizona* (1899), along with two crucial later studies: Henry F. Dobyns, *Spanish Colonial Tucson: A Demographic History* (1976), from the University of Arizona Press; and Kieran McCarty, *Desert Documentary: The Spanish Years, 1767–1821* (1976), from the Arizona Historical Society. Regarding the intrepid Fray Francisco Garcés, see Garcés' *Record of Travels in Arizona and California, 1775–1776*, a new translation edited by John Galvin (1967), an exquisite presentation from John Howell Books in San Francisco that was designed and printed by Alfred and Lawton Kennedy. Concerning the explorations of Fray Silvestre Vélez de Escalante, see Herbert Eugene Bolton, *Pageant in the Wilderness: The Story of the Escalante Expedition to the Interior*

Basin, 1776 (1950), which includes Escalante's diary and itinerary as translated and edited by Bolton, from the Utah State Historical Society. Twenty-six years later, the Brigham Young University Press issued the bilingual *The Domínguez-Escalante Journal: Their Expedition through Colorado, Utah, Arizona, and New Mexico in 1776*, translated by Fray Angélico Chávez and edited by Ted J. Warner (1976).

Regarding the Yuma revolt of July 1781, see Mark Santiago, *Massacre at the Yuma Crossing: Spanish Relations with the Quechans, 1779–1782* (2010), from the University of Arizona Press. See also Vladimir Guerrero, "Lost in Translation: Chief Palma of the Quechan", *Southern California Quarterly* 92, no. 4 (Winter 2010–2011): 317–50.

Regarding the founding of Los Angeles, see Edwin A. Beilharz, *Felipe de Nave: First Governor of California* (1971), from the California Historical Society; and *The Founding Documents of Los Angeles*, edited by Doyce B. Nunis (2004), from the Los Angeles Historical Society. See also William D. Estrada, *The Los Angeles Plaza* (2008), from the University of Texas Press.

10. Santa Barbara

For the life of Fray Francisco García Diego y Moreno, see the entry in Father Geiger's *Franciscan Missionaries in Hispanic California* as well as Francis J. Weber, *A Biographical Sketch of Right Reverend Francisco García Diego y Moreno, First Bishop of the Californias, 1785–1846* (1961).

For the development of the missions following the death of Serra, see Francis F. Guest OFM, *Fermín Francisco de Lasuén (1736–1803): A Biography* (1973), from the Academy of American Franciscan History. For the development, life, and times of a Catholic laity, see Douglas Monroy, *Thrown among Strangers: The Making of Mexican Culture in Frontier California* (1990), from the University of California Press. See also the oral histories gathered in *Testimonios: Early California through the Eyes of Women, 1815–1848*, translated and with an introduction and commentary by Rose Marie Beebe and Robert M. Senkewicz (2006), from Heyday Books and the Bancroft Library. See also *Three Memoirs of Mexican California*, translated by Vivian C. Fisher and others (1998), from the Friends of the Bancroft Library. For biographies of Californios mentioned in this chapter, see Susanna Bryant Dakin, *The Lives of William Hartnell* (1949), from Stanford University Press; Robert Ryal Miller, *Juan Alvarado: Governor of California, 1836–1842* (1998), from the University of Oklahoma Press; and Carlos Manuel Salomon, *Pío Pico: The Last Governor of Mexican California* (2010), from the University of Oklahoma Press.

11. Port-Royal

The online *Dictionary of Canadian Biography* is crucial to this and the following chapters on French Canada as a source of biographical detail and bibliographical reference. Indeed, it is difficult to imagine how anyone, particularly a nonspecialist, could enter the tangled thicket of the history of New France without the constant assistance of this comprehensive research tool sponsored by the University of Toronto and Université Laval. Articles from the *Dictionary of Canadian Biography* are cited below by author, subject, and the designation *DCB*. Also of value is *The Oxford Companion to Canadian History*, edited by Gerald Hallowell (2004), with online version 2012. Of continuing usefulness to these chapters are *The Concise Oxford Companion to Canadian Literature*, edited by William Toye (2001); and the *Literary History of Canada*, Carl F. Klinck, general editor (1970), from the University of Toronto Press.

Special mention must be accorded to the talented and tirelessly productive William J. Eccles and the authority and relevance of such studies as *Frontenac: The Courtier Governor* (1959; revised edition, 2003), *Canada under Louis XIV* (1964), *Canadian Society during the French Regime* (1968), *The Canadian Frontier, 1534–1760* (1969; revised edition, 1990), *France in America* (1972; revised edition, 1990), and *Essays in New France* (1987). As with other notable historians who have devoted themselves to the chronicling of an emergent region and society, the oeuvre of W. J. Eccles, as he signed himself, has become identical with the epic canvas of New France and has provided my chapters with guidance, authority, factual basis, and interpretation.

General histories of Canada that have guided these chapters include Joseph H. Schlarman, *From Quebec to New Orleans: The Story of the French in America* (1929); Arthur R. M. Lower, *Colony to Nation: A History of Canada* (1946); Gustave Lanctot, *A History of Canada*, translated by Josephine Hambleton and Margaret M. Cameron (3 volumes; 1963, 1964, 1965), from Harvard University Press; J. Bartlet Brebner, *Canada: A Modern History*, a new edition revised and enlarged by Donald C. Masters (1970), from the University of Michigan Press; *The Illustrated History of Canada*, edited by Craig Brown (1987); Kenneth McNaught, *The Penguin History of Canada* (1988); and the eminently useful J. M. Bumsted, *A History of the Canadian Peoples* (4th edition, 2011), from Oxford University Press.

As a teenager, I enjoyed the historical novels of Thomas B. Costain, and in high school I read his nonfiction *The White and the Gold: The French Regime in Canada* (1954). A number of years later, I renewed my interest in the epic of French Canada with my purchase (forty-eight years ago from the Starr Bookshop in Cambridge, Massachusetts) of the twenty-volume Champlain edition of *Parkman's Works* from Little, Brown and Company (1897–1898), which includes Charles Haight Farnham's *Life of Francis Parkman* (1901) as its twenty-first volume. I read selectively from these volumes during graduate school and returned in later life to study and take pleasure in all twenty-one volumes; recently I made my reacquaintance with their contents through the superb three-volume Library of America edition of Parkman's works edited by David Levin and William R. Taylor (1983 and 1991). Regarding Parkman as a primary and secondary source, I have depended on him for information and for the sheer enjoyment of his asides on matters Catholic; he provides the sort of commentary that only a grand nineteenth-century historian can exercise as a form of droit du seigneur. Like Samuel Eliot Morison, another Yankee Protestant chronicler of Catholic achievement, Parkman has the ability to scold or satirize as a mode of backhanded compliment.

David Hackett Fischer, in contrast, makes every effort to understand, and even to sympathize with, traditions that are not his own. Fischer's *Champlain's Dream* (2008) from Simon and Schuster reactivated in me a conviction that French Canadian history is of commanding importance to the history of Catholicism in the United States. Fischer's magisterial biography of Samuel Champlain—to which I make every possible acknowledgment—led me to the equally classic *Rise and Fall of New France* by George M. Wrong (2 volumes, 1928), from Macmillan. I thoroughly enjoyed this foundational history, which is at once literary and leisurely in its narrative expansiveness and extremely useful as a resource of bibliographical reference to early twentieth-century sources. Also of value to me for general background is Mason Wade, *The French Canadians, 1760–1945* (1955), from Macmillan. As a reader, I much appreciated Stephen Leacock's two volumes of the Chronicles of Canada series, *The Dawn of Canadian History* (1914) and *The Mariner of St. Malo: A Chronicle of the Voyages of Jacques Cartier* (1914). Of greater scholarly weight but equally enjoyable is H. P. Biggar, *The Voyages of Jacques Cartier*, published from the original with translations, notes, and appendices (1924), issued under the auspices of the Archives of Canada.

Champlain's importance as a writer is perfectly evident in French and English texts of *The Works of Samuel de Champlain*, reprinted, translated, and annotated by six Canadian scholars under the general editorship of H. P. Biggar (6 volumes, 1922), from the Champlain Society (and reprinted by the University of Toronto Press in 1971). The Founder of New France receives due tribute as a writer in this sumptuously edited and annotated edition. Also of value is *Voyages of Samuel de Champlain, 1604–1618*, edited by W. L. Grant (1907), from Charles Scribner's. Regarding Champlain as an explorer, see Samuel Eliot Morison, *Samuel de Champlain, Father of New France* (1972), from the Atlantic Monthly Press–Little, Brown and Company. Already cited, Morison's two-volume *European Discovery of America* continues to serve as a source in this and following chapters.

Regarding the elusive Marc Lescarbot, I had recourse to H. P. Biggar, *The Early Trading Companies of New France* (1901), from the University of Toronto; and the magnificent edition of Lescarbot's three-volume *History of New France*, translated by W. L. Grant, with an introduction by H. P. Biggar (1911), from the Champlain Society, reprinted in a facsimile edition in 1968 by the Greenwood Press. See also René Baudry's biography of Marc Lescarbot in the *DCB*; and H. P. Biggar, "The French Hakluyt: Marc Lescarbot of Vervins", *American Historical Review* 6, no. 4 (July 1901): 671–92. Concerning Lescarbot's *Theater of Neptune in New France*, I had recourse to the bilingual edition translated by Harriette Taber Richardson (1927) for the Riverside Press of Houghton Mifflin and the translation by Eugene Benson and Renate Benson in *Canada's Lost Plays*, edited by Anton Wagner (1982), the fourth volume covering Quebec from 1606 to 1966, from Canadian Theatre Review Publications. The online Gutenberg Project provided me access to the original editions of Lescarbot's poetry, to which Dr. Cyriaque Beurtheret provided me even further access via his translations from the original text. P. Erondelle's translation of the first edition of Lescarbot's *History of French Canada* appeared from Harper and Brothers in 1928 as *Marc Lescarbot, Nova Francia: A Description of Acadia, 1606*, with an introduction by H. P. Biggar. As background to Lescarbot's thought, see *America in European Consciousness, 1493–1750*, edited by Karen Ordahl Kupperman (1995), from the University of North Carolina Press; and Anthony Pagden, *Lords of All the World: Ideologies of Empire in Spain, Britain, and France, ca. 1500– ca. 1800* (1995), from Yale University Press.

Regarding the Huguenot factor, see Geoffrey Treasure, *The Huguenots* (2013), from Yale University Press, a tour de force of scholarship, fine writing, and elegant book design; and J. F. Bosher, "Huguenot Merchants and the Protestant

International in the Seventeenth Century", *William and Mary Quarterly* 52 (January 1995): 77–102. The following *DCB* biographies are relevant to this chapter: René Baudry on Marc Lescarbot; George MacBeath on Pierre Du Gua, sieur de Monts; Huia Ryder on Jean de Biencourt, sieur de Poutrincourt, and Charles de Biencourt, baron de Saint-Just; Marcel Trudel on Francois Gravé, sieur du Pont; R. La Roque de Roquebrune on Jean-François de La Rocque, sieur de Roberval; and Lucien Campeau on Nicholas Aubry.

12. Quebec

The previously cited David Hackett Fischer's *Champlain's Dream* and H. P. Biggar's six-volume edition of *The Works of Samuel de Champlain* from the Champlain Society dominate this chapter and are fully acknowledged as constant sources of information and reference. I have drawn upon the various volumes of *The Works* for specific topics: volume 1, for example, for Champlain's experiences of the Spanish treatment of Indians; volume 2, regarding Champlain's marriage; volume 3, Champlain's sponsorship of the Recollects; volume 4, Champlain and Acadia; volume 5, Hélène Champlain's sojourn in Quebec; and volume 6, the conquest of Quebec by England and its evacuation by the French. Of value as well is Marcel Trudel's biography of Champlain in the *DCB* as well as his *Beginnings of New France, 1524–1663*, translated by Patricia Claxton (ca. 1973). See also two other *DCB* biographies, Marie-Emmanuel Chabot OSU on Champlain's wife, Hélène Boullé, and Albert Tessier on Eustache Boullé, Champlain's brother-in-law.

Regarding religious orders in this era, see *Religious Orders of the Catholic Reformation*, edited by Richard L. DeMolen (1994), from Fordham University Press. Of comprehensive value to an understanding of religious orders and missionary effort in New France during these years are Luca Codignola, "Competing Networks: Roman Catholic Ecclesiastics in French North America, 1610–58", *Canadian Historical Review* 80 (December 1999): 539–85; and the brilliant essays gathered in *Decentering the Renaissance: Canada and Europe in Multidisciplinary Perspective, 1500–1700*, edited by Germaine Warkentin and Carolyn Podruchny (2001), from the University of Toronto Press. Based on papers presented at a conference at Victoria College, University of Toronto, in March 1996, the works in *Decentering the Renaissance* constitute cutting-edge perspectives on the foundations of French Canada. These essays are individually and collectively crucial to my understanding of this era, especially in the matters of settlement patterns, missionary effort, clerical culture, religious practice, Indian-language study, and the tentative development of a French Canadian identity. Of special regard are the essays by Natalie Zemon Davis and Deborah Doxtator on time, history, change, and decentering; Luca Codignola on competition among religious orders; Peter A. Goddard on missionary practice; and Lynn Berry on an emergent connection to Canada as positive place.

Jesuits, Recollects, and Ursulines dominate the first phases of ecclesiastical development. See Elizabeth Jones, *Gentlemen and Jesuits: Quests for Glory and Adventure in the Early Days of New France* (1986), from the University of Toronto Press. See also Jean Delanglez SJ, *Frontenac and the Jesuits* (1939), from the Institute of Jesuit History at Loyola University Chicago; and Robert Aleksander Maryks, *The Jesuit Order as a*

Synagogue of Jews: Jesuits of Jewish Ancestry and Purity-of-Blood Laws in the Early Society of Jesus (2010), from Brill Publishers. See also the *DCB* biographies by Léon Pouliot on Charles Lalemant and Paul Le Jeune. Regarding the evolution of the Ursulines from a pious association of laywomen to a cloistered teaching order, see Mother Francis d'Assisi OSU, *Sant' Angela of the Ursulines* (1934); Marguerite Aron, *The Ursulines*, translated by Mother M. Angela Griffin OSU (1946); Philip Caraman, *St. Angela* (1963); Mary-Cabrini Durkin OSU, *Angela Merici's Journey of the Heart: The Rule, the Way* (2005); and Querciolo Mazzonis, *Spirituality, Gender, and the Self in Renaissance Italy: Angela Merici and the Company of St. Ursula, 1474–1540* (2007), from the Catholic University of America Press.

The beginnings of the involvement of Franciscan Recollects in French Canada can be traced through the following *DCB* biographies: Frédéric Gingras on Denis Jamet, Jean Dolbeau, and Joseph Le Caron; and G. M. Dumas on Pacifique Duplessis, Nicolas Viel, Paul Huet, and Georges Le Baillif. Recollect missionary, explorer, travel writer, and historian Gabriel Sagard, a lay brother, left behind as his literary legacy *Le grand voyage du pays des Hurons* (1632) and *L'histoire du Canada* (1636). In 1939 the Champlain Society published Sagard's *Long Journey to the Country of the Hurons*, edited and with an introduction and notes by George M. Wrong and translated by H. H. Langton, which Greenwood Press reissued in 1968. See also the *DCB* entry on Sagard by Jean de la Croix Rioux.

As a librarian and an aspiring antiquarian, I respect the value of older books as sources of color and context. In this regard, I have been guided in this and the following chapters by Gilbert Parker, *Old Quebec* (1903); Samuel Edward Dawson, *The Saint Lawrence, Its Basin and Border-Lands* (1905); and James Douglas, *Old France in the New World: Quebec in the Seventeenth Century* (1906). Recently published guidebooks of relevance to this and following chapters include Mazo de la Roche, *Quebec, Historic Seaport* (1946); Joan Elson Morgan, *Castle of Quebec* (1949); and W. P. Percival, *The Lure of Quebec* (revised edition, 1965). For the pioneering settlement of Quebec by the Hébert family, see the *DCB* entries by Ethel M. G. Bennett on Louis Hébert, his wife, Marie Rollet, and his daughter Guillemette. Regarding the commissary general of the Company of One Hundred Associates, see the *DCB* entry by Raymond Douville on François Derré de Gand.

Concerning efforts to revive and upgrade the Acadian venture, see George MacBeath's *DCB* entries on Isaac de Razilly and Nicolas Denys. Regarding the civil war in Acadia, see M. A. MacDonald, *Fortune and La Tour* (1983), along with George MacBeath's entries in the *DCB* on Claude de Saint-Étienne de La Tour, his son Charles, and Charles' heroic wife, Françoise-Marie Jacquelin de Saint-Étienne de La Tour. For an antiquarian investigation of efforts to establish a baronetage in Acadia, see Francis W. Pixley, *A History of the Baronetage* (1900).

13. Ville-Marie (Montreal)

For the religious background on the founding of Ville-Marie, see H. L. Sidney Lear, *The Revival of Priestly Life in the Seventeenth Century in France* (1877); Abbé Henri Huvelin, *Some Spiritual Guides of the Seventeenth Century*, translated and with an introduction by Joseph Leonard CM (1927); Pierre Pourrat SS, *Father Olier, Founder of St. Sulpice*, translated by W. S. Reilly SS (1932); and Eugene Aloysius Walsh SS,

The Priesthood in the Writings of the French School: Bérulle, De Condren, Olier (1949), from the Catholic University of America Press.

For the *Jesuit Relations* that played such an important role in inspiring the foundation of Ville-Marie/Montreal, I was privileged to have the use of the magisterial first edition of *The Jesuit Relations and Allied Documents*, edited by Reuben Gold Thwaites, secretary of the State Historical Society of Wisconsin, published in seventy-three volumes by the Burrows Brothers Company, Cleveland, between 1896 and 1901. This French-English publication (sometimes Latin-English or Italian-English) constitutes a grand and heroic documentation of Jesuit effort in New France between 1632 and 1702 and was reissued by Vanguard Press in 1954 and Pageant Books in 1959; it has now been digitized and uploaded to the Internet by Creighton University at http://puffin.creighton.edu/jesuit/relations/. Guides to this vast reportage have been, most notably, Reuben Gold Thwaites himself and Edna Kenton. Kenton's 1925 anthology of selections from the *Jesuit Relations*, entitled *The Indians of North America*, was published by Albert and Charles Boni and included Thwaites' original introduction. Two years later Harcourt, Brace and Company issued an expanded, two-volume version of this anthology, which was republished with a preface by George Shuster in a one-volume edition in 1954 by Vanguard Press. Two years later, Longmans, Green and Company issued this anthology under the title *Black Gown and Redskins: Adventures and Travels of the Early Jesuit Missionaries in North America, 1610–1791* (1956), with a new preface by David B. Quinn added to those of Kenton and Thwaites. In 2000, as a contribution to the Bedford Series in History and Culture from Bedford/St. Martin's, University of Toronto historian Alan Greer edited and provided an introduction to *The Jesuit Relations: Natives and Missionaries in Seventeenth-Century North America*. This volume offers an important new interpretation of the *Jesuit Relations* as a genre of interactive reportage structured and cross-referenced within itself so as to constitute— almost!—a unified instance of a collectively produced literature at once diverse and unified, like the contemporaneous opera of the Baroque era.

Regarding my narration of the founding of Ville-Marie, I have been guided by Gustave Lanctot's *Montreal under Maisonneuve, 1642–1665*, translated by Alta Lind Cook (1969), the authority on this subject. I have also been guided by the scholarly annotations of Ralph Flenley in his edition of *A History of Montreal, 1640–1672, From the French of Dollier de Casson* (1928), a beautifully produced book from J. M. Dent and Sons of London and Toronto, to be discussed in its own right in chapter 16. For *DCB* biographies of the founders, see Marie-Claire Daveluy on Paul de Chomedey, sieur de Maisonneuve, and Jean Mance. See also Marie-Claire Daveluy's entries on the dévot Ville-Marie pioneer Louis d'Ailleboust and his wife, Marie-Barbe de Boullongne; and the early owner of the island, Pierre de Puiseaux. See also Antonio Drolet's brief entry on the pioneer surgeon Louis Chartier concerning the prior ownership of the island. Regarding the indefatigable Marie-Madeleine de Chauvigny de La Peltrie, cofoundress and benefactor of the Hôtel Dieu of Quebec and Ville-Marie, see the *DCB* entry by Marie-Emmanuel Chabot OSU. For the role played by the Order of Malta in the early governance of New France, see the following *DCB* entries: Jean Hamelin on Charles Huault de Montmagny; and Raymond Douville on Achille de Bréhaut de L'Isle.

14. Saint-Ignace

The Native American background to this chapter has been guided by Bruce G. Trigger's *The Children of Aataentsic: A History of the Huron People to 1660* (1976), from McGill–Queen's University Press. See also Elisabeth Tooker, *An Ethnography of the Huron Indians, 1615–1649* (1964), from the Smithsonian Institution; Daniel K. Richter, *Ordeal of the Longhouse: The Peoples of the Iroquois League in the Era of European Colonization* (1992), from the University of North Carolina Press; and Richard White, *The Middle Ground: Indians, Empires, and Republics in the Great Lakes Region, 1650–1815* (1991), from Cambridge University Press.

Thomas Joseph Campbell SJ's *Pioneer Priests in North America, 1642–1710* (3 volumes, 1908), from Fordham University and America Presses, remained the standard Catholic presentation of the North American martyrs for most of the twentieth century. In this category as well is Francis Xavier Talbot, *Saint among the Hurons: The Life of Jean de Brébeuf* (1949). More sophisticated but still pro-Jesuit histories include James T. Moore, *Indian and Jesuit: A Seventeenth-Century Encounter* (1982), from Loyola University Press; and Takao Abé, *The Jesuit Mission to New France: A New Interpretation in the Light of the Earlier Jesuit Experience in Japan* (2011), an installment in the Studies in the History of Christian Traditions from Brill Publishers. In *The Death and Afterlife of the North American Martyrs* (2013), from Harvard University Press, University of Ottawa historian Emma Anderson chronicles the usefulness and deployment of the North American martyrs story across the centuries. An equally sophisticated and critical study is Carole Blackburn, *Harvest of Souls: The Jesuit Missions and Colonialism in North America, 1632–1650* (ca. 2000), from McGill–Queen's University Press.

My own sense of the shared patterns and cross-references of the Jesuit missionary effort in New France has been enhanced by numerous *DCB* entries. Regarding the Acadian pioneers, see Lucien Campeau on Enemond Massé, Gilbert Du Thet, and Pierre Biard. Regarding Jesuit superiors, see Lucien Campeau on François-Joseph Le Mercier and Martin Bouvart; Léon Pouliot on Paul Le Jeune; Honorius Provost on Barthélemy Vimont and Paul Ragueneau; and Micheleine D. Johnson on Pierre de La Chasse. Regarding the North American Martyrs, see Georges-Emile Giguère on Isaac Jogues; René Latourelle on Jean de Brébeuf; Léon Pouliot on Antoine Daniel; and Florian Larivière on Charles Garnier. Portraits of two important Jesuit diplomats include Lucien Campeau on Gabriel Druillettes and Léon Pouliot on Simon Le Moyne. Prototypical missionary careers include J. Monet on Jacques Frémin and André Surprenant on Pierre-Joseph-Marie Chaumonot. Faithful missionary workhorses can be represented by François Du Peron as recorded by J. Monet. Two Jesuit missionaries were lost at sea; see J. Monet on Philibert Noyrot and Lucien Campeau on Jean Dolebeau.

15. The Abbey of Saint-Germain-des-Prés

Regarding Francis-Xavier de Montmorency-Laval, the biography *Bishop Laval* (1910) by A. Leblond de Brumath, part of the Makers of Canada series from Morang and Company, remains the most complete and authoritative. In 1926 the Abbé H. A. Scott produced the shorter and spirited *Bishop Laval*. As is true of many

Dictionary of Canadian Biography entries, the portrait of Laval by André Vachon in volume 2 of the *DCB*, 367–370, is a tour de force of useful fact. Regarding Laval's successor, Jean-Baptiste de la Croix de Chevrières de Saint-Vallier, see the *DCB* entry by Alfred Rambaud. Regarding the social and political background to these years, see W.J. Eccles, *Canada under Louis XIV, 1663–1701* (1964), from Oxford University Press; and Eccles' *Canadian Society during the French Regime* (ca. 1968). See also Alan Greer, *Peasant, Lord, and Merchant: Rural Society in Three Quebec Parishes, 1740–1840* (1987); and Richard Colebrook Harris, *The Seigneurial System in Early Canada: A Geographical Study* (1984), from McGill–Queen's University Press.

For the fused royal and ecclesiastical structures of this era, see Mack Eastman, *Church and State in Early Canada* (1915), from Edinburgh Press. See also the illuminative Wayne J. Hankey, "From St. Augustine and St. Denys to Olier and Bérulle's Spiritual Revolution: Patristic and Seventeenth-Century Foundations of the Relations between Church and State in Quebec", *Laval théologique et philosophique* 63 (October 2007): 515–59.

Regarding the governors interacting with Laval, see the following *DCB* entries: Jacques Mathieu on Pierre de Voyer d'Argenson; W.J. Eccles on Augustin Saffray de Mézy, Pierre Dubois Davaugour, and Jacques-René Brisay, marquise de Denonville; and Yves F. Zoltvany on Louis Hector de Callières. Regarding the formidable Alexandre de Prouville de Tracy, see the *DCB* entry by Léopold Lamontagne. See also the *DCB* entry on Tracy's colleague Daniel de Rémy de Courcelle by W.J. Eccles.

Concerning the imposing Louis de Buade, comte de Frontenac, see W.J. Eccles' comprehensive and revisionist *Frontenac, the Courtier Governor*, with an introduction by Peter Moogk (2003), from the University of Nebraska Press. See also Eccles' *DCB* entry on Frontenac. Already cited but of relevance to this chapter as well is Delanglez, *Frontenac and the Jesuits*.

Regarding the intendants of relevance to this and the following chapter, see the *DCB* entry on Jean Talon by André Vachon; and the *DCB* entry on Jacques Duchesneau de la Doussinière et d'Ambault by Léopold Lamontagne. For the background to the marriage program put into effect by Talon, Colbert, and Louis XIV, as well as multiple other details of life in New France during this era, see Raymond Douville and Jacques Casanova, *Daily Life in Early Canada*, translated by Carola Congreve (1967), from Macmillan. For information regarding the role and place of women in New France, see *Women and Colonization: Anthropological Perspectives*, edited by Mona Etienne and Eleanor Leacock (ca. 1979), from Praeger; and *Women, "Race," and Writing in the Early Modern Period*, edited by Margo Hendricks and Patricia Parker (1994), from Routledge. See also the reader *The Cultural Identity of Seventeenth-Century Woman*, compiled and edited by N.H. Keeble (1994), from Routledge. For a contrary view of the entire question, see Karen Anderson, *Chain Her by One Foot: The Subjugation of Women in Seventeenth-Century France* (1991), from Routledge.

By the end of the seventeenth century, the Diocese of Quebec contained more than one hundred priests. The *DCB* is crucial in presenting the background and careers of these men. Regarding secular priests who appear in this and ensuing chapters, the following *DCB* entries are of relevance: Honorius Provost on Jean Le Sueur, Jean Dudouyt, Charles de Lauson, and Louis Ango Des Maizerets;

Arthur Maheux on Henri de Bernières; Gérard Morrisset on Hugues Pommier; Noel Bélanger on Charles de Glandelet; Nieve Voisine Etienne Boullard on Pierre Hazeur de L'Orme; and Noel Baillargeon on Joachim Fornel. André Vachon contributed the entry on the Sulpician pioneer Gabriel de Thubières de Levy de Queylus. See also Olga Jurgens' entry on Guillaume Vignal, another early Sulpician. Biographies of pioneering Recollects include Jacques Valois on Henri Le Roy, Adrian Ladan, Valentin Leroux, and Joseph Denys; and G.-M. Dumas on Chrestien Le Clercq. Regarding the saintly Recollect lay brother Didace Pelletier, see the *DCB* entry by Alan Gowans.

Regarding the Augustinian Canonesses of the Mercy of Jesus, commonly referred to as the Hospitaller Sisters of the Hôtel-Dieu de Québec, see the following *DCB* entries: Jean-Guy Pelletier on Marie Forestier (Saint Bonaventure de Jesus); and Martin Saint-Jeanne-de-Chantal OSA on Marie Guenet (de Saint Ignace). Regarding the first Canadian-born Hôtel-Dieu sister, see the *DCB* entry by Marie-Jean-d'Ars Charette CSC on Marie-Françoise Giffard (de Saint Ignace). For portraits of pioneering Ursulines, see the *DCB* entries of Marie-Emmanuel Chabot OSU on Marie de Savonnières de La Troche (de Saint Joseph) and Marie-Catherine de Simon de Longpré (de Saint Augustine).

The Autobiography of Venerable Marie of the Incarnation OSU, Mystic and Missionary [1654] was translated by John J. Sullivan SJ, with a preface by James Brodrick SJ (1964), from Loyola University Press of Chicago. See also *Word from New France: The Selected Letters of Marie de l'Incarnation*, translated and edited by Joyce Marshal (1967), from Oxford University Press; and *Marie of the Incarnation: Selected Writings*, translated by Irene Mahoney OSU (1989), from Paulist Press. Also of value to this chapter is the *DCB* entry on Marie Guyart (Marie de l'Incarnation) by Marie-Emmanuel Chabot OSU. Other biographical studies of this formidable woman, canonized in 2014, include Natalie Zemon Davis, *Women on the Margins: Three Seventeenth-Century Lives* (1995), from Harvard University Press; and Anya Mali, *Mystic in the New World: Marie de L'Incarnation (1599–1672)* (1996), from E.J. Brill. Also of value in documenting the growing devotion to Marie de l'Incarnation in the United States is Agnes Repplier, *Mère Marie of the Ursulines: A Study in Adventure* (1931).

Crucial to an understanding of New France as it enters its maturity are Peter Moogk, *La Nouvelle France: The Making of French Canada—A Cultural History* (2000), from Michigan State University Press, especially chapter 7, "Group and Institutional Loyalties: Social Rank, Occupation, and Parish", 117–214, and chapter 8, "The Sovereign Family", 215–33. See also the equally crucial Janet Noel, *Along a River: The First French-Canadian Women* (2013), from the University of Toronto Press.

16. New Orleans

Researching and writing this chapter and the chapter that follows have depended on my access to the *History and General Description of New France by Rev. P. F. X. de Charlevoix, SJ*, translated from the original edition and edited with notes by Dr. John Gilmary Shea, with a new memoir and bibliography of the translator by Noah Farnham Morrison (6 volumes, 1900), from Francis P. Harper of New

York. Acquired by Saint Ignatius College of San Francisco, this rare set includes
Charlevoix' journal and his history. I also enjoyed access to the *Journal of a Voyage to
North America. Translated from the French of Pierre François Xavier de Charlevoix*, trans-
lated and edited with a historical introduction, notes, and index by Louise Phelps
Kellogg (2 volumes, 1923), from the Caxton Club of Chicago, digitally accessed
from the University of Illinois Library at Urbana-Champaign. The 1761 English
translation of *Journal of a Voyage to North America* printed in London for R. and J.
Dodsley is in the Countess Bernardine Murphy Donohue Rare Book Room of the
Gleeson Library at the University of San Francisco. Also of value to this chapter
is *Charlevoix's Louisiana: Selections from the History and Journal*, edited by Charles E.
O'Neill (1977), from the Louisiana State University Press. Regarding Charlevoix
himself, see the *DCB* entry on Pierre-François-Xavier de Charlevoix by David M.
Hayne. From the University of Illinois Library I was also able to access relevant
portions of *Lahontan's New Voyages to North America* [1703], edited by Reuben Gold
Thwaites (1905), from the A. C. McClurg and Company series Library Reprints of
Americana. The Gleeson Library owns Louis-Armand de Lom d'Arce de Lahontan's *Un outre-mer au XVIIe siècle: voyages au Canada du baron de La Hontan, avec une
introduction et des notes par M. François de Nion* (1900), from Plon-Nourrit, Paris. See
also the *DCB* entry on Lahontan by David M. Hayne.

This chapter follows Charlevoix' account as he proceeds from Quebec to Three
Rivers to Montreal. *DCB* entries on representative citizens of Quebec of this era
include J. P. Monet on Grand Seneschal Jean de Lawson; Lucien Campeau on merchant Jean Juchereau de la Ferté; Jean Hamelin on engineer and public official Jean
Bourdon; Alan Gowans on builder Claude Baillif; and C. J. Russ on lawyer and
councilor Jean-François Hazeur.

Regarding the continuing development of the Hôtel-Dieu in Quebec and the
early writing of its history, see the *DCB* entries of C. J. Jaenen on Jeanne-Françoise
Juchereau de la Ferté (de Saint Ignace) and Marie-Andrée Regnard Duplessis (de
Sainte Hélène). Concerning the removal of the chaplain at the Hôtel-Dieu on
grounds of false teachings, see the *DCB* entry of Helmut Kallmann on André-Louis
de Merlac. Regarding the psychological ordeal of one Hôtel-Dieu nun, see the
DCB entry of Marie-Emmanuel Chabot OSU on Marie-Catherine de Simon de
Longpré (de Saint Augustine). For background on the question of diabolical possession in the seventeenth century, see Peter A. Goddard, "The Devil in New France:
Jesuit Demonology, 1611–50", *Canadian Historical Review* 78 (March 1997): 40–62;
Michel de Certeau, *The Possession at Loudun*, translated by Michael B. Smith, with
a foreword by Stephen Greenblatt (2000), from the University of Chicago Press;
and Brian P. Levack, *The Devil Within: Possession and Exorcism in the Christian West*
(2013), from Yale University Press.

For citizens of Three Rivers, see the *DCB* entry of André Vachon on interpreter
and trading clerk Jean-Paul Godefroy; and Raymond Douville on surgeon Jacques
Dugay. Regarding Three Rivers' most distinguished citizen, Pierre Boucher—
indeed, the most prominent Canadian-born layman of his era—see the *DCB* por-
trait of Boucher by Raymond Douville. See also the extensive discussion of
Douville's utopian Catholic seigneury in Douville and Casanova's *Daily Life in Early
Canada*. Crucial to my understanding of Boucher's importance is Lynn Berry, "The
Delights of Nature in This New World: A Seventeenth-Century Canadian View

of the Environment", in *Decentering the Renaissance*. See also Keith P. Luria, "The Counter-Reformation and Popular Spirituality", in *Decentering the Renaissance*. Also of interest is William Bennett Munro's dated but useful *The Seigneurs of Old Canada: A Chronicle of New World Feudalism* (1914), volume 5 of the Chronicles of Canada series from Glasgow, Brook and Company of Toronto.

As pointed out in the text, Charlevoix' *Journal* entries on Montreal are minimal. Still, they provide this chapter with an opportunity to evoke the extraordinary Catholic vitality of this Sulpician seigneury. For Montreal as a fur-trading center, see Louise Dechêne, *Habitants and Merchants in Seventeenth-Century Montreal* (1993), from McGill–Queen's University Press. See also the *DCB* entries of Robert Lahaise on fur trader Jean-Baptiste Legardeur de Repentigny and of Yves F. Zoltvany on Jacques Le Ber. For a demythologizing interpretation of the Dollard massacre, see the *DCB* entry by André Vachon on Adam Dollard des Ormeaux.

The following *DCB* entries on pioneering Sulpicians of Montreal proved useful: Olivier Maurault on Gabriel Souart and François de Salignac de la Mothe-Fénelon; Noel Baillargeon on Claude Trouvé; Armand Yon on François-Saturnin Lascaris d'Urfé; and Jules Bélanger on Bertrand de Latour. The career of François Dollier de Casson is documented in *A History of Montreal, 1640–1672, From the French of Dollier de Casson*, translated and edited, with a life of the author, by Ralph Flenley (1928), from J. M. Dent & Sons. See also the *DCB* entry on Dollier de Casson by Jacques Mathieu.

The career of Marguerite Bourgeoys, the foundress of the Congrégation de Notre-Dame of Montreal, is chronicled by Patricia Simpson in *Marguerite Bourgeoys and Montréal, 1640–1665* (1997), from McGill–Queen's University Press; and in the *DCB* entry on Marguerite Bourgeoys (de Saint Sacrement) by Hélène Bernier. See also the *DCB* entry on Marie Barbier (de l'Assomption) by M. Eileen Scott.

Regarding the founding of the Religious Hospitallers of Saint Joseph at La Flèche and their arrival in Montreal, see the *DCB* entries by Esther Lefebvre RHSJ on Judith Moreau de Brésoles, Catherine Macé, and Marie Maillet. See also the *DCB* entry of Hélène Bernier on Marie Morin, analyst and first native-born Canadian to join the Hospitaller Sisters of Saint Joseph. Regarding François Charon de La Barré, the founder of the Brothers Hospitallers of the Cross and Saint Joseph, see the *DCB* entry by Albertine Ferland-Angers.

17. Natchez

Tracy Neal Leavelle, *The Catholic Calumet: Colonial Conversions in French and Indian North America* (2012), from the University of Pennsylvania Press, is central to this chapter. See also Gilbert J. Garraghan SJ, *The Jesuits of the Middle United States* (3 volumes, 1938), from America Press; and John Anthony Caruso, *The Mississippi Valley Frontier: The Age of French Exploration and Settlement*, with maps by Neil E. Bolyard (1966), from Bobbs-Merrill. Regarding Jesuit missionary alternatives by the late seventeenth century, see three essays in *Decentering the Renaissance*: Peter A. Goddard, "Canada in Seventeenth-Century Thought: Backwater or Opportunity?"; André Sanfaçon, " 'A New Loreto in New France': Pierre-Joseph-Marie Chaumonot, SJ, and the Holy House of Loreto"; and Wallace Chafe, "The Earliest European Encounters with Iroquoian Languages". Concerning the importance of Catherine Tekakwitha to the Jesuits, see Allan Greer's masterful *Mohawk Saint: Catherine Tekakwitha and the Jesuits* (2005), from Oxford University Press.

DCB entries regarding three important Jesuit missionaries in the late seventeenth century include Léon Pouliot on Claude Allouez; Marie-Jean-d'Ars Charette CSC on Claude Dablon; and Maud M. Hutcheson on Pierre-Gabriel Marest. André Vachon profiles Louis Jolliet, and J. Monet profiles Jacques Marquette, for the *DCB*. In *Discovery and Exploration of the Mississippi Valley* (2nd edition, 1903), John Gilmary Shea translated and edited five journals of missionaries (Marquette, Allouez, Membré, Hennepin, and Douay) from this era. An abundant scholarship focused on Marquette provides background not only on Marquette and Jolliet but also on the Jesuit missionary effort in the Mississippi valley. See Reuben Gold Thwaites, *Father Marquette* (1902), from D. Appleton; and Raphael N. Hamilton SJ, *Marquette's Explorations: The Narratives Reexamined* (1970), from the University of Wisconsin Press. Once again, I turned to Agnes Repplier to get a sense of the growing devotion to Marquette in the Catholic heartland. In this regard, see Repplier's *Père Marquette* (1929), from Doubleday-Doran.

As is true of all of his histories, Francis Parkman's *La Salle and the Discovery of the Great West* [1869], which I read for the third time in the Library of America edition (1983) edited by David Levin, commands the subject and is fully acknowledged in every detail and interpretation, save for Parkman's suspicion of Roman Catholicism. To balance Parkman, I had recourse—thanks to the Gleeson Library of the University of San Francisco—to a first edition of John Gilmary Shea's relatively rare debut as a historian, his *History of the Catholic Missions among the Indian Tribes of the United States, 1529–1854* (1857). For a useful contemporary biography of La Salle, see Anka Muhlstein, *La Salle: Explorer of the North American Frontier*, translated from the French by Willard Wood (ca. 1994), from Arcade. See also Céline Dupré's extensive *DCB* entry on René Robert-Cavelier, sieur de La Salle. Regarding La Salle's mistaken sojourn in Texas and tragic death, see Robert S. Weddle, *Wilderness Manhunt: The Spanish Search for La Salle* (1973), from the University of Texas Press.

Concerning La Salle's envious sometime colleague Louis Hennepin, see *A New Discovery of a Vast Country in America, by Father Louis Hennepin, Reprinted from the Second London Issue of 1698, With Facsimiles of Original Title Pages, Maps, and Illustrations, and the Addition of Introduction, Notes, and Index by Reuben Gold Thwaites* (2 volumes, 1903), from A. C. McClurg and Company of Chicago. See also the *DCB* biography of Louis Hennepin by Jean-Roch Rioux. Regarding the French Recollects in Illinois country and Hennepin's pessimistic view of Indian conversion, see Ellis, *Documents of American Catholic History*, 1:74–84. Regarding the form of Indian slavery Hennepin experienced, see Brett Rushforth, *Bonds of Alliance: Indigenous and Atlantic Slaveries in New France* (2012), from the University of North Carolina Press and the Omohundro Institute.

In her edition of Charlevoix' *Journal*, Louise Phelps Kellogg annotates a number of the seminary and Paris Foreign Missions Society missionaries at work in the Mississippi valley during this period. See also Kellogg's *Early Narratives of the Northwest, 1634–1699* (1917), from Charles Scribner's Sons. Regarding the ill-fated Jean-François Buisson de Saint-Cosme, see the *DCB* entry by Céline Dupré as well as a letter by Saint-Cosme in Kellogg's *Early Narratives*, 337–61. Concerning priests of the Paris Foreign Missions Society in the Mississippi valley, see the *DCB* entry by Noel Baillargeon on François de Montigny. Regarding the installation of Paris Foreign Missions Society priest Albert Davion as the founding pastor of the Church of the Immaculate Conception at Fort Louis, forerunner of present-day Mobile, Alabama, see Ellis, *Documents of American Catholic History*, 1:81–84; and the *DCB* entry on Albert Davion by Noel Baillargeon.

Regarding the French conquest of lower Louisiana and the founding of New Orleans, see N. M. Crouse, *Lemoyne d'Iberville: Soldier of New France* (1954), from Cornell University Press. See also the extensive *DCB* entry on Pierre Le Moyne d'Iberville by Bernard Pothier. Regarding the developing ecclesiastical culture of French Louisiana, see Claude L. Vogel OFM Cap, *The Capuchins in French Louisiana, 1722–1766* (1928), from the Catholic University of America Press; and Jean Delanglez SJ, *The French Jesuits in Lower Louisiana, 1700–1763* (1935), also from the Catholic University of America Press. See also Charles E. O'Neill SJ, *Church and State in French Colonial Louisiana: Policy and Politics to 1732* (1966), from Yale University Press. Regarding the brief but important sojourn of Jesuit Paul du Ru, see the *Journal of Paul du Ru*, translated by Ruth Lapham Butler (1934), from the Caxton Club of Chicago. Regarding the arrival of the Ursulines in New Orleans and the establishment of the first convent and convent school in the present-day United States, see Catharine Frances Galvin SSJ, *The Convent School of French Origin in the United States, 1727–1843* (1936), from the University of Pennsylvania Press; and Henry Churchill Semple, *The Ursulines in New Orleans and Our Lady of Prompt Succor: A Record of Two Centuries, 1727–1925* (1925), from P. J. Kenedy and Sons.

18. The River Boyne

I began my study of the founding of Maryland at Harvard University under the guidance of the late and very great Alan Heimert, Powell Cabot Professor of American Literature. From that encounter I still retain the *Narratives of Early Maryland, 1633–1684*, edited by Clayton Colman Hall (1910), reissued by Barnes and Noble in 1946 and 1959. As part of the Original Narratives of Early American History series, this volume contains the major writings of the second Lord Baltimore and the Jesuit Andrew White, the letters of Jesuit missionaries to the English Province, and such important statements as Leonard Strong's *Babylon's Fall* (1655), John Langford's *Refutation of Babylon's Fall* (1655), and John Hammond's *Leah and Rachel or The Two Fruitful Sisters, Virginia and Mary-land* (1656). In 1874 the Maryland Historical Society republished Father White's *Declaratio coloniae Domini Baronis de Baltimore* and White's *Relatio itineris in Marylandiam* with Latin text and an English translation by E. A. Dalrymple on facing pages.

In this chapter, I am guided in matters of subject, interpretation, and bibliography by the all-inclusive and commanding Robert Emmett Curran, *Papist Devils: Catholics in British America, 1574–1783* (2014), from the Catholic University of America Press. In terms of chapters 18, 19, and 20 of this narrative, I acknowledge any and all dependence and guidance, factual and interpretive, on this comprehensive, gracefully written, and useful monograph. Also proving of continuing use was the brief but pioneering anthology, Francis Xavier Curran SJ, *Catholics in Colonial Law* (1963), from Loyola University Press of Chicago.

Each of these studies sent me back to reconsider a historical environment in which I—along with an entire generation of American Catholics nurtured on Evelyn Waugh's *Brideshead Revisited* (1945)—had a lifelong interest: namely, the English Catholic tradition. I was already familiar with Monsignor Peter Guilday's monumental *English Catholic Refugees on the Continent, 1558–1795* (1914), from Longmans, Green and Company, as well as studies by Aidan Gasquet OSB, Hilaire Belloc, Archbishop David Matthews, David Knowles OSB, Monsignor Philip Hughes, and other English Catholic historians of the late-Victorian and Edwardian eras— Dom Bede Camm's *Tyburn and the English Martyrs* (1924), from Burns, Oates and Washbourne, comes immediately to mind—plus Monsignor Robert Hugh Benson's powerful novel *Come Rack, Come Rope!* (1912).

Papist Devils, however, sent me to a whole new generation of scholarship on the English Catholic origins of Maryland during this era, beginning with John Bossy's pioneering and semirevisionist *The English Catholic Community, 1570–1850* (1976), from Oxford University Press, which launched four decades of increasingly nuanced insights into the survival and subsequent transformation of Catholicism in England in the sixteenth and early seventeenth centuries. Of relevance to the English Catholic origins of Maryland in this regard are Thomas H. Clancey, "English Catholics and the Papal Deposing Power, 1570–1640", *Recusant History* 6 (October 1961): 114–40; Peter Holmes, *Resistance and Compromise: The Political Thought of the Elizabethan Catholics* (1982), from Cambridge University Press; Patrick McGrath, "Elizabethan Catholicism: A Reconsideration", *Journal of Ecclesiastical History* 35 (July 1984): 414–28; Kenneth L. Campbell, "English Catholics and Religious Toleration", in *The Intellectual Struggle of the English Papists in the Seventeenth Century: The Catholic Dilemma* (1986), 157–187; and Andrew R. Muldoon, "Recusants, Church Papists, and 'Comfortable' Missionaries Assessing the Post-Reformation English Catholic Community", *Catholic Historical Review* 86 (April 2000): 242–57.

How this more subtly nuanced English Catholic world influenced George Calvert and his successors as barons of Baltimore can be traced through Thomas O'Brien Hanley SJ, *Their Rights and Liberties: The Beginnings of Religious and Political Freedom in Maryland* (1959), from the Newman Press; R.J. Lahey, "The Role of Religion in Lord Baltimore's Colonial Enterprise", *Maryland Historical Magazine* 72 (Winter 1977): 492–511; John B. Krugler, "'With Promise of Liberty in Religion': The Catholic Lords Baltimore and Toleration in Seventeenth-Century Maryland, 1634–1692", *Maryland Historical Magazine* 79 (Spring 1984): 21–43; Maxine N. Lurie, "Theory and Practice of Religious Toleration in the Seventeenth Century: The Proprietary Colonies as a Case Study", *Maryland Historical Magazine* 79 (Summer 1984): 117–25; Edward Terrar, "Was There a Separation between Church and State in Mid-Seventeenth-Century England and Colonial Maryland?" *Journal of Church and State* 35 (Winter 1993): 61–82; and John D. Krugler, *English and Catholic: The Lords Baltimore in the Seventeenth Century* (2004), from Johns Hopkins University Press.

Early English interests in North America can be glimpsed in the Madoc legend. See Thomas Stephens, *Madoc: An Essay on the Discovery of America by Madoc ap Owen Gwynedd in the Twelfth Century* (1893), from Longmans, Green and Company; and Richard Deacon, *Madoc and the Discovery of America: Some New Light on an Old Controversy* (1967). For an anthology of memoirs and chronicles relating to the reconnaissance of North America, see *Early English and French Voyages Chiefly from Hakluyt, 1534–1608*, edited by Henry S. Burrage (1932), in the Original Narratives of Early American History series, from Charles Scribner's Sons. Regarding the voyages of Sebastian Cabot, see Francesco Tarducci, *John and Sebastian Cabot: Biographical Notice with Documents*, translated from the Italian by Henry F. Brownson (1893); Raymond Beazley, *John and Sebastian Cabot: The Discovery of North America* (1898), reissued by Burt Franklin, New York, in 1964; and James A. Williamson, *The Voyages of the Cabots and the English Discovery of North America under Henry VII and Henry VIII* (1929), from the Argonaut Press of London. Of great use are R. A. Skelton's *DCB* biographies of John Cabot (Giovanni Caboto) and his son Sebastian Cabot.

In his chapter entitled "The English Catholics and America, 1581–1633", in his magisterial *England and the Discovery of America, 1481–1620* (1974), from Alfred A. Knopf, David Beers Quinn gives an extensive history of early Catholic efforts to found a colony in the New World. This chapter is crucial to my discussion. Regarding George Calvert's Newfoundland venture, see Thomas M. Coakley, "George Calvert and Newfoundland", *Maryland Historical Magazine* 71 (Spring 1976): 1–18; and Luca Codignola, *The Coldest Harbour of the Land: Simon Stock and Lord Baltimore's Colony in Newfoundland, 1621–1649*, translated from the Italian by Anita Weston (1988), from McGill–Queen's University Press. *DCB* biographies of relevance to Calvert's efforts to colonize Ferryland include Allan M. Fraser on George Calvert; Gillian T. Cell on Sir William Vaughan and Edward Wynne; and E. Hunt on Erasmus Stourton. See also Basil Morgan's *Oxford Dictionary of National Biography* (*ODNB*) entry on Sir Arthur Aston.

Histories of colonial Maryland can with some legitimacy be divided into two categories. The first category consists of early works by Catholic authors who possessed a strong sense of Maryland as a Roman Catholic sanctuary. These titles include James McSherry, *History of Maryland* (1904); William T. Russell, *Maryland: The Land of Sanctuary* (1907); Thomas Patrick Phelan, *Catholics in Colonial Days* (1935), from P.J. Kenedy and Sons; J. Moss Ives, *The Ark and the Dove: The Beginning of Civil and Religious Liberties in America* (1936); and Daniel Sargent, *Our Land and Our Lady* (1939), from the University of Notre Dame Press. Matthew Page Andrews, *The Founding of Maryland* (1933), is not in the Catholic category but is sympathetic to Maryland as a Catholic haven. Later nonsectarian histories, the second category, include *Maryland: A History, 1632–1974*, edited by Richard Walsh and William Lloyd Fox (1974), from the Maryland Historical Society; Aubrey C. Land, *Colonial Maryland, a History* (1981); and Robert J. Brugger and others, *Maryland, a Middle Temperament, 1634–1980* (1988), from Johns Hopkins University Press and the Maryland Historical Society. Of use as a continuing reference is *Maryland, a Guide to the Old Line State* (1940, republished 1973), from The Writers' Program of the Work Projects Administration's American Guide series.

For a detailed account of the voyage of the *Ark* and the *Dove*, see William W. Lowe, "The Master of the *Ark*: A Seventeenth-Century Chronicle", *Maryland Historical Magazine* 95 (Fall 2000): 261–89. For a full description of landing and first settlement, see the anthology of essays *Early Maryland in a Wider World*, edited by David Beers Quinn (1982), from Wayne State University Press. See also J. Frederick Fausz, "Present at the Creation: The Chesapeake World That Greeted the Maryland Colonists", *Maryland Historical Magazine* 79 (Spring 1984): 7–20. For the first phase of Maryland settlement, see Garry Wheeler Stone, "Manorial Maryland", *Maryland Historical Magazine* 82 (Spring 1987): 3–36. See also Russell R. Menard, "Maryland's 'Time of Troubles': Sources of Political Disorder in Early St. Mary's", *Maryland Historical Magazine* 76 (June 1981): 124–41. Regarding the leading Lord of the Manor in the colony, see George Boniface Stratemeier OP, *Thomas Cornwaleys: Commissioner and Counsellor of Maryland* (1922), from the Catholic University of America Press. Regarding the developing socioeconomics and lifestyles of postmanorial Maryland, see Gloria L. Main, *Tobacco Colony: Life in Early Maryland, 1650–1720* (1982), from Princeton University Press; Russell R. Menard, "Population, Economy, and Society in Seventeenth-Century Maryland", *Maryland Historical Magazine* 79 (Spring 1984): 71–92; Lorena S. Walsh, "Land, Landlord, and Leaseholder: Estate Management and Tenant Fortunes in Southern Maryland, 1642–1820", *Agricultural History* 59 (July 1985): 373–96; Lois Green Carr, Russell R. Menard, and Lorena S. Walsh, *Robert Cole's World: Agriculture and Society in Early Maryland* (1991), from the University of North Carolina Press; and Lois Green Carr and Russell R. Menard, "Wealth and Welfare in Early Maryland: Evidence from St. Mary's County", *William and Mary Quarterly* 56 (January 1999): 95–120. Regarding the legal requirements for indentured servitude, see Christopher Tomlins, *Freedom Bound: Law, Labor, and Civic Identity in Colonizing in English America, 1580–1865* (2010), from Cambridge University Press.

Two specialized studies of two separate Maryland revolutions are in a class by themselves: Timothy B. Riordan, *The Plundering Time: Maryland and the English Civil War, 1645–1646* (2004), from the Maryland Historical Society; and Lois Green Carr and David William Jordan, *Maryland's Revolution of Government, 1689–1692* (1974), from Cornell University Press. See also the unsigned *Dictionary of American Biography* (*DAB*) biographies of Leonard Calvert, William Claiborne, and Richard Ingle.

Regarding the English background to these anti-Catholic crusades, see Antonia Fraser, *Faith and Treason: The Story of the Gunpowder Plot* (1996), from Doubleday; and the superb anthology *The Years of Siege: Catholic Life from James I to Cromwell*, collected and edited by Philip Caraman (1966), from Longmans.

Concerning the archaeology of Saint Mary's City, see Henry Chandlee Forman, *Jamestown and St. Mary's: Buried Cities of Romance* (1938), from Johns Hopkins University Press. Regarding Saint Mary's City as an assertion of value and identity, see Henry M. Miller, "Baroque Cities in the Wilderness: Archaeology and Urban Development in the Colonial Chesapeake", *Historical Archaeology* 22 (1988): 57–73.

Regarding the rise and fall of the Duke of York/James II as proprietor of New York, see Robert C. Ritchie, *Duke's Province: A Study of New York Politics and Society, 1664–1691* (1977), from the University of North Carolina Press. Regarding the efforts of Charles II and James II to reestablish a Catholic presence in England, see Hilaire Belloc's vividly presented arguments in *The Last Rally: A Story of Charles II* (1940) and *James the Second* (1928). See also Kenneth L. Campbell, "Catholic Thought under James II", in *The Intellectual Struggle of the English Papists in the Seventeenth Century*, 189–228. Of recurring importance to this chapter is W. A. Speck's lengthy and comprehensive entry in *ODNB* of James II. See also Randall Balmer, "Traitors and Papists: The Religious Dimensions of Leisler's Rebellion", *New York History* 70 (October 1989): 341–72; and Jason K. Duncan, *Citizens or*

Papists? The Politics of Anti-Catholicism in New York, 1685–1821 (2005), from Fordham University Press.

19. Annapolis

Important as investors, founders, and evangelizers in early Maryland, Jesuit missionaries of the English Province expanded their numbers and their ministries in the eighteenth century prior to the suppression of the Society of Jesus in 1773. While the story of English Jesuit involvement began in Maryland and was covered in the previous chapter, I thought it best to bring together in one place all Jesuit sources that proved of value to this narrative.

First of note is the heroic seven-volume (volume 7 contains two volumes) *Records of the English Province of the Society of Jesus*, compiled by Brother Henry Foley SJ (1811–1891) and published between 1877 and 1883 by Burns and Oates, London. Organized into volumes of narrative and volumes of documents, this collection—the life's work of a dedicated temporal coadjutor (lay brother)—constitutes an extensive archive of the English Province since its founding in the early 1620s. Brother Foley does not simply cover the Maryland effort; he conveniently places it in a separate category. Of total value as well is the two-volume biographical dictionary of English Jesuits included within this collection.

Likewise heroic in ambition—although it extends across a mere four volumes, in contrast to Brother Foley's seven—is the *History of the Society of Jesus in North America, Colonial and Federal,* by Thomas Hughes SJ (1849–1939), published between 1907 and 1917 by Longmans, Green and Company, London. Like Brother Foley, Father Hughes divides his volumes into narrative and primary documents; yet his rich and detailed narrative abounds in documentary, archival, and biographical references. These two monuments of Victorian and Edwardian scholarship will remain useful for hundreds of years to come, for it is hard to believe that any one individual will again undertake the completion of such vast and exhaustive works. For modern readers who lack time to climb these Mount Everests of scholarship, the elegant and witty writer Bernard Basset SJ provides *The English Jesuits: From Campion to Martindale* (1967), from Burns and Oates, London. Father Basset is superb on the Elizabethan and recusant eras. In this regard, the following *Oxford Dictionary of National Biography* biographies are relevant to this narrative: Victor Houliston on Robert Parsons; Eamon Duffy on William Cardinal Allen; Paul Arblaster on George Blackwell; Peter Holmes on William Bishop; Joseph Bergin on Richard Smith; and Thompson Cooper on Andrew White.

Regarding White's efforts among the Piscataway and the relationship of the Piscataway to early Marylanders, see James H. Merrell, "Cultural Continuity among the Piscataway Indians of Colonial Maryland", *William and Mary Quarterly* 36 (October 1979): 548–70. See also the chapter "Maryland: 'A Fine Poor Man's County'", in Nicholas P. Cushner's *Why Have You Come Here?: The Jesuits and the First Evangelization of North America* (2006). Of relevance as well is Luca Codignola, "Roman Catholic Ecclesiastics in English North America, 1610–1658: A Comparative Assessment", *Historical Studies* 65 (January 1999): 107–24. Regarding Jesuit efforts at self-support, see Joseph Zwinge SJ, "The Jesuit Farms in Maryland," *Woodstock Letters* 42 (1913): 1–13. Of major importance concerning this issue is Thomas Murphy SJ,

Jesuit Slaveholding in Maryland, 1717–1838 (2001), from Routledge. See also Joseph S. Rossi SJ, "Jesuits, Slaves and Scholars at 'Old Bohemia' 1704–1756, as Found in the *Woodstock Letters*", *U.S. Catholic Historian* 26 (Spring 2008): 1–15.

In 1960 Edwin Warfield Beitzell self-published the extraordinarily researched and thorough *Jesuit Missions of St. Mary's County, Maryland*. Sixteen years later Beitzell brought out a revised and expanded edition, sponsored by the St. Mary County Bicentennial Commission. Despite their unpretentious formats, these two typescript volumes, particularly the revised and expanded edition, constitute eminently readable and useful sources of information regarding first-generation Maryland Jesuit foundations. Appendix A, "Natives of Maryland in Religious Houses and Seminaries Abroad from 1684 to 1788", compiled by Thomas W. Spalding CFX, contributes substantially to our understanding of the trans-European dimensions of Maryland Catholicism. See also Caroline Barieteau, "Recusant English Families and 'American' Priests 1633–1780", *St. Austin Review* 10 (March/April 2005): 18–22. Another pioneering classic, whose timeline and biographies are especially helpful, is William P. Treacy, *Old Catholic Maryland and Its Early Jesuit Missionaries* (1889).

In terms of biographies, the great Jesuit Ferdinand Farmer is beautifully chronicled by John M. Daley SJ in "Pioneer Missionary: Ferdinand Farmer SJ, 1720–1786", *Woodstock Letters* 75 (June 1946): 103–15, 207–31, 311–21. See also Edward I. Devitt SJ, "Letters of Father Joseph Mosley, 1757–1786", *Woodstock Letters* 35 (1906): 35–55. Regarding the post-Suppression period, see Ronald Binzley, "Ganganelli's Disaffected Children: The Ex-Jesuits and the Shaping of Early American Catholicism, 1773–1790", *U.S. Catholic Historian* 26 (Spring 2008): 47–77.

Regarding Jesuit spirituality and practice of ministry, see *American Jesuit Spirituality*, edited by Robert Emmett Curran SJ (1988), from Paulist Press. See also Beatriz Betancourt Hardy, "Religious Practices of Maryland Catholics, 1689–1776", *American Catholic Studies Newsletter* (Spring 1993): 10–12; and Tricia T. Pyne, "Ritual and Practice in the Maryland Catholic Community, 1634–1776", *U.S. Catholic Historian* 26 (Spring 2008): 17–46. For a more ecumenical perspective, see Michael Graham, "Meetinghouse and Chapel: Religion and Community in Seventeenth-Century Maryland", in *Colonial Chesapeake Society*, edited by Lois Green Carr, Philip Morgan, and Jean B. Russo (1988), from the University of North Carolina Press for the Institute of Early American History.

Concerning Jesuit preaching during this period, see *American Catholic Preaching and Piety in the Time of John Carroll*, edited by Raymond J. Kupke (1991), from the University Press of America and the Department of Church History at the Catholic University of America; and Joseph C. Linck CO, *Fully Instructed and Vehemently Influenced: Catholic Preaching in Anglo-Colonial America* (2002), from St. Joseph's University Press. See also Linck's " 'The Example of Your Crucified Saviour': The Spiritual Counsel of Catholic Homilists in Anglo-Colonial America", in Linck's *Building the Church in America* (1999), 13–29, from the Catholic University of America Press.

For background on the all-important role of women in support of home worship in the colonies, see Lois Green Carr and Lorena S. Walsh, "The Experience of White Women in Seventeenth-Century Maryland", *William and Mary Quarterly* 34 (October 1977): 542–71; and Debra Meyers, *Common Whores, Vertuous Women, and Loving Wives: Free Will Christian Women in Colonial Maryland* (2003), from Indiana University Press. See also Edith Ziegler, "The Transported Convict Women of Colonial Maryland, 1718–1776", *Maryland Historical Magazine* 97 (Spring 2002): 5–32.

Regarding Catholics' migration to the Eastern Shore and the three counties of Delaware, see Thomas Joseph Peterman, *Catholics in Colonial Delmarva* (1996), which guides my discussion of this topic. See also C. H. A. Easling, "Catholicity in the Three Lower Counties, or the Planting of the Church in Delaware", *Records of the American Catholic Historical Society (RACHS)* 1 (1884–1886): 117–60. Of value as well is Lorena S. Walsh, "Staying Put or Getting Out: Findings for Charles County, Maryland, 1650–1730", *William and Mary Quarterly* 44 (January 1987): 89–103. See also John A. Munroe, *History of Delaware* (1979), from the University of Delaware Press; and *Delaware: A Guide to the First State,* compiled and written by the Federal Writers' Project of the Works Progress Administration (1938), from Viking Press.

For Catholicism in Virginia, see Gerald P. Fogarty SJ, *Commonwealth Catholicism: A History of the Catholic Church in Virginia* (2001), from the University of Notre Dame Press. Regarding the saga of the Brent family in Virginia, see Bruce E. Steiner, "The Catholic Brents of Colonial Virginia: An Instance of Practical Toleration", *The Virginia Magazine of History and Biography* 70 (October 1962): 387–409. See also the *DAB* biography of Margaret Brent.

For general background on colonial Pennsylvania, see Edwin B. Bronner, *William Penn's "Holy Experiment"* (1962), from Temple University Publications; and James T. Lemon, *The Best Poor Man's Country: A Geographical Study of Early Southeastern Pennsylvania* (1972), from Johns Hopkins University Press. See also Wayland Fuller Dunaway, *A History of Pennsylvania* (1935), from Prentice Hall. The complex and evolving attitudes of William Penn toward Catholicism and Catholics' ability to practice their religion in colonial Pennsylvania has remained a topic for scholarly inquiry over the years. See two articles from the *Pennsylvania Magazine of History and Biography*: J. William Frost, "Liberty in Early Pennsylvania", 105 (October 1981): 419–51; and Joseph J. Casino, "Anti-Popery in Colonial Pennsylvania", 105 (July 1981): 279–309. See also two articles from *Pennsylvania History*: Sally Schwartz, "William Penn and Toleration: Foundations of Colonial Pennsylvania", 50 (October 1983): 284–312; and Paul Douglas Newman, " 'Good Will to All Men ... from the King on the Throne to the Beggar on the Dunghill': William Penn, the Roman Catholics and Religious Toleration", 61 (October 1994): 457–79.

Regarding the Jesuit ministry in southeastern Pennsylvania, see Leo Gregory Fink, *Old Jesuit Trails in Penn's Forest* (1933), from Paulist Press. Concerning the arrival of German Catholics in this area, see Lambert Schrott OSB, *Pioneer German Catholics in the American Colonies, 1734–1784* (1933), from the United States Catholic Historical Society. For background on Conewago, see John Poist Keffer, *The Keffers of the Conewago Valley* (1960) and *Catholic Colonial Conewago* (1974). See also the pioneering John T. Reily, *Conewago: A Collection of Catholic Local History* (1885), published by the author at his print shop in Martinsburg, West Virginia.

For general background, see James T. Lemon, *The Best Poor Man's Country: A Geographical Study of Early Southeastern Pennsylvania* (1972), from Johns Hopkins University Press. Regarding the founding of Goshenhoppen (later Bally) and the spread of Catholic settlement in the Perkiomen Valley, see Leo Gregory Fink's *From Bally to Valley Forge* (1953). Also of relevance are three articles from the

Records of the American Catholic Historical Society (hereafter cited as *RACHS*): Philip S. P. Conner, "The Early Registers of the Catholic Church in Pennsylvania", 2 (1886–1888): 22–28; Francis T. Furey, "Father Schneider's Goshenhoppen Registers 1741–1764", 2 (1886–1888): 316–32; and Thomas C. Middleton OSA, "Goshenhoppen Registers 1765–1786", 3 (1888–1891): 295–398.

Regarding the intersection of French Catholic Fort Duquesne and western Pennsylvania, see Solon J. Buck and Elizabeth Hawthorn Buck, *The Planting of Civilization in Western Pennsylvania* (1939), from the University of Pittsburgh Press; and the symposium essays published in *Catholic Pittsburgh's One Hundred Years* (1943), from Loyola University Press of Chicago. Also relevant is A. A. Lambing, *A History of the Catholic Church in the Diocese of Pittsburgh and Allegheny* (1880), from Benziger Brothers; and Henry A. Szarnicki, *Michael O'Connor: First Catholic Bishop of Pittsburgh* (1975).

From Pennsylvania, Jesuits in the eighteenth century served New Jersey and New York. Regarding New Jersey, see Joseph M. Flynn, *The Catholic Church in New Jersey* (1904); and Wallace N. Jamison, *Religion in New Jersey: A Brief History* (1964). For general background, see John Edwin Pomfret, *Colonial New Jersey: A History* (1973), from the History of American Colonies series of Charles Scribner's Sons; and Richard P. McCormick, *New Jersey: From Colony to State, 1609–1789* (1981), from the New Jersey Historical Society. Regarding settlement patterns in New Jersey, see John E. Brush, *The Population of New Jersey* (1958), from Rutgers University Press; and Rudolph J. Vecoli, *The People of New Jersey* (1965), a supplementary volume to the New Jersey Historical Series from D. Van Norstrand Company. Also of continuing value is *New Jersey: A Guide to Its Present and Past*, compiled and written by the Federal Writers' Project of the Works Progress Administration (1939), from Viking Press.

Concerning Catholicism in New York, see the woefully underestimated *Brief Sketch of the Early History of the Catholic Church on the Island of New York*, by James Roosevelt Bayley, first bishop of New Jersey and eighth archbishop of Baltimore (2nd edition, revised and enlarged, 1870); and William Harper Bennett's even more detailed *Catholic Footsteps in Old New York* (1909). Regarding Governor Thomas Dongan, see John H. Kennedy OMI, *Thomas Dongan, Governor of New York, 1682–1688* (1930), from the Catholic University of America Press. See also Edward Channing, "Colonel Thomas Dongan, Governor of New York", *Proceedings of the American Antiquarian Society* (October 1907): 336–45; and P. W. Browne, "Thomas Dongan: Soldier and Statesman: Irish-Catholic Governor of New York, 1683–1688", *Studies: An Irish Quarterly Review* 23 (September 1934): 489–501. See also the *ODNB* biography of Dongan by Piers Wauchope and the unsigned *DAB* biography.

Regarding fears of a slave revolt and the brutal executions that followed, including the execution of John Ury on grounds of being a Catholic priest, see the ever-authoritative Edwin G. Burrows and Mike Wallace, *Gotham: A History of New York City to 1898* (1999), from Oxford University Press. Regarding fears of a slave revolt at the same time in Montreal, see Afua Cooper, *The Hanging of Angélique: The Untold Story of Canadian Slavery and the Burning of Old Montréal* (2006), from HarperCollins. For general guidance and reference, see Florence D. Cohalan, *A Popular History of the Archdiocese of New York* (1983), from the United States Catholic

Historical Society. Regarding Connecticut, see Stephen Michael DiGiovanni, *The Catholic Church in Fairfield County, 1666–1961* (1987). See also James H. O'Donnell, *History of the Diocese of Hartford* (1900). Regarding Maine, see William Leo Lucey SJ, *The Catholic Church in Maine* (1957). See also Thomas Charland's biography of Sébastien Rale in the *DCB;* and John Lenhart OFM Cap, "The Capuchins in Acadia and Northern Maine", *RACHS* 28 (1917): 46–63. For a magisterial evocation of the entire New England scene during the colonial era, see the first volume of Robert H. Lord, John E. Sexton, and Edward T. Harrington, *History of the Archdiocese of Boston in the Various Stages of Its Development, 1604 to 1943* (3 volumes, 1944), from Sheed and Ward.

20. London

Regarding the life and times of the Carrolls of Maryland, see the authoritative Ronald Hoffman in collaboration with Sally D. Mason, *Princes of Ireland, Planters of Maryland: A Carroll Saga, 1500–1782* (2000), from the University of North Carolina Press on behalf of the Omohundro Institute of Early American History and Culture. In 2001 the University of North Carolina Press, the Omohundro Institute, the Maryland Historical Society, and the Maryland State Archives published the first volume of the collected letters of Charles Carroll, *Dear Papa, Dear Charley: The Peregrinations of a Revolutionary Aristocrat, as told by Charles Carroll of Carrollton and His Father, Charles Carroll of Annapolis with Sundry Observations on Bastardy, Child-Rearing, Romance, Matrimony, Commerce, Tobacco, Slavery, and the Politics of Revolutionary America*, edited by Ronald Hoffman, Sally D. Mason, and Eleanor S. Darcy. See also Hoffman, "The Carroll Family of Maryland", *Proceedings of the American Antiquarian Society* 117 (October 2007): 331–50.

Regarding Charles Carroll of Carrollton, the following publications proved of use in this chapter: Kate Mason Rowland, *The Life of Charles Carroll of Carrollton, 1737–1832, With His Correspondence and Public Papers* (2 volumes, 1898), from the Knickerbocker Press of G. P. Putnam's Sons; *Unpublished Letters of Charles Carroll of Carrollton*, edited by Thomas Meagher Field (1902), from the United States Catholic Historical Society; Ellen Hart Smith, *Charles Carroll of Carrollton* (1942), from Harvard University Press; Thomas O'Brien Hanley SJ, *Charles Carroll of Carrollton, The Making of a Revolutionary Gentleman* (1982) and *Revolutionary Statesman: Charles Carroll and the War* (1983), from Loyola University Press of Chicago; Scott McDermott, *Charles Carroll of Carrollton, Faithful Revolutionary* (2002); and Bradley J. Birzer, *American Cicero: The Life of Charles Carroll* (2010). Of crucial importance to my understanding of the relationships between Carroll and his parents is Pauline Maier, "Charles Carroll of Carrollton, Dutiful Son and Revolutionary Politician", in Maier's *The Old Revolutionaries: Political Lives in the Age of Samuel Adams* (1980), from Alfred A. Knopf.

Regarding Joshua Reynolds' 1763 portrait of Carroll, see the comprehensive and authoritative Fintan Cullen, "Charles Carroll of Carrollton: Painting the Portrait of an Irish-American Aristocrat", *Eighteenth-Century Ireland* 25 (2010): 149–60. Regarding Reynolds as celebrity portraitist, see *Joshua Reynolds and the Creation of Celebrity*, edited by Martin Postle, with essays by Tim Clayton and Stella Tillyard (2005), from the Tate, London. See also Postle's lengthy entry on Reynolds in the *Dictionary of National Biography*. Also of value to this chapter is Ellis Water-house, *Reynolds* (1973), from Phaidon Press. Regarding the disreputable proprietor of Maryland, with whom Charles Carroll dined and attended the races, see Wallace Shugg, "The Baron and the Milliner: Lord Baltimore's Rape Trial as a Mirror of Class Tensions in Mid-Georgian London", *Maryland Historical Magazine* 83 (Winter 1988): 310–30.

Concerning the rise of elites, Protestant or Catholic, in eighteenth-century Maryland, see Charles G. Steffen, *From Gentlemen to Townsmen: The Gentry of Balti-more County, Maryland, 1660–1776* (1993), from the University Press of Kentucky; Trevor Burnard, "A Tangled Cousinry? Associational Networks of the Maryland Elite, 1691–1776", *Journal of Southern History* 61 (February 1995): 17–44; Burnard's *Creole Gentlemen: The Maryland Elite, 1691–1776* (2002), from Routledge; and Lorena S. Walsh, *Motives of Honor, Pleasure, and Profit: Plantation Management in the Colonial Chesapeake, 1607–1763* (2010), from the University of North Caro-lina Press.

Regarding the dynamics of the Glorious Revolution in Maryland, see Richard A. Gleissner, "Religious Causes of the Glorious Revolution in Maryland", *Maryland Historical Magazine* 64 (Winter 1969): 327–41; Lois Green Carr and David William Jordan, *Maryland's Revolution of Government, 1689–1692* (1974), from Cornell Uni-versity Press; Michael Graham, "Churching the Unchurched: The Establishment in Maryland, 1692–1724", *Maryland Historical Magazine* 83 (Winter 1988): 397–426; and Michael Graham, "Popish Plots: Protestant Fears in Early Colonial Maryland, 1676–1689", *Catholic Historical Review* 79 (April 1993): 197–216. On Catholic efforts to maintain status in the colony following the Glorious Revolution, see David William Jordan, "A Plea for Maryland Catholics", *Maryland Historical Magazine* 67 (Winter 1972): 429–35; Michael J. Graham SJ, "'The Collapse of Equity': Catholic and Quaker Dissenters in Maryland, 1692–1720", *Maryland Historical Magazine* 88 (Spring 1993): 5–25; and Tricia T. Pyne, "A Plea for Maryland Catholics Recon-sidered", *Maryland Historical Magazine* 92 (Summer 1997): 162–81. Regarding the unusual and ecumenical case of Richard Bennett III, see Beatriz Betancourt Hardy, "A Papist in a Protestant Age: The Case of Richard Bennett, 1667–1749", *Journal of Southern History* 60 (May 1994): 203–28.

My understanding of the Maryland Catholic elite of the eighteenth century has been guided by a number of critical essays. Regarding the consolidation of the Catholic elite vis-à-vis outmigration from Maryland, see the already cited Walsh, "Staying Put or Getting Out". Concerning the reaction of this elite to political dis-enfranchisement, see Michael Graham, "Roman Catholics, Not Papists: Catholic Identity in Maryland, 1689–1776", *Maryland Historical Magazine* 92 (Summer 1997): 138–61. Regarding the Catholic argument for civil rights based on property, see Gerald P. Fogarty, "Property and Religious Liberty in Colonial Maryland Catholic Thought", *Catholic Historical Review* 72 (October 1986): 573–600.

The Maryland Catholic elite's dependency on slavery can be traced in general terms through Jonathan L. Alpert, "The Origin of Slavery in the United States: The Maryland Precedent", *American Journal of Legal History* 14 (July 1970): 189–221; Whittington Johnson, "The Origin and Nature of African Slavery in Seventeenth-Century Maryland", *Maryland Historical Magazine* 73 (September 1978): 238–45; and Allan Kulikoff, *Tobacco and Slaves: The Development of Southern Cultures in the*

Chesapeake, 1680–1800 (1986), from the University of North Carolina Press. For insights into tobacco culture on a less-than-elite basis, see Lou Rose, "Ebenezer Cooke's *The Sot Weed Factor* and Its Uses as a Social Document in the History of Colonial Maryland", *Maryland Historical Magazine* 78 (Winter 1983): 272–77.

Regarding Catholic practice in this period, see Pyne's already cited "Ritual and Practice in the Maryland Catholic Community". On the loss of the right to public worship, see John D. Krugler, " 'Scandalous and Offensive to the Government': The 'Popish Chappel' at St. Mary's City, Maryland, and the Society of Jesus, 1634–1705", in Krugler's *English and Catholic: The Lords Baltimore in the Seventeenth Century*, 233–250. Regarding the Maryland Catholic elite and its religious responsibilities to the slave population, see Beatriz Betancourt Hardy, " 'The Papists ... have shewn a laudable Care and Concern': Catholicism, Anglicanism, and Slave Religion in Colonial Maryland", *Maryland Historical Magazine* 98 (Spring 2003): 4–33.

An early and still relevant investigation regarding the Academy at Old Bohemia is Thomas Hughes SJ, "Educational Convoys to Europe in the Olden Time", *American Ecclesiastical Review* 29 (1903): 24–39. Also of importance to this chapter are E. I. Devitt SJ, "Bohemia—Mission of St. Francis Xavier, Cecil County, Maryland", *RACHS* 23, no. 2 (June 1913): 97–139; Edmund J. Goebel, *A Study of Catholic Secondary Education during the Colonial Period Up to the First Plenary Council of Baltimore, 1852* (1936), from the Catholic University of America Press; and Rossi's already cited "Jesuits, Slaves, and Scholars at 'Old Bohemia' ". Regarding young women who traveled from Maryland to Europe to enter convents or attend school, see Joseph T. Durkin SJ, "Catholic Training for Maryland Catholics 1773–1786", *Historical Records and Studies* 32 (1941): 70–82. See also Spalding's all-important "Natives of Maryland in Religious Houses and Seminaries Abroad from 1684 to 1788", in Beitzell, *The Jesuit Missions of St. Mary's County, Maryland*, 313–321.

My investigations into Catholic Philadelphia began with the superb text, maps, and bibliography of Monsignor James F. Connelly's *History of the Archdiocese of Philadelphia* (1976), a model of its kind. Monsignor Connelly's history sent me to an even earlier classic, *Catholicity in Philadelphia* by Joseph L. J. Kirlin (1909), a priest of the archdiocese. In terms of general histories, the heroic J. Thomas Scharf and Thompson Westcott's *History of Philadelphia, 1609–1884* (3 volumes, 1884)—which is exhaustively detailed, clearly written, beautifully organized, and extensive and generous in its coverage of Catholic Philadelphia—is one of the finest nineteenth-century urban histories to be produced in these United States. If these volumes were not enough, the history of Philadelphia has been graced more recently by two further classics: the brilliantly analytic *Private City: Philadelphia in Three Periods of Its Growth* by Sam Bass Warner Jr. (1968), from the University of Pennsylvania Press; and the magisterial *Philadelphia: A Three-Hundred-Year History*, edited by Russell F. Weigley, Nicholas B. Wainwright, and Edwin Wolf II, with Joseph E. Illick and Thomas Wendel serving as editorial consultants (1982), a Barra Foundation book from W. W. Norton and Company. My descriptions of Saint Joseph's and Saint Mary's Churches are based on Dennis C. Kurjack's essay in *Historic Philadelphia from the Founding until the Early Nineteenth Century: Papers Dealing with Its People and Buildings with an Illustrative Map* (1953), issued as volume 43, part 1, of the *Transactions of the American Philosophical Society* 43 (1953):

199–209. See also *Famous American Churches and Shrines: Catholic Edition*, edited by Walter T. Murphy (1969). The pioneering publication by the American Catholic Historical Society of Philadelphia of eighteenth-century registers has its own incantatory way of suggesting the lives and deaths of the Catholics who attended these churches. In this regard, see articles in *RACHS* for 1893: "List of Marriages and Baptisms Registered at St. Joseph's Church, Philadelphia", 125–93; "Minute Book of St. Mary's Church, Philadelphia, 1770–1811", 253–459; and "List of Baptisms Registered at St. Joseph's Church, Philadelphia", 37–76. Also of relevance to this chapter is John K. Alexander, "The Philadelphia Numbers Game: An Analysis of Philadelphia's Eighteenth-Century Population", *Pennsylvania Magazine of History and Biography* (July 1974): 314–24.

Regarding the arrival of the French Acadians in Philadelphia, see John Mack Faragher, *A Great and Noble Scheme: The Tragic Story of the Expulsion of the French Acadians from Their American Homeland* (2005), from W. W. Norton and Company. See also John Bartlet Brebner, *New England's Outpost: Acadia before the Conquest of Canada* (1965). Henry Wadsworth Longfellow's "Evangeline: A Tale of Acadie" can be found in Henry Wadsworth Longfellow, *Poems and Other Writings*, edited by J. D. McClatchy (2000), from the Library of America.

Envoy

Monsignor Peter Guilday produced the pioneering *Life and Times of John Carroll, Archbishop of Baltimore, 1735–1815* (1922). Of equal importance is Annabelle M. Melville, *John Carroll of Baltimore, Founder of the American Catholic Hierarchy* (1955). The University of Notre Dame Press has issued *The John Carroll Papers*, edited by Thomas O'Brien Hanley SJ (3 volumes, 1976). Guilday, *The Life and Times*, 43–56, and *The John Carroll Papers*, volume 1, 26–31, each present Carroll's letters to Thomas Ellerker SJ. Regarding Carroll's friend and classmate Henry, eighth Baron Arundell of Wardour, and the chapel at Thorndon, see Mark Bence-Jones, *The Catholic Families* (1992); and Leanda de Lisle and Peter Stanford, *The Catholics and Their Homes* (1995).

INDEX

Abbey of Saint-Germain-des-Prés (Paris), 336, 364–68

Abenaki people, 358–59, 376, 435–36, 524–25

Accault, Michel, 451

Ácoma massacre (1598), 122–27

Acuña y Bejarano, Juan de, the Marquis of Casa Fuerte, 162

Adam of Bremen, 10

Addison, Henry, 531

Addison, John, 498

Ades people, 158–59

Adrian IV, Pope, 5

Adrian VI, Pope, 71

African slavery: Anglican colonies, 535; French Louisiana, 456, 457; Jesuit slave-holding, 506–7, 534; Las Casas and, 34–35, 36, 37; Maryland's slave-based economy, 506–7, 528, 529–30, 534–35; New France, 534; New Spain, 34–35, 36, 37, 72–73; Philadelphia, 538–39; slave revolt hysteria in New York, 521–23; Virginia, 535

Aguayo, Governor (José de Azlor y Virto de Vera), 159–62

Aguirre, Don José Antonio, 247

Aigron, Pierre, 377

d'Aiguillon, duchesse, 311, 323, 333, 339–40, 383

d'Ailleboust, Louis, 347, 348–49

Alana, Joseph Xavier de, 111

Alarcón, Don Martín de, 142, 148

Alarcón, Hernando de, 177

Alberoni, Giulio, 145, 159

Alemán, Juan, 62

Alencastre Noroña y Silva, Fernando de, Marquis of Valdefuentes, 154, 192

Alexander, William (Earl of Stirling), 316–17

Alexander VI, Pope, 17–18, 78, 81

Algonquian people, 330, 345, 376, 413–14, 418, 524

Allande y Saabedra, Don Pedro de, 250

Allen, William Cardinal, 470–71, 479

d'Allet, Antoine, 369, 425

Allouez, Claude, 439–41, 446

Almazán, Fernando Pérez de, 161

Alta California (New Spain), 203–25, 226–29, 247–75, *266*; civil settlements, 228–29, 249–54, 262–63, 272–73; final years of Franciscan system, 267–75; founding of Mission San Luis Rey and San Fernando Rey, 265–67; Franciscan competition to replace Jesuits, 175, 203–6, 208–9; Franciscan diocesan organization, 248–49; Franciscan friars' rebelliousness and misbehavior, 269–70; Gálvez and the Franciscan entrada (Sacred Expedition), 203–13, 218; Gálvez's administrative reforms, 203–4, 205–6, 207–8; García Diego y Moreno as first bishop, 247–49, 265, 269–70, 273–75; Indian labor, 222, 271–72; Indian resistance and attacks, 203, 206, 212–13, 223–25, 258–59; Lasuén years, 259–63; mission irrigation systems, 225; Mission Santa Barbara and establishment of the diocese, 247–49; Monterey Bay search, 204, 210–12, 218; Neve's governance, 250–54, 255; Portolá's overland party, 205, 209–13, 218, 250, 255; Rivera's governance, 222–23, 224–25, 228–29, 245, 251; seaborne expeditions, 204, 205, 209, 210, 212, 218; Serra and civil/military tensions, 221–25, 234, 250–54; Serra as father president of missions, 148, 214, 218–25, 227, 234, 250–54, 259–60; settlements and missions, *266*; soldiers' sexual exploitation of Indian women, 221, 222, 224, 227, 234, 251; the Spanish Crown's ambitions, 221–23; transition from Spanish jurisdiction to Mexican republic, 265, 268–69, 272–75; Yuma-Spaniard alliance, 256–58

Altamirano, Juan de la Cabezas, 101–2, 104

Altimira, José, 269

Alvarado, Hernando de, 64

Alvarado, Juan Bautista, 269–70, 273

Alvarado, Pedro de, 61

Amadís de Gaula cycle (Montalvo), 54

Amamix, Agapito, 267

Ambris, Doroteo, 269–70

American Catholicism, contemporary, x–xii

American Philosophical Society, 519, 538

Ana, Doña, 99

André, Louis, 441, 446

Andrés, Juan, 218

Ángel, Pablo Ventura, 522

Anglesey, Earl of (Christopher Villiers), 478

Ango, Jean, 284

Ango Des Maizerets, Louis, 388–89, 393, 401

Anheuser, Gabriel, 515

Les annals de l'Hôtel-Dieu de Quebec, 1636–1716, 412

Annapolis (Maryland), 500–502, 531

Anne, Queen of Great Britain, 502, 529, 536

Anne of Austria (queen regent), 322, 323, 339, 347, 364

Anunciación, Domingo de la, 80–81

Anza, Juan Bautista de, 223, 232–45; Bolton's *Anza's California Expeditions*, 235–36, 241; and Chief Palma's memorandum, 256–58; first Sonora-California expedition, 234–39, *238*; and Garcés, 232–34, 235, 237; second expedition and San Francisco settlement, 226, 227, *238*, 239–46, 249, 256–58

Anzar, José Antonio, 265

Apache people: and Anza expeditions, 239; and Franciscan missions in Texas, 165, 166, 167; and Pimería Alta missions, 186, 231, 232, 233, 250, 257; and Pueblo uprisings, 135, 136, 139, 140

Apalachee people, 99–101, 105

Apostolic College of Our Lady of Guadalupe at Zacatecas, 146–47, 156, 248, 265, 268; *Libros de los Decretos*, 147

Apostolic College of San Fernando in Mexico City, 146–47, 165, 175, 204–6, 220, 226–27, 237, 253, 263, 267–68

Apostolic College of Santa Cruz (Holy Cross) at Querétaro, 146–47, 154, 169, 204–5, 232, 237, 241–42

Apostolicum Pascendi Minis (papal bull) (1765), 551

Arana, Juan de, 76–77

Arballo, Feliciana, 242–43

Argall, Samuel, 306

d'Argenson, Pierre de Voyer, 375–76, 391

Arguelles y Miranda, Doña Josefa de, 174

Argüello, José Darío, 255

Argüello, Juan Antonio de, 207

Argüello, Luis Antonio, 269

Arizona. *See* Southern Arizona (Pimería Alta country), New Spain's northward advance out of

Arminius, Jacobus, 473

Armona, Francisco de, 207

Arnauld, Antoine, 301

Ars veritatis inventive (Lull), 215

Arteaga, Juan de Matías, 164

Artur, Ricardo, 96–97

Arundell, Anne, 475, 485, 548

Arundell, Lord (Charles), 475, 548, 555

Arundell, Lord (Henry), 555–56

Arundell of Wardour, Lord, 470, 475, 481

Ascensión, Antonio de la, 178, 210–11, 218

Ascham, Roger, 467

Asisara, Lorenzo, 271

Aston, Arthur, 476

Atkinson, Geoffrey, 295

Atondo y Antillón, Isidro, 182, 183

Atwood, Peter, 504, 532

Aubry, Nicholas, 286, 301

Audiencia of New Spain, 38–39, 41, 53, 63, 119

Auguel, Antoine, 451

Augustinian Canonesses Regular (Quebec), 333, 372, 381, 383–84

Aunon, Miguel de, 98

Avalon (Newfoundland colony), 474, 475, 476

Aveiro, Duchess of, 181–82

Ávila, Francisco de, 98

Ayala, Juan Manuel de, 228

Ayeta, Francisco de, 138

Ayllón, Lucas Vázquez de, 71–73

Azanza, Miguel José de, 207

Aztecs, 45, 53, 117, 132–33, 176

Babonneau, Renée, 422

Badajoz, Antonio de, 98

Baegert, Jakob, 196, 197, 199

Baez, Domingo Agustín, 89, 99

Bagot, Jean, 365–66

Baillif, Claude, 402

Bailyn, Bernard, 497

Baker, John, 548–50

Baker, Louisa, 548–50

Baker, Mary Ryan, 548–50

Balboa, Vasco Núñez de, 176

Balcárcel, Antonio, 149

Bancroft, George, 236

Bancroft Library at the University of California–Berkeley, 180, 236, 271

Bandini, Juan, 247, 273

Bandini family of San Diego and Los Angeles, 273

Barco, Miguel, 196

Baron, Denis, 515

Baronius, Caesar Cardinal, 288

Barré, Charlotte, 333–34, 383

Barrenche, Juan, 259

Barrientos, Bartolomé, 85–86

Barrington, Daines, 547

Barrington, Lord (William Wildman), 547

Battle of Ravenna, 45

Battle of the Boyne (1690), 464–65

Battle of the Wilderness (1755), 540

Bauer, Franz, 229

Beatriz de Estrada, Doña, 55

Beaubois, Nicholas Ignatius, 457

Bede, Father (John Hiccocks), 477

Beebe, Rose Marie, 211–12

Belderrain, Juan Bautista, 263

Beleña, Eusebio Ventura, 206

Bellin, Jacques-Nicolas, 452

Belloc, Hilaire, 468

Beltrán, Bernardino, 116–17

Benavides, Alonso de, 127–28, 134

Bendito, Antonio de, 522

Benedict XIV, Pope, 143, 146, 544

Bennett, Elizabeth Rousby, 533

Bennett, Henrietta Maria, 532–33

Bennett, Richard, 494–95, 532

Bennett, Richard, III, 503, 504, 532–34, 539

Bering, Vitus, 261

Berkeley, John (Lord Lieutenant of Ireland), 510

Berkeley, William, 509–10

Bermejo, Pedro, 98

Bernières, Henri de, 379, 391, 393, 401

Bernières-Louvigny, Jean de, 333–34, 367, 378, 379, 384

Bernini, Gian Lorenzo, 143

Berrio, Luis de, 37–38

Berry, Lynn, 416–17

Bérulle, Pierre de, 336, 382, 422

Beteta, Gregorio de, 76–77, 80–81

Biard, Pierre, 304, 306

Biencourt, Charles de, 301, 305–6

Bienville, sieur de (Jean-Baptiste Le Moyne), 455, 456–58

Biggar, H.P., 295

Bigotes, 60–61, 65

Bischoff, Johann, 196

Bishop, William, 480

Bjarni Herjólfsson, 9–12, 13

Black Death, 9, 12, 17

Black Robes in Lower California (Dunne), 193, 208

Blackwell, George, 472, 479

Blakiston, Nehemiah, 500, 529

Blount, Richard, 480

Bobadilla, Francisco de, 27

Bodega y Quadra, Juan Francisco de la, 261

Bohemia Academy (Maryland), 541–42

Boisvert, Rapine de, 339

Boleyn, Anne, 467

Bolton, Herbert Eugene, 64, 66, 235–36, 257; and Anza's California expeditions, 235–36, 239, 241; on Font's Complete Diary, 241;

on Franciscan missions in Texas, 150, 153, 164, 165; on Jesuit mission system in western Borderlands, 180, 182, 250; on Kino, 180, 182, 188, 235, 250

Bons Amis circle, 365–66, 379, 388–89

Book of the Lover and the Beloved (Lull), 215, 216

Bordoy, Antonio, 153

Borgia, Francis, 87, 89, 91–92, 185, 303, 508

Borgia, Rodrigo, 17–18

Borica, Diego de, 262–63

Borromeo, Charles Cardinal, 288

Boscana, Gerónimo, 268

Bosque, Fernando del, 149–51

Bossuet, Jacques-Bénigne, 367, 381, 401

Boswell, James, 527

Boucher, Gaspard, 414

Boucher, Jeanne Crevier, 415

Boucher, Pierre, 413–17, 419–21; and Iroquois attacks on Three Rivers, 414–15; lobbying efforts and audiences with Louis XIV, 415–16; the seigneur of Boucherville (model community), 413–14, 419–21

Boudart, Katherine Mercier, 348

Boullé, Eustache, 280, 309, 320

Boullé, Nicolas, 309

Bourdon, Jean, 324, 384

Bourgeoys, Marguerite, 371–73, 424

Braddock, Edward, 540

Bras-de-Fer de Chateaufort, Marc-Antoine, 323–24

Bravo, Jaime, 192

Brazil, French in, 283–84, 312

Breakspear, Nicolas, 5

Brébeuf, Jean de, 413; Jesuit evangelization of Huronia, 315, 327–29, 343–44, 352–57; and Jesuits' return to Quebec, 314; martyrdom, 343–44, 352–57, 362; and Mother Catherine de Saint-Augustin, 409–10; mysticism, 354; reconnaissance expeditions in Huron country, 315, 327–28

Breen, T.H., 547

Bréhaut de L'Isle, Achille de, 323–24

Brendan the Voyager, 3–5, 13, 465

Brent, Catherine, OSB, 508

Brent, Fulke, 508

Brent, George, of Woodstock, 510–11

Brent, Giles, 485, 492–93, 508–10

Brent, Giles, II, 510

Brent, Margaret, 508–10

Brent, Mary, 508–9

Brent, Richard, 508

Brent, Robert, 541, 542

Brent family of Virginia, 508–11

Brésoles, Judith Moreau de, 373–74, 422

Brevis narratio (Le Moyne de Morgues), 86

Brevísima relación de la destrucción de las Indias (Las Casas), 27–28, 55

British North America, 469–73; Cabot's two voyages, 465–66; Chesapeake colonies, 497; Delaware, 507; legendary journey of Madog and Welsh settlers, 465; Maine, 523–25; Maryland colony, 463, 481–99, 500–507; New Jersey, 520–21; New York, 511–12, 521–23; Newfoundland ventures, 474, 475, 476–78; Parsons and the Winslade plan, 472–73; Pennsylvania, 513–19, 535–39; Virginia, 478, 507–11. *See also* Jesuits in British North America

Brittin, Lionel, 535

Brockholes, Anthony, 512, 520

Brooke, Robert, 500–502

Brooke, Thomas, 533

Brooke (Carroll), Elizabeth, 545–47, 549

Brothers Hospitallers (Montreal), 423

Brothers of the Common Life, 33

Brulé, Etienne, 318

Bryant, Sturgis and Company, 267, 273

Bucareli y Ursúa, Antonio María de, Viceroy: and Anza's California expeditions, 234–35, 237–39, 241, 256; and Chief Palma's request for Spanish-Yuma alliance, 256–58; and Serra's complaints about civil-military relations in Alta California, 222–23, 225, 234, 251; as viceroy of Alta California's Franciscan missions, 171, 222–23, 225, 232, 234–35, 237–39, 245, 256–58, 261

Buckingham, first Duke of (George Villiers), 475, 476

Bueno, José González Cabrera, 211–12

Buisset, Luc, 450

Bullion, Angélique Faure de, 339–40, 346, 349, 350, 371, 423

Burel, Gilbert, 314

Burgess, Anthony, xi

Burke, Edmund, 526–27

Burrón, Manuel, 223

Burrows Brothers Company (Cleveland, Ohio), 331

Burton, Mary, 522–23

Bustamente, Anastasio, 248

Byllynge, Edward, 520

Byrd, William, 468

Caballero y Ocio, Don Juan, 184

Cabeza de Vaca, Álvar Núñez, 44–53, 54, 75; defending the Indians from slavery, 51–53; early life, 45; as governor of Río de la Plata, 51–53; journey across the Borderlands, 48–53; as naked pilgrim, 47,

48, 50; *Narrative* (*La relación* and *La relación y comentarios*), 44–45, 47–51; Narváez expedition, 45–48, 73; portrayal of Indians, 47–50; religious healing ministry, 49–51, 53, 75

Cabot, John, 465–66

Cabot, Sebastian, 466

Cabrera, Juan Márquez, 105

Cabrillo, Juan Rodríguez, 59–60, 177

Caddo confederacy, 150

Cadillac, sieur de (Antoine de La Mothe), 154, 453–54

Caën, Émery de, 300, 312, 314, 315–16

Caën, William de, 300, 312, 326

Cahokia Mission (East Saint Louis), 397, 453

Cahuilla people, 244

Calderón, Gabriel Díaz Vara, 102–4

Calderón de la Barca, Pedro, 128

Califia, Queen, 54, 176

California. *See* Alta California (New Spain); Lower California (New Spain)

California Company, 267

Callières, Louis Hector de, 428

Calusa people, 87–88

Calvert, Benedict Leonard, fourth Lord Baltimore, 500

Calvert, Cecil, second Lord Baltimore, 475, 478–79, 481–99; Maryland colony and proprietorship, 463, 481–99, 516, 529–30

Calvert, Charles, fifth Lord Baltimore, 503

Calvert, Charles, third Lord Baltimore, 463, 465, 497, 503

Calvert, Frederick, sixth Lord Baltimore, 527

Calvert, George, first Lord Baltimore, 473–81, 548; Anglican background, 473–74; and the archpriest controversy, 480; conversion to Catholicism, 475–76; marriages, 474, 476, 479; Newfoundland ventures, 474, 475, 476–78; petition for a Virginia proprietorship, 478; promotion to Irish peerage, 476–77; proposal to bring English Jesuits to North America, 480–81, 489

Calvert, Leonard, 478, 481, 483–84, 485, 489, 491–94, 508–9

Calvert, Philip, 498

Calvert, William, 498

Calvinism, 284, 289, 301, 312–13, 315–17, 326, 473–74

Cambón, Pedro Benito, 226–28

Campa y Cos, Miguel de la, 205, 218

Campbell, John, second Duke of Argyll, 504

Campion, Edmund, 471

Campos, Joseph Agustín de, 229

Canary Islands: civilian settlers in New Spain's Texas province, 161–62, 163; conquest of Gran Canaria, 45; Menéndez armada departure, 68

Cancer de Barbastio, Luis, 55, 75–77

Cañizares, José, 209, 228

Cano, Juan Sebastián del, 176

Canzo, Gonzalo Méndez de, 97, 98

Cape Cod people, 279, 283

Capuchin Franciscans: French Canada, 311, 318, 325, 368, 448–49; Louisiana, 456–57

Carayon, August de, 331

Carbonariis, Giovanni Antonio de, 466

Cárdenas, García López de, 60–62, 115

Cardenas, Juan Inigo, 164

Carignan-Salières regiment, 403, 417–19, 420, 425

Carlos III: defense of Borderlands, 168, 254–55; Franciscan missions in New Spain, 206, 258; Jesuit missions in New Spain, 173, 183, 231; and New Orleans, 167; and Spain's Pacific ambitions, 261

Carmel mission at Monterey Bay, 218–20

Carmelites: English, 475, 476–77; Maryland Catholics, 540–41, 542; Vizcaíno expedition, 178, 218

Carolina colonies, 106–8, 154; Charleston, 107; Irish indentured servants, 506; Stone Rebellion in South Carolina, 521

Carranco, Lorenzo, 195

Carranza, Bartolomé, 470

Carroll, Anthony, 543–44, 545

Carroll, Charles, of Annapolis, 526, 527–28, 533, 539–40; delayed marriage, 527–28, 545–47; son Charles, 526–28, 545–47, 548, 549–50

Carroll, Charles, of Carrollton, 526–28, 543–50; Catholicism, 527; and his father, 526–28, 545–47, 548, 549–50; Jesuit education, 526, 541, 543–45; law studies, 498, 526, 547; libertinage, 527–28; mother, 527–28, 545–47, 549; philosophy studies, 543–45; return to Maryland, 548–50; Reynolds portrait, 526–28, 547, 550; search for a Catholic heiress, 548–50

Carroll, Charles, the Settler, 498, 500–505, 526, 532, 533, 542

Carroll, Daniel, 541, 542, 551

Carroll, Henry, 542

Carroll, James, 504, 539–40

Carroll, John, 542–43, 551–56; Grand Tour of Europe, 552–54; Jesuit education and career, 527, 528, 541, 542–43, 551–52; Maryland chaplaincy, 556

Carroll family, 516, 526–28, 533, 552

Cartier, Jacques, 81, 284–85, 296, 321

Carvalho, Paulo de, 554

Casa de Contratación (Seville), 22, 83–84, 111

Casañas, Francisco, 153

Casgrain, Henri, 331

Castañeda, Carlos E., 149

Castañeda, Pedro de, 62

Castaño de Sosa, Gaspar, 117

Castillo, Juan del, 89

Castillo Maldonado, Alonso de, 44, 47–50, 54, 58

Cathedral of Notre-Dame (Paris), 322, 336, 337

Catherine de Saint-Augustin, 408–10

Catherine of Aragon, 467

Catherine of Braganza, 496–97

The Catholic Calumet: Colonial Conversions in French and Indian North America (Leavelle), 446

The Catholic Church in Colonial Days (Shea), ix–x, xii, 74, 452

Catholic Emancipation Act (1829) (England), 556

Catholic Relief Act (1778) (England), 556

Catholic Revival (France), 382, 390; and founding of Montreal, 334–35, 350–51; and French Catholic humanism, 294–95, 300–301; and Gallicanism/ultramontanism, 390; and good relations with Huguenots, 294–95, 300–301, 306; and Laval, 365, 367; and Marie de l'Incarnation, 335, 382

Cazot, Jean-Joseph, 362

Ceballos, Francisco, 174–75

Ceballos, José, 165–66

Cecil, Robert, first Earl of Salisbury, 469, 473–74

Celestial Favors (*Favores celestiales*) (Kino), 188–91

Celtic Christianity, 3–5

Cermeño, Sebastián Rodríguez, 178

Cervantes, Miguel de, 128

Chabanel, Noël, 345

Chabot, Marie-Emmanuel, 410

Challoner, Richard, 505, 518, 523–24, 555

Champdoré, Pierre, 279

Champlain, Hélène Boullé de, 300, 308–10, 320

Champlain, Samuel, 280, 289, 295, 304, 319–20, 321, 337, 417; battle for Quebec, 318; conversion to Catholicism, 300; de Monts' first and second expeditions, 285–87; death, 319–20; final years and Catholic piety, 320; French Catholic humanism, 290–91, 293, 295; and the Huguenots, 300–301, 309, 318; and Jesuits in New France, 316, 320; marriage, 300, 308–10, 320; and Poutrincourt party's return to Port-Royal,

280, 297; recruitment of Recollects, 299–300, 306; writings, 290–91, 293, 295, 309

Champlain's Dream (Fischer), 280

Chapel of San Miguel (Santa Fe), 136–37

Charay people, 206

Charles Edward Stuart (Bonnie Prince Charlie, the Young Pretender), 514, 532

Charles I, 106–7, 317, 433, 463, 474–76; marriage to Henrietta Maria, 317, 475, 477, 490, 509–10

Charles II, 128, 432–33; and anti-Catholicism in England, 432–33, 463–64; Carolina colony, 106–7; Catholic friendly, 496–97; Penn's Quaker colony, 513

Charles V (Charles I of Spain), 34, 36, 37, 41, 81, 83; and Ayllón's Florida settlements, 72; and Cabeza de Vaca, 44; and Ponce de León's Florida settlements, 71; *Sublimis Deus* on mistreatment of Indians, 54, 75–76

Charlevoix, Pierre–François–Xavier de, 295, 397–400, 410–13, 430–31, 439, 445, 452–53, 458–59, 524; among the Natchez people, 397–99, 430–31; Enlightenment influences, 445–46, 452; *History*, 399, 439, 447, 459; Jesuit background, 399–400, 439, 445; *Journal*, 399, 421, 430, 439, 452, 456, 459; on New Orleans, 397–99, 456; in the Pays d'en Haut (Upper Country), 439–40; on Quebec City, 410–12, 439; and Sulpician Montreal, 421–22; on Three Rivers, 412–13; trek to French Canada, east to Great Lakes, and the lower Mississippi to New Orleans, 397–99, 452–53

Charon de La Barré, François, 423

Charton, François, 314

Chateaubriand, François-René de, 459

Châtel, Edmée, 373

Chauchetière, Claude, 447–48

Chaumonot, Pierre-Joseph-Marie, 332, 352, 438

Chefdeville, Abbé, 166

Chesapeake Bay: colonies of British North America, *497*; Jesuit mission, 89–90; Spanish claim, 72, 84, 89–90, 180

Chevrier, Pierre, the baron de Faucamp, 337, 338

Chicagou, Chief, 458

Chichimeca people, 115–16

Chicora, Francisco de, 72–73

Cholenec, Pierre, 447

Chomedey, Louise de, 372

Chumash people, 265, 271

Church of England (Anglican): and African slavery, 535; Elizabeth I's anti-Catholicism,

468; Fletcher and first services in North America, 179; High Church Anglicans and Catholic thought, 475–76; James I, 473–74; Maryland colony, 500–502, 529, 530–31, 539–40; Newfoundland ventures, 474, 475, 476–78

Church of Saint-Pierre de Montmartre (Paris), 332

Church of San Fernando (Texas), 163–64, 165, 169–70

Church of the Immaculate Conception (Santa Fe), 136–37

Church of the Immaculate Conception at Fort Louis, 455–56

A Church That Can and Cannot Change (Noonan), 34, 506

Cistercian Order of Calatrava, 36–37

Ciudad Rodrigo, Antonio de, 55

Claiborne, William, 483–84, 488–89, 491–95, 509

Clark, George, 522

Claros, Juan, 123

Clavigero, Francisco Javier, 199

Cleland, John, 527

Clement IX, Pope, 390

Clement VII, Pope, 81

Clement XI, Pope, 110

Clement XIII, Pope, 551–52

Clement XIV, Pope, 209, 362, 459, 553–55

Coahuila (Nuevo Estremadura), 149

Coke, Edward, 473

Coke, John, 482

Colbert, Jean-Baptiste, 378, 388–91, 402, 403, 415–16

Cole, Robert, 543

Colegio de Cristo Crucificado (Antigua), 155, 156

Colegio de Nuestra Señora de Guadalupe. *See* Apostolic College of Our Lady of Guadalupe at Zacatecas

Colegio de San Gregorio de Valladolid, 43

Colegio de Santa Cruz de Querétaro. *See* Apostolic College of Santa Cruz (Holy Cross) at Querétaro

Coligny, Gaspard de, 81–82, 86

Collectanea of the Society of Jesus in England (1882), 551

Coloma, Don Manuel, 528

Colorado River expeditions, 187, 203, 236

Columbus, Christopher, 26, 27

Columbus, Diego, 21, 28–29, 38, 39

Columbus, Fernando, 38

Comanche people, 136, 140, 141, 166–67, 188

Communauté des Habitants (Quebec company), 325, 369–70

Compagnie des Prêtres de Saint-Sulpice, 370, 371, 424–25

Company of Louisiana, 456

Company of New France (Company of One Hundred Associates), 300, 312, 313, 317–18, 319, 323, 325–26, 330, 332, 338, 349, 378

Company of Saint-Sulpice (Gentlemen of Saint-Sulpice), 286, 348, 370, 371, 389, 422, 423, 424, 446, 448

Company of the Holy Sacrament, 367

Company of the West, 431, 456

Comunero Revolt (1520), 45

Concepción, Pedro de la, 156

Concepción Argüello, Doña (Sister Maria Dominica), 249

Concepción de Ayubale (Florida), 109

Concepción Quijas, José Lorenzo de la, 270

Condé, prince of, 300, 309, 415–16

Condren, Charles de, 336, 367

Congrégation de la Sainte Vierge, 365

Congrégation de Notre-Dame de Montreal, 424; Notre-Dame Sisters of Montreal, 386, 421, 424

Congrégation de Notre-Dame in Troyes, 372, 373

Contreras, Juan de, 81

Convento San Francisco, 214–15

Conventual Franciscans, 116

Converting California: Indians and Franciscans in the Missions (Sandos), 214, 216

Coode, John, 500, 511, 512, 528

Cook, James, 261

Cooke, Ebenezer, 530

Cooper, John, 493

Copart, Juan Bautista, 182

Copley, Lionel, 465, 500, 529

Copley, Thomas, 490–91, 493, 498

Corbie, Henry, 543

Cordero, Manuel Rivero, 204

Córdoba, Pedro, 21–23, 30, 31, 43

Cornwaleys, Thomas, 485–87, 489, 490–91, 492

Coronado, Don Francisco Vásquez de, 55–67, 115, 177; Seven Cities expeditions and reconnaissance, 55–67; Zuñi rejection of, 60–63

Corpa, Pedro de, 97–98

Corry, John, 522

Cortés, Hernán, 45, 53, 117, 176

Cortés Moctezuma, Isabel Tolosa, 117

Costansó, Miguel, 204, 210–11, 218, 234

Coton, Pierre, 302, 304, 315, 316

Cotton, Robert, 474

Couillard, Guillaume, 310, 380

Couillard, Guillemette Hébert, 308, 310, 380

Council of the Indies (Seville), 51, 93, 207; and Anza's first overland expedition, 234; and Florida settlements and missions, 70–71, 72, 76, 106, 110; and Indian labor/enslavement, 22, 43, 55, 77; Las Casas' presentations, 31–34, 37–38; Laws of the Indies, 43, 55, 70–71, 77, 170, 196, 223, 229, 245, 252, 254, 255; sending Canary Islanders to settle Texas, 161

Council of Trent (1545–1563), 217, 248–49, 336, 381, 449

Council of Virginia, 306

Counter-Reformation: breakdown of Catholic-Huguenot détente, 312–13, 315–19; and Jesuits (ultramontane), 390–91; in New France, 300–301, 306, 312–19, 324, 390; and Philip II of Spain, 78; Richelieu's anti-Huguenot campaigns, 313, 316

Courcelle, Rémy de, 418

coureurs de bois (rangers of the forest), 323, 403, 422, 427, 435

Coxe, Daniel, 520

Cramoisy, Sebastien, 331

Creek people, 109

Crespí, Juan, 209–13, 218, 220, 255

Crespo, Don Benedict, 229

Croix, Carlos Francisco de, 173, 204, 205, 254

Croix, Teodoro de, 254, 258

Crolo, Catherine, 373

Cromwell, Oliver, 488, 494–95

Crookshanks, Alexander, 548

Crosby, Harry, 208

Crouch, Ralph, 541

Croy Seigneur de Clièvres, Guillaume de, 37

Crozat, Antoine, 456

Cruzado, Antonio, 264

Cruzate, Domingo Jironza Petriz de, 139, 151

Cullen, Fintan, 547

Culpeper, Lord (second Baron of Thoresway), 510

Cumaná colony (Pearl Coast), 35–42

Cusabo people, 98–99

Da Costa, Mathieu, 285

Dablon, Claude, 441, 443

Daniel, Antoine, 328, 343

Daniel, Robert, 108

Dare, Virginia, 14

Darnall, Henry, II, 504

Darnell, Henry, 502, 503

D'Aunay, Charles de Menou, 325

Dauversière, Jérôme Le Royer de la, 337–38, 340–41, 374, 423

Davaugour, Pierre Dubois, 370, 377, 415

Davion, Albert, 456

Davis, Natalie Zemon, 385

Davoist, Ambroise, 328

de Gourgues, Dominique, 92

de la Cruz, Antonio, 522

de la Cruz, Francisco, 93

de la Cruz, Juan, 63–64, 66

de la Cruz, Manuel, 149

de la Cruz, Sor Juana, 182

de la Guerra family of Santa Barbara, 273

de la Haye, Georges, 383

de la Roche, marquise, 285

de la Silva, Juan, 522–23

de la Tour, Charles de Saint-Étienne, 325

de la Vega, Francisco la Guerra y, 106

de la Warr, Baron (Thomas West), 507

De Legibus (Suárez), 35

de Monts, sieur (Pierre Du Gua), 279, 285–87, 288, 291–92; first and second expeditions to New France, 285–87, 288, 296; and French Catholic humanism, 279, 285–88, 290, 291–92; trading company, 300, 305

de Nobili, Roberto, 132, 133, 180

de Paul, Vincent, 333, 334, 336, 339, 367, 388

de Renty, baron (Jean Baptiste Gaston), 338

de Sales, Francis, 335, 336, 382

de Soto, Francisco, 51, 54; Florida expedition, 73–75, 99; insurrection at Cumaná, 41–42; lower Mississippi exploration, 74, 442

de Soto, Pedro, 470

Dedal, Adriaan Florensz, 33

Deerfield massacre (1704), 436–37, 524

La défaite des sauvages Armouchiquois (Lescarbot), 293

Delaware colony, 497, 507

Denonville, marquise de (Jacques-René Brisay), 434

Denys, Joseph, 391–92, 395

Descartes, René, 337

Descriptio insularum aquilonis (Adam of Bremen), 10

Description de la Louisiane (Hennepin), 450, 451

Dethunes, Exupère, 392

Detroit (Michigan), 453–54

devil and demons, French Catholics' beliefs in, 408–10, 445

dévot movement (New France), 290, 322–23, 330–41, 369, 371–72; Bons Amis circle, 365–66, 379, 388–89; and *Jesuit Relations*, 330–32, 333; Ville-Marie/Montreal, 322–23, 337, 339–40, 369, 371–72

Deza, Diego de, 31, 43

Dias de la Barrera, Don Ygnacio, 191

Díaz, Juan, 235

Díaz, Melchor, 177

Díaz de León, José Antonio, 171–72

Díaz de Salcedo, Antonio, 97

Dictionary of Canadian Biography, 279, 431

Dictionnaire de la langue huronne (1636), 319

Didacus of Alcalá, 211

Diego, García, 223

Diego, Juan, 145–46

Digges, Charles, 504

Digges, Dudley, 516

Digges, Ignatius, 534

Digges, John, 516

Diocese of Évreux (France), 364, 365, 379

Diocese of Guadalajara (Texas), 148, 162–63

Diocese of Monterrey, 171

Diocese of Quebec, 387–96, 400–402; Laval as first bishop, 386–96; Laval's creation of a cathedral chapter for Notre-Dame-de-Québec, 393–94; Laval's creation of permanent parishes, 389, 392–94; local devotions/saints, 374–75, 393–95; Saint-Vallier as bishop, 395–96, 400–402, 411, 423; Saint-Vallier's episcopal palace, 401–2, 411; Saint-Vallier's quarrels, 400–401

do Campo, Andrés, 63, 66–67

The Documentary History of New York (ed. O'Callaghan), 331

Dolbeau, Jean, 299, 339

Dolbeau, Nicolas, 339

Dollier de Casson, François, 322, 425–29; Iroquois ministry, 446–47; role in development of Montreal, 426–29

Dolores, Mariano de los, 169

Domínguez, Francisco Atanasio, 257

Dominican Friars Preachers: Bishop Altamirano's visit to Franciscan missions in Florida, 101–2, 104; Carlos III's reorganization of Alta California missions, 254–55; Española (Santo Domingo), 21–28, 31–35, 43; Florida missionary expeditions, 75–77, 79–81, 90; Las Casas, 42–43, 75–76; Lower California mission system, 220–22; millenarianism of de la Cruz, 93; Montesinos' campaign against Indian enslavement and genocide, 21–26, 30–34, 72–73, 75–78

Dominicus ac Redemptor Noster (1773), 199

Dongan, Thomas, 463, 511–12, 513, 535, 541

Dorantes de Carranza, Andrés, 44, 47–48, 54, 58

Doutreleau, Stephen, 431–32

Drake, Francis, 96, 178–79, 261

Druillettes, Gabriel, 357–60, 441

Du Fay, Polycarpe, 306

du Pont, Robert, 279

du Pont, sieur (François Gravé), 279, 288

Du Thet, Gilbert, 305–6
du Val, Jean, 280
Dubuc, Peter, 513, 535
Duchesneau, Jacques, 389, 428
Ducrue, Franz Benno, 175, 196
Dudley, Paul, 525
Dudouyt, Jean, 389, 393
Duglas, Valentin, 288, 290
Duhaut-Cilly, Auguste, 267
Dumas, Alexandre, 310, 475
Dunne, Peter Masten, 187, 193, 199, 208
Duns Scotus, John, 215–16
Duplessis, Marie-Andrée Regnard (Mère
    Marie-Andrée de Sainte Hélène), 411–12
Duplessis, Pacifique, 299
Duplessis de Mornay, Louis-François, 456
Dupré, Céline, 431
Durán, Narciso, 268, 274
Dutch West India Company, 512

East India Company, 474
Eccles, W.J., 378, 390–91
Echeandía, José María de, 265, 273
Echeverría y Orcolaga, Don Agustín de, 257–58
Edict of Nantes, 81, 289, 301, 312–13, 432–33;
    revocation of, 316, 432–33, 435, 510
Edmonds, Father (Virginia colony), 511
Edward VI, 467
Ehrman, Sidney M., 236
Einar Thorisson, 1
Eixarch, Tomás, 235, 240
El Paso settlement, 138, 139, 151
Eliot, John, 359
Elizabeth Farnese, Princess, 159
Elizabeth I of England, 83, 287; anti-
    Catholicism, 464, 467–68, 471–72;
    excommunication by Pope Pius V, 178–79,
    468
Ellerker, Thomas, 553–54
Eltonhead, William, 494
England. See British North America;
    Protestant England
English Civil War, 488–89, 491–94
English College at Douai-Rheims (France),
    470, 471, 505
English College in Rome, 470, 471, 472, 475,
    477, 479
Enlightenment: Charlevoix' influences, 445–
    46, 452; and evolution in Jesuit missionary
    approaches, 445–46; Franciscan mission
    system in Texas, 143–45, 146–47, 150, 155;
    Jesuits and, 173, 181, 189–90, 196–97, 400;
    and New Spain, 241–42, 251; and Sacred
    Congregation for the Propagation of the
    Faith, 143–46

Erasmus, Desiderius, 289, 449
Eric Gnupson, 1, 9
Eric the Red, 7, 8–9, 11, 15
Erondelle, Pierre, 294–95
Escalante, Silvestre Vélez de, 257
Escalona, Luis de, 63–64, 66
Escandón, José de, 221
Escobar de Sambrana, Diego, 96
Escobedo, Alonso, 97
Española (Santo Domingo), 21–28, 31–35, 43;
    Dominicans and abolition of Indian slavery,
    21–26, 30–34, 72–73, 75–78; massacre at
    Xaragua, 27–28, 29. See also Las Casas,
    Bartolomé de
Espejo, Antonio de, 116–19
Espinal, Alonso del, 22–23
Espinosa, Alonso Ignacio Benito, 231
Espinosa, Isidro, 157, 158, 160
Espíritu Santo (Mission Nuestra Señora del
    Espíritu Santo de Zúñiga) (Texas), 160–61,
    165
Espronceda, Juan Francisco de, 170
Esselen people, 264
Estebanico, 44, 48, 50, 54, 56–58
Estrada, Alonso de, 55
Estudillo, Rosario, 247
État present de l'Église de la colonie de la Nouvelle-
    France (Saint-Vallier), 395
Eudes, John, 336, 367
Eure, Ralph, 485
Evangeline (Longfellow), 538
La expulsión de los jesuitas de las provincias
    de Sonora, Ostimuri y Sinaloa en 1767
    (Pradeau), 208

Fages, Pedro, 210, 218, 221–22, 251
Faillon, Étienne-Michel, 363
Farmer, Ferdinand (Steinmeyer), 519–21
Faure de Berlise, Guichard, 339
Faveau y Quesada, Antonio, 204
Fawkes, Guy, 469
Fénelon, François, 401
Fénelon, François de Salignac de la Mothe-,
    425, 428, 429, 447
Fenwick, Cuthbert, 492, 498
Ferdinand of Spain, 22–23, 43, 70, 129, 142;
    and California island theory, 176; Las Casas'
    presentation at Council of Indies, 31–34
Ferdinand V, 167
Feria, Pedro de, 79
Ferland, Jean-Baptiste-Antoine, 363
Fernández de Oviedo, Gonzalo, 74
Fernández Pecha, Pedro, 33
Ferrer, Bartolomé, 177
Ferryland (Newfoundland colony), 474, 476–78

Feuillant Fathers (Tours), 382–83

Figueroa, José, 274

filles du roi (daughters of the king), 403–7, 424, 438

Fischer, David Hackett, 280, 293, 309, 323

Fitzhugh, William, 510–11

FitzRedmond, William, 504

Fléché, Jessé, 301, 303–4, 305

Fleet, Henry, 483–84

Flenley, Ralph, 426

Fletcher, Francis, 179

Florida, Spanish, 68–92, 80, 93–111; Apalachee people, 99–101; Ayllón and North Florida coast, 71–73; Bishop Tejada, 110–11, 148; bishops' visits, 101–4; chapels and churches, 97; de Soto's treatment of Indians, 74–75; Dominican missionary expeditions, 75–77, 79–81, 90; English attacks on Spanish missions, 96, 106–9, 111; and English Protestants, 78, 96, 106–9, 111; forced Indian labor, 77–78, 100–101, 104–5; Fort Caroline confrontation with French Huguenots, 68, 84–87, 284; forts and settlements, 71–75, 80; Franciscan diocesan structure, 69–71, 93–96, 102–6, 110–11; Franciscan mission networks, 93–111, 100; French Protestant Huguenot settlements, 68–69, 78, 81–87; Indian revolts and rebellions, 97–98, 99, 100, 105; Indian slavery, 72, 74–78; and the Inquisition, 95–96; Jesuit missions, 87–92; Menéndez expeditions, 68–69, 83–92; Saint Augustine, 68–92, 96–98, 101–9; Tejada and Diocese of Florida, 110–11, 148; Velasco's settlement at Point Saint Helena, 78–81; and the Wars of Religion, 81–87

La Florida (Escobedo), 97

Fogarty, Gerald, 511

Foley, Henry, 551

Fonseca, Juan Rodríguez de, 32–33, 37–38

Font, Pedro: Complete Diary, 241, 242, 243–46, 252; disputes with Anza, 242–43; as historian of Anza's second expedition, 240–46, 251–52

Foote, Cheryl, 132

Forbes, Alexander, 267

Fornel, Joachim, 393

Fort Caroline (Florida), 68, 82–87, 284

Fort Frontenac (Lake Ontario), 433, 434, 449–50

Fort Orange (Albany), 342, 353

Fort Rosalie, Natchez massacre at, 431, 457–58

Fort Saint Louis (Gulf Coast), 151–52, 165

Fort Sainte-Françoise (Quebec), 319

Fort Sainte-Marie-de-Grâce (Quebec), 319

Fort Saint-Louis (Quebec), 324, 333, 343–45, 392, 433

Fourier, Peter, 372

Foxe, John, 467

France: Catholic humanism, 279–98; Catholic-Huguenot relations and revocation of the Edict of Nantes, 316, 432–33; continental ambitions, 323; Counter-Reformation, 300–301, 306, 312–19, 324, 390; French Catholic beliefs in the devil and fallen angels, 408–10, 445; French-Indian attacks on the English in New England, 434–37; history of reconnaissance in New France, 283–87; incursions into New Spain's Borderlands, 151–52, 158, 160; intentions to establish a port on the Gulf of Mexico, 160; Quebec colony and conflicts with England, 316–19, 357, 401; rivalry with Protestant England for North America, 433–37, 454; and Spanish governance of New Orleans after Treaty of Paris, 167–68. See also New France

Francis, Pope, xii, 148, 213–14

Francis I, 81, 284

Francis of Assisi, 207, 213, 214, 215, 242, 255, 311

Franciscan explorations of southern edge of North America: Compostela and New Mexico, 59–60; Coronado and the Seven Cities reconnaissance, 55–67; Narváez expedition, 45–48, 73; Niza expedition, 56–59; and Quivira myth, 61, 66–67, 119, 128

Franciscans: devotions to Mary, 94, 127–28, 145–46, 153, 157, 216, 242, 269, 328; Enlightenment influences, 143–45, 146–47, 150, 155; explorations of southern edge of North America, 45–48, 55–67; millenarianism, 93–96, 105–6, 116; missionary colleges in New Spain, 146–47; missions in Alta California, 266; missions in Spanish Florida, 100; Observant, 32, 38, 116–17; and the Spanish Inquisition, 95–96, 119–20, 128, 129–30, 135. See also Capuchin Franciscans; Franciscans in Alta California; Franciscans in New France; Franciscans in New Mexico Borderlands; Franciscans in Spanish Florida; Franciscans in Texas Borderlands; Recollect Franciscans in New France

Franciscans in Alta California, 203–25, 231–34, 247–75, 266; architecture of mission churches, 263–67; Carlos III's Provincias Internas reorganization, 254–55; diocesan clergy and first ordinations, 248–49;

diocesan organization at Mission Santa
Barbara, 247–49; and Dominicans, 254–55;
final years, 267–75; first bishop (García
Diego y Moreno), 247–49, 265, 269–70,
273–75; first nun and girls' school, 249;
friars' rebelliousness and misbehavior,
269–70; Gálvez and the Sacred Expedition,
203–13, 218; Indian baptisms, 216; Indian
labor, 222, 271–72; Lasuén years as father
president, 259–63; and Mexican republic,
265, 268–69, 272–75; Neve's reglamento,
252–54; post-Jesuit expulsion, 175, 203–6,
208–9; Rivera's governance, 222–23,
224–25, 228–29, 245, 251; secularization of
the mission system, 272–75; Serra as father
president, 148, 214, 218–25, 227, 234,
250–54, 259–60; Serra's disputes with the
military, 221–25, 234, 250–54
Franciscans in New France: Capuchins, 311,
318, 325, 368, 448–49, 456–57; local
saints, 395; quarrels with Laval, 391–92;
Recollects, 299–300, 306–7, 313–14, 318–
19, 325, 368, 381, 391–93, 411, 448–52;
Saint Lawrence Valley, 299–300
Franciscans in New Mexico Borderlands,
115–41; churches and chapels, 130–31,
134; daily aspects of missions, 134;
diocesan structures, 116, 134; Indian
baptisms, 128–29, 134; Mariology, 127–28;
millenarianism, 116; missions among the
Pueblos, 119–21, 130–35; Observants, 116–
17; and Oñate, 119–21; Pueblo uprisings
against, 122–27, 135–40; and the Spanish
Inquisition, 119–20, 128, 129–30, 135
Franciscans in Spanish Florida, 93–111, 100;
Bishop Tejada and Diocese of Florida,
110–11, 148; bishops' visits, 101–4; chapels
and churches, 97; diocesan structure,
69–71, 93–96, 102–6, 110–11; English
Protestant attacks, 96, 106–9, 111; failures,
109–11; golden age, 102–6; Indian
bartering and food gifts, 105–6; Indian
labor, 100–101, 104–5; and Juanillo revolt,
97–98, 99; millenarianism, 93–96, 105–6;
Omnimoda of 1522, 70, 95, 116; Saint
Augustine, 96–98, 101–6; secular diocesan
clergy and religious clergy, 69–70, 93, 102;
and Spanish Inquisition, 95–96
Franciscans in Texas Borderlands: Church
of San Fernando, 163–64, 165, 169–70;
conversion rates, 148, 165; diocesan
structures, 148, 162–64; end of mission
system and secularization of missions,
171–72; Enlightenment influences,
143–45, 146–47, 150, 155; Fernandan,

146–48; first missions among the Tejas
people, 156–59; Indian labor, 163; legacy
and Catholic Texas, 169–70; Margil and
Zacatecan missions, 147, 148, 155–59,
170; midcentury expansion, 164–67;
mission system, 146–48, 153–54, 162–71;
missionary colleges, 146–47, 155; Our
Lady of Guadalupe devotions, 145–46,
153, 157; Querétarans, 146–48, 152–53,
154–55, 157, 165, 166, 169; reconnaissance
expeditions and founding encounters,
148–53; refoundation and renewal of
formal commitment, 153–54; and Treaty of
Paris, 166–71; Zacatecans, 146–48, 155–56,
157–59, 165, 166, 171
Franklin, Benjamin, 416, 515, 539
Frasquillo (Tano Indian), 138, 139
Fredin, Jean, 423
French, Freedom (Marie Françoise), 437
French and Indian War (Seven Years' War)
(1756–1763), 166, 515, 539
French Canada (Quebec colony), 299–429,
398; African slavery, 534; artisans' families,
402–3; brandy trade, 374, 376–77, 389–90,
421–22; Capuchin Franciscans, 311,
318, 325, 368, 448–49; Catholic Revival
influences, 294–95, 300–301, 306, 334–35,
350–51, 382, 390; Catholic-Huguenot
relations, 294–96, 300–301, 312–13, 315–
19; conflicts between France and England,
316–19, 357, 401; Counter-Reformation,
300–301, 306, 312–19, 324, 390; coureurs
de bois, 323, 403, 422, 427, 435; dévots
in, 290, 322–23, 330–41, 369, 371–72;
Diocese of Quebec, 386–96, 400–402;
disease epidemics, 352, 375, 376; domestic
life, 405–7; earthquake (1663), 377–78;
filles du roi (daughters of the king), 403–7,
424, 438; founding of Ville-Marie, 321–22,
325, 334–41, 346; Franciscan Recollects,
299–300, 306–7, 313–14, 318–19, 325, 368,
381, 391–93, 411, 448–52; French Catholic
humanism and foundation of, 279–98;
French settlement (1608), 321; governor
general Mézy, 378, 380; Hospitaller Sisters,
322, 332–34, 356, 368, 371–74, 383–84,
407, 408–10, 411–12, 422–23; Iroquois
attacks on French and their Huron allies,
342–63, 372–73, 414–15, 418–19, 433–35;
Jesuit evangelization of Huronia, 318–19,
327–30, 350–52, 438; Jesuit martyrdom,
342–45, 352–57, 362–63; Jesuits' first
Acadian missions, 301–6, 325, 524; Jesuits
in, 301–6, 313–16, 318–20, 322–34,
347–48, 350–63, 368–69, 438–39; Laval and

the Indians, 376–77; Laval as first bishop, 386–96; Laval as vicar apostolic, 364–80; Laval's disputes with Quebec's governors, 375–76, 378; local saints, 374–75, 393–95; marriages and family life, 307–10, 350, 402–7; Montmagny and, 323–25, 346, 349, 414; Notre-Dame-de-Québec, 393–94, 400; nuns, 332–34, 351, 381–87; Order of Malta, 311–12, 319, 323–25, 330; recruiting settlers and boosting population, 347, 349–50, 371–74, 402–7, 438; Richelieu's authority, 310–12, 314, 316, 318–19, 323–24, 350; Roberval-Cartier settlement, 284–85; Saint-Vallier as Laval's successor, 395–96, 400–402; seigneurial system, 313, 349, 406, 413–15, 419–21; Sulpician/Jesuit quarrels over vicar apostolic, 364, 368–71; Sulpicians, 421–29; trading companies (and fur trade), 300, 303, 316, 318–19, 323, 325–26, 421–22; Ursuline school for Indian girls, 332, 333–34, 384–86, 394; Ursulines, 327, 332–34, 351, 355–56, 368, 375, 381–87, 394–95, 405; women, 286, 347, 350, 371–74, 403–7. *See also* Diocese of Quebec; Montreal (Ville-Marie); Quebec City

French Catholic humanism, 279–98; and Catholic-Huguenot relations, 290, 294–96, 300–301, 306; de Monts, 279, 285–88, 290, 291–92; descriptions of the Indians of Arcadia, 292–95; founding of Quebec colony, 279–98; Lescarbot, 281–83, 287–98, 304, 316; Port-Royal settlement on Saint Lawrence River, 286–87; Poutrincourt, 279–82, 286, 287–93, 295–96, 303

French Oratory and Oratorians, 336, 382, 390

Freydís Ericsson, 1, 10, 15–17

Frías Salazar, Juan, 119–20

Frontenac, Comte de (Louis de Buade), 389, 391, 392, 401, 428, 435, 442

Fuentes, Brother (Spanish Florida expedition), 76

Fuentes, Pedro, 169–70

Fuller, William, 495

Furgler, Francis, the hermit of Burlington, 521

Fuster, Vicente, 224–25

Gadsden Purchase, 186

Gage, Charles, 512, 520

Gali, Francisco de, 177–78

Galinée, René Bréhaut de, 426, 446–47

Galinier, Dominique, 369, 425

Gallegos, Juan de, 73–74

Gallicanism, 364, 370–71, 374, 376, 387–88, 390–91

Galloway, Edward, 544

Gálvez, José de, 173, 203–8, 251, 257; administrative reforms, 204, 205–6, 207–8; mental instability and psychotic episodes, 206–8; Sacred Expedition (Franciscan entrada into Alta California), 203–13, 218

Gamache, marquise de (Nicholas Rohault), 332

Ganganelli, Lorenzo, 209, 553–54

Gannendaris, Celine, 385

Gannon, Michael V., 97–98, 104

Garcés, Francisco Tomás Hermeneglido, 232–37, 250, 259; and Anza's California reconnaissance expeditions, 235, 237, 240, 244; Franciscan background and missionary journeys, 232–33; and San Xavier del Bac, 232–33, 263; Santa Fe-Monterey route expedition, 257; and Yuma uprising, 258–59

Garceto, Juan, 41

García, Juan, 76–77

García de Trujillo, Rodrigo, 96

García Diego y Moreno, Francisco, 247–49, 265, 269–70, 273–75

Garnet, Henry, 469, 473

Garnier, Charles, 345

Garrick, David, 526, 531

Garza, José de la, 163, 170

Gaspar Melchior Baltasar de la Cerda Sandoval y Mendoza, conde de Galve, 139, 152

Gasteiger, Joseph, 196

Gastón, Juan Ignacio, 205

Gaudais, Louis, 378

Gaus people, 66–67

Gay, John, 531

Geiger, Matthew, 520

Geiger, Maynard, 102, 208, 213, 224, 263, 267–68

George I, 504

George III, 556

Gerard, Richard, 485, 496

Gerard, Thomas, 469–70, 485, 500

Gervase, Thomas, 482

Gibson, Edmund, 535

Giffard, Marie-Françoise, 411

Giffard, Robert, 402, 414, 420

Gifford, Bonaventura, 505

Giffs, Margaret, 490

Gilbert, Humphrey, 470

Gilby, Thomas, 355

Gilí, Bartolomé, 270

Giménez Fernández, Manuel, 28–29

Glandelet, Charles de, 401

Glorious Revolution (1688) and aftermath, 433, 500–507, 510–11, 514, 528–29, 532
Goddard, Peter, 408
Godefroy, Jean-Paul, 360, 402
Goldsmith, Oliver, 526
Gómez, Doña Josefita, 247
Gómez, Francisco, 73
Gómez, Fray Francisco, 210, 213
Gómez, Gabriel, 90
Gómez, Miguel, 248
Gondomar, Count (Diego Sarmiento de Acuña), 475
Goñi, Matías, 182
Gonneville, Binot Palmier de, 283–84
González, Manuel, 188
González, Tirso, 184, 185, 187, 188
González de Mendoza, Pedro, 32
Gonzalo, Francisco, 229
Gordillo, Francisco, 72
Gordon, William, 196
Gorry, Jean, 350
Gotter, John, 505
Goupil, René, 353, 354
Grace Cathedral (San Francisco), 179
Grajales, Don Martín Francisco López de Mendoza, 69, 70–71
Gran Chichimeca, 115–16, 117, 122
Granada (Spain), 26, 27, 129, 146
Le grand voyage du pays des Hurons (Sagard), 318–19
Grandier, Urbain, 408
Gravener, John (Altham), 482, 490, 496
Gravier, Jacques, 453
Great Lakes expeditions: Allouez's evangelical outreach, 439–41; Charlevoix, 439–40; French Jesuits in Pays d'en Haut and Illinois country, 439–41, 440; Recollect Franciscans Hennepin and La Salle, 449–52
Greaton, Joseph, 516–18, 536, 538
Green Bay, Wisconsin, 413, 441, 443, 454
Greene, Thomas, 485, 493
Greenland settlement, 1–2, 8–9, 17–18
Greer, Allan, 447
Gregory XIII, Pope, 336
Gregory XV, Pope, 143, 365–66, 390
Gregory XVI, Pope, 147
Grijalva, Pablo, 240
Grimaldi, marqués de, 204
Grisi, Benito, 192
Grollet, Jacques, 152
Groves, Sylvanus, 547
Guadalupe (Jesuit mission in Lower California), 193, 205
Guale people, 73, 98–99, 101–2, 107

Guaraní people of Paraguay, 51–53, 133, 230, 327, 438
Gudrid Thorbjarnardóttir, 8, 14
Gueiquesal people, 149–50
Guercheville, marquise de (Antoinette de Pons), 302, 303, 304–5
Guerin, Jean, 358–59
Guerra, Ana, 156
Guerra, Salvador de, 135–36
Guilday, Peter, 553
Guilford, Francis, 503–4
Guillén, Clemente, 192
Gunpowder Plot (1605), 468–69, 470, 472, 473
Gurlick, Nicholas, 500
Gutiérrez, Agustín, 522
Gutiérrez, Ramón A., 131, 135
Guyart, Marie. See Marie de l'Incarnation
Guzmán, Doña María Andrea, 184

Haakon the Elder, 9
Haakon the Good, 5
Hakluyt, Richard, 56, 179, 289, 295
Hakluyt's Voyages, 179
A Half-Century of Conflict (Parkman), 436
Hall, Benjamin, 504
Hamilton, Alexander, 531
Hammond, George P., 117
Hammond, John, 509
Hankey, Wayne, 422
Hanna, Edward J., 236
Hanna, James, 261
Harding, Robert, 519, 538
Hardy, Beatriz Betancourt, 534–35
Harlay de Champvallon, François II de (archbishop of Rouen), 364, 368, 370, 388, 389
Harmon, Johnson, 525
Harriman, Henry, 512
Harrison, William, 479
Hart, John, 504, 533
Hartnell, William, 273
Hartwell, Bernard, 493
Harvard College, 380, 525
Harvey, John, 478, 483
Harvey, Thomas, 512, 513, 520, 535
Hathersal, Thomas, 541
Hatton, Thomas, 494
Hawkins, John, 78, 82
Hawley, Jerome, 485
Hay, Daniel, 279–80
Hayes, Timothy, 490
Heath, James, 502, 503
Hébert, Louis, 279, 307–8, 402, 413
Hébert, Marie Rollet, 307–8, 310, 402
Helluland (Baffin Island), 9, 11–12

Hennepin, Louis, 448–52

Henri II, 284

Henri IV: and Champlain, 309; and Edict of
    Nantes, 301, 312–13, 432; expulsion and
    readmittance of Jesuits in France, 302;
    French Catholic humanism and Catholic-
    Huguenot relations, 290, 295, 301; and
    New France, 279, 281, 283, 285, 287,
    408

Henrietta Maria (Catholic queen), 317, 475,
    477, 490, 509–10

Henry III, 310

Henry IX, 554

Henry of Navarre, 289

Henry the Navigator, Prince, 37

Henry VII, 466

Henry VIII, 467, 489

Hermitage at Caen, 379, 389, 396

Herrera, Antonio de, 34–35

Hidalgo, Francisco, 153, 154, 156–57

Hidalgo, Nicolás, 135

Hieronymites, 33–34, 78

Hildreth, Joseph, 523

Hill, Clement, 504

Hiou, Anne, 373

Histoire de la Nouvelle-France (Lescarbot), 289,
    293–97, 298

Histoire de l'isle espagnole (Charlevoix), 458

L'histoire du Canada (Sagard), 318–19

*Histoire et description générale de La Nouvelle
    France* (Charlevoix), 399, 439, 447, 459

Histoire notable (Laudonnière), 83

*Histoire véritable et naturelle des moeurs et
    productions du pays de la Nouvelle France
    vulgairement dite le Canada* (Boucher),
    416–17

Historia de la Nueva México (Villagrá), 122

Historia de las Indias (Las Casas), 35, 39–40, 43

Historia de las Indies Occidentales (Herrera),
    34–35

Historia eclesiástica indiana (Mendieta), 93

Historia general y natural de las Indias (Fernández
    de Oviedo), 74

History of Alta and Baja California (Forbes), 267

*History of the Catholic Missions among the Indian
    Tribes of the United States* (Shea), 331, 422

History of the Discovery and Settlement of America
    (Robertson), 34–35

Hobart, Basil, 511

Hogarth, William, 527

Hollahan, Cornelius, 507

Hôpital Général (Montreal), 423

Hôpital-Général (Quebec City), 411–12

Hopkins, Gerard Manley, x

Horsmanden, Daniel, 521–22

Hospitaller Sisters in French Canada, 322,
    332–34, 356, 368, 371–74, 383–84, 407,
    408–10, 411–12, 448; Hôpital-Général
    (Quebec City), 411–12; Hôtel-Dieu
    (Quebec City), 362, 372, 375, 381, 389,
    408–9, 411–12; Montreal's Hospitaller
    Sisters of Saint Joseph, 322, 373–74,
    422–23, 427, 448; Mother Catherine de
    Saint-Augustin, 408–10

Hostell, Lambert, 196

Hôtel-Dieu (Montreal), 372, 422–23

Hôtel-Dieu (Quebec City), 362, 375, 381,
    389, 408–9, 411–12; Laval's residence, 375;
    Mother Catherine de Saint-Augustin, 408–9

Hôtel-Dieu at Dieppe, 333, 411

Houssart, Hubert, 396

Houston, Sam, 171

Howard, Francis (fifth Baron of Effingham),
    510, 511

Howe, Irving, xii

Hozes, Francisca de, 63

Hubert, Nicolas, 403

Hudson's Bay, 454–55

Hudson's Bay Company, 249, 267

Huet, Paul, 299

Hughson, John and Sarah, 522–23

Hughson's tavern (New York City), 522–23

Huguenots (French Protestants): and Catholic
    Revival, 294–95, 300–301, 306; Catholic-
    Huguenot relations in Quebec, 294–96,
    300–301, 312–13, 315–19; Champlain
    and, 300–301, 309, 318; and Counter-
    Reformation, 312–13, 315–19; Edict of
    Nantes, 81, 289, 301, 312–13, 432–33;
    and French Catholic humanism, 290,
    295–96, 301; Menéndez and confrontation
    at Fort Caroline, 68, 84–87, 284; north
    Florida settlements, 68–69, 78, 81–87,
    284; revocation of the Edict of Nantes,
    316, 432–33; Richelieu's anti-Huguenot
    campaigns, 313, 316; Saint Lawrence River
    and Canada expeditions, 284–85

Huízar, Don Pedro, 170–71

Humanae Vitae (Paul VI), xi

humanism. *See* French Catholic humanism

Hunter, George, 534

Hunter, William, 500–502

Huron people: apostate Hurons, 343–44;
    Brébeuf among the Bear People, 327–28,
    345; Brébeuf's reconnaissance expeditions,
    315, 327–28; epidemics and disease, 352;
    Iroquois attacks on, 342–63, 372–73;
    Iroquois destruction of Jesuit mission, 342–
    45, 348, 352–63; Jesuit evangelization of,
    318–19, 327–30, 350–52, 438; Jesuit mission

at Sainte-Marie-aux-Hurons, 328, 345; Recollect Franciscan ministries, 299, 307; Sillery mission (Jesuit), 330, 351, 353–54

Hutchinson, Thomas, 524, 525

Hyland, Nicholas, 542

I Moscoviti Nella California (The Russians in California) (Torrubia), 261

Ibarbo, Antonio Gil, 171

Iberian New Christians, 302–3

Iberville, Pierre Le Moyne d', 454–55

Iceland settlement, 2–3, 5–10

Icelandic Catholic Church, 8

Ignatius of Loyola, 87, 130, 217, 302, 354, 408, 496

Illinois people, 443, 444

Illius Fulciti (papal bull) (1504), 29

Imbert, Simon, 305

Immaculate Conception, doctrine of, 94, 128, 145–46, 216–17, 269, 328

Inama, Franz, 196

indentured servants (Maryland), 487–88, 504, 506, 529–30

Index of Forbidden Books, 128, 216, 367, 544–45

Indian labor and encomienda system: Cabeza de Vaca's opposition, 51; Española (Santo Domingo), 21–26, 30–34, 72–73, 75–78; forced labor and enslavement, 77–78, 100–101, 104–5, 126–27, 135; Franciscan missions in Alta California, 222, 271–72; Franciscan missions in New Mexico, 127, 134–36, 141; Franciscan missions in Spanish Florida, 100–101, 104–5; Franciscan missions in Texas, 163; Jesuit missions of Lower California, 183, 190; Lás Casas and campaign against, 26–43, 54–55, 75–78; Montesinos and campaign against, 21–26, 30–34, 72–73; New Laws of the Indies outlawing Indian slavery, 43, 55, 77. *See also* Indian slavery

Indian slavery: Dominicans and abolition on Santo Domingo, 21–26, 30–34, 72–73, 75–78; forced labor, 77–78, 100–101, 104–5, 126–27, 135; Las Casas' slaves, 26–27, 28; New Laws of the Indies outlawing, 43, 55, 77; Spanish Florida, 72, 74–78

Indies, Spanish Empire in: Española (Santo Domingo), 21–28, 31–35, 43; Las Casas and campaign against Indian enslavement, 26–43, 54–55, 75–76; Las Casas' first expeditions, 26–28; Montesinos and campaign against Indian enslavement, 21–26, 30–34, 72–73, 75–78. *See also* Council of the Indies (Seville); West Indies

Infante Jaime II, 215

Ingle, Richard, 491–93

Ingoli, Francesco, 143

Ingstad, Helge, 12

Innocent X, Pope, 366, 401

Innocent XI, Pope, 432

Inquisition, Spanish, 34, 129–30; and Franciscan evangelization of Pueblos, 119–20, 128, 129–30, 135; and Franciscan missions in Florida, 95–96; and Loyola, 302

Inscrutabili Divinae (papal bull) (1622), 143

Inter Caetera (papal bull) (1493), 81

Ireland: Delaware immigrants, 507; English Catholic colony in Antrim, 469; English Protestant colonization, 467; James II and, 464–65; Pennsylvania Irish population, 515, 517; redemptioners, 517

Iriarte, Juan Pedro de, 220

Iroquois people: Christianized Mohawks of the Montreal area, 447–48; Druillettes' idea for anti-Iroquois league, 357–60; Franco-Iroquois alliance, 515; French Catholic evangelization among the Five Nations, 446–47, 511, 515; French invasions to subdue, 418–19, 433, 434; French Jesuit ministries, 511, 515; Frontenac's negotiation of peace, 435; Jesuit martyrdom, 342–45, 352–57, 362–63; Lachine massacre (1689), 434, 436, 454; Mohawks, 342, 343, 346, 348, 353, 356, 360–62, 418–19, 447–48; Senecas, 342, 345, 433; Sulpician ministries, 446–47; war against the French and their Huron allies, 342–63, 372–73, 414–15, 418–19, 433–35

Irving, Washington, 236

Isabella, Queen, 27, 31, 32, 129

Islendinga Book (Ari Frode), 10

Iturbide, Agustín de, 268

Jacobite uprising (1745), 514–15

Jacques, Cristóvão, 284

Jager, Claude, 332

James, John, 518

James, Richard, 474

James Francis Edward Stuart (the Old Pretender), 504, 554

James I of England (James VI of Scotland), 316–17, 468–69, 472, 473

James II of England (Duke of York), 497, 505, 507, 511, 520, 532–33; defeat at Battle of Boyne, 464–65, 514; ousted from Protestant England, 464; pro-Catholic policies, 433, 463–65, 510, 513–14

James of Santiago, Saint, 127–28, 146

Jamestown settlement, 106–7, 282–83, 483, 508
Jamet, Denis, 299, 306–7
Jansen, Cornelius Otto, 401
Jansenism, 301, 401, 407, 453
Japan, Jesuit missions in, 180, 185, 327, 329–30, 351
Jaramillo, Juan de, 63
Jayme, Luis, 224–25, 245
Jeanne-Françoise de Saint Ignace, 411
Jenison, John, 548
Jesuit Collège de Clermont (Paris), 326, 361, 364, 365, 403
Jesuit Collège de La Flèche (Paris), 326, 337, 364, 365, 459
Jesuit college in Bruges, 543, 552, 554–55
Jesuit college in Liège, 518, 543, 555
Jesuit college in Quebec, 438–39, 541
Jesuit Collège Louis-le-Grand (Paris), 397, 400, 458, 526, 543–44, 547
Jesuit Relations: and Le Jeune, 327, 328, 331–32, 333, 334–35; publication history, 331; *Relation of 1654* and Marie de l'Incarnation, 381–83, 385, 387; story of Catholic Mohawks of Kahnawake, 447
Jesuits (Society of Jesus): anti-Jesuit Pope Clement XIV, 553–55; archpriest controversy, 479–81; China, 132–33, 180, 181–82, 366, 453; and the Counter-Reformation, 390, 551; and doctrine of the Incarnation, 180–81, 189; and the Enlightenment, 173, 181, 189–90, 196–97, 400, 445–46; expulsion from Paris (1762), 543; India, 132–33, 180, 181–82; Japan, 180, 185, 327, 329–30, 351, 366; martyrdom, 342–45, 352–57, 362–63; in Protestant England during Elizabethan persecutions, 470–73, 479–80; Reductions of Paraguay, 133, 180, 438; suppression and dissolution of the order, 95, 199, 209, 459, 551–55. *See also* Jesuits in British North America; Jesuits in French Canada; Jesuits in New France's interior frontier; Jesuits in New Spain
Jesuits in British North America: African slavery, 506–7, 534; Annapolis trial of Brooke and Hunter, 500–502; banishment from Maryland colony, 500–503; captured during English Civil War, 492–93, 509; Chesapeake region missions, 505–7; Delaware, 507; and Jesuit education, 541; Maryland colony, 480–82, 485, 489–93, 496, 500–503, 505–7; missions to local Indians, 496; New Jersey, 519–21; New York, 512, 519; Oxford College dons,

470–71, 505; Pennsylvania, 516–19, 538–39; property in Maryland, 480–81, 489–91, 496, 502–3, 506, 532; property ownership (mortmain), 480–81, 489–91; and suppression of the order, 555; Virginia, 508
Jesuits in French Canada, 301–6, 313–20, 322–34, 350–63, 368–69, 438–39; anti-Semitism against, 302–3; belief in the devil, 408, 445; Brébeuf, 315, 327–29, 343–44, 352–57, 362; Charlevoix, 397–400, 410–13, 439, 445, 452–53, 458–59; dévots, 330–32, 333; donnés (lay volunteers), 329, 375; evangelization of Huronia, 318–19, 327–30, 350–52, 438; first Acadian missions, 301–6, 325, 524; fur trade, 316, 323, 325–26; Iroquois destruction of Huronia missions, 342–45, 348, 352–63; Iroquois ministries, 511, 515; *Jesuit Relations*, 322, 326, 328, 330–32, 333, 342, 362, 381–83; Lalemant, 314–18, 320, 326–27, 337, 343–44, 356, 362; martyrs, 342–45, 352–57, 362–63; Montmagny's relations with, 324–25; Noyrot, 313–14, 316, 317–18; opposition to Saint-Villier, 453; Poutrincourt's resistance to, 301–6; quarrels with Sulpicians, 368–71; in Quebec, 313–16, 319–20, 323, 325–27, 347–48, 350–52; Quebec college, 438–39; at Sainte-Marie-aux-Hurons, 328, 345; Sillery mission, 330, 351, 353–54
Jesuits in New France's interior frontier, 439–46, 452–54; Allouez's evangelical outreach, 439–41; Charlevoix, 439–40; Enlightenment influence on missionary approaches, 445–46; exploration of Illinois country and the interior waterways/Mississippi River regions, 441–45; Jolliet-Marquette party, 442–44; missions in Great Lakes region (Pays d'en Haut and Illinois country), 439–41, *440*; New Orleans, 457; Ottawa mission in Illinois homeland, 441
Jesuits in New Spain: case for exemption from tithes, 196; challenges and dificulties, 192, 197–99; Chesapeake Bay massacre, 89–90; expulsion/removal, 173–75, 199, 203–6, 208–9, 231; farming and stock raising projects, 186–87, 190; Kino and Pimería Alta missions, 181, 182–83, 186, 190–91, 229–31; Lower California, 95, 173–75, 180–99, *198*, 229–31, 250; Menéndez expeditions, 87–92; missionary model and mission system, 87, 95, 180–94, 229–30; post-1734 generation and renewed mission efforts, 196–99; post-expulsion transition

to Franciscan missions, 175, 203–6, 208–9; pre- and postsuppression histories and memoirs, 199; relations with Indians in the Borderlands, 175, 182–83, 190–91, 194–96, 203, 229–31; Spanish Florida, 87–92

The Jesuits in North America in the Seventeenth Century (Parkman), 327, 331

Jesús, Juan de, 138

Jesús, Simon de, 138

Jesús Pico, Pío de, 275

Joan of the Angels, Mother, 408

Jogues, Isaac, 342–43, 348, 352–54, 356–57

John of the Cross, 355, 382

John Paul II, Pope, 146, 148

Johnson, Samuel, 526–27

Jolliet, Louis, 442–44

Jón Árnason (Smyrill), 2

Jones, Hugh, 542

Jonquet, Etienne, 308

Journal de Trévoux, 458

Joyce, James, xii

Joyeuse, François de, 299

Juanillo revolt, 97–98, 99

Juchereau, Jeanne-Françoise, 411–12

Julime people, 151

Julius II, Pope, 45

Jumano people, 151

Junta Magna (1568), 70, 95–96, 116

Kahnawake (Christianized Mohawk village), 447

Karankawa people, 160–61, 166, 171

Keats, John, 176

Keller, Ignacio Xavier, 230

Kellogg, Louisa Phelps, 452, 459

Kelly, Margaret, 507

Kent Island (Chesapeake Bay), 488–89, 491–92, 496, 508

Kerry, Margaret (Peggy), 522, 523

King George's War (1744–1748), 166, 539

King Philip's War (1675–1676), 136, 137, 360

King William's War (1689–1697), 166, 434–35, 539

Kino, Eusebio Francisco, 180, 181–91; and Catholic New France, 188–89; *Celestial Favors*, 188–91; China mission, 181–82; early life and Jesuit studies, 181–82; Jesuit missions of Lower California and Pimería Alta, 181–91, 208, 229–30, 249–50; and Salvatierra, 180, 181, 182–86; search for land route to Lower California, 187, 203

Kino's Historical Memoir of Pimería Alta, 188

Kirke, David, 317, 318

Kirke, Jarvis, 317, 318

Knatchbull, Robert, 533

Knights Hospitaller of Saint John of Jerusalem, 36–37

Knights of Malta (Order of Malta), 171, 180, 222, 311–12, 319, 323–25, 330

Knights of the Golden Spur, 36–37, 39

Knights of the Order of Santiago, 53, 83, 262

Knights Templar, 173

Kumeyaay people, 209–10, 223–25, 260

La Barre, Joseph-Antoine Lefebvre de, 433–34

La Chaise, François de, 389–90, 401

La Motte de Lucière, Dominique, 450

La Peltrie, Marie-Madeleine de Chauvigny de, 375; marriage, 333–34, 379, 384; Montmagny expedition to found Ville-Marie settlement, 321–22, 334, 341, 346–47; and Ursulines of Quebec, 321, 332–34, 351, 383, 384–85, 394

La Pointe du Saint-Esprit (Lake Superior), 440–41

La Purísima Concepción (Lower California), 186, 193, 205, 230, 258–59, 264–65

La Purísima Concepción (Texas), 157–58, 163, 164, 165

La Ribourde, Gabriel de, 391, 450, 451

La Rue, Pierre de, 545

La Salle, sieur de (Réne-Robert Cavelier), 151–52, 444–45; and Catholic evangelization among the Iroquois, 446–47; discovery of Niagara Falls, 450; establishment of Fort Saint Louis, 151–52; expedition with Hennepin and Recollect Franciscans, 448–52; Mississippi valley and French Louisiana, 151–52, 444–45

La Salle and the Discovery of the Great West (Parkman), 451

Labazares, Guido de, 79

Lachine massacre (1689), 434, 436, 454

Ladan, Adrian, 392

Lafitau, Joseph-François, 445–46

Lafora, Nicolás de, 168

Lahontan, Louis-Armand de Lom d'Arce de, 404, 433, 439

Laínez, Diego, 302

Lalande, Jean, 342–43, 348, 356

Lalemant, Charles, 314–18, 320, 326–27, 337, 343–44, 356, 362; breakdown of Catholic-Huguenot détente, 315–16; and founding of Montreal, 338, 339; Jesuit education, 326; Jesuits' return to Quebec, 314, 326–27; martyrdom, 343–44, 356, 362

Lalemant, Jérôme, 352, 356, 358, 450

Lambert, Florentin, 416

Lamberville, Jacques de, 448

Langford, John, 485

Lapérouse, comte de, 260
Laplace, Cyrille, 269
Lara, Casimir López de, 164
L'Archevêque, Jean, 152
Larios, Juan, 149–51
Larkin, Thomas Oliver, 273
Las Casas, Bartolomé de, 23, 26–43, 54–55;
    and African slavery, 34–35, 36, 37;
    becoming a Dominican Friar Preacher,
    42–43; Cumaná venture (utopian colony),
    35–42; Dominican campaign against Indian
    enslavement, 26–43, 54–55, 75–78; first
    expeditions to the Indies, 26–28; Indian
    slaves of, 26–27, 28; and Narrative of
    Cabeza de Vaca, 47; ordination, 28–29;
    presentation to Ferdinand, 31–34; and
    Sublimis Deus on mistreatment of Indians,
    54, 75–76
Lascaris d'Urfé, Françoise-Saturnin, 425
Lasuén, Fermín Francisco de, 223, 252–53,
    259–63
Laud, William, archbishop of Canterbury, 475,
    491
Laudonnière, René Goulaine de, 82, 83, 293
Lauson, Charles de, 379, 393
Lauson, Jean de, 338, 415
Laval, François de (François-Xavier de
    Montmorency-Laval), 364–68, 400; arrival
    in New France, 368, 379; and Bons Amis
    circle, 365–66, 379; and the brandy trade,
    374, 376–77, 389–90; and the Catholic
    Revival, 365, 367; creation of a Quebec
    seminary, 378–80; death, 400; disputes
    with Quebec's governors, 375–76, 378; as
    first bishop of Diocese of Quebec, 386–96;
    and the Indians of Quebec, 376–77; Jesuit
    clerical career, 365; and Jesuit missions in the
    interior frontier, 440–41; as Monseigneur
    L'Ancien, 374, 396, 400; and Montmorency
    family, 364–65; and the Recollect
    Franciscans, 391–92; as secular clergy, 365,
    366, 368, 371; successor, 395–96, 400–402;
    and Sulpician/Jesuit quarrels over the vicar
    apostolic, 364, 368–71; and the Ursulines,
    386–87; as vicar apostolic, 364–80
Laverdière, C. H., 331
Law, John, 399, 456
Laws of Burgos, 22–26, 69
Laws of the Indies, 70–71, 170, 196, 254; on
    civil settlements and churches/missions,
    70, 223, 229, 245, 252, 255; New Laws
    outlawing Indian slavery, 43, 55, 77
Lazaga, Juan de, 256
Le Ber du Chesne, Jean, 423
Le Ber du Chesne, Pierre, 423

Le Blond de la Tour, Pierre, 456
Le Boesme, Louis, 441
Le Caron, Joseph, 299, 307, 308, 310, 319
Le Clerc, Alix, 372
Le Clerc, Jacques (Pie de Palo), 83
Le Clercq, Maxim, 166
Le Gardeur de Tilly, Charles, 402
Le Gaudier, Antoine, 326
Le Jeune, Oliver, 310
Le Jeune, Paul, 300, 337, 416; and the
    Catholic Revival, 334–35; and Champlain,
    300, 319–20; and Jesuit missions in
    Huronia, 328; and the Jesuit Relations, 327,
    328, 331–32, 333, 334–35; and Jesuits'
    return to Quebec, 319–20, 327
Le Jumeau, Renée, 422
Le Maistre, Jacques, 425
Le Moyne, Charles, 350, 454
Le Moyne, Simon, 360–62
Le Moyne de Morgues, Jacques, 86
Le Normant de Mézy, Sébastien-François-
    Ange, 545
Le Roy, Henri, 392
Le Sueur, Jean, 384
Leavelle, Tracy Neal, 446
Leclerc du Tremblay, François (Father Joseph
    of Paris), 311
Legauffre, Thomas, 348
Legazpi, Miguel López de, 177
Leglay, Claude, 338
Leif Ericsson (son of Eric the Red), 1, 2–3, 7,
    10, 11–13, 17, 132
Leisler, Jacob, 512
Lenox, James, 331
Leo X, Pope, 81
León, Alonso de, 152–53
León, Juan Recio de, 161, 170
Leroux, Valentin, 391–92
Léry, Jean de, 293
Lescarbot, Marc, 281–83, 287–98, 304, 316,
    417; French Catholic humanism and
    settlement of New France, 287–98, 304,
    316; Histoire de la Nouvelle-France, 289,
    293–97, 298; and Jesuits of New France,
    304, 316; life and education, 288; poem
    "Adieu à la France," 291–92; at Port-
    Royal, 281–83, 290–91, 293, 297–98; The
    Theater of Neptune masque, 281–83, 288,
    297, 301
Lesdiguières, duchesse de, 399, 458
Leutze, Emanuel, 483
Lewger, John, 492–93
Lewis, William, 485, 494
Lewis and Clark expedition (1803–1806), 235,
    397

Leyva de Bonilla, Francisco, 117, 119
Liancourt, marquise de, 339, 349
libertinage, eighteenth-century, 527–28
Life and Times of Fray Junípero Serra (Geiger), 208
Lilly, Samuel, 516
Linares, Gertrudis, 243
Linares, Pedro de, 90
Linares, Salvador Ygnacio, 243
Linck, Wenceslaus, 175, 196
Lingendes, Claude de, 342
Llewellyn, John, 498
Llorens, Juan Bautista, 263
Lloyd, Philemon, 533
Loaysa, Alfonso de, 22–23
Locke, John, 544
Lodowick, Dom Laurence, 508
Logan, James, 536
Longfellow, Henry Wadsworth, 538
Longville, Thomas, 477
Lope de Vega, Félix, 128
López, Baltazar, 98, 99
López, Diego, 62
López, Francisco, 116–17
López, José Francisco, 171
López, Juan, 76
López, Melchor, 155
López, Nicolás, 151
Lorenzana, Francisco Antonio, 207
Los Adaes (Texas), 160–61, 164, 168–69, 171
Los Angeles (California), 249, 250, 255–56
Loudon, Earl of (John Campbell), 538
Loudun incident of mass hysteria (1633), 408
Louis XIII, 300, 313, 317
Louis XIV: and Boucher, 415–16; and Catholic New France, 323, 364, 387–88, 390, 401, 402, 415–16, 423, 424, 433–34, 444; and the Huguenots in France, 432; and Saint-Vallier as bishop of Diocese of Quebec, 401; and War of Spanish Succession, 456
Louis XV, 543
Louisiana (French), 107, 154, 158, 166–67, 397, 444–45, 454–58; Charlevoix on, 397–99, 456; Iberville's explorations, 454–55; La Salle and, 151–52, 444–45; New Orleans, 455–58; Palatinate German Catholics, 517; reliance on African slaves, 456, 457; Spanish governance and French settlers' revolt, 167–68; Treaty of Paris and ceding to Spain, 166–67
Lowe, Richard, 482
Lower California (New Spain), 95, 173–99, *174, 198*; Dominican mission system, 220–22; Indian labor, 183, 190; Indian resistance and rebellions, 185, 186, 194–96, 203, 229–31; Indians' amenability to evangelization and Hispanicization, 191, 193–94, 229–30; Jesuit farming and stock raising projects, 186–87, 190; Jesuit missions, 95, 173–75, 180–99, *198*, 229–31; Jesuit missions of Pimería Alta, 181, 182–83, 186, 190–91, 229–31; Jesuit missions post-1734, 196–99; Jesuit-Indian relations, 175, 182–83, 190–91, 194–96, 203, 229–31; Jesuit's expulsion and removal, 173–75, 199, 203, 208–9, 231; Kino, 181–91, 208, 229–30, 249–50; Kino's search for land route, 187, 203; Mission San Xavier del Bac, 186, 229–31, 250; Northern Pima people, 182–83, 229–31, 249–50; Santa Rosa/Todos Santos, 192–93, 194–95, 205; transition from Jesuit to Franciscan missions, 175, 203–6; Tubac presidio founding, 230–31
Lull, Raymond, 215
Lullian University (Palma de Mallorca), 214–15
Luna, Pedro de, 106
Luna y Arellano, Tristán, 79–80
Luxembourg, Marie Liesse de, 314

Macé, Catherine, 373, 422
Macé, René, 374, 422
Maclin, Marguerite, 373
Madog ab Owain Gwynedd, 465
Magellan, Ferdinand, 176
Maier, Pauline, 546
Maillet, Marie, 373–74, 422
Maine, 523–25; Acadia border disputes, 524–25; early plans for English Catholic colony, 470
Maintenon, marquise de (Françoise d'Aubigné), 388, 401
Maisonneuve, sieur de (Paul de Chomedey): defense against Iroquois attacks, 346–47, 348–49; governor of Ville-Marie/Montreal, 322, 334, 338–39, 340–41, 346–47; Montmagny expedition to found Ville-Marie, 321–22, 334, 340–41
Majorca, 214–15
Maldonado, Rodrigo, 61–62
Maleta, Pedro, 142
Malspina, Alejandro, 260
Mance, Jeanne, 321–22, 339–41, 427; as female dévot and hospital volunteer, 339; founding hospital at Ville-Marie, 321–22, 334, 339–41, 346, 349, 350, 371–74, 422; Montmagny expedition and founding of Ville-Marie/Montreal, 321–22, 334, 339–41

Manners, Matthias (Sittsenberger), 519, 545

Mansell, Thomas (Harding), 502–3

Mar, Earl of (John Erskine), 504

Marefaschi, Cardinal, 554

Margil de Jesús, Antonio, 147–48, 155–59, 170, 218

María de Ágreda (María de Jesús Coronel), 127–28, 152, 216–17

María de Toledo, 28–29

Marie de l'Incarnation, 344, 355, 381–87; Catholic Revival influences, 335, 382; devotion to the Sacred Heart of Jesus, 382; dream visions, 381–82, 383; her son Claude Martin, 377, 381–82, 386–87; and *Jesuit Relations of 1654*, 381–83, 385, 387; and Laval, 375, 386–87; letters, 377, 381, 385, 386–87; life, background, and marriage, 382; as local saint of Quebec, 394–95; on Tracy, 417, 419; Ursuline school for Indian girls, 333–34, 384–86

Marie de Saint Bonaventure de Jésus, 332–33, 383, 411

Marie de Saint Ignace, 332–33, 356, 383

Marie de Saint Joseph, 332–33, 383, 394–95

Marillac, Louise de, 339

Marlborough, first Duke of (Lord John Churchill), 464

Marmolejo, María, 45

Marquette, Jacques, 441, 442–44

Márquez, Diego, 119

Márquez, Gerónimo, 128

Márquez, Juan Menéndez, 107

Marrón, Francisco, 96–97

Martin, Dom Claude, 377, 381–82, 386–87

Martin, Felix, 331

Martín, Francisco, 65

Martín, Pedro, 81

Martínez, Alonso, 121, 123, 127

Martínez, Esteban José, 261–62

Martínez, Pedro, 89

martyrdom, Jesuit, 342–45, 352–57, 362–63

Mary, Franciscan devotions to: doctrine of the Immaculate Conception, 94, 128, 145–46, 216–17, 269, 328; early Spanish expeditions and La Conquistadora, 146; in New Mexico Borderlands, 127–28; Our Lady of Guadalupe, 145–46, 153, 157, 242; in Spanish Florida, 94; Texas Borderlands, 145–46, 153, 157

Mary, Queen of Scots, 83, 284, 287, 467–68, 469

Mary of Modena, 463

Mary of Orange (Mary II of England), 433, 463–65

Mary Stuart, Queen of Scots, 83, 284, 287

Maryland colony, 463, 481–99, *497*, 500–507, 528–35, 539–43, *552*; African slaves, 506–7, 528, 529–30, 534–35; Anglican, 500–502, 529, 530–31, 539–40; Annapolis culture, clubs, and entertainment, 531; anti-Catholic crusades and legislation, 465, 488–89, 491–95, 500–505, 528, 532, 539–40; Brent family, 508–10; Carroll family, 516, 526–28, 533, *552*; Catholic communities on the Eastern Shore, 502–3; Catholic restoration of the early 1700s, 503–4; Claiborne's attempts to end the hereditary proprietorship, 488–89, 491–95; clergy and connection to Catholic Europe, 540–41; corn cultivation and exports, 486–87, 488; disease and health, 487–88, 496; early local economic development, 486–87; elite property interests and property ownership, 532; English Civil War (Plundering Time), 488–89, 491–94; English manor gentry and Catholic elite, 485–87, 490, 529, 531–35, 541–42; first Catholic settlers, 482–88; founding and first governor Calvert, 463, 481–99, 516, 529–30; fur trade, 486; Glorious Revolution and aftermath, 500–507, 528–29, 532; governor Leonard Calvert, 481, 483–84, 485, 489, 491–94, 508–9; indentured servants, 487–88, 504, 506, 529–30; Jesuit property ownership, 480–81, 489–91, 496, 502–3, 506, 532; Jesuits, 480–82, 485, 489–93, 496, 500–503, 505–7, 540, 541–42; local Indians, 483–84; manorial era settlements, 495–96; Pennsylvania-Maryland border dispute, 515–16; Protestant seizure and banishment of Catholics (1689), 465, 500–502, 528–29; Puritans, 493–95; Quakers, 529; religious freedom, 463, 481–82, 493–94, 528–29; reorganization as royal colony, 528–29; Saint Mary's City, 484, 489, 492, 495–99, 500, 528–29; students' Catholic educations, 541–43; tobacco cultivation and export, 486–87, 488, 530–31; Toleration Act (1649), 463, 493–95, 499, 528, 532; trial of Jesuits Brooke and Hunter, 500–502

Maryland Toleration Act (1649), 463, 493–95, 499, 528, 532

Mason-Dixon Line, 515–16, 524, 535

Massachusetts, 358–59, 524–25

Massanet, Damián, 152–53

Massé, Enemond, 304, 306, 314, 337

Mateos, Bartolomé, 81

Mather, Cotton, 412

Matienzo, Tomás de, 43

Matthews, John, 500

Mazarin, Jules Cardinal, 323, 348, 367, 388
McGuire, Thomas, 520
Medici, Allesandro de', 288
Médicis, Catherine de, 81–83, 307–8
Médicis, Marie de, 304, 313, 330
Medina, Alonso de, 43
Megapolensis, Jan, 361
Meléndez, Doña María, 99
Melgosa, Pablo de, 62
Membré, Zénobe, 166, 450
Mémoires de septentrionale (Lahontan), 404
Memorial de los abusus (Las Casas), 28
Ménard, René, 440
Méndez, Juan Bautista, 90–91
Mendieta, Gerónimo de, 93, 105
Mendizábal, Bernardo López de, 130
Mendoza, Don Antonio de, 53–67, 76, 115, 177
Mendoza, Don López de, 89
Mendoza, Juan Antonio de, 231
Mendoza, Juan Domínguez de, 151
Mendoza, Manuel de, 109
Menéndez de Avilés, Pedro, 117; and
    Chesapeake Bay, 72, 84, 89–90; Florida
    expeditions, 68–69, 83–92; and Fort
    Caroline, 68–69, 82–87, 284; founding
    Saint Augustine, 68–69, 107; and Jesuit
    missions in Spanish Florida, 87–92; life of,
    83–84
Meras, Solis de, 85
Mercado, Lorenzo, 156
Mercado, Vásquez del, 270
Mercier, Jean-Paul, 453
Le Mercure de France (Paris newspaper), 399
Merici, Angela, 381
Merlac, André-Louis de, 401, 407
Merritt, William, 512
Mesa, Bernardo de, 23–26
Metézeau, Clément, 382
Mexía, Juan Ruíz, 109
Mézy, Augustin Saffray de, 378, 380
Michel, Jacques, 317, 318
Micheltorena, Manuel, 274
Michilimackinac (Michigan's Upper
    Peninsula), 441, 443, 450–51
Middendorff, Bernhard, 231
Miera y Pacheco, Bernardo, 257
Migeon de Branssat, Jean-Baptiste, 428
Mi'kmaq people (Souriquois Confederacy),
    376; baptisms, 303–4; and the French
    humanists of Port-Royal, 281, 287, 298,
    301; the sagamore Membertou, 280–81,
    298, 301, 303–4, 305
millenarianism, Franciscan, 93–96, 105–6, 116
Miller, Henry M., 499
Miller, Perry, xii

Miranda, Ángel de, 109
Miranda, Pedro de, 135
Miruelo, Diego, 46
Mission Dolores (Jesuit mission of Lower
    California), 182–83, 185, 186, 205
Mission Dolores (San Francisco de Asís) at
    San Francisco Bay, 223, 226–29, 264, 269;
    Anza's expedition and establishment of a
    presidio and mission, 226–29, 245–46
Mission Dolores de los Ais (Texas), 159
Mission Nuestra Señora de la Candalaria de la
    Tama (Florida), 106
Mission Saint-François-Xavier (Wisconsin),
    443, 444
Mission Santiago (Lower California), 195, 205
Mississippi valley explorations (New France),
    441–45, 452–58; Charlevoix' trek to
    the lower Mississippi and New Orleans,
    397–99, 452–53; Fort Saint Louis,
    151–52; French Louisiana, 151–52, 454–58;
    Iberville, 454–55; Jesuits, 441–45, 452–53;
    Jolliet-Marquette party, 442–44; La Salle,
    151–52, 444–45; New Orleans founding,
    455–58
Mixtón War, 115
*Moeurs des savages Américains comparés aux
    moeurs des premiers temps* (Lafitau), 445
Mohawks of the Iroquois Confederacy, 342,
    343, 346, 348, 353, 356, 360–62, 418–19;
    story of Catherine Tekakwitha, 447–48
Molína, Miguel, 166
Molyneux, Robert, 519
Monaco, Joseph Mary, 111
Monastery of Belém in Lisbon, 33
Monastery of Saint Jerome outside Madrid, 33
Monastery of San Lorenzo del Escorial outside
    Madrid, 33
Monastery Yuste in the province of
    Guadalajara, 33
Montagnais people, 299, 330, 358
Montalvo, Garci Ordóñez de, 54, 176
Montáñez y Patiño, Don Juan de Ortega
    Cano, 184
Monterey (California): Anza expedition and
    journey to San Francisco, 226–28, 245–46;
    development and home architecture, 273
Monterey Bay: Carmel mission, 218–20;
    search for, 204, 210–12, 218; Vizcaíno
    expedition, 178, 210–11
Montero, Don Gerónimo, 195
Montesino, Alonso Gómez, 125
Montesinos, Antonio de: and Ayllón's north
    Florida expeditions, 72–73; campaign
    against Indian enslavement and genocide,
    21–26, 30–34, 72–73, 75

Montesinos, Reginaldo de, 34

Montesquieu (Charles-Louis de Secondat), 544–45

Montielo, María Ana, 259

Montigny, François Jolliet de, 456

Montizambert, Edward Louis, 416

Montmagny, Charles Huault de: expedition party to found Ville-Marie/Montreal, 321–22, 341, 414; at Fort Saint-Louis, 324; governance of Quebec as Knight of Malta, 323–25, 349; Quebec colony, 323–25, 346, 349, 414; relations with Jesuits, 324–25

Montmorency, Charlotte-Marguerite de, princesse de Condé, 339

Montmorency, Henri II duc de, 314

Montmorency, Mathieu de, the Great Constable of France, 364

Montreal (Ville-Marie): African slavery in, 534; Bourgeoys' educational work and school, 371–73; Brothers Hospitallers, 423; Christianized Mohawk village Kahnawake, 447; dévots movement, 322–23, 337, 339–40, 369, 371–72; Dollier's reconnaissance expeditions, 425–29; Dollier's role in development of, 426–29; founders' religious visions and dreams, 335–38, 346; founding, 321–22, 325, 334–41, 346; fur-trading history, 421–22; Hôpital Général, 423; Hospitaller Sisters of Saint Joseph, 322, 373–74, 422–23, 448; Iroquois attacks, 345–49, 372–73; Jesuit-Sulpician quarrels over appointment of vicar apostolic, 368–71; as lay-dominated autonomous colony, 347–50, 369–70; Maisonneuve's governorship, 322, 334, 338–39, 340–41, 346–50, 371; Mance and hospital fund, 321–22, 334, 339–41, 346, 349, 350, 371–74, 422; marriages, 350; Montmagny expedition party, 321–22, 340–41, 414; Notre-Dame Sisters, 386, 421, 424; Recollect ministries, 299; recruitment of settlers, 347, 349–50, 371–74, 402–3; secular clergy, 336, 348, 368, 371; and Society of Our Lady of Montreal in Paris, 322–23, 334, 338, 340, 346–49, 368, 370–71, 402; Sulpicians, 421–29. See also French Canada (Quebec colony)

Montúfar, Alfonso de, 79

Moore, James, 108–9

Moraga, José Joaquín, 226–28, 235, 240

More, Thomas, 35, 477, 490

Morell, Pedro Agustín, 111

Morin, Marie, 422–23

Morison, Samuel Eliot, 2, 11, 12, 14, 51, 236, 241, 280

Morris, Robert, 538

Mosley, Joseph, 534

Mourelle, Francisco Antonio, 261

Moya y Contreras, Pedro de, 177–78

Mumford, Lewis, 539

Muñiz, Andrés, 257

Muñoz, Juan, 76

Muñoz, Manuel, 171

Murphy, Francis Xavier, 355

The Mystical City of God and the Divine History of the Virgin Mother of God (María de Ágreda), 128, 216–17

Nachrichten von der Amerikanischen halbinsel Californien (Baegert), 197, 199

Nadal, Jerónimo, 302

Nájera, Manuel, 205

Narrative and Critical History of America (Winsor), 74

Narváez, Pánfilo de, 29–30, 45–48, 73, 99

Natchez people: Charlevoix' journey among, 397–99, 430–31; massacre of the French at Fort Rosalie, 431, 457–58

Navigatio Sancti Brendani Abbatis (Voyage of Saint Brendan the Abbot), 3–5

Neale, Henry, 517–19

Neale, James, 485, 532

Neale, Leonard, 541

Neri, Philip, 336

Neve, Felipe de, 250–54, 255

New France: de Monts' first and second expeditions (and Champlain), 285–87, 288, 296; history of French reconnaissance in, 283–87; Kino's linking Jesuit missions of Lower California with, 188–89; Mississippi valley explorations, 151–52, 441–45, 452–58. See also French Canada (Quebec colony); Jesuits in French Canada; Jesuits in New France's interior frontier

New Jersey, 519–21

New Mexico (New Spain), 115–41, 126; Ácoma massacre and retaliation, 122–27; encomienda system and Indian labor, 127, 134–36, 141; Espejo expedition, 116–19; Franciscan diocesan structures, 116, 134; Franciscan millenarianism, 116; Franciscan missions among the Pueblos, 119–21, 130–35; Indian baptisms, 128–29, 134; Indian conversions, 121, 132; mestizos and population with mixed bloodlines, 131, 136–37, 140–41; mission churches and chapels, 130, 134; Oñate's colonization, 117–29; Pueblo religion and culture, 121–22, 131–38, 141; Pueblo Revolt of 1680, 136–38, 148, 151, 186, 191, 203; Pueblo uprisings, 122–27, 135–40; Pueblos in the sixteenth century, *126*; Santa Fe capital city, 129, 136–40; Spanish Inquisition, 119–20, 128, 129–30, 135; Tewa warriors and Popé (medicine man), 137–38

New Orleans: Capuchins in, 456–57; Charlevoix on, 397–99, 456; founding, 455–58; Governor Bienville, 456–58; Jesuits in, 457; Palatinate Germans, 517; Spanish governance and French settlers' revolt, 167–68; Ursulines in, 457

New Spain: Alta California, 203–25, 226–29, 247–75, *266*; Lower California, 95, 173–99, *174*, *198*; New Mexico, 115–41, *126*; Pacific ambitions, 176–80; Southern Arizona (Pimería Alta country), 229–45, 249–50; Spanish Frontier, circa 1550–1600, *118*; Texas, 142–72, *144*. See also Jesuits in New Spain

New Toledo, 39, 40–41

New York colony, 463, 511–12, 521–23; anti-Catholic Leisler rebellion, 512, 535; Catholic governor Dongan, 463, 511–12, 513, 541; Catholic proprietor, 463; Charter of Liberties (1683), 463, 512; English Jesuits, 512, 519; French Jesuits' mission to Iroquois, 511; guarantee of religious liberty/toleration, 463, 465, 512; Jesuits, 512; New York City, 463, 521–23; slave revolt hysteria and rumored of Catholic conspiracy, 521–23

Newfoundland: and England's Northwest Passage expeditions, 476–77; Markland and early Scandinavian Christianity, 9, 11, 12; Province of Avalon and Ferryland colony, 474, 475, 476–78

Newfoundland Company, 474

Niagara River and Niagara Falls, 450

Nicholas V, Pope, 17, 18

Nicholson, Francis, 499, 500, 529

Nicolas, Louis, 441

Nicollet, Jean, 413

Nixon, George, 513, 535

Niza, Marcos de, 55–63, 65, 115; *Relación*, 55–63, 115

Nocedal, José, 228

Noonan, John T., Jr, 34, 506

Nootka Sound Convention, 262

Norfolk, Duke of, 552, 556

Northwest Passage, 177; to Asia, 284, 296; Cabot expedition to Hudson Bay, 466; Cartier expeditions along Saint Lawrence River, 284; Drake expedition, 179; England's Newfoundland ventures, 476–77

Noticia de la California (Venegas), 199

Noticias de la Nueva California (Palóu), 208, 227

Notley, Thomas, 498

Notre-Dame de la Victoire (Quebec City), 410

Notre-Dame Sisters of Montreal, 386, 421, 424

Notre-Dame-de-Bon-Secours (Montreal), 372

Notre-Dame-de-la-Récouvrance (Quebec), 320

Notre-Dame-de-Lorette (Huron mission), 438

Notre-Dame-de-Québec, 393–94, 400

Notre-Dame-des-Anges (Quebec), 306–7, 391–92, 414, 449

Noüe, Anne de, 315

Le nouveau horizons de la Renaissance française (Atkinson), 295

Nouveaux voyages dans l'Amérique septentrionale (Lahontan), 404

Nouvel, Henry, 441

Nouvelle découverte d'un très grand pays (Hennepin), 451

Nova Scotia (New Scotland), 316–17. See also Port-Royal (Acadia)

Noyrot, Philibert, 313–14, 316, 317–18

Nuestra Señora de Guadalupe (Texas), 157, 160

Nuestra Señora de la Candelaria (Texas), 165–66

Nuestra Señora de la Luz (Texas), 164–65

Nuestra Señora de la Soledad (Saint Augustine hospital), 97

Nuestra Señora de Loreto (Jesuit mission of Lower California), 192

Nuestra Señora de Regla, monastery of (Cádiz, Spain), 94

Nuestra Señora del Pilar de la Paz (Lower California), 192

Nuestra Señora del Refugio (Texas), 165, 171

Nuestra Señora del Rosario (Texas), 165, 166

Nueva Galicia, 55, 59, 63, 115, 117–19

Nuevas Filipinas (Texas), 149, 158

Nuevo León (Borderlands), 51, 148–49

Nuevo Santander (Borderlands), 149

Oacpicagigua, Luis, 230

Oates, Titus, 433, 464

Observant Franciscans, 32, 38, 116–17

O'Callaghan, E.B., 331, 363

Ocampo, Gonzalo de, 38–39

Occidentalis Americae partis . . . (1594), *24–25*

Oconor, Hugo, 232, 250

O'Daniell, Marian and Margaret, 502

Oglethorpe, James, 110, 522, 523

Ohlone (Castañoan) people, 264

Ojeda, Alonso de, 38

Olaf Haraldssön, 5, 132
Olaf Tryggvason, 3, 5, 7
Olier, Jean-Jacques, 334–48, 367; education and missionary career, 335–36, 337; and founding of Montreal, 334–38, 341; and secular clergy, 336, 348
Olivares, Antonio de San Buenaventura y, 142, 154, 160
Omnimoda of 1522, 70, 95, 116
Omnipotens Deus (papal bull) (1517), 116
Oñate, Cristóbal de, 117
Oñate, Juan de: Ácoma massacre and council of war, 122–27; colonization of New Mexico, 117–29; as Last Conquistador, 119, 122; and Pueblo religion and culture at Ácoma, 121–22
Onondaga Iroquois, 349–50, 361–62, 372–73
Opera omnia (Duns Scotus), 215
Ordaz, Blas, 270
Order of the Minims, 320
Ordóñez, Isidro, 129
O'Reilly, Alexander, 167–68
Ormeaux, Adam Dollard des, 372–73
Ortega, José Francisco, 209, 210–12, 222–23, 260
Ortiz, Juan, 74
Ortiz de Matienzo, Juan, 72
Otermín, Antonio de, 138–39
Ottawa mission (Jesuit), 441
Ouebadinskoue, Marie (Marie-Madeleine Chrestienne), 414, 415
Our Catholic Heritage in Texas (Castañeda), 149
Our Lady of Guadalupe (devotions), 145–46, 153, 157, 242
Outpost of Empire (Bolton), 235
Ovando, Nicolás de, 27
Owen, Nicholas, 468
Owings, Robert, 516
Oxford College, 470–71, 505
Ozon, Potentien, 391

Pacific ambitions of New Spain (Gulf of California-Pacific coast region), 176–80; and British Royal Naval expeditions, 261–62; California island theory, 54, 176–77, 178, 186–87; Cortés exploration of the Pacific and Lower California shoreline, 176; efforts to find an Upper California harbor, 178; and Manila galleons, 177–78, 189, 195, 204; Nootka Sound crisis, 261–62; Russian threats, 261; Sacred Expedition's seaborne expedition and maritime crew, 204, 205, 209, 210, 212, 218; Spanish-English competition, 178–79,

261–62; three foundational efforts, 59–60, 177–78; Vizcaíno expedition, 178, 204, 218
Padilla, Antonio Lorenzo de, 104
Padilla, Juan de, 63–67, 115
Paine, James, 555
Palacios, Juan de, 184
Palatinate Germans, 517–19, 536
Pallu, François, 366
Palma, Salvador, 235, 237, 256–59
Palóu, Francisco, 205, 208, 213, 226–27, 259, 260
Pames people, 218
Papal Donation of 1493, 81, 83
Pareja, Francisco, 98
Parga Araujo, Juan de, 109
Paris, Archdiocese of, 388
Paris Foreign Missions Society, 145; New Orleans, 455–57; Quebec, 286, 371, 374, 378–80, 389, 401, 448–49, 453
Parkman, Francis, 84, 236, 459; on Champlain, 280; and Charlevoix, 459; on the Deerfield massacre, 436–37; on discovery of Niagara Falls, 450; on Hennepin-La Salle expeditions and Hennepin's Sioux captivity, 451; on Jesuit mission to Huronia, 327, 352, 357; and Jesuit missions in New France, 327, 331; on New France (French Canada), 86–87, 324, 327, 331, 334, 346, 352, 357, 363, 374, 402; on wars of religion and French-English rivalry for North America, 433, 436–37
Parrilla, Diego Ortiz, 230–31
Parrón, Fernando, 213
Parsons, Robert, 470–73, 479, 541
Pasamonte, Miguel de, 21
Pascal, Blaise, 301, 303, 401
Patrón, Agustín, 157, 160–61
Pattie, James Ohio, 267
Patuxent people, 484, 490, 496
Paul III, Pope, 54
Paul V, Pope, 381
Paul VI, Pope, xi
Payeras, Mariano, 272
Paz, Matías de, 23
Peasley, William, 477–78, 485
Peckham, George, 470
Pelletier, Didace, 391–92, 395
Peña, Tomás de la, 228, 270
Peña Saravia, Tomás de la, 228
Peñalosa, Diego de, 76
Penn, William: and Delaware, 507; distrust of Catholics' loyalty, 513–14; imprisonment as suspected Catholic sympathizer, 529, 536; and James II, 513–14; Philadelphia charter, 535–36, 539; proprietary Quaker colony

of Pennsylvania, 491, 513–15, 520; and Quaker New Jersey, 520
Pennington, Francis, 500
Pennsylvania, 513–19, 535–39; African slavery, 538–39; border dispute and first Catholic colony in Conewago Valley, 515–16; Catholic Philadelphia, 535–39, 537; Catholic population, 515, 517–19, 538; Fort Duquesne, 515, 540; Glorious Revolution and aftermath, 514; Irish immigrants, 515, 517; Jesuit missions and settlements, 516–19, 538–39; Palatinate Germans (Pennsylvania Dutch), 517–19, 536; Penn's distrust of Catholics' loyalty, 513–14; Penn's proprietary Quaker colony, 491, 513–15, 520
Pennsylvania State House (Philadelphia), 537, 539
Peoria people, 443
Peralta, Francisco, 192
Peralta, Pedro de, 129, 136
Pérez, Juan, 209, 218
Pérez, Melchior, 63–64
Pérez de la Cerda, Sebastián, 96
Pérez de la Torre, Diego, 55, 63
Péricard, François de, bishop of Évreux, 365
Perrot, François-Marie, 428
Petre, Benjamin, 505
Petre, Lord, 555
Peyrí, Antonio, 265–67, 268
Philadelphia, Pennsylvania, 535–39, 537
Philip II of Spain, 33, 76, 116, 386, 467; authorizing Velasco's colonization enterprise in Florida, 78–81; and Cabeza de Vaca, 44; and the Counter-Reformation, 78; and ecclesiastical/diocesan organization in the Indies, 70, 93, 95, 116; on the Jesuits, 303; and Las Casas, 43; and Menéndez de Avilés in Florida, 83, 85, 86, 89
Philip III of Spain, 98, 102, 129
Philip V of Spain, 107–8, 110, 188; and Franciscan missions in Texas, 143, 159, 161, 163; and War of Spanish Succession, 143
Philippe, duc d'Orléans, 397
Philippines: Magellan's expedition, 176; Manila galleons and New Spain's Pacific ambitions, 177–78, 189, 195, 204; Spanish conquest of, 177–78; Spanish missions, 96; and Texas, 149, 158
Phips, William, 401, 410
Piazza di Spagna (Rome), 143
Picany, Blanca, 215
Piccolomini, Celio, 364

Pícolo, Francisco María, 185–86, 192
Picques, Bernard, 366
Pima people, 182–83, 206, 229–31, 249–50
Pima Revolt of 1751, 229–31
Pimería Alta. See Southern Arizona (Pimería Alta country), New Spain's northward advance out of
Pine, Robert Edge, 547
Pino, Miguel del, 208
Pioneers in the New World (Parkman), 86–87
Pious Fund of Californias, 184, 185, 192, 274
Pius IX, Pope, 83
Pius V, Pope, 116, 178, 468, 479, 514
Pius VI, Pope, 555
Pizarro, Francisco, 54
Pizarro, Gonzalo, 54
Plessis, Joseph Octave, 437
Plunkett, Oliver, 464
Polanco, Alfonso de, 302
Polanco, Francisco Manuel, 170
Pole, Anthony (Father Smith), 477, 479
Pole, Reginald Cardinal, 467, 470
Pombal, Marquis of, 554
Pompadour, marquise de (Jeanne Antoinette Poisson Le Normant d'Étiolles), 543
Ponce de León, Juan, 68, 71
Poncet de La Rivière, Joseph-Antoine, 332–33, 369
Poole, Stafford, 146
Poor Clare Franciscans, 127–28, 152
Popé (Tewa medicine man), 137–38, 139
Portolá, Gaspar de, 175, 205, 208, 209–13, 218, 223, 250, 255
Port-Royal (Acadia), 279–83, 286–87, 290–91, 293; English destruction of (1613), 308, 319; Jesuit arrival at, 305; Lescarbot's The Theater of Neptune masque, 280–83, 297, 301; Order of Good Cheer, 297–98, 301; Poutrincourt party's return to, 279–82, 297; Scots Calvinists in, 316–17
Potgravé, Robert, 280
Potomac River, 483, 484
Pott, John, 478
Poulton, Ferdinand, 496, 498
Poulton, Thomas, 503, 541–42
Poutrincourt, sieur de (Jean de Biencourt), 279–82, 286, 287–93, 295–96, 303, 308; de Monts' expeditions, 286, 295–96; French Catholic humanism, 287–93, 303; resistance to Jesuits in French Canada, 301–6; return to Port-Royal, 279–82, 297
Pradeau, Alberto Francisco, 208
Prat, Pedro, 212, 218
Prescott, William Hinckling, 236
Prideaux, Magdalen, 490

Priestley, Herbert Ingram, 206, 208
The Private City (Warner), 539
Protestant Association (Maryland), 500, 528,
    529
Protestant England: Champlain and the battle
    for Quebec, 318; competition for control
    of Pacific coast, 178–79; contests for
    control of North America, 178–79, 357,
    433–37, 454; destruction of Port-Royal
    (French Acadia), 308, 319; and New France
    (Quebec colony), 316–19, 357, 401, 410;
    and Spanish Florida, 78, 96, 106–9, 111. *See
    also* Protestant England and the persecution
    of Catholics
Protestant England and the persecution of
    Catholics, 432–33, 463–73, 532; archpriest
    controversy, 479–81; and Catholic Spain,
    471–72, 474–75; Catholic supporters
    of Spanish intervention and removal of
    Elizabeth, 471, 472; Elizabeth I, 464,
    467–68, 471–72; English Civil War,
    488–89, 491–94; Glorious Revolution
    and aftermath, 433, 500–507, 510–11,
    514, 528–29, 532; Gunpowder Plot and
    aftermath, 468–69, 470, 472, 473; and
    James II's pro-Catholic policies, 433, 463–
    65, 510, 513–14; Jesuits during Elizabethan
    persecutions, 470–73, 479–80; Maryland
    colony anti-Catholicism and legislation,
    465, 488–89, 491–95, 500–505, 528, 532,
    539–40; oaths of allegiance and loyalty,
    465, 472, 482, 514, 529; William and Mary,
    463–65
Protestant Reformation, 178; England, 467,
    514; Icelandic Church, 8; and Jesuit
    missions, 185
Protestants, French. *See* Huguenots (French
    Protestants)
Province of Jalisco (Franciscan), 204–5
Prudhomme, Louis, 349
Pueblo people: baptisms, 128–29, 134;
    conversions, 121, 132; and Franciscan
    missions in New Mexico, 119–21, 130–35;
    gift-giving rituals, 131–32; Katsina dance,
    133–34, 136, 141; Oñate's council of war
    and the Ácoma massacre, 122–27; Pueblo
    Revolt of 1680, 136–38, 148, 151, 186,
    191, 203; religion and culture, 121–22,
    131–38, 141; Tewa medicine man Popé,
    137–38; Tewa pueblos, 60–63, 64, 116–17,
    137–38
Pueblo Revolt of 1680, 136–38, 148, 151, 186,
    191, 203
Puente y Peña, José de la, the Marquis of
    Villapuente, 192–93

Puiseaux, Pierre de (sieur de Montrénault),
    321–22, 341, 347
Puritans: English Civil War, 488–89, 493;
    Maryland colony, 494–95

Quakers: Anglican Maryland, 529; New
    Jersey, 520; Penn's proprietary colony of
    Pennsylvania, 491, 513–15, 520
Quarenghi, Giacomo, 555
Quebec City: Charlevoix' account of,
    410–12, 439; ecclesiastical history, 410–11;
    episcopal palace/cathedral, 402, 411;
    Hôpital-Général, 411–12; Hôtel-Dieu,
    362, 372, 375, 381, 389, 408–9, 411–12;
    Jesuit college, 438–39; Jesuits in, 327, 330,
    332, 438–39; Recollect Franciscans, 381,
    391–92, 411; social life, 412; Ursuline
    convent and school, 386, 411. *See also*
    French Canada (Quebec colony); Montreal
    (Ville-Marie)
Queen Anne's War (War of Spanish
    Succession), 107–9, 143, 153–54, 166, 397,
    410, 411, 436–37, 456, 524–25, 539
Quen, Jean de, 369
Quentin, Jacques, 305, 306
Querétaran Franciscan missionary colleges in
    New Spain, 146–47
Quevado, Juan, 37
Quexos, Pedro de, 72
Queylus, Gabriel de Thubières de Levy
    de, 369, 379, 422, 425, 426; as Sulpician
    candidate for vicar apostolic, 364, 368,
    369–71
Quinn, Arthur, 179
Quintana, Andrés, 271
Quirenza, Giacomo, 555
Quiroga, Diego de, 106
Quirós, Fernando, 228
Quirós, Luis de, 90–91
Quivira myth and expeditions, 61, 63–67, 119,
    128, 149, 150, 177

Rábago, Felipe de, 165–66
Ragueneau, Paul, 317–18, 342, 345, 362,
    408–9, 450
Raisin, Marie, 373
Rale, Sébastien, 524–25
Rallvau, Jean, 280
Ramírez, José Antonio, 266
Ramón, Domingo, 156–58, 160–61
Rasilly, Claude de, 325
Ravaillac, François, 305, 313
Razilly, Isaac de, 311–12, 316, 318, 319, 320,
    323, 325
Razilly–Condonnier company, 319

Rebolledo, Diego de, 106

Recollect Franciscans in New France, 299–300, 306–7, 313–14, 318–19, 325, 368, 381, 391–93, 448–52; Hennepin and La Salle's Great Lakes expeditions, 449–52; Montreal, 299; Notre-Dame-des-Anges (Quebec), 306–7, 391–92, 449; Quebec City, 381, 391–92, 411

Reconquest (Spain), 27, 36–37, 146, 216

redemptioners, Irish, 517

Redondo, Cristóbal, 90

Reed, Edward, Lord of Tusburie and Witten, 508

Reed, Elizabeth, 508

Reformation. *See* Protestant Reformation

Regnans in Excelsis (papal bull) (1570), 468, 471, 479, 514

Regnault, Christophe, 343, 362

Relación histórica de la vida y apostólicas tareas del venerable padre Fray Junípero Serra (Palóu), 208, 227

religious freedom: Edict of Nantes and Huguenots, 81, 289, 301, 312–13, 432–33; Maryland colony, 463, 481–82, 493–94, 528–29; New York colony, 463, 465, 512; revocation of Edict of Nantes, 316, 432–33, 435, 510

Repentigny, Pierre Legardeur de, 322

Repplier, Agnes, 213

El Requerimiento (The Requirement), 60, 66, 69

Reséndez, Andrés, 46

Resino, Dionisio, 110

Retz, Francis, 518–19

Retz, George, 196

Rey, Acapito, 117

Reyes, Antonio de los, 254–55

Reynolds, Joshua, 526–28, 547, 550, 555

Rezanov, Nikolai Petrovich, 249

Rhodes, Alexandre de, 366, 367

Ribadeneyra, Pedro de, 302

Ribault, Jean, 68, 82, 84, 85–86

Ricci, Laurence, 555

Ricci, Matteo, 132, 133, 180

Richardson, Samuel, 527

Richelieu, Armand Jean du Plessis Cardinal de, 310–11, 480; anti-Huguenot campaign, 313, 316; authority in New France, 310–12, 314, 316, 318–19, 323–24, 350; and conflicts between France and England, 317

Rigby, Roger, 493

Rim of Christendom (Bolton), 180, 235

Ripoll, Antonio, 265

Ritter, John Baptist de, 520

Rivera, Fernando, 255–56, 258

Rivera, Pedro de, 161–62

Rivera y Moncada, Fernando de, 175; disputes with Serra, 222–23, 224–25, 251; as military commander of Franciscan missions in Alta California, 222–23, 224–25, 228–29, 245, 251; the Sacred Expedition, 205, 209–10, 212–13

Roanoke colony, 14, 106

Robertson, William, 34–35

Robineau de Portneuf, René, 435

Robinson, Alfred, 267

Roche-d'Aillon, Bonaventure de la, 315

Rodríguez, Agustín, 115, 116–17

Rodríguez, Blas, 97–98

Rodríguez, Estevan, 192, 195

Rodríguez, Juan, 159

Rodríguez de Fonseca, Juan, 23

Rogel, Juan, 89, 92

Rojas, Carlos, 229

Rolfe, John, 437

Roman Oratory, 336

Romanus Pontifex (papal bull) (1511), 29

Romero, Sebastián, 185–86

Ronceray, Andrée de, 422

Roper, Margaret, 490

Roquemont de Brison, Claude, 317–18

Rosas, Luis de, 135

Rouen, Archdiocese of, 388. *See also* Harlay de Champvallon, François II de (archbishop of Rouen)

Rousby, Ann, 533

Rousseau, Marie, 337–38, 339

Rouville, Hertel de, 436, 437

Royal and Pontifical University of Mexico, 78

Royal Ordinances of 1573, 116–17, 119, 125, 128–29

Rubí, Mariano, 270

Rubí, marqués de, 168–71, 231–32

Rubio, José María de Jesús González, 275

Ruhen, Henry, 230

Ruiz, Manuel, 263

Sabeata, Juan, 151

Sable Island colony (New France), 285

Sacred Congregation for the Propagation of the Faith, 143–46, 475; and Enlightenment principles in Catholic missions, 143–46; Laval's consecration as vicar apostolic of New France, 364–66, 367–68, 375, 376; and Lord Baltimore's request for secular priests in Maryland, 491; Spain and

Portugal's rights to evangelization in Asia
and the Indies, 365–66
Sacred Expedition (Franciscan entrada into
Alta California), 203–13, 218
Saeta, Francisco, 186
Saga of Eric the Red, 2, 3, 13
Sagard, Gabriel, 306–7, 318–19, 417
Saint Augustine (Florida), 68–92, 96–98,
101–9; Bishop Altamirano's visit, 101–2,
104; Castillo de San Marcos (fortress),
96, 100, 107; Convent of Saint Francis,
104, 105, 108; English Protestant siege of,
96, 106–9; Franciscan diocesan structure,
69–71, 102–6; Grajales' ministry, 69, 70–71;
Menéndez expeditions, 68–69, 83–92
Saint Bartholomew Day massacre (1572),
81–82
Saint Bernard, Anne de, 332–33, 334, 383
Saint Denis, Louis Juchereau de, 154, 156–57,
160
Saint Helena (Florida), 79–80, 82, 89
Saint Inigoes Manor (Maryland), 496
Saint Joseph's Church (Philadelphia), 536–39
Saint Mary's chapel (Philadelphia), 536–39
Saint Mary's City (Maryland), 484, 488–89,
495–99, 500, 528–29
Saint Omer's College (France), 477, 502, 503,
519, 536; and Maryland Catholic students,
526, 527, 528, 533–34, 541, 542–44
Saint Xaverius mission (Maryland), 502–3
Saint-Bernard, Dom François, 383
Saint-Cosme, Jean-François Buisson de,
430–31, 453, 456
Saint-Cosme II (Great Sun of the Natchez
people), 431
Sainte Croix, Cécile de, 332–33, 334, 383
Sainte-Anne de Beaupré, shrine of (Quebec),
394, 395, 419
Sainte-Marie-aux-Hurons (Jesuit mission),
328, 345
Saint-Ignace (Jesuit mission), 343–45
Saint-Jure, Jean-Baptiste, 339–40
Saint-Lusson, Simon-François Daumont de,
442
Saint-Sulpice Church (Paris), 286, 341, 348,
369, 396
Saint-Vallier, Jean-Baptiste de la Croix de
Chevrières de: as bishop of Diocese of
Quebec, 400–402, 411, 428–29, 439;
episcopal palace, 401–2, 411; Jesuit
opposition to, 453; as Laval's successor,
395–96, 400–402; and religious orders in
Montreal, 423–24
Sakki Thorisson, 1
Salamanca, Miguel de, 37

Salas, Juan de, 127–28
Salazar, Domingo de, 81
Salières, sieur de (Henry de Chapelas), 417
Salvatierra, Juan María de, 180, 181, 182–87,
192, 229
San Antonio, Matías Sáenz de, 157
San Antonio de Padua (California), 223
San Antonio de Valero (the Alamo) (Texas),
142, 263; as Catholic city, 170; Church
of San Fernando, 163–64, 165, 169–70;
founding, 142, 148, 159; Franciscan
mission, 142, 148, 159, 164, 165–66, 171;
San Fernando de Béxar (villa), 142, 159,
161–62, 163–64, 169–70
San Blas (California), 204, 209, 222
San Borjo (California), 193
San Buenaventura (California), 220, 225, 248,
264
San Carlos Borromeo (California), 220, 223,
226, 227, 264
San Diego Bay, 177, 178, 193, 204, 209, 212
San Diego de Alcalá (California), 193, 211,
218, 220, 223–25, 237, 264; Indian uprising
(1775), 223–25; Lasuén at, 259–60
San Esteban del Rey (Ácoma, New Mexico),
130
San Fernando at Velicatá (California), 206,
218, 220–21
San Fernando de Béxar (villa at San Antonio),
142, 159, 161–62, 163–64, 169–70
San Fernando Rey de España (California),
265–67
San Francisco Bay, 178, 211; Anza's
expedition, 226–29, 245–46. *See also*
Mission Dolores (San Francisco de Asís) at
San Francisco Bay
San Francisco de Asís. *See* Mission Dolores
(San Francisco de Asís) at San Francisco
Bay
San Francisco de la Espada (Texas), 163, 165
San Francisco de los Tejas (Texas), 153, 154,
157
San Francisco Solano (California), 221, 269
San Francisco Xavier de Nájera (Texas), 159
San Gabriel Arcángel (California), 222, 223,
225, 226, 227, 237, 255, 264
San Ildefonso (Texas), 165
San José de Comondú (Jesuit mission of
Lower California), 193, 205
San José de Guadalupe, pueblo of (first civil
settlement in Alta California), 228–29, 249,
250, 252, 253–54
San José de los Nazones (Texas), 157–58
San José del Cabo (Jesuit mission of Lower
California), 192, 195

San José y San Miguel de Aguayo (Texas), 159, 160, 165, 170–71

San Juan Capistrano (California), 223, 225, 264

San Juan Capistrano (Texas), 163, 165

San Lorenzo (Texas), 165

San Lucas, Diego de, 135

San Luis Obispo (California), 248, 264

San Luis Rey de Francia (California), 265–67

San Miguel de Linares (Texas), 158–59, 160

San Miguel Island (California), 177

San Xavier del Bac (Franciscan mission), 232–33, 250, 263; church architecture, 263

San Xavier del Bac (Jesuit mission): foundation of, 186, 229, 250; founding of Tubac presidio, 230–31; Pima Revolt of 1751, 229–31; ranchería of San José de Tucson, 231

San Xavier missions (Texas), 165–66

Sánchez, Benito, 157

Sandos, James, 213, 214, 216, 224, 268, 270–72

Santa Ana (mining camp), 175, 205

Santa Ana, López María, 274

Santa Barbara (California): church, 265; diocesan organization, 248–49; first bishop (García Diego y Moreno), 247–49; and secularization of the mission system, 274–75

Santa Catalina (Saint Catherine's Island) (California), 107

Santa Clara de Asís (California), 223, 228–29, 248, 252, 253–54, 264

Santa Cruz de San Sabá (Texas), 165, 166

Santa Fe, New Mexico, 129, 136–40

Santa Gertrudis (California), 193, 205

Santa Inés (California), 264–65, 274

Santa María (California), 193

Santa María, Juan de, 116–17

Santa María y Mendoza, Pedro, 157

Santa Rosa/Todos Santos (Jesuit mission of Lower California), 192–93, 194–95, 205

Santiago de los Caballeros (Antigua), 155

Santiesteban, José, 166

Santo Domingo, Jaime de, 81

Santo Domingo el Real in Jerez de la Frontera, 45, 53

Santos, José de los, 270

Sarmiento y Valladares, José, conde de Moctezuma y Tula, 184

Sault Sainte-Marie (Lake Superior), 353, 360, 441, 442–43, 447

Saunders, John, 485

Scandinavian Christianity, 1–18, 132; Celtic Christianity and travels of Brendan the Voyager, 3–5, 13; de-Christianization of Greenland, 17–18; the fourth and fifth voyages to Vinland, 14–15; Freydís Ericsson and Vinland expedition, 15–17; Garðar complex in Greenland East Settlement, 1–2, 15, 17–18; Greenland settlement, 1–2, 8–9, 17–18; Helluland (Baffin Island), 9, 11–12; Iceland, 2–3, 5–10, 132; L'Anse aux Meadows, 11, 12, 15; Leif Ericsson's expedition, 11–13; maps, 3, 6, 11; Markland (northern Newfoundland), 9, 11, 12; the Norse diaspora, 5–7, 6; the North American settlements, 9–18; Norway becoming Christian, 5–7; settlement sagas, 2–3, 7, 9–10, 12–14, 15–16; skrælings (indigenous Eskimos and Indians), 10, 13–15, 18; Thorvald Ericsson's expedition, 13–14; Vinland (Nova Scotia), 9–17

Schneider, Thomas, 518–20

Scholasticism, 215

Scotland, Protestant, 466–67, 504, 532

Second Anglo-Powhatan War, 483, 484

Second Vatican Council, x–xi

Sedeño, Antonio, 89

Séguier, Pierre, 337, 338

Segura, Juan Bautista de, 90–91

Seignelay, marquise de (Jean-Baptiste Antoine Colbert), 433–44

Selvagio, Juan, 34

Seminole War, 111

Señán, José, 269

Senecas of the Iroquois Confederacy, 342, 345, 433

Senkewicz, Robert, 211–12

Las sergas de Esplandián (The deeds of Esplandián) (Montalvo), 54, 176

Serra, Junípero, 181, 213–25, 237; asceticism and self-punishment, 217–18, 220; biographers, 208, 213; canonization, 148, 213–14, 236; and Carlos III's Provincias Internas reorganization, 254–55; church building, 218; death, 254–55, 259; disputes with military commanders, 221–25, 234, 250–54, 260; and doctrine of Immaculate Conception, 216–17; as father president of Franciscan missions, 148, 214, 218–25, 227, 234, 250–54, 259–60; founding of Alta California missions, 148, 214, 218–25, 227; Franciscan Catholicism, 213–17; and Indian attack on Mission San Diego, 223–25; Jewish ancestry, 214, 218; Majorcan influences, 214–15; and Neve, 250–54; and Portolá's expulsion of Jesuits from Lower California, 208–9; and the Sacred Expedition to Alta California, 205, 209–10, 213; Scotist influences, 215–16; and soldiers' sexual exploitation of Indian

women, 221, 222, 224, 234, 251; *Writings*,
    208, 213
Serrano, Doña Ana Regina, 240
Seven Cities of Cíbola myth, 53–67, 115, 149,
    177, 188
Sewall, Henry, 497, 503
Sewall, Jane Lowe, 497
Sewall, Nicholas, 504
sexual violence against Indian women by
    Spanish soldiers, 181; in Franciscan
    missions of Alta California, 221, 222, 224,
    227, 234, 251, 271; in Texas province, 148,
    153, 165–66
Seymour, Jane, 467
Seymour, John, 500–502, 532
Shackel, Sandra, 132
Shaftesbury, first Earl of (Anthony Ashley
    Cooper), 464
Shea, John Gilmary, ix–x, xii; and Charlevoix'
    Journal, 452, 459; on de Soto's Florida
    expedition, 73–74; on Franciscan mission
    networks in Spanish Florida, 104, 110; on
    Franciscan missions among the Pueblos,
    130–31, 134, 138; on Fray Marcos de Niza,
    56; French Canadian historiography, 331,
    363; on Jesuit missions in interior North
    America, 452, 453–54; on Menéndez
    and Spanish attack on Huguenots at
    Fort Caroline, 85, 86; on Sulpicians and
    founding of Montreal, 422
Sidney, Henry, 469
Sierpe, Don Pedro Gil de la, 184, 185
Sigurd Jorsala-Ari, 1
Sillery, Madeleine Brûlart de, 339
Sillery, Noël Brûlart de, 330–31
Sillery mission (Jesuit), 330, 351, 353–54
Silva, Francisco Xavier, 166
Silva, Manuel, 171
Silvy, Anthony, 441
Simpson, George, 249
Sioux people, 451–52, 458
Sixtus IV, Pope, 129
slavery. *See* African slavery; Indian labor and
    encomienda system; Indian slavery
Sloughter, Henry, 465
smallpox: California, 256; Indians of Quebec,
    333, 352; New Mexico, 134, 141; Texas,
    153
Smith, John, 179, 295
Smith, Richard, 480
Society for the Propagation of the Gospel, 535
Society of Jesus. *See* Jesuits (Society of Jesus)
Society of Our Lady of Montreal (Paris),
    322–23, 334, 338, 340, 346–49, 368,
    370–71, 402

Solís, Gabriel de, 90–91
Sorie, Jacques, 83
Sotolongo, Francisco de, 103–4
Souart, Gabriel, 369, 425
Sousa, Mathias de, 486
Southern Arizona (Pimería Alta country), New
    Spain's northward advance out of, 229–45,
    249–50; Anza expedition from Monterey
    and San Francisco, 226–28, 245–46; Anza's
    California reconnaissance expeditions for
    overland route, 232–45, *238*; Anza's first
    expedition (Sonora-California), 234–39,
    238; Anza's second expedition, *238*, 239–
    46, 249, 256–58; Font's *Complete Diary*,
    241, 242, 243–46, 252; partnership of Anza
    and Garcés, 232–34; presidio and Mission
    Dolores at San Francisco Bay, 223, 226–29,
    245–46; relocation of Tubac to Tucson,
    231–33, 250; Rubí's recommendations for
    Borderlands defense and reorganization,
    168–71, 231–32; women settlers in the
    Anza party, 240–41, 242–43
Southey, Robert, 465
Spain: fall of Granada, 27, 129, 146; and
    Protestant England, 471–72, 474–75;
    Reconquest and expulsion of the Moors,
    27, 36–37, 146, 216. *See also* New Spain
Spalding, Thomas, CFX, 542
Spanish exploration of southern edge of North
    America, 44–67, *52*; Cabeza de Vaca,
    44–55; Coronado expeditions, 55–67, 115;
    Franciscan missionary reconnaissance of
    the Seven Cities, 55–67; Marcos de Niza,
    56–59; Mendoza expeditions and the Seven
    Cities myth, 53–67; Narváez expedition,
    45–48, 73; Quivira myth and expeditions,
    61, 66–67, 119, 128; siege and destruction
    of Moho pueblos, 62–63; the Tewa
    pueblos and Tewa resistance, 60–63; Zuñi
    rejection of Coronado, 60–63
The Spanish Frontier in North America (Weber),
    74
The Spirit of the Laws (Montesquieu), 544–45
Stafford Rangers, 510
Statutes of Mortmain, 480–81, 489–91
Stefnir Thorgilsson, 7
Stiger, Kaspar, 229
Stock, Simon (Thomas Doughty), 475, 476–77
Stone, William, 493, 494–95
Storia della California (Clavigero), 199
Stourton, Charles, 552
Stourton, Charles Philip, 552–54
Stourton, Erasmus, 477–78
Suárez, Francisco, 35, 302, 544
Suárez del Real brothers, 269–70

INDEX

637

Sublimis Deus (papal bull) (1537), 54, 75–76, 77
Sucinta relación, 174–75
Sulpicians in New France, 421–29; Charlevoix on, 421–22; Compagnie des Prêtres de Saint-Sulpice, 370, 371, 424–25; Dollier's reconnaissance expeditions, 425–29; Dollier's role in development of Montreal, 426–29; fur-trading history, 421–22; Gentlemen of Saint-Sulpice, 286, 370, 371, 389, 422, 423, 424, 446, 448; Iroquois ministry, 446–47; Montreal, 421–29; quarrels with Jesuits, 364, 368–71; Queylus as Sulpician candidate for vicar apostolic, 364, 368, 369–71
Surin, Jean-Joseph, 408
Susquehannock people, 483–84, 486, 493, 496
Swift, Jonathan, 472

Tac, Pablo, 267
Tadoussac (Saint Lawrence River), 285, 299, 321
Talbot, John, 535–36
Talbot, Robert, 477–78, 485
Tale of the Greenlanders, 12–13
Talon, Jean (Intendant), 402, 403–4, 418–19, 438–39, 442
Tamaral, Nicolás, 194–95
Taos people, 135
Tarabel, Sebastián, 235
Taraval, Sigismundo, 194–95
Tatham, John (Gray), 513, 520–21, 535
Tegonhatsihongo, Anastasia, 448
Teja, Jesús de la, 169–70
Tejada, Francisco de San Buenaventura y, 110–11, 148, 162–64
Tejas people, 150–51, 152–53, 156–59
Tekakwitha, Catherine, 447–48
Tello, Tomás, 230
Tempis, Antonio, 196
Tenorio, Gonzalo, 93–94, 96
Terán de los Ríos, Domingo, 153
Teresa of Ávila, 128, 130, 217, 382, 386
Terreros, Alonso Giraldo de, 166
Tessier, Urbain, 403
Tewa pueblos, 60–63, 64, 116–17, 137–38
Texas (New Spain), 142–72, 144, 167–68; Alarcón's civilian/military expedition, 142, 148; Canary Islanders in, 161–62, 163; conversion rates, 148, 165; Diocese of Guadalajara, 148, 162–63; early Franciscan reconnaissance expeditions, 148–53; end of mission system and secularization of missions, 171–72; Enlightenment influences, 143–45, 146–47, 150, 155;

first missions among the Tejas, 156–59; Franciscan diocesan structures, 148, 162–64; Franciscan legacy and Catholic Texas, 169–70; Franciscan mission system, 146–48, 153–54, 162–71; Franciscan missionary colleges, 146–47, 155; French incursions and threats, 151–52, 158, 160; Indian attacks, 166; Indian baptisms, 150, 166; Indian labor, 163; Margil and Zacatecan missions, 147, 148, 155–59, 170; midcentury expansion of mission system, 164–67; Mission San Antonio de Valero, 142, 148, 159, 164, 165–66, 171; as Nuevas Filipinas, 149, 158; Our Lady of Guadalupe, 145–46, 153, 157; Rubí's recommendations for defense, 168–71, 231–32; San Fernando de Béxar, 142, 159, 161–62, 163–64, 169–70; second cluster of missions, 159–61; sexual assaults on Indian women, 148, 153, 165–66; Tejas people and culture, 150–51, 152–53, 156–59
Thangbrand, 7
Thaumur de La Source, Dominique-Antoine-René, 453
The Theater of Neptune (Lescarbot), 280–83, 288, 297, 301
Thirty Years' War (1618–1648), 315, 327, 339, 517
Thorfinn Karlsefni, 14–15
Thorgeir Thorkelsson, 7
Thornstein Ericsson, 10, 13–14
Thorpe, John, 555
Thorvald Kodransson, 6–7
Thorvard Ericsson, 1, 10, 15–17
The Three Musketeers (Dumas), 310
Three Rivers (Trois-Rivières) (Quebec), 299, 321, 324, 368, 391, 395, 401–2, 412–15
Thwaites, Reuben Gold, 331, 363, 447
Tibesar, Antonine, 208
Tiguex War, 62–63
Timucuan people, 68, 71, 98–99, 101–2
Tirsch, Ignacio, 196
Toledo Herrera, Francisco de, 302
Tonge, Israel, 464
Tongva (Gabrielino) people, 264
Tonigiano, Luigi, 551
Tonnetuit, sieur de (Pierre de Chauvin), 285
Tony, Henri, 455
Torcapel, Jean, 379
Torquemada, Tomás de, 129
Torres Perea, Joseph de, 229
Torrubia, José, 261
Tovar, Pedro de, 64
Tracy, marquise Alexandre de Prouville de, 386, 417–19, 433

Tranchepain, Mary, 457
Treaty of Dover (1670), 432, 464
Treaty of Fontainebleau (1762), 166–67
Treaty of Paris (1763), 111, 166–68, 362, 424
Treaty of Ryswick (1697), 455
Treaty of Saint Germain–en–Laye (1632), 318
Treaty of Utrecht (1713), 397, 456, 524
Treaty of Vervins (1598), 288, 290
Treaty of Westminster (1674), 463
Treviño, Juan Francisco, 137
Tronson, Louis, 426, 428
Trouvé, Claude, 429, 447
Trudel, Marcel, 323
The True Doctrine of God (Ricci), 132
True Relation (Smith), 179
Tubac presidio, 230–33, 250
Tucson, 231–33, 250
Tuesday Club of Annapolis, 531
Tuite, Nicholas, 549
Tupatír, Luis, 137
Turk (El Turco), 61, 63, 65–66
Tyrconnell, Earl of, 464

Ubaldini, Roberto, 300
Uchitíes people, 194–95, 196
Ugarte, Juan de, 184–85, 192
Ulloa, Francisco de, 176
University of Paris, 37, 215, 288, 311, 335, 364
Urango, Don Ferdinand, 78–79
Urban College of Propaganda Fide (Rome), 145, 146–47
Urban VIII, Pope, 134, 353, 390
Ursuline Convent of Faubourg Saint-Jacques (Paris), 320
Ursulines in French New Orleans, 457
Ursulines of Quebec, 327, 332–34, 351, 355–56, 368, 375, 381–87, 394–95, 405; and Brébeuf, 355–56; convent monastery, 384–86; and the filles du roi, 405; foundress La Peltrie, 321, 332–34, 351, 383, 384–85, 394; as local saints, 394–95; Marie de l'Incarnation, 381–87; Marie de Saint Joseph, 394–95; school for Indian girls, 332, 333–34, 384–86, 394
Ury, John, 522–23
Ute people, 139, 140, 141
Utopia (More), 35

Valdés, Fernando de, 98
Valdés, Juan Bautista, 235, 237
Vallejo, Mariano Guadalupe, 273
Van Sweringen, Garrett, 498
Vancouver, George, 260
Varennes, René Gaultier, 420

Vargas, Diego de, 139–40
Vaudreuil, marquise de (Philippe Rigaud), 436
Vaughan, William, 474
Velarde, Juan, 124
Velasco, Luis de, 78–81, 89–91, 119
Velásquez, Don Diego, 31
Venegas, Miguel, 199
Ventadour, duc de (Henri de Lévis), 313–14
Vergara, Gabriel, 157
Verger, Rafael, 220
Vergerano, José María, 213
Vernal, Doña María, 99
Verrazzano, Giovanni da, 81, 284
Viel, Nicolas, 306, 421
Vignal, Guillaume, 424–25
Vila, Vincente, 204, 209, 213
Villa Branciforte, 262–63
Villafañe, Ángel de, 80, 89–90
Villagrá, Gaspar Pérez de, 122
Villareal, Francis de, 89
Villegagnon, chevalier de (Nicolas Durand), 284
Villegas, Juan de, 61
Vimont, Barthélemy, 321–22, 332, 341, 352, 384
Viniegra, Juan Manuel, 206, 207
Virginia colony, 478, 483–84, 497, 507–11; African slavery, 535; anti-Catholicism, 509–10; Brent family, 507–11; Calvert's petition for a proprietorship, 478; and Catholic settlers of Maryland, 483; Glorious Revolution and aftermath, 510–11; Jamestown, 106–7, 282–83, 483, 508; Second Anglo-Powhatan War, 483–84; Spanish claim, 72, 179, 507–8
Virginia Company, 474, 476
Vivero, Martín de, 131
Vizarrón y Eguiarreta, Juan Antonio, 196
Vizcaíno, Juan, 213
Vizcaíno, Sebastián, 178, 204
Voltaire, François-Marie Arouet, 143, 400, 459, 543, 545
von Brunegg, Philip Segesser, 229

Wadding, Luke, 215
Wagner, Franz Xavier, 196
Walker, Hovenden, 410
Walpole, Horace, 143
Wappeler, Wilhelm, 518–19
War of Austrian Succession, 110, 521–22
War of Jenkins' Ear (1739–1748), 110, 539
War of Spanish Succession (Queen Anne's War), 107–9, 143, 153–54, 166, 397, 410, 411, 436–37, 456, 524–25, 539

War of the Quadruple Alliance, 159–60
Wardour Castle (England), 548, 555
Warner, Sam Bass, Jr., 539
Wars of Religion (Europe), 81–87, 287, 312–13, 433–37, 454
Waugh, Evelyn, 555
Waugh, John, 510–11
Waymouth, George, 470
Webb, Joseph, 523
Weber, David J., 74, 125
Welsh mythology, 465, 474
West, Benjamin, 536, 547
West Indies, 417–18, 455
Wharton, Henry, 504
White, Andrew, 480, 482–84, 490, 493, 496, 509, 529
Whitefield, George, 514–15, 521
Willcox, Thomas, 520
William of Orange (William III of England), 433, 463–65, 528
William the Conqueror, 315, 508
Williams, John, 436–37
Willing, Thomas, 536
Winslade plan, 472–73
Winslow, Edward, 358
Winslow, John, 358–59
Winsor, Justin, 74
Winter, Edward and Frederick, 485
Wiseman, Henry, 485
Writings of Junípero Serra, 208

Wyatt, Thomas, 467
Wynne, Edward, 474, 476

Xaragua massacre (Española), 27–28, 29
Xavier, Francis, 181, 329, 502–3
Ximénez de Cisneros, Francisco, 32–34

Yamasee people, 107, 108, 109
Yaocomaco people, 484, 487
Yazoo people, 431–32
Ybarra, Pedro de, 98
Ye, Juan, 138
York, Henry Cardinal, the bishop of Frascati, 554
Yuma people (Quechans), 186–87, 235, 237, 244, 256–59

Zacatecan Franciscan missionary colleges in New Spain, 146–48
Zaldívar, Juan de, 122
Zaldívar Mendoza, Vicente de, 123–27
Zamet, Sebastien, 339
Zeballos, Sancho, 90
Zuazo, Alonso de, 34, 37
Zumalde, Don Mateo, 195–96
Zumárraga, Juan de, 55, 115, 145
Zuñi pueblos, 60–63, 135
Zúñiga, Don Baltasar de, 142, 158
Zúñiga Acevedo y Fonseca, Gaspar, 119–20, 178